Professional Series

GROUP INSURANCE

Fifth Edition

Principal Editor
William F. Bluhm

Associate Editors
Robert B. Cumming
Alan D. Ford
Jerry E. Lusk
Peter L. Perkins

Request for permission should be addressed to:
ACTEX Publications, Inc.
P.O. Box 974
Winsted, CT 06098

Manufactured in the United States of America

10 9 8 7 6 5 4 3 2 1

Cover Design by Christine Phelps

Library of Congress Cataloging-in-Publication data

Group insurance / principal editor William F. Bluhm ; associate editors
Robert B. Cumming... [et al.]. -- 5th ed.
     p. cm.
Includes bibliographical references and index.
ISBN 978-1-56698-613-7 (pbk. : alk. paper) 1. Insurance, Group--
United States. 2. Insurance, Group--Law and legislation--United States.
I. Bluhm, William F., 1952- II. Cumming, Robert B.

  HG8058.G748 2007
  368.300973--dc22

                                                            2007013340

ISBN: 978-1-56698-613-7

PREFACE

The first edition of Group Insurance began in a conceptual stage around 1987, as an outgrowth of my involvement in the Society of Actuaries' Education and Examination Committee. The second and third editions were 'nudges' in the direction of the changing landscape of group insurance and actuarial practice. The 4th might better have been called a full-fledged 'shove.' This 5th edition is somewhere in between, I think. I encourage readers to contact me with comments and suggestions on the content and direction – particularly actuarial students, and particularly while the material is fresh in your minds.

There are many people who have contributed to each of the editions in different ways. This includes some technical support, but mostly moral support. I will not try to list all of them here – the list would be overly long, I would end up always wanting to add more, and, of greater concern to me, would miss someone whom I don't want to hurt. However, to each of you who has given encouragement and support, I give you my sincere and heartfelt thanks.

There are, however, a few people who stand out far and away above the rest.

The first is my dear friend Dick London. Dick founded ACTEX, and nourished it unselfishly to its impressive position today. Along the way, he got excited about this book, championed it in a way no one else has, and, most of all, respected my desire to maintain creative control over it. Dick is one of those few friends I have found through my life that I know I can count on, who has rejoiced in my journey, and who values the friendship as much as I do.

I also want to acknowledge the contribution of two other ACTEX people; Gail Hall, who continues in Dick's tradition, and Marilyn Baleshiski, the format editor.

Christine, Samantha, and Joey (my family): Thanks for your love and understanding. You continue to be the most precious part of my life, as you have each been since you became part of it.

I wish all of you the satisfaction and joy I have found in being able to pass on my knowledge in such a visible (and apparently useful) way. Thanks for buying the book, and thanks for reading it. Thanks to the authors (current and past) for your time and effort. Most especially, thanks to the section editors, who have (generally) made my life a lot easier.

St. Paul, Minnesota   William F. Bluhm, FSA, MAAA
March 2007   Principal Editor

TABLE OF CONTENTS

◄SECTION THREE►
OVERVIEW OF LEGAL AND REGULATORY ENVIRONMENT

◄SECTION FOUR►
ACTUARIAL PRACTICE IN A REGULATED ENVIRONMENT

◄SECTION FIVE►
UNDERWRITING AND MANAGING THE RISK

◄Section Six►
Funding and Rating

◄SECTION EIGHT►
MANAGEMENT

SECTION ONE

INTRODUCTION

1 THE GROUP INSURANCE MARKETPLACE

Kara L. Clark

OVERVIEW OF GROUP INSURANCE

Group Insurance is an effective and efficient means of providing protection from the adverse financial impact of unforeseen events, to individuals who share a common bond. Group insurance, as used throughout this text, means a benefit program where coverage is provided to a group of individuals. This includes not only traditional coverage provided under insurance policies, but also includes self-insured benefit programs provided by employers, associations and labor unions, government programs, and health service corporations such as health maintenance organizations.

Group insurance is provided to a group of individuals who are connected to one another through some common characteristic. Typical groups include employees of a single employer or group of employers, debtors to a common creditor, members of professional or trade associations, labor unions, or individuals eligible under a government plan.

A fundamental principle underlying all insurance is the pooling of risk. The risks covered by insurance policies are typically infrequent and potentially costly events. The policyholder pays a relatively small, predetermined amount in the form of the insurance premium to the provider of the insurance coverage. In return, the provider of the coverage pays for the cost of the insured's covered event, or provides services directly, should the event occur. In this way, the participants in any particular insurance program share in the financial risk of the covered event.

Another key principle underlying insurance programs is the concept of insurable interest. That is, the policyholder and beneficiaries of a program must experience loss or hardship if the covered event should occur, and therefore have a vested interest in mitigating the risk. Insurable interest on behalf of the policyholder and beneficiaries is required for an insurance program to be financially, and often legally, viable.

Group insurance shares these basic principles with other types of insurance. Group insurance differs from individual insurance in that the provider of the insurance coverage considers the entire group of eligible individuals as a whole in evaluating the risk, deciding whether or not to insure the risk, and in setting the price for the risk. Group insurance allows a more efficient means of issuing coverage than individual insurance, since greater numbers of insureds are added to the insured pool at any one time. However, the insurer still must protect itself against antiselection, and therefore, will require that certain standards be met before offering coverage to the group. For example, the insurer may require that at least 75% of the group participate in the insurance program. Likewise, for employer-sponsored plans, the insurer may require that the employer pay for some minimum percentage of the employee's premium, so that employees have a greater incentive to join the group insurance program. These requirements encourage greater participation in the program, which in turn helps to establish an appropriate level of risk.

Group plans also provide a more efficient means of marketing and delivering insurance programs. The primary level of marketing is to the plan sponsor, which can be an employer, association or other entity. A secondary level of marketing is to eligible individuals, and is typically accomplished in a common setting, either in the workplace or through other regular communications to the group, such as association newsletters. Group plans are marketed through a variety of distribution networks, including agents, brokers, consultants, and by direct sales. However, instead of needing to make the sale with every potential insured, the primary sales effort can be focused toward the sponsor decision-makers. Therefore, the cost of the marketing effort is typically lower on a per-participant basis than for individual insurance. Likewise, administrative expenses are typically lower on a per-participant basis for group insurance, because individual premium billing is not required, and plan sponsors often provide low-cost access to participants for communication and information distribution.

The group insurance market includes a diversity of product lines. Medical coverage represents a large portion of group coverage in the United States, and may include medical indemnity insurance, Preferred Provider Organization (PPO) plans, Point of Service (POS) plans, and Health Maintenance

Organization (HMO) plans, as well as the government-sponsored Medicare and Medicaid programs, which are available only to certain disabled, needy and older Americans. In Canada, where nearly all residents are covered by the provincially sponsored healthcare system known as Medicare, private group medical plans cover only those benefits not generally available under the public system. Therefore, while group medical coverage is widespread in Canada, it is not as large a part of the total group insurance market as it is in the United States. In both the United States and Canada, a variety of other coverages are also sold on a group basis, including indemnity and managed dental plans, short and long term disability income coverage, life insurance, vision and hearing coverage, long term care insurance, pre-paid legal, group property and casualty, and other special risk coverages such as accidental death and dismemberment and travel accident.

HISTORY OF GROUP INSURANCE

Group insurance has its roots in ancient times, as far back as the Romans. Medieval craft guilds used insurance concepts in their operation. Then, late in the nineteenth century, the industrial revolution contributed to the growth of group insurance concepts. As transition occurred from an agricultural to an industrial economy, many workers moved from self-employment to larger employers. Employer liability law began to develop, and employee benefit programs began to emerge.

Academics of the early 1900's also began to identify the economic security needs of individuals related to accident, illness, old age, and death. Interest in socially based solutions to these issues began to grow.

Group plans began to be offered before 1870, and were typically cash accident and sickness (disability) plans. These were followed by group prepaid medical services plans. Group insurance began to be issued in the 1890's. A number of group insurance plans were already in place by the 1940's, when United States governmental price-wage controls limited employers' opportunities to increase wage scales to attract and retain employee talent. In order to differentiate themselves in the marketplace, employers looked to other benefits, including group insurance coverages that could be provided to employees without violating the wage control regulations. The 1950's brought additional governmental price-wage controls, further spurring the growth in group insurance coverages. Additional support for group insurance growth was provided through a landmark court decision in 1949 (the *Inland Steel* decision), which allowed for pension and other employee benefits to be included in the scope of collective bargaining.[1] Tax policy has also often favored benefits provided through group insurance coverages, further contributing to their proliferation. For all these reasons, insurance coverages became an integral part of many employee compensation packages.

By the mid-20th century, major medical plans emerged as a melding of the prepaid medical services approach used by early Blue Cross/Blue Shield carriers ("the Blues") and the indemnity (fixed dollar) reimbursement approach used by traditional insurance carriers. Self-insurance became popular in the 1970's among larger employers, who viewed the concept as a way of saving some group insurance costs, through the elimination of premium taxes and the opportunity for control of invested assets.

In the United States, Internal Revenue Code Section 125 was established by the Revenue Act of 1978, which stipulated that otherwise nontaxable benefits provided under Section 125 plans would not be subject to the doctrine of constructive receipt (and therefore taxed), even if the plan participants could have elected to receive cash instead.[2] In the 1980's, medium and large-sized employers began offering their employees flexible benefit plans under Section 125, as a means to limit employer cost while providing employees the appeal of choice. Under flexible benefit plans, employers provided employees with some predetermined amount of funds or credits, which the employee could then use to purchase coverage from among a range of benefit offerings that would best suit the employee's particular financial needs.

Rapid increases in health insurance costs instigated the move toward more managed health plan offerings in the 1980's and 1990's, including Health Maintenance Organization (HMO), Preferred Provider Organization (PPO), and Point of Service (POS) plans. Plan sponsors gave up some freedom of choice in provider selection and agreed to care guidelines, in return for much lower premiums than available under traditional indemnity plans. The 1990's also saw the emergence of laws and regulations designed to increase access to health care insurance coverage, including the extension of coverage to individuals for whom the period of coverage would have typically terminated, as well as limitations on health status underwriting. Late in the 1990's, the public's dissatisfaction with restrict-

---

[1] *Employee Benefit Planning,* 3rd Edition, Jerry S. Rosenbloom and G. Victor Hallman.

[2] *Employee Benefit Planning,* 3rd Edition, Jerry S. Rosenbloom and G. Victor Hallman.

ive managed care increased. This dissatisfaction, in conjunction with less willingness from provider groups to accept managed care payment discounts, and the concern of employers over potential liability, led to a move toward less restrictive managed care plans, such as POS and PPO plans. Today, 61% of employees with health coverage are enrolled in a PPO plan, compared to 21% in HMOs and 15% in POS plans.[3]

Health Savings Accounts and Health Reimbursement Accounts have received considerable industry, government, and media attention. While there are many variations, these arrangements often involve an employer-provided set amount of funds (the "account") for each employee, combined with a high-deductible health plan. Funds in the account can then be used by the employee to cover their out-of-pocket costs (for example, the deductible, coinsurance amounts, or possibly care not covered by the insurance plan at all). These plans are intended to involve the employee more closely in healthcare purchasing decisions, and often include access to consumer education and other support tools specific to these decisions. These plans are relatively new and there is considerable debate over their effectiveness in controlling health care costs. They have not yet been broadly adopted, but many employers are considering them as a possible alternative option.

In Canada, the public healthcare system was initiated with the passage of the Hospital Insurance and Diagnostic Act of 1957 and the Medical Care Act of 1968. These two Acts established the health insurance programs that covered medically necessary services for nearly all Canadian residents. The Canada Health Act of 1984 replaced the two prior acts, although it maintained their basic premises. In addition, the 1984 Act included provisions to discourage user fees and extra billings as related to insured health care services.[4]

Flexible benefit programs in Canada received increased attention in the 1980's for many of the same reasons these programs became popular in the United States. These reasons included the change in workforce demographics since the origin of employee benefit programs, as well as government rulings that enhanced the ability of employers to offer choice to meet different employee needs and manage benefit costs.[5]

---

[3] *Employer Health Benefit Survey, 2005,* Kaiser Family Foundation and Health Research and Educational Trust

[4] Canada Health Act Overview, at http://www.hc-sc.gc.ca/medicare/chaover.htm

[5] *Canadian Handbook of Flexible Benefits*, Second Edition, Robert J. McKay

Regulation of group insurance occurs at both the state and federal level in the United States. Federal regulations apply to employer benefit plans, which include those plans provided on a self-insured basis. State law generally applies to the business of insurance. Therefore, insured benefits provided by an employer must comply with state laws, since the state regulations will apply to the insurance company providing the insurance program. On the other hand, self-insured benefits provided by an employer are not considered "the business of insurance" and are therefore not subject to state regulations. However, the line of distinction is blurring, as the federal government has implemented legislation which impacts health insurance, especially with regard to the availability and continuation of coverage.

Insurance companies in Canada may also be subject to both federal and provincial regulations. Companies that elect to be federally registered because they operate in more than one province are subject to federal law. Companies must also have a license from each province in which they do business, no matter where they are registered.

BUYERS OF GROUP INSURANCE PRODUCTS AND SERVICES

State or provincial laws and regulations may define valid groups eligible for group insurance. The National Association of Insurance Commissioners' (NAIC) model law provides a typical list. In general, the individual members of a group share some common characteristic or trait with each other, independent of being covered by the same insurance policy. That is, the group should already have a purpose and should not be formed solely for the purpose of obtaining insurance coverage. The NAIC model law has been adopted by all states, and is described in detail in a later chapter.

Different categories of group insurance purchasers include:

SINGLE EMPLOYERS

Group insurance plans issued to a single employer cover the employees and their dependents. The employer is usually the policyholder, although in some cases a trust may be established and becomes the policyholder. Single employers may choose to purchase coverage from an insurer or managed care organization in return for a fixed premium, or in the case of larger employers, may elect to self-insure some or all of the risk. In fully insured plans the employer pays premiums, but employees are often required to contribute to the cost. In self-insured plans, the employer may similarly require the employees to contribute to the cost of the coverage. Self-insured employers may administer their own insurance plans, but more commonly purchase Administrative Services Only (ASO) contracts from an insurance company or third-party administrator.

MULTIPLE EMPLOYER TRUSTS

Two or more employers may join together to form a multiple employer trust for the purpose of buying and funding group insurance for their employees. In this case, the trust is the policyholder, and the employers are known as participating employers. As with single employers, coverage may either be purchased on a fully insured basis, or be self-insured. Employees may be required to contribute toward the cost of coverage, whether the plan is fully insured or self-insured. Participating employers usually elect to join the trust because they anticipate greater purchasing power or spreading of risk if they combine their covered workforce with that of other employers. In some cases, the participating employers may have found it difficult to be accepted as an individual employer by an insurer, given their particular risk status. Joining a multiple employer trust allows for a greater pooling of risk that an insurer may then be willing to accept. Some multiple employer trusts are formed by insurance companies or third party administrators in order to make coverage available to smaller employers more efficiently. In addition, participating employers might also have unique administration requirements (such as an employee hours bank), and a multiple employer trust may provide a more efficient means of providing for those needs.

ASSOCIATIONS

An association may also offer group insurance coverage to its individual members. Associations are defined as groups of individuals or institutions that share common professions, interests, activities, or goals. Associations include, among others, professional organizations, trade organizations, and alumni organizations. Other groups, often known as affiliation groups, also may be purchasers of group insurance. These groups are formed because members have a common interest. Examples are the American Automobile Association (AAA) and the American Association of Retired Persons (AARP). The association or a trust formed by the association is the policyholder.

Most often, the full cost of coverage is borne in some manner by the association member. The association member may remit the premium directly to the association for payment to the insurance provider, to a third party administrator working on behalf of the association, or directly to the provider of the insurance coverage.

Associations may automatically provide their members with some types of group insurance coverage, such as group accident or term life, and the premiums may be included as part of the membership dues. Associations may be in the market for group insurance coverage simply to provide an additional benefit to their membership for the dues that members pay.

LABOR UNIONS

A labor union may be the policyholder of a group insurance plan. A union may also negotiate benefits with employers participating in a Taft-Hartley multiple employer trust (named after the U.S. federal law which authorized such trusts), in which case the trustees are the policyholders. Coverage may be fully insured or self-insured. Benefits and employee contributions, if any, are generally provided for in a collective bargaining agreement. Premiums may be required of the union, the employers, and/or the union members. Benefits are paid directly to the union members or their dependents, or may be assigned to a provider of medical services.

GOVERNMENT EMPLOYEE GROUPS

Collectively, the United States government is the largest employer in the country, and is consequently the largest purchaser of group insurance for employees and their dependents. Some of the most prominent plans are the Federal Employees' Group Life Insurance (FEGLI) and Federal Employees' Health Benefit Association (FEHBA) plans, in addition to numerous smaller agency plans and state and local government sponsored plans.

TRICARE provides health benefits to the retired members of the United States military and their dependents, as well as dependents of active service personnel. The program covers services rendered outside of military treatment facilities, and includes medical, dental and other services. TRICARE was commonly referred to as CHAMPUS prior to the introduction of expanded managed care features and options.

At the federal level, employees often have a choice of plans. At the state level, plans are often established for state employees and local governments are given the option to join. The governmental sponsor is the policyholder, and the plans may be insured or self-insured, and trusts are often used.

GOVERNMENT SOCIAL INSURANCE PROGRAMS

In the United States, the government also provides group insurance coverage as a sponsor of many social insurance programs, including Medicare (health care for the aged and disabled), Medicaid (health care for the financially indigent), and Social Security disabled-worker and survivor benefits (disability and life benefits for disableds and their dependents). These programs are typically self-insured, although some Medicare and Medicaid-related fully insured managed care programs can also be found.

In Canada, the vast majority of the general population is covered by provincial government sponsored health coverage, also known as Medicare. The costs of these social insurance programs are paid through a combination of payroll taxation, general revenues, and insured premiums. These programs are discussed in detail in later chapters.

CREDITOR GROUPS

Creditor organizations, including banks and other lenders, may purchase group insurance coverage on those to whom they have lent funds. Coverages purchased typically include life and/or disability income coverage. The creditor organization is usually the policyholder, and charges the premium to the debtor. Should the insured become disabled or die, the insurance company would pay the benefits to the creditor organization to reduce the amount of the insured's outstanding debt.

DISCRETIONARY GROUPS

Groups are sometimes established primarily for the purpose of providing insurance or self-insured group benefits. Some of these programs are sponsored by insurance companies for reasons of efficiency in delivering coverage to small employers. Similar plans are also sponsored by administrators, and may be either insured or self-insured. These plans are generally issued to trusts. Purchasing alliances formed under state programs for the purpose of providing medical coverage are examples of closely regulated discretionary groups. Often, these groups obtain coverage from insurance companies, health service corporations and HMOs, and offer coverage to interested parties who then choose to join the program. Discretionary groups are much more common in the United States than in Canada.

SELLERS OF GROUP INSURANCE PRODUCTS

Group insurance products are sold by a variety of entities. Some of the products are sold on a self-insured basis, by (1) insurance companies under ASO contracts, (2) third party administrators, or (3) health service corporations.

INSURANCE COMPANIES

In both the United States and in Canada, group insurance products may be sold by life, health, or property and casualty companies. Insurance companies may offer the full range of group insurance products, including indemnity medical plans, PPO plans, POS plans, capitated or subcapitated medical plans, dental, disability, life, and long term care. Many insurance companies do not offer medical coverages, and the trend in the United States has been to withdraw from the medical market, leaving the market to a smaller number of companies who specialize in this coverage. Insurers also provide Administrative Services Only (ASO) contracts or provide services that offer some blend of insurance and administration to self-insured employers or multiple employer trusts. ASO is generally limited to medical and dental coverages, with some ASO disability plans in place as well.

In the United States, insurers have some advantages over other group sellers to the employer market, in that they often have a national presence, are licensed in most states, and can offer policyholders a full range of benefits from a single source. Further, with respect to health coverages, an insurer can often establish national networks of providers for their many customers more effectively than most single employers can. The ability to offer a range of benefits is an advantage not only to the purchasers of the insurance products, but also to the insurance companies. Multiple product offerings provide for efficient product distribution, and the earnings from multiple coverages can be more stable in total.

Insurance company ownership may be structured in stock or mutual form. The majority of companies are stock companies, owned by stockholders. There has been a trend over the past few decades for mutual companies, owned by their policyholders, to convert to the stock form. Stock insurance companies are typically in the group insurance market to make a reasonable return on investment for their shareholders, and have some advantages over mutual companies and not-for-profit organizations in access to capital in the financial marketplace. Mutual companies allow for any positive financial experience to be returned to the participating policy-holders. They are limited in their ability to raise capital, and must rely on surplus and earnings to finance growth opportunities.

Commercial insurers typically do not have as significant a local market share as Blue Cross/Blue Shield plans and local managed care organizations. Thus, they may not be able to negotiate provider payment discounts and other cost management features as effectively in local markets.

HEALTH CARE SERVICE CORPORATIONS

Health care service organizations are not-for-profit entities, and are often exempt from state premium or income tax. The majority are Blue Cross / Blue Shield or Delta Dental plans, although not all Blue Cross / Blue Shield plans are health care service organizations. Blue Cross / Blue Shield plans are all independent organizations operating under a common trade-mark. In recent years, many Blues organizations have explored alternative corporate arrangements or joint ventures, including for-profit subsidiaries. Others have converted to stock ownership, as described above.

Health service corporations generally sell only medical and dental products, including indemnity, PPO, POS, or capitated plans, but many offer other coverages through affiliated companies. They also typically offer ASO (or a similar product called Administrative Service Contracts, which passes along all claim risk to the policyholder but all tax dollars still flow through the plan as premium) and other alternative funding contracts. They often have a strong local presence, and may only be licensed in a single state.

Local market penetration relative to other providers of group medical products is often quite high. This may allow health service corporations to enjoy deeper provider payment discounts than those available to other types of organizations. Long-term relationships with physicians and hospitals contribute to this favorable position.

Health service corporations sell to employers, union trusts, associations, and other groups. To the extent the buyer also provides other group products to its membership, such as disability or life, those products need to be purchased from another carrier. Penetration in some markets is significant, with these plans especially popular with collectively bargained plans.

Health service corporations tend to be closely regulated, particularly with respect to individual products. Some states treat these companies as insurers of last resort, and require that they accept all risks. Rates are subject to approval in some jurisdictions.

HEALTH MAINTENANCE ORGANIZATIONS

Health Maintenance Organizations (HMOs) are typically licensed as different entities from insurance companies or health service organizations. They have a variety of types of owners, including the public, insurance companies, Blue Cross/Blue Shield organizations, and provider groups. They may be organized as for-profit or not-for-profit, although for-profit is more common.

HMOs contract with providers of care, such as hospitals and physicians or physician groups, to form networks. HMOs may own hospitals and directly employ physicians. HMOs are also directly involved in the management of health care. HMOs tend to be local. They typically provide only medical benefits, although some dental and vision benefits may also be provided. Benefits provided to participants are generally comprehensive, but the participants are often limited to receiving care from only the providers with whom the HMO has contracted, except in the case of emergencies. The public's level of satisfaction with HMOs has received considerable media attention. Concerns about cost savings at the expense of quality of care, choice of provider, and selection of treatment plans, has led to the movement away from restrictive HMO plans to those providing more choice.

PROVIDER OWNED ORGANIZATIONS

In the 1990's, provider owned organizations such as physician hospital organizations (PHOs), provider-sponsored organizations (PSOs), and provider-sponsored networks (PSNs) began to form. These organizations often emerged due to providers' increased interest in more control of their own delivery of medical care and in the reimbursement of provided services. These organizations consist of provider groups, usually a hospital or hospital system and the associated group of physicians with admitting privileges. The group accepts a scheduled payment, known as global capitation, in return for accepting the risk of providing specified health care services. They may contract directly with employers, government, insurance companies or managed care organizations.

The local focus of these organizations, as well as their direct affiliation with providers, may offer marketing advantages relative to other types of organizations. However, these groups may also not be as well prepared to accept risk (in terms of both capital and management expertise) or perform administrative services as well as other types of organizations. The number of these "integrated" delivery systems has been on the decline in recent years.

SELF-INSURED EMPLOYERS

Self-insured employers do not provide group insurance coverage in the same way as insurance companies or Blue Cross/Blue Shield organizations, but they do accept risk. Self-insured benefits most often include medical, dental, and short-term disability. Due to the lower frequency and higher severity of life and long-term-disability coverage, and also because of income tax considerations, these benefits are often insured. Employers may elect to self-insure for a variety of reasons. Self-insured plans are not generally subject to state premium tax or state mandated benefit provisions. Also, since the self-insured plan pays claims as they are submitted, the sponsor retains the use of the funds until they are paid and benefits from investment return on those monies. Self-insured employers often contract with an insurance company or third-party administrator to provide for the administrative aspects of the plan.

In Canada, group insurance products and services are offered by insurance companies and Blue Cross plans, which tend to operate more like insurance companies than Blue Cross/Blue Shield plans found in the United States. Canadian Blue Cross plans may offer other group insurance products, such as disability plans, besides group medical coverages. Because the mix of public and private care is different than in the United States, managed care organizations such as HMOs and other provider owned organizations are rare in Canada. Self-insured employer plans are common in Canada as in the United States.

GOVERNMENT INSURANCE PROGRAMS

UNITED STATES MEDICARE

Medicare provides health coverage to the eligible aged and disabled in the United States. Part A coverage, which is mandatory, provides for inpatient hospital, skilled nursing facility, and home health benefits. Providers of Part A services must accept the government's payment as payment in full. Part B coverage provides for outpatient hospital benefits, physician services, durable medical equipment, ambulance, and other non-physician providers. Participation in Part B is voluntary, and eligible and interested beneficiaries must pay a premium to enroll. In addition to the premium, beneficiaries are also subject to some cost sharing provisions for Part B services. Physicians are not required to accept the government's payment as payment in full, although many do, and there are limits to the amount they can charge in excess of the government's payment. Medicare Part D, providing prescription drug coverage, was added to Medicare in 2006. Participation in Part D is voluntary, although eligibles who do not enroll within certain timeframes may be subject to late enrollment penalties. Medicare Part D may be offered through a stand-alone prescription drug plan ("PDP") or a Medicare Advantage ("MA") plan (discussed below). The benefits and premiums vary by plan and plan sponsor. Eligibles may have many options of stand-alone PDPs or MA plans from which to choose. Funding for Medicare is provided through payroll taxes, general revenues, and beneficiary premiums.

Many Medicare eligibles also have the opportunity to forego traditional Medicare coverage and participate in a Medicare Advantage plan. The majority of MA plans are managed care plans, such as HMOs or PPOs. The government provides a payment to the MA plan for each enrolled beneficiary. The MA plan then assumes the risk of providing services for the covered insured. Some MA plans may offer additional benefits beyond those normally provided by Medicare Parts A, B, and D. Insureds covered by an MA plan pay Part B premiums to Medicare, as well monthly premiums to the MA plan.

UNITED STATES MEDICAID

Medicaid provides health coverage to the financially indigent in the United States. Medicaid coverage is very comprehensive, with many benefits covered at 100%. Medicaid is also very broad, including benefits such as dental, vision, and custodial nursing care, in addition to traditional health benefits. Cost-sharing levels for beneficiaries are very low. Medicaid reimburses providers at rates that often represent deep discounts from standard charges, which must be accepted as payment in full. Physicians are not required to participate in Medicaid, although hospitals frequently must participate. Medicaid programs are administered by state governments and are funded by state and federal general revenues. States may pay providers on a fee-for-service basis, or may provide for services through prepaid programs such as HMOs. The number of Medicaid beneficiaries in managed care plans has grown from 14 percent of enrollees in 1993 to 59 percent in 2003.[6]

CANADIAN MEDICARE

Provincial government sponsored healthcare programs known as Medicare cover the majority of the population of Canada. Medicare provides coverage for a variety of medical services, such as hospital services, inpatient and outpatient physician services, as well as extended health care services, which include long-term residential care. Benefits are on a service basis, meaning that Medicare provides medical services and that patients do not need to pay first and then submit a claim. Federal standards for provincial programs discourage user fees. Although they are not required to do so, a vast majority of physicians participate in the Medicare program. Under Medicare, physicians are generally compensated on a fee-for-service basis. Medicare is funded by the provinces through payroll taxes, general revenues, and in some provinces, premiums. Provincially sponsored Medicare plans that meet federally established criteria for portability, universality, comprehensiveness, accessibility, and public non-profit management are eligible for a federal funds transfer to offset some of the costs of the provincial program.

---

[6] Centers for Medicare and Medicaid Services, Medicaid: Technical Summary, from http://www.cms.gov

2 OVERVIEW OF SALES AND MARKETING

William A. Raab

INTRODUCTION

A textbook on group insurance would not be complete without a description of how sales and marketing fits with the other group functions. A company can have state-of-the art systems and efficient administration. The actuaries can develop competitive rates and funding alternatives, but nothing will happen until and unless products have been properly developed, marketed, and sold.

The terms "marketing" and "sales" are often used interchangeably. Departments named "marketing" are often really "sales." "Sales" departments frequently encompass both the sales and marketing functions. It is helpful to distinguish between the two activities.

The American Marketing Association defines marketing as "the process of planning and executing the conception, pricing, promotion, and distribution of ideas, goods, and services to create exchanges that satisfy individual and organizational objectives."[1] This is a broad description of the process that begins with the original product or service concept, and concludes with an exchange of something of value for the product or service – the "sale" to the customer. Although this is the technically correct definition, a different perspective may be helpful.

It is more common in practice to separate the marketing and sales functions. That separation is not because there is a dichotomy between marketing and sales, but rather because there is a close relationship that can be explained with the analogy, "marketing is to sales as strategy is to tactics."

---

[1] E.N. Berkowitz, *Essentials of Health Care Marketing,* (Gaithersburg, Md., Aspen Publicaions, 1996) p. 4.

17

Using this frame of reference enables us to see marketing as an overall process, with distribution and sales as the implementing component.

MARKETING

This is not a marketing textbook, but rather a chapter on marketing and sales. There will be an overview of some basic marketing concepts, not an in-depth analysis. Many fine books exist on the subject. When necessary, an explanation will be given relating these concepts to group insurance.

MARKETING FUNCTIONS

As stated above, we are looking at marketing as the process of preparing the way for sales. In keeping with this, we will look at some of the marketing functions, and at how they fit into the overall strategic planning process.

Strategy is conventionally viewed as the overall game plan or blueprint that guides the company toward achieving its stated goals and objectives. The marketing area plays a key role in this strategic plan by providing important information about the company's current position in the market, as well as possible future opportunities. The marketing area can also participate in the overall planning process by developing strategies and tactics for specific products, customers, distribution channels, and so forth.[2]

Marketing research is an important part of this overall planning process. The role of research is, quite simply, to focus on understanding customers. Who are the potential customers for our products, what features do they wish to purchase, where are they located, how much are they willing to pay, and from what types of distribution arrangements do they wish to buy? What are our competitors doing?[3] Scientific survey techniques and sophisticated statistical analysis are employed. In fact, market research is a profession in itself, with its own trade organization. It is not unusual for a company to supplement the efforts of its own research department by using an outside specialty firm.[4]

---

[2] A. Hiam and C.D. Schewe, *The Portable MBA in Marketing*, (New York, NY, John Wiley and Sons, Inc., 1992) p.24.

[3] Hiam and Schewe, pp. 103-108.

[4] Hiam and Schewe, pp. 108-110.

This type of research is commonplace in the consumer product industry, and is gaining ground in financial services. The traditional group insurance companies may have lagged behind durable goods companies in implementing a research-based approach. This is probably due, at least in part, to their focus on product and distribution. In today's environment that has changed. Insurers and managed care organizations recognize the role research plays in the marketplace.

The development of competitive products is one of the processes identified in the marketing planning process. Common sense tells us that companies need products and services to sell in order to make a profit. How are new products developed? Although there is a general pattern to the process, the specifics are different at every company. Two different approaches are summarized below. The first might be called a traditional product-driven process; the second is market-driven.

The Product Development Process:[5]

The product development process under a traditional, product-driven approach can be conceptualized into seven steps:

- Idea Generation: Ideas can come from a number of sources, such as product managers, a product committee, customers, competitors, or employees.

- Idea Screening: The product ideas are screened to determine which are compatible with the company's strategy, resources, and skills.

- Concept Development and Testing: A team refines the concept into a product, and questions such as "What are the benefits?" and "Who will buy this?" are answered.

- Business Analysis: Costs are projected, and a return on investment (or return on equity) analysis is done.

- Product Development: The actual product is given concrete form.

- Test Marketing: The product is tested in limited real-world markets.

- Commercialization: Full-scale manufacture and distribution.

The Market-Driven Product Process:[6]

The market-driven process can be thought of as having three major steps:

---

[5] Hiam and Schewe, pp. 244-253
[6] Berkowitz, pp. 17-19

- Assessment of Target Market Needs: A target market is chosen, and market research is done to assess the needs of that market. Competitive analysis is a critical part of this research.

- Identification of Differential Advantage: Since the needs of the buyer and the competition's approach are known, a determination is made how to differentiate one's own product or service from the competition, to better serve the customer's need.

- Strategy Formulation: A strategy is developed to build and deliver the product, based upon the differential advantage. This is then followed by one of two rollout processes:

  ○ Pre-Test: A limited market test, or

  ○ Full Implementation: The full product implementation begins.

Either the traditional process or the market driven process can be used in group insurance. The traditional approach has historically been used by most group carriers, while the market-driven approach has been used more often in recent years as markets have become more strategic and complex. Advertising, public relations, and other forms of promotion are also important marketing functions. They are designed to communicate the company's message about its products and services to the public, or to specific customer segments. This can take the form of mass media advertising, mass mailings, trade shows, seminars, public relations events, and so forth. The specific purpose of these campaigns can range from name recognition of the company, to specific product information, to building the value of the company's brand names. As with market research, it is not unusual for outside specialty firms to be retained to assist the company with these advertising and promotional functions.

At this point, the company has developed its strategy and done necessary planning, researched the market, developed products to meet the demands of that market, and implemented an advertising and promotional campaign to build awareness of its products and services.

Although there may be subtle differences from industry to industry, this overall process applies to a broad range of products and services, from laundry detergent to mutual funds to group insurance. The stage is now set to distribute those products. It's time for sales to begin.

Before going on to the sales process, let's look at marketing in a different way.

MARKET-DRIVEN ORGANIZATIONS

In a sense, marketing can be viewed conceptually as much bigger than mere research, development, and promotion. Marketing can be viewed as a culture, which permeates a company and its people "from the mailroom to the boardroom," and launches the company to greatness. These companies are driven by the markets and the customers they serve, not by the products they sell, or by their distribution networks.

Books on this subject abound, but for this chapter the focus will be on one case study: Matsushita Electric. This study shows the value of breaking free from traditional thinking. With a little effort, one can see how it applies to the group insurance business. It is the story of how a particular company – Matsushita Electric (JVC) – rose to dominance in a specific segment of the consumer electronics business – VCRs.[7] This is significant because the VCR helped establish the dominance of Japanese companies in consumer electronics. The authors describe this as a twenty-year "race," beginning in the late 1950s when an American company first produced the video tape recorder. It lasted until the late 1970s when JVC introduced the VHS format and won the race. JVC was not the only company to see clearly the potential for videotape. At least two other competitors made major efforts, but JVC made a corporate-wide commitment.

First, they had to acquire the competencies necessary to reduce the size from large bulky machines to ones that were compact. Next they had to envision what configuration of price, product features, size, and performance characteristics were necessary to appeal to the mass market. (Remember, this was for a machine that no one had ever seen!) Next, JVC was able to establish its video format (VHS) as the industry standard (through licensing the VHS format to strategic partners who manufactured their own machines). Once JVCs standard became the industry standard, they were able to dominate the market through cost reductions and features enhancement. The competing format eventually disappeared from the market.

There are similarities between the JVC story and the history of HMOs in the health insurance market. Although there were several companies involved, and the story played out regionally, the themes are much the same. These companies saw the future potential in the mass market for a product

---

[7] This case study is from G. Hamel and C.K. Prahalad, *Competing for the Future*, (Boston, MA. Harvard Business School Press, 1994), pp. 47-52.

that few people knew existed. They acquired, or invented, the competencies necessary to control health care costs by monitoring physician practice patterns, controlling provider behavior, negotiating discounts, limiting access to expensive technologies, and shifting the financial risk to the providers through capitated reimbursement schemes. This, along with some positive selection bias in their marketing approach, translated into a lower cost basis for their products. (Meanwhile, the traditional health insurance industry was responding to cost issues by raising deductibles and coinsurance limits, and encouraging employers to pass on part of the cost to employees.)

Next, HMOs were able to envision what configuration of product features and price employers and employees would be willing to buy. The products typically featured low out-of-pocket costs to the employee, with a focus on wellness and preventive care, but no benefits outside of the HMO network. Employers were attracted by lower premiums. HMO companies were then able to establish their new standard as a market standard, and in a twenty-year period captured one-third of the market. From that position they have been able to launch product enhancements to keep themselves competitive as the market evolved, even as that evolution included a response to consumer backlash against some of the HMO industry's cost-controlling techniques.

SALES

In a sense, sales can be seen as the culmination of the marketing process. That would be an oversimplification, of course. Ongoing customer service after the sale completes the marketing and sales process. Organizations cannot survive if they must focus their sales efforts on replacing dissatisfied customers who have terminated their relationship. In the context of market-driven organizations, marketing, sales, and ongoing service are all one continuous process.

Group insurance often has two levels of sale. The initial sale is made to the plan sponsor. This entails selection of plans to be offered and their cost, and often includes a discussion of financial management, administration and services offered to the sponsor. Later, a second sale is often made to the participants. This can include selection of a particular plan from among those offered by the sponsor, and for certain products, such as group universal life and long-term care, may be similar to the sale of an individual insurance product. The "second sale" is discussed in more detail later in the chapter.

Historically, group carriers have organized their sales efforts to plan sponsors around a variety of distribution channels. Some of these models and their advantages and disadvantages will be reviewed here. Prior to that discussion, however, it is necessary to have a basic understanding of who the players are, and what their roles are, in the distribution process.

INTERMEDIARIES

Employers tend to rely on third-party advisors to assist them with their employee benefit plans. This assistance includes advice on issues such as plan design, pricing, and comparative analysis of competing carriers' products and services. The advisor usually gets involved in ongoing customer service, and often acts as the employer's representative in resolving disputed billing and claims issues. At renewal, the adviser surveys the marketplace to see if the client would be better served by renewing the plan with the current carrier or by changing carriers. This analysis includes a discussion of plan design alternatives, either with the current carrier or a competitor.

Research conducted by a leading insurance industry organization confirms the employer penchant for using advisors. "Approximately 80% of employers use the services of an outside advisor, and over 47% of these employers have used the same advisor for more than five years."[8]

These advisors fall into three general categories: brokers, agents, and consultants.

"Broker" is somewhat of a generic term. Many states do not specifically recognize nor license insurance brokers. The professional license that is involved is typically a Life and Health Agent license, but the broker may also have a separate license to sell Property, Casualty, and Liability Insurance. Having both types of licenses would obviously create additional sales opportunities with the same business client. Once an individual or corporation has such a license, it can usually be appointed to represent

---

[8] "Marketing Group Insurance and Health Care Benefits: Trends and Insights, Phase Two"; p. 30; LIMRA International, Windsor, CT, 2001.

more than one insurance carrier. The broker's compensation is usually based on sales commissions for products sold. The commissions are a percentage of premium paid, or a fee per covered employee. In either case, the commission is built into the price of the product.

"Agents" are similar to brokers, except that they are typically associated with a single carrier. Their compensation is also based on commissions. Brokers are thought of as representing multiple companies.

"Consultants" typically work only with large employers. Compensation is typically based on a fee for services rendered, as opposed to commissions. The consultant could be paid an annual retainer, and/or could be paid an hourly fee for consulting services. There could also be fees negotiated for specific projects, such as marketing the various benefit packages at renewal (in which case, products are usually quoted net of commissions).. Some brokerage firms operate as consultants in certain instances and as brokers in others.

There has been a wave of consolidation among insurance brokerage firms in the last few years. Some of the major consulting firms have gone through mergers and acquisitions, as have smaller regional and local firms. National banking organizations have begun building insurance sales divisions, often by purchasing existing regional or local brokerage firms. Group insurance is often a logical target for these bank-owned insurance brokers, because of the existing banking relationships with business clients.

In late 2004 the Attorney General of the State of New York announced an investigation into the business practices of several large property and casualty insurance brokerage firms. Among the allegations was bid-rigging, in order to place business with preferred carriers, thus earning contingent commissions. The National Association of Insurance Commissioners (NAIC) got involved, as did several state insurance departments and attorneys-general. Even though the original allegations involved property and casualty coverage, the inquiries were expanded to include other lines, including group insurance. There were numerous civil actions, and the NAIC strengthened commission disclosure requirements in its Producer Licensing Model Act.[9]

---

[9] The NAIC website (www.naic.org) provides archival material on this subject, as does the website of the New York Attorney General (www.oag.state.ny.us).

DISTRIBUTION MODELS

BROKERAGE

Under the brokerage distribution model, the carrier relies on independent brokers to distribute products. These brokers are self-employed entrepreneurs, who are responsible for maintaining their own office space and clerical staff. This method can be used for wholesale distribution (such brokers are often called general agents), retailing, or a combination of both. It is attractive to some companies, especially those with limited resources, because it does not require the large commitment of capital and staff resources necessary to house, train, supervise, and maintain a branch-office field force. A portion of these savings may be given back in the form of higher commission rates, overrides, and expense allowances to the brokers.

This model is characterized by a single, narrow distribution channel. The broker does not have the sale of the company's products as his or her sole responsibility. Other companies' products are also sold. This makes the carrier vulnerable to price competition, since the business will often flow to the carrier with the lowest rate.

As an independent, the broker may choose to specialize in other product lines, such as property and casualty, or financial planning. Even if the broker is specializing in the desired product, distribution can be limited to a local area or a specific client base. In order to maintain sufficient revenue flow, the carrier must support a broad variety of products for many market niches.

This method is most frequently used to distribute individual and small group insurance products, including various types of life insurance, annuities, Medicare supplement coverage, critical illness coverage and long term care policies, where the agent relationship is an important element of the sale. Group products tend to be sold based on price and value, and this model has not been widely used by group carriers.

GROUP FIELD FORCE

The group field force model is the traditional model used for years by most large group carriers. Under this distribution system, the carrier employs a full-time salaried field force of captive group representatives. The group representatives are usually paid an incentive for sales in addition to a base salary. This distribution method is typically a wholesale model, where the carrier representatives call on and sell through brokers and consultants.

This distribution channel is wider than in the pure brokerage model. The sales force is totally dedicated to the sale of the carrier's products. There is no specialization in outside product lines, no distribution of other companies' products, and distribution is not limited to a small local area. Rather, the group sales force tends to operate in as many market niches as possible. Relationships are developed with a large variety of brokers, thereby gaining access to a large, diverse base of prospects. This enables the carrier to generate sufficient sales volume while serving a narrower market with a more focused portfolio of products.

Overhead expenses are higher than in the brokerage model. However, this may be partially compensated for by the loyalty of the field force, which will sell value instead of low price. This permits pricing at levels sufficient to cover expenses while maintaining profit margins. Company growth can be managed by increasing the size of the sales force. Although overhead increases as sales representatives are added, economies of scale are possible. Revenue increases as a result of expansion are more predictable because the sales people are employees, not independent brokers.

DIRECT SALES

Direct selling to employers and other potential plan sponsors has been used with some success, although it has not been the preferred method for most group carriers. For many years, certain Blue Cross-Blue Shield health plans distributed group products directly to plan sponsors through salaried sales employees. These salaried representatives would receive some incentive payments based on sales performance, but no commissions were paid to agents or brokers. One possible reason for the success of this application is the power of the Blue Cross/Blue Shield brand. In certain areas, strong name recognition and dominant market share resulted in consumer demand for the product. When there is consumer "pull" for the product, there is diminished value in paying agents or brokers to "push" that product. This model is still used by some local Blue plans and HMOs. Other direct selling also occurs through mass mailing, telemarketing and website marketing. This is often backed by a skilled fulfillment staff that helps direct the sale after the initial response. These techniques can be used for sales to plan sponsors and to individual participants in a sponsor plan.

MULTIPLE LEVEL

The multiple-level distribution model is the most advanced model currently in use for distribution of group insurance, and is more complex than the others. Under this model, the carrier uses different types of distribution, layered one on top of the other, to sell its products. The layers include a mix of wholesalers, retailers, brokers, life agents, general agents, salaried representatives, telemarketers, and direct sellers.

The distribution channels are extremely broad and enable the carrier to focus specific products into different channels. There is a mixture of low-expense models (like brokers) with higher expense models (like salaried representatives on a sales incentive plan). This permits the carrier to have the advantages of a dedicated field force, without the severe impact on pricing. The expense loads of the field force are blended with the lower-expense methods. Because of the complexity of this system, sophisticated sales management and marketing support are critical to success. This model is widely employed by carriers with a national presence. It gives the carrier the flexibility to exploit whichever channel or channels work in specific marketing areas.

SALES TO PARTICIPANTS

Some group insurance products require that sales be made to individual participants, after the initial sale has been made to the employer. (This is the "second sale" mentioned above.) These sales are usually made by specialized enrollment staff that may be paid by commissions, or by salaried enrollment specialists. The participants may meet with these specialists in the workplace, or respond to printed and website information at their convenience.

Health carriers, including HMOs, often market to participants. This is often needed where plan sponsors offer multiple choices of plans, and where different carriers may offer the plans. This is especially true with competing HMO plans, and where different models such as PPO and POS plans compete with HMOs in cafeteria plans. Once the sales representative has activated the employer group, employee meetings are held at the worksite. Enrollment specialists explain the benefits to interested employees, and assist in completing enrollment applications.

This type of "second sale" may include a situation when the employer offers competing plans from different carriers, such as an HMO and POS from one carrier and a PPO from another. This may happen when there is a strong local or regional HMO plan that would be desirable to the employees, and is offered alongside a competitor's PPO. In situations like these, the person doing the enrollment is surely attempting to "sell" his or her product.

A recent innovation is the "Benefit Fair." At a Benefit Fair representatives from all the carriers whose products the employer is sponsoring, including group life, disability, dental, medical, prescription, are available in a conference room or cafeteria. The carriers use tabletop displays, and give away inexpensive promotional items. Employees visit the carriers they choose, ask questions, and obtain marketing materials, plan information, and enrollment forms. The enrollment forms are usually completed and submitted at a later date.

MARKETING SEGMENTATION

Group insurance carriers often look at sales and distribution from the perspective of target market segments. Segmentation analysis is not de-signed to replace emphasis on distribution channels. Rather, it enables the company to understand its potential customers and focus its distribution efforts appropriately. As a result of the process, management can make specific decisions as to which market segments to pursue, with which products, through which distribution channel(s).

For example, we could look at segmenting by industry. A carrier might focus on public sector employees and dedicate its resources to the specific needs of that market. Certain group LTD carriers, for example, have focused on educators as a sub-segment of the public sector market. A carrier might choose to limit distribution to certain geographic areas. Another carrier might focus on associations and other affinity groups.

One common way for group carriers to segment business is by employer size. This is a convenient way for carriers to look at market segments because it relates to distribution channels. Certain size segments tend to be serviced by specific types of distributors.

SIZE SEGMENTS

Smallest Groups (2 to 50 Employees)

This small group segment is heavily regulated by "Small Group Reform" legislation in the U.S. Carriers are required by the states to operate under a variety of mandates, including such things as required guaranteed issue, community rating, minimum loss ratios, statutory plan designs, and strict limitations on substandard rating practices. In order to remain profitable in this environment distribution expenses must be kept to a minimum. Carriers offering products in this size segment often use the brokerage and general agency distribution methods, with little or no group field force involvement. Agents and brokers who operate in this market usually specialize in small groups only. The clientele tends to be less sophisticated regarding group insurance than in the large group market. Small employers usually do not have the resources to maintain full-time benefit managers or human resource departments, and tend to rely on brokers for advice on benefit plan management.

Smaller Medium Sized-Groups (51 to 100 Employees)

This size segment is not as heavily regulated as the 2 to 50 segment. For example, there are few restrict ions on pricing and underwriting, and no mandatory plan designs. However, to control expenses carriers usually limit their plan design offerings, and many maintain pooled community rating in this size segment. The group field force model would typically be used in this segment, while the brokerage and general agency models would play a more limited role. A carrier operating in both this and the small group segments would probably use the multiple-level distribution model. Employers and brokers are more sophisticated, and the client usually has staff dedicated to benefit issues. The client would typically seek the advice of a small to medium-sized brokerage firm for their benefit programs.

Mid-Market Groups (100 to 500 Employees)

In this size segment, claim experience is usually available, which has a major impact on product pricing for health plans. Flexibility of plan design is necessary. Employers in this size category are relatively sophisticated, and have benefit managers who closely monitor their benefit offerings. They require benefits customized to the needs of their business and the type of employee they hire. Self-insurance is a major consideration for certain types of benefits. These customers typically deal with highly skilled brokers at large local or regional brokerage firms. The process of obtaining and analyzing the information necessary to prepare a proposal requires the expertise of a highly skilled group benefit specialist, both on the broker and carrier side of the equation. Consequently, the group field force model is usually favored by carriers in this size segment. In addition, carriers often have account managers who focus on servicing and renewing these groups.

Large Groups (500 Employees and Up)

What defines a large group? There are no hard and fast rules, so size distinctions are somewhat subjective. Very large groups are usually multi-site and multi-state, and have full-time benefit and risk management departments that manage a complex array of benefit plans. Employees typically have a large number of plan options from which to choose. These customers usually deal only with large employee benefits consulting firms. Many carriers have "national account" or "special account" field forces dedicated to sales and service in this size segment. Locally or regionally competitive health carriers may be unable to provide adequate coverage nationally, and would then be limited to competing for business at specific locations only. Blue Cross Blue Shield companies, separate companies with specific localized service areas, are nonetheless able to market a national network of provider contracts, and can provide local provider discounts and customer service to multi-location groups.

ADDITIONAL DISTRIBUTION METHODS

So far, the discussion of distribution methods has focused on traditional models. However, there are other methods of distributing group insurance, often referred to as "alternative distribution." Alternative methods involve mass-marketing techniques such as television, radio, and newspaper advertising, direct mail solicitation, Internet website sales, and worksite marketing.

With the exception of Internet and worksite marketing, the products distributed through these alternative methods are generally not the same as the employee benefits that have been the focus of this chapter. Among the products sold this way are critical illness coverage (such as cancer-only coverage), hospital confinement benefits, accidental death benefits, and term life insurance. Television, radio and newspaper advertising often include a celebrity endorsement. Direct mail solicitations are usually linked to a credit card or to membership in an association. Since the carrier is marketing the coverage directly to the consumer, there is no broker or group field force compensation. However, there are significant marketing expenses involved, and carriers often retain specialty-marketing firms to do the work.

WORKSITE MARKETING

Worksite marketing of voluntary programs is more closely related to traditional distribution methods. There is usually a broker involved, and sometimes the group field force is involved as well. Employees are solicited at the jobsite in group meetings, which are often followed by individual one-on-one meetings, where the final sale is made and the application taken. In addition to traditional enrollment materials, the enrollment specialist often uses a laptop computer that includes an electronic application for coverage, policy illustrations, and other marketing material.

The coverage is typically paid 100% by the employee through payroll deductions. Sales commissions are higher than under the employer's base plan, because of the expense of an enrollment team. Products distributed in this manner include dental, vision, short and long-term disability, supplemental term life insurance, accidental death, and critical illness coverage. Another product that may be solicited at the worksite is "Gap" insurance, designed to reimburse the deductible and coinsurance under the employer-provided health plan.

Certain products that accumulate benefits over an extended period of time, such as group universal life and long-term care, are also effectively marketed through these enrollment specialists.

INTERNET MARKETING

Another alternative distribution method is Internet marketing, often referred to as e-commerce. E-commerce goes beyond simple product distribution. Companies are using this non-traditional tool for some of the traditional marketing functions: advertising, public relations, product promotion, image building, and brand management, to pave the way for sales. For example, most major carriers have websites where individuals can obtain information about the company, its products and services, local sales offices, charitable and community activities, the current stock price, employment opportunities, and so on. Recent research (primarily focusing on carriers marketing individual products) indicates that carriers specifically view the Internet as a strategic vehicle for effective communications, and for enhancing service to agents, brokers, and customers.[10] It is reasonable to conclude that results would be similar for group products.

---

[10] MarketTrends, *LIMRA's Factbook: 2005 Trends in the United States*; p. 64; LIMRA International, Windsor, CT, 2005

Many carriers are using the Internet for transaction management by giving their customers access to secure websites for plan administration purposes. Plan sponsors can do additions and deletions to their group bill, and participants can obtain information on policy and account values, find primary care physicians, and check on the status of claims. The carrier is in effect using the Internet as a tool to manage the ongoing customer relationship. The cost per transaction using the Internet can be significantly lower than toll-free telephone or Email.[11]

In addition to communication and transaction management, carriers also use e-commerce for product sales. Through the carrier website, consumers can obtain quotes for various forms of insurance coverage. Unless the carrier is a direct writer, the consumer is usually referred to a local sales office for assistance, generating leads for the carrier's agents and brokers. This is particularly true for group insurance coverage.

A recent innovation is group Internet enrollment. The employee enrolls for benefits directly through the Internet, making paper communication and forms unnecessary.

Internet enrollment can be done through the employer's website, through a third-party vendor, or through a link to the carrier website. This creates yet another opportunity to sell voluntary products such as ADB (Accidental Death Benefit), supplemental group term, and universal life. Because of the additional expenses involved, Internet enrollment is more practical for large employers.

Insurance carriers are not the only ones using the Internet for product sales. There are websites operated by insurance brokerage firms where consumers can obtain proposals for various insurance products, including group insurance. This is a variation of the brokerage and general agency distribution methods described above. The consumer would have access to the products of several carriers, and could obtain comparative pricing and benefit information. The brokerage firm would be required to maintain appropriate licensure for the various states where proposals would be delivered. This channel is usually viewed as a supplement to, not a replacement for, the traditional broker intermediary favored by employers for purchasing group insurance. However, brokers who do not adapt to this new environment risk losing a portion of their customer base.

---

[11] Ibid, p. 62.

CONCLUSION

The group insurance landscape has changed significantly in the last twenty-five years. There is no reason to believe that the pace of change will decrease. Government regulation, competitive pressures, the need to achieve scale, changing consumer preferences, and the demographic change of our population will all play a role in the evolution of the insurance industry.

Group companies are currently organized in a variety of ways. Some group operations are separate departments within life insurance companies. Others are primarily group health companies, or managed care companies. Some are dominant regional players, while others are large national players. Other companies are specialized niche players – focusing on certain types of products, or certain types of customers, or specific geographic regions.

It is difficult to predict which method or methods will be successful – consolidation, diversification, specialization, regionalization, or something else. The important thing is to be able to recognize what is going on: companies are developing and executing marketing strategies that they hope will ensure their success. There is one common underlying theme, however: markets must be identified, products developed, sales made, and customers satisfied. The thrill and the challenge are in the execution.

3 HEALTH CARE POLICY AND GROUP INSURANCE

Cori E. Uccello

Health care is regarded by many as a basic human right. Government policy related to the delivery of health care is often at the forefront of the public debate. We debate how health care is provided, how it is financed, and how it is regulated. Laws and regulations constantly change, and health plans closely monitor the changes and adjust their organizational strategies and processes. Strategic and operational direction can be greatly impacted.

To fully appreciate the role and importance of public policy for the health plan and the health actuary, it is helpful to understand:

- The primary policy issues and initiatives under discussion, including: cost, access, quality, and solvency;
- The motivations behind health policy initiatives;
- The environmental factors affecting the health policy debate;
- The various players (or interest groups) participating in the debate; and
- The differences in impact on health insurance customer segments.

The following discussion addresses health care policy issues from a U.S. perspective. The primary health policy issues of cost, access, quality, and financial viability are just as relevant from the Canadian as well as global perspective. Also, many of the environmental factors, such as rapidly escalating costs, are key issues in Canada as well. However, significant environmental factors, such as the Canadian medical financing systems and regulatory systems, are quite different. A more detailed discussion of health policy issues from a Canadian perspective is provided in the later chapter entitled *Health Benefits in Canada*.

Proposals for comprehensive health care reform stretch back to the 1960's, with the milestone establishment of the Medicare health insurance pro-

35

gram for the elderly. However, President Clinton's 1993 Health Security Plan proposal was the most recent attempt at comprehensive reform. More recently, health reform proposals have been more incremental in nature.

Growth in medical costs, a major health policy driver, was reduced to moderate levels during the 1990's. However, the first years of new century brought a return to double-digit medical claim cost growth. Although the increases have abated somewhat since then, health spending continues to grow faster than overall inflation, and faster than the economy as a whole. The enormous financial cost of providing health care services to the U.S. population is a key reason for such close public attention. National health expenditures, $1.9 trillion in 2004, make up almost one-sixth of the U.S. economy.[1] Health insurance premiums and direct health spending make up a prominent portion of the budgets of many individuals, families, corporations, state governments, as well as the federal government.

Perhaps a more basic and compelling reason for the importance of health care policy is the universal need for health care services. Common life experiences such as birth, injury, sickness, and death all give rise to varying levels of health care needs. The direct personal impact, combined with high levels of financial expenditure, assures that health care policy is likely to remain on the public policy agenda far into the future.

When evaluating public policy activity, it is important to recognize that the objectives generally pursued are prescriptive in nature. Affected interest groups drive the agenda, and address how health care systems ought to be structured. The activity of determining what is "good" or "bad" health care policy involves not only facts, but also involves political philosophy, core values, and views on ethics. In any public policy analysis, it is essential to recognize the distinction between normative statements of how health care systems "ought" to work and how they actually do work. To be effective, public policy initiatives must be founded on careful, objective analysis of economic principles, health care dynamics, and the behavior of individuals and organizations.

Debates on public policy take place amid a flurry of often contradictory information, undefined health care needs, financial constraints, and unknown program dynamics. Actuaries can add value to the health policy

---

[1] Centers for Medicare and Medicaid Services (CMS), Office of the Actuary, National Health Statistics Group. National Health Expenditure Tables, updated annually at www.cms.hhs.gov.

process by applying dispassionate analysis to health policy issues. This analysis often involves developing and testing financial theories relating to the health care system, and how the health care system would work under alternative circumstances.

The focus of this chapter is on the health care policy process, and recognizes that in the process, there are many players, each with a different perspective. Achieving resolution in a controversial health care policy debate will generally require compromises and tradeoffs from all participants. Providing sound quantitative analysis in the rapidly changing and often confusing arena of health care policy is a key role for the actuarial profession.

HEALTH BENEFITS ENVIRONMENT

To fully appreciate current health policy debates, it is important to understand the environmental context in which issues are debated, modified, rejected, or enacted. This section provides a brief overview of some of the economic and environmental issues affecting health policy.

HEALTH SPENDING RISES AS A SHARE OF THE ECONOMY

Total national health spending, expressed as a portion of the total economy, held fairly stable at nearly 14 percent between 1993 and 2000.[2] During that time, the growth in health spending was fairly similar to that of Gross Domestic Product (GDP). Over the next several years, however, health spending greatly outpaced GDP growth, and by 2003, national health expenditures rose to 16 percent of GDP. Although this ratio has stabilized somewhat since then, probably due to strengthening economic growth, the health expenditure portion of the economy is expected to soon begin rising again. As a result, CMS projects that by 2015, health spending will comprise 20 percent of GDP.

Although nearly all categories of health expenditures experienced accelerated growth in the early 2000's, the growth in prescription drug spending was particularly high, sometimes twice as high as the overall growth in medical spending. For instance, in 2000 prescription drug spending grew

---

[2] Centers for Medicare and Medicaid Services (CMS), Office of the Actuary, National Health Statistics Group. National Health Expenditure Tables, updated annually at www.cms.hhs.gov.

over 15 percent, compared to 7 percent for overall health spending.[3] Several reasons have been provided for this high growth rate. Spending on consumer advertising by the pharmaceutical industry may increase consumer demand, and investment in pharmaceutical research and development requires a pricing structure that will recover that investment. Most recently, however, the growth in prescription drug spending has slowed and now is more in line with growth rates of other health spending components.

The high growth in medical spending, and its resulting impact on health insurance premiums and government spending for health care, is a primary driver of many of the cost-related policy initiatives. As a major contributor to health spending growth, the pharmaceutical component is often a target for political action. However, as the growth in prescription spending has slowed, other components of medical spending, such as hospital costs and physician costs, have once again become targets.

INCREASING NUMBER OF UNINSURED

The number and percentage of Americans without health insurance coverage has been increasing fairly steadily over at least the last two decades. Because individuals age 65 and older have nearly universal access to Medicare, the majority of the uninsured are nonelderly. In 2004, more than 45 million nonelderly individuals (or 17.8 percent) lacked coverage, up from over 39 million (or 16.1 percent) in 2000.[4] The decline in coverage occurred among adults and was due primarily to a decline in employer-sponsored coverage.[5] Although coverage of dependent children also declined in the employer-sponsored segment, an increase in Medicaid and other state coverage among children more than offset this decline.

Increases in the number of uninsured have consequences that many perceive as negative. Those without insurance coverage receive a reduced level of health care, health care providers suffer losses as a result of uncompensated care, and reductions in employer-based and other private coverage place increasing strains on Medicaid and other public programs. As a result, policymakers are facing increased pressure to explore alternative ways to expand health insurance coverage.

---

[3] Centers for Medicare and Medicaid Services (CMS), Office of the Actuary, National Health Statistics Group. National Health Expenditure Tables, updated annually at www.cms.hhs.gov.

[4] U.S. Census Bureau. Historical Insurance Tables, updated annually at www.census.gov.

[5] John Holahan and Allison Cook. 2005. "Changes in Economic Conditions and Health Insurance Coverage, 2000-2004. *Health Affairs* Web Exclusive W5-498 – W5-508. Available at www.healthaffairs.org.

EROSION OF RETIREE HEALTH BENEFITS

The proportion of employers offering health insurance coverage for their retirees has been declining steadily over the past two decades. For instance, among firms with 500 or more workers, 46 percent offered retiree health benefits in 1993, compared with 29 percent in 2005.[6] Coverage rates among smaller employers are even lower. In addition, many employers that do offer coverage have increased the premium and/or cost sharing requirements. There are concerns by policymakers that the decline in retiree health coverage will lead to increases in the uninsured among early retirees (who aren't old enough to be eligible for Medicare).

To help address the decline in coverage, the Medicare Modernization Act of 2003 included a subsidy to employers who offer retiree health coverage. However, these subsidies are available only to retirees who are eligible for Medicare, not for pre-Medicare eligible retirees. Although most eligible employers have chosen to continue offering coverage, and thereby accept the subsidy, they may choose other options in the future. Other policy proposals aiming to address the health insurance needs of early retirees have included proposals to decrease the Medicare eligibility age or to allow early retirees to buy into Medicare coverage.

TAX TREATMENT OF EMPLOYER-PROVIDED HEALTH INSURANCE

The current tax code includes incentives for employers to provide health insurance to their workers. Employer contributions to employee health benefit plans are deductible as a business expense. In addition, employer contributions to health insurance premiums are excluded from a worker's taxable income. Workers can also make their premium contributions on a pre-tax basis if they are made through a cafeteria plan.

Although the tax-favored status for employee health benefit plans has likely played a key role in the widespread availability of health insurance, some are concerned that it has led to overly generous plans, which in turn has contributed to skyrocketing health costs. There are also concerns that the tax subsidies are not targeted effectively, because they provide greater benefits to higher-income households. As a result, there have been calls to re-examine the tax treatment of health insurance.

---

[6] Mercer Human Resources Consulting. *National Survey of Employer-Sponsored Health Plans: 2005 Survey Report.* 2005.

SHIFT TO LESS STRINGENT MANAGED CARE

During the 1990's and continuing in the 2000's, there has been a shift to less stringent forms of managed care. HMO enrollment dropped from approximately one-third of the group market in 1996 to under one-quarter in 2005.[7] At the same time, PPO and Point-of-Service (POS) enrollment increased from 42% to 76%. Only 3 percent of group health plan enrollees are in a conventional plan.

Public policy debate and consumer demand has played a role in this shift to less stringent managed care. A backlash against managed care covered in the media, and policy initiatives, such as those mandating the inclusion of "any willing providers" in managed care networks, have led – directly or indirectly – to an increase in open-access plans, and higher enrollment in less stringent managed care plans. Plans have migrated toward the use of financial incentives to steer consumers to lower cost options, rather than strict utilization controls.

CONSOLIDATION AND COMPETITION WITHIN THE INDUSTRY

The trend of health insurance industry consolidation has continued in recent years. Mergers and acquisitions have led to there being a few very large commercial insurers that, along with Blue Cross/Blue Shield plans, dominate the market. In a majority of states, the largest insurer in that state controls at least one-third of the market share, and the three largest insurers control at least two-thirds of the market share.[8] Insurer consolidation has transformed the competitive environment, and further consolidation is possible.

PLAYERS IN THE HEALTH CARE POLICY ARENA

When analyzing health policy issues, it is important to identify individuals and groups that have an interest in a given issue, and to understand their perspectives. There are many players involved in the health policy process, including the actuarial profession. Although elected officials are the ones

---

[7] The Henry J. Kaiser Family Foundation and Health Research and Educational Trust. 2005. *Employer-Sponsored Health Benefits, 2005 Annual Survey.*

[8] James C. Robinson. 2004. "Consolidation and the Transformation of Competition in Health Insurance." *Health Affairs* 23(6): 11-24.

who formally introduce legislation, other groups often forward their own policy proposals. These groups can include trade or industry organizations such as the Blue Cross Blue Shield Association or the National Association of Insurance Commissioners, research organizations such as the Heritage Foundation or the Urban Institute, or advocacy organizations such as AARP.

Aside from advancing their own policy proposals, trade associations and other organizations play other major roles within the public policy process. These organizations provide data, quantitative as well as qualitative, that help inform the debate and many times are on one side or the other of the debate. These organizations are also a strong force in getting the debate to reach the public. They do so not only by communicating the issues to their membership, but also by communicating directly to the public. A memorable example of this was the efforts of the Health Insurance Association of America (HIAA) in their television campaign against the Health Security Act.

Private research organizations, sometimes referred to as "think tanks," also play an important role in the public policy process. These organizations supplement the information available from resources within the government, such as the Congressional Budget Office, the Congressional Research Service, and state government resources. Private sector organizations analyze the current health benefits environment and how particular policy proposals would impact the status quo. These analyses include examinations of the impacts on individuals and groups, as well as the impacts on the health system and economy as a whole. Research organizations can be either non-profit or for-profit, and can sometimes be oriented toward liberal or conservative principles or funded by organizations supporting one side of the debate.

The actuarial profession, primarily through the American Academy of Actuaries, is also involved in the public policy process. The Academy works in both a reactive and proactive manner on health policy issues, depending on the issue and what the actuarial profession can contribute to the debate. The actuarial profession, through the Academy's staff and volunteers, has provided informal comments, monographs, issue briefs, cost benefit analysis, and testimony to the Congressional staff and the Administration. These interactions have increased the awareness and appreciation of the role of the actuarial profession in providing health care coverage to the public as well in the public policy process, providing nonpartisan technical support and analysis of the consequences of various policy proposals.

Many of these same players are active at the state level, including the actuarial profession. While each state has its own agenda with different players, the issues discussed tend to be similar across state lines, and national organizations are able to provide support and resources to the state organizations. Federal health policy agenda tends to focus more on health insurance expansion proposals, the tax treatment of health insurance, the federal regulation of insurance, and Medicare. State health policy issues tend to focus more on state regulatory issues, including insurer solvency and premium rating rules. The National Association of Insurance Commissioners (NAIC) is a primary resource for the states. The NAIC drafts model laws and regulations for the states to use, with the goal of furthering continuity among state lines. States are not obligated to use the models, and often make changes to the models.

MAJOR HEALTH CARE POLICY ISSUES

Health care policy issues can be organized under a few primary categories:

- Affordability,
- Access,
- Quality of care, and
- Solvency of public and private health plans.

It is difficult to completely isolate each of these issues, since there is a high degree of mutual dependence. For example,

- In a free market economy, affordability in many ways determines access,
- Quality, when there is no access, has little meaning, and
- Affordability and quality can often be in direct conflict.

With these interrelationships in mind, this section will now focus on current health care policy issues and the initiatives intended to address each of them.

AFFORDABILITY OF HEALTH CARE

As discussed above, aggregate spending for health care in the United States is growing at a fairly dramatic rate. As a result, health insurance premiums are also growing, threatening the affordability of health insurance coverage. Average job-related health insurance premiums increased by 9 percent in 2005. Although this is down from the 14 percent rate increases just a couple of years earlier, it is still much higher than overall inflation and wage growth.[9]

There is general agreement that health care costs must be controlled. This is because growing health care expenditures threaten to consume ever-increasing shares of the economy, leaving less available for other spending. It also threatens to make health care and health insurance less and less affordable to consumers.

However, disagreements arise regarding what is the best strategy or combination of strategies that should be used to reduce health care costs. Several approaches have been tried in the past, with varying degrees of success. The advent of managed care helped limit health spending, but rather than slowing the annual rate of spending growth, the savings were mostly one-time reductions in cost. Moreover, consumer backlash has led to a loosening of classical managed care cost controls.

Regulatory efforts at the state level have attempted to address health insurance affordability in the small group and individual markets by compressing the maximum differences in health insurance rates between different risk categories. The effect is to bring down the cost of insurance for those in the high-cost categories and raise if for those in the lower-cost categories. This leads to some increase in the number of lapsed policies, and perhaps in the number of uninsureds. Also, because rating restrictions do not address the underlying costs of health care, they do not help stem the overall growth in costs.

Policymakers are now pursuing a new generation of public policy proposals attempting to address health care and health insurance affordability. These include the consumer directed movement (to increase consumer involvement in their health care decisions), the use of tax credits to subsidize health insurance premiums, small group and individual market reforms, reinsurance strategies to address high-cost cases, and medical liability reform to lower health costs. Many of these approaches would result in only one-time decreases in health costs or health insurance premiums. Unless policies that reduce the rate of growth of health care expenditures are implemented, health costs will continue to rise.

---

[9] The Henry J. Kaiser Family Foundation and Health Research and Educational Trust. 2005. *Employer-Sponsored Health Benefits, 2005 Annual Survey.*

POLICIES TO INCREASE AFFORDABILITY

Consumer-Directed Health Plans (CDHPs)

A criticism of the employment-based health insurance system, and health insurance in general, is that it shields consumers from the true costs of health care. With employers heavily subsidizing health insurance coverage, and the insurance itself covering a majority of health costs, consumers only face their typically modest deductibles, coinsurance, and/or copayments. As a result, consumers have little financial incentive to control their health costs by choosing the most cost-effective providers and treatment options.

To address this concern, there has been a movement to consumer-directed health plans. The goal of these plans is to provide consumers with financial incentives and other tools to choose more cost effective care. The concept of consumer-directed health plans is evolving, and, to date, adoption of these plans in the employer-group market has not been widespread. Nevertheless, there is potential for wider adoption, as many employers are at least considering moving to this type of benefit plan.

Although specific consumer-directed plans can vary from employer to employer, the typical employer consumer-directed health plan combines a high deductible health plan with a health reimbursement arrangement (HRA). Workers can use the balance in the HRA account, which is funded solely by the employer and can accumulate balances over time, toward the deductible and other out-of-pocket costs. This approach provides employees with a better perspective on the true costs of health care and greater incentives to control costs, and provides employers with more explicit control of cost allocations to health benefit plans. Consumer-directed plans also aim to provide educational resources and decision-making tools, such as information on provider cost and quality, to help consumers make more informed health care decisions.

Health Savings Accounts (HSAs)

Health Savings Accounts are essentially a type of consumer-directed health plan. They are somewhat similar to Medical Savings Accounts (MSAs), which had been implemented previously on a limited basis. HSAs were enacted as part of the Medicare Modernization Act of 2003, and first made available in 2004. They combine a high-deductible health plan with a tax-preferred health savings account. Employers can set up plans for their workers, and both employers and workers can contribute toward the HSA. Alternatively, individuals can purchase high deductible health plans and set up their HSAs through the individual health insurance market.

Like Health Reimbursement Arrangements, HSA balances can be used toward deductibles and other out-of-pocket expenses, and any unused balances can be rolled over to the next year. Unlike many HRAs, however, HSAs are completely owned by the individual and are portable on job change. Money not used toward qualified medical expenses is taxed and, for those not yet 65, subject to a 10 percent tax penalty. Individuals age 65 and older can no longer contribute to HSAs, but can use any remaining balances toward medical expenses, including Medicare out-of-pocket costs or retiree medical insurance premiums.

It is too early to tell whether HSAs, and all consumer directed health plans, for that matter, will materially impact health care spending. Other questions that will need to be examined include whether individuals will have enough information to make their health care decisions, whether high deductibles will discourage necessary as well as unnecessary care, and whether consumer-directed plans will experience positive selection, attracting healthy individuals and leaving the less healthy to more traditional plans.

Tax Credits to Subsidize Premiums

Policies to increase the affordability and availability of health insurance have typically focused more on either expansion of public programs, such as Medicaid or the State Children's Health Insurance Program (SCHIP), or on expansions of private insurance coverage. Recently, policymakers have turned their attention more toward ways to increase private coverage.

One way to increase the affordability of private insurance coverage is to offer tax credits for individuals who purchase coverage. This approach was implemented on a small scale when as part of the Trade Act of 2002, health coverage tax credits equal to 65 percent of health insurance premiums became available for workers displaced by international trade and for retirees receiving pension assistance from the PBGC. Participation in this program is fairly low, likely reflecting that the eligible population is unaware of the program and/or finds that the remaining premium is still unaffordable.

Policymakers have advanced various proposals to use tax credits to increase coverage among the broader uninsured population. Specific proposals vary widely in many ways, including: (1) whether credits would be available only for those who purchase coverage in the individual market, or also for those with employer-based coverage; (2) whether the tax credits would be a flat dollar amount or a percentage of the premium; (3) how to define income eligibility for the credit; and (4) whether the credit would be given to individuals who purchase coverage, or to employers that provide coverage. Each of these design elements would impact differently the number of uninsureds who gain coverage, the impact on the current individual and employer group markets, and the cost of the program.

HEALTH INSURANCE MARKET REFORM

Although the vast majority of large employers offer insurance to their workers, small employers are much less likely to do so, in large part because the costs can be prohibitive. Similarly, people desiring coverage through the individual market can find the premiums prohibitive. As mentioned above, existing state regulatory efforts reforming rating and policy issue rules had the effect of increasing premiums for some individuals and small groups. In addition, most states have enacted numerous mandates requiring the coverage of particular services, providers, or persons. These mandates also increase the cost of coverage. Compounding this is the increased administrative costs associated with meeting the differing requirements of different states.

To address the perception that state regulatory efforts have actually worsened the affordability and availability of health insurance, policymakers have put forward various proposed reforms of the health insurance market. These reforms include allowing small groups to band together to purchase insurance. This could then avoid many state mandated benefit requirements and other regulations, allowing insurers to sell insurance across state lines. This would also mitigate state-to-state regulatory variations. Although these approaches have the potential to decrease premiums for some groups, especially younger and healthier groups, they also have the potential to increase premiums for some older and less healthy groups.

REINSURANCE STRATEGIES

Some policymakers have proposed that the government reinsure plans for the costs of their high-cost cases. Under this approach, once the claims for a particular individual exceed a threshold amount, the government would pay all or some of the claims. This scheme would shift the excess claims of the highest cost individuals to government, and would thus reduce premiums. In essence, the government would be providing excess stop loss in-surance. Lower attachment points would reduce premiums more, but at higher costs to the government. Thus, the cost of care isn't really lowered under such proposals, but is shifted to the government.

ACCESS TO HEALTH CARE

Assuring access to health care services is another key public policy issue that is perceived to relate directly to the presence of health insurance. Al-though the key concern is whether people have access to and are receiving the appropriate level of health care services, this can be difficult to meas-ure directly, and the presence of health insurance is often used as a proxy for access to care. Numerous studies indicate a substantial gap in the use of health care services between the uninsured and those with health insurance coverage. The uninsured are less likely to use preventive services includ-ing cancer screenings, more likely to postpone seeking medical care, and less likely to fill prescriptions than those with insurance. As mentioned earlier, 45 million Americans lacked health insurance coverage in 2005.

The Health Insurance Portability and Accountability Act of 1996 (HIPAA) addressed the access issue by requiring major changes in the group and individual health insurance markets. Some provisions aimed at increasing access include: easing portability of coverage from group to individual insurance, restricting pre-existing condition limitations, prohibiting dis-crimination with respect to eligibility or contributions levels on the basis of health status, and guaranteeing coverage for small employers and renew-ability for small and large employers. Notably, however, while HIPAA increased access to health insurance coverage, it did not address afforda-bility issues. (More details on HIPAA provisions are available in chapter eleven, *Regulation in the United States*.)

Some states also implemented any-willing-provider laws in an attempt to increase access to care, particularly for insureds in managed care plans. The foundation of a managed care system is the creation of a health care provider network, and the development of financial incentives to encour-age network utilization by health plan members. However, provider asso-ciations and some consumer groups criticized the restrictions that managed care places on the choice of physician. To address these situations, many states have adopted any-willing-provider laws that require managed care plans to accept into their provider networks all those providers that meet the network's qualifications and are willing to accept the network's reim-bursement rates. Although these laws can ensure that insureds have access to a wider variety of providers, this access also limits the ability of managed care plans to control costs.

Policies to Improve Access

Various options are available to increase the access to health insurance or health care. The policy measures discussed in the previous section that are aimed at improving health care affordability can also be seen to help increase the access to health insurance, by making premiums more affordable to some insureds who might otherwise not be able to afford the coverage.

On the other hand, some proposals aiming to improve access to health care could actually increase health care costs and insurance premiums, due either to expanding coverage requirements or by causing antiselection. If premiums become less affordable as a result, the number of insureds would logically increase.

Thus, any policy proposals in this area need to be examined closely, to determine their impact on both access to care and health care costs. Policy makers must weigh these often conflicting outcomes.

Common approaches to increase access to health care directly include:

- *Expanding community health centers.* The creation of new or expanded centers (typically with limited or no cost to those receiving care) would increase access to health care for the uninsured.

- *Limiting health plans' authority to control access to health care providers or services.* Examples include restricting the use of utilization controls and a wider proliferation of any willing provider laws.

- *Limiting or prohibiting health plan benefit exclusions.* Examples include limitations on pre-existing conditions and requiring coverage for certain services or providers.

Approaches to increase access to health insurance coverage include:

- *Mandate insurance coverage.* Either individuals might be required to obtain insurance, or employers could be required to offer insurance to their employees.

- *Expand guaranteed issue requirements.* Although HIPAA requires guaranteed issue for small groups and certain individuals, not all individuals have access to guaranteed issue coverage.

- *Expanding public health plan eligibility.* Examples include increasing the income eligibility or other eligibility criteria for Medicaid (typically to groups with greater income levels) or expanding Medicare eligibility to early retirees.

- *Expanding High-risk Pools.* Many states operate high-risk pools that offer a way for otherwise uninsurable individuals to obtain health insurance. However, enrollment in these pools is limited, and most temporarily exclude coverage for pre-existing conditions.

QUALITY OF HEALTH CARE ISSUES

Ensuring that insureds receive a high quality of care is one of the most complex health care policy issues. Although it is clear that providing quality care is desirable, and that, absent other factors, increasing the quality of care is also desirable, defining quality care is difficult. Definitions of quality vary, but most include references to efficiency, effectiveness, safety, balance between risks and benefits, and patient satisfaction.[10]

The numerous stakeholders in the health care arena hold different perspectives on what defines quality of care. For instance, patients desire access and responsiveness from health care providers and positive health outcomes. Some physician groups strive to preserve professional judgment (rather than treatment protocols) as to what is the best course of medical treatment for a given situation. Finally, purchasers typically focus on cost efficiency. Finding areas of agreement among the various stakeholders and resolving areas of disagreement are key to establishing a common methodology for evaluating health care system quality.[11]

Also complicating the issue of standardization of quality is that each patient can have variations in physical and psychological characteristics requiring a certain level of customization of care.

An additional complication is that there is no generally accepted methodology for analyzing and quantifying quality of care. It appears that the appropriate use of evidence-based protocols may offer a useful tool in addressing this type of issue.

---

[10] American Academy of Actuaries. 2005. "Pay for Performance: Rewarding Improvements in the Quality of Health Care."

[11] Jill Schield, James J. Murphy, and Howard J. Bolnick provide a more thorough discussion of the various stakeholder perspectives as they relate to quality in managed care in "Evaluating Managed Care Effectiveness: A Societal Perspective," *North American Actuarial Journal*, 5(4): 95-111. October 2001.

Measuring Quality of Care

The challenge of measuring quality of care raises the need for effective health care information technology. Access to information and the development of reliable public information sources is key to maintaining and improving quality of the health care system.

Efforts to measure quality of care fall into three broad categories:

- Determining whether providers or facilities are qualified to provide the necessary level of care,

- Determining whether the practice of medicine in a given situation is in accordance with adopted standards of practice, or with the practice norms in a given community, and

- Determining whether patient outcomes – or population outcomes – are in line with goals and expectations.

Accreditation systems for providers and plans

These systems generally focus on whether a provider or an organization meets applicable minimum qualification standards. For instance, the Joint Commission on Accreditation of Healthcare Organizations (JCAHO) compiles information on health care providers and has developed standardized systems for accrediting hospitals and other provider organizations. Similarly, the National Committee for Quality Assurance (NCQA) compiles information on and accredits managed care plans.

Practice evaluation

In the medical field, quality has traditionally been defined as care that is consistent with community norms. This has led to disparities in the practice of medicine in different geographic regions.

The adoption of national standards for the practice of medicine is a relatively new concept. However, in response to initial efforts of governments, insurers, health care consultants, and health plans to develop practice guidelines, medical specialty societies have begun to actively develop their own practice guidelines, which are more national in scope.

Measurement statistics

In order to evaluate performance, it is necessary to identify criteria that would permit objective evaluations, and ensure that results can be compared fairly.

Requirements in the selection of measurement statistics would include:

- that measures be relevant,

- that a change in practice have the potential to improve medical outcomes or health of a population, and

- that the area be one where stakeholders may be affected for the better.

In addition, measures must be based on objective scientific evidence. For this to be true, repeated measurements must produce the same results, the measures must accurately address quality of care, and factors other that quality must be accounted for in the analysis. Finally, the measures must provide meaningful and statistically valid analysis.

Several organizations have developed clinical quality measures, including the NCQA. The NCQA's Health Plan Employer Data and Information Set (HEDIS) includes information on various quality and performance measures, including member access, use of preventive services, and treatment of acute and chronic illnesses. Using this information, NCQA compiles "report cards" on health plans that facilitate cross-plan comparisons.

STRATEGIES FOR IMPROVING QUALITY OF CARE

Health Information Technology

Advances in health information technology have the potential to increase health care quality, for a number of reasons. They can facilitate better care coordination, help reduce medical errors, and enhance performance measurement. Policymakers have advanced proposals to set standards for health information technology, identify and reduce barriers for the electronic exchange of health information, encourage the sharing of health information across providers and consumers, and promote the adoption of uniform quality measures. Balanced against the benefits of greater sharing of health information are concerns about privacy. Advancements in health information technology will need to adequate address privacy safeguards, especially since many such safeguards are required by law.

Evidence-Based Medicine

As discussed above, clinical practice patterns can vary greatly by provider, without clinical explanation. Often, such patterns will vary across geographic areas. Further, it is often true that more costly treatment doesn't necessarily mean better treatment for a particular condition or procedure. To help better determine the appropriate type and level of care better for a given patient, there is a growing focus on evidence-based medicine. The goal of evidence-based medicine is to use the best available clinical evidence when making individual treatment decisions.

Pay for Performance

Sometimes provider reimbursement methods do not take quality of care directly into account. Some feel, for instance, that fee for service payment methods can encourage over-treatment. Alternatively, capitation methods might encourage under-treatment. Pay for performance programs are a new and growing payment strategy that use financial incentives to reward providers for providing quality care that, at least theoretically, provides the right amount of care. These programs are gaining popularity in the commercial market, and the Centers of Medicare and Medicaid Services has been pursuing the use of pay for performance programs in Medicare. Keys to successful pay for performance programs include the availability of the information needed to assess provider performance on a reliable and comparable basis, the proper balance of financial incentives, and program acceptance by providers.

SOLVENCY ISSUES

Health insurance companies guarantee the reimbursement or the direct provision of covered health benefits. This guarantee is a financial arrangement, which, if poorly managed, could lead to the insolvency of the health plan. Inherent in this financial arrangement are numerous types of risks. The actuarial profession is uniquely qualified to evaluate all types of health insurance risk-bearing entities' financial status, based on the nature of the insurance risks and the increasing volatility of the U.S. economy. In addition, actuaries estimate future contingent liabilities and, based on those estimates, determine whether a health insurance risk bearing entity has adequate surplus and reserves to meet future obligations with sufficient margins.

Solvency laws and regulation are key elements of health care policy because they are primarily in place to protect the public from the consequences of insolvency. With that purpose in mind, many believe that the risk to the public should drive solvency regulation, rather than the risk to the other entities doing business with the insurers. Whether solvency regulation should be a function of who owns or controls a given risk bearing entity, even if insolvency would not impact the financial risk to the public, is one of the primary issues in this public policy debate.

ADDRESSING SOLVENCY ISSUES

One goal of a solvency structure is to provide a regulatory and industry framework to measure, monitor, and ensure that health insurance risk-bearing entities have the financial capacity to provide health care for their insureds. Solvency structures are evolving to directly address the various financial risks inherent in different lines of insurance, and different types of assets held to back those risks. Most of the solvency standards applicable to health insurance risk-bearing entities are part of the current state regulatory framework. These solvency standards include:

- Risk based capital requirements,
- Financial statements based on statutory reporting requirements,
- Licensing requirements,
- The Insurance Regulatory Information System (IRIS),
- Company examinations by state regulators,
- Minimum contingent reserve and liability standards,
- Premium regulation, and
- Capital management policies.

As discussed above, some proposals to address health insurance affordability would reform the insurance market to allow the preemption of some state regulations. One concern arising from such proposals is whether and how state solvency requirements would be applied. When developing health care policy, it is important to understand the impact of having different solvency regulation or capital standards for different risk-bearing entities. Different standards have the potential to create artificial competitive advantages for certain risk-bearing entities.

The regulatory structure for solvency protection should continue to be reviewed in consideration of the evolving health care environment and the role of solvency regulation in protecting the public. Appropriate solvency safeguards with adequate oversight and enforcement can greatly reduce the potential consequences of increased solvency risk.

Actuaries and Future Health Care Policy Considerations

Any improvement to the U.S. health care system must be balanced, and must address the primary issues of affordability, quality, and access. As has been discussed earlier, these issues are not independent, and the system is complex. Any changes in one area can have unforeseen consequences in other areas.

Developing an acceptable proposal for improvement to the U.S. health care system depends on the ability to build consensus for an approach. Consensus building will hinge on the ability to agree on issues involving the relationships between employees, employers, medical providers, private insurance systems, and public/government insurance systems.

Actuaries, as experts in all aspects of the finance and delivery of health benefits, are closely involved in the analysis of health care financing issues. They bring essential analytical expertise to the development of practical solutions to health care issues.

SECTION TWO

GROUP COVERAGES, BENEFITS, AND PLAN PROVISIONS

4 GROUP LIFE INSURANCE BENEFITS

Michael J. Thompson
Frank Cassandra

Group life insurance benefits were first introduced in 1911. The initial focus was on basic group term life insurance on the lives of employees. Coverage was intended to provide for final expenses in the event of an employee's premature death. Benefits were typically defined as simple flat amounts, a simple function of earnings, or a flat amount based on the employee's position in the firm. There was no selection of amounts by individual insureds. Premiums were charged to the employer using a composite rate for the group, mainly to keep administration of the plan simple.

Group life insurance benefits have gradually expanded over time to meet the more varied needs of employees and their dependents. While traditional basic group term life insurance is still the most common form of group term life insurance today, more specialized and tailored coverage has gradually been developed. The most common types of other benefits now offered include:

- Supplemental/Optional Group Term Life Insurance
- Dependent Group Term Life Insurance
- Accidental Death and Dismemberment Insurance
- Survivor Income Benefits
- Group Permanent Insurance
- Group Universal Life Insurance
- Group Variable Universal Life Insurance

A description of the types of group life insurance plans, plan provisions, and related tax and statutory considerations associated with each of these benefits is outlined in the balance of this chapter. There is also a brief description of group credit life insurance.

Basic Group Term Life Insurance

Types of Plans

Basic group term life insurance plans are designed to provide a common level of basic insurance protection for the covered group of employees. Typical plan designs include the following:

- Flat dollar plans, such as a flat $10,000 for all employees.
- Multiple of earnings plans, such as 1 or 2 times earnings. (This is the most common type of plan design).
- Salary bracket plans, such as the plan described in the following table:

Salary	Life Insurance Amount
Up to $20,000	$ 20,000
$20,001 - $40,000	$ 40,000
$40,001 - $60,000	$ 60,000
$60,001 - $80,000	$ 80,000
$80,001 and over	$100,000

- Position plans, such as the plan shown in the following table.

Position	Life Insurance Amount
Hourly Employees	$ 25,000
Non-officer Management	$ 50,000
Officers	$100,000

Such plans are designed to preclude individual selection of amounts and hence minimize antiselection risk.

Many basic group term life insurance plans include age related and/or retirement related reductions in specified face amounts of insurance. Such reduction formulae are designed primarily to reflect the generally reduced need for life insurance at ages greater than 65 and in retirement. Additionally, such reductions help to control the overall cost of the plan to the employer, by mitigating the substantial increase in term insurance costs at higher ages.

A typical basic group term life insurance plan may contain the following type of reduction formula:

For Active Employees	
Ages less than 65	100% of Basic Annual Earnings
Ages 65 through 69	70% of Basic Annual Earnings
Ages 70 and above	50% of Basic Annual Earnings
For Retired Employees	50% of Final Year's Basic Annual Earnings

In the United States, age related reductions must be actuarially cost justified under the Age Discrimination in Employment Act (ADEA).

PLAN PROVISIONS

Basic group term life insurance includes plan provisions relating to eligibility, continuity of coverage, and benefit payment. The following discussion describes the provisions prevalent in most plans.

Eligibility Provisions

Under most basic group term life insurance plans, the eligible class of employees is usually defined as all full time employees working more than a minimum number of hours (typically 20 hours).

Most policies also include an actively-at-work requirement. This provision requires that an employee be actively at work, performing all the usual duties of his job at his normal place of employment, before the life insurance becomes effective.

Basic group term life insurance may be non-contributory (no employee contributions toward the cost of coverage are required) or contributory (employee contributes toward the cost of coverage). Non-contributory plans typically require 100% participation. Contributory plans typically require 75% minimum participation. The participation requirement may be a function of underwriting constraints, the size of the group, and statutory considerations.

Basic group term insurance plans may contain a "medical evidence of insurability" provision. Such a provision typically requires an employee to provide medical evidence of insurability (most typically by means of a medical questionnaire) for amounts in excess of a defined threshold. The threshold is typically a function of the size of the group and the underwriting standards of the insurer. Such provisions are designed to avoid a disproportionate amount of coverage on substandard lives within a group.

Most plans also contain a specified plan maximum amount of insurance. This provision is generally necessary to avoid disproportionate amounts of coverage on a single life or on a handful of highly paid individuals within a single group.

Continuity of Coverage Provisions and Conversion Rights

The insurance laws of virtually every state and province require basic group term life insurance plans to contain a conversion provision. The conversion provision describes the insured's right to convert his group term insurance coverage to an individual life insurance policy upon termination of employment or membership in the eligible class. The individual life insurance policy may have a face amount less than or equal to the amount of the lost group insurance coverage. Premiums are based on rates for a standard individual policy based on the insured's age at time of conversion. The individual policy must be of a form generally made available by the insurer, other than term insurance. A more limited conversion right is available if the group insurance for an insured's class ends due to termination or amendment of the group policy. The insured generally has a specified period (usually 31 days) after group coverage ends to elect a conversion policy. If the insured dies within the conversion period the amount that was eligible for conversion is payable on death.

Disability Provisions

Most basic group term life insurance plans contain one of the following three disability provisions:

- Waiver of Premium. Group term life insurance is continued without premium payment when an employee becomes totally disabled, provided the insured is less than age 60 or 65 when the disability begins, and remains continuously disabled until death.
- Total and Permanent Disability. When an insured become totally and permanently disabled, this provision typically provides a benefit on a monthly installment basis, equal to all or a portion of the life insurance benefit. On death, the original death benefit would be reduced by any disability installments made.
- Extended Death Benefit. Under this provision, a death benefit is payable if an insured's insurance terminates prior to age 60 and dies within a year of the termination date, while being continuously and totally disabled from the termination date to the date of death.

Benefit Payment Provisions

Group life insurance benefits are payable to the beneficiary who is designated by the insured. If a beneficiary has not been designated, the insurance is paid to the insured's estate. In general, the employer may not be named as beneficiary. A facility of payments provision allows for payment of the life benefit to specified persons related to the insured, or in some instances to a funeral home, in lieu of payments to the estate.

On death, several settlement options may be available to the beneficiary including a lump sum, a monthly installment, or a money market account typically with check-writing privileges.

Many plans now contain an Accelerated Benefits Provision, which allows a limited payout of the death benefit prior to death if the insured becomes terminally ill. The insured must typically have a limited number of months (usually 24 or less) to live. Typical plans provide for a payout of 25% or 50% of the face amount, with an overall maximum of $25,000 or $50,000. The trend over time has been for group policies to contain less restrictive limits on accelerated payment amounts. The insurer may pay an actuarially determined, discounted value to cover lost interest and administrative expenses.

Some insurers allow viatical assignment of group term life benefits. In a viatical assignment, the certificate holder "sells" (assigns) all of his incidents of ownership in the group coverage to a third party (viatical settlement provider). The viatical settlement provider pays the certificate holder a lump sum determined as an actuarially discounted value of the specified face amount. Viatical settlement providers are not regulated by state insurance departments, and cases of abuse of terminally ill individuals (by taking inappropriate discounts) and investors (by promising specified rates of return by investing in viatical settlements) have been reported.

FEDERAL INCOME TAX IMPLICATIONS

Deductibility of Premiums

Premiums paid by an employer to provide group life insurance on the lives of its employees are generally deductible on the employer's income tax return in both the United States and Canada. This applies to most basic life, supplemental life, survivor's benefits, dependent life, accidental death and group universal life plans that are described in the following sections.

Taxability of Proceeds

Death benefits payable under basic group term life insurance plans are excludable from a beneficiary's gross income in both the United States and Canada. This also applies to most basic life, supplemental life, survivor's benefits, dependent life, accidental death and group universal life plans. Payments made to a terminally ill insured under an accelerated benefit option are excludable from the insured's gross income, provided that the insured has been certified by a physician to have an illness which can reasonably be expected to result in death within 24 months from the date of the certification.

Taxable Income to Employees

In the United States, under Section 79 of the Internal Revenue Code, employees are taxed on the value of employer provided group term life insurance to the extent that such insurance exceeds $50,000. The first $50,000 of employer provided group life insurance is received tax-free by employees.

IRC Section 79 defines the value of group term life insurance in excess of the first $50,000 using a schedule of uniform premium rates known as Table I. Table I is promulgated by the Internal Revenue Service and is updated from time-to-time to reflect changes in the level and slope of insured mortality in the United States. The most recent version of Table I was published in 1999 and applies to insurance provided after June 30, 1999. It is presented in the following table:

Table I

U.S. IRS Uniform Premium Rates	
5 Year Age Bracket	**Monthly Cost per $1,000 of Coverage**
Under 25	$0.05
25 to 29	0.06
30 to 34	0.08
35 to 39	0.09
40 to 44	0.10
45 to 49	0.15
50 to 54	0.23
55 to 59	0.43
60 to 64	0.66
65 to 69	1.27
70+	2.06

Income is imputed to an employee based on the economic value of the coverage in excess of $50,000. The imputed income is determined as follows:

- The Table I rate for the insured's attained age on the last day of his taxable year is multiplied by the total amount of group term life insurance in excess of $50,000 divided by $1,000.

- Any required employee contributions are then subtracted from the calculated amount.

To illustrate the calculation, suppose an employee age 50 on December 31st of a particular tax year, is covered for $125,000 of group term life insurance, and contributes $0.10 monthly for each $1,000 of coverage. The calculation of imputed income for that employee is then:

- Table I monthly rate per $1,000 for an insured age 50: 0.23

- Table I cost of group term life insurance over $50,000:

$$((\$125,000 - \$50,000 / \$1,000) \times 0.23 \times 12 = \$207$$

- Employee contributions:

$$(125,000 / 1,000) \times 0.10 \times 12 = \$150$$

- Imputed income:
$$\$207 - \$150 = \$57$$

All of an employee's contribution can be used to offset the value that would otherwise be taxable to him, even contributions on the first $50,000.

The favorable tax treatment specified under IRC Section 79 only applies to group term life insurance plans that do not discriminate in favor of "key employees." The term "key employee" has the specific meaning in IRC Section 79. If a plan is found to be discriminatory in favor of key employees, the $50,000 exclusion does not apply to them, and imputed income for key employees is determined using the greater of the Table I rates and the actual cost of the insurance.

In Canada, employer payments for group life premiums including the applicable provincial sales taxes are considered to be taxable to the employee. This applies to all types of plans except accidental death and dismemberment coverage, which is taxed only in Quebec.

STATUTORY CONSIDERATIONS

Federal Regulation

On the Federal Level, the Employee Retirement Security Act (ERISA) provides significant protections to participants in employee welfare benefit plans. In general, it imposes standards of conduct for plan sponsors and imposes certain reporting and disclosure requirements. Group term life insurance plans are subject to many provisions of ERISA. The Age Discrimination in Employment Act (ADEA) prohibits discrimination in the workplace based on age. Particularly for group life insurance, it requires that any applicable age related reductions in group life insurance coverage be actuarially cost justified.

State and Provincial Regulation

In addition to federal requirements, any group term life insurance plan design must consider applicable state or provincial insurance law. Some common state laws govern the contents of group term life insurance policies and certificates. The provisions which may be regulated and some common requirements include but are not limited to the following:

- Requirements which preclude plans which permit individual selection of amount.

- Maximum employee contribution requirements

- Minimum participation requirements

Various other state and provincial statutes or regulations may apply, based on National Association of Insurance Commissioners model laws or regulations. These are discussed further in the chapters on regulation in the United States and Canada.

GROUP SUPPLEMENTAL LIFE PLANS

TYPES OF PLANS

Supplemental or optional life plans provide additional insurance beyond basic group term life, and are typically provided on an employee-pay-all basis. Generally, employee-pay-all optional life plans are written with a unisex, step-rated premium structure. Rates vary by 5-year age brackets. Such supplemental plans may be written with a flat premium structure by age. These plans tend to be provided on an employer subsidized basis, due to selection concerns, and are typically avoided due to tax implications. The amounts of insurance available are usually a choice of flat amounts (such as $25,000, $50,000, or $100,000), or a choice of a multiple of earnings (such as 1 to 4 times basic annual earnings). As many as 3 to 5 options may be available to employees in a typical plan.

PLAN PROVISIONS

Plan provisions for supplemental or optional life insurance are generally the same as basic group term life insurance, however there are a number of potential differences.

If a disability provision is included, it is usually limited to a waiver of premium provision.

Minimum participation requirements tend to be more liberal (lower) than for basic group term life, such as 25% rather than 75%. Also, due to the selective nature of supplemental group term life insurance, evidence of insurability requirements more stringent than for the basic coverage generally apply. Medical evidence of insurability is typically provided by means of a medical questionnaire, commonly referred to as a Statement of Good Health. Many plans may offer no coverage or very modest amounts of coverage without at least limited medical evidence of insurability, via a short-form questionnaire of 4 or 5 medical questions.

Also due to the voluntary nature of the coverage, a suicide exclusion is common in supplemental group life insurance plans. Such provisions exclude deaths caused by suicide within the first two years of coverage and within two years of any employee initiated increase in coverage election.

It is now common for employee-pay-all group supplemental life insurance plans to include a portability option. Portability provisions allow plan participants who terminate employment to continue their group coverage by paying premiums directly to the insurer. Under some portability arrangements, the premium rates paid by portable lives remain the same as those paid by similarly situated individuals under the active group. Under these arrangements, experience on portable lives is combined with the experience of the active group for experience rating purposes. More commonly however, the rates applicable to portable lives are based on a separate schedule of rates applicable to the insurer's "portability pool" and include a monthly administration charge to defray the cost of direct billing. Under these arrangements, the experience on portable lives is usually not included with the experience of the active group for experience rating purposes.

Experience emerging thus far on portable lives has proven to be signifycantly poorer than experience on similarly situated active lives reflecting the antiselective nature of the portability decision.

FEDERAL INCOME TAX IMPLICATIONS

Taxable Income to Employees

Generally, supplemental group life insurance plans are made available on a fully contributory (employee-pay-all) basis.

U.S. IRC Section 79 allows for such employee-pay-all supplemental life insurance plans to be considered outside of IRC Section 79 (thereby avoiding imputed income consequences) provided two conditions are met:

(1) The plan is employee-pay-all with no direct or indirect employer subsidies; and

(2) The optional life premium step-rates are all at or below the Table I premium step-rates; or alternatively, are all at or above Table I premium step-rates. (This comparison of a particular plan's rates to the officially published Table I rates is commonly referred to as the "Straddle Test." If a particular plan's rates do not "straddle" Table I, it is generally held that the plan does not contain any overt subsidy by age); the financial treatment of the optional life plan must be independent of the employer provided plan.

When a particular supplemental plan's premium rates are all at or below the Table I rates, it is generally advantageous for the basic and supplemental group life programs to be treated as separate plans for the purposes of IRC Section 79. This is because income based on the supplemental plan would otherwise be imputed at the Table I level, offset by (relatively lower) employee contributions. Any supplemental plan provided outside of IRC Section 79 is not considered an employer-provided group term life insurance plan and therefore, does not generate imputed income.

The most recent update to Table I (1999) decreased rates by up to 50% for some age bands. The premium rates for many existing supplemental group term life insurance plans may now, as a result of the decrease, be higher than the Table I rates. Plan sponsors may now want to consider this fact in determining whether or not to treat their current basic and supplemental plans as separate plans for the purposes of IRC Section 79.

An alternative approach to keeping an optional life plan outside Section 79 (supported by some IRS private letter rulings) may be to provide the optional life plan through a Voluntary Employees' Beneficiary Association (VEBA). Under this approach, the employer's involvement in the program becomes much more restricted.

STATUTORY CONSIDERATIONS

The same federal laws and regulations that apply to basic group term life insurance also apply to group supplemental term life insurance plans.

While the same state and provincial laws governing basic group term life insurance apply to supplemental or optional life insurance, it is worthwhile pointing out how these laws have generally been interpreted.

- Laws "precluding individual selection of amount" have generally been interpreted as not precluding offering an employee a limited number of selections under each of which an employee is entitled to a specific dollar or multiple of earnings amount of insurance.
- Maximum employee contribution requirements have been viewed in the aggregate where step rate contributions have applied.
- Minimum participation requirements apply to all group term life insurance provided through an employer. Consequently, if the basic group term plan meets a statutory 75% minimum participation requirement, then all the group term life insurance provided through that employer meets the minimum participation requirements (even if less than 75% participate in the supplemental or optional life insurance plan).

GROUP ACCIDENTAL DEATH AND DISMEMBERMENT (AD&D) INSURANCE

Group AD&D insurance is typically offered as a companion coverage to group term life insurance. The AD&D benefit is payable if an employee dies as the result of a covered accident. A percentage of the benefit (commonly 50%) may also be payable if the employee loses a member (defined as a hand, a foot, or the sight of an eye). If more than one member is lost in a covered accident then the full AD&D benefit is typically payable. Most policies provide that no more than 100% of the specified face amount is payable for all losses due to a single covered accident.

Many employers provide a basic AD&D plan where the AD&D face amount is defined as 100% of the basic group life insurance face amount. Supplemental (Voluntary) AD&D plans may also be offered providing supplemental accident coverage on an employee-pay-all basis. The coverage may be either non-occupational (only covering accidents not related to work) or 24-hour. Typically a covered loss must occur within a specified period (usually one year) after the accident. Voluntary AD&D plans may also provide coverage to other family members such as spouses and children.

Business Travel Accident Coverage ("BTA") is a common specialized form of AD&D coverage which provides benefits if an employee dies as a result of a covered accident while traveling on company business. The coverage amount is usually a function of salary (such as 2 times basic annual earnings) as is always 100% employer paid.

This coverage is described in greater detail in the Miscellaneous Benefits chapter.

DEPENDENT GROUP LIFE INSURANCE

TYPES OF PLANS

Dependent group life insurance is designed to provide a lump sum benefit to the employee in the event of death of a covered dependent. This coverage is generally only available when employee group life insurance is in force.

The definition of a dependent has been historically limited to an employee's legally married spouse and the natural and legally adopted children of the employee. Recent societal trends have resulted in employers and insurers increasingly expanding the definition of a dependent to include same-sex domestic partners and the children of the domestic partners. Employees seeking coverage on domestic partners are usually required to demonstrate that insurable interest exists on the life of the domestic partner (such insurable interest is assumed to exist automatically in the case of blood relationships and legal marriage). The demonstration typically involves certifying economic interdependence by means of an affidavit and/or providing documentary evidence of the interdependence. Generally, insurers have begun to accept valid domestic partnership registrations provided by certain local, provincial and state jurisdictions. The insurance laws of several states (including New York State) currently do not permit this more expansive definition of a dependent for group life insurance.

Originally, dependent group life insurance was designed as non-contributory or partially contributory coverage that provided very modest benefits to cover burial and other final expenses. The plan typically provided flat amounts of insurance on the lives of spouses and children. A typical schedule of benefits might have been as follows:

Coverage On	Specified Face Amount
Spouse	$5,000
Each Child age 6 months or older	$2,000
Each Child less than 6 months	$500

Where these limited amounts of insurance were provided, premiums were generally based on a composite rate developed from the age and gender distribution of the employee group. Any required employee contributions were also generally on a flat-rate basis for ease of administration.

Reflecting the greater prevalence of households with two working parents and the desire of employers to provide expanded access to benefits with limited cost to the employer, dependent group life insurance benefits have evolved into predominantly employee-pay-all programs with much more liberal benefit amounts. In many plans, multiple coverage choices (either as flat dollar amounts or as a percentage of the employees base annual earnings) are provided to employees. Maximum benefit amounts up to and in some limited cases exceeding $100,000 on spouses and $10,000 on children are common. To avoid severe antiselection, amounts on the spouse may be limited to some percentage (most commonly 50%) of the employee coverage amount. A typical schedule of benefits might be as follows:

Coverage On	Specified Face Amount
Spouse	Option 1: No coverage Option 2: $ 10,000 Option 3: $ 25,000 Option 4: $ 50,000 Option 5: $100,000
Each Child	Option 1: No coverage Option 2: $ 5,000 Option 3: $ 10,000

Where higher amounts of spousal coverage are permitted, it is common to see premium rates based on age based step rates. To simplify administration, such rates may be based on the age of the employee rather than the age of the spouse, assuming an age distribution of employees and spouses. Such structures are more risky for plans with multiple-choice options and where there are higher maximum amounts.

Coverage on children normally ends when the child attains age 19. Coverage may be extended to some later age, such has 21 or 23, if the child is attending college full time. A recent trend has been to extend coverage even beyond the otherwise applicable limiting age in the case of totally and permanently disabled dependent children.

PLAN PROVISIONS

Eligibility Provisions

The eligibility rules for dependents are usually the same as for health coverage, except that newborn children may not be eligible until they reach a specified age such as 14 days.

A deferred effective date provision may apply that provides that the effective date of coverage on a dependent who is currently confined for medical treatment in an institution or at home is deferred until the dependent is medically released from that confinement.

In addition, where higher amounts of spousal coverage are offered, they may be subject to medical evidence of insurability requirements, typically in the form of a medical questionnaire.

Continuity of Coverage Provisions

Coverage generally continues only while the employee's group term life coverage continues. Dependent coverage usually ends when the employee retires, even if the group term life insurance is continued on the life of the former employee into retirement. Conversion rights, consistent with those required on employee coverage, are generally included for spouse and child coverage. Conversion rights typically also apply when group coverage ends due to divorce or due to a child reaching the limiting age. Disability provisions are generally not available on dependent coverage.

Benefit Payment Provisions

The beneficiary for dependents group life insurance is usually the employee, and benefits are typically payable in a lump sum.

FEDERAL INCOME TAX IMPLICATIONS

Taxable Income to Employees

In the United States, if the amounts of dependent group life insurance available on the lives of spouses, domestic partners, and children are less than $2,000, the benefits are considered an excludable *de minimus* fringe benefit under IRC Section 132 and result in no imputed income to employees.

Where the amounts of dependent group life insurance exceed $2,000, income may be imputed to employees under IRS Notice 89-110. Imputed income is based on the IRS Table I premium rates less any applicable required employee contributions.

In Canada, premiums paid by the employer, including any applicable provincial sales taxes, are considered taxable income to the employee.

STATUTORY CONSIDERATIONS

Some jurisdictions establish a maximum amount of insurance that may be provided on the lives of dependent spouses and children, or place restrictions on children's eligibility. Such laws were adopted out of concern for the welfare of spouses and children. The trend has been for states to liberalize or repeal such restrictions, particularly on spouses, over time.

SURVIVOR INCOME BENEFITS

TYPES OF PLANS

Survivor income benefit plans provide a monthly payment to the employee's spouse and children on the employee's death in lieu of a lump sum death benefit. The benefit is typically expressed as a percentage of the employee's monthly earnings, and is intended to more closely meet the needs of the employee's surviving dependents. An example of such a benefit plan would be (a) a spouse benefit of 25% of the employee's monthly earnings, and (b) a children's benefit of 15% of those earnings.

The duration of the monthly benefit varies by plan. A typical spouse benefit is payable to the earliest of remarriage, attainment of a limiting age such as 62, or death. A typical children's benefit is payable to age 19, or age 23 if still a full-time student.

Survivor benefit plans were developed mainly out of concern for the welfare of financially unsophisticated spouses and were once very common. Such plans have grown much less common in the last 20 years, but remain relatively popular with employers in blue-collar industries and with some union sponsored plans.

PLAN PROVISIONS

Survivor income benefit plan provisions for eligibility and continuity of coverage are similar to group basic term life insurance, with two potential differences: (1) The conversion privilege applies to the commuted value (the present value) of the monthly survivor benefit, and (2) The disability provision is limited to a waiver of premium provision.

Benefit payment provisions are established by the plan and may include the following:

- *Guaranteed Benefit Period.* A period for which the benefit is payable, regardless of the surviving spouse's death or remarriage.

- *Maximum Benefit Period.* Benefits are not paid beyond a maximum number of years, such as ten, or not beyond a limiting age, such as 62.

- *Remarriage Provision.* Benefits may or may not cease on remarriage.

- *Dowry Provision.* A lump sum benefit may be payable on the remarriage of the spouse, to reduce the incentive not to remarry.

- *Social Security Offset.* Some plans may provide for an offset of Social Security survivor benefits.

- *Last Survivor Provision.* Benefits may be defined by the composition of the remaining eligible survivors. A level last survivor benefit would pay the same amount regardless of how many survivors are eligible. A joint and 2/3 last survivor would provide a benefit to a spouse alone or child(ren) alone that is 2/3 of the benefit while both are eligible.

Survivor income benefits are usually paid to the employee's spouse if eligible, otherwise in equal shares to the children.

FEDERAL INCOME TAX IMPLICATIONS

Taxability of Proceeds

With survivor benefit plans, the death benefit is received by the beneficiary in the form of an annuity. Each monthly payment is considered to be composed of a non-taxable portion and a taxable interest portion. In the United States, the portion of each monthly payment that is excluded from taxable income is calculated as the ratio of the commuted value (actuarial present value) of the expected survivor annuity (using the interest basis of the insurer) to the commuted value of the expected survivor annuity using a 0% interest rate for discounting. The mortality tables found in IRC Section 72 are used as the mortality basis for discounting.

Taxable Income to Employees

Survivor income benefits in the United States and Canada are considered group term life insurance. In the United States they may give rise to imputed income for benefits in excess of the $50,000 IRC Section 79 exclusion. Since benefits under survivor income benefit plans are received in the form of an annuity, imputed income calculations are based on the commuted value of the expected payments the insurer is obligated to make to the beneficiary. In the United States, the present value calculation uses a mortality table specified in IRC Section 72 and the interest rate used by the insurer to calculate the amount of insurance held by the insurer.

GROUP PERMANENT LIFE INSURANCE

TYPES OF PLANS

Although once more popular, group permanent life insurance is rarely provided today, largely because of the tax limitations discussed below. The following outlines the types of plans that may be available.

Single-Premium Group Paid-Up Life Insurance

A level death benefit is provided for a fixed premium, based on attained age. This product may be used by an employer to "buy-out" a retiree life insurance benefit, thus avoiding the need for future premium payments. It generally includes a level face amount and growing cash value.

Group Ordinary Life Insurance

This is the group counterpart to individual whole life insurance generally with a fixed life insurance amount, level premiums and a growing cash value.

Group Term and Paid-Up Plans

This coverage provides level insurance similar to group ordinary coverage. This coverage, however, splits the coverage into a combination of group paid-up life insurance paid by the employee and corresponding decreasing group term life insurance paid by the employer. The total face amount (term plus paid-up) is maintained according to the employer's prescribed plan.

PLAN PROVISIONS

Plan provisions for group permanent life insurance are similar to group term life insurance with the following potential differences:

- No continuity-of-coverage provisions are necessary for group paid-up insurance.
- The disability provision is usually limited to waiver of premium on the term portion of group term and paid-up insurance.
- The conversion privilege is limited to the face amount less cash value for group ordinary life insurance.

TAX CONSIDERATIONS

In the United States, employer-provided group permanent life insurance benefits are subject to onerous tax treatment under Section 79. Essentially, since Section 79 imputes income to an employee based on a formula using conservative interest and mortality assumptions (1958 CSO and 4% interest), the imputed taxable income for group permanent life insurance can be substantially *greater* than the economic value provided to the employee using the cash values defined in the policy. Employee-pay-all group permanent life insurance may be excludable from Section 79 and not generate any imputed income under the following conditions:

- The insurer sells the insurance directly to the employee, who pays the full cost.

- The employer's participation is limited to such functions as selection of insurer and type of insurance, providing the insurer with lists of employees and use of premises, and collecting premiums.

- The insurer or employer does not condition the sale on the purchase of other obligations.

GROUP UNIVERSAL LIFE INSURANCE

TYPES OF PLANS

Group universal life (GUL) insurance plans were developed in the mid-1980's as the group insurance counterpart to individual universal life plans started in the late 1970's. In general, they consist of two components, namely term life insurance and a side fund that accumulates with interest, to provide tax-favored savings and long-term life insurance protection. Coverage on dependent spouses and children may also be included under GUL policies.

The death benefit under GUL plans is defined as the sum of the term life insurance component plus the side fund component. The term life insurance component can be designed similarly to an optional life plan (a multiple of salary or a flat amount) with the side fund being added on. This results in an increasing death benefit. Alternatively, the overall GUL death benefit (term plus side fund) can be a level benefit, with the term amount (net amount at risk) decreasing as the side fund grows.

The GUL premium may be credited to the fund net of premium tax and expense charges. The term costs can then be charged to the fund, with the balance accumulating with interest. The GUL premium may be determined flexibly, with the minimum amount allowable being enough to satisfy the cost of the term insurance element, and the maximum amount being defined by the GUL policy. A target premium may be defined as the periodic premium necessary to fund a given level death benefit by a certain age, assuming the current interest crediting rate. The cost of term insurance, or term cost, is typically based on either one-year or five-year step rates, and are subject to change annually. In addition, a schedule of maximum term costs may be included in the GUL policy.

The credited interest rate for the side fund is set by the insurer, generally based on prevailing market conditions and investment performance in the general account segment supporting the GUL product. Rates are most commonly reset annually. There may also be a guaranteed minimum credited interest rate included in the GUL policy, typically 3% or 4%.

Plan Provisions

Eligibility provisions for GUL are similar to group supplemental or optional life plans. GUL may provide for continuity of coverage through some combination of the following approaches:

- A waiver of premium disability provision may apply to the term portion of the premium.
- A portability provision, similar to that described earlier for supplemental life plans, may apply where employees can continue coverage at termination or retirement, on a premium-paying basis.
- The accumulation fund may be used by the certificate holder to purchase paid-up insurance on retirement or termination. The paid-up insurance would generally include a cash value of its own.
- Coverage may continue on a non-premium paying basis, with monthly term costs being withdrawn from the accumulation fund until exhausted.
- A conversion privilege may be provided. The amount convertible may be limited to the total GUL death benefit (term plus fund) prior to termination, less any paid-up insurance purchasable by the fund.

The death benefit payment provisions in GUL certificates are similar to group term life insurance. In addition, all or a portion of the fund may be paid out as a surrender or a policy loan. As a surrender, the amount is directly deducted from the fund. A reinstatement provision is typically also included. As a policy loan, the amount continues to be considered part of the fund earning interest, but an offsetting policy loan interest charge is assessed. The policy loan interest charge is typically 1%-2% higher than the crediting rate. On death, any outstanding loans and interest charges are deducted from the death benefit otherwise payable.

STATUTORY CONSIDERATIONS

Generally, most provincial and state insurance laws and regulations that apply to group term life insurance are also applicable to GUL policies. In addition, many jurisdictions, in the absence of specific laws related to GUL, have extended certain individual insurance regulations to GUL coverage such as non-forfeiture provisions that afford protection to insureds with regard to cash value insurance.

To address past abuses of policy cash value illustrations in the sale and marketing of insurance in the United States, the NAIC has promulgated the NAIC Model Illustration Regulation (1997). In general, the model regulation regulates the form and content of any illustration (defined as any presentation or depiction that includes non-guaranteed elements of a policy of life insurance over a period of years used in the sale of cash value life insurance.) The goal of the Regulation is to ensure that illustrations do not mislead purchasers of life insurance, and to make illustrations more understandable. Insurers must specify which policy forms they wish to market with an illustration. To the extent that an insurer designates any GUL policy as a form to be marketed with an illustration, the GUL illustration must meet the form and content requirements of the regulation.

FEDERAL INCOME TAX IMPLICATIONS

Taxable Income of Employees

The tax implications of group universal life insurance are very favorable, provided the plan is maintained outside of Section 79 (in the United States). They include the following features:

- The interest on the fund accumulates on a tax-deferred basis.

- Cash surrender of the accumulation fund is taxable on the gain on surrender. Gain on surrender is defined as the excess of the cash surrender over the certificate holder's basis in the contract. Basis in the GUL contract is defined as the total deductions from the accumulation that were used to pay cost of insurance charges, premium tax expense charges, and any applicable administrative expense charges. Consequently, interest accumulations are only taxable to the degree they exceed the term costs plus premium tax and expense charges.

- The total death benefit (term plus fund) is payable tax free to the beneficiary.

A GUL plan may be maintained outside of Section 79 similarly to group permanent life plans. A GUL plan that is maintained outside of IRC Section 79 does not generate imputed income. A GUL plan provided under Section 79 (if employer contributions are involved) is subject to the onerous group permanent life insurance tax provisions discussed earlier.

Also in the United States, Section 7702 of the Internal Revenue Code contains certain requirements that assure that an insurance contract contains sufficient protection elements such that the savings elements of the program do not inappropriately dominate.

In order to satisfy the definition of life insurance under IRC Section 7702, the GUL certificate must satisfy either: (1) the cash value accumulation test, or (2) both the guideline level premium test and the cash value corridor test, both specified in that section of the code. If a contract fails to meet the requirements, it is not considered life insurance with the following serious consequences:

- All income in the contract becomes immediately taxable; and

- The contract loses the advantage of tax-free buildup of cash value; and

- Only death benefits in excess of the net surrender value are excludable from the beneficiary's gross income.

To the extent that the cash value of the accumulation fund in a particular GUL certificate exceeds a defined limit in relation to the specified face amount, the certificate may become a Modified Endowment Contract (MEC). A contract may become a MEC if it meets the definition of life insurance specified in IRC Section 7702, but fails to meet the seven-pay test defined in Section 7702A of the Internal Revenue Code. If a certificate becomes a MEC, it is subject to less favorable tax treatment, specifically, policy distributions from the certificate such as withdrawals and policy loans are treated as taxable interest first rather than non-taxable basis first and are subject to an IRS penalty of 10%.

GROUP VARIABLE UNIVERSAL LIFE INSURANCE

TYPES OF PLANS

Group Variable Life Insurance (GVUL) plans were developed in the 1990's in response to the generally superior performance of equity versus fixed income investments during the 1980's and 1990's. GVUL plans are very similar to GUL plans; however, under GVUL plans, there are several investment options available to the certificate holder to invest the cash accumulation fund. The options most commonly include various equity investment fund choices. In addition, most GVUL plans also include a money market or fixed interest rate option in addition to the equity options.

PLAN PROVISIONS

All plan provisions commonly found in GUL plans are found in GVUL plans as well. In addition, certain provisions specific to GVUL are included. Mainly these involve limitations on the amounts and timing of allowable withdrawals and movement of funds among and between the various available investment options and the fixed interest fund option.

STATUTORY CONSIDERATIONS

As is the case with GUL, most state and provincial insurance laws and regulations that apply to group term life insurance, are also applicable to GVUL policies. Similarly, many jurisdictions, in the absence of specific laws related to GVUL, have extended certain individual insurance regulations to GVUL coverage such as non-forfeiture provisions that afford protection to insureds with regard to cash value insurance.

The NAIC Model Illustration Regulation explicitly exempts variable insurance policies, and GVUL illustrations are not required to meet the form and content requirements of the NAIC Model Illustration Regulation.

Unlike GUL or Group Term Life Insurance products, GVUL is considered an investment product as well as an insurance product and is therefore subject to SEC and NASD regulation. Most notably, for example, a prospectus describing the elements of the insurance program and the underlying investment options must be delivered to each prospective insured before an application for insurance is taken.

GROUP CREDIT LIFE INSURANCE

A variation on group life insurance is group credit life insurance that provides a death benefit equal to the unpaid consumer debt of the insured. The creditor (usually a bank) is both the group policyholder as well as the beneficiary of the policy. The amount of insurance is tied directly to the debtor's account balance. The premium is generally paid by the debtor, usually as a component of the cost of servicing the debt. However, dividends payable under the policy are paid to the creditor. This feature can make group credit life insurance very profitable to the creditor, and consequently can lead to potential marketing abuses.

There is considerable regulation of group credit life insurance. Many jurisdictions have promulgated maximum rates in order to avoid excessive charges being made, in order to maximize dividends to the creditor at the expense of the debtor.

5 GROUP DISABILITY INCOME BENEFITS

Michael D. Lachance
updated by Daniel D. Skwire

Disability insurance is an excellent example of a coverage for which the insurance mechanism was created. While it has a relatively low likelihood of occurrence as compared to other employee benefit coverages, an extended period of disability can be financially and psychologically devastating.

Disability insurance is designed to replace lost income resulting from a serious accident or sickness. The purpose of the coverage is generally to enable the insured to meet their basic financial obligations rather than to assure a continuing lifestyle. The proportion of lost income replaced by disability insurance is usually less than 100% of the insured's earnings prior to disability. Unlike other employee benefits where the occurrence of a claim can easily be determined, determining whether someone is disabled can sometimes be quite challenging. Setting the proportion of lost income to something less than 100% of the insured's earnings prior to disability encourages the disabled employee to return to work as soon as they are capable of doing so.

There are two basic forms of group disability income protection that have been marketed in the United States. Group short-term disability (STD) typically protects income for periods of disability lasting up to one year. Group long-term disability (LTD) protects against loss of income for periods of disability lasting two years or longer, up to normal retirement age. STD has been very common among employers for many years while LTD has gained increasing importance in recent years. Both STD and LTD provide valuable protection against catastrophic income loss and are critical elements in a well-designed employee benefits package.

Long-Term Disability

Definition of Disability

The definition of disability is the key element of any group LTD insurance contract because it is used to determine who is eligible to receive disability benefits. A typical definition of disability in an LTD policy might contain the following language:

- During the first 24 months after the elimination period, Disability means that the employee, as the result of sickness or accidental injury, is unable to perform some or all of the material and substantial duties of the employee's own occupation and has a loss of 20% or more of pre-disability earnings.

- Following the first 24 months after the elimination period, Disability means that the employee, as the result of sickness or accidental injury, is unable to perform some or all of the material and substantial duties of any gainful occupation for which the employee is reasonably suited by education, training, and experience and has a loss of 40% or more of pre-disability earnings.

There are several important elements of this definition. First, disability depends not on medical symptoms, but on the insured's ability to perform material and substantial occupation duties (as the result of sickness or accident). Thus, a condition such as a bad back might prove disabling for an occupation that requires heavy lifting, but not for one that requires only office work.

Second, the definition refers to the employee's "own occupation" in the first 24 months following the elimination period (the time period after the date of disability before benefits are payable), but to "any gainful occupation" following that time. It also has a higher loss of earnings requirement after 24 months. The own occupation definition used in the first 24 months is more generous in nature, since it refers to a more specific set of duties and therefore makes it easier to qualify for disability benefits. Once an employee has been disabled for some period of time, however, it is common to use the stricter "any gainful occupation" definition in order to qualify for continued benefits. The stricter definition may encourage some employees to return to work in occupations other than their own. The length of the own occupation period varies for different disability policies. While 24 months is common, some policies use an own occupation definition for the entire benefit period.

Finally, the sample definition may allow someone who is working part-time to qualify for disability benefits (although, as described below, those benefits may be reduced by their work earnings while disabled), as long as the person's income is reduced by 20% or more of pre-disability earnings. This is known as a "partial," "residual," or "loss of earnings" definition of disability. Some policies, known as "total disability" policies, require the insured to be unable to perform any of their occupational duties in order to qualify for LTD benefits.

In recent years, some companies have begun to offer a definition of disability that is based on the insured's inability to perform certain basic activities of daily living (ADLs) such as feeding, bathing, and dressing. These ADL definitions of disability were originally designed for long term care insurance contracts. As a result, the ADL definitions typically require the insured to be more severely disabled to meet this definition of disability than they would have to be to satisfy the "own occ" or "any occ" definitions. This alternative definition of disability was developed to meet the needs of market segments that might otherwise be ineligible for disability benefits and to satisfy basic disability protection needs in price-sensitive markets.

ELIMINATION PERIOD

A second key feature of an LTD contract is the elimination period. The elimination period is the period of time that a covered employee must be disabled before they are eligible to collect disability income benefits. A longer elimination period eliminates the costs associated with paying many short-duration claims and reduces the cost of the disability insurance program. Elimination periods vary from 1 month to 2 years but the most common elimination periods are 3 months and 6 months. These two elimination periods are popular because they avoid gaps and overlaps in coverage when coordinating with 13-week and 26-week sick leave or STD programs typically offered by today's employers.

Due to the competitive nature of the marketplace and the needs of certain groups, LTD insurers offer various enhancements to the elimination period requirement. For example, some contracts allow a disabled employee to satisfy the elimination period with a period of partial disability. Similarly, some contracts allow the insured to return to work for a number of days or months without having to satisfy a new elimination period. This prevents a disabled employee from being penalized as a result of an unsuccessful attempt at returning to work.

Benefit Period

Once an insured has met the definition of disability requirements and satisfied the elimination period, monthly benefit payments can begin. The most common benefit periods are expressed as a number of years (typically 2 or 5 years) or "to age 65." The "to age 65" concept arose from historical traditions of retirement at age 65, even if involuntary. Since Social Security retirement benefits and company pension benefits commenced at this age, the disabled insured would no longer be in need of the income provided by LTD benefits. However, this paradigm is no longer accurate. U.S. citizens are living longer, and choosing to work longer, than ever before. In the United States, the normal retirement age for collecting full Social Security retirement benefits has been gradually increasing. As a result, the "to age 65" benefit period is evolving into a Social Security "Normal Retirement Age" ("NRA") benefit period.

The Age Discrimination in Employment Act (ADEA) requires that the cost of benefits provided to employees must not decline with advancing age of the employees. Currently, the federal government has provided employers with a "safe harbor" for meeting this requirement if they provide a benefit period equal to the longer of "to age 65" or five years. The ADEA also allows for other benefit periods if the employer can demonstrate that the costs of benefits provided to older employees are actuarially equivalent to those provided to younger employees. Most companies offer a Reducing Benefit Duration (RBD), which provides for benefits to be paid until age 65 for disability prior to age 60, and then grading down between ages 60 and 70, with a minimum benefit period of 1 year. The key issue for any employer using the RBD benefit period is to demonstrate that the shorter benefit period at older ages is offset by higher claim rates, so that the total expected cost for a particular age is not lower than that for a younger age.

Benefit Amounts

Monthly benefits payable are typically equal to a defined percentage of pre-disability earnings (such as 60%), not to exceed a predetermined dollar amount or maximum benefit amount. Since group insurance is provided by the employer, the earnings that are used for pre-disability earnings are those from the employer providing the coverage. Depending on the needs of the employer, earnings may include base salary, along with various sources of additional income such as deferred compensation, commissions, or bonuses.

The benefit percentage elected by the employer has a direct impact on the cost of the coverage even beyond the difference in the percentages. Industry claim studies show that claim costs per dollar of benefit increase as the percentage of income insured increases.[1,2]

Additionally, employer-paid premiums generally result in taxable benefits to the employee and employee-paid premiums result in tax-free disability benefits. Therefore, the same benefit percentage will result in a higher percentage of income being replaced when employees pay all or a portion of the premiums. This tax impact must be considered when determining the expected level of income replacement when pricing and underwriting voluntary and payroll-deduction programs.

The maximum benefit amount helps to prevent concentration of risks with one or a few insured individuals. These maximums may vary by industry to reflect the risks of certain occupations, group sizes, and the average salaries within groups.

BENEFIT OFFSETS

The formula benefit, typically expressed as a percentage of pre-disability earnings is often offset by income from certain other sources. This ensures that the sum of disability income benefits plus income received by the disabled employee from other sources does not exceed pre-disability earnings. If not for benefit offsets, the combination of Social Security benefits, retirement benefits, workers compensation, part-time work earnings, and LTD benefits could exceed pre-disability earnings for many insureds. Thus, the employee's disability would result in an increase in net income creating little incentive to return to their pre-disability status as an active and contributing employee.

Integration with Social Security benefits is treated in a variety of ways as selected by the employer: (a) only the primary insurance benefit may be deducted, (b) any family Social Security benefits received may be deducted, or (c) the family Social Security benefits may be deducted only if the combination of the benefit otherwise payable and the Social Security benefit would exceed some higher income percentage such as 70%. This last method is commonly referred to as "all sources" integration, and provides an incentive for the disabled individual to apply for Social Security benefits.

---

[1] Society of Actuaries TSA Reports 1982 & 1984, Committee on Group Life and Health Insurance, Group Long Term Disability Insurance.

[2] Milliman & Robertson, Disability Newsletter, June 1993, "The Impact of Replacement Ratios".

There are many benefits arising from a disabled individual receiving Social Security benefits for the employer and disabled employee:

- It reduces the cost of the insurance program for the employer.
- The employee receives higher replacement of income since Social Security benefits aren't fully taxed.
- It allows continued Social Security credits for the disabled individual.
- It qualifies the disabled person for Medicare benefits.

The are various methods in use to reduce LTD benefits by a disabled employee's earnings:

1. The proportionate loss formula looks at the percentage of lost work earnings due to disability and applies this percentage to the benefit otherwise payable. This is a version of partial or residual benefits, as described earlier.

2. The 50% offset method reduces the benefit by $1.00 for every $2.00 of work earnings received by the disabled employee.

3. The final method ignores all earnings during the first 12 months of disability until the sum of work earnings plus benefits otherwise payable exceed 100% of pre-disability earnings. At that point, the benefit payable is reduced dollar for dollar by the excess amount. After 12 months, either the proportionate or 50% offset is used. This method provides a large incentive to return to work at the end of the first year, and encourages a gradual transition back to work during the first year of disability.

LIMITATIONS AND EXCLUSIONS

LTD contracts typically contain certain limitations and exclusions. These are used to manage the risk of antiselection by an employer or employee and to avoid the potentially costly administration of subjective or abusive claims. As an example, it has been quite common to limit benefits for mental and nervous and/or drug and alcohol conditions to the first two years of disability. This practice has been challenged by claimants asserting that it is not permitted under the Americans with Disabilities Act (ADA). However, legal decisions have upheld the legality of their use by insurance companies in properly managing the LTD risk.[3] The two-year limit is extremely effective in managing the risk for subjective types of disability such as mental and nervous conditions. As a result, some companies have expanded its use to include other disabling conditions, as a way to manage the cost of certain high-risk industries or occupations. This exclusion is typically referred to as the Special Conditions Limitation clause.

For smaller size groups, where antiselection by the policyowner (who is typically also an employee of the company) is common, preexisting condition exclusions may be used. A typical exclusion would not pay benefits for disabilities occurring during the first 12 months of the policy for conditions, which manifested themselves within 3 to 12 months prior to issuance of the policy.

Other common exclusions are for disabilities resulting from an act of war, or those caused by an intentionally self-inflicted injury, or occurring during the commission of a felony. Normal pregnancy was once commonly excluded from coverage; however, in recent years most companies have removed this exclusion. A very high percentage of LTD contracts are written with a 3-month to 6-month elimination period. Thus, as a practical matter, there is little additional cost associated with covering pregnancy as any other disability.

OPTIONAL BENEFITS

The above paragraphs describe the basic benefits provided by LTD policies. However, there are a number of options that may be added to disability contracts, depending upon the needs and desires of the employer and its employees, for example:

- COLA - A cost of living adjustment linked to an inflation index is used to provide inflation protection for benefits received during disability.

- Survivor Benefit - A lump sum benefit payable to the insured's survivors upon the death of the insured.

---

[3] Weyer v. Twentieth Century Fox Film Corp., 198 F.3d 1104 (9th Cir. 2000); Lewis v. Kmart Corp., 180 F.3d 166 (4th Cir. 1999); Ford v. Schering-Plough Corp., 145 F.3d 601 (3rd Cir. 1998): Parker v. Metropolitan Life Ins. Co., 121 F.3d 1006 (6th Cir. 1997): EEOC v. CAN Ins. Co., 96 F.3d 1039 (7th Cir. 1996): EEOC v. Aramark Corp., Inc., 208 F.3d 266 (D.C. Cir 2000): McNeil v. Time Ins. Co., 205 F.3d 179 (5th Cir. 2000); Kimber v. Thiokol Corp., 196 F.3d 1092 (10th Cir. 1999); EEOC v. Staten Island Sav. Bank, 207 F.3d 144 (2nd Cir. 2000).

- Expense Reimbursement – Reimbursement for day care expenses.

- Pension Benefit – This benefit funds pension contributions that otherwise might be lost due to lost earnings caused by a period of disability.

- Conversion Option – This option allows insureds who lose coverage under the LTD plan to covert to either group or individual disability coverage.

- Spousal Benefits – Disability protection for spouses of insured employees.

- Catastrophic Benefits – An additional amount paid for a more serious type of disability, such as one resulting in total paralysis, or in the loss of two or more ADLs.

Election of these options varies dramatically by market segments in which the LTD product is sold. LTD insurers must have a full complement of these features available to meet the needs of employers in the market segments in which they compete.

SELF-INSURED LTD PLANS

Many larger employers choose to self-insure all or a portion of their LTD benefits. For LTD, some employers may choose to insure claims after an extremely long elimination period (during which benefits are self-insured) or to purchase some type of stop-loss coverage, in which they are reimbursed by an insurer for claims that exceed a specified cost. When accommodating self-insurance or providing stop-loss coverage, an insurer must feel confident that the employer has enough funds on hand to handle the volatility that can occur with LTD results. LTD by its nature has a low rate of claims but a high cost amount per claim. Tax reform legislation enacted in 1993, and new GAAP accounting guidelines such as FAS112 (for private employers) and GASB43 and GASB45 (for public employee benefit plans and employers), have made self-insurance less attractive. This is because limits on deductions, coupled with specific rules regarding recognition of liabilities, may adversely impact company earnings.

VOLUNTARY LTD PLANS

The majority of LTD coverage sold in the United States today is non-contributory, meaning it is entirely paid for by the employer. However, there are a number of trends that have contributed to a rise in recent sales of contributary, or voluntary, LTD coverages:

- Rising medical costs are forcing employers to pass some of the costs of employee benefits on to the employees.
- Expansion into new markets where the employers have not typically provided LTD benefits for their employees.
- Greater recognition of the need for disability coverage.

As was discussed earlier, one consideration for contributory or voluntary LTD plan design is the taxability of benefits. Under current tax regulations, if premiums are paid with employee after-tax dollars, then the LTD benefit is non-taxable. This results in higher income-replacement ratios when compared to a non-contributory plan utilizing an identical benefit design.

SHORT-TERM DISABILITY

As mentioned earlier, short-term disability is another commonly available group disability insurance coverage. The primary differences between STD and LTD are:

- STD benefits are paid weekly vs. monthly under LTD contracts.
- The benefit period for STD is considerably shorter than under LTD, typically 13 or 26 weeks.

DEFINITION OF DISABILITY

To be considered disabled, the insured typically needs to be unable to perform all the duties of the insured's own occupation. Also, the disability may be focused only on accidents or sicknesses occurring outside of the workplace. This avoids overlap with workers' compensation coverage.

Partial disability benefits can be found on STD contracts. Historically, disability insurers avoided partial benefits on STD contracts in order to ensure a simplified contract, to limit potential benefit abuse, and to keep administrative costs low. However, STD and LTD are increasingly sold together and this joint sale has forced disability insurers to look differently at some of these plan provisions in order to better coordinate the STD and LTD programs.

ELIMINATION PERIOD

The elimination period for STD is very short. Eight days is fairly common but the elimination period can be as short as 0 days. It is common to have a shorter elimination period for accidents than for sicknesses. Accident claims tend to be less challenging to administer. It is usually easier to verify that a disability was caused by an accident than it is to show that a disability was caused by a sickness.

Due to the short elimination period, STD has a much higher frequency of claim than LTD. It is not uncommon to see incidence rates for STD that are at least 10 times the incidence rates for LTD. Conversely, STD has much shorter claim durations. Overall STD costs tend to be much less volatile than LTD. This results in a greater proportion of STD programs being self-insured by the employer than is common with LTD programs.

BENEFITS

Relative to LTD, STD maximum benefit amounts are typically smaller for two reasons: First, most employees have other sources of funds which they can tap into to meet their basic needs for the short term. Second, an employer sick leave program often supplements the STD plan. This enables the employer to receive the insurance carrier's claim administration services and coordinate sick-leave payments while self-insuring much of the cost of STD benefits.

STD benefit payments are usually not integrated since federal disability programs have long elimination periods and part-time work typically disqualifies an insured from eligibility for STD payments. STD benefits will occasionally be integrated with employer sick leave benefits or with work earnings received.

Again due to the short-term nature of the benefits, exclusions for STD are few. They typically involve excluding certain causes of disability, such as acts of war and intentionally self-inflicted injuries.

MANDATED STATE DISABILITY INSURANCE PROGRAMS

Five states have mandated state disability insurance (SDI) programs. California, New Jersey, New York, Rhode Island, and Hawaii have short-term disability programs for workers in their state. To avoid over-insurance, insurers either offer longer elimination periods for LTD to avoid double payments, or reduce the amount of the STD benefit amount so that the sum of the STD and SDI programs match the benefit desired by the employer. SDI programs require continual monitoring because they vary by state and change frequently. As a result, most carriers offer longer LTD elimination periods and let the SDI program serve as the short-term disability program for employees in a mandated state. For all states except Rhode Island, the employer can elect to cover the mandated benefits under a private program. This can often be done at a lower cost than under the state run plan.

TRENDS

During the 1980's group disability carriers enjoyed a period of solid growth and high profits. As a result, many insurers offering group disability products increased their commitment to disability. Additionally, many insurers that had not previously sold disability products decided to enter the market. In an effort to maintain and increase market share, disability insurers began playing "product leapfrog" with a constant progression of benefit liberalizations: maximum benefits spiraled upwards; own-occ periods lengthened; "specialty" own-occ definitions of disability were introduced; and, other product features were liberalized in order to respond to marketplace needs. Additionally, because profit margins were high, many of these liberal plan features were introduced without rate increases, or at rates that did not adequately reflect the true cost of these benefits.

In the early 1990's, there was a major push by U.S. business to become more competitive in the global market. As a result, many corporations experienced management cutbacks, financial restructurings, downsizing, re-engineering, and every other productivity improvement program one can imagine. At the same time, increasing medical costs in the U.S. forced health insurers to look at alternative ways to manage the utilization of health care expenditures. The result was a period of tremendous economic stress on many professional occupations – the primary markets for disability insurers at the time.

The convergence of these marketplace forces caused many employees to use their disability coverages as never before, increasing claim costs and severely eroding group disability profits. As a result, disability insurers took many actions designed to increase the profitability of their disability lines of business. Rate increases, product changes, underwriting guidelines changes, and investments in more sophisticated claims adjudication systems and methods were all designed to better manage the risk of disability products and increase profits.

Fortunately for group disability carriers, rate guarantees on group disability coverages average about two years. Thus, group disability carriers were able to take needed rating actions, and LTD profits during 1996 and 1997 rebounded from their low point in 1995. Profits have generally remained in the 6% to 8% range every year since 1997. This profit range does not approach the level of profits during the 1980's. However, given the increase in competition since then, it is more reflective of what can be achieved in the LTD market under today's market conditions.

As of 2004, the group disability market totals approximately a $10.6 billion, consisting of $7.8 billion of LTD inforce premiums and $2.8 billion of STD premiums. In the past five years, STD and LTD inforce premiums have grown by an average of about 5-6% per year.[4] Prior to that time, growth in STD inforce premiums had been about double the rate of growth in LTD inforce premiums. That trend was primarily reflective of a major industry push toward insured STD products as insurers tried to develop integrated disability products. However, STD profits were often low or negative during that high growth period, and the slower growth in recent years has coincided with improved profitability.

Many insurers once theorized that packaging STD and LTD benefits would result in lower LTD claim costs due to the opportunity for companies to begin managing complex claims at an earlier date. As a result, they offered discounts to LTD customers who also purchased STD policies. More recently, however, it appears that this type of packaging has not justified the discounts being offered, perhaps because the presence of STD benefits makes it easier for employees to remain out of work during the LTD elimination period, therefore increasing the number of LTD claims. This phenomenon is difficult to measure, but group disability insurers remain focused on balancing the demands of growth and profitability however they can.

---

[4] 2004 JHA Group Disability Market Survey

6 MEDICAL BENEFITS IN THE UNITED STATES

Darrell D. Knapp

Group medical benefits have grown to be the predominant group insurance coverage in the United States, both in terms of premium dollars and covered lives. In 2003, more than 174,000,000 persons received employment-based health insurance. This represents over 60% of the population.[1] Medical benefit plans include all coverages that facilitate the provision of medical services to individuals. This includes plans that provide medical services directly (service benefits) and plans that pay for expenses incurred related to medical care (indemnity benefits).

Service benefits typically involve some restrictions of provider selection and assure no additional cost to the insured beyond the designated deductible, copay, or coinsurance. Blue Cross originated as a service benefit provider, providing for hospital care at designated hospitals in return for a periodic prepayment. Modern day health maintenance organizations (HMOs) are another example of service benefit plans.

As a contrast, *indemnity benefit plans* typically involve limited or no provider restrictions but may reimburse expenses only up to a pre-defined level. Any expenses in excess of that level are the responsibility of the insured.

Medical benefit plans involving the provision of services or reimbursement for services related to dental care, prescription drugs not covered under the main medical care program (often called freestanding prescription drug programs), vision care, and hearing care will be covered in later chapters in the book.

The growth of medical benefit plans has been largely aided by favorable federal income tax treatment of benefits. Under the U.S. Internal Revenue

---

[1] U.S. Census Bureau, *Statistical Abstract of the United States*: 2006.

Code, employer payments for medical insurance or benefits generally do not generate taxable income to the employee. This means that the dollars the employer pays for a group medical plan are of greater value to the employee than dollars paid directly to the employee, which would then be taxable.

This tax advantage has become a double-edged sword. Many employee benefit plans now provide benefits for services that go beyond the theoretical definition of an *insurable event.* Theoretically, an insurance system will only be effective if benefits are provided for events that are random, catastrophic in nature to the beneficiary and outside the control of the insured. If these conditions are not present, there is no insurable event and the system is subject to a level of self-selection that may cause the system to fail. Logically, this requirement would lead the health insurance industry to only provide coverage for non-routine, non-budgetable services that result in the incurral of significant expense. However, the impact of tax policy has led the industry down an entirely different track where benefits are often provided on a first-dollar basis for routine events such as annual physicals and immunizations.

One recent detour from that path is the tax treatment for Health Spending Accounts and Health Reimbursement Accounts. Under those programs a high deductible insurance program is coupled with a spending account that can carry over from year to year. Tax benefits accrue to both the insurance program and the spending accounts. This places this combination of programs on a similar tax footing as a traditional medical program. This primary theory behind these programs is that by returning some of the financial consequences for utilization of health care to the individual, wiser consumption of resources will occur. A side benefit is that the insured portion of the program more clearly has an element of requiring an insurable event.

DIMENSIONS OF A MEDICAL PLAN

As compared to many years ago when all medical benefit plans were somewhat similar, there is currently a wide variety of the types and structures of medical benefit plans available in today's market place. However, in an effort to broadly describe all medical benefit plans, it is possible to define any given medical benefit plan by its position on each of three dimensions or continuums. The first dimension is the definition of covered services and the conditions under which those services will be covered. The second dimension is the degree to which the insured individual participates in the cost of providing coverage or services. The third dimension is the degree to which the provider of services participates in the risk related to the cost of services.

THE FIRST DIMENSION

The definition of services covered and conditions under which they are covered include the following elements:

- Definition of incurral date
- Covered services, limitations and exclusions
- Covered facilities
- Covered professional services
- Other covered services

Incurral Date

In order to receive medical benefits, coverage must generally be in effect on the date on which contractual liability to pay for that service occurs. That date is generally referred to as the incurral date of the benefits.

Medical benefit plans have a variety of definitions of incurral date. The most common definition is the *date of service* (for professional services) and the *date of admission* (for inpatient hospital services). A more limiting definition of incurral date is date of service for all covered services. This definition would result in denying a portion of a hospital charge if coverage lapsed while a covered individual was actually in the hospital.

A less limiting definition would have contractual liability attached at the *date of onset of a disability*. This definition would result in all claims related to a given disability or illness to be said to be incurred at the first date of that disability. Under this type of provision, the definition of disability can vary widely, from being unable to perform the normal functions of a similarly situated person such as returning to work, to requiring continued institutionalization. This type of definition of incurral date is commonly used for plans that provide disability type benefits, such as disability income policies or long-term care policies.

Another alternative definition of liability attachment is connected to the *date a claim was paid*. Excess risk or stop-loss policies commonly attach liability on either a "paid" basis or a "paid and service date" basis. For example, many stop-loss contracts accumulate claims on a basis such as incurred in 12, paid in 15. This definition requires that a valid claim be both incurred during a 12-month period (generally the policy year) and paid or submitted for payment in a coinciding 15-month period (or within 3 months of the end of the policy year).

In addition to the definition of when liability attaches on an ongoing basis, many contracts include a provision that extends benefits in the event that an individual is disabled at contract termination. This type of provision is usually stated either in terms of a number of days from the date of termination, provided an individual remains disabled under a normal activities definition of disability, or until the end of an institutional stay beginning prior to coverage termination. The benefits covered under an *extended benefit provision* are normally limited to medical services related specifically to that disability and subject to the availability of other insurance. For example, if an individual receiving benefits under this provision due to a disability from a heart condition were to be injured in an accident, the charges stemming from that injury would not be covered. Likewise, if an individual has new coverage that replaces the terminated coverage, the extended benefits provision may not be applicable.

Covered Services, Limitations, and Exclusions

In addition to determining whether coverage exists as of the date the claim is incurred, it must also be determined if a given medical service is covered. Many *covered services*, and limitations or exclusions to those covered services, are subject to regulatory requirements that can differ broadly, depending on the regulatory entity that has jurisdiction over a given medical benefit plan:

- Insured medical plans are regulated by the state Departments of Insurance, which have varying mandated benefits in spite of efforts by the National Association of Insurance Commissioners (NAIC) to encourage similar legislation from state to state.

- Self-funded plans are broadly regulated by the Department of Labor under ERISA legislation that has very few specific references to covered services and limitations. Some states regulate certain (non-pre-empted) aspects of self-funded plans.

- The regulatory bodies for HMOs vary from state to state, sometimes being the Insurance Department, and sometimes being another entity such as the Health Department or Department of Corporations. This creates a potentially varying set of benefit requirements for an HMO plan than for an indemnity plan. On a benefit-by-benefit basis, HMO benefit requirements may be either more restrictive or more liberal than those of insured plans.

- The federal government has begun adding an additional level of regulation, through legislation specifying certain benefit provisions and operational practices such as mental health parity bills and minimum stay requirements for maternity.

There are several variations in medical insured plans that have emerged. One is in a *limited benefit policy*, often called a basic plan, which is generally available to uninsured or low-income individuals, sometimes without medical underwriting. These plans are often a result of health care policymakers' concern that the costs of mandated benefits may preclude individuals from obtaining insurance coverage.

Another variation is a *mini-med policy*. With these plans, benefits are very limited and subject to a small overall maximum. A mini-med plan might provide a fixed per diem for hospital stays, a fixed amount for doctor's office visits, and scheduled benefits for surgeries and diagnostic services, with the balance being billed to the insured. These policies limit the insurer's risk as the cost is known and the only risk is the frequency of utilization. These policies have been very popular in certain industries where the provision of some type of health benefits are desired to attract prospective employees but the cost of a full medical policy is prohibitive.

A third variant is a *short-term medical policy*. This is similar in benefits to a normal medical policy but usually requires medical underwriting and provides coverage only for a very limited duration. The underwriting treatment allows this policy to be provided at very favorable premium levels, but the limited duration would result in someone who develops a serious illness to possibly become uninsurable, and thus uninsured, at the expiration of the policy. This coverage does provide an effective bridge for someone who is temporarily without insurance benefits, such as during a change of employers, and may be a less costly option than COBRA continuation, particularly if subsequent coverage is assured.

Specific covered services and some limitations or exclusions are discussed in the subsequent paragraphs. Overall exclusions are discussed in the section on other contractual provisions, presented later in this chapter.

Covered Facilities

Covered facilities can include acute care hospital facilities, emergency room, outpatient hospital and surgery facilities, inpatient or outpatient psychiatric facilities, inpatient or outpatient alcohol and drug treatment programs, skilled nursing facilities or nursing homes, and home health care.

Hospital inpatient services include all charges by a hospital related to inpatient admission for medical stays, surgical stays and maternity admissions. Benefits are typically limited to the cost of average semi-private room and board charges and related ancillary charges. Charges for intensive care units and recovery rooms are often limited to a multiple of those charges for average semi-private. Treatment must occur in an appropriately licensed and certified facility.

As a result of federal labor laws, employers with greater than 15 employees are required to treat maternity as any other illness with respect to their medical benefit plan. For smaller employee groups, no maternity benefits or maternity benefits limited to a specified total dollar amount may be offered where permitted by state insurance law.

Inpatient facility charges may require some sort of *pre-certification* or *concurrent review* by the benefit plan administrator in order to be covered. The pre-certification generally requires that the covered member or their physician contact the plan administrator to obtain pre-approval of the number of days of the hospital stay. Approval is based on the medical appropriateness of the admission and the requested length of stay. Failure to comply with these pre-certification requirements may result in a cutback of benefits payable, ranging from a fixed dollar amount (such as $500) to a percent of the total charges (such as 50%).

Charges related to emergency room use often have some limitations applied, to avoid excess utilization of the hospital emergency room. These limitations frequently involve defining emergency as requiring a treatment event such as the administration of an intravenous needle, life-threatening illness, treatment due to accidental injury, or subsequent admission. In addition, benefits payable for services in the emergency room often require higher deductibles or copays in order to discourage emergency room use. Facility charges for outpatient surgery are normally covered at full charges. Outpatient surgery is often: (1) mandatory for a defined list of procedures, in an effort to discourage unnecessary hospital admissions, and/or (2) subject to pre-certification requirements similar to that previously discussed for inpatient. Another method utilized to encourage the use of outpatient surgery is to increase the percentage benefit payable or to reduce or eliminate deductibles or copays.

Charges related to psychiatric admissions and alcohol and drug treatment are often limited by an annual or a lifetime maximum benefit, and are required to be performed in a facility or by a provider licensed for that particular use. This is one area of coverage that is frequently subject to varying state mandates, ranging from "covered as any other illness" to a small coverage maximum. In 1996 the federal government passed legislation restricting the types of limitations available on many benefit plans. This legislation prohibits fixed dollar benefit maximums. However, the legislation still allows programs to limit the level of reimbursement available or the number of services provided.

Charges related to service provided by a skilled nursing facility are generally covered if performed by a licensed facility providing skilled nursing care as opposed to custodial care. Limitations also include a requirement that the admission in the skilled nursing facility (and continued stay) is in lieu of hospitalization. This is in contrast to a long-term care insurance policy, which often provides coverage based on a deficiency in the ability to perform specified activities of daily living or the medical necessity of custodial (non-acute) care.

Coverage for home health care services are also limited to those services performed in lieu of other treatment being required. The services are often covered on an extra contractual basis approved by a case manager working on behalf of the plan administrator.

Certain programs also attempt to direct the insured to a specific facility through either varying the level of available benefit (such as in a preferred provider organization or PPO) or through limiting coverage only to specified providers (such as in a closed-panel HMO). This redirection is generally coupled with provider contracts favorable to the insurer, which creates a less expensive product for the consumer.

Covered Professional Services

Coverage for professional services is generally limited to licensed or board certified providers. The definition of providers is well defined and may exclude certain provider types such as dentists, chiropractors, naturopaths, or podiatrists. These exclusions are often limited by state mandates requiring coverage for certain providers.

Coverage for professional services related to surgery includes surgeries performed on an inpatient, outpatient, and office basis. Coverage for outpatient or office surgery frequently will include a list of procedures for which surgery is required to be performed on that basis. Other typical limitations include a provision reducing payment for multiple procedures and provisions regarding charges from an assistant surgeon, such as paying at a reduced percentage fee schedule or refusing to pay at teaching hospitals where interns are readily available as assistant surgeons. Charges related to anesthesia are typically covered with similar limitations as surgery.

Covered services provided by physicians may include office visits, home visits, hospital visits, emergency room visits, and preventive care. Hospital visits are generally limited to one visit per day, and are usually assumed to be included in surgical fees if the visit is a follow-up to a surgical procedure. Physicians' charges in the emergency room are often subject to the same restrictions as emergency room facility charges. Visits related to preventive care are not covered by many insurance plans but are generally covered by HMOs. However, certain states have mandated that preventive benefits be covered for young children utilizing pediatricians, guidelines for frequency of visits and the appropriate immunizations. The reason for not covering preventive benefits historically has been that a preventive office visit is a small expenditure in which utilization is controlled by the individual obtaining the service and thus does not meet the definition of an insurable event. This results in coverage for preventive physician visits being somewhat inappropriate for a true insurance contract, but entirely appropriate for an employee benefit plan. Conversely, managed care plans assert that these preventative services, which may not be performed if not covered, ultimately reduce the cost of medical care through prevention and early detection and interdiction of medical conditions. Many indemnity plans are rethinking this position and increasing the availability of preventative coverage due to market demands.

Services for an obstetrician or a gynecologist are generally covered as any other provider. However, most insurance plans exempt routine exams provided by such physicians. Physician services related to a pregnancy are covered comparably to facility charges.

Additional professional services include consultations (which may require referral), outpatient psychiatric treatment, outpatient alcohol and drug treatment, physical therapy (which may include a requirement to establish improvement or anticipated improvement in the defined period of time), and immunizations and injections (which are generally excluded or covered under a defined schedule).

Certain benefit plans attempt to direct the insured to a given set of providers, in a fashion similar to that discussed in the Facilities section above. In addition, some plans require that certain conditions be met before coverage is available. The most common example of this is referred to as a *gatekeeper requirement.* This is where an insured designates a primary care physician. Then all access to other covered services requires a referral from that designated physician.

The selection of providers to be included in an insurer's "preferred" list involves contracting with those providers and a process called *credentialing.* The credentialing process includes assuring the provider meets the licensing, quality and efficiency standards of the insuring organization. After the initial contracting stage, providers periodically go through a similar process of *recredentialing* to assure the standards continue to be met. Today, a number of carriers are using stronger recredentialing requirements than previously, to replace or allow loosening of gatekeeper referral requirements.

Other Covered Services

Other covered services under medical contracts typically include diagnostic, X-ray and lab, prescription drugs, appliances and durable medical equipment, ambulance services, private duty nursing, and wellness benefits.

Medical benefit plans covering prescription drugs are becoming an industry unto themselves. Most often, prescription drug benefits are part of a freestanding drug program that includes a separate deductible or copayment per prescription. Other features common in prescription drug plans include provisions requiring utilization of mail order services for maintenance drugs, and incentives to encourage substitutions of drugs available on a generic basis or on a specified listing of preferred drugs referred to as a *formulary* (the incentives often being to vary the copay or deductible levels). Various methods of managing prescription patterns are used, including on-line databases that compare a physician's prescription patterns against a specified formulary for treatment. Many freestanding drug programs are finding that major pharmaceutical manufacturers are willing to provide significant rebates in exchange for preferred or exclusive positioning in a formulary. Another facet of coverage relating to prescription drugs is the inclusion or the exclusion of oral contraceptives as a covered expense. This is an expense that is typically felt to be an uninsurable event, but yet is considered a valuable benefit in an employee benefit plan. Oral contraceptives are required to be provided in a number of states.

Coverage related to appliances and durable medical equipment is usually centered around a decision whether it would be more economical to rent or to purchase a given apparatus. Durable medical equipment purchases frequently require the approval of a case manager acting on behalf of the plan administrator to assure benefit dollars are spent judiciously.

Coverage regarding ambulance services normally contains a provision providing transportation to the nearest facility and may have special conditions on the utilization of an air ambulance.

Private duty nursing coverage is generally provided only in the event that such service is in lieu of other more expensive services. This coverage is often approved in conjunction with the case manager.

In addition to providing reimbursement for medical services, many employee benefit plans also provide *wellness benefits*. These can include training classes and encouragement for healthy life styles such as smoking cessation, weight loss, and dietary training. In addition, wellness benefits often include profiling of, and recommendations regarding, each covered individual's health status and lifestyle. This profiling may include analysis of questionnaires completed by the covered individuals and medical analysis such as blood work.

Nurse help lines are another benefit growing in popularity. This dial-in service provides the insured contact with a nurse to perform triage for virtually any medical condition. This service includes the dual benefits of providing an additional service to the insured, while helping assure the medical care is high quality and cost-efficient.

Disease management benefits are also rapidly expanding. These are typically non-contractual benefits provided to specifically identified individuals at increased health risk due to the presence of chronic diseases. Some carriers have found have targeting specific additional benefits to individuals with chronic conditions, such as diabetes or heart disease, will result in both better health for these individuals and lower long term costs, as conditions are promptly treated before complications or co-morbidities occur.

THE SECOND DIMENSION

The second dimension in defining a medical benefit plan is the degree to which the insured shares in the cost of medical benefit plan.

Purposes

Generally, having the insured share in the cost of the plan serves the following three basic purposes:

- *Control of Utilization.* It is widely felt that requiring a covered individual to share in the cost of a medical benefit plan has significant utilization controls. Several studies have shown drastic reductions in utilization when an insurance plan is subject to deductibles, copays, or coinsurance.[2] Proponents of this philosophy argue that it is desirable to place cost concerns in the hands of the ultimate purchaser of health care services: the covered individual. Opponents of this philosophy are concerned that the reduced utilization gained through such cost sharing will result in either decreased general health status or increased health care expenditures at a slightly delayed time as untreated medical conditions fester and worsen.

- *Control of Costs.* Requiring the covered individual to share in the cost lowers the premium cost, and can potentially provide more affordable coverage. A counter argument is that federal tax policy which currently provides for full deductibility of employer-provided insurance premiums, and only limited deductibility of medical care costs, actually encourages maximizing the amount to be paid in premiums and minimizing the amount of cost sharing at point of claim.

- *Control of Risk to the Insurer.* As discussed earlier, many covered benefits, although a valuable portion of an employee benefit program, do not truly meet the definition of an insurable risk. Increasing cost sharing on behalf of the covered individual results in a benefit program that more truly represents an insurable risk.

Provisions for Cost Sharing

The individual can share in the cost of the benefit program through contributions (premiums) or participating in the cost of medical care. Sharing

---

[2] The first of these studies was a study by the Rand Corporation entitled "Does Free Care Improve Adults' Health?" published in The New England Journal of Medicine on December 8, 1983. In addition to published studies, many experienced actuaries have observed the phenomena in their company experience. A number of organizations that offer high deductible programs or "medical savings accounts" are also noting this phenomenon.

in contributions primarily addresses the objective of controlling the employer's cost through contributions by the employee. This essentially results in all employees sharing equally, or sometimes proportionally to income level, regardless of the level of health care resources consumed. However, as the contribution sharing grows, the number of people dropping out of an employer's program will likely increase, because some individuals will no longer consider participation as either a reasonable purchase or affordable. As a group, those dropping out will tend to be healthier (the sicker group finding the coverage more valuable), and generally consume fewer health care services. This leaves the remaining participating pool to have a higher average cost.

There are a number of provisions which result in the covered individual sharing in the cost of medical care including deductibles, coinsurance, copays, UCR (usual, customary, and reasonable) charge levels, paying at a fee schedule or per diem (per inpatient day), annual maximum payments, lifetime maximum payments, daily limits on specified services (also called internal limits), and limits on the number of days covered.

A *deductible* may have many forms. It can be a fixed dollar amount, a deductible per hospital admission, or a corridor deductible (a deductible applied after a given level of benefits have been exceeded). It can be stated as a percent of salary or may include family limitations. Deductibles stated as a percentage of salary or family limits (such as a family paying a total deductible of no more than two times the individual deductible) attempt to deal with issues of equity and affordability inside the employee benefit plan.

Another provision relating to deductibles is a *carryover provision* whereby any claims applied to the deductible in the last quarter of a deductible accumulation period (often a calendar year) are also carried over and applied to meet the deductible in the subsequent period. This attempts to correct a perceived inequity that may arise if, for example, an individual has no charges until the end of December in a calendar year deductible plan, and then meets the deductible only to have it reapplied on January 1. This provision is often difficult to administer, and is becoming less common.

Coinsurance refers to the percentage of covered services paid for by the insurer after the insured meets the deductible. The most common coinsurance level is 80% up to a given stop-loss amount. The stop-loss amount is stated either in terms of the maximum out-of-pocket expense of the covered individual or the total covered charges subject to the coinsurance provision. For example, a plan with a $100 deductible and 80% coinsurance of the next $5,000 of charges would require a covered individual to pay the first $100 of covered expenses and 20% of the next $5,000 of charges to a maximum limit of $100 + (.20)(5,000) = \$1,100$.

The coinsurance level can be varied for different services to control or encourage specific behavior. For example, an insurer might provide 100% benefit payment for outpatient surgery but 80% for inpatient surgery. In addition, a severe coinsurance level is often used to control behavior and control the insurer's risk when medical necessity is not clearly definable for a covered service such as for psychiatric care or physical therapy. This severe coinsurance, often as low as 50%, has the double impact of reducing risk to the medical benefit plan as well as creating a significant utilization control on behalf of the covered individual who is personally funding the coinsurance.

Another common method of cost-sharing involving direct payment by the insured is the use of *copays*. Copays are typically a fixed dollar amount required to be paid as of the time each covered service takes place. Copays can vary significantly by service type to create incentives which impact utilization. For example, a plan might include a higher copay for emergency room use than for office visits. Copays are most frequently used in service benefits contracts such as in HMOs, where the concepts of deductibles and coinsurance do not readily apply because no reimbursement actually takes place.

Limiting reimbursement to UCR charges is also a tool that may result in increased cost sharing on behalf of the insured. *UCR maximums* are set by a plan administrator, and generally attempt to represent a reimbursement level that reflects the lowest of a given provider's usual charges, the charges that are customary in that given geographic region for similar procedures, and a charge level that is reasonable in relationship to the specific services provided. These limitations are generally not applicable to plans providing service benefits. The provisions are generally a tool to limit cost. However, some reduction in utilization of specified high cost providers may result from the insured being required to make up the difference between a provider's bill and the UCR reimbursement provided by the insurer. For many network plans, UCR reimbursement, after any copayments, by participating providers, is accepted as payment in full as a requirement for participation in the network.

Varying deductibles and coinsurance are often used to encourage the insured to comply with certain requirements or use certain providers. For example, a *PPO* plan will often waive the deductible and/or reduce the coinsurance if the insured seeks care from a predefined list of providers. Occasionally, use of a given provider is a requirement for any benefit. This is a standard provision for HMOs but is also increasing in use in insurance contracts through both *Exclusive Provider Organizations* (EPOs) and *Centers of Excellence*. EPOs are similar to standard HMOs in that no benefits other than emergency services are provided if care is obtained from a non-network provider. Centers of Excellence have been established by many carriers to provide a high quality cost efficient mechanism of arranging for high intensity services such as transplants. Coverage for those services is often limited to services provided by the Centers of Excellence. Another example of varying deductibles and coinsurance is an open panel HMO or *Point of Service* (POS) program. Similar to a PPO, this program will provide a much higher level of benefits if the insured follows all of the protocols and restrictions of the HMO, and a lower level of benefits if the insured receives care otherwise. A *tiered network* is a variation of this concept where a carrier can define multiple networks inside a given benefit plan with varying copays dependent on which provider is used. With this variation, the insured retains greater choice of providers, but has additional cost sharing if they choose providers deemed to be expensive or inefficient.

A classic example of attempting to modify insured behavior through the use of copays can be found in prescription drug programs. These programs have evolved, from a simple fixed dollar copay per prescription, to multiple tiers of copays and coinsurance levels depending on whether a drug is brand or generic, on or off a carrier's formulary, and whether or not a therapeutically equivalent is available. Although quite complicated, these multi-tier copay prescription drug programs appear to be very effective at modifying consumer behavior.

Annual maximums and *lifetime maximums* are provisions that attempt to provide bounds on the risk undertaken by the insurer. Most often annual maximums are used on covered services where either medical necessity is difficult to define or the course of treatment is vague, such as for chiropractic or mental and nervous disorders. In addition, annual maximums can be used on catastrophic or somewhat experimental items such as certain organ transplants.

Limits on the benefit payable per day of covered services are an effort to control costs, to encourage the insured's awareness of costs, and to encourage wise consumption of health care resources. A limit on the number of days for which services will be covered is an attempt to control utilization. Both *daily limit maximums* and *number of day limits* are most commonly used on benefits such as psychiatric (mental and nervous) benefits, skilled nursing facilities, home health care, and private duty nursing.

In some plans, all of the above provisions may be waived or coverage increased depending on which provider is used or on the completion of certain requirements such as pre-certification. Such provisions again reflect an attempt to influence the behavior of the insured when they make the decision to purchase health care in the open market.

Different combinations of the above limitations have historically been given specific labels. For example, a *base plan* generally provides for first dollar coverage without deductible or coinsurance for hospital coverages. Provisions may include a number of days limit, and a limit to either room and board charges and/or ancillary charges for each day of hospitalization. A *supplementary major medical plan* typically excludes services provided under a base plan, and provides coverage for all other services subject to a corridor deductible and coinsurance limits. In contrast, a *comprehensive program* has all covered services in one program, subject to a deductible and coinsurance.

THE THIRD DIMENSION

The third dimension in defining a medical benefit plan is the degree to which the provider participates in the cost. This may include not only discounts or other modifications to provider payments, but also conditional payments based on some element of plan utilization. Having providers participate in benefit plan costs is intended to both reduce the costs of the underlying plan of benefits through rate concessions, as well as provide incentives for the providers to control utilization, particularly in the areas of referrals to expensive specialists and in hospital admissions.

Providers gain anticipated increases in patient volume by being a provider on a plan's preferred provider list. This type of decision can be either offensive, as part of an effort for a given provider to expand its customer base, or defensive, as part of an effort to prevent erosion of customer base to competing providers.

The algorithm establishing provider cost sharing can take on many forms, each of which has their own subtle impacts on underlying costs and behavioral incentives. These forms include the following:

- Discounts from billed charges
- Fee schedules and maximums
- Per diem reimbursements
- Hospital DRG reimbursement, Ambulatory payment classifications, or global payments
- Bonus pools based on utilization
- Capitation
- Integrated delivery system

Straight *discounts for billed charges* are the simplest form of establishing provider cost sharing. However, this form only acts to reduce costs of the underlying benefit plan and provides no incentives for utilization modifications. In addition, reimbursement based on a predefined percentage of billed charges may have little impact to control health care costs if used extensively, since a provider may increase billed charges to offset reductions due to the discounts.

Reimbursement based on *fee schedules* or *fee maximums,* although simple to implement, also acts only to reduce costs and fails to affect utilization patterns. This reimbursement method has some cost-saving advantage to the insurer over a straight discount from billed charges, however, in that the provider is unable to adjust billed charges to impact the overall level of claims. Under both discounts from billed charges and fee schedules and maximums the provider remains able to increase utilization, either through changes in how procedures are coded on bills, or in an actual increase in the number of services.

Per diem contracts are most commonly used for hospitalization benefits. An amount per day of hospital stay is negotiated. This per diem often varies based on the level of care, such as normal care, intensive care unit, cardiac care unit, and maternity ward. A hospital accepting a per diem contract is undertaking some risk of the intensity of services provided per bed day. Per diem contracts can act both to reduce costs and to have some basic controls on the provision of services ancillary to hospital room and board. However, per diem contracts generally provide no incentive to encourage either outpatient use in lieu of inpatient, or reduced lengths of stay. Many per diem contracts also include some outlier provisions where the longest hospital stays revert to payment of a percentage of billed charges for either charges in excess of the threshold or for total charges. These provisions further complicate any incentives from the payment system, especially if exceeding the threshold results in a modification on the amounts below the threshold.

Reimbursement based on *DRG* (diagnosis related groups) provides a set reimbursement to a hospital for a stay regarding a given diagnosis, regardless of the length of stay or the level of services provided. Some adjustment may be made under these contracts for cases involving inordinately short or long stays as compared to the norm for a diagnosis. This is the reimbursement mechanism used by individuals covered under the Medicare program. The impact of this reimbursement mechanism is that the hospital accepts risk for the length of a given admission as well as the amount of ambulatory services provided during admission. This reimbursement mechanism provides effective utilization incentives regarding charges during a hospital admission, but limited incentives for impacting the number of admissions. In addition, DRG payments are highly sensitive to the coding methodology used in determining diagnosis. Some observers believe that any significant reductions in costs may be offset through aggressive coding. A similar reimbursement mechanism for outpatient charges is reimbursement based on *APCs* (ambulatory payment classifications). Another similar mechanism is *case rate payments* or *global payments*, where a single reimbursement is negotiated to cover all services associated with a given condition (the case payment can include both facility and professional fees). The most common uses of global payments include maternity cases and transplant cases.

Bonus pools based on utilization refer to a contractual provision whereby a provider would receive an additional bonus if personal or overall utilization of medical services was below a pre-defined target or if other quality of care criteria are met. This bonus pool is generally funded out of a percentage of provider payments withheld from initial payment, or a *withhold*. Conceptually, this reimbursement mechanism appears to provide excellent incentives for a provider to have heightened awareness of utilization. However, effective implementation is much more difficult. If the bonus is not a significant proportion of a provider's income, a provider can do more to maximize income by increasing utilization than by controlling utilization and receiving the bonus. In fact, many physicians have stated they view such a withhold program as a benefit which they do not expect to receive, and thus it has little influence on their behavior. If the bonus is developed to be a significant portion of income, it may be difficult to enroll a broad base of providers willing to accept the risk of adverse experience deviations, which may be perceived as beyond their control. Furthermore, this type of bonus pool creates difficult ethical questions when a provider is given a strong financial incentive not to provide medical care to a patient. In addition to providing utilization incentives, bonus pools are probably most popular in their ability to provide an acceptable risk for the insurer. For example, if all reimbursement for medical services is subject to a 25% withhold, the insuring organization has effectively established a 25% cushion for excess utilization above the targets, in which its charges paid to providers will not increase.

A *capitation* model is one in which the insurer subcontracts with a provider to perform a defined range of services in return for a set amount per month per enrollee. This represents the very end of the spectrum in terms of minimizing risk to the insurer, in that virtually all risk is passed along to the provider. Essentially the only risk remaining with the insurer is the solvency of the provider and the ability of the provider to deliver services. Capitation agreements may also effectively reduce costs and provide utilization incentives in that a provider's income will be maximized to the extent they can provide fewer services. This utilization incentive raises the same ethical questions as mentioned above in the discussion on bonus pools.

Capitation contracts have extended beyond the services performed by a single provider, to capitating a provider group for most or all health care services. This type of arrangement is called *global capitation.* Under this arrangement, the provider group essentially replaces the insurer as the primary risk taker. The regulatory status for this type of arrangement is unclear. Some jurisdictions are requiring providers to obtain an HMO license in order to accept global capitation, while some jurisdictions are requiring no regulatory oversight if the entity offering the capitation is regulated.

Another capitation alternative is *specialty capitation.* Under this arrangement a fixed payment is made for all of the medical expenses associated with the treatment of a given condition or for all of the services provider by a given physician specialty. These capitations are often woven into disease management programs by providing a fixed capitation for treatment of chronic conditions such as diabetes or heart disease.

An *integrated delivery system* model is one where the insurer actually owns or employs the providers of care. This is most frequently seen in a staff model HMO but also exists when hospital or physician organizations develop managed care plans that accept insurance risk.

The underlying theme of all of the mechanisms in which providers partici-pate in the insurance risk is to increase the providers' awareness of costs and utilization. It is important to the long-term viability of a plan that such mechanisms be constructed to be beneficial for both the provider and the insurer. If either party is significantly disadvantaged in the contractual ar-rangement, the forces of economics will eventually dismantle that entire program.

OTHER MEDICAL PLAN PROVISIONS

In addition to the three basic dimensions that define a medical benefit plan described in the previous section, there are a number of other provi-sions that are standard in any benefit plan. These may include the fol-lowing:

- Overall exclusions
- Mandated benefits
- Coordination of benefits
- Subrogation
- Preexisting conditions
- COBRA continuation
- Conversions

Most medical benefit plans exclude charges for or services related to the following:

- Services deemed not to be *medically necessary* in order to treat a specific condition. There are several exceptions to this exclusion; the most common of which is preventive care.
- Services which are deemed to be *experimental* by some accepted medical authority. These services are generally excluded because ei-ther the usefulness of the treatment has not been clinically estab-lished or because, as an experimental treatment, alternative funds may be available to provide the treatment.
- Services related to cosmetic surgery. Although possibly excluded under the medical necessity clause, most contracts also have a spe-cific exclusion that limits services related to cosmetic surgery. Re-constructive surgery resulting from accidents or mastectomies is often exempted from this exclusion.

- Other specified services including mental services, hearing services, vision services, care of the feet, and spinal manipulation. These services are often delineated because medical necessity for these types of services is somewhat difficult to establish.

- Transplants are often excluded from coverage or coverage is provided with an inside limit such as a $100,000 maximum for a transplant. In addition, specific plan provisions may cover or exclude costs associated with acquiring a transplanted organ from a donor. Contractual provisions specifically addressing transplants are increasing in popularity, and some court rulings have indicated that transplants can no longer effectively be excluded as experimental procedures.

- Services for which payment is not otherwise required. This exclusion covers a host of situations including free care provided through governmental programs, care provided as part of a controlled group for an experimental program in which no payment is required, and care provided as part of a school or employer-related facility.

- Services required due to an act of war.

- Services provided as a result of a work-related injury. These services are generally excluded from group medical benefit plans because expenses would be reimbursable under a workers' compensation program.

- Services provided by, or charges from, a provider related to the patient.

Medical benefit plans also include provisions for specific benefits mandated by the appropriate regulating bodies. As mentioned previously, these *mandated benefits* vary significantly from state to state, creating administrative difficulty for multi-state insurers. In addition there are non-territoriality issues raised when an insurance contract is written in one state and covers individuals in other states. Some states mandate provisions for individuals covered in that state, whereas some states mandate provisions based on the situs of the contract. An additional issue regarding mandated benefits is the preemption claimed by self-funded benefit plans regulated under ERISA. ERISA provides exemption from any state laws for employee benefit plans that it regulates.

Most employee benefit plans also contain a provision discussing *coordination of benefits* procedures. Coordination of benefits refers to the process used to adjudicate claims when a service is covered under multiple benefit plans. Such a clause will designate one carrier as primary and responsible for coverage as if they were the only insurer. The alternative carrier is designated as secondary and is responsible for any additional benefits that their plan may provide. The secondary carrier can coordinate based on either total charges or total benefits. The most common approach is coordination based on total charges in which the secondary carrier will pay the total benefits it would have normally paid, less any benefits covered by the primary carrier, up to a maximum of the total charges incurred. When coordinating based on benefits, the secondary carrier will first calculate the normal level of benefits it would have provided had it been primary, and they reduce those benefits for any benefits provided by the primary carrier. The current NAIC model bill on coordination of benefits specifies the primary carrier based on the following hierarchy:

- The benefit plan not containing a coordination of benefit clause in the event one of the plans does not contain such a clause.
- The carrier covering the covered individual as an employee.
- If both carriers cover the individual as a dependent, the benefit plan for which the covered employee (not the dependent) has the birthday that falls earliest in the calendar year.
- If both benefit plans cover an individual as an employee, or if both employees covering a dependent have the same birthday, the plan that has had coverage in effect the longest.

Benefit plans covering individuals as employees, or as dependents of active employees are primary with respect to Medicare for employers with more than 20 employees. Benefit plans covering individuals as retirees or as dependents of retirees are secondary if Medicare can be a primary carrier.

Medical benefit plans generally contain a *subrogation clause* that assigns the right of recovery from any injuring party to a carrier that has provided services or reimbursed charges for medical services. In addition, this clause generally gives the carrier the full right to act on behalf of the covered individual in seeking such damages, and is often referred to as *third party liability*. Subrogation clauses most commonly come into play when addressing workers' compensation claims or automobile accidents. As a result of subrogation clauses, the 9/11 terrorist strikes had relatively little impact on the health insurance industry because most of the injuries occurred while individuals were actively at work and subject to workers' compensation coverages.

Medical benefit plans generally have a *preexisting exclusion* clause that either precludes or limits coverage for services related to any condition that was defined to be preexisting at the date coverage began. A preexisting condition is generally defined as a condition for which treatment was received within a specified number of days prior to the effective date of coverage. There may be a required number of days free of treatment to consider a condition no longer preexisting, and a defined period of time after which the preexisting exclusion would not longer apply. The most common preexisting condition definition is for conditions arising within six months prior to the effective date, and requiring either six months treatment free or 12 months to exempt the exclusion. This is referred to as a 6-6-12 provision. If the condition is deemed to be preexisting, this exclusion will either specify no coverage is available or designate a small maximum benefit available for preexisting conditions. Frequently this provision is waived when a group changes carriers so that there is no discontinuity in coverage. In such a case, a no loss/no gain provision may be used, where an insured's benefits will match those of the prior carrier where preexisting conditions exist. The *Health Insurance Portability and Accountability Act of 1996* (HIPAA) significantly restricted the application of preexisting exclusions. Under this act, if an individual has prior qualifying coverage, preexisting exclusions cannot be reapplied.

The *Consolidated Omnibus Reconciliation Act* (COBRA) requires employers with 20 or more employees to offer continued coverage beyond a person's normal termination date. This can arise when a dependent loses eligibility due to either divorce or death of the employee, when an employee or a dependent loses eligibility due to termination of employment, or when a dependent loses eligibility due to no longer meeting the definition of a dependent child. Continued coverage is required to be offered for a period between 18 and 36 months. The length of the continuation period varies dependent on the terminating event. The employer may charge the individual insured up to 102% of cost for the coverage. Although not required in an insurance contract, most carriers are offering to accept these risks and administer this coverage due to competitive requirements.

Another common provision of medical benefit plans is a *conversion privilege* to either an individual insurance plan or a group conversion trust if an individual is no longer eligible for coverage under the group medical plan. These conversions may have limited benefits and vary significantly according to specific state requirements. They may also be rated at a premium level that would discourage anyone from accepting this coverage unless they were absolutely unable to acquire coverage elsewhere. Some states limit the applicable rates. However, this provision does provide a last resort assurance of some continued availability of medical benefit coverage.

SPECIAL SITUATIONS

The three dimensions of a medical benefit plan described earlier in this chapter broadly categorize any medical benefit plan. However, specific combinations of these descriptions have been referred to as a given type of program. As the group medical benefit market has matured over the past decade, there has been considerable lack of strict definition of what is an HMO, what is a PPO, and what is a traditional indemnity plan.

MANAGED CARE PLANS

An *HMO* is a service benefit plan that broadly involves significant provider sharing in costs and minimal insured sharing in costs. The general philosophy of the HMO is that providers control the utilization of health care and the end consumers have little input into the purchasing decisions. Therefore, to effectively manage costs the provider component must be controlled. A common benefit plan would require a $10 or $20 copay for an office visit, varying copays for prescription drugs (depending on the drug), and a $50 copay for emergency room utilization. However in order to receive coverage, an insured may have to follow specific guidelines including having all care managed by a primary care physician, who would provide referrals to specialists, as necessary, except in the event of an emergency. HMOs typically have restrictive provider networks involving a small proportion of physicians and hospitals in a given community. In return, the physicians and hospitals agree both to conform with the HMO's utilization protocols and to provide care at a reduced fee level.

An *Exclusive Provider Organization* (EPO) generally has a similar design to an HMO. The primary distinction is that an EPO is regulated as an insurance contract or self-funded plan while an HMO may be subject to different regulatory requirements.

A *Point-of-Service* (POS) program is a hybrid of an HMO where the insured selects a primary care physician and has low copayment benefits similar to that described above if guidelines are followed. However under this program the insured also has the alternative of seeking care outside of the network with additional cost-sharing requirements.

Preferred Provider Organizations (PPO) are plans that offer an insured the freedom to use either a designated panel of providers or their provider of choice. To encourage the insured to use the preferred provider panel, a lower level of coinsurance is often used and deductibles are waived if participating providers are used. PPOs typically involve significant provider sharing in the cost, although generally less than HMOs. A typical PPO plan would involve a deductible (such as $200) that would be waived if the preferred provider panel were used, and a 10% coinsurance if the preferred provider panel was used and 20% if the panel were not used. Unlike an HMO, a PPO is typically an indemnity benefit plan with more emphasis on acute care and less emphasis on preventive services. The provider cost sharing in a PPO is generally more focused on reducing the overall costs to the benefit plan than on attempting to impact provider utilization.

FLEXIBLE SPENDING ACCOUNTS

Another example of a medical benefit plan is a *flexible spending account* *(FSA)*. An FSA is a benefit plan whereby an employee contributes pre-tax dollars on an annual basis that are then used to provide reimbursements for their own medical expenditures. The amount of reimbursement is limited to the amount contributed. There are virtually no limitations in a flexible spending account regarding benefits or providers. There would be no insured cost sharing beyond their initial funding of the account, and there is no provider cost sharing. The impact of an FSA is basically the opportunity for an insured individual to shift pre-tax dollars into after-tax reimbursements for medical care.

MEDICAL SPENDING ACCOUNTS

A hybrid of a flexible spending account is a *medical spending account* *(MSA)*. This plan combines a high deductible indemnity program with a reimbursement account to fund routine and budgetable expenditures. Proponents of MSAs assert that this combination provides catastrophic protection for truly insurable events while, if allowed, retaining the tax preferential treatment of expenditures for routine care. The high deductible program is one end of the insured cost-sharing spectrum targeted at impacting individual consumption patterns. Proponents believe that this type of program will create a more astute consumer of health care resources, ultimately leading to a more efficient marketplace. Opponents are concerned that if the reimbursement account is allowed to grow from year to year, the program effectively creates an additional tax loophole that may even encourage individuals to defer or decline appropriate medical care.

Recent tax law changes have significantly clarified the viability of such programs through Health Spending Accounts (HSAs) and Health Reimbursement Accounts (HRAs).

DEFINED CONTRIBUTION PROGRAMS

As a mechanism for limiting the total cost of medical benefit programs, many employers are looking at *defined contribution programs*. These programs are also commonly referenced as *consumer driven health plans*. Under a defined contribution program, the employer would determine the amount that would be provided for the medical benefit program and then the employee would select a program from a menu of offerings or design a plan of benefits that met their personal needs. If the amount provided by the employer were insufficient to cover the cost of the selected program, the employee would make additional contributions. Defined contribution programs vary from simply providing the employee with a limited number of choices all the way to essentially allowing the employee to tailor their own unique set of benefits. Many defined contribution programs are incorporating a medical savings account or health reimbursement account option, where some of the employer contribution can go into the reimbursement account.

Recent tax law changes have significantly clarified the viability of MSAs by allowing carry forward of unused balances from year to year through Health Spending Accounts (HSAs) and Health Reimbursement Accounts (HRAs). Currently most major employers either offer or are contemplating offering an HSA or HRA option.

MEDICARE SUPPLEMENT AND RETIREE BENEFIT PLANS

Medicare supplement policies include little provider cost sharing. The benefits can be defined as either a specific delineation of benefits covered, or simply as those normally covered benefits not reimbursed by Medicare. The degree of insured cost sharing under these programs ranges broadly from none to a significant portion of the cost Medicare does not pay. Recently, some retiree medical plans include managed care and flexible spending features.

LONG-TERM CARE

A *group long-term care plan* provides coverage for long-term care that may not be provided under a normal medical benefit plan. Long-term care typically involves little provider cost sharing, but involves significant insured cost sharing in an effort to encourage the insured to control utilization. Covered services differ significantly from normal benefit plans, in that coverage for long-term care requires both a triggering event and the utilization of services. The triggering event can include medically necessary confinement; the deficiency in a specified number of activities of daily living such as eating, dressing, toileting, walking, bathing; or the approval of a case manager. Long-term care policies typically include coverage for custodial care including care in a skilled nursing facility and home health care. Benefits are generally stated in terms of reimbursement for services provided, subject to a fixed dollar maximum per day. Long-term care is discussed in detail elsewhere in this text.

7 HEALTH BENEFITS IN CANADA

Bruno Gagnon

THE CANADIAN MEDICARE SYSTEM

Nearly every person who lives in Canada is covered by the Medicare program of his or her province of residence. The program is very similar from one province to another. It provides service benefits mainly for physician care, surgery and hospitalization in a public ward in Canada.

Since the most expensive services (physician care and surgery) are already covered by Medicare, there are no comprehensive managed care organizations such as HMOs, large-scale PPOs, and Blue Shield in Canada. There are seven regional Blue Cross Organizations, who act mostly as insurers. Some of them are registered as insurers and pay premium taxes. As a result, nearly all private plans are underwritten or administered by insurers (whether on an insured or self-insured basis).

THE CANADA HEALTH ACT

Under the Canadian Constitution, matters related to health, including regulation of hospitals and licensing of physicians, fall under provincial jurisdiction. However, the federal government, which has a greater taxing power than the provinces, can initiate social security measures in areas that fall under provincial jurisdiction by setting national standards and subsidizing provinces that set up programs that conform to these standards.

The federal government initiated Medicare in 1958 for hospital insurance, with all provinces and territories having their plans in effect by 1961, and in 1967 for medical insurance, with all provinces and territories having their plans by the beginning of 1972. The federal subsidy was initially approximately 50% of the cost of these plans.

To be eligible for the federal subsidy, provincial Medicare plans have to comply with the following five principles of the Canada Health Act.

- *Comprehensiveness*:
  All medically required hospital and physician services must be covered under the plan.

- *Universality*:
  All legal residents of a province or territory must be entitled to the insured health services provided for by the plan on uniform terms and conditions.

- *Accessibility*:
  Reasonable access by residents to hospital and physician services must not be impeded by charges made to them.

- *Portability*:
  The plan may not impose a waiting period in excess of 3 months for new residents and coverage must be maintained when a resident moves or travels within Canada or is temporarily out of the country.

- *Public Administration*:
  The plan must be administered and operated on a non-profit basis by a public authority.

Extra-billing and user charges are discouraged by provisions of the Canada Health Act that reduce federal grants to a province by one dollar per dollar collected in that province by physicians through extra-billing or user charges.

Although an overwhelming majority of physicians contract with their provincial Medicare Board, and do provide services within the framework of the provincial plan, neither the Canada Health Act nor the provincial laws force them to do so. As a result, some physicians have chosen to practice outside Medicare and charge their patients whatever amount they consider reasonable for their services. This is not considered as charging user fees or practicing extra-billing, since services provided by a physician practicing outside Medicare are not covered by it. Moreover, the patients can still obtain these services free of charge merely by seeing a doctor who is enrolled in Medicare. The system is a quasi-monopoly as there is little incentive for patients, except those on waiting lists for care, to seek treatment outside Medicare.

Until recently, several provinces prohibited private insurance of hospital and medical services obtained outside their provincial Medicare program, if these services were available under the provincial program. The other provinces allowed private insurance to cover these services. The prohibition of private insurance for these services was based on an interpretation of the Canada Health Act under a contentioning that private insurance would undermine the objectives of the *Canada Health Act,* especially accessibility, by diverting resources from the public sector.

This prohibition was challenged in Chaoulli v. Quebec where the Supreme Court of Canada ruled, by a 4 to 3 majority, that, because of long waiting lists, the anti-insurance prohibition in the Quebec law infringed the rights to life and personal inviolability guaranteed by the Quebec Charter of Rights and Freedoms.

Due to concerns that the Chaoulli judgment could jeopardize its entire public health system, the Quebec government requested and obtained a stay of the judgment. The government came to the conclusion that it must allow private insurance, but only for the procedures for which the waiting list is too long. At this writing, these procedures are elective hip, knee and cataract surgery.

Private insurance is minimal at this time, due to the limited number of procedures that can now be privately insured. In the longer run, a wider demand for private coverage of health care offered under Medicare may be created if the provinces are not able to manage their waiting lists.

PRIVATE HEALTH CARE

There are two different areas where private health care can exist in Canada.

The first area is services that are available free of charge under Medicare but are rendered by physicians who practice outside Medicare. Even after the Chaoulli case, these services are not covered by group insurance plans, because private insurance for the vast majority of these services is illegal in most provinces, and covering these services where legal may make a plan difficult to administer and also might raise questions about equity between employees living in different provinces. Furthermore, group insurance plans usually exclude any services that may be available to the insured free of charge.

The other area of private health care in Canada includes all services that are not available under Medicare. These services are the main focus of group health insurance plans.

Provincial Medicare Plans

Officially, there are two different plans: hospital insurance and medical insurance. However, provinces tend to centralize the administration of both plans, so they can be considered as the two main features of a single plan. Coverage is provided on a service basis (except for out-of-Canada coverage, which is on a reimbursement basis) with most physicians (95%) being paid by the provincial board on a fee-for-service basis.

Any resident of any province can choose to be treated by any physician who practices in his or her province of residence, as long as the physician is enrolled in the system in some way. Most of these physicians charge their fees directly to the provincial plan. Other physicians (in rare instances) may collect their fees (as long as these fees are those agreed between the provincial plan and the physicians' association) directly from the patient who, in turn, will be reimbursed by the provincial plan. On the other hand, services provided by physicians practicing outside the system are not reimbursed.

Due to the lack of the most modern technology in some parts of the country, some specialized services are not available in every province. In this case, the provincial board usually pays the cost of those services if they are obtained in another province.

Eligibility and Coverage

All permanent residents of a province or territory are eligible for coverage. Coverage for services other than prescription drugs is available without charge, except in Alberta and British Columbia where a small premium is charged.

Reciprocity agreements among provinces allow a person who moves from one province to another to become eligible in his or her new province of residence as soon as coverage terminates under the Medicare plan of his or her former province of residence. Coverage may be continued for up to 12 months when a resident is temporarily absent from his or her province.

Benefits

Benefits are similar in all jurisdictions, with only minor differences. The following services are generally covered in most jurisdictions:

- Hospital services:

  ○ Room and board in a public ward;

  ○ Physicians' services, diagnostics, anesthesia, nursing, drugs, supplies and therapy. (These services are available on either an inpatient or an outpatient basis);

  ○ Room and board in a nursing home or long term care hospital (partial coverage in most provinces);

- Physicians services, including services of a general practitioner, specialist, psychiatrist, surgeon, anesthetist, or obstetrician;

- Other professionals, such as optometrists, chiropractors, osteopaths, podiatrists and physiotherapists (coverage varies considerably among provinces);

- Prescription drugs for social assistance recipients and residents over age 65 in most provinces (British Columbia, Saskatchewan, Manitoba and Ontario also have a high-deductible prescription drug plan for other residents. Quebec has a compulsory plan for everyone not covered under a group insurance plan);

- Prostheses and therapeutic equipment;

- Other diagnostic services, such as laboratory tests and X-rays performed outside a hospital;

- Dental care:

  ○ Medically required oral and dental surgery performed in hospital. Extractions and fillings are usually not covered except for medical complications;

  ○ Diagnostic, preventive, and minor restorative services performed out of hospital are covered for young children and social assistance recipients in some provinces;

- Out-of-province coverage:

  ○ Hospital and medical expenses incurred in other provinces are usually paid according to the amount payable in the province where the person is treated; and

  ○ Hospital expenses incurred out of Canada are reimbursed only in part (on a per diem basis); medical expenses out of Canada are reimbursed up to the amount that would have been paid for the same treatments in the province of residence.

FINANCING

In 2003, health expenses in Canada amounted to approximately 123 billion dollars, or 9.9% of the GDP (up from 9.1% in 2000 and equal to the peak of 9.9% of the GDP in 1992).[1]

Most provincial Medicare plans are financed through general revenues, along with special payroll taxes and transfer payments from the federal government. The Federal transfer payments take two forms; cash transfers and tax point transfers. (Tax point transfers occur when the federal government agrees to lower its tax rate so that the provinces and territories can raise theirs by the same amount.[2])

During the 1980s and early 1990s, the huge size of the Canadian federal debt (70% of GDP) and repeated budget deficits prompted the federal government to restrain its expenses. The federal cash transfer payments to the provinces for maintaining their Medicare plans did not keep pace with inflation on health costs. As a result, the federal cash subsidy proportionally decreased until it represented only 24% of the cost of provincial Medicare plans in 1995 and was expected to continue decreasing even faster.

This could have led to a situation where the federal cash subsidy would have become a marginal component of funding, with the consequence that a province might have been able to collect much more money through user fees and extra-billing than the amount of the federal subsidy that would have been forfeited as a result of the provisions of the Canada Health Act, as the reversal of tax point transfers for non-conforming provinces would have been difficult.

In 1996, to avoid such a situation and make sure that the provinces would still conform to the requirements of the Canada Health Act, federal grants for Medicare were combined with all other social transfer payments (for services such as education) into the Canada Health & Social Transfer. As a result, a province that would allow user fees or extra-billing could be penalized up to the full amount of the Canada Health & Social Transfer.

It is noteworthy that in 2002, federal funding (Health component of total Federal Transfers and Health component of federal tax points transfers) represented approximately 44% of the cost of physicians and hospitals.

---

[1] Canadian Institute for Health Information: *Health Care in Canada, 2005 Edition*

[2] Canadian Department of Finance; www.budget.gc.ca/transfers/taxpoint/taxpoint_e

The federal transfers represented only 27.5% of the total provincial health expenses in 2002, compared with 37.5% in the early 1970's, prompting the provinces to ask for more federal health care funding.[3]

In 2004, the Canada Health & Social Transfer was replaced by two new transfers, the Canada Health Transfer and the Canada Social Transfer. Having a federal transfer specifically devoted to health was a recommendation of the Romanow Commission.[4]

CHALLENGES FOR THE CANADIAN MEDICARE SYSTEM

In recent years, the provinces were caught in a situation where they had less money to spend on their Medicare plan, while at the same time they were prevented from sharing the cost of these plans with patients through user fees or extra-billing. Raising taxes was not an option (due to the already very high level of taxes and major increases to the Canada/Quebec Pension Plans contribution rate), so the provinces had to cut their spending on health care.

This prompted provincial boards to cut or reduce benefits not required under the Canada Health Act, such as out-of-Canada coverage, dental services, optometric services and prescription drugs. At the same time, various rationing schemes were put in place, such as reducing the number of physicians and nurses providing services within the provincial plans, limiting their compensation, reducing or limiting the number of services that they can perform, or reducing with the number of hospital beds. This resulted in queuing and longer delays, mostly for non-emergency care.

In recent years, the Medicare system has continued deteriorating. The following concerns were raised in reports[5,6] published in early 2002:

- Waiting for months to see a specialist is common, because of a shortage of some specialists, poor scheduling practices, and inappropriate assessments of need;

---

[3] Commission on the Future of Health Care in Canada: *Building on Values: Final Report, November 2002, page 312*

[4] Federal Commission on the Future of Health Care in Canada, *Romanow Report, November 2002*

[5] Commission on the Future of Health Care in Canada: *Shape the Future of Health Care: Interim Report, February 2002, page 30*

[6] Commission on the Future of Health Care in Canada: *Canadians' Thoughts in their Health Care System: Preserving the Canadian Model Through Innovation, pages 5-6 & Figure 32*

- Shortages of equipment, specialists, and technicians cause waiting for diagnostic procedures such as MRI;
- Waiting for elective and non-emergency surgery is common, due to a lack of operating room time and a shortage of hospital beds;
- Emergency rooms are overcrowded, due to the unavailability of after-hours clinics, the non-emergency use of emergency rooms, the inability to transfer patients to regular wards, and poor distribution of caseloads with neighboring facilities;
- People who need long-term care tend to wait in hospital because of a shortage of beds in long-term care, insufficient community care and housing alternatives, and non-standardized admission criteria;
- Technology-intensive services are not available everywhere;
- The demand for services exceeds the supply, resulting in rationing; and
- Some services that are essential to the treatment of a medical condition, such as prescription drugs for chronic illnesses, are not covered by Medicare.

When Medicare was implemented, hospital and physician services were the two major components of health care. Now, these services account for less than half of the total cost of the system. More money is being spent on drugs than on physicians.

RESPONSE TO THESE CHALLENGES

The 10-year period between 1995 and 2005 was characterized by an unprecedented number of committees, commissions, and reports on how to fix the problems of Medicare. These include the National Forum on Health[7] (F), the Federal Commission on the Future of Health Care in Canada[8] (R), the Alberta Premier's Advisory Council on Health[9] (MZ), the Standing Senate Committee on Social Affairs, Science and Technology[10] (K), and the Quebec Working Committee on the Permanence of the Health and Social Services System[11] ME). The most important recommendations formulated in these reports are shown below, using letters above to indicate the reports in which the recommendation appears.

---

[7] National Forum on Health, *Final Report, 1997*

[8] Federal Commission on the Future of Health Care in Canada, *Romanow Report, November 2002*

[9] Alberta Premier's Advisory Council on Health, *Mazankowski Report, December 2001*

[10] Standing Senate Committee on Social Affairs, Science and Technology, *Kirby Report, October 2002*

[11] Quebec Working Committee on the Permanence of the Health and Social Services System, *Menard Report, July 2005*

Scope
- Keeping the requirements of the Canada Health Act unchanged or expanding them (F, K, R);
- Maintaining a "single payer" universal healthcare model for the provincial public healthcare programs (F);
- Expanding the scope of publicly funded provincial public healthcare programs to include home care and prescription drugs (F, R);
- Expanding Medicare to cover the portion of the cost prescription drugs that exceeds 3% of total family income (K);
- Expanding Medicare to cover post-acute and palliative home care (K, R);
- Establishing a partially pre-funded national long term care insurance program (ME);
- Redefining comprehensiveness under the Canada Health Act to avoid putting Medicare under the obligation to cover the full range of health services, treatments or technologies available today or in the future (MZ).

Philosophy
- Reforming primary care to focus on patients instead of services (F; MZ)
- Emphasizing prevention of illness and injury and promotion of good health (R);
- Promoting health by changing the compensation of physicians from a fee-for-service basis to a more appropriate basis, such as capitation (F, K, MZ, R)
- Providing incentives to attract, retain, and best utilize health providers (MZ, K);
- Basing health care spending on Canadian values (R).

Delivery
- Creating multi-disciplinary primary health care groups, providing a wide range of services 24 hours a day, 7 days a week (K);
- Re-configuring the health system to encourage more choice, competition, and accountability (MZ);
- Making quality a top priority (MZ);
- Using the private sector to deliver health services, within the framework of the public Medicare system (ME);
- Removing barriers to expansion of care initiatives (R);
- Expanding use of nurse practitioners (R);
- Delivering more health services in communities or at home (R).

Administration

- Using information technology and computerized databases, including electronic health records, for making health-related decisions, while guaranteeing privacy (F, MZ, K, R);
- Giving more powers and responsibilities to regional health authorities (MZ, K);
- Providing residents with a guarantee of access to selected health services within a reasonable time frame (R, MZ, K);
- Appointing a National Health Care Commissioner who would report annually on Canada's health care system (K).

Research and Analysis

- Appointing a National Health Council to measure the performance of the health care system, collect information, report publicly on efforts to improve quality, access and outcomes in the health care system, and coordinate activities in health technology assessment (R);
- Developing indicators to measure performance of the system and health outcomes (R);
- Determining what the community can afford to spend on health care (ME).

Treatment

- Implementing new and more effective diagnostic tests (R);
- Developing evidence-based decision-making, including clinical guidelines (R).

Funding

- Shifting from lump sum funding of hospitals to service-based funding (K);
- Increasing or finding other sources of revenues for the health care system (MZ, K, ME, R);
- Establishing a new dedicated cash-only federal transfer as part of the Canada Health Act, with increased federal funding and an escalator provision set in advance for 5 years (R);
- Implementing stable, predictable, long-term funding arrangements with clearly defined rules (R).

Some of these recommendations are clearly in direct conflict with others, and illustrate the diversity of views on the future of Medicare in Canada.

The Quebec Prescription Drug Act

In January, 1997, Quebec implemented mandatory coverage of prescription drugs for all residents of the province. Any resident who is eligible for coverage, either as a worker or as a dependent, under a private group insurance plan set up by an employer or trade association, must be covered by such plan. All other residents must enroll in a prescription drug plan managed by the province. The only exception is for persons aged 65 or older, who may choose to be covered under the plan of their employer or former employer, if they are eligible to such plan, or under both, with the provincial plan being primary. All private plans must at least cover the drugs covered by the provincial plan.

Since the plan was implemented in 1997, premiums have more than tripled (as of mid-2006), despite a deductible increase of 45% and an out of pocket maximum increase of 17.5% in 9 years. This is due to increases in the cost and utilization of prescription drugs.

PRIVATE MEDICAL PLANS

Due to the comprehensive coverage already provided by provincial Medicare plans, private medical plans, usually called extended health plans, typically cost from 2.0% to 2.5% of payroll (before tax), depending on their richness.

Extended health plans usually include five types of benefits: hospital expenses, prescription drugs, health practitioners, miscellaneous expenses, and out-of-Canada emergency care. The expression "major medical" is sometimes used to refer to the last four types. This latter expression may be misleading since major medical plans in Canada are not superimposed on any extensive basic plan, as might be the case in US, but only on a modest hospital plan and, of course, the provincial Medicare plan.

In recent years, prescription drugs and out-of-country medical have evolved toward becoming more or less separate from the remainder of health insurance, with their own cost containment features (deductible, co-payment and/or coinsurance and maximums). Hospital benefits were already treated somewhat differently from the other health benefits.

Hospital and prescription drug benefits are usually provided on a direct-pay basis (the plan pays the provider directly) while other benefits are generally provided on an indemnity basis, with coverage for reasonable and customary charges, except for health practitioners who may be covered for a scheduled amount per treatment. Out-of country benefits are typically provided at 100%, and may include a limit on the number of days covered.

Coverage is based on the date of incurral, which is the date when services are provided. Benefits are paid according to the coinsurance level, after satisfying the deductible.

DEDUCTIBLE

Deductibles for extended health plans in Canada are much lower than in the United States. Typical deductibles vary from $25 to $50 per person or per family, and usually apply to all covered expenses except hospitalization, out-of country, and prescription drug. Flexible plans tend to offer options with higher deductibles such as $100, $250, or $500.

Deductibles in many plans have not been increased for the last 25 years, despite sustained inflation on covered expenses. As a result, many deductibles are now lower than the average cost of a single claim. Such deductibles have lost much of their efficiency as a cost containment feature, since they no longer cause insureds to self-pay small "nuisance" claims. This is why several plans now have no deductible.

Some employers have been successful in increasing or indexing the deductible under their extended health care plan. In addition, some employers have implemented high deductibles, along with the introduction of health care spending accounts to be used to pay for the smaller claims. This approach requires extra care, as high deductibles tend to be more vulnerable to inflation leverage than smaller ones.

COINSURANCE

Coinsurance levels vary from 80% to 100% and are not necessarily the same for the five types of coverage. Hospital charges are usually paid in full, with no deductible. Other eligible expenses are reimbursed at 80% or 90% (with or without a deductible), or at 100% (with a deductible), except for psychologists where a lower coinsurance (typically 50%) is usually applied. Out-of-Canada emergency expenses are generally covered at 100%. Plan sponsors and insurers have been reluctant to provide plans that pay the full cost of prescription drugs with no deductible. Some plans (typically flexible benefits plans) have recently implemented progressive coinsurances (such as 70% of the first $1,000 and 100% of the remainder). As an attempt to control the ever-increasing cost of prescription drug coverage, some plans have implemented a two-tier coinsurance, where generic drugs are reimbursed at 100% while other drugs are reimbursed with a lower coinsurance.

OVERALL LIMITS

By contrast with the United States, there is generally no overall limit to insured benefits payable for expenses incurred in Canada by an active employee, since insured plans are not exposed to catastrophic claims, with the most expensive treatments being covered by the provincial Medicare plan. There is, however, a maximum (typically $1,000,000) applicable to charges incurred out of Canada. For retirees, there is frequently an overall maximum, which is expressed either on a 1-year, 3-year, or 5-year basis, or as a lifetime limit (generally no more than $10,000 to $50,000).

ELIGIBLE EXPENSES

Hospital Charges

Medical plans usually pay charges for room and board, up to a maximum per diem which is expressed either as a flat dollar amount or, more frequently, as the difference between the cost of a semi- private or private room and the cost of public ward (which is paid by the provincial Medicare plan. Such charges must be incurred in Canada for the treatment of an acute condition or for pregnancy. (Out-of-Canada hospital charges are often covered in miscellaneous expenses, along with out-of-Canada medical expenses.) There is no maximum benefit, either in dollars or as a total number of days of hospital confinement. Chronic care is usually not covered.

Prescription Drugs

In Canada, prescription drugs represent approximately 65% to 70% of the cost of medical plans. This area of coverage has therefore been the focus of much attention from both insurers and plan sponsors. As a result, various definitions of eligible drugs have been designed, such as the following:

- All drugs prescribed by a physician
- All drugs for which coverage is mandated by law
- All drugs that require a prescription from a physician
- All drugs prescribed by a physician, up to the cost of the lower-priced generic drug that is an acceptable substitute (found only in direct-pay drug plans)
- All drugs prescribed by a physician, up to the cost of the highest-priced substitute that would be covered by the provincial Medicare plan if the patient were a social assistance recipient (found mostly in direct-pay drug plans)

The following substances are generally not considered to be prescription drugs, and thus are excluded from most plans: any substitute of food or household products (salt, sugar or milk, dietary products, vitamins, proteins, minerals, hormones, cosmetics, soaps, shampoos, antacids, and laxatives), so-called "natural" products, vaccines, and contraceptives other than oral contraceptives. However, intrauterine devices are often included with prescription drugs.

Direct-pay drug plans have become prevalent in recent years, as most providers are now able to provide real-time claims adjudication. This feature is quite attractive since it allows the plan sponsor to set up its own list of covered drugs. With on-line claims adjudication, the pharmacist can tell the patient whether a drug is covered or not and whether a substitute is covered or not. Hence, generic and therapeutic substitutions are encouraged. This also allows the plan sponsor to decide which new products (nicotine patches, for example) should be covered and to what extent.

A popular variant is deferred-pay drug plans, where adjudication is on-line and the insurer makes payment to the insured afterwards (within 10 days for large claims and 3 months for very small claims). The main advantage of these plans is that they typically cost 10% to 15% less than direct-pay plans for a similar coverage. This difference has been linked to utilization, but the exact reasons why utilization is lower with a deferred-pay plan are not clear. It is thought that, for a patient with a particular medical condition, physicians may prescribe several drugs, one of which is aimed at curing the conditions and others that are aimed at enhancing the patient's comfort. With direct payment, it is felt that the patient will buy all prescribed drugs while with deferred payment, the patient would first buy the main drug and then buy the other drugs only if they are really needed.

Mail-order drugs are now available in most provinces and generate some savings, most occurring on so-called "maintenance drugs" such as contraceptives and drugs for chronic conditions such as insulin.

Health Practitioners

Practitioners can be classified in two categories: those whose services are covered only if prescribed by a physician (physiotherapist, audiologist, speech therapist and dietitian), and those whose services do not require a prescription (optometrist, psychologist, psychoanalyst, chiropractor, naturopath, osteopath, podiatrist and acupuncturist).

Eligible expenses for health practitioners are usually subject to inside limits. For all practitioners, there is a limit of one treatment per day, and a maximum number of treatments per year or an annual dollar maximum.

Also, for practitioners whose services are eligible without a prescription, there often is a maximum dollar amount per treatment, which typically represents approximately 50% to 75% of the average cost of a treatment. Such a limitation is necessary because of the elective nature of the treatments.

Limits usually apply separately to each type of practitioners. However, as a cost containment measure, some plan sponsors have begun grouping several practitioners (such as chiropractors, osteopaths and physiotherapists who all work on the musculo-skeletal system) under a single inside limit of, say, $500 per year.

Miscellaneous Expenses

While prescription drug expenses and practitioners' fees are frequently claimed for the treatment of minor conditions, miscellaneous expenses are much less frequent, and generally incurred for serious illnesses. These expenses are usually eligible only if prescribed by a physician and include almost any insurable medical expense that is not otherwise covered in the plan or by the provincial Medicare plan, such as the following:

- Ambulance transportation (including air travel where ground transportation is either unavailable or inappropriate)
- Laboratory tests, X-rays, electrocardiograms
- Radiotherapy
- Oxygen
- Blood and blood products
- Serums injected by a physician
- Needles, syringes and glucometers, including reagent strips, for control of diabetes
- Ostomy supplies
- Rental or purchase of medical equipment such as wheelchairs, hospital-type beds, and respiratory devices
- Purchase of artificial limbs and eyes
- Prostheses (including mammary prostheses)
- Casts, splints, trusses, braces and crutches
- Other orthopaedic apparatus
- Therapeutic apparatus
- Elastic support stockings
- Hearing aids (up to a maximum per 36- to 60-month period)

- Orthopaedic shoes (only part of the cost is normally eligible)
- Confinement in a convalescent home
- Home care

Miscellaneous expenses also include private duty nursing out of hospital (up to an annual limit such as 20 shifts or $4,000 to $25,000) and dentist's fees for treatments required because of an accidental injury to the mouth (with a stated maximum per injury such as $1,000). Confinement in a convalescent home is also included in this benefit, subject to a maximum number of days (typically 120) per confinement or per calendar year.

No maximum or inside limits generally apply to miscellaneous expenses other than those already mentioned.

Out-of-Canada Coverage

Out-of-Canada coverage has been the focus of much attention in the recent years, due to cutbacks and limits in many provinces of reimbursement for out-of-Canada medical expenses under the provincial Medicare plan. Eligible expenses typically are the expenses beyond what is reimbursed by the provincial plan, and may be subject to inside limits.

There are two main areas of Out-of-Canada coverage: emergency coverage (travel insurance and travel assistance) and referrals.

Emergency coverage was formerly included in miscellaneous expenses, but is evolving into a special class of benefits due to greater insurer sophistication and increased exposure related to cutbacks under the provincial Medicare plans. Covered expenses are for emergency care only, during a short (usually less than 3 months) trip outside Canada, and include hospitalization and medical care provided by a physician or a surgeon.

The deductible is often waived on emergency coverage because it would have no impact on the cost or utilization of the plan. It is so small (typically $25) as to be negligible compared with the cost of a claim, which can easily exceed $10,000. Because of the usually large size of claims, coinsurance is frequently 100%. It is felt that the application of a coinsurance percentage would cause undue hardship to the insured. There is usually a very high maximum benefit, such as $1,000,000 per trip or per calendar year, often set by a reinsurer.

The insured employee must be covered by their provincial Medicare plan, otherwise the private plan will pay only the expenses over what the provincial plan would have paid if the insured had been covered under this plan.

Most plans provide out-of-Canada coverage in the form of travel insurance. This includes repatriation expenses and travel assistance in addition to the usual coverage. Travel assistance is aimed at reducing the cost of travel insurance by directing the patient to the most cost-efficient resources.

Referrals for services not available in the province of residence of the insured person are rarely covered by private plans, since most referrals are already covered by the provincial Medicare plan. Referral must be in writing, and obtained from a doctor located in the province of residence. Services must be rendered in Canada, or out of Canada only if they are not available in Canada. In the latter case, the provincial Medicare plan must approve the treatment and pay its part of the cost. Coinsurance on referrals may be lower than for emergency treatments.

EXCLUSIONS

All services covered by the provincial Medicare plan generally are excluded, except to the extent that the law allows private plans to pay for expenses in excess of those paid by provincial plan.

Other exclusions are similar to those in United States: expenses other than usual, customary and reasonable charges; or resulting from self-inflicted injuries, insurrection, war, or service in the armed forces; cosmetic surgery or treatment (except for accidental injuries); and experimental drugs or treatments.

OTHER PROVISIONS

The Canadian Life and Health Insurance Association has adopted guidelines for coordination of benefits. These guidelines recommend that the "Total Allowable Expenses" approach be used whenever possible. This approach is the predominant method used in the United States, and is the NAIC method used for insured plans. It provides that total benefits payable to an individual cannot exceed total allowed charges, and specifies the order in which carriers pay.

Some plans provide for an extension of benefits to dependents for up to two years after an employee dies. Benefits may also be paid for a number of months (usually 3 months) after insurance terminates, if the employee or dependent is disabled at the time of termination. These provisions are becoming less common, being replaced by a restricted waiver-of-premium provision.

Premiums are frequently waived after a 3-month to 6-month elimination period (usually the same period as for long term disability income benefits and waiver of premium for life insurance), if the insured employee is totally disabled. This continues for as long as the insured employee remains totally disabled, provided that the group insurance policy remains in effect. Provisions relating to termination of coverage due to retirement or attainment of a specified age continue to apply.

FUNDING

Most large employers self-insure a part of their group medical benefits, along with their dental and short-term disability insurance benefits. The main reasons why self-insured plans are popular are the cost savings on the premium tax (except in three provinces, including the largest ones) and the cash flow advantages, just as in the United States. Another reason, for employers with employees in Quebec, was the fact that, from 1985 to 1991, the Quebec sales tax was not charged on the employer's contribution to a self-insured plan. Many employers then chose to self-insure to avoid this tax. Also, compared with the United States, the claims that would be most subject to large fluctuations are covered by the provincial Medicare plan in Canada. As a result, the experience of group medical and dental insurance plans covering more than 100 employees tends to be fairly stable.

Flexible benefits plans are getting popular among employers with at least 100 employees. Because these plans are perceived as being part of a total compensation package, and since the experience of medical and dental plans for groups of this size is fairly stable, the medical and dental component of many flexible benefits plans is provided on an ASO basis. These plans are typically supplemented by aggregate, and sometimes specific, stop-loss insurance, especially for medical services outside Canada.

Because the provincial Medicare plan pays the greater part of medical expenses, the cost of private medical plans is much lower in Canada than in the United States, and the scope of medical plans is much more limited. Consequently, an employer who wishes to set up a flexible benefits plan has less leeway in the design of the various options to be included in the plan. Most flexible benefits plans in Canada use a modular, or a "core-plus" approach, rather than a pure cafeteria approach, mostly because employers feel that they ought to provide a minimum safety net to their employees in most types of benefits. Also, the workforce of most "large" Canadian employers is too small to justify the higher administrative expenses under a pure cafeteria plan.

DENTAL PLANS

The only dental benefits provided under the Canadian Medicare system are medically required oral and dental surgery performed in hospital and, in some provinces, preventive and minor restorative services for young children. Thus, dental coverage remains mostly a private matter. As a result, dental care coverage has evolved with the same pattern as in the United States.

Virtually all plans use a type of scheduled approach, under which the eligible expenses are based on the fee guide published by the Dentists' Association of the employee's (or employer's) province of residence. In a significant minority of cases, the eligible expenses are not based on the current edition of the fee guide, but on the previous year's edition, or even on an earlier edition.

In the fee guide, a code is assigned to each procedure that can be performed by a dentist, along with the description of the procedure and the suggested fee. Some guides also show the relative value units assigned to a procedure. Plans define their eligible expenses either as a list of dental procedures or as a specific list of codes from the fee guide. The latter approach used to cause problems with plans covering persons in different provinces, since at some point every provincial dentists' association had its own coding systems. These systems were quite similar among provinces, but the differences forced insurers to develop extensive conversion systems. To solve this problem, a new Canadian Dental Association Procedure Coding System was adopted in 1990 by all provinces except Quebec.

There are five main areas of dental coverage in Canada:

- Diagnostic and preventive care (oral exams, X-rays, fluoride application)
- Minor restorative care and surgery (fillings, extractions, repairs to dental prostheses)
- Periodontal and endodontal treatments (such as root canal therapy)
- Prostheses and major restorative treatments (crowns, inlays, bridgeworks, dentures)
- Orthodontia

Diagnostic, preventive and minor restorative care are often combined with periodontal and endodontal treatments and referred to as routine care. Prostheses and major restorative treatments, sometimes combined with periodontal and endodontal treatments, are often known as major care. Orthodontia generally remains distinct from the other components of dental care. Most dental plans cover the first four areas of coverage, while approximately half the plans also cover orthodontia.

DEDUCTIBLE

The deductible on a dental plan is quite similar to that applicable to the medical plan, although combined deductibles (that apply to both medical and dental care) are rare. This similarity may be related to the fact that the average premium per capita for a dental plan is generally comparable to the premium for the medical coverage. A typical deductible is $25 to $50 per person, or $50 for the whole family. It usually applies to all covered expenses except orthodontia and, frequently, diagnosis and preventive care.

As for accident and sickness insurance, deductibles in most dental plans have remained stable for a long time, despite sustained inflation on covered expenses. The average deductible is now lower than the cost of the minimum claim that can be incurred. As a result, it is now seen more as a user's fee than as a utilization disincentive. A certain number of plans have eliminated their deductible.

OTHER COST-SHARING AND LIMITS

Coinsurance varies among the five main areas of coverage. Diagnostic and preventive care is usually paid in full, with no deductible. The rationale is that, by encouraging prevention, the plan sponsor will avoid being faced with more expensive claims for extensive restoration later. Minor surgery and restorative care is reimbursed at 80% to 100%, generally after satisfying a deductible. Prostheses and major restorative treatments are reimbursed at 50% to 80% after the deductible. The coinsurance on periodontal and endodontal treatments varies depending on their classification, from 80% to 100% if they are included in routine care or from 50% to 80% if included in major care. Orthodontia is typically reimbursed at 50%, with no deductible.

There is usually a $1,000 to $2,000 annual maximum reimbursement for all eligible expenses except orthodontia, which is subject to a separate, lifetime maximum (generally $1,000 to $2,000). There is also a limit on the frequency of diagnosis and preventive services, with some services such as X-rays and scaling being eligible only when a number of months at least have elapsed since a prior, similar, treatment. A six-month delay was the standard practice until recently, when several major plan sponsors implemented a nine-month delay. This longer delay has met some opposition from the dentists, who consider it too long. The replacement of a prosthesis is usually eligible expense only if at least five years have elapsed since the prosthesis has been installed.

COST CONTROLS

Some cost control features are typical of dental plans, such as pre-certification, the alternative treatment clause, and the missing-tooth exclusion.

The alternative treatment clause is found in nearly all dental plans. It allows the insurer to pay only the cost of the least expensive appropriate treatment. To avoid resentment from the claimant, this clause is usually associated with a pre-certification clause that requires advance approval by the insurer of the treatment if it is expected to cost more than a specified sum of money (usually $300 to $500). After receiving the treatment plan, the insurer informs the claimant of the amount of reimbursement to which he or she is entitled, and may eventually propose an alternative, less expensive, treatment.

The missing-tooth exclusion is intended to exclude the cost of a dental prosthesis that replaces a tooth that has been extracted before the claimant became insured under the plan. The rationale behind this clause is that the plan does not have to indemnify the insured for an event (the loss of the tooth) that occurred before coverage began. This rationale has been somewhat contested on the ground that a problem which is left untreated (due to this exclusion) may lead to another problem which would be covered, but might be more expensive to solve.

FUNDING

Dental plans in Canada typically cost from 1.0% to 1.5% of payroll (before tax), which is less than the cost of a medical plan. Insurers write smaller plans, either on a fully pooled basis (for very small plans) or on a retention basis. Large employers usually self-insure their dental plans, along with their medical plan. They retain the services of an insurer on an ASO basis, often with an aggregate stop-loss policy. Large amount pooling is rare since the largest possible claim for a dental treatment is limited to the annual maximum that is much lower than the cost of a large medical claim.

Capitation

In the end of the 1980s, insurers and insurer-sponsored organizations tried to take advantage of the rapidly increasing number of dentists competing for a limited number of insured patients, by introducing capitated plans. These plans were patterned after American plans, and were not necessarily adapted to the Canadian market. In particular, the choice usually given to employees was either to join the capitated plan or to remain with a less generous traditional plan. This forced employers to maintain two concurrent dental plans. This was not very practical for the average Canadian employer.

Several dental associations were strongly opposed to capitation, and exerted pressure on their patients not to join capitated plans and on insurers not to offer such plans. After a few years most insurers ceased to offer capitated plans, and very few such plans remain in effect.

Direct-pay Dental Plans

While capitated plans floundered, direct-pay dental plans have become increasingly popular. Under this type of plan, the insured person is given an identification card that includes information relative to the dental plan, along with an expiration date.

When the insured has dental treatments, the dentist uses the card to submit a claim to the insurer. The claim is adjudicated by a computer that informs the dentist of the amount payable by the plan. This amount is paid directly by the insurer to the dentist. The insured person only has to pay the difference between the total cost of the dental treatment and the amount payable by the plan.

VISION CARE PLANS

Eye examinations by an optometrist are usually included in the medical plan. Prescription glasses or contact lenses may either be included in the medical plan, using the same deductible and coinsurance percentage or be provided on a stand-alone basis, generally with no deductible and with a high level of coinsurance. Two approaches can be used to determine the eligible expenses: the traditional approach and the scheduled approach.

TRADITIONAL APPROACH

Under the traditional approach, eligible expenses are limited to a flat amount that does not exceed the cost of a standard pair of glasses, including the frame. This maximum amount of eligible expenses is the same whether the insured person chooses eyeglasses or contact lenses, and is usually limited to one occurrence per 24-month period (or often on a 12-month period for children). Since the maximum is usually low, the traditional approach tends to be equivalent to paying the same amount to every insured person.

A plan that uses the traditional approach can be improved through discounting. Under this modified approach, the plan sponsor chooses an insurer that has entered into an agreement with a network of opticians (a form of Canadian PPO) to negotiate a discount (up to 20%) on the price of eyeglasses and contact lenses for its insureds. Since the cost of the glasses or lenses is generally greater than the maximum benefit payable under the plan, the discount becomes net savings to the employee. The extra premium charged by the network to the insurer (and charged back) to the group is typically very low, and represents only an administration fee.

SCHEDULED APPROACH

The scheduled approach is similar to that used for dental care. Eligible expenses for glasses are determined by reference to the schedule published by the optometrists' association. Thus, the insurer applies the deductible and the coinsurance to the eligible expenses for the glasses, which vary according to the strength and the type of focus, if any. Eligible expenses for the frame are generally limited to a small allowance, which can vary with the number of years elapsed since the last claim. Eligible expenses for contact lenses are equal to the expenses that would have been eligible for eyeglasses. Eligible expenses are also limited to one pair of glasses or contact lenses per claim period (such as 3 years), except if the insured's vision varies by more than 1/2 dioptry. Due to its complexity, this approach is used only for large plans.

The scheduled approach has several advantages. Every insured person is covered according to his or her needs since the eligible expenses recognize the fact that different persons have different visual problems, instead of being based on some uniform amount. The benefit is indexed since it is based on a schedule that is adjusted each year to recognize the variation in the cost of eyeglasses.

However, the insured is encouraged to wait as long as possible before changing his glasses, or to keep the same frame, since the allowance for the frame increases with the time elapsed since the last claim. By contrast with some traditional plans, there is no need for two different maximums, one for eyeglasses and the other for contact lenses.

Tax Environment

A premium tax is charged on the net premiums (premiums less refunds) of insured plans in all provinces. The tax rate varies from 2% to 3%, except in Newfoundland where it is 4%. This tax must be included in the gross premium. This tax is also charged on benefits paid by self-insured plans (also called Administrative Services Only (ASO) plans) in Quebec, Ontario, and Newfoundland.

In addition, Quebec and Ontario apply a sales tax on group insurance premiums or their equivalent in self-insured plans.

The 6% federal Goods and Services Tax (GST) does not apply to insurance premiums but is charged on administrative expenses billed by an insurer or a third party administrator on ASO contracts which are not supplemented by stop-loss. The GST also applies to the supplies (computers, paper, and so on) used by insurers and by providers of health care. Hence, even though the GST does not apply directly to insurance premiums, it does increase slightly the cost of group insurance.

Quebec applies income tax to employer contributions for health and dental plans, whether such plans are insured or not. All other provinces have their income tax collected by the federal government and do not tax employer contributions to health and dental plans. The federal government and all provinces charge their income tax on employers' contributions to group life insurance coverage.

8 DENTAL BENEFITS IN THE UNITED STATES

Herschel Reich

INTRODUCTION

Dental coverage is one of the most popular employee benefits in the United States. According to the National Association of Dental Plans, more than 162 million people were estimated to have dental benefits as of 12/31/04, or 55% of the population.[1] This represents a significant increase from the twelve million individuals covered in 1970 (and the nearly one million people covered by the benefit in 1960). The overwhelming majority of these individuals are insured in the private commercial market, with the balance covered by Medicaid, the military and government institutional programs. Dental coverage is not included in the traditional U.S. Medicare program, but Medicare Advantage plans often include basic dental services as a means of distinguishing themselves in their product offerings.

This chapter will focus on group dental benefits, the largest component of the private commercial market. Individual dental insurance is not widely available, largely due to the antiselective nature of the benefit which makes appropriate pricing difficult, and because most insurers don't see enough potential reward to make the product worthwhile, given the complex regulatory environment of individual accident & health insurance. Discount cards, which are growing in popularity, are often geared to the individual market.

Group dental plans are generally provided through employers, and offer coverage to both employees and their dependents. The main advantages over individual plans are the spread of risk as well as economies of scale in administration over a wider base. The employer's role can range from

---

[1] NADP / DDPA 2004 Joint Dental Benefits Report: Enrollment Model

paying the full cost of the plan (non-contributory to the employee) to just serving as a coverage facilitator by sponsoring a worksite-based voluntary employee-pay-all plan. Most dental plans with a contributory component are usually wrapped under a Section 125 or payroll deduction plan, allowing for payment of premium with pre-tax dollars. In addition to the traditional employer – employee relationship, multiple employer trusts, unions, associations, and chambers of commerce also provide group dental insurance plans to their respective members.

Group dental coverage is available as both an insured product and an administrative services only contract. Partial self-funding vehicles with aggregate stop loss are available, particularly when benefits are aggregated with medical benefit plans.

OVERVIEW OF THE DENTAL INSURANCE INDUSTRY

The dental insurance concept was first proposed as early as 1945 by the American Dental Association (ADA), the main association for dentists in the United States. Pilot programs developed throughout the 1950's, with the first group dental plan offered by the Continental Casualty Company in August 1959. Initial growth was primarily confined to the West Coast.

Dental benefit plans grew quickly from that point, and are now one of the most frequent employer sponsored benefits. The 2000 Mercer / Foster Higgins National Survey of Employer-sponsored Health Plans indicated that 51% of all employers with 10 or more employees offer a dental benefit plan.[2] With the rise in voluntary coverage, the number of employers sponsoring dental plans has grown rapidly. The NADP 2005 Purchaser Behavior Study reports 71% of employers of six or more employees offer dental coverage. For employers with more than 10,000 full-time employees, coverage is nearly universal with 96% offering coverage. By comparison, 79% of firms with 100 to 249 employees offer coverage and 40% of employers with 6 to 24 employees do so.[3] With the dental market reaching maturity, the future market potential remains largely in the voluntary small group market.

For employers that do not offer a plan, the primary reason appears not that they fail to recognize the value such a plan might offer their employees,

---

[2] 2000 Mercer / Foster Higgins National Survey of Employer - sponsored Health Plans
[3] NADP 2005 Purchaser Behavior Study

but rather the additional cost of such plans. With medical premiums steadily increasing, employers are increasingly being squeezed as to where they can spend their benefit dollars. This phenomenon is also contributing to the growth of the voluntary market.

Penetration of the market also varies by region. For example, 71% of the population in the New England region of the U.S. is covered by dental benefits, making that region the one with the highest density. The regions defined as Mountain and West South Central by the Census Bureau had the lowest density, with rates of approximately 43% and 44% respectively.[4] Surveys also show dental plans to be most popular in the Health Care industry and least popular in the Transportation/Utilities sectors.[5]

Dental insurance has been effectively shown to play a vital role in improving the oral health of Americans. Surveys sponsored by Delta Dental Plans Association reported that the presence of dental coverage has helped reduce the incidence of cavities and extractions while encouraging patient visits to the dentist for regular checkups and cleanings.[6] A report published by the Surgeon General in 2000 stated clearly that lack of dental insurance is a barrier to care.[7] According to a survey by the ADA, 63% of dental patients have private dental insurance.[8] And, according to a Harris Interactive May 2000 Omnibus Survey, the top reason for not visiting a dentist was lack of dental insurance.[9]

Initially, most employers in the U.S. offered dental benefits under a comprehensive medical plan. Under such integrated plans, dental expenses were combined with major medical benefits in the calculation of plan benefits. Subsequently, product designs shifted to freestanding dental plans, with almost all plans offered this way today, especially among fully insured plans. With the emergence of consumer-driven health plans, there is potential for the return of integrated dental and medical benefits. Early evidence does not yet show much impact.

Group dental benefits are similar in most fundamental characteristics to other forms of group benefits. Coverage is provided through a master

---

[4] NADP / DDPA 2005 Dental Benefits Joint Report: Enrollment

[5] 1994 Foster Higgins National Survey of Employer - sponsored Health Plans

[6] 2000 DDPA survey

[7] Oral Health in America: A Report of the Surgeon General, U.S. Public Health Service, 2000

[8] American Dental Association, 1998 Survey of Dental Practice

[9] Research! America: Harris Interactive May 2000 Omnibus Survey

policy or contract issued to the policyholder or sponsor, and employees receive individual booklets or certificates of coverage. Both documents outline the details of the group-specific plan design and the eligibility rules to receive coverage.

Dental insurance is marketed by a wide variety of organizations, including insurance companies, dental service corporations such as Delta Dental, Blue Cross and Blue Shield plans, Dental Health Maintenance Organizations (DHMOs), dental referral plans and third party administrators. The primary distribution vehicle is independent brokers and consultants working in conjunction with insurer sales representatives. Some plans are sold direct to larger employers. Increasingly the Internet is being used to help distribute product, either directly, as an electronic intermediary), or in support of traditional intermediaries and brokers.

THE BASIC COMPONENTS OF DENTAL PLAN DESIGN

Dental benefits are designed to provide coverage for the prevention, diagnosis or treatment of dental disease or injury. Dental problems affect people of all ages and can be as acute in childhood as they are in old age. A primary emphasis in dental plans is on preventive care through checkups, cleanings and examinations. It is cheaper in the long run to prevent or treat dental problems in the early stages of disease. Plans encourage such care by minimizing the expense to the patient for seeking treatment before problems can get any worse. In this aspect, dental plans have been far ahead of medical plans, which, until recently, largely did not cover preventive medicine.

Dental plans differ from medical plans in the fairly moderate nature of claim levels. According to CMS, per capita consumer expenditures for dental services were roughly $273 in 2004, compared to $3700 for Hospital, Physician and Drug expenditures.[10] Dental disease is not a catastrophic risk. While medical bills can reach hundreds of thousands or even millions of dollars over a short time period, dental costs are usually limited in even the most extreme circumstance to several thousand dollars of treatment.

---

[10] Centers for Medicare and Medicaid Services, Office of the Actuary, National Health Expenditures by Type of Service and Source of Funds: Calendar Year 2004

On the other hand, dental services are often more elective than medical services, increasing the difficulty in underwriting and pricing a plan of benefits. The key to designing an effective dental plan is to include a wide variety of plan design provisions and underwriting requirements to help guard against the elective nature of dental benefits. Dental treatment can often be planned over time without affecting the appropriateness of care. Many plan provisions have been incorporated into dental plans to limit the antiselection resulting from the elective nature of such benefits, especially in the first year of a plan when patients will often seek dental work to correct problems arising from past neglect.

Dental conditions can also be treated by a wide variation of treatment plans, often at a substantial cost difference. Most plans, in an effort to reduce costs, will reimburse the patient for the least expensive form of adequate treatment.

Dental plan designs have been structured to include substantial out-of-pocket cost sharing, which helps ensure that participants choose and use care appropriately, while still receiving a meaningful benefit.

Dental benefits are usually divided into three classes of benefit, by type of service:

Type I (Preventive and Diagnostic) procedures include:

- Diagnostic services: Oral exams, x-rays (sometimes Type II, sometimes just bite-wings covered as Type I), diagnostic tests and laboratory exams (sometimes Type II) and emergency treatment.
- Preventive services: Prophylaxes (cleanings) fluoride treatments, sealants (sometimes not covered, or Type II), space maintainers (sometimes Type II or only covered when Orthodontia is covered).

Type II (Basic) procedures include:

- Restorative services such as amalgam, silicate, acrylic and resin restorations (filings).
- Endodontics (root canal treatments – sometimes all Type III, sometimes endodontic surgery is moved to Type III)
- Periodontics (gum treatments – sometimes Type III, sometimes periodontal surgery is moved to Type III).
- Repairs to prosthodontics (sometimes Type III)
- Oral surgery (extractions – sometimes more complex cases are Type III, sometimes all Type III)
- Adjunctive general services such as general anesthesia.

Type III (Major) procedures include:

- Restorative services including inlays, onlays and crowns, and posts made from various materials such as porcelain and precious metals.

- Prosthodontic services, including fixed and removable bridges, and full and partial dentures.

As dental insurance has increased in cost through inflation, it has become routine to shift services from either Type I to Type II, or from Type II to Type III, as described above.

Medical plans in the U.S. continue to cover treatment required because of accidental injury to natural teeth, removal of impacted teeth and surgical treatment for jaw (TMJ) disorders. Coordination-of-benefit provisions are used to avoid duplication of coverage with dental plans.

Each type of dental service is governed under the plan by a coinsurance percentage that splits the fee between the insurer and the patient. Plans are designed to encourage prevention and require significant costs sharing on more expensive and/or elective procedures. A typical plan design might reimburse 100% for Type I, 80% for Type II, and 50% for Type III. Such a plan is often described as a 100/80/50 plan.

Plans will typically have a calendar year deductible, which is often waived for Type I services, and an annual maximum. The typical deductible is $50 or less, and is usually on a calendar year basis. A policy year or lifetime deductible option is also available. Other common deductible provisions include: (1) a family deductible limit that sets the family deductible maximum to be three times the individual deductible maximum, and (2) a deductible credit provision that allows a credit in the first year of the plan for amounts used to meet a deductible in the employer's previous plan. On the other hand, a deductible carryover provision (a credit to the current year's deductible for expenses incurred in the last three months of the prior year which are used to satisfy the prior year's deductible), often found in medical plans, is not as common in dental plan, primarily because of the minimal nature of the deductible.

The typical plan maximum is $1,000, with a range from $500 to $2,500. The low maximums are in sharp contrast to the unlimited maximums typical in medical plans. These maximums are applied to each individual. Family maximum provisions are rare.

A fourth type (Type IV) of services that is often added to a dental plan is orthodontics. Orthodontia services are often given its own lifetime deductible and maximum. The typical amount is $1,000, and is set to cover between 25% and 50% of the typical costs because of the elective nature of the treatment.

Dental plans often contain plan provisions aimed at limiting plan cost and overall antiselection. These provisions include:

- *Exclusions*: Dental plans often include exclusions for services that are elective, not essential for good dental care, or covered by other plans. The most frequently used exclusions include care for cosmetic reasons, experimental treatments, services for non-dental items such as filling out claim forms, broken appointment fees, and benefits related to on-the-job accidents.

- *Pre-existing conditions limitations*: Most plans will not cover any charges incurred by a covered person before they are insured. This would not only include treatment started before the effective date, but would also include coverage begun after the effective date for conditions existing before the effective date. The most common example would be a missing tooth. Plans generally do not pay for prosthetic devices replacing teeth which were lost before a covered person became insured, but they will pay for a device to replace those teeth if it also replaces other teeth lost or extracted while insured.

- *Benefits after insurance ends*: Dental plans contain a very limited set of extended benefits after termination. The typical plan provision will pay for work stated before the termination date and finished within 31 days of termination.

UNDERWRITING AND RATING PARAMETERS

Underwriting, or the selection of risks to be covered, is extremely important for dental plans due to the elective nature, as well as the relatively modest cost, of dental coverage. Dental plans often employ underwriting controls that serve to limit costs and control antiselection. Plan provision and the nature of the groups covered are reflected in pricing structure. This section will describe these underwriting controls and some of the rating variables. More detail on the determination of expected claims is discussed in the chapter on "Estimating Dental Claim Costs" in another chapter.

GROUP SIZE

Dental plans generally have a minimum group size to which coverage can be offered. This limit is typically five, although some plans are offered to groups as small as two. Groups that fall below the minimum group size can be terminated. Since dental services are highly elective, this provision should be strictly enforced.

In general, the larger the group, the lower the price, because of both economies of scale and decreased risk variability. Once groups reach a certain size level, their experience is considered credible, and rates are based on the experience data. Groups of smaller size are charged manual, or book, rates. Partially credible groups are rated as a combination of the book rate and the experience rate.

ELIGIBLE INDIVIDUALS

Generally, plans will cover employees and their dependents. Dependents can include spouses and legally dependent children, including foster children and stepchildren. Dependent children are usually covered up to age 19, or 23 if a full-time student. Disabled children can be covered beyond the age limit.

Most group plans are sold to active employees only. Retirees may be included in a plan if they represent a small percentage of the risk. In general, employees are covered until the earlier of the termination of their employment or the group's cancellation date. Dependents are similarly covered until the earlier of the end of the employee's eligibility or the cessation of dependency status. For example, a spouse's coverage will usually cease on divorce. COBRA continuation provisions are applicable to dental as with medical, although fewer people elect to continue their coverage.

PARTICIPATION

Dental plans generally include minimum participation requirements. Plans sold to groups with less than 75% participation may have their rates loaded or benefits reduced to adjust for the increased antiselection inherent in the group's low enrollment. Some plans may exclude employees and dependents covered by a spouse's plan from the calculation of the participation percentage. It is common to require enrollees in both medical and dental plans to be enrolled under the same enrollment options. For example, an employee enrolled under an "employee only" medical plan (even though that employee may have eligible dependents) would be required to enroll as an employee only option under the dental plan.

Voluntary plans may allow participation as low as 25% of eligible employees, or have a minimum number of employees selecting a plan. Pricing may be adjusted to account for the actual participation percentage. Preferably, the anticipated participation percentage is accurate, so that the rates don't have to change after the enrollment. Benefits can also be downwardly adjusted to avoid a price adjustment, often by deferring certain benefits.

EMPLOYER CONTRIBUTIONS

Most non-voluntary plans require a minimum level of employer contribution, usually 50% of the single employee premium. This helps to have employees meet the participation standard mentioned below. Plans that are non-contributory, because they have 100% participation, are often available at a rate discount.

OTHER COVERAGES

The presence of other coverages in the options available to the participant is the most favorable situation from an underwriting perspective. For example, the participant might be given a choice of medical plans, with dental being available only on some of the options. Unpackaging allows the participant to more readily select against a plan.

DEMOGRAPHICS

Age and gender are important pricing variables. Groups with higher female content receive rate loads. For example, an all-male group might have a factor of 1.00 and an all-female group might be 1.15. The age slope for dental is much flatter than medical, but generally claim costs increase by age. The most sophisticated pricing models would vary both age and gender slopes by the category of coverage.

Another important pricing variable is location. Companies have area factors that vary by state, service area, or zip code.

Restricted industry lists are not as extensive in dental as in medical. Rate loads and discounts are often applied by occupation or industry, taking into account observed differences in utilization. Some occupations with the high levels of utilization include actors, teachers, and sports teams. Also, those employees with strong union affiliations are usually more aware of their dental benefits than other employees, and tend to have higher than average utilization.

Premium rates are developed by family structure tiers. Two tier (employee and dependent), three tier (employee, employee plus one dependent, ee plus two or more dependents) and four tier (employee, employee plus spouse, employee plus child(ren), employee plus spouse and child(ren), are all common.

Waiting and Deferral Periods

Dental plans often impose a waiting period before a new employee is eligible to join the plan. Often the eligibility date is expressed as the first of the month following X months from the date of hire. Closely aligned with the waiting period is an eligibility provision that contains a limit on certain Type II and Type III services. These limits can apply to new entrants and to late entrants, or those who join a plan more than 31 days after first becoming eligible. Some plans will limit benefits in the first year (for late entrants) to coverage for preventive services and other services due to accidental injury only. For some groups, especially those without prior dental coverage, Type III services may be deferred for the entire group for a period of one year or more. Voluntary plans also work this way. These provisions are extremely important, because many dental services are highly elective and can be postponed.

Incentive Coinsurance

Another approach to guard against poor experience in the first few years of a dental plan, especially on plans with no prior coverage, is an incentive coinsurance approach. Under incentive coinsurance, benefits are initially provided at a lower coinsurance level for Type II and III services, and increase each year, as long as an individual uses preventive services each year. For example, benefits may start out at 100/70/35 in the first year and go up 10 percentage points for Type II services and five percentage points for Type III services each year that a specified series of preventive procedures has been performed, until an ultimate benefit level of 100/100/50 is reached. If in any year, an individual fails to see a dentist, then benefits are reset to the Year 1 level.

TRANSFERRED BUSINESS

Dental plans will generally pay for certain charges incurred before the plan's effective date, as long as the plan is a replacement of another plan, without any break in coverage. Payment is usually limited to the lesser of the old plan benefit and the new plan benefit, less any benefits paid under the old plan's extension provision.

In the first year of a plan, it is also common to reduce the deductible by the amount of covered charges applied against the old plan's deductible. Also, in the first benefit year the new plan will charge benefit payments by the old plan against its payment limits.

REIMBURSEMENT MODELS AND DELIVERY SYSTEMS

The three general types of delivery systems for dental benefit plans are indemnity (traditional fee-for-service reimbursement), PPO (preferred provider organization, generally reimbursed with discounted fee-for-service) and DHMO (dental HMO, generally prepaid or capitated). Dental plans have generally moved through the same product continuum as their medical counterparts. As of calendar year 2004, 52% of individuals were covered by PPO plans, 29% by indemnity plans, 12% by DHMO plans and 7% by Discount Card plans (a combined 71% in dental network-based plans). Comparable 1994 figures were 70% indemnity, 10% PPO and 15% DHMO and 5% in Discount Card plans.[11] New sales are more even heavily weighted toward PPO plans, and continued substantial shifts in in-force business are predicted by most observers.

FUNDING MECHANISMS

Most dental plans are structured as fully insured plans. However, as group size increases, self-insurance becomes a realistic alternative. Thus, all the funding mechanisms common to group medical insurance are available, with the exception of individual stop loss, which is not a concept that extends itself to dental insurance because of the low maximum benefits.

Direct Reimbursement, which is a concept endorsed by the American Dental Association (ADA), encourages employers to administer their own

---

[11] NADP / DDPA 2001 Dental Benefits Joint Report

dental programs, potentially reducing overall plan cost. Even if the risk is manageable to the employer, the insurer's claim paying capabilities and cost control procedures argue strongly for administration provided by a third party. Direct contracting or reimbursement plans have not materially gained in popularity, despite the ADA endorsement.

A prepaid dental plan, which is also called a Dental HMO (DHMO) has a per member per month (PMPM) payment to cover dental health services, even if no care is required. Thus, the indemnity and PPO model of fee-for-service reimbursement is replaced with a capitation mechanism.

INDEMNITY PLANS

"Scheduled indemnity plans" cover services up to a maximum per procedure set by the plan. All dentists are eligible to render care, and those that charge above the maximum reimbursement will often bill the patient for the balance. The schedule is often fairly low. These plans were quite popular in the past, and are still common in the voluntary market, but have generally been replaced by Usual, Customary and Reasonable (UCR) plans, because it is cumbersome to update the scheduled benefits each year. However, with the rise in employee-pay-all-plans in recent years, the low cost of scheduled plan design is once again appealing.

"UCR plans" are the typical traditional fee-for-service plans that are common in today's market. Services are covered up to the UCR limit, subject to deductibles, coinsurance and maximums.

PREFERRED PROVIDER PLANS (PPO)

"Managed indemnity plans," or "passive PPOs," are plans that take advantage of contracted fees with participating dentists. Plan design is the same whether in-network or out-of-network. Participants are encouraged only by reduced out-of-pocket expenses to use network dentists.

"Discounted fee-for-service PPO plans" provide incentives (or disincentives) to participants to seek care from in-network providers, who have agreed to a set percentage discount (15% to 35%) from their standard charges. Care is available out-of-network on a reduced benefit basis, usually with greater coinsurance requirements.

"Fee schedule PPO plans" are the same as discounted fee-for-service plans, but require that in-network dentists agree to a specific fee schedule, rather than a discount. Fewer dentists will agree to this, but the discounts are often greater. Most plans use this approach today in building their networks. Fee schedules are based on average charge data in a geographic region, where credible, and relative values elsewhere. Certain procedures that are of greater priority to a particular dentist may be negotiated.

"Discount Card plans" are not insurance products, but are available to individuals or groups, and allow members to receive discounts from participating providers. Under these plans, the participant pays the dentist directly, and there are no claims. These plans only have value for an employer that does not have compensation dollars available to spend on dental insurance.

"Exclusive provider organization plans (EPOs)" are in-network-only PPO plans. In exchange for more steerage, more select panels are set up with greater discounts expected. Not all states allow EPO plans.

"Point of Service (POS) plans" are a hybrid of the indemnity, PPO and DHMO concepts. The patient can pick (by choosing their dentist) between receiving benefits from an in-network HMO provider, a PPO provider, or any other provider, at different levels of benefit. This choice is made either once a year (most common), once a month, or in rare instances at the true point-of-service.

DENTAL MAINTENANCE ORGANIZATIONS PLANS (DHMO)

"Independent provider association (IPA) DHMO plans" construct their panels from independent dentists who agree to capitation reimbursement. The amount the dentist is paid is not directly tied to the frequency or value of services performed. In essence, the dentist assumes the majority of the financial risk involved in treating patients. Specialists, available on referral, are typically compensated on a discounted fee-for-service basis. Primary care and specialty dentists are chosen from a limited panel of participating providers. In order for capitation to work, providers need to have a minimum number of patients to spread their risk.

"Staff model DHMO plans" employ their own dentists, and offer the greatest control over cost of care.

COMPARING THE THREE PLAN TYPES

The table below highlights the key differences between the three plan types. Further detail is given in the discussion that follows.

Plan Type	Indemnity	PPO	DHMO
Premium	High	Medium	Low
Patient Access	Highest	Fair	Limited
Benefit Richness	Least	Fair	Highest
Reimbursement	UCR/Schedule	Schedule	Capitation
Cost Management	Least	Fair	Most
Utilization	High	High	Low
Quality Assurance	Least	Fair	Highest
Fraud Potential	High	Moderate	Low
Provider Contracting	No	Yes	Yes

Premium

Dental HMO premiums are generally 15% to 25% below PPO plans, and 30% to 40% below traditional indemnity plans.

DHMO rates are low primarily due to the gatekeeper approach and capitation mechanisms, features that control utilization and limit plan costs.

Patient Access

In an indemnity plan, a patient can pick any dentist, and there is no limit on access. In PPO plans, access is more limited, but out-of-network options are still available. DHMO plans generally restrict access to network only.

The major handicap any managed care plan will face in a particular market is the adequacy of its network. The provider panel in a DHMO is usually relatively small in comparison to its PPO counterpart.

Benefit Richness

PPOs use the same basic plan designs as previously described for indemnity plans. The major difference is the difference in benefits between an in-network and out-of-network provider. Plan designs might be structured as in the following examples:

- 100/100/60 in-network, 100/80/50 out-of-network – rewards patient for going in-network in comparison to standard indemnity 100/80/50 design.

- 100/80/50 in-network, 80/70/40 out-of-network – penalizes patient for not going in-network in comparison to standard indemnity 100/80/50 design.

- 100/80/50 in and out-of-network – with only balance billing on out-of-network services encouraging patients to use a network dentist.

Large differentials in PPO and EPO plan benefits are rare, and generally prohibited by state PPO laws.

The typical DHMO plan will include coverage for the same services provided for under indemnity and PPO models, but often with a lower out-of-pocket expense to the patient. Although perceived as the richest of the plans, even HMOs will not cover purely cosmetic procedures.

The typical DHMO plan also has no deductible, and no annual or lifetime maximum. DHMO benefit plans often contain richer benefits for major and orthodontic benefits than is typical in other plans. Patient out-of-pocket costs are often expressed as a copay for each service.

Most dental HMO plans do not pay benefits for out-of-network services, other than a small emergency services benefit. This is changing, however, as the dental HMO industry mirrors the increasing popularity of medical point-of-service (POS) plans.

Cost Management

Indemnity programs manage cost through UCR, LEAT ("least expensive alternative treatment," discussed later), clinical logic, and predetermination. PPOs use many of the same techniques, and additionally reap the benefits of the extensive credentialing programs that are set up to find cost-effective quality dentists. DHMO plans, in addition to the above techniques, have the gatekeeper approach and the specialty referral process to control utilization (and thus cost.)

Utilization

The tendency in indemnity plans and PPO plans is to over-use services – because of fee-for-service reimbursement. Some PPOs experience higher utilization because some dentists "make up" the discounts by performing more procedures. An effective utilization management program employing predetermination and claim review may limit these potential abuses. HMOs on the other hand, are perceived to promote an underutilization of services. Critics contend that office waits are longer, scheduling is more difficult, and more costly care is withheld.

Quality Assurance

Indemnity plans offer very little chance of assuring that quality care is received. This is the "price" of free choice. PPOs and HMOs, with their selective screening processes, offer higher assurance of quality. On the other hand, many plans are criticized as utilizing cost-efficient, as opposed to quality, dentists. Plans have responded by issuing patient satisfaction report cards indicating overall satisfaction with provider dentists. Despite this, most participants and plan sponsors still have negative biases against managed care.

Fraud Potential

Dental insurance is extremely susceptible to fraud. While the effectiveness of combating fraud is really a function of the insurer's utilization management efforts, and not of the particular plan types sold, HMOs, and their capitation approach, minimize many of the incentives to commit fraud from either the dentist or participant.

Provider Contracting

Both PPOs and DHMOs use a contract to arrange for services to be provided at agreed-on rates. Indemnity plans that allow full services from all dentists do not. Most contracts are for a one-year term, and are automatically renewable. In the contract, the dentist agrees to abide by the plan's quality assurance and utilization management programs, and to discounted charges or a fee schedule. In return, the insurer promises to encourage patients to use network providers. The contract also spells out the grievance, review and provider relationship functions. DHMO contracts will also spell out specialty referral guidelines.

Contracts are generally offered to providers who have undergone an extensive credentialing process. This process is repeated every several years. In addition to collecting biographical and practice information, dentists are asked to reveal potential problems, such as criminal offenses and past malpractice situations. HMOs often conduct on-site reviews of a dentist's practice, checking the office OSHA compliance, and reviewing sample patient records. The credentialing process is usually much more extensive in DHMO plans than other plans.

Recruitment of dentists is often a face-to-face process, with a knowledgeable dental care professional representing the insurer. Companies employ a wide variety of techniques, such as practice management, training and other perks, to attract dentists into their programs. Dentist resistance is, of course, a function of geography and provider to patient relationships.

Managed care plans are becoming more popular with dentists. According to NADP estimates, approximately 60% of dentists participate in PPO plans and 15% plus in DHMO plans.[12]Growth in capitated plans has clearly stalled. Dentists are becoming more selective in joining HMO plans, as the capacity equation moves in their favor. (The ratio of private practitioners per U.S. resident has begun to decline, and is projected to continue to decline through 2020.) Trends also vary by general dentist and specialist. 80% of dentists are general practitioners. This is the reverse of the medical field, where 32% are engaged in primary care.[13] Also, the number of yearly dental school graduates has declined 20% since 1980.[14]

Dental networks have low rates of provider terminations, which are under 5% in most instances. Thus, once a dentist is sold on the PPO or DHMO concept, the dentist is likely to join and stay with the concept.

CLAIM PRACTICES

Dental costs are relatively modest when compared with medical benefits, but the elective nature of many services can cause claim costs to vary significantly. Acceptable treatment plans can vary widely, and proper coding of procedures is important. In order to control the cost of dental plans, claim administration procedures unique to dental are necessary. The chapter on Claim Administration and Management that follows later in this text gives details for many of the claim practices common to all health plans. Here, those practices that are important for dental claims are discussed.

PREDETERMINATION OF BENEFITS

Most plans suggest that patients about to undergo a treatment plan with expected costs more than a specified limit, such as $200 or $300, submit the plan for pre-treatment review to verify coverage under the plan. While mainly intended as a protection against surprises, this policy also services as a deterrent against over-utilization of services. Predetermination often

---

[12] NADP / DDPA 2005 Joint Dental Benefits Report: Network Statistics

[13] American Dental Association, 1998 Distribution of dentists in the U.S. by Region and State; U.S. Census Bureau, Health and Nutrition, *Statistical Abstract of the United States: 2000, No. 186*

[14] U.S. Census Bureau, Health and Nutrition, *Statistical Abstract of the United States: 2000, No. 188*

requires that x-rays and diagnostic models be submitted, to evidence the necessity of treatment and services rendered.

LEAST EXPENSIVE ALTERNATE TREATMENT (LEAT)

Predetermination is crucial to plan success, because dental problems can often be treated with differing procedures varying widely in cost. Plans are generally written to cover the cost of the least expensive alternate treatment, so long as it meets clinically and professionally accepted standards of practice. The principal area where the alternate benefit provision is cost-effective is with Type III services, especially crowns and fixed partial dentures.

Each of the services under the plan is governed by an extensive series of age and time limitations. For example, oral exams, cleanings and fluoride treatments will be limited to twice a calendar year. X-rays will have separate frequency restrictions. Sealant treatments may be limited to children under age 16. The purpose of these limitations is to lower overall plan costs within the framework of clinically accepted standards of dental practice.

COORDINATION OF BENEFITS

Plans will not pay for charges to the extent that they are also paid by another health or dental plan sponsored by the plan holder, or by Medicare. If a covered person also received benefits from another plan (other than the ones mentioned above), the plan will generally coordinate benefits from that plan. In this way, the patient will not receive benefits that exceed the charges incurred. Benefits from other plans cannot be used to meet the plan's deductible. Dual coverage for dental coverage can be relatively more valuable than for medical coverage, because reimbursement can be much higher with the luxury of two annual maximums.

In addition to all of the above-mentioned provisions, several claim administration provisions are typically included in group contacts and in the administrative guidelines that govern the claim paying process.

Since dental is such a high frequency insurance coverage, speedy and accurate claim administration is a vital aspect of good customer service. Advances in claim paying ability through electronic claim filing and adjudication are expected to be a high priority for all dental claim payers in the years ahead.

DENTAL REVIEW

Proper administration of a dental plan requires a sophisticated claim payment system to properly adjudicate claims. The system must automatically check eligibility, age and frequency limitations. ADA service codes can also be manipulated in some situations by unbundling certain charges to the dentist's advantage. Good systems will re-bundle these procedures.

Most dental plans also employ dental professionals serving in a consultant capacity to review difficult claims, ensure dental necessity, and evaluate and approve the prescribed treatment plan.

MAXIMUM ALLOWABLE CHARGE

Maximum Allowable Charge (MAC or Usual Customary and Reasonable (UCR) provisions limit covered expenses for a particular service to the lesser of:

- The dentist's usual fee for the procedure,
- The fee level set by the plan administrator based on charges submitted in the same geographical area, and
- The reasonable fee charged for a service, even when unusual circumstances or complications exist.

Most payers use a percentile approach, typically covering expenses in the range of the 80th to 90th percentile, to assure that they are establishing a reasonable level of MAC. (This means that charges will be 100% recognized or covered, for 80% to 90% of dentists in the area.)

FUTURE OF DENTAL BENEFITS

With employers facing large medical plan cost increases once again, dental insurers are increasingly developing low-cost products to meet employer needs.
Voluntary plans will continue to grow in popularity. Among non-voluntary plans, the employee's contribution percentage will continue to grow.

Additionally, the consumer-driven healthcare phenomenon is spreading to dental insurance, with greater access to information and benefit choice becoming important to plan participants. Plans are adding treatment cost estimators to websites so patients can know in advance their out- of-pocket costs and compare fees of in-network and out-of-network providers. Stand alone dental Health Reimbursement Accounts plans are also becoming more common.

Defined contribution plans represent both an opportunity for dental insurance as well as a threat. Since dental expenses tend to be manageable, they lend themselves well to flexible spending accounts, medical savings accounts, and health reimbursement arrangements. Plans are being designed that will allow employees to use employer funding dollars to buy a core benefit and to buy-up additional amounts of coverage with their own dollars. Several newly developed defined contribution health plans include dental and vision benefits in their scope, potentially eliminating the need for stand-alone insurance.

Employees seek larger networks to provide choice to their employees, boding well for the continued popularity of PPO plans. Many carriers are beginning to allow more on-line self-service to employees and employers, including online access to data about providers and claim payment information.

Shortages in dentist capacity and supply will put pressure on building and maintaining dental networks. Providers will likely be more selective in the networks they join.

9 PRESCRIPTION DRUG BENEFITS IN THE UNITED STATES

Audrey Halvorson
John Watkins

INTRODUCTION

Prescription drugs are an increasingly important part of health care. New drugs are regularly introduced which improve the health and quality of life for many. Through the use of drugs, physicians are increasingly able to treat conditions before they require acute care. Prescription drugs are truly changing the face of medical care in the twenty-first century.

Prescription drugs have been covered by many health benefit plans, either as an eligible charge as part of a major medical program, or as a separate benefit provided through a drug card. Prescription drug benefits are usually available through Medicaid. The Medicare Modernization Act (2003) created a federally funded drug plan that is available to all Medicare beneficiaries, either through a stand-alone Part D prescription drug program or as an integral part of a managed Medicare Advantage plan.

Prescription drug benefit costs as a percentage of total medical claim costs increased rapidly in the late 1990's into the early 2000's. The trend has slowed somewhat, more recently. Retail drug costs represented 11% of all U.S. health care spending in 2004. Their 8.2% growth rate that year was the first single digit increase in a decade. The slowing of price growth has been driven by over-the-counter availability of two very popular prescription drugs, promotion of generic drug use by payers, and a wave of patent expirations that will lower overall spending in several popular drug classes.[1] It is very possible that this trend rate will increase in the future.

There were several reasons for the 1980's large and accelerating increase in costs; reasons that could again push trends up:

---

[1] Smith C, Cowan C, Heffler S, et al. National Health Spending In 2004: Recent Slowdown Led By Prescription Drug Spending. *Health Affairs* 25, no. 1 (2006): 186–196. (Data from CMS.)

- *Prescription drug pipeline*: Research brings powerful new drugs to market, providing new solutions for patients. Some of these new drugs represent completely new therapies, offering hope to patients with diseases that were previously untreatable. Others provide increased convenience in dosage, and fewer side effects than older drugs. Companies often have a significant investment in research and development for new drugs, and are anxious to recover these costs.

- *Biologics*: These drugs are particularly expensive, costing at least ten times as much as the older ones they replace. The current price range is $1,000 to $50,000 per patient per month. Biologics are produced by complex manufacturing processes that are not easily replicated. For this reason, we are not likely to see generic biologics any time soon.

- *Patents*: New drugs are covered by patents that protect the original manufacturer from competition for a period of time. Generics, using the clinical formula for the new drug, are not allowed to be sold until after the patent expiration. This allows drug manufacturers to cover costs for research on the drug, as well as provide additional monies for other ongoing research. In recent years, manufacturers have been able to extend the profitable life of popular drugs, through litigation against generic competitors and by creating modified versions of the original product that retain patents for several years after the original molecular patent has expired.

- *Direct to consumer advertising*: Marketing to consumers through television, radio, print, and other media has increased consumer awareness of these new, high cost drugs. We have all heard the ads that encourage patients to ask their doctors about the benefits of a certain drug, or even to ask for free trial samples. Physicians are not only feeling pressure from the drug manufacturer's sales force, but are also feeling pressure from their patients to use certain drugs. Studies have shown that this pressure is effective,[2] and that both physicians and the public are divided as to whether they believe the net effect is beneficial.[3]

---

[2] Kravitz RL, Epstein RM, Feldman MD, et al. Influence of patients' requests for direct-to-consumer advertised antidepressants: a randomized controlled trial. *JAMA*. 2005 Apr 27;293(16):1995-2002.
JAMA. 2005 Apr 27;293(16):1995-2002.
Free Full Text Influence of patients' requests for direct-to-consumer advertised antidepressants: a randomized controlled trial.
JAMA. 2005 Apr 27;293(16):1995-2002.

[3] Robinson AR, Hohmann KB, Rifkin JI, et al. Direct-to-consumer pharmaceutical advertising: physician and public opinion and potential effects on the physician-patient relationship. *Arch Intern Med*. 2004 Feb 23;164(4):427-32.

- *Faster approval process:* The approval process by which the Food and Drug Administration (FDA) approves drugs for use in the market has been streamlined. This increase in the speed of approval for drugs increases the number of high cost drugs coming to the market, adding additional upward pressure on the trend in both average cost of drugs and utilization of the new drugs. Recent concerns about the safety of several FDA approved drugs may reduce this effect.

- *Brand name advertising*: Marketing of brand name drugs after generics become available is designed to maintain the sales levels of these more expensive drugs. Patients are encouraged to ask for the brand name, even when less expensive alternatives are available.

- *Aging population*: As the proportion of the population at the older ages increases, the demand for drug therapy increases.

- *Increase in testing for disease*: Recent years have shown a greater awareness of conditions which, often without symptoms, result in drug therapies. Examples are bone density tests and cholesterol screening, which often result in drug therapies to avoid acute illness and complications. Genomic testing, still in its infancy, will further increase this trend.

Thus, the average cost of covered drugs remains at risk for accelerating increases, while the number of prescriptions per patient and the number of patients using prescriptions continues to increase.

The concern that claim trends of prescription drug benefits can help to drive double digit health care cost increase, have caused health plans offering these benefits to look closely at ways of designing prescription drug benefits, contracting with vendors and managing utilization to temper those trends. Plan sponsors, unable or not willing to accept these trends in costs, are also pressuring health plans to design ways to control these costs.

COVERAGE TYPES

The two most common forms of prescription drug benefit coverage are a drug card program or coverage through a sponsor's major medical plan.

Prescription drug card programs generally do not integrate the drug benefit with the medical benefits. Thus, although the card program can contain a deductible amount, only prescription drug claims are counted toward that deductible. These are sometimes called "freestanding" drug benefit programs. Card programs are self contained, and are generally administered separately from the medical benefits, often times using a pharmacy benefit manager (PBM), or other third party administrator type of arrangement. This does not necessarily mean that the drug program is a separate employee benefit program or insurance contract, rather that the drug benefits are adjudicated separately, without the need to coordinate with the base medical program.

Access to benefits under a card program is obtained through the use of a card, which allows the pharmacist to verify eligibility and plan information electronically, through the PBM or other drug administrator. Drug card plans usually provide access to a pharmacy network with discounted prescription pricing that has been negotiated by the PBM or the health plan.

A typical major medical plan covers drugs subject to a deductible and coinsurance, and is integrated with the medical benefits. For example, a $250 deductible, 80%/20% coinsurance plan would count prescription drug claims toward the deductible, just like any other medical expense. Once the deductible is met, later prescription drug claims would have a participant cost share of 20% coinsurance. Other combinations of benefits are available under the major medical integrated plan, with the main feature being the integration of the deductible. In the new high deductible major medical plans designed for use with health savings accounts (Consumer Driven Health Plans), the member pays both drug and medical costs up to the deductible amount from the health savings account or out of pocket. Once the deductible has been reached, drugs are covered under the major medical benefit.

Both of these types of coverage often include a mail order program, which allows for purchasing drugs by mail order or by e-commerce, and is discussed in more detail below.

PLAN DESIGN ISSUES

Benefit designs are structured to control costs by encouraging the efficient use of available drugs. Current benefit designs of drug programs include the use of formularies, copays, coinsurance, minimums of copays and coinsurance, and even limits to coverage of lifestyle drugs.

FORMULARIES

Formularies are lists of preferred drugs, identified either by a health plan or by a PBM. Whether a drug is on the list may affect member cost sharing and access to the drug. Formulary design is discussed in another section.

The following formulary-related benefit designs currently exist in the prescription drug coverage market:

- *Closed*: Closed formularies only cover those drugs listed on the formulary. If used in a Medicaid plan, the participant cost share is very small or nothing. If used in a group commercial plan, the participant cost share may vary by generic versus brand name, or may be flat for all drugs on the closed formulary. Closed formulary plans must have a process to allow coverage of non-formulary medications for individual patients based on medical necessity.

- *Open*: Open formularies do not affect whether or not a drug is covered, but usually affect the cost share. Typical designs have two tiers of drugs: tier 1 (generics) and tier 2 (brand name drugs). Tier 1 drugs generally have a low participant cost share amount, and tier 2 drugs will have a higher participant cost share. For example, an open formulary benefit design might have a $10 copay for generics, and $20 copay for brand name drugs. Another variation is 10% coinsurance for generics, and 20% for brand name drugs.

- *Three tier*: Three tier formularies, also known as incentive formularies, have become popular in the last few years. Tier 1 is typically defined as generic drugs, and is similar to tier 1 of the open formulary. Tier 2 is defined as preferred drugs, chosen for clinical efficacy, cost, or otherwise, and tier 3 is considered non-preferred drugs, that is, not "on formulary" although still covered under the benefit plan design. How drugs are determined to be preferred or non-preferred is briefly discussed below in the section entitled "Formulary Design." Participant cost share levels increase as the tier level increases. For example, tier 1 (generics) may have a $10 copy, tier 2 (preferred) may have a $20 copay, and tier 3 (non-preferred) may have a $40 copay. If coinsurance is included in the design, the participant cost shares may be 10%, 20% and 40%, for the respective tiers. This design is intended to help manage costs, by encouraging patients and their physicians to use the preferred tier of drugs, through the higher participant cost shares for the non-preferred drugs.

- *Four tier*: Four tier formularies have recently been seen. One such plan identifies a separate tier for chronic use, maintenance drugs. This tier of drugs may have a cost share level between the generic drug tier and the preferred drug tier. Another four tier design may put lifestyle drugs (drugs that are not medically necessary but add value to someone's lifestyle, such as Viagra) at a 100% participant cost share, while providing the drugs at the health plan's discounts with pharmacies. Recently some plans are taking specialty pharmaceuticals (biologics and other very high cost drugs that are usually dispensed by specialty pharmacies) out of the standard three tier benefit and placing them in a fourth tier with a cost share that is commensurate with their high cost. Other four tier formulary designs are sure to be tried.

PARTICIPANT COST SHARING

Participant cost share options include: copayments, coinsurance, deductibles, and combinations.

Copay plans, often seen with managed care plans, are also available with PPO, POS, and indemnity plans. Copay plans typically have different copay amounts for different formulary tiers.

Coinsurance plans may have a deductible for drugs along with the coinsurance in the plan design. With a tier based formulary design, the coinsurance will often increase with the tier of the formulary. If the coinsurance plan is part of a major medical integrated plan, the plan's medical deductible must be met before the coinsurance takes affect. In these situations, the prescription drug claim is applied to the plan deductible.

If the coinsurance plan is not integrated with a major medical plan, a separate prescription drug deductible may apply. If there is a prescription drug deductible, only drug claims are counted in meeting the drug deductible. Once the deductible is met, coinsurance is then applied to the drug claims.

Coinsurance plans are also available with managed care, PPO, POS, and indemnity plans.

Another prescription drug plan design uses the larger of a copay value or percentage coinsurance as the participant cost share. For example, a plan might have a cost share of the greater of $10 or 10% of the drug cost. A drug costing $75 would require a participant payment of $10, and a drug costing $170 would require a participant payment of $17.

Cost sharing maximums can occur as well, such as percentage coinsurance with a dollar value maximum, which protects the participant from the high cost of certain drugs such as AIDS drugs. Here, a participant might pay 10% of the cost to a maximum of $25. A drug costing $50 would require a $5 participant payment, and a drug costing $400 would require a $25 participant payment.

As pharmacy benefit premiums rise, member cost sharing is also increasing in the private employer-funded sector. This may preserve affordability of these benefits for a while, but there is a limit to how far this strategy can reasonably be pursued. Studies have shown that members will indeed use less medication as the out-of-pocket cost increases, but unintended conesquences of this may adversely affect the outcomes of health care.[4] Since the money that members use to pay the cost share amount usually comes from their pay, there is ultimately a limit to how much an employer can cost shift before the employee's total compensation package becomes unaffordable.

LIMITATIONS ON USAGE

Limitations will often exist with respect to the amount dispensed and frequency of refills. For example, a typical prescription dispensed at a pharmacy will provide 30 to 35 days supply of a drug. With this limit, refills can only be made close to the expected time when the previous prescription will have been used up. In the example above, a participant may only be allowed to get a refill after 28 or 30 days.

MAIL ORDER PROGRAMS

Mail order programs are often available, under either a card program or a major medical integrated program. New Consumer Driven Health Plans tied to a Health Savings Account are limited by law to retail programs only, and cannot use mail order programs. Mail order programs are best used for maintenance drugs, such as those used by long term therapy patients. Typically, a mail order program will dispense up to three months worth of prescription drugs, and often at a participant cost share of one or two times the cost share if dispensed at a retail pharmacy. For example, a three tier formulary copay plan design of $10/$20/$40, may have mail order copays of $20/$40/$80, with a mail order limit of three times, or 90 days supply. This provides lower cost to participants, and encourages the use of the mail order program.

---

[4] Gibson TB; Ozminkowski RJ and Goetzel RZ. The Effects of Prescription Drug Cost Sharing: A Review of the Evidence. *Am J Manag Care*. 2005;11:730-740.

Average costs of prescription drugs, however, have been increasing faster than the rate of the participant cost share under copayment plans. Thus, for health plans with certain plan designs, the cost of mail order drugs can become higher than retail dispensed drugs. As the proportion of mail order drugs increases for a health plan, this problem worsens. Thus, it may not be long before mail order copay factors increase to as much as 2.5 times a retail prescription copay.

MANDATORY GENERICS AND "DISPENSE AS WRITTEN" BENEFIT ISSUES

Another benefit plan option for reducing drug cost is to mandate generic dispensing when a generic product is available. Most states' generic substitution laws permit a physician to mark the prescription "dispense as written" or "DAW," which requires the pharmacy to dispense the brand name drug rather than the generic substitute. There are three possible benefit approaches in dealing with this:

- *Mandatory generics without exception*: With this benefit, the generic is covered at tier 1 and the brand is always tier 3, regardless of the physician's instructions regarding substitution. In some benefits, the member must also pay the difference in cost between the brand and its corresponding generic.
- *Mandatory generics unless physician writes "DAW"*: With this benefit, the generic is covered at tier 1 and the brand is tier 3. However, if the physician orders the brand to be dispensed, the member does not have to pay the cost difference between brand and generic.
- *Voluntary generics*: The member does not pay the cost difference, regardless of how the prescription is written, but still pays the third tier copay if brand is dispensed unless the brand is a preferred brand (tier 2).

However, if no generic exists, these provisions would not apply. Many plans will also make temporary exceptions when the generic equivalent is unavailable to pharmacies due to manufacturing shortages.

FORMULARY DESIGN

ASSIGNMENT TO TIERS

Formulary design, or determining which drugs should be preferred drugs and which should be non-preferred drugs, can vary widely between health plans. Most hospitals and some medical provider groups have their own formularies as well. Physicians do not always have information on formularies when they prescribe a medication for a participant. Thus, confusion can occur when a participant goes to the pharmacy. This can be rectified if computerized physician order entry is available to the physician at the point of prescribing the drug. Prescribing tools such as ePocrates, a PDA-based drug information system, may include formulary information. Some health plans are making this type of information available through such tools on their own Web sites.

Three-tier benefit plans were originally designed to help manage costs. Assume that a three-tier program has a formulary design that includes generics in tier 1, preferred brand name drugs in tier 2, and non-preferred brand name drugs in tier 3. One might think that the average cost of drugs in tier 2 would be less than the average cost of drugs in tier 3. This is not always the case, as will be shown below. Some health plans may have formularies like this, which may have been based on the cost of each drug.

However, many health plans have formularies based on clinical safety and effectiveness and availability of single source drugs, rather than the cost of the drug.

Brand name drugs can be broken down into two categories – single source brands and multi-source brands. Single source brand drugs are those where there is no other drug available that has the same chemical formula that can be considered "generically equivalent." Generic equivalence is determined by the FDA, based on bioavailability studies that show that the generic product delivers the same amount of active ingredient as the brand.

Multi-source brand drugs are those that have generics available. Multi-source drugs become available after a patent expires.

When there is no generic equivalent, a plan may still reduce drug cost by encouraging substitution of a therapeutically interchangeable drug. Therapeutically interchangeable drugs are those drugs that have the same therapeutic effect to treat a condition, despite the fact that their chemical structure differs.

For example, a three-tier formulary might be designed as follows:

Tier 1) Generics
Tier 2) Preferred brands
Tier 3) Multi-source brands and single source brands that are non-preferred

The philosophy behind the often higher cost single source drugs and the preferred multi-source drugs being on tier 2 (or "on formulary") is to provide participants with the drugs they need at the lower brand name cost share level. Thus, if a drug is the only one of its kind, and it is judged to be safe, effective and cost-effective, they can get it at the tier 2 cost share. This can result in the average cost of drugs in tier 2 being higher than the average cost of drugs in tier 3. However, the formulary design was built with the participant in mind. A well-designed formulary should generally include drugs that cover 90-95% of the medication needs of the participants.

PHARMACY AND THERAPEUTICS (P&T) COMMITTEES

The choice of which drugs to put on the formulary is usually not based purely on cost, but rather on clinical value and cost-effectiveness. These formulary decisions are typically made by the organization's Pharmacy and Therapeutics (P&T) Committee. These committees typically consist of respected pharmacists and physicians representing the geographical area served by the organization. Others, such as nurses, physician assistants, laypersons, and ethicists, may be included. In some plans, only members that are not employed by the organization have voting rights, while the organization's staff attends the meetings as non-voting members. In these cases, the staff establishes the committee charter, selects voting members and plans the agenda but does not control the resulting decisions.

The P&T committee determines whether a drug under consideration should be added to the formulary. Figure 9.1 appended to this chapter shows a schematic of one health plan's formulary process.[5]

On the left side of the diagram, under the heading of "Clinical Processes," is a description of the decision process of the P&T committee. The three possible decisions out of the P&T committee are "Don't Add," "Add," and "Interchangeable/May Add." Once a decision is made to categorize a drug as "Add" or "Interchangeable," the process goes back to the health plan to determine the budget impact of the "add" or "may add" decision and how it will be implemented.

In this process, the P&T committee first answers the question, "Is it safe and effective?" If the answer is yes, they then answer, "Is it worth the additional cost, compared to existing alternatives?" If the answers are affirmative, the business decisions are passed to an internal committee of

[5] This diagram was developed by John Watkins, Premera.

the health plan that determines the financial impact of implementing the formulary decisions, answering the question, "How can we afford to pay for it?" This committee may conduct a bidding process among the alternative products that have been declared interchangeable by the P&T committee, making the final product selection based on budget impact modeling of the different choices. This is done at this particular health plan by a cross functional group including the pharmacy services department, the actuarial department, and the PBM. The pharmacy department and PBM then oversee the implementation and communication to stakeholders of the resulting formulary changes.

VALUING FINANCIAL IMPACT OF FORMULARY DECISIONS

To determine the financial impact of formulary decisions, financial modeling using various sets of assumptions is necessary, to project net plan cost of changing the formulary.

"Cost" must consider the average wholesale price (AWP), the discount from the AWP contracted, the dispensing fee, participant cost share, and the rebates for drugs "on formulary."

Rebates (payments from manufacturers for preferred status of their drugs on a formulary) are the most difficult portion of "cost" to project. Rebates can be aggregated, based on the total sales of that manufacturer's products, or paid to the health plan by the PBM as an amount per script for a particular drug. Rebates are calculated using an agreed on formula, usually based on formulary status, accessibility as compared to competitor products, and market share within the therapeutic class of that manufacturer's products. Rebates can thus vary depending on how many other therapeutically interchangeable drugs are on formulary and the relative ease of member access and cost share. Rebates may vary depending on whether or not a manufacturer "bundles" drugs in a rebate formulary – that is, rebates may be lost for a group of drugs from a particular manufacturer if one drug out of the group is taken off formulary or not added to formulary. Rebates are discussed in greater detail below.

Thus, detailed financial projections should be performed for an entire therapeutic class of drugs when determining the financial effect of adding or deleting drugs to a formulary. It may also be necessary to project beyond the therapeutic class, depending on the terms of the rebate agreement pertaining to a specific drug or set of drugs. In some cases, movement to a product in a different pharmacologic class that can be used for the same purpose should also be modeled.

Formulary budget impact model inputs include assumptions about formulary status, market shares, rebates, inflation and future availability of generics in the class. Discussion of the details of a financial projection model for formulary decisions is beyond the scope of this chapter.

PHARMACOECONOMIC ANALYSIS

A new type of financial analysis is being used by P&T committees to determine the medical cost effectiveness of drugs during the clinical review. Pharmacoeconomic analysis attempts to determine the entire medical cost of treating a patient with a specific clinical problem with various drugs, diagnostics and other treatment strategies including surgery. This type of modeling is called decision analysis.

A decision analytic model is built around a decision tree. The problem will be framed as a choice of "treatment A" or "treatment B." For each treatment choice, a "care path" is determined, based on probabilities of occurrence derived from clinical studies. Costs for each service are estimated, including physician services, hospital stays and other medical services, as well as the cost of drugs in the care path. The total cost of the care path is determined based on these probabilities and costs. Care paths are then compared to determine the cost variation between paths.

The Academy of Managed Care Pharmacy (AMCP) has developed the Format for Formulary Submissions, a template for manufacturers to submit an evidence dossier that summarizes the clinical and economic evidence for their drug under consideration by a P&T committee. The information is then reviewed by staff pharmacists who typically also conduct their own literature search, and may prepare a monograph for the committee to review when deciding whether to add the drug to formulary. Staff may also review and critique the pharmacoeconomic analysis technique.

The Format process was adopted by AMCP in 2000,[6] and the organization has now trained pharmacists and physicians representing a number of health plans and PBMs around the country. Most manufacturers are now submitting their information in the required format, though the quality of models submitted does not always meet the Format standards.

Because the economic analysis to be used has been left to each manufacturer to define, the information provided by different manufacturers

---

[6] For the current Format document, see www.amcp.org under "Professional Resources."

for therapeutically interchangeable drugs may not be directly comparable. Results of clinical studies are included as part of the form, and many of the studies have shortcomings such as a short duration and a small sample size. In some situations, modeling can help infer some of the missing information from existing clinical data. This process also allows the modeler to examine things from a more realistic perspective than is normally found in clinical trials. For example, patients outside of such studies probably do not take their medication as regularly as those who know they are being observed by the investigators.

Translating the information into a form that can be understood by the business (non-clinical) side of a health plan – and by brokers, employers and members—is just beginning. This is an area where actuaries can add significant value by bringing their expertise to the process.

PHARMACY PAYMENTS

Payments to pharmacies for dispensing of prescription drugs include a dispensing fee along with a reimbursement amount for the drug dispensed (typically a discounted average wholesale price). The pharmacy collects the participant cost share at the point of sale.

If no PBM is used, a health plan will pay the pharmacies at the contracted rates of discounted AWP plus the dispensing fee that they can get through direct contracting. If a PBM is used, the PBM pays the pharmacy the contracted amounts, and the health plan reimburses the PBM.

When retail pharmacies provide prescription drugs to participants under integrated medical plans without a card, the individual will typically pay for the prescription and later submit a claim for reimbursement. This process is cumbersome and does not provide complete integration of pharmacy and medical claims data for optimal management of utilization. As biologic drugs increase in number and cost, it will become imperative that health plans and PBMs improve the integration of the various claim systems involved.

PBMs AND PHARMACY NETWORKS

When a PBM is used by a health plan, the PBM/health plan contract will typically state a discount level and a dispensing fee for use of the PBM pharmacy network. Discounts from AWP will vary between mail and retail, with mail discounts often being higher than retail, and will vary between generic and brand name.

Generic discounts may be based on the use of a MAC (Maximum Allowable Cost). The Center for Medicaid Services (CMS) has its own defined MAC. Most PBMs will also have their own defined MAC. It is important to identify which MAC is being used when contracting with a PBM. The CMS MAC is often used to charge the health plan, whereas PBM-defined MACs may or may not be used by the PBM to reimburse the pharmacy. Thus, specific identification in the PBM contract will help clarify confusion.

MAC discounts for generics can range from approximately 48% discount from AWP to over 60% discount, depending on the drug under consideration. Brand name discounts can range from 10% discount from AWP to over 20%, depending on the region, rural versus urban area, and the rebate arrangement with the PBM. Rebates are discussed later in this chapter.

Dispensing fees will also vary between mail and retail, with mail being close to $0 per script, and retail ranging from below $2.00 to over $3.00 per script. Dispensing fees do not typically vary between brand name and generic drugs.

The PBM may have more than one network, and thus, may have more than one set of contracted rates.

The PBM contracts separately with each pharmacy for discounts and dispensing fees. These rates may determine in which network the PBM puts each pharmacy. Each pharmacy, just as in contracting with various provider groups, may have slightly different discounts and dispensing fees.

A PBM may have a single set of discounts and dispensing fees with a health plan. The PBM/pharmacy contracts may differ from the PBM's contract with the health plan. Thus, there is the possibility that the amounts the PBM pays the pharmacies may be different from what the health plan pays the PBM, due to the fact that two separate sets of contracts are being used.

Sometimes the pharmacy discounts are passed directly to the health plan from the PBM. If this is the situation, it is important to monitor experience to make sure the health plan and PBM contracted rates are being met in the aggregate. If they are not being met, settlements between the health plan and PBM may be required.

In other cases, the pharmacy discounts are not passed directly to the health plan, but rather the health plan (and the participants) receive the PBM/health plan contracted rates for each drug dispensed at each pharmacy. This process called, "Level Billing," does not require after-the-fact settlements, since the PBM/health plan contracted discounts and dispensing fees are used to reimburse the PBM. In this situation, the PBM reimburses the pharmacies based on its own contracts, which may be different from what the health plan pays the PBM. The concept is similar to a contract with an IPA medical group, where the IPA is paid based on its contract with the health plan, and the IPA pays its physician participants based on the rate it has contracted to pay the physicians (which may or may not be different from the health plan contracted rate).

REBATES

Rebates are payments from manufacturers for preferred status of their drugs on a formulary. Rebates, as mentioned earlier, can be amounts per script sold, or aggregates based on the formulary status, market share and volume of a particular drug or group of drugs sold by a health plan or even a PBM.

When health plans contract directly with a manufacturer without the use of a PBM, it is often thought that the volume of a particular health plan is probably not large enough to get a favorable arrangement. Thus, PBMs may be considered to get better rebate arrangements. However, this is not always the case. A PBM is an intermediary, and unless separate administrative charges are used to pay the PBM, often times the PBM's source of revenue from the health plan is a percentage of the rebates earned. This gives the incentive to the PBM to increase rebates. This incentive, however, may be contrary to the health plan's objectives in providing the most clinically effective and least costly drug to participants.

The health plan will earn a share of these total rebates, with the other portion going to the PBM for their costs of administration. The share percentages will vary depending on the benefit plan design (closed, two-tier, three-tier, or four-tier). The minimum guarantees may also vary by benefit plan design.

Some PBMs are not willing to disclose the rebate contracts with manufacturers to the health plan. Thus, some arrangements, such as bundling of drugs where rebates can be lost if one drug out of a handful made by a manufacturer is taken off of preferred status on a formulary, may not be made known to health plans until a formulary change is considered.

When using a PBM, rebates may include a minimum guaranteed rebate per rebateable drug, per brand name drug, or per drug dispensed. Rebates per rebateable drug are difficult to track, as the drugs earning a rebate will change over time. Rebate guarantees based on something that is trackable are encouraged, either per brand name script or per script. Rebates may also vary by mail versus retail, with mail rebate guarantees generally being higher.

PBMs can balance the minimum rebate guarantee with the discount from AWP and dispensing fees. As the minimum rebate guarantee increases, the contracted AWP discount often decreases. If a PBM cannot contract with pharmacies to meet the AWP discount included in the PBM/health plan contract, they can balance the cost by decreasing the minimum rebate guarantee. The PBM may also increase the retained PBM percentage share of rebates, to balance with a higher than achievable AWP discount.

The minimum guaranteed rebate is often paid to a health plan on a quarterly basis. The total earned health plan rebate is typically determined six months after a fiscal year ends. Total earned health plan rebates include the manufacturer rebate deals, per script, per market share, and other agreements made by the PBM. As these agreements are often not disclosed fully to the health plan, nor are they dependent solely on a health plan's market share, these total rebate values are difficult to project and monitor. Reliance on the PBM for calculation is often required.

When contracting with a PBM for multi-year contracts, a health plan should consider an inflation factor on the minimum guarantee if it is on a per script basis, as it is expected that the cost per script will be increasing over time. Without an inflation factor, the minimum rebate guarantee per script will actually decrease as a percentage of the script cost.

It is not necessarily true that contracting through a PBM maximizes either rebates or total net cost saving to the plan. Health plans willing to establish their own contracting process have also proven quite successful. The willingness of a manufacturer to offer deep discounts depends not only on the number of pharmacy lives covered, but also on the ability of the plan to move market share, shifting prescription volume from interchangeable competing products to the product(s) being contracted. A plan with as few as 500,000 pharmacy lives can obtain excellent rebates if they have demonstrated effective control of market shares in similar situations in the past.

Rebates can be very troublesome for a health plan. As rebates are paid after some period of time after a participant receives a prescription at the pharmacy, an adjustment to the cost to the plan sponsor should be considered to account for the value of rebates received by the health plan. If a PBM is involved, the PBM's motivation is to maximize rebates, as their revenue is often a percentage of rebates. This can be in direct conflict with a health plan's goal of minimizing net plan cost, minimizeing cost to the participant, and maximizing use of generics and clinically effective drugs.

Once a P&T committee determines that a drug may be added, financial projections can best determine the effect on the net plan cost (cost after discounts, dispensing fee, cost share, and rebates), the cost to the participant, and the value of rebates.

"Transparency" of prescription drug contracts, including discounts and rebates, is often required by large employer group clients. From a health plan perspective, this might affect how a plan contracts with a PBM or with pharmacies and manufacturers. Or, the plan may develop a communication and pricing plan that provides transparency as to how the contracts affect the group's claim costs.

LEGAL ISSUES ARISING WITH RESPECT TO PBMS

There have been recent legal concerns with PBMs that are owned by manufacturers, to the point where no PBMs are now owned by manufacturers. At the time when PBMs were owned by manufacturers, these PBMs were sometimes seen as using anti-competitive pressures, in that they might have pushed health plans to add drugs from the owner manufacturer as preferred drugs on the health plan's formulary.

Merck was the first pharmaceutical company to purchase a PBM, acquiring Medco in 1993. Other manufacturers quickly followed suit, thinking this would be a smart way to market their products. Most of these ventures were short-lived, due to regulatory scrutiny and adverse publicity. With the exception of Merck, the drug companies that purchased PBMs sold them within less than five years at a considerable loss.

No matter the ownership of the PBM, it is recommended that, when contracting with a PBM, it be made clear that the health plan "owns" its formulary, and that the health plan develop a well documented process for formulary design that shows no undue conflict of interest pressure from the perspective of the PBM or any manufacturer.

Overview of the One Health Plan's Formulary Process

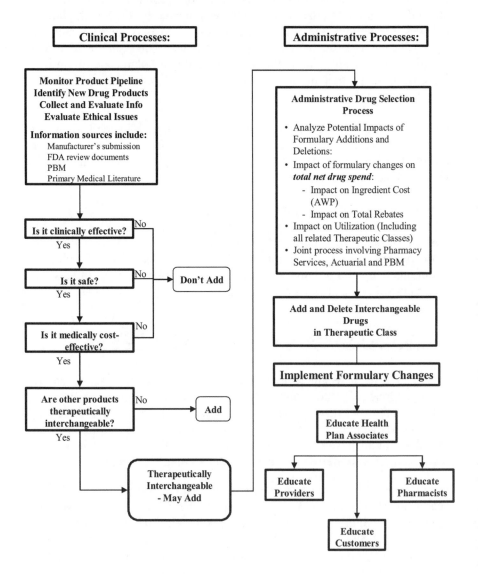

Figure 9.1

10 GROUP LONG-TERM CARE INSURANCE

Malcolm Cheung

GROUP MARKETPLACE OVERVIEW

HISTORY AND OUTLOOK FOR THE FUTURE

Group long-term care insurance (GLTCI) is a relatively new group coverage that has been marketed to employers and associations since 1987. Although the GLTCI market is still relatively small, it is a growing and effective way of providing coverage through group techniques.

The market for long-term care insurance is more advanced in the United States than in Canada. This is because Canadian Medicare covers certain long-term care expenses, and there is less perceived need. At this time, Canadian insurers are only beginning to show interest in long-term care insurance on a group basis, although that interest may increase in the future. The discussion that follows is based on long-term care insurance in the United States.

Long-term care insurance (LTC) addresses an individual's need for protection against the high costs of long term care services, services that are generally custodial in nature that an individual may need to perform the basic activities of daily living (ADLs). The need for LTC services may be the result of an accident or an illness, or may be due simply to the effects of aging. Interest in LTC insurance in America has grown significantly over the past decade, due to a number of factors that should continue to drive the product's growth for many years to come.

Increasing life expectancies have resulted in a larger proportion of Americans reaching those ages where chronic illnesses and disabilities and the need for long-term care services are much more likely. The aging of 75 million baby boomers, many of whom are currently approaching retirement age, will increase the demand for LTC services. Combined with Americans' concern about outliving their retirement savings and assets, interest in LTC insurance will continue to increase.

Most of the cost of LTC services in the United States is paid by those needing the care or by their families. Although the government, primarily through Medicaid, also pays a significant share of long term care costs, governmental entities at both the federal and state levels recognize that public funding will not be able to keep pace with the increased demand for LTC that is anticipated in the future. Consequently, Congress enacted tax incentives for the purchase of private LTC insurance in 1996, as have a number of states.

One development that has sparked additional interest in GLTCI is the introduction in the fall of 2002 of a voluntary GLTCI plan for all federal employees, retirees, and their eligible family members. As of early 2005, almost 220,000 individuals have enrolled in the plan, making it the largest single employer group LTC plan in the nation.

Market Size

As of the end of 2005, almost 7,400 employers and associations have sponsored GLTCI plans for their employees or members, as well as for their qualified family members. These plans have almost 2 million participants and generate approximately $1.3 billion in annualized premium. In-force employer-sponsored GLTCI premiums have grown at an average annual rate of 19% from 2000 to 2005.[1] The GLTCI market is still relatively small when compared to the market for individual LTC insurance (ILTCI), for which there are 4.4 million in-force policies and $7.3 billion of annualized premium as of the end of 2005.[2]

The Sales and Marketing Process

The GLTCI sales and marketing process has two distinct components – the selection of the LTC insurer/administrator by the plan sponsor (the first sale), and then the execution of an education and marketing campaign to convince the sponsor's employees or members to enroll for coverage (the second sale).

---

[1] LIMRA U.S. Group Long-Term Care Insurance – 2005 Sales and In-Force Survey

[2] LIMRA Individual Medicare Supplement and Long-Term Care Insurance –2005 Sales and In-Force Survey

FIRST SALE

Insurers typically market GLTCI to potential plan sponsors by working with the brokers and benefits consultants who handle the sponsor's other employee or member benefit coverages. This process would include educating the broker or consultant about a particular insurer's GLTCI product and features, as well as about the value of GLTCI to potential plan sponsors. This value includes:

- Keeping its benefit portfolio current and competitive with no cost to the sponsor if offered as a voluntary coverage;
- Helping to attract and retain quality employees, particularly in a competitive job market;
- Reducing productivity losses through missed or distracted work time; and
- Responding to the needs and expectations of employees and association members.

Requests for proposals (RFPs) are typically distributed to qualified GLTCI insurers by brokers/consultants on behalf of potential plan sponsors. Occasionally, RFPs are issued directly by potential plan sponsors without the use of an intermediary.

When a broker is involved, commissions based on the premium generated by the GLTCI plan are usually paid and incorporated into the pricing. These commissions are typically in the range of 10% to 15% of first year premium and 5% to 15% of renewal premium. Benefit consultants are usually compensated directly by the plan sponsor on a fee-for-service basis for assisting in the RFP process.

Although most employer-sponsored GLTCI plans are employee-pay-all, some employers may subsidize the cost of GLTCI coverage for their employees. This is usually done in one of three ways:

- The employer buys a basic, or "core" level of coverage for all of its employees and gives employees the option to voluntarily "buy up" to a richer level of coverage;
- The employer makes a contribution to the cost of coverage if the employee elects to enroll. This contribution can be either a percentage of the premium cost or a flat dollar amount; or
- The employer buys comprehensive coverage for a subset of its employees, which is typically the management group only. This is called an executive carve-out.

After assessing the competing proposals submitted by interested insurers, the plan sponsor can either select a carrier, or it can identify finalists and then select a carrier based on a finalist presentation and/or a site visit.

SECOND SALE

Once selected, the carrier and the plan sponsor work together to implement the plan, and to develop and execute an enrollment campaign designed to educate the eligible population about the need for LTC, the costs of LTC services, and the potential benefits of LTCI. Such a campaign will include discussion of:

- Protecting retirement savings and assets from potentially catastrophic LTC expenses;
- Preserving one's freedom of choice and independence when and if LTC services are needed; and
- Avoiding becoming a burden to one's family, financially and for caregiving.

This enrollment campaign typically lasts one to two months, and can utilize a number of marketing tools and media, including:

- Informational articles in company news publications,
- Announcement letter from the plan sponsor mailed directly to the home,
- Lead generator brochures,
- Reminder postcards,
- A toll-free telephone number to request additional information and to ask questions about the plan,
- An educational website customized to reflect the sponsor's plan and which could allow on-line enrollment,
- A printed enrollment kit that would include plan details, application forms, premium rates, as well as consumer disclosure documents that are mandated by law (NAIC Shopper's Guide and Outline of Coverage),
- Group enrollment meetings conducted at the worksite,
- E-mail reminders,
- Payroll stuffers, and
- Videos

Since GLTCI is usually offered as a voluntary benefit, the success of the enrollment campaign in generating high plan participation is critical to the financial viability of the plan. This is due to the need to recover up front marketing and acquisition costs, as well as the need to control any antiselection if coverage is made available on a guaranteed issue basis. Currently, typical plan participation rates are relatively low, averaging less than 5% of eligible employees and retirees. Participation rates do, however, vary significantly from group to group, and are driven by a number of factors, including employee demographics (age, income, gender, marital status), the level of employer sponsor support and advocacy for the plan, the simplicity and affordability of the offered plans, and the effectiveness of the educational and marketing campaign during the initial enrollment. A good participation rate would be 10% or higher.

THE INDIVIDUAL MULTI-LIFE MARKET

As the individual LTC insurance market shifts its focus to the baby boomers, many of whom are still working, group LTCI plans using individual policy forms have increased in popularity, especially in the small to mid size group (fewer than 500 employees) marketplace. Under an individual multi-life arrangement, individual policies are issued to each plan participant, and there is no need for a contract between the plan sponsor and the insurer. Compared to true group plans, individual multi-life plans generally offer greater flexibility in available plan designs and options. The solicitation and enrollment process is typically driven by the agent or broker, targets key segments of the eligible population, and is more consultative in nature than a true group enrollment campaign, often including on site one-on-one meetings.

Individual multi-life underwriting of active employees is often abbreviated and less rigorous than individual product underwriting, as the employer sponsor can verify an employee's actively-at-work status. Individual product premium rates are used, but a multi-life or group discount is usually applied, to reflect administrative and marketing efficiencies or reduced sales compensation.

Plan sponsors often prefer individual multi-life to true group plans, if they do not want the plan to be subject to ERISA requirements. Producers often prefer the individual multi-life approach because of the higher levels of compensation paid by individual policies in the first year. This compensation is often used to recoup enrollment and marketing costs incurred by the producer to install the plan.

Plan Eligibility

Employer sponsors usually make GLTCI coverage available not only to employees and retirees, but also to their spouses, parents, grandparents, and in some cases to adult children (and their spouses) and to domestic partners (where permitted by law). The individual underwriting applicable to the various members of the eligible class varies, and will be discussed in detail in the section on underwriting. Coverage provided on a guaranteed issue basis is typically restricted to full time, actively-at-work employees.

Insured Demographics

Individuals who purchase GLTCI coverage are typically in their early-forties to mid-fifties in age. The typical buyer is a married college graduate who earns at least $50,000 per year, and who has significant assets to protect. Women are somewhat more likely to purchase GLTCI than men, as women typically outlive their spouses and consequently may have a greater need for this coverage. Married people are also more likely to purchase GLTC than those who are single, and it is very common for both spouses to enroll for coverage at the same time.

Types of GLTCI Plans

There are several types of GLTCI plans that are distinguished by the manner in which plan benefits are paid to the insured. These variations are described below.

Service Reimbursement Model

Currently the most popular type of GLTCI plan is the service reimbursement model. Under this model, the insurer reimburses the cost of LTC services for the insured after the benefit trigger and the waiting period is satisfied. This reimbursement is subject to fixed limits that are specified in the group certificate and that vary by type of service received. These limits can be applied on a daily, weekly, monthly, annual, or lifetime basis, depending on the particular plan purchased. For example, a typical plan might reimburse up to $100 per day for nursing home care, $50 per day for care provided in an assisted living facility or in the insured's home, and up to $750 per year for informal care, all subject to a total lifetime maximum reimbursement of $200,000. Bills and receipts from qualified LTC providers, as defined in the group certificate, are submitted for review by the insurer before reimbursement is authorized. Payment can be made directly to the provider, or to the insured. As mandated by HIPAA for a tax-qualified plan, most insurers require that every claimant have a formal plan of care developed by a qualified health care practitioner, and only LTC services consistent with that care plan are eligible for reimbursement.

SERVICE INDEMNITY MODEL

Under the service indemnity model, once the benefit trigger and the waiting period has been satisfied, a fixed benefit payment is made for any day or week that formal LTC services are received, regardless of the actual charges incurred for those services. For example, if a plan has a $50 per day home health care benefit, the insured would receive $50 per each day he or she received home health care services, even if the cost of those services were less than $50 per day.

DISABILITY OR CASH MODEL

Under a disability or cash model plan, a predetermined benefit is paid for each day an insured is eligible for benefits, having met the benefit trigger and satisfied the waiting period, whether or not the insured is actually using formal LTC services. This model provides the insured with maximum flexibility in how plan benefits can be utilized and is the simplest to explain. Although there should be administrative savings associated with this model because bills and receipts do not need to be reviewed and processed, the additional benefit utilization and faster benefit payout make the premiums for this model significantly higher than those for the other models. Cash models are also more susceptible to antiselection and claim fraud, as cash benefits can exceed the actual cost of LTC services received, and can come to be viewed by the claimant and the claimant's family as an additional source of income.

UNDERWRITING GLTCI

Most GLTCI plans offer coverage to actively-at-work, full time employees on a guaranteed issue basis if they enroll during the open enrollment period.

This means that applicants do not have to provide the insurer with any health-related information to enroll for coverage. The open enrollment period is typically a one to two month period during which the insurer and plan sponsor conduct the enrollment campaign. Limiting the availability of guaranteed issue coverage to a finite period of time helps to reduce any potential antiselection that may occur. The full time, actively-at-work requirement also serves as an underwriting screen that can help limit antiselection.

Employees who are eligible to enroll during the initial open enrollment period but who decline to do so can enroll in the plan after the open enrollment period ends, but they would have to submit full evidence of insurability. This helps minimize ongoing adverse selection against the plan. New employees hired after the open enrollment period are typically given between 30 and 90 days from the date of hire to enroll for GLTCI on a guaranteed issue basis. Subsequent to the initial open enrollment period, many insurers are willing to conduct open re-enrollment campaigns to help increase plan participation. To limit adverse selection, it is important that such open re-enrollments not be too frequent or regular and not be pre-announced.

Members of the eligible group other than full time, actively-at-work employees are usually required to complete a fairly lengthy health questionnaire (also known as a long form) in order to qualify for coverage. This form includes information related to the applicant's height and weight, prior health history, medications, and primary and specialty care physicians. Telephone interviews are commonly used to verify the information provided in the long form.

When indicated by the applicant's responses to the questionnaire, the insurer will request health-related information directly from the applicant's physician on an attending physician's statement before completing the underwriting review. Commonly, applicants over the age of 70 are also interviewed either by telephone or in person to screen out those who may already be cognitively impaired Insurers have begun to use new tests to identify individuals who are mildly cognitively impaired. These new tests include the AQT Test of Cognitive Speed, the Minnesota Cognitive Acuity Screen (MCAS), and the Enhanced Mental Skills Test (EMST), among others. Since the most common reason for an LTCI claim is severe cognitive impairment, many insurers are now requiring these tests even when underwriting applicants younger than age 70.

Some GLTCI plans allow spouses of active employees to enroll for coverage with "simplified" underwriting. This usually means that spouses fill out a short form questionnaire with typically 3 to 5 questions that screen out those who have medical conditions or current care needs that would make them uninsurable. The Federal LTCI Plan actually uses a short form questionnaire for both active employees as well as their spouses.

GLTCI coverage is usually issued on an accept or decline basis, with little or no use of substandard or rated coverage. This is in contrast to the ILTCI market, where preferred and substandard risk/premium classes are common, as are modified, reduced coverage offers to substandard risks.

GLTCI PREMIUMS

Unlike premiums for other group health benefits, which are usually group-rated or based on the insured's attained age, premiums for GLTCI coverage are based on the age of the applicant at issue. They are intended to remain the same over the lifetime of the insured. The older an individual is at issue, the higher the premium. The combination of level premiums and a morbidity risk that increases significantly with age results in the need for the insurer to hold significant policy reserves to pre-fund anticipated future claims.

LTCI coverage is guaranteed renewable, and insurers reserve the right to adjust rates prospectively on a class basis if plan experience warrants, and if the appropriate regulatory authorities approve. GLTCI premiums are typically guaranteed for a limited period of time after the effective date of a group contract. Guarantees usually last at least 3 years, but no more than 10 years.

Premiums for GLTCI coverage currently average approximately $650 per enrollee per year. Policy premiums are usually waived if the insured is benefit eligible or receiving plan benefits.

PLAN PROVISIONS

BENEFIT TRIGGERS

To become eligible to receive benefits under a LTCI plan, the insured individual must satisfy the plan's benefit trigger. Benefit triggers have evolved considerably over the years that LTCI has been marketed.

Many policies issued in the 1980's required that an insured be confined in a hospital for at least three days and that the need for LTC services commence within two days of the hospital stay in order for plan benefits to be payable. Other early plans included a medical necessity trigger, which required that a physician certify that LTC services are needed. Plans sold in the late 1980's and the early 1990's typically included benefit triggers based on the inability to perform Activities of Daily Living (ADLs) or the presence of a significant cognitive impairment.

ACTIVITIES OF DAILY LIVING

In 1996, the Health Insurance Portability and Accountability Act (HIPAA) established minimum standards that an LTCI plan must meet in order to receive the same income tax treatment under the Internal Revenue Code as medical insurance policies. This preferential tax treatment is discussed in the "Regulation in the United States" chapter later in this text. Under HIPAA, the benefit trigger of a tax-qualified LTCI policy must be the inability to perform (without substantial assistance from another individual) at least two activities of daily living (ADLs), or a cognitive impairment that requires substantial supervision to protect the health and safety of the insured. Since the passage of HIPAA, LTCI benefit triggers on new GLTCI policies have basically conformed to the HIPAA standard, as almost all GLTCI plan sponsors require a tax-qualified plan design.

The ADLs allowed by HIPAA and most commonly used in GLTCI benefit triggers are bathing, dressing, eating, toileting, maintaining continence, and transferring from bed to chair. The definition of what an insured needs to be able to do to be considered independent in any particular ADL can vary from plan to plan. Typical ADL definitions are:

Bathing – washing oneself by sponge bath or in either a tub or shower, including the task of getting into or out of the tub or shower;

Continence – the ability to maintain control of bowel and bladder function; or, when unable to do so, the ability to perform associated personal hygiene (including caring for catheter or ostomy bag);

Dressing – putting on and taking off all items of clothing and any necessary braces, fasteners or artificial limbs;

Eating – feeding oneself by getting food into the body from a receptacle (such as a plate, cup or table) or by a feeding tube or intravenously;

Toileting – getting to and from the toilet, getting on and off the toilet, and performing associated personal hygiene; and

Transferring – moving into or out of a bed, chair or wheelchair.

COGNITIVE IMPAIRMENT

Federally tax-qualified LTCI plans are also required to trigger benefits if there is a severe cognitive impairment that requires substantial supervision to protect the insured from threats to health and safety. Examples of behaviors that can be used to qualify insureds for benefits include wandering and getting lost, combativeness, inability to dress appropriately for the weather, and poor judgment in emergency situations. Common tools that are used by insurers to assess degrees of cognitive impairment include the Short Portable Mental Status Questionnaire developed at Duke University in 1978, and the Folstein Mini-Mental State Examination.

ELIMINATION/WAITING PERIOD

Once benefit eligibility has been triggered, most GLTC plans have an elimination period or waiting period, during which the insured needs to remain disabled and benefit eligible, before benefits are paid.

This waiting period is usually expressed in days and varies from zero to 365 days. The most common waiting periods are 30, 60, 90, and 100 days. The purpose of this waiting period is to ensure that benefit payments are only for long-term chronic disabilities, and thereby to moderate the premium cost of the plan.
Most GLTCI plans are marketed with a single waiting period option, the most common of which is 90 days.

How the waiting period is satisfied varies from plan to plan. Some plans simply count the calendar days that an insured has been benefit eligible. In other plans, only days in which formal LTC services are actually received count toward satisfying the waiting period. One variation of this approach is to count a full week towards the satisfaction of the waiting period if formal services were received during any single day of that week. There are also different ways for plans to handle those situations in which the waiting period starts but is not totally satisfied before an insured recovers, or in which there are multiple periods of disability. Some plans will require that a full waiting period be satisfied again if two periods of disability are separated by more than 180 days, while others will require that the waiting period be satisfied only once in a lifetime, even over multiple periods of disability.

It is common for the waiting period to be waived for certain types of benefits, such as respite care, care management services, hospice care, and caregiver training benefits. These benefits will be described fully later in this chapter.

Covered Services

LTCI plans utilizing the service reimbursement or service indemnity models can provide coverage for a relatively narrow set of covered services, or for a broader and more comprehensive range of services. In the early years of LTCI, many, if not most, LTCI plans only provided benefits for care provided in a nursing home. As other types of LTC services emerged, and as consumer interest in these care alternatives increased, LTCI insurers in the late 1980's and early 1990's started to develop LTCI products that also provided benefits for home and community-based care, assisted living facility care, and informal care provided by an unlicensed or uncertified provider. Plans that cover a full range of LTC services are called comprehensive plans and are the most commonly sold LTCI plans. There are even some plans that provide coverage only for home and community-based care.

Although the definition of the types of covered services can vary from plan to plan, generally speaking, the following types of LTCI services can be covered:

Nursing Home Care – care provided in a facility that provides skilled, intermediate, or custodial care, and is either Medicare-approved as a provider of skilled nursing care services, or is state-licensed as a skilled nursing home, intermediate care facility, or a custodial care facility.

Assisted Living Facility Care – care provided in a facility that is state-licensed or certified as an Assisted Living Facility (ALF). For states that do not license or certify such facilities, an ALF is a facility that meets the following minimum criteria:

- Is a group residence that maintains records for services to each resident;

- Provides services and oversight on a 24 hour a day basis; and

- Provides a combination of housing, supportive services, and personal assistance with the Activities of Daily Living.

Home and Community-Based Care – medical and non-medical services provided to ill, disabled, or infirm persons in their residences or in a community-based facility, like an adult day care center. Such services may include assistance with ADLs, homemaker services, and respite care services, and are typically provided by a home health care agency, a licensed nurse registry, or by an informal care provider.

Hospice Care – services and supplies provided through a state-licensed or certified facility or community-based program designed to provide services to the terminally ill.

Caregiver Training – training and educational programs designed to help informal caregivers obtain state licensure or certification as a home health care provider.

Respite Care – formal, paid care provided to relieve an informal care provider.

Independence Support Services – services designed to allow an individual to remain at home, rather than have to be institutionalized. Such services would include personal emergency alert systems and home modifications such as the installation of wheelchair ramps or grab bars in the bathroom, and the widening of doorways.

Care Management Services – services provided by a geriatric case manager or a nurse to develop an insured's plan of care, identify local provider resources, and coordinate all necessary LTC, medical care, personal care, and social services.

ALTERNATE PLAN OF CARE

Many GLTCI plans have a provision that allows the insurer to pay benefits for services that may not be explicitly defined or covered by the group contract and certificate. This provision is typically called an alternate plan of care provision, and allows the plan to continue to provide meaningful benefits even as new ways to provide LTC emerge over time. Determination of eligibility for this benefit is usually at the sole discretion of the insurer.

BENEFIT LIMITS

Almost all GLTCI plans impose limits on the amount of benefits that will be paid for any given day, week, month, or year, as well as over the entire lifetime of the insured. These limits usually vary by the type of LTC service received.

Almost all plans have daily limits for institutional care (nursing home and ALF care). Although home and community-based care limits are also usually applied on a daily basis, it is not uncommon to see these applied on weekly or monthly basis. When GLTCI plans are marketed to the eligible population, the enrollee selects the level of institutional care daily maximum benefit that he or she would like in the plan. A choice of three or four alternative institutional daily maximums is typically offered (such as $100/day, $150/day, $200/day, and $250/day). The daily maximum benefit for home and community-based care is expressed as a percentage of the institutional daily maximum. In group plans, that percentage is typically 50% or 60%, but higher percentages are becoming more common.

Limits for other covered services, such as caregiver training and independence support, are usually expressed as a flat dollar amount or as a fixed multiple of the institutional daily maximum benefit amount, and are applied on either an annual or a lifetime basis.

Although the prevalence of plans with unlimited lifetime benefits is increasing, most group plans have a lifetime maximum benefit limit that is applied to all benefits that are paid to an insured. Although it is common to refer to the lifetime maximum in terms of the number of "years" of institutional benefit available, most of these limits are administered as a "pot of dollars" that is drained as benefits are utilized. For example, consider a plan that pays up to $100 per day in a nursing home, $50 per day for home and community-based care, and that has a 5 year lifetime benefit maximum. Expressed in dollars, the lifetime maximum would be 5 years multiplied by 365 days per year multiplied by $100 per day, or $182,500. This lifetime maximum benefit would last significantly longer than 5 years (20 years, in fact) if the insured only uses home health care every other day and received a reimbursement of $50 per day.

INFLATION PROTECTION

In light of the limits that are usually imposed on the level of benefits provided by GLTCI plans, most plans have an inflation protection feature that would increase these limits as LTC costs increase over time. There are two major ways that this inflation protection can be provided, as follows:

1. **Periodic Increase Offers**
   Under this approach to inflation protection, the insured is periodically given the opportunity to voluntarily purchase additional amounts of coverage on a guaranteed issue basis. The most common period between offers is 3 years. For protection against adverse selection, some insurers either cease making these offers or require full underwriting if an insured declines two or three consecutive offers. The amount of each inflation offer is typically equal to the difference between the existing policy benefit (institutional daily maximum benefit) and the benefit equal to the original benefit purchased at issue compounded annually at a rate of 5% for the period beginning with policy issue and

ending in the year in which the inflation offer is made. However, some insurers will only offer adjustments that reflect the impact of inflation since the last offer, so if an insured declines an offer, there is no opportunity to "recover" that adjustment in the future without providing evidence of insurability.

An insured is usually given 30 days to accept an inflation offer on a guaranteed issue basis. If an offer is accepted, the premium for the policy will increase by an amount equal to the premium, based on the insured's age at the time the offer is accepted, for the increase in coverage. On acceptance of the offer, all benefit limits that are linked to the institutional daily maximum benefit would increase proportionally.

Although this approach to inflation protection keeps the premium cost of initial coverage low, premiums will increase significantly over time as inflation adjustments are added and as the insured ages.

2. Automatic Inflation Protection

Under a policy with automatic inflation protection, all benefit limits increase automatically each year by a preset percentage, usually 5% on either a compound or a simple basis. The premium for this increasing coverage, however, is level over time and is based on the insured's age at issue. As a result, the premiums for a policy with automatic inflation protection are significantly higher than the initial premiums for a policy with periodic increase offers, although that relationship will reverse over time if the periodic inflation offers are consistently accepted.

NONFORFEITURE BENEFITS

GLTCI plans are often sold with a nonforfeiture benefit available as an option, or included in the base coverage. A nonforfeiture benefit allows an insured who voluntarily terminates or lapses coverage to receive a reduced, paid-up benefit without having to continue to pay premiums. This option is particularly appealing in the GLTCI market, since the average issue age is relatively low, and there may be many years before claims can be expected to occur.

The most common nonforfeiture benefit in current GLTCI plans is the "Shortened Benefit Period" (SBP). The SBP nonforfeiture benefit is the minimum standard for a tax-qualified LTCI plan as established by HIPAA, and pays the same benefits in both amount and frequency as are in effect at the time of lapse. However, the lifetime maximum benefit is reduced to an amount equal to the sum of all premiums paid prior to lapse, less plan benefits paid to date. This benefit is usually not available until a policy has been in effect for at least three years. A minimum SBP benefit of 30 times the institutional daily maximum is usually provided. When offered as an enrollee level option, there is an additional premium if this option is selected.

Some older GLTCI plans provide nonforfeiture benefits on a reduced paid up benefit basis or on an extended term benefit basis. Under a reduced paid-up benefit, both the daily and lifetime benefit maximums are reduced and coverage is extended for the life of the insured. Extended term nonforfeiture benefits do not reduce the inside benefit limits of the coverage, but only cover disabilities that commence within a limited period of time after lapse.

Increasingly, plans now include a contingent nonforfeiture benefit if an optional nonforfeiture benefit is not selected by the insured. This contingent nonforfeiture benefit is only provided to an insured if he or she lapses coverage due to a "substantial" premium increase. The NAIC Model LTCI Regulation specifies the triggers for a "substantial" premium increase. The nonforfeiture benefit provided is the same as the SBP benefit described above.

OTHER PLAN FEATURES

DEATH BENEFIT

Many GLTCI plans include a death benefit. Typically, this provision would pay the spouse of an insured (or, if the insured does not have a spouse, the estate of the insured) an amount equal to a percentage of the cumulative plan premiums paid prior to the insured's death, less any plan benefits paid. The percentage paid is usually a function of the age of the insured at the time of death and decreases to 0% if death occurs after age 70 or 75. A typical death benefit would pay 100% of cumulative premiums paid, less benefits, for death occurring prior to age 65, decreasing in 10% increments for each year of increasing age at death until no benefit is paid for death occurring at age 75 or older.

Like the nonforfeiture benefit, this feature is particular appealing to younger insureds who may have many years until they are likely to receive benefits and may value the ability to recoup their premiums should they die prematurely before utilizing the plan.

BED RESERVATION BENEFIT

Most GLTCI plans have a bed reservation benefit that will continue to reimburse the insured for institutional care even if he or she needs to temporarily transfer out of the LTC facility to an acute care facility due to a medical condition. The purpose of this benefit is to help ensure that the LTC facility bed will be available to the insured on return from the acute medical facility, as many LTC facilities have long waiting lists and will not hold a bed for a patient temporarily without payment. Most plans limit the bed reservation benefit to 21 days per calendar year or per hospital stay.

SPOUSAL RIDERS AND DISCOUNTS

Most employer plan sponsors prefer not to offer voluntary GLTCI coverage to married employees on a more preferential basis than to unmarried employees. However, group plans are available with a premium discount for individuals who are married. This marital discount can be as large as 40%, and is quite common in the ILTCI and individual multi-life markets. It can be actuarially justified by the fact that married people would have a natural live-in informal care provider, and that married people tend to be healthier than those who are not married.

Some group plans also include a spousal waiver of premium benefit or a survivor waiver of premium benefit. Under a spousal waiver of premium provision, if both spouses are insured under the group plan, the premiums for both policies would be waived if one of the spouses becomes benefit eligible. Under a survivor waiver of premium provision, if both spouses are insured and one spouse dies, then the premiums for the surviving spouse would be waived for life. The survivor benefit is usually only paid if both policies have been in-force at least 10 years and neither policy has paid any benefits.

RESTORATION OF BENEFITS

Many currently offered plans include a restoration of benefits provision. This plan feature restores the lifetime maximum benefit limit if an insured who is on claim recovers before exhausting the plan's benefits. Most plans require that the insured not satisfy the benefit trigger for a specified period of time (typically 90 days to up to a year) before benefits are restored. Some plans will also limit the number of times the lifetime maximum benefit limit can be restored in an insured's lifetime.

This feature would be of greatest value to younger insureds, who may initially use plan benefits as a result of an accident and still be able to access the full lifetime maximum benefit to cover a chronic condition later in life.

International Coverage

Some group plans will only pay benefits if the care is provided within the United States. Others, however, will also provide benefits if care is received abroad. There are some special considerations that insurers need to address if they are to effectively manage claims abroad. These would include how to determine whether an insured located in another country has satisfied the benefit trigger, and whether a foreign care provider has the qualifications required by the policy. Claim administration would also be complicated by language and currency differences. Given these issues, insurers typically limit the amount and/or duration of benefits payable for care received abroad.

Shared Lifetime Maximum Benefit Pools

A plan design feature that was first introduced in the ILTCI market, but has found its way into some GLTCI plans, is the shared lifetime maximum. Shared lifetime maximum benefit pools allow an insured who uses up all of his or her benefits to tap into any remaining lifetime benefits of a spouse's policy, or to leave any unutilized benefits at death to a surviving spouse.

Independence Support Benefits

Independence support benefits are paid for home modifications and personal emergency alert systems that would enable an insured to remain in the home for a longer period of time. Qualifying home modifications would include the installation of entrance ramps, the widening of doorways, and the installation of grab bars in the bathroom. Often, independence support benefits will also pay for the training of informal caregivers to enhance the quality of the care that they are able provide.

Policy Exclusions

Like all insurance policies, GLTCI policies do not pay benefits in certain situations. The most common policy exclusions are those that are allowed to be included in a tax-qualified plan, as defined by HIPAA and the NAIC LTCI Model Regulation. These are:

- Pre-existing conditions or diseases.

- Mental or nervous disorders (other than Alzheimer's Disease).

- Alcoholism and drug addiction.

- Illness, treatment, or medical condition arising out of

  ○ war or an act of war,

  ○ participation in a felony, riot, or insurrection,

  ○ service in the armed forces,

  ○ suicide, attempted suicide, or intentionally self-inflicted injury, or

  ○ aviation (as a non-fare-paying passenger).

- Treatment provided in a government facility or services for which benefits are available under Medicare or other governmental program (except Medicaid).

- Services provided by a member of the insured's immediate family or for which no charge is normally made in the absence of insurance.

- Expenses for services paid under another LTCI or health insurance policy.

- Expenses for services or items that are reimbursable under Title XVIII of the Social Security Act, or would be so reimbursable but for the application of a deductible or coinsurance amount. This applies to tax-qualified LTCI policies only.

REGULATORY FILING CONSIDERATIONS

EXTRATERRITORIAL APPLICATION OF STATE REQUIREMENTS

LTCI is tightly regulated and monitored at the state level, and all states have adopted statutes and regulations concerning LTCI.

Many regulators view LTCI as having a high potential for abuse since it is primarily a senior product. As with Medicare supplement insurance regulation, LTCI regulation addresses product design, the way the product is sold, and what needs to be disclosed to the consumer in the sales process. LTCI regulation also has some additional features that are intended to protect consumers who purchase a product that has a long tail for claims. These regulations typically mandate non-forfeiture benefit and inflation protection offers.

Similar to the group A&H eligibility laws, the LTC regulations usually define the types of groups to whom LTCI can be sold, as well as any specific requirements concerning the type of group. Most states require submissions of certificate forms and rates for out-of-state LTC group contracts that are issued to discretionary groups, with supporting documentation that the benefits are reasonable in relation to the premiums charged. Some states have a section within the LTC law or regulation that specifically addresses out of state filing requirements, indicating the types of groups that are subject to the requirement.

Some states have extra-territorial authority stemming from their A&H insurance code or regulation, or from their definition of conducting the business of insurance.

More and more states are expanding extra-territorial authority, especially for products like LTCI, that regulators feel may be sold in an inappropriate manner. While the numbers are in transition and may depend on each insurer's own interpretation of a particular state's regulations, approximately 30 states extend extra-territorial authority over LTCI to association groups, and roughly 20 states extend that authority to employer/employee groups. Filing requirements vary, from informational copies of the certificates to prior approval of the forms and rates. Typically, there are additional filing requirements and assurances that must be made for affinity associations. If the extra-territorial requirements of a particular state are at odds with the LTC requirements of the situs state of a GLTC plan, it may be necessary to offer a different plan to residents of the extra-territorial state than to those of the group plan's situs state. This can complicate the marketing and administration of the plan. Ongoing legislative and regulatory efforts to create an optional federal charter for insurers (similar to how the banking industry is regulated) and to create an Interstate Insurance Product Regulation Compact may improve the speed at which new LTCI products can be brought to market, and also lower product administration costs by eliminating or reducing product variations by state.

A point of interest concerning the Federal employee LTCI plan is that this plan is not subject to state regulatory review. The review and approval of the Federal employee plan and rates were performed by the Federal government's Office of Personnel Management. This results in streamlined product design and administration, since there are no state variations due to extra-territorial authority.

NAIC MODEL LTCI REGULATION

The National Association of Insurance Commissioners (NAIC) has developed legislative and regulatory language relating to LTCI that is consistent for all states. The current version of the NAIC Model LTCI Regulation was adopted by the NAIC in 2000. Most states have used the NAIC Model LTCI Regulation as the basis for their LTCI regulations. Consequently, there is a considerable amount of consistency between states in their requirements surrounding LTCI minimum benefit standards, definitions, and rating requirements, although some significant variations do exist. The NAIC Long-Term Care Insurance Model Act and Regulation are discussed in detail in the "regulation in the United States" chapter later in this text.

The same state LTC statutes and regulations address both group and individual coverages. Loss ratio requirements may differ between group and individual. Regulation of LTCI rates overall is changing very quickly since the NAIC included rate stabilization standards in the version of the Model LTCI Regulation adopted in 2000. These standards are designed to help ensure that insurance companies set LTCI premium rates that are reasonably expected to remain level, even under moderately adverse experience conditions.

Disclosure requirements are the same in most states, with outlines of coverage, buyer's guides, and cautionary language relating to suitability required. A few states exempt employer/employee groups from the outline requirements under certain circumstances. Historical rating practices are required to be disclosed under the new rate stabilization regulations noted above.

The disclosure and delivery provisions do not explicitly recognize that, for employer/employee group business, the average age of the insured is much younger than for the individual market, and that the group delivery system is not agent based.

TERMINATION PROVISIONS

INDIVIDUAL PORTABILITY

GLTCI coverage is usually portable, which means that if an insured's relationship with the sponsoring organization terminates, coverage can be continued.

Many group contracts allow such insureds to continue coverage under the same group plan with the same premium rates. Other group contracts move these "portables" to a pooled group conversion plan or offer an individual LTCI conversion policy. In these latter situations, the conversion coverage needs to be as good as the insured's existing coverage, but the conversion premiums may not necessarily be the same as the current premiums.

GROUP CONTRACT TERMINATION

If a GLTCI contract is terminated, and the plan sponsor is replacing the initial insurer with a successor insurer's plan, contracts (especially those involving the larger group plan sponsors) will often allow existing insureds to be transferred to the new insurer's plan with an associated transfer of plan reserves or assets. This would allow these transferred insureds to pay premiums under the successor insurer's plan on an original issue age or close to an original issue age basis. The amount of assets transferred in such a situation is typically defined in the initial insurer's master group contract or administrative agreement with the plan sponsor. Not all group contracts, however, include such a transfer of reserve or assets provision.

If a group contract is terminated and the plan sponsor does not choose a successor insurer, then the insureds must be given the right to convert their coverage to a comparable individual LTCI policy.

CLAIM ADMINISTRATION

An LTCI insurer or administrator needs to be consistently fair and objective in the administration of LTC claims without creating an unnecessary burden on the insured or the insured's family. The two major components of the claim administration process are benefit eligibility assessment and care management.

BENEFIT ELIGIBILITY ASSESSMENT

The benefit eligibility assessment process typically begins with the insured or the insured's family contacting the insurer, either by submitting a claim form or by telephone. In those situations where there is clear written documentation of the insured's condition from the insured's attending physician or LTC service providers, the process can generally be completed without an on-site assessment. Otherwise, the insurer, at its own expense, will arrange for an assessor (typically a geriatric nurse or social worker) to conduct an on-site assessment and interview at the insured's home. This interview is particularly important in determining whether significant cognitive impairment exists. The information gathered by the assessor, who is usually an external contractor to the insurer, is then reviewed by the insurer to determine whether the benefit trigger has been satisfied.

Benefit eligibility reassessments are conducted periodically, but no less frequently than once a year, as required by HIPAA for tax qualification.

CARE MANAGEMENT

Once deemed eligible, the insurer will usually require that a licensed health care provider develop a plan of care. The insurer will confirm that the plan is appropriate and will monitor future claim activity to ensure that the care being received by the insured is consistent with the established plan of care.

Care management in the LTCI environment is quite different than care management in the medical insurance environment. Medical care management is focused on cost and utilization containment. In the medical insurance world, care management involves the imposition of restrictions as to which health care providers an insured can use, as well as to the types of medical procedures and medications that an insured can receive. Long term care management, however, is not focused on cost containment, but rather on helping the insured find and coordinate the LTC services that will allow him or her as much independence as possible.

Although LTC care managers can make recommendations with respect to available care providers that the insured can use, the insured typically has complete freedom to choose any appropriately licensed or certified provider and receive full plan benefits.

TAX ISSUES

THE HEALTH INSURANCE
PORTABILITY AND ACCOUNTABILITY ACT

As mentioned earlier in this chapter, the Health Insurance Portability and Accountability Act of 1996 (HIPAA) provided tax incentives to individuals who take financial responsibility for their own LTC needs by purchasing qualified LTCI policies. There are several tax benefits associated with a qualified LTCI policy. Generally, these include deductibility of premiums paid by employers and employees (subject to general medical expense rules), employer contributions not being treated as taxable to the employee, and benefits not being considered taxable income to the beneficiary. LTCI premiums are an acceptable expenditure for Medical Savings Accounts (MSA) that are available to the self-employed as well as to employees of small businesses, but LTCI is not permitted in a Section 125 Cafeteria or Flexible Spending Account Plan.

Qualified LTCI policies that provide benefits on a "per diem" basis, such as under a service indemnity or a disability model, are treated differently for tax purposes than reimbursement policies. The tax free receipt of per diem benefits is limited, so that policyholders are taxed on the amount of benefits exceeding the greater of a daily dollar limit that is indexed for inflation and published annually by the IRS, and the amount of qualified LTC expenses incurred by the insured. If the periodic payments exceed this cap, the benefit amounts in excess of the cap are included in gross income.

More detail on the requirements for qualified LTCI plans is found in the "Regulation in the United States" chapter later in this text.

STATE TAX INCENTIVES

An increasing number of states have also enacted state income tax incentives for the purchase of LTCI. States are increasingly interested in promoting the purchase of private LTCI because state Medicaid budgets are straining under the burden of rapidly increasing LTC costs. These state tax incentives can take the form of either a tax deduction or a tax credit for qualified plan premiums. At the end of 2005, twenty-two states had enacted an LTCI tax incentive.

PUBLIC-PRIVATE LONG-TERM CARE PARTNERSHIP

The Deficit Reduction Act of 2005 (DRA) includes provisions that tighten Medicaid eligibility rules, and allow for an expansion of the Partnership LTCI concept to all 50 states. Partnership LTCI policies allow individuals who apply for Medicaid LTC benefits to protect an amount of personal assets that is greater than the amount normally permitted by state Medicaid programs. The additional asset protection is equal to the dollar amount of benefits received from the Partnership LTCI policy. Medicaid programs will also be able to extend reciprocal asset protection to those who currently reside in a state that is different from the state in which a Partnership policy was issued. The DRA also establishes a National Clearinghouse for LTC Information, which will help consumers make educated choices regarding their LTCI coverage. This legislation is expected to significantly heighten public interest in LTCI as a means to help achieve retirement security.

BLURRING DIFFERENCES BETWEEN GLTC AND ILTC PRODUCT DESIGN

In addition to currently being a significantly larger market than that for GLTCI, the ILTCI market is characterized by a more consultative one-on-one marketing and sales process, as well as significantly higher initial commissions. First year commissions for ILTCI are typically in the range of 50% of premium for the writing agent or broker, with another 25 to 35% of first year premium paid as a management override. ILTCI policies are usually fully underwritten with long form questionnaires, although simplified short form underwriting is sometimes used for employer groups. The target market for ILTCI has been somewhat older (60 years and higher) than for GLTCI, but that difference is shrinking as ILTCI producers have begun prospecting to pre-retirement baby boomers.

The traditional differences between the GLTCI and ILTCI products are summarized in the table below.

Despite these differences, there are similarities as well. Both are rated on a level premium basis where the premium is a function of the insured's age at issue. Furthermore GLTCI coverage is typically fully portable, so if an insured's relationship with the sponsoring organization terminates, coverage can continue as long as premiums continue to be paid, often with no change in benefits or rates. If coverage is not continued under the original group contract, coverage can be extended through an individual conversion policy.

	GLTC	**ILTC**

Sales Compensation	Broker
	   15% First and Renewal Years
	     No override
	     Not Vested
	
	Insurer funds marketing
	Group Sales Representative
		Agent/Broker
		   45-55% First Year
		   25-35% First Year
		Override
		   5-15% Renewal Year
		   Vested
		Producer funds marketing

Application Forms	Single state situs with extra-territorial variations	State specific forms
Rating	Field/Home Office Enrollment Kit/Website Single risk class Some spousal discounts Payroll deduction	Producer Web quote generator Multiple risk classes Spousal/Group discounts Direct billed
Underwriting	Guaranteed issue for active employees Short form for active spouses Long form for others Accept or decline	Long form health questionnaire for all applicants Modified offers made

Benefit Features	Limited benefit choices
	   2-4 Daily benefit levels
	   Inflation protection
	   Non-forfeiture
	Home Health at 50-75%
	Lifetime max: 3 years to Unlimited
	Periodic inflation protection most common
	Death Benefit
	No spousal riders
		Full design flexibility
		
		Home Health at 100%
		Unlimited lifetime max common
		Automatic inflation protection most common
		No Death Benefit
		Spousal waiver/death benefit riders available

Rapid expansion of LTCI distribution channels and increasing public awareness of LTC and LTCI has resulted in much more comparison-shopping by consumers. As ILTCI and GLTCI products increasingly compete directly with each other, the traditional product design and marketing differences between the two products have begun to blur.

For instance, several ILTC insurers have developed simplified issue products that are used for multi-life employer groups. These products allow active employees of these employers to obtain ILTCI coverage using a shortened health questionnaire. Some companies even guarantee that those applicants who do not meet the simplified underwriting standards will receive an offer of reduced coverage. These ILTC programs also limit the number of plan options that are available, which is a common practice in GLTCI plans.

On the other hand, the number of plan options that are typically made available in GLTCI plans is increasing. Multiple waiting period options, lifetime maximum benefit limit options (including an unlimited option), and home and community based care coverage level options are being offered with greater frequency in GLTCI plans. To address the increasing complexity of the GLTCI plan, insurers have resorted to using personalized rate quotes (either on paper or via the internet), as well as to placing some of the available options "in front of the curtain" for marketing purposes, while other options are kept "behind the curtain" and only available on request.

SUMMARY

GLTCI is a group benefit with tremendous growth prospects. Increasing life expectancies, the maturing of 75 million Baby Boomers, heightened concerns about outliving one's assets, constraints on the continued public funding of long-term care services, and state and federal tax incentives will all contribute to GLTCI's continued growth. This growth will undoubtedly be accompanied by a continuing evolution in plan design, and in how this relatively new group coverage is sold and marketed.

11 MISCELLANEOUS BENEFITS

William J. Thompson

INTRODUCTION

In addition to the most visible employee benefits, namely life insurance, medical care, dental benefits, and disability coverages, there are a variety of additional benefit programs that are typically written as group insurance plans. Some of them, such as vision and hearing benefits, AD&D, critical illness, group legal, and group property and casualty, may be offered as part of an employer's employee benefits program. With the use of flexible benefit dollars that many employers provide in a "cafeteria program," several of these types of benefits have appeal as optional coverages.

Other benefits written as group coverages may be offered through other distribution channels, such as banks or credit card companies, associations or clubs (such as motor clubs, alumni associations, and schools) or as supplemental products to group health insurance plans to meet specific needs, such as short-term medical coverage.

With the continued rise in the cost of providing healthcare benefits, employers are looking for ways to manage the cost of their other benefit programs. One approach is the use of voluntary coverages, under which the employer makes certain benefits available via payroll deduction, sometimes on a pre-tax basis, but the coverage is 100% employee paid, sometimes through individual policies.

VOLUNTARY COVERAGES

Because medical coverage consumes such a large share of the employer's budget for benefits, employers have at times felt forced to cut back on the funding for other benefits, such as life insurance and disability plans. It is

207

becoming increasingly common for employers to allow employees to "top up" their benefits – benefits that may not be as rich as the employer once provided – by purchasing additional coverage on a voluntary basis through payroll deduction.

For example, an employer may limit long term disability benefits to 50% of covered pay, but allow the employee to "top up" their coverage to 60%, 67%, or even more at the employee's expense. The employer might limit the benefit from their contribution to life insurance coverage to one times salary, but allow the employee to purchase up to two or three times salary. Dependent life (spouse and/or dependent children) are other common voluntary benefits.

These programs are sold as part of the employer's group plan, and are rated on an attained age basis using the group's demographics. Insurers normally require a certain participation rate (typically from 10% to 20%) by eligible employees before implementing this coverage.

CRITICAL ILLNESS BENEFITS

Historically known as "cancer insurance" or "dread disease insurance," critical illness (CI) policies have become mainstays in many countries that have national health insurance programs, where the CI coverage can be used to supplement the national program. In addition, CI may be used to cover services not provided by the insurance program, such as providing a lump sum benefit in the event of a qualifying condition, travel expenses for family members who travel to a center of care with the patient, or possibly some income replacement coverage.

Critical Illness insurance is a popular benefit in Canada, Europe and other countries. Over the past several years, it has become more common in the United States, with several insurers beginning to offer this coverage.

BENEFIT DESIGN

In Canada, these programs are often referred to as "living benefits" policies. Most provide a lump sum benefit upon the diagnosis of certain specified conditions, such as cancer, heart attack, or stroke. With benefits that average close to $100,000, they are most commonly sold as stand-alone policies as opposed to riders on other policies. In Canada, this coverage is typically sold as non-cancellable insurance and usually as an individual policy.

In the United States, there are examples of both group and individual CI policies. Individual programs are commonly offered through an affinity arrangement. Group programs are commonly voluntary programs, under which each employee can decide whether to purchase the coverage through payroll deduction. Benefits range from lump sum payments upon the diagnosis of specified conditions, similar to the Canadian approach, to indemnity benefits to cover deductibles or services not covered by the employer's group medical program.

SELECTION AND PRICING ISSUES

Since CI programs are either sold to individuals or on a voluntary basis in a group or association setting, the opportunity for individuals selecting against the insurer is obvious. It is common to require a short form medical application for group coverage and sometimes a more thorough medical application for individual coverage. Policy language commonly employs a strong pre-existing condition limitation clause. Some carriers carefully re-underwrite at the time of a claim, if it occurs during the first couple of years after the coverage is issued. In a group setting, some insurers require a minimum participation rate of at least 10% to as much as 20% before putting the coverage in place.

Other product design approaches to protect against antiselection include graded benefit provisions and attained age benefit limits. Graded benefit provisions provide only a very limited benefit if the specified condition is diagnosed during the first two years. Attained age benefit limitations reduce the amount of benefit when the specified illness is diagnosed after a certain age. For example, the policy may pay only 50% of the face amount if the diagnosis occurs after age 70.

CI benefits are most commonly designed with a level premium based on the participant's issue age. Therefore, pricing requires projections of assumptions far into the future. Morbidity and mortality data that directly relate to CI insurance are not readily available. Therefore, it is common to rely on government publications and population data to obtain baseline information. The actuary must make adjustments for antiselection, with the adjustment based on the questions contained in the application, the marketing approach, and policy provisions such as pre-existing condition limitations.

Because of the level premium feature, CI policies can produce substantial policy, or active life, reserves, and because of this, investment income is an important assumption with this type of business. Persistency assumptions are also very important, since the release of active life reserves on terminating policies contributes to the stream of earnings. High persistency can have an adverse affect on this business, since the expected reserve release into earnings may not occur as anticipated.

Some Canadian policies are issued as non-cancellable, so substantial margins on top of expected claims are necessary to protect against pricing risk. Because rates are locked in on non-cancellable business, the insurer has no ability to increase rates if experience emerges at a worse level than anticipated. The actuary needs to test this business regularly to determine if a premium deficiency reserve is needed.

Most CI policies provide either fixed amount lump sum or indemnity benefits upon the occurrence of the prescribed insurable event. Medical inflation is not a factor in the pricing of these plans, but changing patterns in utilization of healthcare services is a risk that should be addressed. During the 1990's, when HMOs in the United States were practicing aggressive care management, inpatient utilization trends were negative. CI plans that provided indemnity benefits for each day of hospitalization saw favorable results, as this negative trend in inpatient days translated into fewer and shorter claims.

VISION AND HEARING BENEFITS

Though some coverage for routine vision and hearing exams may be provided as part of a physical exam within a traditional group medical benefits program, it is becoming more common to find separate riders that provide for hardware and supplies, along with coverage for examinations. Some states mandate coverage for hearing or vision exams for children up to a certain age. In those instances, hearing and vision exams are covered as part of an insured medical program. When hearing benefits are not mandated, vision benefit riders tend to be more popular.

BENEFIT DESIGN

The most common benefit designs provide for periodic examinations to detect any problems with vision or hearing. One exam per year is a common limitation. The benefit may have a prescribed dollar maximum, or the patient may be required to receive care from a participating vision or hearing provider who has agreed to a negotiated reimbursement schedule. Should the examination detect a serious medical problem, the regular medical plan covers the follow-up care for the treatment of that problem.

Corrective devices are also typically covered. A vision plan will normally provide for one set of lenses each year or two, and for frames every two years. A hearing plan will typically provide for new devices about every five years, and adjustments more frequently. Normally, benefits are subject to scheduled dollar amounts.

Occasionally, employers will offer an "affinity" vision program that looks like an insurance benefit; however, it is actually just a discount arrangement with certain optical providers, normally offering a discounted eye examination and discounts on glasses and contact lenses. These arrangements are not insurance plans.

Though most insurers and HMOs offer hearing and vision programs, there is a rapidly growing number of independent companies that contract with insurers, and sometimes directly with large employers, to provide vision or hearing benefits. With the expected growth of defined contribution health-care, and resulting individual selection, it is likely there will be further growth in these specialized companies.

SELECTION AND PRICING ISSUES

The most significant issues that need to be addressed in the pricing of hearing and vision benefits are risk selection and demographics. Both coverages show rapid increases in both cost and incidence with age. Because of this, it is important to recognize the demographic characteristics of the covered population. For example, the expected utilization of both vision and hearing services roughly doubles between age 35 and 55.

Individual selection greatly contributes to the cost of the program. Smaller groups, separate employee premium payments, and cafeteria plan election of the benefit all contribute to higher utilization and higher than average costs. There may also be a first year spike in cost for a group that did not have the coverage before. This is the "pent up demand" phenomenon that is also often seen in new dental programs.

TRENDS

These benefits are fairly commonly offered. With the aging of the population and the workforce, employee demand for vision and hearing services may increase, adding further to the availability of these benefits. On the other hand, when healthcare costs are rising rapidly, employers may look for ways to cut back on services. When hearing and vision benefits are viewed as optional riders, they are more vulnerable to being eliminated.

Because of the predictable nature of hearing and vision services, these benefits lend themselves to coverage through flexible spending accounts and health reimbursement arrangements.

GROUP LEGAL

Group legal coverage got its start through collectively bargained plans, such as those for the major automakers, and through plans sponsored by local bar associations. It is not a commonly offered benefit.

BENEFIT DESIGN

Benefit designs vary from limited to comprehensive. A very limited benefit design offers a certain number of hours of telephone consultation per year for a narrow range of services, such as preparation of a will. A more comprehensive plan covers a wider array of common legal services, such as real estate transactions for primary residence, and preparation of wills, leases, and adoptions. Some plans may cover divorce and legal separations. More extensive services, including business and investment matters and criminal law, are normally excluded.

The structure is often a PPO-like plan, under which certain attorneys agree to accept negotiated fees. Out of "network" benefits may be payable, with the employee responsible for costs in excess of the negotiated rates.

SELECTION AND PRICING ISSUES

As indicated above, group legal has traditionally had a relatively small market, primarily through large organizations. In collectively bargained arrangements, the employer often pays premiums. As a result, individual selection is relatively small. However, if the employee has an option to purchase the benefit with employee dollars, or if the plan is offered through smaller groups, individual selection issues must be addressed.

GROUP PROPERTY AND CASUALTY

Some large employers make arrangements with a property and casualty insurer to offer auto or homeowner's coverage to their employees. Homeowner's protection normally extends to condominium or rental coverage.

The property and casualty insurer may issue a group policy through the employer with certificates to the employee; another alternative is to issue individual policies.

Employees normally pay 100% of the premium via payroll deduction. Premiums may be lower than individually purchased insurance, due to savings in commissions and some administrative cost savings to the insurer. Payroll deduction also makes premium payments more convenient. Risks are individually underwritten and priced accordingly. Due to the group nature of the offerings, some marginal risks may be accepted that would otherwise be declined.

Employers value the benefit because it provides a valuable benefit to employee with limited expenses, generally tied to the cost of setting up payroll deduction plans. This can serve as an employee recruitment and retention advantage over other employers.

SPECIAL RISK COVERAGES

Certain limited risk benefits are offered to employers, educational institutions, or affinity groups (such as motor clubs) to provide specific limited coverage to eligible persons. Among the most common of these are travel accident insurance, accidental death and dismemberment (AD&D) coverage, student medical plans, and hospital indemnity plans (HIP).

TRAVEL ACCIDENT INSURANCE

As its name implies, travel accident insurance provides coverage only for accidental death (and sometimes injury) while traveling according to the terms of the policy. This coverage is very inexpensive. Employers may purchase such coverage for employees while on business travel, with amounts tied to salary or job title. Benefit amounts may be several hundred thousand dollars. In some instances, an accidental medical benefit of several thousand dollars may be added to the coverage, normally applying after a deductible of several hundred dollars to eliminate incidental claims. The employer typically pays premiums, although employee paid coverage is possible.

Credit card companies sometimes offer similar coverage that applies if airline tickets are purchased using the credit card. Motor clubs also provide their members with similar coverage, which is paid for as part of the annual membership fees. These organizations sometimes provide a base amount and invite participants to enroll for higher optional amounts.

ACCIDENTAL DEATH AND DISMEMBERMENT (AD&D)

Typically an employee paid option, AD&D is an inexpensive benefit that provides protection in limited circumstances. It is popular with employees because of its low cost, often around $.03 per $1,000 of coverage per month. Employees normally have some choice as to benefit amounts, choosing from a variety of options that may range from around $25,000 to $500,000 or more. Coverage might be extended to dependents as well, for an additional premium.

Death benefits require that death be caused by an accident and that death occurs within a certain time period, often six months, of the date of the accident.

Dismemberment benefits require either the complete severance of an arm or leg, or the complete and permanent loss of use of an arm, leg, sight, or hearing. Payment of 50% of the principal amount is commonly paid for loss of use of one member, with payment of 100% for loss of two or more members. No more than 100% of the face amount is payable for all losses from a single accident.

STUDENT MEDICAL PLANS

Student medical plans can take a variety of forms. At one extreme is a limited student accident program, typically offered to elementary, middle school, and high school students. A school district makes this coverage available at the parent's cost. Benefits are limited to certain accidental medical claims that occur at school, or on the way to or from school. Scheduled benefits are common with relatively low limits, sometimes with a deductible. Parents complete a simple application at the beginning of the school year, and submit a single premium with the application for coverage during the year.

The other common form of student medical plans is a more comprehensive program, typically offered by colleges and universities. Protection is more comprehensive, covering both accidents and illnesses that occur during the semester. Coverage is normally paid secondary to any other medical insurance the student may have. In some instances, the insurance makes payments to the student health clinic on campus for visits there. Premium bills normally come with each semester's tuition bill. Coverage is usually mandatory, unless the student (or parent) can provide evidence of other comprehensive healthcare coverage. Since most group medical plans extend eligibility to dependent children who are attending college, the majority of students opt out of this program.

Usually, a licensed insurance company underwrites student coverage, on a group platform. For enrollment purposes, the educational institution identifies the covered persons to the insurer, who then issues certificates to the covered students. Claims are administered by the insurer.

Hospital Indemnity Protection (HIP)

HIP is commonly offered through affinity groups to supplement traditional medical coverage. These programs offer a limited daily benefit while the participant is confined in an acute care hospital. The benefit period is often limited, with 30 days being typical. Some policies offer an additional benefit when confinement is in an intensive care unit, with the regular benefit being increased by 50 to 100% for those intensive care days. The benefits provided by these policies are paid in addition to any benefits paid under the participant's regular group medical program.

Typical affinity groups that offer hospital indemnity protection include travel clubs, credit card companies, and the American Association of Retired Persons (AARP). The plans are written as a group contract, with certificates of coverage for participating members. Participation is voluntary, with monthly or quarterly premium payments being required. Coverage continues as long as premiums are paid and the participant remains a member of the sponsoring affinity group. Coverage can also terminate if the affinity group ceases to sponsor the program.

Pre-existing condition limitations are commonly used as the principal underwriting tool for this benefit.

Benefit amounts are usually under $100 per day of inpatient care. Therefore, in pricing HIP, there is no need to recognize trends in the unit cost of the benefit provided. Over the past decade, hospital utilization has been declining due to the effects of medical management programs under managed care plans. As a result, there have been negative total utilization trends for HIP programs. However, hospital inpatient utilization has begun creeping upwards again, with admission rates growing around 1% per year and length of stay growing by 2-3%, producing a total utilization trend increase of as much as 3-4%. These utilization trends must be monitored and managed to ensure that the pricing of the HIP program recognizes those changes in utilization of inpatient services.

Credit Insurance

Credit insurance pays benefits, upon occurrence of an insured event, which help pay off debt of the insured. The most common form of credit insurance is life insurance. Somewhat less common is credit disability protection. Credit insurance is made available when a consumer takes out a loan (such as a mortgage, home equity loan or line of credit, or a new or used car loan) or when opening a new credit card.

The creditor (often a bank) is both the group policyholder and the beneficiary. Premiums are normally paid by the debtor, either as a single premium when money is borrowed, or as a monthly charge that is added to the cost of the debt. Though the debtor pays the premiums, experience refunds or dividends (as well as commissions) are paid to the policyholder, which is the bank or other creditor. Consequently, low premium rates are not important to the policyholder. In fact, the higher the rates, the more the experience refund. To manage this situation, credit insurance is tightly regulated. Many jurisdictions have established maximum rates in order to avoid excess premium charges, and by limiting the amount of dividend that the creditor may receive and retain.

Credit Life Insurance

Credit life insurance pays a lump sum benefit to the creditor on the death of the debtor. The benefit amount is directly tied to the debtor's outstanding account balance. The purpose of credit life insurance is to pay any remaining debt on the death of the debtor.

Credit life is priced as a decreasing term benefit. The length of the term is the number of years for which the loan has been taken out. The rate of decrease is tied to the loan's rate of interest. As indicated above, the debtor pays a fixed rate for this insurance, while the group policyholder (the creditor) has either a guaranteed rate with a commission payment or an experience-rated policy with experience refunds or dividends. In either case, the pricing is typically set at or very close to the statutory maximum rates that are allowed to be charged for credit life insurance.

Credit Disability

Though less common than credit life insurance, credit disability is regularly available through consumer lending institutions, such as banks, credit card companies, and credit unions. Unlike credit life insurance, the loan is not paid off in the event of a covered disability. Instead, credit disability makes a monthly payment equal to the minimum payment required to keep the debtor's account current.

When it is issued on an account with a revolving line of credit, such as a credit card, both credit life and credit disability premiums are charged monthly based on the balance on the account that month.

CAFETERIA PLANS

As its name suggests, a cafeteria plan is an arrangement under which an employee is allowed to select from a menu of various benefit plan offerings. Cafeteria plans are regulated under Section 125 of the Internal Revenue Code. That code allows employees to either receive cash, which is taxable income, or to receive non-taxable fringe benefits of equal value on a before-tax basis.

There are two primary benefits that arise through the use of a cafeteria plan. First, both the employer and employee can achieve tax savings through the use of pre-tax purchasing of benefits. Second, the employee has more options among benefits, thereby receiving a program of benefits that matches their personal needs.

Tax savings are achieved in the following way: The value of the benefits provided is not included in the employee's gross income before taxes, thereby reducing the employee's taxable wages. The employee's federal income taxes and, in most states, state income taxes are reduced because the wage base has been lowered. Similarly, the employer's basis for certain payroll taxes is also lowered as a result of the salary reduction.

More detail on the legal requirements for a cafeteria plan is included in the chapter on "Regulation in the United States."

The types of benefits that may be offered to an employee in a cafeteria plan include:

- Group term life insurance (though the cost of benefits in excess of $50,000 are added to the employee's income),
- Medical coverage,
- Dental coverage,

- Prescription drug coverage,
- Vision benefits,
- AD&D,
- Disability income benefits,
- Travel accident coverage,
- Dependent care assistance plans (offered under Section 129),
- Flexible Spending Accounts,
- Participation in a qualified cash or deferred 401(k) plan, and
- Paid vacation days, under certain circumstances.

Each year, the employer typically establishes a certain dollar amount or credit that the employee can use to purchase benefits from the cafeteria plan. Historically, those credits have been sufficient to cover the employer's expected contribution to the group life and health insurance benefits, though, with the recent shift toward more employee cost-sharing, those credits may start dropping. The employee selects the benefits that are most appropriate for their personal circumstances. If the employee's selections cost less than the employer contribution, the balance can be taken in cash, which is treated as additional taxable income. If the cost of the selections exceeds the employer's contributions, the excess is treated as a salary reduction from the employee's gross income. As indicated above, this salary reduction results in an income tax saving for the employee.

Because each employee is allowed to choose the benefits that are most appropriate for their own situation, the pricing of benefits in a cafeteria plan requires anticipation of a degree of antiselection that would not otherwise exist. More detailed discussion on this topic is contained in the chapter "Managing Selection in a Multiple-Choice Environment."

12 GOVERNMENT OLD-AGE, SURVIVORS, AND DISABILITY PLANS IN THE UNITED STATES

Bruce D. Schobel

The United States Government provides a variety of entitlement and other benefits under the authority of the Social Security Act. The most familiar such benefits are retired-worker benefits payable by the Old-Age, Survivors and Disability Insurance (OASDI) program, which is what the public ordinarily calls "Social Security." These retired-worker benefits are similar to group pension benefits. Other benefits authorized by the Social Security Act are similar to group insurance benefits. These may be categorized as cash benefits and medical benefits.

The most important such cash benefits are Social Security disabled-worker benefits and survivor benefits. These benefits are described in this chapter. The most important such medical benefits are (1) Medicare, a federal entitlement program primarily for the aged and long-term disabled, and (2) Medicaid, a federal/state welfare program for the poor. Those programs are described in the following chapter.

SOCIAL SECURITY CASH BENEFITS (OASDI)

COVERED POPULATION

Today, about 97% of workers in the U.S., both employees and the self-employed, are covered by Social Security. The only notable exceptions are the following:

- Federal workers hired before 1984 (a closed group).
  About one-fourth of state and local government workers (those covered by retirement plans that are comparable to Social Security are not compulsorily covered).
- A very small number of people who object to receiving governmental benefits on religious grounds (such as many Amish).

- Railroad employees, who have a separate government-run system that is financially integrated with, and in many ways equivalent to, Social Security.

Workers in covered employment pay Social Security taxes under the Federal Insurance Contributions Act (FICA) in the case of employees, or under the Self-Employment Contributions Act (SECA) in the case of the self-employed, on their earnings up to an annual maximum. They receive coverage credits (formerly known as quarters of coverage) on the basis of these earnings.

In 2007, workers receive one coverage credit for each $1000 of covered earnings in the year, up to a maximum of four credits for $4000 or more in covered earnings, regardless of when those earnings occurred during the year. The amount of earnings required to earn coverage credits has changed annually since 1978 and will continue to do so in the future, based on changes in the national average wage.[1] Workers with enough coverage credits establish insured status for various types of benefits.

INSURED STATUS

Disability-Insured Status

To become eligible to receive disabled-worker benefits in the event of disability, a worker must have disability-insured status. The number of coverage credits required for this status varies, depending on the worker's age at disability onset, from six coverage credits at ages in the early 20s, to 40 coverage credits at ages 62 or older (in 1991 and later). In addition, some or all of the coverage credits must have been earned recently (the "recent-attachment" test). For those required to have 20 or more coverage credits, at least 20 of them must have been earned in the 40 calendar quarters ending with the quarter of disability onset. For those required to have fewer than 20 but more than 6 coverage credits, at least half must have been earned after age 21. For those required to have only 6 coverage credits, they must have been earned in the 12 calendar quarters ending with the quarter of disability onset.

Fully-Insured or Currently-Insured Status

The family of a deceased worker may receive survivor benefits if the worker was either fully insured or currently insured at the time of death.

---

[1] Section 213 of the Social Security Act (42 U.S.C. 413).

Fully-insured status, which provides eligibility for the full range of survivor benefits, requires that the deceased worker have been credited with coverage credits generally equal to the calendar age at death less 22, with a minimum of 6 and a maximum of 40 coverage credits. These need not have been earned at any particular time. Currently-insured status, which provides eligibility for young-survivor benefits only, requires just 6 coverage credits in the 13 calendar quarters ending with the quarter of death.

OTHER ELIGIBILITY CONDITIONS

Disabled-Worker Benefits

A worker with disability-insured status can receive disabled-worker benefits if he or she becomes unable to engage in any "substantial gainful activity" (SGA) because of a physical or mental impairment that has lasted or is expected to last for 12 months or to result in prior death. The level of earnings that represents SGA has varied over the years, and is currently subject to automatic adjustment. The level for 2007 is $900 per month.[2] To be disabled, a worker must be judged unable to earn that much in any job that exists in the national economy, regardless of whether he or she would be hired for such a job, if it exists. In many but not all cases, the determination of disability takes into account the worker's age, education and work experience.

Initial disability determinations are made by state agencies on behalf of the Social Security Administration (SSA), under agreements authorized by federal law. A large percentage of initial claims are denied, for a variety of reasons. Many claims are appealed and result in hearings before administrative law judges employed by SSA. About one-fourth of all disability benefit awards are made by these administrative law judges.[3] Unfavorable decisions can ultimately be appealed to the federal courts, and many are.

Disabled-worker benefits are paid after a waiting period of 5 full calendar months. Thus, for example, a worker who becomes disabled on March 15 cannot count March toward that waiting period. The 5 relevant months would be April through August. Benefits would be payable for the month of September, and the payment would ordinarily be made on the designated payment date in October, usually the 3rd. Of course,

---

[2] Federal Register, 71 FR 62636.

[3] See, for example, the chart on p. 48 of the "1998 Green Book" issued by the House Committee on Ways and Means (WMCP: 105-7, May 19, 1998).

because of the time needed to collect medical evidence and to handle appeals, many disabled-worker claims are not processed quickly enough to permit benefits to begin so soon after disability onset. In those cases, retroactive benefits are paid in a lump sum.

Disabled workers are periodically reviewed to see whether they remain disabled according to the definition in the law. Typically, these reviews are required every 3 years, but they can be done more or less frequently, depending on the medical condition. In general, the government must establish that a disabled beneficiary's condition has improved before he or she can be removed from the benefit rolls. In other words, the government is bound by its previous determinations, absent some change in circumstances.

Disabled-worker benefits are automatically converted to retired-worker benefits when the disabled worker attains normal retirement age (NRA). The NRA is age 65 for workers born before 1938 and rises gradually to age 67 for workers born after 1959. Disabled-worker benefits cannot be received by people at or above their NRA.

Survivor Benefits

The family of a deceased worker can receive survivor benefits if the worker met the insured-status requirements described above at the time of death. Surviving spouses and surviving ex-spouses must establish that the marriage relationship existed or was deemed to exist for the required length of time. Children must establish dependency, which is deemed to exist for most natural and adopted children. In very rare cases, parents age 62 or older can receive survivor benefits, if they were financially dependent on the deceased worker and not receiving larger benefits in their own right.

BENEFIT AMOUNTS

Disabled-Worker Benefits

Disabled-worker benefit amounts are computed using essentially the same procedures as are used to compute Social Security retired-worker benefit amounts. The worker is treated as if he or she had reached age 62, the earliest eligibility age for retired-worker benefits, but no early-retirement reduction factor is applied to the benefit. Cost-of-living benefit increases are effective every December, starting with the year of entitlement.

Under certain circumstances, the spouse and each child (under age 18, generally, or themselves disabled) of the disabled worker can receive additional monthly benefits. The amount payable to a family member is nominally 50% of the worker's primary insurance amount (PIA); however, the total benefits payable to the family, including the disabled worker, are limited by a maximum family benefit that never exceeds 150% of the worker's own benefit.

Social Security disability benefits are integrated with Workers' Compensation and certain other public disability benefits. In general, the total benefits from all such programs cannot exceed 80% of "average current earnings" (as defined in the law), with triennial redeterminations to reflect inflation. In 37 states and the District of Columbia, the disabled-worker benefit is reduced to bring the total within the limit, and in 12 states, usually the reverse occurs. Nevada is a special case.

Survivor Benefits
The deceased worker's PIA is computed using the standard procedures, but treating young deceased workers as if they were age 62 at the time of death and not applying any actuarial reduction. In addition, earnings in the year of death are used in the computation before the end of that year (which is not allowed in the computation of retired- or disabled-worker benefits). Survivors receive a percentage of the deceased worker's PIA, ranging from 75% for eligible children (under age 18, generally, or disabled) to 100% for a widow(er) first claiming benefits at or above his or her own NRA. The widow(er) cannot generally receive more than the worker was receiving, if the worker was already receiving a benefit. A widow(er) claiming benefits before his or her NRA has an actuarial reduction. This reduction causes the benefit percentage to grade linearly from 71.5% of the deceased worker's PIA at age 60 to 100% at the widow(er)'s NRA. A widow(er) can "inherit" delayed-retirement credits from a deceased worker who had earned such credits at the time of death. A *disabled* widow(er) at ages 50-59 can receive 71.5% of the deceased worker's PIA. An eligible surviving parent receives 82.5% of the PIA, and 75% each if both parents receive benefits.

A maximum family benefit applies to survivor benefits. It ranges from 150% to 188% of the PIA, with most families being limited to 175%. Surviving ex-spouses of the deceased worker are excluded from the family for this purpose.

13 GOVERNMENT HEALTH CARE PLANS IN THE UNITED STATES

John W. Bauerlein
updated by Leigh M. Wachenheim

MEDICARE AND MEDICAID

From the 1930's through the early 1960's, government health insurance was proposed periodically, but never fully established, other than limited federal funding of state payments to cover medical services to the poor. Private health insurance, mostly through group insurance offered as an employee benefit, grew to be the predominant form of health care coverage. Over time, Congress perceived an increasing need to improve access to medical care for the elderly, the disabled, and individuals on public assistance. Legislation passed in 1965: Title XVIII and Title XIX of the Social Security Act, created the Medicare and Medicaid programs – Medicare for the elderly, and Medicaid for the poor.

Medicare is a federal program, while Medicaid is a joint federal and state program. Currently, the programs are administered at the federal level by the Centers for Medicare & Medicaid Services (CMS), a unit of the Department of Health and Human Services. Individual states have significant control over the management, design, and administration of their state Medicaid program.

A large percentage of the U.S. population receives health care coverage through these programs. Medicaid covered 15% of the U.S. population in 2004. At that time, Medicare covered about 14% of the U.S. population and just over 97% of the population age 65 years and older. The following table shows recent population and enrollment figures:

Medicare and Medicaid Enrollment Relative to U.S. Population		
	Enrollment (1,000s)	% of Population
Total U.S. Population – 2004 Estimate[1]	293,657	100%
Medicare Beneficiaries – 2004[2]	41,882	14%
Medicaid Beneficiaries – 2004[3]	44,356	15%

Note: Some beneficiaries participate in both Medicare and Medicaid.

Medicare and Medicaid have achieved their goals to expand access to health insurance coverage and protect those who cannot afford the cost of catastrophic events. Both programs have helped increase life expectancy and reduce the poverty rate for the elderly. However, Medicare particularly continues to face funding and cost challenges that will only grow worse in the future. Health care cost trend, rapid increases in the number of beneficiaries, and longer life expectancy will require substantial changes to keep the Medicare program solvent.

Costs for Medicare and Medicaid have grown much more than anticipated at the time they were established, putting a significant strain on Federal and state budgets. Total expenditures for the fiscal year ending September 2004 were $301.5 billion under Medicare[4] and $296 billion under Medicaid.[5] Total Medicare cost, about 2.7% of 2004 GDP, is projected to increase to just under 8% of GDP over the next 35 years under the intermediate Board of Trustees assumptions if the program is kept in its current form. Medicare enrollment, which has already increased from 19 million beneficiaries in 1966 to about 43 million today, will rise rapidly as the baby boom generation reaches eligibility age.

MEDICARE

Medicare covers most persons over 65 years of age, some disabled individuals under 65, and most individuals with end-stage renal disease (ESRD). Eligibility for coverage is available to the following:

---

[1] Population Division, U.S. Census Bureau, Table NC-EST2005-01

[2] 2006 Annual Report of the Board of Trustees of the Medicare Trust Funds

[3] 2004 Medicaid Managed Care Enrollment Report, Centers for Medicare & Medicaid Services

[4] September 2004 Monthly Trend Report, Office of the Actuary, CMS

[5] CMS-64 Quarterly Expense Report, FY2004

- Persons at least age 65 and eligible for Social Security or Railroad Retirement benefits.

- Individuals entitled to Social Security or Railroad Retirement disability benefits for a period of at least two years.

- Insured workers with ESRD, including spouses and children with ESRD.

- Some other aged and disabled individuals who pay mandatory premiums.

Medicare is not scheduled to change the eligibility age of 65 as the Social Security normal retirement age increases from 65 to 67.

Medicare consists of three "Parts." Part A provides Hospital Insurance (HI), Part B provides Supplementary Medical Insurance (SMI), and Part D provides outpatient prescription drug insurance. An alternative to Part A and B Medicare, available to beneficiaries in some locations is Medicare Advantage, a program whereby Medicare enters into contracts with voluntary private sector managed health plans. Medicare Advantage is sometimes called Part C and is discussed more below.

Eligible persons receive HI coverage automatically at no premium charge. HI services include:

- Inpatient Hospital benefits cover semi-private room and ancillary services and supplies.

- Skilled Nursing Facility benefits cover semi-private room, meals, skilled nursing and rehabilitative services, and other services and supplies (only after a related three-day inpatient hospital stay).

- Home Health Agency benefits generally cover services following discharge from a hospital or skilled nursing facility.

- Hospice Care is provided to terminally ill patients with life expectancies less than six months.

HI does not cover custodial services such as nursing homes or long-term care deemed medically unnecessary.

Unlike most private sector health plan design, Medicare HI coverage is tied to a "benefit period" starting at admission date and ending sixty days after discharge from the hospital or skilled nursing facility. There are no

HI beneficiary premiums. However, there are cost sharing provisions and limits on coverage when care is provided. The cost sharing amounts change each calendar year, and the amounts for 2007are shown in the table below:

2007 HI Cost Sharing and Coverage Limits		
Type of Service	**Cost-Sharing**	**Coverage Limits**
Inpatient Hospital	• $992 deductible per benefit period • $248 per day for $61^{st} - 90^{th}$ day each benefit period • $496 per day for the $91^{st} - 150^{th}$ day each lifetime reserve day	• Total of 60 lifetime reserve days, which are non-renewable • No coverage beyond the lifetime reserve (maximum coverage of 150 days per benefit period)
Skilled Nursing Facility	• Up to $124 per day for $21^{st} - 100^{th}$ day of each benefit period	• No coverage beyond 100 days each benefit period
Home Health Agency	None	None
Hospice Care	None	None
Blood	• Beneficiary pays first 3 pints of blood	None

SMI coverage requires a monthly premium subject to change each calendar year. The standard 2007 monthly premium is $93.50, which is automatically deducted from the Social Security payment. In 2007, higher income individuals will be subject to an additional premium ranging from 35% to 80% of the base premium, depending on income. A beneficiary can decline SMI coverage. However, if a beneficiary elects SMI coverage at a later date, the monthly premium increases 10% for each 12-month period that coverage available was declined. Nearly all beneficiaries receiving HI coverage also elect SMI coverage.

SMI covers most medically necessary services not covered by HI insurance. SMI also covers certain preventive care services. The following list describes specific SMI covered services:

- Outpatient Hospital (includes services such as emergency room and outpatient surgery);
- Medical Care (covers services provided by physicians and other qualified health practitioners. Also covers cost of diagnostic tests, supplies, durable medical equipment and ambulatory surgical center fees);

- Clinical Laboratory and Radiology services;
- Physical and Occupational Therapy services;
- Speech Pathology services;
- Outpatient Rehabilitation, including partial hospitalization services;
- Radiation Therapy services;
- Transplants;
- Dialysis;
- Certain Drugs and Biologicals (SMI only covers those that cannot be self-administered, except certain cancer drugs);
- Certain Preventive Services, including bone mass measurement, colorectal cancer screening, diabetes services, mammogram screening, Pap test and pelvic exam, prostate cancer screening, and vaccinations.

Similar to HI coverage, SMI does not cover services that are custodial or deemed medically unnecessary (except as noted above). SMI also does not cover dental care, eyeglasses, hearing aids, and most retail pharmacy prescription drugs.

Beneficiaries pay a $131 deductible once per calendar year (in 2007). After the deductible, beneficiaries pay, with some exceptions, coinsurance of 20% of the Medicare-approved amount. The beneficiary coinsurance varies for certain outpatient hospital services, and the coinsurance does not apply for clinical lab and certain preventive care services. The coinsurance is 50% for outpatient mental health care. Again unlike most private sector health plan, there is no annual limit on the amount of out-of-pocket costs incurred by beneficiaries.

Medicare Advantage plans are also available as an option in many locations, typically with much lower out-of-pocket costs, increased coverage limits, and some services not covered by Medicare such as retail prescription drugs and physical exams. The Medicare Advantage program is described in detail later in this chapter.

Coverage for outpatient prescription drugs became available starting on January 1, 2006, as a result of the Medicare Prescription Drug, Improvement, and Modernization Act (MMA), passed in 2003. "Part D" provides some coverage for most prescription drugs used by Medicare enrollees. Medicare provides this coverage exclusively through contracts with private sector insurers. Most contracts are made with two types of carriers: (1) Prescription Drug Plans (PDP) which provide prescription drug coverage on a stand alone basis and (2) Medicare Advantage-Prescription Drug plans (MA-PD) which provide prescription drug coverage along side other Medicare HI and/or SMI benefits.

Each year, Medicare determines the monthly rate it will pay contractors to provide coverage, and a basic premium to be paid by beneficiaries. The cost of each plan in excess of these amounts is passed along to beneficiaries in the form of a supplemental premium. Premium rates vary significantly by carrier and plan, ranging in 2006 from $0 to over $100 per month. Premium subsidies are available for low income beneficiaries.

The law defines "standard" Part D coverage in terms of Medicare and enrollee liabilities, relative to annual drug costs. The table below summarizes standard coverage in 2007. In 2007, beneficiaries were subject to a $265 annual deductible and then were responsible for 25% of costs up to an "initial coverage limit" of $2,400. Beneficiaries were then responsible for 100% of costs, until reaching the "out-of-pocket threshold" of $3,850. (This part of the benefit, where the beneficiary is fully responsible for costs, has become colloquially known as the "donut hole.") The $3,850 of out-of-pocket cost corresponded to total drug costs of $5,451. Each year, the deductible, coverage limit, and out-of-pocket threshold are subject to inflationary adjustments.

2007 Part D Cost Sharing and Coverage Gap		
Annual Drug Cost	Medicare Pays...	Enrollee Pays...
$ 0 to $265(Deductible)	0%	100%
$265 to $2,400	75%	25%
$2,400to $5,451 (Coverage Gap)	0%	100%
$5,451 +	95%	5%*

* or, if more, a $2.15 copay for generics and preferred multiple source drugs and $5.35for other drugs, subject to inflationary adjustments after 2007.

Some drugs are specifically excluded from standard Part D coverage, including drugs covered by Part A or B, drugs used to treat anorexia and weight loss, fertility drugs, drugs used for cosmetic conditions including hair loss, drugs used to relieve cough and cold symptoms, barbiturates, benzodiazepines, vitamins and minerals (except for prenatal vitamins and fluoride), and over the counter drugs. Participating carriers are permitted to define their own formularies within certain parameters.

Each plan offered by an insurance carrier must provide at least the Standard Part D coverage outlined above. However, contractors may enhance their plans to include coverage for drugs not covered by Part D, or to reduce or eliminate cost sharing or fill in the coverage gap.

Beneficiaries often purchase private Medicare Supplement or "Medigap" insurance, to fill in out-of-pocket costs, and provide benefits not covered by Medicare. This coverage is usually purchased on an individual policy basis and is only available to beneficiaries enrolled in Medicare. Twelve standardized plans, "A" through "L," are available in all states. Medigap carriers are prohibited from selling a Medigap policy to beneficiaries enrolled in a Medicare Advantage plan.

PROGRAM FINANCING

Medicare is funded on a pay-as-you-go basis. There is no prefunding of premiums, set aside as reserves, to fund future benefit payments. The HI program is financed primarily through payroll taxes paid through employment. These taxes paid by current employees bear no direct relationship to those employees' future Medicare costs, and employees have no ownership of their past contributions. The SMI program is financed through a combination of contributions from the general fund of the Treasury and beneficiary premiums. In fiscal year 2005, 75% of SMI funding was from general revenues and 24% came from beneficiary premiums. Part D is financed through a separate account within the SMI trust fund. Like Part B, Part D is funded through appropriations from general revenues, so that appropriations plus premiums equal expenditures. These monies are deposited to the individual HI and SMI trust funds. Additional funding sources are earnings on relatively small amounts of assets invested in Treasury securities, and income taxes on Social Security benefits paid to high-income beneficiaries. These other funding sources contributed about 1% of SMI revenues in FY 2005.[6] Benefit costs and administrative expenses are charged against the funds.

The HI payroll tax rate is 1.45% of earnings, with a matching amount paid by the employer (self-employed individuals pay the full 2.9%). Unlike payroll taxes that fund Social Security income benefits, there are no earnings caps on application of the HI tax. The tax rate can only be changed by an act of Congress, which has occurred periodically to ensure solvency, at least in the short term. Similar to Social Security, the HI

---

[6] 2006 Annual Report of the Board of Trustees of the Medicare Trust Funds

program is intended to be self-supporting. Medicare costs and annual increases have been relatively unpredictable, making accurate long-range projections of the HI program's solvency status difficult.

A board of trustees manages the HI and SMI funds. The board must report to Congress on the financial status of the trust funds by April 1 of each year. The CMS chief actuary issues annually an opinion certifying that the assumptions and cost estimates used in determining the financial status are reasonable. In the 2006 Trustee's report, the chief actuary affirms that assumptions and cost estimates are "reasonable in their portrayal of future costs under current law," but that there is a "strong likelihood that actual Part B expenditures will exceed the projections" due to legislative action to avoid reductions in the physician fee schedule. According to the 2006 report, the HI trust fund fails both the short-range and long-range measures of financial adequacy, using an intermediate set of assumptions. Assuming other program provisions remain the same, the report states that the tax rate would need to immediately increase from its current level of 2.9% to 6.4% to keep the program in actuarial balance through 2080. The changing demographics, high medical cost trend, and pay-as-you-go financing approach will make it difficult to achieve intergenerational equity.

Aside from higher taxes, other approaches to improving Medicare solvency include the following:

- Reduce or eliminate some covered services;
- Increase Medicare cost sharing through higher deductibles and co-pays;
- Raise the eligibility age for benefits to age 66 or 67; or
- Adjust reimbursement to providers of care.

The American Academy of Actuaries Medicare Reform Task Force concluded that Medicare faces urgent financial problems that demand action. These problems will accelerate around 2010 and any delay in implementing solutions will make the required changes that much more difficult.

MEDICARE PROVIDER REIMBURSEMENT

Medicare uses a complex system of reimbursement to pay hospitals, physicians, and ancillary providers. During the past decade, Medicare has implemented numerous reimbursement methodologies designed to reduce cost, encourage appropriate utilization, and lower Medicare cost trends.

Currently, hospitals are reimbursed on a prospective payment system (PPS) basis. Hospitals are paid a set amount for each admission based on the diagnosis-related grouping (DRG) methodology, which classifies each admission based on the patient's condition and the services performed by the hospital. There are just over 500 defined DRGs. Hospitals can also receive additional reimbursement for some outlier hospital stays, graduate medical education costs, and disproportionate share (DSH) adjustments. Hospitals qualify for DSH adjustments depending on the portion of overall hospital services delivered to uninsured and low-income patients. The DRG approach encourages hospitals to provide services efficiently (once a patient is admitted), as reimbursement generally does not increase with each additional day in the hospital.

Beginning January 1992, a complex fee schedule was implemented for physician services reimbursement. The fee schedule uses a resource-based relative value scale (RBRVS) to assign relative values to medical services. The fee reimbursed for a particular service is based on the following elements:

- Nationwide Conversion Factor. This factor is updated annually. The nationwide conversion factor is based on certain budget and growth rate targets for Medicare expenditures. The factor in 2005 and 2006 was $37.8975. This factor applies to all services except anesthesia, which has a different conversion factor and unit values set by the American Society of Anesthesiologists.

- Units for the procedure. Medicare has assigned a unit value to each physician procedure. Separate unit values apply to the components representing the resources needed to deliver a service. These components are described below:
  - Work Value, measuring the physician's time and skill needed to perform the service;
  - Practice Expense, reflecting the cost of rent, staff, supplies, equipment, and other overhead requirements; and
  - Malpractice Value, measuring the professional liability costs associated with the service.

  Unit values are also adjusted annually.

- Geographic Area. Medicare-defined factors for each of the three practice components are applied to them, producing area adjusted unit values.

Reimbursement for a particular service is equal to the sum of the area-adjusted unit values, multiplied by the nationwide conversion factor. Most physicians accept Medicare reimbursement as full payment for services. Physicians that are not "participating" may bill patients an additional amount, subject to about a 10% limit above the Medicare reimbursement amount.

Hospital outpatient services are reimbursed based on an outpatient prospective payment system (OPPS), which became effective on August 1, 2000. This system, also called Ambulatory Payment Classification (APC), covers facility charges only. The APC system works in many ways like a fee schedule but with "packaging" of some services to control overall reimbursement to the hospital for delivering care to a patient.

MEDICARE+CHOICE AND MEDICARE ADVANTAGE

The Tax Equity and Fiscal Responsibility Act of 1984 introduced risk contracting between Medicare and private health plans. In exchange for a defined capitation payment, private health plans, generally HMO's, are obligated to offer benefits at least as generous as basic Medicare and to return any excess capitation payments. Alternatively, plans can use excess payments to provide additional benefits, an approach that nearly all participating plans choose. HMO payment rates for aged and disabled beneficiaries were initially set at 95% of the projected Medicare fee-for-service program costs for the average beneficiary. Payment rates were established on a county-specific basis, and adjusted to a beneficiary's demographic, Medicaid eligibility, working aged, and institutional status.

Enrollment in HMOs grew rapidly, particularly during the 1990's, such that by 1998, there were 346 risk contracts with enrollment at about 6 million Medicare beneficiaries. In 1998, 74% of Medicare beneficiaries resided in an area with at least one HMO option, and in many counties the majority of Medicare beneficiaries had opted for an HMO instead of original fee-for-service Medicare coverage.[7] HMO plans were, and continue to be, attractive to beneficiaries because of richer benefits and lower out of pocket costs offered at little to no additional premium. In many areas, HMO plans include prescription drug coverage, a benefit not available through original Medicare but one valued by the elderly.

---

[7] CMS Fact Sheet, 8/29/01

The Balanced Budget Act of 1997 (BBA) created the Medicare+Choice program, which significantly altered how HMOs were paid. The Act attempted to address the belief that HMOs had been overpaid due to favorable selection by healthier-than-average beneficiaries. Legislators also saw cutbacks in HMO payments as a source of savings, as they worked towards a balanced budget. HMOs would no longer be paid at 95% of the average Medicare beneficiary cost but at a reduced level.

The net effect for HMOs was that annual increases in payment rates were curtailed to levels much lower than the underlying cost trends. HMO's responded by reducing benefits, increasing out-of-pocket amounts, and requiring supplemental premium payments from beneficiaries.

The result of the BBA payment rate adjustments is not surprising. After the 1998 peak, Medicare+Choice enrollment had declined substantially. Most HMOs had withdrawn from counties with low payment rates, or exited the Medicare+Choice line of business entirely. As of September 2002 there were only 155 Medicare Advantage plans, and enrollment was at about 5 million.[8] The Medicare Prescription Drug, Improvement and Modernization Act of 2003 (MMA) reversed this trend.

MMA triggered monumental changes to the Medicare program. Perhaps most significant, the legislation created the Part D outpatient prescription drug benefit described earlier. The legislation, which renamed the Medicare+Choice program Medicare Advantage, also revitalized the interest of the insurance industry in this line of business. Payment rates in some areas of the country were increased significantly. Moreover, trends in payment rates are required to keep pace with fee-for-service Medicare cost trends going forward.

The legislation also introduced new market opportunities including regional PPOs and Special Needs Plans (SNPs). Regional PPOs must offer PPO coverage across an entire region, with the goal of increasing managed care offerings in rural areas. SNPs are plans designed to meet the needs of specific groups, such as the institutionalized, the dually eligible (Medicaid and Medicare), and beneficiaries with severe chronic conditions.

Finally, the legislation introduced a bidding approach to the contracting process between Medicare and private Medicare Advantage contractors. In this process, contractors prepare a bid for each of their plans. The bid

---

[8] CMS Fact Sheet, 9/02

is compared to a benchmark rate developed by CMS. If the bid comes out under the benchmark, the plan keeps 75% of the difference (the "rebate"), which it may use to increase benefits, reduce cost sharing, or reduce Part B or Part D premiums. The government keeps the other 25% as savings. A bid over the benchmark results in a premium. A similar bidding process is used for Part D coverage.

Another change to payment rates made by the BBA, and not welcomed by the HMO industry, was risk adjustment. The Act mandated risk adjustment by January 2000, but gave the Secretary broad discretion to develop a methodology whereby capitation payments would recognize the health status of HMO enrollees. CMS' original methodology, called the Principal Inpatient Diagnostic Cost Group Model (PIP-DCG), relied on inpatient hospital diagnoses to assign Medicare beneficiaries to risk categories. Inpatient hospital data, rather than all inpatient and outpatient diagnoses, was used initially to ease the administrative burden on HMOs and moderate the immediate impact of risk adjustment. Under risk adjustment, HMOs were paid a base amount (varying by age and gender) with potential add-ons for the following:

- Medicaid enrollment
- Originally eligible for Medicare due to disability
- Health status – defined using PIP-DCG groups

A new methodology, the Centers for Medicare & Medicaid Services Hierarchical Condition Categories (CMS-HCC) model was implemented in 2004. This model uses both inpatient and outpatient diagnostic data. The model includes 70 diagnostic categories (HCCs). In addition to health conditions, the payment model takes into account age and sex, Medicaid eligibility, originally disabled status, working-aged status, and institutionalized status. The CMS-HCC model is additive in that it will recognize and incrementally increase payment for multiple conditions that are not closely related in the same beneficiary. By contrast, the PIP-DCG model recognized only the "principal" diagnosis for each beneficiary. Conditions that are closely related are placed in hierarchies, and only the most costly condition is recognized.

The transition from the prior demographic method to risk-adjusted payments was gradual. From 2000 through 2003, HMO payments were based on a blend of 90% demographic method and 10% risk adjustment. The risk adjustment blend was then increased from 30% in 2004 and is scheduled to be to 100% in 2007.

A separate risk adjustment model was developed for Part D prescription drug coverage. This model is similar to the CMS-HCC model, but designed to reflect Part D costs instead of costs for Part A and B services.

MEDICAID

Medicaid provides medical assistance for individuals and families with low income and resources. The Federal and State governments finance the program jointly. Most poor people in the United States receive medical coverage through Medicaid.

The Federal government sets national guidelines. Within these guidelines, states determine provider reimbursement rates, eligibility criteria, and the level and scope of covered services. Unlike the Federally administered Medicare program, the states administer Medicaid. There is substantial variation in Medicaid program provisions from state to state, leading to 56 distinct Medicaid programs – one for each state, territory, and the District of Columbia. Although states have broad discretion over many aspects of the program, they must follow Federal requirements to receive matching funds.

ELIGIBILITY

Individuals can qualify for Medicaid under many categories of eligibility. The Federal government sets the minimum criteria and States are free to expand eligibility. The two broad categories of eligibility linked to federally assisted cash payments are:

- Aid for Families with Dependent Children (AFDC): Children and adults in poor, single-parent families that qualify for cash assistance are eligible for Medicaid. During the 1980s, eligibility was expanded to certain low-income pregnant women and children not receiving cash assistance, subject to income limits at a defined percentage of the Federal Poverty Level (FPL).

- Supplemental Security Income (SSI): Low-income aged, blind, and disabled individuals on cash assistance are Medicaid-eligible. Some states extend Medicaid eligibility to certain other elderly and disabled individuals not eligible for cash assistance.

Other required categories of eligibility are recipients of foster care and adoption assistance, and low-income Medicare beneficiaries. States have the option to expand eligibility to other groups such as working disabled, long-term care patients, and those medically needy but with income or assets above the maximums.

In addition to "categorical" requirements (generally the aged, blind, disabled, or members of a single-parent family with dependent children), certain income and asset requirements must be met. Income requirements are defined as a percentage of the FPL. For example, states must cover all pregnant women and children under age 6 with incomes below 133% of the FPL. The FPL in 2006 for a family of one was $9,800 in most states. Minimum eligibility criteria for SSI and other categories are set by the Federal government, with states having the option to set income and asset limits at a higher level. Flexibility in eligibility rules has helped states substantially in their coverage and reform efforts.

The above requirements refer to the *categorically* needy. States also often extend coverage to the *medically* needy. These individuals can qualify for Medicaid when their medical expenses reduce income below defined limits. Such coverage may have less extensive eligibility and benefit provisions. However, to receive Federal matching funds, certain groups and medical services must be covered. Most states have programs for medically needy individuals.

Medicaid enrollment was fairly stable through 1989. Then, eligibility expansions led to a rapid rise, so that 1995 enrollment was about 50% higher than 1989 enrollment. In the latter half of the decade, enrollment declined or held steady for all eligibility groups except the blind and disabled, which grew at about 3%. This shifted the proportion of disabled enrollees from 14% of total enrollment in 1990 to more than 17% in 1998. The proportion of blind and disabled enrollees has important financial implications, due to these beneficiaries' high medical costs. Although blind and disabled persons were 15% of beneficiaries in fiscal year 2003, they represented 44% of Medicaid program costs.

Besides a strong economy, the most likely cause of this decline in enrollment is welfare reform. The Personal Responsibility and Work Opportunity Reconciliation Act of 1996, known as the welfare reform bill, affected eligibility for many individuals. The most important provision replaced the open-ended AFDC with Temporary Assistance for Needy Families (TANF). TANF limits cash benefits to a maximum of five years, and allows States to impose other employment-related requirements.

From 2000 to 2002, Medicaid enrollment increased dramatically among families, largely due to the recession of 2001. Since then, growth has moderated, largely due to states tightening eligibility requirements under budget pressure, while among the aged and disabled it has continued to grow at about 3%. Going forward, Medicaid enrollment is expected to increase, as is the proportion of aged and disabled enrollees. Consequently, Medicaid spending is also expected to grow, especially when the first year of the baby boom generation reaches age 65 in 2011.

The majority of Medicaid beneficiaries are children. Title XXI of the Social Security Act, known as the State Children's Health Insurance Program, was initiated by the Balanced Budget Act of 1997. SCHIP allows States to expand coverage, with support from Federal Funding, to substantial numbers of uninsured low-income children not eligible for Medicaid. The upper income limit for eligibility is typically 200% of the FPL. As of June 12, 2006, each state has an approved SCHIP plan in place.

FINANCING

Each state finances its own Medicaid program, with substantial support from the Federal government. The source of Federal funding is general revenues; there are no earmarked payroll taxes or beneficiary premiums, as there are for Medicare. Since Medicaid is an entitlement program, total financing requirements are driven by the number of recipients and the cost of services provided.

The Federal government finances between 50% and 76% of each state's Medicaid program costs.[9] The level of Federal support to each state depends on the state's average per capita income. The lower a state's average per capita income, the higher the federal support percentage. In general, the Federal government funds 50% of the state's cost to administer the program. The average Federal match percentage was 60% in fiscal year 2006,[10] with an average annual cost of $4,487 per person

[9] CMS Medicaid At-a-Glance 2005
[10] Ibid.

served.[11] In spite of the Federal match, Medicaid program costs are a significant portion of overall state budgets. In fiscal 2004, Medicaid costs were 22.3% of total state general funds.[12]

COVERED SERVICES

States must offer a broad range of basic medical services to categorically needy individuals. Covered services include:

- Inpatient and outpatient hospital,
- Physician,
- Lab and x-ray,
- Skilled nursing facility and home health care,
- Preventive care, prenatal care, screening and vaccines for children,
- Family planning,
- Services at federally qualified health centers and rural health clinics, and
- Transportation.

Other optional services, which nearly all states offer, are:

- Dental,
- Outpatient prescription drugs,
- Prosthetic devices and hearing aids,
- Optometric services and eyeglasses, and
- Rehabilitation and physical therapy.

States are required to pay Medicare Part B premiums and cost sharing for low-income Medicare beneficiaries. States can require that some individuals share in the cost through premiums and copayments. However, significant cost sharing is prohibited by Federal regulations. Most Medicaid beneficiaries pay little to no cost when they access medical care.

PROVIDER PARTICIPATION AND REIMBURSEMENT

Participating providers must accept the state's defined reimbursement as payment in full. Providers may not bill Medicaid patients additional

[11] CMS Fiscal Year 2003 National MSIS Tables
[12] National Association of State Budget Officers, 2004 State Expenditure Report

amounts, and are forbidden from withholding services if the patient is unable to pay the requisite cost-sharing amounts. State provider reimbursement rates must be sufficient to enlist enough providers such that access and availability is comparable to that received by the general population. Due to low reimbursement and other restrictions, Medicaid programs often do not achieve this objective, as providers are not required to accept Medicaid patients. Medicaid reimbursement is generally lower (often substantially lower) than Medicare or private health plan reimbursement. State budget limitations often restrict their ability to reimburse providers at reasonable rates.

Hospital Payments: States reimburse hospitals in a variety of ways. Many states use a prospective payment approach similar to that used by Medicare. Others reimburse based on the cost to deliver services. Some hospitals with a high proportion of Medicaid, low income, and uninsured patients, receive additional reimbursement known as the disproportionate share hospital (DSH) adjustment.

Physician Payments: States typically reimburse physicians according to a fee schedule. Medicaid physician reimbursement is very low, with levels often much lower than private payers and Medicare. Many physicians limit their participation in the Medicaid program, almost entirely because of the low reimbursement rates. Physicians have also expressed concern over continuity of coverage and litigation issues with Medicaid patients.

In addition to covering medically necessary treatment provided by hospitals and physicians, Medicaid also pays for the long-term care needs of qualifying individuals. Long-term care costs represent nearly one third of nationwide Medicaid costs.

MEDICAID COSTS AND MANAGED CARE

Utilization of services under Medicaid, particularly for aged/blind/disabled recipients, is higher than for the commercial population. Total costs of medical services for aged/blind/disabled recipients are often 5 to 10 times higher than the cost for a typical commercial member. The following table shows fiscal year 2003 average Medicaid payments per person served[13]:

---

[13] CMS Fiscal Year 2003 National MSIS Tables

Eligibility Category	FY 2003 Annual Cost
Adults	$2,285
Children Under 21	$1,462
Blind and Disabled	$13,303
Age 65 and Older	$13,677
Total	$4,487

For decades Medicaid costs have escalated at a very high rate. Medicaid's share of national health expenditures, 2.9% in 1966, has grown to 15% in 2004.[14] At expected cost trends, Medicaid expenditures will grow to $621 billion in fiscal year 2015. The growth in expenditures is due both to high medical cost trends and growth in the number of beneficiaries.

Rising Medicaid costs and state budget limitations have encouraged states to pursue alternatives to the traditional fee-for-service delivery system. Federal government waivers allow states to contract with managed care organizations, which include HMO's, prepaid health plans, and primary care case management programs. States contract with HMO's and prepaid health plans to provide medical services for a fixed payment rate per member (often varying by category of eligibility, location, and demographics). As required by the waiver, payment rates in aggregate are less than expected Medicaid program costs, and the participating health plans are responsible for providing, delivering, and administering services to Medicaid recipients.

Since the 1990's, states have aggressively introduced new programs to enroll recipients in managed care. The types of programs and managed care penetration vary significantly by state. Managed care penetration is lower in those states that have retained the traditional fee-for-service program, where managed care enrollment is voluntary. The percentage of Medicaid recipients enrolled in some form of managed care program nationally was 61% in 2004.[15] Most Medicaid managed care enrollment consists of children and non-disabled adults. The elderly and disabled have generally not been as actively enrolled in managed care.

Health plans participating in Medicaid waiver programs have experienced mixed results. In many states, health plan payments rates were set at ag-

---

[14] CMS Office of the Actuary, National Health Statistics Group
[15] CMS 2004 Medicaid Managed Care Enrollment Report

gressively low levels and annual rate increases have not kept up with underlying medical cost trend. As a result, many Medicaid health plans have exited certain states or gone out of business entirely. Nationwide the number of health plans participating in Medicaid waivers steadily decreased from 2000 through 2003, and then increased slightly in 2004.

Medicaid Managed Care in California

California has introduced into its Medicaid program, called Medi-Cal, a mix of comprehensive managed care programs. The type of program varies by region within the state.

"Geographic Managed Care" (GMC) has been introduced in Sacramento and San Diego counties. GMC is a program where the state contracts with independent managed care medical and dental plans. Beneficiaries are informed of the plan options, and then make their selection. Plans are then responsible for providing all mandatory benefits and services, plus any additional benefits they choose to offer. The state negotiates payment rates with each plan. Family aid categories, medically needy, and medically indigent are required to enroll in GMC. Other categories of eligibility such as SSI and foster care may voluntarily enroll in a GMC plan or remain in traditional fee-for-service Medi-Cal. As of June 2003, 5.3% of Medi-Cal beneficiaries are enrolled in GMC.[16]

The "Two-Plan Model" is the other common managed care program in Medi-Cal. Under this model, two HMO plans are offered in each county. One plan, named the "Local Initiative," is run by the county government or community-based organization. This was designed to support the hospitals and physicians that traditionally serve the Medicaid population. The other plan, named the "Commercial Plan," is a commercial HMO selected by the state through a competitive bid. Payment rates to the plans are set by the state. Similar to GMC requirements, family aid categories, medically needy, and medically indigent are required to enroll in the Two-Plan model. Other categories of eligibility, such as SSI and foster care, may voluntarily enroll in a GMC plan or remain in traditional fee-for-service Medi-Cal. As of June 2003, 37.7% of Medi-Cal beneficiaries are enrolled in the Two-Plan model.[17]

---

[16] Managed Care Annual Statistical Report published August 2004 by the Medical Care Statistics Section of the California Department of Health Services

[17] Ibid.

The Future of Medicare and Medicaid

Many feel Medicare and Medicaid have not kept up with changes in health care, and encouraging appropriate utilization and access to health care services. Government leaders will be challenged to adopt changes to improve the programs while making difficult and unpopular moves to address financial solvency.

Despite the dire outlook for the long-term financial status of Medicare and Medicaid, these programs enjoy broad public support. Program costs will undoubtedly take up an increasing share of government expenditures, which may require higher payroll and other taxes, always an unpopular step politically. However, the public expects Medicare will be there for them during their retirement years, and believes that Medicaid fulfills its mission to provide needed health care to the poor and disabled.

SECTION THREE

OVERVIEW OF LEGAL AND REGULATORY ENVIRONMENT

14 PRINCIPLES OF HEALTH INSURANCE REGULATIONS

Julia T. Philips
Leigh M. Wachenheim

INTRODUCTION

This chapter presents some of the principles underlying insurance regulation, particularly of health insurance and group life insurance. In this introduction, we describe the problems that can occur in an unregulated market, the goals of regulation, and the means used to regulate. The rest of the chapter presents examples to illustrate the means that can be used. The examples are mostly drawn from real situations in the United States, although they are chosen to illustrate broad principles, and therefore should be useful in aiding the understanding of any system of insurance regulation.

PROBLEMS IN AN UNREGULATED MARKET

It is possible to envision an insurance marketplace that does not need any kind of government regulation. Insurers have managers, actuaries, customer service representatives, and agents who act together in the best interests of policyholders and potential policyholders. They voluntarily make sure that their customers have the most complete information possible in order to purchase the most suitable policies at a fair and adequate price, and they hold sufficient reserves to be certain to have enough assets to pay any future claims or other obligations.

This fantasy is actually not too far from the truth. We probably would all agree that most people, working for insurance companies and other insuring organizations such as HMOs, are honest people interested in the welfare of their customers. However, that unregulated market would be a very unstable one, because one dishonest company could gain a competitive advantage. If just one company entered the market with misleading marketing materials, an unfair price, and inadequate reserves, they would be sure to attract a substantial number of customers from the other companies. Those customers do not have the time or expertise to investigate companies and establish which ones are operating in a fair and safe manner.

In an unregulated market, a customer may purchase a policy that is based on fraudulent claims and misleading presentations by a company. Or, a company may become insolvent with no warning, leaving the policyholder without the promised insurance protection. In still a third case, the customer may purchase a policy that only appears to be a good value, but in fact returns more profit to the company than protection to the policyholder.

Almost all of the specific insurance laws that are on the books of any jurisdiction were originally written in response to a problem that some consumers encountered with their insurance policies.

GOALS OF INSURANCE REGULATION

The primary goal of insurance regulation is to prevent serious problems for the consumer such as those listed above. Secondarily, regulation is often used to accomplish four other goals: (1) to prevent other, less serious problems for the consumer, (2) to maintain fairness among competing companies, (3) to raise tax money, and (4) to advance social goals. This chapter will focus on the primary goal described above – how regulation is designed to address serious consumer problems.

Serious consumer problems can be divided into two main categories: (1) insolvency or financial problems of the insurer, and (2) the purchase of policies that are a poor value or that don't provide the benefits the consumer expected.

One of the most serious problems an insurance policyholder can face is the loss of benefits due to the insolvency of the insurer. Sometimes, even monetary compensation would not fix the resulting problem, such as a delay in urgently needed medical treatment or an inability to purchase a new policy due to a decline in healthiness. In addition to the actual loss of benefits, the worry about possible insolvency and the long aftermath of insolvency can be frightening and stressful to consumers.

Another serious problem faced by consumers is the purchase of a policy that is not a good value. This may be the result of such problems as a bad match between the customer's needs and the policy benefits, or an unreasonably high premium rate. Sometimes the customer realizes soon after purchasing the policy that it is not a good value, and sometimes the customer realizes this many years later or never. It is the rare customer that has enough knowledge of the marketplace to identify the overpriced or unsuitable policy.

Unfortunately, even the best regulation cannot prevent all insolvencies and problems. Insurance regulation is aimed at accomplishing as much as possible, given existing constraints such as budget and social acceptance.

Preventing consumer problems is important, but there are other necessary characteristics of regulation, as well. Regulations should also be fair, honest, and cost-efficient.

LEGAL BASIS

One philosophical decision that must be made in any regulatory system is its level of complexity. Both simplicity and complexity have advantages and disadvantages in different situations.

Simplicity may be effective where regulation can rely on other standards. For example, in the United States a state may require insurer's reserves be certified by a Member of the American Academy of Actuaries. This simple requirement rests on the complex qualifications to be a member of the Academy, and the potential for professional discipline if the actuary does not follow prescribed actuarial standards. Therefore, the complex details are elsewhere. Simplicity may also be effective where there is general understanding and agreement on the standards. For example, it may be sufficient to state that a company's advertising may not be misleading. It is unnecessary to list the possible misleading statements if a consumer and a regulator can identify what is misleading based on a common understanding.

Complexity may be necessary in cases where the markets themselves are complex, or where simple requirements have not been effective in cases where the markets themselves are complex, or where simple requirements have not been effective in preventing problems. Some complexity in regulation just accumulates over time, as more and more requirements are added to the body of regulation. Although it seems possible to go back and rewrite such laws to be simpler, in practice that doesn't usually happen. First, there is no compelling reason to invest the effort, and second, many laws are controversial and cannot be simplified without raising arguments over their meaning.

A typical regulatory body of law may have different categories of requirements in order to give some form to the complexity. For example, a government may have a constitution, laws, regulations, and administrative directives or bulletins. The constitution is simple, stating broad principles. The laws are still simple, but there are many of them addressing specific issues. The regulations may be detailed and complex. The administrative directives address very specific and timely issues. Each of these levels of regulation generally gain their authority from prior levels. For example, the legislature gets its authority to pass laws from the State's constitution. A state's Insurance Department gets its authority to enforce the state's laws from the legislature.

In the states, generally insurance *laws* are enacted by elected governments, written to set forth general standards of protection that are intended to be implemented or administered by the state's executive department. Such laws are likely to stand without change for many years. Accompanying *regulations* are promulgated by agencies to implement those laws, and give specific standards that are likely to change from time to time.

REGULATORY ENFORCEMENT OF LEGAL FRAMEWORK

The means, or steps, of regulation can be divided into these five categories: (1) licensing, (2) information gathering, (3) prior approval, (4) enforcement, and (5) receivership.

LICENSING

The first and most fundamental step in regulation is licensing. This establishes which companies are subject to regulation. If a company does not agree that its business subjects it to insurance regulation, the issue must be decided in the judicial system. Licensing involves giving a unique legal name to each company. Licensing can be as simple as providing the company's name for a list, or as complicated as submitting detailed financial projections and product information for scrutiny before a license is issued.

In addition to licensing companies, regulators often license agents in order to monitor sales practices more closely.

Any company that wishes to be licensed must demonstrate that it is not likely to become insolvent any time soon. It must also agree to follow the rules of the jurisdiction in which it wishes to be licensed. Generally the company must have a minimum level of capital available. In addition, it must have a reasonable business plan that projects financial success.

Generally, it is required that an insurer must first exhaust any administrative remedies (such as a hearing by the Insurance Department) before instituting judicial proceedings.

INFORMATION GATHERING

After licensing, information gathering is the next step. The type of information gathered varies widely among regulatory bodies and for different types of coverage. In some cases, no information is gathered until an apparent violation is found.

However, often much time and effort is devoted by regulators to gathering information (either on a preset schedule or on an ad hoc basis) for purposes such as the following:

- Monitoring financial soundness of companies,
- Confirming compliance with regulatory requirements,
- Providing information to consumers, and
- Designing new regulatory requirements.

PRIOR APPROVAL

A third step in regulation is prior approval for business activities, such as issuing policies or changing premium rates. This step is useful in cases where prevention is more effective than cure of a regulatory problem. For example, if an unfair insurance policy has been issued, it can be too late for the consumer to acquire a different policy. Therefore, legislation may require that the exact policy language be scrutinized for compliance with statutory requirements, before the policy can be issued to consumers.

Prior approval has been required in some jurisdictions for policy form language, premium rate levels, reinsurance arrangements, dividend payments, mergers, investments, and other actions of companies.

ENFORCEMENT

The fourth step in regulation is enforcement. This is a critical step. Regulation without enforcement ultimately can be ignored by the regulated. In order to protect the vast majority of insurers who operate with integrity, a regulatory structure must include penalties for those who violate the law. Enforcement often relies on consumer complaints to discover violations, and then requires the company to make the consumer whole. Sometimes the regulator imposes fines or other penalties on the company. If the company disputes the violation, an investigation must take place. Sometimes the dispute must be settled in the judicial system. Ultimately, the most extreme penalty is to withdraw the company's license to sell insurance in the jurisdiction.

Another circumstance leading to a complaint can occur when the company is complying with the law, but the policyholder does not understand the legal requirements. Thus, a major task of enforcement is determining whether a violation has taken place, and if it has not, educating the policyholder. Some regulation puts the burden on the company to make sure the customer understands the policy and its provisions before buying it.

RECEIVERSHIP

The last step involves regulating companies that are financially impaired. This can range from receiving and reviewing special reports on financial condition to taking over an insolvent company and running it until it is liquidated.

FEDERAL REGULATION OF INSURANCE IN THE UNITED STATES

This chapter includes a very brief discussion of federal regulation, as it is covered in detail elsewhere in this book.

From the mid-1800's to the present, there has been controversy over the roles of the states and the federal government in the regulation of insurance. Currently the division of regulation is set by the federal law that was passed in the McCarran-Ferguson Act of 1945, which gives the states authority over insurance except where there is a specific federal statute that preempts state authority.

Some of the federal regulation that applies to insurance includes:

- The Age Discrimination in Employment Act (ADEA),
- The Americans with Disabilities Act (ADA),

- The Balanced Budget Act (BBA),
- The Consolidated Omnibus Budget Reconciliation Act (COBRA),
- The Employee Retirement Income Security Act (ERISA),
- The Family Medical Leave Act (FMLA),
- The Health Insurance Portability and Accountability Act (HIPAA),
- The HMO Act,
- The internal revenue code,
- Medicare as secondary payor laws,
- The Mental Health Parity Act (MHPA),
- The Newborns' and Mothers' Health Protection Act (NMHPA),
- The Omnibus Budget Reconciliation Act of 1990 (OBRA 90), and
- Sex and pregnancy discrimination under Title VII of the Civil Rights Act.

ERISA

The federal law that arguably has the greatest impact on state regulation of insurance is ERISA, which took effect in 1974. Although ERISA is primarily concerned with regulation of employer provided pensions, one section contains the "ERISA preemption." This section provides that state regulation of insurance does not apply to benefits provided directly by an employer to his employees as part of an employee welfare plan.

This type of self-funded insurance has grown, until around half of all employees who are covered by group medical plans are in these self-funded plans. These plans are exempt from most state regulation, including licensing, mandated benefits, market conduct, premium tax and other assessments, pre-approval of rates and forms, and solvency requirements.

One argument in favor of this preemption is that large employers will find it difficult and costly to comply with state laws in several states, and that uniform federal regulation will make more sense. Although the federal government has recently passed some legislation protecting employees against certain abuses in these plans, the federal regulatory structure for employee benefits other than pensions has so far not been nearly as active as state regulators in adopting rules to protect employees.

HIPAA

The Health Insurance Portability and Accountability Act (HIPAA) contains an extensive and complex set of requirements on insurance. One major change as a result of this law was that self-funded employer plans had to comply with some consumer protections, such as 'portability' (the ability of consumers to change insurers without losing coverage). The law includes requirements for portability of medical coverage from one group to another, and also from group coverage to individual coverage. It also addresses long term care insurance, setting up standards for federally qualified policies, which entitle the purchaser to a modest tax advantage. HIPAA also includes significant privacy and security protections. It applies to both insured plans and self-insured plans, and for most provisions does not prevent the states from imposing more stringent regulation on the insured plans.

STATE SOLVENCY REGULATION IN THE UNITED STATES

A primary focus of insurance regulation is on safeguarding the solvency of all types of insurers. In this section, we discuss actions commonly taken in state law and regulations to help prevent insolvency and to protect the interests of policyholders, insureds, and beneficiaries when an insurer impairment or insolvency occurs. Regulators charged with enforcing such laws include a variety of governmental entities, including Departments of Insurance, Departments of Health, Departments of Corporations, and other agencies.

CAPITAL REQUIREMENTS

All insurers need capital to protect against adverse deviations in experience for which current reserves may be insufficient. 'Capital' for this purpose refers to the difference between an insurer's assets and liabilities. It is equivalent to 'net worth,' 'surplus,' or free reserves. Insurers are generally required to meet minimum capital requirements before beginning operation in a particular regulatory jurisdiction.

Insurers that are going concerns typically need capital amounts that are related to the risk characteristics of the lines of business they insure and the types of assets they hold. Regulators review their capital in relation to those considerations. For example, in the United States state regulators use "risk based capital" formulae to estimate needed capital. These formulae have been adopted by the National Association of Insurance Commissioners

(NAIC) as part of the instructions for insurers' annual statements. They vary somewhat for life insurance companies, property/casualty insurance companies, and various types of managed care organizations, although there is an ongoing effort to create uniformity among the formulae over time. The formulae are discussed in some detail elsewhere in this book.

Once the company has used a risk based capital formula to determine the ratio of total adjusted capital (TAC) to risk-based capital (RBC), regulatory response is based on state law. The results of the formula are used as a simplified analysis that is a "red flag" for potential financial problems. (The lower the ratio, the more severe the corrective action called for.) Once the formula indicates problems, the state uses expert financial examiners to analyze the company. That analysis may find that the problems are not as severe as indicated by the formula.

GUARANTY FUNDS

In the United States, one method of protecting insureds from insurer insolvency is the use of 'guaranty funds,' after the solvency takes place. In this situation, a monetary assessment of all similar insurers in order to cover some of the financial consequences of the insolvency. In order to help establish uniformity among the states, the NAIC has adopted the *Life and Health Insurance Guaranty Association Model Act* (Model) as a guide to the states. Most states have enacted legislation based on the Model. The purpose of this Model is to protect against loss of two general categories of benefits: (1) payment of current claims and cash values and (2) continuation of coverage. The second is of particular importance for insureds covered by health policies, since underwriting standards or pre-existing condition provisions may make it difficult or impossible to obtain similar coverage.

The Model establishes separate accounts for two types of insurance offered by life and health insurance companies: (1) life insurance and annuities and (2) health insurance. An association is established and is empowered to make two types of assessments, one for the purpose of covering administrative, legal, and other such expenses and the other for the purpose of paying claims and providing continued coverage.

Certain types of insurers, such as hospital and medical service organizations and health maintenance organizations, may be exempted from participation in these funds. Also, certain insurance arrangements may not be covered by the fund, such as employer-funded plans that are exempt from state regulation.

RESERVES

Another important regulatory method to protect solvency is requiring adequate levels of reserves for future payment of current liabilities. A detailed source of information about regulatory requirements for health insurance reserves in the United States is the *Health Reserves Guidance Manual,* developed by the Accident and Health Working Group of the NAIC with the assistance of the American Academy of Actuaries.

The manual provides a summary of statutory guidance regarding the following types of health insurance reserves, along with explanatory material:

- *Claim reserves and liabilities,* which are a measurement as of the valuation date of an insurer's contractual obligation to pay future benefits (including capitation payments);

- *Contract reserves,* which are a measurement of the portion of premium payments in early policy years that is needed to pay for higher claim costs in later years;

- *Provider liabilities,* which are a measurement of an insurer's obligation to make future payments to providers under a risk-sharing arrangement; and

- *Premium deficiency reserves,* which are a measurement of the extent to which future premiums and current reserves are not expected to be sufficient to cover future contractual claim payments and expenses.

STATE CONSUMER PROTECTION REGULATION IN THE UNITED STATES

The large body of consumer protection law in the states grew over time in response to specific perceived problems. Typically, a state legislature will choose to investigate a particular consumer problem, and have witnesses testify about the issue. Therefore, some areas have little regulation and some have a lot. For example, in most states, consumer protection regulation varies significantly by type of coverage. For coverage such as dental insurance, medical stop loss sold to employers, and many types of group insurance, regulation is minimal. For other coverage, such as comprehensive medical, Medicare Supplement, and long-term care insurance, regulation is extensive and complex, dealing with marketing, rating, policy forms, and consumer education.

Consumer protection regulation can be divided into categories of disclosure, reasonableness, and fairness. There is much disagreement on the appropriate type and level of consumer protection regulation. In the fifty states, four territories, and one district whose insurance commissioners are members of the NAIC, there is wide variation in consumer protection regulation.

DISCLOSURE

Many state laws require disclosure to the potential customer of key features of the insurance policy. The insurance company may be required to provide a standardized "shopper's guide," an outline of coverage, a summary of the benefits, and/or an illustration of the results of the policy under different future scenarios. Sometimes the wording of these disclosures is specified by regulation, or is subject to prior approval.

The actual policy language is also regulated in the interest of disclosure. The policy must include certain information in a prominent place in typographic fonts of at least a certain size. The policy may be required to have the application form attached, and may have to contain tables of future guaranteed costs or benefits under the policy.

REASONABLENESS

Many states require that some types of policies include certain benefits or do not include certain exclusions. These requirements are usually considered part of a general requirement that benefits be 'reasonable,' or that they aren't unfair, unjust, inequitable, or discriminatory. For example, a medical policy may be required to provide mental health treatment with deductibles or co-payments by the insured that are no greater than those required for any other medical service. This is a "mandated benefit," and is referred to as "mental health parity." As another example, a Medicare supplement policy may be prohibited from excluding coverage for emergency medical treatment provided in foreign countries.

Many states also require that health benefits be reasonable, usually "in relation to premiums," at least for small groups. Almost the only method of measuring reasonableness that state regulation uses is the loss ratio. The loss ratio is the ratio of claims to premiums. The typical minimum loss ratio for small groups is 65-70%, and is managed from year to year by companies, with regulatory oversight.

Larger group rates are generally not as big a concern to regulators.

Fairness

Some regulations are designed to prohibit discrimination among classes of policyholders. For example, many states prohibit different premium rates by gender, even though statistical analysis shows a meaningful correlation between gender and claim cost for many types of insurance.

Insurers generally try to use techniques such as underwriting and "risk classification" as much as possible, setting their rates differently for many different classes of policyholders or refusing to issue coverage to some applicants. They do this for three reasons. First, the insurer who uses more risk classification has a competitive advantage over one who uses less. For example, an insurer who gives a discount for nonsmokers will attract more of them, and fewer smokers. A competitor who does not have a nonsmoker discount may find that claim costs are higher than expected, due to the higher proportion of smokers purchasing its policies relative to the proportion of smokers in the general population.

Second, failing to use such techniques can actually destroy a market, in certain circumstances. As an extreme example, if an insurer issues cancer indemnity insurance, which pays a fixed benefit upon diagnosis of cancer, without screening out those applicants who already know they have cancer, it is impossible to set a correct rate. Paying claims on those who have cancer will drive the rates up so high that the only purchasers will be those who know they have cancer. Then the rate will have to be higher than the benefit to cover administrative costs, and nobody will buy the policy.

Third, some feel it is fairer to charge insureds premiums based on the risk they are at issue, rather than intentionally subsidizing higher cost risks. Others feel that social fairness requires such subsidizations.

However, there is a clear public opinion that everyone should be able to purchase insurance at an affordable price. Therefore, regulation must strike a balance between prohibiting discrimination and preserving the private market for insurance.

15 REGULATION IN THE UNITED STATES

Edward P. Potanka
Keith M. Andrews

Insurance is a regulated business. Historically, the business of insurance has been regulated by the states. In 1944, the pre-eminent role of the states in regulating insurance was cast in doubt. In *U.S. v South-Eastern Underwriters Ass'n.*, the United States Supreme Court ruled that insurance transactions crossing state lines were regulated by the federal government under the commerce clause of the Constitution. Congress quickly responded in 1945 by enacting the McCarran-Ferguson Act that confirmed the pre-eminent role of the states in regulating insurance:

> *"The business of insurance, and every person engaged therein, shall be subject to the laws of the several States which relate to the regulation and taxation of such business... No Act of Congress shall be construed to invalidate, impair, or supersede any law enacted by any State for the purpose of regulating the business of insurance..." 15 U.S.C.A. 1012(a) and (b)*

Although the McCarran-Ferguson Act left to the states the regulation of insurance, insurance companies and the group insurance business are, nonetheless, profoundly impacted by the federal regulation of employee benefit plans.

This chapter outlines the salient features of state and federal regulation of group insurance, including HMOs. State regulation is discussed in Part 1, while federal ERISA benefit plan regulation is discussed in Part 2.

PART ONE✦

STATE REGULATION

Every state has enacted comprehensive laws regulating virtually all aspects of the business of insurance. In fact, few businesses are as heavily regulated as the business of insurance. Part One summarizes the salient features of state regulation of group insurance and HMOs. While all lines of group health insurance are regulated by the states, the regulatory requirements relating to group health insurance and HMOs are far more extensive than those relating to the other major group insurance lines (Life, Accidental Death & Dismemberment, Disability, and Long Term Care). This disproportionate regulatory attention to group health insurance is reflected in this summary.

STATE REGULATION OF GROUP INSURANCE GENERALLY

ORGANIZATION OF STATE INSURANCE DEPARTMENTS

All state insurance laws provide for the creation of an Insurance Department or Bureau in the executive branch, to administer the laws regulating insurers and the business of insurance. State insurance laws typically establish a single Commissioner or Superintendent as the head of the Insurance Department (in a few cases there is an Insurance Board). In addition to overseeing the operation of the Insurance Department, the Commissioner is empowered by statute to interpret the insurance laws, make regulations implementing the insurance laws, and to license insurance companies, authorized reinsurers, and third-party administrators, as well as insurance agents, brokers, and consultants. The Commissioner is also empowered to conduct examinations of the operations of licensed insurers, and to assess penalties (including termination of licensure) for violations of insurance laws and regulations.

ORGANIZATION AND LICENSING OF INSURANCE COMPANIES

In order to engage in the insurance business in a state, a company must obtain an insurance license from that state's insurance commissioner. The license pertains to specific lines of business, and must be renewed annually. The requirements for a license vary, depending on whether the insurer is a domestic insurer (domiciled in that state), a foreign insurer (a United States company domiciled in another state) or an alien insurer (domiciled outside the United States). The licensing requirements for foreign and alien insurers are more stringent than for domestic insurers. Imposing more stringent licensing requirements on non-domestic insurers encourages insurers to domicile in the state, and provides policyholders and consumers greater protection from abuses by foreign and alien companies, over which the Insurance Commissioner has less regulatory control.

POLICY/CERTIFICATE FORM AND RATE FILING REGULATIONS

Either by law or regulation, virtually all states require the filing of group life and health policy and certificate forms used in the state. Some states require that the Commissioner approve the policy and certificate forms prior to use ("prior approval" states). Others, so-called "file and use" states, require only that the forms be filed prior to use. Some states require annual filing of forms initially used during the prior year. Many states also require the filing of group health premium rates or rating formulas.

LICENSING PRODUCERS

Most states require that producers, including insurance agents, brokers, and other insurance intermediaries, be licensed in order to conduct business in the state. Many states require that agents pass tests before licenses are granted. In addition, there are state laws that require agents to take continuing education classes in order to maintain their licenses. The Commissioner may revoke or suspend a license, or impose financial penalties, for violations of regulatory requirements. As a result of perceived abuses, many states have recently begun to enact laws imposing upon producers the obligation to disclose to their clients the compensations they may be entitled to receive from the insurance companies whose products they recommended to a client.

ADVERTISING REGULATION

Most states have adopted by statute or regulation the National Association of Insurance Commissioners ("NAIC") model regulations relating to advertisements for life and health insurance products. These laws and regulations are intended to protect consumers from unfair, inaccurate, deceptive, and misleading advertisements, and to prevent disparaging, unfair, or incomplete comparisons with other insurance companies or their products.

What is "advertising" material? That is often a question faced by insurers in attempting to apply these laws to their business. At least one state has taken the position that the term "advertising" is so broad as to embrace an insurer's web site.

REGULATION OF BUSINESS PRACTICES

Virtually all states have adopted, in some form, the NAIC Unfair Trade Practices and Unfair Claim Settlement Practices Model Acts. These regulations govern the conduct of insurance companies by prohibiting specified unfair practices relating to the issuance, renewal and termination or underwriting of coverage, advertising, rebating, and claim practices. Repeated violations indicating a pattern or practice that is in violation of the prohibitions can subject the insurer to a cease and desist order from the insurance regulator, as well as fines or license revocation.

PROMPT PAY LEGISLATION

In the past decade, health care providers have successfully lobbied state legislators to enact laws requiring that insurers and HMOs pay "clean" claims within a specified period of time (typically 30-45 days). Interest charges, at relatively high annual rates, are required for claims not paid within the required timeframe. State laws requiring that insurers pay interest on delayed claim payments are nothing new. What is new is that insurance regulators in some states have embraced enforcement of these laws against health insurers and HMOs more aggressively, and in some instances, imposed seven figure fines for violation of prompt pay laws.

REGULATION OF INSURER SOLVENCY

One of the most important duties of the Insurance Commissioner is to assure the financial soundness of the licensed insurers doing business in the state. The financial soundness of the insurance company is assessed initially during the licensing process. Once licensed, insurers must maintain adequate reserves, specified minimum levels of capital and/or surplus, and in some cases, deposits for the protection of policyholders. To facilitate monitoring of the financial condition of insurers, financial reports are required to be annually filed with the Commissioner.

The financial statements prepared by insurers were first designed by the NAIC in 1871 and have undergone many revisions over time. The last major revision was in the 1950's. Each year minor revisions are made.

These statements are commonly referred to as the "NAIC Blank." Every three years, the information submitted in the financial statement is subject to on-site financial audit review by the insurance department, through a "triennial exam." These audits are directed by the insurance department, but are at the expense of the insurer subject to the audit.

Investments

In keeping with the purpose of assuring the solvency of licensed insurers, even the types of investments that an insurer may make are regulated. The regulatory restrictions depend on the type of investment. Capital may be invested in conservative and secure investments, such as government bonds and mortgages. Capital investments are required for funds that are equal to the legal minimum surplus for the particular line of insurance. Reserve investments may be made with all of the other funds available to insurers. In addition to the conservative investments allowed for capital investments, other investments are allowed for reserve investments. Regulatory restrictions pertaining to investments do vary by state, with some states requiring more conservative investment strategies than others. State laws or regulations typically require that any investments be approved by the board of directors or another committee charged with the insurer's investment operations. Persons charged with approval are permitted no interest in the investments or their sale to the insurer.

The Insurance Commissioner sets the asset valuation standards at a level that is consistent with NAIC rules.

Reserves

Adequate reserves must be established by insurers to deal with prospective claim liabilities. Life insurers must establish a minimum life insurance reserve by law. The NAIC has developed model requirements for this purpose. Although reserves are required, determination of their adequacy is usually left to the insurer. Most states require that reserve levels be certified as being adequate at the end of each calendar year, by an actuary that is a member of the American Academy of Actuaries and is considered as the appointed actuary for the insurer.

Surplus and Dividends

Mutual insurers are limited by law in many cases as to how much surplus can be accumulated. The purpose of this is two-fold. First, it limits the amount that is available for use as excess funds. Second, it allows for the payment of reasonable dividends. State insurance laws also require that the dividends be paid annually and not be deferred.

Similarly, some not-for-profit organizations have their respective levels of surplus (called "free reserves") limited by state statute, regulation, or regulatory practice.

Liquidation and Rehabilitation

If a licensed insurer is in jeopardy of becoming insolvent, state insurance laws authorize the Commissioner to apply to a state court for an order allowing the Commissioner to assume the insurer's assets. An insurer's impending insolvency may initially come to the attention of the regulator in a variety of ways, and is usually confirmed by means of an on-site financial examination of the insurer. There must be actual evidence of financial insufficiency or wrong-doing to support the application for an order assuming an insurer's assets. The grounds for assuming the assets of an insurer include:

* Non-cooperation with examiners,
* Refusing to remove questionable officers,
* Charter violations,
* State law violations, or
* Endangered capital or surplus or technical insolvency.

The insurer may apply for a court hearing to appeal the take-over; however, during this process the Commissioner will have control of the company's assets.

The NAIC has developed a Model Insurers Supervision, Rehabilitation and Liquidation Act. By the terms of this act, the Commissioner may seek reorganization of the insurer to preserve its tangible assets. In this instance, the name is usually changed and the company is returned to the hands of private management.

If the Commissioner determines that rehabilitation is impossible, then liquidation is proposed. The Commissioner obtains another court order asking for liquidation of the insurer's assets. The same grounds as are used to assume the assets are used to obtain the court order for liquidation. The Commissioner is named as the liquidator, collects all assets and pays all obligations that are due. An attempt is often made to have a reinsurer assume some or all of the obligations of the company. Notices advising of the liquidation are sent to other commissioners, guarantee funds, insurance agents, providers, and any others with claims against the insurer.

Guaranty Associations

States have enacted laws creating so-called guaranty associations to protect insureds when life and health insurers fail to perform their contractual obligations due to financial impairment or insolvency. To provide this protection, an association of insurers licensed in the particular line of business is created to pay the claims and continue the coverages of the impaired or insolvent insurer up to specified limits. To fund these continuing obligations, association members (usually all insurers licensed in the particular line) are required to pay a periodic assessment. Generally, HMOs are not subject to guaranty fund laws.

Insurance Regulatory Information System (IRIS)

The NAIC has developed an early warning testing system designed to reveal indications of financial problems and insolvency. It is called the Insurance Regulatory Information System (IRIS).

The NAIC will conduct an IRIS test series for insurers that voluntarily submit their annual statements for the tests and pay the required fee, and those insurers with a history of financial problems.

Under IRIS, an annual statement is subjected to tests where certain ratios are developed. These ratios are meant to indicate future financial problems that could potentially result in insolvency. When these results are combined with other factors, such as the results of previous examinations, the insurance department and the insurer are better able to assess the company's financial future.

GROUP LIFE AND HEALTH DEFINITIONS

The vast majority of states have laws that define what constitutes a group for the purposes of issuing a group life or health insurance policy. These "group definition" laws typically permit an insurer to issue a group insurance policy to the following groups:

- Single-employer groups covering their employees and their dependents,
- Labor union groups covering their members,
- Association groups covering their members,
- Multiple-employer trust groups (METs) made up of employers, unions or a combination of the two, covering employees of the employer or members of the union, and
- Creditors of financial institutions.

There is often a "catch-all" category referred to as discretionary groups. These are groups not within any of the other defined groups to which an insurance company may issue a group insurance policy at the discretion of the Commissioner. Not all states allow all of these groups, and the laws are by no means uniform or consistent from state to state.

STANDARD CONTRACT PROVISIONS

State insurance laws often require that group insurance policies contain specified standard provisions, or provisions which (in the opinion of the Commissioner) are more favorable to the persons insured, that typically relate to:

- *Grace Period.* There must be a 31-day grace period provision for the payment of premium during which time the benefits will remain in force. The policyholder is liable for payment of a pro rata premium payment for this period.
- *Incontestability.* There must be a provision that provides that the validity of the policy shall not be contested after it has been in force for two years, except for nonpayment of premium. The provision must also state that no statement made by any insured, relating to his or her insurability, shall be used to contest the validity of the person's insurance after it has been in force prior to the contest for two years nor unless the statement is in writing and signed by the insured.
- *Application and Statements.* A provision is required to the effect that the application has to be made a part of the policy and the insured's statements are to be considered representations and not warranties.
- *Evidence of Insurability.* There must be a provision indicating when evidence of insurability, if any, would be required.
- *Misstatement of Age Provision.* If premiums or benefits vary by age, there must be a provision stating how premiums or benefits will be adjusted due to a misstatement of age.
- *Certificates.* A provision must be included stating that the insurer will issue certificates to the policyholder for delivery to each insured.
- *Benefits/Eligibility.* Policy provisions must set forth the benefits, identify to whom they are payable and include specific terms of eligibility for coverage.

POLICY PROVISIONS FOR GROUP HEALTH PLANS ONLY

- *Preexisting Conditions.* A provision must be included in the policy describing the exclusions or limitations that apply to medical conditions which existed prior to the person's coverage under the policy. Any such provision must be limited to conditions for which advice or treatment was received within 6 months of the person's coverage effective date, and cannot generally apply for longer than 12 months after the coverage effective date. (See the discussion on the federal HIPAA law in Part Two of this chapter for more information on pre-existing conditions.)

- *Notice and Proof of Claims.* A group health policy must include a provision that specifies the periods of time following the occurrence of a "loss" in which a notice of claim and proof of loss must be provided to the insurance company. This is waived if it is not reasonably possible to give it. The insurer must furnish the appropriate claim forms to the insured.

- *Legal Actions.* A provision specifying the periods of time when a legal action may not be brought on a claim must be included in the policy. For example, a legal action may not be brought any earlier than 60 days nor later than 2-3 years following submission of a claim.

POLICY PROVISIONS FOR GROUP LIFE PLANS ONLY

- *Beneficiaries.* There must be a provision identifying the designated beneficiary.

- *Conversion Rights.* The group policy must give the insured the right to convert his or her group life insurance to an individual life insurance policy, if his or her group life coverage ceases due to termination of employment or termination of membership in an insured class. The amount that can be converted cannot exceed the amount in effect immediately prior to termination. Conversion must be offered without evidence of insurability, and at the insurer's customary rate for the person's class of risk and attained age. The person must make application and pay the first premium within a specified time following termination of group coverage.

  The conversion privilege is also available to insured dependents whose group life insurance ceases due to the employee's death or because they no longer qualify as a dependent.

If termination of group life insurance is due to termination of the group policy or the covered person's class, the person may also convert to an individual policy if he or she was covered under the group policy for at least five years prior to termination. However, the amount that can be converted is limited to the lesser of the amount in effect immediately prior to conversion or $10,000.

- *Death During the Conversion Period.* A provision must be included which states that if a person dies within the 31-day conversion period, the amount which could have been converted will be paid as a claim under the group policy, regardless of whether he/she has applied to convert.

- *Disability Continuance.* There must be a provision stating that if an active employee becomes totally disabled while insured, he or she may continue coverage under the group policy by payment of the premium for up to six months. Coverage will cease, in any case, when (a) the person is approved for coverage under a premium waiver provision of the policy, or (b) the policy terminates.

MANDATED BENEFITS

Legislative mandates that group insurance policies include certain benefits (so-called "mandated benefits") focus principally on health insurance. States mandate benefits primarily to meet the perceived needs of their citizens or to satisfy the demands of interest groups such as health care providers. Mandated benefits have been viewed by state legislatures as politically attractive since they allow legislators to demonstrate a benefit to specific constituents at no direct cost to the state. As a result, mandated benefit laws have proliferated and there is little in common from state to state except that most states require minimum levels of coverage for alcohol and drug treatment. Even where states mandate a particular benefit, there is little consistency between states as to the specifics of the coverage required. The list of coverage mandates is extensive. The more common mandated benefits include coverage mandates for

- mental disorders,
- alcoholism and drug dependency,
- newborn children from birth,
- well-child care,
- handicapped children beyond their normal termination age,
- mammography,

- recognition of a variety of health care practitioners (such as chiropractors, and podiatrists), to provide services that are within the scope of their respective licenses and would be payable under a policy to other licensed medical providers, and

- coverage of children under policies covering non-custodial parents.

Some mandates apply only to policies issued or delivered in the state. Others apply extra-territorially to the citizens of a state even if covered under a group policy that is issued in another state. As a result, insurers covering people in multiple states under a group insurance policy must include the mandated benefits of the state where the contract is issued and offer people living in other states any extra-territorial benefits. Employees covered under the same employer sponsored group health plan may be entitled to different benefits depending on where they live.

Although mandated benefit laws are politically attractive to state legislators because they come at no cost to the state, they certainly have a cost. In recognition of the additional cost of mandated benefits for employers, some states have permitted insurers to offer the mandated benefits at an additional cost. Coverage for domestic partners, for example, is often only required to be offered as an optional benefit to a group. In instances of this nature, the cost of adding the additional coverage or benefit is often very high due to selection considerations. Increased awareness of the cost of mandated benefits has in some instances resulted in state legislatures imposing a moratorium on additional mandates.

COORDINATION OF BENEFITS

It is not uncommon for an individual covered under a group health plan (insurance or HMO) to have other insurance coverage for health care expenses. For example, a person may be covered under his/her employer's group plan and covered under his/her spouse's plan as a dependent. With more than one plan in force, there is the possibility of duplication of benefit payment and of the person profiting from the injury or sickness. This leads to unnecessary increases in the cost of group insurance coverage. During the 1960's, group insurers attempted to develop rules for coordinating their coverages to avoid duplication of claim payments. In 1970, the NAIC adopted a Group Coordination of Benefits Model regulation to establish rules for insurers to use in determining which insurer would be primary and which would be secondary in duplicate coverage situations. The model act has been continually updated and adopted by all but a handful of states.

The coordination of benefit ("COB") rules apply to group and group-type plans only. Individual plans (other than automobile no-fault plans) would not be included in the list of plans with which a group plan could coordinate its benefits. The COB rules establish a precise order of benefit payment determination. The COB rules are typically included in the group insurance policy or HMO service agreement. In application, the COB administration rules can be very complex.

REQUIREMENTS FOR CONTINUATION OF COVERAGE

Continuing coverage when a group health policy terminates or a person's coverage under the group policy terminates has been dealt with in the insurance laws or regulations in about two-thirds of the states which have adopted some form of the NAIC Group Health Insurance Mandatory Conversion Privilege Model Act. These laws require that group health insurers offer individuals, who have been covered for at least three months under a group policy, and whose coverage has terminated, the option of converting their group coverage to an individual major medical health insurance policy. The person losing coverage must exercise the conversion option within 31 days after termination of the group plan coverage, and the policy must be issued without evidence of insurability. However, if the person is eligible under another plan that, together with the benefits of the converted policy would cause over-insurance, the insurer may refuse to issue the conversion plan.

These respective state insurance laws specify the minimum benefit levels that must be provided under conversion policies. They may also require that the premium rates for the conversion policy be the same as those that apply to the insurer's individually underwritten standard risks. In recognition of the fact that insurers will be anti-selected against for this conversion coverage, the experience under converted policies cannot normally be used to establish rates. However, the insurer may be allowed to amend its rates so as not to exceed a specified minimum loss ratio.

DISCONTINUANCE AND REPLACEMENT OF COVERAGE

Employers frequently discontinue coverage under one group insurance policy (life or health) and replace it with coverage under another group insurance policy issued by another company. This discontinuance and replacement situation can pose a number of problems. Because many group life and health insurance policies exclude from eligibility the replacement coverage for persons with pre-existing conditions or not actively at work, some people would be left without coverage as a result of the change in insurance companies. This poses a dilemma for employers desiring to ensure the continuity of coverage for their employees and their dependents. Some employers, on the other hand, attempted to take advantage of these limitations in the replacement carrier's policy in order to preclude seriously ill or injured people from continuing coverage that adversely affected their premium.

To address these issues, the NAIC developed a Group Coverage Discontinuance and Replacement Model Regulation, which has been implemented in some form in half the states. (Also refer to the later discussion of COBRA.) The model regulation addresses these issues by defining the responsibilities of both the prior carrier and the succeeding carrier. Under this model, the prior carrier must provide an extension of benefits to the following extent:

- For life insurance, if a disability extension is included, it will not be terminated by the policy's discontinuance.

- For long- and short-term disability, termination of the plan during an existing disability will not affect benefit payments for the disability.

- For major medical benefit plans, 12 months of continuation for the disabling condition while disabled. For basic benefit plans, 90 days for the disabling condition while disabled. An extension does not need to be provided for dental and maternity expenses.

These rules help assure a smooth transition to the succeeding carrier's plan in a transfer of coverage situation. The prior carrier is only responsible to the extent of its contractual extension of benefits provisions and any accrued liabilities. The succeeding carrier's responsibilities with regard to persons eligible under its plan (who were also covered under the prior carrier's plan on its termination date) are also specified:

- Each person eligible for the succeeding carrier's plan who satisfies that plan's actively-at-work/non-confinement/on-disability rules shall be covered by that plan as of its effective date.

- The succeeding carrier must provide an alternative benefit plan for transferring persons who do not satisfy the actively-at-work/non-confinement rules of the new plan. Those rules are not waived for these persons.

- The minimum level of benefits of the alternative plan shall be the applicable level of benefit of the prior carrier's plan, reduced by benefits paid by the prior carrier. Thus, this combination provides that the extension of the prior carrier covers the disabling condition, and the alternative benefits of the succeeding carrier cover other conditions. This alternative coverage must be provided until the earliest of the following dates:

○ The date the person becomes eligible for benefits under the succeeding carrier's plan. This means that when the employee returns to active work, or the dependent ceases to be hospital confined or disabled for the length of time necessary to be insured under the new plan, they will be covered under the new plan.

○ The date the individual's coverage would terminate in accordance with the succeeding carrier's plan provisions that apply to termination of coverage.

○ If the person was disabled prior to the change, the date as of the end of the appropriate extension period for the disabling condition under the prior carrier's plan. If the prior carrier is not required to have an extension of benefits, then the date as of the end of the period which would have been required if the law had applied.

Transferring persons are given credit for satisfaction or partial satisfaction of waiting periods under the prior plan. The same is true of deductibles; however, the credit need only apply to expenses incurred during the 90 days prior to the change in carriers. Also, only those charges need to be taken into account that would count towards the deductible of the succeeding carrier.

There are times when a person has reached the prior plan's out-of-pocket limit, and is receiving 100% of covered charges incurred under the prior plan. What happens when there is a change in carrier? This is not a subject which is addressed in the Model. This issue may be dealt by agreement between the succeeding carrier and the group policyholder.

SMALL GROUP REFORM

During the late1980's and early 1990's, national attention was focused on the plight of the working uninsured and the perceived abuses occurring in the small employer health insurance market. To promote the availability of health insurance coverage to small employer groups, and to prevent abusive underwriting and rating practices, most states enacted so-called "small group" legislation during the early 1990's. A small employer group is generally defined as one with 50 or fewer employees, although the state laws vary somewhat in their definitions.

These small group laws require insurers and HMOs to issue coverage to small employers on a guaranteed issue basis. Insurers may choose to withdraw from the small group market, but they are then restricted from re-entering the small group market for a period of time (typically five-years). The small group laws provide for mechanisms to cover high-risk groups through reinsurance mechanisms or through the allocation of claim losses to carriers participating in the small group market. In addition, small group carriers are required to renew small groups except in limited situations (non-payment of premium, fraud or misrepresentation on the part of the employer, non-compliance with the plan's provisions, or failure to meet the insurer's participation requirements). Renewal rate increases above specified amounts are restricted, and rating practices must be disclosed to customers. These small market reforms have resulted in many insurers and HMOs withdrawing from the small group market in many states.

REGULATION OF MEDICARE SUPPLEMENT INSURANCE

Medicare Supplement insurance is coverage that is designed and marketed as a supplement to reimbursement under Medicare. It fills in the deductible and co-insurance amounts not paid by Medicare, and increases its benefits as Medicare's deductible and co-payment requirements rise.

The NAIC Medicare Supplement Insurance Minimum Standards Model Act outlines uniform standards for Medicare supplement insurance benefits, and for its advertising, marketing and disclosure. The coverage may be issued on an individual or group basis. Virtually all states have enacted some form of the NAIC Model Act.

REGULATION OF LONG-TERM CARE INSURANCE

The NAIC Long-Term Care Insurance Model Act and the Long-Term Care Insurance Model Regulation have been adopted in some form in the vast majority of states.

The common elements of all long-term care laws and regulations applicable to group plans include:

- benefit "triggers" (the physical or mental failures that cause benefits to start),

- continuation or conversion options on termination of group coverage,
- protection against unintentional lapse of coverage,
- offer of automatic increase in benefits to offset the impact of inflation,
- standards for advertising, marketing and the applicant's suitability for coverage,
- limits on preexisting conditions and other restrictions to benefits,
- type used in printed material, and
- form and rate filing requirements.

Long-term care insurance is defined in the NAIC Long-Term Care Model Act as insurance designed and marketed to provide at least 12 months of coverage for necessary diagnostic, preventive, therapeutic, rehabilitative, maintenance or personal care services, not provided in an acute care unit of a hospital. The most striking difference between long-term care and medical care is that long-term care is driven by the insured's need for maintenance or custodial care, while medical care is designed to cover the costs incurred for treatment of illnesses and injuries.

HIPAA includes a provision that makes premiums for "qualified" LTC plans deductible for federal tax purposes and for state income tax to the extent the state tax is based on federally-taxable income. Prior to HIPAA, deductibility of LTC coverage premium was not addressed in the law. The law applies to contracts issued after December 31, 1996 and "grandfathers" many contracts issued prior to 1997.

STATE REGULATION OF PREFERRED PROVIDER ARRANGEMENTS

Insurers and others have sought to emulate HMOs by developing arrangements that include the quintessential feature of HMOs – a relationship with providers. This has led to the development of preferred provider arrangements (PPAs) which are currently the fastest growing health care delivery alternative. These are more often but less precisely called preferred provider organizations (PPOs), although this term sometimes is limited in meaning to a network of providers which does not actually take insurance risks, but rather contracts with insurers to provide services.

A preferred provider arrangement involves a group of health care providers that have contracted directly or indirectly with an insurer. These providers become "preferred" by virtue of the insurer providing a meaningful financial incentive for plan participants to use the providers in its provider network. Typically, insurers encourage the use of their panel of preferred providers by means of lower co-insurance requirements when preferred providers are used. However, even health insurance plans with no coinsurance differential between preferred and non-preferred providers can still afford a meaningful economic incentive for insureds to utilize preferred providers, since their coinsurance is calculated on the provider's discounted charge.

Preferred provider arrangements take many forms. To achieve its objectives, a preferred provider arrangement should have both a carefully selected network of efficient providers and negotiated compensation arrangements with those providers.

It is no accident that these elements of successful PPOs are also the building blocks that are critical to the success of an HMO. An HMO gatekeeper feature can easily be added to the basic preferred provider arrangement, making the PPA look even more like an HMO.

The resemblance to an HMO is closer yet with an exclusive provider arrangement (EPA or EPO) in which coverage is limited to services provided by the panel of preferred providers (except in emergencies). Add to this restricted access feature paperless claim processing and capitated compensation arrangements with providers, and the coverage is, for all practical purposes, indistinguishable from the coverage offered by an HMO. (The feature that distinguishes this arrangement from an HMO is that it is indemnity-based. Insurers *reimburse* or *indemnify* an insured for covered expenses. HMOs, by statutory definition, *provide* or arrange for the provision of covered services.)

To actually implement preferred provider arrangements, the insurer can either contract with providers directly or with third party vendors with established networks (often referred to as rented networks). An insurer may even secure the necessary building blocks by contracting directly with an HMO which can sell to an insurer its network services.

As the preceding discussion suggests, PPAs are really hybrids which combine traditional features of indemnity insurance products and the managed care features typically associated with HMOs. As a result of insurance products mimicking HMOs, the once clear distinctions between HMOs and insured plans have become blurred. Indeed, by emulating HMOs, insurers have switched from a passive to an active management of health care, with a direct contractual relationship with providers.

All of these changes take place in a heavily-regulated environment. While the alternatives for preferred provider arrangements are virtually limitless, in the real world the form that these alternatives take is shaped by the preferences of plan sponsors and the restrictions imposed by laws, regulations, and regulatory attitude.

Many of the state laws and regulations applicable to PPAs predate them by decades, and rarely contemplated them. Moreover, the state regulatory environment cries out for uniformity. There is no federal PPA law from which the states can take their lead. As a consequence, PPAs that may be acceptable in one state may not be permissible in another state. Efforts to develop insured PPAs which are unaffected by state boundaries are often doomed to fail. As a consequence, the guiding principle for insurers in developing PPAs is to do whatever works. This general rule has an important caveat – what works today may not work tomorrow. The regulatory context is quickly changing, as legislators and regulators attempt to keep pace with product changes.

Determining what will work requires an understanding of the interplay of a spectrum of laws and regulations, which are discussed in the following section.

INSURANCE LAWS AND REGULATIONS AFFECTING PPAs

To date, approximately 30 states have enacted specific PPA laws or promulgated some form of PPA regulation. Even in states with no PPA law or regulations (New York, for example), insurance regulators have developed informal policies regarding permissible PPA activities. Most state PPA laws and regulations are based on the NAIC Preferred Provider Arrangements Model Act.

While PPA laws are frequently referred to as enabling laws, this is a misnomer. It is true that such laws may clarify doubt as to the applicability of existing freedom-of-choice or anti-discrimination laws (discussed subsequently) that never contemplated PPAs. However, in the absence of any express prohibitions, insurers have always had the right to contract with providers and alter policy provisions to provide benefit incentives. In many states, PPA arrangements operate in the absence of PPA enabling laws and regulations. PPA laws and regulations generally serve to affirm insurers' rights to engage in particular activities, rather than create such rights. In fact, the salient feature of most so-called PPA enabling measures is that they regulate and restrict the activities of insurers. These restrictions are generally intended to afford protection to providers and consumers.

Provider Protections

Some state statutes reflect successful efforts of physicians and other health care providers to prevent insurers from excluding from their panel of preferred providers any providers willing to meet the insurer's terms for participation in the panel. For good reason, these so-called any-willing-provider laws are not favored by insurers offering PPOs. Restrictions on an insurer's ability to selectively limit its preferred provider panel can pose a serious threat to the effective operation of a PPA. They can, for example, undermine the insurer's ability to negotiate volume-based discounts with providers, and impair the insurer's ability to control utilization and assure quality. In addition, if any willing provider is permitted to participate in the preferred provider network, the management of the larger panel can result in increased administrative costs.

Most states have enacted some form of any-willing-provider law, although in many instances their scope is limited to pharmacies or other provider categories.

Another significant provider protection feature commonly found in PPA laws and regulations is a restriction on differences in benefit levels (usually measured in terms of coinsurance percentages) applicable to covered charges of preferred and non-preferred providers. The following provision in the NAIC Preferred Provider Arrangements Model Act reflects this protectionist attitude:

> *If a Health Benefit Plan provides differences in benefit levels payable to Preferred Providers compared to other providers, such differences shall not unfairly deny payment for current services and shall be no greater than necessary to provide a reasonable incentive for Covered Person to use the Preferred Provider.*

More than a dozen states have imposed limitations on benefit differentials between preferred and non-preferred providers, generally in the range of twenty to thirty percent. The language of these state enactments usually goes beyond the Model Act. This reflects successful lobbying efforts by providers to *require* that preferred provider plans reimburse non-preferred providers. North Carolina's PPA law is a good example:

A person enrolled in a preferred provider plan may obtain covered health care services from a provider not participating in the plan. The preferred provider plan may, however, limit the coverage for health care services obtained from a provider not participating in that plan, except that payments for services rendered by such non-participating providers may not be reduced by more than twenty percent (20%) of the payments that would be made to participating providers under coverage for the same services.

By requiring coverage of non-preferred providers, these provisions effectively preclude an insurer from offering an EPA. Some states expressly forbid EPAs. EPAs are expressly recognized by statute or regulation only in a few states (California, Indiana, Florida and Pennsylvania).

Benefit differentials are, by design, behavior modification devices. Regulatory restrictions on benefit differentials obviously impair an insurer's ability to create incentives for insureds to seek care from preferred providers. Of course, that is the whole point of these provider protection measures; they are designed to benefit providers that do not participate in a PPA.

Other provider protection provisions that infrequently show up in laws and regulations include requirements that allied medical practitioners (such as chiropractors, dentists, optometrists) be included in preferred provider arrangements.

Consumer Protections

Provisions designed to protect participants in preferred provider plans are also reflected in the NAIC Preferred Provider Arrangements Model Act and in numerous state statutes and regulations. The Model Act seeks to assure that PPA mechanisms that seek to limit provider choice will, at the same time, assure the availability and access to all appropriate care. Section 4 of the Model Act requires an insurer to "assure reasonable access to Covered Services available under the Preferred Provider Arrangement and an adequate number of Preferred Providers to render those services." Most state PPA laws and regulations reflect this concern. The freedom of insureds to go to any provider, that is preserved by restrictions on benefit differentials, largely assures the accessibility and availability of health care services to participants in insured PPAs.

EPAs are a different matter. Like an HMO, an EPA severely limits the participant's provider choice. Assuring the availability of, and access to, a full range of health care providers and services is far more important in the EPA context. Not surprisingly, therefore, the few states that expressly recognize EPAs have extensive requirements or review processes (similar to requirements imposed on HMOs) to assure the adequacy and accessibility of health care services available through the EPA.

A related concern is quality. This is a difficult issue to deal with through regulation. It is relatively easy to assure availability and accessibility by reviewing the number, type and location of providers. But how do you measure quality? Because it is difficult to measure, legislators and regulators have attempted to deal with it only in the most general terms. Georgia's PPA law, for example, simply requires that a preferred provider arrangement "not ... have an adverse effect on the ... quality of services." A few states have attempted to come more directly to grips with quality assurance. Massachusetts has promulgated comprehensive PPA regulations under which the Commissioner, in reviewing each insured health benefit plan submitted for approval, must be satisfied that "there is a quality assurance program that includes organizational arrangements and ongoing procedures for the identification, evaluation, resolution and follow-up of potential and actual problems in the administration or delivery of covered health care services for covered persons." The regulation requires that this quality assurance program meet eight enumerated criteria.

The PPA Model Act has also recognized that attempts to influence patient behavior through benefit differentials may be unfair in cases of emergency. Accordingly, Section 5(A)(1) of the Model Act mandates inclusion in preferred provider policies of "a provision that if a Covered Person receives emergency care for services specified in the Preferred Provider arrangement and cannot reasonably reach a Preferred Provider that emergency care rendered during the course of the emergency will be reimbursed as though the Covered Person had been treated by a Preferred Provider."

While many state PPA laws and regulations reflect this concern, some insurers have concluded that it is inappropriate to offer a preferred benefit for emergency care. Benefit differentials are intended to influence the behavior of insureds in selecting providers. While appropriate for elective care, it may be inappropriate to influence an insured to do anything but go to the nearest appropriate facility or provider in an emergency. Indeed, offering benefit differentials that create incentives to use preferred providers in cases of emergency may increase the insurer's potential liability exposure. Accordingly, some insurers have concluded that all emergency care should be covered at the same level. The question of whether emergency care provisions like the NAIC Model permit all emergency care charges to be uniformly covered (at the non-preferred level) has been the subject of some debate between insurers and regulators.

While no two PPA laws and regulations are precisely alike, most are mildly restrictive and very general in nature. Though many states include some or all of the provider and consumer protections discussed, few offer a truly comprehensive scheme of regulation.

In an attempt to overcome the lack of uniformity in state laws and regulations relating to PPAs, some consideration has been given periodically by the insurance industry to federal legislation that would preempt state laws restricting the development of PPAs. To date, no such legislation has been enacted.

Other Insurance Laws

In the absence of any specific PPA laws or regulations, it is necessary to determine whether there are any other insurance provisions that may restrict an insurer's ability to offer preferred provider arrangements. Existing anti-discrimination and freedom-of-choice laws have frequently been cited as possible impediments to PPA development, but rarely have they actually impeded PPA development.

Two-thirds of the states have enacted statutes which prohibit insurance policy provisions requiring that a medical service be rendered by a particular doctor or hospital. Georgia's is fairly typical:

> *Any group accident and sickness policy may provide that all or any portion of any indemnities provided by any policy on account of hospital, nursing, or medical or surgical services may, at the insurer's option, be paid directly to the hospital or person rendering such services; but the policy shall not require that the service be rendered by a particular hospital or person.*

These "freedom-of-choice" laws are patterned after an old NAIC Model Act that did not contemplate PPAs. It was adopted decades ago to address a concern that workers' compensation policies might limit reimbursement to certain physicians and hospitals. While insurance policies incorporating benefit differentials do channel insureds toward certain providers, and away from others, the insureds in a PPA still retain the freedom to select any provider. This fact has, until now, enabled insurers offering PPAs to avoid application of freedom-of-choice statutes. However, they remain a basis which regulators may seize on, in the absence of PPA legislation, to preclude PPA provisions in insurance policies if they are so inclined. The greater the benefit differential, the greater the risk that an insurance regulator may attempt to apply a freedom-of-choice statute in this way. A group insurance policy incorporating an exclusive provider arrangement is particularly vulnerable to freedom-of-choice statutes.

Virtually all states have adopted, either by statute or regulation, the NAIC Model Act Relating to Unfair Methods of Competition and Unfair Deceptive Practices in the Business of Insurance. Included in its prohibitions is "making or permitting any unfair discrimination between individuals of the same class and of essentially the same hazard ... in the benefits payable" under a policy of accident and health insurance. However, the language of the Model Act (which has been adopted with great uniformity by the states) does not prohibit all discrimination, only unfair discrimination. While "unfair" is not defined, the fact that the discrimination in benefits payable is a result of the insured's free choice of providers would seem to eliminate any element of unfairness. Under a typical insured PPA arrangement, every insured has the same opportunity to receive reimbursement at the preferred level.

These potentially restrictive freedom-of-choice and anti-discrimination laws are rendered inapplicable in states with specific PPA laws, which typically affirm the right of insurers to engage in such arrangements notwithstanding any other contrary provisions of law.

Corporate Practice of Medicine

To date, the common law prohibition against the corporate practice of medicine has not been an important consideration for insurers and others in developing preferred provider arrangements. In part, this may be attributable to the fact that most insurers, and certainly most insurance regulators, are not even aware of the doctrine or because the doctrine has lost its persuasive value. Nonetheless, as arrangements between insurers, employers and provider entities continue to evolve, the doctrine may assume greater importance. The doctrine evolved because of the public policy concern that corporations may influence the decisions of medical care professionals in their employ. It seems possible that a regulator might invoke the doctrine where, for example, the utilization review or incentive compensation mechanisms in a preferred provider arrangement were seen to influence the decisions of health care professionals. Unlike HMO laws, moreover, no state PPA laws contain an exemption from the prohibitions on corporate practice of medicine.

Antitrust Laws

The application of state and federal antitrust laws to various health care delivery alternatives is a complicated subject. Whenever selective contracting arrangements exist involving competitors (in this case, health care providers) and payers, and those contracts deal with issues related to price, the basic ingredients for anti-competitive behavior exist.

While any alternative health care delivery systems like PPAs must be structured with due consideration of the antitrust laws, the fact is that they have not, to date, been a significant impediment to their development. This may be attributable to the care with which various arrangements have been structured. In addition, the courts have been cautious to condemn arrangements that appear to offer lower prices to consumers. Similarly, the Department of Justice and the Federal Trade Commission have, on several occasions in the past, indicated their view that PPAs have a potentially beneficial procompetitive effect and should, therefore, not be discouraged.

Many insurers have attempted to include provisions in their agreements with health care providers guaranteeing that the provider will not afford any more favorable financial terms to any other payor. The so-called "most favored nation" clauses can have a pro-competitive or anti-competitive effect depending upon the insurer's market share. In fact, federal anti-trust regulators have successfully challenged the use of "most favored nation" clauses by some Blues with very high market shares, because of their anti-competitive effect.

HMO Laws

HMOs have what any PPA needs – a network of providers with negotiated compensation agreements. Can an HMO contract with an insurer to rent its provider network to the insurer to establish a PPA? Under both federal and state HMO laws, the answer is yes.

The federal HMO Act (discussed later in this chapter) and its implementing regulations do not specifically address whether an entity which has qualified under the federal HMO Act may engage in PPA activities. In a 1983 Program Information Letter, the Office of Health Maintenance Organizations indicated that it was favorably disposed toward qualified HMOs acting as the preferred (or exclusive) provider organization for insured and self-insured plans, at least on a fee-for-service basis. Indeed, in recent years, the Office of Prepaid Health Care has condoned the expanded role of qualified HMOs in insured and self-insured plans, including the following:

- Acting as a third-party administrator in the collection of premiums and processing and paying of claims.

- Providing pre-admission certification, continued stay review, and other utilization management services.
- Providing and maintaining a panel of providers to serve as the preferred providers for insured or self-insured health care plans.

There would appear to be no need for the qualified HMO to establish a separate corporate entity to engage in these activities, in view of the 1988 HMO Act amendments and the supporting legislative history.

Whether or not state HMO laws actually contemplate HMOs acting as PPAs, most can be read to permit such activity. For example, the introductory clause to the powers section of the NAIC Preferred Provider Arrangements Model Act states that an HMO's powers "include, but are not limited to" those enumerated. Thus, the Model Act language does not limit the powers which the entity licensed as an HMO may otherwise possess. The entity licensed as an HMO will usually be a general business corporation. Whatever its status, its basic organization documents (charter, certificate of incorporation, and so forth) will determine whether there are limitations on the entity's powers that would preclude it from contracting in a non-HMO capacity.

State PPA laws and regulations often provide additional legal support for the proposition that HMOs may contract to serve as a preferred provider organization for insurers. The NAIC Preferred Provider Arrangements Model Act recognizes the right of insurers to contract with "Health Care Providers" and thereby establish PPAs. A health care provider is defined to mean "providers of Health Care Services licensed or registered in this State." In turn, the NAIC Model Health Maintenance Organization Act empowers any entity licensed as an HMO to act as a provider of health care services.

There are valid policy reasons for permitting licensed HMOs to operate as preferred provider organizations. Having been licensed as an HMO, the entity will already have met certain minimum standards regarding solvency and quality of care and it continues to be under the State's regulatory oversight.

Contracting with an HMO offers many obvious advantages to an insurer desiring to establish a PPA. An HMO can provide the services of an established provider network with built-in utilization and quality control mechanisms and discounted provider compensation arrangements.

Questions of Identity

What is it? That is a question that regulators have asked with increasing frequency in recent years with the development of PPAs. It is a critically important question, and determines whether and how an arrangement will be regulated.

At what point does an insured PPA look so much like an HMO that it ceases to be insurance and becomes subject to HMO regulation? An insurer that acts like an HMO, in all relevant aspects, will be subject to regulation as such. The PPA regulations in some states specifically contemplate this possibility. The PPA laws in Pennsylvania and Massachusetts require regulators, when reviewing insured PPA filings, to determine whether the insurer is engaging in the business of an HMO, and therefore required to be licensed as such. At what point does the insurer step over the line? Only one state, Pennsylvania, has attempted to address in its laws or regulations the point at which a preferred provider arrangement becomes an HMO. Ohio has taken the position that all entities performing similar functions should be licensed and regulated similarly. As a result, insurers offering PPO plans similar to traditional HMO plans are all licensed and regulated under the same managed care organization statute.

Even where an insurer's emulation of an HMO falls short of making it an HMO, it may still raise basic questions concerning whether its arrangements are permissible for an insurer.

A feature commonly exhibited by HMOs is capitated compensation arrangements with providers. Under a capitated compensation arrangement, the provider agrees to provide certain services to members for a fixed periodic charge. By shifting the utilization risk to the provider, capitation has the inherent potential to curb excessive utilization.

Capitated arrangements with providers can offer insurers many advantages. But is it insurance? State regulators have wrestled with this question in connection with preferred provider arrangements. It is a question that is not susceptible to easy resolution. Where an insurer or employer enters into a capitated arrangement with providers, the question is whether the insurance contract, in covering those capitated charges, is providing "services," which is outside the scope of its licensure. Generally, the test is whether the plan, when viewed as a whole, has "service" or "indemnity" as its principal purpose or object and whether there is a shift in the risk of loss. So long as the principal purpose of an insurance contract remains to indemnify, an element of capitation would seem to be permissible.

The NAIC Preferred Provider Arrangements Model Act contains an express recognition of capitated arrangements between insurers and providers, as do the PPA laws in a few states.

The precise boundaries of insurance remain unclear. The regulators' and courts' answer to the question of "what is it" will either permit or inhibit the continued development of non-traditional health care alternatives. The key will undoubtedly be whether insurers demonstrate that the public can be protected if they are given additional flexibility.

STATE REGULATION OF HEALTH MAINTENANCE ORGANIZATIONS

Like insurers, HMOs are heavily regulated. Currently, all jurisdictions have laws which regulate aspects of HMO operations. Even in the absence of specific HMO laws, HMOs could be established. However, the absence of specific HMO enabling laws leaves HMOs subject to general corporation law, insurance or health service corporation laws, malpractice laws, and common law prohibitions on corporate practice of medicine. These laws do not specifically contemplate HMOs and can impair their operation. Thus, the enactment of comprehensive HMO laws has generally had the intended effect of promoting the formation and operation of HMOs.

HMO laws vary considerably from state to state. However, nearly 30 states have based their HMO laws on the NAIC Model Health Maintenance Organization Act originally adopted in 1973. Reviewing the Model Act serves as a useful framework for examining state HMO regulation.

DEFINITIONS

Health Maintenance Organization

Only entities meeting the definition of a health maintenance organization are subject to HMO regulation and can derive the benefits of HMO legislation. Most state HMO laws define an HMO along the lines of the NAIC Model:

> *"Health Maintenance Organization" means any person that undertakes to provide or arrange for the delivery of basic health services to enrollees on a prepaid basis, except for enrollee responsibility for co-payments and/or deductibles.*

This definition reflects the fact that an HMO is predicated on three basic principles:

1. It is an organized system that *provides or arranges for the provision of health care services* to enrollees. Unlike insurers, which simply reimburse health care expenses incurred by insureds, HMOs combine the delivery and financing of health care. HMOs accomplish this by establishing relationships with providers. These relationships may either be direct (employing or owning providers) or indirect (independent contractor arrangements).

2. It makes available all basic health services that the enrollee might reasonably require. (Note that an entity providing less than all "basic health care services" on a prepaid basis typically will not qualify as an HMO.) Moreover, as the name health *maintenance* organization suggests, an HMO emphasizes the promotion of health and the prevention of illness.

3. The payments for coverage are only on a *prepayment* basis, whether made by individual enrollees, employer groups, Medicare or Medicaid.

Basic Health Care Services

Most state laws include in the definition of basic health care services preventive care, emergency care, in-patient and out-patient hospital and physician care, diagnostic lab and diagnostic and therapeutic radiological services. At a minimum, an HMO must provide these basic health care services. State laws typically exclude dental services, vision services, mental health or alcohol/substance abuse services, and long-term rehabilitation services from the definition. HMOs are, however, free to supplement their basic mandated coverage with these additional services.

Because the definition of basic health care services is so broad to begin with, most HMO laws do not include many of the state mandated benefits commonly applied to insured plans.

REGULATORY OVERSIGHT OF HMOS

The definition of an HMO evidences the fact that the HMO arrangement combines the provision and financing of health care services to enrollees. Thus, HMOs exhibit both provider and insurer characteristics. Not surprisingly, therefore, states have had to grapple with the issue of where HMO regulatory oversight should properly reside. Logically, state health departments are more capable of overseeing the provider aspects of HMO operations, and insurance departments are more capable of overseeing the insurer aspects of HMO operations. While the majority of states have resolved this problem by assigning all regulatory responsibility to the insurance regulator, in some cases it is shared by the insurance and health regulators (although the primary responsibility is usually assigned to the insurance regulator). California is notable for having assigned HMO regulatory responsibility to neither.

REQUIREMENTS FOR CERTIFICATE OF AUTHORITY

In order to operate as an HMO, state HMO laws require the HMO entity to secure a certificate of authority. To obtain a certificate of authority, the HMO must generally submit a detailed filing including the following eight major categories of information which demonstrate initial compliance with various ongoing regulatory requirements:

- *A Description of the HMOs organization, governance, and management.* This includes information reflecting the form of organization (including the articles of incorporation or the articles of association or trust agreements), bylaws or rules, and biographical information on the people responsible for the affairs of the HMO (the board of directors or trustees, and the principal officers or partners). In addition, evidence of a fidelity bond covering these people is often required.

- *Contracts with Providers.* This includes copies of standard forms of contracts between providers, third-party administrators, and other third-party vendors. State laws typically identify several requirements for provider contracts. For example, most states require that provider contracts contain a "hold harmless" provision which requires the provider to look solely to the HMO for payment for services and supplies, and likewise prohibits the provider from seeking payment from an HMO enrollee except for copayment amounts. In addition, advance notice of termination of the contract by the provider is often mandated for inclusion in provider contracts.

- *Coverage Agreements.* This includes copies of individual and group contracts and evidence of coverage forms, which the HMO proposes to use. Again, HMO enabling laws typically contain very detailed requirements for contracts and evidence of coverage forms, designed to ensure full disclosure of the coverage.

- *Financial Information.* Financial statements and a detailed financial feasibility plan (business plan) demonstrating the viability of the organization are required.

- *Provider Information.* This includes a map or description of the HMO's geographic service area and a list, with addresses, of all providers having employment or contractual arrangements with the HMO. HMOs are also required to give this information to enrollees.

- *Grievance Procedure.* Most state HMO laws require the establishment of an internal grievance procedure. This takes the form of a system to resolve written complaints by enrollees concerning health care services provided or arranged by the HMO. Some HMO laws require an arbitration procedure, but most do not. A description of the HMOs grievance procedure conforming to the requirements of the law must be included in the filing and reflected in the materials given to enrollees.

- *Quality Assurance Program.* HMOs are typically required to submit a detailed description of their program for credentialing providers, evaluating the care rendered to enrollees, initiating corrective action, and reevaluating deficiencies. HMO enabling laws typically contain detailed requirements for quality assurance programs.

- *Insolvency Protection Measures.* This is an area of heightened concern following recent insurance company and HMO insolvencies. HMOs must satisfy minimum net worth requirements identified in the HMO law, and thereafter continually maintain that minimum net worth. A deposit of cash or securities is usually required. This deposit is made with the regulator, or a trustee acceptable to the regulator, and is required as a reserve against unfunded claims. Additional protections against the risk of insolvency (such as reinsurance or corporate guarantees) are typically required. Many state laws require HMOs to cover the enrollees of other HMOs that become insolvent. Very few states have guaranty funds applicable to HMOs.

Given the detail of the information required, the process for obtaining a certificate of authority can be a long one, taking many months to complete. Even after the HMO receives its certificate of authority, it is generally required to continue to comply with the requirements applicable to the items it submitted as part of its original application. Any subsequent material changes (referred to as "material modifications") must usually be reported, either annually or prior to such change. Thus, these initial organizational requirements also represent the chief requirements of ongoing HMO regulation.

HMO RATE REGULATION

While some states do not regulate the rates that an HMO may charge, most do. Generally, no rate may be used until a schedule of premium rates or a methodology for determining premium rates has been filed with and approved by the designated regulatory agency.

Most state laws regulating rates require simply that premium rates be actuarially sound and not be "excessive, inadequate or unfairly discriminatory." This is the same general requirement imposed on insurance company rates.

To compete with insured plans, HMOs have desired to experience rate. Following the 1988 amendments to the federal HMO Act, which for the first time allowed federally qualified HMOs to prospectively experience rate specific groups, states began to take a more flexible attitude toward HMO experience rating. The vast majority of state HMO regulators will now allow HMOs to prospectively experience rate specific groups. Many will even permit retrospective experience rating, although this seems inconsistent with the basic definition of an HMO as a prepaid arrangement. A minority of states, however, do impose more stringent requirements on rates. New York, for example, generally requires that HMOs community rate.

Notwithstanding the flexibility allowed by most state regulators, those HMOs that are also federally qualified must contend with the stiffer federal law requirements discussed subsequently.

FINANCIAL REGULATION

All state HMO laws require the filing of financial statements annually (more frequently in some states). In addition, the majority of states require that annual reports include identification of any material changes in information submitted with the original application for a certificate of authority, as well as information regarding the enrollee population. A number of states also require that the annual report include information regarding grievances, utilization patterns, and other matters.

HMOs are subject to periodic examination of their operations by their regulator(s). Most states require that HMOs be examined at least every three years.

Approximately one-third of the states subject HMOs to premium taxes or a similar assessment.

POWERS

State HMO laws enumerate the powers of HMOs, which typically include the following:

- The purchase, lease, construction or operation of hospitals, other medical facilities and other property necessary for the conduct of the business;
- Transactions with affiliates such as loans or transfer of responsibility;
- Furnishing health care services through providers, provider associations, or agents or providers which are under contract with or employed by the HMO;
- Contracting with third parties for the performance of functions such as marketing, enrollment, and administration;
- Contracting with licensed insurance companies or hospital or medical service corporations for insurance, indemnity, or reimbursement against the cost of health care services provided by the HMO;
- The offering of health care services in addition to basic health care services on a prepaid basis, either alone or as a supplement to basic health care services; and
- The joint marketing of products with a licensed insurer or hospital or medical service corporation.

Most state HMO laws make clear that the powers of an authorized HMO are not limited to those specifically enumerated in the statute. Thus, HMOs can engage in non-HMO activities such as preferred provider arrangements in conjunction with insurers, third party administrators, or plan sponsors. Moreover, most HMOs are corporations or partnerships having a legal existence quite apart from their licensure as HMOs. An entity that is licensed as an HMO, if it is also incorporated, will generally have the power to engage in any business transaction that any other business corporation can under applicable state law. The powers conferred by the HMO law are in addition to those that the HMO entity may have as a general business corporation or partnership. These powers may, however, be limited in the HMOs organizational documents (such as articles of incorporation, charter, partnerships agreement or articles of association).

REGULATION OF PRODUCERS

HMO producers are generally subject to similar or the same licensing requirements applicable to insurance agents.

POINT-OF-SERVICE PRODUCT RESTRICTIONS

Following the 1988 amendments to the federal HMO Act, a number of states, by statute, regulation, or regulatory discretion, began to permit HMOs to offer reimbursement for care received outside the HMOs network of providers. These "point-of-service" or "open-HMO" products offer HMOs the ability to compete with insurers and others that offer open access products such as PPOs. However, some states have questioned whether offering non-emergency care outside the HMO network to indemnity subscribers constitutes engaging in the business of insurance, which would require licensure of the HMO as an insurance company. This is one area where the state laws and the views of regulators are still evolving. A growing number of states by regulation, statute, or administrative discretion have authorized HMOs to begin offering open-HMO products.

CORPORATE PRACTICE OF MEDICINE

State laws restrict the practice of medicine to persons who satisfy various professional licensing requirements that typically include graduation from an accredited medical school, successful completion of residency requirements, and passing a state examination. Because a corporation is incapable of meeting these licensing requirements, the courts have uniformly held that corporations or other non-human legal "persons" are precluded from engaging in the practice of medicine. The corporate practice prohibition evolved because of the public policy concern that corporations may influence the decisions of medical care professionals in their employ. As a provider of medical care services, it is critical for an HMO to be free of the common law prohibitions against the corporate practice of medicine. Section 27.C. of the Model Law does this:

> *Any health maintenance organization authorized under this Act shall not be deemed to be practicing medicine and shall be exempt from the provisions of [citation] relating to practice of medicine.*

Many HMO laws incorporate a similar provision. It is important to note that this exemption from the prohibitions on corporate practice of medicine applies to the entity authorized as an HMO, and arguably frees the entity from these strictures even when the entity engages in non-HMO activities. This is important in the development of alternative delivery systems when the HMO provider network is used in a preferred provider arrangement.

ANY-WILLING-PROVIDER LAWS

Health care providers, faced with the threat of being excluded from HMO provider networks, have fought back. They have succeeded in persuading legislatures to enact various forms of any-willing-provider laws, which impair the ability of HMOs to selectively contract with providers. As applied to HMOs, any-willing-provider laws have often been challenged as preempted by ERISA with respect to ERISA-governed group plans. However, in 2003, the Supreme Court indicated that such laws were not pre-empted by ERISA.

STATE REGULATORY FOCUS

While state HMO laws regulate most aspects of HMO operation, most HMO regulators would probably view their chief roles as (a) protecting consumers in those areas where marketplace forces do not offer adequate protection, and (b) establishing and maintaining ground rules for competition among rival entities. The marketplace does not offer consumers protection against the risk of insolvency. Thus, assuring the fiscal solvency of HMOs is a critical focus of HMO regulators. Similarly, the closed delivery systems of HMOs create unique risks for consumers, including a limited choice of providers, gatekeeper mechanisms, and financial incentives for providers that may result in under-treatment or poor quality care. Accordingly, quality assurance and accessibility of care are also major concerns of regulators.

UTILIZATION REVIEW REGULATION

Beginning as early as the mid-1970's, state legislators and regulators began to consider the merits of various forms of utilization review (UR). Until very recently, most legislation and regulation has either been permissive or actually sought to promote UR activities by insurers. Several states were apparently so taken with the promise of various forms of UR services that they actually required insurers to abandon their role as passive indemnitors and include UR provisions in their policies. Florida, for example, enacted a statute that required a health insurance policy to include procedures or provisions to contain health insurance costs, such as UR, and required second opinions for surgery. Nevada enacted the following requirement:

The commissioner shall not approve any proposed policy of health insurance unless he determines that the insurer has adopted and is using three or more practices in administering benefits that control or reduce the cost of health care.

As early as 1976, New York required insurers to cover second opinions for surgery, and other states have enacted measures promoting various forms of cost containment activity. The PPA laws in some states require that the insurer offering preferred provider arrangements have in place standards for assuring appropriate utilization.

By the end of the 1980's, the regulatory environment had begun to change dramatically. By then, virtually all health insurers had incorporated some form of UR into some of their policies, and many had developed the capacity to provide UR services to third parties. In addition, numerous independent companies providing utilization management services had sprung up. Even HMOs began to sell UR services. Utilization management programs proliferated to the point where surveys indicated that, by 1989, half of all large employers included utilization management provisions in their health benefit programs, up from just 5% in 1984. As a result, the American Hospital Association reports that individual hospitals now routinely deal with 50 to 250 different review organizations.

Utilization management firms had clearly complicated life for hospitals and for physicians. They responded by pushing for regulation of utilization management firms. This provider backlash was first manifested in 1988, when Maryland enacted the first comprehensive law regulating utilization management firms. The Maryland law became a model advanced by hospital associations in other states. By 1998, approximately 35 states had enacted comprehensive UR laws and/or regulations. It is evident that the pendulum has swung away from regulation that promotes utilization management activities. In addition to requiring licensure of firms engaged in providing utilization management services, these new laws have imposed requirements including the following:

- Restrictions on the use of UR procedures and criteria used by firms;
- Restrictions on the type or qualifications of personnel to qualify for licensure to carry out UR;
- Payments to providers for the cost of responding to requests for information;

- Mandates on the hours of operation;
- Restrictions on access to medical information;
- Restrictions on the location at which UR must be performed;
- Burdensome regulatory filings of UR data;
- Requirements that medical necessity denials be made by a physician in the same or similar specialty as the attending physician; and
- Requirements that the physician making the UR determination be licensed in the state where the member resides.

There have even been attempts to define UR as the practice of a health care profession, thereby invoking professional licensing requirements and prohibitions against corporate practices of medicine. Several state medical boards have attempted to initiate licensing actions against physicians employed by HMOs and engaged in UR activities.

Not surprisingly, these measures have sparked heated debate between providers and utilization management firms. This promises to be an area of continued contention during the years to come.

OPEN PHARMACY LAWS

Another example of provider backlash to managed care arrangements is the enactment of open pharmacy laws backed by state pharmacy associations. These open pharmacy laws typically take one of three forms:

- Any-willing-provider laws, which require the inclusion of any pharmacy willing to meet the HMOs or PPAs terms and conditions in the HMO or PPA provider network. Nearly 20 states had passed any-willing-provider laws, as of 1998.
- Nearly half of all states have enacted laws directly or indirectly limiting the use of mail order drug firms.
- At least sixteen states require out-of-state pharmaceutical vendors to become licensed in order to do business.

UNITARY DRUG PRICING LAWS

Because of their ability to "steer" members to particular drugs through the use of formularies (restricted lists of drugs that are covered), drug manufacturers have been willing to extend discounts on drugs to hospitals, HMOs and other organizations. Pharmacies do not "steer" business in this way and have been unable to secure similar discounts. They have fought back by lobbying state legislatures to enact "unitary pricing" laws which require manufacturers to offer the same discounts to every purchaser on the same terms. To date, few states have enacted such laws.

RECENT STATE LAW CHANGES

Managed Care "Backlash"

In the past decade, state legislatures have considerably broadened the scope of regulatory oversight over HMOs, PPOs, and other managed health care plans. One clear trend at the state level is to depart from the NAIC HMO Model Act, to impose regulation on all facets of HMO operations. Not surprisingly, these reforms have focused chiefly on assuring consumer rights and protections as an increasing number of Americans receive coverage through managed care plans, and as perceived abuses gain notoriety. The following consumer oriented reforms are illustrative:

- Most states have now enacted patient protection laws that, among other things, create an external appeal process for appealing plan benefit decisions to an independent third party.

- Several states (including Virginia, Tennessee, and Maryland) have enacted laws which require HMOs to offer point-of-service plans to employees, so as to assure access to non-network providers.

- Texas and Missouri have stripped away the malpractice protection of corporate practice of medicine laws that are enjoyed by HMOs in most states. (Since corporations cannot practice medicine, these laws have been interpreted as insulating HMOs from malpractice liability - they do not practice medicine.) The Texas legislation has gone further than any other state, in creating a statutory cause of action for failing to use "ordinary care" in denying or delaying payment for care recommended by a physician. (It should be noted, however, that other states have gone just as far in court decisions.)

There is a growing sense that dramatic changes in the regulation of HMOs and other managed care plans are needed. The managed care industry is, literally, under siege by regulators and lawmakers as a result of increased activism by consumers and providers. The future holds the promise of far more regulation for insurance companies and HMOs offering managed care plans.

PHOs

Physician hospital organizations (PHOs) are organizations formed by physicians and hospitals to enhance their bargaining position with HMOs, insurers, self-funded plan sponsors, and other payors. The formation of PHOs also allows the participating physicians and hospitals to share administrative expenses.

Legislators and regulatory agencies are struggling to determine how, if at all, PHOs should be regulated. A basic concern involves their ability to assume risk. For example, if a PHO accepts capitation and does not pass on risk to the individual providers via sub-capitation arrangements, it functions much like an HMO. Currently, only a handful of states have laws that to any extent included PHOs within their jurisdiction, and each has taken a different approach.

While PHOs are not yet specifically contemplated by laws or regulations in the vast majority of states, they may nonetheless be subject to existing state laws and regulations, depending on the activities in which they engage. For example, PHOs that perform utilization review functions will be subject to existing laws and regulations applicable to utilization review firms. Statutory and common law prohibitions on the corporate practice of medicine may apply. Assumption of risk, particularly for services not provided by physicians or hospitals participating in or contracted with the PHO, would trigger application of licensing and regulation as an insurer.

How PHOs will ultimately be regulated is yet to be determined. However, as the states struggle to keep up with the development of PHOs, one thing is certain. Competing HMOs and insurers will lobby hard to ensure that these newly emerging organizations do not achieve a regulatory advantage. In this regard, the NAIC is considering a Model Uniform Licensing Act, that would require integrated health care delivery systems engaged in similar activities to be regulated in a similar fashion.

Risk Shifting

The various reimbursement arrangements that shift risk away from regulated entities like HMOs and insurers toward unregulated provider entities are a source of concern for state regulators. Such arrangements raise issues regarding sufficiency of capitalization, reserve adequacy, adequate information systems, and sufficiency of administrative capacity. The concern of regulators is that the inability of these unregulated entities to assume risk or added administrative responsibilities can result in the denial of access to medical care and/or disruption in the continuity of medical care for patients.

Existing laws may already deal with some risk shifting arrangements. For example, if a provider group, hospital, or vendor enters into a capitated arrangement with an HMO or insurer, for services rendered by it or by other providers, it would seem that it is acting as an insurer or reinsurer, and that it should be regulated as such. Similarly, a provider organization that agrees to provide health care services on a capitated basis may fall within the ambit of the HMO definition, in those states where an HMO is defined in terms of providing less than all basic health care services (as in California and Texas).

State regulators are trying to come to grips with how, if at all, to regulate provider groups that assume varying degrees of risk. In August of 1995, the NAIC sent a notice to all state insurance commissioners suggesting that providers who accept risk may be required to be licensed as insurers. A similar notice was sent again in 1997. A handful of insurance commissioners have issued bulletins reflecting the position articulated in the NAIC letters. A minority of the states have regulations or laws that apply to these "downstream" risk arrangements. Typically, they require that financial solvency standards be met by the risk-assuming entity, and that their contracts with group insurers and HMOs be filed. The fact that increasing numbers of risk-assuming provider entities have failed to meet their obligations to pay providers assures that this will be an area of legislative focus in the future.

Collective Provider Activities

Physicians complain that they are at a disadvantage when negotiating with large HMOs and insurers over reimbursement and other terms. In response to intense lobbying by the American Medical Association and state medical societies, Texas and New Jersey have enacted laws granting physicians an exemption from state anti-trust laws in order to negotiate on a collective basis with HMOs and insurers. While these state efforts are of doubtful effectiveness unless and until changes are made in federal anti-trust law, this will be an area of tension between HMOs/insurers on the one hand and health care providers for some time to come.

✦PART TWO✦

THE ROLE OF FEDERAL REGULATION

In the McCarran-Ferguson Act, Congress clearly expressed its intent to leave to the states the regulation of the business of insurance. Although most federal laws do not directly regulate the activities of insurers and HMOs, they do directly regulate employers and the group plans they sponsor. Because insurers and HMOs provide the funding mechanisms and administration of employer sponsored group insurance plans, these federal laws have a profound impact on insurers and HMOs. These federal laws are the subject of this section.

THE FEDERAL HMO ACT OF 1973

In 1973, Congress enacted the federal HMO Act to promote the development of the then fledgling HMOs. To accomplish this, the federal HMO Act conferred a number of distinct advantages on those HMOs that met the requirements of the act and, thereby, became "federally qualified." However, HMOs are not required to become "federally qualified." In order to obtain the advantages of federal qualification, HMOs must voluntarily comply with the requirements of the Act, but there is no requirement that they do so. In this sense, the federal HMO Act does not really regulate HMOs in the way that state law does.

ADVANTAGES OF FEDERAL QUALIFICATION

Many of the advantages of federal qualification under the original federal HMO Act were stripped away by 1988 amendments to the Act. Congress had, by then, concluded that HMOs had become a viable alternative to insurance, and no longer needed the advantages originally conferred under the Act to promote their growth.

One of the last remaining vestiges of the original Act is the "equal contribution requirement." Employers that happen to offer a federally qualified HMO as a benefit option may not financially discriminate against persons enrolling in a qualified HMO. The regulations give five examples (which are illustrative only) of employer contributions that would be considered non-discriminatory:

- Equal dollar contributions for HMO and non-HMO plans;
- Equal contributions for demographic classes of employees;
- Contributions of an equal percentage of premium for all plans;
- Contributions of a negotiated amount mutually acceptable to the employer and the HMO; or
- If the employer requires employees to contribute to all health plans, it may require employees to make a contribution to a qualified HMO that does not exceed 50 percent of the employee contribution to the principal non-HMO alternative. (This would be useful in cases where the HMO would otherwise be available to employees at little or no cost.)

Employers must, therefore, be careful to examine their contribution strategy if they offer their employees coverage through a federally qualified HMO. Any federally qualified HMO can challenge the employer's contribution strategy if it feels that the employer financially discriminates against it through its contribution strategy. The penalties for non-compliance can be severe – a civil fine of up to $10,000 for the initial violation, and a like amount for each additional month of non-compliance. Enforcement is the responsibility of CMS (formerly called HCFA).

Federal qualification can be an advantage to HMOs desiring to contract with government plans. Federal qualification or qualification as a certified medical plan (as defined in 42 CFR 417) is required in order for an HMO to contract as a Medicare or Medicaid carrier.

In the past, many employers looked on federal qualification as a "seal of approval" with respect to the quality of the HMO. As a result of more active state regulation, and the development of independent certifying organizations (most notably, the National Committee on Quality Assurance (NCQA)), federal qualification has largely lost its luster as a measure of quality.

The federal HMO Act contains a provision which preempts all state laws which prevent the federally qualified entity from operating as a health maintenance organization in accordance with the terms of the federal HMO Act. At one time, this provision may have been important in permitting the establishment of HMOs in the face of state law prohibitions on the corporate practice of medicine. However, the fact that all states statutorily recognize HMOs, and most such statutes specifically exempt HMOs from the restrictions on the corporate practice of medicine, significantly reduces the importance of the preemption provision. However, the preemption provision may still be useful in thwarting state anti-managed care legislation. While there is no case law on the subject, the Department of Health and Human Services issued a letter in 1995 which concluded that a Virginia law requiring HMOs to cover out-of-network ancillary health care services was preempted.

Most HMO business involving employer groups is subject to the Employee Retirement Income Security Act (ERISA). ERISA requires that employee benefit plans implement procedures for appealing denied claims for plan benefits, and ERISA identifies minimal claim appeal procedures. Employers purchasing HMO coverage for their employees typically expect their HMOs to satisfy these claim appeal requirements in the administration of their plans. The ERISA regulations make an exception for federally qualified HMOs. A federally qualified HMO which satisfies the claim appeal requirements in the federal HMO Act is automatically deemed to comply with the somewhat less stringent claim procedures required by ERISA.

At one time, state laws gave preferential treatment to federally qualified HMOs. For example, Connecticut law permitted only federally qualified HMOs and Blue Cross plans to negotiate rates with hospitals. Few state laws remain that give any advantage to federally qualified HMOs.

DISADVANTAGES OF FEDERAL QUALIFICATION

Becoming federally qualified and maintaining federal qualification means subjecting the HMO to additional regulatory requirements which may, in some cases, outweigh the advantages derived from being federally qualified. These disadvantages include:

- The necessity of establishing a separate line of business for any non-qualified HMO business (such as insurance, PPO, or third party administration);
- The requirement that specified minimum coverage be offered. This has the effect of a benefit mandate for qualified HMOs. The federal minimum may exceed the state law requirements;
- Restrictions on the use of anything more than "nominal" co-payments, which limits benefit design; and
- Restrictions on rating that may be more restrictive than state requirements.

The once powerful allure of federal qualification has greatly diminished. As a result, some HMOs that were once federally qualified have voluntarily relinquished their federal qualification.

THE EMPLOYEE RETIREMENT INCOME SECURITY ACT OF 1974 (ERISA)

ERISA imposes broad reporting and disclosure requirements on parties (generally employers) sponsoring employee welfare benefit plans.

APPLICABILITY OF ERISA

There is a misconception that ERISA applies only to self-insured plans. In reality, ERISA governs any employee benefit plan established or maintained by an employer or by an employee organization, or by both, to the extent that such plan was established for the purpose of providing the following benefits for its participants or its beneficiaries:

- Medical, surgical, or hospital care or benefits in the event of sickness, accident, disability, death or unemployment,
- Vacation benefits,
- Apprenticeship or other training programs,
- Day care centers,
- Scholarship funds,
- Prepaid legal services, or
- Any benefit (other than pensions at retirement or death, and insurance to provide such pensions) described in Section 302(C) of the Labor Management Relations Act of 1947.

ERISA applies to these types of plans regardless of whether the group plan is funded by means of a group insurance policy, a group service agreement from an HMO, or the plan is self-insured. Only the following types of benefit plans are exempted from ERISA's requirements:

- Government plans maintained by the federal, state or local governments or agencies for their employees,
- Church plans maintained by a tax-exempt church for its employees,
- Plans required by state law such as worker compensation, unemployment compensation, and disability insurance laws,
- Plans which are maintained mainly outside of the United States which substantially cover nonresident aliens, and
- Plans covering self-employed persons such as sole proprietors and partners and their spouses.

In view of the fact that ERISA applies to the vast majority of group benefit plans, insurers and HMOs administering such plans must be prepared to ensure compliance on behalf of their customers sponsoring such plans.

PLAN OPERATION

The party establishing and maintaining an employee benefit plan (typically an employer or union) is called the plan sponsor. The plan sponsor is responsible for designating a plan administrator that is identified to plan participants as the party responsible for the administration of the plan. Normally, the plan sponsor serves as the plan administrator.

ERISA establishes standards of conduct for plan "fiduciaries." A fiduciary is a party that:

- Exercises any discretionary authority or control respecting management of the plan or disposition of its assets;
- Renders investment advice for a fee or other compensation, direct or indirect, with respect to any moneys or other property of the plan, or has any authority or responsibility to do so; or
- Has any discretionary authority or responsibility in the administration of the plan.

Each plan must designate one individual to act as the "named fiduciary" of the plan, usually the plan sponsor or the plan administrator. However, any party meeting the definition of "fiduciary" is considered a fiduciary, and subject to the rules governing fiduciary conduct regardless of whether the party is identified in plan documents as a "named fiduciary." ERISA requires that a fiduciary:

- Act in the sole interest of the plan and for the exclusive purpose of providing benefits to participants and their beneficiaries and defraying reasonable administrative expenses;
- Act with prudence and care in carrying out his or her duties;
- Diversify the investments of the plan to minimize risk and loss, unless circumstances show that this is not prudent; and
- Adhere to the plan documents in discharging its duties.

PLAN DOCUMENTS

The most basic requirement reflected throughout ERISA's various provisions is disclosure. Among other things, ERISA requires that every employee benefit plan maintain written plan documents including a Summary Plan Description ("SPD") which must be provided to plan participants. The SPD must be written in a manner that is understandable by the average plan participant, and must disclose to participants the benefits under the plan, the appeal process when a claim for plan benefits is denied, and other information regarding the parties responsible for the administration of the plan. The SPD need not be a single document. Typically, employers treat the insurer's group policy or HMOs group service agreement as the benefit description component of its SPD.

PREEMPTION OF STATE LAW

ERISA's requirements apply to employee benefit plans. They do not directly apply to insurers or HMOs (except to the extent that they are considered plan fiduciaries, in which case the fiduciary standards apply). Nonetheless, because insurance companies and HMOs provide the funding vehicle and administrative services for group plans, there are many opportunities for conflict between the ERISA requirements applicable to the plans they administer and the laws regulating insurance companies and HMOs. Congress contemplated these conflicts between ERISA and state law, and included in ERISA a provision (Section 514) stating that ERISA pre-empts any state law that "relates to" an employee benefit plan. In so doing, Congress recognized that most people were covered by benefit plans of larger employers covering people in multiple states.

To ensure the uniform application of these benefit plans for all participants in these plans, the preemption provision was added to insulate these plans from inconsistent state laws affecting plan administration. However, mindful of the fact that the McCarran-Ferguson Act left the regulation of insurance to the states, the preemption provision excluded from preemption "any law of any State that regulates insurance." This is known as the insurance "savings" clause. ERISA also makes clear that employee benefit plans shall not be deemed to be insurance companies for purposes of the "savings clause."

As a result of the preemption provision, no state insurance law which regulates the business of insurance may apply *directly* to an employee benefit plan. However, state insurance law can apply *indirectly*, as a result of the plan being funded and administered by an insurance company or HMO that is subject to state regulation. Self-funded plans are not subject to state insurance laws, and the states are prohibited from considering these plans to be insurance companies for the purposes of making state laws apply to them. The fact that stated mandated benefits had to be included if an employer chose to fund its employee benefit plan through an insurance policy or group service agreement created an incentive for employers to self-insure their benefit plans, to escape the additional costs of these mandated benefits.

Smaller employers, too small to self-insure their employee benefit plans, also sought to avoid state mandated benefits by participating in self-funded multiple employer welfare arrangements (MEWAs). States challenged the right of MEWAs to escape insurance regulation under the "deemer" clause, especially after several MEWAs failed in the early 1980's. In an attempt to clarify the situation, in 1983 Congress passed the Erlenborn-Burton Act, which defined a MEWA for the first time in ERISA. It allows self-funded MEWAs that obtain an exemption from the DOL, and are subject to state laws that relate to reserves and contribution levels, to void state insurance regulation. Those who don't obtain the DOL exemption are subject to all state laws. As a result of this clarification as to the status of MEWAs under ERISA, state insurance regulators have been more aggressive in requiring self-funded MEWAs to become licensed as insurance companies.

Insurers and HMOs have also attempted to take advantage of ERISA's preemption provision. Attempts by insurers and HMOs to avoid various state laws by application of ERISA's preemption provision have been the source of considerable litigation and an inordinate number of these cases have been decided by the United States Supreme Court. For example, state laws imposing punitive damages on group insurers for "bad faith" denials of employee benefit plan claims has been held preempted. On the other hand, the Supreme Court has held that state external review laws and any-willing-provider laws are not preempted by ERISA.

Claim Review Procedures

ERISA requires that an employee benefit plan establish a reasonable procedure for plan participants to appeal a decision to deny, in whole or in part, a claim for plan benefits. A claim procedure is deemed "reasonable" if it meets the minimum standards for review of a denied claim set forth in the law and regulations promulgated by the Department of Labor. In 2000, the DOL published final regulations that set comprehensive new standards for processing claims under ERISA covered plans. The new claims procedure regulation applies to all ERISA governed plans. HMOs and insurers administering ERISA governed plans must adapt their claim adjudication and appeal processes to satisfy the ERISA requirements, in order for their employer customers to satisfy their obligations under ERISA.

The DOL regulations establish timeframes for claim and appeal determinations (which vary depending on whether an urgent, pre-service, concurrent care, or post-service claim is involved) and set standards for the content of denial letters. Unlike the earlier DOL claim appeal regulations, the new regulations contemplate managed care coverage determinations as claims subject to the ERISA procedural requirements.

COBRA

The Consolidated Omnibus Budget Reconciliation Act of 1985 (COBRA) gives certain persons the right to continue their group health benefits beyond the date that their coverage would otherwise terminate. The entire cost (plus an additional administration fee of 2%) must be paid by the COBRA continuant.

Generally, COBRA applies to employers with 20 or more full or part-time employees. Federal workers have their own continuation law similar to COBRA. State and municipal workers are usually subject to COBRA. Only church plans are exempt from COBRA or COBRA-type coverage extensions.

BENEFITS AFFECTED BY COBRA

Benefits that may be continued under COBRA are:

- *Core Benefits*. These include hospital, surgical, and medical benefits (other than vision care and dental benefits). Any COBRA continuance option must include core benefits for which the person was covered just prior to the COBRA qualifying event. (A COBRA "qualifying event" is an event which qualifies a person for continued coverage under COBRA).
- *Non-Core Benefits*. These include dental benefits, vision care benefits and flexible spending accounts under Section 125 (cafeteria-type) plans.

Even if the qualified beneficiary (a person eligible for COBRA continuance) was covered by these non-core benefits prior to termination, he or she may, but is not required to, continue them under COBRA. Which non-core benefits, if any, are to be continued will be indicated by the qualified beneficiary at the time of COBRA enrollment.

Group life insurance, accidental death and dismemberment, and short or long-term disability coverage are not required to be continued.

MAXIMUM TIME PERIODS

Continuation will be available for a qualified beneficiary up to a maximum time period of 36 months after the original qualifying event. When the qualifying event is "entitlement to Medicare," the 36-month continuation period is measured from the date of Medicare entitlement. Under COBRA, coverage may be continued:

- Up to 18 months for an employee and covered dependents when coverage terminates due to reduction of hours worked, or termination of employment for reasons other than gross misconduct. An individual who is disabled at the time of termination may have COBRA coverage extended 29 months provided (a) he /she is considered disabled for Social Security purposes, and (b) he/she notifies the plan administrator within 60 days of the Social Security Administration's determination of disability; and

- Up to 36 months for (a) a child who ceases to be a covered dependent, (b) a covered dependent of a deceased employee, (c) a former covered spouse whose coverage ceases due to divorce or legal separation, or (d) a covered dependent when the employee's coverage ceases due to eligibility for Medicare.

There are special rules for continuing retired employees and their dependents when the employer declares Title 11 bankruptcy.

TERMINATION OF COBRA CONTINUANCE

Continued coverage may cease before the maximum period is reached, on the earliest of the following:

- The date the employer ceases to provide a group health plan to any employee;

- The date that the qualified beneficiary first becomes, after the date of election, (a) covered under any other group health plan (as an employee or otherwise), or (b) entitled to benefits under Medicare (except when eligibility is due to end-stage renal disease. In this case, coverage must be allowed to continue until the maximum period is reached. Medicare will pay secondary to the plan for the first 18 months and primary thereafter). A qualified beneficiary who becomes covered under a group health plan with a pre-existing condition limitation must be allowed to continue his or her COBRA coverage for the length of the pre-existing condition limit;

- The employee's right to COBRA continuation has been unclear when the employee has other group coverage on the date of the qualifying event. This occurs most often when an employee is covered under a spouse's group health plan at the time of the qualifying event. This was clarified by the IRS in Treasury Regulation 54.4980B-7, which provides that an employer may terminate COBRA continuation coverage of a qualified beneficiary based upon coverage under another group health plan or entitlement to Medicare benefits only if the qualified beneficiary first becomes covered under the other group health plan or becomes entitled to Medicare benefits after the date of the COBRA election; and

- The date the employer fails to receive a timely payment for the cost of the person's COBRA coverage.

When coverage terminates due to an employee's death, termination, or eligibility for Medicare, the employer has 30 days in which to notify the plan administrator of the qualifying event. When coverage terminates due to divorce or change of dependent status, the qualified beneficiary has 60 days from the qualifying event in which to notify the plan administrator that the qualifying event has occurred.

Complete instructions on how to elect continuation must be provided by the plan administrator within 14 days of receiving notice of the qualifying event. Qualified beneficiaries then have 60 days in which to elect continuation. The 60-day period is measured from the later of the date coverage terminates or the date the person receives notice of the right to continue. If continuation is not elected in that 60-day period, the right to elect continuation ceases.

An excise tax of $100 per day for each qualified beneficiary is imposed when the employer fails to comply with COBRA. The tax can be fully or partially waived if the failure to comply is due to reasonable cause and not willful neglect. If the failure was inadvertent, the start of the tax period can be delayed. Also, it will not usually apply if corrected within 30 days and due to a reasonable cause.

The maximum tax liability for a plan during a year due to reasonable cause and not willful neglect is the lesser of (a) $500,000, or (b) 10% of the amount paid or incurred by the employer (or trust in the case of multi-employer plans) during the preceding tax year for the employer's group health plan.

As an additional note, some states extend COBRA provisions to include smaller employers (less than 20 employees, the minimum size required by federal law) and for longer periods (such as the standard 18 months).

Continuation, Conversion, and COBRA

When both COBRA and state law continuation provisions apply, the person must be given the choice of which benefits he/she wishes to take, those of COBRA or those of the state continuance law. The state continuance period and the COBRA continuance period are to run together. If the state period is longer than that of COBRA and COBRA's period is exhausted, the part of the period remaining on the state continuation is still available to the continuant.

Civil Rights Act of 1964

Both sex and pregnancy discrimination in the workplace are generally prohibited by the Civil Rights Act of 1964, Title VII. This law applies to employers which (a) are engaged in an industry affecting [interstate] commerce, and (b) employ at least 15 employees for each working day in each of 20 or more calendar weeks in the current or preceding calendar year. The Civil Rights Act was subsequently amended to include the Pregnancy Discrimination Act. This act provides that employers must treat disabilities and medical claims that arise from pregnancy to the same extent as they are treated for any other disability.

Americans with Disabilities Act (ADA)

The ADA prohibits employers of more than 15 employees from discriminating based on disability in employment.

Employers and labor organizations cannot discriminate against qualified disabled persons regarding the terms, conditions, and privileges of employment, including (among other things) fringe benefit plans, whether or not employer-administered.

Insurance plans may continue to underwrite, classify, or administer risks based on state law. Also, an organization's bona fide benefit plan may use these practices whether or not based on state law. However, when the plan is not based on state law it cannot use the practices as a subterfuge to avoid ADA.

Coverage limits are permissible under health care plans, but the plan may not discriminate against disabled participants. For example, a plan may limit coverage for mental and nervous disorders; however, a person with such a disorder cannot be refused benefits for other conditions covered under the plan simply because of his/her mental or nervous disorder.

Pre-existing condition limitations are not affected by ADA provided that they are not a subterfuge to avoid ADA.

MEDICARE AS SECONDARY PAYOR LAWS

When Medicare was enacted there was a question as to how its benefits would be paid in relation to hospital and medical expense benefit plans. Initially, there was no federal guidance and Medicare was considered the primary payor. After Medicare had paid its benefits, other benefit plans would consider their obligation as secondary payor. Changes in the law over the years have resulted in Medicare being treated as the secondary payor in nearly all situations.

THE HEALTH INSURANCE PORTABILITY AND ACCOUNTABILITY ACT OF 1996 (HIPAA)

Following the failure to enact the significant health care reforms proposed during President Clinton's first term, incremental reforms have been enacted by Congress. The most important is the Health Insurance Portability and Accountability Act of 1996 ("HIPAA"). HIPAA made reforms in three general areas: insurance portability and availability, administrative simplification, and health care fraud and abuse prevention.

"PORTABILITY" AND AVAILABILITY REFORMS

To facilitate access to health insurance coverage for individuals who lose group coverage because they change jobs or their employer changes insurers, the following reforms were implemented:

- Group health plans or health insurance issuers providing coverage to groups may not impose a pre-existing condition exclusion (PCE) on a plan participant unless (1) the PCE relates to a condition for which medical advice or care was received within 6 months prior to the enrollment date; (2) the PCE extends no more than 18 months after the enrollment date; and (3) the PCE period is reduced by the aggregate periods of creditable coverage under other plans (employer sponsored group plans, Medicaid, Medicare, and the Federal Employees Health benefit Plan) as of the enrollment date. If there is a break in creditable coverage for any 63 day period after a creditable coverage period began, that period of creditable coverage will not count towards the PCE period. In addition, PCEs are not applicable to certain newborns and adopted children and may not be imposed on conditions relating to pregnancy. To facilitate the administration of this requirement, benefit plans and their insurers and HMOs must provide certification that an individual was covered and other information, at the time the individual ceases to be covered under COBRA and at the timely request of an individual. Certain small group and disability plans are not subject to the PCE provisions. States are free to impose shorter periods limiting PCEs.

- A group health plan and a group insurer or HMO may not establish eligibility rules based on "health status-related" factors. Requiring evidence of insurability is prohibited.

- A group health plan or group insurer/HMO may not require higher premiums than those charged people "similarly situated" on the basis of any health-status related factors.

- Special enrollment periods are required to permit eligible employees or dependents to enroll after they lose other coverage.

- Multi-employer health plans and MEWAs may not deny an employer whose employees are covered under such plan continued access to the same or different coverage, except for such things as nonpayment of contributions, fraud, and noncompliance with material plan provisions.

- Health insurers and HMOs that offer health insurance in the small group market (2-50 employees) in a state must accept every small employer group in that state that applies for coverage, and must accept for enrollment every eligible individual that applies for coverage in the initial enrollment period. (Plans with limited provider network service areas can limit to those in the service area.) An insurer or HMO can deny coverage in the small group market if it demonstrates that it does not have the financial reserves necessary to underwrite such coverage, and if it applies its decision uniformly to all groups applying for coverage. If an insurer or HMO denies coverage on this basis, it is excluded from writing any new coverage in the small group market for a period of time. Insurers can, however, establish employer contribution and group participation rules as conditions of coverage.

• With certain limited exceptions, group insurers and HMOs that offer coverage in the small or large group market must renew or continue in force such coverage for all groups at the option of the plan sponsor. Coverage may only be terminated by the insurer or HMO for nonpayment of premiums, fraud or misrepresentation, uniform modification or withdrawal of a particular product from the market, or discontinuance of all health insurance coverage (provided specified notice is given to policyholders

• Insurance companies and HMOs issuing individual health insurance policies or service agreements are also required to offer coverage to eligible individuals without limits based upon pre-existing conditions.

PREVENTING HEALTH CARE FRAUD AND ABUSE

HIPAA establishes a new Health Care Fraud and Abuse Control Program designed to coordinate federal, state and local law enforcement activities to control fraud with respect to *all* "health plans," not just Medicare and Medicaid.

ADMINISTRATIVE SIMPLIFICATION AND PRIVACY

In order to encourage more widespread adoption of electronic data interchange (EDI) technologies and uniform standards for financial and administrative data, HIPAA directed the Secretary of HHS to adopt standards for electronic information transactions and data elements for such transactions as well as security standards relating to the transfer of individually identifiable health information; standards relating to electronic signatures and standards necessary for transferring COB information. Compliance with the regulations will require extensive changes by insurers and HMOs at great expense. However, the objective is to reduce cost in the healthcare system through the use of uniform data sets and the increased use of electronic transfers of information.

Final privacy regulations became effective in 2001. These regulations cover all aspects of the health care delivery system, and address the use and disclosure of individually identifiable health care information in any form, whether communicated orally, electronically or in writing. The regulation affords a patient the right to education about privacy safeguards, access to their medical records, and a process for correction of records. It also requires the patient's permission for disclosure of personal information for purposes unrelated to health care. Compliance with the regulations was required by April of 2003. The regulation does not preempt state laws that afford more stringent privacy protections. Thus, group insurers and HMOs have to contend with multiple layers of federal and state privacy laws.

EFFECT OF HIPAA ON COBRA

HIPAA included three changes to the provisions of COBRA, as follows:

- Qualified beneficiaries under COBRA who are determined to be disabled under Social Security during the first 60 days of COBRA continuation are eligible for an additional 11 months of COBRA continuation. Previously, the law required the person to be disabled at the time of the COBRA qualifying event.
- The additional 11 months of continuation is also available to the disabled person's spouse and dependent children.
- Children born or adopted during the COBRA continuation period are qualified beneficiaries under COBRA.

NEWBORNS' AND MOTHERS' HEALTH PROTECTION ACT OF 1996

The Newborns' and Mothers' Health Protection Act of 1996 requires group health plans to extend coverage for hospitalization for childbirth. Health plans must provide coverage for at least 48 hours of hospitalization following a normal delivery, and for 96 hours following a cesarean delivery.

MENTAL HEALTH PARITY ACT OF 1996

The Mental Health Parity Act of 1996 mandates parity in dollar limits for mental health benefits and medical-surgical benefits. The Act does not specifically require health plans to provide mental health benefits. However, when coverage for mental health conditions is included, any lifetime or annual dollar limits applied to mental health benefits must at least be equal to those applicable to medical-surgical benefits of the same plan.

The law applies to employers with over 50 employees. An exemption from the law may be claimed if, after providing the required parity for at least six months, an increase of at least one percent in plan costs can be demonstrated. The law has raised debate over whether it will encourage or discourage plans to include parity between mental health benefits and other health benefits. Proponents claim it will make much-needed coverage more widely available at modest cost. Others believe it will increase claims costs substantially and will result in plans eliminating all mental health benefits. In early 1998 the Clinton Administration ruled that plans subject to the law must comply for at least six months prior to claiming an exemption based on increased plan costs. That is, the plans must have actual rather than projected experience to substantiate cost increases that result from complying with the law.

THE FAMILY MEDICAL LEAVE ACT (FMLA)

FMLA allows eligible employees to take unpaid leave for specific family and personal situations. It applies to employers who employed 50 or more employees, including public agencies and schools. Eligible employees are those who have worked 12 months or more for the employer. An employee may take up to a total of 12 weeks of family medical leave time during a 12-month period.

SUMMARY OF FEDERAL REGULATION

The federal laws enacted within the past decade represent attempts to incrementally reform the health care system following the demise of President Clinton's proposal for a national health insurance program. These incremental reforms reflect two trends that have significance for group insurers/HMOs:

1. For the first time, the federal government has begun to mandate substantive coverage requirements, a role historically eschewed by Congress since enactment of the McCarran-Ferguson Act.

2. For the first time, the federal regulations do not attempt to preempt state laws. A number of the federal reform acts contemplate states imposing more stringent requirements. This attitude is also reflected in the Supreme Court's recent holding *Rush Prudential HMO, Inc. vs. Moran.*

The combination of these trends will make more difficult the job of compliance for group insurers and HMOs.

16 REGULATION IN CANADA

Nicola Parker-Smith

In Canada, insurance companies are governed by various Insurance Acts at both the federal and provincial level, as well as numerous provincial regulations, industry guidelines and codes of business standards. At the federal level, the 1992 Insurance Companies Act consolidated the Canadian and British Insurance Companies Act and the Foreign Insurance Companies Act. In addition, it included other matters previously in the Canadian Business Corporations Act, relating to the governance of insurance companies.

In 1999, the federal government passed legislation allowing mutual life and health insurance companies to demutualize. The legislation required that the insurance company remain widely held (no individual can hold more than 10% of the shares of a company) for two years following demutualization. This was known as the transition period.

In 2001, legislation was passed which set December 31, 2001 as the end of the transition period for demutualized companies. After this date companies with equity of less than $5 billion were eligible to be closely held. Demutualized companies with more than $5 billion in equity would continue to be widely held, but investors could now purchase up to 20% of voting shares.

Large banks are not permitted to acquire or merge with large demutualized insurance companies, and vice versa.

The legislation also allowed life and health insurance companies access to the Canadian Payments System, enabling them to offer payment and other services to customers. The Financial Consumer Agency of Canada will enforce consumer related aspects of the legislation.

FEDERAL REGULATION

Federal legislation applies to companies that choose to be licensed federally because they operate in more than one province. The legislation

313

deals primarily with matters relating to financial soundness and solvency, investment limitations, and corporate powers. This legislation is subject to review every 5 years. The most recent review in 2006 did not result in any significant changes.

The Office of the Superintendent of Financial Institutions (OSFI) is responsible for supervising federally regulated life and health insurance companies, to ensure they meet requirements pertaining to capital resources, large exposure and commercial lending criteria, liquidity, loan loss provisions, systems and controls, and the board of directors and management.

In ensuring financial soundness, OSFI measures capital adequacy by applying the Minimum Continuing Capital & Surplus Requirements (MCCSR) guidelines. Insurance companies are expected to maintain a target capital level of 150% or more of their MCCSR requirement, with a minimum requirement of 120 % of MCCSR. Capital is comprised of Tier 1 (or Core Capital) and Tier 2 (or Supplemental Capital). OSFI expects each financial institution to maintain ongoing Tier 1 Capital at 105 %.

Insurance companies are required to provide corporate and financial information to OSFI on a regular basis. Certain rules apply to the valuation of assets as well as the basis for reserve liabilities. With the 1992 Act, a shift took place toward reporting on a generally accepted accounting principles (GAAP) basis. The Canadian Institute of Actuaries (CIA) has developed standards of practice for the valuation of policy liabilities of life insurers, which provide guidelines in determining reserve liabilities.

In 1999, OSFI developed a Supervisory Framework, which outlines a process for assessing safety and soundness of regulated financial institutions. OSFI evaluates the institutions' risk profile, financial condition, risk management process and compliance with laws and regulations.

A provincially incorporated company comes under provincial authority for its powers as a corporation as well as its contracts and authority to transact business. For a federally incorporated company, its contracts and authority to transact business come from provincial law. An insurance company incorporated outside Canada must obtain a federal license to operate, but its contracts and authority to transact business are subject to provincial law. More than 90% of the premium income in Canada is sold through companies that are federally registered.

PROVINCIAL REGULATION

PROVINCIAL INSURANCE ACTS

Each province has enacted legislation affecting the operation of insurance companies and the activities of agents and brokers. This includes the licensing and marketing of insurance company products, standards of competence for insurance agents, and consumer protection. Provinces have attempted to keep their respective insurance legislation uniform to avoid inconsistencies. For example, Quebec has adopted reforms with the objective of greater harmonization and standardization with federal companies, to improve the stability of provincial companies and to assist such companies in their future growth. All provinces continue to pursue further harmonization.

The provincial Insurance Acts cover many aspects of group life and health insurance, including the following:

- Rights and obligations of insured and beneficiary,
- Designation of beneficiaries,
- Content of contracts and member certificates,
- Administration of contract including payment of premiums,
- Payment of claims,
- Requirements on termination, and
- Requirements on takeover or change of carrier.

In Quebec, legislation requires that employers extend a given level of prescription drug coverage to employees who are residents of Quebec if the employer is offering other health related benefits. The legislation requires employer sponsored prescription drug coverage to pay at least 71.5% of the cost of each prescription and 100% of the cost of prescriptions in a year which exceed $881 for each insured adult.

GROUP INSURANCE GUIDELINES

Guidelines established by the Canadian Life and Health Insurance Association (CLHIA) provide the minimum standards for group insurance practices. The guidelines apply to life and accidental death and sickness (including health and dental) insurance. Where provincial legislation covers matters dealt with in the guidelines, such legislation takes precedence. In particular, the guidelines include the following:

- *Group Insurance Plan Description for Members.* Requires an insurer to issue to each member a plan description which outlines the principal benefits and conditions under the contract.

- *Conversion/Continuation Privileges.* Describes the conditions under which a member may continue life insurance coverage on an individual. Every contract of group insurance must permit a member to convert his or her insurance without evidence of insurability prior to age 65, in the case of termination of employment and in the case of termination of the plan. Certain limits apply to the amount that may be converted. Conversion can be to a one-year term plan, term to 65 or to any individual contract of insurance under any regular plan then being issued by the insurer. The premium paid by the member would be the premium then in effect for the individual insurance. In the event a plan which contains a disability provision is terminated, insurance for any person disabled at the time of termination is to be continued as if the plan was still in effect. It is interesting to note that a contract of group health insurance does not have to provide a conversion privilege.

- *Change of Insurer.* Rules regarding replacement of a group contract are designed to ensure that no member loses coverage or has to requalify for certain coverages solely because of not being actively at work on the date the replacing coverage comes into effect. Outstanding benefits are paid either under the old contract or the replacing contract depending on the financial arrangements that have been made.

- *Coordination of Cost-of-Living Adjustments in Government Plans.* The disability benefit payable to an insured under a contract of group insurance is not to be reduced because of a government sponsored plan or support program cost-of-living adjustment occurring after the date on which the benefit becomes payable under the contract.

- *Creditor's Group Insurance.* The Guideline with respect to creditor's group insurance has been developed to assist insurers in protecting the interests of debtors insured under group insurance contracts and in response to concerns that have been expressed by consumers and regulators. It does not seek to regulate the premiums or charges to consumers, either directly or through minimum loss ratios or limits on commission and expense payments. Specific provisions covered include the following:

  o Amount and Duration of Creditor's Group Insurance

  o Cancellation or Non-renewal

- ○ Application Requirements and Information Provided to the Debtor
- ○ Content of Certificates
- ○ Refunds
- ○ Claims

While the guidelines are not enforceable by law, and are still considered voluntary, CLHIA members are expected to follow the guidelines during their normal course of business.

OTHER GOVERNMENT LEGISLATION

HUMAN RIGHTS

Human Rights legislation has been in place in most provinces since 1970. Generally, any business or industry registered or incorporated in a province is governed by the Human Rights Code of that province. In Ontario, the Employment Standards Act applies as well as the Human Rights Code. The federal government has authority to regulate certain types of businesses such as banking, transportation, communications and radio and television broadcasting. Federally regulated industries are governed by the Canadian Human Rights Code. Human Rights legislation is considered as "fundamental," so it will often take precedence over any other legislation that may conflict with it. Individuals may not make private contracts in which they agree to waive the rights accorded by Human Rights Statutes.

The intent of the legislation is to provide for equal treatment without discrimination in several areas of daily life, including housing, employment, and the provision of goods and services to the public. Employee benefits such as life and health plans are considered to be "a term or condition of employment," and insurance contracts are characterized as "goods or services to the public."

Characteristics such as sex, age, marital and family status, mental and physical handicap, and criminal conviction are "prohibited grounds of discrimination" frequently found in the codes of many jurisdictions. Statutes, however, may contain explicit exceptions to the various prohibited acts and bases of discrimination. This permits, for example, employer contributions to a group insurance plan to vary by age or sex, in order to provide equal benefits. Regulations and guidelines for employee benefits passed in conjunction with Human Rights Acts also make further exceptions to the Act's protection, defining with more precision which groups the Act may not apply to and which activities do not come within the scope of the Act.

The Ontario Human Rights Commission released a report which urges the insurance industry to avoid discrimination in its pricing and risk assessment on the basis of genetic testing. This could limit an insurers ability to apply a preexisting condition clause.

Most Human Rights Acts are administered by locally appointed Commissions, which investigate individual complaints and attempt to settle them by negotiation. If settlement fails, a Board of Inquiry may be appointed to hear both sides. The Board's decision may be appealed to the appropriate court.

Human Rights codes reflect changing social conditions. As a result, they are frequently amended with new grounds of prohibited discrimination and new definitions coming into force, and existing grounds are tested before the courts.

In May of 1999 the Supreme Court of Canada ruled that the definition of spouse in the Ontario Family Law Act violates the guarantee of equality in a case called M v. H. The Act defined spouse as someone of opposite gender. As a result, Ontario passed Bill 5, effective March 2000, extending rights to same-gender partners. In July 2000, federal tax legislation was amended to change the definition of common-law partners to include same-sex, common-law couples, and to treat them equally under the Income Tax Act. The legislation became effective in the 2001 tax year.

Effective December 2006, the Ontario Human Rights Code was amended to prohibit employers from forcing employees to retire at or beyond age 65. This amendment does not affect group insurance plans. The provision of group insurance benefits to employees over age 65 continues to be at the discretion of employers.

EMPLOYMENT STANDARDS ACT

The Labour or Employment Standards Acts set out the rights and responsibilities of both employees and employers, including minimum wage, hours of work, overtime pay, paid public holidays, pregnancy, prenatal and emergency leave, and termination notice and severance pay.

The Acts of all provinces require an employer to provide individual notice of termination of employment to an employee. The notice periods range from one week to a maximum of eight weeks, depending on an employee's length of service. In lieu of the required notice, an employer may choose to pay wages, usually representing the length of the notice period. In Ontario, an employer is required to continue employee benefits during the notice period, even if the employee is not at work. Temporary layoffs, variously defined in terms of periods ranging from 60 days to 13 weeks, are not covered.

Most jurisdictions have group termination provisions requiring the employer to give notice to the Minister of Labour in the event that particular numbers of employees are terminated at the same time or within a specified number of weeks. The length of notice period depends on the number of employees terminated, and ranges between 8 and 16 weeks.

Changes to the Employment Standards Act in Ontario eliminated the ability of employers to suspend disability benefits during maternity leave. Employers and insurers who provide benefit plans are required to deliver the same level of benefit to individuals who are experiencing a health related absence from work due to pregnancy as they do for other health related absences.

LABOUR LEGISLATION — CHILD CARE LEAVE OF ABSENCE

All jurisdictions have labour legislation requiring employers to provide unpaid maternity leave to qualifying pregnant employees and to protect their jobs while away on leave. The legislation also prohibits an employer from terminating an employee solely because of her pregnancy. The employee must have worked for that employer between 5 and 12 months in most provinces, to qualify for leave ranging from 17 to 52 weeks.

The labour laws of several jurisdictions require employers to provide unpaid child care leave to fathers of newborns or to adopting parents.

The federal government passed privacy legislation in April of 2000. This legislation is intended to balance an individual's right to privacy of personal information with the need of organizations to collect, use, or disclose personal information for legitimate business purposes. The Personal Information Protection & Electronic Documents Act (Bill C-6) is effective January 1, 2001 and comes into force in three phases. The first phase, which applies to personal information other than personal health information collected or used by federally regulated organizations, comes into force on January 1, 2001. The second phase, which extends to include personal health information for organizations included in the first phase, comes into force January 1, 2002. The final phase, which extends to all organizations, came into force January 1, 2004. This legislation applies to all provinces without similar legislation. Quebec, Alberta and British Columbia have introduced similar privacy legislation.

GOVERNMENT PROGRAMS

EMPLOYMENT INSURANCE

Canada's Employment Insurance is a federal benefit program governed by the Employment Insurance Act (EI), and administered by Human Resources Development Canada. The Employment Insurance Act, which was fully implemented in January 1997, was a fundamental restructuring of the old Unemployment Insurance Act 1971. As federal legislation, EI is applied consistently throughout Canada, with special variations on eligibility and benefit durations due to regional levels of unemployment. In 2006, Quebec introduced the Quebec Parental Insurance Plan which replaces the Federal Employment Insurance Plan for maternity, parental and adoption benefits.

The legislation requires employers and employees to contribute premiums. As of January 1, 2007, the weekly employee contribution was $1.80 per $100 of insurable earnings subject to maximum annual earnings of $ 40,000. The weekly contribution rate for employers not participating in the Employer Premium Reduction Program is 1.4 times the employee premium or $ 2.52 per $100 of insurable earnings. The weekly contribution rate for employers participating in the Employer Premium Reduction Program is 1.248 times the employee premium. In Quebec, the weekly contribution effective January 1, 2007 is $ 1.46 for employees and $ 2.04 for employers, per $ 100 of insurable earnings. Also effective January 1, 2007, the weekly contribution to the Quebec Parental Insurance Plan is $ 0.416 for employees and $ 0.586 for employers per $100 of insurable earnings, to maximum annual earnings of $ 59,000. EI compensates employees for interruptions of earnings caused by unemployment, illness, and the birth or adoption of a child. More than one type of special benefit (maternity, parental, or sickness) may be claimed within one benefit period, up to a maximum of 50 weeks.

- *Regular Benefit.* To be eligible for regular benefits an individual must have worked between 420 and 700 hours of work within the last 52 weeks, or since the start of their last claim, if shorter, depending on the unemployment rate in their region. The basic benefit rate could be adjusted if an individual has drawn regular benefits in the past (intensity rule). Regular benefits are paid from 14 to 45 weeks. The maximum EI benefit is $423 per week. Regular EI benefits must be repaid if net annual income exceeds $48,750. The repayment is equal to 30% of the lesser of (net income in excess of $48,750) and (the total regular benefits).

- *Sickness Benefit.* To be eligible for sickness benefits, an individual must have worked and paid EI premiums for at least 600 hours in the last 52 weeks, or since the start of the last EI claim. Also, regular weekly earnings must have decreased by more than 40%. The basic benefit rate is 55% of average insured earnings up to a maximum of $423 per week. If an individual is in a low-income family with children, and receives the Child Tax Benefit, the benefit rate could be higher but subject to the same maximum benefit. EI is second payer and the benefit is reduced by the amount of disability payments received from group insurance for sickness or loss of income. The benefit is paid for a maximum of 15 weeks after a 2-week waiting period.

- *Maternity Benefit.* Pregnant women who have worked a minimum of 600 hours in the past 52 weeks, or since the start of their last claim, are eligible for benefits. The benefit amount is the same as for the Sickness Benefit. The 15 weeks of benefit can be taken up to 8 weeks before birth is scheduled but cannot be received later than 17 weeks after the baby is due or born, unless the infant is confined to a hospital.

- *Parental Benefit.* Parental benefits can be collected for up to 35 weeks by both natural or adoptive parents while they are caring for a newborn or adopted child. Benefits are only available within the 52 weeks following the child's birth, or for adoptive parents from the date the child arrives home.

- *Compassionate Benefit.* Compassionate benefits are payable for up to 6 weeks to a person who has to be absent to care for a gravely ill family member at risk of dying within 26 weeks. Other eligibility requirements and the benefit amount are the same as those for the sickness benefits.

- *Employer Premium Reduction Program.* An employer may reduce EI premiums by establishing a wage loss replacement plan that provides benefits at least equivalent to the EI benefit. The plan must be approved by HRDC who have established minimum requirements for a qualifying plan. The employer must share the reduction with employees according to a prescribed schedule and must inform them of their right to this share. Premium reductions are for one year and annual registration is required.

- *Supplemental Unemployment Benefit (SUB).* An employer may set up a SUB plan to add to EI's payments under the unemployment, sickness, pregnancy and/or adoption benefits. HRDC must approve the SUB plan prior to its implementation and has established detailed requirements for a qualifying plan. Without approval, payments are considered earnings for EI purposes, and will be deducted from any benefits paid to employees.

WORKER'S COMPENSATION

Worker's compensation (WC) is a program regulated by each province's Worker's Compensation Act, providing benefits to an employee or the employee's family in the event of injury, illness or death arising from or in the course of employment. Benefits include loss of income payments, death benefits and medical benefits. WC Acts apply to most businesses, and cover approximately 70% to 90% of the work force. Boards or commissions in each province administer the Act and determine a claimant's eligibility for benefit payment. Employers pay the entire cost of WC by their contributions to the compensation fund. Most classes of industry participate in collective liability, and are assessed contribution rates on the basis of all injuries related to that collective class of employers. Private insurers are not involved in insuring WC benefits.

WC legislation establishes mandatory coverage for most industries. All full-time or part-time employees of industries with coverage are eligible for benefits. Executive officers, partners and sole proprietors in covered industries are not automatically covered, but may apply for coverage. Any individual covered by WC loses their right to sue their employer for injuries resulting from employment.

WC loss of income benefits are salary related and are payable to compensate for earnings lost during the period the injured worker is unable to work. Most compensation schemes have a waiting period between the injury date and the commencement of eligibility of benefits. Once the waiting period has elapsed, benefits in many cases are backdated to the date of injury. Most short-term disability (STD) and long-term disability (LTD) benefits are reduced directly by WC benefits.

Death benefits generally include an immediate lump sum, funeral costs, transportation of the deceased when required, a monthly pension, and lump-sum payments on remarriage. The monthly pension payments in many provinces are earnings related. They are generally set at 80% to 90% of the deceased worker's net average earnings for a sole dependent spouse, and from 10% to 15% of earnings for a dependent child. There is a maximum on covered earnings, which varies by province.

All provinces pay the cost of medical care arising from a WC claim for as long as it is needed. For these cases, no benefits are payable under insured health plans.

CANADA/QUÉBEC PENSION PLANS

The Canada/Québec Pension Plans (C/QPP) are contributory, earnings-related Government programs providing retirement pensions and supplementary benefits. The supplementary benefits include surviving spouses' pensions, disability pensions, benefits for the disabled contributor's children as well as a death benefit. Almost all working people are covered by the C/QPP, with the legislation exempting a few categories of seasonal, part-time and government workers.

The employee and the employer make matching contributions. In 2007, this is 4.95% of the employee's salary and wages, up to the Year's Maximum Pensionable Earnings (YMPE) of $40,000 reduced by the Year's Basic Exemption (YBE) which has been frozen at $3,500. Self-employed people pay the combined contribution of 9.9 %.

A CPP contributor under age 65 is eligible for a disability pension if their mental and physical disability is 'severe and prolonged,' such that they can not support themselves by regular employment at any job. A QPP contributor under age 65 is eligible for the disability pension if their disability prevents them from working at their own occupation. In the past, the application of the definition was generally less restrictive than the wording implied. Effective in 1998, the administration of disability benefits has been tightened.

Although practices do vary, an insured LTD benefit is normally reduced by the basic disability benefit under the C/QPP. Generally, benefits for dependent children are not a direct offset to the LTD benefit but are included in the 'all source' maximum. Cost-of-living increases in C/QPP are not taken into account for benefit payment purposes.

Disability Determination Boards make findings with respect to eligibility for disability. The minimum qualifying period is calculated on the basis of several factors, but in general for those considered to be disabled in 1998 and later there must have been contributions in four of the last six years. The disability benefit is made up of a flat monthly amount and a component related to earnings. There is a three-month waiting period which may be waived for a disability that reoccurs within five years. Benefits are paid to recovery, death or age 65, after which it is replaced by a retirement pension. The retirement benefit is based on the YMPE at the time disability occurs and then indexed to CPI until age 65.

Survivor benefits are payable to survivors of contributors who have met the requirement of the minimum qualifying period. Survivors who are at least 45 or less than 45 and either disabled or with dependent children are entitled to the benefit.

The fuller funding of the CPP means the reserve fund is expected to grow to an equivalent of five years of benefits over the next two decades. Funds not required to pay benefits, which previously have been invested in non-marketable securities of provincial governments, will now be invested in a diversified portfolio of securities. This change will put the CPP on the same basis as most other pension plans as well as the QPP.

AUTOMOBILE INSURANCE

In Canada, automobile insurance is governed by various provincial acts and regulations as well as by CLHIA Guidelines. Most auto insurance policies have a common structure and common provisions. Accident benefits, which include medical, funeral, rehabilitation and loss of income compensation, must be included in auto insurance in most provinces.

An auto insurer is required to compensate the accident victim first, before any finding of fault. Benefits are similar to those provided under employer sponsored group plans, so coordination of benefits is used to avoid duplication. Unfortunately, this practice does vary by province. In most cases, a group disability plan pays first, with the auto insurer paying only if the benefit does not meet the minimum statutory amount.

PROVINCIAL MEDICAL PLANS

All provinces have their own medical and hospital plans in place. Private insurance plans are designed to supplement these provincial plans. The services covered by private plans vary by province, and it is the provinces that decide what can be covered. Standard contracts exclude expenses for which benefits are payable under a government plan. When claims are paid, the assumption is made that a claimant is covered by a provincial plan. To the extent that the full cost of a service is not covered by a provincial plan, the balance can be insured where permitted.

There has been considerable cost shifting from provincial medical plans to private insurance health care plans over the past five years, as health care costs have increased at rates which significantly exceed rates of general inflation. As a result of rising health care costs, the federal government and many of the provincial governments are evaluating the health care system and are considering health care reforms.

TAXATION

INCOME TAXES

The Income Tax Act of Canada governs the taxation of employee benefits. Interpretation Bulletins published by Revenue Canada (Taxation) explain how the law will be administered. Section 6 of the Act outlines all the amounts which are included as income from employment for tax purposes. Paragraph 6(1)(a) provides for certain exclusions, including employer contributions to a group sickness or accident plan, private health services plan, supplementary unemployment benefit plan, or group term life insurance plan.

As of July 1, 1994, all employer contributions for group life insurance premiums are considered taxable income to an employee. Prior to the July date, an exception was available for employer-paid premiums with respect to the first $25,000 of insurance coverage.

Death benefits paid under a group life insurance plan are not included in a person's income for tax purposes when settling their estate, nor are such benefits considered taxable income to the beneficiary.

Premiums paid by an employer on behalf of an employee for loss of income benefits (STD & LTD) are not taxable to the employee if the benefits are provided under a group sickness or accident plan, private health services plan, or supplementary unemployment plan. The tax status of any loss-of-income benefits depends on who has paid the premiums. In the case of an employee-pay-all plan, the benefits paid are not taxable to an employee. Where the employer has made a contribution, the benefits are taxable regardless of the amount of the employer contribution. When loss of income benefits are taxable, an employee is allowed to deduct contributions made to the plan by the employee before the end of the tax year.

Except in Québec, premiums paid by an employer on behalf of an employee to a supplementary health plan or a dental plan are not included in the employee's income for tax purposes. The change in Québec was made with the Québec budget of 1993. Premiums paid by the employee may be included in medical expenses to determine the amount that can be deducted for tax purposes. Any benefits received under a health or dental plan are not taxed.

Some social benefits must be repaid if net income for the year exceeds a certain level. This is done through the tax system and applies in the case of Employment Insurance benefits and the Old Age Security pension.

SALES TAX

In 1985, Québec imposed a 9% sales tax on all insurance premiums. In the case of self-funding (ASO) arrangements, the tax is applied to the claims paid. Expenses of operating the plan are taxed at a lower rate of 7.5%. Employees who are Québec residents pay the tax.

In 1993, Ontario began assessing an 8% Retail Sales Tax on group insurance premiums and ASO equivalents. Any person residing or conducting business in Ontario is required to pay tax on group life and health premiums. For plan sponsors, the tax is based on where the employee reports to work each day. In the case of self-funded arrangements, the tax base depends on whether the plan is considered as being funded. To be funded, contributions must be sufficient to cover benefits and expenses foreseeable and payable within the next 30 days. The sales tax is applied to the contributions for a funded plan and to the claims plus expenses for an unfunded plan.

PREMIUM TAXES

All provinces impose premium taxes on group life and accident and sickness insurance premiums. The tax is applied to the gross premiums paid, less any dividends that are declared. Premium tax rates in effect on January 1, 2007 are as follows:

- Newfoundland – 4%
- Prince Edward Island – 3.5%
- Nova Scotia, Saskatchewan, North West Territories, Nunavut – 3%
- Québec – 2.35%
- Other provinces – 2%

GOODS AND SERVICES TAX

The Goods and Services Tax (GST) was introduced January 1, 1991. It is more complex and comprehensive than the federal sales tax it replaced. Group insurance premiums are exempt from the tax and most services provided for under a group insurance policy do not attract GST. Administrative fees paid under a self-insured plan are subject to GST. Where a self-insured plan has an insurance element, such as stop-loss coverage, the fees paid under the self-insured plan would be exempt from GST. The GST rate in effect on January 1, 2007 is 6%.

In Newfoundland, New Brunswick and Nova Scotia, the GST and the provincial sales tax have been harmonized and are referred to as the Harmonized Sales Tax (HST). Administrative fees paid under a self-insured plan are subject to HST where services are rendered in these provinces.

COMPCORP (ASSURIS)

In January 1990, a consumer protection plan was established to protect both policyholders and group certificate holders against the loss of benefits due to the insolvency of an insurance company. The plan, now called Assuris, is administered by the CLHIA, and is funded by most of the insurance companies operating in Canada. In the event of an insolvency, the plan provides for coverage of $200,000 for life insurance, $60,000 for cash accumulation plans and health benefits, and $2,000 per month for disability and annuity benefits. In order to deal effectively with various issues that arise, CompCorp incorporated its own insurance company.

GENERAL SUMMARY

The following tables provide a summary of government benefits, effective January 1, 2007 (unless otherwise stated). Note that some of the benefits are adjusted quarterly to reflect increases in the cost of living.

SUMMARY OF GOVERNMENT BENEFITS (2007)

I. Canada/Québec Pension Plan

	CPP	QPP
Year's Maximum Pensionable Earnings	$43,700.00	$43,700.00
Year's Basic Exemption	3,500.00	3,500.00
Maximum Contributory Earnings	40,200.00	40,200.00
Maximum Employer/ Employee Contribution (4.95% each of contributory earnings)	1,989.90	1,989.90
Death Benefit Maximum Death Benefit	2,500.00	2,500.00
Maximum Monthly Spouse's Pension		
(age 45-55)	482.30	729.84
(age 55 but less than 65)	482.30	729.84
(age 65 or older)	518.25	518.25
Monthly Orphan's Pension	204.68	64.99
Disability Benefit Maximum Monthly Contributor's Pension	1053.77	1,053.74
Monthly Children's Pension	204.68	64.99
Maximum Monthly Retirement Benefit		
(age 60)	604.63	604.63
(age 65)	863.75	863.75

II. Employment Insurance (2007)

Maximum Insurable Earnings	
per week	$ 769.23
per annum	40,000.00
Maximum Annual Contribution	
Employee (1.8% of insurable earnings)	720.00
Employer (1.4 times employee contributions under non-qualified plan)	1,008.00
Maximum Weekly Benefit	
Regular Claimants (55% Benefit)	423.00

III. Worker's Compensation

Province	Maximum Earnings Covered *	Weekly Benefits for Temporary Disability	Maximum Monthly Benefits for Permanent Disability
B.C.	$64,400	90% average gross earnings	90% average gross earnings
Alberta	61,200	90% net earnings	90% net earnings
Sask.	55,000	90% net earnings	90% net earnings
Manitoba	62,050	90% net earnings	90% net earnings
Ontario	71,800	85% net average earnings	85% net average earnings
Québec	57,000	90% net income	90% net income
N.B.	50,900	85% net income	85% net average earnings
N.S.	43,200	75% net earnings for 26 weeks, 85% after	75% net earnings for 26 weeks, 85% after
P.E.I.	44,700	80% of net for 38 weeks, 85% after	80%/85% of average earnings
Nfld.	48,425	80% net earnings	80% net earnings
N.W.T. & Nunavut	67,500	90% net earnings	90% net earnings
Yukon	69,500	75% gross earnings	75% gross earnings

* According to figures currently available.

IV. Old Age Security

(Effective January 1, 2007)	Maximum Monthly Benefit Level
Basic Benefit	$ 491.93
Allowance	901.97
Allowance for Survivor	999.81
Guaranteed Income Supplement (GIS)	
Single	620.91
Spouse –non pensioner	620.91
Spouse – pensioner of allowance recipient	410.04

OAS pensioners with annual income which exceeds $63,511 must repay part or all of their OAS pension. Pensioners with annual income greater than $102,865 are required to repay all of their OAS pension. Allowance benefits cease when annual income exceeds $27,600. Similarly, GIS payments cease when annual income exceeds $35,712.

V. Taxation of Employee Benefits

Government Plan	Employee Contributions Tax Deductible?	Employer Costs Tax Deductible by Employer?	Employer Contributions Taxable to Employee?	Benefits Received Taxable to Recipient?
C/QPP	Yes	Yes	No(1)	Yes
Old Age Security				
Basic Benefit	N/A	N/A	N/A	Yes
Spouse's Allowance	N/A	N/A	N/A	No
GIS	N/A	N/A	N/A	No
Employment Insurance	Yes	Yes	No(1)	Yes
Worker's Compensation	N/A	Yes	No	No
Provincial "Medicare" Plans: Alberta, B.C.	No	Yes	Yes	No

(1) Taxable benefit is conferred if employer pays employee's portion, but employee can claim the corresponding amount as a tax deduction.

V. Taxation of Employee Benefits (cont'd)

Employer Sponsored Plans	Employee Contributions Tax Deductible?	Employer Costs Tax Deductible by Employer?	Employer Contributions Taxable to Employee?	Benefits Received Taxable to Recipient?
Group Life				
Member	No	Yes	Yes	No
Dependent	No	Yes	Yes	No
Group AD&D	No	Yes	No	No
Survivor Income Benefit (1)				
Combined Coverage	No	Yes	Yes	Interest element only
Group Health (EHIP and Dental)	No(1)	Yes	No	No
Group Income Replacement (WI and LTD)	No	Yes	No	Yes(2)
Salary Continuance (sick pay)	N/A	Yes	N/A	Yes

(1)   Employee contributions deductible only under allowable medical expense deduction.

(2)   Benefit is not taxable (a) if employee-pay-all policy, or (b) until benefit payments exceed an employee's contributions.

VI. Provincial Health Care Programs

	Monthly Premium Rates (2007)		
Province	Single	Couple	Family
British Columbia	$54.00	$96.00	$108.00
Alberta (excl. seniors)	$44.00	$88.00	$88.00
Quebec, Ontario	Premium is per adult, dependent on income and collected through income tax returns		
Other Provinces	No premiums are required		

SECTION FOUR

ACTUARIAL PRACTICE IN A REGULATED ENVIRONMENT

17 GROUP INSURANCE FINANCIAL REPORTING: U.S.

James T. Blackledge
updated by Dick Glatz and Tim Harris

This chapter provides an overview of group insurance financial reporting, with particular attention to actuarial aspects. This chapter will not be a complete discussion of financial reporting issues, nor will it be a "recipe" for financial reporting. The discussion is generally from the point of view of a commercial insurance company. However, most of the concepts presented for commercial group insurers are also applicable to other carriers, such as HMOs, Blue Cross type corporations, and provider-sponsored organizations.

We will first discuss the various types of group insurance financial reporting, present group specific considerations involved in preparing financial reports, detail some of the specifics of annual statement financial reporting for group coverages, and present some of the recent developments affecting group financial reporting.

This chapter is written from the U.S. point of view. Specific Canadian issues are discussed in the next chapter.

TYPES OF GROUP INSURANCE FINANCIAL REPORTING

The major types of group insurance financial reporting include the following:

- Group Carrier Financial Reporting
  - Statutory (required under state laws and regulations)
  - GAAP (under generally accepted accounting principles)
  - Tax (U.S. federal income tax)
  - Managerial
- Policyholder Financial Reporting
- Provider Reporting

These six types of reporting are discussed in the following paragraphs.

STATUTORY

Statutory financial reporting refers to the accounting conventions required to be used by all life and health insurance companies to complete the NAIC annual statement blank. These annual statements are required to be filed with the state insurance departments of every state in which the insurer does business. Life insurance companies, HMO's, health service (Blue Cross / Blue Shield) corporations, and property-casualty companies write health insurance in the United States. Each company must report financial results on the life, the health, or the property-casualty annual statement blank. The domiciliary state has the discretion to decide which annual statement blank a company must file. If a life insurance or property-casualty company writes predominantly health lines of business, that company should file a health blank. According to the annual statement instructions, the state is guided by the Health Statement Test to determine if a company should file the health blank. This chapter discusses reporting from both the life blank and the health blank point of view.

The focus of these financial statements is to demonstrate the solvency of the insurer. As such, these financial reports have a balance sheet orientation, and conservative standards of asset and liability valuation are mandated.

Following are the major examples of this conservatism on the asset side of the balance sheet:

- Certain items are nonadmitted assets (assets not allowed in the determination of statutory solvency). These include agents' balances (amounts which are owed the insurer by agents), furniture and equipment, and properties used in business.
- The NAIC prescribes asset values to be used, rather than allowing flexibility.
- Deferred acquisition costs, which GAAP accounting allows as an offset to reserve liabilities, are not allowed.

There are a number of examples of conservatism on the liability side of the balance sheet, as well:

- The Commissioner's Reserve Valuation Method limits the recognition of expense allowances in life insurance and annuity reserves.

- Lapses may be assumed in policy reserve calculations only in specific circumstances, including certain health policy reserves. (This is of limited relevance to group insurance, since most group insurance doesn't generate policy reserves. Exceptions include group permanent life insurance and long term care benefits.)

- Minimum morbidity and mortality tables, which generally include material conservatism, are typically required when determining reserves.

- Maximum interest rates (to be used in setting reserves) are usually specified.

- AVR and IMR (Asset Valuation Reserve and Interest Maintenance Reserve), required reserves intended to provide a cushion against investment losses and interest rate fluctuations. (The AVR and IMR replace the Mandatory Securties Valuation Reserve, or MSVR. Not all of the entities providing health insurance are required to hold these reserves.)

Historically, actuaries have been more concerned with the liability side of statutory financial reporting. An actuarial opinion as to the adequacy of actuarial items is required to be filed with the annual statement. Generally, the items on which the opinion is based are included in Exhibit 5 (life insurance and annuity reserves), Exhibit 6 (health insurance reserves), Exhibit 7 (deposit-type contract reserves), Exhibit 8 (claim liabilities), and Page 3 (total liabilities and surplus) of the annual statement. This perspective has changed with the advent of asset adequacy analysis requirements, required by the current NAIC Standard Valuation Law (SVL) and the Actuarial Opinion and Memorandum Regulation (AOMR). The Model NAIC Valuation Law has been adopted by all states, but at the time of this writing there were two versions of the AOMR in use by states.

The major actuarial assumptions and methods of statutory financial reporting are generally specified in the SVL. In the past, these assumptions and methods have been viewed as a "recipe" for the actuary to follow that would allow him or her to opine that the reserves are adequate. The valuation actuary concept is a departure from this "cookbook" approach toward more responsibility and freedom for the actuary, to ensure that the reserves are, indeed, adequate. A continued departure from the cookbook approach is anticipated in the proposed Principles Based Reserve approach currently being developed. At the time of this update the elements of this approach are still in discussion.

GAAP

Group GAAP financial reporting refers to the accounting conventions adopted by the Financial Accounting Standards Board (FASB) in its Statement of Financial Accounting Standards (SFAS) No. 60: Accounting and Reporting by Insurance Enterprises. Additionally, SFAS No. 97 details GAAP for universal life type policies. Life and health insurers whose stock is publicly traded are required by the Securities and Exchange Commission (SEC) to prepare financial reports on a GAAP basis. Mutual companies have been required by the AICPA to use GAAP for statements ending December 15, 1997 and later, or risk having their audit opinion qualified as not conforming to GAAP.

GAAP financial reporting standards provide a consistent framework for comparing the financial results of different entities and attempt to more accurately reflect the earnings during a reporting period. The focus of GAAP is on the income statement. Accurate reporting of income by year and the trend in these numbers are important, since they are often used in securities valuations.

Statutory financial reporting emphasizes solvency and produces a conservative valuation of both assets and liabilities. As such, it can distort both the current level of earnings and the historical trend in earnings. The major modifications to statutory reporting necessary to produce GAAP financial results are as follows:

- Removal of some of the conservatism in reserving assumptions (GAAP reserves still include some conservatism, referred to as "provision for adverse deviation");
- Full recognition of deferred taxes;
- Recognition of the market value of most assets;
- Recognition of lapses in reserves;
- Capitalization of deferred acquisition costs;
- Recognition of all receivables and allowances; and
- Removal of the AVR and IMR

Conceptually, GAAP financial reporting attempts to match the incidence of revenues and expenses, while statutory financial reporting tends to accelerate expense recognition and delay revenue recognition (or at least offset revenue recognition with corresponding liabilities producing the same effect).

Statutory financial reporting attempts to determine the value of the insurer if it was forced to liquidate. GAAP financial reporting attempts to determine the value of the insurer on a going concern basis. In addition, the conservative assumptions required in many statutory reserve items can be replaced by a much less conservative GAAP margin for adverse deviation.

TAX

Tax financial reporting refers to the accounting conventions required by the various taxing authorities in the determination of the tax liability of life and health insurance companies. The discussion that follows will focus mainly on the impact on actuarial items of U.S. federal income tax requirements. State premium taxes and assessments will not be discussed. State income taxation exists in a minority of states, but is often offset by premium taxes.

In general, statutory financial reports are the starting point for tax reporting, with certain adjustments of reserve items. The most obvious example of these adjustments is the required use of minimum interest rates for tax reserves. These rates exceed the statutory maximum interest rates, and thus lower the recognized tax reserve and increase taxable income.

A related item which affects the taxable income of life and health insurers is the deferred acquisition cost (DAC) tax. The DAC tax is basically a requirement that insurers delay the recognition of certain expenses when calculating current taxable income. The expense deferred is not related to any real expense related to sales efforts or results, but is merely a specified percentage of in-force premium. The purported justification for the deferral is that the expense approximates the actual acquisition expenses which should have been deferred (in order to better match revenues and expenses). This provision has been compared to an interest free loan to the federal government, since the capitalized costs are recouped over a ten-year period. The DAC tax rate varies by product and applies to group life insurance, group annuities, and those group products which are treated as guaranteed renewable or non-cancelable H&A policies for tax purposes. Group long-term care contracts are often subject to this tax.

For tax basis calculations, group carriers must also reduce their provisions for refunds and unearned premiums by 20% for the purpose of determining their taxable income. Again, the intent of this provision is more relevant to insurance coverages with high acquisition expenses, but is applied to group business as well.

The reader should consult current tax laws before reviewing tax basis financial reports. Such a review will ensure an understanding of the current requirements and the information being reported to comply with them.

MANAGERIAL

Managerial financial reporting can be described as modifications of other financial reporting methods to provide a more accurate picture of the impact of management decisions on the value of the insurer.

Generally, managerial financial reporting starts from a GAAP basis, making adjustments to address GAAP's limitations. Examples of these limitations are the artificial limit on the deferrable acquisition costs, the use of reasonable and conservative reserve valuation assumptions rather than best estimates, and the lock-in of assumptions.

Following are several possible reasons to produce managerial financial reports:

- To measure financial results in alternate ways, such as by product, by cost center, or by strategic business unit.
- To relate financial results to pricing methods.
- To improve communication of results to management.
- To include projections of future experience, in order to determine the true "value" added by management during a reporting period.

Management reporting is discussed further in the chapter on experience analysis.

POLICYHOLDER

Policyholder financial reporting generally provides information for three purposes: information on the results of any risk-sharing arrangements, information to fulfill government reporting requirements, and information necessary for the policyholder to complete his or her own financial reports. Reporting of the financial consequences of risk-sharing arrangements provides the policyholder with documentation of the flow of funds involved in the insurance arrangement. The form and content of these reports depends upon the nature of the risk-sharing arrangement, and are discussed later in this chapter.

Government reporting requirements include reporting for ERISA (the federal law governing employer-sponsored plans) and Internal Revenue Service (IRS) reporting for Voluntary Employee Benefit Associations (VEBAs, or 501(C)9 trusts.) ERISA plans are generally required to complete Form 5500 annually, to be filed with the Department of Labor (DOL) and the IRS. VEBAs are required to file IRS Form 990, which is essentially a tax return for non-profit organizations. A VEBA may be subject to tax on non-exempt function income. Interest income on excess actuarial reserves may be considered non-exempt function income, but safe harbors are provided within the regulations.

Policyholders often need certain information in order to complete their own financial reports. Actuarial reserves for self-funded policies and reserveless policies are an example. Some policyholders may also desire estimates of retrospective premium liabilities or refunds payable. The proliferation of self-funding arrangements, and the rapid increase in medical costs increase the need for regular redetermination of actuarial reserves. Reports that assist policyholders with determining their liabilities arising from post-retirement benefits (required by SFAS No. 106) and from post-employment benefits (required by SFAS No. 112) are examples.

PROVIDER

Provider reporting generally provides information for two purposes: provider risk-sharing arrangements and medical management reporting.

Provider risk sharing refers to the practice of making a portion of the provider's reimbursement contingent upon the occurrence of certain events. It is a concept that is central to the operation of many Health Maintenance Organizations (HMOs). For example, the provider might enter into a contract with the HMO, trading fee-for-service reimbursement for capitation with a risk-sharing payment. The risk-sharing payment might be partially funded through a withhold, and partly out of current profits.

The risk-sharing payment is often linked to the level of utilization or the average cost per member of services over which the provider is felt to exercise some degree of control. Often, stop-loss mechanisms are used to reduce the impact of large claims on the provider's risk sharing payment.

The retrospective settlement of the risk-sharing payment and the financial implications to both the provider and the HMO create a need for reporting capabilities which support the settlement. In addition, providers who assume the risk associated with providing services may need to establish reserves in their own financial statements. Often, data for specific insureds or facilities must be tracked separately, in order to administer the settlement.

In addition to provider risk-sharing, medical management reporting is receiving more attention. Medical management reports may include reporting to regulatory entities, reporting to industry groups, and reporting to providers. Such reports are starting to contain increasing clinical information, including outcomes and other quality measures.

Several states have started requiring financial information related to health care in addition to the information found in the NAIC annual statement blank. With the concern over the impact of cost reduction on the quality of care, financial reporting to industry groups has increased. Finally, as health care payors become more aware of the impact of medical management on utilization, costs, and quality of care, reporting will increase.

SPECIFIC CONSIDERATIONS FOR GROUP INSURANCE

The major considerations in financial reporting for group insurance are the following:

- Alternative funding methods
- Policyholder accounting
- Administrative arrangements
- Excess coverages
- Regulatory requirements
- Other liabilities

ALTERNATIVE FUNDING METHODS

The introduction of alternative funding methods for group insurance complicates the various types of financial reporting previously discussed. In a pure insurance arrangement, the policyholder remits a fixed premium as consideration for complete indemnification of the covered benefits under the policy. From the insurer's standpoint, the financial results of all policies written this way can be aggregated. Thus, many of the actuarial items can be determined in the aggregate, or for groupings of policies with substantially similar characteristics. This means, for example, that the actuary may only need to determine one reserve to cover the incurred but unpaid claims for an entire block of business. By utilizing a large volume of data, the reserve can be more credible and require less margin for adverse deviation.

With some alternative funding methods, claim reserves must be determined at the policy level in order to determine the premium refund reserve associated with the policy. By segmenting claims data to the policy level, some credibility is lost. However, any increase in the margin in the claim reserves included in the refund calculation may simultaneously understate the refund reserve. (Some carriers avoid this problem by creating an explicit margin to claim reserves which is not included in the refund calculation.) Also, misestimation of the claim reserve can have a major adverse impact if the insurer refunds or releases funds to the policyholder that are eventually required to pay higher than anticipated claims runout.

Alternative funding methods span the risk transfer continuum from the fully-insured contract to a fully self-insured contract. In looking at financial reporting of alternative funding arrangements, administrative service fee income becomes a material element of reporting.

Where there is a retrospective premium rider, retrospective premiums create due and unpaid premiums on the financial statement. Under this type of contract, a group policyholder agrees to remit additional premiums (up to a cap) after a policy year is over, based on a retrospective look at the group's financial results. Generally a due and unpaid premium asset is calculated as of the valuation date, based on interim estimates of financial results. These financial results require estimates for claim reserves and expenses charged to the policyholder. Misestimation of these items can cause positive or negative financial results to emerge, once the final policyholder accounting is issued.

Retrospective experience rating refunds (or dividends, if the insurer is a mutual company) require calculation of an additional liability, generally called a refund reserve, dividend liability, or a rate credit reserve. An insurer may agree to let the policyholder share in any positive results generated by the policy (much like a dividend in individual participating life insurance). Similar to retrospective due and unpaid premiums, interim estimates of financial results are required to estimate the amount of any refund, and the current estimate is held as a liability on the financial statement.

Experience combinations refer to the practice of combining several policies of one policyholder prior to the determination of the financial results, allowing surplus under one policy to offset deficits on another. This can be accommodated on the financial statement by creation of category of assets and liabilities referred to as transfers.

Reserveless agreements refer to the situation where the policyholder holds the actuarial reserves for a policy. While the insurer must still set up claim reserves to cover this liability (because it is their contractual obligation to pay those claims), the policyholder promises to pay for those claims if the policy ever cancels. The policyholder may present a letter of credit to the insurer to secure this obligation. These agreements are often called terminal premiums, as they only become due and payable if the policy terminates. These terminal premiums are accounted for as offsets to the actuarial reserves, either as an asset or a negative liability. Terminal premiums can be used with nearly all forms of alternative funding methods. If used with refund arrangements, due and unpaid premiums or refund reserves can be affected. Unsecured terminal premiums can create some financial reporting problems. The valuation actuary needs to determine the level of security needed to allow terminal premiums to offset actuarial reserves for financial reporting. One possible approach would be to discount the value of the terminal reserve to reflect the probability of being able to collect it upon termination of the policy. This treatment requires ongoing evaluation of the financial risk of the policyholder.

In a minimum premium plan, the policyholder funds the claims portion of the policy with funds held in their own bank account, or reimburses the insurer for claims paid on the insurer's bank account. In most jurisdictions, the policyholder can avoid premium taxes on the claims portion of the premium by doing so. The self-funded portion of claims are often referred to as equivalents. The NAIC annual statement does not require the reporting of premium equivalents within the income statement. This is important to remember when comparing the annual statements of different group insurers. Minimum premium plans can be used in conjunction with other alternative funding methods (often retrospective refunds). The accounting for these plans is similar to that of the reserveless arrangements: claims are charged against the policyholder's funds first, and excess claims are then charged to the insurer.

Fee income can arise in a number of ways. Insurers may unbundled certain expense charges, and charge the policyholder for these on an "as used" basis. Examples would be fees charged for utilization review or preferred provider organization (PPO) access fees. Some policyholders use third party administrators to perform administrative duties for the insurer. In these instances, the insurer collects premiums paid by the policyholder and remits service fees to the third party administrator. A third type of fee income arises when the policyholder contracts with the insurer on an administrative services only (ASO) basis.

Accounting for fee income is similar to premium accounting. The main difference is that the fee income is often not immediately determinable. Fees are often charged in relation to the expense involved in the tasks performed. An example would be a claim administration expense, charged on a per draft basis. Such a charge would require knowledge of the number of drafts issued during an accounting period. For these reasons, estimates of fee income may be used in financial reports. ASO fees are reported as part of Exhibit 2 (General Expenses) for companies filing the NAIC annual statement blank for life and accident and health companies. (The net effect of ASO fee income and expenses associated with the administration of these contracts is typically disclosed in the Notes to Financial Statements section.)

POLICYHOLDER ACCOUNTING

In many alternative funding methods the policyholder participates in the insurance risk to some degree. This creates the need for financial reporting to the policyholder. It also requires special calculations whenever the insurer prepares its own financial reports.

As discussed previously, alternative funding arrangements generally require the estimation of policy level financial results on the valuation date, in order to determine the financial impact on the insurer. A simplified calculation of such policy level financial results might follow the following format:

Gain = (Collected Premium, less Pooled Premium)

    less (Paid Claims, less Pooled Claims)

    less (Ending Claim Reserve, less Beginning Claim Reserve)

    less (Expenses, Risk and Profit Charged, less Interest Credited)

When the bottom line is a loss, the insurer will determine if other funds are available to use as premium, which will depend on the funding arrangement. For example, if the policyholder agreed to provide an additional 5% of billed premium as a retrospective premium, the insurer would set up a due and unpaid premium reserve to cover the loss up to that 5% amount. This increases the amount of reported earned premiums. When the bottom line is a gain, the insurer will determine if the policyholder is eligible for a refund. The amount of the anticipated refund is a liability to the insurer, and is held as a refund reserve. The refund reserve lowers the reported earned premiums. (This reserve is often reported in Exhibit 6 of the NAIC annual statement under "reserve for rate credits.")

Since the policyholder is sharing in the risk of the policy, a financial report must be prepared detailing the results of the policy period. Typically, these reports are produced within two or three months after the end of the policy period. If the policy cancels, many insurers retain the right to wait up to fifteen months before issuing the final accounting. This reduces the risk of misestimation of any remaining claim reserves.

Producing policyholder reports soon after the policy period closes makes it necessary to estimate reserves for incurred but unpaid claims. These estimates are generally not the same as the estimates used in the insurer's financial statements, since the insurer has the benefit of greater hindsight regarding the claim runout. Since these estimates differ from the ones used in the insurer's financials, a gain or loss in the insurer's own financial reports may be recognized at the point the policyholder statement is issued.

Another consideration arises because of the insurer's distribution of policies by renewal date, which is often skewed toward the beginning of the year. This happens because many policyholders prefer January 1 as their renewal date. In the first quarter, the insurer may have a higher than normal amount of policyholder accounting statements issued. This can create a reported gain or loss in the first quarter, which probably was attributable to the prior calendar year and ideally should have been reported on the prior year's annual statement.

For certain funding arrangements in a positive financial position, increasing the claim reserve within certain limits will merely decrease the refund reserve, and vice versa. This phenomena provides an automatic source of margin in setting claim reserves, at least until issuance of the policyholder's statement. However, once a refund is paid, a loss may not be recoverable, at least until the next policy period.

ADMINISTRATIVE SERVICE AGREEMENTS

In addition to alternative funding methods, policyholders may enter into administrative service agreements with a insurer. Some of these arrangements were discussed under the heading of fee income. The main types of administrative arrangements are the following:

- Self-administration,
- Third-party administration,
- Funds held by the insurer,
- Funds held by the policyholder, and
- Premium billing.

Self-administration refers to the transfer of responsibilities normally performed by the insurer (such as premium billing or eligibility functions) to the policyholder. Transferring these responsibilities to the policyholder may make it more difficult to estimate assets and liabilities for the financial statements. For example, if the policyholder is responsible for determining the amount of premium owed to the insurer, the insurer may not be able to accurately estimate the amount of any due and unpaid premium. Claim reserves may be similarly affected by policyholders that pay their own claims or determine eligibility for claim payments.

Third-party administration refers to the transfer of responsibilities normally performed by the insurer (usually claims payment, but sometimes also premium billing or eligibility functions) to a third party. The same financial reporting concerns as with self-administration apply. In addition, the introduction of a third party into the chain of correspondence may lengthen the period from the point that a claim is incurred until it is eventually paid. Thus, the claim reserve estimate may need to be adjusted. The actuary should be aware of differences in the method of processing claims, the definition of incurred dates, and differences in claim adjudication, and how these impact the financial statements.

In both self-administration and third-party administration, the insurer will generally reserve the right to audit the functions performed. This provides some protection against inappropriate practices which may adversely affect the financial results of the insurer.

Funds held by the insurer refer to policyholder money left on deposit in an account with the insurer. These usually take the form of premium stabilization reserves or funds (PSRs or PSFs), also called Rate Stabilization Reserves, or straight deposits. An insurer may require a PSR as a margin against adverse experience, before agreeing to certain funding arrangements. Generally, PSRs are considered in the calculation of refund reserve. Straight deposits are usually not available to the insurer, and are not considered in the refund reserve calculation.

Deposits will also impact financial reporting when interest is credited to the policyholder. The insurer will recognize a gain or a loss depending on the difference between net investment income earned on these funds and the interest credited.

Funds held by the policyholder refer to reserves, self-funded claims, or other items held by the policyholder but subject to the insurance contract. The policyholder may establish a line of credit to ensure payment of retrospective premiums or terminal premiums. These items are accounted for as if the insurer had possession of the funds.

Premium billing methods can affect the calculation of due and unpaid premiums or refund reserves. Examples are non-monthly premiums and delayed premiums (premium drags). Non-monthly premiums create administrative difficulties, but otherwise do not pose a problem. Delayed premiums can introduce the risk of non-payment and so the financial solvency of the policyholder should by underwritten at issue and renewal.

Stop-loss coverages (specific or aggregate) are generally written to limit the policyholder's exposure to losses on an underlying policy administered by the insurer, the policyholder or a third party. If the coverage is sold with level premiums, the durational nature of the claim liabilities (heavily increasing as the duration increases) suggests an unearned premium or policy reserve may be appropriate, in addition to normal reserves.

REGULATORY REQUIREMENTS

Certain regulatory requirements can impact the liabilities of group insurers. The valuation laws of each state specify reserve assumptions and methodologies. In the past, it was generally sufficient to satisfy the requirements of the state of domicile of the insurer. More and more, states are revising their requirements to cover any insurer doing business in their state. To the extent these laws differ, an insurer might be required to use the most conservative state's law as the basis of its statutory financial reporting.

The NAIC has developed a model Actuarial Opinion and Memorandum Regulation that has been adopted, presently in two different forms, by the states. This regulation sets forth the requirements for an actuary who signs a statement of opinion as to the adequacy of annual statement reserves in light of the underlying assets. It also provides sample wording for the actuarial opinion. The regulation also specifies when asset adequacy analysis is required for insurance companies.

Asset adequacy analysis has been an annual statement requirement since 1992. Basically, the actuarial opinion must include a statement as to whether or not asset adequacy analysis was done as part of the determination of the adequacy of the reserves. Companies may need to set aside aggregate reserves beyond the statutory based minimum reserves, based on their asset adequacy analysis. The valuation actuary will typically disclose the type of asset adequacy analysis that was done as part of the actuarial opinion on reserves, which accompanies the annual statement. Most group coverages seem to be relatively insensitive to asset adequacy scenarios.

State specific health care reform initiatives may also create new financial reporting requirements for insurers. Some states use assessments to fund risk pools and to subsidize payors using community rating techniques. Financial reporting is typically required to determine both the total assessment and the amount to be allocated to each payor.

MISCELLANEOUS

Provider Incentive Arrangements

These arrangements are most common in HMOs, but have also been used with PPOs and other managed care products. Generally, these arrangements involve financial rewards for providers tied to specific performance objectives. These arrangements require estimates of their value on the valuation date, to measure their impact on the financial results of the insurer. A liability must be shown to reflect the amounts that may eventually be paid to providers under the terms of the incentive arrangement.

Another complicating factor is in the way provider incentives are administered. The incentives are generally calculated based on the specific insureds a provider treats, rather than at a group level. This requires a mechanism to allocate the provider's incentive payment to each of the insurer's groups. This is a particular problem with policyholder accounting for alternative funding contracts.

Capitated Provider Contracts

These are quite common in HMOs, and may require unique treatment in the HMO financial statement. Under a capitation contract the insurance risk is transferred from the HMO to the provider, which would generally eliminate the HMO's liability for the capitated services. However, in some situations the capitated entity may not have the financial strength to assume the capitated risk, and the HMO may end up assuming some of the capitated risk. Therefore, a reserve may need to be established, even though the HMO has capitated a provider.

Uncovered Expenditures

These are costs to an HMO or managed health care plan that are the obligation of the HMO, for which the HMO enrollee may also be liable in the event of the HMO's insolvency. Statutory requirements for HMOs generally require that the HMO allocate its liabilities between uncovered and covered expenditures.

Deficit Carryforwards

These arise from alternative funded groups which incur a deficit and renew their policy for another period. If these are recognized on the financial statement, they can be a significant source of gain in future periods. An important issue is whether to anticipate recoveries of these deficits in determining financial results. GAAP accounting principles seem to imply that these deficits be carried as assets at their realizable value. Statutory financial reporting practice is to ignore these deficit carryforwards, unless there is a contractual agreement between the insurer and an employer that requires the employer to pay deficit carryforwards in case of termination of coverage.

Interest on Policy Funds

Interest on policy funds held by the insurer on behalf of the policyholder creates a liability to the insurer, to the extent these funds must ultimately be credited to the policyholder. Interest earned in excess of that credited to the policyholder will be a gain to the insurer. In alternative funding contracts, interest on policy funds may be accounted for as a separate item to policyholders, or it may be used as an offset to expenses.

Policy Year Accounting

This will often differ from the statutory accounting period (calendar year) or the fiscal accounting period. We have already mentioned that the timing of the issuance of the policyholder accounting may impact the financial results where policyholder accounting items differ from the estimates included in the statutory or GAAP financial reports.

Multi-Year Rate Guarantees

In response to competitive pressures, many payors offer rate guarantees that extend beyond the more typical one-year term. The payor needs to check whether regulatory approval of multi-year rate guarantees is required. In addition, the actuary needs to consider whether multi-year rate guarantees require additional reserves. The main consideration is whether a significant component of current premiums is related to an advance funding of future claims. If so, the actuary may consider establishing an unearned premium or active life reserve.

Retention Formulas

Retention represents charges made to a policyholder by an insurer for all items other than claims themselves, such as risk, taxes, and expenses. Retention may be determined using factors or formulas, or based on an actual accounting. Retention charges are an important part of the accounting for alternative funding methods. Retention may be difficult or impossible to determine for certain insurers, such as staff model HMOs, where the line between claims and expenses is hazy.

In order to determine whether a policy is generating a gain or a loss for the period, each element of gain or loss, including expenses, must be estimated. Interim estimates of expenses may differ from what actually gets charged to the policyholder in policyholder accounting. These differences will be gains or losses in the insurer's financial reports in the period in which accounting is finalized.

SPECIFIC ANNUAL STATEMENT CONSIDERATIONS

There are different annual statement blanks required for life companies, HMOs, health service corporations, and property-casualty companies. The following describes the specific pages in the life and health blanks that deal with actuarial reserves and liabilities.

LIFE BLANK

The following items refer to particular pages, exhibits, and schedules in the life company blank.

Liabilities, Surplus, and Other Funds (Page 3)

Page 3 of the annual statement summarizes the company's total liabilities. Items of particular note include the following:

- Line 9.2, provision for experience rating refunds, which arise from policies subject to retrospective experience rating agreements.
- Line 12, general expenses due or accrued, including the loss adjustment expense reserve. This is a reserve for the expense cost of administering the claims represented by the claim reserve.

Other actuarial items are also included on page 3, but are provided in greater detail in other exhibits discussed later.

Analysis of Operations (Page 6)

The analysis of operations by line of business details the statutory operating results. Items specific to the group line include the group conversion expense, transfers between lines of business, interest on policy or contract funds, and loadings on life policies.

Group conversions often create losses, which may be more appropriately charged to the group line of business than the individual line, as a cost of doing business. Transfers between lines of business, such as for conversions, allow greater accuracy in reporting each line's results.

Analysis of Increase in Reserves during the Year (Page 7)

Group insurance practices create several difficulties in completing this analysis. For instance, the majority of group life products do not require active life reserves. Also, tabular premiums in the same sense as for individual life products are not determined. Rather, premiums are determined on an aggregate basis.

Generally, Exhibit 5 reserves are used as the basis for this analysis. These include reserves for paid up life policies and waiver of premium riders, as well as annuity active life reserves. Tabular premiums are often assumed to be a percent of Exhibit 1 premiums.

Exhibit 5

Exhibit 5 details aggregate reserves for life policies. As mentioned, active life reserves are less significant for group insurance. Secondary benefits such as reserves for waiver of premium, total and permanent disability benefits, and survivor benefits are included.

Exhibit 6

Exhibit 6 details aggregate reserves for A&H policies. These include active and disabled life reserves, unearned premium reserves, reserves for rate credits, and reserves for future contingent benefits. Unearned premium reserves for group A&H policies are generally less significant than for individual A&H policies. Many group policies have monthly premium modes with premium due on the first of the month.

Additional or policy reserves are also generally less significant for group policies than for individual policies, due to the yearly renewable term nature of most group coverages and the associated ability to increase rates annually.

Exhibit 7

Exhibit 7 shows deposit funds and other liabilities. The major group items are typically for guaranteed investment contracts (for insurance companies that offer these) and other deposit funds.

Exhibit 8

Exhibit 8 details liabilities for the accrued but unpaid portion of incurred policy and contract claims. Incurred but not reported (IBNR) and claims in course of settlement (ICOS) are reported separately.

As a practical matter, most group insurers determine the sum of ICOS and IBNR liabilities. This calculation is based on as up-to-date statistics as possible and is reconsidered carefully at each valuation. The total is then allocated between ICOS and IBNR based on percentages which are determined less frequently.

Schedule H

Schedule H is the A&H Exhibit. Among other things, the exhibit includes a test of adequacy of the previous year's claim reserves.

A major consideration for group insurance is the impact of alternative funding methods on the reserve adequacy. As mentioned earlier, refund reserves are generally available as a margin against high claims runout until the refund is actually payable. These refund reserves are not considered in the reserve test. Although not specific to the group line, the practice of ignoring investment income on reserves adversely affects this test.

Schedule O

Schedule O is the Development of Incurred Losses. The exhibit presents reported incurred claims by calendar year and tracks them over subsequent calendar years. Generally, a decreasing amount shows redundancy in the prior year's reserves.

LTC Experience Statements

Experience statements on Long-Term Care insurance are required as a supplement to the annual statement filing. These exhibits attempt to show the development of long-term care claims experience relative to the pricing assumptions.

Actuarial Opinion and Memorandum

As discussed previously, the NAIC's Actuarial Opinion and Memorandum model law creates additional requirements for the actuary who signs the opinion on reserves for the annual statement filing. These additional requirements may include asset adequacy analysis.

There are a number of Actuarial Standards of Practice (professional standards of practice, promulgated by the Actuarial Standards Board) that directly relate to these topics, including: (1) ASOP No. 7, "Analysis of Life, Health, or Property/Casualty Insurer Cash Flows," (2) ASOP No. 22, "Statements of Opinion Based on Asset Adequacy Analysis by Actuaries for Life or Health Insurers," and (3) ASOP No. 28, "Compliance with Statutory Statement of Actuarial Opinion Requirements for Hospital, Medical, and Dental Service or Indemnity Corporations, and for Health Maintenance Organizations."

Management's Discussion and Analysis

A somewhat related supplement to the annual statement filing is Management's Discussion and Analysis. Although not necessarily actuarial in its focus, the actuary may be prevailed upon to assist with or to complete this analysis. This analysis is intended to enhance the regulator's understanding of the insurer's financial condition. The discussion focuses on material changes in the annual statement from year to year and on known material events that may affect the insurer's future financial position or operating results. Further information related to this analysis is included in the annual statement instructions, and can be obtained from the NAIC's Publications Department.

HEALTH BLANK

The health blank replaced the HMO blank and the Health Service Corporation blank for the 2001 annual statement. Generally, an actuary will only be concerned with the Liabilities, Capital and Surplus page and the Underwriting and Investment Exhibits. However, the following list of exhibits may be of interest:

- Liabilities, Capital and Surplus (page 3),
- Analysis of Operations by Lines of Business (page 7),
- Underwriting and Investment Exhibit, Part 2 (pages 9-13),
- Exhibit 4 – Claims Payable (page 20),
- Exhibit 7 – Summary of Transactions with Providers (page 23),
- Notes to Financial Statements (page 25),
- General Interrogatories (pages 27-28.1),
- Exhibit of Premiums, Enrollment and Utilization (page 30),
- Schedule S (pages 44-49), and
- Supplemental Exhibits and Schedules Interrogatories.

Liabilities, Capital and Surplus

Page 3 of the annual statement summarizes the company's total liabilities, capital and surplus. This page has been recast and now more clearly delineate the actuarial and related items. The first seven items are of particular note: claims unpaid, accrued medical incentive pool and bonus payments, unpaid claims adjustment expenses, aggregate health policy reserves, aggregate life policy reserves, property/casualty unearned premium reserves, and aggregate health claim reserves. These seven items as well as any actuarial liabilities included as a write-in item are typically included when an actuary is asked to certify the reserves in the annual statement.

Analysis of Operations by Lines of Business

Also known as the Gain and Loss Exhibit, the Analysis of Operations by Lines of Business provides the income statement details for various health products. The product detail is much greater than with prior statement blanks, particularly with respect to dental, stop loss, disability income, and long term care. There are several actuarial items displayed, including: incentive pool and withhold adjustments, net reinsurance recoveries, claim adjustment expenses, and the increase in reserves for accident and health contracts.

Underwriting and Investment Exhibit

This exhibit, in addition to a number of other purposes, replaces Schedule H from the former statement blank. Part 2A - Claims Liability End of Current Year shows the detail of the net reserve included on Line 1 of the Liabilities, Capital and Surplus page. The sufficiency of last year's reserve for unpaid claims can be seen in Part 2B - Analysis of Claims Unpaid - Prior Year - Net of Reinsurance. Part 2D - Aggregate Reserve for Accident and Health Contracts shows the details of Line 4, aggregate policy reserves, and Line 7, aggregate claim reserves from the Liabilities, Capital and Surplus page.

Exhibit 4 – Claims Payable

The Claims Payable exhibit shows the detail of the total claims payable including an aging schedule for known claims.

Exhibit 7 – Summary of Transactions with Providers

The Summary of Transactions with Providers shows the amount of payments made to providers by the type of reimbursement, such as capitation, fee-for-service, contractual fee payments, bonus/withhold arrangements, and salaries. This information is used in the calculation of risk-based capital for the health company.

Notes to Financial Statements

The Notes to Financial Statements include remarks on several items of interest to actuaries:

- health cost recognition,
- contingencies,
- reinsurance,
- retrospectively rated contracts and contracts subject to redetermination,
- change in incurred claims and claim adjustment expenses, and
- premium deficiency reserves.

General Interrogatories

Part 1 (Common Interrogatories) of the General Interrogatories includes the name and the address of the actuary who provides the statement of actuarial opinion/certification. Part 2 (Health Interrogatories) contains additional detail on items including stop loss reinsurance and premium rate guarantees.

Exhibit of Premiums, Enrollment and Utilization (page 30)

For each of the medical product lines along with vision and dental, the Exhibit of Premiums, Enrollment and Utilization shows:

- membership for the prior year and each quarter of the statement year,
- annual utilization data for physicians, non-physicians, hospital days and admissions,
- premiums collected and earned, and
- claims paid and incurred.

Schedule S (pages 44-49)

Schedule S shows reinsurance information for the health plan.

Supplemental Exhibits and Schedules Interrogatories

The Supplemental Exhibits and Schedules Interrogatories asks several questions that may be of direct interest to actuaries, generally related to whether the supplemental exhibits (actuarial certifications, risk-based capital calculations, management's discussion and analysis, and the long-term care experience reporting forms) will be filed timely.

RELATED ISSUES AND RECENT DEVELOPMENTS

A number of related issues and recent developments deserve comment as they impact financial reporting.

PREMIUM DEFICIENCY RESERVES

Premium deficiency reserves have been receiving more attention in recent years. The codification of statutory accounting principles set forth specific requirements for premium deficiency reserves. (Codification is discussed in more detail in the following section.) In general, codification requires that premium deficiency reserves be established when expected claim payments and administrative costs exceed premiums for the remainder of a contract period. Premium deficiency reserves are discussed in more detail in chapter 20 on Actuarial Certification of Reserves.

SFAS NO. 97

GAAP accounting principles, as described in SFAS No. 60, were developed prior to the proliferation of universal life policies. In order to handle the unique flexible product features, SFAS No. 97 was developed.[1]

SFAS NO. 106 AND NO. 112

SFAS No. 106 is FASB's statement on accounting for post retirement benefits other than pensions. The rapid increase in health care costs and promises to provide retirees medical care for life have combined to create very large unfunded liabilities for many employers. These benefits have traditionally been funded on a pay as you go basis. SFAS No. 106 generally requires that the liability for these benefits be determined and expensed according to a recognized actuarial funding method. This will not only impact the financial statements of insurers' clients, but of the insurers themselves as employers.[2]

SFAS No. 112 is FASB's statement on accounting for post-employment benefits. Post-employment benefits include severance pay, continuation of life and health insurance, outplacement assistance, and so on. The post-employment benefits covered by SFAS No. 112 do *not* include pensions or other postretirement benefits. According to SFAS No. 112, employers must accrue annually over time the costs associated with post-employment benefits that meet certain conditions.

THE VALUATION ACTUARY

The valuation actuary concept will increase the public's reliance on the actuary to ensure the solvency of the carrier. Implementation of the concept may impact financial reporting as actuaries move away from defined reserve assumptions towards more appropriate assumptions based on circumstances specific to the insurer. Also, statutory reporting requirements may become less conservative, leaving the valuation actuary responsible for determining a reasonable level of conservatism.

---

[1] SFAS No. 97, "Accounting and Reporting by Insurance Enterprises for Certain Long-Duration Contracts and for Realized Gains and Losses for the Sale of Securities," Financial Accounting Standards Board.

[2] SFAS No. 106, "Accounting for Post-Retirement Benefits Other than Pensions," Financial Accounting Standards Board.

ASSET ADEQUACY ANALYSIS

As mentioned earlier, asset adequacy analysis has been required in some actuarial certifications since 1992. Asset adequacy testing can impact statutory financial reporting in that testing may indicate the need for greater reserves.

RATING AGENCIES

Financial reporting can be impacted by the desire of insurers to gain the highest possible rating from the various rating agencies. Risk-based capital and assigned surplus formulas are often used to determine the appropriate level of surplus that should be maintained.

CODIFICATION (STATUTORY ACCOUNTING PRINCIPLES)

The National Association of Insurance Commissioners codified Statutory Accounting Principles effective January 1, 2001. The codification is contained in the "Accounting Practices and Procedures Manual." As of each March, the Manual is updated for that year. The text is a wealth of information for accountants and actuaries alike. Of particular interest to actuaries are SSAP No. 51, "Life Contracts," SSAP No. 54, "Individual and Group Accident and Health Contracts," and SSAP No. 55, "Unpaid Claims, Losses and Loss Adjustment Expenses." In addition, "Appendix C – Actuarial Guidelines," provides a single reference source for the NAIC's guidance to actuaries.

SUMMARY AND CONCLUSIONS

In conclusion, there are special considerations to financial reporting for group insurance, primarily due to the flexibility in financing of group products. The group market has continued to evolve with new funding arrangements and products. It is important that anyone attempting financial reporting for group insurance understand the current environment, keeping up with the changes taking place.

18 Group Insurance Financial Reporting: Canada

J. Harvey Campbell
Pierre Saddik

Financial Reporting in Canada

This chapter is a summary of group insurance financial reporting from a Canadian perspective, from the point of view of a domestic federally licensed life insurance company. Other group carriers will have basically similar reporting requirements.

The evolution of regulatory financial reporting continues unabated as Canadian GAAP converges to the International Financial Accounting Standards. The latest significant change was the introduction of Section 3855, Financial Instruments – Recognition and Measurement into the handbook of the Canadian Institute of Chartered Accountants. Section 3855 gives companies choices for classifying their financial assets and financial liabilities, each option having different measurement and recognition requirements. Life insurance policies are not considered as financial liabilities with the exception of certain financial reinsurance agreements.

The major considerations in financial reporting for group insurance in Canada are very similar to those in the U.S. There are, however, significant differences in the regulatory environment

Types of Group Insurance Financial Reporting

Financial reporting can be for the insurance company or to policyholders. Company reporting can be on various bases: statutory, tax (according to the Canadian Income Tax Act), management, and consumer protection plan.

Statutory

Statutory financial reporting refers to the accounting policies used to complete the Life-1 annual statement. A life company is required to file this

357

completed statement with the Office of the Superintendent of Financial Institutions of Canada. It is important to note that an insurer can only publish financial statements which are based on statutory accounting, although the large Canadian stock companies are showing US GAAP results in a note to the financial statements. The use of two financial statements on different bases, such as occurs in the United States, is not allowed. This arises from the requirement of the regulatory authorities to use Canadian GAAP in the preparation of the annual statement except as otherwise specified by the Superintendent.

Generally accepted accounting principles for Canada are published in a handbook prepared by the Canadian Institute of Chartered Accountants (CICA). Specific items applicable to insurance companies are contained in Section 4211. The GAAP approach in Canada emphasizes the consistency of the income statement and an accurate matching of expenses to revenue, in a similar fashion as GAAP in the United States. The new rules for asset values require a classification of assets into one of the following: Held to Maturity (HTM), Loans and Receivables (Loans), Available for Sale (AFS), Held for Trading (HFT), and Real Estate (RE). Assets are valued at fair value except for Loans and HTM, which are valued at amortized cost. Income taxes are on an incurred basis, using the asset and liability method of accounting for income taxes.

Actuarial liabilities should be calculated according to the recommendations of the CICA Handbook. The handbook calls for a determination of actuarial liabilities using the *Canadian asset liability method*. This method defines reserves to be the amount equal to the carrying value of the insurance enterprise's assets that, taking into account the other pertinent items on the balance sheet, will be sufficient without being excessive to discharge the enterprise's obligations over the term of the liabilities for its insurance policies (including annuity contracts), and to pay expenses related to the administration of those policies. Most insurance companies are classifying assets which back liabilities as either AFS or HFT, which effectively causes actuarial liabilities to be valued at fair value, and introduces the possibility of significant volatility in the value of the actuarial liabilities.

All elements which can impact the financial results should be included in the valuation.

In performing the calculation of actuarial liabilities, the general principles that should be adhered to, according to the CICA Handbook, are the following:

- Liabilities should be computed on a going concern basis.

- The use of expected experience and a separate provision for adverse deviation (PFAD) whenever an assumption about future events is required. The PFAD should be limited and reasonable. This is quite different from U.S. statutory reporting in that there are no mandated bases for reserve calculations.

- All acquisition costs, without arbitrary limits, should be incorporated in the computation of actuarial liabilities.

- Most costs should be included, except for income taxes, marketing overhead, and shareholder transfer.

- Surrender privileges and policy lapsation should be considered.

These principles have been accepted by regulatory authorities but with strengthened solvency safeguards. A description of the safeguards can be found in the Regulatory Requirements section of this Chapter.

Tax

An insurance company is subject to a variety of taxes such as federal income tax, investment income tax, provincial income tax, taxes on capital (federal and provincial), other general business taxes, and premium tax. Of these taxes, only federal income tax and investment income tax will be discussed. Provincial income tax is usually based on the federal calculation. The other taxes are calculated in a straightforward manner.

Federal income tax starts with the income based on statutory accounting, and is then adjusted by modifying a number of income and expense items. For group insurance, the four most important items are: (1) changes in actuarial reserves, (2) reserves for incurred but unreported claims, (3) provisions for deferred policy acquisition costs and (4) provisions for experience rating refunds. Various sections of the income tax act ensure that the deductions for the increases in these items are reasonable, justified, and not more than the corresponding statutory expense. For group term insurance that provides coverage for a period not exceeding 12 months, the actuarial reserve is limited to an unearned gross premium reserve determined by apportioning the premium paid equally over the policy period. Tax reserves for amounts due after the valuation date on known claims incurred prior to that date are generally limited to 95% of the statutory reserves. The reserve for incurred but unreported claims is limited to 95% of the statutory reserve. Expenses incurred on account of the acquisition of an insurance policy (other than a non-can or guaranteed renewable accident and sickness policy or life policies except group term life with a coverage period of 12 months or less) must be capitalized and amortized over the term of the policy where the term extends beyond the end of the taxation year. The provision for experience rating refunds is limited to amounts which will ultimately be paid or unconditionally credited to the policyholder but not greater than 25% of the annual premium, a reasonable amount, or the amount of the statutory reserve. Investment income tax, at the rate of 15%, is paid by life insurers on investment income earned on assets supporting the following liabilities:

- Group life insurance contract rate stabilization reserves
- Group life active life reserves (paid-up, level premium, conversions)
- Experience rating refund liabilities which are not due within twelve months

Management

The same considerations as apply to U.S. management reporting apply in Canada.

Consumer Protection Plan

The life insurance industry in Canada established a consumer protection plan in 1990 (known as Assuris) which indemnifies (within certain limits) the policyholders of an insurance company in the event of the insolvency of the company. Assuris is a not-for-profit organization funded by the entire life insurance industry in Canada. All direct writing companies are obligated to belong to the plan and are required to file with the industry organization which administers the plan, the statutory calculation of minimum surplus requirements (see MCCSR calculation below). The minimum surplus standard is based on risk factors applied to the actual asset mix and liabilities of the company. This is similar to RBC calculations as they now exist in U.S. financial reporting.

Policyholder Reporting

Policyholder financial reporting in Canada is similar to the United States, with the exception of governmental reporting requirements. In Canada, the insurer must issue to the policyholder income tax forms (T-4) for taxable disability income benefits and interest earnings forms (T-5) for death-related benefits, including lump sum and survivor income benefits. In addition, an insurer must issue T-5 for any interest earned on rate stabilization reserves if such reserves exceed 25% of the policyholder's annual premium.

Finally, interest credited to refund deposit accounts is to be reported to tax authorities, as it represents income taxable in the hands of the policyholder.

REGULATORY REQUIREMENTS

The federal law requires that an insurer's board of directors appoint an actuary who must be a Fellow of the Canadian Institute of Actuaries (the appointed actuary). The actuary must value the actuarial and other policy liabilities of the company, as well as any other matter specified by the Superintendent. The actuary's valuation must be done in accordance with generally accepted actuarial practice with such changes as may be specified by the Superintendent.

Generally accepted actuarial practice is the responsibility of the Canadian Institute of Actuaries (CIA), and current practice is to be found in the Standards of Practice. The General Standards, Section 1000 edicts that the standards are the only explicit articulation of accepted actuarial practice. Explanations, examples, and other useful guidance may be found in educational notes, historical standards, and other actuarial literature. The Practice-Specific Standards for Insurers, Section 2300, Life and Health Insurance articulate the standards which apply to insurers including group insurance. . This standard requires reserves to be calculated using scenario projections of asset and liability cash flows, including margins for adverse deviation, rather than the discounting of expected benefits at predetermined interest rates. The reserve is equal to the carrying value of a group of assets necessary to provide sufficient cash flow to meet the total liability cash flows as they become due.

There are no specific articles related to group insurance. The concepts and methods are considered to be universal in their application. There are examples of how concepts should be applied in specific types of group contracts. A significant concept in the standard is the term of liabilities. For group policies with no constraints, the term of the liabilities is the first renewal after the valuation date.

There are a number of other solvency safeguards contained in the legislation, especially Sections 368 and 369 of the Canadian Insurance Companies Act. These include the following.

- The actuary is required to examine the current and future solvency position of the company.

- The actuary is required to report to the chief executive officer and the chief financial officer any matters that have come to the actuary's attention in the course of carrying out the actuary's duties and in the actuary's opinion have material adverse effects on the financial position of the company and require rectification.

- A copy of the report referred to above is to be provided to the directors.

- If, in the opinion of the actuary, suitable action is not being taken to rectify the matter, the actuary shall send a copy of the report to the Superintendent.

ANNUAL STATEMENT CONSIDERATIONS

The current version of the annual statement provided to the regulator (Life-1) was introduced in 2005, and the description that follows is based on this version. This statement does not have exhibit or statement identifiers, but rather page numbers are used which are intended to be permanent for each statement and exhibit. The annual statement is divided into several sections including corporate information (pages starting 10.00), consolidated financial statements (pages starting 20.010), detailed insurance and financial information (pages starting 21.010, 22.010, 23.01, 35.01, and 45.01), segregated fund information (pages starting 60.01), non-consolidated financial statements (pages starting 70.02), and miscellaneous exhibits (pages starting 75.01 and 95.01). Consolidated financial statements would include ancillary corporations which could include other insurance companies. Non-consolidated exhibits relate only to the life company. A reasonably complete instruction guide for filling out all the pages is available. The major items, which concern group insurance, are given in the following paragraphs.

Pages 20.020, 35.070, and 70.020: Liabilities, Policyholders' and Shareholders' Equity Consolidated, Consolidated by Territory, and Non-Consolidated
(The line numbers below refer to page 20.020)

- *Line 010, Net Actuarial Liabilities.* The calculation of actuarial reserves is detailed on pages 22.010 and 22.020, which are discussed below. These reserves include the present value of payments to lives already disabled, survivors benefit reserves, active lives reserves and unearned premiums. Reserves for accident and sickness business are included in this line.

- *Line 040, Other Insurance Policy & Contract Liabilities.* This would include provisions for premiums paid in advance, policy-holder dividends, amounts on deposit, experience rating refunds, and outstanding reported claims which are normally accounted for on an exact basis. The provision for unreported claims is estimated using appropriate techniques. Greater detail is developed on page 22.020. There is no separate reporting for claims in course of settlement.

Pages 20.030 and 70.030: Income Statement Consolidated and Non-Consolidated

All lines of business are grouped together on these pages with details by line on supplementary pages.

Page 20.080: Appointed Actuary's report

The appointed actuary's report is as prescribed by the Canadian Institute of Actuaries and is as follows:

To the policyholders [and shareholders] of [the ABC Insurance Company]:

I have valued the policy liabilities of [the Company] for its [consolidated] balance sheet at [December 31 xxxx] and their change in the statement of income for the year then ended in accordance with accepted actuarial practice, including selection of appropriate assumptions and methods.

In my opinion, the amount of policy liabilities makes appropriate provision for all policyholder obligations and the [consolidated] financial statements fairly present the results of the valuation.

Page 22.010 Actuarial Liabilities by Line of Business – Canada and U.S.A. (Consolidated) and Page 75.030 Actuarial Liabilities by Line of Business – In Canada (Non-consolidated)

These exhibits give a summary of the direct, assumed, ceded, and net reserves for each line of business, which includes non-par group life, non par group annuity, and non-par group accident and sickness.

Page 22.020 Other Insurance Policy and Contract Liabilities

The liabilities are shown separately for provisions for premiums paid in advance, policyholder dividends, amounts on deposit, experience rating refunds, and outstanding reported claims. However there is no separation by line of business.

Page 35.010 Analysis of Income by Line of Business- Canada
Page 35.020 Analysis of Income by Line of Business- U.S.A.

A development of income for the major lines is required, including non-par group insurance, non-par group annuity, and non-par group accident and sickness for Canadian Business (Page 35.010) and US business (Page 35.020). Accounting ledgers will provide the totals for most of the items, except for net investment income and general expenses. These two items must be approximated in a reasonable and consistent manner. Fee income for administrative services must be distinguished from premium income.

Page 35.030 Analysis of Income by Line of Business- Summary

The insurance lines including all group insurance are combined by territory on this page. The territories are Canada, & U.S.A., Europe, and Asia/ Other.

Page 35.040 Analysis of Sales (premiums and Deposits) by Major line of Business and Territory

This page details the new annualized premiums on new policies sold in the reporting period or the equivalent for deposit and fee income. The group business is divided into protection type business, deposits, and ASO fees. The reporting is by territory using the same territories as for page 35.030.

Page 45.010 Premiums and Commissions – Canada
Page 45.020 Premiums and Commissions – U.S.A.

These pages require information on single premiums, first year premiums and renewal premiums for the non-par group life, the non-par group annuity, and the non-par group accident and sickness lines of business. The same information is required for commissions. The information for Page 45.010 relates to policies issued in Canada as defined in the Insurance Companies Act. The information for page 45.020 relates to policies issued to residents of the United States.

Page 75.04 Analysis of Amounts of Life Insurance – Effected and In Force

For both inforce and new effected, the amounts of life insurance for direct business, for reinsurance assumed business and for reinsurance ceded business are required for group par and group non par.

Page 75.060 Movement of Annuities (Gross) – Group Annuities

The exhibit shows the beginning and ending inforce, and the movements in the year, for accumulation, payout, and disability group annuities. Inforce reinsurance accepted and ceded at year end are also shown. The exhibit is a simple summary of complex products and is intended to reconcile the count of annuity contracts between years, as well as verify the components of the variation where applicable. It is also a control mechanism for the setting up of actuarial liabilities for annuity contracts and for any payable that is outstanding on the annuities.

Page 95.01 Premiums
Page 95.02 Policyholder Benefits Paid and Incurred
Page 95.02 Experience Rating Refunds (direct)
Page 95.04 Movement of Insurance – Life – Group (Direct)

These 4 pages give information split by current residence of the certificate holder, irrespective of whether the contract is issued in or out of Canada. The current residence can be one of the thirteen provinces or territories. There is also a miscellaneous column for policyholders no longer resident in Canada, and a total for out of Canada business. Companies are required to establish procedures for the maintenance of current addresses for certificate holders. For premiums and benefits, information is required for group life, group annuity, and group accident and sickness on a direct, assumed, and ceded basis. The information for experience rating refunds is on a direct basis only for the three lines of business. The 'movement of insurance' exhibit is for direct group life only, and reconciles the beginning of year inforce with the end of year inforce with the usual movement categories.

Quarterly Reports

Companies are required to file quarterly financial reports with OSFI. The return is an abbreviated version of the Life-1, containing only 9 pages. The analysis of income, pages 35.01 through 35.04, are required, so the group lines will need to report the information indicated above for these pages on a quarterly basis. The other pages are not group specific, but give consolidated financial information for the company as a whole.

Actuarial Report: To Accompany OSF154 Annual Statement

The actuary is required to file a report with the annual statement which provides the regulatory authorities with the following:

- A description of all the assumptions used, and a full and complete justification for each assumption.
- A description of any approximations used.
- Any changes in the assumptions and the effect thereof.
- A signed statement which affirms compliance with the Standards of Practice of the Canadian Institute of Actuaries.
- A description of how the actuary is compensated and a signed statement to the effect that the actuary has performed his duties without regard to personal considerations.
- A signed copy of the opinion of the actuary as it appears on page 20.080 of the Life-1 report.
- Any other information that the Superintendent may require.

The instructions for completing the actuary's report exceed 50 pages and the report itself will often run to hundreds of pages.

MCCSR Calculation: To Accompany Life-1 Annual Statement

The company must prepare the Minimum Continuing Capital and Surplus Requirement (MCCSR) form and the completed form must be signed by the appointed actuary and a senior company officer. The MCCSR is the amount of capital which the supervisory authorities require. The amount of capital required is based on factors applied to the risk elements involved in the company's business. For group insurance, these factors relate to the risk of mortality and morbidity (both short and long term). The factors recognize the length of premium guarantees and the existence of rate stabilization reserves. For disability benefits, the factors vary by duration since disablement and by benefit period. There are also risk factors for short term benefits such as dental, accidental death and dismemberment or medical.

Dynamic Capital Adequacy Testing

The actuary is required by section 368 of the Insurance Act to meet once a year with the directors of the company (or with the audit committee, if the directors so choose) and present a report on the financial position of the company and its expected future financial condition. The actuary must conform to the Standard of Practice on Dynamic Capital Adequacy Testing promulgated by the Canadian Institute of Actuaries. The Standard of Practice requires the actuary to test the effect of plausible adverse scenarios on the insurer's forecasted capital adequacy. The purpose of the exercise is to identify plausible threats to satisfactory financial condition, to identify actions which lessen the likelihood of those threats, and to identify actions which could mitigate a threat if it materialized.

A company's group insurance portfolio must be included in the investigation of capital adequacy. To the extent that there are future guarantees as to mortality, morbidity, expenses or other risk factors, the actuary must assess the company's position with respect to those guarantees and the impact they may have on the capital position in the event of possible deterioration.

The Superintendent of Insurance requires that the Dynamic Capital Adequacy Report be filed with the regulatory authorities.

RECENT DEVELOPMENTS

The Canadian Institute of Actuaries is in the process of creating a practice certificate which would be mandatory for appointed actuaries. To obtain the certificate, an actuary would need a minimum level of practical experience and would have fulfilled the continuing education requirements both generally and specifically for valuation of policy liabilities.

There is considerable activity related to the development of international accounting standards and international standards of regulatory capital for insurers. Canadian actuaries and Canadian regulators are actively involved. The modifications to Canadian reporting practices have already commenced with the new rules for asset measurement conforming to international standards, and it is clear that more changes are coming.

19   RISK-BASED CAPITAL FORMULAS

Rowen B. Bell
Robert B. Cumming

This chapter describes risk-based capital formulas, including their structure, development, and use. Risk-based capital formulas are important tools in the financial assessment and management of insurance companies. Under a broad definition, risk-based capital formulas would include any formula that calculates a target capital based on factors that reflect the level of financial risk for an organization. However, in more common usage, risk-based capital refers specifically to the formulas used by state regulators in the U.S. to set minimum capital requirements for insurance companies and to determine when to take regulatory actions.

HISTORY OF RBC FORMULAS

The National Association of Insurance Commissioners (NAIC) adopted separate risk-based capital formulas for life insurance companies and property & casualty insurance companies in the early 1990's. Prior to this, various states including New York, Minnesota, and Wisconsin had experimented with risk-based capital formulas and requirements.

Some companies whose business includes significant amounts of group health insurance were, for historical reasons, organized as either life insurers or P&C insurers. However, many other group health insurers were organized under other portions of state insurance codes, such as HMO statutes. By the mid-1990s, some issuers of health insurance were calculating RBC, while others were not.

To rectify this, in 1998 the NAIC adopted a risk-based capital formula for health organizations. Today, the RBC formula that applies to an insurer is determined based on which statement blank that insurer files.

The Health RBC formula is used for companies that file the NAIC's health annual statement ("Orange blank"), while the Life RBC formula is used for companies that file the NAIC's life/A&H annual statement ("Blue blank"), and the P&C formula is used for property and casualty companies ("Yellow blank").

By 2001, a mild frustration had emerged among regulators over the fact that two identical health insurers could have different risk-based capital results, due solely to the fact that one company files the Blue blank, and hence uses the Life RBC formula, while the other files the Orange blank and uses the Health RBC formula. To rectify this, the NAIC adopted rules by which the health insurers who had traditionally filed the Blue blank or Yellow blank were encouraged to migrate to the Orange blank, implying that these insurers would file Health RBC going forward.

Consequently, by 2006 the vast majority of companies specializing in group medical insurance now file the Orange blank, and use the Health RBC formula. However, most of the companies that write disability income, long term care, and group life insurance continue to file the Blue blank and the Life RBC formula.

NAIC RBC MODEL ACTS

The NAIC has developed model laws for states to use in implementing risk-based capital requirements for insurance companies.

In 1998, the NAIC developed and adopted the "Risk-Based Capital (RBC) for Health Organizations Model Act." This model act is very similar to the life and P&C model act which was adopted by the NAIC in 1993. The life and P&C model act has now been adopted in nearly all states. The health model act was adopted by 25 states in the first 5 years following its adoption by the NAIC.

The RBC model act specifies the regulatory actions available to or required of the Insurance Commissioner. The level of action depends on the ratio of the insurance company's actual capital to the required capital based on the risk-based capital formula. However, the model act does *not* specify the actual RBC formula other than stating that it should depend on the insurance company's assets, credit risk, underwriting risk, and other business risks. The actual formula is specified by the NAIC. This allows the NAIC to modify and refine the formula over time without requiring each state to take action to adopt the changes.

According to the model act, each insurance company compares their Total Adjusted Capital (TAC) to their authorized control level (ACL) capital requirement calculated according to the risk-based capital formula. TAC includes statutory capital and surplus of the reporting entity, plus certain adjustments for life and P&C subsidiaries. If the ratio of TAC to ACL RBC falls below 200%, then varying degrees of regulatory action are available to or required of the Commissioner, as summarized in Table 19.1 below.

Table 19.1

Regulatory Actions	
TAC-to-ACL Ratio	**Regulatory Action**
≥ 200%	None
150% to 200%	Company Action Level Event
100% to 150%	Regulatory Action Level Event
70% to 100%	Authorized Control Level Event
< 70%	Mandatory Control Level Event

Each of these regulatory actions is further described below:

Company Action:
Company must submit a corrective action plan to the Commissioner.

Regulatory Action:
Company must submit a corrective action plan, and the Commissioner may examine the company and issue an order specifying corrective actions.

Authorized Control:
Commissioner may take the actions identified above or may place the company under regulatory control if deemed to be in the best interests of the policyholders and creditors of the company.

Mandatory Control:
Commissioner must take regulatory control of the company.

Formally, this schedule of regulatory actions applies only in states that have adopted the RBC model act. As noted above, the Health RBC model act has been adopted in approximately half of the states to date.

Nevertheless, the influence of Health RBC has been pervasive throughout the country, for three main reasons.

First, all companies filing the Orange blank are required to calculate Health RBC and disclose the results of the calculation in the "Five Year Historical Exhibit" of the annual statement, even if their domiciliary state has not adopted the Health RBC model act. Due to this, every health insurer's RBC position is a matter of public record.

Second, even in states that have not adopted the Health RBC model act, regulators are very familiar with the RBC concept and are likely to express formal concern over health insurers whose TAC-to-ACL ratio falls below 200%.

Third, the concept of Health RBC has been embraced by organizations with quasi-regulatory functions, such as the Blue Cross Blue Shield Association (which requires Blue Cross/Blue Shield plans to maintain a minimum TAC-to-ACL ratio in order to retain their ability to use the Association's trademarks) and the various rating agencies.

HEALTH RBC FORMULA

The Health RBC formula defines a capital requirement based on the key factors that affect the level of uncertainty in a company's future financial results. These key factors include the amounts and types of insurance products sold by the company, the methods used to reimburse healthcare providers, and the amounts and types of assets held by the company.

In developing an understanding of the Health RBC formula, one should keep two items in mind.

First, Health RBC is an example of a "standardized approach" to a capital formula, in that the capital requirement is determined by applying fixed factors to information available from an insurer's balance sheet or income statement. The factors used in the formula are intended to represent an aggregate perspective on risk that can be applied uniformly across companies and across time periods.

Recently, there has been increasing interest in the regulatory community towards capital formulas that are based on company-specific internal models – often referred to as the "advanced approach" to capital formulas. Such formulas should better reflect the risk factors pertaining to a company at a point in time. As of this writing, while certain aspects of the NAIC Life RBC formula (e.g., C-3 Phase II) reflect an advanced approach, the Health RBC remains based on a standardized approach.

Second, Health RBC was designed to identify financially weak companies, rather than to be a barometer by which to assess the relative financial strength of companies. It is generally acknowledged that a company having a TAC-to-ACL ratio of 100% is at greater risk of financial distress than a company having a TAC-to-ACL ratio of 150%. However, it does not follow from this that a company having a TAC-to-ACL ratio of 400% is less financially sound than a company having a TAC-to-ACL ratio of 600%. If one were building a formula to measure financial strength, rather than one designed to detect financial weakness, the result might look somewhat different than the NAIC RBC formula.

In light of these items, while it is important for every company to understand its NAIC Health RBC in light of regulatory consequences, the company may want to develop its own internal risk-based capital formula, reflecting company-specific risks, for use as a management tool.

The NAIC's RBC formulas are refined over time. The formula structure and parameters described below are applicable for 2006.

CALCULATION OF RBC AFTER COVARIANCE

In the Health RBC formula, the RBC after covariance (RBCAC) is defined as:

$$RBCAC = H_0 + \left\{ H_1^2 + H_2^2 + H_3^2 + H_4^2 \right\}^{1/2}$$

where:

H_0 is the Asset Risk for Affiliates

H_1 is the Asset Risk for Other Assets

H_2 is the Underwriting Risk

H_3 is the Credit Risk

H_4 is the Business Risk

The authorized control level (ACL) risk-based capital, referenced earlier, is defined as one-half of the RBC after covariance.

The covariance adjustment refers to the impact of using the square root of the sum of the squares as opposed to simply adding all the pieces together. The covariance adjustment is made due to the independent nature of the major categories of risk identified above. That is, it is perceived as unlikely that each of the risks listed above will result in financial losses simultaneously. Accordingly, the covariance adjustment lowers the level of capital required.

In practice, the covariance adjustment has a profound impact on how one should view the Health RBC formula, due to the distribution of a health insurer's risks by major risk category. The figures in Table 19.2 below are derived from the author's study of the aggregate risk profile of all Blue Cross/Blue Shield plans as of 2001[1]:

Table 19.2

Risk Category	Relative Risk (indexed to $H_2 = 100$)	Marginal Impact on RBCAC of $1000 Increase in Risk
H_1	34.9	$325
H_2	100.0	$931
H_3	8.6	$80
H_4	15.9	$148

The "relative risk" column indicates, for example, that for every dollar of H_2 risk, the typical BC/BS plan had 34.9 cents of H_1 risk. The "marginal impact" column is calculated by assuming that the risk categories are distributed as shown in the relative risk column and then observing that, for $i \neq 0$,

$$\frac{\partial RBCAC}{\partial H_i} = \frac{H_i}{RBCAC - H_0}$$

The implication of Table 19.2 is that, for most companies filing the Health RBC formula, the H_2 category will dominate the output of the formula, and the H_1, H_3, and H_4 risk categories are of significantly diminished importance.

In light of this observation, we will focus our discussion of the Health RBC formula on the H_2 risk category, with lesser coverage of the other categories.

---

[1] http://library.soa.org/library/record/2000-09/rsa02v28n240pd.pdf

For complete details on the Health RBC formula, we refer the reader to the *NAIC Health Risk-Based Capital Report Including Overview and Instructions for Companies*, which is published by the NAIC and updated on an annual basis.

UNDERWRITING RISK (H_2)

This reflects the risk of having inadequate premium rates in the future due to fluctuations in claim levels. As discussed above, this factor dominates the RBC requirement for most health insurers.

In general, underwriting risk is calculated separately for each health insurance product by applying a risk factor against some measure of the insurer's exposure. The exposure measure is usually either earned premium or incurred claims, measured on an annual basis and net of any ceded reinsurance.

As noted earlier, generally the risk factors for each product are common across all companies, rather than being fine-tuned to reflect company-specific circumstances. There are two exceptions to this. First, in some cases the factors are tiered by size, implying that a large company achieves a lower average risk per exposure unit than a small company. Second, some risk factors are adjusted in order to reflect the nature of the insurer's provider reimbursement contracts.

The RBC formula subdivides underwriting risk into Claim Experience Fluctuation Risk versus Other Underwriting Risk. Each of these components is described in detail below.

Claim Experience Fluctuation Risk

The Claim Experience Fluctuation Risk portion of the formula covers medical insurance and similar products, with some exceptions. As of 2006, there are five product groupings:

- *Comprehensive Medical & Hospital.* This covers all group and individual medical products, including Medicaid risk and Medicare Advantage products, but excluding the FEHBP and TRICARE programs and excluding ASO/ASC coverages;
- *Medicare Supplement;*
- *Dental;*

- *Medicare Part D*. This was added in 2006 and covers standalone Medicare drug products only; Medicare Advantage products that include drug benefits are reported in Comprehensive Medical & Hospital; and

- *Other*. This catch-all category includes standalone drug products (other than Medicare Part D) and standalone vision products.

Within each product grouping, the risk charge is calculated as (Incurred Claims) times (Risk Factor) times (Managed Care Risk Adjustment Factor). However, there is a floor on the risk charge; this floor is referred to as the 'alternative risk charge,' and it reflects the risk that exists from catastrophic claims on individual members regardless of how few members the company insures. In practice, the alternative risk charge is only relevant for small insurers or for insurers writing a very small amount of business in one of the product groupings.

As mentioned above, the Risk Factor varies based on the type of coverage and the amount of Underwriting Revenue. Table 19.3 shows the risk factors. A weighted average Risk Factor is calculated based on the amount of underwriting revenue (annual earned premium) in each tier. For example, an insurer having $250 million of premium in the Comprehensive Medical grouping would have a weighted average risk factor of 9.6% for that grouping.

Table 19.3

Underwriting Risk Factors by Underwriting Revenue Tier			
Coverage	$0-3 Million	$3-25 Million	$25+ Million
Comprehensive	15.0%	15.0%	9.0%
Medicare Supp.	10.5%	6.7%	. 6.7%
Dental	12.0%	7.6%	7.6%
Medicare Part D	14.1%	14.1%	10.9%
Other	13.0%	13.0%	13.0%

The relative level of factors by product grouping is intended to reflect differences in the relative volatility of experience. For example, the risk from catastrophic claims is clearly less for dental insurance than it is for major medical. Therefore, it is logical that dental should have a lower capital requirement per dollar of premium than medical.

The purpose of the Managed Care Risk Adjustment Factor is to reflect the fact that certain contractual reimbursement arrangements with providers lead to greater predictability of future claim levels, thus reducing the need for capital to support fluctuations in experience.

In order to calculate this factor, the insurer takes all of the claims paid over the previous 12 months, and assigns those claims to one of the following 5 managed care categories:

Category 0:

This is the default category and includes payments made on a fee-for-service basis (with or without a percentage discount from charges), or according to a UCR (usual, customary and reasonable) schedule. It also includes payments made to capitated providers under contractual stop-loss provisions.

Category 1:

This category includes payments made based on such contractual arrangements as provider fee schedules, hospital per diems or case rates, and non-adjustable professional case and global rates. The common element here is that there are contractual protections to the insurer regarding the level of allowed charges.

Category 2:

This category includes payments that would normally fall under Category 0 or Category 1, but that also fall under the scope of a withhold or bonus arrangement with the provider.

Category 3:

This category includes capitation payments, so long as those payments are contractually fixed (either as a percentage of premium or as a dollar amount per member) for a period of at least 12 months. Arrangements that include a provision for prospective revision within 12 months, or a provision for retroactive revisions, do not qualify and are classified as category 1 or 0, respectively. Also, capitated payments to non-regulated intermediaries are subject to a special limitation: If payments by the intermediary to providers with no contractual relationship to the inter-mediary exceed 5% of total payments, then the excess is reported as Category 0 instead of Category 3.

Category 4: This category applies primarily to a staff model HMO, and includes non-contingent salaries to persons directly providing care and facility-related medical expenses generated within a health facility that is owned and operated by the health plan.

Table 19.4 below shows the risk adjustment factor associated with each of these managed care categories.

Table 19.4

Managed Care Risk Adjustment Factor		
Category	Description	Factor
0	Arrangements not included below	1.00
1	Contractual fee payments	0.85
2	Bonus/withhold arrangements	Variable (0.75 to 1.00)
3	Capitation	0.40
4	Non-contingent expenses	0.25

The overall Managed Care Risk Adjustment Factor is calculated as a weighted average of the factors for each category, where the weights are the proportions of total claim payments by category. The overall factor is then applied to all product groupings, except Medicare Part D and Other.

For Medicare Part D, there is a risk adjustment factor component to the RBC calculation, but it is not related to managed care techniques; instead, it relates to risk-mitigation provisions that may exist in the Part D contract between the insurer and the federal government.

Other Underwriting Risk

This portion of the formula includes health insurance coverages not included in the Claim Experience Fluctuation Risk portion, as well as some additional adjustments.

Disability Income: Table 19.5 shows the Health RBC factors for disability income coverages, which are applied against earned premium. The factors vary by group vs. individual coverage, and by amount of premium. Within group, the factors also vary by long-term vs. short-term; within individual, the factors also vary by renewability provision. There are also separate factors for three distinct types of credit disability coverages, not shown in the table.

Table 19.5

RBC Factors for DI by Earned Premium Tier		
Coverage	$ 0-50 Million	$ 50+ Million
Non-Cancelable	35%	15%
Other Individual	25%	7%
Group Long-Term	15%	3%
Group Short-Term	5%	3%

For purposes of applying the earned premium tiers, all individual products are combined, and all group products are combined, but the individual and group products are not combined with one another, and the ordering of products is RBC-maximizing. For example, if a company has $40 million of LTD premium and $40 million of STD premium, then all the LTD premium receives the 15% factor, while the STD premium receives an average factor of 3.5% ($10 million at 5%, making $50 million in total group premium at the higher factors, and then $30 million at 3%). If this company also has $40 million of non-cancelable individual DI premium, then all of that premium receives the 35% factor.

Long Term Care: Historically, the Health RBC approach for LTC insurance was very similar to that used for disability income insurance. More recently, the approach has been thoroughly revised and now includes three components; one based on premium, one on incurred claims, and one on claim reserves.

In the premium component, a factor of 10% is applied to the first $50 million of earned premium, with a factor of 3% applied to the excess. An additional 10% factor applies to non-cancelable premiums.

In the incurred claim component, one factor is applied to the first $35 million of claims, and a lesser factor is applied to the excess. As long as earned premiums are positive, the factors are 25% and 8%. Else, higher factors of 37% and 12% are used, in order to compensate for the absence of a premium component in this case.

The final component is equal to 5% of the LTC claim reserves.

Other Coverages: Table 19.6 summarizes the RBC factors for other miscellaneous types of accident & health insurance.

Table 19.6

RBC Requirements for Miscellaneous Coverage Types	
Coverage	**RBC Requirement**
FEHBP and TRICARE	2% of incurred claims
Stop Loss and Minimum Premium	25% of premium
Hospital Indemnity and Specified Disease	3.5% of premium plus $50,000
AD & D	5.5% of premium less than $10 million plus 1.5 % of premium in excess of $10 million plus 3 times the maximum retained risk*
Other Accident	5% of premium

* The amount representing 3 times the maximum retained risk is subject to a maximum of $300,000.

The factor for FEHBP and TRICARE is lower than for other medical business due to the financial safeguards that are built into these federal programs. The risk factor used for stop loss reflects the higher variability of this coverage. The premiums for these coverages are not included in the Comprehensive Medical product grouping.

Rate Guarantees: When a health insurer guarantees premium rates for future periods on a product whose claim costs increase with healthcare inflation, the risk of future underwriting losses is increased. In recognition of this risk, Health RBC includes additional charges on the earned premium from such policies where the rate guarantee exceeds 15 months. The factor is 2.4% for guarantees of 15 to 36 months, and 6.4% for longer guarantees.

Premium Stabilization Reserves: These reserves usually consist of accumulated experience rating refunds that can be drawn upon in the event of poor future experience, thus helping to reduce the insurer's risk. No credit is provided for premium stabilization reserves for FEHBP business, since the impact of such reserves is already reflected in the lower RBC factor for this business. For other premium stabilization reserves, the insurer's underwriting risk is reduced by 50% of the amount of the reserves held.

ASSET RISK – AFFILIATES (H_0)

This reflects the risk that an investment in the stock of an affiliated company may lose some or all of its value. Separate approaches are used for affiliates that are subject to RBC versus those that are not.

For investments in affiliates that are subject to risk-based capital, such as directly or indirectly owned insurance subsidiaries, the RBC is calculated on a "see-through" basis. That is, the RBC requirement for a stock investment in such affiliates is based on the RBC after covariance for the subsidiary, prorated for the percentage ownership of that subsidiary. There are limits and adjustments based on how the affiliate's RBC compares to the affiliate's surplus and the book value of the affiliate.

The see-through approach, combined with the fact that H_0 risk is not subject to the covariance adjustment, tends to imply that in situations where one insurer owns another, the RBC after covariance of the parent will be similar to what it would be if the two insurers were merged.

For other investments in affiliates, the RBC requirement is calculated as a factor times the book value of the stock of those affiliates. The factor is 30%, except for non-U.S. insurance subsidiaries where the factor is 100%.

The H_0 risk category also includes a provision for certain off-balance sheet items, including contingent liabilities, non-controlled assets, and guarantees for affiliates. The RBC requirement is calculated as 1% of the reported value of these items.

ASSET RISK – OTHER (H_1)

This reflects the risk that investments may default or decrease in value. In general, the risk-based capital requirement for an asset is calculated as the book value of the asset times a factor. The factor varies depending on the type of asset, ranging from 0% to 30%. In addition, the factor is doubled (but capped at 30%) for certain assets held in the 10 largest issuers, reflecting the additional risk to the company of having a high concentration of assets from a single issuer.

Not all of the assets on an insurer's balance sheet are covered within the H_0 or H_1 risk categories. As discussed later, some assets, such as reinsurance receivables, are handled in the credit risk (H_3) portion of the formula; others, such as due & unpaid premium, are not contemplated within the RBC formula.

As discussed earlier, the important of asset risk within Health RBC is somewhat diminished by covariance. What follows is a brief discussion of asset risk factors for those asset classes most commonly held by health insurers. There are risk factors for other classes of invested assets besides those discussed below (e.g., preferred stock).

Cash and Bonds: U.S. government bonds are considered to be risk-free and hence have a risk factor of 0%. Cash, money market mutual funds, and corporate bonds that are rated Class 1 (high investment grade bonds) by the NAIC's Securities Valuation Office (SVO) receive a risk factor of 0.3%, reflecting the minimal default risk of these assets. Other bonds have risk factors based on their SVO rating, from 1% for Class 2 (low investment grade) up to 30% for Class 6 (in default).

Common Stock: Investments in unaffiliated common stock, including most mutual funds, receive a risk factor of 15%.

On the surface, it seems the risk charge for an investment in the stock of a non-affiliate is one-half of that for a comparable investment in the stock of an affiliate (for which the risk factor is 30%, as discussed above). However, that analysis ignores the impact of covariance. Since affiliated stock lies outside the covariance adjustment while unaffiliated stock lies within, in reality the effective risk charge per dollar invested is considerably smaller for unaffiliated stock than for affiliated stock.

Property & Equipment: All property and equipment owned by the insurer, including health care delivery assets, receives a 10% factor. However, it is important to note that this factor is applied against the admitted asset balance only, and that statutory accounting places considerable restrictions on the admissibility of these types of assets.

CREDIT RISK (H_3)

This reflects the risk that amounts owed to the health insurer will not be recovered. This risk is common to all types of businesses, although some receivables are unique to health insurers, such as pharmacy rebate receivables. Also, the calculation of H_3 contemplates the possibility that capitated providers will not fulfill their contractual obligations.

As discussed earlier, for most health insurers the impact of the H_3 risk category is marginalized by covariance. However, for an insurer that makes very heavy use of capitation arrangements, it is possible that the H_2 and H_3 categories will be in closer balance, implying that both would play a significant role in determining RBC after covariance.

The credit risk for capitation reflects that capitated providers may not provide the agreed-upon services and the health insurer will incur additional expenses in arranging for alternative coverage. The RBC requirement is 2% of the annual capitations paid directly to providers, and 4% of the annual capitations paid to intermediaries. If the health insurer receives acceptable letters of credit or has withheld funds for a particular provider, then the capitations for that provider are exempted.

For other types of credit risk, the current RBC requirements are 0.5% of reinsurance receivables from non-affiliates, 1% of investment income receivable, 5% of health care receivables, 5% of amounts due from affiliates, and 5% of receivables relating to uninsured plans.

BUSINESS RISK (H_4)

The business risk category of the Health RBC formula includes several miscellaneous types of risk not included elsewhere, each of which is discussed below. The practical importance of these risk categories, however, is severely limited due to the impact of covariance.

Administrative Expense Risk: Administrative expenses for health insurance are subject to misestimation just like claim expenses, but the degree of misestimation should be somewhat less. Thus, the risk factors applied to administrative expenses are somewhat less than the factors applied to claims. The risk factor varies between 4% and 7% of annual administrative expenses, depending on premium volume.

Risks from ASC/ASO Business: Administrative services contract (ASC) and administrative services only (ASO) are both contracts where the health insurer agrees to provide administrative services for a third party, typically a large employer, that is at risk for medical expenses. The NAIC defines the distinction between the two as follows. Under an ASC contract, benefits are paid from the health insurer's bank account and the health insurer receives reimbursement from the third party. Under an ASO contract, benefits are paid from a bank account owned or funded by the third party, or alternatively, benefits are paid from the health insurer's bank account, but only after the health insurer has received funds from the third party to cover the benefit payments.

Under both types of contracts, there is a risk that the insurer may misestimate the amount that it charges the customer for administrative services. For this reason, a risk factor of 2% is applied against the annual administrative expenses for ASC/ASO contracts.

Under an ASC contract only, there is some additional risk since the health insurer is fronting the cash for the benefit payments. If the third party goes bankrupt, the health insurer might not be able to collect these amounts. Accordingly, there is a 1% risk factor applied to annual benefit payments administered under ASC contracts.

Guaranty Fund Assessment Risk: A 0.5% risk factor is applied against premiums that are subject to state guaranty fund assessments, reflecting the risk that future assessments will be higher than expected.

Excessive Growth Risk: The RBC requirement for excessive growth only applies if a health insurer's RBC increases from one year to the next by more than the sum of 10% plus the insurer's percentage growth in underwriting revenue. The excessive growth RBC requirement is 50% of growth in RBC beyond this safe harbor amount. Since the safe harbor includes the growth in revenue, this is really not an adjustment for excessive growth in the amount of business a health insurer has. Rather, it is an extra adjustment that applies if the health insurer changes to a significantly more risky mix of business or provider reimbursement arrangements.

RESERVING RISK

Theoretically, a capital provision for reserving risk would be appropriate to reflect the possibility that the insurer's future surplus will be impaired due to unfavorable development in the claim liabilities and reserves established as of the valuation date.

However, the Health RBC formula does not contain such a provision (except for long term care, as noted previously). Instead, the formula implicitly assumes that the insurer's claim liabilities are accurately stated. This reflects that the actuarial opinion accompanying the Orange blank includes a statement by the opining actuary that the recorded reserves make "good and sufficient provision" for the company's liability.

The absence of reserving risk from the Health RBC formula has two interesting implications.

First, it implies that an insurer's capital requirement is disconnected from the level of conservatism in its actuarial reserves. This is a counter-intuitive result. If two insurers bear the same risk profile, but Company A holds more conservative reserves for those risks than Company B, then in theory Company A needs less capital than Company B, since the additional conservatism in the reserves is functioning as capital. However, under Health RBC, the two companies would have the same capital requirement.

The second implication is related but is somewhat subtler. Recently, the phrase "Total Asset Requirement" (TAR) has been introduced into actuarial jargon, as a synonym for the sum of an insurer's statutory reserves and required capital. Conceptually, one might want the insurer's TAR to be adequate with high probability, say 95%. In this case, since the required capital (i.e., Health RBC) contains no provision for reserving risk, it would be necessary for the statutory reserves to be set at such a level so that the reserves themselves would be adequate 95% of the time.

This argument has been used by some actuaries to justify the level of conservatism typically found in group medical claim liabilities. If, instead, there were a capital requirement for reserves, then the desired level of confidence on the insurer's TAR could be achieved without needing the reserves themselves to be set at a 95% confidence level. Indeed, from a theoretical perspective, one might argue that medical claim liabilities should be set at a 50% confidence level, and that a significant capital requirement should be imposed on the liabilities in order to achieve the desired high level of confidence (such as 95%) from a TAR perspective.

DEVELOPMENT OF THE HEALTH RBC FORMULA

The initial work on the current Health RBC formula started in late 1993, when the NAIC sent a request to the American Academy of Actuaries for assistance in developing a RBC formula for health insurers.

The American Academy of Actuaries set up a work group that prepared a set of recommendations for the NAIC. The group's work focused on the structure and parameters for the calculation of the underwriting risk, since this component tends to dominate the RBC requirement for health insurers, and since this was an area where the treatment of health insurance in the existing Life and P&C RBC formulas was overly simplistic.

RUIN THEORY MODEL

To develop risk parameters for underwriting risk, the work group developed a stochastic "ruin theory" model. This model was used to determine the level of capital needed to give a 95% probability that an insurance company would not become insolvent over a five year time horizon. The model projected financial gains and losses on a year by year basis. This model was used to determine how capital requirements should vary for different volumes of business and for different types of coverage.

The key factors that impacted the risk for a given scenario included:

- The risk of catastrophic claims and other statistical fluctuations in claim levels.
- The risk of misestimating trends or other pricing errors.
- The length of time needed to recognize a pricing error, implement an adjustment, and have that adjustment become effective.

To model the risk of statistical fluctuations in claim levels, a claim probability distribution for an individual person was developed for each type of coverage. A Monte Carlo method was then used to develop a distribution of total claims for a portfolio of business.

To model the risk of misestimating trends and other pricing errors, the work group studied the fluctuation in loss ratios over time for different types of coverage. This information was used to develop a probability distribution for pricing errors. This distribution, along with the individual claim distribution, became the basis for the model's stochastic simulation.

EVOLUTION OF RBC FORMULA

After the Academy provided its initial recommendations, the formula went through a series of changes, many of which were intended to make it easier to perform and audit the calculation. Some of the more significant changes made by the NAIC are summarized below:

- *Capitation to providers*: The Academy recommended a 40% credit but the NAIC increased this to 60%.
- *Capitation to non-regulated intermediaries:* The Academy recommended no credit, but the NAIC used a 60% credit (the same as for direct capitation of providers), with some restrictions as discussed earlier.
- *Staff model HMO:* The Academy recommended a 50% credit but the NAIC increased this to 75%.
- *Premium stabilization reserves:* The Academy recommended a 100% credit to be applied on a contract-by-contract basis (meaning

that each contract's reserve could be used to fully offset the underwriting risk associated with that contract, but not to offset risk arising from other contracts). The NAIC used a 50% credit applied on an overall basis.

- *Business subject to prior approval:* The Academy recommended an increased risk factor for business subject to prior regulatory approval of rate increases, which the NAIC did not adopt.

- *Excessive growth risk:* The Academy recommended an extra charge for growth in total RBC of over 20%. The NAIC applies an extra charge only if RBC growth exceeds the growth in premium plus 10%.

- *Self-insured (ASO) business:* The Academy recommended a RBC requirement of 0.5% of premium equivalents (administrative expenses plus benefits paid). The NAIC uses 2% of administrative expenses.

The NAIC Health RBC formula continues to evolve. In recent years, Academy work groups have been formed to provide recommendations to the NAIC on revisions to the original RBC treatment of disability income and long term care insurance, and to develop an appropriate RBC treatment for the Medicare Part D program. The RBC approaches for these products have changed over time, and reflect the recommendations of these recent Academy work groups.

LIFE RBC FORMULA

As discussed earlier, today most companies whose primary business is group medical insurance file the Orange blank, and therefore use the Health RBC formula. However, most companies writing disability income, long term care, or group life insurance file the Blue blank, and therefore use the NAIC's Life RBC formula.

The Life RBC formula is significantly more complex than the Health RBC formula, and its level of complexity has increased in recent years. Because of this, we will not attempt to provide a comprehensive review of the Life RBC formula, but will instead discuss some highlights relevant to group insurance. For a full description, the reader is referred to the *NAIC Life Risk-Based Capital Report Including Overview and Instructions for Companies.*

As of 2006, the Life RBC formula for RBC after covariance is:

$$RBCAC = C_0 + C_{4a} + \{(C_{1o} + C_{3a})^2 + (C_{1cs} + C_{3c})^2 + C_2^2 + C_{3b}^2 + C_{4b}^2\}^{1/2}$$

where:

C_0 = Asset risk – Affiliates

C_{1cs} = Asset risk – Unaffiliated common stock and affiliated non-insurance stock

C_{1o} = Asset risk – All other

C_2 = Insurance risk

C_{3a} = Interest rate risk

C_{3b} = Health credit risk

C_{3c} = Market risk

C_{4a} = Business risk

C_{4b} = Health administrative expense component of business risk

We noted previously that, for a typical health insurer, the underwriting risk component (here called "insurance risk") tends to dominate RBC after covariance. For a typical life insurer, however, this is not the case. Other risk categories, such as asset risk and interest rate risk, tend to be more important for a life insurer than insurance risk. This implies that life insurers who also write health insurance may enjoy a lower effective capital requirement for health insurance than monoline health insurers, thanks to the so-called "diversification benefit" provided by the covariance adjustment.

INSURANCE RISK FACTORS

In general, the approach to the C_2 component of the Life RBC formula is heavily based on the Health RBC treatment of the H_2 component, as discussed above. The following summarizes some of the key differences in insurance risk factors between the Life and Health RBC formulas.

- *Individual Medical:* The Life formula applies a 20% load to the RBC requirement for individual comprehensive medical coverage, in recognition of the risk arising from the additional time needed to get premium rate increases filed and approved for individual products.

- *Vision:* The Life formula combines vision insurance together with dental insurance, whereas in the Health formula vision falls under Other rather than Dental.

- *Claim Reserves:* The Life formula applies a 5% charge against all health claim reserves reported in Exhibit 6 (reserves for unaccrued benefits, as opposed to liabilities for unpaid claims), whereas the Health formula does this only for long term care claim reserves. This charge does not resolve the issues discussed above regarding reserving risk for health products that have claim liabilities rather than claim reserves, such as medical insurance.

- *Disability Income and Long Term Care:* Superficially, the risk factors in the Life formula for disability income and long term care insurance appear to be materially higher than those found in the Health formula. This reflects a complex series of tax adjustments that have been implemented in certain portions of the Life formula. Once tax effects are netted out, the treatments of these products are consistent between the two formulas.

- *Group Life*: The Life formula includes a provision for group life insurance. The RBC requirement is based on a factor times the net amount at risk. The factor is tiered based on premium volume. For example, the factor is 0.18% for the first $500 million and grades down to 0.08% for amounts over $25 billion. The net amount at risk is based on life insurance face amount in force, less reserves.

- *Workers' Compensation Carve-Out*: During the late 1990s, it was common practice among P&C insurers to carve out the portions of workers' compensation risk that represented health/disability risk rather than liability risk, and cede that portion to life insurers. At the time, the RBC requirement in the Life formula for such risks was considerably less than that found in the NAIC P&C RBC formula. (Thus, the assumption of WC carve-out risk by life insurers may be partially attributable to the desire to minimize capital requirements.) More recently, the Life formula has been modified to include special factors for this type of risk that are more consistent with the treatment in the P&C formula.

20 ACTUARIAL CERTIFICATION OF RESERVES

Robert B. Cumming
updated by Dick Glatz and Tim Harris

INTRODUCTION

This chapter covers regulatory requirements, guidance, and practices related to certifying actuarial reserves for group business for statutory reporting. This chapter is intended to supplement the chapter which discusses the calculation of claim liabilities and reserves, as well as the chapter which covers group insurance financial reporting.

When filing the statutory annual statement, companies must include a statement from a qualified actuary, setting forth his or her opinion relating to the actuarial liabilities and reserves included in the financial statement. In preparing this opinion, actuaries should be familiar with the requirements and guidance provided by the following items:

- State laws and regulations,
- Accounting Practices and Procedures Manual,
- Statutory Annual Statement Instructions,
- Actuarial Standards of Practice,
- Health Reserves Guidance Manual, and
- Actuarial Practice Notes.

The remainder of this chapter discusses each of these, as they relate to the actuarial opinion.

STATE LAWS AND REGULATIONS

Many states have adopted laws and regulations which relate to the actuarial opinion regarding reserves. The laws and regulations often prescribe

391

certain requirements for the calculation of the reserves, or particular language to include in the actuarial opinion. The laws and regulations vary by state, and by life insurance company versus health insurance company. (Health insurance company refers to Health Service Corporations, such as Blue Cross Blue Shield plans and Health Maintenance Organizations (HMOs)). Most states have very specific laws and regulations that apply to life insurance companies. However, this is not the case for health insurance companies.

The first step in preparing the actuarial opinion should be to review the state laws and regulations that are applicable to the type of organization for which the opinion is being prepared. States often adopt, either verbatim or with some modification, the model laws and regulations developed by the National Association of Insurance Commissioners (NAIC). (The NAIC is an association of state insurance regulators. The NAIC facilitates many projects related to the regulation of the insurance industry.)

LIFE INSURANCE COMPANIES

For life insurance companies, the following NAIC model laws and regulations might apply:

- The Standard Valuation Law,
- The Actuarial Opinion and Memorandum Regulation,
- The Minimum Life and Annuity Reserve Standards, or
- The Health Insurance Reserves Model Regulation.

Actuarial Opinion and Memorandum Regulation (AOMR). The AOMR specifies the language to be included in the actuarial opinion for life insurance companies. The AOMR also specifies the need for an actuarial memorandum in support of the opinion, and the need for asset adequacy analysis as part of the analysis of reserves and liabilities.

Minimum Life and Annuity Reserve Standards. The Minimum Life and Annuity Reserve Standards applies mainly to individual coverages. This model law specifies minimum standards for the valuation of life insurance. The minimum standards include interest rates, mortality rates, and the commissioners reserve valuation method. For group life insurance, the model law indicates that the minimum standard for calculating reserves is to be based on "tables which provide for an adequate reserve."

Health Insurance Reserves Model Regulation. The Health Insurance Reserves Model Regulation applies to individual and group health insurance. The regulation specifies requirements for claim reserves, premium reserves, and contract reserves.

For claim reserves, the regulation discusses interest rates, morbidity requirements, and methodology. For group disability income, morbidity tables are specified, although, carriers with credible experience may use their own experience for the early durations. For other group benefits, the regulation specifies that "the reserve should be based on the insurer's experience, if the experience is considered credible, or upon other assumptions designed to place a sound value on the liabilities." The regulation specifies that "a generally accepted actuarial reserving method ... may be used to estimate all claim liabilities."

Unearned premium reserves, determined on a pro-rata basis, are required by the regulation. The minimum unearned premium reserve is determined based on the valuation net modal premium (if contract reserves apply) or the gross premium (if no contract reserves apply). For group coverages, typically no contract reserves are required so the gross premium requirement applies.

Under the regulation, contract reserves are required for all individual and group contracts for which: (a) level premiums are used or (b) due to the premium structure at issue, the value of future benefits at any time exceeds the value of future valuation net premiums. In general, if rates are designed to pre-fund some part of future years' costs, then contract reserves will be required. Contract reserves are rare for group health insurance coverage. Situations where contract reserves might be held include: (a) multi-year rate guarantees where it is expected that future rates will not be sufficient to cover future costs, (b) pre-funding of the increase in claim levels for small group medical coverages when claim levels are expected to increase faster than premiums, and (c) coverages where level premiums might be used, such as group long term care coverage.

For contract reserves, the regulation discusses minimum standards for morbidity, interest, termination rates, and methodology. For group disability coverages, the regulation specifies particular tabular morbidity standards. For other group coverages, the regulation specifies that the tables shall be established by a qualified actuary and acceptable to the commissioner. For coverages other than long term care and return of premium, the minimum reserve is based on the 2-year full preliminary term method. For long term care and return of premium contracts, the minimum reserve is either a 1-year or 2-year full preliminary term, depending on the circumstances.

The regulation requires that a gross premium valuation be performed whenever "a significant doubt exists as to reserve adequacy" for any major block of contracts. The gross premium valuation should take into account "all expected benefits unpaid, all expected expenses unpaid, and all unearned or expected premiums…"

HEALTH INSURANCE COMPANIES

There is a wide variation in the extent of state laws and regulations related to actuarial reserves and liabilities for health insurance companies, such as Blue Cross Blue Shield plans and HMOs. Many states have very little in the way of laws or regulations that provide specific requirements for actuarial reserves and liabilities. However, some states, such as Texas and Colorado, have very specific requirements for reserve items such as premium deficiency reserves.

In states with limited specific requirements, many actuaries look to other sources for guidance. These sources include the Accounting Practices and Procedures Manual, Statutory Annual Statement Instructions, Actuarial Standards of Practice, Health Reserves Guidance Manual, and Actuarial Practice Notes.

For health insurance companies, there often is no state regulation that specifies the wording of the actuarial opinion. In such situations, the actuary often uses the standard wording from the NAIC Annual Statement Instructions. (For life insurance companies, the wording of the actuarial opinion is specified in the AOMR, which most states have adopted.)

ACCOUNTING PRACTICES AND PROCEDURES MANUAL

The Accounting Practices and Procedures Manual (APPM) provides a comprehensive guide to statutory accounting principles and requirements. The APPM is produced by the National Association of Insurance Commissioners (NAIC), and is updated periodically. The manual is intended to "establish a comprehensive basis of accounting recognized and adhered to if not in conflict with state statutes and/or regulations, or when the state statutes and/or regulations are silent." This manual is especially important for health insurance companies since, as described above, state laws and regulations are often silent with respect to specific requirements for actuarial reserves.

The comprehensive codification of statutory accounting principles was first incorporated in the APPM in 2000 and effective January 1, 2001. Some of the requirements of particular interest to group health actuaries include the following Statement of Statutory Accounting Principles (SSAP) and Issue Papers (IP):

- SSAP #54 & IP #54: Individual and Group Accident and Health Contracts
- SSAP #55 & IP #55: Unpaid Claims, Losses and Loss Adjustment Expenses
- SSAP #84 & IP #107: Certain Health Care Receivables and Receivables Under Government Insured Plans

Each of these SSAPs is discussed below.

SSAP #54: INDIVIDUAL AND GROUP ACCIDENT AND HEALTH CONTRACTS

SSAP #54 covers reserve requirements including policy reserves, claim reserves, and premium deficiency reserves. (Policy reserves are also referred to as contract reserves or active life reserves.) For specific reserve requirements, SSAP #54 refers to Appendix A-010 "Minimum Reserve Standards for Individual and Group Health Insurance Contracts." This appendix is nearly identical to the NAICs "Health Insurance Reserves Model Regulation" discussed above. In addition, SSAP #54 refers to the Health Reserves Guidance Manual. The manual is discussed later.

Premium Deficiency Reserves

SSAP #54 includes a specific requirement for premium deficiency reserves. Premium deficiency reserves are similar in general concept to the gross premium valuation requirement included in the "Health Insurance Reserves Model Regulation." However, the specific language in SSAP #54 differs from the "Health Insurance Reserves Model Regulation" and may be interpreted differently. SSAP #54 states:

> *"When the expected claims payments or incurred costs, claim adjustment expenses and administrative costs exceed the premiums to be collected for the remainder of a contract period, a premium*

> *deficiency reserve shall be recognized by recording an additional liability for the deficiency ... For purposes of determining if a premium deficiency exists, contracts shall be grouped in a manner consistent with how policies are marketed, serviced and measured. A liability shall be recognized for each grouping where a premium deficiency is indicated. Deficiencies shall not be offset by anticipated profits in other policy groupings. Such accruals shall be made for any loss contracts, even if the contract period has not yet started."*

The requirement for premium deficiency reserves is a controversial topic and a significant change in group health reserving for most health insurance companies. (This is not as significant of a change for life insurance companies, which often were subject to the gross premium valuation requirement in the "Health Insurance Reserves Model Regulation.") There are a variety of opinions regarding the appropriate determination of premium deficiency reserves, and a variety of interpretations of the wording in SSAP #54.

(Historically, the term "deficiency reserves" was used in life company reserving. When a contract's gross level premium was less than a statutorily defined valuation net premium, deficiency reserves were required to fund the difference. The meaning of the term in the health context has obviously changed.)

Some of the key issues and considerations in calculating premium deficiency reserves include:

- Grouping of contracts,
- Time period for the projection,
- Expenses: marginal vs. fully allocated,
- Investment Income (from allocated surplus),
- Margin/conservatism, and
- Closed block vs. open block.

Grouping of contracts
That is, how fine should you slice and dice the business? This is a key issue, since deficiencies in one grouping can not be offset by profits in other policy groupings. The more groupings that are used, the more likely it is that you will have a significant deficiency in one of the groupings. One extreme would be to have a separate grouping for each combination of

product type, group size category, marketing method, geographic area, policy form, and perhaps other categories. The other extreme would be to have one grouping for the entire health business. Typical groupings for a health insurance company might include: Medicaid, Medicare+Choice, individual medical under 65, Medicare Supplement, small group, and large group. The actual groupings for a particular company might vary significantly from this, based on their situation and their interpretation of SSAP #54. Some of the issues include: If, due to regulation or otherwise, it is expected that one market segment will subsidize another market segment, does it make sense to establish a deficiency reserve if the overall result is positive?

Time period for the projection
SSAP #54 requires that a projection be made for the "remainder of the contract period." For large group business, this generally means a projection to the next policy anniversary, or for simplicity, a projection to the end of the next calendar year. For small group business, due the guaranteed renewability provisions, this might or might not be interpreted as requiring a long term projection (until most of the business lapses.) For individual guaranteed renewable business, a long term projection is often viewed as appropriate. Some of the issues related to the time period include: Do you allow future long term gains to offset losses in the short term? If losses are expected in future years, but you could cancel the entire block of business, do you need to recognize the loss?

Expenses: marginal vs. fully allocated.
Should each line of business be expected to cover marginal expense levels or fully allocated expenses? The NAIC's Health Reserves Guidance Manual states that "If other lines of business can cover overhead expenses, the test for deficiency and the calculation of the deficiency reserve can be performed using only direct costs."

Investment income
Some actuaries have argued that investment income from allocated surplus should be allowed as an offset in the calculation of the premium deficiency.

Margin/conservatism
Should one use best estimate assumptions or include a margin for adverse deviation?

Closed block vs. open block
Should the projection include new business or only those groups/contracts that are inforce as of the valuation date? Traditionally, reserve analysis is

performed for that business which is inforce as of the valuation date. The language in SSAP #54 implies a closed block approach. However, some argue that an open block projection is more comprehensive and realistic since it includes the impact of expected sales of new business.

SSAP #55: Unpaid Claims, Losses and Loss Adjustment Expenses

SSAP #55 covers liabilities for unpaid claims and claim adjustment expenses, for life insurance contracts and accident and health contracts. SSAP #55 specifies that the following items should be considered in determining liabilities:

- Liability for unpaid claims: This includes due and unpaid claims, claims in course of settlement, and incurred but not reported claims. This includes additional unpaid medical costs resulting from failed contractors under capitation contracts;
- Claim adjustment expenses;
- Liabilities for withholds from payments made to contracted providers; and
- Liabilities for accrued medical incentives under contractual arrangements with providers and other risk sharing arrangements.

The liability for unpaid claims and related items is required to be based on the estimated ultimate cost of settling claims, using past experience adjusted for current trends. The liabilities are not to be discounted unless authorized for specific types of claims by specific SSAPs.

SSAP #55 also specifies that "management shall record its best estimate of its liabilities" for unpaid claims. This language appears to be in conflict with the standard actuarial practice of including a margin for adverse deviation in the statutory claim liability. (Some actuaries have interpreted this language as requiring a best estimate of the appropriate statutory claim liability where the statutory claim liability includes an appropriate margin.)

Interpretation 01-28 (INT 01-28) of the Emerging Accounting Issues Working Group (EAIWG), entitled "Margin for Adverse Deviation in Claim Reserve," addresses the best estimate language. (The NAIC's EAIWG is responsible for responding to questions related to application, interpretation, and clarification of statutory accounting principles.) INT 01-28 allows for, but does not require, a margin to be included in the liability estimate. It states, "The working group reached a consensus that the concept of conservatism is inherent to the estimation of reserves and as such should not be specifically prohibited in the consideration of management's best estimate." In interpreting the statutory requirements in the APPM, actuaries should also be cognizant of the preamble which states that "In order to provide a margin of protection for policyholders, the concept of conservatism should be followed when developing estimates as well as establishing accounting principles for statutory reporting."

SSAP #84: CERTAIN HEALTH CARE RECEIVABLES AND RECEIVABLES UNDER GOVERNMENT INSURED PLANS

This SSAP deals with accounting for receivables related to pharmacy rebates, claim overpayments, advances to providers, provider risk sharing, and government insured plans. In general, the SSAP requires that these receivables be reported on a gross basis rather than a net basis. (Under the gross basis, a separate asset would be established, subject to admissibility requirements. Under the net basis, the receivable would be implicitly or explicitly netted out of the liability for unpaid claims.) The reporting basis will impact the appropriate liability for unpaid claims. Depending on interpretation, this SSAP could be in conflict with the common actuarial practice of implicitly recognizing some level of claim recoveries in the calculation of the liability for unpaid claims. (Recoveries are often implicitly reflected in the calculation, since claim triangles often include some negative claim payments due to recoveries or corrections of claim overpayments.) The issue relates to whether the SSAP applies only to specifically identified past overpayments, or also to the implicit recognition of overpayments reflected in the claim triangles. Actuaries might want to consider the materiality requirement, discussed in the Preamble of the APPM, when determining if a change in practice is required or appropriate.

NAIC ANNUAL STATEMENT INSTRUCTIONS

The NAIC produces and updates the forms and instructions used for reporting the financial condition of insurance companies. The forms are referred to as the annual statement blanks. There are separate blanks for life insurance companies, health insurance companies, and property & casualty companies. The blanks are discussed in more detail in the chapter on financial reporting.

Actuaries should be familiar with the blanks and instructions when preparing actuarial opinions regarding reserves. The instructions specify what should be included in various line items on which the actuary expresses an opinion.

The health instructions also include standard wording for the actuarial opinion. The standard wording consists of an identification paragraph, scope paragraph, and opinion paragraph. The identification paragraph identifies the actuary and his or her relation to the company. The scope paragraph identifies the items on which an opinion is to be expressed. The items should include, but are not necessarily limited to, the following:

- Claims unpaid (page 3, line 1),
- Accrued medical incentive pool and bonus payments (page 3, line 2),
- Unpaid claims adjustment expenses (page 3, line 3),
- Aggregate health policy reserves (page 3, line 4),
- Aggregate health claim reserves (page 3, line 7),
- Experience rated refunds, and
- Any actuarial liabilities included in Page 3, Line 21 (Aggregate write-ins for other liabilities).

The opinion paragraph includes the following language:

"In my opinion, the amounts carried in the balance sheet on account of the items identified above:

A. *Are in accordance with accepted actuarial standards consistently applied and are fairly stated in accordance with sound actuarial principles,*

B. *Are based on actuarial assumptions relevant to contract provisions and appropriate to the purpose for which the statement was prepared,*

C. *Meet the requirements of the laws of (state of domicile)*

D. *Make a good and sufficient provision for all unpaid claims and other actuarial liabilities of the organization under the terms of its contracts and agreements,*

E. *Are computed on the basis of assumptions consistent with those used in computing the corresponding items in the annual statement of the preceding year-end,*

F. *Include appropriate provision for all actuarial items that ought to be established."*

The opinion paragraph should also include a statement that: (1) the Underwriting and Investment Exhibit – Part 2B (follow-up study on last year's estimate of the claim liability) was prepared in accordance with Actuarial Standard of Practice No.5 and (2) the methods, considerations, and analyses used in forming the opinion conform to the relevant Actuarial Standards of Practice.

ACTUARIAL STANDARDS OF PRACTICE

Actuarial Standards of Practice are developed and promulgated by the Actuarial Standards Board of the American Academy of Actuaries.

For group health coverages, the following actuarial standards might be directly relevant:

- No. 5. Incurred Health and Disability Claims;
- No. 28. Compliance with Statutory Statement of Actuarial Opinion Requirements for HMDI Corporations and HMOs; and
- No. 42. Determining Health and Disability Liabilities Other Than Liabilities for Incurred Claims.

The following provides a brief summary of some of the requirements in these ASOPs.

ASOP #5 has a fairly broad scope; it applies to all practice involving the analysis of health claim liabilities. Some of the particular requirements in ASOP #5 include:

- Margin: The actuary should consider what margin, if any, is appropriate. If margin is included, it should be reasonable to cover moderately adverse developments, not all conceivable adverse developments;
- The actuary should recognize and reflect the impact of benefit plan provisions, company practices, and environmental factors;
- The actuary should review the impact of any changes in benefits, measurement of exposure, provider contracts, claim filing, claim processing, and coding of payment and incurral dates;
- The actuary should consider the impact of carve-outs, such as mental health, chiropractic, or prescription drugs;

- The actuary should account for reinsurance and coordination of benefits;
- The actuary should perform follow-up studies of prior estimates; and
- The actuary should consider alternative approaches and assumptions.

ASOP #28 applies specifically to the actuarial opinion on reserves and related actuarial items. This ASOP includes the following requirements:

- The actuary should be familiar with the NAIC blanks and instructions and state laws and regulations;
- The actuary should be satisfied that reserves and related items are adequate to cover obligations under moderately adverse conditions; and
- The actuary should ensure that provision has been made for all actuarial items that ought to be established.

ASOP #42 broadly applies to health coverage liabilities other than claim liabilities. Some of the items discussed in ASOP #42 include:

- General considerations when determining health coverage liabilities. These considerations include: plan provisions, benefit management, premium guarantees, risk-sharing arrangements, economic factors, business practices, and reinsurance;
- Specific considerations when determining health coverage liabilities for contract reserves, premium deficiency reserves, and provider-related liabilities.

The actuary should also be familiar with the following ASOPs if they apply to situation at hand:

- ASOP # 7: Analysis of Life, Health, or Property/Casualty Insurer Cash Flows, and
- ASOP # 22: Statements of Opinion Based on Asset Adequacy Analysis by Actuaries for Life or Health Insurers.

Other ASOPs of a more general nature might apply as well, such as, ASOP No. 23 on data quality and ASOP No. 41 on actuarial communications. Copies of these and other ASOPs are available on the website of the Actuarial Standards Board[1].

---

[1] www.actuarialstandardsboard.org

HEALTH RESERVES GUIDANCE MANUAL

The NAIC's "Health Reserves Guidance Manual" provides guidance regarding the calculation and documentation of health liabilities and reserves for statutory financial statements. The guidance manual is intended to assist actuaries that estimate health reserves, as well as examiners who review statutory financial statements on behalf of state regulatory agencies. The initial version of the manual was prepared by an American Academy of Actuaries work group for the NAIC.

The manual was developed in response to some of the reserve requirements in codification. In particular, the requirement for a premium deficiency reserve was a significant change in statutory accounting practices for many HMOs and Blue Cross Blue Shield plans. (Many life insurance companies were already subject to the NAIC's Health Insurance Reserves Model Regulation, which includes a gross premium valuation requirement. The gross premium valuation requirement is similar in concept to a premium deficiency reserve.)

The Health Reserves Guidance Manual (HRGM) covers claim reserves (including claim liabilities), contract reserves, provider liabilities, and premium deficiency reserves. The HRGM is referenced in SSAP #54 of the Accounting Practices and Procedures Manual. This reference gives greater authority to the HRGM. The following provides a brief discussion of some items in the HRGM which are not covered in other chapters. (For a more in-depth discussion on the methods used to calculate reserves, refer to the chapter on short term claim reserves and liabilities. For a more in-depth discussion on specific statutory financial reporting requirements, refer to that chapter.)

CLAIM RESERVES

Definition of Claim Reserves

The Health Reserves Guidance Manual (HRGM) defines a claim reserve as "a measurement of a reporting entity's contractual obligation to pay benefits as of a specified date." "Benefits" include those covered by a capitation arrangement with a medical provider. Accordingly, the claim reserve should include provision for any capitation payments that are due as of the valuation date but have not been paid.

Data Reconciliation and Quality

The HRGM states that "all claim data used to calculate reserves should be reconciled, to the extent possible, with paid claims reported by the carrier in its financial statement." The reconciliation might be prepared by another person, but should at least be reviewed by the actuary. Documentation should be prepared by the actuary that covers data quality and data reconciliation.

Conservatism

The HRGM states that "To the extent that assumptions are made at the expected level, an overall load for conservatism should then be added to this average reserve." The HRGM states that support should be provided for the adequacy of the margin. The HRGM states that "The best support will be an analysis of historical data, indicating how frequently the underlying method produces inadequate reserves ..." An example of this type of analysis is included in the chapter on applied statistics. The level of conservatism might vary by type of coverage and size of block of business. However, the main concern is the adequacy of the reserves in the aggregate for a reporting entity.

Follow-up Studies

Follow-up studies are used to determine the accuracy of prior reserve estimates. A follow-up study involves comparing (a) the prior reserve estimate, to (b) the actual claim runout plus a reserve for any remaining claim runout. The HRGM states that follow-up studies should be performed for each category of business used in establishing reserves. The HRGM also states that follow-up studies should be performed at a minimum for each year-end, but preferably at the end of each reporting period (monthly or quarterly).

CONTRACT RESERVES

Definition of Contract Reserves

The HRGM defines a contract reserve as "a reserve set up when a portion of the premium collected in the early years is meant to help pay for higher claim costs arising in the later years." In general, contract reserves are required when the present value of future benefits exceeds the present value of future valuation net premiums. This typically occurs for issue age rated policies, which might include coverages such as individual disability income, long term care, and Medicare Supplement. Some companies might also hold contract reserves for products with multi-year rate guarantees, or for attained-age rate medical products where the premiums in the early durations are intended to prefund some of the cost increases due to the wear-off of underwriting selection and for cumulative antiselection.

The APPM and the Health Insurance Reserves Model Regulation provide additional details and requirements regarding the calculation of contract reserves.

Special Issues

The HRGM discusses some issues that are not explicitly addressed in the APPM or in the Health Insurance Reserves Model Regulation. These issues include: (a) recognition of inflationary cost increases in the development and updating of contract reserve factors, and (b) the morbidity basis for business that does not have a specifically required morbidity table.

PROVIDER LIABILITIES

The HRGM defines a provider liability as "the reporting entity's obligation to make future payments to providers under some form of risk-sharing arrangement." A risk-sharing arrangement is an arrangement where payment is contingent upon certain financial or operating goals being achieved. This does not include capitation or fee-for-service payments, unless subject to such a contingency.

PREMIUM DEFICIENCY RESERVES

The HRGM provides a definition of premium deficiency reserve and discusses the calculation methodology, key assumptions, and general considerations. Many of these general considerations were also discussed above in the section on SSAP #54. The general considerations include: how to group the contracts, time period for the projection, and use of marginal versus fully allocated administrative expenses.

Definition of Premium Deficiency Reserve

The HRGM defines a premium deficiency reserve as "a reserve that is established when future premiums and current reserves are not sufficient to cover future claim payments and expenses for the remainder of a contract period."

GROUPING OF CONTRACTS

The HRGM indicates that groupings should "reflect how premium rates are developed and applied" and that "this will usually result in groupings by product type and case size." Companies often group policies based on the line of business definitions in the annual statement. According to the HRGM "Other criteria that may be considered include...marketing methods, geographic rating areas, and length of rate guarantee." Some actuaries prefer broad groupings for the purpose of testing for premium deficiency reserves, since the actuarial opinion is really focused on the overall solvency of the company. The HRGM does state that "each grouping should be large enough to be material relative to the size of the reporting entity."

Product groupings might include: comprehensive medical, Medicare Supplement, Medicare+Choice, Medicaid, dental, and stop loss. Group size categories might include: individual, small group, large group, and mega group. Some actuaries might combine some or all of these segments related to group business.

Time Period for the Projection

The beginning of the time period is the valuation date. Regarding the end point for the time period, the HRGM states "The ending of the time period is more difficult to determine, and requires a substantial amount of judgment in many cases." Some actuaries interpret the requirement in SSAP #54 to require a projection to the end of the current contract year. However, for some segments of business, the HRGM suggests a longer term time horizon. The HRGM states "there may be a block of business that renews annually, but for which the premiums are subject to regulatory restrictions. In that case, the contract period implicitly lasts until the business can be restored to profitability or lapses completely." The HRGM also discourages using long term gains to offset short term losses.

Administrative Expenses

The HRGM states that the "expenses considered for a particular grouping should represent a reasonable allocation of all the reporting entity's expenses." However, the HRGM also states that it is acceptable to use marginal expense assumptions if other lines of business can support the overhead: "If other lines of business can cover overhead expenses, the test for a deficiency and the calculation of the deficiency reserve can be performed using only direct costs."

ACTUARIAL PRACTICE NOTES

Actuarial Practice Notes are developed by the American Academy of Actuaries to provide information to actuaries on current actuarial practices in new or developing areas. Practice Notes are not interpretations of Actuarial Standards of Practice (ASOPs), nor do they convey generally accepted actuarial practices in the same sense that ASOPs do. Practice Notes have not been promulgated by the Actuarial Standards Board, nor are they binding on any actuary.

The Health Practice Notes relevant to reserving include:

Health Practice Note	Title
1995-1	General Considerations
1995-3	Large Group Medical Business
1995-9	Long-Term Care Insurance Business
2003	Long-Term Care Insurance Compliance with the NAIC LTCI Model Regulation Relating to Rate Stability
August 2005	Individual Major Medical Business
October 2005	Small Group Medical Insurance Reserves and Liabilities
March 2006	Medicare Supplement
March 2006	Statutory Reserves for Individual Disability Income Insurance
August 2006	Group Long-Term Disability Income Insurance

The Practice Notes listed above represent a description of practices believed by the work group to be commonly employed by health actuaries in the United States. Although some of these Practice Notes are focused on individual coverages, they are included in the list for completeness.

These Practice Notes were developed in response to the requirements in the NAIC's Actuarial Opinion and Memorandum Regulation, the Standard Valuation Law, and the Accounting Practices and Procedures Manual. They are intended to provide guidance to health actuaries regarding determining adequate reserve levels and complying with asset adequacy requirements.

The Practice Notes are available on the web site of American Academy of Actuaries at www.actuary.org.

21 SMALL GROUP RATE FILINGS AND RATE CERTIFICATIONS

James T. O'Connor

INTRODUCTION

In the early 1990's the National Association of Insurance Commissioners (NAIC) and most states introduced regulatory reforms related to the underwriting, marketing, and rating of small employer group insurance. The extent of these early reforms varied somewhat from state to state, but most laws shared common elements. In 1996, the federal government enacted the Health Insurance Portability and Accountability Act (HIPAA), which set uniform requirements for small employer medical insurance carriers related to the underwriting and marketing of such insurance.

Most states require that each small group insurance carrier provide an annual rate certification, signed by a qualified actuary, attesting that the carrier's rates, and, in some states, underwriting and marketing procedures are in compliance with state law. Many states also require the filing of small group premium rates before they can be used. This chapter discusses these important laws and related regulations, as well as the required rate certifications.

NAIC MODEL LAWS AND REGULATION

The first of the NAIC model laws was adopted in December of 1990. This was followed in December, 1991, by the model law which many states enacted and which is today the basis for most of the small employer group rating laws. This model law is entitled "Small Employer Health Insurance Availability Model Act." There are two versions, one for "Prospective Reinsurance With or Without an Opt-Out" and the other "Allocation With or Without an Opt-Out." The differences between these two versions are not

409

related to the topic of this chapter. In March of 1993, the NAIC adopted the "Model Regulation to Implement the Small Employer Health Insurance Availability Model Act." Few states have enacted this model, although many states have included parts of the model regulation. Later, the NAIC adopted a new model law intended as a more restrictive alternative to the 1991 model. This model entitled "Small Employer and Individual Health Insurance Availability Model Act" governed the rating and underwriting of individual medical insurance, as well as small group insurance. Few states have revised their small group laws to this latest model.

Because the most common provisions of the states' small group rating laws are based upon the 1991 NAIC model, this is the model law upon which this chapter will concentrate. Its most salient features will now be discussed.

APPLICABILITY

The laws apply to health benefit plans that provide medical coverage to employees of small employers issued by health insurance carriers and HMOs. This includes coverage on individual policy forms, as well as group forms, if the employer sponsors the plan by paying or reimbursing the employee for a portion of the premium or by receiving a federal tax benefit.

While the NAIC model originally applied to groups of 2 to 25 employees, today a small employer is most commonly defined as one with 2-50 eligible employees. This coincides with the HIPAA definition of a small group, to which all states and insurers needed to adhere in order to comply with the marketing and underwriting requirements of HIPAA. However, it should be noted that several states still define a *small employer* for rating purposes as having 2-25 eligible employees or a range somewhat different than that of the HIPAA definition. A few states also extend the rating restriction down to a group of one employee (sole proprietorships and self-employed).

THE AFFILIATE RULE

The model law requires carriers that are affiliated companies, or eligible to file a consolidated tax return, be treated as a single carrier with respect to rating and other restrictions of the law. This can be a significant consideration for corporate groups that acquire business through the purchase of new companies. The intent of the rule was to limit the use of a strategy of moving less healthy business out of one carrier into another in order to minimize the impact of the model law's rating limitations. HMO affiliates may be treated as an exception to this rule.

Many states have not adopted this rule as part of their small group law. Several states have included language that allows the corporate group to treat affiliates separately as long as no small group business is transferred from one related carrier to another. This approach effectively limits potential gaming abuse without discouraging legitimate acquisition of small employer insurance companies by other companies.

CLASSES OF BUSINESS

The NAIC model law allows carriers to classify their small employer group business in up to nine classes. However, these classifications may only reflect substantial differences in expected claim experience or administrative costs, and only if certain criteria are met. Those criteria include business being sold through different distribution systems, acquiring a block of small group business from another carrier, or providing coverage to members of legitimate associations. States vary considerably in their adoption of class limitations. Under the NAIC Model, the use of business classes can legitimately allow up to an additional 20% rating differential between blocks of small employer business. There are additional comments later in the chapter regarding the use of classes.

Consumer-driven health plans (CDHP) introduce a new consideration for a carrier in determining its classes of business. A few carriers have argued that CDHP plans should be considered a separate class However, at this point, it appears that most carriers have included CDHP plans in the same class as their traditional medical business.

ALLOWABLE CASE CHARACTERISTICS VERSUS OTHER RISK CHARACTERISTICS

One of the most critical aspects of the small employer rating laws is the recognition of certain case characteristics as allowable rating factors, not subject to premium range limitation tests of the law. The Model Law defines *Case Characteristics* as follows:

"Case characteristics" means demographic or other objective characteristics of a small employer that are considered by the small employer carrier in the determination of premium rates for the small employer, provided that claim experience, health status and duration of coverage shall not be case characteristics for the purposes of this Act.

The Model Act continues in Section 6A.(10) to limit allowable case characteristics to age, gender, geographic area, family composition, and group size, unless prior approval of the commissioner is received for others. Furthermore, it limits the use of industry as a rating factor to a spread of 15% between the lowest and highest industry rating factors. The NAIC model regulation limits the use of group size to a maximum of 20% between the highest and lowest factors.

There exists a lot of variation between states in their limitations as to what can or cannot be used as an allowable case characteristic. Many follow the NAIC model (but some without the 20% group size limitation). Some simply require that allowable case characteristics are objective and applied consistently, but otherwise do not list what can or cannot be used, other than disallowing claim experience, duration of coverage, and health status. A number of states no longer allow gender as an allowable case characteristic rating factor. Many do not allow industry. Others do not allow group size, while a few recognize differences due to group size only to the extent that administrative expenses differ, but not for expected morbidity variation. Almost all states allow rating variation by geographic area, but a couple states limit the number of rating areas or the amount of rating variation by area.

It is important to a carrier's rating strategies to know what each state will or will not allow. For example, the state of Florida recognizes "tobacco usage status" as an allowable case characteristic, while many other states consider it as a health status characteristic. There are other case characteristics that may be allowed in less restrictive states. These are discussed in the chapter in this text on "Underwriting Small Groups." One new case characteristic that some carriers may use is the presence of a health savings account (HSA) or other CDHP features, since such a structure can impact claim experience and premium rates. The more case characteristics that can be justified for use as "allowable" will provide the carrier with more rating flexibility and a greater total spread of rates between groups. Due to rating system limitations, compliance concerns, and market habits, most carriers have not employed many of these other objective characteristics in their rating structures.

Variance in coverage characteristics (the benefits) of the plan are allowable differences, that do not need to be included as part of the rate range variation that is limited by the law. Certain aspects of allowed variance for this are discussed in the testing section of this chapter.

Most state insurance departments require that the rating factors used for case and coverage characteristics be reasonable and based on actuarial analysis. The NAIC has published a guidance manual for implementation of the Model Act, providing ranges deemed to be reasonable for various benefit and case characteristics.

THE INDEX RATE

Under the Model Act, an index rate is to be determined for each class of business for each rating period, for small employers with similar case characteristics. The index rate is the arithmetic average of the applicable base premium rate and the corresponding highest premium rate. The base premium rate is the lowest rate charged or that *could* be charged under the rating system. Very often the base rate is the new business rate the carrier uses, although this is not necessarily the case. The index is calculated only after all the rates have been adjusted to account for all the allowable case characteristics and benefit design variations. Benefit design includes expected managed care impact and preferred provider negotiated discounts.

Use of a "unified" rating manual for all plans sold within a class generally makes it easy to determine the index rate, provided that the carrier does not make exceptions to the manual. The base rate would be the lowest possible rate (after case characteristic and benefit adjustment) that could be charged under the rating manual. The corresponding highest rate would be 67% higher than the base rate, under the NAIC model law. (The 67% factor comes from a comparison of the highest to lowest rates allowed under the ±25% rule, described further below) The model law requires that the insurer maintain a rating manual for each class of business. It leaves the structure of the rating manual up to each carrier. Some are more complicated than others.

RATING RESTRICTIONS BETWEEN CLASSES

While the use of classes for business of differing risk as described above provides the carrier with additional rating and underwriting flexibility, the rating differential between classes is limited to 20% between the lowest to highest class index rates.

Rating Restrictions within a Class of Business

Under the Model Act, within a class of business, premium rates charged during a rating period (to groups with similar case characteristics and similar coverage) cannot vary from the index rate by more than 25%. (This rule varies in some states.) This means the highest rate cannot exceed the base rate by more than 67% $\left((1+.25) \div (1-.25) - 1 = .67\right)$. Again, the premium rates referred to are those after adjustment for allowable case and benefit plan characteristics.

Rate Increase Limitations

The Model Act limits rate increases applied to each group, to the sum of the following:

1. The percentage change in the new business rate measured from the first day of the prior rating period to the first day of the new rating period;

2. 15% annually for experience, adjusted pro rata for rating periods of less than one year (this also varies by state); and

3. Any adjustment due to change in coverage or case characteristics.

The Model Act and most of the state versions of the law specify the rate increase limit as the *sum* of the three items. Many actuaries feel that a literal interpretation of this was not intended by the drafters of the Model Act. This non-literal interpretation is supported by drafters of the NAIC Model Regulation as discussed later in this chapter.

However, the actuary certifying compliance should be aware that some states insist on the literal interpretation, particularly for the first two items.

Rating Consistency

The Model Law and many of the states' laws require that rating factors be consistently applied. This means that rates for groups with similar allowable case characteristics and the same benefit plan will be identical, except for the risk factor applied to each group. Even the choice of risk factor should be objectively and consistently applied. One way to demonstrate such application is the use of a well-organized rate manual and objective application of an underwriting manual.

One area of rating methodology that states have allowed under such requirements is the use of a composite (average per employee) rating approach for larger groups, while person-by-person, or "list billed" rating is used for smaller sized groups.

The use of different family composition rating structures (the rate tier structure) based upon choice by the employer is another example of inconsistent rating that is sometimes used by some carriers and condoned by many states.

ANNUAL RATE CERTIFICATION

Section 6.E(2) of the Model Act requires each small employer carrier to file with the commissioner an annual actuarial certification, certifying that the carrier is in compliance with the Act. Most states require such a filing. The due date for submission of the certification is March 15th in the Model Act and in many states. However, the due dates vary somewhat by state.

The certification generally needs to be signed by a qualified Member of the American Academy of Actuaries. Professional standards require that it be in accordance the Actuarial Standards Board's promulgated Actuarial Standard of Practice (ASOP) No. 26. The certification generally addresses the business over the past calendar year, but also may need to address the "actuarial soundness" of the rates both retrospectively and prospectively.

While the laws generally presume that the opinions will be "clean" (without language which qualifies the opinion), the actuary needs to indicate in the certification whether or not there are any exceptions to compliance.

Applicability as to what the actuary certifies varies from state to state. Some states, like the NAIC Model Law, require that the certification address compliance with the requirements of the entire Act. This includes not only the premium rates charged, but also the underwriting and fair marketing provisions of the law. Included in the opinion regarding the premium rates is a certification concerning their actuarial soundness. On the other hand, many states simply require that the certification address only the premium rates, often without the need to address their actuarial soundness. Therefore, before issuing the certification, the actuary needs to be familiar with what each state requires, and qualify the opinion to the extent certain aspects have not been reviewed in the process of certification (such as underwriting or fair marketing procedures of the company). Depending on the state's requirements, the information and data available from the carrier, and the timeframe in which to conduct the review, the amount of time and work needed to responsibly sign a certification can vary considerably.

ACTUARIAL SOUNDNESS OF RATES

As mentioned above, the Model Act and the laws of a number of states require the actuary to certify that the rating methods of the small employer carrier are "actuarially sound."

Certifying to "actuarial soundness" of the rates is perhaps the most controversial part of the certification process, for two reasons. First, the work involved to do a thorough review can be immense, especially if the certifying actuary has also not done the prior pricing of the plans. Reliance upon loss ratio reports and expected pricing targets is the most practical approach for testing for actuarial soundness. Second, many actuaries feel that, in at least some states, certain plans or benefit options cannot be priced on an actuarially sound basis, due to the restrictions imposed on the rating and underwriting by the state laws. ASOP No. 26 allows the opinion to be based upon an expectation of the aggregate adequacy of all the small group plans. Methods for testing for actuarial soundness are discussed later in this chapter.

COMPLIANCE TESTING

DATA NEEDS

ASOP No. 26 provides a data list that is likely to be needed in the certification review process. The extent of the data list for a specific state is dependent upon the requirements of the state regarding what the certification must address (such as premium rates, underwriting procedures, and fair marketing procedures). The needed information is also dictated by the numbers and types of business classes the carrier has, and the structure of its rate manuals.

Generally, the data and information needed include the following:

- The small group rate manual(s) used during the rating period being reviewed;
- The small group rate manual(s) used during the prior period;

- The policy and certificate forms used for the business; and
- Listing of groups in force during the testing period, by effective month or renewal month; this listing should include groups that lapsed during the testing period as well. There is a fair amount of information needed for each of these groups, including:

  ○ Actual rates charged at time of issue or renewal;

  ○ Actual rates charged during the previous rating period;

  ○ Group size (number of eligible employees, number of insured employees, and the number of dependents during the period being tested and the previous period);

  ○ The value of allowable case characteristics for each group, including detailed demographic census data, and their change from the prior year; and,

  ○ The value of any change in benefit from the previous year (such as an increase in plan deductible).

If the actuary also needs to opine on actuarial soundness, marketing processes, and/or underwriting procedures, the following would also be needed:

- Loss ratio and claim experience reports,
- Sales brochures and other solicitation materials,
- Description of the underwriting procedures,
- Underwriting results for each new group,
- Marketing materials, and
- Underwriting manual.

The amount of detail required for the review of these items will need to be determined by the certifying actuary based upon discussions with company management and his or her knowledge of the carrier's business.

SAMPLING

Ideally, 100% of the cases should be tested to determine compliance, especially for intra-class testing. However, there are situations that may require using sampling techniques for performing the tests. The need can occur for various reasons: the company has a long history of in force business that had used various rating approaches over time and may never have been converted to a unified rating system; the carrier may have a number of different classes of business with distinct rating manuals and rating methodologies; the insurer may simply have too large of a volume of group cases to do 100% testing; or the carrier's limited system capabilities prevents complete testing.

The NAIC Guidance Manual discusses sampling techniques in a broad sense. It refers to both random sampling and stratified sampling techniques. The determination of the sample size is best based upon a statistical analysis, choosing the likelihood of discovering non-compliant cases given $p\%$ of the total population cases are non-compliant. That likelihood should provide the actuary a high comfort level that the testing approach will expose non-compliant cases if any exist. If non-compliant cases are uncovered, sampling techniques do not necessarily indicate the magnitude of the problem, but do provide an indication of the existence of non-compliance.

INTRA-CLASS RANGE TESTING

Intra-class range testing is the verification that each group's rate is within ±25% (or whatever percentage is applicable in the state) of the index rate for groups with similar case characteristics and benefit plans. Technically, the law states that only such similarly situated groups need to be compared. However, it is not really practical to compare rates without using a rate normalization process to adjust rates for case and coverage characteristics, so that the groups' rates are then based on similar case and coverage characteristics.

The main challenge for intra-class range testing is expressing each group's rate on a consistent basis, since the case and coverage characteristics can vary considerably from group to group within a class. Normalization is fairly straightforward when rates are calculated using rating factors for each allowable case and coverage characteristic applied to a starting manual rate. Since these rating factors must be consistent for each group within a class, rates can readily be adjusted to remove the effect of these factors.

If the lowest rate that theoretically could be charged (the base rate) can be determined directly from the new business rating manual, the index rate can be calculated as the average of the lowest and the highest allowed health status adjustment factors. For example, if the lowest allowed rate in the rating manual equals 90% of the standard manual new business rate, and the highest allowed rate is 66% higher than the lowest rate, the index rate (ratio) will be: $\left[.90 + (.90 \times 1.66)\right] \div 2 = 1.197$.

However, not all carriers have systems that can normalize all rates for all characteristics. A testing method has been developed to address such a situation, provided that the carrier can provide two pieces of information: (1) the group's current rate, and (2) the new business rate for the group's current case characteristics and benefit plan. This method can easily test every group's rate for compliance for within class or intra-class rate compliance through computerized analysis. It assumes that the certifying actuary has already verified that the carrier is applying reasonable rating factors in a consistent manner to all groups in the class. Listings of actual and new business rates for each group can be compared, and then ratioed to a normalized rate, from which the index rate and then index ratios can be determined. A step-by-step description follows:

1. For each group, the carrier needs to provide the following rate data:

    a. The previous year's actual rate for the group, adjusted for changes between the previous year's census and the current year's census;

    b. The previous year's new business rate, for the most similar benefit design available at the group's date of rate renewal;

    c. The current year's actual rate for the group;

    d. The current year's new business rate on the group's date of rate renewal.

    This data will allow for not only the intra-class test, but also for the rate increase test. For the intra-class test, only items c and d are needed.

2. Sort cases together by rate renewal month (or by whatever rating periods are used).

3. For each rating period, calculate the ratio of the actual group rate to the corresponding applicable new business rate. This ratio automatically normalizes each rate charged for applicable case and benefit characteristics, and therefore puts each case on a comparable basis with all the other cases being renewed for that period. (This methodology is reasonable only if the case and benefit characteristics factors of the new business rates are consistent between plans. This consistency is a requirement of the small group laws.)

4. The index rate for each renewal month can be calculated as the arithmetic average of the minimum and maximum "ratios" for that renewal month calculated in Step 3.

If there are serious compliance problems, certain outlier case ratios could distort the calculation of the index rate, and may need to be excluded from the calculation. These outlier cases cannot be excluded from the determination of compliance, only from the determination of the index rate.

5. Divide each group's ratio calculated in Step 3 by the Index Ratio.

6. Any case whose ratio is outside the range of .75 to 1.25 (1.00 ± 25%) should be tagged for possible non-compliance. For states with test criteria different than 25%, the appropriate percentage should be used.

7. The rates for those groups that are tagged for possible non-compliance should then be reviewed thoroughly to see if there is a plausible and acceptable explanation as to the deviation (such as mid-year census changes for a composite rated group).

This methodology can easily process large blocks of business, and easily identify any groups with rates out of compliance. It does have certain limitations of which the actuary needs to be aware, particularly in regard to census and benefit changes that may not immediately be reflected in the rates when composite rating methods are used.

REASONABLENESS OF RATING FACTORS

As mentioned earlier, the approach described above assumes that the certifying actuary has already verified that the carrier is applying reasonable rating factors, in a consistent manner, to all groups in the class. The NAIC has published a guidance manual for implementation of the Model Act, providing ranges deemed to be reasonable for various benefit and case characteristics. This is useful to consult, but some of the factor ranges may be outdated since the NAIC does not regularly update the manual.

While many carriers base reasonableness of their factors on their experience data, for some coverage (benefit) characteristics, this may not be appropriate if inherent in the data is the impact of health status selection, which the Model Law does not allow to be reflected as an allowable difference. For example, groups selecting $2,500 deductible plans tend to be somewhat healthier than groups with $250 deductible plans. This difference in health status gets imbedded in the claim experience data. Therefore, if the ratio of the benefit factors for the two plans is calculated as the ratio of raw claim costs between the two sets of claim experience, health status differences would be imbedded in that benefit factor, which is contrary to what is allowed in the Model Law. However, if the deductible difference is calculated based on construction of a claim probability table from the experience of all of the carrier's business combined, health status differences would be eliminated for the most part. Alternatively, use of deductible differences from a consultant's pricing manual may provide an unbiased benefit factor. This issue is one of the reasons that all business in a class for a given rating period is combined and normalized for testing, rather than just testing each set of benefit options.

CDHPs introduce a similar issue to the testing. Many believe that people who opt for CDHPs tend to be healthier than those who choose traditional plans. While this may be true, it is not clear that they are healthier than people who opt for plans with the same deductible level without account funds. The certifying actuary will want to know how the benefit factors for the CDHP were developed and whether they are biased or not.

One characteristic to note about HSA plans is that they require aggregate family deductibles, unlike most traditional plans. This distinction should be identified in the normalization process.

CLASS RATE INCREASE TESTING

The Model Law and most state laws are very specific that the limitation applied to small group rates is based upon "the sum of" the three measures described previously. However, many actuaries have challenged the practicality and the reasonableness of applying a sum of all three. The NAIC responded to this reaction by clarifying in its Small Group Rating Regulation that:

A change in premium rate for a small employer shall produce a revised premium rate that is no more than the following:

(a) the base premium rate for the small employer (as shown in the rate manual as revised for the rating period), multiplied by

(b) one plus the sum of (i) the risk load applicable to the small employer during the previous rating period and (ii) 15%.

This interpretation allows the change in case and benefit characteristics to be multiplicative with the change in the base rate, with the 15% additive. However, the implication is that the new business rate is the base premium rate, which is not necessarily true.

In practice, carriers will determine the change in the new business rate for each given group's current demographics and benefit plan, and then add

15% to this ratio to determine the maximum allowable rate increase. This may involve the ability of the carrier to be able to state each group's previous rate for the group's current demographics and benefit plan. Similarly, the new business rates for both the previous rating period and the rating period being tested need to be determined for the group's current demographics and benefit plan. If systems are in place to perform this calculation, then the testing can be very straightforward. Alternatively, if the rating structure and manual are well organized, and rate increases for both new business and renewals are very well defined (a set percentage increase defined by specific case characteristics), the testing may be achieved through review of the application of the percentages and reasonable sample testing.

BETWEEN CLASS TESTING

As stated earlier, in states where separate rating classes are permitted, the rate differentials are limited generally to a maximum of 20% between the highest and lowest index rates. Testing for compliance with this requirement can be the most complex and time-consuming aspect of small group compliance testing, depending upon the structures of the rating manual for each class. The laws do not require consistency of rating factors or rate structures between classes. Because of this, a methodology to derive index rates on a comparative basis needs to be used.

If the rating formulas and the rating factors for each class are exactly the same, except for the starting normalized manual rates which differ by a fixed percentage, the verification of compliance can be very straightforward. However, in practice this is often not the case, especially when one of the classes is acquired business from another carrier. In these situations, the testing is more complex, requiring the normalization of the rate manuals or rate tables to a consistent basis.

The index rate is defined in terms of groups with similar case and coverage characteristics. To verify compliance, theoretically each and every group within a rating class would have to be rated according to the criteria of each and every one of the carrier's other rating classes. This extensive type of testing is usually not practical or feasible. The NAIC Guidance Manual suggests a methodology in which a minimum sample of 100 groups from each class is tested in this manner. If the resulting rates for each tested group in every class are within 20% of each other, then compliance is deemed to be demonstrated.

Another approach, not recommended by the NAIC Guidance Manual, is to test the rating manual of each class by developing rates for one or more sample censuses and plans of benefits. The resulting census rates for each class cannot exceed that of any other class by more than 20%. The limitation of this methodology is that there are very many possible combinations of censuses and benefit plans and this approach does not provide a high comfort level that the tested artificial census/benefit design combinations are necessarily representative of all such combinations.

Except for the first situation in which identical rating manuals are used, varying only by a class rating factor (from 1.00 to 1.20), no method is totally satisfying in assuring compliance.

TESTING PREMIUM RATES FOR ACTUARIAL SOUNDNESS

Some states have included in their laws the NAIC provision for certifying that the premium rates charged were or are actuarially sound. A definition of "actuarial soundness" is not provided in the NAIC model act, its model regulation, or its guidance manual. However, a definition is provided in Section 2.1 of ASOP No. 26.

> *"Actuarial Soundness – Small employer health benefit plan premium rates are actuarially sound if, for business in the state for which the certification is being prepared and for the period covered by the certification, projected premiums in the aggregate, including expected reinsurance cash flows, governmental risk adjustment cash flows, and investment income, are adequate to provide for all expected costs, including health benefits, health benefit settlement expenses, marketing and administrative expenses, and the cost of capital.*
>
> *For either a retrospective or a prospective certification, the determination of actuarial soundness is based on information available at the time the premium rates were established."*

This requires an analysis of the expected profitability of the premium rating manual and pricing methodology during the period of certification. This analysis might include a review of experience reports upon which the rates were based. Prospectively, it can include review of loss ratios or claim costs relative to expected levels during the period. Certifying to actuarial soundness is usually easiest if the certifying actuary is also the person who was involved in the pricing. It should be noted that financial losses do not necessarily mean that the rates were not set to be sound. The carrier may have reasonably expected the rates to be adequate based upon the information available at the time of pricing. For example, if the carrier had the misfortune of having more than its expected share of large claims, losses could result even though the rates had been set to be sound. Actual claim trend could prove to be considerably greater than expected. While premium stabilization reserves (claim fluctuation reserves) are not very common for small group business, the presence of such reserves should also be considered in determining the soundness of the rates.

UNDERWRITING REQUIREMENTS VERIFICATION

The NAIC model requires adherence to certain underwriting practices. Chief among these are the following:

- Guaranteed issue except for certain allowed exceptions (a HIPAA requirement);
- Guaranteed renewability except for certain allowed exceptions (a HIPAA requirement);
- Prohibition against singling out individual employees or dependents for special treatment (good or bad); and
- Application of rating factors and underwriting procedures on a consistent basis for every group.

The certifying actuary needs to review the carrier's underwriting guidelines, a set of reasonably selected applications, and the underwriting decisions for those cases based on the underwriting guidelines. It is best if the carrier has a set of published guidelines and protocols for its underwriters in making issue and rating decisions (this does not mean that underwriting judgment is eliminated). The actuary needs to feel comfortable that the underwriting practices are compliant with the intent of the law.

There are two particular areas of rating methodology that can prove to be challenging in deciding whether the rating has been consistently applied. These are:

- The use of composite rating for larger sized small groups while mini-groups are rated on a "list bill" basis;
- The use of multiple dependent tiering options for groups. Two-tiered (single and family), three-tiered (single, two-person, and family), four-tiered (single, couple, employee and children, and family);

Technically, the use of either of these might result in different rates for otherwise similarly situated groups. However, states have generally recognized the practical aspects of allowing both of these, provided that they are applied consistently. The actuary should verify each specific state's practice, particularly for allowance of family tiering choices.

ADHERENCE TO FAIR MARKETING REQUIREMENTS

The NAIC law also has a section on standards to assure fair marketing. The key points that would need to be certified to, if required, are the following:

- Under HIPAA, any plan offered for sale by a carrier to a small employer (with certain exceptions primarily related to association plans) within a class must be available to all small employers within the same class. There are specified exceptions based upon consistently applied employee participation and employer contribution rules, geographic location outside of the provider network area, provider network capacity limits, and carrier financial capacity. The last two require a cessation of marketing for 180 days.
- Under the NAIC Model Act and the laws of many states, carriers actively selling in the state must offer certain benefit plans mandated by state regulation, often referred to as "Standard" and "Basic" plans. These benefits are usually determined by a state sponsored board of directors, subject to the approval of the insurance commissioner.
- As part of its solicitation and sales materials, the carrier needs to make reasonable disclosure regarding four aspects of the rating and coverage:
  - The extent to which premium rates are related to the health status of the employees and their dependents;
  - The carrier's right to change premium rates and the factors that affect such changes;
  - The provisions relating to any pre-existing condition provisions; and,
  - The provisions relating to renewability of the policy and contracts.
- Commissions and other sales compensation cannot vary by the health status, claim experience, industry, occupation, or geographic location of the small employer within a state.
- Commissions and other sales compensation for sale of the state mandated plans must be reasonable. ("Reasonable" is not defined.)

- Carriers may not make the terms of a producer's contract subject to the health status, claim experience, occupation, or geographic location of the small employer business the producer sells.
- No carrier or producer may encourage an employer to exclude an employee from coverage.
- Denial of an application for coverage must be in writing with the reason(s) for denial stated.
- Third party administrators (TPA) retained by small group carriers are also subject to these rules.

Documentation of Compliance Testing

The ability of an actuary to certify adherence to these marketing requirements can be difficult, and is highly dependent upon the quality of documentation maintained by the carrier. Most states recognize that verification of marketing compliance is not an actuarial function, and therefore do not require the actuary to certify to it. Where required, at a minimum the carrier should be able to present a log of all applications received, the underwriting action on each applicant, sales compensation contracts in effect, required disclosure statements in the sales materials, and evidence of the disclosure of the availability of the state mandated plans.

The small group carrier is required to maintain at its office a complete and detailed description of its rating practices and renewal underwriting practices. Included should be the documentation of the compliance testing of the certifying actuary.

Premium Rate Certifications

As mentioned throughout this chapter, most states require that a qualified actuary certify to the compliance of at least the premium rates and rating methodology used by the carrier for its small group business. While a few states prescribe a format for the certification, most do not. ASOP No. 26 does provide a list of items that should be included in the certification.

It is very important that the actuary clearly indicate whether the statement of opinion is non-qualified or qualified. If qualified, the actuary should describe the sections of the law that are not in compliance, and state any actions that are being taken by the carrier to bring its rates and practices into compliance. Some actuaries provide detailed lists of groups failing the rating range and rate increase tests; others provide just summary disclosure of the failures.

The actuary may not be in a position to opine on all the requirements of the law. As such, the opinion statement must disclose that the actuary is providing a limited certification, pointing out which sections of the regulatory requirements are addressed and those which are not.

STATE VERSIONS OF THE LAWS

Most states adopted the second-generation model laws introduced by the NAIC, but only a few states enacted laws similar to the later NAIC model law. Most of the statutes and regulations enacted by the states contain at least some variation from the model laws. For this reason, each insurance carrier needs to be familiar with not only the NAIC models, but also the variations from the model in each state in which they operate.

PREMIUM RATE FILING REQUIREMENTS

Many states today require that policy forms, certificates, applications, disclosure statements, and premium rates to be used for small employer plans be filed with the states. Some require state insurance department approval before business can be sold in the state. Others require informational filings and do not have approval authority over the rates. The amount and type of information required also varies by state. Thus, rules for each state need to be reviewed before implementing the rates.

PRICING CONSIDERATIONS AND STRATEGIES RELATED TO COMPLIANCE REQUIREMENTS

In order to succeed in the small group marketplace, it is important that a carrier lay out a strategy for success before implementing a small group program. The strategy needs to begin with identification of the company's philosophy of how aggressively it will interpret and implement the small group requirements of each state and what risk characteristics it will reflect in its rating structure. There are system and actuarial resource implications to these decisions due to the wide range of variance of the laws by state.

Some carriers have implemented "middle of the road" strategies to be able to keep business fairly uniform among the states in terms of rating structures and case characteristics employed, while others have implemented local market strategies in which they make variations based upon each state's rules. Many carriers have decided to exit certain states that have very restrictive laws or in which the carriers' market share was too small to merit the administrative expense of complying with the state's rules. Quite a few carriers decided to withdraw from the small group market entirely, feeling the underwriting and rating restrictions made other venues more attractive for use of the company's capital.

22 FILINGS AND CERTIFICATIONS FOR MEDICARE-RELATED GROUP COVERAGES

Patrick J. Dunks
Eric P. Goetsch

INTRODUCTION

Even prior to the passage of the Medicare Prescription Drug, Improvement, and Modernization Act of 2003 (MMA), employers had numerous options for providing Medicare-related coverage to Medicare-eligible retirees and Medicare-eligible dependents. However, historically, most employers provided coverage through products that wrapped around Medicare's primary coverage. With the creation of Medicare's Part D prescription drug benefit, and an increasingly aggressive Medicare Advantage (MA) market following MMA, most employers providing coverage to Medicare-eligible retirees are now considering different approaches to providing these retiree health benefits.

EMPLOYER OPTIONS

Employers or unions can provide retiree medical benefits that add to traditional Medicare's Part A/B benefits by providing coverage that wraps around Medicare coverage, or they can replace and enhance Medicare's Part A/B benefits through an MA plan. The latter approach, whether through a plan sponsored by an employer or union, or through one purchased from an MA organization, requires an Actuarial Certification of the MA Part A/B bid underlying the plan. (The bid is a filing prepared for CMS, and uses a standardized format that shows the development of the premium rate and various other key financial measures.) Employers and unions are often interested in MA plans, because it is possible to realize reduced costs and/or increased benefits without additional cost.

Employers or unions can provide prescription drug benefits to Medicare-eligible beneficiaries in various ways, by: (1) wrapping coverage around retiree-purchased Medicare Part D plans, (2) providing primary coverage without a federal retiree drug subsidy (RDS), (3) providing primary coverage with a federal RDS, or (4) purchasing coverage on behalf of the retiree through a Part D plan. A Part D plan can be either a stand-alone prescription drug plan (PDP) or a Medicare Advantage plan with Part D (MA-PD). The third and fourth options listed above require actuarial certifications. The first, third, and fourth options provide value to employers by, respectively, reducing benefit costs, offsetting costs with a tax-free subsidy from the federal government, or providing premium reductions through Part D plan subsidies.

MA and PDP options that reduce costs for employers could also reduce employer liabilities (Financial Accounting Standards Board 106 or Government Accounting Standards Board 45) for post-retirement benefits other than pensions.

Insurer Appeal

In the Medicare-related group market, most insurers provide employers with support for their prescription drug RDS programs. Insurers not providing such support risk losing commercial group accounts.

MA organizations and PDPs tend to seek group enrollment because, in addition to the fundamental objective of growing their plan, marketing costs for group enrollment are substantially lower compared to those for a similar number of individual Medicare beneficiaries.

Medicare Advantage Plans

MA group products are part of the MA program administered by the Centers for Medicare & Medicaid Services (CMS), and described in Chapter 13. However, several CMS waivers for certain employer groups allow MA group products more flexibility than MA individual products.

Employer Group Waivers

In each service area, an MA organization must submit Part A/B and Part D bids for each MA-PD individual benefit plan and Part A/B bids for each MA-only individual plan. For MA-PD group plans, the MA organization only needs to submit two Part A/B and Part D bids, one each for calendar year and non-calendar year plans. For MA-only group plans, only one Part A/B bid needs to be submitted. MA organizations usually submit their employer group plan Part A/B bids with traditional Medicare benefits plus non-specific additional employer group benefits. Part D employer group bids are filed with standard Part D benefits.

For each employer group, the MA organization may build a benefit plan tailored to that employer, as long as: (1) the benefit plan is, on average, at least as rich as traditional Medicare benefits and (2) the MA organization maintains an actuarial development in their files demonstrating how they spent the non-specific additional benefit cost (contained in their Part A/B group bid) to benefit Medicare-eligible retirees. Such additional benefit costs often include one or more of: reducing A/B cost sharing, relaxing Medicare benefit limits, adding non-Medicare benefits, enhancing Part D benefits, or reducing Part D premiums for employer groups. MA organizations and employers negotiate employer-specific premiums, just as they do with other group coverage. Medicare-eligible retiree contributions are limited, so that retirees are not disadvantaged relative to the filed bid premiums and benefits.

In general, MA organizations are allowed to expand their employer group product service areas to include all Medicare-eligible retirees residing in the state for network products, as long as: (1) the majority of the employer's employees reside in the MA organization's individual plan service area and (2) the MA organization agrees to reimburse non-contracted providers at Medicare allowable fee levels. Beginning in 2008, MA organizations can expand non-network employer group products to retirees residing anywhere in the United States. Changes and further details about MA employer group waivers may be found at the CMS website[1]

PART A/B EMPLOYER GROUP BIDS

As actuaries develop Part A/B bids for MA organizations, they estimate risk-adjusted benchmark CMS revenue, develop medical and administrative cost estimates for traditional Medicare benefits, add a target profit load to the cost estimates, and then subtract those cost estimates from the benchmark revenue estimate to project savings. as defined by CMS. To maintain actuarial soundness, the revenue and cost estimates need to reflect the same underlying population characteristics.

CMS requires the MA organization to provide additional benefits that, together with a relative administrative and profit load equal to that used for the traditional Medicare benefit bid, have value equal to or greater than seventy-five percent of savings. CMS retains the remaining twenty-five

---

[1] http://www.cms.hhs.gov

percent of savings. For employer group bids, however, the MA organization can simply file a placeholder benefit rather than precisely defining the additional benefits as the organization must do for individual plan bids.

When developing employer group Part A/B bids, actuaries consider available base period experience, other data sources, expected cost trends, anticipated population characteristics (and associated risk scores), administrative costs, and target profit loads. Base period experience must be reported on the bid form.

For many MA organizations, employer group enrollment may be relatively low, so risk score and medical cost experience could be less than fully credible. So, employer group bids are often based on individual MA plan experience, with appropriate adjustments for group plan characteristics. If the MA organization doesn't have credible experience under the MA program, risk scores and cost estimates are often developed based on CMS projections, sample Medicare beneficiary experience under traditional Medicare, or other research. Even when experience is credible, risk scores and cost estimates are often used to test experience data.

Adjustments applied to experience reflect recent experience trends, expected provider reimbursement changes, changes resulting from care management modifications, expected traditional Medicare trends, and other factors. For organizations with MA provider contracts that mirror traditional Medicare reimbursement, expected provider reimbursement changes often mirror traditional Medicare trends.

Part A/B bids include estimated Part A/B risk scores for the expected enrollment, and these should be consistent with the underlying medical cost estimates, whether based on actual experience or manual rating approaches. The estimated risk scores should also be adjusted for anticipated improvements in provider disease coding, the organization's capture of such coding, and any announced changes in the CMS-HCC risk adjustment mechanism.

The Part A/B bids should also reflect the service area, any expected utilization changes due to benefit level changes, the impact of care management, expected administrative costs, and target profit levels.

CMS indicates that administrative cost targets should generally be consistent with the plan's most recent budgets and appropriate GAAP methodology, to the extent this is consistent with the organization's standard accounting practices. CMS expects target profit levels to be consistent with return on investment for the organization's other products.

Many considerations for MA organization Part D bids are similar to those for Part A/B bids. We discuss Part D considerations for MA organizations and stand-alone PDPs later in this chapter. One consideration specific to MA-PD plans is that administrative costs common to Part A/B and Part D, such as enrollment and overhead, should be allocated in proportion to risk revenue under the Part A/B and Part D components.

CMS issues electronic bid forms, instructions, suggested actuarial certification language, and filing directions in early April each year. Part of the bid includes a certification by the actuary that the bid conforms to Actuarial Standards of Practice (ASOP), as promulgated by the Actuarial Standards Board. The instructions ask the actuary pay particular attention to ASOPs 5, 8, 16, 23, 25, and 31.

Bids and actuarial certifications are submitted on or before the first Monday of each June for the following calendar year. The first review, a "desk review" of the bid, looks at reasonableness and consistency, and focuses on that year's areas of emphasis as determined by CMS. CMS also performs audits on bids, which are in-depth reviews of them. CMS is required under current law to audit one-third of MA organizations every year.

SPECIAL NEEDS PLANS FOR EMPLOYER GROUPS

MA organizations can create special needs plans (SNPs) to restrict enrollment to members with particular characteristics. SNPs can be created for dual eligible (Medicare/Medicaid) members, institutionalized members, and members with specific diseases. Disease-specific SNPs have been created to target members with diseases such as diabetes, chronic heart failure, chronic obstructive pulmonary disease, or HIV-AIDS. Organizations that offer disease-specific SNPs must create care management programs that target that disease. Their planned care management programs must be approved by CMS as part of their SNP application.

Except as noted above, MA rules and regulations apply to SNPs. However, all SNPs must include prescription drug coverage. Similarly to regular MA plans, SNPs can be offered as employer group coverage. SNP bids should reflect the expected SNP population and any special care management or other programs offered. Other considerations are similar to those for regular MA plans.

MEDICARE SUPPLEMENT PLANS

Group Medicare Supplement health policy forms must be filed with state insurance departments. Employer group Medicare Supplement rates must be filed and approved in some states while association group rates must be approved in all states. Typically, rate filings require actuarial memorandums or statements. Each state sets its own requirements for insurance products so actuaries can check with each state for particulars.

When developing Medicare Supplement rates, actuaries consider available experience, other data sources, expected cost trends, anticipated population characteristics, administrative costs, target profit loads, loss ratio requirements, if any, and competitive issues.

For many Medicare Supplement insurers, employer group enrollment may be relatively low, so experience may be not be fully credible. For this reason, group rates are sometimes developed based on individual Medicare Supplement plan experience, with appropriate adjustments for group characteristics (such as underwriting differences). If the Medicare Supplement insurer doesn't have credible experience, cost estimates are often developed based on rating manuals available for purchase, rate filings available for other carriers, or other sources. Even when experience is credible, alternate cost estimates are often used to test experience data.

Adjustments applied to experience reflect recent experience trends, expected traditional Medicare trends, and other factors.

Other employer group health products for Medicare-eligible retirees that are not legally Medicare Supplement policies, often called Medicare Wrap or Retiree Health plans, are not subject to rate approval authority although a few states still require submission of the rates for their records. Employers and insurers negotiate rates for these types of plans.

PRESCRIPTION DRUG PLANS UNDER PART D

Prescription drug coverage through stand-alone PDP or MA-PD group products are part of the Part D program administered by CMS, and described in Chapter 13. However, similarly to the MA plans described earlier, numerous CMS employer group waivers have allowed group products with Part D coverage to be more flexible than similar individual products.

EMPLOYER GROUP WAIVERS

In each service area, a PDP or MA-PD organization must submit Part D bids for each benefit plan sold to individuals. For employer group plans, however, PDP organizations may submit just two Part D bids for their business across the nation; one for calendar year plans, and one for non-calendar year plans. MA-PD organizations must submit group bids in each service area due to A/B bid requirements. CMS instructs insurers to file employer group Part D bids with standard Part D benefits.

For each employer group, the PDP or MA-PD organization may build a benefit plan tailored to that employer as long as the benefit plan meets CMS' Part D equivalence requirements. Those requirements are that: (1) group-specific benefits must be, on average, at least as rich as standard Part D benefits, (2) the plan deductible must be no greater than the standard Part D deductible, and (3) catastrophic coverage must be at least as rich as standard Part D catastrophic coverage. Most employer group plans meet the first two requirements easily, but many plans must improve catastrophic coverage. PDP and MA-PD organizations and employers negotiate employer-specific premiums.

In general, PDPs are allowed to expand their group product service areas to include all Medicare-eligible retirees residing in the United States. CMS' website[2] should contain any modifications or further details. MA-PD group waivers are generally limited by MA requirements discussed earlier in this chapter.

PART D EMPLOYER GROUP BIDS

As actuaries develop employer group Part D bids for PDPs or MA-PDs, they develop prescription drug and administrative cost estimates for standard Part D benefits, add a target profit load to the cost estimates, and estimate Part D risk scores consistent with the cost estimates.

When developing employer group Part D bids, it is important to consider available experience, other data sources, expected cost trends, expected rebates, formularies, anticipated population characteristics and associated risk scores, administrative costs, and target profit loads. Base period experience must be reported on the bid form.

---

[2] http://www.cms.hhs.gov

As with MA plans, for many PDPs and MA-PDs, employer group enrollment may be relatively low, so risk score and drug claim cost experience could be less than fully credible. Even if overall drug claim cost experience is credible, the drug claim cost distribution critical to Part D bid development may not be. Thus, as described before, employer group bids are often based on individual experience, with appropriate adjustments. If a PDP or MA-PD organization doesn't have credible Part D experience, risk score and drug cost estimates are often developed based on other available data. Even when experience is credible, such risk score and cost estimates are often used to test experience data.

Adjustments applied to experience reflect many thing; recent experience trends, expected pharmacy or pharmacy benefit manager (PBM) reimbursement changes, expected drug cost trends, utilization trends, expiration of patents on high cost drugs (leading to introduction of generic equivalents), expected utilization shifts from generic to new brand drugs, the release of new drugs, the impact of the experience's underlying benefit levels on utilization, formulary changes, drug utilization review modifications, medication therapy management modifications, and other factors. The design of the Part D benefit (deductibles, initial coverage periods, coverage gaps, and catastrophic coverage) requires consideration of the potentially different impact of the above factors on each segment of the pharmacy claim cost distribution, in addition to the impact on overall cost.

Total drug rebates must also be estimated as part of the bid process. Rebate contracts with PBMs or pharmaceutical manufacturers, and many of the above factors, influence those rebate levels.

Part D bids include estimated Part D risk scores for the expected enrollment, and those estimates should be consistent with the underlying pharmacy estimates, whether based on actual experience or manual rating approaches. The estimated risk scores should also be adjusted for anticipated improvements in provider disease coding, the organization's capture of such coding, and any announced changes in the Part D risk adjustment mechanism.

Part D bids should also reflect expected administrative costs and target profit levels. As with MA bids, administrative cost targets should be consistent with recent budgets and appropriate GAAP methodology. Target profit should be consistent with the return on investment for other products.

The timing, certification, ASOP concerns, and review process are the same as for Part A/B group bids.

SPECIAL NEEDS PLANS FOR EMPLOYER GROUPS

As discussed earlier, MA-PD organizations can create SNPs to restrict enrollment to members with particular characteristics. SNP Part D bids should reflect the expected SNP population and any special care management or other programs offered. Other considerations are similar to those for regular MA-PD plans.

RETIREE DRUG SUBSIDY FOR PLAN SPONSORS UNDER PART D

In order to encourage employers and unions to maintain prescription drug coverage under their retiree health programs, the MMA provides for a tax-free subsidy to qualified plans. The subsidy is 28% of drug claim costs within a claim interval defined by indexed endpoints. In order to receive the subsidy, a plan sponsor must provide prescription drug coverage that is actuarially equivalent to standard Part D coverage. Actuarial equivalence for the RDS is relatively simple, compared to the approach described for PDPs and MA-PDs.

To receive the RDS, a plan sponsor must apply for the RDS each year and then report drug claim cost to CMS. The applications require an actuarial attestation that the plan meets the "gross" and "net" tests defined in CMS regulations. Additional details are available on CMS' website[3]

The gross test examines whether the plan's prescription drug benefit provides coverage that is, on average, at least as rich as standard Part D coverage. The gross test must be performed separately for each benefit option within a group health plan. The gross test includes all Part D covered drugs. In other words, when performing the gross test, a benefit option's coverage of non-Part D drugs cannot contribute to the benefit value compared to standard Part D's benefit value, and similarly, its lack of coverage of Part D covered drugs counts against it.

The net test examines whether the portion of the group health plan benefit paid for by the plan sponsor is at least as great as the value of the standard

---

[3] http://www.cms.hhs.gov/EmployerRetireeDrugSubsid

Part D benefit paid for by CMS. The net test must be performed separately for each group health plan.

When performing the gross and net tests, actuaries consider available experience, other data sources, expected cost trends, expected rebates (if any), formularies, the cost of drugs not covered by Part D, and anticipated population characteristics.

For many group health plans, enrollment may be relatively low, so drug cost experience might not be fully credible. Even if overall drug cost experience is credible, the drug claim cost distribution critical to comparing the plan's benefits to standard Part D benefits may not be. Thus, tests may use a blend of group health plan prescription drug experience and other data sources.

Adjustments applied to experience are similar to those described in developing Part D bids. The design of the Part D benefit (deductible, initial coverage corridor, coverage gap, and catastrophic coverage) warrants consideration of the potentially different impact of all relevant factors on the employer's design plan, across different segments of the pharmacy claim cost distribution, in addition to the impact on overall cost.

If drug rebates on Part D drugs are shared with the group health plan, the extent to which they reduce plan sponsor drug expenditures should be considered.

The gross and net tests are pass/fail tests. Given the lack of precision inherent in actuarial projections, test results that are initially close to the pass/fail line often warrant additional testing using alternate assumptions or methods. In the end, the actuary should be prepared to defend the selection of final assumptions supporting the attestation.

Actuarial Standards of Practice 5, 6, 8, 16, 23, 25, 31, 41, and 42 may provide guidance when performing RDS attestations. The American Academy of Actuaries issued a Health Practice Note that provides additional discussion concerning attestation issues.

The RDS application and attestation are administered entirely through CMS' website.[4]

---

[4] ibid

Plan Sponsor Creditable Coverage Notices

MMA requires plan sponsors to send creditable coverage notifications to all Medicare-eligible covered individuals (whether actively employed or retired), by November 15 prior to the upcoming calendar year of coverage. Individuals maintaining creditable coverage will not be penalized if they later join Part D. Individuals without creditable coverage, if they do not initially elect Part D coverage but wish to do so later, will be charged a lifetime late enrollment penalty (1% of the nationwide average premium for each month without coverage prior to joining Part D.)
Coverage is considered creditable if the benefit plan passes the gross test described above. In other words, the benefit plan is as least as rich as standard Part D coverage, on average. The net value test is not required for determining creditable coverage.

CMS regulations offer safe harbors for plan sponsors to determine creditable coverage without the assistance of a qualified actuary. The previously footnoted CMS website contains details. If the creditable coverage determination does not fall under a safe harbor, a more rigorous application of the gross test described above is anticipated.

SECTION FIVE

UNDERWRITING AND MANAGING THE RISK

23 INFORMATION MANAGEMENT

Robert E. Worthington
William R. Lane

INFORMATION MANAGEMENT

WHAT IS IT? WHY IS IT SO IMPORTANT?

Information management is the discipline of planning, creating, presenting, and applying information to improve business performance and decision-making processes. More than data management, it includes the steps necessary to put meaning and relevance to data. If done well, it also finds new insights about the company, it's consumers, and it's industry.

Real business advantages emerge from effective information management. Early, insightful knowledge and action about consumer buying patterns, performance trends of suppliers, and opportunity within an industry, is an acute competitive advantage for any business.

Health care companies use information management in much the same way as other businesses. They seek to preempt competition with unique knowledge about markets, providers, competitive pricing, the quantity and quality of health care services being delivered, and what consumers want from their health care plans.

Today, health plans strive to improve the quality of care, as well as to manage health care costs. To do this, health plans must firmly understand the factors driving health care demand, delivery, and costs, and what constitutes quality care. Information management provides techniques and tools to help develop this knowledge base.

The integration of quality and cost eventually leads to value-based results, such as pricing for services based on outcomes. The cycle of: (1) defining

441

practice guidelines, (2) using the guidelines for caregiving, measuring and recording results, and (3) adjusting guidelines, is being used to constantly refine the cost/quality relationship.

To achieve effective information management, companies must first practice effective data management. Data gathering, quality, grouping, storage, and retrieval activities must be dependable and routine. Most companies are using some type of data warehouse approach to make pertinent data available to anyone in the business who needs it and is authorized to use it.

THE DATA WAREHOUSE AND RELATED TOOLS

Data begins to become information as *content* becomes the focus. Users (often business units) define the data they need, and the IT/IS (information technology or information systems) area pulls it from various sources to a common storage medium, usually a data warehouse or data repository. Once users define their need, IT/IS is the principal driver of data content in the data warehouse.

The next step is to ensure the integrity of the data. This is accomplished in a variety of ways, including validity and completeness checks (called "edits") in data collection systems, and balancing of the "loads" (transferal of data) to the data warehouse. Building greater integrity into the data warehouse is an iterative effort between users and IT/IS. The users are uniquely qualified to know whether or not data looks reasonable. This step takes a surprisingly long period of time in most data warehouse projects.

Next, the meaning or context of the data is supplied by the users. This critical third step is the transformation of data into information or business intelligence. Someone determines what the manipulated, arranged data means, and uses the results to judge business performance or gain knowledge about business conditions. At this point, a management information system is born. This stage is reached only after the right data, confidence in the data, and interpretation and communication come together.

Health organizations have begun gathering both financial and clinical data into their data warehouses. The combination of these two types of data allows broad analysis of the cost and quality of health care. Clinical data can be derived from claims if diagnosis and procedure codes are captured and stored. Innovative companies are targeting the capture of patient medical records to get the most direct and complete clinical data.

The technique for discovering hidden meanings buried deep in data is called *data mining*. Using sophisticated algorithms to display both widespread trends and interesting deviations or relationships in their data, companies are finding opportunities to grow and differentiate themselves from their competitors.

INFORMATION MANAGEMENT GROUPS (IMGS)

In information-based processes, companies tend to decentralize information management directly to the business units. This is based on the premise that business needs are best met by the people on the 'front line' who use the information.

An information management group's charge is to make business measurement routine, and to develop information that is useful for business insight, direction, and optimizing business performance. These groups tend to be function-oriented, rather than process-oriented, although the latter is the ultimate goal of the business. A functional focus, such as membership or finance, lets a company refine key business measurements before combining them across functional areas, for a bottom-up approach to information management.

Some of the critical first steps for the successful implementation of information management programs within a company include the following:

- Corporate direction about the role and responsibilities of information management groups,
- A robust and dependable data warehouse operation,
- Trained and skilled staff,
- An approach to deal with the proverbial 'gray' areas of overlap, when there is no clear owner of the data and related reporting,
- Standard terminology and definition of corporate terms,
- Standard calculation sets used to generate the most often used measurements, and
- Common, centralized technical services to support information management.

INFORMATION PRODUCTS

Some companies are realizing that empirical and insightful health care information is marketable. They are producing and selling information as a new line of business. Pharmaceutical companies have been doing this for years. They have been joined by numerous utilization management companies to produce regionally based information products for a wide range of health care services.

Most recently, physician and hospital profiling, which shows how physicians or facilities rank among their peers and national norms on utilization rates, costs, quality of care, and customer satisfaction, has set the stage for more informed consumer participation in health care delivery.

THE STATE OF MANAGEMENT INFORMATION SYSTEMS IN HEALTH CARE

Integration of previously diverse information systems is a key factor in the effectiveness and efficiency of health care delivery and administrative services. However, such integration is an enormously daunting task, largely dependent on the ability and willingness of all parties to integrate processes, systems and technologies.

Hospitals have many unconnected systems and technologies, and are faced with the herculean task of linking them through common interfaces to make them useful across the continuum of care. Admissions, order entry, scheduling, laboratory, radiology, pharmacy, nursing care plan, patient medical record, and discharge planning systems, to name a few, must all work together for effective caregiving and administration.

Health care practitioners also have various practice management systems and technologies in their offices. Hundreds of different practice management systems are in use today. These systems are purchased and used independently of other systems, unless the practitioner is part of a larger organization that requires the use of a common system.

System integration on the provider side of health care is happening, but it will take years before integrated management information systems dominate the provider community.

The MIS environment on the payer side is similar. The rapid changes in health insurance, particularly those brought about by managed care, third-party benefit administration, and mergers have left their mark on payer MIS. It is common for payers to have multiple claim payment systems, based on the type of health plan being serviced or as a result of mergers and acquisitions.

In today's world, payer information systems must provide for the integration and reporting of financial and clinical data, as well as support for managed care functions that are linked to sophisticated network, reimbursement, and incentive arrangements. Many payers have new technology platforms, and their management information systems are in the throes of major change.

NEW INFORMATION SYSTEMS AND TECHNOLOGIES

Just as integration is a key factor for better, less costly health care, new technologies are critical to making integration happen and managing the complexity of health insurance administration.

There are a number of technologies used to integrate health care MIS systems. Each technology fills a unique role in the integration process, and is briefly described below:

- *Client Server systems.* By adopting an "open system architecture," the elements of such systems permit interaction and communication between platforms with a minimum of problems.

- *Integration software tools.* Often called 'integration engines,' they allow mapping of data between systems with different file types and data layouts, making it easier for data passage and data sharing.

- *Internet, , mobile, and Web-based technologies.* These offer a common electronic connection for all systems and users at the point of service.

- *Document imaging.* Documents are electronically stored and made available instantly to any one who is authorized to access them. Early patient medical record systems used imaging technology.

- *Workflow management software.* Provides instructions for how work is done at each step in a business process and automatically stages and tracks work as it flows through the company. Allows images of pertinent documents to be part of each workflow and for quick process adaptation as the business changes.

- *Expert systems.* Captures a base of knowledge, applies the knowledge base to the process at hand, "learns" from the results, and applies what is learned to the next case.

- *Data warehousing, data mining, and business intelligence tools.* Brings all kinds of data together from different systems for integrated reporting and analysis, trend (including exception event analysis), and business performance monitoring.

These technologies, and newly built or redesigned core application systems, are enabling a greater degree of health care MIS integration.

Health care application systems are rarely built in-house any more. Custom system development has given way to purchased systems and system integration. Purchased systems offer a quick solution for companies, but have some unique challenges too. It is very unlikely that a purchased system will support all of a company's current processes and practices, so the business must decide whether to adjust to the system or whether to modify or augment the system. Especially for large organizations, this can be a fundamental cultural change, for both the business itself and for its IT/IS area.

BASIC ELEMENTS OF MANAGEMENT INFORMATION

INFORMATION: A BASIS FOR ACTION

Although it sounds simplistic to say that management information is only useful if it can be used as a basis for making a decision, this seemingly obvious statement is all too often overlooked. Thus, before discussing management information reports, we will start by considering the types of questions normally asked and the type of actions typically available to management.

In the realm of group insurance, management questions tend to center on the financial performance of a block of business. Typical questions include the following:

- Is the block of business making or losing money?
- How much is it making or losing?
- How consistent has its performance been?
- What can be reasonably expected to happen in the near future?
- What might be expected if certain factors change?

Perhaps the most important question is the following:

- How do the results differ from what management expected?

There are usually multiple options for action if management is seeking to effect changes in financial performance. The most obvious and most frequent response is to increase premium rates. It is at this point that the difference between management information and simple data reporting become apparent. Reports which produce financial data, but don't give enough information for management to make appropriate rate changes are simply data reporting.

KNOW YOUR AUDIENCE

It is impossible to list in advance all possible questions that management might ask and how to produce reports which answer these questions. Thus, the first step in developing management reporting is to know your audience. Find out the expectations and knowledge levels of the people requesting the information. Each of them will have different expectations for information and different levels of knowledge. This usually means producing different reports for different audiences.

Who are the audiences with a vested interest in the information? The audiences are both internal and external to the organization. Internally, they are managers or decision makers with line or business unit responsibilities. Some of the functions include financial analysis, product development, sales and marketing, network management, actuarial, and service management. External audiences include alliance partners, suppliers, regulators, investors, and the general public. Although a challenging task, it is necessary to know how to address these audiences.

The most important consideration in knowing your audience is knowing *why* they need the information. It helps to determine *what* information needs to be delivered. The same information may be used for different purposes. For example, financial results for self-funded customers might be shown in several places, such as under claim processing fees, stop-loss insurance, and managed care services. If a report is to be used to evaluate the financial performance of self-funded groups, it should show all profit and loss components together. There would be no need for this treatment if management is using the report only to determine if managed care fees are sufficient to cover the associated expenses.

Knowing your audience must also translate into knowing *how* the information will be used. Some individuals wait for results to change over several reporting periods before they take action. Others do not want to see results unless some form of action is needed.

While there are no hard and fast rules, the value and usefulness of management information is directly related to how well the audience is known, and how well that knowledge is used to meet their specific reporting and work style needs.

TIMEFRAMES: PAST, PRESENT, AND FUTURE

Management information has three timeframes: the past, the present, and the future. Each of these timeframes has a purpose and presents its own unique challenges.

Past

Past period reporting is usually intended to provide a broad overview of results and to spot trends and long-term changes. For many purposes, past period reporting should be made as accurate as possible by restating amounts which had to be estimated when first reported. For example, incurred but unreported claims must be estimated for current reporting. Later, actual claim payments can replace the estimates, providing a different but more accurate picture.

Consistency can become a major issue in reporting past time periods and should always be considered in historical reporting. Trends or changes in results can be caused by a change in the manner in which data was collected or reported. It is critical to put all reporting on a single basis whenever possible. Otherwise broad caveats as to the content and usefulness of the reports should be included.

Present

Current period reporting is the most frequent and useful form of reporting. As much as possible, management should be made aware of any discrepancies and sensitivity that exist between reported results and prior estimates. For example, financial results are relatively insensitive to estimated due and unpaid premiums, but claim reserve estimates have a very significant and direct impact on profit and loss.

Future

Projections of results into the future are useful tools for financial planning and goal setting. The challenge in projections is in developing models which take all significant factors into consideration. It is difficult to balance available resources and knowledge against the sophistication usually desired from projections. Many important management decisions, such as budgeting, staffing, and systems development are based heavily on projections of future results. To the extent that overly simplified models are used, totally inappropriate decisions could result.

COMPONENTS OF MANAGEMENT INFORMATION

FINANCIAL: REVENUE, COSTS, AND PROFIT

The first question in financial reporting is what basis of accounting will be used. The typical choices are statutory or GAAP. Statutory numbers must be developed for filing with states, and GAAP numbers must be developed for reporting financial performance under generally accepted accounting principles. Federal income tax also has its own accounting basis. In general, each company should decide which accounting basis will be used for their internal financial evaluation and consistently use it for management reporting.

Revenue is usually reported at the most aggregate level of detail, and includes premiums, investment income, and service fees. Premium deposit funds, also known as premium stabilization reserves or a similar term, often exist to accumulate monies held for clients and may be drawn upon to pay future premiums for these clients. Since they are not yet "premium," they aren't included as premium, although they may represent potential revenue in the event of unusually high losses. Similarly, policyholder dividends, experience rating refunds, and transfers from other lines of business may be used to reduce reported premiums, but would potentially be available as revenue if losses had been higher than reported.

When a financial statement is only used to determine how much profit was earned, as might be the case in a historical trend study, then little detail for premium is needed. If the financial statement is also used to see if margins are eroding and if future time periods might produce losses, then revenue details should be included. An insurance carrier that refunds all premium in excess of claims plus an expense allowance, and reduces reported premium by those refunds, will find that loss ratios (incurred claims divided by earned premium) will change only slightly while the block is profitable. A financial statement which shows total earned premium without supporting detail provides little or no clues as to how the business is performing until after losses have been incurred.

Claims and expenses are the two major components of costs. Since most large carriers have a significant amount of self-insured business, it is important to show claim equivalents, and corresponding premium equivalents, as part of internal financial statements, otherwise it may be difficult to know how the self-insured block of business is performing. This is particularly true when the business is partially self-insured as with minimum premium or limited liability arrangements. Also, financial results are stated in a more consistent way from time period to time period, and ratios such as expense to claims are more meaningful.

Premium equivalents are often set exactly equal to the self-funded claim equivalents. The information becomes more meaningful if premium equivalents also include margin within the premium. For example, on a totally self-insured case, premium equivalents would equal expected claims, claim equivalents would equal actual claims, and a refund equivalent would be a balancing item. This gives valuable insight into whether or not aggregate attachment points were more or less likely to be breached in the future.

Expenses are the other major component of costs. It is important that proper expense accruals be made not only for outstanding bills which are owed, but also to cover the cost of processing claims for which claim reserves have been established. Various approaches can be taken with regard to service fees. Some companies reduce expenses by the amount of service fees they receive from self-funded clients. Other companies keep expenses at the full level and show the fee income as 'other' or 'miscellaneous' income in revenue. Some companies pay third-party administrators to administer some of their business and show TPA service fees as expense. Other companies let TPAs bill clients directly, and the service fees never appear in the insurance company's financial statements. These differences in business practice can cause financial statements to look different from carrier to carrier.

Investment income is an important source of revenue and needs to be considered when evaluating financial results. Too often, capital gains, a major component of investment income, is excluded when reporting investment income by product line. This is the approach required by the statutory basis of accounting. It has become apparent, however, that the liabilities of a block of business cannot be considered separately from the assets underlying those liabilities. When investment strategies rely heavily on capital gains, financial reporting should include them.

Insurance accounting is fundamentally accrual accounting. Credit is taken for business transactions even though cash has not changed hands. This means that reserves must be held for events which occurred recently but for which actual payment may not be made for some time to come. There are different types of reserves. It is valuable to show beginning and ending reserves as financial statement details. Reserves based on proven formulas should be shown separately from reserves that are based on an actuary's judgment. Margins in the first type of reserves are often different from those in the latter.

Financial reporting should also reflect reinsurance transactions. While small transactions can be absorbed in operations with little impact, substantial reinsurance transactions can significantly affect financial experience. Although profit or loss may be absorbed by the reinsurer for several time periods, it won't necessarily continue, so management needs to know how reinsurance is affecting the business.

Many group operations are composed of several corporate entities. Eventually, results must be consolidated into a company total. It's not uncommon for different entities within an enterprise to show financial results in different formats. It is tempting to consolidate results at a high level with little detail. However, the information will be much more valuable if key operating factors continue to be reported with the consolidated financial statement.

EVENTS: FREQUENCY, IMPACT, CAUSES, AND CORRELATIONS

Financial information is paramount to management reporting, but as discussed earlier with respect to provider information, non-financial information must be used too. Frequency and intensity or size of claims are two other key operating measurements. Since frequency and intensity do not always convey their significance directly, such as, is it good or bad if mortality is 4.5 deaths per thousand, they should be compared to expected values or trends and industry norms or other benchmarks.

Management information is designed to show 'what' has happened in the business but not necessarily 'why' it happened. In order to discover what caused the results, information must be analyzed and correlated to other information. The reporting approach must be able to support this analysis. For example, a high loss ratio for a line of business might need to be traceable to a particular group policy, categories of service, places of service, providers, or treatments, with associated costs.

Some variation in business results is caused by demographic differences. Reporting by market or service regions is especially effective for uncovering and documenting variations, and refining actions that can improve undesirable results.

One of the keys to managing insurance is being reasonably accurate about predicted future results. Correlations must be drawn between benefit plans, pricing, provider contracting, care management disciplines, customer behavior, and future results. Management information should strive to make it easier to find such correlations and, once found, report the results in an understandable and useful manner.

PEOPLE: SELF-INTEREST AND OTHER MOTIVATORS

People make decisions based on what they value. Generally, individuals will select insurance options with the highest level of benefits for the least amount of money. These choices are influenced by the type of health care services the individual expects to consume, such as wellness benefits for children or frequent vision care. This individual adaptation is a common characteristic of flexible benefit programs. It is important to report and monitor the correlation between health plan selection, use of the plans, and any subsequent disenrollment from the plans. Individuals expecting large claims will tend to choose health plan options with high benefit levels, a type of antiselection. This effect and individual behavior should be closely monitored, due to the potential financial impact on the company.

Group insurers, large employers, employer group coalitions and health care providers usually behave in ways that protect their own best interests too. Management information systems need to account for purchaser, consumer and provider behavior. Such behavior can significantly influence financial results.

People usually act in a predictable rather than random manner. When factors prompting individual decisions are understood, then monitored, and the decisions are correctly translated into their financial impact, carriers can better manage their financial performance.

CHALLENGES OF MANAGEMENT INFORMATION

There are certain challenges to producing management information which should be kept in mind whenever designing or producing reports. As with most of the concepts discussed here, they are reasonably self-evident, but all too often overlooked.

CONSISTENCY

A general concern with reporting is the consistency of information. Inconsistent data causes wrong conclusions. This is true for numerical reports, such as consistently including or excluding various sources of gain in a profit statement. It is also true for graphical reports, such as using consistent bar graph scales when showing profits. Inconsistently reported data are very difficult to compare to each other. The amount of consistency that is needed is dependent on the audience. Generally, unless there is strong reason to vary reporting approaches, it is best to report information in a consistent manner.

Several ways typically exist for reporting the same results, and different approaches have their own unique strengths and weaknesses. It is usually preferable to settle on one approach for management reporting, unless there is a special need and the audience is well-educated on how it varies from other reports.

Insurance companies generally rely on accrual accounting, and more rarely on cash basis numbers. Certain reports, however, such as bank account balances of self-funded clients, are usually shown on a cash basis. Even then, while the cash data must be made available to the client so they know their current cash position, accrual reporting is needed to know the account's outstanding liability.

Another accounting question which should be answered in a consistent way is the question of when a claim is considered paid. Some companies consider a claim to be paid when a check or draft has been issued, others when the check clears the bank. Neither approach is wrong, but only one approach should be used, if possible, once a method is chosen.

Since claim reserve estimates are so important to financial results, and may include varying degrees of professional judgment, some reporting systems automatically report historical results on a "restated" basis. (This means that claim reserves for prior periods are revised to the most current estimate of what they should have been at the time they were set.) The restating of claim reserves is a widely accepted basis for reporting because it corrects prior misjudgments.

If the restated claim reserve method is used, care must be taken when explaining results. For example, if reserves are set on a conservative basis, even a profitable line of business can appear to be consistently losing money in the most recent time period. This anomaly does not occur when reserves are frozen at their original level.

A question often asked by management is, "How do we compare to our competition?" Whenever reports compare results from different companies, special care should be taken in developing the reports. Each company's approach is bound to be different. The reporting approach itself may be why results look different between competitors. Certain results, such as expense levels and sales, appear to be so simple that cross comparisons ought to be easy. In the real world, however, even items such as these are treated so differently by different companies that care should be taken in making comparisons. If possible, try to find out how results are developed before making such comparisons.

Availability of Data

It is always useful to consider the source of data being reported. How and from where is it being captured? Is it on an electronic database? Is someone else already putting together a similar or identical report?

The reverse should be considered. Is it realistically possible to assemble the data from any source? If the data must be obtained on a manual basis from an area which is already over-worked (and what functional areas are not?) then that area must either agree that the data is worth capturing or you'll never get the data you want.

Reliability of Data

It is virtually never prudent to simply use data as you find it without checking its validity. Some data is reasonably self-correcting, such as billing addresses. (If the address becomes incorrect, then either the policy will soon lapse or someone will intervene to correct the address.)

Whenever the same data item is held by two separate systems, there is a possibility that the data will become inconsistent and one or the other system will contain incorrect data. This argues for the importance of comparing sources and explaining differences.

One of the most useful checks on data validity is to check data against itself. For example, gross disability benefits less social insurance offsets should equal net benefits. By incorporating "edits" (validity checks) into a reporting system to compare the data against itself, many errors can be caught before any inaccurate reports are released. Sometimes the data are not expected to match exactly but certain values should be within reasonable ranges of each other.

It cannot be overemphasized that inaccurate input will result in inaccurate output. ("Garbage in, garbage out.") No matter how timely and easily understood reports may be, if they are not accurate, they should not be accepted. The world is constantly changing, and a reporting system which was accurate last year may not be accurate this year without modification.

VALUE OF DATA

If the purpose of management information is to give management a basis for action, then it is worth asking if any actions could be taken based on a given report.

When an operation runs into financial difficulty, there is usually a flurry of activity to discover what caused the problem. Many new reports are created. Usually only one or two reports actually highlight the problem areas, but often all the reports are continued long after the crisis has passed. It is generally worth the effort to quickly retire the non-actionable reports.

Last, but certainly not least, the cost of producing the report should be considered. Some reports can be very expensive to produce, or they might require significant input from key personnel who are already overbooked. While the report might be of some value, is it worth the cost to produce it?

EXTRACTING INFORMATION FROM DATA

While information comes from data, data is not automatically information. It is possible to have all the right data but little or no information. The manner in which data is presented goes a long way in determining whether or not the audience actually receives information. Data can be presented in a variety of ways depending on the needs of the audience: Text, numbers or graphics.

An important consideration is how much time the audience will have to review the reported information. Graphics work best for quick assessment of trends. Numbers work better if analysis is needed for fine-tuning a work process. In most cases, the more concise the package, the better, as long as it contains the information that the audience requires.

COMMON TYPES OF REPORTS

The following reports are presented as examples of typical reports used by many companies to provide management information. There are always differences from one company to another which will be reflected in the data or the manner in which it is shown. Sample reporting elements are included for many of the report types at the end of this chapter.

Historical Studies

Financial Results

The most frequent form of historical study is a display of financial results. The purpose is to find or examine trends in key factors. It may not be necessary to include all of the components which produce the final profit or loss figure. For example, if investment income or fee income are modest, then they may not be displayed.

The most important items to report are often ratios. The ratios shown depend on what management views as critical, but it might be the ratio of incurred claims to earned premium or total expenses to earned premium. For a block of self-funded clients, it might be the ratio of fee income to claim equivalents.

The critical factors for monitoring operational success in health insurance lines of business have expanded with managed care. It is important to report key factors in terms of averages per member per month (PMPM). (Some insurers still measure using historically more prevalent measures like "per employee" or "per subscriber.") Such factors as average operating expense PMPM or average medical cost PMPM should be calculated and displayed. Often, these values are presented in great detail, and form part of the actuarial information needed to manage the business.

The use of graphics is frequently helpful for these reports. A line or bar chart can quickly show how key ratios have changed over a period of time. Critical levels, such as the target for the factor, can also be shown. (See: Appendix for sample reporting elements)

Persistency Studies

Persistency studies for group insurance typically focus on lapses during the current time period. Each duration is rarely considered separately, except possibly from small group business. Lapses typically occur on or near the renewal date. Thus, reporting often shows only the business which has gone past the renewal date and is still in force.

The basis for persistency reporting is usually premium or insured lives. Often, separate reports are needed by size of case and product type, since these are major factors that heavily influence persistency. (See: Appendix for sample reporting elements.)

Mortality Studies

Mortality studies of group insurance tend to be less refined than similar studies for individual insurance because a group carrier typically lacks the detailed exposure data which most carriers collect on individual insurance policyholders and applicants.

To the extent possible, the following factors should be included in the report: Industry, type of schedule (flat and scheduled, or subject to significant individual selection), age, sex, type of underwriting, and life style status, such as smoker/non-smoker, regular exercise, etc.. Data on claims is usually available. Data on exposures is often more difficult to obtain.

Pooled life insurance is often a significant profit source for carriers and its experience should be considered separately.

Since liabilities for disabled lives involve estimates of both mortality and recovery, these exposures require a more analytical approach. A run-out approach, where one compares the initial reserve plus interest against payouts plus remaining reserves is needed to fully report on disabled lives.

Disability Studies

Fully understanding disability results involves knowing more than the frequency and initial severity of claim. Recovery from disability has a major impact on financial results and must be considered in any full reporting package. There are several ways in which recoveries from disability (or duration of claim) can be measured. A detailed comparison of expected recoveries to actual recoveries can be performed. Recovery statistics should be separated into reasonable risk classes. Many companies look at claim terminations from all causes combined, rather than studying mortality and recoveries separately.

Another method of evaluating claim duration is to report "claim run-outs." This involves taking a block of claim reserves as of a historical point in time, and carrying the reserves forward based on actual claim experience. In essence, the reserve for each year of incurral can be restated at the end of every following calendar year. The full stream of any given incurral year gives a picture of the adequacy of total initial reserves. Accumulating all incurral years during a given calendar year can illustrate the impact of global, external trends, such as a recessionary period, on reserves. (See: Appendix for sample reporting elements.)

Claim Lag Statistics

One form of historical reporting which is extremely common is that of reporting claim paid split according to the date the claim was incurred and the date on which it was paid. Such reports are sometimes called run-outs, claim lags, or reserve triangles.

These types of reports are essential to evaluating reserve requirements for claims which are paid within a relatively short time after incurral, such as medical claims. They can be used on a block of business, or for individual cases if the case is large enough to be credible.

These reports are described more fully in the chapter on claim reserves.

CURRENT REPORTING

Income Statements

A current income statement typically has much more detail than a historical report of financial results. In addition to the types of line items shown, detail may also be given as to the cash amount actually collected or paid, and the beginning and ending asset or reserve. For GAAP reporting, amounts receivable may be reduced by the probability of actually collecting over-due amounts.

As always, the detail to be shown will depend on the business being analyzed. In general, groups with retention accounting or a minimum premium arrangement will require the greatest amount of detail.

Other components which are not listed in the sample reporting elements at the end of the chapter but might be of interest include the following:

- Due and unpaid premium
- Premiums paid in advance
- Unearned premiums
- Premium stabilization funds (non-ledger)
- Target surplus

Fee income should be split into those separate components that represent separate functions. This allows management to see the growth in service business. Fees which are simply collected from a client in order to pay a third party vendor should also be shown separately.

Not all companies show all types of detail. Small numbers may be rolled up into one composite figure such as "other premium reserves."

Expenses

Expense reporting is becoming more critical as the group insurance business tends toward a service business as opposed to risk assumption. Management information with regard to expenses requires several different kinds of reports. First, there is a need to report on expenses from a total enterprise perspective. Management needs to know the total cost of operations broken down by its chief components.

In many group operations, risk assumption is no longer the primary product. Employee benefit services, spanning a wide range of managed care services, flexible benefits administration, and claims processing service, have become a dominant product. A service orientation requires more thorough reporting of expenses and fee income.

For many operations, critical expenses can be split into people related (salaries and benefits), corporate overhead, computer systems (both hardware usage and software development and maintenance), and external fees to vendors and provider networks.

One quick check on expense levels is to consider them as a ratio to premium and equivalents. The next step is to break these expenses into groupings that can be managed and monitored against specific activity levels.

The global expense categories shown in the sample report must be redistributed into functional activity centers, if they are to be managed. The format depends on the organizational structure of the operation, but reconciling global expenses with the expenses of the functional activity centers is required. Some categories, such as corporate overhead, can be ignored at this point, but will eventually need to be allocated to products in some reasonable manner. This reconciliation is essential to link the monitoring of total expenses with the monitoring of unit costs.

An important category of expense monitoring is usually the budget. Budget reports are very common and standardized. They simply split expenses into functional categories such as base salaries, overtime, employee benefits, printing, travel, supplies, dues, and others. They are usually done as shown in Exhibit 5 of the annual statement but with further detail.

The columns on a budget report will typically show current budget, prior budget, prior actual expenses, variance amounts and percentages, and remaining estimates. Budget reports are often split by organizational structure, since the intended use of a budget is to monitor and control costs by organizational area. A budget report might be produced for a specific department, summarized for a division, and summarized again for the entire company.

While it is very common to have expense budgets, it is just as important to have work effort budgets or projections. The anticipated total expenses for an area ought to correspond to an anticipated future work effort so that unit costs can be projected and monitored. Although the reason to compare budgets to work efforts seems clear, it is often not performed except for the most production oriented areas such as claims processing and sales.

If work efforts are anticipated in setting a budget, then it is possible to report not only actual expenses and budgeted expenses, but also the expense load which can be sustained if all target unit costs are applied to the actual work effort for the time period. This allows management to determine if larger or smaller expenditures are warranted based on growth or shrinkage. (See: Appendix for samples of reporting elements.)

Unit Costs

Expenses are meaningless unless reported in terms of the results produced. The cost of operating a claims processing unit, for example, needs to be compared with a measure of work effort. This measure could be the number of claims (perhaps weighted for degree of difficulty), the number of payment transactions (including "zero pays"), or something similar. The intent is to measure the workload and compare it to the cost. In order to use the unit costs which result, the measure of work effort must be measurable on a client by client basis, so that costs can be accurately allocated and prices set appropriately.

The base for measuring work effort is not always clear cut. What measurement should be used for home office marketing overhead? It is a real expense but does not easily translate into a specific work unit. A frequent measure for this and similar direct overhead items is a graded premium scale. Such scales allocate more effort to larger cases but on a declining marginal basis as the case size grows.

Reporting to Policyholders

Policyholders (and their representatives) tend to ask two questions: "How much money did I spend?" and "Where did I spend my money?" The first question is answered by accounting reports, and the second question is answered by benefit analysis reports.

The accounting reports show premiums coming in, including any deferred premiums under alternative financing arrangements, and costs going out, including benefit payments, expense charges, charges for pooled coverages, and so forth. These reports vary too widely in their structure to be shown here, and are very dependent upon the financial arrangements made for funding benefits. For example, a minimum premium product will require reporting of the client's benefit account, while a fully-insured product will only show premiums. On the other hand, some ASO reports ignore premiums entirely and focus solely on benefits.

The other frequent question can be answered in a more standardized fashion. A report for medical coverage, for example, would start with the submitted charge amounts, and shows the various reasons why the full charges were not paid. This gives an overview of the benefit payments to the policyholder on a reasonably global level. This type of report might show various employer locations in separate columns, or various time periods with percentage increases. It might also show dollars on a per member or per employee basis as opposed to reporting dollars in aggregate. Each employer will have their own internal reporting needs and will want to view the data differently. (See: Appendix for samples of reporting elements.)

The next level of policyholder reports will typically break down the submitted charges into various sources. This type of reporting ignores the plan design features such as deductibles and coinsurance, and reports charges before any reductions for usual and customary limits, provider network negotiated prices, and coordination of benefits. These reports can easily be compared across time periods, between various sub-groups, or against the normative, combined results of many employers. They facilitate the ability to compare one set of results with others, allowing judgments to be made regarding the overall program.

Further detail is needed to answer typical questions asked by employers. For example, hospital services and charges could be broken down in to diagnostic related groupings (DRGs). Companion reports should be produced which show utilization of services and the average charge per service rendered. When expressed on a per member basis, this type of data lends itself well to graphical display. A bar chart can display the average charge per member for in-patient hospital services for several sequential time periods. The reader can quickly and easily assimilate large quantities of data and visually note any program trends. (See: Appendix for samples of reporting elements.)

Policyholders typically request several other relatively simple reports. These include the following:

- *Bank reconciliation reports* which allow the policyholder to monitor and control the bank account upon which the insurance company is drawing for benefit payments. The format will vary by the type of banking arrangement, and the type of information needed to balance the account.

- All *large claims* within the most recent time period. This is usually in alphabetical order by member name or in decreasing order by size of claim. Pending claims may also be reported.

- *Claim payment details,* sorted alphabetically by member name.

- *Claim payment lag reports*, detailing the time taken to pay currently submitted claims. In many cases, carriers are making financial guarantees with respect to service, and these reports demonstrate whether the guarantees are being met.

- *Ad hoc reports* may be requested for specific areas, such as the charge per provider for each type of procedure, or the number of hospital admissions split by the day of the week on which admission and discharge occurred

Many carriers also produce reports which demonstrate the effectiveness of their managed care programs. These reports might focus on price discounts, utilization savings, network effectiveness, or drug utilization. Such reports are, as one would expect, heavily dependent upon the type of managed care network being used.

Provider and Network Monitoring

It is important to monitor the effectiveness of providers and networks, and develop profiles of practice patterns. Clinical practice guidelines are rapidly emerging and being used to evaluate practitioners and rank them with their peers and regional norms. Due to increased emphasis on the quality of care, under-utilization of services is as important to monitor as over-utilization of services.

Carriers are in varying stages of implementing provider profiling reporting systems. Competition, as well as the demand to balance the cost and quality of care, requires that provider profiling become an integral part of managed care reporting.

Companies that do not yet have fully implemented provider and network reporting systems can list providers by the percentage of services and dollar amount of services which are outside of normal expectations for a given diagnosis. This basic information can give management a tool to educate outlying providers and, when appropriate, help them adjust their patterns of practice.

Some of the measurements used to track provider and network performance are: Credentialing/recredentialing compliance, pathway/guidelines compliance, number of peer complaints, number of member complaints, and repeat procedure rate. More specifically, tracking number of office visits, number of referrals to specialists, high frequency/high dollar service categories, inpatient and outpatient utilization, PMPM, and most frequently used laboratory tests by provider is a good starting point for profile reporting. (See: Appendix for a more complete list of reporting elements.)

Data analysis for monitoring providers and networks is becoming much more sophisticated than just a few years ago. Data must be adjusted or grouped into more meaningful types of information to be useful and accepted by the provider community. This process is called *normalization*. It is a way to group items together to better reflect their true meaning and circumstances.

The most common methods of data normalization used for provider and network monitoring, as well as how they are applied, are as follows:

- Case mix adjustment, used for adjusting statistics related to provider case loads for complexity, severity, and case mix.
- Diagnostic Cost Groups (DCGs), used for predicting the level and relative cost of treatment of members using diagnosis codes.
- Diagnostic Related Groups (DRGs), used for grouping hospital inpatient stays into categories based on diagnosis.
- Episode Treatment Groups (ETGs), used for identifying and grouping individual episodes of care and patient classification.

Sales and Marketing Monitoring

Sales and marketing activities directly affect three vital corporate areas: revenue, customer relations, and public image. It is imperative that management be attuned to results and status in all three areas.

Important interactions occur between clients and the company right from the start of the selling process. Information about products, prices, services, and value is exchanged and potential sales begin to materialize. Agents, brokers, and consultants are often involved, and have their own information needs. What types of information does management need to monitors sales and marketing activities?

Sales-in-process reporting gives visibility to the new sales activity, and alerts management to status and issues for each new sales opportunity. The reports would include information about prospects, sales calls, number of quotes and proposals delivered, notes regarding client meetings and negotiations, new earnings estimates, and decision time lines.

Producer performance is monitored through reports that show closing ratios (sold business / quoted business), actual sales against sales force quotas, revenue generated from new sales, persistency rates for renewing existing business, and commissions. Agent and broker performance is judged by these same measures. It is also necessary to make sure that business sold by these agents and brokers is good business, and falls into a normal distribution curve for risk.

Reporting on top accounts, jeopardy accounts, customer call types, product performance, and brand strength helps management stay informed about the quality and effectiveness of its marketing, sales, and service activities.

Consumer Information

Health plans and other information intermediaries are now publishing information to help people make good health care choices and wisely spend their health care dollars. As high deductible health plans and health spending accounts become more common, consumers are seeking cost and quality information regarding potential caregivers, facilities, and physicians alike.

For hospitals, the information includes overall quality and cost ratings as compared to other hospitals in a region, morbidity rates by major diagnoses and treatments, average cost by treatment, readmission rates, and infection rates. Patient (or consumer) comments are also available and translated into satisfaction scores regarding the hospital's service and quality of care.

For physicians, the information includes average cost of office visits and treatments and patient satisfaction scores. Outcomes-based quality ratings are being developed, and will likely appear in the next wave of cost and quality information.

PROJECTING THE FUTURE

Cash Flow and Asset Projections

Reporting historical data is much more standardized than projecting future results. Most commonly, projections use the same format as historical reporting because the purpose is to predict what those "historical" reports will look like at some time in the future.

Cash flow and asset projections are one form of projecting the future. They do not have a counterpart in past experience reporting. They are focused on future profits or losses, the timing of such gains and losses, and their impact on surplus and cash flow.

Increasingly, considerations of cash flow are becoming more prominent as cash flow testing, or asset/liability matching, is being required by a growing number of state insurance departments.(See: Appendix for samples of reporting elements.)

Other Projections

Projections are needed for a variety of reasons. These reasons include tax planning, strategic planning, and acquisitions / mergers, or sales of blocks of business. The details behind the business activity will strongly influence the type of reporting necessary. It is impossible to show all the potential variations and formats associated with these types of business activities.

In general, however, reports use a familiar format, such as a financial statement, and add detail for special purpose reporting. Tax planning looks carefully at those items which vary from regular accounting and impact tax liabilities. Strategic planning tends to focus on the impact of changing the mix of business, or on the impact of spending large sums of money either acquiring business or building resources such as systems. Acquisitions or mergers focus on the financial results of the purchase, and often require intense focus on tax implications as well.

HEDIS: STANDARD FOR MANAGED CARE REPORTING

The Health Plan Employer Data and Information Set (HEDIS) developed by a coalition of HMOs, large employers and an employee benefits consulting company, has evolved into a widely accepted industry standard for information reporting by managed care organizations. It is a necessary part of any managed care reporting system and compliments the National Committee for Quality Assurance (NCQA) accreditation process. HEDIS goes well beyond traditional reporting and implementation requires a significant investment and work effort.

Two significant industry trends are inherent in the widespread acceptance of HEDIS reporting standards. First, carriers or health plans are becoming more accountable for the health care experience. Second, benefit managers are requiring quality measures as well as performance guarantees as a condition for doing business with them. HEDIS provides a reporting framework for both.

Separate HEDIS reporting for Medicaid, Medicare, and commercial populations is required. A further breakout by product for commercial populations is also required.

HEDIS reporting currently falls into eight categories with over eighty measures: Effectiveness of care, access/availability of care, satisfaction with the experience of care, health plan stability, use of services, cost of care, informed health care choices, and health plan descriptive information. This is further confirmation that health plans need to collect and integrate clinical data with traditional data and that health plans are being held more accountable for the health care experience.

HEDIS is expected to evolve in to a comprehensive quality management system. The National Committee for Quality Assurance continues to make periodic updates to HEDIS reporting requirements. Any implementation of HEDIS should be based on the current standards release and be as flexible as possible to accommodate further refinements and updates.

CONCLUSION: MASTERY OF MANAGEMENT INFORMATION - A CORE COMPETENCY

It is not a simple task to provide quality management information. It requires considerable thought and effort. However, few things are as valuable as knowledge, and a management information system that truly increases knowledge, and the subsequent ability of a company to effectively compete in its markets, is well worth the effort to build and maintain.

APPENDIX: SAMPLES OF REPORTING ELEMENTS

Financial Results Report

Premium	Expenses
Interest	Profit (Loss)
Fees	Loss Ratio
Revenue	Expense Ratio
Claims	Profit Ratio

Persistency Studies

Year End In-force
Up for Renewal
Renewed
Percent Renewed

(Separately for each of First Year,
Years 2-5, and Over 5 years)

Disability Studies

Frequency	Claim Run-outs
Covered Income	Initial Reserves:
Covered Lives	Unreported Claims
Expected Gross Income	+ Known Claims
Expected Net Benefits	− Expected Offsets
Expected No. of Claims	= Total Reserve Funds
Actual Gross Income	
Actual Net Benefits	Thereafter:
Actual No. of Claims	Starting Funds
Act/Exp by Income	+ Interest Earned
Act/Exp by Benefits	− Claim Payments
Act/Exp by Lives	= Funds Remaining
Act/Exp Reserves	

Policyholder – Benefit Analysis Reports

In Patient Hospital	Psychiatrist's Fees
Out Patient Hospital	In patient
Physicians Fees	Out patient
In patient	Office
Out patient	Anesthesia
Office	Radiology
Routine Exams	Pathology
Surgeon's Fees	Drugs
In patient	Dental Injury
Out patient	All Other

Office

Total Charges

Income Statements

Premium	Claims
Regular Earned	Incurred
+Transfers	+ Equivalents
− Refunds	
+ Equivalents	Interest Paid

Investment Income	Expenses
Fees	Commissions
Processing	General
Managed Care	Taxes and Fees
Pass Through	Loss Ratios
Other	Profit (Loss)

Change in Reserves	Federal Income Tax
Active Life	
Deficiency	Operating Gain

Policyholder - Accounting Reports

Charges Submitted	Normal Benefits
Expenses Not Covered	Medicare COB
U & C Reductions	Other Plan COB
Negotiated Reductions	Prompt Pay Discounts
Deductibles	Other Adjustments
Coinsurance	Drafts Used
Other Plan Reductions	

Expenses (by Line of Business)

Commissions	Premium Taxes
Overrides	Licenses and Fees
General Expenses	Total Expenses
Salaries and Benefits	Earned Premium
Computer Operations	Premium Equivalents
Service Fees	Expenses/Premium and Equivalents
Provider Fees	
Corporate Overhead	
All Other	

Cash Flow and Asset Projections

Collected Premium	Investments
Interest Credited	
Paid Claims	Cash
Cash Surrenders	
Expenses	Assets Due Year 1
Net Cash Flow	Annual Cash Income
Cash Balance	Assets Due Year 2
+ Premium Due	Annual Cash Income
− Claim Reserves	
− Other Reserves	Assets Due Other Years
	Total Assets
Net Surplus	Total Annual Income

Provider and Network Monitoring

General Measures	Profiling
Office visits	Top 10 Rx's
Specialist referrals	Physician ETG / efficiency
High frequency/High dollar categories	Encounters per patient
In/Out patient utilization PMPM	Direct & Indirect billed services
Rx PMPY	Relative clinical complexity index
% Generic Rx	Expected/Actual cost per patient
Admissions per 1000	Standard deviation from mean %
ER visits per 1000	
Outpatient surgeries per 1000	
Most frequently used tests	
Repeat procedure rate	

Compliance and Member Satisfaction	Network Effectiveness and Monitoring
Credentialing/recredentialing compliance	Physician, specialist, facility coverage areas
Pathway / guidelines compliance	Member / Specialist per county ratios
Peer and member complaints	Network access standards
	Network stability
	Network reimbursement rates
	Hospital / Total paid comparison
	% Change in office utilization and unit cost
	Utilization and cost by Place of Service
	% of Physician dollars by CPT code

24 UNDERWRITING LARGE GROUPS

James T. Lundberg
Ann Marie Wood

INTRODUCTION

The mission of large group underwriting is simply to help the insurer achieve its strategic goals and financial objectives in the large case market. The methods include risk selection, thoughtful plan design, and a myriad of rating and analytic techniques. Large employers and their carriers have increasingly come to view their relationship as a partnership, and the role of the underwriter is often to devise risk and financial alternatives that satisfy mutual needs and goals. Additionally, the continued evolution of managed care plan alternatives has dramatically increased the complexity of the large group underwriting processes.

THE MARKET

The term "large group" can refer to as few as 50 or 100 employees, up to the largest health and welfare plan in the private or public sector. In the 1990's, most states passed small group reform laws that generally apply to groups with fewer than 51 employees. This leaves three larger case market segments:

- Pooled groups (typically 51 to 200 employees)
- Experience-rated groups (200 to 1,000 employees)
- Large groups (1,000 or more employees)

Eligible groups are defined by law, and include single-employer plans, associations, labor unions, multiple-employer trusts, employer coalitions, and government plans. The most common coverages include life, disability, medical, and dental benefits. Plan designs are flexible and often customized to meet the specifications of larger groups. Employees may be able to choose from among several coverage or benefit options, either within a single risk pool, or divided among competing carriers, as is often the case with managed care plan alternatives.

The major focus of this chapter is underwriting of single-employer group medical plans in the U.S., with most of the emphasis being on groups with over 200 employees. We will highlight some unique challenges posed by "jumbo" groups (over 5,000 lives) and by a broad range of managed care options available to most large groups.

SOME BASIC PRINCIPLES

The underwriting of large groups involves risk selection and financial projections, based on aggregate data and historical trends, for a specific group plan or for a class of plans with similar characteristics. The very nature of group insurance offers some inherent risk/underwriting protection, in that the employee risk pool consists largely of individuals who are sufficiently healthy to retain full time employment.

Key risk factors include demographics, industry, financial outlook, work force stability, work site location(s), carrier persistency, and levels of employee and dependent participation in the plan. For managed care plans, case risk assessment includes an analysis of provider access (that is, how accessible will the provider network be to the members?) and projected in-network usage and cost savings.

Prior loss ratio or utilization data of a particular group are often considered in pricing. The degree of credibility given to prior experience data varies according to the size and nature of the group and type of coverage.

Fully insured experience rating is quite common for medical and dental plans with as few as 100 enrollees, usually with pooling of large medical claims. Retrospective experience rating is less common, but can appeal to groups with 500 to 1,000 employees. Minimum case size requirements are usually higher for life and disability, where claim experience is more volatile due to lower frequencies of loss, and varying amounts of coverage by employee.

The prior claim experience of a large group has traditionally been the major factor used to project future costs, especially for health care. This is still true, but today's pricing models must also consider the dynamics of managed care plans, multiple-choice scenarios, relaxed rules for plan participation, defined contribution strategies, and the resulting antiselection implications.

In many respects, the employer and carrier often have similar goals; for example, both want to see low claim costs, high quality, and satisfied employees. They may have somewhat different views on other aspects of the program, such as profit margins or funding methods. One of the underwriter's primary goals is to offer financial arrangements that enable both parties to accomplish their objectives.

SALES INTERACTION

It is important to involve the sales representative in the process of determining the best rate to be offered. One approach may be to structure a component of the incentive compensation program to encourage selling the value of the carrier rather than just price. Another is to reward the sales representative for selling rates at full margin, as determined by the underwriting and actuarial areas, instead of negotiating a lower rate just to increase the likelihood of closing the renewal or sale.

It is also important for the sales representative to appropriately qualify a prospect. This involves first determining the minimum information necessary for quoting experience rated business, and then communicating the purpose and value of obtaining the information to the prospective account. The effective date, current and requested benefits, prior carrier information, census, employer contribution, waiting periods, industry, sole carrier vs. multiple carriers, large claim data, active/retiree information, current rates, and fees are some of the categories to consider.

NEW BUSINESS UNDERWRITING

CHARACTERISTICS OF THE GROUP

A number of criteria are used to screen, approve, and classify large group prospects. They vary by carrier, coverage and size of group but this section will focus on seven key dimensions: (1) age and gender, (2) location or area, (3) type of industry, (4) financial strength, (5) ease of administration, (6) level of participation, and (7) prior persistency.

Age and Gender

Demographic content is one of the most important risk characteristics of a group. Age is the single best overall indicator of future mortality and morbidity. Gender mix also impacts both life and health claim costs, and composite age-gender factors are good predictors for several specific medical conditions, such as pregnancy and heart disease. Average family size, and resulting adult/child mix, can be an important risk factor for medical plans. Plans with a high percentage of retirees will have higher claim costs for group life and medical (prior to Medicare offsets) and often require more intense administrative services.

Location or Area

Geographic location(s) can also be a risk factor for most group coverage. There are significant regional and local differences in health care practices and prices. This can be attributed at least partially to the level of competition resulting from an over- or under-supply of providers. In many urban areas, costs are higher due to cost shifting from Medicare, Medicaid, HMOs, and other preferential programs.

Type of Industry

Type of industry is often a major factor in assessing new groups. Some industries expose employees to health hazards or to high stress levels. More commonly, industry risk appears to be related to the lifestyles and socio-economic content of the insureds.

Some industries pose substandard risk and administrative challenges, due to unstable employment levels, seasonal nature of their work, low wages, or high turnover rates. This is compounded by requirements imposed by COBRA, HIPAA, and similar state laws. Certain industries have a reputation for particularly rich or lean benefit plans or contribution levels. Others tend to sponsor employee wellness programs. While there is little statistical evidence linking such programs to lower employee benefit costs, most underwriters view them favorably.

Financial Stability

Financial strength and credit rating are important risk criteria. Some important questions include: Does the group have a history of making timely payments? Is there a risk of insolvency? If there are alternate funding methods, who will bear the risk for claim runout liabilities? Who will hold the monies? Is the business cycle trending up or down? Does the employer plan an expansion or merger?

Business downturns often lead to reductions in staff. Since downsizing tends to be uneven among job classes, age groups, or locations, it can result in dramatic shifts in demographic factors. Also, the anticipation of layoffs often produces a spike in disability claims, and in utilization of elective medical and dental services. After the lay-offs, studies show that the true cost of COBRA is at least 25% higher than medical benefits for at-work participants. Caveats are often included in quotes that reserve the right to reprice if the enrollment changes by ± 10% or more from the enrollment that the quote is based on. Life plans tend to see antiselection in the form of either premium waiver claims, requests for portable benefits, or applications for conversion policies.

Ease of Administration

Administrative costs (and prices) are a major consideration for the group underwriter (and client). Larger groups offer the opportunity for higher productivity and economies of scale. On the other hand, this advantage can be offset by added complexity, if there are multiple sub-groups, plan designs, work sites, unions, vendors, procedures, or points-of-contact.

The larger a group is, the greater the emphasis on administrative services and costs. Jumbo groups tend to have highly customized services, so the underwriter must work closely with his or her administrative experts to assess the costs. A major component of the case review is devoted to evaluating the customer's ability to provide accurate and timely data on employee enrollment, terminations, and status changes. Does the employer or carrier prepare and distribute benefit summaries, ID cards, claim forms and other communication materials? If the employer has several affiliated companies or work sites, do they have uniform and adequate HR and information technology resources?

Level of Participation

Insurers usually require that the employer pay a minimum portion (such as 50%) of the premiums for each benefit plan, to keep the cost attractive for healthier employees and their respective dependents. The traditional 75% minimum participation rule is still common, but is often modified to consider all health plan options offered by an employer, or through a spouse's employer.

Adequate plan participation is an important risk factor for a group, but can be difficult to assess in an environment of multiple options, dual-income families, and defined contribution packages. The large case underwriter should review the entire employee benefit program, including competitors' plans, and attempt to balance underwriting principles with market demands for consumer choice. To the extent that credible claim experience reflects the current participation levels, the underwriter has to anticipate future enrollment changes in developing prices or caveats.

Carrier Persistency

Installation and setup of a very large new group account can be extremely expensive, and competitive pricing pressures do not allow room to recoup these costs in the first or second contract year. Therefore, underwriters should carefully review a prospective client's track record of persistency with their prior carriers. Groups that go to market every year, or every time a rate guarantee expires, may find fewer and fewer bidders.

Large employers must also consider the internal costs associated with implementing and communicating a new plan, and the potential disruption of patient-provider relationships due to changing managed care networks. Depending on the situation, these factors may result in a bias for the status quo, requests for multi-year contracts, or adding new carrier options to fill in geographic "gaps" or to foster member choice.

Other Considerations

Larger employers often opt for self-funded ASO (administration services only) contracts for health plans, to obtain financial benefits (premium taxes, risk margins, and cash flow) and an ERISA preemption from state-mandated benefits. Minimum premium plans are hybrids that offer most of the financial benefits of self-funding, along with risk protection that is similar to retrospective-rated insured plans. These funding alternatives are less common for HMOs, due, in part, to regulatory restrictions and complications of provider participation in risk when capitation arrangements are involved.

The underwriting of large groups has placed little emphasis on the health status of individuals, with the main exceptions being review of applications for large amounts of life insurance and pricing or pooling adjustments for medical "shock" (or catastrophic) claims.

HIPAA, and related state laws, prohibit discrimination based on health status, and promote health care access and portability. HIPAA includes provisions that:

- Prohibit use of evidence of insurability for late entrants;
- Mandate that "special enrollees" (late entrants who experience a qualifying event) be treated as "on time" enrollees; and

- Limit pre-existing condition exclusions (in part to allow credit for other prior coverage).

The portability section of HIPAA requires insurers to issue a certificate of prior coverage to employees who terminate employment. HIPAA also includes Administrative Simplification and Privacy sections, designed to standardize the electronic exchange of health care data and protect the security and privacy of individual's health records. These are major initiatives, and some insurers make employer surcharges to cover HIPAA developmental costs.

Since most large employer groups allow for employee choice among HMOs and other health care options, employees are typically able to switch between plans during an annual open enrollment period, without any underwriting or benefit restrictions.

The emergence of portability and consumer choice tends to level the playing field among competing carriers, but the cost impact varies from group to group, and year to year, and should be part of the case risk assessment.

Plan Design

Effective plan design can help to keep the total plan affordable to both the employer and the employees. The trend among larger employers has been to offer employees a broad menu of choices, with the employer making a fixed dollar maximum contribution toward the cost. Some larger employers are now scaling back the number of benefit plan and carrier choices, while many smaller employer groups are adding more plan options. Health care options often feature a dual choice scenario, where carriers compete at the individual employee level based on relative benefits, price, access, quality and other factors. Therefore, underwriters should review the design and features of their proposed plan(s) in relation to competing options, with a goal of optimizing enrollment and controlling antiselection.

Group term Life Insurance plan designs have become extremely flexible. Employees are often free to select an amount of insurance ranging from zero to several times annual earnings with few, if any, underwriting restrictions if they are actively at work. Underwriting safeguards include a balanced spread of risk (by age/gender, income, and plan option), minimum participation or "packaging" rules, age and retirement reductions, and (at least short form) evidence of insurability for abnormally large amounts ($500,000 or more). Optional Life plans often use attained age step rates.

Plan design is an important factor in evaluating group short or long term disability benefit plans. Key elements include the length of the elimination period, the percentage of compensation to be replaced, benefit offsets for other sources of disability income (such as Social Security and Workers Compensation), and the maximum duration of benefit payments.

The underwriter must look at features of a group disability plan in the context of overall economic conditions, the specific job skills of a particular industry, and the employment outlook for that job or geographic area, as well as the employer's commitment to assist and accommodate the return to work of rehabilitating employees. Special hazards might be addressed by providing limited benefits, either overall or for certain risks such as mental, nervous, and substance abuse.

Traditional fee-for-service health plans try to control costs by a combination of deductible and co-insurance features, contractual limitations and exclusions, limits on negotiated provider fees, or similar plan design features.

HMO plans often have rich benefits for preventive and routine care by primary care providers in a network setting, with modest member co-pays. More expensive specialty and facility care may be subject to pre-approval, higher out-of-pocket payments, and/or benefit maximums. Open access HMO plans address consumer demand for self-referral by relaxing pre-authorization rules, in exchange for higher member co-pays, or premiums. A preferred provider plan (PPO) or a point-of-service (POS) plan will usually allow a patient to use either a network or a non-network provider, but pay significantly lower benefits for non-network care.

Managed care plan design and network access must be viewed together. The underwriter has to project plan participation and in-network usage for all competing plans. This entails a geographic match of employee residences (or work sites) to network provider offices. For the larger groups, it is also common to prepare a disruption analysis of the providers who participate in each network to determine how a new carrier or new type of plan would affect existing physician relationships.

The variety and customized nature of large group insurance plans presents a significant challenge to the underwriter, who must assess the relative value and effectiveness of all available plan designs, utilization controls, and health care delivery systems. Then, he or she must try to anticipate the impact of employee choice.

EVALUATING THE EXPERIENCE

The access to, and the use of, group-specific prior experience data is a unique feature of underwriting large groups. The larger the group, the more critical this information becomes. At the low end of the larger case market, an employer group with 100 employees might see manual or community rates. Through the mid-sized range, the underwriter will apply more and more credibility to prior experience data. For very large groups, it is common to apply full credibility to prior experience, especially for health benefits. Intense competition for the most attractive groups may sometimes tempt the underwriter to use a credibility factor that may not be actuarially sound.

Prior experience reports come in many forms, formats, and degrees of accuracy. The underwriter is looking to answer two basic questions:

- Can I identify meaningful past results and trends?
- How can I apply this information to projected costs for the proposed plan(s) and eligible group(s)?

The ideal goal in evaluating prior experience data is to know the risk as well as the existing carrier. While this is often impractical, there are many techniques to help determine if the information is valid, reliable, and useful. Is the information current? Is it accurate? Is it consistent over time? Is it based on the most appropriate plans and population? Does it reflect underlying business trends and cycles? Are claim data provided on a cash basis or incurred basis? Are there any fees included in the claim data? Do the reserve levels appear to be adequate? Are they redundant? Are claims reflective of enrollment for the given time period? Were there benefit changes during the given time period? Do claims include or exclude high dollar or catastrophic claims? The answer to any of these questions may provide a key piece in the underwriter's puzzle.

Various internal checks may be used to determine whether prior experience information is accurate and reliable. For example, reported premiums can be tested in relation to past premium rate and exposure data. Reserves for incurred but unreported claim liabilities may be compared to prior claim run-out data. Reviewing month-by-month data may reveal distortions due to unusual claim patterns or administrative problems. Using an independent source such as Equifax to obtain employer related information is often very helpful to the underwriter in verifying the accuracy of information.

Group Life

Group life claim experience tends to be relatively volatile, due to a low frequency of loss, and often wide variations in amounts of coverage. Even for jumbo groups, many carriers try to smooth out the blips in claim experience by looking at several years of data or by using a blend of case and book of business experience. Pooling of large claims is common, with the pooling point tending to increase with the size of the group. Claim experience is usually more stable for basic life plans (due to employer contributions and uniform amounts of insurance) than for optional life plans, which tend to be employee-paid, and to offer more choices.

Life evaluations are complicated by the fact that industry practices vary with respect to pooling, disability reserves, conversion charges, portability, report close-out dates, interest payments to beneficiaries, and in other ways. The underwriter must know the competition to understand how these things will affect the experience.

Disability Income

Group disability income (especially LTD) experience also may reflect low claim frequencies but large potential liabilities. As with life coverage, the underwriter will review multi-year data, and will often use blending and pooling techniques to increase the statistical confidence of his or her projections. Reserves for future benefit payments are so critical, and industry methods so varied, that the disability underwriter wants to have sufficient information about each open claim (including age, duration, and diagnosis) to validate reserve levels. The experience data will also be reviewed to detect any abnormal patterns that may be due to business cycles or industry risks.

Medical Plans

For a large, stable group, most carriers consider one year of medical claim experience to be an adequate sample to project future costs. For indemnity plans, this may merely involve adjusting incurred claims for large claims, then inflating for trend. The proposal underwriter might also make adjustments to reflect differences in cost containment programs, claim controls, or provider discounts.

Managed care and multiple plan options can complicate the evaluation process. If the experience data reflect another carrier's managed care plan, the challenge is to understand the underlying price and utilization dynamics, and to attempt to quantify the effects of replacing (or co-existing with) that program with your proposed plan(s) and delivery system(s). To do so, the underwriter must be able to build a model that compares the two offerings in terms of:

- Service area,
- Size of network,
- Ease of access (for these employees),
- Projected enrollment (for HMO, or if multiple options),
- In-system usage (for POS or PPO),
- Provider payment/reimbursement contracts (by type of service or provider), and
- Utilization management.

Service area and network size data are usually readily available. Ease of access can be measured by matching provider locations to a census of employees' home (or work) ZIP codes. Software tools can be used to determine the degree of access for urban, suburban and rural areas. Another method is a disruption analysis, where you match prior claims (or provider selections) to the bidder's contracted network. Enrollment and in-system usage for the proposed plan will depend on network area, size and access, and other factors such as employee contributions and competing HMO options. These estimates involve both art and science, but the tools have become quite sophisticated.

Provider contracts are usually proprietary, so determining the value of a competitor's provider reimbursement arrangement can be a difficult step in evaluating managed care experience data. It is very desirable to maintain a database that precisely defines a carrier's own network contracts and corresponding provider discounts. When possible, the database should be used on an area-specific basis to compare discounts of the incumbent insurer. This type of comparison takes on many forms, and is generally referred to as "re-pricing."

Large case RFPs often provide experience reports that summarize billed charges, plan payments (after provider discounts and patient liability), utilization statistics, or other forms or combinations of claim experience. The data may be aggregated, or split by network area, type of service or provider, or benefit plan. Managed care claim experience often includes capitation payments, or various other forms of non-traditional provider compensation. The challenge for the underwriter is to identify the services that are included in these charges, in order to project the corresponding cost of care under the proposed plan(s) and compensation method(s).

In addition to any case-specific experience data, the underwriter may have access to plan-wide data for other carriers. Over time, an underwriter tends to develop a working knowledge of major competitors' provider arrangements and utilization results through experience and networking.

Beyond different prices per unit of care, utilization of services varies widely by type of health plan, network efficiency, and intensity of utilization management. The underwriter must try to quantify the value of "healthcare management" inherent in the prior claim experience, and try to estimate the relative impact of tighter or looser controls for each proposed plan type. The looser end of the spectrum includes rich fee-for-service indemnity plans, with little financial incentive for either providers or patients to be concerned about "third party payer" costs. At the tighter end, an HMO plan might have restricted access, pre-authorization rules for most non-primary care, and provider compensation methods that reward low utilization rates for expensive services. Most modern healthcare plans fall between these extremes, and feature varying degrees of compromise between optimal cost savings and consumer demand for access, choice, and minimal hassle.

The methods used to project claim costs under a new plan, using claim experience from a different plan, will depend on the types of provider reimbursement used. If both plans pay discounted charges for service, then one could merely adjust the current claim cost data for differentials in the plans' discounts, utilization management savings, and in-system usage, with appropriate consideration for trend. On the other hand, if the current plan pays on a discounted fee-for-service basis for care that would be capitated under the proposed plan, or vice versa, then the underwriter may have to use different pricing methods by type of service or provider.

In general, the first step is to look at each component of the prior experience data to identify the pieces that provide credible information about the utilization patterns of the employer group, or sub-group. The next step is to identify which cost of care components under the proposed new plan should be adjusted to consider the prior experience data, and the amount of the adjustments. The cost for capitated services might be a fixed amount per head, or adjusted for age and gender, with little or no consideration given to prior claim data. On the other hand, the pricing of non-capitated services might be highly influenced by the prior experience data. So, the underwriter should have a good working knowledge of provider compensation methods-- and the types of providers or services they cover – for both the old and the new plan.

Today, evaluating and projecting managed care claim costs for large groups invariably requires dealing with multiple choice scenarios. The table below shows the type of format that might be seen in large group RFPs to illustrate the key assumptions made by the underwriter in projecting claim costs for multiple plan options. This example is of a large employer who currently offers one comprehensive major medical plan for all employees, and will be offering the three new options shown – HMO, PPO, and high deductible indemnity plans. In the illustration, initial relative benefit values were determined as if all participants enrolled in each option as though 100% of employees choose that option. Provider discounts and utilization savings are relative to the base year claim data, which reflects no discounts and minimal cost containment or utilization management. Selection and antiselection assumptions are based on the drivers discussed in the chapter titled "Managing Selection in a Multiple-Choice Environment." While the "selection and antiselection" assumptions produce a composite factor of 1.023, the projected annual cost of care is reduced from $5,980 to $4,919 per employee or

$$[.35(\$4,168) + .60(\$5,536) + .05(\$2,768)] = \$4,919$$

after applying all factors. Of course, the total cost for any of the proposed plans would have to consider administrative expenses, risk charges, taxes, and other retention items.

Projecting Multiple Option Claim Costs					
			Proposed Flexible Options		
	Current Major Medical Plan	HMO	Point-of-Service		High Deductible Indemnity
			In-Network	Out-of-Network	
Prior Year Claims per Employee	$5,200	$5,200	$5,200	$5,200	$5,200
Adjust for:					
Relative Benefit Value	× 1.00	× 1.15	× 1.05	× .95	× .65
Provider Discount Savings	× 1.00	× .75	× .82	× 1.00	× 1.00
Utilization Savings	× 1.00	× .91	× .96	× 1.00	× 1.00
Trend	× 1.15	× 1.11	× 1.12	× 1.15	× 1.17
Mix of Network Usage	N/A	N/A	80%/20%		N/A
"100% Enrollment" Claim Cost	$5,980	$4,530	$4,987		$3,955
Projected Enrollment	N/A	35%	60%		5%
Selection and Antiselection	1	0.92	1.11		0.70
Projected Claims per Employee	$5,980	$4,168	$5,536		$2,768

This illustration is simplistic in two major ways. First, it assumes that there is no existing managed care plan, while most large employers are likely to offer one or more managed health care plans. If such a plan is reflected in the prior year claim experience, the factors to adjust for the changes in plan benefits, provider discounts, and utilization savings would change for each of the proposed plan options. For example, if the prior claim data reflected an average discount savings of 15%, then the relative adjustment factor for the proposed HMO plan would be about .88 (.75/.85). An alternative method is to add an extra step to build the estimated savings for existing managed care plans back into the prior claim data to approximate the cost of a pure indemnity plan and then proceed with the cost projections for all proposed plans using the full managed care adjustment factors as shown in our illustration.

Another over-simplification is that our example does not contemplate the common scenario where an employer's plan offers competing dual choice plans. If we were to complicate our example by assuming two current carriers, with separate claim experience and demographic data available, then the underwriter might perform a separate claim cost projection for each of the two groups, and then calculate composite costs for each proposed plan option based on a best estimate of any enrollment changes. If the new benefit program will include dual choice competition, then the factors to adjust for selection and anti-selection should attempt to anticipate changes in the risk pool. In general, dual choice options tend to increase the impact of anti-selection. One key to project the impact for a given plan or carrier is to understand the method used to calculate employee contributions.

Medicare Part D

The Medicare Modernization Act created the biggest change in Medicare Programs since 1965. Beginning January 1, 2006, Medicare beneficiaries are able to have a new prescription drug benefit – Medicare Part D. The availability of this benefit is causing many employers to reconsider their current healthcare options offered to their retirees and carriers to reconsider the pricing of medigap and medicare carve-out contracts.

Wellness

The impact of wellness (such as health screenings or on-site flu shot clinics) and disease management programs on claim experience are difficult to measure. Most underwriters give little, if any, significant credit to premium rate projections for these programs on a prospective basis. Any impact is perceived to be reflected in claim experience further in the future than the time represented in a renewal projection. It is not uncommon to add the direct administrative expense for these programs to rates in advance of any potential impact on claim experience.

Dental and Vision Plans

These plans carry an inherent risk of antiselection, since insureds often have discretion over the nature and timing of the services provided. Much of the care is elective, and the insured or provider may be able to select among plan options, schedule appointments, and select courses of treatment that will maximize benefit payments.

Most group dental plans have several features designed to reduce antiselection. Patients' out-of-pocket sharing is often low or nil for diagnostic and preventive procedures, moderate for basic restorative work, and substantial for expensive major services like crowns or orthodontia. Age or frequency limits are common for some procedures, such as X-rays. Most plans have "missing tooth" exclusions and restrictions on replacement work. The majority of plans now feature access to a dental PPO, and many employers offer a DHMO option, a dental managed care plan.

Traditional underwriting rules require strict minimum participation requirements for dental plans, or that they be packaged with group medical plans to limit antiselection. However, market changes toward defined contributions and consumer choice are driving rapid growth in voluntary dental plans, where the employer contribution is small or none. The underwriter's main defenses are higher premium rates, reduced benefits, and various types of contractual or underwriting protections. Premium loadings for new voluntary dental plans can be +5% to +25%. To keep the price down, these plans usually have higher out-of-pocket costs, lower benefit maximums (such as $500 to $1,000 per year), and more restrictive contract provisions. A wide range of special protections includes an extended waiting period for most major services, and "lock-in" or "lock-out" provisions designed to prevent jumping in and out of the plan.

New business pricing methods for existing dental plans are similar to medical. Claim experience data is credible for stable groups down to 200 or so employees, since dental claim experience is much less volatile than medical. With the growth of PPO and DHMO plans, dental pricing must consider adjustments for different networks, dual choice options, and antiselection not unlike those required for medical plans. Virgin groups, with no prior dental plan, require special underwriting care to offset accumulated neglect and a likely utilization blip in the first plan year.

Traditional group vision plans include frequency limits (such as two years between covered routine eye exams) and feature a closed list of covered benefits based on a fixed payment schedule. In the past, most such plans were packaged with medical plans, and the risk was predictable and stable. With new technology and wider choices in vision care, the trend is to replace traditional vision care plans with employer sponsored discount programs, HMO rider plans, or pre-tax health spending accounts.

DEVELOPING THE PROPOSAL

Basic Considerations

Large group RFPs are often correspondingly large, with lengthy questionnaires and highly detailed financial exhibits. No matter how complex the task may be, the essence of the proposal process is to take all that has been learned about the group, plan design, and prior experience, and present a package that is both financially sound and attractive to the buyer.

Most large case RFPs include specifications for the proposed plan design(s) which are frequently highly customized. The specifications for a jumbo group may include the option to "carve out" benefits or services to specialty vendors. Traditionally, large national employers place a high value on providing uniform benefits in all locations, which can be a challenge with varying state laws and regulations (one reason many favor ASO). However, it is also common for the RFP to request bidders to propose alternate plans, if they believe this would improve their offer. Indeed, several of the Fortune 500 companies subscribe to "the best local plan(s)" philosophy in purchasing managed care, especially for HMOs.

In order to complete the proposal exhibits that relate to claim risk, the underwriter must address plan design, funding arrangements, and enrollment patterns that may be unique to a group. In theory, most rating and funding methods are similar (albeit with different risk charges) for groups with 1,000 or 50,000 employees. In practice, the larger the group, the more likely it is that the underwriter will encounter risk issues that are not covered in their company' standard rate manuals.

Thoughtful underwriting requirements and caveats are equally as important as careful rate analysis. Where feasible, the major assumptions behind the claim projections should become stated conditions of the offer. Such caveats might address specified employer contributions, minimum participation (perhaps by plan option), stable demographics, major acquisitions or divestitures, restrictions on any competing plans, or many other factors. Large employer groups are ever changing, so it is especially important to use caveats to cover contingencies that are beyond the carrier's control.

Comparing and validating competing carriers' likely projected claim costs for a managed care plan is a difficult task for employers and their consultants. Most of the larger broker/consulting firms send periodic surveys to health plans, and maintain extensive databases with cost and utilization figures by plan, location and component of care. They also examine HEDIS reports, and other public sources. Also, the RFP may include detailed questions and exhibits related to plan performance in managing health care costs. It is common to be asked to provide negotiated fees for sample procedures for several major worksite locations. An RFP for a self-funded plan may include an alternate request for insured premium rates, just to keep the bidders honest. Conversely, an RFP for a fully insured plan may request a quote for a self-funded plan, to obtain more detailed information on the rate buildup.

Another approach is to request a risk-sharing arrangement in an ASO RFP. Basically, each bidder is asked to project their annual (per head) claim costs (the "target"). If actual claims exceed the target, then the carrier shares a percentage of the risk for excess claims up to a specified maximum, in the form of a year-end payment to the employer. Risk-sharing is typically based on incurred claims, often with deferred settlements to reduce the need to estimate IBNR liabilities.

A well-designed risk-sharing agreement should include a fair formula and reasonable caveats, such as:

- Adjustments for changes in demographics, or similar factors that are beyond the control of the carrier/ network manager,

- A symmetric gain/loss sharing formula, or a risk charge,

- A risk-free corridor around the target claim cost (such as 3%), and

- Some form of pooling of experience, especially for non-jumbo groups.

Development of administrative expense charges might start with the carrier's standard expense allocation tables. These charges vary by product, and the tables usually group (at least direct) costs into major functional components, such as claim processing. The tabular charges are then modified to consider client-specific characteristics or services.

For jumbo groups, client-specific adjustments to expense charges may become more refined. If and where the administrator uses dedicated client service teams, the tabular expense charges for those functions might be replaced by the actual cost estimates. Cost accounting might also be used to determine the incremental expenses for extraordinary processes or services. Services provided by vendors or outsourcing firms may reduce the carrier's costs, but the savings may be offset by the cost of multiple interfaces. A thorough proposal should clearly define the type, scope, and intensity of services contemplated in the quoted price. It may be appropriate to remove charges for certain types of services from the base premiums or fees, and direct-bill based on actual emerging costs. Frequent direct-bill items include large (and hard to predict) printing and distribution jobs and pass-through charges (such as dedicated toll-free lines).

Of course, expense charges should also include provisions for premium taxes, interest, risk charges and profit. For managed care plans, there may be charges for network access, or other payments to third parties. Again, for larger groups, most of these charges tend to be case-specific.

Performance Guarantees

Very large groups often have less perceived need for insurance protection, so the quality and price of administrative services take on ever more importance as the size of the group increases. This has created the phenomenon of performance guarantees. This entails negotiating pre-set standards and metrics for customer service, and a schedule of premium or fee penalties (or far less often, rewards) if actual results deviate from the targets. Performance guarantees have been commonly used for ASO health plans, but they now pop up in RFPs for all types of products and funding methods. Also, a bidder may proactively offer a performance guarantee to highlight a competitive strength.

Performance standards can cover the gamut of services and customer outcomes, but most often deal with the speed or accuracy of claim processing and customer service teams. Others might target specific concerns, such as prompt issue of employee ID cards, or responsiveness of the account manager. Managed care standards may encompass network size or access, distribution of provider directories, or member satisfaction surveys. Jumbo employers (with large fiduciary responsibilities) often request performance guarantees relating to quality of care, such as board certification, NCQA accreditation, and HEDIS clinical/utilization data.

The underwriter should include a sensitivity analysis of the likelihood of performance guarantee settlements. One question to consider is whether, and to what extent, the existence of performance guarantees is likely to improve service results. This may depend on many factors, such as:

- The degree to which services are centralized,
- Whether the client has dedicated service teams,
- Timeliness and management use of tracking reports,
- Accountability for results, and
- Ability to influence the behavior of third parties (including providers).

Ideally, a performance guarantee should be structured to encourage prompt identification and resolution of problems.

Funding Alternatives

Another major component in developing the proposal is to settle on the funding method(s) that will be offered. Funding methods requested in an RFP may or may not be a good fit with the bidder's risk tolerance, capabilities, and strategic goals. Sometimes, bidders may emphasize a funding option to give them a competitive advantage.

Another consideration is the extent to which the employer offers multiple choices among plans and vendors, and the employer's contribution strategy in relation to the cost of those options. The amount that the employee pays out of pocket in premium, in combination with the benefits, drives their selection of plan. High Deductible Health Plans (HDHP) may be offered as the sole product, or as an option with other products. When offered as an option, the spread of rate relativities will introduce an additional selection impact to consider. HDHP programs such as Health Reimbursement Accounts (HRA) and Health Savings Accounts (HSA) may also include contributions toward the deductibles by the employer which, again, introduces selection considerations. A highly fragmented risk pool may render some funding methods less attractive. If the employer is considering a wide range of potential plans and carriers, a bidder may hedge an offer of a given funding option with minimum "packaging" requirements.

Once the price has been determined, and the benefit, administrative, and funding options have been reviewed, then the challenge is to put together a package that produces the best synergy between the buyer's needs and objectives, and the carrier's strengths and strategic goals. This is where proposal underwriting becomes an art. The secret is to listen to the customer, and read between the lines of the RFP.

Depending on a group's size and the amount of financial risk they are willing to assume, there are a variety of funding alternatives available. Carriers assume all the risk in fully insured funding, and employers assume all the risk in self-funded arrangements. Employers may purchase reinsurance coverage on their self-funded programs, to mitigate the impact of high dollar claims per participant (specific stop-loss) or overall higher claims than projected (aggregate stop-loss). The characteristics, basic features, and billing options will provide a range of advantages and disadvantages that can be used in determining which funding best meets the carrier's and employer's needs.

As the market moves from managed care programs to consumer driven health plans (CDHPs) like HRAs and HAS's, underwriters will need to consider different criteria than in the past. HRAs and HSAs have different regulatory bases and may be offered as either full replacement programs or as options. Benefit design, employee cost, strength of competition, and the enrollment process are a few of the factors affecting the selection and pricing.

RENEWAL UNDERWRITING

EVALUATING THE CASE

The first renewal of a new case elicits two common questions; "what happened here?" and "Why?" Other questions can be asked to help find the answers. Was the required participation level verified at time of issue? Did the enrollment rise, fall, or remain stable? Is there any evidence of antiselection? At what point did paid claims attain a mature level? Were there any catastrophic claims? What is the required reserve for incurred but not reported claims? Were cost control measures effective? Are administrative procedures efficient? Are they expensive? What do I know now that I wish I had known a year ago?

The renewal evaluation focuses on the same types of risk characteristics and experience data used in the proposal process, but now there is access to more information. Claim data can be analyzed by age, gender, diagnosis, location, frequency, duration, network, and so forth. The prior carrier's reserving levels can be tested. Premiums can be reconciled to covered lives and volumes of insurance. Sources of data aberrations (such as claim backlogs) can be investigated.

Renewal data can be compared to assumptions regarding the intensity and cost of administrative services. At a minimum, the underwriter should be able to better predict the number of claims and other transactions. For a jumbo group, the actual costs for some functions or services may have been documented.

A common dilemma faced by the renewal underwriter is timing. In order to give the employer adequate notice of the new rates, claim data are often not on a mature basis, especially in the first plan year. Case-specific patterns that may impact IBNR calculations can not be fully quantified in time to validate first-year reserves. Should you apply full credibility to your own data or also consider prior experience? What if the two are quite different? This can be an especially difficult question if there are any catastrophic claims early in the claim history.

DEVELOPING RENEWAL RECOMMENDATIONS

The usual first step in renewal discussions for insured plans is to present the new premium rates for the existing program. Hopefully, the employer has received periodic experience reports, so there are no major surprises. If the renewal premium is abnormally large, the underwriter must decide whether to remedy the situation all at once or over a period of two or more years. Sometimes introducing a funding alternative, such as a retrospective premium agreement, can help offset the need for higher rates.

Renewal recommendations may involve proposed plan design changes. This might be prompted by an analysis of utilization data, or by employer budget pressure. Approaches include increasing employee cost-sharing, adding a utilization review program, adopting a managed care plan, or finding ways to shift health care to more cost-effective models. Jumbo employers tend to have a high level of interest in issues relating to quality of care, to the point where quality and price are closely linked in renewal recommendations and negotiations.

Some large employers who have been in business for many years have a strong interest in reducing their liabilities for retiree benefits. This interest is spurred by an aging population and accounting rules. The renewal analyses of health plan benefits often include ways to reduce the cost of retiree plans, without undue cost-shifting to the retirees. One common strategy is to tweak retired health plan benefits and contributions to try to encourage over-age-65 participants to enroll in Medicare Risk plans.

For other types of plans and products, renewal recommendations often include an analysis of alternate rating and funding methods. Funding options may include stabilization reserves, retrospective premiums, extended payment periods, or various forms of full or partial self-insurance.

In one sense, the renewal process is much like the proposal process, except that the underwriter should know a good deal more about the case, and about the customer.

REVISION UNDERWRITING

An interesting aspect of underwriting large cases, especially jumbo groups, is that their needs and benefits are constantly changing, and the underwriter may have frequent, even daily, involvement with the account. Revisions for jumbo groups tend to stretch the underwriter's resources and imagination.

Revision underwriting includes developing cost estimates for any potential changes in plan design(s) or composition of the group. The latter might be required due to collective bargaining, enrollment shifts, acquisitions or divestitures, or downsizing.

RENEWAL MONITORING

The large case underwriter's role includes tracking of emerging claim experience and of other risk factors throughout the contract year. The underwriter might review premiums and claims each month, and do a more formal analysis of emerging trends, and re-projection of full year results, two to four times per year. Depending on the type of plan, the analysis might include a review of claims by diagnosis, type of provider, type of service, geographic area, business unit, demographic category, or others. Often, the underwriter will review patterns of claim submission and processing, and will project incurred but unreported liabilities.

One purpose of renewal monitoring is for internal control and financial reporting requirements. Due to the size and varied funding methods used for large cases, accurate projection of experience is an important part of a company's financial reporting. It also enables the underwriting department to manage their book of business. Depending on the funding method, these reviews often include updating projections of insurer and employer settlements and liabilities. One example is year-end returns or retrospective premiums due under a participating contract. Another is the need to project employer and insurer liabilities under a minimum premium plan, or a self-funded plan with stop-loss coverage.

Renewal monitoring is also used to quickly identify emerging issues or problems, and to take corrective actions. The options often depend on the severity of the problem, the product and funding method, and the customer relationship. For example, one option may be to meet with the client to pre-sell a large upcoming renewal, or to propose benefit changes. If the funding method is such that the employer bears, or shares, the risk, the discussions may be more open-ended, with each party sharing ideas of how to address their mutual problem. The key is early communication of the issues, as large group customers are not fond of year-end "surprises."

SPECIAL RISKS

ASSOCIATION PROGRAMS

Most states permit group insurance contracts to be issued to associations of specific types. These programs generally fall into two categories:

- An Association of individuals, covering the bona fide members of an organization, such as a medical society or a bar association, that was formed to further some common interest or occupation.
- A multiple-employer trust (MET), where the policy is issued to the trustees of a fund established by two or more employers in the same industry and covers their employees.

Of the two, the association of individuals poses the greater risk of antiselection. In fact, there are few such plans being marketed today as group insurance (although there are many individual plans of coverage in effect). Most programs are limited to life or disability insurance coverage and rely heavily on medical evidence of insurability. The spread-the-risk safeguard normally inherent in group insurance programs is not found in these plans, where participation rarely exceeds 5% of the eligible members.

The second category, multiple-employer plans, offers many of the underwriting safeguards found in single-employer groups. Most such plans require substantial employer contributions and have minimum participation rules for each employer. The primary marketplace for multiple-employer groups is among small employer groups bound together in a strong trade association.

Successful multiple-employer plans almost always display the following characteristics:

- The sponsoring association is a strong entity, with a high percentage of eligible firms participating as dues-paying members. These associations also provide many other services to their members.
- A large pool of eligible members.
- A relatively small average employer size. Member firms with more than 50 or so employees tend to find their coverage elsewhere.

As with any small employer group, successful underwriting of multiple employer programs includes preexisting condition exclusions, age rating, closely monitored premium collection, limited plan designs and often limited evidence of insurability.

Many multiple-employer plans are self-insured. These are referred to as Multiple Employer Welfare Associations (MEWAs). Several states have promulgated strict rules designed to protect the members of MEWAs from the risk of insolvency, in response to a somewhat spotty financial history for these plans.

TAFT-HARTLEY GROUPS

In addition to the restrictions imposed by the Taft-Hartley Act, state laws differ widely with respect to eligibility rules, types of coverage permitted, minimum size requirements, and employee contributions. The underwriters must be satisfied that the trustees have established adequate facilities for administering the plan, and that the income of the fund is sufficient to cover the cost of administration as well as the cost of the insurance. Generally, successful programs have required that coverage be noncontributory, and 100% of the eligible employees of each contributing employer are insured at all times. Special care is needed to ensure coverage is limited to full-time employees, and the minimum number of hours worked requirement is high enough to exclude employees who will not earn enough employer contributions to cover the cost of their insurance. Termination and reinstatement of coverage also present unique problems.

PURCHASING ALLIANCES

Purchasing alliances are formed when two or more non-affiliated large groups come together to solicit insurance bids via a common RFP. The groups may have secondary motives, such as to share the cost of hiring a consultant, but the main purpose of such alliances is to enhance their purchasing power through economies of scale and added negotiating leverage.

These groups typically purchase fully insured plans, in order to avoid issues of co-mingling employers' funds. Some of the first purchasing alliances were formed by political sub-divisions, backed by enabling legislation. The individual groups might pay the same premium rates, or simply receive comparable size discounts off their separate rates.

A more recent form of purchasing alliance is a coalition of (usually very) large employers who combine forces to purchase managed care plans, sometimes directly from providers. This phenomenon has been largely localized, but there are a few national coalitions. The passage of federal Association Health Plan legislation (AHPs) would likely increase the number of, and interest in, national coalitions.

Firms participating in coalitions usually have to agree to abide by ground rules that are set by the coalition in order to foster consistency and team-work among the member firms, and to elicit more attractive rates from bidding carriers. Examples of typical ground rules include:

- Common plan designs.
- Restrictions on offering plans not sponsored by the coalition.
- A limited number of sponsored plans in any one area.
- Favored status for the best (or least expensive) local plan.

Large employer coalitions may focus on issues other than price.

One of the side benefits that is most attractive to these sophisticated buyers is the added ability to monitor and influence quality of care issues. Again, the major objective is to negotiate lower rates. The incremental economies of scale may be quite small for these already jumbo buyers. The combined negotiating leverage of the coalition can be substantial, particularly in lo-cations where the participating firms employ a high percentage of a plan's total membership.

Some employer coalition RFPs mandate identical premium rates for all participating employers. This compounds the underwriter's biggest chal-lenge with alliance plans: to help ensure that his or her plan attracts and retains a fair share of healthy enrollees, and a fair share of enrollees from the more desirable employer groups. The fact that contribution formulas usually favor low cost plans creates some delicate trade-offs.

UNDERWRITING GROUP DISABILITY INCOME

Group disability income provides benefits that require special underwriting consideration. Successful underwriting of group disability income starts with the recognition that disability claims are a subjective and volatile risk. The decision of whether to submit a claim for disability, or to stay on claim, often depends upon the claimant's motivation, which is frequently related to their occupation, and is influenced by the amount of benefit be-ing paid. Careful underwriting and claim management is necessary to con-trol this selection, as well as to properly classify the insurance health risk involved.

LTD is more risky to the insurer than most other health insurance cover-ages, because it involves a low frequency of claims for large amounts, mak-ing financial results less stable and less predictable than for medical care.

Classification of groups for disability income rating purposes is generally by occupation and industry. These two elements may be handled in combination or may be treated separately, depending upon the company philosophy, the particular plan, and the characteristics of the group. Rates also vary by age and gender, and occasionally a plan is given rate credits for lower replacement ratios. Because of the very long-term nature of claims and the volatility that could be caused by a single claim, there tends to be a high degree of pooling. Experience rating is only used for very large groups, and case credibility factors are low.

The underwriter must be careful in designing the plan limitations exclusions, and benefit formula, so as to avoid overinsurance. Overinsurance is when the benefit is so high as to influence the submitting of a claim or to encourage malingering.

One example of this principle is to fully offset (deduct from benefits otherwise payable) both primary and dependent Social Security benefits if the LTD gross benefit exceeds 50% of pre-disability earnings. In general, offsets of income from all social programs, both state and federal, is advised if the replacement ratios are over 50% of gross pay.

A second way to avoid excessive replacement ratios is to 'step down,' or have lower benefit percentages for higher amounts of coverage. The definition of 'high' depends upon many factors, including the industry, the size of the group, the extent of top-heaviness (since a high benefit on only one or two top executives is more questionable than high benefits for 25 or 50 executives), and whether the plan is contributory.

Liberal definitions of disability, such as own occupation to age 65, or use of a residual disability clause, should be restricted to white collar groups in otherwise select situations. Industries which are cyclical, seasonal, or subject to high turnover should be avoided. This is because layoffs generate higher incidence rates, and STD is subject to possible misuse as unemployment insurance.

Growing firms are lower risk. Firms with a history of employment fluctuation are higher risk. A company which has reduced its work force recently is not necessarily a bad risk, but a company which is over-staffed in relation to recent orders and projected revenue can be a very poor risk.

A commercial rating report on the financial status of the employer should be ordered on large groups. Danger signs include a drop in revenues exceeding 25% in the past year, or excessive debt, or a history or prospect of financial instability. Again, the underwriter is concerned that the STD or LTD might be used for unemployment benefits.

Single-employer groups, which include hourly workers or union members, can be insured for disability income, but with suitable loadings in the rates for any extra risk. Disability plans covering the members of a union-sponsored plan can be poor risks, unless the union is interested in controlling claim costs and has a good record in administering welfare benefit plans.

Groups with substantial proportions of commissioned salesmen can be insured, subject to careful determination of the amount of benefits and a well defined statement of eligibility for benefits. The disability benefits can be based on monthly earnings, which include commissions, using 1/12 of the earnings in the twelve month period prior to disablement. This is conservative for recently hired sales persons, and is designed to reduce the impact of a jumbo sale shortly after enrolling for LTD. Eligibility for commissioned persons is sometimes difficult to determine, because it is difficult to tell when they are actually losing money due to a disability, or even when they return to work.

Non-contributory plans are especially desirable for LTD since individual selection is minimized, and a better spread of risk is assured.

Insurers in the LTD market must be sure to accumulate adequate surplus when experience is good, in order to carry them through the down cycles. An underwriting response to a downturn can be perceived as more flexible than a rate increase. Underwriting can be quickly tightened in those industries and geographic regions which are most impacted by rising employment.

UNDERWRITING GROUP LIFE

Group term life underwriting risks share certain similarities with disability. Claim frequencies are low, and the amount at risk on any individual can be quite high. The potential for antiselection can be a concern with some plan designs, and allowing employee choice greatly increases the average cost per participant. A high percentage of plan participation is the best way to ensure a balanced spread of risk.

Fully insured experience rating is usually based on several years' experience, and applies low credibility to case data, except for very large groups.

Retrospective experience rating is usually reserved to basic life plans with significant employer contributions; optional life plans are almost always non-participating (in part, to preclude the possibility of ERISA problems).

Life coverage may be continued into retirement. It is standard within the industry to require reduction of benefits provisions and to limit maximum allowed retiree benefits, since they are often effectively guaranteed (continued until death). Special attention is given to certain concerns when evaluating retiree risk, including: (1) the financial stability of the group, (2) the historical and potential impact of lay-offs on the retiree liability, and (3) the anticipated aging of the retiree population. This last point is critical when either a multiple year rate guarantee or one rate for both actives and retirees is requested.

Alternate funding options may be limited to retrospective premium arrangements, and a few approaches to reduce carrier reserves. Self-insurance is not feasible, due to adverse tax implications for beneficiaries. Large employer group life plans also reflect the trend toward defined contribution and multiple choice (or cafeteria) plans. This results in employee-paid optional life plans with very large amounts of insurance. In many modern life plans, the concept of choice has been extended to include annual flex plan enrollments and qualifying life events. Underwriting safeguards include participation requirements, benefit formulas related to earnings, age based rating, evidence of insurability for very large amounts of insurance, and limits (such as an additional one times earnings) on open enrollment benefit increases.

Group life carriers have added new benefit features in recent years, in part to differentiate their product and to reduce the impact of intense price competition. These include living benefit provisions that allow for payment of a portion of the death benefit in the event of a terminal illness, and beneficiary financial counseling that offers investment and disbursement advice from an independent financial counselor. Group universal life plans also offer the combination of life insurance protection and tax-favored investment gains. Group variable universal life plans are also available and provide greater individual choice and control regarding the investment funds used. Universal life plans can also help to reduce the need for the employer to provide expensive retired life coverage on a group basis, a good fit with the defined contribution focus. Of course, new features can mean new risks.

Living benefit payments can represent added risk if a "terminal" claimant later recovers (which is more common than one might expect). The portability provision that is common to group universal plans, and is now being seen in some group term life plans, can result in antiselection, which can be especially intense if a large employer experiences a downsizing. Despite the challenges presented by intense competition and liberal plan provisions, a well-designed group life plan can still generate excellent underwriting and investment gains.

25 UNDERWRITING SMALL GROUPS

James T. O'Connor

INTRODUCTION

The term "small group health insurance" typically refers to comprehensive medical expense plans offered and sold to employers with up to 50 employees, although some refer to groups with up to 100 employees as small employer groups. Traditionally, the underwriting techniques used for small groups vary depending upon the size of a group. Groups with fewer than 10 employees are often underwritten using methods similar to those used for individual insurance. Large group underwriting techniques begin to apply increasingly as group size increases.

While the advent of state small group rating and underwriting laws and regulations in 1990 introduced a legal definition of *small employer group*, it was the enactment of the federal Health Insurance Portability and Accountability Act (HIPAA), effective in July 1997, that better standardized this definition. HIPAA and all states define a *small employer group* as an employer group of 2-50 eligible employees for purposes of guaranteed availability and renewability. Some states also include employer groups of 1 (self-employed persons) as being subject to the small employer group rating laws. Several states continue to apply rating laws to groups up to only 25, but their underwriting rules apply to groups up to 50 in compliance with HIPAA. These laws are critical to understanding the rating and underwriting considerations and methods used by health insurers.

Numerous small group carriers have chosen to exit the market since HIPAA was enacted, due to a combination of the risks and expense associated with compliance, the increased competition of managed health care plans, and the intense pressure to negotiate competitive payment rates with network providers. Blue Cross and Blue Shield plans and several large nationwide commercial carriers, along with local managed health care plans, have established themselves as key competitors in the small group market. This has influenced the competitive marketplace in terms of premium rates, plan design, approaches to health care delivery, and the underwriting of the insured. In response, carriers have introduced consumer-driven health plans (CDHPs) to employers as a means of reducing premium rates and making their employees more aware of the high costs of health care. The introduction of Health Savings Accounts (HSAs) by the federal government in 2004 has provided new impetus to CDHPs due to the attractive tax benefits of HSAs, although these have been slow to catch on. These are particularly attractive to small professional partnerships.

New approaches to rating and underwriting small groups are also developing, primarily through the use of risk adjustment analyses, new risk predictor tools, and continually increasing technological improvements, particularly related to web-based, telephonic, and other electronic underwriting and enrollment capabilities. These new capabilities allow greater precision and faster processing in medically underwriting applicants. They also allow agents and brokers to concentrate on prospecting and sales, rather than spending administrative time with a prospect gathering application information.

This chapter looks at the nature of the small group market and the approaches used by insurance carriers and health plans to underwrite and set premium rates for this marketplace.

THE SMALL GROUP MARKET

DEMOGRAPHICS OF THE MARKET

Small employer groups represent 75% of U.S. business establishments, but only 28% of employees, according to a U.S. Agency for Healthcare Research and Quality tabulation. The following table illustrates this fact and presents the distribution of firms by size.

Number of Employees	Distribution of Establishments	Distribution of Employees
< 10	58.3%	13.0%
10-24	12.1%	8.8%
25-49	4.8%	6.5%
50-99	3.4%	7.1%
100-999	7.2%	18.7%
1000+	14.2%	45.9%
Total	100.0%	100.0%

Source: 2003 Medical Expenditure Panel Survey (MEPS), Agency for Healthcare Research and Quality, published in July, 2005

These statistics include establishments with only 1 employee, which are typically not subject to small employer group rating and underwriting laws.

Although small groups comprise a large market, many do not offer group medical plans to their employees (57% in the 2003 MEPS survey). Those groups that offer a plan often include substantial cost-sharing for their employees (in both premiums and benefits), frequently without any employer contribution for dependents of employees. This is primarily due to basic cost considerations and to comparatively high rates of employee turnover.

A small business owner must carefully consider the purchase of group medical insurance in terms of its impact on the success of the business. Since medical insurance is a relatively expensive item, a small employer may elect to cover only the owner and perhaps a few key employees through individual insurance. As with all insurance coverage, owners are much more likely to purchase medical coverage if they suspect their employees or dependents are more likely than average to incur medical expenses. Cost pressures on small business, often coupled with greater first-hand knowledge of the medical status of employees and dependents, create a market with substantial potential for antiselection.

If there were no barriers to buying insurance when needs are greatest, small employers would, if acting rationally, select against insurance programs by purchasing only when they knew they would collect benefits. Insurance companies have reacted to such opportunities for antiselection, as well as a perceived demand for lower costs, by underwriting potential insureds, both as a group and as individuals within the group. Rates for the group are often based on an assessment of each employee's health status, particularly for the smallest groups. The opportunity for antiselection tends to be less for larger sized groups and where a greater percentage of employees are enrolled in the medical plan.

Opportunities for antiselection increased significantly with the enactment of the Health Insurance Portability and Accountability Act (HIPAA) in 1997. This law not only set a standard for the definition of a *small employer*, but more importantly requires small group health insurance carriers and health plans to offer all of their major medical and comprehensive health insurance products on a guaranteed acceptance and renewal basis (with very limited exceptions). A carrier cannot reject an applicant on the basis of health status or prior health experience. Furthermore, an individual employee or dependent cannot be singled out for special rating treatment due to their health. Also, HIPAA requires that preexisting condition limitations or exclusions cannot be imposed on individual employees who have had continuous coverage for more than 12 months.

These market characteristics create a volatile market that presents immense risk to insurers who do not fully understand the nature of the market. Such volatility, coupled with the increasing costs of insurance, has led to increasing numbers of employed uninsured and to carriers exiting the market. In response, rating, underwriting, and product design restrictions, which continue to vary noticeably from state to state, have changed the nature of the risks faced by insurers operating in the small employer market. These risks need to be addressed strategically by each insurer to assess its long-term viability and strategy in this marketplace.

PRODUCT CHARACTERISTICS

The small business owner generally has the ability to select from similar types of coverage as those offered to large employers. This section looks at those product characteristics.

Medical Plans

Generally, medical plan offerings include a selection of deductibles, coinsurance amounts, co-payments, and out-of-pocket limits. Many of the cost-saving ideas common to large group programs are also offered to small groups. These include various cost containment provisions, such as hospital pre-admission certification, preferred provider options, and other managed care features. Insurance companies and Blue Cross and Blue Shield plans are major players in the small group medical market. HMOs continue to increase their presence in this market. There are a plethora of PPO (Preferred Provider Organizations) and POS (Point of Service) arrangements, as well as indemnity and HMO coverage. Very few plans remain available in the marketplace without some cost management features.

The increase in the presence of managed care and HMO plans, that are geographically concentrated, has resulted in commercial carriers having to consider pricing, underwriting, and plan design on a local market basis rather than on a general nationwide basis with only area factors to differentiate area.

HIPAA introduced a number of challenges to rating and underwriting small employer plans. First, it dictates that pregnancy cannot be considered a preexisting condition. Also, the law requires that all plans be available to any eligible group. In combination, this hobbles a carrier's ability to limit maternity benefits for very small groups, as was the practice prior to HIPAA. Carriers responded to these requirements by restructuring their maternity benefits for mini-groups to "same as any illness" coverage. Some continue to offer maternity as optional coverage, particularly in the mini-group market, but many now include it as a standard benefit. For groups with 15 or more employees, U.S. federal law requires the employer to provide maternity coverage. Supplemental accident benefits and prescription card benefits are also common options.

Consumer-Directed Health Plans

Almost all small group insurers have now introduced consumer-directed health plans (CDHPs) to employers. CDHPs can be generalized into two types: 1) health reimbursement account (HRA) health plans, and 2) HSA high deductible health plans (HDHPs). These plans are similar to those offered in the large group market and are discussed in more detail in chapter 4 of this book. Employer groups have introduced these CDHPs as a means of reducing premium rates and making their employees more aware of the high costs of health care.

These programs, through their cost-sharing structures, are intended to incent employees to be more cost-conscious about medical expenditures. Employees are expected to be more satisfied, because there is less management of care by the insurer, so that choices are made only by the employee and his or her doctor. Costs to the employee can be lower if the employee uses preferred providers (who have agreed to discount pricing). Some of these self-directed health plans make use of a tiered co-payment design, in which services from more costly providers are subject to higher co-payments than lower cost providers. These plans are sometimes promoted as also being less costly to the employer, due to a combination of lower administrative costs, more cost-conscious usage by employees, and the impact of the corridor deductible.

The introduction of Health Savings Accounts (HSAs) by the federal government in 2004 was expected to provide new impetus to CDHPs due to the attractive tax benefits of HSAs, although they have been slow to catch on. These plans are particularly attractive to small professional partnerships. Under the law, the HDHP must have a deductible of at least $1,050 for employee-only coverage and $2,100 for family coverage in 2006, and is scheduled to increase each year. There are maximum out-of-pocket limits of $5,250 and $10,500, respectively. Other than preventive care, all benefit services must be subject to the high deductible, including outpatient prescription drugs and doctor office visits.

Typically, an employer contributes an amount to the HRA or HSA account, and the medical plan will have a high deductible. HRAs have the advantage of being more flexible in plan design, including offering copays for drugs and office visits. Also, the HRA account contribution is actually an accounting entry, and does not actually need to be funded until used. In contrast, HSA contributions by an employer immediately become owned by the employee to do with whatever he or she desires, even use it for non-medical purposes. If an employee leaves the employer, the money contributed by the employer into the HSA goes with the employee. With relatively high employee turnover rates for small employers, this limitation, along with the others mentioned above, have made HSA/HDHP benefit plans relatively slow to catch on in the small group market. However, they are attractive to small professional firms and partnerships in which the tax benefits of the HSAs overshadow the limitations of the health plans.

Critics of CDHPs claim that such plans discriminate against less healthy people, since their out-of-pocket costs are likely to increase. These plans are relatively new on the market, and there are many variations offered at the present time. Time will tell if CDHP plans prove to be successful and become an important part of the market.

Ancillary Benefit Programs

The employer is offered employee life, accidental death and dismemberment, dependent life, short-term and long-term disability insurance, and dental insurance, as well as a full range of medical expense insurance plans. These ancillary coverages can be issued on an accept/reject basis, independent of the medical guaranteed issuance.

Most programs offer only modest amounts of life insurance. These life insurance programs may be either non-contributory or contributory, depending upon the benefit level desired and the employer money available. Benefit schedules are either a flat amount (such as $10,000), flat amounts by class, or some multiple of salary (such as two times salary). In addition, carriers can offer supplemental amounts of insurance, with each employee having the ability to choose within a range of optional amounts and paying the full cost of coverage.

Modest life insurance benefits included in combination with medical benefits usually are not separately medically underwritten, due to cost considerations. Those plans that offer large amounts of life insurance require underwriting considerations similar to the requirements for an individual life policy. Greater underwriting attention is required for greater amounts and for groups with fewer lives insured.

Both long-term disability income insurance (LTD) and short-term disability insurance (STD) are available to small groups, in standard benefit combinations. Benefit amounts are offered as flat amounts, or as benefit schedules based upon occupation class or a flat percentage of salary. To avoid over-insurance, carriers generally will limit disability income benefits to no more than 50-70% of earnings. In addition, disability income benefits are usually coordinated with Social Security disability benefits and state cash sickness plans, as well as with employer sick-pay plans and Worker's Compensation.

Many small employers, especially new or struggling companies, cannot afford complete employee benefit programs. Since purchasing medical insurance is usually perceived as the most important priority, optional coverages are frequently not sold. STD benefits are rarely purchased by small businesses, unless they are required to do so by state law. Although regular LTD plans are available to them, small business owners who wish to purchase LTD benefits often do so through individual policies or combination sales. Combination LTD sales are programs that provide LTD for small amounts (such as 40% of gross pay) plus level premium individual policies to cover the additional amounts. The amount of guaranteed issue, and thus the degree of underwriting, varies by the amount of benefit and the number of lives insured. Programs with fewer than 10 lives are generally individually underwritten.

DISTRIBUTION SOURCES

Small group insurance is distributed mainly though general agents and brokers. In the larger end of the small group market, group service representatives are sometimes used by carriers that also sell in the larger group markets. Competitive compensation schedules are critical to the sale of small group insurance, particularly at the smaller size end of the market.

The majority of carriers employ a level commission schedule which varies by group size. However, in the mini-group market, some carriers vary the commission rates by policy duration, with a higher first year rate and then level rates for subsequent durations. Generally, the first year differential will not exceed 5 percentage points (such as 15% first year, 10% renewal). However, in the group association market, commission rates for groups of fewer than 5 employees can have much higher first duration rates, similar to the individual A&H comprehensive medical market.

During periods of high medical inflation and rate increases, many carriers paid commissions based upon original issued premium levels; that is, the portion of premium arising from rate increases is not commissionable. As trend decreased, many carriers reverted back to paying on a collected premium basis.

Often, compensation is structured to encourage positive field underwriting by the agents, especially in a guaranteed issue environment. Due to fair marketing rules in many states' small group laws, the compensation arrangement cannot vary by the health status or claim experience of a specific group, but generally can differ based upon such criteria as renewal persistency. It is important that laws regarding fair marketing be adhered to in structuring sales compensation packages. Sometimes there is a fine line between fair marketing and incenting the agents to best represent the carrier's interests. The commission structure as well as the experience of the distribution force can influence what part of the small group market will be prospected. The use of group service representatives will motivate sales at the upper end of the size range, while the use of agents and brokers who also sell to the individual or association markets will tend to result in sales to smaller, baby groups.

Electronic and telephonic capabilities allow carriers to shift much of the application and enrollment processes away from the agent. This allows the the agent to concentrate on prospecting and sales, rather than spending administrative time with a prospect to gather the application information.

A number of small group carriers are also selling coverage through the internet. At this point, such activity is generally limited to the information and sales process, still requiring traditional off-line underwriting before policy issue. As insurers become more comfortable with the internet process, and are able to minimize antiselection through more reliable on-line underwriting processes, we may likely begin to see instant on-line underwritten quotes for most uncomplicated cases. The introduction of risk predictor software based upon a prospective insured's medical conditions or the prescription drugs being used by the prospect may make internet underwriting more feasible in the future. State regulation may also need to be updated in order to make direct internet sales possible.

Commercial insurers generally provide small group medical plans through multiple employer trusts (METs). Other carriers, such as Blue Cross/Blue Shield Plans, that are geographically concentrated, may use direct group policy forms. Most carriers will sell to small employers through associations, particularly for employers with fewer than 10 employees (the "baby group" size). Some carriers market individual medical forms to baby groups in states where benefit mandates are more onerous or riskier for group forms. HIPAA and state laws generally apply the small employer rating and underwriting requirements based upon whether the coverage was sponsored by the small employer, not based upon whether the policy is an individual or group filing form. Because the small employer rating and underwriting requirements are significantly different from coverage sold to individuals, carriers need to be able to verify which set of laws applies to a given sale. This requirement was introduced to discourage carriers from avoiding the rating and underwriting rules for one market by using the other.

Most METs are insured, although some are self-funded and managed by an organization that sponsors and markets the plan (usually a third party administrator, or TPA). Commonly referred to as MEWAs (Multiple Employer Welfare Arrangements), many of these plans have been organized under the ERISA exemption from state regulated mandates. These plans tend to be viewed negatively by most state regulators and agents who sell small group plans, due to a history of failures over the years.

In establishing an insured MET, an insurer appoints a trustee and establishes a trust in compliance with state law. A group insurance policy will be issued to the trust to provide coverage to participating employers who join the trust. Employers are not issued a separate policy covering their group. Rather, employees who elect coverage are issued certificates of insurance. Trusts are issued in one state (situs state) that is selected by the insurance company. The policy will comply with the laws of the state of situs. In addition, other states will also require that certain laws be met with respect to plans sold to their residents, such as mandated coverage and premium restrictions. The trust policy will generally include a range of benefit plans. Each employer chooses a plan to purchase (subject to underwriting rules established for the trust) and the actual certificate issued to each employee will reflect the options applicable to that employer.

THE COMPETITIVE ENVIRONMENT

The competitive environment in the small group market has not only changed in terms of the products offered, but also regarding the nature of the players in the market.

National carriers still play a crucial role in offering coverage to small group carriers, but the companies involved have changed. While several of the old-line companies still are influential in this market, the large national managed care companies have become market leaders. This is also true of regional carriers, particularly the Blue Cross and Blue Shield plans, as they continue to merge with each other. These carriers often dominate large group markets and bring significant market power to their provider negotiations for the small group market. Local HMO and small managed health plans also compete in the market, although to a lesser extent than the large national managed care companies and Blue Cross and Blue Shield plans. What they have brought to the competitive landscape is realization of the need to consider the local environment in competing for business through provider negotiation, knowledge of the local businesses, plan design, and their knowledge of the competition. For larger carriers to thrive in a specific geographic market, they too must consider these competitive characteristics on a local basis. The "one size fits all" formula is no longer an effective marketing approach for small groups.

This local landscape, coupled with the risks and expense of complying with each state's laws and regulations, has made it challenging for midsize and smaller insurance companies to compete effectively in the small employer market. For this and other reasons, many of these carriers have withdrawn from the small employer group market, deciding that their capital can be more successfully invested in other activities and markets.

The enactment of HIPAA required carriers to offer all of their medical insurance products to small groups of all sizes on a guaranteed issue basis with guaranteed renewability. States have required that the premium rates also be limited in terms of the range of rates between groups with similar characteristics and in the differences in premium rate increases that can be implemented. States differ significantly in the details of these limitations, with resulting variation in allowing carriers to forestall antiselection.

UNDERWRITING THE GROUP

Underwriting of small groups traditionally takes place on two levels: (1) evaluating the business entity, and (2) examining the health status and other characteristics of each individual to be covered. With the passage of HIPAA and other small group reform laws, the approach carriers take to underwriting the group has become much more important. This is due to the limitations imposed on a carrier's ability to reject or rate-up (increase rates to reflect worse than average risks) specific individuals within a group. Today the emphasis for underwriting is on proper rating rather than on accept/reject decisions, benefit limitations, or exclusions.

In underwriting the group, both the characteristics of the insured and of the employer itself should be considered. The rating structure used by the carrier, which is more and more often dictated by small group law, has an important bearing on the significance placed upon certain characteristics.

FINANCIAL VIABILITY

The carrier incurs substantial costs in selling, underwriting, and issuing the group. In order to retain the group as a client long enough to recoup these acquisition expenses, it is important that the business be financially viable. Such concern cannot be taken lightly in the small group market because of the significant number of business failures in the market.

While financial underwriting is common in the large group markets, it is not always feasible in this market. Employers are not often willing to discuss financial information. Alternative underwriting considerations can include the number of years of operation and the level of employee turnover. Employers with high employee turnover tend to be unfavorable groups for health coverage because of higher administrative costs. Groups with seasonal employment can have higher costs both from administration expenses and antiselection. At a minimum, the carrier should verify that the group is in fact a true commercial business.

INDUSTRY/OCCUPATION

The type of business and the duties performed by its employees are also related to expected future claim costs. Certain types of businesses are exposed to higher health risks. Some of these risks are clearly work-related, such as a job which requires handling hazardous chemicals. Other risks are related to lifestyle issues. For example, employees of a motorcycle dealership are more likely to ride motorcycles and might present a greater risk than employees of an accounting firm. In the past, certain industries or occupations would not be eligible for insurance by some small group carriers; others would receive a premium surcharge. Under HIPAA, there cannot be ineligible industries. The only way to reflect industry morbidity differences is through rate surcharges and discounts. However, it should be noted that many states no longer allow *industry rating,* and others limit the size of the surcharge to a maximum of 15%. There is a wide variety of industry rating factors used by carriers. There has not been widely accepted research done in this area. There are differences of opinion as to how predictive the use of industry rating is for reflecting higher morbidity costs.

GROUP SIZE

Group size is another important group characteristic, affecting both expected claims levels and per capita acquisition and maintenance expenses. The larger the group, the more lives over which the morbidity risk can be spread. An individual employee's health status in a larger group will be a smaller factor in the decision to purchase insurance and the level of benefits chosen. Also, the administrative expenses incurred in writing a group of 35 are lower on a per capita basis than those for a group of 10.

Historically, carriers offered coverage at lower rates and used less stringent underwriting as employer group size increased. However, one typical objective of small group reform laws is to force small group carriers to pool the group size risk over their entire small group portfolios, by either disallowing group size rating variation or by limiting it. For example, the NAIC model regulation allows only up to a 20% variance. States requiring modified community rating generally do not allow any adjustment for group size. Some states limit rate variation by group size to only legitimate administrative expense differences, but do not allow any recognition of morbidity variation correlating to group size. These limitations can create additional risk for a carrier intending to write business in both the baby group market and the larger small group market. This is actually a marketing risk, since many carriers tend to have sales forces that gravitate to either the baby group market or the larger end of the small group market.

An advisable underwriting practice is for the small group insurers to verify the actual size of the group applying for new coverage or renewing its coverage. HIPAA guaranteed issue requirements apply only to groups with 2-50 employees. A group with more than 50 employees, even if fewer than 50 apply for coverage, is not subject to guaranteed issue rules, nor states' rating limitations. Small groups often can change size over a plan year, particularly baby groups. It is prudent to verify the group size at renewal time to be sure that the group is still subject to small group laws. A group of 2 or 3 employees can frequently be downsized to a group of 1 in poor economic times.

Workers Compensation

An important aspect of group underwriting is to recognize the impact of workers compensation programs on insured costs. Most plan designs exclude claims that are covered or could be covered under workers compensation. Some carriers require employers to have all employees eligible for workers compensation to have such coverage as a condition for offering non-workers compensation health benefits. Like participation and contribution rules, the lack of workers compensation coverage could qualify as grounds for rejection, even in today's guaranteed issue environment.

Participation

In order to qualify for medical coverage, a small group is expected to meet certain participation requirements set by the carrier. At point of sale, these requirements provide the insurer some protection against antiselection by prohibiting a significant number of employees (presumably the most healthy) from opting out of coverage. Participation requirements also help protect the insurer after issue from *case stripping*, where a few employees and/or dependents with expected high medical costs remain under the plan, with the remainder dropping coverage, or purchasing less expensive group coverage elsewhere.

In determining participation, the employer may carve out specified classes of employees, such as non-union employees or management employees. Employees who are not members of these classes will not be considered in determining whether participation requirements are met. In some cases, employees who have coverage elsewhere (such as through a spouse's plan) will not be considered in determining participation.

The majority of states continue to allow participation as a requirement for insurance, even where coverage is otherwise guaranteed issue. Often the participation requirements are limited by law, such as limiting the requirement to be no greater than 70% of eligible employees. Some states, however, require that employers who have coverage from other sources such as a spouse's plan, even if it is HMO coverage of the same employer group, either cannot consider them in determining participation, or must include them in both the numerator and denominator of the participation formula. This latter requirement poses a risk to the insurer that the healthiest employees subscribe to another plan (such as an HMO) and it is left with less healthy lives to insure. Where permissible, participation rules that do not allow more than one carrier's health plan to be in force help protect the insurer from antiselection, especially for groups of less than 15 employees.

It is important that participation is rechecked periodically after initial enrollment, such as on renewal dates, to assure that the plan is not being selected against by having healthy lives move to other plans after issue.

EMPLOYER CONTRIBUTIONS

Another underwriting consideration is the employer's contribution to the cost of insurance. The more the employer pays of the total cost, the higher the employee participation tends to be. Generally, carriers require that the employer make some contribution to the cost. Although large employers frequently contribute 80 percent or more of the cost of insurance, small employers typically cannot afford such high contributions. It is not uncommon for small employers to pay a portion of the employee's premium (say 50 percent), but require the employee to pay the full cost of dependent coverage.

This requirement often results in an employer not sponsoring a health insurance program for its employees due to the employer's concern of affordability of coverage. The lower the contribution rate (and therefore the participation rate), the more likely it is that the insureds will be less healthy than the entire group as a whole. Some states will not allow a small group to be insured unless the employer contributes a minimum level of the premium and the group meets minimum participation levels.

The use of a contribution requirement, including contribution for dependents, can help limit a carrier's exposure to the baby group market if it wishes to discourage sales to this market segment.

PRIOR COVERAGE AND EXPERIENCE

In underwriting a group as a whole, it is important to gather and review information regarding the prior coverage and experience of the group. If this is the first time the group is obtaining coverage, discovering the reasons for seeking coverage at this time can point to other areas that should be investigated more fully. For example, the spouse of a valued executive may have contracted what is likely to be a costly medical condition. The business may be new and its financial stability may need to be reviewed more closely.

If the group is changing carriers, information regarding the prior coverage is an important underwriting consideration, particularly because of the requirements for portability of coverage (usually without regard to the differences in benefits) which eliminate much of the protection offered by a preexisting condition provision. Therefore, reviewing the health status and experience of the group is a paramount consideration in deciding what premium rate to offer a group. However, it must be recognized in reviewing the experience of small employer groups that the experience will tend to lack statistical credibility, and that a single past routine hospital claim can result in the appearance of poor experience. Ideally, the experience should be investigated for the likelihood that a similar morbidity level will continue. However, this is usually not administratively feasible for very small groups, where it would have the most impact.

The motives of the group for changing carriers should be investigated to the extent possible. Is the group increasing benefits or just seeking more competitive premium rates? Is the group seeking to add employees who were not covered under the prior carrier and would have been considered "late entrants?" Are certain dependents being added who were not covered by the prior plan? There are other antiselective motives which might also be detected by soliciting information about the prior coverage.

ELIGIBILITY RULES AND CLASSES

As mentioned above, an employer can establish certain rules regarding eligibility for its health plans. These rules generally include such criteria as the number of weekly hours an employee works and the number of months the employee has been with the company. Many employers have a waiting period of one to three months before an employee's coverage can begin. They also usually only cover their full-time employees, although some states have now defined a full-time employee for the purpose of health care coverage to be one working as few as 20-25 hours per week.

Some small groups (usually toward the larger end of the small group range) may subdivide their employees into two or three classes. This is most often seen in those companies which have union labor. The union employees may have a collectively bargained plan, while the non-union employees may have a separate eligibility class with its own health plan. Other examples of eligibility classes are exempt versus non-exempt employees and hourly employees versus salaried employees.

For groups with less than 20 employees, active employees eligible for Medicare should be required to have both Part A and Part B of Medicare to minimize expected claims since Medicare will be the primary insurer. For groups of 20 or more, Medicare will be the secondary insurer.

INDIVIDUAL UNDERWRITING CONSIDERATIONS

The key to successfully underwriting a block of small employer health programs is to assure a reasonable mix of healthy and unhealthy lives. If rating and underwriting is too liberal compared to that of the competition, the carrier's program will be easily exposed to antiselection, attracting a disproportionate share of unhealthy insureds.

The degree of individual underwriting had become stricter and stricter over the years, as each carrier sought to gain a competitive edge. As one carrier introduced tougher underwriting criteria, other carriers felt pressured to do the same. This cycle led to many employees and small groups being rejected for medical coverage or being offered rates at prohibitively high levels. As the number of uninsured began to increase, state insurance departments and the federal government grew concerned with the problem, resulting in the enactment of laws such as HIPAA restricting underwriting and rating practices. In particular, the ability of a carrier to single out individuals within an employer group by rejecting them or by charging them higher rates was eliminated. Although individual risk evaluation techniques continue to be used, they are now employed in making a decision about the rate level for the group rather than for a particular individual.

ENFORCEMENT OF ELIGIBILITY

The underwriter, through the application and wage and tax statements, checks for the eligibility of each employee and his or her dependents. To be eligible, the employee generally will need to be actively at work for the employer and work a minimum number of hours per week (usually 30 hours, although some states require coverage for employees with as few as 20 hours). If the employer has elected to cover only specific categories (classes of employees), the employee must be in one of the eligible classes.

Eligibility checks tend to be more critical for underwriting baby groups due to the pervasiveness of family businesses and the temptation to present unhealthy relatives for coverage. Eligibility of dependents may also be verified. Dependent eligibility is usually limited to children under age 19 (extended to age 24 if a full time student).

Post-claim underwriting of eligibility may be a more cost-effective approach for an eligibility check than investigating each employee's and dependent's eligibility at renewal. However, such practice can also lead to litigious disputes.

PREEXISTING CONDITION LIMITATIONS

Most small group plans restrict benefits for preexisting conditions when allowed by law. A preexisting condition is usually defined as a condition that was treated during some period of time prior to coverage (a maximum of six months under HIPAA). Benefits are then limited for some period of time after issue (maximum of 12 months, except up to 18 months for late entrants). For HMOs, a waiting period of up to 2 months (3 months for late enrollees) can be substituted for the preexisting condition limitation period. Preexisting condition limitations provide protection for a short period of time for some self-limiting types of conditions, and allow additional flexibility at the time of underwriting to cover groups that might otherwise be deemed too risky. They do not effectively limit the insurer's risk for other more serious conditions. Some believe that preexisting condition limitation provisions discourage people from waiting until an illness strikes to seek out insurance.

One of the reforms enacted by HIPAA was the requirement of portability of medical insurance coverage. This action was taken in response to a perceived growing problem where employees are reluctant to change employers for fear of loss of health insurance, at least during the new preexisting condition period that would have accompanied enrollment in a new employer's plan. The imposition of portability introduced new underwriting considerations for carriers. Where previously a carrier might have accepted a group knowing that the preexisting condition limitation period would provide adequate short-term protection to make the case profitable, with portability such a group would need to be reassessed since the carrier would essentially be buying claims at the outset of issuance. Such a group might now need to be issued with a substandard rate-up.

Accordingly, the underwriter needs to evaluate the applicability of the preexisting condition limitation provision for each group underwritten, including the amount of creditable coverage applicable to each employee and dependent.

TREATMENT OF NEW ENTRANTS / LATE ENTRANTS

The enactment of portability laws effectively limits preexisting condition limitation provisions to be applicable only to new and late entrants. The laws typically vary in their treatment between new and late entrants. Generally, the period is limited to 12 months for new entrants, but 18 months for late entrants. Therefore, it is important to distinguish between new and late entrants to avoid the extra antiselection risk introduced by late entrants.

INDIVIDUAL MEDICAL ASSESSMENT

Both the employees of a small group and their dependents are usually individually medically underwritten, particularly for the smallest sized groups. This continues to be true even though an individual employee cannot be singled out for rejection or substandard premium rate-ups. This remains the central focus of the small group underwriting process.

In the absence of laws mandating otherwise, underwriting standards are strictest for the smallest groups. Some medical conditions that may not be acceptable in a two-life group, because of the high expected claim cost, could be acceptable when compared against the premiums generated by a 20 life group. In the extreme, a one-life employee group must be underwritten comparably to an individual program, since it is, in fact, an individual applying for insurance. Even in a 25 life group, a single expensive on-going claim can assure that the group will be unprofitable at any reasonable and allowable premium level.Underwriting criteria need to be applied in an objective and non-discriminatory manner, regardless of group size. These criteria need to be designed in a manner that will assure objectivity and yet recognize the risk implications inherent in groups of different sizes.

Different carriers use various underwriting approaches. Some applications use a short-form questionnaire that asks a few broad questions; others ask a long list of detailed questions. As mentioned earlier, web-based, electronic, and telephonic capabilities allow carriers to shift much of the application and enrollment processes away from the agent (and their potential coaching in how to complete the application). These approaches allow for faster processing, since the systems automatically generate drill-down questions specific to a disclosed condition, saving follow-up time by an underwriter to get this information. Paper applications cannot solicit this level of detail on a condition. These processes also allow for direct contact between the underwriter and the applicant. Telephonic approaches are more practical for very small groups. Web-based health statements make more sense for larger small groups, since telephoning every employee can be cost-prohibitive. Telephone verification though can be effective for groups of all sizes.

The information obtained from the applicants is often supplemented by information from other sources which include the following:

- Medical records
- Attending Physician Statements (APS),
- Medical Information Bureau (MIB),
- Follow-up telephone verification,

- Follow-up clarifications,
- Physical examinations, particularly urine and blood testing,
- Prescription drug usage or other predictive analysis, and,
- Web-based prescription drug usage reporting services.

The use of various underwriting information and procedures needs to be considered in terms of its costs, compared to the expected claim reductions and ultimate impact to aggregate profits (in dollars).

Most states require that small group plans set manual rates without regard to the anticipated health status or claim experience of the groups expected to enroll in the plans. Reflection of health status and claim experience could be an adjustment to the manual rates, recognizing that many states have placed limits on these "morbidity" adjustments. Therefore, a carrier needs to determine for itself an acceptable balance between the level of underwriting it needs to be competitive without exposing itself to a disproportionate share of high risk business.

The key to individual underwriting is the ability to gather the information gathered on each individual and to convert it to a numerical measure for assessing and establishing the employer group's premium rate. This is most often done through use of a debit point underwriting manual, which provides guidance to the underwriter on the debit points to assign for a particular condition. The debit points for all employees and dependents are combined and then translated into an underwriting adjustment for the entire group. While this was once a very manual process for medical underwriters, several consulting firms now offer electronic and web-based underwriting debit tools. These tools assist the underwriter in evaluating each applicant by providing background information on each condition, including points to consider related to the development of the condition. They also provide debit points, based upon such criteria as elapsed time since the onset or treatment of the condition and the severity of the condition. These tools typically also collect statistics on the groups and conditions being underwritten that can be useful in evaluating the underwriting process.

The use of predictive models based upon analysis of diagnostic information and prescription drug usage data are beginning to emerge in today's market as sophisticated approaches to help more accurately determine initial and renewal rates needed for a group. Vendors offer small group carriers web-based, real time access to large outpatient prescription drug usage databases to verify drug usage disclosed by employees on their applications, along with additional information that may not be included on the application.

Some states require modified community rating which prohibits a carrier from rating for health status and for prior claim experience. Federally qualified HMOs also must rate on a community rating basis. This requirement does not necessarily eliminate the need for individual underwriting. It can still be important for determining the level at which to set the community rate. Relying strictly on emerging claim experience could take too long before credible results can be attained.

POST-ISSUE UNDERWRITING

In some instances, most conveniently during the claim adjudication process, carriers discover that the information provided by the insured at the time of underwriting materially misrepresented the facts. In the case of fraud or material misrepresentation, coverage may be rescinded; that is, all premiums are returned and both the insurer and the group are returned to the same position as if coverage had never been issued. Rescission rights in some states are affected by case law or by statute.

While carriers are sometimes criticized for post-issue underwriting during the claim adjudication process, it is a sensible, cost effective process in the interest of not only the carrier, but also of the other insureds, as it can contribute to lower premiums.

UNDERWRITING OPTIONAL BENEFITS

Carriers also establish special underwriting rules and procedures regarding the issuance of optional benefits. This is necessary to limit the additional antiselection that can take place when benefits are offered on an optional basis.

A common example is optional maternity coverage or prescription drug coverage offered in the baby group market. (Maternity coverage is mandatory, due to federal law, for groups of 15 or more employees.) Carriers generally require all employees of the group to be covered by the optional benefit.

Optional benefits are usually available only at issue to avoid self-selection for when the benefit is needed. Increases in deductibles and other cost-shares are usually allowed at any time, but decreases are not.

Rates for optional benefits can vary by group size where allowed by law. This can help minimize antiselection by rating based on actual claims expected by group size.

RATING APPROACHES

Medical coverage for a small group, particularly a baby group, is usually priced by calculating the rates applicable to each employee and then summing over all employees. Each employee, and often each dependent, has a specific rate that applies. For larger small groups, carriers will often use a composite rating methodology, which takes into account average group characteristics rather than specific characteristics.

The small group laws have forced some carriers, especially those using composite methods, to revise their rating methodology. This is because of their exposure to greater volatility in terms of small groups' case characteristics, together with the requirement that rating factors must be applied consistently to all groups within a class of small group business. This prohibits one rating methodology being used for baby groups and another for larger small groups. However, most states have allowed the continued use of composite rating for larger sized small groups while at the same time using detailed (list bill) rating for baby groups.

This section discusses initial and renewal rating practices for small groups. Such practices are an integral part of the underwriting process of an insurer.

RATING PARAMETERS

Rating parameters can typically be viewed in two parts: those which comprise the manual rate (allowable benefit and case characteristics), and adjustments for health status, claim experience, duration, and other characteristics. The parameters which comprise the manual rate typically include the following:

- *Age.* Carriers usually rate using quinquennial attained age rating bands, although some employ rates for each individual attained age, and others use decennial bands. The majority of states require that the age rating factors be actuarially sound, although many states limit the spread between the highest and lowest rates. These limits have typically ranged from 2:1 to 3:1, where the actual ratio of a male age 64 to a male age 24 is in the range of 4:1 to 7:1, depending upon benefit plan and the degree of underwriting. This forced compression results in younger insureds subsidizing older insureds' premium rates.

  Such subsidization introduces additional demographic risk to small group carriers, which is best underwritten. If a greater proportion of older insureds is assumed than realized, the rates may prove to be non-competitive, particularly at the younger ages, and vice-versa.

Affordability issues at the younger ages are heightened by forced subsidization, resulting in relatively fewer such insureds. This tends to increase the average age of small groups being covered. This is particularly true since the employee contribution portion is typically larger than that for large group business.

- *Gender.* The use of gender as a rating factor varies among carriers. Those that write baby groups usually set rates by the gender mix of the group. Others that write larger small groups will often use a unisex two, three, or four tier (employee only, employee and spouse, employee and child, and family) rating structure where the actuary assumes an expected aggregate block gender mix by age group.

  While most states still allow gender-distinct rating, a fair number have either limited the rate differentials allowed between gender rates or require unisex rating.

  Unisex rating also creates a demographic risk that needs to be recognized in the pricing, as males at most ages subsidize higher cost females. Actual age/gender distributions need to be periodically compared to the mix assumed in pricing to assure adequate unisex rates.

- *Geographic Area.* Medical costs vary considerably by geographic area. For this reason, carriers usually apply geographic area factors to their rates. These factors vary by carrier in terms of relative magnitude to nationwide or manual rates. The area factors are usually determined by 3-digit ZIP code or by county within each state. The factors may be intended to compensate for all or some of the following:

  o Expected claim cost variation by area,

  o PPO provider discounts, which can vary significantly by area,

  o Area variation in the impact of managed care programs,

  o Surcharges to price for state mandated benefits, marketing, or administrative expense differences by area,

  o Competitive posturing by area, or

  o Variances in loss ratio minimums by state.

  Because most states require that rating factors be applied consistently, it is necessary to be able to identify the area factor components, particularly the PPO discounts, the managed care impact, and expense components that could vary by plan.

- *Group Size.* Carriers have varied rates by group size to reflect both the ability to spread risk and the lower per insured costs as size increases. However, many states have limited this rating factor through rating laws, allowing expense adjustments of only 20% (NAIC model regulation), and limiting claims difference recognition as part of the allowable variance from the index rate. Other states, particularly those requiring modified community rating, do not allow variation by group size. Some states allow group size variation only for justifiable administrative expenses, but not for expected morbidity differences. Furthermore, as stated earlier, underwriting criteria and procedures are to be applied consistently without regard to group size.

- *Industry.* Carriers sometimes vary rates by industry, recognizing that some industries tend to experience higher claim levels due to greater risk of accident or due to riskier lifestyles of typical industry employees. State reform laws have significantly limited a carrier's ability to rate by industry today. Those that allow industry as an allowable case characteristic generally limit the range from lowest to highest to 15%.

  Some actuaries contend that industry rating is not necessary if medical risk assessments are being performed on each group member. While this may in part be true, use of industry rating also reflects the likelihood of risks related to avocations, accidents, and health problems related to the work environment that have not yet become evident.

  Since the enactment of HIPAA and its guaranteed issue requirements, there appears to have been an increase in the use of industry rating factors in order to obtain additional rate variation for industries previously on a carrier's ineligible list.

- *Managed Care and Negotiated Discounts.* Most of the small group rating laws are silent regarding treatment of managed care effects and provider discounts as allowable benefit and case characteristics. Carriers have generally treated these rating factors as benefit factors.

  As with other rating factors, the adequacy and competitiveness of the plan's rates are dependent upon accurate assumptions as to the impact of managed care, the provider discounts, and the relative use of network providers and out-of-network care. Using more detailed managed care and provider discount assumptions by category of care, type of provider, geographic area, and provider network can result in the best match of risk and rate. This relates to the local pricing referred to earlier in this chapter.

- *Plan of Benefits.* Pricing for the specific plan of benefits is, of course, a critical component of rating. In the past, there was relatively little regulation in the small group market on how benefits were priced. Reliance on market forces generally produced reasonable rates relative to the benefits provided.

  With the advent of small group reform, many, if not most states, introduced a brief clause in their law that states "Rating factors shall produce premiums for identical groups which differ only by the amounts attributable to plan design and do not reflect differences due to the nature of the groups assumed to select particular health benefit plans."

  This was intended to have significant impact on the competitive posturing among carriers. Instead of competing by underwriting selection and risk aversion, the focus would turn to competition based on service and efficiency. No longer can plans be priced based upon differing experience for plans with a given combination of benefit parameters such as deductible, coinsurance, and out-of-pocket limit. Claim studies show that higher insured cost-sharing plans tend to generate claim costs lower than otherwise expected due to the combination of behavioral incentives and their greater attraction to healthier people. Conversely, richer benefit plans are more attractive to less healthy people, and tend to induce higher utilization. Despite the fact that any insured, healthy or unhealthy, can opt for the higher cost-share plan, states require that they be priced without bias to the health status of the insured anticipated to enroll. This was done with the intent of broadening the risk pool subsidy of the less healthy by the healthier.

- *Family Composition.* Carriers have traditionally varied family composition rating structures by plan, distribution source, and/or group size. The following family composition tiers are typically used:
  - Two Tier: 1) Employee Only or 2) Employee and Family. Family includes a covered spouse and/or covered children.
  - Three Tier: 1) Employee Only or 2) Employee and either a spouse or child, or 3) Employee and Family. Family includes more than one other family member.
  - Four Tier: 1) Employee Only or 2) Employee and Spouse or 3) Employee and Children or 4) Employee and Family. Family includes a spouse and children.

  Some carriers, particularly baby group carriers, use variations of these, charging for each child up to 2 or 3. In order to avoid being selected against by large families, several have structures which freeze the rate after 2 or 3 children, but then charge for each additional child after the fifth or sixth.

The rates for each tier used can be applied on an exact basis (the sum of the individual rates applicable to each covered member), or through use of average family composition loading factors, applied to a composite PMPM rate. These loading factors generally are determined using the exact age/gender distribution for the group or an expected age/ gender distribution by family composition tier. A pricing risk is introduced when expected distribution factors are applied.

- *Participation Levels.* While not widely used, some carriers have considered varying rates by participation level within group size. Some state laws and regulations would make the approach infeasible, but, where allowed, the approach could be used to help mitigate the risk of accepting groups with lower than ideal participation levels.

- *Tobacco Use.* The ability to use an insured's tobacco use status as an allowable case characteristic varies from state to state. Some states explicitly disallow or allow its use. Many state insurance departments consider rating based upon tobacco use as health status rating, since morbidity tends to be greater for tobacco users, and therefore not an allowable case characteristic.

- *Other Possible Case Characteristics.* While numerous states limit allowable case characteristics to an explicitly stated list of 4 or 5, other states are more flexible and allow reasonable and objective characteristics to be used. While few, if any, carriers use the following, these might be legitimate characteristics:

  o The presence of dual plans with an employer,

  o Participation level,

  o Employer contribution level,

  o Evidence of prior coverage,

  o Full-time vs. part-time employee content, or

  o Percentage of enrollees on COBRA continuation.

There undoubtedly could also be others. The use of such case characteristics might provide a competitive advantage to a carrier. However, many feel that the lack of research in these areas or the added administrative costs to use them minimize the advantages that might be gained.

RATING STRUCTURES

A result of the tight underwriting and preexisting condition limitations previously used by small group carriers was a very steep durational claim cost (aging) curve. Initial claim costs per insured started out very low, but increased rapidly as the selection and preexisting condition limitations wore off, until leveling off after the third year. There is an opinion among some actuaries that an ultimate level of claim costs does not exist, and that cumulative anti-selection continues to cause experience to deteriorate by duration. A Society of Actuaries study conducted in 1991 indicated that experience tends to become at least somewhat level after several years after issue.

With HIPAA's guaranteed issue and portability requirement, the durational curve has become flatter, but still exhibits a significant difference in the first duration (for example, 25% below third duration costs). This is due in part to the impact of the preexisting condition limitations that can still be applied to some insureds, to the durational impact of applying a calendar year deductible in the year of issue (especially if there is no carryover provision), and to the initial underwriting and rating structures that are in place

Most states now limit durational and tiered rating to a specified maximum range (67% in most states, which is the ratio of 125% to 75% of the indexed rates), and some states disallow durational rating altogether, while still permitting limited tiered rating. These rating ranges do not include the impact of allowable case characteristics such as age, gender, and geographic area. Therefore, actual rating ranges from the youngest age to the oldest and from rural areas to metropolitan areas can easily exceed 67%. Some states have been compressing the allowable rate ranges, and other states have moved to modified (or adjusted) community rates.

Modified community rates typically allow the carrier to vary rates for a plan only by age, geographic area, and family composition. All other risk parameters need to be recognized in the pricing assumptions. New issues will generally subsidize renewals; males will subsidize females; the healthy groups will be pooled with the less healthy.

Many states allow a carrier to establish different rating classes, provided that they meet certain criteria. Those criteria require an expectation that one class will have higher morbidity or administrative expenses than another class, and fall into one of several situations such as being 1) an acquired block of business; 2) a legitimate association; or, 3) sold by different marketing organizations. Index rates between such classes are generally limited to a 20% differential.

Small group rating and underwriting requirements have caused carriers to re-evaluate their approaches to rating and underwriting. Corporate strategies for operating in a highly regulated small group environment are needed. Discussion as to the potential profitability of remaining active in each specific state or area within a state is a process conducted by successful carriers.

THE RATE MANUAL

The majority of states expect carriers to maintain a rate manual for each class of business from which all rates can be determined. The rate manual might be a set of rate sheets for each plan, each sheet having rates which vary by allowable case characteristics (such as age, gender, and family composition), and with rating factors to be applied for other rating characteristics, like geographic area, group size, industry, trend factor, and morbidity factors. Alternatively, it might simply be a single composite PMPM rate, to which tables of rating factors apply including plan benefit relativity factors. It is important to keep allowable case characteristics separate and distinct from other rating factors in order to enable proper testing for compliance with state rating laws. These allowable case characteristics, as well as the limit placed upon other rating factors, can vary by state. Because of this, an organized rate manual that details variations by state is important for both compliance purposes as well as for encouraging that maximum advantage of rating and underwriting allowances is taken. Most states require an annual actuarial certification that the carrier's rates and underwriting procedures are in compliance with state laws and regulations. By organizing the rate manual as stated above, it is relatively simple to determine the variations from the manual rate. It also enhances the carrier's ability to perform experience analysis by rating factor enabling better actual-to-expected studies.

One of the rating decisions a carrier must make in developing its rate manual is at what point within the range of allowable rates (usually a 67% range) it should place its standard new business rates. Often the new business rate is the lowest rate available, but some carriers leave room below the standard new business rate for preferred new business and renewal rates. A carrier must also decide as to how low the new business rate can be set without setting the highest tiered rates too low for the overall block to be profitable.

UNDERWRITING INTENSITY RELATIVE TO RISK TRANSFER

Most small group insurance coverage in today's market is comprised of PPO plans. HMO-sponsored health plans typically include more managed care features than PPO plans. However, these managed care plans usually involve less risk sharing with providers than what was common several years ago. Reimbursement approaches vary in terms of the degree of risk that is shared. Most typical in the market are discounted fees for service through schedules (for example, percentage of RBRVS for physicians or per diems for hospitals), which involve little or no risk transfer. However, HMO and POS plans sometimes have negotiated true risk transfer through capitation arrangements with provider groups.

The carrier should consider the interrelationship between its underwriting intensity and its transfer of risk. If the capitation rate is based upon non-underwritten expected utilization levels, the underwriting intensity can be relaxed to reflect that basis. However, two points need to be considered:

- Generally, not all benefits are capitated and therefore some risk remains with the insurer. It may be in the carrier's interest to maintain a higher level of underwriting to minimize its risks.
- The long term success of a managed care plan is dependent on creating a win-win-win-win situation for the providers, the insurer, the employers, and the insureds. Adequate underwriting is generally needed to assure that the network providers are not selected against by a greater than expected number of unhealthy enrollees.

Conversely, in determining capitation rates, or if PPO access fees are based upon a fee per member or per certificate in force, it is important to recognize that utilization of services will be lower in the first policy year for underwritten plans, and this lower utilization probably should be recognized in the fees paid to the providers and PPOs.

RE-RATING RENEWAL BUSINESS

Carriers employ different methods for determining rates for renewing business. Some apply general rate increases equally to all renewals. A few may bring renewals only up to the new business rate. Others set the rates based on a durational formula (although many states disallow durational rating). Most carriers today use a tiered rating method based upon a review of the experience of each renewing group, or based upon another predictive model.

In setting tiered renewal rates, many carriers simply use each group's claim experience, either as is or with large claims pooled, and categorize them according to their adjusted loss ratio experience to determine each group's renewal rate level. The experience used may or may not have been adjusted for IBNR and pending claims. There have been many variations of this type of renewal rating approach. It is an expedient methodology that provides some differentiation among groups to try to retain healthy groups. However, the approach ignores the fact that there is little statistical credibility in using only a given small group's claim experience. These methods often result in: (1) giving unnecessarily large rate increases to groups that will prove to be healthy in the future, because of a poor past experience year, and (2) awarding inadequate rate increases to past healthy groups that may be destined to have high future claims.

Yet, when such analysis is coupled with consideration for the diagnoses of the insureds or their prescription drug usage, it is felt that the predictive confidence of future experience is greatly improved. In the past, this may have been done by determining if the cause of claim was due to an accident, an acute condition not expected to recur, or an ongoing chronic condition. Disregarding claim experience on covered persons who have left the group and including new underwriting information on new entrants is an advisable approach, although more administratively burdensome. It also demands that the carrier be diligent in collecting such information during the renewal process.

Today, carriers and vendors are developing risk predictive software tools that are based on detailed diagnostic (ICD9 codes) and/or pharmaceutical usage information. The expected future cost of specific conditions can be estimated based upon actuarial studies and factored into the determination of the group's renewal premium (as well as initially issued premium). These risk predictor methods have become an integral part of small group rating systems for a number of carriers, particularly larger insurance companies. The Society of Actuaries conducted a study of these risk adjuster tools in 2002 and is currently in the process of updating the study. Other organizations have also performed studies on their effectiveness. One such study done specifically for the small group marketplace concluded that optimal renewal rating results were attained when risk adjuster analysis was combined with a loss ratio approach. It also found that applying credibility factors by service category to a group's experience is almost as effective as a diagnostic risk adjuster method. The study also noted that the advantages of the use of more sophisticated predictive methods, such as risk adjusters, diminish as state rating ranges become tighter. They also diminish as group size increases. As such, a carrier needs to weigh the expected advantages of the use of a predictive modeling system with the cost of developing, leasing, or purchasing these systems.

Because of the antiselective tendencies in the small group market, the renewal process should include a review of the eligibility, participation, and contribution levels of the group to ensure that they still meet acceptable criteria. While these plans are guaranteed renewable, they do not need to be renewed if they fail to meet acceptable underwriting criteria. These renewal procedures must be applied consistently however, irrespective of claim experience.

Unless the policy contract language restricts the carrier, plans which are out-of-date can be replaced at renewal with similar benefit plans that may have more state-of-the-art managed care features or other cost containment provisions.

In setting renewal rates, the carrier must assure that such rate increases are in compliance with state law. Most states restrict the size of renewal increases to be no more than 15% in addition to the annual increase in the new business rates. Furthermore, the renewal rates cannot exceed the allowable ranges for the class of business (often ∀25% of the index rate). More detailed discussion of rating strategies are discussed in the chapter on small group compliance issues.

Other renewal underwriting considerations include allowance to change benefits after the initial effective date. Generally, benefit downgrades (such as moving to a higher deductible) do not present a problem. However, the carrier should be wary of benefit upgrade requests (for example, moving to a lower deductible, or adding an optional benefit such as maternity coverage or prescription drug coverage). Usually, such upgrades are not allowed for fear of antiselection. Under guaranteed issue requirements, the employer can reapply for the coverage desired, but should be treated as a new issue and not a renewal. In this case, the 15% rate increase limitation would not necessarily be applicable.

RISK POOLING

Many states have established specific risk pooling programs for small group business. They can be categorized into (1) reinsurance programs, and (2) risk-adjustment formula programs.

REINSURANCE PROGRAMS

Many of the states have established a small employer health insurance reinsurance program in order to help distribute the added risks of guaranteed issue. This program is a reinsurance pool into which a carrier can place entire groups or individuals enrolled in a group plan.

Typically, the reinsurance premiums are loaded by a factor of 1.5 for entire groups and a factor of 5.0 for an individual. The base reinsurance premiums are representative of typical small employer group rates adjusted for the reinsurance benefits. The reinsurance benefits generally require a $5,000 reinsurance deductible and a cost-share of 10% of the next $50,000 of benefits incurred up to benefits of statutorily defined plans (often called Basic and Standard Plans). Any shortfalls in the pool are funded through assessments of the participating carriers.

As part of the underwriting process, a small group carrier needs to decide if a group or individual will be placed in the pool. Typically, that decision must be made within 60 days after issue. The decision should be based upon a consideration of whether the expected annual claim payout will exceed the sum of the reinsurance premiums, the $5,000 deductible, and the anticipated 10% coinsurance. This needs to be done for both the entire group and for the unhealthy individuals of the group, to determine which is the more cost effective approach. For groups of two or three employees, placing the entire group may be more cost effective, depending on the age, gender, and family composition mix of the group. Criteria can be developed for the underwriters to recognize viable candidates for the pools, especially with the introduction of risk predictor software systems.

RISK-ADJUSTMENT FORMULA PROGRAMS

A couple of states have developed risk-adjustment formulas to be applied to all small group carriers to redistribute premiums or claims in an attempt to somewhat normalize the risk of guaranteed issue. These formulas tend to break the risk-sharing into two pieces: (1) demographic risk, and (2) catastrophic case risk. A complete discussion of risk adjustment formula programs is included in another chapter of this text.

SUMMARY

This chapter has presented various methods, criteria, and considerations which carriers employ in underwriting and rating small groups. Underwriting is evolving more and more from a risk-selection and risk-aversion process into a risk-assessment process to be incorporated into the rating and servicing of the plans.

26 MANAGING SELECTION IN A MULTIPLE-CHOICE ENVIRONMENT

Clark E. Slipher

MULTIPLE-CHOICE ENVIRONMENT DEFINED

A multiple-choice environment is any situation where individuals have a choice among insurance plans. This chapter will focus on the multiple-choice environment created when an employer allows its employees to choose among two or more medical insurance options.

FAVORABLE VS UNFAVORABLE SELECTION

An informed and rational individual will usually choose the insurance plan that best meets his or her individual needs, so a multiple-choice environment usually leads to selection. The selection can be favorable or unfavorable to the insurer:

- *Favorable selection* (also known as positive selection) occurs when "low-risk" employees tend to choose the insurer or plan option. Low-risk employees are those that have a lower than average expected claim cost due to their age, gender, contract type (e.g., single or family) or other aspect of their risk profile.

- *Unfavorable selection* (also known as antiselection, negative selection, or adverse selection) occurs when "high-risk" members tend to choose the insurer or option.

In a multiple-choice environment, if one or more options experiences favorable selection, then the remaining options experience unfavorable selection.

WHY OFFER CHOICE IF IT COSTS MORE?

The overall combined cost in a multiple-choice environment is typically higher than the cost in a single-choice environment, because:

- individuals use the opportunity to choose as a way to minimize their out-of-pocket costs, at the expense of the insurer or employer (this is the cost of selection);

- there is less economy of scale and less negotiating leverage with healthcare providers due to fragmentation of a group; and

- communications are generally more complex, and administrative expenses are greater.

Despite the additional costs and complexity, multiple-choice provides opportunities for an insurer or employer to offer insurance options that better fit customer or employee needs. The following situations illustrate how insurers and employers take advantage of a multiple-choice environment (even with the additional cost):

- *Introducing a new option.* Insurers and employers are often reluctant to totally replace a proven incumbent plan with an untested new product. Offering a new product as an option to the incumbent plan allows time for testing and transitioning to a new product.

- *Taking advantage of favorable selection.* Some insurers create plan features and pricing to attract the low cost risks. For example, healthy employees (without strong ties to particular providers) may be willing to choose a lower cost, limited provider network. Active and fit employees may be drawn to wellness or sports medicine benefits.

- *Encouraging consumerism.* Offering a variety of health plan options is a natural extension of consumerism. Americans demand choice in every other product they purchase, so why not in health care? Many insurers and employers believe they can provide information and distinguishing plan features that can entice employees to choose their option, even at a higher price.

- *Implementing a defined contribution concept.* Some employers desire to switch their health benefit commitment to employees from providing a defined medical plan benefit to a defined monthly contribution toward the premium. Under the defined contribution concept, the employer lets the employees choose from a variety of health plans. The employers' contribution to the premium is a fixed dollar amount, regardless of the option the employee chooses. The employee must pay the difference between their option's total premium and the employer's fixed contribution. The defined contribution strategy allows employers to avoid making tough decisions between increasing monthly employee contributions or increasing employee cost sharing (deductibles and copays). The employer can let each employee decide by offering a generous plan (with higher employee contributions) or a lower cost plan (with higher employee cost sharing).

• *Choice for the sake of choice.* "Choice" itself has intrinsic value. Offering choice distinguishes an insurer or employer as flexible and leading edge.

WHAT FACTORS INFLUENCE EMPLOYEES' CHOICE?

In a multiple-choice environment, many factors influence an employees' choice of a health plan option, including:

• *Inertia* (employees tend to stay with a prior plan option unless new information becomes available or something significant changes to compel the employee to consider other options).

• *Plan provisions and costs*, such as: covered benefits, employee cost sharing amounts, benefit exclusions, underwriting requirements, eligibility restrictions, waiting periods and pre-existing condition exclusions.

• *Employee and dependent demographics*, such as: age, gender, health status, family size, income, degree of risk aversion and education.

• *Employer actions and attitudes*, such as: employee contributions, attitude toward managed care, communications to employees, enrollment process (and plan defaults) and eligibility for retiree medical coverage (which may be limited to certain options).

• *Information available* about options, such as: employee communications, advertising, selection tools and word-of-mouth. A basic tenant of consumer-driven products is providing additional information. Of course, increasing employee knowledge about their choices and health care treatment is good, but it increases the selection potential.

- *Provider and provider network attributes*, such as: provider availability, access restriction, reputation, fees, quality, and medical management restrictions (e.g., specialist referral requirement).

- *Insurer and administration issues*, such as: claim administration, customer service and reputation.

Employee's choices are governed by a complex combination of the above factors and other factors, which sometimes makes employee choices hard to predict.

MULTIPLE-CHOICE SCENARIOS

The degree of choice that an employer or insurer makes available to employees in a multiple-choice environment can vary significantly. The following situations provide a few scenarios:

- *Choice between medical coverage and no coverage.* An employee's most basic health plan choice is whether to be covered by the employer's plan. Large monthly employee contributions or high cost sharing levels (e.g., deductibles) may deter an employee from taking an employer's plan. Also, employees in dual income families are often eligible for medical coverage from their own employer and from their spouse's employer (as a dependent). Some employers will pay cash (e.g., $100 per month) to employees who waive the employer's coverage to take the coverage from the spouse's employer. An insurer should be aware that the choice between coverage and no coverage creates anti-selection because an employee who waives the employer coverage often has lower average health costs than the employee who takes the employer's coverage.

- *Choice based on member cost sharing.* Options may differ by levels of deductible, coinsurance, copay, out-of-pocket limit and other member cost sharing features. Traditionally, employees could choose between two or three cost sharing levels for their entire family. However, the increased emphasis on consumerism and improved technology have prompted some plan sponsors to allow employees to customize their cost sharing levels using dozens of options. The plan sponsors also often provide computer selection models to assist the employee in optimizing their plan choice. More option and better selection tools help the employee, but increases the insurer's anti-selection risk.

- *Choice based on provider networks or medical management.* Choice between an open network product (e.g., PPO) and a restricted network product (e.g., an HMO) has existed for some time. Now, emerging provider fee, efficiency and quality evaluation tools are causing insurers and employers to develop new provider network products. For example, new network products may use narrow provider networks, special provider fee schedules, additional medical management or tiered benefit levels to distinguish themselves. The level of provider choice, the degree of medical management, and the presence of specific providers (a Children's hospital, for example) drive employee selection decisions.

- *Choice among insurers.* Two or more insurers may offer health plan options to the same employee of one insurer. For example, a large employer may offer employees a choice among a self-insured PPO option and two fully-insured HMOs. The insurers compete for employees at multiple levels, such as: price, cost sharing feature, provider network, covered services, customer service, insurer name recognition, and other features. Splitting the risk pool of employees among more than one insurer creates a dangerous anti-selection situation because the losses caused by anti-selection against one option cannot be easily offset by gains of favorable selection for another insurer.

- *Optional riders added to core coverage.* Some insurers or employers subsidize a core medical plan and allow employees to buy additional coverage or riders (e.g., vision) at the employee's expense. The anti-selection opportunity varies by the predictability of the service covered by the rider. For example, a vision care rider may be highly selected against by employees who know they need glasses. However, a rider that provides additional levels of long-term disability coverage may be less subject to anti-selection.

- *Choice by each family member.* Traditionally, most employers require each employee to choose one option for themselves and their covered dependents. Some insurers and employers are now allowing employees to choose a different option for each covered family member. This additional flexibility is appreciated by employees, but increases the selection opportunities.

• *Choice between consumer-directed plans and traditional plans.* New consumer-driven plans combine a high deductible health plan (HDHP) with a savings account (e.g., healthcare reimbursement arrangement or qualified health savings account or HSA) that can be used to pay for medical expenses below the high deductible. Unused account balances can roll over to the next year. Employers often allow employees to choose between the new account based plan and the employer's traditional medical plan, which may represent a dramatic difference in plan design (thus an opportunity for anti-selection). Some critics of consumer-driven plans speculate that their savings are caused by favorable selection rather than changes in behavior. Initial results regarding the impact of selection have been mixed.

In practice, an employer or insurer often uses a combination of the above scenarios (or creates new types of choice) to create unique multiple-choice environments.

MEASURING SELECTION AND HEALTH STATUS

An underwriter pricing options in a multiple-choice environment must measure the current health status and/or estimate the future health status of employees expected to choose each option.

Traditionally, insurers estimated the impact of selection based on employees' age and gender. The age and gender mix of each option or a change in the mix over time is one indicator of the selection bias of an option. Even small shifts in members from one plan to another can greatly influence the financial results of each of the programs because the expected claims levels for a 64-year-old male employee may be up to seven times that of a 23-year-old male employee. Age and gender analysis is still prevalent because the information on each employee is usually readily available.

More recently, insurers are supplementing the traditional age and gender analysis with new risk and health status evaluation models, such as:

- **Health risk assessments**, which use questionnaires and employee self-reporting to identify health risk attributes of an employee. The assessment assigns a health risk score to each employee based on risk attributes, such as smoking status, body mass index, exercise habits, seatbelt usage, and alcohol usage.

- **Risk adjusters**, which use a member's medical claim information (such as diagnoses, medical services, prescription history) to make statistical predictions of future claim costs. Many commercially-available and proprietary risk adjusters are emerging and being implemented for premium rate development, experience analysis and disease management applications.

Similar to the factors associated with an age and gender mix of members who are in a particular plan option, the average health risk assessment score or risk adjuster score of those members are also a measure of selection.

SELECTION IMPACT OF EMPLOYEE CONTRIBUTIONS

The amount of monthly employee contributions for each option in a multiple-choice environment has a significant impact on an employee's choice of plan. An employee is willing to pay a higher employee contribution if he or she expects that the option will provide better benefits, lower cost sharing (deductible, copays), access to key providers or some other value.

Many employers set employee contributions using a "defined contribution" model in which the employer contributes a fixed dollar amount on behalf of each employee to any of the health plan options. The employee contribution is then calculated as the difference between the total premium rate for the option the employee selects and the employer's fixed contribution.

This defined-contribution model creates opportunity for employee selection that the insurer should contemplate when setting the premium rates. The following example illustrates the selection potential:

- An employer offers three health plans (A, B and C) to employees. Plan A benefits are lean (20% less than Plan B); Plan B benefits are moderate; and Plan C benefits are rich (20% more than Plan B).

- The insurer sets the Year 1 premium rates for each plan based only on the expected benefit differences among the plans and does not account for selection.

- The employer contributes a defined contribution amount equal to 100% of Plan B premium in Year 1. Employees pay an employee contribution (or receive a cash credit) equal to the difference between the premium rate for the plan they choose and the employer's fixed contribution.

- The employees have the following relative health status (or morbidity).

	Number of Employees	Relative Health Status (Morbidity)
Low Risk	50	50%
Average Risk	30	100%
High Risk	20	225%
Composite	100	100%

If we assume the high risk employees always choose the richest plan (C), while the low risk employees always choose the leanest plan (A), then the Year 1 results are:

Year 1				
			Monthly Contributions	
Plan	Monthly Insurer Premium Rates	Number of Employees	Employer (Does not Vary by Plan)	Employee (Premium – Employer)
A	$200	50	$250	$ (50)
B	250	30	250	0
C	300	20	250	50
Total Employer Contribution ($)			$25,000	$(1,500)
Total Employer Contribution (%)			100%	0%

Note: The negative employee contributions are actually funded by the employer in this example.

The average cost adjusted morbidity in the above example is 1.106, and is determined as follows:

Year 1 Costs – Adjusted for Health Status			
Plan	Monthly Insurer Total Premiums	Actual Insurer Cost	Relative Health Status
A	$10,000	$5,000	50%
B	$ 7,500	$7,500	100%
C	$ 6,000	$13,500	225%
	$23,500	$26,000	110.6%

Note: The actual cost is determined as follows:

$$\text{Plan A: } \$6,250 = 0.50 \times \$200 \times 50$$
$$\text{Plan B: } \$7,500 = 1.00 \times \$250 \times 30$$
$$\text{Plan C: } \$13,500 = 2.25 \times \$300 \times 20$$

This example suggests the anti-selection risk (or the "average cost adjusted morbidity") is +10.6%($26.000/$23,500). because actual costs are 10.6% greater than the costs the insurer expected in the original premium rate development. The employer also paid an additional $1,500 per month in the form of the net credits given those employees choosing Plan A ($2,500 credit paid for Plan A offset by $1,000 in Plan C contributions).

In Year 2, we assume premium rates increase 25% (based on prior year experience results and reflecting expected annual trend increase), and the employer reduces its contribution to 80% of the base plan cost. As a result, the younger and healthier employees choose one of the lower cost plans to avoid an increase in their respective contribution rates. The less healthy employees stay in the higher cost plans.

Year 2 Adjusted for Health Status				
			Monthly Contribution	
Plan	Monthly Insurer Premium Rates	Number of Employees	Employer (Does not Vary by Plan)	Employee (Premium – Employer)
A	$250.00	60	$ 250	$ 0
B	312.50	30	250	62.50
C	375.00	10	250	125.00
	Total Employer Contribution ($)		$25,000	$3,125.00
	Total Employer Contribution (%)		89%	11%
	Contribution Dollars Compared to Year 1		+0%	$(4,625)

Using the same methodology and assumptions discussed above, the cost adjusted morbidity in Year 2 is 1.083.

Year 2 Costs – Adjusted for Health Status			
Plan	Monthly Insurer Total Premiums	Actual Insurer Cost	Relative Health Status
A	$15,000	$ 8,750	0.583
B	$ 9,375	$13,281	1.417
C	$ 3,750	$ 8,438	2.250
	$28,125	$ 30,469	1.083

Note: The actual cost is determined as follows:

Plan A: $8,750 = (0.50 × $250.00 × 50) + (1.00 × $250.00 × 10)
Plan B: $13,281 = (1.00 × $312.50 × 20) + (2.25 × $312.50 × 10)
Plan C: $8,438 = 2.25 × $375.00 × 10

Even with a large increase in premiums (based on prior year observed experience), actual costs have once again been greater than expected costs. As a result, the employer can expect another large increase in premium rates in the next contract period.

The example illustrates how anti-selection spiral can be encouraged, or even caused, by employer contribution rules and benefit plan design and content. To compensate for the anti-selection cost, an insurer needs to anticipate the mix of subscribers choosing the respective plan options and include a selection loading in the premium rate calculations. The selection loading can be spread as an even percentage load across all plans. However, some insurers may vary the percentage by plan, and often are greater for the higher cost plans and lower for the least costly plans. This tends to "encourage" subscribers to choose the lower cost plans and imposes a penalty on those subscribers choosing the higher cost plans.

UNDERWRITING MULTIPLE-CHOICE SITUATIONS

An underwriter can use several techniques to assist in managing selection and its financial impact in a multiple-choice environment:

- *Additional premium margin.* The pricing example in the employee contribution discussion of this chapter shows a method of determining a selection loading to be added to premium to pay for the additional cost of selection. An insurer may also want to add an additional margin (1% to 3%) to the premium to account for the potential that the underwriting may not be able to perfectly predict the selection pattern and costs when determining prospective premium rates.

- *Employee Contributions or Plan Design Limits.* Reasonably limiting some of the cost and benefit differential among plans can help manage selection:

- Limit the spread in monthly employee contributions from the lowest cost option to the highest cost option (e.g., maximum monthly spread of $40 for single coverage and $100 for family coverage). Options with very high employee contributions, relative to other options, tend to draw only a few, very unfavorable risks.

- Limit the spread in benefits so that difference in relative value of the richest benefit option is not more than 20% to 30% of the lowest option.

- Mixing favorable and unfavorable cost sharing or benefit provisions among options to avoid one option being labeled as the "best plan" if you expect high health costs.

- Avoiding options with obvious selection potential (e.g., only one option covers infertility benefits and others do not).

- *Participation requirements: One insurer offering multiple-choices.* One insurer can offset anti-selection from one option from favorable selection in another option in a multiple-choice environment. Therefore, the standard minimum participation requirement that 75% of a large group's eligible employees enroll in one of the employer's options is often sufficient. The minimum participation may increase as group size decreases for groups less than 100 employees (down to 100% participation for the smallest groups). Employees who waive the employer's coverage and opt for coverage in a spouse's plan are often excluded from the count of eligible employees in this calculation.

- *Participation requirements: Multiple insurers offering multiple-choices.* When an employer's risk pool is split among multiple insurers, one insurer may attract an unexpected, unfavorable risk mix and not be able to offset the losses from a favorable risk mix from another option (which is insured by someone else). In these situations, additional participation rules may be imposed:

- An insurer requires that all insurers in the multiple-choice environment can have consistent underwriting, eligibility or pre-existing condition requirements. This rule assures that another insurer does not "dump" unfavorable risks to other insurers.

- An insurer imposes an additional minimum requirement (e.g., must obtain 50% of total employees) and reserves the right to withdraw the premium quote (or requite) if the additional participation is not obtained.

- All insurers agree to a redistribution of income among the insurers based on the health status (measured by risk adjusters, or age/gender analysis) of the employees who actually select each insurer option. Multi-employer purchasing pools (and Medicare Advantage) sometimes use similar risk adjustment programs

- An insurer who expects a favorable risk mix may be willing to waive some participation rules to take advantage of a situation.

PRICING STRATEGIES

A multiple-choice environment places additional pressure on the underwriting staff to anticipate selection among options and the resulting impact on insurer costs. Careful study of existing accounts may provide insights into the selection dynamics. Once the selection can be predicted, actions can be initiated to influence future selection patterns.

The basic pricing strategy employed in multiple-choice situations is to determine the aggregate premium necessary to cover the aggregate cost of claims for all plan options. While each plan option should be priced on a somewhat independent basis, it is the aggregate result that should be the most important consideration.

Development of premium rates for each of the plan options includes the following six steps: (*The tables included in this example are based on research for the situations described and may or may not be applicable to a particular environment. They should be considered as illustrative in nature and only used as a guide to the actuary developing selection tables for a specific purpose.*)

Step 1. *Determine the actuarial value of each benefit option*, taking into consideration:

(a) the actuarial value of the benefits
(b) provider reimbursement arrangements
(c) medical management differences, and
(d) administrative expense and margin requirements.

The actuarial value of each benefit option should be determined prior to considering any impact on the aggregate claims due to selection. These values reflect the required premium rates as if every employee in the group participated in the option.

Step 2. *Estimate the enrollment mix by plan option.*

Employee contribution rates can serve as a basis for estimating the enrollment mix. Increasing contribution rates for specific options will tempt employees to choose other lower cost plan options. Each employee will decide if the option differences (benefits, network, managed care restrictions, and so forth) offset the employee contribution differences.

The following table presents a simple model for estimating enrollment mix in a multiple-choice environment, which consists of only two options: a new generation plan (e.g., HMO or consumer-directed health plan, CDHP) and a traditional plan (e.g., indemnity, PPO or point-of-service):

Contribution Differential (Per Employee per Month)*	Enrollment Mix	
	Traditional Option	New Generation Option
Less than $50	85%	15%
$50 - $75	80	20
$76 - $100	70	30
$101 - $125	55	45
$126 - $150	45	55
More than $150	30	70

* Difference between the traditional and new generation options, assuming traditional option is more expensive.

Step 3. *Estimate the relative health status factor for each option based on the expected enrollment mix from Step 2.*

The relative health status factor estimates the average expected costs for employees in the traditional or new generation option relative to the overall cost of the group (100% is the overall relative costs for a group) based on their age/gender and other health status or morbidity differences.

The relative cost factor can be estimated based on the expected enrollment mix between the traditional and new generation options. Generally, younger and other low risk factor employees are the first to venture to new generation plans. As the new generation plans become more familiar and their membership increases, the selection factor decreases. Eventually, the new generation membership will gravitate toward the average characteristics of the total group membership. A sample table of relative cost factors follows:

Traditional Option Enrollment	Traditional Option Relative Health Status Factor	New Generation Relative Health Status Factor	Overall Health Status Factor
Less than 20%	151%	94%	100%
20% - 39%	139%	83%	100%
40% - 49%	132%	74%	100%
50% - 59%	127%	67%	100%
60% - 79%	119%	56%	100%
More than 79%	108%	24%	100%

For example, if the traditional plan expected enrollment is 70%, the employees selecting the traditional option are expected to have costs of 119% of the overall group average and the other 30% of employees that select the new generation option are expected to have costs that are 56% of the overall group average. The overall health status is 100% (by definition, but for checking purposes: $(70\% \times 119\%) + (30\% \times 56\%) = 100\%$)

Step 4. *Calculate the preliminary selection adjusted rates for each option.*

The selection adjusted rates equal the Step 1 actuarial rates multiplied by the Step 3 relative health status factors for each option. The resulting selection adjusted rates would be self-sustaining for each option if the expected mix of employees by option is exactly correct and does not change. However, static participation is unlikely if the employer uses the defined contribution model for setting employee contributions (described earlier in this chapter). The difference in employee contributions between the traditional and new generation plans is likely to expand significantly using the Step 4 rates. This would cause further employee selection and a selection spiral.

Step 5. *Calculate average selection loading.*

Calculate the average selection loading as the ratio of the average of the Step 4 selection adjusted rates and the average of Step 1 actuarial rates.

Step 6. *Calculate blended selection adjusted rates.*

Calculate the blended selection adjusted rates by multiplying the Step 1 actuarial rates by this average selection loading from Step 5. This step assumes that a single insurer insures both options. These Step 6 blended rates are appropriate for a single insurer environment because they are self-sustaining for the entire group, and they do not create additional selection. However, in a multi-insurer environment, the Step 4 preliminary selection adjusted rates may be more appropriate because each option may be required to be self-sustaining since one insurer will not insure all employees.

The following table shows how results are calculated using this model on a per member per month basis (PMPM).

Option	(1) Actuarial Rates Before Selection	(2) Expected Enroll-ment	(3) Relative Health Status Factor	(4) = (1) x (3) Preliminary Selection Adjusted Rates	(5) = (4) Avg. / (1) Avg. Average Selection Loading	(6) = (1) x (5) Blended Selection Adjusted Rates
Traditional	$300.00	70%	119%	$357.00	102.9%	$308.74
New Generation	$240.00	30%	56%	$134.40	102.9%	$247.00
Average	$282.00	100%	100%	$290.22	102.9%	$290.22

Step 1: The New Generation option is estimated to have a cost that is 80% of the Traditional option before any selection bias is considered

Step 2: Estimated by underwriter, perhaps based on employee contribution differences

Step 3: Estimated by underwriter, perhaps based on expected enrollment %

Step 5: $290.22 / $282.00 = 1.029

MONITORING RESULTS

Monitoring of experience for both specific employers and product lines is essential to effective product management in a multiple-choice environment. Effective management requires knowledge of selection preferences and the likely cost impact of these preferences. Key factors and statistics that an insurer should monitor are:

- Claim to premium loss ratios for various multiple option situations (e.g., total replacement, consumer driven vs. traditional option. Loss ratios should be monitored for all options combined and on an option-by-option basis.

- Comparison of actual-to-expected selection patterns and health status indicators, segmented by anticipated selection variables (e.g., employee contribution, cost sharing options available, network options).

- Comparison of changes in health status by employer group and by multiple-choice options over time.

- Monitoring of competitor and marketplace pricing and underwriting practices to the extent reliable public information is available. Also comparisons of an insurer's health status versus industry or community benchmarks to help assess whether the insurer is receiving favorable or unfavorable selection relative to other insurers.

- Market research of current and potential insureds about what specific factors, preferences and information influence their choices of health options

Information learned from analysis of this information should be used to modify the insurer's multiple option pricing and underwriting strategy and models.

SUMMARY AND CONCLUSIONS

Today's group health marketplace is significantly more complicated than in the past. The health insurance companies who succeed will be those who understand the dynamics of the multiple-choice environment and act accordingly. Effective actuarial and underwriting analysis and the development of appropriate pricing strategies will be essential. A thorough understanding of the impact of selection on overall plan costs is important to the long-term financial success of any health insurer operating in this environment. Employers will continue to become more knowledgeable in this environment and will be seeking solutions to meet their specific cost and benefit coverage requirements.

27 CLAIM ADMINISTRATION AND MANAGEMENT

Jeffrey L. Smith
Sheila K. Shapiro

OBJECTIVES OF THE CLAIM ADMINISTRATION FUNCTION

The administration of claims is an integral part of the entire risk management process. It is also a central function in providing the product and service purchased by a group on behalf of its members. As such, the primary concern of claim management is to fulfill the intent of the insurance contract or administrative service contract. Claim management does not mean claim avoidance, nor is it merely a check writing facility to compensate members for any and all financial losses. The objective is to provide precisely the payment prescribed by the contract, no more and no less.

It is with the contract that the claim management process begins. A clear, concise and unambiguous contract is critical to an effective and efficient claim administration function. In actuality, however, no contract, despite the most careful drafting, can possibly include specific directions for every possible set of facts and circumstances encountered in the adjudication of claims. Still, the contract is the governing document. No actions in the claim adjudication process should contradict the provisions of the contract, unless by legislative or regulatory mandate. Where the contract lacks specificity on a particular issue, the role of the claim management process is to produce a result consistent with the intent of the contract. This consistency will provide results that are likely to withstand audit scrutiny. Thus, a key element of the claim management process is the interpretation and application of a contract under varying circumstances and facts. In this context, the additional requirements of equity and consistency become important objectives of the claim adjudication process.

Knowledge of and adherence to regulatory requirements at the federal and state level is another key area of claim management. Claim audits examine

549

timeliness, accuracy, and contract interpretation, and withstanding this scrutiny has become a critical component of the claim function. Additionally, performance guarantees for commercial customers, interest payments for providers (for claims that are not paid timely), and regulatory fines for noncompliance have become more commonplace. This oversight is intended to ensure that the insured or beneficiary receives the appropriate contracted benefit. Additionally, these audits are intended to ensure that the provider of service also receives the appropriate compensation in a timely fashion.

Effective management requires claim payment data that satisfies diverse internal needs of the insurance company. Many of these needs are statistical, and are used both to evaluate and monitor risk. In tandem with clinical staff, they also measure and help determine effective use of premium dollars. The data acquisition process is as important to the organization as the accuracy of the claim payment itself.

INFORMATION REQUIREMENTS

Certain basic information is necessary for the proper handling of a claim. Although the specifics will vary with the type of insurance coverage, the information needed generally falls into the following categories:

- Identification of the policyholder and claimant. This will include identifying the contracting group entity, the individual insured and, in the case of dependant coverage, the relationship of the claimant to the insured. This will be used to determine eligibility of the claimant under the contract.
- Proof of loss. That is, proof of death, disability, medical expense, and so on, consistent with the contract definition of an insured loss.
- Date(s) of loss. As the insurance contract is in force for only a specified period of time, the date of the incident or loss is necessary to determine whether the contract was in force on that date.
- Information to determine the amount of the contractual liability for the loss, if any. This information will vary greatly depending on the type of coverage.
- The individual or entity to which payment should be made. This would include identification of the beneficiary, for example, or an indication of assignment of medical benefits to a health care provider.
- Additional information regarding other coverage for coordination of benefits, required to ensure that the claim being paid is being processed at the correct rates.

As noted earlier, the primary use of information in the claim adjudication process is to assure that proper payment is made to the appropriate party; however, there are numerous purposes for the data compiled in the claim adjudication process. These include such functions as financial and management reporting, pricing, establishing claim reserve liabilities, health care provider monitoring, and fraud and abuse control. Additionally, external reporting of claim data may be utilized by self insured clients and governmental agencies.

LIFE AND ACCIDENTAL DEATH AND DISMEMBERMENT

In relative terms, the claim process for life and AD&D is a simple and objective determination of pertinent facts: verification of death, the eligibility of the deceased, the date of death, and so on. Policy provisions may also require information regarding the circumstances of the death. That is, was the death accidental, from natural causes, or self-inflicted? Many policies have specific clauses specifying incontestable periods and exclusion of coverage for suicide.

The existence of disability provisions within a group life contract can add significantly to the complexity of the claim management process. This often involves obtaining evidence of disability and medical opinions as to the extent and probable duration of disability. Periodic follow-ups may be required to determine whether an insured remains totally disabled.

The process of assuring that payment is made to the appropriate party should be a straightforward procedure where a named beneficiary is present. The process can become quite complex, however, when no beneficiary has been named or when the named beneficiary is no longer living.

Policy provisions such as living benefits riders add an additional consideration to the claim management function. These policy provisions may specify circumstances under which a portion of the policy proceeds are to be disbursed prior to death, to pay for medical costs associated with terminal illness, or for custodial or maintenance expenses.

DISABILITY

The management of a disability claim is a complex process that can potentially span a number of years. Historically, claim management techniques varied significantly, between short-term disability (accident and sickness) coverage and long-term disability insurance, which often provides benefits to age 65 or beyond. Although some differences remain, plan sponsors and insurers are beginning to see both as parts of the same disability claim management process.

The process begins with an initial determination of the potential liability. This process includes assessing the claimant's condition relative to the contractual definition of disability, reviewing the contractual provisions, and determining the amount due the policyholder as a result of these factors. This can vary from contract to contract and, in fact, may vary within a contract based on the duration of the disability. For example, it is not uncommon for the initial disability determination to be made on the basis of an individual's ability to perform the specific functions of their own occupation and, after an initial period of coverage, to have the definition shift to an "any occupation" type of standard.

The next step is the establishment of the disability status of the claimant. This process begins by obtaining an assessment from the claimant's own physician. The insurer's claim management staff, often including nurses and physicians, then reviews that assessment. For complicated or contentious situations, the insurer may require an independent medical examination. Occasionally, the process requires investigation and surveillance to be sure that the actual activities of the insured are consistent with the claim of disability, through "field investigations."

As a direct result of the investigation into the claimant's health status, the insurer will establish a plan for managing the disability. This plan may be as simple as an expected timeline for recovery, as in the case of a broken bone, or it may be a very complex program of vocational rehabilitation and workplace accommodation designed to hasten the claimant's return to work.

The determination of the appropriate level of periodic benefit payments usually begins with a determination of the claimant's pre-disability salary. Most benefits are calculated as a percentage of salary. This gross benefit will usually be offset against benefits available from other sources such as Social Security, Worker's Compensation or other employer-sponsored plans. The group contract will specify the specific offset provisions. Thus the claim examiner must monitor and coordinate the payments with a number of external sources.

A key role of the claim examiner is to make sure that the claimant is taking advantage of all other benefit sources that will produce offsets to the insurer's payments. Some insurers provide direct assistance for their claimants in applying for social insurance benefits and appealing any negative decisions.

The ongoing nature of the disability claim also requires ongoing claim management, including periodic review and monitoring to assure that the claimant remains disabled.

Since the desired conclusion of any period of disability is the return of the claimant to full-time work, the management of disability claims often involves provisions and services designed to ease the transition from total disability back to active employment. If full recovery is not possible, consideration is made for partial recovery, the type of work that can be done, and the differential in work earnings. In this instance, partial benefits may be provided. Many large disability insurers also provide for rehabilitation services to actively support the insured's return to active employment. These services are usually coordinated with the plan sponsor, and can include such things as employee re-training for another activity, or work site accommodation for the physical needs of the employee. The company can be proactive in spending in this area, as a trade-off for lower continued disability payments.

There are several other considerations for disability claim managers dealing with long term claims. For example, it is typical for a group policy to provide for benefit limitations for certain types of disability (such as psychiatric disability). In such cases, it is important that these limitations be communicated with the employee, so that as the termination of benefits approaches, the employee can plan accordingly. In addition, some group disability contracts will also provide for indexing of benefits over time, or for cost of living adjustments. These are additional calculations to be managed by the claim adjustor.

If the disability will be present for the long term, the claim management process becomes less intensive; however, periodic updates need to occur to verify continued eligibility for benefits. If other solutions are not available, the company may wish to investigate alternatives to continued periodic benefit payments. If, for example, the disability is truly long term and not subject to significantly increased mortality, the company can consider alternatives such as a lump sum payment.

This might give the employee the opportunity to pursue other options for either working or accommodating their modified lifestyle, while affording the company the ability to terminate the claim. Some claimants use lump sum payments to fund a new business or for re-education.

HEALTH INSURANCE

The cost of group health insurance is a significant and rapidly escalating expense for most employers. Thus, much attention is now focused on the controlling of health care claim cost. As with all other coverages, the contract specifies the level and scope of coverage. Although there remain some indemnity plans paying a specified amount for a specific occurrence (such as a fixed amount per day in the hospital), most group health plans are reimbursement programs. These plans pay for the actual costs of providing necessary health care.

CLAIM ADJUDICATION PROCESS

The claim adjudication process generally consists of four steps, as described below. With the significance of changes brought about by managed care, notable exceptions to this general process exist. They will be described in detail in the next section.

Step 1. *Benefit Eligibility and Proof of Loss.*

The basic step, in addition to the question of eligibility for benefits, is obtaining proof of loss resulting from a covered illness or accident. This will normally include the compilation of itemized bills from hospitals, doctors and other health care institutions and professionals. In each instance it will be necessary to have the dates on which each expense was incurred (the date on which services were rendered) and what illness or accident generated the expense.

Individuals covered by group benefit plans may have a variety of benefit options. Today's systems must be flexible enough to determine eligibility and coverage selected at the patient level. This eligibility determination is the first step in the claim adjudication process. Health contracts vary greatly in the level and scope of coverage. Different benefit parameters sometimes apply to different diagnoses within the same contract; however, this differentiation seems to be disappearing due to legislation enacted in response to the proponents of "parity" of payment for all types of illness or injury.

The next step in applying the contract to the medical expenses that have been presented for payment is a determination of which expenses are eligible for coverage. This would include a review of the specific scope of the contract. For example, does the contract cover expenses related to diagnostic tests or prescription drugs or organ transplants?

A claim examiner must also determine the individual's eligibility to receive benefits based on the presence of a pre-existing condition. This determination has become more complex since the passage of the Health Insurance Portability and Accountability Act (HIPAA). The claim examiner needs to have information relative to the continuity of coverage from one employer to another or from individual to group coverage. The specific group coverage may include a "no gain/no loss" rule governing the situation where coverage has been moved from one insurer to another. Each of these circumstances must be addressed.

Step 2. *Determine Eligible Charges.*

The next step in the basic health claim process is the determination of the amount of eligible charges. Often, with respect to traditional group health indemnity insurance, this will simply be billed charges for institutional providers and some form of usual and customary charge structure for professional charges. These usual and customary type structures generally reflect the prevailing charge levels in the community based on a compilation of actual past charges. Most usual and customary schedules set payment at a percentile (such as 90th) of the actual distribution of charges for each specific procedure or diagnosis. Thus, it is critical to obtain the proper coding of claim charges by procedure.

Most health care benefit plans have moved or are moving to some form of managed care program. The variety and complexity of these programs makes it imperative that the adjudicator access information that will determine whether the payout will be by schedule of allowance, grouping of charges (DRGs) or network allowances. Payment levels will differ based on the managed care philosophy that is exercised.

Step 3. *Determine Gross Benefit Level.*

Once the total dollars of eligible charges have been determined, it is then possible to apply the basic contract parameters to determine the gross benefit level. This includes the application of copayments, deductibles, coinsurance, out-of-pocket expense limitations and policy maximums. The contract will specify the claim basis for these applications, gross charges, net allowances or other mechanisms.

Step 4. *Determine Net Payment Level.*

To arrive at a net payment level, the claim examiner must also consider the existence of other plan liability (OPL). The two major forms of OPL are coordination of benefits (COB) and subrogation (SUB).

COB provisions recognize the eligibility of family members who have benefits available from two health plans as a result of both adults in the family (husband and wife or, in some cases, domestic partners) having family coverage. In the case of coverage for the adult, the group plan covering the adult as the employee is the primary plan and the plan covering the other adult is the secondary plan. In the case of the dependent children, the predominant method (and the method contained in the NAIC model regulation) of determining primary plan eligibility is the "birthday rule." The plan maintained by the adult whose birthday falls earlier in the calendar year becomes the primary plan for the dependent children.

When benefits are paid under COB provisions, the primary plan first makes the benefit payment according to the terms of that contract. The secondary plan can use one of two common methods for determining benefit payment:

1. *Maintenance of Benefit.* Under this arrangement, the secondary plan pays the difference between the total eligible charges determined by the primary plan and the actual payment made by the primary plan. The only limitation, which is seldom reached, is that the payment made by the secondary plan does not exceed what the secondary plan would have paid if it were primary.

2. *Non-Duplication.* Under this arrangement, the secondary plan determines what it would have paid if it were primary and then subtracts what the primary plan paid. In this case, the patient would likely not receive payments totaling 100% of the eligible charges under the primary plan unless the secondary plan was a 100% plan (not too likely in the current environment).

While the NAIC model regulation is silent with regard to these two methods, some states have written specific provisions in their administrative code identifying the approach to be used in that state. The prevalent approach seems to be the Maintenance of Benefit approach; however, employers are increasingly trying to find ways to contain the rapid rise in health care costs and may begin to move to approaches such as Non-Duplication.

As is the case with most benefit provisions, self-funded plans administered under the provision of ERISA have much more flexibility in the administration of COB provisions. These plans can opt to follow the NAIC model regulation or adopt an alternative approach. The major issue in adopting a provision that differs from the NAIC model is coordinating with primary plans administered by insurers that do use the NAIC model regulation. Differences in COB administration have the potential to create "loopholes" into which employees fall, creating employee relations problems. Accordingly, most of these self-funded plans voluntarily follow the NAIC model regulation and adopt the Maintenance of Benefit approach.

There are other methods that have historically been used to administer COB provisions. These variations were designed to avoid plan liability and most of these methods have been defined by state insurance departments as "Unfair and Deceptive Practices."

While most plans recognize COB provisions, there are some that do not contain COB provisions, and that make benefit plan payments without consideration for COB. These plans typically provide limited benefits and include such plans as school accident plans, individual plans, some supplemental sickness and accident policies, and hospital indemnity plans that provide a limited indemnity payment per day of hospitalization.

SUB provisions generally are the result of integration of health insurance plans with automobile insurance policies containing a medical payments provision. Payment for claims that arise as a result of an automobile injury are commonly paid under the health insurance plan, and recoveries are then made against the auto insurer.

It is common practice for health insurers to "pursue and pay" COB claims and "pay and pursue" SUB recoveries.

To carry out the COB component of claim adjudication, first the examiner determines which coverage is primary and which is secondary or supplemental. If the coverage is primary, then the gross benefit determined above becomes the amount payable. If, however, the coverage is secondary, the examiner modifies the gross payment level according to one of the methods identified above. The existence of payment mechanisms such as DRGs has further complicated the coordination process, especially, as is most likely the case, when the two carriers use different reimbursement systems.

In actually making the benefit payment, the claim examiner must determine to whom payment is to be made. Often, especially in the case of high dollar amount claims, the benefits have been assigned to the institution or professional providing the medical care.

Managed Care and the Claim Adjudication Process

There are two basic items that tend to make managed care plans unique in terms of claim adjudication. The first is a network of providers under contract to the insurance company or other risk assuming entity. The second is the use of some degree of health care management, usually prospective to, or concurrent with, the delivery of health care services. Under typical managed care arrangements, claim payments are made directly to the network providers. Providers are responsible for collecting any patient liability, either at the time services are rendered or upon receiving a remittance advice from the health plan describing the amount that can be collected from the patient.

Medical appropriateness and medical necessity are integral parts of the claim adjudication process for most managed care plans. Designed to review both the services provided and the most appropriate setting for those services, criteria of medical appropriateness are used to determine whether the payment of a claim is acceptable as submitted, requires some modification, or is denied.

Claim payment adjudication under managed care arrangements can take many forms, and is typically governed by contract agreements with network providers. Discounts from billed charges, DRGs, per diems, and fee schedules are all reimbursement alternatives still used by health plans in certain situations. In some cases, providers are paid a pre-determined amount per member per month (referred to as capitation) for the delivery of the services specified by the provider contract. In most cases, claims are still required to be submitted by these providers for services delivered under these contracts. These "claims" (typically referred to as encounters) are processed in the same fashion as noted above; however, there are no actual "payments" made to the providers. The claims are used for statistical and quality reporting purposes, and for retrospective review of the providers' service delivery.

In an attempt to create and maintain reasonable standards, most health plans have developed care protocols by diagnosis to establish acceptable and reimbursable treatment patterns. These provide guidance to the claim examiner as to whether the medical care expenses are reasonable and appropriate or whether further investigation is required. Given the additional complexity and ambiguity introduced by the inclusion of appropriateness and necessity concepts, it is common for a health plan to have a mechanism for claimants and providers to establish payment levels in advance of incurring the expense. Some states have required specific appeal mechanisms, as well as health plans' commitment to follow the determination of a review by an outside organization.

Current managed care benefit programs (especially PPO and POS plans) commonly provide different payment levels for use of designated or preferred providers.

This differentiation may also extend to referrals from preferred providers. The claim management process must routinely have data with respect to the status of providers, as well as the status and source of referrals, to properly adjudicate a claim in the managed care setting. In some instances the financial responsibility for a referral may (based on the contract between the insurer and the provider) be that of the referring physician.

In extremely complex or expensive claim situations, the health plan may become directly involved in determining the plan of treatment, the place of treatment and consideration of treatment alternatives. This case management function often involves the authorization of payment for expenses outside the scope of the group contract if the net result is quality care and cost effectiveness. For example, this could involve the use of specialized outside vendors for rehabilitation services or could provide for installation of specialized medical equipment at the patient's home. The key is that effective case management should produce a better result for the claimant while lowering the overall cost of care.

Another issue that complicates the claim adjudication process is the continued trend toward specialization of service. These specialized arrangements (generally referred to as "carve-outs") have changed the claim adjudication process. Examples of these carve-outs are pharmacy benefits administered by Pharmacy Benefit Managers (PBMs), behavioral healthcare provider networks, cardiology networks, and others. Some of these carve-out networks process and pay their own claims (PBMs routinely pay the pharmacy claims), while others rely on the health plan to process claims.

Banking Arrangements for ASO and Minimum Premium Plans

With an Administrative Service Only (ASO) contract, plan sponsors can opt to have their claims processed by an "administrator" (often a health plan), and pay a fee for the services rendered. This fee covers the administrator's costs to administer the claim adjudication process, which may also include the fees for the use of the health plan's network or other services. Additional services might include (among others) the maintenance of eligibility records, actuarial support, and the administration of supplemental benefit plans.

For most ASO accounts, a separate banking account is set up and is funded directly by the plan sponsor to cover the actual benefit payments. A bill is usually sent from the administrator on a monthly basis for the administration fees.

In the case of a Minimum Premium plan, a set rate is charged by the insurer each month to cover administration charges. A limit is also set each month on the amount of claims that can be charged against the bank account, which is funded directly by the plan sponsor. When claims exceed the limit on an accumulative basis for the contract period, the insurer/administrator pays claims using their own funds. There are many variations of minimum premium type arrangements and the administration can also vary significantly.

Ancillary Health Products

The claim adjudication process for most ancillary products (including dental and vision care plans) is much the same as for the medical plan. Issues of eligibility, determination of benefits to be paid, and identification of patient liability are much the same as that described for the medical plans. Techniques used to manage or limit the insurer's liability for these plans include indemnity payment schedules and annual benefit maxima. Dental and vision care plans typically use a UCR fee schedule, but carry varying coinsurance payment levels by type of service, and have annual dollar benefit limits. Some expensive dental services, or services where the patient has a choice of materials to be used in the restoration process, are subject to a pre-determination of benefits in order to better manage the cost of those services.

The separation of the pharmacy benefit from the basic medical plan and the emergence of the PBM was largely a creation of HMOs that wanted a separate management and administrative system for this component of the benefit plan. Their objective was to make the plan more "customer-friendly" and be able to use different cost-sharing features than were available under the medical plan. Often, the most expensive drugs are subject to pre-authorization. In other cases, a mandatory generic substitution provision is included. Most all of these plans have an electronic point-of-sale device that transmits the prescription data on a real-time basis to the PBM. The PBM can electronically determine eligibility and transmit to the pharmacy any provisions that must be followed regarding coverage and payment for the drug prescribed. At that point, alternatives can be discussed with the patient or corrections to the prescription can be made.

Consumer Driven Health Plans ("CDHPs") and the Administration of Health Savings Accounts ("HSAs")

The administration of CDHPs and HSAs presents additional challenges to the overall premium billing, enrollment, and claim adjudication processes. In the case of CDHPs, subscribers within an employer group are typically given three or more health plan options from which to choose, usually with varying levels of contribution requirements. With CDHPs, it is critical to accurately record the choices of each member on the enrollment and billing records. As long as this is done, the back end claim adjudication processes should follow standard procedures. There could, however, be some customer service issues as different members within the same employer group receive different levels of claim payments for their respective option of choice.

HSAs present the additional complication of dealing with a bank account as part of the overall administration process. While most services are still paid under the standard insurance arrangement, some benefit payments are paid directly from a member's Health Savings Account. This functions much like a checking/savings account for each member. The member and/or employer will pre-fund the account with a set amount each year (usually paid monthly). Certain non-covered services such as deductibles, copays, coinsurance amounts, dental services, etc. will be paid from the account. Balances can be carried forward from year-to-year, and used to pay for future services, including the cost of long term care programs.

In general, the normal claim adjudication process for a health plan functions the same for CDHPs and HSAs as it would for standard benefit programs. There are, as noted above, additional administrative complexities for these types of arrangements that increase the overall cost of administration.

OTHER ISSUES IN CLAIM ADJUDICATION

Claim History Database

An additional and important part of the claim function is the creation and maintenance of a claim history database. As medical bills are presented, this database is necessary to keep track of accumulation of deductibles, out-of-pocket expense limits, and benefit period maximums. It also provides a record for avoiding the payment of duplicate claims. Even under fully capitated programs, it has become important to track utilization of services in order to manage the contractual relationship with providers.

With increased competition in group health insurance, and increased regulatory intervention focused on the activities of health insurance underwriters, claim information is being used to a much greater extent in the risk assessment process. The claim information in these databases is being organized by diagnosis, by type of medical service (including the type of drugs prescribed) and by episode of care. The relationship between an individual's past claim history and future potential claims has been the subject of a great deal of research. Uses for this more refined claim data are numerous. This data is being used as a predictive modeling tool to supplement the traditional methods of assessing risk in the small group and individual markets. Medicare is using "risk adjusters" based on this data in setting premium rates for Medicare + Choice plans. Predictive modeling using information from the claim history database has become an essential tool for risk assessment and pricing.

Experimental Procedures

Continuing advances in medical technology are also creating new issues in the claim management process. Medical advances are constantly creating new treatment approaches not contemplated by current insurance contracts. The most common problem for the claim administrator is in the area of experimental or investigational procedures. Some of these procedures may ultimately prove to be effective treatments, while others will prove to be ineffective or possibly even harmful. Most insurers still exclude coverage for experimental and investigational procedures. Individuals with life threatening or serious illness, however, do not want to be denied the opportunity to receive any treatment that may provide a cure for their condition. Thus, the handling of these claims has become an increasingly difficult task. Many insurers are now looking to national professional or governmental agencies to specify the safety or acceptability of specific procedures as non-experimental.

Upcoding and Unbundling

Another area requiring constant vigilance in claim management is the changing claim submission practices of physicians and other professionals. As insurers develop claim systems, screens, and edits to deal with these changes, providers continue to change the way they code claims, combining or unbundling services to maximize their reimbursement. Some insurers have now established sophisticated claim adjudication systems to capture and repackage unbundled services which produce a higher than intended reimbursement when billed as separate procedures.

Claim Processing Systems

Given the constant innovations in the areas of cost containment, managed care, medical technology and benefit complexity, claim administration is becoming much more challenging. Computer software has become central to the claim adjudication process. The newest systems have extensive on-line, interactive capabilities. The software has been developed with artificial intelligence to facilitate complex and detailed edits, and minimize intervention by the claim examiner. Getting all the necessary data into the system has also been a focus of improved technology. Many claim submissions now are received electronically directly from hospitals and physicians or are submitted on machine-readable forms. Document imaging is also used extensively to enter information submitted in hard copy to the insurer.

Many new technologies are now being used by health plans and insurance companies. Some of these technologies allow for a high degree of automation, while some components still require a high degree of human intervention and judgment.

The major components of the claim processing workflow are typically grouped as follows. Many different vendors provide some of these services, but no one solution exists on the market today, although many of these systems are able to be integrated with each other:

1. Receipt processing - This consists of various systems which receive claims and the supporting documentation via a variety of sources. Claims can be received electronically or by facsimile from claim clearing houses, physician groups, and hospitals. Paper claims are also received, and some organizations scan these documents, transferring them to an electronic medium. Once the claim is received, it is logged into a system and given a unique identifier.

2. OCR - Scanned paper claims and paper faxes also can be processed using Optical Character Recognition (OCR) technology. This allows for each document, once scanned, to be translated to data without the need for human intervention. It should be noted that not all scanned documents nor claims will process without human intervention, due the aberrations and variations of documentation submitted.

3. Repair - Once claims are in an electronic format, they are processed into the health plan's "core processing" system. Here claims are either able to make a match on all of the necessary fields required to process a claim and then are auto-adjudicated (see #4), or they are rejected and manual intervention is necessary.

4. Auto-Adjudication – If all of the necessary fields are present on the claim, the system can adjudicate the claim and it is then ready for payment.

5. The payment process – Some plans transmit funds directly into providers' bank accounts, while others still print checks and remittance advices (the details of the payment of each claim associated with that check) and send them by mail to the members and providers.

These new systems have greatly enhanced the efficiency of the claim administration function, and have improved the timeliness of service to the claimant. The entire process will likely continue to improve in efficiency as new systems are developed and integrated with existing processing systems. The move toward a paperless environment will continue, as electronic integration with providers develops, and as systems become more interactive with internet access (via both members and providers).

The claim administration function has become increasingly reliant on the insurer's medical department, legal department and managed care specialists. Common or interactive databases and systems have been created to manage the constant exchange of information between all of these areas as well as with medical care providers and group administrators.

Fraudulent Claims

There are several ways that an insurer can be the target of fraudulent claims. The two most visible have been: (1) fraud on the part of an employer or employee of an enrolled group, and (2) fraud on the part of an employee of the insurer. However, there are other types of fraud that may not, on the surface, be considered fraud but achieve the same result. That result is the payment by the insurer (or other health care organization) for claims for which it would otherwise not be responsible.

Fraudulent claims on the part of a person covered by a policy issued by the insurer, or the employer applying for group coverage, are generally the result of misleading or inaccurate information on the application for coverage, or inaccurate information supplied by the employer in order to obtain coverage for the employee.

There have been numerous examples of cases where a claim examiner authorized payment of a claim, and had a check sent to an "organization" established by the claim examiner or a collaborator in the company who was authorized to set up company customer accounts.

Activities more transparent to the employer or covered employees and dependents, but equally egregious, are actions by providers that result in increased payments by insurers. Upcoding and unbundling (both mentioned earlier in the chapter) could arguably be called fraudulent. Closer to the classic definition of fraud is the practice of billing for services which haven't been provided. This could simply be the billing of more services than were provided, or billing for visits that did not occur. It could also include billing for services that the provider extends to the patient as "free," but results in a bill for a multitude of services to the insurer. It could also be interpreted to include those cases where a provider agrees to accept whatever the insurer will pay as "payment in full," waiving co-pays and/or deductibles, implicitly inflating the amount charged to the insurer to cover the amount for which the patient would have ordinarily been responsible.

The relatively subjective nature of the determination of eligibility for some forms of disability presents additional sources of fraud. Cases of fraud include misrepresenting the employee's ability to work, not disclosing part-time work or earnings from other sources, and not disclosing benefits received from other sources (such as Social Security).

SECTION SIX

FUNDING AND RATING

28 HEALTH RISK ADJUSTMENT

P. Anthony Hammond
Robert B. Cumming

INTRODUCTION

Health risk adjustment can be defined as the process of adjusting payments to health plans or health care providers in order to reflect the health status of the members. Health risk adjustment is commonly described as a two-step process. The first step involves *risk assessment*, which refers to the method used to assess the relative risk of each person in a group. The relative risk reflects the predicted overall medical claim dollars for each person relative to an average person. The second step in the risk adjustment process is *payment adjustment,* which refers to the method used to adjust payments in order to reflect differences in risk, as measured by the risk assessment step. It is common to refer to a particular risk assessment method as a *risk adjuster.*

The use of health risk adjustment continues to grow, especially those methods based on medical diagnosis codes from claim data. The federal government uses medical diagnosis codes to adjust payments to Medicare Advantage and Medicare Part D contractors. Numerous states have implemented methods that use medical diagnosis codes to adjust payments to managed care plans for Medicaid enrollees. Some states have implemented diagnosis-based methods to transfer money among carriers in the individual or small group market.

Diagnosis-based methods of health risk adjustment are being used by employers in analyzing how employee contributions should vary by choice of health plan. Health insurers are increasingly using diagnosis or pharmacy-based methods of risk assessment for provider profiling, case management, provider payment, and rating/underwriting.

Need for Health Risk Adjustment

The use of health risk adjustment reflects the desire to provide equitable payments to health plans and health care providers and make fair comparisons among plans and providers. Risk adjustment is necessary since the health status of enrollees can vary significantly across health plans and health care providers. One major goal of risk adjustment is to induce health plans and providers to compete on the basis of efficiency and quality, rather than selection of healthier risks. A second major goal is to preserve choice for consumers and have consumers pay an appropriate price for their choice of health benefit plan or provider.

The following provides additional discussion of the major policy arguments for instituting health risk adjustment.

First, it is felt by many to be in the public's interest to have health plans compete just on the basis of efficiency, and not risk selection. When employers and consumers compare premiums for group health insurance plans offering similar benefits in today's market, they cannot distinguish an efficiently run plan from an inefficient one. Plans that enroll a greater proportion of healthy individuals than their competitors will generally have lower premiums/costs. Thus, although some of these plans may appear to be more efficient than others because they offer lower premiums, they actually may not be managing the health care costs of their enrollees any better. In fact, they simply may be insuring people who, on average, cost them less. One of the main policy goals for health risk adjusters is to encourage plans to be more efficient by risk adjusting their premiums to reflect the plan's relative efficiency.

Second, there is the recognition that under certain reforms, plans with a disproportionate share of high-risk enrollees may need to be compensated. Legislation requiring plans to issue coverage to all applicants ("guaranteed issue") often contains restrictions on health plan premiums. Those restrictions limit what risk characteristics can be used to adjust a plan's premiums, and often include limits on the ratio between the highest premium and the lowest. Restrictions on risk characteristics almost always disallow risk adjustments for health status or prior health claim experience, yet may allow premiums to vary on the basis of age, sex, geography, family status (such as single, couple, single-parent family, or two-parent family). Some laws and health care reform proposals go so far as to call for *flat community rating*, whereby no premium variation is allowed for any risk class other than geography or family status.

Whenever laws and proposals require carriers to guarantee issue and, at the same time, limit the premiums a carrier can charge, they disassociate the premiums that carriers charge their customers from the risks the carriers assume and the claim costs they will incur. These limits on premiums become problematic when, intentionally or unintentionally, carriers enroll very different mixes of risks but are unable to vary their premium rates to adequately reflect the variation in risk. Furthermore, the more rates are restricted, the greater the need for health risk adjustment. A health risk adjuster may then be put in place, to pool the high-risk individuals of all carriers in a market, thereby protecting the solvency and competitive position of carriers that enroll a more than proportional number of high-risk individuals.

Other proposals express similar goals but may state them in a slightly different way. For example, in a report from the Bush Administration's White House Task Force on Health Risk Pooling,[1] the stated goal is "to reduce premium differentials between the healthy and the sick." New York's Regulation 146 adds another goal for health risk adjusters: "to encourage insurers to enter, remain in, and compete vigorously in the small employer group and/or individual health insurance market."[2] Meanwhile, private employers have been calling for health risk adjusters to operate within the purchasing cooperatives that they are forming or joining.

Whatever the policy goals, risk adjustment mechanisms are designed to make monetary transfers from plans covering lower-than-average risk populations to plans covering higher-than-average risk populations. In effect, a health risk adjuster increases the average premium for plans covering lower-than-average risks and decreases the average premium for plans with higher-than-average risks.

AVERAGE PREMIUM REFLECTS ENROLLEES' RELATIVE RISK

As noted earlier, in the absence of a health risk adjustment mechanism, a plan's average claim cost (and premium) will reflect the relative risk of the population it insures, not just its relative efficiency.

As an example of how this works, we assume Carrier A and Carrier B each enroll 1,000 adults from one community in similar health insurance plans, and that their risk profiles are as follows:

---

[1] *Health Risk Pooling for Small-Group Health Insurance*, White House Task Force on Health Risk Pooling, January 1993.

[2] Insurance Department of the State of New York, Regulation No. 146 (11 NYCRR 361), *Establishment and Operation of Market Stabilization Mechanisms for Individual and Small Group Health Insurance and Medicare Supplement Insurance.*

Proportion of Enrolled Adults by Risk Category			
	Low Risk	**Average Risk**	**High Risk**
Carrier A	.45	.50	.05
Carrier B	.35	.50	.15

In this case, Carrier B has a greater proportion (15 percent) of high-risk enrollees compared with Carrier A (5 percent). Assume that low-risk, average-risk, and high-risk adults in the community have average claim costs of $100, $200, and $600 per month, respectively. The average claim cost per enrollee for each carrier is the weighted average of these costs and the proportion of enrollees in each risk category.

Average Claim Cost for Each Plan		
	Calculation	**Weighted Average**
Carrier A	.45(100) + .50(200) + .05(600)	$175
Carrier B	.35(100) + .50(200) + .15(600)	$225

Even if the two carriers were equally efficient in administering their benefits, the monthly cost for an enrollee covered by Carrier A would be $50 less per month, solely because it enrolled healthier people on average than did Carrier B. If each of these carriers were risk-rating their policies so that low-risk enrollees were charged a premium rate based on their average cost ($100 per month), average risks were charged a premium based on their cost ($200 per month), and the high-risk enrollees were charged premiums based on their cost ($600 per month), neither of the carriers would have difficulty collecting sufficient premium in aggregate to cover its costs, because any change in enrollment would result in an appropriate change in aggregate premium. However, if insurance law or regulation limited what carriers could charge, premiums charged to high- or low-risk individuals would no longer reflect their respective risks.

For example, if flat community rating were required, each carrier would have to raise its premium for low-risk individuals. Some of the low-risk individuals would choose to move from Carrier B to Carrier A because its community rate would be lower. At the same time, high-risk individuals tend to migrate less than low-risk individuals, perhaps because they fear a change in plans or providers. The net effect is greater migration by low-risk individuals.

When migration of low-risk individuals occurs, Carrier B loses $125 toward its expected claim cost, for each low-risk individual leaving, and Carrier A picks up $75 for each new low-risk enrollee. The net effect is that Carrier B's cost rises, while Carrier A's drops further – exacerbating the difference in average cost between the two plans. It is exactly this problem that health risk adjusters are intended to rectify. With health risk adjusters, monetary transfers among carriers are designed to mitigate the financial impact of such migration.

HEALTH RISK ASSESSMENT

There are many definitions of health risk, both technical and nontechnical. People speak of themselves as being in good health or poor health, and actuaries speak matter-of-factly of good risks and bad risks. The example above delineates three categories of risk: low, average, and high. Of course, how such risk categories are defined can be very subjective. For purposes of risk classification, actuaries need to define health risk in objective, quantifiable terms. Thus, health risk is defined and measured in terms of the expected cost of medical care usage.

Risk assessment, the first step in health risk adjustment, is the process of determining the relative health risk of individuals in a particular risk class. Risk assessment involves risk classification, the traditional insurance practice of pooling individuals with similar risk characteristics, as well as risk measurement, which applies the statistical and actuarial methods for quantifying the level of risk of individuals within a risk class.

Health risk adjustment mechanisms present new challenges with respect to risk classification and risk measurement. Risk adjustment mechanisms ultimately involve monetary transfers, explicitly or implicitly, among carriers on the basis of the relative health risk of their enrollees. If the risk classification or risk measurement methods used do not accurately predict claim costs, the monetary transfers among carriers will be inadequate, and the goals of risk adjustment will not be met. Furthermore, to eliminate any financial incentive insurers may have for seeking the better risks in a market requiring them to "guarantee issue," the risk assessment method employed must be at least as predictive as any method a carrier might employ to select risks.

RISK ASSESSMENT METHODS[3]

To date, most research related to health risk adjustment has focused on the first step, risk assessment and the risk classification schemes used for risk assessment. If a risk classification scheme is too broad, the average claim cost of individuals in a risk class will vary significantly. Wide variation in average claim cost of individuals in a risk class makes risk measurement for that class less accurate, and the entire risk adjustment mechanism becomes more susceptible to gaming.

Risk Classification Schemes

Risk classification schemes are generally based on one or more of the following criteria: demographics, prior utilization or claim expenditures, diagnosis and/or pharmacy information from administrative claim data, medical information or history, perceived health status, functional health status, and behavior and lifestyle factors. We will discuss each of these classification criteria.

Demographics. Today's risk classification schemes based on demographics generally classify individuals by age, gender, family status, or geographic location. Demographic factors such as age, gender, and geographic area are often incorporated in diagnosis based risk assessment methods.

Utilization Measures or Claim Expenditures. Utilization measures and/or claim expenditures are often used for risk assessment for rating purposes for employer groups. However, the use of claim expenditures or utilization measures is generally viewed as inappropriate for health risk adjustment, as defined earlier. For the purpose of health risk adjustment, the goal for risk assessment is to use only the impact of a person's health status on future expected costs. That is, when we assign a score to a person's health risk, we want to exclude the impact of factors such as provider fee levels, provider practice patterns, and health plan care management.

Diagnosis and Pharmacy Information. These methods use diagnosis codes and/or pharmacy codes from administrative claim data for health risk assessment. Some of the common diagnosis and pharmacy based methods are discussed in the following section.

---

[3] Some of this summary of risk assessment methods was originally prepared as part of a draft discussion paper for the Health Insurance Association of America's Risk Adjustment Work Group. The research noted is cited in full in a bibliography at the end of this chapter.

The use of diagnosis based methods of risk assessment is growing significantly. Medicare and many state Medicaid agencies have started to use diagnosis based methods of risk assessment. Large employers are using diagnosis based methods of risk assessment to evaluate health plans and adjust employee contribution levels by health plan. Health insurers are using diagnosis based risk assessment methods for provider payment, provider profiling, case management, and rating/underwriting.

Medical Information or History. Risk classification schemes based on medical information or history classify risks on the basis of biomedical measurements or medical history questionnaires. Biomedical measurements that might be used include blood pressure, serum cholesterol level, height, weight or similar medical information. Medical history questionnaires solicit information from individuals on general health statistics (height, weight) and prior medical conditions for which the individual has (or should have) sought medical attention. This approach is currently used by some carriers for underwriting determinations for life insurance and small-group and individual health insurance.

Perceived Health Status. Risk classification schemes may be based on the self-assessment of an individual's health status as determined through a questionnaire. One example of this is the 36-question health survey developed by Rand Health Sciences Program. Research on the survey's application for health risk adjustment has been conducted at Kaiser Permanente's Center for Health Research.

Functional Health Status. Risk classification schemes may be based on an individual's ability to perform various basic activities of daily living (such as bathing, dressing, transferring, toileting, continence, and feeding). This approach to risk assessment is frequently used to determine eligibility for long-term care benefits.

Lifestyle and Behavior Factors. Risk classification schemes may be based on certain behaviors or social habits such as smoking, fitness level, substance abuse, or diet. The results of the study[4] on health behaviors conducted by Milliman & Robertson, Inc. and Staywell Health Management Systems, Inc. indicated significant differences in per capita claims cost between defined risk classifications. For example, current smokers were found to have 31% greater claim costs than individuals who do not currently smoke. Similarly, individuals with 'weight 20% or more above or

---

[4] *Health Risks and Their Impact on Medical Costs,* a study by Milliman & Robertson, Inc, Staywell Health management Systems, Inc, in conjunction with the Chrysler Corporation and the UAW, 1995.

below the midpoint of frame-adjusted desirable weight range' were shown to incur claims 37% higher than for individuals within 20% of the weight range.

Blended Methods. In practice, it is common to blend to together one or more of the above approaches. For example, for health plan payment purposes, most risk assessment schemes blend together both diagnosis and demographic information. In fact, almost all commercially available risk assessment tools use both diagnosis and demographic information in an integrated fashion to assign risk scores to each member. Risk assessment tools that have been designed for renewal rating purposes generally blend together even more information including diagnosis, pharmacy, demographic, claim expenditure, and claim utilization data.

Risk Measurement

Once a risk classification scheme is developed, it should be a relatively straightforward matter to calculate the average claim cost and relative risk of individuals in each risk class using classical methods. The average claim cost for all enrollees in a risk class is then divided by the average claim cost of all enrollees to calculate the relative risk. The relative risk of individuals in a specific risk class may not be the same for each carrier, however. For instance, in the prior example, the relative risk factors for each carrier would be as follows:

	Carrier A		Carrier B	
Risk Class	Average Claim Cost	Relative Risk Factor	Average Claim Cost	Relative Risk Factor
Low	$100	.571	$100	.444
Average	200	1.143	200	.888
High	600	3.429	600	2.667
Total	$175	1.000	$225	1.000

When each carrier determines its relative risk factors and calculates its premium rates from its own risk factors, it will generate rates appropriate for the average costs in each of the risk classes. Neither of the carrier's relative risk factors would be appropriate for the risk adjustment mechanism, however, because the risk adjustment mechanism needs to reflect the relative risk factors for the entire market, that is, for all carriers combined.

When calculating relative risk factors for the entire market, the experience from all carriers must be combined. This process is complicated by data collection and timing issues. The data must be collected from all carriers on the same basis, which is difficult to do unless the risk classes are such that data can be collected easily. Further, there must be no room for discretion in determining whether an individual belongs in a specific risk class. For example, an individual's age is easily and unambiguously determined, but whether an individual is considered a cancer patient or a diabetic may be more difficult – especially if the enrollee has both conditions – but the risk classification scheme must clearly define in which category the individual belongs.

Timing is also an issue, because the actuary needs to collect data from all carriers in the market. This is not always possible, so approximations may be made by using large employer data, for example, which might be reasonably predictive of claim costs, until data from all carriers were available. For research purposes, that approximation probably is adequate for comparing one risk assessment method against another. For actual administration of a risk adjustment mechanism, such approximations may need to be adjusted as soon as credible data are received from all carriers in the risk pool, so that retrospective adjustments can be made to correct initial inaccuracies in the relativities.

If we revisit the prior example, and assume carriers A and B are the only two carriers in the market, the market-wide relative risk factors for the three risk classes and each carrier would be determined as follows:

Proportion of Enrolled Adults by Risk Category			
	Low Risk	Average Risk	High Risk
Market Total	.40	.50	.10

Average Claim Cost for Market Total		
	Calculation	Weighted Average
Market Total	.40(100) + .50(200) + .10(600)	$200

Using the weighted average cost for the market, the actuary can then calculate the relative risk factors for each carrier:

Relative Risk Factors by Carrier		
	Weighted Average Claim Cost	Relative Risk Factor
Carrier A	$175	0.875
Carrier B	225	1.125
Market Total	$200	1.000

The risk assessment process has determined that Carrier A is 12.5 percent less risky than average, and Carrier B is 12.5 percent more risky than average. But how accurate was the risk assessment? The performance of risk assessments will be discussed later in this chapter.

DIAGNOSIS AND PHARMACY BASED RISK ASSESSMENT

The following describes some of the common diagnosis and pharmacy based risk assessment models, including:

- Adjusted Clinical Groups (ACGs)
- Chronic Illness and Disability Payment System (CDPS)
- Clinical Risk Groups (CRGs)
- Diagnostic Cost Groups (DCGs)
- Episode Risk Groups (ERGs)
- Impact Pro
- Medicaid Rx
- Pharmacy Risk Groups (PRGs)
- RxGroups
- RxRisk

The models are revised and updated periodically. The risk assessment models differ in terms of:

- Type of data: diagnosis vs. pharmacy vs. procedure codes
- Site of data: Inpatient vs. all-encounters
- Additive vs. mutually exclusive categories
  Population for which the model was calibrated
- Number of diagnosis codes used
- Number of medical condition categories
- Cost of product, vendor/developer support, and user interface and related tools

Adjusted Clinical Groups. The ACGs is a diagnosis-based risk assessment model developed by Jonathan Weiner and other researchers at Johns Hopkins University. This model was originally based on ambulatory diagnoses. Later versions use both inpatient and ambulatory diagnosis codes. The model groups diagnosis codes (there are about 15,000 diagnosis codes) into Adjusted Diagnosis Groups (ADGs). ADGs are then combined with age and gender to produce mutually exclusive Adjusted Clinical Groups. ACGs differ from most other models in that the ACG categories are mutually exclusive; that is, a member is classified into only one ACG category. In general, this makes custom calibration by the end user much easier but results in a decrease in predictive performance and some loss of clinical granularity.

Chronic Illness and Disability Payment System. The CDPS is a diagnosis-based risk assessment model developed by Richard Kronick and other researchers at the University of California, San Diego. Although this model was originally developed for use with Medicaid populations, it can also be used with commercial populations. The CDPS model is an update and expansion of a prior model developed by Kronick and published in 1996 called the Disability Payment System (DPS). The DPS model was developed for the Medicaid disabled population.

The CDPS model assigns each member to one or more medical condition categories based on diagnosis codes. Each member is also assigned to demographic category based on age and gender. For each member, the model predicts total medical costs based on the medical condition categories and age/gender category assigned.

Clinical Risk Groups. The CRGs were developed by 3M Health Systems. The CRGs use diagnoses and a selected set of procedure codes, considered non-discretionary, to calculate a risk score for each member.

Diagnostic Cost Groups. The DCG model is a diagnosis-based risk assessment model originally developed by researchers including Randall Ellis and Arlene Ash at Boston University. The DCG models include a number of variations depending on the type of population being analyzed (commercial, Medicaid, Medicare), the source of the diagnosis data (inpatient only versus all encounters) and the purpose of the model (payment versus explanation).

The DCG model assigns each member to one or more medical condition categories (called hierarchical condition categories (HCCs)) based on diagnosis codes. Each member is also assigned to a demographic category based on age and gender. Based on these medical condition and age/gender categories, the model predicts the total medical costs for each member.

CMS uses a simplified version of this model for risk adjusting the payments to Medicare Advantage plans. The simplified model includes about 70 condition categories.

Episode Risk Groups. The ERGs were developed by Symmetry Health Data Systems, which is now part of Ingenix. The ERGs are based on the Episode Treatment Groups (ETG) model also developed by Symmetry.

The ETGs group together claim expenditures based on an 'episode of care' concept using clinically similar condition categories. The main purpose of the ETGs is to facilitate provider profiling. The ETGs allow users to compare the efficiency of physicians, clinics, and hospitals. For provider profiling and care management purposes, the ETGs provide more actionable information since the expenditures and utilization data is organized by episode, medical condition, and type of medical service, such as radiology use, emergency room use, and hospital inpatient use. This allows users to identify the drivers of potential excess utilization, since the tool allows one to drill down by physician, condition, and type of medical service. The tool can be used to identify where utilization and/or cost are outside of the norm and what is driving the variance.

The ERG model assigns each member to one or more medical condition categories (called episode risk groups). The medical condition categories assigned to a member depend primarily on that member's diagnosis codes and pharmacy data. In a small number of cases, the ERGs assigned to a member depend on the presence of a defining surgery code.

Impact Pro. Impact Pro is a tool specifically designed for underwriting and rating, and for identifying potential high cost members for case management. It is based on the ERGs, but includes other markers (beyond diagnosis and demographic information) that are predictive of high future medical expenditures but would be inappropriate to include in a risk adjuster used for payment purposes.

Medicaid Rx. Medicaid Rx is a pharmacy-based risk assessment model developed by Todd Gilmer and other researchers at the University of California at San Diego. The model was originally designed and calibrated for a Medicaid population, but has been used for commercial populations. The model is an update and expansion of the Chronic Disease Score model developed by researchers at Group Health Cooperative of Puget Sound.

The Medicaid Rx model assigns each member to one or more medical condition categories based on the prescription drugs used by each member and to one demographic category based on age/gender.

Pharmacy Risk Groups (PRGs). The PRGs is a pharmacy-based risk assessment tool developed and sold by Ingenix.

RxGroups. RxGroups is a pharmacy-based risk assessment model developed by DxCG Inc in conjunction with Kaiser Permanente and clinicians from CareGroup and Harvard Medical School. RxGroups can be used alone to predict total medical costs for each member or it can be used in conjunction with hospital inpatient diagnosis codes.

RxGroups assigns each member to one or more drug therapy categories and to one demographic category based on age/gender. RxGroups is somewhat different than the other pharmacy-based risk adjusters, in that it uses drug therapy categories as opposed to medical condition categories.

RxRisk. RxRisk is a pharmacy-based risk assessment model developed by Paul Fishman at Group Health Cooperative of Puget Sound. RxRisk is a combination of the original Chronic Disease Score model, designed for adults, and the Pediatric Chronic Disease Score model.

The RxRisk model assigns each member to one or more medical condition categories and to one demographic category based on age/gender.

EVALUATING RISK ASSESSMENT METHODS

A health risk adjuster needs to be accurate, practical, predictable, and inviolable (not subject to gaming). Since risk adjustment monetary transfers depend on the relative risk factors, any risk assessment method must be accurate and unbiased, in order for the risk adjustment mechanism to be applied fairly.

Risk assessment methods may be very accurate but, at the same time, quite impractical for use as a market-wide risk adjustment mechanism. Thus, there generally has to be a trade-off made between accuracy and practicality. To be practical, a risk assessment method must be understandable and cost-effective.

In addition, if a health risk adjuster is not also predictable, carriers cannot reasonably estimate expected costs for developing health plan premiums. Further, if a risk adjuster is subjective or too simplistic, it could be gamed, and the integrity of the entire risk adjustment mechanism could fall apart.

Whereas some researchers and actuaries advocate using other criteria for evaluating risk assessment and risk adjustment methods, their additional criteria generally boil down to one of the four mentioned above. For example, some would require that a risk adjuster cost little to implement, protect the privacy or confidentiality of policyholders' records, and be one that all stakeholders – anyone affected by the risk adjuster – agree is "fair." These additional criteria, however, come under the criterion that a health risk adjuster must be practical.

Upon evaluation, demographic risk assessment is an objective method; the factors are readily available and easily understood. The method's drawbacks may be that it cannot explain enough of the variation in risk, and managed care plans may prefer a method that is based on specific medical conditions.

Risk assessment methods using diagnosis and/or pharmacy data are objective, and such data can be readily collected and verified. In using these methods, it is important to use only those diagnosis, pharmacy, and procedure codes that are least susceptible to discretionary usage. Most models do not use procedure codes due to concern about the risk score being impacted by physician practice patterns. However, some models (ERGs and CRGs) use a few procedure codes that they view to be non-discretionary. Similarly, there is concern that pharmacy based risk assessment models might be unduly influenced by physician practice patterns.

Risk assessment methods based on medical information and treatment history may directly reflect broad classes of health status, such as high blood pressure; however, such data may be difficult to collect, as it is not routinely available for most health plans. It may also be very expensive to start collecting this information on large populations.

Perceived health status and functional health status methods are necessarily subjective measures that could easily be gamed. The data is not currently collected by carriers and would require surveys and other expensive data collection efforts. Since this data is subjective, its collection would need to be carefully designed and controlled to avoid gaming.

Whereas behavioral and lifestyle factors can be obtained either through surveys or at the time a policyholder enrolls, this approach to risk assessment has some of the same problems as methods based on perceived health status. While some factors such as smoking and drinking have a direct impact on health care costs, the available data may be insufficient for risk assessment unless applied in combination with one or more other methods.

MEASURING PREDICTIVE PERFORMANCE

A study sponsored by the Society of Actuaries compared the performance of seven common diagnosis and pharmacy based methods of health risk assessment.[5] In this study, a variety of measures were used to compare the predictive accuracy of risk adjusters. In general, these measures compare actual claim dollars with predictions from the risk adjuster models. The comparison is performed on two levels: (1) by individual and (2) by group.

Measures of Predictive Accuracy – Individual Level

The individual measures of predictive accuracy include:

1. Individual R-squared,

2. Mean absolute prediction error, and

3. CPM (Cumming's Prediction Measure), a new measure, which has certain advantages over existing measures.

Individual R-squared is described as the percentage of the variation in medical claim costs explained by the risk adjuster model. Variation refers to the difference in medical costs for a given individual compared to the average medical cost for all individuals.

Individual R-squared is a standard statistical measure for assessing model results. It is commonly used for measuring predictive accuracy of risk adjusters. It is a single summary measure on a standardized scale of 0 to 1, where 0 indicates that the model explains 0% of the variation in cost among the individuals and 1 indicates that the model explains 100% of the variation i.e., 100% accuracy in the predictions. The standardized scale helps with comparability between studies.

Individual R-squared has certain drawbacks. Because it squares each prediction error, it tends to be overly sensitive to the prediction error for individuals with large claims.

Mean absolute prediction error is calculated as follows. First, the prediction error for each individual is determined by calculating the difference between predicted medical costs and actual medical costs. Next, the absolute value of each of these prediction errors is calculated, and, finally, the mean of the absolute prediction error across all individuals is determined.

The mean absolute prediction error is also a single summary measure of predictive accuracy. On the positive side, it does not square the prediction errors, so it is not overly sensitive to large claims. However, it is not

---

[5] "A Comparative Analysis of Claims-based Methods of Health Risk Assessment for Commercial Populations" by Robert B. Cumming, David Knutson, Brian A. Cameron, and Brian Derrick dated May 24, 2002.

expressed on a standardized scale, so comparisons across studies are difficult to make.

Cumming's Prediction Measure (CPM) is defined as follows:

$$CPM = 1 - \frac{\text{Mean Absolute Prediction Error}}{\text{Mean Absolute Deviation from Average}}$$

CPM combines the best qualities of R-squared and mean absolute prediction error. Like R-squared, CPM is a single, summary statistic expressed on a standardized scale of 0 to 1. However, CPM is not as sensitive to large claims since it uses the absolute value of the prediction error rather than the square of the prediction error.

Measures of Predictive Accuracy – Group Level

A group level measure of predictive accuracy involves adding up the total predicted claims for a group of individuals and comparing that value to the actual claims for the same group. This comparison gives a *predictive ratio*. A predictive ratio that is closer to 1.0 indicates a better fit. The predictive ratio is the reciprocal of the common actual-to-expected (A to E) actuarial ratio.

The group level measures differ in terms of how the groups are determined. There are two general approaches: (1) *non-random groups* and (2) *random groups*. Non-random refers to grouping individuals based on selected criteria. The common criteria used for analyzing risk adjusters include groups based on medical condition or amount of claim dollars. Non-random groups can also be defined based on other criteria, such as being part of a particular employer group. This is sometimes referred to as using *real groups*. Random groups refer to groups created by selecting individuals at random from the study data set.

R-Squared and CPM Results

Table 28.1 below shows some results from the study. This table shows a summary of the R-squared and CPM measures for a prospective application (using diagnosis/pharmacy data from 1998 to predict 1999 medical expenditures) with claims truncated at $100,000. Results are shown using both offered weights and recalibrated weights. The offered weights are the standard risk weights that were provided with the models. The recalibrated weights were calculated as part of the study based on the data set used for the study.

Table 28.1

Summary of R-Squared and CPM (Prospective Model) Claims Truncated at $100,000					
Risk Adjuster	Type of Risk Adjuster	R-Squared With		CPM With	
		Offered Weights	Recalibrated	Offered Weights	Recali-brated
ACG	Diag	NA	.140	NA	.171
CDPS	Diag	.125	.186	.128	.183
DCG	Diag	.180	.198	.172	.198
Medicaid Rx	Rx	.098	.165	.123	.186
RxGroups	Rx	.181	.185	.200	.205
RxRisk	Rx	.148	.154	.168	.175
ERG	Diag+Rx	.193	.197	.216	.218

Summary of Results

The following provides a summary of the results from the SOA study:

- For prospective applications, the pharmacy based models perform similar to the diagnosis based models.

- For concurrent applications, the diagnosis based models perform better than the pharmacy based models.

- Recalibration of the risk weights resulted in a significant increase in performance for some of the risk adjusters (CDPS and Medicaid Rx).

- The predictive performance of the models has increased significantly since the prior SOA study in 1995.

- The models still significantly overpredict for those people who are low cost in the future, and significantly underpredict for those people who are high cost in the future.

For a complete discussion of these results refer to the Society of Actuaries study. The full study is currently available on the health section page of the Society's web site, www.soa.org.

EVALUATING RISK ADJUSTERS

In addition to what was discussed under the evaluation of risk assessment methods, risk adjusters (including the transfer formula) should not be statistically biased in any way. Introducing factors that are not directly related to risk into the method will make it more difficult to determine how well the true risk adjustment is working. Generally, a risk adjuster that is easily understood and practical will be easier and more cost-effective to implement. The cost of implementing it should not exceed its benefit to plans and to the market as a whole in terms of efficiency and savings. Any perception of unfairness by the marketplace may be highly contentious.

If a risk adjuster can be gamed, the market will question whether it is equitable, and possibly raise legal challenges. Similarly, if the risk adjuster does not provide sufficient incentive for carriers to manage their costs, it will be perceived as unfair. Thus, risk adjustment transfers should be based on expected costs rather than on actual costs, to encourage efficiency.

Carriers are apt to prefer a health risk adjuster that allows them to determine, with reasonable certainty, what their payments will be at the time they set premiums.

RISK ADJUSTMENT IN NEW YORK

Risk adjustment is prescribed by New York State's Regulation No. 146. New York's health risk adjustment mechanism applies to individual and small-group health insurance products and Medicare Supplement policies. Much can be learned from New York State's experience in implementing a health risk adjuster.

NEW YORK REGULATION 146

New York Regulation 146 promulgated a two-component approach to risk adjustment, which it described as a "market stabilization process." The two components include: (1) a demographic pool which applies only to Medicare Supplement policies and (2) a specified medical conditions pool that applies only to individual and small group policies other than Medicare Supplement.

The demographic pool uses an age/sex factor prospectively to assess and adjust for relative risk differences among carriers' insured populations. In the words of the regulation, "Insurers and HMOs with relative risk factors less than the average contribute money to regional pools; insurers and HMOs with relative risk factors greater than the average receive money from the pools."

Separate demographic pools are established in each of seven geographic areas across the State of New York. Transfers to and from the demographic pools are based on age, sex, and geographic location of a carrier's insured population. (Originally, the demographic pool also applied to individual and small group policies other than Medicare Supplement. However, this was phased-out when the specified medical conditions pool was revised and expanded in 1999.)

The specified medical conditions pool is used to transfer money among carriers based on the average health risk of each carrier's enrollees. A separate pool is used for each of the seven geographic areas. If the average health risk of a carrier's enrollees is less than the regional average, then that carrier pays into the pool. If the average health risk of a carrier's enrollees is more than the regional average, then that carrier collects from the pool. For 1999 to 2002, there is a limit on the amount a carrier has to pay into the pool. The limit is five percent of the carrier's incurred claims in each year.

The average health risk for each carrier is measured using a set of relative risk factors specified in the regulation. For each of the specified medical conditions (specified by ICD-9 diagnosis code), there is a relative risk factor. For members without a specified medical condition, there is a default relative risk factor. The risk assessment is based on claims paid during the 6 months prior to the assessment date. For the claim to be eligible, the person must have had an overnight inpatient hospital stay or, for certain conditions, have had paid claims exceed $5,000 in the six month period.

(Prior to 1999, the specified medical conditions pool operated differently and was more limited in terms of the number of covered conditions. Under the prior structure, carriers made a prescribed contribution to the regional pool for every individual or family they insured. Carriers then collected prescribed lump-sum payments from the pool for each covered occurrence of a listed medical condition C but not more than the carrier had to pay in claims for the specified condition. In addition, carriers would collect monthly payments from the fund for certain chronic medical conditions, such as muscular dystrophy with long-term ventilator dependency.)

ANALYSIS OF NEW YORK REGULATION 146

Several lessons can be learned from the experience with New York Regulation 146. The first is that health risk adjusters can be implemented and can work. While only redistributing about 5% of total premiums, New York's demographic risk adjuster is adequately adjusting for some, but not all, of the risk differences among carriers. After some initial confusion, carriers have been able to report the necessary data reasonably accurately. The pool's administrative costs have been under 1% of claims.

On the other hand, legal challenges have jeopardized the efficiency and viability of New York's health risk adjustment mechanism. For example, a suit brought by self-insured employer plans in the state was not upheld, but a considerable portion of the pool's funds were put into escrow during similar legal challenges. These and other problems continue to hamper the risk adjustment mechanism.

RISK ADJUSTMENT IN MEDICARE

The Medicare program is certainly the most well known example of health risk adjustment using diagnosis information. The federal government uses diagnosis codes to measure health risk and adjust payments to Medicare Advantage and Medicare Part D contractors. For further details on the risk adjustment in Medicare, please refer to Chapter 13 "Government Health Care Plans in the United States" and Chapter 22 "Filings and Certifications for Medicare-Related Group Coverage."

BIBLIOGRAPHY

Anderson, Gerald F., et al., "Setting Payment Rates for Capitated Systems: A Comparison of Various Alternatives," *Inquiry*, 27: 225-233, Fall 1990.

Ash, Arlene, et al., "Adjusting Medicare Capitation Payments Using Prior Hospitalization Data," *Health Care Financing Review*, Vol. 10, No. 4, Summer 1989.

Brown, Robert, et al., "An Evaluation of Risk Assessment Methods," HIAA Internal Memorandum, August 1993.

Cumming, Robert B., et al, "A Comparative Analysis of Claims-based Methods of Health Risk Assessment for Commercial Populations," Society of Actuaries, May 2002.

Epstein, Arnold M. and Edward J. Cumella, "Capitation Payment: Using Predictors of Medical Utilization to Adjust Rates," *Health Care Financing Review*, Vol. 10, No. 1, Fall 1988.

Hornbrook, M.C., et al., "Adjusting the AAPCC for Selectivity and Selection Bias Under Medicare Risk Contracts," *Advances in Health Economics and Health Services Research*, Vol. 10, pp. 111-149, 1989.

Robinson, James C., Harold S. Luft, et al., "A Method for Risk-Adjusting Employer Contributions to Competing Health Insurance Plans," *Inquiry*, 28: 107-116, Summer 1991.

Robinson, James C., "A Payment Model for Health Insurance Purchasing Cooperatives," *Health Affairs*, Supplement 1993, pp. 65-75.

Weiner, Jonathan P., et al., "Development and Application of a Population-Oriented Measure of Ambulatory Care Case-Mix," *Medical Care*, Vol. 29, No. 5, pp. 452-472, May 1991.

Weiner, Jonathan P., "Johns Hopkins Ambulatory Care Groups (ACGs): A Case-Mix System for UR, QA, and Capitation Adjustment," *HMO Practice*, Vol. 6, No. 1, March 1992.

Society of Actuaries, "A Comparative Analysis of Methods of Risk Assessment; Final Report," December 21, 1995.

29 ESTIMATING CLAIM COSTS FOR LIFE BENEFITS

Stephen T. Carter
Dan Skwire

RISK SELECTION

The typical group covered for group life insurance consists of the employees of a single employer. However, other groups – such as multiple-employer trusts, negotiated welfare funds, union groups, and professional, public and fraternal associations – can be provided group life insurance with appropriate underwriting and pricing safeguards. The important considerations are that insurance be incidental to the group's existence and to the insured's membership in the group.

Risk selection considerations for group life are very different from those for individual policies. Individual life insurance is sold to people who essentially have total freedom of choice as to when to buy, amounts of insurance, and type of coverage. Only the underwriting practices of the insurance company prevent those with terminal illnesses from buying new or additional insurance. As a result, the health of the applicant, insurable interest, and background investigations are all an integral part of the individual life underwriting and pricing processes.

By contrast, group life insurance is usually sold with various features designed to minimize the effect of selection. These features include eligibility rules, benefit design, and rate structure. Group life insurance is generally sold under a plan of insurance, which precludes individual selection of amounts. However, a growing number of plans allow an employee some freedom of choice by offering several benefit options and allowing the employee to select one. Typical plans provide for a flat amount of insurance, a multiple of earnings, or a schedule of amounts based on occupational titles. Participation (the percentage of eligible employees in a group insured under the plan) minimums are usually established to minimize antiselection.

Additionally, most plans require that an employee be actively at work on the date coverage is to become effective. If dependent coverage is offered, coverage for a dependent hospitalized on the effective date of the plan is not effective on that person until the day following the date of discharge. New employees are usually not eligible for the plan until after they have completed a waiting period, typically one month of employment.

By insuring a group of actively working individuals, there is a degree of risk selection in the very fact that daily employment requires a minimum state of physical health. Aged and impaired lives tend to drop out of the workforce. Also, some companies require prospective employees to pass a physical examination or undergo drug testing.

It is presumed that few unhealthy individuals join most groups, and automatic election of amounts, participation minimums, waiting periods, and actively-at-work requirements all serve to minimize the effects of antiselection. Thus, group life insurance for medium and large groups is generally offered without evidence of insurability provided the amount of insurance is moderate and coverage is elected at the earliest opportunity. Some level of individual medical underwriting is usually required for high amounts of coverage, late entrants, small groups (less than 25 employees), some multiple-employer and association plans, and for certain optional benefits.

Medical underwriting usually consists of an individual health statement – a health questionnaire that requests information about the applicant's current health status and medical history. Depending on the information submitted, the insurer might require additional information, including a physical examination. A physical examination may be required for applicants who do not enroll at their earliest opportunity.

Because group life insurance is not normally individually underwritten, it does not exhibit the select and ultimate mortality patterns found in the individual life insurance. The mortality rate among persons insured under group policies covering non-hazardous industries is comparable to the rate of mortality among standard ordinary life insurance policyholders after the benefit of individual underwriting wears off.

PREMIUM STRUCTURE

The premium for the group life insurance product is composed of the expected claim cost, a margin for adverse claim fluctuations, the expenses attributed to the product and the specific group, and a risk charge and a profit charge. There is an interrelationship among these elements, so they need to be considered in total as well as separately. Risk charges may not be included for completely pooled business, but groups which participate in their own experience through some form of cash refund require risk charges that vary by the size of the risk involved.

The most significant part of the pricing process is the development of the expected claim cost. In general, unisex treatment of employees is legally required for virtually all aspects of employment. This means that, while the recognition of gender in developing rates is necessary and appropriate (because gender is a proven indicator of expected claim experience), the final employee contributions must be the same for both males and females.

Typically, group life insurance rates are expressed as an average monthly premium rate per $1,000 of insurance, such as $0.14 per month per $1,000. This average premium rate depends upon the age and gender composition of the group. Once calculated, however, it applies to each $1,000 of insurance regardless of the insured's age or gender.

Because of the volatility of group life insurance, where a single claim can often exceed the group's annual premium, companies generally use a manual table for pricing. There are two different approaches to this.

MANUAL PREMIUM TABLES

The first approach is to develop a manual premium table. For fully-pooled business, the rate charged is usually established by first calculating the manual rate, then adjusting it for group size, reflecting the margin (if any), risk and profit, and expense elements appropriate for the size of the case, relative to the averages built into the table. For cases which participate in their own experience through alternate funding or some form of cash refund, the rate charged is usually established by calculating the manual rate, multiplying it by an average expected claim factor to get an expected claim rate, and then adding the appropriate expense, risk and profit, and margin elements.

For larger groups, the charged rate may be based on a combination of the manual rate (with appropriate adjustments) and the group's own experience. The more credible a group's own experience is, the more weight is given to its own experience in developing the rate. To better predict a group's experience, several prior experience years are often combined with the current experience year.

For the very largest groups, the rate charged is developed solely from its own past experience, adjusted for any benefit and demographic changes. These adjustments can be developed by comparing the relationship of manual rates for the old plan and old demographic basis to those for the new plan and new demographic basis.

MANUAL CLAIM TABLES

The second method used by some companies is to directly develop a manual claim table. Under this approach, for either fully-pooled or cash refund business, the charged rate is established by calculating the manual claim rate and then adding the appropriate expense[1], risk[2] and profit, and margin elements. For larger groups, the claim rate may be based on a combination of the manual claim rate and the group's own experience.

Manual claim tables will typically show expected monthly claim costs for each age and sex. Table 29.1 is an example.

Table 29.1

Monthly Claim Rate per $1,000 of Coverage					
Age	Male	Female	Age	Male	Female
15	$0.09	$0.04	40	$0.16	$0.08
20	0.09	0.04	45	0.22	0.15
25	0.09	0.05	50	0.34	0.18
30	0.09	0.08	55	0.64	0.29
35	0.12	0.08	60	0.83	0.45

To calculate the expected claims for a group, the volume of group life insurance is split into amounts for each age-sex category, then multiplied by the corresponding claim rate, as shown in Table 29.2.

---

[1] Practices differ widely in the extent to which expenses are recognized as percentages of premiums, percentages of expected claims, amounts per group, amounts per life, or combinations of these variables. Because premiums are typically small, these assumptions significantly affect a company's competitiveness in different market segments and for groups with different characteristics.

[2] Company practices also vary widely in whether a risk margin is included in expected claims tables and whether the risk margin is expressed as a percentage of expected claims, a constant per $1,000 of insurance, or a combination of both.

Table 29.2

Employee	Sex	Age	Insured Amount	Monthly Rate	Expected Claims
A	M	25	$ 72,000	0.09	$6.48
B	M	35	90,000	0.12	10.80
C	F	30	130,000	0.08	10.40
D	F	50	180,000	0.18	32.40
E	M	40	270,000	0.16	43.20
		Total	$742,000		$103.28
Average Expected Claim Rate: $.139 per Month per $1,000					

In this example, the average expected claim rate is $0.139 per month per $1,000.

To illustrate the combination of manual claim rate and a group's own experience, suppose the group had an actual experience claim rate of $0.10 per month that was considered 20% credible. An adjusted claim rate would then be developed by multiplying $0.139 by 80% and $0.10 by 20%, for a final rate of $0.131. Expected monthly claims would be calculated by multiplying $742,000 by $0.131 per $1,000, or $97.20. Of course, in this particular illustration, the case is far too small to have any credibility and therefore only the manual rate would be used. This process is described in more detail in the chapter on experience rating.

DEVELOPING A MANUAL CLAIM TABLE

Developing a manual claim table for group life insurance is quite difficult. A major problem is finding appropriate and current group mortality experience. For individual life insurance, the underwriting process that is used identifies many characteristics of the individual insureds that can be retained and used to analyze mortality experience. In group insurance, detailed information about individuals insured under larger group plans may not be recorded and tracked. In fact, group insurance for large groups may be self-administered for billing purposes. That is, the insurer relies on the employer to report aggregate insured volumes each month, and all the insurer may receive on the billing reports is the total volume of insurance, the average life rate, and the total premium. While the insurer may attempt to get individual census data annually or biennially, many larger groups are not able to submit information, and when they do, it may cover only a portion of the group.

As a result, it is difficult even for a large insurer to obtain substantial amounts of exposure data on its own group mortality experience. To develop a manual claim table, most carriers must rely on studies done by the Society of Actuaries and the Canadian Institute of Actuaries, together with studies of their own experience and the use of population statistics.

When using these studies, special attention must be paid to any inherent limitations in the studies being used. Typical limitations include treatment of disability claims, completeness of accidental death experience, combined male and female data, experience only on single employer groups, and improvements in mortality. In developing the manual claim tables, group mortality trends must be recognized, along with the costs of reinsurance and conversion policies.

NATIONAL STUDIES

Society of Actuaries Studies

The principal sources of group life insurance mortality data are intercompany studies produced by the Group Life Insurance Experience Committee of the Society of Actuaries. The most recent study includes experience from 1999 through 2001 and was published by the Society of Actuaries in 2006 (referred to as the 2006 Study).[3] The prior study included experience from 1985 through 1989 and was published in 1996 (referred to as the 1996 Study).[4] The exposure base for the 2006 Study was 18.6 million life-years and $723 billion of insurance submitted by 12 companies. Experience is analyzed by amounts of insurance as well as by lives.

While the exposure base may appear to be substantial, the 2005 *Life Insurance Fact Book*[5] reveals that the type of groups covered by the study had $7.6 trillion of group life insurance inforce in 2004 alone. Although this total includes some types of policies excluded from the 2006 study, the disparity indicates the difficulty insurers have in developing substantial amounts of exposure data.

The 2006 Study excluded the following types of business: group universal life, group variable universal life, groups for all which all business was medically underwritten, conversions, waiver reserve buyouts, paid up coverage (including retirees), experience under portability or continuation of coverage provisions, dependent coverage, mass-marketed

---

[3] Report of the Society of Actuaries Group Life Experience Committee, August 2006.

[4] 1985-89 Intercompany Group Life Insurance Experience, August 1995.

[5] *Life Insurance Fact Book*. Washington: American Council of Life Insurance, 2005.

business, standalone AD&D, and reinsurance assumed. The study included business with a variety of disability provisions. For credibility reasons, separate results were provided for only two types of disability provisions:

1. The insured becomes disabled prior to age 65 or 70 and benefits are provided for the lifetime of the claimant

2. The insured becomes disabled prior to age 65 or 70, and benefits are provided to age 65 or 70.

The 1996 study computed waiver incidence rates by using an adjustment factor of 75% to reflect the average present value of death benefits due to disabled lives. The 2006 Study, however, provides unadjusted waiver incidence rates, and permits users to assign their own claim costs to the waiver benefits. Other studies indicate that the 75% factor is high, especially when coverage cancels or reduces at a specified age.[6]

The experience in the 2006 Study is available for a wide range of categories (age, sex, industry, disability provision, exposure type, coverage type, and case size) through a pivot table that can be downloaded from the Society of Actuaries website. Ratios of the 1999-2001 experience to the 1985 – 1989 experience, as well as crude claim rates, are presented.

Canadian Institute of Actuaries Studies

The Canadian Institute of Actuaries (CIA) also conducts studies of group life insurance experience. The last published report includes experience for 1989-91. The Canadian experience is published both on number of lives and amounts of insurance.

Tabulations of experience are given for three different disability provisions: waiver of premium to age 60, waiver of premium to age 65, and total and permanent disability.

Ratios of actual to tabular are given, with tabular represented by the 1968-72 Canadian Basic Group Life Tables with waiver of premium adjustment. Tabulations of data are displayed by group size, sex, disability provision, and region. Disability and accident claims are shown separately.

---

[6] Krieger, Raymond B., "Reserves for Lives Disabled under Group Insurance Extended Death Benefit Provisions of the Premium-Waiver Type," TSA XXIII, 1971.

Use of Actual to Expected or Tabular Ratios

Actual to expected ratios are very useful for coverages, like group term life, with low claim frequencies. For example, to see which size groups have better experience, Table 29.3 can be constructed from the 1985-89 SOA study.

Table 29.3
2006 SOA Group Life Study
Annual A/E Mortality Rates by Group Size
(Expected Basis is Overall Experience from 2006 Study)

Group Size	A/E by Lives	A/E by Amount
< 10	142%	155%
10 - 24	100%	115%
25 - 49	93%	99%
50 - 99	90%	97%
100 -249	88%	87%
250 - 499	89%	87%
500 - 999	100%	90%
1,000 - 4,999	112%	108%
5,000 +	185%	162%
All Groups	100%	100%

According to the 2006 study, mortality experience is worse for the smallest and largest groups and most favorable for groups with 100-500 lives. Ratios of actual to expected claims must be used carefully, however, because expected claims may not reflect all of the variables known to influence claim rates.

The 1960 CSG Table

The National Association of Insurance Commissioners (NAIC) perceived a need for a group life mortality table in 1958. This need arose primarily because individual life tables, mainly the 1941 CSO table, were being used as a standard for group life insurance minimum premium rates. It was widely recognized that individual life experience differs significantly from group experience and that an individual life table should not be used as their basis. Also, mortality improvements over the 1940's and 1950's were so great they deserved recognition.

The Commissioners 1960 Standard Group Mortality Table (1960 CSG), adopted in November 1960 by the NAIC, was the result. The Society of Actuaries intercompany study was used as a basis for the 1960 CSG table. The study was published in the *Transactions* of the Society of Actuaries,[7] and was based on the experience of standard employer-employee groups with 25 or more employees for calendar years 1950 to 1958. The data used included 59 million life years of exposure and approximately 400,000 claims.

At the working ages, margins were added to the mortality rates calculated from this data. Rates for ages under19 and over 70 were obtained from various loadings of the 1958 CSO Table.

The 1960 CSG was originally intended as the basis for group life minimum premium rates. Historically, some states imposed minimum premium rate requirements for group life insurance. These minimums were intended to help insurers maintain financial integrity by preventing insurers from using inadequate rates. Since no state has minimum premium rate provisions at this time, the use of the table is principally as a tabular base when comparisons of actual to expected experience are made. Its documentation remains a valuable resource for actuaries who need to construct tables based on their own company or intercompany experience.

The 1960 Basic Group Mortality Table

A basic group life table was constructed from the 1960 CSG, and is known as the 1960 Basic Group Mortality Table. This table generally represents the smoothed experience, without margins, underlying the 1960 CSG. However, at ages 18 and below, the rates were merged into 85% of the 1949-1951 total population rates.

The principle uses of the 1960 Basic Group Mortality Table are as a standard when comparisons of actual to expected claims are made and as the classic reference source for construction and graduation of group life tables.

Population Statistics

Population statistics are not entirely appropriate for generating expected claim levels, since mortality levels in the general population tend to be higher than the mortality levels of group plans, except for certain hazardous occupations. There are a number of reasons for this.

Generally, there is a flow of healthy individuals into a group, while aged and impaired lives tend to drop out. Prospective employees must pass a physical exam at many companies. Actively-at-work and waiting periods

---

[7] Miller, J.D., "The Commissioners 1960 Standard Group Mortality Table and 1961 Standard Group Life Insurance Premium Rates," *TSA* XII (1961), 586.

are required by most group plans, and individual medical underwriting is required for certain risks.

However, population statistics can be very useful in estimating annual improvements in mortality, in determining ratios of mortality by age bracket, in comparing male and female mortality, and in developing rates for the very young and the very old.

For example, the 1985-89 SOA study has limited data for ages 65 and over. In fact, the combined total of years exposed for all ages 65 and over is less than the figure for the 60-64 age-bracket alone. An extension of a claim table for ages 65 and over can be accomplished by using the 1985-1989 SOA data. However, this approach may produce rates for the older ages that are not consistent with general population mortality data.

A scale of ratios can be selected for extending claim rates can be devised by comparing ratios of three sources that represent national data: the National Center for Health Statistics (NCHS), the Social Security Administration, and U.S. Decennial Life Tables.

COMPANY EXPERIENCE

Data can also be obtained from studies of a carrier's own business. Claim tables can be constructed from a carrier's experience by determining the number of claims per unit exposed in a study cell (age, sex, and so forth). Exposure units can be based on either lives or amounts of insurance. When available, these studies are the best source of mortality assumptions because they reflect the carrier's underwriting and marketing practices.

Since most results require graduation and interpolation (for rates at individual ages), a published table that has already been smoothed can be used as a basis for graduation, or the experience data itself can be graduated. The ratio of the total study results to a tabular base can be used to adjust the results into a smooth progression.

The relationship between a carrier's experience and intercompany experience is also useful for assessing current business practices. It can also be used to evaluate changes in marketing focus or benefit design. For example, if existing business is concentrated in small groups, but the company plans to increase emphasis on larger groups, the experience-to-expected relationships can be an indicator of future results for the company.

CHANGES IN MORTALITY

Changes in overall mortality levels since the experience data was developed need to be considered. If a carrier has used a study of its own experience to develop a manual claim table, it may be possible to recognize group mortality trends by studying its emerging experience. By doing ongoing studies of experience, a carrier could adjust its manual claim table every two to four years.

Another approach is to calculate average annual improvements in mortality between two known mortality tables for each age bracket, and use these as an estimate of future mortality improvements.

Table 29.4 shows the ratio of the monthly mortality rates in the Society of Actuaries 2006 Study (central year 1987) to the monthly mortality rates in the 1996 Study (central year 2000), along with a calculation of the average annual rate of improvement implied by those results:

Table 29.4

Estimated Annual Improvement from SOA Studies				
Central Age	Ratio of 2006 / 1996		Annual Improvement	
	Male	Female	Male	Female
27	63%	36%	3.49%	7.56%
32	66%	34%	3.15%	7.96%
37	58%	65%	4.10%	3.26%
42	63%	76%	3.49%	2.09%
47	66%	64%	3.15%	3.37%
52	73%	95%	2.39%	0.39%
57	54%	82%	4.63%	1.51%
62	70%	84%	2.71%	1.33%

The estimated annual improvements shown above should be read with caution. For example, the 2006 Study contains the following comments related to mortality improvements:

"As in prior studies we continue to see mortality improvements of over 1% per year; however, the rate varies by age and gender. These results have not been adjusted for changes in the underlying mix of industries or any other factors. The ratio of the 2006 death rates by lives for males is relatively stable, but for females it is much more variable. The progression of female mortality rates is relatively smooth by age in the 2006 Study. The prior study contained some anomalous results for female mortality at certain ages that could not be resolved." (p. 5)

Another approach is to approximate group mortality trends by analyzing changes in general population mortality. It is reasonable to expect that changes in general population mortality will be comparable to changes in insured group mortality over a given period. Table 29.5, prepared by the American Council of Life Insurers,[8] presents the average annual change in mortality for the general population derived from data provided by the Social Security Administration (SSA).

Table 29.5

Average Annual Percentage Improvements in Mortality 1982 through 1993					
Age Group	Male	Female	Age Group	Male	Female
25 - 29	−1.0	0.6	55 - 59	1.8	1.2
30 - 34	−2.5	−0.1	60 - 64	1.5	0.5
35 - 39	−2.0	1.5	65 - 69	1.7	0.4
40 - 44	−0.2	2.0	70 - 74	1.2	0.4
45 - 49	1.1	2.4	75 - 79	0.9	0.9
50 - 54	1.4	1.6	80 - 84	0.3	0.7

The SSA data for 1982-85 is based on actual mortality; 1986 mortality is based on preliminary national data; the 1987-1993 mortality rates are projections under SSA's intermediate mortality scenario that incorporates estimates of the impact of AIDS on the general population. Based on the ACLI/HIAA AIDS survey and a LIMRA survey, the incidence of AIDS in the population covered by group life insurance is only about 67% of the incidence of AIDS in the general population. Thus, the mortality improvement factors were modified to reflect only 67% of the SSA AIDS estimates.

The impact of new developments on mortality also needs to be considered. While new treatments for illness and heroic measures are likely to increase longevity, in many instances they may replace death claims with disability claims. On the other hand, the advent of AIDS has increased both death and disability claims. Very often, these developments affect specific age or gender groups more than the general population.

---

[8]"ACLI Again Urges the IRS to Update Section 79 Table I during 1990," General Bulletin of the American Council of Life Insurance, No. 4163, January 11, 1990..

The AIDS epidemic has placed insurers in a difficult position. The use of specific testing in individual medical underwriting is being severely restricted by a number of states. While this is of more concern for individual insurance than for group insurance, where medical underwriting is not usually practiced, it is very important for those situations where medical underwriting is used, such as late entrants. Additionally, employers may not be in a position to deny employment, and therefore coverage, to someone who has AIDS. The advent of AIDS has accentuated the need for conservatism in projecting mortality improvements.

REINSURANCE

Many small and medium-size group carriers limit the amount of coverage that they will retain on any one individual, and they usually reinsure a portion of their life risks.

Prior to the terrorist attacks of September 11, 2001, nearly all carriers purchased catastrophic coverage to protect against the adverse financial effect of a catastrophic event causing multiple deaths among their insureds. Following those events, however, the availability of catastrophe reinsurance was greatly reduced, and deductibles and prices have increases by 5 to 10 times. Now many carriers have chosen to self-insure that risk or to participate in various forms of pooling mechanisms in order to reduce the concentration of risk inherent in group life insurance.

The net cost of reinsurance should be factored into the claim table or into the expense charges used in the pricing of group life, and should reflect whatever reinsurance the company elects to use, including self-insurance for catastrophic risk.

CONVERSIONS TO INDIVIDUAL LIFE POLICIES

Under most group life policies, if group coverage terminates insureds can convert to an individual permanent life insurance policy (other than term insurance) at standard rates. Many companies do not provide disability benefits or accidental death benefits under the converted policy, allow conversion of reductions due to retirement or attainment of a specified age, or pay commissions on converted policies.

This benefit is subject to severe antiselection. Generally, unhealthy lives are more likely to convert than healthy lives and the standard rates for an individual policy are not enough to cover this antiselection. The excess cost needs to be recovered from the group policies, since the individual business line typically charges the group line for them. Additionally, many insurers permit a dual application system and issue regular individual coverage to those who qualify. This further exacerbates the situation since only the truly impaired lives will receive a conversion policy.

The manual claim table should be adjusted to include the anticipated excess cost of conversions, which may range as high as 1% to 1½% of total claims. When conversions occur, the present value of expected excess cost over the life of the conversion policy is usually charged to groups that are experience rated. A typical charge is in the neighborhood of $100 per $1,000 of coverage converted, although many carriers have introduced schedules of conversion charges that vary by age.

Some companies offer a portability provision along with the conversion option. This feature, which is gaining in popularity, allows the employee to keep his or her group life coverage in force after termination of employment. There is the same anti-selection concern as with conversions; however, because of the lower cost of term insurance versus a permanent policy, the portability feature should also attract some of the healthier terminating employees. There is currently little published information on the expected mortality level for this feature.

MANUAL CLAIM TABLE ADJUSTMENTS

Once a manual claim table has been developed, the manual claim rates determined from that table are adjusted based on the characteristics of the group such as industry, geographic location, marketing considerations, employee contributions, plan options, effective dates, and disability provisions.

DISABILITY FACTORS

The manual claim table usually assumes that group life insurance on totally disabled employees is subject to a standard waiver of premium disability benefit provision. Under the standard approach, once a disability claim has been approved, a disabled life reserve is established for that claim. The disabled life reserve may be established through a direct calculation using assumptions regarding future interest rates, recovery rates, and mortality rates, or it may be determined in simpler fashion by multiplying the amount of group life insurance by a reserve factor such as those in Table 29.6.[9]

---

[9] See TSA XXIII. The factor varies by gender, age at disablement, and with the interest rate assumed.

Table 29. 6

Coverage after Disability Continues	Reserve Factor
Lifetime	75%
Lifetime but Reduces at Age 65	65%
Terminates at Age 65	50%

Recent experience pertaining to disability provisions on group life insurance is contained in the Society of Actuaries 2006 Study, including a detailed mortality study on disabled lives.

If the group is experience rated, the reserve is charged against the plan's experience. If the employee recovers, the plan is credited with the reserve. If the employee dies, the reserve is released to pay part of the claim and the remaining amount (25%, 35%, 50%) is charged against the plan's experience. If the group terminates, many carriers will charge the remaining amount against the plan's experience for all of that group's disabled employees for whom the carrier retains liability.

The 1975-79 SOA study showed that plans with an extended death benefit provision have better experience than plans with a waiver of premium disability benefit provision. For this reason, many companies multiply manual rates by a factor of 0.90 when an extended death benefit provision applies.

Where there is no waiver provision in the plan, but life insurance for disabled employees is provided by means of the employer continuing to pay premiums, the expected claims are initially lower than under the waiver of premium approach because no disabled life reserve is created when a disability occurs. However, as the case matures, the ultimate claim level will be the same as if reserves were funded at the time of disability. Theoretically, in this situation the manual claim rates could be multiplied by a factor of 0.90 initially, grading to 1.00 by the end of the seventh year. For simplicity, one company multiplies the manual claim rates by 0.92 for the first two years that the arrangement is in effect, and by 1.00 after that.

EFFECTIVE DATE ADJUSTMENT

Employee ages are normally determined by subtracting the employee's year of birth from the current year. Thus, assuming a central birth date of July 1 in each year, the manual claim table is appropriate for rates effective on a July 1 central date, or for policy years that coincide with the calendar year. If the plan's rates are effective on another date, the rates should be adjusted by multiplying the manual claim rates by a factor. For example, if the plan began on April 1, then the central effective date is October 1, which is ¼ of a year later than the ages being measured. Therefore, the claim rates should be adjusted for ¼ year older mortality. One set of such factors is illustrated in Table 29.7

Table 29.7

Central Date	Factor
January	0.97
February – March	0.98
April – May	0.99
June – July	1.00
August - September	1.01
October - November	1.02
December	1.03

INDUSTRY FACTORS

Different industries reflect varying mortality patterns, in part because of the hazards of the particular industry and its occupations, and in part because of the socio-economic status, leisure time activities, and general health of those employees.

The typical method of adjustment for industry mortality is to multiply the manual claim rates by a factor. Factors are usually assigned by Standard Industry Classification (SIC) Code and may range from a 25% discount for groups such as banks and insurance companies, to a 50% load for mining companies. For extremely hazardous industries, such as mining, the characteristics of a particular group need to be carefully studied for a proper appraisal of the risk, and the group may be declined. Table 29 .8 illustrates sample industry factors:

Table 29. 8

SIC Code	Industry	Factor
1230-1239	Anthracite Mining	1.50
6011-6059	Banking	.75

Most industry adjustments are based on studies, such as the 2006 SOA study. However, white-collar workers tend to exhibit better mortality than blue-collar workers, even within a given industry. If only white-collar workers are to be covered, the factor for that industry should be adjusted. If a particular group has employees in several different industries, a single industry factor is usually determined by weighing the various industry factors by the volume of insurance in each industry.

REGIONAL FACTORS

United States and Canadian population statistics and comparisons show regional differences in mortality patterns. Differences at working ages are small, and most carriers assume they are covered by the differences implicit in industry adjustments. Some carriers make a specific adjustment to the manual claim rates based on the geographical location of the group's employees. Table 29.9 illustrates a regional factors table.

Table 29.9

State	Metropolitan Area	Counties	Monthly Claim Rate Adjustment
Kansas	Kansas City	Johnson, Wyandotte	−$0.03
Kansas	Elsewhere		− 0.09
Louisiana			None

LIFESTYLE FACTORS

A few companies have adopted a distinction between smokers and non-smokers. This distinction can only be applied on groups where information on smoking can be obtained, which may require that insureds sign a form indicating whether they smoke or not. Since a group with more smokers will generate higher mortality and disability claims, the method provides for a more favorable rate for groups with fewer smokers. A typical pricing pattern is to reduce each manual claim rate by about 5% for non-smokers, and to increase it by about 30% for smokers. Under those assumptions, a group with 15% or fewer smokers will have a lower manual claim cost than would have been produced without the smoker/non-smoker distinction.

There has been some experimentation with lifestyle rating. A carrier will offer discounts for a group with healthy lifestyles with respect to smoking, drinking, and exercise habits. These experiments have met with limited success because of the difficulty in obtaining experience data for evaluating risk factors, and the extreme difficulty in obtaining data from employees to price a group. Additionally, part of the reason different industries have different mortality patterns is because of the lifestyles of their employees.

Marketing Considerations

Experience is sometimes influenced by the source of business. Sometimes, business produced by captive agencies will have more favorable results than other business, provided that special underwriting concessions are not made. Welfare funds and union groups tend to have worse experience than single employer groups. For this reason, some carriers adjust manual claim rates to reflect the source of business.

Competition in the group life business has increased the frequency and duration of rate guarantees. Normally, rates are guaranteed for one year. If rates are guaranteed for a longer period, an additional charge should be made. A typical charge would be a 5% increase in the rate for a two-year guarantee.

Contribution Schedules

Where an employer pays the full cost of the group life insurance plan (the plan is *non-contributory*), antiselection is minimized because all employees, both healthy and unhealthy, participate. Consequently, the best experience usually emerges under a non-contributory plan. Some carriers apply a discount of up to 5% to the manual claim rates if the plan is non-contributory.

If contributions are required, either a flat contribution approach or an age-rated approach is used. Under a flat contribution approach, everyone pays the same rate per $1,000 of coverage. This discourages the younger, healthier employees from enrolling in the plan since they often can buy individual policies at a lower cost; older employees who are receiving a bargain tend to enroll and remain in the plan. Generally, these programs produce less favorable results than non-contributory plans. However, if the amount of insurance is modest, fewer employees waive coverage, and the experience should be similar to a non-contributory plan.

Under an age-rated approach, the rates that employees are required to contribute vary by age groupings, such as ages 20 to 24, 25 to 29, and so forth. This type of approach is more equitable to all employees. As a result, the experience under this type of plan tends to be closer to the experience of a non-contributory plan.

Typically, insurers require 75% or higher employee participation in a group life plan.

CASE SIZE FACTORS AND VOLUME ADJUSTMENTS

Many group life insurance plans contain adjustments for case size, premium volume, or both. Case size factors are generally based on the number of insured lives, and they are designed to reflect anticipated differences in underlying mortality based on the size of the case. Premium volume adjustments generally consist of discounts for cases with higher total premium amounts, and they are intended to reflect the lower expenses (particularly commissions) associated with larger cases.

PLAN OPTIONS

Plan options may also cause experience to vary from standard. For example, a plan might allow an employee to choose group life coverage of one, two, or three times earnings. Usually, these plans are completely paid for by employee contributions. To minimize anti-selection, it is imperative that an age-rated approach be used. Employee participation of 25% or higher is generally required for these plans.

The number of options offered and the frequency with which elections are permitted will influence the experience results. If everyone has only a single option, the experience will tend to be more favorable than a plan that permits the election of different coverage levels.

Plans that permit frequent changes by an employee from one plan option to another without requiring evidence of insurability will tend to experience a higher claim level than plans which do not. If the elections are tied to modules in a flexible benefits program where, for example, an employee must choose between high life insurance amounts and a lower medical deductible, the results will tend to be better than under plans that allow an independent life election.

OTHER COVERAGES

DEPENDENT LIFE

Dependent group life coverage is often offered to groups with employee life coverage. Usually the amounts are modest, but there has been a recent trend toward substantial amounts on spouses. Child amounts are usually small, often with a reduced amount during the first year of life. A typical benefit might provide $5,000 or $10,000 on the spouse, and $1,000 or $2,000 of coverage on each child.

The expected claims level will generally not be as favorable as group employee experience, for a number of reasons. First, dependents need not be actively-at-work to obtain coverage. Second, dependent life coverage is virtually always employee-pay-all due to federal tax considerations, and is therefore subject to the antiselection factors of optional coverages. If significant amounts of insurance are provided, the contributions are generally age-rated. Most companies price dependent group life coverage rather conservatively.

SURVIVOR INCOME BENEFIT

Survivor income benefits provide for payment of a monthly benefit to an eligible survivor of an employee who dies while insured. It differs from group term life insurance principally in that a benefit is payable only if there is an eligible survivor, and continued payment of the benefit is contingent on the continued eligibility of the survivor.

A typical survivor benefit might provide a monthly benefit of 10% to 40% of the employee's monthly salary to a spouse until age 65, or remarriage if earlier, and 5% to 15% to each dependent child, with a total spouse and children benefit limit of 50%. Determining the present value of this benefit requires assumptions about interest, number and ages of dependents, mortality, remarriage, and salary information. Manual claim rates are then applied to the present values as if they were regular group life insurance amounts.

The survivor benefit has not been widely accepted by either employees or employers. As a result, new business in this area is seldom written.

ACCIDENTAL DEATH AND DISMEMBERMENT BENEFIT

Accidental death and dismemberment is offered in conjunction with a group term life plan or on a stand-alone basis. Usually, both occupational and non-occupational accidents are covered, which is called 24-hour coverage. For some riskier industries, insurers may provide only non-occupational coverage.

Experience with respect to accidental death is available in various Society of Actuaries studies and may be used as a basis for developing manual claims. These claim rates are typically increased by 10% to allow for dismemberment claims.

The type of industry is the most significant rating factor for the more hazardous industries. While this is primarily because of on-the-job hazards, the experience still tends to reflect the lifestyles of the employees insured, even for non-occupational deaths.

Gender is also an important rating factor because female accidental death claim rates are less than half of the male claim rates for most ages. Accidental death claims also tend to vary with age – high at the younger ages, lower in the middle years and high again at the older ages. At the older ages, it is often difficult to determine whether a death was due to an accident, so coverage normally terminates when the employee retires.

Although most insurers do not vary AD&D rates by age, all carriers vary the AD&D rates by industry. Some also vary the rates by female content, as shown in Table 29.10.

Table 29.10

Percent of Volume on Females	Monthly Premium Rate per $1,000 of Coverage by Industry Classification				
	AA	A	B	C	D
0 - 14	0.05	0.06	0.09	0.11	0.15
15 - 29	0.04	0.05	0.08	0.10	0.14
30 - 44	0.03	0.05	0.07	0.09	0.12
45 - 69	0.03	0.04	0.06	0.08	0.11
70 - 100	0.02	0.03	0.04	0.06	0.08

AD&D is a popular coverage with group members because of its high benefits and relatively low cost. Because of the volatility of the experience, it is normally sold on a fully-pooled basis.

GROUP UNIVERSAL LIFE (GUL)

In recent years, universal life insurance has been introduced as a group product on two different bases. The first product is term insurance with a side fund, where the employee has the option of electing term insurance alone or term insurance with a side fund. The side fund continues to grow with interest earnings and as additional contributions are made.

The second product is an individual universal life product based on group mortality and marketed on a group basis. The fund account is an integral part of this package, and the employee cannot elect to omit it. Under this approach, the employees have less latitude in determining the amount of their contributions.

Both product types are portable; that is, an employee can choose to keep coverage inforce upon termination of employment. These products are virtually always employee-pay-all because of federal tax considerations, and are generally offered in addition to the regular, employer-paid group life plan, either to employees only or to employees and their dependents.

To encourage good participation and thus better mortality experience under the GUL plan, the underlying employer-paid group life plan should ideally provide no more than one times earnings. At this level, it will be apparent to many employees that they need more insurance. The level of the underlying group life plan and other underwriting requirements, such as actively-at-work requirements, multiple of earnings options, level of guaranteed issue, and type of health statement, must all be considered in establishing appropriate mortality levels.

LIVING BENEFITS

The growth of AIDS marked the beginning of recognition that the terminally ill need to have early access to their life insurance proceeds, to pay for medical expenses and improve the quality of their remaining life. Companies were formed by entrepreneurs to buy the life policies of the terminally ill at a discount from the face amount. These events spurred both the regulators and the insurance industry into action.

Now, living benefits (also called accelerated death benefits) coverage is being added to individual life products, group universal life, and group term life. Coverage generally falls into three basic models, and combinations of these, which primarily differ as to the event that triggers benefits: long-term care, catastrophic illness, or terminal illness.

Long-term care benefits typically provide for a monthly benefit of 2% of the face amount beginning with permanent confinement in a nursing home. Some plans also include additional services, such as permanent home health care, as benefit triggers. The monthly benefit is paid until a specified portion of the death benefit is paid, ranging from 50% to 100%. The remaining portion of the death benefit is paid to the beneficiary upon the insured's death.

Catastrophic illness benefits pay a single amount, typically 25% of the face amount, upon the occurrence of a listed disease; such as heart attack, stroke, cancer, coronary artery surgery, and renal failure. Other conditions are often included. After a claim, the policy is typically rewritten to 75% of its previous amount.

It can be difficult to precisely define some of the diseases and to develop claim assumptions. For example, a state may require AIDS to be added to the list, but how is AIDS defined and when is the benefit triggered? Different answers to these questions have different impact on claim assumptions.

Terminal illness benefits pay a single amount, from 25% to 50% of the face amount, when the insured has been diagnosed with a terminal illness by a physician who certifies the insured has less than 6 (or 12) months to live. The remaining portion of the death benefit is paid to the beneficiary upon the insured's death. The benefit cost is either factored into the manual claim rates or a separate premium charge is made.

In other terminal illness plans, carriers discount the advance payment for interest, and may also make an administrative charge of $100 to $300. There are no premium charges under this approach. The beneficiary and the insured pay the cost of this feature out of the death benefit. Regulations limit the level of the interest rate but not the discount period. Some carriers with a "less than six months to live" requirement will use a twelve-month discount period. It is argued that this is justified because of antiselection, errors in physicians' opinions, and fraud.

If living benefits coverage is added to a group's life plan, it should apply to all insureds, to avoid antiselection and administrative problems. To further avoid antiselection, a 30-day waiting period could be used before coverage becomes effective.

30 ESTIMATING MEDICAL CLAIM COSTS

Gerald R. Bernstein
Shelly S. Brandel

Medical claim costs are the essential element in the pricing of medical benefit products. The cost of medical care is by far the largest component of medical plan premiums. This chapter will discuss the development of the estimated claim cost (cost of care) that is used in establishing the price of a medical care plan.

The wide range of available health insurance products means that various risk-bearing entities assume the cost of providing health insurance, from insurance companies to HMOs, employers, and provider groups. Over the past few decades, there has been a shift from pure indemnification for medical costs to prepayment of services, and in many cases, back to pure indemnification. Yet the essential problem of estimating the cost of care remains.

Insurers often produce a "group rate manual" which contains detailed claim cost information. This manual enables the actuary to make pricing adjustments for variations in plan design, demographic characteristics, level of utilization management, size of group, geographic area, and other factors which are likely to impact future costs. The use of a group manual allows a company to adjust their own historical data to be more reflective of the specific population being rated. This manual can be developed from a company's own experience, but is often supplemented by data from public sources or purchased from industry sources. Group manuals are also available from actuarial consulting firms.

This chapter will describe the development of a company's average medical cost (or manual rate) which serves as the key component of the group rate manual. The group manual, in turn, is used in pricing either traditional indemnity or managed care benefit programs. The chapter will discuss the

613

entire process of developing the manual rate, including the collection of experience period data, the adjustment or normalization of the data to a set of "standard" characteristics, the projection of the data to the rating period, and the adjustment of the manual rate to a specific situation.

This chapter concentrates only on the process of developing the medical cost portion of the manual rate. Other chapters in this text discuss the issues involved in adjusting the manual rate to include administration and other premium loadings, as well as other group-specific rating methodologies.

Although the methods and techniques described in this chapter are framed in the context of medical benefits, they may easily be applied to other benefits. Programs that provide vision care, prescription drugs, and dental benefits may be priced using similar methods. These programs have many characteristics similar to medical programs, such as a high frequency of claims with relatively low dollar amounts.

DATA CONSIDERATIONS

Summarizing medical claim data is a complex process for several reasons, including the multitude of benefit plans, variations in provider claim coding conventions, and varying group characteristics. In the past it has been difficult to capture all the information necessary to adjust for all these variables. However, improvements in information systems and database technology enable the actuary to manipulate complex data more efficiently.

Estimating medical claim costs is a process that involves projecting historical claim information to a future period, recognizing factors such as case characteristics, demographic data, and provider contracting details. This process begins with the selection of an appropriate data source. There are many factors to consider when selecting the appropriate data source, several of which are described below.

IS THE DATA APPROPRIATE FOR ESTIMATING CLAIM COSTS?

The source data should generally reflect the characteristics of the company's population and benefits. For example, commercial data should not be used to estimate claim costs for a population aged 65 and over. Any data will need to be adjusted, or normalized, for several factors, including the insurer's demographic mix, benefit levels, provider contracting details, and the rating period, among many others.

WHAT LEVEL OF DETAIL IS NEEDED?

Aggregate data is usually sufficient to estimate medical claim costs. In other words, data is summarized into broad service categories and across all benefit plans and other group characteristics. For example, in the process of renewal pricing for a large, stable group or a stable block of small groups, the process often starts with a comparison of actual to expected loss ratios or a comparison of actual to expected claim costs per person (or per employee).

If developing manual rates, the insurer's data for the entire line of business is typically used. If developing an experience rate for a particular group, then data for that group is used.

As the ability to handle large volumes of data has expanded, and the focus on controlling medical costs has grown, aggregate methods are often supplemented with more detailed analyses. Further, an increasing number of plans allow employee choice between multiple plan options, causing greater need for more detailed analysis. In the past, a group may have covered all employees through one medical program, and historical medical costs per employee may have been a reasonably stable predictor of future medical costs. Now, many groups offer multiple plan choices, including HMOs and PPOs, and the age, gender and health characteristics of those covered by the different plans may be constantly changing. The broad range of emerging consumer-driven products will only complicate matters further.

In general, the more stable the block of business being rated, and the fewer differences between the experience period and the rating period in terms of population and delivery system characteristics, the more likely it is that using aggregate data is an appropriate option. Conversely, the less stable, and greater differences in case characteristics between the experience period and the rating period, the greater the need for more detailed data.

DATA SOURCES

The best source of data is usually a company's own experience, as long as there is sufficient volume for the data to be credible. This data will reflect the company's cost patterns as well as administration, risk selection, and other characteristics. Sometimes, however, this information is not appropriate for projecting future costs, especially in situations where changes are occurring in benefit design, type of group, provider contracts, utilization management, underwriting practices, or claim administration. Additionally, insurers do not always track information at the detailed claim level, since individual claims are not always the basis for benefit payments.

Movement to managed care plans or to consumer-driven plan options only compounds this issue. In situations of significant change, or if the volume of a company's own claims data is not sufficient to be credible, it must be supplemented with other data. The other data can be from public sources such as the Centers for Medicare & Medicaid Services (CMS) and the Bureau of Labor Statistics (BLS), or purchased from industry sources or actuarial consulting firms.

COLLECTING DATA FOR MANUAL RATES

Data to develop medical claim costs should be collected in a level of detail that is consistent with the company's rating methodology. The variables discussed below should be considered, both in collecting data to use in the development of the manual rate and in adjusting the manual rate for a group-specific rate development.

Companies will often only capture data that is needed to facilitate prompt claim processing. As data entry techniques and the ability to handle data files continue to improve, the amount of information collected is also increasing. The increase in the amount of available information is improving the ability to analyze data and project medical claims. (On the other hand, insurers are growing steadily more protective of their data, making it less available publicly. HIPAA's privacy standards will likely greatly strengthen this trend.) The following section describes variables that should be considered in the collection process.

FINANCIAL INFORMATION

When collecting financial data in order to estimate medical claim costs, there are a few important considerations. One is to define the type of claim dollars to be collected. If benefit plans or provider reimbursement arrangements are changing, it will be useful to collect not only paid claim amounts, but also billed and allowed claim dollars. The billed and allowed amounts, similar to the paid amounts, should reflect only services covered by the insured arrangement.

The difference between paid and allowed amounts normally reflects the value of any insured cost sharing (deductible, coinsurance, or copayments). The difference between allowed and billed amounts normally reflects the negotiated provider reimbursement arrangements.

Other items that must be clearly defined in the data include the treatment of reinsurance recoveries and coordination of benefit (COB) recoveries. The preferred situation is to have the claim information reflect 100% of the claims for covered services, before reductions for reinsurance and COB recoveries. It is also important, however, to be able to identify these recoveries and, potentially, adjust for them as part of the rating process.

EXPERIENCE PERIOD

If possible, data should be collected for a period of at least twelve months. A twelve-month period ensures the data being studied includes a complete seasonal cycle of incurrals and payments. Capturing the complete seasonal cycle is important. This is because claim levels vary over the year. One main reason is that the months of November and December often have claim levels lower than average, due to people avoiding elective care during the year-end holidays.

Claims may be analyzed on either an incurred basis or a paid basis. In either case, care should be taken to capture the corresponding exposure information (number of covered members or contracts during the experience period). Further, assuming claims are being analyzed on an incurred basis, the claims should be "completed," or reflective of all claims incurred by the exposed lives over the designated experience period. This can be done by collecting data for a specified incurral period with payment dates extending far enough beyond the incurral period that most claims incurred during the service period will have been paid. Alternatively, the historical payment patterns can be analyzed to estimate completion factors to apply to the data in order to "complete" the claims.

EXPOSURE BASIS

Exposure units, or employee and dependent units, are monthly counts of insureds summarized over the experience period. Exposure units were historically defined as one of the following:

- Number of employees,
- Number of contracts,
- Number of subscribers, or
- Number of covered persons (members).

Claim costs calculated on the first three bases are subject to misestimation when the covered family composition changes. The third basis requires exposure counts for spouses and each child, which historically have not been available for many traditional plans.

In some cases, spouse and children exposure counts are estimated in order to calculate costs per member per month (PMPM), as is traditionally done in HMO and other managed care calculations. PMPM-based analyses have become much more prevalent in recent years as carriers have integrated their managed care and traditional operations.

FREQUENCY OF DATA COLLECTION

If a company does a detailed study on an annual basis, the results can be used to study trend and the impact of cost containment programs, plan design changes, or utilization management improvement efforts. When a detailed study cannot be performed annually due to timing, budget, or other constraints, a less detailed study can be performed to evaluate overall medical costs and trends.

NORMALIZING DATA FOR IMPORTANT RATING VARIABLES

In most cases, the historical data must be normalized for a number of factors, including demographic mix, geographic area, benefit plan, group characteristics, utilization management efforts, and provider reimbursement arrangements. Then, when calculating a rate for a specific group, the manual rate must be adjusted to reflect the characteristics specific to that group. This section describes important rating variables to consider when normalizing historical data.

AGE AND GENDER

The variation in claim cost by age and gender can be substantial. For example, adult males under age 25 have roughly 20% of the claim costs of men and women ages 55-64. These age/gender cost relationships do not change significantly from year-to-year, so it is common only to perform age/gender studies relatively infrequently, perhaps every few years.

In the development of a manual rate, the historical costs reflect the demographics of the block of business being analyzed. The actuary may adjust the historical costs to a "standard population" using appropriate age/gender factors. Alternatively, the actuary may treat the historical experience as representative of a standard population. In other words, the population underlying the historical experience is defined, by default, as the standard population. The latter is the simpler approach.

Separate age/gender factors may be appropriate for major service categories such as hospital, physician, or prescription drugs, particularly if such benefits are sold independently of other coverages (an optional drug rider, for instance). Also, since the incidence of low claim dollars can be different by age or gender than the incidence of high claim dollars, it can be worthwhile to develop separate age/gender factors for high deductible plans. Typically 5-year or 10-year age bands are used for age/gender factors.

When developing a group specific rate from the manual rate, the manual rate is adjusted to reflect the actual age/gender composition of the group being rated.

GEOGRAPHIC AREA

In many cases data may be collected from a broad geographic area where significant differences in claim costs by finer geographic area exist. The variation in claim costs by geographic area for a comprehensive benefit plan can vary widely, even ± 50%. When collecting experience period data, therefore, it is important to adjust the raw data to reflect one specific geographic area.

As with age/gender factors, area factors can be studied at either a detailed level or in aggregate. Many companies lack sufficient volume to credibly study their own claim cost variations at the ZIP code, county, or metropolitan statistical area (MSA) level in all states where they do business. A company might use area factors from a competitor or from an actuarial consultant, and then monitor loss ratios by area as experience emerges. Higher variation between the actual loss ratio and the expected loss ratio indicates areas that require adjustment.

Separate utilization and charge area factors at a detailed level are often difficult to establish because of limited amounts of data. For details on selected services, one might focus on a fine level of service, while keeping the area dimension broad, such as by state. For details at a fine level of geography, such as ZIP code, one might focus only on total claim costs. Computer statistical packages can be helpful in evaluating such data.

Benefit Plan

Different benefit plans can produce significantly different claim costs, even when all other variables are identical. Claim costs often must be adjusted to reflect a different benefit plan from the average plan included in the claim data.

Plan design variations in traditional plans often include deductibles, co-insurance, out-of-pocket limits, and plan benefit maxima. Other variations can include wellness benefits, prescription drug cards, inside limits on specified services (such as mental, nervous, and substance abuse benefits), and the definitions of family deductibles and carry-over provisions.

Managed care benefit plan variations often include varying member co-payments, dollar maxima for specific benefit categories, and covered services. More recently, managed care plans have emerged that include combinations of copayments on some services and deductibles and coinsurance on other services. In addition, high deductible health plans (HDHPs) have become more common as another means of cost control and are often coupled with an HSA or HRA.

Different benefit plans are likely to experience different utilization patterns depending on the degree of insured cost sharing. For example, a group with a $5,000 deductible may have lower utilization than a group with a $100 deductible simply because the higher deductible often acts as a deterrent to an individual seeking medical care. Further, data on a $5,000 deductible plan is not likely to have information collected on many physician office visits, because relatively few office visit claims are paid on claims in excess of that amount, and people are less likely to submit such claims if they know they fall under the deductible. Similarly, a plan that does not cover chiropractors is not likely to have data on chiropractic charges. Other information or assumptions will be needed to assess the value of benefit changes in those instances.

Once again, it is important to adjust the experience period data to reflect a common benefit plan. In many cases it is most practical to adjust all experience data to reflect the richest benefit plan. This process normally involves using allowed charge data, and adjusting utilization to reflect the estimated impact on utilization if all insureds had the richer benefit plan. The adjustments may be made on either an aggregate basis, if aggregate data is used for a traditional indemnity insurer, or on a more detailed basis, which is normally the preferred approach for a managed care plan.

HDHPs can have an additional level of complexity, as utilization (and thus cost) of benefits under plans with identical benefits may vary based on how much money from an underlying account (either an HSA or an HRA) is available to pay for benefits.

Finally, there are often situations where not all insureds are covered for certain services. It is important in these cases to match the claim experience to the appropriate exposure base. This situation most often arises when estimating claim experience for both base plans and benefit riders, such as prescription drug benefits or vision benefits. Very often only a portion of the total exposed population is covered by the rider. In these cases it would be appropriate to use a different exposure base for the rider than is used for the base plan experience.

GROUP CHARACTERISTICS

When developing group specific rates, the manual rate is adjusted to reflect the characteristics, such as industry and group size, of each group being rated. The manual rate should represent the "average group." Therefore, historical experience must be adjusted to reflect average group characteristics.

Industries with above average costs typically involve physical labor, such as mining or construction, or those where employees tend to be highly aware of available benefits and services, such as educational institutions and health care providers.

Group size can also be a significant rating factor. As the size of a group decreases, the influence of individuals with serious conditions is magnified, and the cost per exposure unit can increase significantly, with even just one of these high cost individuals. As the size of a group increases, the impact of individuals with serious conditions is dampened.

There is some tendency for smaller employers to provide medical coverage in a way that selects against insurers. The employer can be aware of specific health conditions of their employees, and may choose the plan most beneficial to covering a particular condition. Claim cost studies on blocks of small cases are often made on a durational basis, because the impact of employer selection, underwriting (where allowed), and coverage limitations for pre-existing conditions is greatest in the first year of coverage. However, the guarantee issue requirements and pre-existing condition limitations of the Health Insurance Portability and Accountability Act of 1996 (HIPAA) has, in many cases, changed the durational pattern of claim costs for small group medical coverages.

For example, in a small group medically underwritten block of business, first year claims can be as little as 60% of the claims expected in the sixth and later years. With HIPAA's restrictions, the first year claims are often much closer to ultimate years' claims. Additionally, the number of years to reach ultimate claim levels is less, since initial underwriting savings are less.

UTILIZATION MANAGEMENT PROGRAMS

Most managed care plans use a process known as utilization review or utilization management (UM) to assess the necessity of a given treatment or the appropriateness of the setting in which care is delivered. A well-designed UM program helps ensure timely delivery of appropriate care by qualified providers in an efficient setting.

Conceptually, UM can take place either before, during, or after care is delivered. The focus of prospective UM is typically on necessity of proposed treatment and appropriateness of setting. During the delivery of care, UM involves monitoring patient progress and planning for conclusion of care. Post-treatment, or retrospective, UM focuses on ensuring that all reported care was actually delivered, to see if charges for required care were appropriate, or to assess whether certain care was necessary. A more detailed discussion of UM programs can be found elsewhere in this text.

The source data should be adjusted for any significant changes in UM programs, either during the experience period or between the experience period and the rating period.

PROVIDER REIMBURSEMENT ARRANGEMENTS

Compensation arrangements between insurers and healthcare providers take a wide variety of forms. For example, hospital reimbursement can be based on discounts from billed charges, per diems, case rates, Medicare payment levels, capitation, or other arrangements.

If any provider reimbursement arrangements changed during the experience period, it is important to adjust the experience to reflect a common reimbursement level. An obvious example would be if a managed care organization had a capitation arrangement with their primary care physicians that terminated during the experience period. There would most likely be little or no information on the capitated services prior to the change, but the capitated services would appear in the data after the arrangement was terminated. In this case, an adjustment would be necessary to reflect the claim amounts on a non-capitated basis throughout the entire experience period.

Similar adjustments would be required if a physician fee schedule, per diem schedule, or even a discount arrangement changed during the experience period.

Additional information on provider contracting arrangements can be found elsewhere in this text.

PROJECTING EXPERIENCE PERIOD COSTS TO RATING PERIOD

Claim costs are trended from the manual's experience base time period (for manual rating) or the group's base experience period (for experience rating) over which data is collected, to the rating period (the period over which rates will be effective). For purposes of estimating medical claim costs, measuring and projecting trend is a critical component of the process. When projecting experience from a base period to a rating period, it is usually necessary to estimate cost increases for a period of fifteen months or more.

For our purposes, trend includes all elements that may influence the average medical claim costs. These elements include not only changes in the average unit cost per service, but also changes in the utilization of services, as well as changes in medical practice patterns, changes in the mix of services, and provider reimbursement arrangements. New technologies, drugs, and services also have an impact on trend. Finally, plan design can impact trends due to deductible and copay leveraging.

In establishing appropriate trend adjustments to reflect all these elements, the actuary should separate the elements between secular trends and other factors. Secular trends are defined as the percentage change in average claim costs resulting only from those factors that affect a static population with first dollar, 100% benefits. The two major components of secular trend are changes in the utilization of services and changes in the average unit cost per service.

Secular trends can be estimated by examining historical changes in both utilization and average unit costs, as well as by reviewing external information such as health care market studies, surveys, or econometric models.

Historical changes in claim costs can be reviewed in various levels of detail, depending on the detail available in the experience data and the desired precision in the trend assumptions. Trends can be examined by comparing total medical costs for all services combined or can be reviewed by individual types of service (hospital inpatient, hospital outpatient, physician, and prescription drugs), or even in more detailed categories. Within each of these categories, historical trends can be separated further between changes in utilization and changes in unit costs.

Whatever level of detail is used in the analysis of historical trends, it is useful to measure trends over three month and twelve month rolling periods. The pattern of twelve month trends indicates the magnitude of annual trends, while the three month pattern can be a leading indicator of trend direction. When reviewing historical trend patterns, it is important to keep in mind the historical changes in provider reimbursements, utilization management efforts, and average benefit levels. Changes in these factors over time could explain some of the historical trend patterns.

When negotiated arrangements include scheduled reimbursements such as inpatient per diems, case rates, or physician fee schedules, the secular trend on unit costs can be estimated by examining the changes in these arrangements between the experience period and the rating period. However, negotiated arrangements based on discounts off billed charges are less useful in estimating trend, as the unit costs will also be heavily impacted by changes in provider discount levels.

Managed care plans have historically been able to moderate health care trends to some extent, through a combination of utilization management efforts and negotiated reimbursement arrangements. However, the managed care backlash in recent years has caused increases in managed care trends, as utilization management efforts have softened and providers have become more aggressive in reimbursement negotiations.

Furthermore, cost shifting among payors has resulted in disproportionate provider cost increases to commercial plans. For example, as government programs such as Medicare and Medicaid limit payments to providers, the providers raise charges for indemnity and managed care patients to make sure their costs are covered.

Finally, trends are influenced by plan design. Deductibles and copayments can create trend leveraging which increases the impact a secular trend has on claim costs. This is discussed in greater detail in another chapter.

METHODS OF ADJUSTING MANUAL BASE RATES

Once the data has been collected, properly normalized, and trended to the rating period, it represents a standardized set of claim costs. The insurer is then ready to calculate the manual rate for a specific group or situation. The method chosen to calculate claim costs depends most importantly on the style of benefit plan. Benefit adjustments for traditional insurance products with deductibles and coinsurance are calculated very differently from benefit adjustments for traditional managed care products, which likely have first dollar coverage and fixed copayments on specified services.

CLAIM PROBABILITY DISTRIBUTIONS

Claim probability distributions (CPDs) are typically used to estimate the impact of deductibles, coinsurance, out-of-pocket maximums, and annual benefit maximums on claim costs. CPDs are also sometimes called "continuance curves" if continuous, or "continuance tables" if discrete. They are used by traditional insurance or indemnity type plans. CPDs can also be used for plans whose reimbursement methodology and benefit design are similar, such as many PPO plans. They are also used in the development of claim costs for high deductible plans, such as those used with health savings accounts (HSAs) or health reimbursement accounts (HRAs).

In this method, the estimated medical claim costs are determined using a CPD from an established database. As discussed above, there are many factors that might change between the experience period and the rating period. Further, where data is obtained from sources other than the block for which claims are being estimated, there may be differences in these factors.

An example of a CPD and its use is shown in Table 30.1 below. To construct a CPD, the annual claims are first summarized on a per member basis. The members are then grouped into cost ranges based on their annual claim payments. The data in columns (2) and (3) are calculated on a per member per year basis, and these two columns define the CPD. The remaining columns are calculated to help ease the use of the CPD, and are developed as follows:

- Column (4) is the product of Columns (2) and (3)
- Column (5) is the backsum of Column (2)
- Column (6) is the backsum of Column (4)

Table 30.1

(1)	(2)	(3)	(4)	(5)	(6)
Range of Claims	Fre-quency	Average Annual Claims	Annual Cost	Accumu-lated Fre-quency	Accumu-lated Annual Cost
$0	0.250000	$0	$ 0.00	1.000000	$3,000.00
$0.01-50.00	0.050000	40	2.00	0.750000	3,000.00
$50.01-150.00	0.100000	100	10.00	0.700000	2,998.00
$4,000.01-5,000.00	0.025000	4,500	112.50	0.150000	2,500.00
$5,000.01-6,000.00	0.020000	5,400	108.00	0.130000	2,387.50
$900,000.01-1,100,000.00	0.000005	1,050,000	5.25	0.000005	10.00

Consider a plan with a $100 deductible, 80%/20% coinsurance to an out-of-pocket limit of $1,100 (including the deductible) and a $1 million calendar year maximum benefit. Thus, the plan covers 0% of the first $100, 80% of the next $5,000, and 100% of the next $996,000. From the claim probability distribution in Table 30.1, the values of the appropriate deductible levels can be developed, as illustrated in Table 30.2 below:

Table 30.2

Deductible	Value of Claims Over Deductible	Value of Deductible
$0	$3,000.00	$0.00
100	2,998.00 − 0.70(100) = 2,928.00	72.00
5,100	2,387.50 − 0.13(5,100) = 1,724.50	1,275.50
1,001,100	10.00 − 0.000005(1,001,100) = 4.99	2,995.01

The estimated claim cost for this plan is calculated as follows:

$$
\begin{aligned}
&(\$72.00) &\times\ &0.00 \\
+\ &(\$1,275.50 - \$72.00) &\times\ &0.80 \\
+\ &(\$2,995.01 - \$1,275.50) &\times\ &1.00 \\
&&=\ &\$2,682.31
\end{aligned}
$$

This method is most useful for pricing comprehensive or major medical coverages, where there is a comprehensive deductible, coinsurance, and an out-of-pocket limit. When member cost sharing varies by detailed type of service, an "actuarial cost model" is useful, as described in the next section.

ACTUARIAL COST MODELS

The actuarial cost model method builds an estimated total claim cost by developing a claim cost for each detailed type of service category. This method is used by many HMOs, and is also useful for PPO, POS, and other plans utilizing copayments. The actuarial cost model method is most useful where there are copayments and limits which apply to specific services, rather than to all services combined.

The actuarial cost model method utilizes a per member per month (PMPM) cost estimate for various medical service categories which collectively reflect all the services covered under the benefit plan. This method projects the annual utilization (or frequency) of services provided and the cost per service for each category.

The gross benefit cost is typically quoted as a PMPM cost, and is calculated as one-twelfth (for a monthly rate) of the product of: (1) the annual frequencies and (2) the average allowed charges per service. The gross benefit cost is then reduced by the value of any plan copayments, to arrive at the net benefit cost PMPM for each type of service. A total net benefit cost PMPM is then derived.

In developing the estimated cost per service targets, applicable provider arrangements should be recognized. For example, if an HMO had a fully capitated arrangement with all network physicians, the net benefit cost would be known in advance, and actual utilization and cost per service would not affect the capitation rate. However, if a capitation rate had a risk sharing element, an estimate of the results of the risk sharing arrangement would have to be developed.

In practice, an HMO might have a fully capitated rate with one group of physicians, a risk sharing arrangement with another, and discount arrangements with others for the same set of services. In this case, the cost model would reflect a weighted average of such arrangements. Additionally, if the HMO had a per diem arrangement with network hospitals, the per diem rate would be used to develop the associated unit costs for inpatient hospital services.

Table 30.3, shown on the following page, illustrates the operation of the cost model method. In this example, the total net benefit cost is $279.30 PMPM, comprised of $87.70 for hospital services, $132.00 for physician services, and $59.60 for ancillary services. In this table, the net benefit cost is developed by major service category: hospital, physician and ancillary services. When applying the cost model method, assumptions and methods must be chosen to be consistent with the plan provisions and contract arrangements, which may vary by service category. For example, a special form of utilization review may apply to a particular benefit. Further, contractual limitations and benefit restrictions may apply, each of which should be reflected in the calculations.

USING COST MODELS TO ESTIMATE
THE IMPACT OF BENEFIT PLAN CHANGES

Many changes in benefit design can be evaluated based on the actuarial cost model described above. For example, the impact of a proposed increase in an office visit or prescription drug copayment can be most precisely predicted in terms of average utilization and average cost per service.

Unless a change in benefit design actually influences the use of resources or the cost of care delivered, the total cost of care is not changed, but simply allocated differently between the insured and the health plan. One basic question that follows is whether costs should be measured with or without member cost sharing. In setting rates, insurers will often measure cost changes net of copayments and other items for which they are not responsible. Unless utilization is affected, however, a change in copayment is really cost shifting, not cost savings. Providers will tend to measure the effect of any change in terms of their total compensation, including carrier payments, copayment revenue, and recoveries from other parties.

Table 30.3 shows the estimated cost impact of increasing prescription drug copayments from $10 to $15. All values shown are illustrative.

Table 30.3

(1)	(2) Annual Utilization per 1,000	(3) Gross Cost per Script	(4) Copay	(5) Net Cost per Script	(6) Gross PMPM (2) × (3) ÷ 12,000	(7) Net PMPM (2) × (5) ÷ 12,000
Before	10,100	$75.00	$10.00	$65.00	$63.13	$54.71
After	9,700	$75.00	$15.00	$60.00	$60.63	$48.50
Difference	(400)	$0.00	$5.00	($5.00)	($2.50)	($6.21)

As can be seen, the $5 increase in the per prescription copay is assumed to decrease gross costs (the total cost of the prescription) by $2.50 PMPM and net costs (the cost to the plan sponsor) by $6.21 PMPM. The change in gross costs is due entirely to assumed changes in utilization, while the net cost savings reflects both utilization changes and cost shifting.

This example includes several simplifying assumptions that are not likely to be precisely satisfied in practice. First, it is implicitly assumed that all prescriptions cost at least $15. Second, it is assumed that the average cost per script remains the same following the change in utilization. Depending on the time available and the degree of precision desired, the simplified pricing shown above could be expanded to reflect these factors.

Some expected utilization changes are fairly obvious while others are more subtle. If the office visit copayment is increased, for instance, it is likely that overall office visit utilization will decrease somewhat, as the increased copayment provides a larger disincentive for members to seek care. What is less obvious is that the cost of prescription drugs might also decrease when the office visit copayment is increased, since the decrease in office visits is likely to lead to a decrease in the number of prescriptions written.

For POS and PPO plans, the net cost of care to an insurer or plan sponsor might seem intuitively lower when care is delivered out-of-network. That is, since members bear responsibility for a greater portion of total costs for out-of-network care, it seems probable that the carrier's or employer's cost would be lower. However, depending on the ability of in-network providers to deliver efficient care, and depending on reimbursement and benefit levels, the net cost to the plan sponsor of in-network services might actually be lower.

The cost impact of changes in benefit design might also be affected by the contractual arrangement in place. For example, if the cost of a certain benefit is covered under a capitation arrangement, a change in the copay for that benefit will not have any rate impact unless the capitation payment can be adjusted accordingly.

31 ESTIMATING CLAIM COSTS FOR DISABILITY BENEFITS

Roy Goldman
John C. Antliff
Daniel D. Skwire

This chapter describes how average expected claim costs can be determined for long and short-term disability income insurance offered on a group basis. This includes net manual premium rates for standard plans covering standard groups. It also includes manual rate adjustments for variations in benefit provisions and underwriting and variations in characteristics of covered groups. Group disability income coverages, benefits, plan provisions, and underwriting are described in other chapters.

Usually several data sources are researched in insurer's own claim experience. If the insurer's own experience data are unavailable or insufficiently reliable or credible, frequently used alternative sources include the following:

- Intercompany experience studies compiled by committees of the Society of Actuaries and published in the *Transactions* and the *Reports.*

- Rate filings made by other insurers in various states, which are public information.

- Basic research through governmental and business publications and discussions with experts in various fields.[1] An increasing amount of information is available on the Internet.

Consulting firms and reinsurers can often be helpful. When sources other than an insurer's own experience are used, appropriate adjustments should be considered to reflect the insurer's underwriting approach and benefit management. Manual rate development can be a good test of an actuary's judgment and creative ability.

---

[1] An example of a government publication relevant to long-term disability claim costs is "Social Security Disability Insurance Program Worker Experience," Actuarial Study No. 118 (June, 2005), Social Security Administration, Office of the Actuary (SSA Pub. No. 11-11543). It includes disability incidence rates and claim termination rates.

LONG-TERM DISABILITY

The determination of expected claim costs or net manual rates for LTD is more complicated than for other group insurance coverages, because it involves the present value of a disabled life annuity as well as a claim incidence rate. The present value of the disabled life annuity depends on factors such as the assumed interest rate, the claim termination rates reflecting claimants' deaths and recoveries, the maximum duration of benefits, and the likelihood and amount of benefit offsets such as Social Security and Workers Compensation benefits. Usually the assumed interest rate and claim termination rates are the same as those used in calculating claim reserves, unless a risk or profit margin is built into these pricing assumptions which differs from the conservatism in the reserving assumptions. The margin in the assumed interest rate and claim termination rates is in addition to any margin built into the claim incidence rates assumed in calculating net premiums and any explicit margin built into the gross premium.

The pricing and reserving interest assumptions should reflect the insurer's investment strategy for assets used to back the reserves—generally investment grade bonds and mortgages with investment durations consistent with liability durations. Increasingly, claims adjudication practices have used negotiations to settle disputed claims and provide other claimants with alternative payment schemes. These practices may impact the expected duration of claims, the reserve assumptions and possibly the reserving interest assumption.

SOURCES OF DATA

Insurer Studies

Studies of an insurer's own LTD claim experience can take the form of loss ratio studies, actual-to-expected (A/E) claim incidence studies, or A/E claim termination rate studies.

Loss ratio studies can be performed in two basic ways. A **calendar year loss ratio study** computes the ratio of incurred claims to earned premium for a given calendar year, where incurred claims are defined as paid claims plus the increase in claim reserves during the year for all claim incurral years combined. This type of loss ratio study bears the closest relation to a company's financial statements, but it may not provide the clearest picture of historical trends, because the results for each calendar year are affected by payments and changes in reserves pertaining to claims that may have been incurred long ago. Calendar year loss ratio studies may also overstate morbidity costs unless the change in reserves is adjusted to remove that portion of the increase attributable to the required interest on reserves.

An **incurral year loss ratio study** addresses these issues by using a different type of calculation. Incurral year loss ratios are computed as incurred claims divided by earned premium for a specific claim incurral year, where incurred claims are defined as the present value of claim payments made to date plus the present value of the current claim reserve, all discounted back to the year of incurral. The earned premium in the denominator is the earned premium for the year of incurral. Incurral year loss ratios, though they do not correspond directly to financial statements, do provide a better historical trend, by attributing the full cost of a claim to the year in which that claim is incurred. Because an incurral year loss ratio is computed using present values, no further interest adjustment is required.

When performing any type of loss ratio study, an insurer should include the reserves for incurred but not reported (IBNR) claims. In the case of an incurral year loss ratio study, it will be necessary to estimate what portion of the total IBNR reserve applies to each incurral year (the largest portion will apply to the most recent incurral year). Failure to include IBNR reserves in a loss ratio study will result in understated values for recent years in which claims have not been fully reported.

A/E claim incidence rate and claim termination rate studies measure a company's actual claim incidence rates or claim termination rates relative to expected rates. The results are often expressed as ratios, where 100% signifies actual experience equal to the expected basis. Expected values are often based on a published table such as the Society of Actuaries 2000 Basic Group Long Term Disability Table (Table 2000) or the 1987 Commissioners Group Disability Table (1987 CGDT), A company with a large block of business may rely on its own historical experience as an expected basis, rather than a published table.

Loss ratio studies and A/E studies can be segmented into many classifications, including age group, gender, elimination period, benefit percentage, type of social security offset, employee contribution percentage, size of group, industry, area, or others. This type of analysis is very useful in identifying experience trends that can be reflected in pricing.

TSA Reports

Last performed for the 1984 Reports, the intercompany LTD studies in the Society's *Reports* series contain annual claim incidence rates per 1,000 by age group, gender and elimination period and ratios of actual to tabular (A/T) incidence rates for many other plan and group characteristics, as well as aggregate-age-gender rates per 1,000, and actual-to-tabular ratios by year of incurral for a number of years. They also contain annual termination rates per 1,000 claims exposed to death or recovery, (by age group, gender, duration of disablement and elimination period), and aggregate-age ratios of actual-to-expected claim terminations by calendar year of disablement (and by duration of disablement).

Expected terminations are based on the 1964 Commissioners Disability Table (1964 CDT), varying by age and duration of disablement. Tabular incidence rates are the crude rates of disablement by age group, gender and elimination period for non-jumbo groups (fewer than 5,000 employees).

There are a number of observations which can be drawn from the 1984 *Reports*,[2] which should be kept in mind, when using this source:

- Table I-6A, in the *1984 Reports*, shows A/T ratios separately for groups containing over 50% salaried and over 50% hourly employees, for thirteen industry categories. This confirms the Table I-5 relationship between salaried and hourly claim ratios in virtually every industry. This indicates that the salaried/hourly split of each group is useful as a pricing factor, in addition to a rating factor based on industry.

  Most LTD insurers have attempted to develop tables of industry rating factors which are based on more refined industry categories than those in Table I-6A (based on the first two digits of the 1972 Standard Industrial Classification codes), although these tables may be based as much on subjective judgment as on actual experience.

- Table I-7 shows that the A/T ratio for employee-pay-all plans is 7% higher than for plans where the employer shares the cost. It also shows an A/T ratio of 102% for employer-pay-all non-contributory plans, which is inconsistent with the intercompany experience in previous reports. This statistic is inconsistent with the experience of two of the leading LTD insurers, who do not participate in the Society studies, who show loss ratios for non-contributory plans that are lower than the loss ratios for contributory plans by more than 10%. This apparently reflects more than the adverse selection which results from less-than-100% enrollments under contributory plans. It may

---

[2] "Report of the Committee on Group Life and Health Insurance: Group Long-Term Disability Insurance," *TSA* 1984 Reports, 243.

also be caused by a greater sense of entitlement on the part of employees who contribute toward the cost of their benefits, as opposed to an interest in cost containment on the part of employers who pay the entire cost. Also, employer-paid benefits are taxable, which lowers the income replacement ratio for the disabled employee.

• There is a disturbing degree of fluctuation in the A/T ratios in many cells of various Tables from one Report to the next, even though successive Reports have four of five experience years in common (1977-81 in 1984 *Reports* versus 1976-80 in 1982 *Reports* for the same insurers), and even if groups of more than 5,000 employees are excluded. Some of the relationships between T/A ratios are illogical, which casts doubt on the reliability of the relationships that seem logical. If the pricing actuary is unable to rationalize relationships in the experience studies, he is well-advised to substitute his best judgment.

• With regard to claim termination rates, the study shows persistent reductions in termination rates from 1962 to 1981. The actual termination rates were much lower than those expected according to the 1964 Commissioners Disability Table, especially in the first year of disablement. This had been recognized for a long time by LTD insurers, who have been using suitable modifications of 1964 CDT for reserving and pricing.

The information contained in the TSA Reports is now quite dated and should therefore be used with caution. Because there are no recent studies with as much detail, however, the information may still have some use in estimating group disability claim costs.

1987 Commissioners Group Disability Table

In December 1987, the National Association of Insurance Commissioners adopted the 1987 Commissioners Group Disability Table, which was published in *TSA* XXXIX as the GLTD Valuation Table (Table E-1).[3] This table is based on group experience, unlike the 1964 CDT, which was previously used for LTD claim reserves.

The 1987 CGDT has the further advantage that its claim incidence and termination rates vary by gender and elimination period, whereas the 1964 CDT did not include incidence rates and its termination rates varied only by age and duration of disablement.

---

[3] Society of Actuaries Committee to Recommend New Disability Tables for Valuation, "Group Long-Term Disability (GLTD) Valuation Tables," *TSA* XXXIX (1987), 393.

The 1987 CGDT claim termination rates are equal to 90% of the termination rates in the basic table (Table D-1), signifying an explicit margin for valuation purposes. Some actuaries may prefer to use the 1987 CGDT termination rates for pricing, in order to have the same claim termination margin in the gross premiums as will be included in reserves (assuming that 1987 CGDT will be used to value future claims).

Appendix G of the report of the Committee to Recommend New Disability Tables for Valuation in *TSA* XXXIX offers suggestions on how to modify the termination rates of the GLTD Tables to recognize differences by occupation of claimant, industry of employer, income replacement ratio or other specific factors (such as union groups or members of other organizations).

SOA 2000 Basic Experience Table

Several intercompany studies were performed by the Society of Actuaries Disability Experience committee during the 1990's to supplement the Reports. One formal table was released for review and testing and was referred to as the Table 1995A. It provided for a longer select period, based on elimination period, and broke total claim termination rates into separate rates for deaths and recoveries. It also incorporated an adjustment for the own occ/any occ transition found in most LTD contracts.

A modified table was considered for recommendation to the NAIC. Subsequent testing of the table on current experience indicated that the overall termination rates were too high, and the modified table was not recommended. Revisions to the table resulted in the most recent version, known as Table 2000. This table remains available, but users are advised to be careful of its application, especially for valuation purposes. With appropriate modifications and sufficient strengthening of termination rates, it may be adequate for GAAP accounting and general pricing.

NET MANUAL PREMIUMS FOR STANDARD PLANS

Once a company has developed morbidity assumptions using the types of studies and reports described in the previous sections, with possible modifications for the company's underwriting and claim practices, it is then possible to compute net manual premium rates. The net monthly premium is calculated as

$$(IncidenceRate) \times \sum_{\substack{Benefit \\ Period}} Benefit_t \times Continuance_t \times InterestDiscount_t.$$

Depending on the sophistication desired, the incidence rate can be separated into various components. Three common components are mental disorders, maternity, and all remaining diagnoses. This is done because the current experience levels of mental disorders and maternity claims did not occur to a similar degree in the experience underlying most claim cost tables. AIDS was formerly a fourth component that had different experience initially, but improvements in treatment have drastically reduced the termination rates of this diagnosis, and the experience of AIDS now closely follows the underlying table. Table I-4 of the *1984 Reports* provides a basis for separating incidence into various components.

Incidence tables useful for pricing can be found in *TSA* XXXIX and in the *1984 Reports*. The tables are somewhat outdated, however, and modifications should be made, at a minimum, for the emergence of the AIDS risk and for generally higher levels of mental disorders. Some companies use an aggregate incidence rate for all causes, while others separate incidence into various components based on cause of disability. Maternity, for example, is often treated as a separate cause of disability from other conditions.

Termination assumptions can be taken from the 1987 CGDT or Table 2000. Once again, some adjustments may be necessary. Maternity costs should reflect a high recovery rate and produce approximately a six week claim (for the 30 day elimination period plans). Improvement in the treatment methods for AIDS and HIV mean that disabilities from those causes generally follow the same claim termination rate patterns as other causes. Some companies assume lower termination rates for claims due to mental disorders – an assumption that is incorporated in Table 2000.

Social Security Offsets

After the elimination period, most LTD benefits are reduced by state disability plans and workers compensation awards during the first six months of disability. After six months, Social Security offsets can be anticipated.

One precise approach to reflecting these offsets in premium calculations would be to calculate the expected Social Security award directly, according to a table of probabilities of Social Security disability awards (varying by age and gender), the formula for primary and family Social Security disability benefits, and the various features of the plan. Those features include the gross benefit percentage, plan minimums and maximums, and the type of Social Security offset (direct offset of family or primary benefits or indirect offset of family benefits via a "backdoor" or "all source" limit, such as 70%, which is higher than the gross benefit percentage).

The Social Security probabilities should represent the chance that an LTD claimant will receive a disability benefit, after exhausting all levels of appeal (see page 193 of *TSA* XLII).[4] The table below shows some illustrative probabilities. For a female, age 30-39, there is a 35% chance a Primary award will be made and a 15% chance a Family award will be made. When pricing Social Security offsets, many carriers also consider the timing of Social Security approvals. Many claimants are denied for Social Security on their first application, and the ultimate approval rates may not be achieved for several years after the claim is initially filed.

The amount of the primary Social Security disability insurance (SSDI) benefit depends on "bend points" which are adjusted for inflation each year. For example, the Primary Insurance Amount (PIA) in 2006 is 90% of first $656 of AIME, plus 32% of next $3,955 plus 15% of AIME in excess of $3,955 where AIME is the Average Indexed Monthly Earnings over the worker's entire career covered by Social Security.

Ages	Primary Benefit		Family Benefit	
	Male	Female	Male	Female
0-29	.35	.30	.15	.10
30-39	.40	.35	.20	.15
40-49	.50	.45	.20	.15
50-54	.60	.60	.20	.10
55-59	.65	.70	.20	.05
60-64	.70	.80	.20	.05
65+	.75	.85	.20	.05

Family SSDI is 150% of the PIA for a claimant with a spouse or child (although the family benefit cannot exceed 85% of AIME), and AIME can be assumed equal to current salary, at least for males. One desirable refinement would be to set the assumed PIA for females at about 90% of the PIA for males, recognizing that historically many females have extended periods of zero or low earnings while raising children. This historical adjustment may make less sense in the future as male and female earnings records converge. Another possible refinement would be to vary the PIA by age, using statistics published by the SSA,[5] recognizing that AIME is not equal to current salary and that it decreases with age (for a given current salary) because older workers have longer earnings records and the upward trend in earnings is generally greater than the indexing in AIME.

---

[4] Goldman, Roy, "Pricing and Underwriting Group Disability Income Coverages," *TSA* XLII (1990), 171.

[5] For example, see 10-25-91 *Federal Register*, Vol. 56, No. 207, pp. 55327-28.

The ratio of the PIA at males ages over 59 to the PIA at male ages under 30 ranges from 97% for a current monthly salary of $1,500 to 83% for a salary of $4,000.

The gross benefit percentage and the type of Social Security offset (and other features of the plan which determine the income replacement ratio) will also affect claim incidence rates and claim termination rates. Such effects are discussed later in the chapter.

CANADIAN INTEGRATION

In Canada and Quebec, integration occurs with disability benefits from the Canadian Pension Plan (CPP) and Quebec Pension Plan (QPP). These benefits are generally available after five months of disability. Both CPP and QPP benefits vary somewhat from Social Security benefits, in amounts and likelihood of receipt. Generally, primary awards under CPP and QPP are less than Social Security, but dependent awards can be larger. Pricing and reserving based on U.S. models should be modified for earlier integration and level of likely awards.

Some insurers provide LTD benefits that are based on an after-tax replacement level. Hence, the level of integration with CPP and QPP benefits may depend on the claimant's expected income tax rate. This can be approximated, based on salary.

ADJUSTMENTS FOR PLAN VARIATIONS

Adjustments of manual rates will be needed for variations from standard plans in benefit provisions and underwriting.

Benefit Percentage

Table I-5A of the 1984 *Reports* shows that claim incidence is lower for 50% gross benefits than for higher benefit percentages. One would expect higher incidence for 66 2/3% and 70% benefits than for 60% benefits (as shown in the 1982 Table I-5A), and claim termination rates which decrease with increasing benefit percentage. Higher income replacement ratios provide greater incentive to claim disability and less incentive to return to work. These effects could be represented by an income replacement factor as a rating multiplier, such as the following:

Gross Benefit	Rating Factor
50%	0.880
60%	1.000
66 2/3%	1.067
70%	1.100

In addition, the savings from Social Security and other offsets become proportionately smaller as benefit amounts increase (since the size of the savings remains unchanged while the gross benefit increases), resulting in higher rating factors for plans with higher benefit percentages.

Maximum Benefit

When the actual maximum benefit issued without evidence of insurability exceeds the underwriting guideline, it would be prudent to charge a higher rate for the excess, on the grounds that higher claim rates will result from the incentives implicit in large benefits, in spite of the favorable high income class of risk.

Minimum Benefit

Rating adjustments are needed for non-standard minimum benefits. Social Security 'freeze' regulations prevent offsetting with Social Security cost of living increases, hence the minimum benefit does not have to consider the leveraging of Social Security offsets.

Elimination Period

The claim incidence and termination rates of 1987 CGDT (or the GLTD Basic Table) afford a reliable basis for varying manual premium rates among 3, 6 and 12 month elimination periods. Some sort of interpolation is appropriate for other elimination periods between 3 and 12 months.

Not many insurers offer LTD with 1 or 2 month elimination periods, and this experience is not readily available. One approach in setting premium rates for 1 or 2 month elimination periods would be to extrapolate from the 3 and 6 month 1987 CGDT tables, relying heavily on short-term disability experience, and recognizing that pregnancy claims are significant for short elimination periods. The 1987 CGDT tables reflect experience prior to 1981 when normal pregnancy was generally excluded from LTD contracts.

Benefit Period

Variations in the benefit period from the traditional benefits to age 65 can be reliably priced by doing routine net premium calculations on the basis of 1987 CGDT. This includes variations in the extension of benefits above 65 to satisfy the Age Discrimination in Employment Act, or to replace age 65 with the Social Security normal retirement age (for persons born after 1937).

Definition of Disability

Theoretically, the 1987 CGDT reflects the "any reasonable occupation" definition of disability. Loadings are needed if this is liberalized to inability to perform the material duties of the claimant's own occupation. One such set of loadings might be as follows, recognizing that the elimination period is included in the "own occupation" period, and assuming that the standard provision is "any reasonable occupation":

Own Occupation Period	Loading
2 years	8%
3 years	11
5 years	14
to age 65	25

It is also important to consider whether the elimination period may be satisfied with total or partial disability. A plan that permits the EP to be satisfied with partial disability is more generous and should have a higher cost.

Social Security Offsets

Rate calculation procedures to recognize Social Security offsets have been described previously. An additional rate adjustment factor is desirable to reflect the effect of various types of Social Security integration on claim incidence and termination rates. For example, Table I-5A of the 1984 *Reports* shows a ratio of primary offset to family offset claim incidence rates equal to 124% (102/82) while Table I-8 shows a ratio of indirect offset to direct offset claim incidence rates equal to 120% (110/92).

Other Offsets

In addition to offsets for Social Security benefits, most LTD plan contain offsets for other sources of income, including state cash sickness plans (in five states and Puerto Rico), workers' compensation, pension benefits, sick pay, and part time work. These offsets are priced with varying degrees of sophistication.

The impact of sick pay and part time work earnings is generally included implicitly, by ensuring that premium rates are consistent with historical experience – unless a company's block of business has unusual characteristics, such as a high proportion of insureds with large amounts of accrued sick leave.

The percentage of LTD claimants receiving Workers' Compensation (WC) income replacement benefits has been increasing and ranges between 3% and 12% for different industries. State-specific rate credits are not generally necessary for WC offsets, because WC is provided for occupational disability in all states with considerable uniformity (such as two-thirds of covered wages or 80% of spendable wages, although there is substantial variation in the maximum benefit). Texas permits an employer to opt-out of coverage so the actuary must consider loading the LTD rates when an employer does not have separate Worker's Compensation benefits. The effect on over-all LTD claim costs is reflected in the insurer's loss ratio studies.

Specific rate credits are generally unnecessary for offsets of retirement benefits under employers' pension and profit sharing plans. Credits for disability benefits under retirement plans are determined on an ad hoc basis, recognizing the specifics of that case. These calculations can be extensive, but it is not practical to standardize them. Approximations are often warranted, although the credits are usually large, ranging from 20% to 60% of the LTD premium otherwise payable.

Specific LTD rate credits are desirable for offsets of the temporary disability benefits mandated by Hawaii, New Jersey, New York, Puerto Rico and Rhode Island if the elimination period is shorter than 6 months, and are competitively necessary for UCD offsets in California if the elimination period is shorter than 12 months. These benefits extend for up to 52 weeks in California, 30 weeks in Rhode Island and 26 weeks in the other three states and Puerto Rico.

Limits on Mental and Nervous Conditions, Alcoholism and Drug Abuse

The incidence of mental and nervous claims has been increasing. Their proportion of total LTD claims is probably 15% to 30% higher than in the 1962-1981 intercompany data from the 1984 *Reports*.

Most LTD plans impose a lifetime limit of 24 months on benefits for disabilities due to mental and nervous conditions when not confined to an institution. Many LTD insurers impose a similar limit on alcoholism and chemical dependency. Some plans subject all of these non-confined disabilities to a single, combined lifetime limit of 24 months.

If an insurer's standard provision is two separate 24-month limits, illustrative rating adjustments for variations regarding non-confined disabilities would be as shown in the table below. All of these loadings and credits should be greater for certain industries where disabilities due to mental and nervous conditions, alcoholism, and drug problems are more prevalent.

Variation	Percentage of Total LTD Cost
No limits	+ 8%
M&N unlimited, A&D 24 months	+ 5
M&N 24 months, A&D unlimited	+ 3
M&N unlimited, A&D excluded	+ 2
M&N 24 months, A&D 24 months	0
Combined 24 month limit	− 1
M&N 24 months, A&D excluded	− 3
M&N excluded, A&D unlimited	− 3
M&N excluded, A&D 24 months	− 6
No coverage	− 6

The purpose of the 1990 Americans with Disabilities Act (ADA) is "to provide a clear and comprehensive mandate for the elimination of discrimination against individuals with disabilities." It specifically addresses insurance and states that "this Act shall not be construed to prohibit or restrict an insurer...from underwriting risks, classifying risks, or administering such risks that are based on or not inconsistent with State law." The Equal Employment Opportunity Council (EEOC) has brought numerous suits against insurers and employers, arguing that the two year limitation for mental nervous benefits violates the ADA. Disability actuaries need to be aware of recent court decisions affecting the two year mental nervous limitation.

Optional Features

Determining the extra premium for a pension supplement is simply a matter of evaluating the amount of additional disability benefit represented by the pension contributions. Each case must be analyzed according to its unique characteristics.

Survivor benefits also must be evaluated to determine the equivalent LTD monthly benefit, which involves probabilities of LTD claimants dying and having eligible dependents.

Cost-of-living adjustment (COLA) riders typically involve rather extensive tables of rate loadings which depend on the terms of the COLA, CPI-related or flat percentage adjustment; the annual limit on recognized changes in the CPI (such as 5%); the cumulative limit on recognized increases in the CPI; and the limit on the number of years of adjustment after disablement. These loading percentages can be determined for various ages, elimination periods and benefit periods.

Catastrophic disability riders that pay benefits if the insured suffers the loss of two or more activities of daily living or experiences a cognitive impairment may be priced using assumptions similar to those used for pricing long-term care insurance.

Underwriting Variations

Many variations in the details of actively-at-work requirements, evidence of insurability (EOI) requirements, and preexisting condition limitations (PEL) are possible, for various group size ranges. We will consider the effect on LTD claim costs of variations in PEL rules. We will assume that evidence of insurability (via short health questionnaires) is required for groups of fewer than 10 employees and for late entrants in all groups and that the employee is not eligible until actively at work for one day on or after the date of normal eligibility.

Preexisting condition limitations are typically described with three numbers, such as 6-6-24. The first 6 indicates that a condition is defined as preexisting if treated during the 6 months prior to the effective date of LTD coverage. The second 6 indicates that the exclusion expires after the employee goes 6 months without treatment for the preexisting condition (or a related condition). The final number, 24, indicates that the exclusion expires after the employee has been insured for 24 months, regardless of treatment.

The following table illustrates rate adjustments for changes in PELs from 6-6-24 for 10 to 24 employees, 3-3-12 for 25 to 99 employees, and no PEL for 100 or more employees.

Number of Employees	6-6-24	3-3-12	No PEL
First Year Adjustment re Original Entrants (non-transfer cases)			
10-24	0%	+ 12%	EOI
25-99	− 8	0	+ 16%
100+	− 8	− 4	0
All Years Adjustment re New Hires (percent of entire premium for all employees)			
10-24	0	+3	EOI
25-29	− 2	0	+ 4
100+	− 2	− 1	0

Requests for liberalized PELs on a case basis should usually be refused, unless the underwriter is persuaded that adverse selection is not an important reason for the request. If an insurer is considering the effect of a change in its standard PEL, the above first year adjustment can be divided by 4 and added to the all years adjustment (which happens to also equal the all years adjustment in this illustration).

EMPLOYEE CONTRIBUTION/PARTICIPATION

The level of pre-tax employee contribution affects the taxability of the LTD benefit. For plans paid with pre-tax dollars, disability benefits are taxable. For plans paid with after-tax dollars, which is often the case with employee-paid plans (called "contributory" or "voluntary" plans), disability benefits are non-taxable. For a plan that pays non-taxable benefits, a 60% benefit may effectively replace 70% or more on an after-tax basis. Likewise, a 66⅔% benefit may provide replacement of over 85% on an after-tax basis, which is why benefit ratios in excess of 60% are written less often and only on select groups. Hence, one rating factor for contributory plans should reflect the level of after-tax replacement: a 60% contributory plan may need to be rated using the loads discussed in the section on Benefit Percentages.

Increased employee awareness is also an argument for loading contributory plans.

Finally, contributory plans should reflect the level of participation by employees in the plan. Presumably, the least healthy employees will be the most likely to participate, resulting in antiselection and requiring a rate load. This load increases as participation decreases. At participation levels below 25%, the load should be replaced by individual underwriting. Alternatively, a voluntary product should be offered, with strict pre-existing limitations and lower benefit levels. The table below illustrates how the level of employer participation can be introduced into the rating of business.

Employee Participation	Rate Factor
90-100%	1.00
80-89	1.07
70-79	1.17
60-69	1.29
50-59	1.44
40-49	1.67
25-39*	2.00

*If participation is lower than 25%, consider re-enrollment or cancellation (unless EOI was obtained from all enrollees). Alternatively, a voluntary product should be offered.

ADJUSTMENTS FOR GROUP CHARACTERISTICS

Age and Gender

The claim incidence and termination rates of 1987 CGDT (or the GLTD Basic Table) afford a reliable basis for varying manual premium rates by age and gender. To the extent that maternity benefits are included on plans with elimination periods less than 90 days, however, adjustments to female claim costs may be necessary.

Occupation

Before considering variations in LTD claim costs by industry, it is desirable to establish rate adjustment factors for broad categories of occupation, such as (a) hourly and salaried employees, (b) blue collar, grey collar, and white collar occupations, (c) union members and non-union employees, and (d) commissioned sales personnel.

The blue-grey-white-collar classification involves many subjective judgments, whereas the hourly-salaried classification is objective and simple in practice.

The analysis of Table I-5 of the 1984 *Reports* shows that the theoretical loading for hourly employees is 114% versus salaried employees. If an insurer is willing to complicate its rating system somewhat, greater accuracy in pricing can be obtained by using both a loading factor for hourly employees and a loading factor for blue collar employees, instead of simply loading hourly employees 114%. For example, the hourly loading could be cut to 65% (times the hourly proportion) and the blue collar loading could be 30% (times the blue collar proportion) where 1.65(1.30) = 2.14. A loading of 15% could be used for borderline occupations (grey collar), and the concept could be expanded to use the same 30% blue collar loading for union members and for employees compensated more than 50% by commissions. The 30% loading would apply to an employee who is in one or more of these three categories. The 65% loading for hourly employees could be further reduced if a portion of the needed loading is built into the industry rating factors. However, the determination of an industry factor for each case will be simplified if none of the hourly loading is built into the industry factors, because then the industry factor for each case will not depend on the hourly percentage of the group.

Industry

Some LTD insurers use occupational rating factors which depend on a detailed classification of occupations, similar to those found in rate manuals of individual disability income insurers. However, for group insurance it seems more appropriate to charge premiums according to the industry of the group, rather than the occupation of the individual, other than very broad categories of occupations suggested above. Often industry rating factors are based more on underwriting judgment than on credible experience.

Pure industry factors are discussed above with the hourly factor completely excluded (and the blue collar-union-commissioned factor also excluded). Likewise, if an earnings factor is used, this will have a theoretical impact on the industry factors. Care must be taken to avoid double-counting.

Average Earnings per Employee

There is a fairly widespread belief that disability rates are better for higher paid workers. Therefore, a sophisticated LTD manual rate structure might also incorporate an adjustment factor based on the average earnings of the group. For example, the following earnings factors might be appropriate (and would be presented as discounts for highly-paid groups, although they would cause the overall level of basic LTD rates to be higher):

Average Monthly Earnings per Employee	Earnings Factor
Less than $1,800	1.00
$1,800-2,199	.98
2,200-2,599	.96
2,600-2,999	.94
3,000-3,499	.92
3,500-3,999	.90
4,000 or more	.88

Not all industries experience more favorable claims with higher average earnings, however. For example, surgeons and stockbrokers (occupations in the medical and financial services industries), while enjoying high income, may have high rates of disability due to the physical requirements, economic uncertainty, or stress associated with their professions. Therefore, insurers should carefully consider how average earnings factors interact with occupation and industry factors.

Area and AIDS

Credible experience by geographical area is not nearly so available for LTD as for medical coverage. However, the few insurers who have sufficient LTD experience for this purpose have apparently concluded that area variations in LTD claim costs are quite significant (perhaps half as significant as the variations in medical claim costs). Insurers who have introduced area factors in their LTD manual rates generally distinguish only between entire states, although there are a few exceptions such as within California.

An insurer who lacks meaningful data on LTD experience by state or region may get some idea of appropriate area adjustments by looking at the rate filings of a few of the leading carriers, which are available from several state insurance departments as a matter of public record.

Some companies use a 5% load in Louisiana and Nebraska because their courts interpret "any reasonable occupation" to be the same as "your own occupation."

Reasons for the very adverse experience of most insurers in California (or at least southern California) seem to include the entitlement culture, litigiousness, and the attitudes of lawyers and judges, including the threat of punitive damages against insurers or plan sponsors. Variations by state or by sales office territory can also be caused by varying quality of field underwriting.

In 1994 AIDS accounts for about 4% to 5% of LTD claims. This incidence rate appears that it may have peaked. AIDS affects all earnings classes. The reserve per $100 of net benefit for an AIDS claimant is lower than for other claimants after disability has lasted for more than six months because of high AIDS mortality. However, AIDS reserves are initially higher than non-AIDS reserves because of low or zero recoveries.

The risk of AIDS does vary significantly by geographic area. The high risk cities include San Francisco, New York, Newark and Washington. In those cities the load might range from 10% to 25% on males at ages 30-39, with lower percentages at ages 20-29 and 40-49, and perhaps no load at ages 50 and above. An alternative approach is to develop area adjustment factors which do not vary by age or gender, and thereby allow the effects of AIDS claims to emerge in the experience by area.

Size of Group

Table I-3 of the 1984 *Reports* show that ratios of actual-to-tabular rates of disablement increase with increasing case size as follows:

Number of Employees	A/T Incidence
Less than 100	88%
100-249	99
250-499	101
500-999	103
1,000 or more	104

The table shows the higher blue collar incidence associated generally with larger cases.

Insurers generally provide volume discounts, based on the size of the group. The volume discount reflects the LTD commission scale (which itself varies by size) and the greater spreading of fixed expenses. The influences of higher incidence may offset volume discounts. However, keeping these two influences separate in the rate structure permits greater accuracy in pricing and facilitates analytical studies.

MISCELLANEOUS FACTORS AFFECTING LTD CLAIM COSTS

Economic Cycle

Increasingly, LTD insurers are becoming aware of the significant impact the economy can have on LTD experience.

Tables I-2 and II-2 of the 1982 *Reports* shows a pronounced rise in rates of disablement in 1976. For example, the A/T ratio for non-jumbo groups with a 6-month elimination period was 105%, compared with 89% in 1971-75 and 99% in 1977-80. This was apparently a reflection of the rise in unemployment during the 1974-75 recession. A similar effect of the 1980 recession is less apparent in the 1984 *Reports*. The 1982 recession failed to have an adverse impact on LTD profits.

The adverse effect of the 1980 and 1982 rises in unemployment may have been offset by the effect of double-digit inflation, which discouraged potential claimants from going on disability and relying on a fixed income (except for the Social Security COLA).

Most insurers have an overall rate adjustment factor used to change all LTD manual rates simultaneously, to reflect changes in overall profitability due to the economic cycle or for other reasons. On the other hand, many insurers recognize that LTD is a volatile risk and try to avoid overreacting to cyclical swings. Surplus accumulated during favorable periods can be used to absorb some increase in claim costs during unfavorable periods. A tightening of underwriting posture in certain regions or industries may be a more flexible response than an increase in manual rates because it can be quickly relaxed when the external picture brightens.

Distribution System

A group insurer's distribution system will affect its LTD claim costs, although not as much as the quality of its home office underwriting and claim administration. Claim costs are usually higher on groups covered under association programs because adverse selection is greater than under single employer cases, unless the underwriting is tight enough to overcome this tendency.

Terrorism Risks

On September 11, 2001, the United States suffered an enormous loss from terrorist attacks on the World Trade Center and the Pentagon. Although property-casualty insurers and life insurers suffered massive losses as the result of these attacks, the impact on disability insurers was much smaller.

It is important, however, for disability insurers to consider the potential impact of catastrophic events in the pricing of their products. An event such as a chemical or biological terrorist attack could result in very significant morbidity with comparatively small mortality, for example. Since 2001, the cost of catastrophe reinsurance, which many companies use to protect themselves from catastrophe risk, has increased significantly and may need to be considered explicitly in the pricing of disability insurance.

It will be increasingly important for disability actuaries to consider concentrations of risk and exposure to potential terrorism in the pricing and reserving of disability costs in the future.

SHORT-TERM DISABILITY

Determination of net manual rates for short-term disability (also called STD, weekly indemnity, and accident and sickness) is not much different from other group life and health insurance coverages, when based on an insurer's studies of its own experience. Unlike LTD, it is not necessary to separately determine rates of disablement (claim incidence rates) and disabled life annuities (claim reserves). An insurer's studies of its own short-term disability experience will generally be based on loss ratio studies. Manual rates can be adjusted periodically, using the incurred loss ratios multiplied by ratios of actual premium to manual premium.

Manual loss ratios may be available separately by STD plan, and perhaps by size of group and industry, but usually not by age or gender. The original determination of net manual rates according to all of these parameters must be based on data from other sources, either from special, detailed studies of the insurer's own experience (if sufficiently credible), or outside sources as discussed below.

SOURCES OF DATA

Due to the high frequency and low severity of STD claims relative to LTD claims, historical STD experience gains statistical credibility much faster than LTD business, and it is possible to make pricing decisions based on much smaller volumes of inforce business for STD than for LTD. Therefore, the best source of data for pricing STD is generally a company's own experience.

There has been little useful information published regarding historical STD experience. If a company has none of its own data available, however, or wishes to supplement its own data with industry statistics, the following sources may be helpful, though less than ideal.

1947-49 Tabular Claims

The tabular claim rates still being used for A/T ratios in the inter company studies (last published in the 1983 *Reports*), were developed in the paper by Morton D. Miller in *TSA* III[6] and summarized in the 1962 *Reports*.

TSA 1983 Reports

The 1983 *Reports* contain the thirty-sixth and final annual report of intercompany experience under group weekly indemnity insurance contracts.

Experience by Industry

The 1980 *Reports* contains exposure and A/T ratios for each of 83 industry classifications, according to the first two digits of the 1972 Standard Industrial Classification codes. This was the last quinquennial report on intercompany STD experience by industry. It combines policy years ending in 1975 through 1979 for all plans, with and without maternity, using 40% of the $3.42 tabular for the six-week maternity benefit. It does, however, separate experience on groups smaller and larger than 1,000 employees.

This is the best available source of STD experience by industry since an insurer's own experience will probably have statistical credibility for few industries, even for the largest insurers.

1985 Commissioners Individual Disability Table A (1985 CIDA)

The 1985 CIDA table was adopted by the NAIC to replace the 1964 Commissioners Disability Table as the basis of active life reserves and

---

[6] Miller, M.D., "Group Weekly Indemnity Continuation Table Study," *TSA* III (1951), 31.

claim reserves for individual policies issued after 1986. The 1985 CIDA tables are published in *TSA* XXXVII.[7]

Despite the fact that individual experience will differ from group STD (and LTD) experience in frequency and duration, the 1985 CIDA tables can be of considerable value in developing rate adjustment factors for group STD (and LTD) – especially by age and occupation class – although not in establishing the overall level of claim costs. 1985 CIDA incidence and termination rates vary among four occupation classes.

In using data from 1985 CIDA for pricing STD, it is critical to note that normal maternity claims, which represent a very high proportion of total STD claim costs, are excluded from 1985 CIDA.

Individual Disability Experience Committee 1990-1999 Study

The Society of Actuaries Individual Disability Experience Committee recently published an intercompany study of individual disability experience from 1990 to 1999. Although there are many important differences between individual and group policies that affect the usefulness of this information in pricing STD benefits (including underwriting methods and offset formulas), the wealth of detailed experience on short benefit period and occupation groupings is of significant interest to STD insurers. As with the 1985 CIDA table, however, it is critical to note that this study excludes claims due to normal maternity.

ADJUSTMENTS TO EXPERIENCE STUDIES

The experience of a group insurer with short term disability (or any other coverage, for that matter) will depend on its marketing strategy, distribution system, field and home office underwriting, and claim administration, as well as the accuracy of its pricing. The STD experience available from the sources described above can be used as guides in developing manual rates, but the overall level of claim costs or net manual rates must be adjusted to the insurer's own actual or anticipated experience.

Adjustments are usually required to graduate or smooth crude data, so that the final rates have reasonable internal relationships. Any significant trends should be recognized, whether unique to the particular insurer or applicable to all STD insurers.

---

[7] "Report of the Committee to Recommend New Disability Tables for Valuation," *TSA* XXVII (1985), 449.

Two specific examples include the treatment of AIDS and maternity claims. The frequency and severity of AIDS claims has changed significantly since the onset of the epidemic, through the development of more modern forms of treatment. Companies should ensure that their pricing assumptions are consistent with current claim patterns. Likewise, many sources of published data have little detail on maternity claims, and companies must be sure that they have made appropriate allowance for maternity costs, which can be quite significant for STD.

STATE MANDATED CASH SICKNESS BENEFITS

The only available data on these plans are probably certain statistical reports published by government agencies, such as a report produced on New York's DBL by the New York State Insurance Department. However, unless there is a major exposure of these coverages, an insurer can probably use its regular STD manual rates for these plans, including adjustments for any unusual features. Some insurers already have accumulated significant data and may be open to requests for assistance.

CREDITORS DISABILITY INSURANCE

Creditors disability insurance is purchased in conjunction with a consumer credit transaction and provides a monthly benefit equal to the required repayment of the debt, while the insured is disabled during the term of coverage.

Credit disability premium calculations are typically much simpler than those for credit life insurance. They are usually single premiums specified in the prima facie rates specified by regulation or law in the state. Prima facie rates are the maximum rates an insurer may charge, unless the insurer can demonstrate a need for higher rates. They are usually promulgated by each state's insurance commissioner in credit insurance regulations. The prima facie rate is intended to produce a loss ratio at least equal to the benchmark loss ratio, which is 50% in most states. The practical result is that most insurers charge the prima facie rates of each state. Therefore, there is not much need for extensive experience data and actuarial ingenuity in devising more accurate pricing.

If creditors and their insurers were more able and willing to reduce their profit margins by competing on price, they would have a greater need of accurate pricing and their actuaries would need claim experience extensive enough to be statistically significant when analyzed according to various parameters, such as type of lender (which involves different characteristics of borrowers). The large disability credit insurers may have sufficient data for this purpose.

32 ESTIMATING DENTAL CLAIM COSTS

Leigh M. Wachenheim

The basic techniques and considerations involved in developing claim costs for dental insurance plans are very similar to those for medical plans. In this chapter, the data sources commonly used as a basis for developing claim costs for dental plans are discussed, as well as the factors that affect claim costs, including characteristics of both the benefit plan and the insureds. Additional considerations related to voluntary plans, plans offered in a multiple option setting, and experience rating are also discussed.

This chapter includes numerical examples, which are based on a typical comprehensive benefit plan, as outlined in Table 32.1.

Table 32.1

A Typical Comprehensive Dental Plan			
Class	**I: Diagnostic and Preventive**	**II: Basic**	**III: Major**
Coinsurance	100%	80%	50%
Covered Benefits	Oral Evaluations Prophylaxis Fluoride Treatments X-Rays Laboratory and Other Diagnostic Tests	Emergency Treatment Space Maintainers Simple Extractions Surgical Extractions Oral Surgery Anesthesia Services Restorations Periodontics Endodontics	Inlays/Onlays/Crowns Dentures and Other Removable Prosthetics Bridges and Other Fixed Prosthetics Denture and Bridge Repair Other Prosthetics
Deductible	$100		
Annual Maximum	$1,500		

While the results discussed in this chapter could be expected to change somewhat with the plan, the general principles they illustrate still apply.

This chapter covers only the development of claim costs – the amounts paid to the dentists and ancillary providers who deliver dental care. In order to turn these claim costs into premium, provision must be added for other costs, such as sales commissions, administration, network access fees, premium taxes, and risk margins, as well as profit.

DATA SOURCES

Estimated claim costs for dental plans are typically developed by analyzing and adjusting experience from some recent past period. If available and credible, a carrier's own historic data may well be the best experience base. This data reflects not only the carrier's particular benefit plans, negotiated fee levels, and population demographics, but also its specific business practices in critical areas such as underwriting, claims adjudication, and utilization management. In addition, a carrier is likely to be aware of any problems or biases in its data.

Sometimes, however, historic experience is not available or is not appropriate for the purpose of developing expected claim costs. For example, a carrier may be planning to enter a new geographical area or market segment, develop an unusual benefit plan, or simply may not believe that its own data is credible. In those cases, there are a number of other data sources that can be used as a supplement or primary source.

Several databases are available which contain fee level information, including:

- Prevailing Health Care Charges System® (PHCS) and MDR Payment System®: These databases contain fee data by CDT procedure code and geographic area. Both of these databases are maintained by Ingenix, a private company.

- National Dental Advisory Service®: This database includes fee percentiles by CDT code and three digit zip code. It is based on surveys of practicing dentists.

- American Dental Association "Survey of Dental Fees": This survey includes mean, modal, and percentile fee levels for close to 200 CDT codes. Data is also provided separately by region.

Detailed utilization data is more difficult to obtain. The Milliman Inc. *Dental Cost Guidelines* includes utilization statistics by CDT code, as well as average charge data. The manual also includes adjustment factors for age and gender, industry, area, and other variables that affect dental claim cost. Other consulting firms may have manuals for a similar purpose.

Another source to consider is the actuarial memoranda and rate filings of other carriers, which are publicly available in some states. These filings can contain fairly detailed information regarding both covered benefits and the rating factors being used to reflect various risk characteristics, such as those discussed in this chapter. While the rates and factors included in these filings may not be appropriate for general use, they can provide a broad overview of how other insurers are reflecting these risk factors in their premium rates.

Finally, insurers may be able to get both charge level and utilization information from third party administrators or reinsurers, particularly where an existing or proposed business relationship exists.

As a general principal, it is important to consider the source and quality of any information before using it to develop claim costs or premium rates. The American Academy of Actuaries has issued an Actuarial Standard of Practice on Data Quality (ASOP No. 23). Although it was written with actuaries in mind, this ASOP provides helpful guidance to anyone who is faced with selecting, analyzing, or relying on data for the purposes of developing claim costs. The ASOP recommends that data be selected with due consideration of:

- the appropriateness of the data for its intended use;
- the reasonableness and comprehensiveness of the data;
- limitations of the data and modifications or assumptions needed to use the data;
- the cost and feasibility of alternatives; and
- the sampling methods used to collect the data.

CLAIM COST FACTORS

The factors that impact claim costs for dental plans can be divided broadly into two categories: (1) those that have to do with the plan, and (2) those that have to do with the covered population (the insureds). Each of these will be discussed below in detail. It is important to keep in mind that the factors that impact dental claim costs do not always operate independently. For example, many carriers use rate manuals that include separate adjustments for group size and participation level, although these are both intended to capture the impact of anti-selection. As another example, trend factors based on billed charge levels may not be appropriate for plans that include negotiated fees. Therefore, when developing or using claim cost adjustment factors, it is necessary to document and understand how they have been adjusted to reflect these relationships.

THE PLAN

Plan characteristics that impact claim cost include covered benefits and cost sharing provisions, the period of coverage, provider reimbursement levels, and care management practices.

COVERED BENEFITS AND COST SHARING PROVISIONS

It is essential to keep in mind the highly discretionary nature of dental services when developing claim costs for these plans. Preventive and basic dental services, which can easily account for one-third to one-half the claim costs of a typical comprehensive dental plan, are entirely elective. Furthermore, there is often a wide range of options available for treating dental disease and disorders, both in terms of cost and timing. For example, the cost of acceptable treatments for a one surface posterior restoration could range from $65 for an amalgam filing to $600 for a crown.[1] For this reason, the cost sharing provisions of dental plans (deductibles, coinsurance, and copays) are significant drivers of claim cost. In particular, coinsurance on Class III services tend to be substantial, with 50% or more of the cost frequently paid by the patient.

In the case of employer plans, it is also important to take into account any interaction with an existing group medical plan, both in terms of cost sharing and covered services. For example, an integrated deductible, where both dental and medical costs can be used to satisfy the deductible, will lessen the impact of the value of the deductible in reducing claim costs from the impact of a stand alone deductible of the same amount. As another example, if certain surgical services, such as the removal of

---

[1] Mayes, Donald S., *Dental Benefits: A Guide to Dental PPOs, HMOs and Other Managed Plans.* International Foundation of Employee Benefit Plans, Inc. (2002)

impacted teeth, are also covered under a medical plan, a reduction in dental claim costs may be warranted. This is particularly the case if patient cost sharing is likely to be less under the medical plan than it is under the dental plan.

Coverage for specific benefits can have a material impact on costs. Examples include coverage of:

- the replacement of teeth missing prior to the plan effective date (often excluded);
- the replacement of existing dentures (often limited to once every 5 to 7 years); and
- sealants for children.

Insureds are usually required to share some of the cost of covered dental services with the insurer through deductibles, coinsurance and copays, and annual and lifetime maximums. Cost sharing provisions have a significant impact on claim cost for at least two reasons: (1) they reduce the cost to the insurer of the services that are provided and (2) they incent the insured to choose less expensive services where possible. Many payers believe that encouraging preventive care is cost effective, because it reduces the need for more expensive restorative services. This reduces claim costs. For this reason, cost sharing is often waived for Class I (preventive and diagnostic) services.

In plans that feature a provider network, cost sharing is frequently lower if a participating provider is used. The claim cost for these plans is usually calculated by estimating the claim costs separately for in- and out-of-network services (on a stand-alone basis), and weighting them together using expected usage for weights. Also, some plans will require more cost sharing if a specialist is used for certain services, although this is relatively uncommon, as it can be difficult to administer and may cause confusion among insureds.

The impact on claim costs of deductibles, coinsurance, and plan maximums on a typical comprehensive plan is discussed below.

Deductibles

Deductibles typically vary between $25 and $100, and may be waived for Class I services. A $0 or $50 deductible might easily increase claim costs for a typical comprehensive plan (such as that outlined in Table 32.1) by 40% and 20%, respectively, from a plan with a $100 deductible. The vast majority of this impact will come from reductions in the cost to the insurer of services that have been provided (rather than from reductions in utilization).

Some employer plans feature a single deductible that applies to both dental and medical expenses (a/k/a an "integrated" plan). In this case, the impact of the deductible on dental expenses is somewhat reduced, as part of the deductible is met by paying medical expenses.

Coinsurance and Copays

The level of coverage for one class of dental services can significantly affect the utilization of other covered classes. In particular, richer benefits for basic restorative dental services are frequently tied to higher utilization of preventive and diagnostic services. For example, utilization of Class I services (diagnostic and preventive) under a 100/100/100 (Class I/II/III) coinsurance plan could easily be 20% higher than utilization of the same services under a 100/80/50 coinsurance plan. This is because patients would be much more likely to visit a dentist to take care of Class II and III work and, as long as they are at the dentist, much more likely to catch up on Class I services.

"Scheduled" plans are also available, which pay a fixed, pre-defined amount for each procedure. In determining the effective coinsurance on these plans, it is important to take into account the ability of providers to "balance bill" patients the difference between billed charges and any negotiated fee level.

Maximum Limits

Annual and lifetime maximums are also common features of dental indemnity style plans, with annual maximums frequently applied to Class I, II, and III services, and lifetime maximums applied to orthodontic services. In some cases, annual maximum limits are applied only to Class II and III services. Annual maximum limits typically vary between $500 and $1,500, which is the range where they have the most impact. For example, increasing the annual maximum on a comprehensive plan from $500 to $1,500 might easily increase expected claim cost by over 40%. However, increasing the maximum from $1,500 to $2,500 or more will have a relatively minor impact – increasing expected claims by less than 5%.

It is important to keep in mind that some expensive dental procedures can be done in stages over a period of years to work around annual maximums. Maximum limits also have a "dampening" impact on trend, as discussed below.

PERIOD OF COVERAGE

Estimating claim costs usually involves projecting changes in cost and utilization levels from some base period into the future period of coverage. Therefore, both the rate of change and the length of time between the experience period and the projection period need to be recognized.

Trends in dental costs have generally been lower than trends in medical costs in recent years. Figure 32.1 shows dental and medical cost trends from 2000 through 2005, according to research by Milliman, Inc. Dental cost trends have been in the range of 4% to 7% annually, while medical trends have been in the range of 7% to 10%.

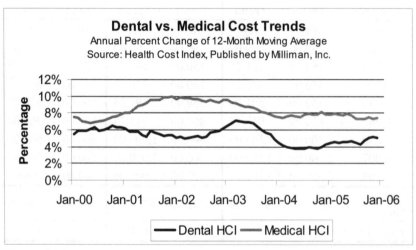

Figure 32.1

The rate of change of claim costs for any specific dental plan will also be a function of many other factors, including changes in negotiated reimbursement levels or the method or data used to determine usual and customary levels, covered benefits or other policy provisions (such as preauthorization requirements), provider networks, and general dental practice.

Dental trend is also impacted by the "leveraging" impact of deductibles, a well-known phenomenon in the world of medical insurance pricing. In the case of dental insurance, it is also important to consider the related "dampening" impact of maximum benefit limits, which are common features of these plans.

For example, consider a comprehensive dental plan with the distribution of insureds by annual claims shown in Table 32.2. Column (a) is the percentage of insureds in each "bucket." Columns (b) and (c) are annual claims for each bucket before and after applying a 7.5% annual trend factor, assuming no limit on benefits. Columns (d) and (e) and columns (f) and (g) show the same experience, with a $1,000 and $500 maximum on annual claims. As the annual maximum decreases, the impact of trend decreases.

Table 32.2

Impact of Annual Maximums on Claim Cost Trend

Percent Insureds	No Maximum		$1,000 Maximum		$500 Maximum	
	Before Trend	After Trend	Before Trend	After Trend	Before Trend	After Trend
(a)	(b)	(c)	(d)	(e)	(f)	(g)
0.400	$0.00	$0.00	$0.00	$0.00	$0.00	$0.00
0.350	150.00	161.25	150.00	161.25	150.00	161.25
0.120	350.00	376.25	350.00	376.25	350.00	376.25
0.030	550.00	591.25	550.00	591.25	500.00	500.00
0.060	850.00	913.75	850.00	913.75	500.00	500.00
0.030	1,400.00	1,505.00	1,000.00	1,000.00	500.00	500.00
0.007	2,000.00	2,150.00	1,000.00	1,000.00	500.00	500.00
0.003	3,500.00	3,762.50	1,000.00	1,000.00	500.00	500.00
Average Claim	$228.50	$245.64	$202.00	$214.15	$159.50	$166.59
Annual Trend		7.5%		6.0%		4.4%

PROVIDER REIMBURSEMENT LEVELS

The methods insurers use to reimburse dentists can be broadly separated into two categories: (1) fee-for-service and (2) capitation. In some cases, a combination of these methods is used to reimburse dentists in a given plan. When analyzing the impact of reimbursement levels on provider incentives, it is important to keep in mind that, for dentists, patient payments for coinsurance and non-covered services is also a critical component of revenue. This is quite different from the medical market, where insurer reimbursement tends to comprise a significant majority of a provider's revenue among commercially insured patients.

Fee-for-Service

Fee-for-service is the traditional and still most commonly used method of reimbursing dentists. The fee-for-service method of reimbursement is appealing due to its simplicity: a dentist performs a service for a covered member and is paid for that service. When fee-for-service reimbursement is used, the dentist is compensated only when services are actually performed. Dental insurers typically use two variations of the fee-for-service reimbursement methodology. These include: (1) UCR/RC and (2) fee schedules and tables of allowance. Each of these is described below.

UCR (Usual, Customary, and Reasonable) or *RC (Reasonable and Customary)*: UCR and RC were the traditional methods used to reimburse dentists and are still very common. Although the definition of UCR can vary somewhat from plan to plan, it typically refers to a fee which is: (1) the provider's usual fee for the service, (2) does not exceed the customary fee in that geographic area, (3) and is reasonable based on the circumstance.[2] Customary fees are frequently defined as the 80th or 90th percentile of fees being charged locally, based on a specified data source – although lower levels, such as the 50th percentile, are sometimes used. This methodology is subject to high inflationary trends as providers have a strong financial incentive to make their usual fees equal to customary fees.

Plans based on UCR reimbursement may also permit the provider to "balance bill" the patient for any excess between his or her fee and UCR. This effectively increases the insured's coinsurance and should be considered when choosing utilization adjustments to expected claim costs based on cost-sharing levels.

Fee Schedules and Tables of Allowance: A fee schedule is a list of covered services and the amounts the plan will pay for each service. Fee schedules are commonly used in network based plans, and the participating dentist is usually required to accept these fees as payment in full. That is, while payment may be split between the insurer and the patient according to the cost sharing provisions of the plan, the dentist is not permitted to "balance bill" the patient for any difference between his or her usual charge and the amount in the fee schedule.

Fee schedules are typically chosen by insurers based on an analysis of the distribution of fee levels in the local community, usually in terms of percentiles. (Percentiles can be used to estimate what percentage of dentists charge at or below a given fee level for a given procedure.) There are a number of data sources available that provide percentiles by CDT procedure code and zip code, including some of those mentioned above.

---

[2] *Fundamentals of Employee Benefit Programs*, Fifth Edition. Employee Benefit Research Institute, (1997)

Historically, large national insurers have used fee schedules that are between 15 and 25% lower than the 50th percentile or the community average.[3] Fee schedules that are too deeply discounted will impair the insurer's ability to attract providers to the network.

When analyzing the impact of fee schedules on claim cost, there are several factors to take into account. First, providers may tend to use the fee schedule to determine the *minimum* amount they will charge for a service, instead of the *maximum* amount they are allowed to charge, as intended by the insurer. Table 32.3 illustrates the impact this might have on claim costs for periodic oral examinations, one of the most common dental procedures and frequently reimbursed by the insurer at 100%.

Table 32.3

Average Charges Under a Fee Schedule Procedure: Periodic Oral Examination (CDT 0120) Fee Schedule Amount: $33 (60th Percentile)			
Percentile	Average Charge	Dentist's Fee Using the Schedule as a	
		Maximum	Minimum
0 - 20	$22	$22	$33
20 - 30	25	25	33
30 - 40	27	27	33
40 - 50	29	29	33
50 - 60	32	32	33
60 - 70	34	33	33
70 - 80	37	33	33
80 - 100	42	33	33
Average		$29	$33

In this example, using the fee schedule as a minimum instead of a maximum increases the average fee paid for services by 14%. The potential impact of this practice on claim costs for a given procedure will depend on the range of fees and the fee level that is chosen for the schedule. In reality, providers are not likely to act uniformly in treating the fee schedule either as a minimum or a maximum and the impact would be somewhere in between. Also, there are insurers who, if they are in a position to do so, choose not share the actual dollar amounts in their fee schedule with the providers, in order to mitigate the tendency to charge the maximum.

---

[3] Mayes, Donald S., *Dental Benefits: A Guide to Dental PPOs, HMOs and Other Managed Plans.* International Foundation of Employee Benefit Plans, Inc. (2002)

Second, many insurers increase their fee schedules only every two to four years. This may result in a few years of constrained charge level trends, followed by a spike when the schedule is modified.

Finally, while fee schedules do control cost levels at the procedural levels, they do nothing to control utilization rates or the intensity of the services provided. In order to meet their own revenue needs, some dentists may attempt to offset the financial impact of fee schedules by providing more services or by substituting a more expensive service for a less expensive service.

A table of allowances is similar to a fee schedule. However, the insured may be required to pay the difference between the dentist's charge and the amount allowed by the plan.

Capitation

Capitation is commonly associated with dental HMO plans. When dentists are reimbursed on a fee-for-service basis, they are paid for services actually performed. However, a dentist reimbursed on a capitated basis is paid a fixed amount per member enrolled with that dentist, or a "per capita" amount, even if no services are performed.

The capitation payment made to the dentist on a periodic basis (usually monthly) is negotiated with the dentist before the coverage period. The calculation of the capitation payment, therefore, is of major importance. If the capitation is set too low, the dentist may lose money and become dissatisfied. If the capitation is set too high, the plan will lose money if it is able to market the plan at all.

The primary components making up the capitation rate per member are:

- the assumed utilization of services by members (the number of times a member will use each service during the covered period), and
- the allowed average payment per service when a procedure is performed.

Table 32.4 illustrates the calculation of a monthly capitation rate to be paid to a participating dentist by a hypothetical dental plan. This dentist will be paid a capitation for diagnostic and preventive services as well as certain simple restorations. All other services will be reimbursed according to a significantly discounted negotiated fee schedule.

Table 32.4

Development of a Per Member Per Month Capitation Rate					
Procedure	Assumed Annual Services per 1,000	Allowed Cost per Service	Gross PMPM Benefit Cost	Coinsurance	Net PMPM Benefit Cost
I. Diagnostic					
A. Oral Exams	700	$28	$1.63		$1.63
B. X-Rays	630	25	1.31		1.31
II. Preventive					
A. Prophylaxis	650	50	2.71		2.71
B. Fluoride	200	20	0.33		0.33
III. Restorations					
A. Amalgam	250	85	1.77	0.35	1.42
B. Resin	220	100	1.83	0.37	1.46
Capitation Per Member Per Month					$8.86

Adjustments may be needed to historic fee-for-service data before it is used to develop capitation rates, as capitated arrangements often lead to reductions in the utilization of certain services and increases in others. For example, the frequency of major restorations might be expected to decrease when dentists are reimbursed on a capitated rather than fee-for-service basis. However, the utilization of other less costly services may be expected to increase, as dentists are incented to use less expensive alternatives where possible.

Providers who accept capitation from insurers may ask for some downside protection, in case the services required by the members assigned to them turns out to be more expensive than was assumed in the capitation rate calculations. Sometimes this protection takes the form of a periodic alternative minimum revenue calculation, based on a significantly discounted fee schedule and the actual mix of services. This type of guarantee may lessen the inherent financial incentives to the provider to avoid more costly services which capitation might otherwise create. These guarantees need to be taken into account when estimating potential variance in claim costs.

A risk margin may also be appropriate in this situation.

Key to making this reimbursement method feasible is assigning a sufficient number of members to the capitated provider (usually 200 or more where the provider is capitated for a comprehensive set of services).[4]

---

[4] Mayes, Donald S., *Dental Benefits: A Guide to Dental PPOs, HMOs and Other Managed Plans.* International Foundation of Employee Benefit Plans, Inc. (2002)

CARE MANAGEMENT

Care management, focused on ensuring that patients receive professionally appropriate treatment at a reasonable cost, has the potential to reduce claim costs significantly. The care management program that will be most effective in any particular plan depends on the methods being used to reimburse dentists. Dentists paid on a fee-for-service basis, have a financial incentive to over-treat their patients – to provide more services or more expensive alternatives than may be strictly needed or reasonable. Dentists paid on a capitated basis may have an incentive to under-treat their patients, since they are paid the same amount by the plan regardless of the number or type of services provided.

Preauthorization

The primary technique used to manage the utilization of dental services in traditional fee-for-service plans is the "preauthorization" or "predetermination" provision. Preauthorization requires insureds to submit a treatment plan to the insurer for review and prior authorization before services are delivered, whenever costs are projected to exceed some specified level, such as $200 - $300.

The impact of preauthorization depends heavily on how the insurance carrier administers the provision. Carriers who actively enforce the provision, and who limit payment for expensive procedures to the cost of less expensive alternatives, will realize the biggest reductions in claim costs. Claim costs for a plan with a preauthorization requirement which is vigorously enforced can be 10 - 20% lower than costs for a plan with no such provision, all other things being equal.

Provider Profiling

Some plans are able to develop and maintain high quality networks, composed of providers who practice "conservative" dentistry, favoring lower cost, but still professionally appropriate options for their patients. As a group, such a network will not only lower claim costs, but will also likely generate lower administrative expenses. Some plans will use a higher level of reimbursement to attract such providers, which would offset the savings associated with conservative practice patterns, to some degree.

Self-Management under Capitation

Dr. Donald Mayes has indicated that a well-designed and administered dental HMO can be expected to cost 15 - 40% less than a fee-for-service plan with comparable benefits.[5] In part, this is because capitated providers may be managing themselves differently than they would under a fee-for-service plan, due to the different financial incentives. Capitated dentists may have more incentive to recommend less expensive treatment where a range of alternatives exist (depending on patient cost-sharing), and they have little incentive to "upcode" or "unbundle" their charges. In addition, Dr. Mayes mentions that, due to the rigor of the provider selection process, dental HMOs may tend to favor dentists who are better business managers, which may also lead to lower costs.

On the downside, capitated dentists may also have more incentive than fee-for-service dentists to under treat their patients, since their reimbursement from the plan does not depend on the number or type of services performed (although this is not true of patient cost sharing payments). Many dental HMOs use quality assurance mechanisms to guard against this problem.

THE INSUREDS

Characteristics of the insureds that impact claim cost include age and gender, geographic area, group size, prior coverage and preannouncement, employee turnover, occupation or income, and participation.

AGE AND GENDER

Dental costs can vary significantly depending on the age and gender of the patient. For example, expensive major restorative services, such as bridges and dentures, are provided to adults much more frequently than to children. For that reason, premium rates are frequently adjusted, at the policy level, to reflect the age and gender composition of the covered insureds. For group plans, particularly large group plans, age and gender information for dependents may not be available, in which case rating factors based on general assumptions may be used.

Table 32.5 shows the relative cost at various ages for males and females, by major service category before cost sharing, for a standard commercial population. The relative cost is a ratio of the average claim costs for each category of people compared to the total insured population.

---

[5] Mayes, Donald S., *Dental Benefits: A Guide to Dental PPOs, HMOs and Other Managed Plans*. International Foundation of Employee Benefit Plans, Inc. (2002)

Table 32.5

Relative Dental Costs by Age and Gender				
Demographic Group	Class			
	I: Diagnostic/ Preventive	II: Basic Dental	III: Major Dental	Total I, II, and III
Younger Male (under 40)	0.859	1.047	0.714	0.898
Older Male (over 40)	0.954	1.092	1.805	1.232
Younger Female (under 40)	1.098	1.153	0.952	1.083
Older Female (over 40)	1.106	1.067	2.105	1.350
Child	0.983	0.835	0.118	0.697
Member Average	1.000	1.000	1.000	1.000

Source: 2005 Milliman, Inc. *Dental Cost Guidelines*

GEOGRAPHIC AREA

The cost of dental services can vary significantly by geographic area. For example, Table 32.6 shows relative charge levels in selected cities, based on typical billed charge levels, assuming a typical mix of dental services in a comprehensive plan.

Table 32.6

Average Billed Charge Levels as a Percent of National Average Charge Levels	
City	Billed Charge Levels as a Percentage of National Average
Fairbanks, AK	145%
Miami, FL	120%
Charlotte, NC	101%
Midland, TX	85%

Source: 2005 Milliman USA *Dental Cost Guidelines*

In addition, different area adjustments may be appropriate for different service categories. For example, a lack of oral surgeons in a particular area may make those services relatively more expensive than basic diagnostic and preventive services in that same area. Therefore, if Class III services (including surgery) are not covered by a plan, an adjustment to the numbers in Table 32.6 may be appropriate.

Finally, many dental plan services today are delivered by providers who have agreed to accept negotiated reimbursement levels. These might also vary dramatically from billed charge levels by area. In those cases, the development of expected claim cost levels should include an analysis of the impact of these agreements, as described above.

GROUP SIZE

As with medical insurance, smaller groups are more likely than larger groups to make benefit decisions based on detailed information regarding the specific needs of their employees. It would not be surprising to see claim costs for very small groups (and individuals) be 30% - 40% higher than claim costs for larger groups (100+ employees), for the same benefit plan.

PRIOR COVERAGE AND PRE-ANNOUNCEMENT

Because of the discretionary nature of most dental services, utilization rates within a group that has not had prior coverage can be expected to be high relative to a group that has had such coverage. Sometimes benefit design is used to control utilization, as described below under voluntary coverage.

The pre-notification period given to employees that they will be enrolled in a dental plan is particularly important where there was not prior coverage, or where benefits are being upgraded. This is because employees who require dental work are more likely to postpone treatment until the plan becomes effective. A significant preannouncement period (7+ months) can easily increase claim costs 10% in the first year over what they would have been with no preannouncement. On the other hand, where there is no (or a short) preannouncement period, claim costs in the second year may be slightly higher than they would be with a longer preannouncement period, as treatment may be postponed.

EMPLOYEE TURNOVER

A corollary to the principle mentioned above is that claim costs among groups with higher turnover can also be expected to be higher than those with lower turnover – since some portion of new employees will not have had prior coverage. Some carriers make an explicit adjustment to premium rates to recognize this.

OCCUPATION OR INCOME

There is a positive correlation between the utilization of dental services and occupation. Entertainers and professionals (such as accountants, writers, doctors, and others) are, as a group, higher than average users of dental services. Semi- or unskilled workers tend to be lower than average users. Another consideration is the benefit awareness level of the group.

For example, some union groups may be better informed than other groups about their coverage and, consequently, more likely to use the plan. Claim costs between groups can easily vary by as much as 50%, depending on occupation, all other things being equal. Some carriers adjust expected claim cost based on income or education instead of (or along with) occupation.

PARTICIPATION

Again due to the highly elective nature of dental work and the significant risk of anti-selection, groups that do not have 100% participation are typically expected to generate higher claim costs than those that do. Appropriate loading factors can vary significantly, depending on the level of participation and options from which the employee is allowed to choose. For example, if employees are required to choose dental coverage on the same contract basis (for example single or family) as their medical coverage, the risk of anti-selection will be reduced.

ADDITIONAL CONSIDERATIONS

VOLUNTARY PLANS

Employers use voluntary group products as a way to provide access to certain insurance benefits. While the employee usually pays the entire premium for these benefits, the group vehicle does offer certain advantages. These include the availability of group rate discounts, the use of group underwriting standards, and pre-tax payroll deduction of premiums.

Since coverage is voluntary and employee paid, voluntary products are subject to significant anti-selection, particularly in the first year or two of coverage. Sometimes carriers use alternative benefit designs to control the impact of this selection. These include tiered coinsurance and maximum benefit structures, which vary by year of coverage as illustrated by example in Table 32.7.

Table 32.7

Tiered Dental Plan			
Plan Year	Coinsurance by Class		Maximum Benefit (All Classes)
	I	II	III	
1	70%	50%	50%	$500
2	90%	65%	50%	$1,000
3	100%	90%	50%	$1,500

Carriers will also use elimination (or waiting) periods, to discourage prospects from enrolling with the intention of having significant dental problems treated in the first year and then dropping coverage. The elimination period is the period between the time a person is enrolled in the plan and the time he or she becomes eligible to receive benefits. For example, a plan may include no elimination period for Class I services, a 3-month elimination period for Class II services, and a 12 month elimination period for Class III services. Orthodontia benefits, if they are offered at all, may be subject to a fairly long elimination period, such as 12 - 24 months.

Other techniques used to control selection in voluntary situations include participation requirements. Frequently, carriers require: (1) a minimum number of employees to be enrolled, typically 5 - 10, but sometimes fewer and (2) a minimum percentage participation level, frequently in the range of 20% - 25%. Additionally, the plans may include restrictive networks or capitation payment arrangements to control costs.

Sometimes voluntary dental benefits are made available on an employer paid basis through a "cafeteria plan." In this case, dental insurance may be offered, along with a number of other options including vision, disability, or life insurance. While selection may be somewhat tempered in this case, since employer dollars are being used, it is still significant to the extent that dental is being chosen instead of other attractive benefits.

MULTIPLE OPTION SETTINGS

Sometimes employers will be offered a choice of more than one dental plan, with differing levels of benefits and/or provider access. Insureds can be counted on to select the plan that is the most advantageous to them – those who are likely to use more dental services will tend to choose a richer plan, while those who are not aware of any exceptional dental needs will tend to choose the leaner plan, especially where there is an difference in required contributions.

Key drivers of selection in a multiple option environment which should be considered when projecting claim costs include:

- Differences in the actuarial value of the benefits. Cost sharing levels on Class II and III benefits and maximum limits are particularly important. Availability of orthodontic benefits in only one plan would also be a key driver;
- The relative cost to the employee of the various plan options; and
- Access to current providers.

Methods used to control selection might include minimum participation levels, "sole carrier" requirements, and underwriting loads.

EXPERIENCE RATING

The experience rating process for dental plans is similar to the process used for medical plans, as described in Chapter 35. However, there are a few differences worth mentioning here.

First, as a general rule, dental insurance experience tends to be much more credible than medical insurance experience at the same group size. (Credibility is a measure of the degree to which a group's own past experience can be relied on as a statistically valid basis for projecting future experience. For most insurers, credibility is primarily a function of group size – the larger the group, the higher the credibility, other things being equal.) This increased credibility is primarily due to the relatively narrow range between the lowest and highest annual claims that might be experienced by any insured under most dental plans.

A major element of credibility is the extent to which random statistical fluctuation causes deviations in experience. This is the element of credibility that is driven by group size. This is illustrated in Figure 32.2, which shows the expected distribution of aggregate claim costs for a group of 500 members around the expected (0.00) level due to random fluctuations. Separate curves are shown for a comprehensive dental plan and a comprehensive medical plan, with the dental curve being much "tighter" than the medical curve.

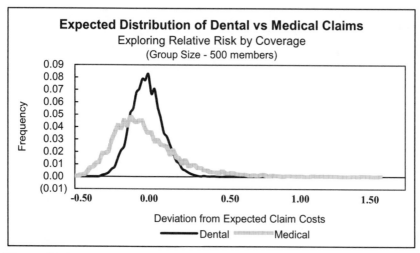

Figure 32.2

Another way of looking at these results is to measure the probability that claims will exceed a given percentage of the expected level, as shown in Table 32.8.

Table 32.8

Probability Aggregate Claims will Exceed Expected Level Comprehensive Coverage - 500 Members		
Aggregate Claims as a Percentage of Expected	Dental	Medical
110%	16%	25%
115%	6%	18%
120%	2%	13%

Even so, there may also be reasons a dental carrier would choose not to rely completely on a group's own experience, even if it is a very large group. For example, due to the elective nature of most dental procedures, even a sizable group may require manual adjustments if they have high turnover or low participation.

Second, an important part of experience rating in the medical arena is the removal of large claims and assignment of pooling charges. Because very large claims are unusual in dental insurance, large claims analysis and pooling is generally not a part of the experience rating process.

33 PRICING GROUP LONG-TERM CARE INSURANCE

Deborah A. Grant
Amy Pahl

INTRODUCTION

This chapter provides an overview of pricing group long-term care (GLTC) insurance. It will serve as an introduction to the issues inherent in the pricing of this product line.

Long-term care is a unique group insurance product for three major reasons. First and foremost, it is entry age (or issue age) rated, and is the only group insurance product provided on this basis. Entry age rating is required by the NAIC LTC model regulation for ages 65 and greater. Even though younger issue ages may be attained age rated, there are virtually no products offered in the United States with attained age rating. It remains to be seen if term rating would make the product more popular at younger ages.

Second, the product is overwhelmingly offered as optional coverage, where employees pay 100% of premium. There are examples of employer paid GLTC, typically with the employer providing the premium for a minimum benefit level with optional upgrades, but America's Health Insurance Plans (AHIP) estimates only about 2% of GLTC plans have employer contributions to premium.

Third, GLTC has a unique set of eligible insureds. It is offered to actively-at-work employees, their spouses, parents, grandparents (including in-laws), and retirees. It is also becoming more common to include adult children and siblings in the family member offering. The ability to offer the coverage to such a broad class of eligibles hinges on the different underwriting protocols used for each subset. In turn, this introduces unique pricing challenges.

These three characteristics make the actuarial issues faced in pricing and managing the product more akin to traditional individual health insurance than group health insurance. However, there are very special issues to consider in the group product line that do not occur in individual, with the most significant being the decreased ability to predict the risk characteristics of the block of business at the time of pricing. Additional issues not present in individual insurance are experience rating, policyholder reporting, and handling reserves when the group changes carrier or the individual changes groups.

This chapter will discuss regulatory issues, policy design features from the point of view of the employer, employee, carrier, and broker, and the resulting pricing asset share model and assumptions. Background on policy types and plan features in group LTC policies are included in another chapter.

REGULATORY ISSUES

The GLTC pricing actuary should thoroughly understand the National Association of Insurance Commissioners' (NAICs) LTC Insurance Model Act and Regulation, and the portions of the Health Insurance Portability and Accountability Act of 1996 (HIPAA) that relate to LTC. In addition, the actuary should understand the current regulatory issues and concerns regarding the GLTC product line.

The most recent federal regulatory advancement includes provisions in the 2005 Deficit Reduction Act (DRA) designed to reduce federal entitlement spending by tightening qualification rules for Medicaid benefits and providing funding to expand LTC partnership programs. Both of these initiatives are expected to encourage personal responsibility by consumers for funding their LTC needs through private insurance.

The DRA revised the eligibility rules for Medicaid benefits by changing qualification rules relating to asset transfers allowed prior to Medicaid benefit eligibility, and excluding individuals with more than $500,000 in home equity from qualifying for Medicaid benefits.

Expansion of the state LTC partnership programs is expected to encourage the purchase of private LTC partnership policies. Under a partnership policy, if a consumer exhausts the benefits in the contract, the amount of assets equal to the benefits paid under the policy are protected against Medicaid "spend-down" rules. Although the initial motivation for these

DRA provisions was to reduce federal government spending, they also provide an incentive for consumers to purchase private LTC insurance.

The most recent state regulatory issue is rate stabilization legislation, coming from the adoption of the revised LTC model regulation in 2000. This model changed the focus of state regulation from ensuring a minimum loss ratio is met to one of ensuring that rate increases will not be necessary.

Subsequent to the 2000 rate stability regulation, the NAIC adopted revisions to the LTC Model Act and Regulation to include new consumer protections. The Model Act includes a new section on required producer training, covering the LTC insurance product as well as information about Partnership programs. The amendments also provide consumers more options when new services or providers become available in the market and greater flexibility to reduce coverage in order to make premiums more affordable.

NAIC LONG -TERM CARE MODEL ACT AND REGULATION

The NAIC Model Regulation and Act provide the legislative basis for LTC insurance. Like most NAIC models, not all states pass the regulation exactly as written. The version of the LTC model regulation adopted in October, 2000, made significant changes to the required actuarial certification made by the LTC pricing actuary at the time of rate filings.

Employer groups do not typically self-fund long-term care insurance benefits. LTC is a classic insurance risk with low frequency and high claim amount, and is therefore not an appropriate coverage for self-funding. Even the Federal Employee's LTC plan, contracted in December 2001 with over 20 million persons eligible for coverage, elected to insure. The model regulation is therefore the governing document for virtually all long-term care policies in the United States.

The Model Act provides the definition of LTC insurance, and applies to all health business sold by any organization. The Act and Regulation cover renewability, policy exclusions, unintentional lapses, minimum benefit standards, and standards for disclosure, reporting, advertising and marketing. They also require that the policyholder be offered compound inflation protection (which, in most states, may be offered to the group policyholder as opposed to each certificate holder) and non-forfeiture benefits.

There are several sections in the Act and Regulation of particular interest when pricing group LTC insurance, which did not change with the adoption of the 2000 Model Act and Regulation. First, the regulation requires that GLTC be issued with a basis for continuation and conversion that preserves the entry age of the individual, and does not require additional underwriting for similar benefits. In combination with the entry age premium structure, the result is that once certificate holders are in a carrier's risk pool, they are expected to remain (unless the group changes carrier). This is an unusual feature in group health insurance, where it is typical for individuals to frequently enter and leave a group.

The model act also defines extraterritorial jurisdiction. In this context, "extraterritoriality" is a state's claim that the coverage of its residents must comply with its requirements, regardless of the requirements of the state in which the group policy is sitused. For those states who adopted the model act, group LTC coverage may not be offered to a resident in a given state under a group policy issued in another state, unless the second state has statutory and regulatory long-term care insurance requirements substantially similar to those adopted by the first. There are many state variations of the requirement in the Model Regulation.

The major changes in the October 2000 LTCI model regulation apply to both individual and group long-term care insurance, and these changes had a significant impact on pricing. The intention is a change in focus away from minimum loss ratio requirements toward rate stability. The regulation requires disclosure of rating practices, requires an actuarial certification at the time of initial rating that rates will be adequate in the event of moderately adverse experience (among additional items), and eliminates minimum loss ratio requirements in the initial rate filing. It also places limits on expense allowances in the event of a rate increase, requires reimbursement of unnecessary rate increases, and provides policyholders the option to escape the effect of rising rate spirals by guaranteeing the right to switch to currently sold insurance without underwriting. The regulation authorizes the commissioner to ban companies that persist in filing inadequate initial premiums from the marketplace for five years.

Disclosure of Rating Practices

Disclosure of rating practices must be made to the applicant at the time of application. The required elements to be disclosed are i) a statement that the policy may be subject to rate increases in the future, ii) an explanation of potential future rate revisions, iii) the premium rates or rate schedules currently effective, iv) a general explanation for applying premiums or rate schedule adjustments, and v) information regarding each premium increase on the policy or similar policy forms over the past ten years. The insurer may add explanatory information, and has the right to exclude from disclosure certain premium rate increases on business acquired from other insurers.

Actuarial Certification at Initial Rate Filing

At the time of the initial rate filing, the prior NAIC standard required an actuarial certification that a minimum 60% loss ratio would be met over the life of the policy. The 2000 Model NAIC regulation is designed so that the need for future rate increases will be minimized, although the commissioner may ask for a demonstration that premiums are reasonable in relation to benefits. The actuary must certify:

- That the initial premium rate schedule is sufficient to cover anticipated costs under moderately adverse experience,

- A statement that policy design and coverage have been reviewed and taken into consideration,

- A statement that the underwriting and claims adjudication processes have been reviewed and taken into consideration, and

- A complete description of the basis for contract reserves that are anticipated to be held under the form, including sufficient detail or a sample calculation, a statement that the assumptions used for reserves contain reasonable margins for adverse experience, a statement that the net valuation premium does not increase, and a statement that the difference between the gross and net valuation premium for renewal years is sufficient to cover expected renewal expenses.

As of 2006, 34 states have approved the 2000 model regulation. This being the case, the pricing actuary is in the difficult position of having to certify to the minimum 60% loss ratio in approximately one-third of the some states, and for others that the rates are sufficient under moderately adverse experience.

The pricing actuary is also challenged to define "moderately adverse" experience. The American Academy of Actuaries completed a Practice Note in May 2003 to provide guidance to a pricing actuary when completing an actuarial certification under moderately adverse experience.

Premium Rate Schedule Increases

The 2000 Model regulation makes a distinction between exceptional rate increases and other increases. Exceptional rate increases are those required due to i) changes in laws or regulations applicable to long-term care coverage, or ii) due to increased and unexpected utilization that affects the majority of insurers of similar products. Examples of other reasons for rate increases that are not "exceptional" would be lower lapses than assumed in pricing, or lower investment income earnings than assumed in pricing.

The requirements for rate increases state that the sum of accumulated value of incurred claims and the present value of future incurred claims (without the inclusion of change in active life reserves) will not be less than the sum of:

(i) the accumulated value of initial earned premium times fifty-eight percent,

(ii) eighty-five percent of the accumulated value for prior premium rate schedule increases on an earned basis,

(iii) the present value of future projected initial earned premiums times fifty-eight percent, and

(iv) eighty-five percent of the present value of future projected premiums not included in iii, on an earned basis.

In the case where both exceptional and other rate increases are present, the amounts in (ii) and (iv) will be seventy percent for the exceptional rate increase amounts. Accumulations and present values are calculated using valuation interest rates specified in the Health Reserves Model Regulation.

**Unnecessary Rate Increases and
Replacement of Coverage in Rate Spirals**

The model regulation includes the requirement that, in the event of revised premium schedules being greater than 200% of the initial rating, lifetime projections must be submitted to the commissioner of insurance every five years. In the event that actual experience does not match projected experience, or that minimum loss ratio requirements are not met following rate increases, the commissioner may require premium rate schedule adjustments or other measures to reduce the difference between projected and actual experience.

In the event that antiselective lapsation is anticipated in a rate filing, or is evidenced by actual experience following rate increases, the commissioner may determine that a rate spiral exists. The insurer may then be required to offer replacement coverage without underwriting.

Groups of 5,000 or more eligible employees where 250 or more are insured, or groups where the employer pays more than 20% of premium are exempted from the requirements of the refund or reduction of unnecessary rate increases, and from the requirement to offer replacement coverage in the event of rate spirals.

HEALTH INSURANCE PORTABILITY AND ACCOUNTABILITY ACT (HIPAA)

The major effects of HIPAA on LTC insurance were to define qualified plans, clarify taxation of premium and benefits, standardize benefit triggers, and allow tax reserves to be calculated on a one year preliminary term basis.

The stated intention of HIPAA is to make health insurance coverage available, portable, and guaranteed renewable for individuals. However, portability and guaranteed renewability were already universal for GLTC insurance. This was because the LTC model regulation requires guaranteed renewability, and also requires conversion or continuation of coverage. Even without the compelling legislation, market forces would seem to require GLTC to be portable.

HIPAA did, however, have a major impact on the LTC market with respect to availability of coverage. HIPAA included: (1) codification of the taxability of benefits, and (2) the benefit triggers of a tax-qualified policy. HIPAA Section 321 settled a longstanding question on the taxability of premium and benefits, by defining that a qualified long-term care insurance contract shall be treated as an accident and health insurance contract. Therefore, premium paid by an employer is not taxable income to the employee. Premium paid by individuals is a qualified medical expense, and is deductible from their income once the 7.5% of income threshold is met. Benefits provided by a qualified LTC policy, as with other medical insurance, are not taxable income.

HIPAA Section 321 also defines the benefit triggers (that is, the insurable event which causes benefits to be paid) of a qualified policy. HIPAA has had the effect of rapidly moving the LTC industry to standardized triggers. Qualified long-term care services are defined as the "necessary diagnostic, preventive, therapeutic, curing, treating, mitigating, and rehabilitative services, and maintenance or personal care services" of a "chronically ill individual" provided "pursuant to a plan of care prescribed by a licensed health care practitioner." A person must be certified by a licensed health care practitioner as

(i) being unable to perform at least 2 activities of daily living (ADL) for a period of at least 90 days,

(ii) having a level of disability similar to that described in (i), or

(iii) requiring substantial supervision to protect such individual from threats to health and safety due to severe cognitive impairment.

Prior to 1996, there was great variation in the benefit triggers in LTC policies.

Another change due to HPAA that has pricing implications is the change of the tax reserve basis. One year preliminary term tax reserves are now allowed for tax qualified LTC policies. Since many states already previously required one-year preliminary term for contract reserves, this creates better timing between contract and tax reserves. This raises the return on investment for LTC insurance from prior levels. Tax reserves are required to be two-year preliminary term for other health insurance products.

NAIC HEALTH INSURANCE RESERVES MODEL ACT AND REGULATION

The NAIC Health Insurance Reserves Model Regulation provides the basis for LTC reserves: claim reserves, premium reserves, and contract reserves. For group or individual long-term care insurance, the mortality table is specified (the 1994 Group Annuity Mortality Table, without projection,, but morbidity tables are not.

The model regulation adopted in July 1998 by the NAIC changed the total termination rates (voluntary lapse plus the mortality table) that may be included in the reserve basis for LTC insurance. The change in the model regulation explicitly recognized that mortality is a significant portion of total termination in LTC insurance, unlike other health coverages, and not being able to include 100% of the mortality assumption at the older ages resulted in reserve redundancy. In 2005 the model regulation was revised to limit voluntary lapse rates to a maximum of 6% in policy year one, 4% policy years two through four and 3% (2% for individual) in policy years five and later.

Another departure from other heath lines is the requirement that the contract reserves be one-year preliminary term. Other health lines, and LTC policies issued prior to December 31, 1991, may use a two-year preliminary term method.

PROFESSIONAL ACTUARIAL ISSUES

LTC pricing actuaries have been criticized in the past for aggressive rating practices that, while technically meeting the requirements of the LTC rate regulations and the applicable Actuarial Standard of Practices (ASOPs), do not meet the spirit of the requirements.

The following ASOPs are most relevant to group LTC pricing:

- ASOP Number 5, Incurred Health and Disability Claims, discusses the data, methods, assumptions, and other aspects of calculating or reviewing health and disability claims;

- ASOP Number 18, Long Term Care Insurance, is a general standard discussing designing, pricing, funding, and calculating liabilities of LTC products; and

- ASOP Number 23, Data Quality, discusses selecting and reviewing data to be used, and disclosures with respect to data limitations.

POLICY DESIGN AND PROVISIONS

Policy design and provisions of a group long-term care offering obviously have major implications on pricing. There are four major stakeholders in the policy design process of GLTC: the employer group (the policyholder), the insurance company (carrier), the employees (certificate holders), and the insurance broker. The concerns and goals of each group should be understood by the pricing actuary.

THE EMPLOYER GROUP

A major pricing assumption is the choice of participation rates expected to be obtained by voluntary employer groups. Enrollment participation of 5-10% is considered good, but may be too low to overcome issues relating to high start-up costs and antiselection.

There are various ways to increase the participation rate, including: (1) underwriting for suitability, and (2) vigorous enrollment, including enrollment of eligible relatives of employees.

The offered benefits should be tied to the cost of services and availability of services in the geographic area. A typical offering has three or four pre-packaged plans with varying levels of benefit period, daily benefit amount, and home health care percentage. Often only one elimination period is offered. Of special importance is the offer of inflation protection. The NAIC model regulation requires that 5% annual inflation protection must be offered to the policyholder, but it is not necessary to make the offer to each individual certificateholder.

Another appeal to employers is that LTC complements other products. It can be seen as an extension of the group's long-term disability coverage, 401k benefits, and life insurance. In contrast to major medical plans, which are perceived as very expensive and are subject to rate increases every year, employers may provide a minimal LTC benefit at low cost and with stable pricing to employees.

The level of underwriting rigor applied to the actively-at-work requirement is a decision for the employer group and the carrier to make together. Employer groups are used to offering all benefits without underwriting, other than an actively at work requirement. However, many people with a diagnosis or condition that is predicted with high certainty to lead to a future LTC claim may be actively-at-work. These high frequency claims must be accounted for in the premium rates, and this may require premium levels that are higher than what healthy employees could obtain in the individual market. Because of this problem, "modified guaranteed issue" is often used, meaning employees must i) be actively at work, ii) not have been ADL dependent in the past one to two years, and iii) not have received any LTC services in the past one to two years. In addition, other questions are often included about specific diagnoses, the use of assistive devices and prescription drug use.

Modified guaranteed issue allows an affordable LTC product for the group, but does exclude some employees, and this may be problematic for employers. This is a difficult issue that must be addressed by the employer group and carrier together. Not all employer groups are willing to give up the benefit of guarantee issue.

Carriers

The concerns of carriers in GLTC include the need to sell both to employers and employees, up-front marketing and distribution costs, and the risk of low enrollment in this voluntary product. A major pricing problem is the level of participation to assume, and therefore the morbidity level to assume. Morbidity can vary significantly by the level of participation. Some carriers can distinguish claim cost patterns that differ by participation groupings, such as $\leq 3\%$, 5% or $\geq 10\%$. Others report similar claim costs for all groups with less than 10% participation. The current practice is to price to the average expected participation rate, and monitor experience to make sure this level is achieved.

The size of the group is also a consideration in the overall morbidity. The group LTC market, like its counterparts of other group health lines of business, consists of many markets of varying group size, from association groups, small groups, to mid-size and to large groups. The premium rate structure may include discounts for group size, but unless discounts are based on commission and expense savings, this is only appropriate to the extent that the premium structure reflects the level of antiselection anticipated, or reflects the underwriting tools and procedures used with groups of different sizes.

Another pricing strategy is to use an individual policy form and its premium rates with group discounts based on commission and expense savings, and expected relative morbidity. This means issuing an individual policy to each employee. This strategy has the advantage of a premium rate structure that allows the matching of appropriate rate levels to the risk. Parents and parents-in-law may be offered spousal discounts along with individual underwriting. This strategy is often not understood by employer groups, however, who may believe the group vehicle to be intrinsically better.

The carrier faces a cash outlay to implement a group case. Costs include integration of the product into the employer's payroll deduction plan, and the enrollment and education of eligible prospects. The carrier must work closely with the employer group to ensure a level of participation that will recover these costs, as discussed above.

EMPLOYEES

For employees, the concerns are two-fold. First, a group insurance offering may be their first introduction to long-term care, and their first awareness of the risk that this insurance is designed to cover. Employees may have aged from providing for young families, where the desired ancillary benefits may be supplemental life insurance and dental, to planning retirement, where the desired benefits are disability insurance and long-term care.

The second major concern is cost. Employees typically pay 100% of LTC premiums, and the premiums may be significant. Issue-age premiums for younger ages may be lower than for individual insurance, due to lower commission and underwriting costs. However, it is a pricing challenge to retain this differential at older ages, due to the fact individual products may be able to offer spousal discounts and preferred rating, and are basing their rates on full underwriting.

BROKERS

Brokers have found that group LTC insurance provides an opportunity to open the door to the competitive life and disability markets with a product that is less familiar. There is then an opportunity to extend the market to parents and grandparents.

EXPERIENCE RATING

As in other types of group health insurance, groups of a certain size may choose to experience rate. To have a high degree of confidence that claims are credible in LTC insurance, groups should probably contain at least 32,000 participants, which, with an expected participation rate of about 10%, implies about 300,000 eligible employees.

Prospective experience rating is fairly unusual in group LTC, since these products are relatively new, and due to the regulatory pressures described earlier.

A hallmark of retrospective experience rating is the employer taking some risk in the outcome of the group. An experience fund may be established to track emerging results.

The actual level of the fund may depend upon emerging claims, expense, lapse, investment and mortality experience, though pricing assumptions may be used for some of these elements. Experience that lowers the fund may necessitate the carrier reaping less profit than expected. Should the fund fall significantly lower than expected levels, the program should be reviewed for possible corrective actions, either administrative (for example, tighter underwriting and care management) or as rate increases. Likewise, better than expected experience allows the carrier to reap greater than expected profits. Some contracts require that a portion of such better than expected experience be returned to the group certificate holders, through improved benefits or lower premiums.

Additionally, many large group contracts include performance standards with respect to underwriting and claims adjudication, account servicing, and data reporting. If performance standards are not met, the experience fund may be assessed penalties, or there may be a one-time premium reduction.

Poor experience and subpar performance compared to standards may cause the group to open the case to a rebidding process. Transfer of groups under such scenarios is discussed in the next section.

GROUP TRANSFER

The possibility of changing carriers is present for both small and large groups. Early group contracts often did not contain terms to cover what happened in the event that group desired to change carriers. The industry quickly learned that transfer issues should be included in the RFP and the group contract. A group may wish to transfer from one carrier to another when the following items fall outside of target performance levels:

- Claim experience,
- Enrollment penetration,
- Return on investment,
- Administrative expenses, or
- Customer service.

Because of potential problems in changing carriers, this action is only taken if the group feels that performance measures can be improved by such a change.

The RFP should address which certificate holders will transfer in the case of carrier change. It may be elected to transfer only new issues, although the employer group may not wish to leave any part of the group behind if administrative or service issues are the reason for the change. The advantages of leaving existing insureds with the original carrier are that the administrative transfer difficulties are avoided, and the existing carrier pays for any past mistakes. Most often, the individuals are given the choice of whether to "stay or go," and this creates antiselection challenges for both old and new carriers. The RFP should also consider the time of the transfer, and the asset segregation for the group.

Upon transfer, the active life reserves (that portion of premium set aside for future claims) or the experience fund (if applicable) should be transferred to the assuming carrier. Problems that may occur with transfer include:

- Difficulties in determining the actual experience of the group,
- Inadequacy of the statutory reserves held, due to inappropriate assumptions or methods,

- Inadequacy of the experience fund, or
- Difficulties in data and record transmission.

An important consideration is that the reserves to be transferred are not necessarily the statutory active life reserves. If the group is large enough, the experience fund is probably the best measure of the amount to transfer. This fund measures premium, less benefits paid less a provision for profits and expenses accumulated to date. Many contracts, especially those for smaller groups, use the statutory active life reserve as the amount to be transferred. The problem with transferring the statutory active life reserves is that these reserves reflect the requirements of the state of domicile of the current carrier, which may not be the requirement of the assuming carrier. In addition, statutory reserving methods vary from company to company, and may not reflect actual experience.

Finally, the RFP should consider how the amount to be transferred relates to the assets supporting the reserves. Should these actual assets or cash be transferred? Do assets need to be liquidated for a cash transfer? Are the assets for the particular group segregated, and if so, may actual securities be transferred, and at what market value?

The RFPs for large groups should consider these issues at the time of initial bidding, to avoid later conflicts. Periodic rebidding may be built into the contract, but generally at not less than five to seven year intervals.

PRICING MODELS

Long-term care pricing is typically based on lifetime asset share projection models. This section provides a general overview of such asset shares, and a discussion of assumption setting for pricing.

The general pricing problem in LTC is to set premium rates that are appropriate for the life of the business. This is typically done through a multi-cell model, where each cell is a projection of future financial results for a representative policy with a given set of rating characteristics (options and demographics). These cell-based results are then composited and averaged, assuming a distribution of options and demographics. Compositing and averaging may result in subsidization of one option or demographic group by another, and if so, introduces a pricing risk if the assumed distribution is not achieved.

ASSET SHARES

An asset share model is used to project the financial income and outgo for a given cell. Assumptions are made in order to build the year-by-year projection, and premium rates are then determined that will result in the required profit criteria, given the income and outgo modeled over the lifetime of the policy. The asset share technique is an important pricing tool because of the steep nature of LTC claim cost slopes, the level premium structure, and the extended length of time a certificate holder is expected to remain in the risk pool.

Because of the low lapse rates that occur with this line of business, and the very steep slope of the claim costs over time, projections must be fairly long. For certificates issued to those in their fifties, projections should be longer than 30 years.

The first pricing step is choosing the model's cells. The asset share model is defined by cells that vary by risk characteristic. Premium is either taken directly from the model, or is interpolated. Enough cells should be modeled in order to capture the different possible relationships between claim costs and premium slopes. In addition to different cells for different benefit plans (such as different home health care benefits, inflationary options and other benefit options), this means creating cells by different sex, issue age, and underwriting method.

The process of selecting model cells is extremely important. Pricing to averages can lead to inappropriate premiums, and then to misleading expected results against which emerging results are measured.

MODEL ASSUMPTIONS

The major assumptions needed to define the pricing model include lapsation, mortality, morbidity, selection, expenses, interest, and the reserve basis for the asset share model.

Lapsation

Voluntary lapse rates are much lower in a block of LTC than with other types of health insurance. This result is logical when the entry age and level premium structure is considered, but was misestimated by the LTC industry when the product was first introduced. Group LTC voluntary lapse rates in duration one may be as high as 10% to 14%, compared to a much lower initial duration rate of 6% to 7% for individual LTC. The group LTC ultimate voluntary lapse experience is slightly higher than individual, running 1.5% to 2.5%, compared to some company's individual rates of .5% to 1.0%. Employer paid groups experience higher lapse rates, as expected, due to employees dropping the coverage when they leave the employer and must begin to pay on their own.

Because of the steep claim cost slope, and entry age rating, the premium rates are very sensitive to changes in lapse assumptions. This is especially true for products with inflation protection. Changing from a typical set of assumptions used in the early to mid 1990's (for illustration, 15% grading to 7.5%), to lapse experience seen in the late 1990's and into the early twenty-first century (6% grading to 3%) requires a significant change in premium, especially at younger ages. The premium change required for issue age 62 is about 10% for non-inflationary products, and about 19% for inflationary products. For a forty-seven year-old, the required increases are 13% and 43%, respectively. The impact is quite dramatic, and illustrates the importance of this assumption. Although many companies were fortunately conservative in setting morbidity assumptions in the early generations, they had difficulty predicting the lapse behavior of purchasers of LTC. The greater impact on inflationary products has led to smaller profit margins on these options. Due to competitive pressures, companies have been reluctant to increase inflationary rates, and subsidization of inflationary benefits by non-inflationary benefits has resulted.

Mortality

At this writing, the 1994 Group Annuitant Mortality table ('94 GAM) is the mortality table required for statutory reserves by the NAIC's Health Insurance Reserves Model Regulation. Because of this, and because of state insurance department expectations, the '94 GAM is often used in pricing. However, this table was chosen because it was expected to be conservative, not because it was demonstrated to be the appropriate mortality model for those who purchase LTC insurance.

Some companies have observed better than '94 GAM mortality on underwritten business in individual lines. For those segments where good individual underwriting is performed, use of selection factors should be considered. Other companies have an easier time measuring total termination rates, and set their voluntary lapse rates equal to the total termination rate with the '94 GAM, or the chosen pricing mortality basis, backed out. However, the risk with this latter method is that if mortality is set too high, the effect is leveraged at the tail.

Morbidity/Claim Costs

Developing appropriate claim costs is a major task for the pricing actuary. Claim costs are developed both from public data and insured data, whether the company's own or obtained through a consultant or reinsurer.

Claim costs can be thought of as the product of: (1) frequency of claim, times (2) length of stay, times (3) the daily benefit amount. Other assumptions needed for home health care claims are the percentage of claims made up of each type of service; the expected number of services used each month, and the expected cost of each service. The usual technique used to create claim cost tables is to measure prevalence of ADL deficiencies and cognitive impairment, measure the continuance and prevalence of care on various care paths, and back into claim frequency from the two. For plans with integrated benefits, that is with a single benefit period or maximum and a single elimination period applicable to multiple types of benefits, transfer from one type of care to another should be considered, in order to avoid overstating claim costs.

Salvage adjustments, or adjustments made to claim costs to account for when the actual expense incurred by claimants is less than the maximum daily benefit per day, are not usually made for nursing home services. It is assumed that most policyholders purchase the appropriate level of daily benefit, or even purchase a lesser amount as a form of coinsurance. It is also assumed that inflation takes care of any overinsurance before the time of claim. However, salvage should be considered in pricing the home health care portion of claims, and in order to price the relativity of daily limits to benefits, versus weekly or monthly limits.

Public data is very beneficial in a young industry where emerging experience is not credible in all model cells. This is particularly true at attained ages over 90 where credible insured experience is not yet available. In using such population data, it must be adjusted for the presence of the Medicaid population, benefit eligibility criteria, and the fact that some discharges are for short returns to home during a period of care that would be considered one claim on a policy. In general, population data includes higher frequencies and shorter stays than insured data. Population data must therefore be modified for expected insured utilization.

Claim costs may be expressed on the basis of total exposure, or non-institutional exposure, and the asset share model may be developed for either exposure basis. Care must be taken, however, when extrapolating claims for use with total exposure. It is tempting for the pricing actuary to use slopes developed to extrapolate claim costs at extreme ages where credible experience is not yet available. However, if the claim costs for use with a total exposure base are built by extending the available curve with no modification to slope, the claim costs could imply 100% institutionalization by insureds in their mid-nineties, which is obviously not a valid outcome.

Choosing claim costs for benefits that will not be used until well into the future is a pricing challenge. This challenge is helped by the continual morbidity improvement that has been observed, both in population and insured data. The difficulty lies in predicting the norm of the medical delivery system that will be providing benefits thirty years or more from when the policy is purchased. This problem is illustrated by the industry's experience with covering assisted living facilities (ALFs). ALFs, which provide supervision and assistance in an independent living setting, were introduced in the 1990's. For some policies, such as stand-alone nursing home, covering ALFs represented a significant increase in claim costs. Policy language may not have addressed ALFs, and, in some cases, companies determined either to cover ALFs extra contractually or that they had no basis to deny coverage. For other policies, such as comprehensive policies, the ALF represented a shift in claim costs, but not a significant increase in total.

There are many important variables that dictate the level of claim costs, or the choice of adjustments to make to claim costs.

Marital Status: LTC claim costs may be differentiated by marital status or by the presence of another potential caregiver (such as by two siblings living together). Marital discounts are common in individual LTC for this reason, and discounts for unrelated persons living together are becoming popular. Marital discounts are not popular in GLTC, but the affect of marital status should be considered when developing composite claim costs.

Gender: Claim costs vary significantly by gender, with females having a much steeper slope, and significantly higher ultimate costs than males. Some of this differential is due to the sociological phenomenon that females are usually younger than their partners, and are more inclined to be caregivers. Females tend to provide care for their older spouses, but do not have a caregiver available to them, due to infirmity or death. Because of the large gender differential in claim costs, it is important to model males and females separately, and composite results to obtain unisex premiums. Note that, with the exception of a few states, unisex premiums are not required by law or regulation; however, virtually all LTC policies are offered with unisex premiums.

Benefit Trigger: Policies with different benefit triggers have different claim cost patterns. A trigger of medical necessity is more difficult to price because of its less objective nature. The standardization of benefit triggers by HIPAA has made the pricing actuary's job easier, as data will be more uniform going forward. Since HIPAA, over 90% of all group and individual LTC insurance policies are issued with the standard tax-qualified trigger.

Area. Utilization patterns of LTC services do vary by geographic area. Of special note is the increased utilization of nursing homes in the upper Midwest, most likely due to the decreased availability of home health care services in more rural and remote areas. Also of note is the increased utilization of home care services in Florida, most likely due to attitudinal differences regarding outside caregivers, and, in some cases, to fraudulent overutilization. Area rating is not common in the individual LTC market, much less the group market. The problem for the group actuary is that it is harder to predict the area distribution of risks. A single large group with specific geographic concentration could skew results from pricing assumptions.

Case Management: LTC case management is a benefit included in many policies, and is provided by a professional care manager. This person coordinates paid care with informal and community based care, in order to maintain the highest level of independence possible for a patient with ADL deficiencies, or cognitive impairment. Because the purpose of the case manager is to help the insured maintain independence, and also because it is very difficult for patients and their families to know and optimize the possible solutions to LTC needs, policyholders tend to be very receptive to the use of care planners and case managers. Companies that incorporate a case manager into the claim adjudication process usually experience lower claim costs. Partially offsetting these lower claim costs; however, is additional expense associated with ongoing case management.

Selection

Selection refers to the adjustments by policy duration made to claim costs tables, for input into the asset share model. Selection is a measurement of underwriting, and the wear-off of initial selection. In LTC, selection might also measure a comparable "marriage wear-off," as the effect of having a companion caregiver changes durationally. The durational changes in claim costs are much longer in LTC insurance than with other health insurance products, and part of this is due to the change in available caregiver status.

Appropriate selection factors can vary significantly due to the level of underwriting performed on the product. Some actuaries feel that there are permanent changes in the ultimate claim costs due to the degree of underwriting, but others feel that morbidity ultimately returns to an average level. It is important for the actuary to have a thorough understanding of the underwriting performed in order to model selection, and the new model regulation requires a certification that underwriting has been considered in determining the premium rates.

The GLTC actuary has an especially difficult time modeling selection relative to the individual actuary. The group LTC actuary may have three distinct underwriting styles used in the development of the risk pool: guaranteed issue or modified guaranteed issue for employees actively at work, short-form or simplified for spouses, and full individual style used for other eligibles. The expected risk pool must be determined at each issue age from a composite of all three styles. While this is simpler at the extreme ages, at the very critical issue ages of about 50 to 65, the mix of applicants must be monitored frequently to make sure the premium rates determined by pricing assumptions match actual emerging experience.

Expenses

As with other coverages, the LTC pricing actuary models the overall expense of issuing and administering the policy, and develops a method to allocate expenses to each pricing cell. Generally, expenses are modeled as the sum of expenses expressed as a percent of premium, per policy year exposed, percent of claims paid or incurred, and per application or policy issued.

A difficulty with LTC insurance is the high start-up expenses relative to other blocks of business. With individual LTC, one component of the high initial expenses is heaped commissions. Group LTC typically has lower and more level commissions, but has higher initial enrollment expenses. The "per enrollee" cost of the significant fixed expense of enrollment is heavily dependent on the participation rate of the group, which is not known at the time of pricing.

Initial underwriting expenses are also part of the high start-up expenses relative to group health lines. The group LTC actuary has the same difficulty with setting underwriting expense assumptions as he does with setting the appropriate selection factors: determining the mix of underwriting styles, and therefore the cost of underwriting, at each issue age.

Interest

Interest is used in three ways in the asset share model. First, it is used to model the investment income on the assets that support the reserves. Because of the large amount of additional reserves held on this line of business, this is a very important assumption. This assumption is usually set as the anticipated new money rate over the anticipated sales life of the policy.

Second, interest is used to choose a discount rate for the present value calculations. Usually the investment income earnings rate is chosen.
Third, an interest rate is used in the statutory reserve calculation, which is, by the current regulation, the interest rate use in the valuation of a whole life policy. During times of extreme interest rates, or in a rapidly changing interest environment, the pricing actuary may need to choose an average rate over the anticipated sales life of the policy.

Reserve Basis

As noted earlier, premium rate filings must include a "complete description of the basis for contract reserves that are anticipated to be held under the form, including sufficient detail or sample calculation, a statement that the assumptions used for reserves contain reasonable margins for adverse experience, a statement that the net valuation premium does not increase, and a statement that the difference between the gross and net valuation premium for renewal years is sufficient to cover expected renewal expenses."

Because a high level of policy reserves is generated at early durations, and the valuation interest rate is typically lower than the investment earnings rate, there are two important considerations. First, the level of margins to include in the reserve basis must be determined, and whether to provide this margin through changes in lapse assumptions, in morbidity (including the level of selection), or in interest rates. Second is the impact, on a present value basis, of the way these margins are included.

Other Assumptions

There are other pricing considerations in LTC that could lead to significantly different rate structures. The average daily benefit chosen by the policyholder can vary greatly by individual and by group, depending upon affordability, and the attitude towards purchasing a lower daily benefit amount as a form of coinsurance. This affects the amount of premium needed to cover fixed policy expenses. Individual LTC often has a significant proportion of insureds paying annually, and the modal load structure needs to be reviewed to avoid dichotomies between the group and individual lines. Marital discounts and tiering by rate class is unusual in group insurance, but common in individual, and may also lead to dichotomies between the group and individual lines.

PROFIT CRITERIA

The asset share model is used to calculate the premium rates needed to achieve the pricing profit criteria. Typically, long-term care rating is based on lifetime goals of pre-tax profits, post-tax profits, or return on investments (ROI), or a criterion that examines all three measures. Some companies also consider GAAP return on equity (ROE) in conjunction with these statutory measures. Loss ratios are not typically used as criteria in pricing, even before the change in model regulation; however, resulting lifetime loss ratio expectations should be examined carefully to make sure regulatory restraints are met, and also as a measure of the degree of relative risk levels between pricing cells.

SUGGESTIONS FOR FURTHER READING

The reader is encouraged to refer to the following materials on long-term care insurance.

NAIC Publications

- The NAIC Long-Term Care Insurance Model Act, October 2000
- The NAIC Long-Term Care Insurance Model Regulation, October 2000
- The NAIC Guidance Manual for Rating Aspects of the Long-Term Care Insurance Model

Actuarial Standards of Practice and Practice Note

- ASOP Number 5, Incurred Health and Disability Claims
- ASOP Number 18, Long Term Care Insurance
- ASOP Number 23, Data Quality
- Practice Note, May 2003, Long-Term Care Insurance Compliance with the NAIC LTCI Model Regulation Relating to Rate Stability

References on Asset Shares

- *Individual Health Insurance*, edited by Francis T. O'Grady, SOA, 1988. This text provides a general overview of asset share calculations.
- *Life Insurance Products and Finance*, David B. Atkinson and James W. Dallas, SOA, 2000. This text provides discussion on cash-flow projections for Life Insurance
- *Actuarial Mathematics*, Bowers et al., SOA, 1997. This text provides the foundation for setting premium and reserves.

Experience Reports

- *1984 - 2001 Long-Term Care Experience Committee's Intercompany Study*, SOA, 2004
- *Long Term Care Insurance Persistency Experience*, LIMRA International and SOA, 2004
- *Long Term Care Insurance Experience Reports*, NAIC, published yearly.

34 CALCULATING GROSS PREMIUMS

Richard S. Wolf
Jay Ripps

GROSS PREMIUM DEVELOPMENT

For any group coverage, gross premium represents the cost of the coverage to the customer. It is composed of estimated claim costs; plus certain expenses, and less investment credits.

Where the coverage is self-insured, or on an administrative services only (ASO) basis, the term "gross premiums" is replaced by "contribution rate" or "premium equivalent."

The rating process begins with the development of claim costs. For purposes of this chapter, we assume that claim costs have already been determined, with appropriate reflection of pooled claims and pooling charges, since these topics have been covered elsewhere in the text. We will concentrate on the other elements of gross premiums. We first discuss pricing assumptions, including expense assumptions and expense allocations. Then the specifics of manual rate development and subsequent adjustments for group specifics are presented.

PRICING ASSUMPTIONS

Gross premiums consist of the expected claim costs, loaded to reflect:

- Administrative expenses,
- Commissions and other sales expenses,
- Premium and other taxes, plus
- Contributions to surplus (which typically reflect the level of risk and the profit expectation for the assumption of that risk),

Less:

• Credit for investment income on assets and cash flow.

Some companies explicitly build up claim costs into gross premiums by adding amounts for each cost element, while others use target loss ratios to develop gross premiums, which are calculated as projected claims divided by target loss ratios. In either method, each cost element must be considered and quantified.

ADMINISTRATIVE EXPENSES

To be viable in the long run, the premium structure for a group insurance product must make adequate provision to cover the expenses of designing, developing, selling, underwriting, and administering the product, including allocations of overhead expenses not directly attributable to the administration of the product (for example, salaries and benefits of executive/corporate staff, or maintenance of information technology infrastructure supporting multiple products). Design and development expenses are generally amortized over a number of years; it is important to quantify and consider such expenses explicitly in developing gross premiums. These expenses vary significantly by product, group size, and from company to company.

Expenses associated with the development and administration of provider networks for medical or dental coverages may be recovered with a network access charge. This type of charge may also be used to recover the expenses associated with utilization management. Some companies account for access fees and/or utilization management expenses as claim costs – reasoning that these expenses reduce claims by more than the amounts of the expenses, resulting in a net reduction in claim costs as compared to claim costs in the absence of such discounts or programs.

As part of the company's strategy and marketing plan, a company may ignore overhead expenses for a new product or market segment, in order to offer introductory products at a lower price. This is called "pricing on the margin," where only expenses associated directly with the new product are included. Usually, the company intends eventually to cover an appropriate portion of overhead expenses, once the new product reaches a sufficient level of membership.

Expenses frequently vary between first year and renewal years. Administrative expenses are higher in the first year due to the time involved in setting up a new group on computer systems and issuing participant ID cards.

Marketing expenses are also higher in the first year with the expense of sales brochures, time spent on the sales activity, and possibly higher first year commissions. As with design and development expenses, a company may choose to amortize first year expenses over a number of years, in order to promote the growth of a new product.

Amortization of design and development expenses, amortization of first year expenses, and pricing on the margin should be used with caution, because they can result in unrealistically low initial premiums that require unsaleable rate increases in later years to maintain the financial viability of the product.

Considerations

In developing the administrative expense component, there are a number of considerations:

- How are expenses allocated to the product? A corporate strategy of equitable overhead allocation is needed, or one product or business segment can inadvertently subsidize the expenses of another, distorting the profitability of both. There are many allocation methods, most of which are combinations of the following:

    o *Activity Based Allocation.* This method allocates expenses according to some measure or estimate of use for the products or functions. For example, a transfer charge approach may be established for mailing expenses-- one that charges the actual postage expense back to a particular function or product.

    For the processing of mail, a transfer charge arrangement may be set up that establishes a processing charge per unit of mail, based on the budgeted expenses and volumes for the mail processing area. In this group, the transfer charge is established at the beginning of the year, and may be updated during the year to keep the charges in line with the expenses.

    o *Functional Expense Allocation.* The functional expense allocation process involves determining how total expenses for an organization are split by major and minor activity categories, by line of business for new and renewal business. The process requires surveying each employee (or category of employees) to determine how time is allocated to the various tasks being performed. This can be done either by recording information about activities as tasks are performed, or by retrospectively estimating how time was spent.

- How should administrative expenses be allocated to groups? Expenses can be expressed in a variety of ways, the primary objective often being to achieve equity among group customers without unduly complicating the process. Sometimes the equity objective is secondary to an overriding strategic objective of the company. Expenses are generally expressed on one or more of the following bases, differentiating between first year and renewal year expenses for each coverage:

  o Percent of premium

  o Percent of claims

  o Per policy

  o Per employee (certificate)

  o Per claim administered

Certain expenses may best be charged separately to the customers who use them, rather than being spread over all customers via the expense allocation formula. Some customers are particularly demanding concerning service and special reporting. If possible, it may be better for overall premium equity if the expenses of these special services are charged separately.

It is generally preferable to charge administrative expenses on a basis that best reflects the activities that generate the expense. For this reason, a basis that combines a number of factors is generally used, since some expenses vary by members or certificates, some by number of groups, some by number or amount of claims, or by other units. Competitive considerations must be reflected in choosing the basis for charging expenses, since the choice may determine the relative competitiveness of rates. The example below is a simple illustration of this consideration.

Contract issuance total expense:	$1,000,000
Number of contracts issued:	1,000
Cost per contract issued:	$1,000 / contract
Premium collected:	$30,000,000
Cost as a percent of premium:	3.3%

If Company A charges the $1,000 per contract and Company B charges the 3.3%, there will be a tendency for company A to attract groups with larger premium. This occurs because the fixed $1,000 per contract diminishes as a percent of premium as the premium per group grows. For example, the $1,000 charge represents five percent of premium for a group with $20,000 in premium, while it represents only one percent of premium for a group with $100,000 in premium.

- What does the competition include as expenses in its pricing? If the competition charges extra for special services or is subsidizing one block with the profits of another, an adjustment may be needed to accommodate the market place.

Sources of Data

In general, the data for determining expense factors could come from either internal or external sources. Internal sources show what is needed to cover company operating costs, and external sources show what the market demands.

Internally, the main data source is a functional cost study that systematically measures how many resources (such as employees or computer systems) are used in to performing each function for various categories of group size, coverage, or line of business.

External sources include (a) studies by industry associations, (b) published expense data from annual statements, (c) competitive feedback (primarily based on competitive quotes or state rate filings), and (d) special surveys. External sources must be interpreted with extreme caution, first because the data itself may not be accurate, and secondly because comparisons with other companies are subject to distortion from differences among companies in defining or accounting for expenses.

Internal sources are generally the company's accounting systems. These systems usually record all expenses of the company by type of expense and by area or function of the company. The types of expenses include expenses for salary, bonuses, benefits, rent, postage, travel, office and computer equipment, and a number of other types of expense. The level of detail to be recorded is typically driven by expense distinctions required for the company's annual statement or tax calculations.

Expenses can be categorized as either direct or overhead expenses. The direct expenses can be attributed to products by a number of expense attributions or allocations.

Once the allocation method is determined, as discussed above, either the accounting system automatically allocates expenses as they accrue to product lines by using time accounting and account codes on payments or expenses, or by doing end of period allocations. In some cases expenses cannot be automatically allocated by the accounting system, and special surveys or reports of time spent, number of policies issues, amount of premium earned etc. must be used to allocate total costs at the end of the accounting period.

COMMISSIONS AND OTHER SALES EXPENSES

Group insurance products are generally marketed by agents or brokers who are compensated on a commission basis. Some carriers use only salaried representatives or use a combination of salaried representatives and brokers. Often there are commissions paid to general agents who are responsible for managing a number of agents. These are known as commission overrides.

Commissions should in some way reflect the value of the services being performed. This value is based on the volume and complexity of work being performed, general payment practices among other companies' brokers, and what customers are willing to pay for the services.

Companies typically pay special bonuses as incentives to salaried representatives or brokers. Bonuses can be based on persistency, volume, types of groups sold, or other measures that align with company marketing goals.

In addition to commissions and salaries paid to sales personnel, other sales expenses may include advertising or promotional expenses, which can be significant. These expenses may include both expenses directly related to the product as well as an allocation of expenses attributable to promotion of the company in general, such as advertising to promote brand name recognition.

Commissions are generally expressed as a percent of premiums, with the percent decreasing with group size. For example, the commission may be a flat percent of total premiums of the group, but with the percent varying by expected group size. Alternatively, commissions may be expressed on a sliding premium scale basis. Some companies pay commissions as a flat dollar amount per member; in this way, commissions do not automatically increase in proportion to health premiums, which may result in excessive commissions over time.

Under either approach, commission rates for large groups will generally not vary between first and renewal years. This is not true in the small group area, where there are sometimes higher first-year commissions and production bonuses. Commission structures may be one of the major reasons that gross premiums vary by group size.

PREMIUM TAXES

Premium taxes vary by state, generally 1% to 3% of premiums. Accordingly, rates for large groups generally reflect the distribution of memberships by state. Alternatively, a simpler treatment for pricing is to set the tax assumption at the average premium tax in the states where the company operates, weighted by the business volume distribution by state. For smaller groups, pricing generally varies by state to reflect each state's tax rates.

OTHER TAXES

Companies are subject to other taxes – notably federal and state income taxes. These taxes are generally levied on the company as a whole and must be allocated to its various products. Allocations may be a common percentage of premiums across all products, or the allocations may reflect the pre-tax operating results of each product or product segment.

RISK AND PROFIT CHARGES

The chosen level of risk and profit charges should, in theory, reflect the degree of risk involved, the amount of company capital allocated to support the coverage, and the return expected on the capital. The degree of risk varies by group size, depending on the benefits provided, the funding vehicle, and the degree of resources required to administer the account. In practice, risk and profit charges reflect not only the appropriate risk considerations but also competitive market prices.

For the smallest groups, coverages are often pooled. The company's risk is largely one of underestimating claims in the pricing of the pool, or in underwriting a specific group. This underpricing can be due to either statistical fluctuations, such as shock or catastrophic claims, or misestimation.

Small group rate and benefit regulations introduce additional risks that premiums may not be sufficient. Risks resulting from new benefit mandates or from regulations that restrict underwriting flexibility may be hard to estimate. Also, rate regulation may restrict rate increases so that premiums cannot be increased sufficiently to cover costs.

For larger groups, which may involve financial arrangements other than full assumption of insurance risk by the carrier, the risk is a combination of underestimating claims and financial risk. If the company carries forward experience deficits for recovery in later years, there is less risk to the carrier than under a fully insured arrangement, but there is a risk of the customer terminating its contract while it is still in a deficit position.

For self-insured accounts, where the insurance company or HMO provides only administrative services there is a risk that administrative fees are not adequate to cover costs. There is also a risk that the customer, although self-insuring, might be unable to meet its financial obligations under the plan. If this occurs, the customer, its employees, or regulators may look to the insurance company or HMO for help.

For jumbo accounts, there is a risk that the company will be unable to reduce its expenses rapidly enough in response to a termination of the account to avoid losses until its expenses are appropriately reduced.

The following table illustrates a possible return-on-surplus approach to setting risk and profit margins:

Coverage	Required Surplus	Required Return on Surplus	Target Risk/ Profit Margin
Small Groups	25% of annual premium	18% before tax	4.5%
Large Groups	12.5% of annual premium	15% before tax	1.875%
ASO	5% of annual premium equivalents	12% before tax	0.6%

Note that risk/profit charges should reflect profit margins built into expense charges, investment income credits, and pooling charges. That is, to the extent that profits may be expected from those sources, additional explicit risk and profit charges may be reduced, such that the total of all expected profit sources equals target margins. With the advent of state risk-based capital (RBC) requirements, companies are using RBC to further evaluate needed return on capital. These analyses typically involve allocations of capital in proportion to RBC requirements by line of business or by subsidiary. Returns are then measured against target returns on RBC requirements.

INVESTMENT EARNINGS

Investment earnings are typically thought of as being earned on assets related to medical claim reserves, other reserves (such as life insurance premium waivers or present value of amounts not yet due on LTD), and on cash flows.

An insurer may provide the customer cash flow advantages under an insured arrangement by such as allowing the customer to hold their own medical claim reserves. If so, the amount of investment earnings available will typically be substantially reduced.

Unless the company uses the investment year method of calculating returns, or otherwise segregates assets by product line, the rate of return credited in the premium formula is generally based on the company's portfolio rate of return, which represents the composite return on the company's general portfolio of investments. The credited interest rate may also take into account the investment strategy, and the character of liabilities involved, especially the type and timing of the liabilities. If either presents significant risk, a margin may be retained by the company as a return for assuming that risk.

Investment earnings can be reflected in pricing (a) as an explicit rate component, (b) as an offset to expenses, or (c) as an offset to the provision for risk or profit. Some companies do not explicitly reflect investment earnings, but rather adjust target loss ratios or profit margins to reflect them.

MANUAL PREMIUM RATES

For a particular coverage, manual premium rates for a whole block of business are often determined as part of the overall rating structure. These are the rates that would be charged in the absence of any credibility being given to past claim experience or health underwriting of the group. Often, these are averaged in some way (as described in the Experience Rating chapter) with a group's own experience to establish the gross premium for a particular group.

RATING CHARACTERISTICS

The manual rate structure reflects all of the major variables affecting cost that the company intends to include in its rate structure. These variables could include plan characteristics, age, gender, geographic adjustments, industry adjustments, group size, period for which the rates are being set, and others.

The average gross premium rate for a product will then be adjusted to reflect various rating characteristics. These rating adjustments are done using rate factors that may have been calculated many years earlier, but which are evaluated regularly to verify that they are still appropriate.

The U.S. federal government restricts the use of gender-based employee contribution rates for groups, other than very small groups. However, the rate charged to the group can be based on a number of rating characteristics. Common rating characteristics include:

- age,
- gender,
- health status,
- rating tiers,
- geographic factors,
- industry codes,
- group size, and
- length of premium period.

Age and gender are used as rating characteristics to reflect differences in morbidity. The gender-based elements of rates can be averaged out of the final rate quote provided to the group, so that even though the quoted rates *depend* on the gender mix, the rate structure quoted to the group does not reflect it.

Rates can also be loaded for specific substandard health conditions. This individual medical underwriting generally occurs in setting premium rates for small groups but does not occur in larger groups, where the rates are more often based on the group's past claim experience.

Another decision in setting rates includes choosing how the dependent rate will be expressed, and how many rating tiers there will be. The common rating tier choices are:

One Tier: Composite

Two Tier: Employee only, family

Three Tier: Employee only, employee and one dependent, family

Four Tier: Employee only, employee with one dependent, employee with children, family

Five Tier: Employee only, couple, employee with child, employee with children, family

Geographic location is an important consideration since claim costs can vary considerably by geographic location, expenses tied to claim costs may result in overstated expenses in high cost areas and understated in low cost areas. Regulatory factors and risks mentioned earlier vary by state, and may be built into geographic factors.

The group's industry type (commonly designated by SIC code) can be an element of setting premium rates, since significant variation is found in the medical costs between different industries.

Since expenses and risk charges vary significantly by group size, group size is a common rating characteristic.

Most group premium rates are set on a one-year term basis, so that claim costs, expenses, taxes, commissions, investment income, and any other premium elements, must be projected for the next year only (typically, this involves projections 15-18 months beyond the period of the data on which they rely, since rates must be set well in advance of the date they become effective). Rates for some coverages, however, are established for more than one year – generally as a level premium over a number of years. This category includes long-term care insurance and some forms of group life insurance. Premium rates for periods larger than one year require projections over a longer time period; therefore, they involve greater risk and require greater risk charges. Investment income assumptions and persistency assumptions are typically more important elements in setting multi-year rates than in setting one-year term rates.

MARKETING, COMPETITIVE, AND REGULATORY ISSUES

Typically, manual rates are ultimately adjusted for competitive and market strategy considerations. Manual rates are often determined separately for different group size categories and different products. There needs to be a rational relationship between these categories. For example if the small group division of an insurer rates groups from groups size 11-100, and the large group division rates groups from size 100+, the rates for comparable products for a group size 95 and for a group size 105 should not differ significantly.

Differences in premium rates between products should generally reflect differences in expected costs (their "actuarial value") although for strategic, competitive or selection reasons premium rates may deviate from strict actuarial equivalence. Each company must match its financial plan and market strategy with the competitive forces to determine where it wants its gross premiums to be relative to the competition.

Also, state or provincial group insurance laws restrict how rates can vary due to differences in rating characteristics, as well as by how much rates can increase from year to year. This is discussed in more detail elsewhere in Section 3.

GROUP SPECIFIC ADJUSTMENTS

Manual rates are often used as a reference point for a particular group. The premium rates for a group may be expressed as a percentage of the manual rates (such as "manual + 10%," or "manual − 5%.") The determination of the appropriate percentage of manual rates involves determining the ratio of expected claim and other costs for the particular group to the comparable costs expected under manual rates.

Premium rates for large groups are based entirely on the group's own experience. For other groups whose rates are based on manual rates, adjustments are made to manual rates for new business discounts and credible prior claim experience.

New business discounts are sometimes used to encourage a group to change carriers. Discounts are often justified based on lower claim expectations due to the effect of group underwriting or other reasons. Such discounts should be supported by analysis of claim experience by duration. Caution must be used in the level of first-year discounts, since renewal rates will then have to be increased for trend plus the discount, which may result in upset customers and the loss of the group in the second year. This practice may be limited by group rating restrictions in some states.

A group's past or estimated claim experience can be used in adjusting manual rates. The larger the group, the more consideration is given to the past claim history of the group. A thorough discussion of this process can be found in the chapter on experience rating.

Expected claims for a group may represent a blend of actual claims based on that group's prior claim experience with the claim component of manual premiums. The blending process may involve use of pooling, with the level of pooling being a function of the coverage and the spread of risk involved. This depends on the coverages, risks involved, and the insurer's overall risk strategy. This topic is discussed further in the chapter on experience rating.

For jumbo groups, there may be strong pressure to reduce rates as much as possible to make a sale. Such groups may sometimes be perceived to offer a measure of prestige that provides a marketing advantage. Additionally, they may increase a company's negotiating power with providers, which could lead to larger provider discounts. There may also be significant economies of scale with jumbo groups in enrollment, billing, and general administration. On the other hand, these groups can demand a lot of special attention. They often work through consultants who require special reporting, and may even suggest dedicated claim processors or other special services. It is important to quantify as much as possible the net effect of these considerations in setting premium rates.

For self-insured groups, contribution rates are determined in a similar fashion, but loadings are based on the cost of administrative services and stop-loss insurance provided by the carrier.

MONITORING OF EXPERIENCE

As discussed in this chapter, gross premiums are based on a wide range of assumptions regarding claim costs, expenses, taxes, sales expenses, and investment income. Actual experience will never conform precisely to these assumptions; therefore, an essential element of pricing is to develop and implement systems and procedures to monitor actual experience in a manner that allows for ready comparison of actual experience to pricing assumptions, so that pricing assumptions can be appropriately modified in light of emerging experience.

35 EXPERIENCE RATING AND FUNDING METHODS

William F. Bluhm

Experience rating is the process whereby a policyholder is given the financial benefit of, or held financially accountable for, its past claim experience in insurance rating calculations.

Prospective rate calculations are the evaluation of probable experience for a future rating period, leading to gross premium rates to be charged. The coverage period is most often (but by no means always) an upcoming policy year. In the absence of experience rating, rates are based on manual rates or community rates, which are prospective rates based on the demographic or other underwriting characteristics of the group, but not on its specific claim experience. Community rates are often defined to limit the demographic factors being recognized. When manual rates are based on the combined experience of a pool of similar policies, they are called pooled rates.

Retrospective rate calculations are the evaluation and measurement of financial experience for a past period of time, for use in determining the cost of providing insurance for that period to the policyholder. This is necessary because of special rating arrangements where a policyholder is held, at least in a limited way, financially responsible for that cost, rather than for the prospective cost only.

In this chapter the use of experience rating methods and formulas, and their interrelationship with the rating of group policies, will be addressed. The use of human judgment in setting a rate for a particular policy, more properly addressed under the subject of underwriting, is beyond the scope of this chapter.

This chapter has four major sections. This first section is introductory. The second section describes prospective experience rating, the third describes retrospective experience rating, and the last section describes alternative funding methods in use today. These practices are often combined with one another, but often are not. The reader should keep in mind that these different practices serve different purposes in group insurance, despite their frequent use of similar theory and techniques.

INTRODUCTION

REASONS FOR EXPERIENCE RATING

There are a number of reasons for the use of experience rating. Group policyholders often prefer to pay a premium based on the unique experience of their own group, rather than having their experience pooled with other groups.

Pooling of experience is, in a sense, the opposite of experience rating – a number of groups' experience is averaged together for rating purposes into an experience pool. Some groups in a pool will have higher than average claims, so that if their premium rate were based solely on their own experience, they would have higher than average claims, so that if their premium rate were based solely on their own experience, they would have to pay a higher than average premium. By averaging their experience with that of other groups, their premium will be closer to the average. This then means that groups with lower than average claims will have to pay premiums higher than that dictated by their experience, which they may view as a subsidization of the groups with higher claims.

The insurer, on the other hand, would generally like to quote and charge premiums which are as competitive (low) as possible, while still meeting profit objectives. If a group requests a quote for insurance from the insurer, and if the insurer believes the group truly to have lower than average claim expectations, the insurer would prefer to base its quote on that group's characteristics, rather than on an average claim expectation. Obviously, however, the insurer cannot charge the lower than average claim group a lower than average premium without offsetting this by charging the higher claim groups a higher premium.

The insurer may not want to credit a group with its good experience where this is not theoretically justified, since this would require the parallel crediting of unjustified bad experience to other groups. Competitive pressures, however, may cause this to happen, despite the theoretical justification.

The setting of the level at which past claim experience is considered statistically credible usually involves a balance between theoretical and practical considerations.

Theoretical: In developing theoretical models of group claims, one common assumption in the past has been the stochastic independence of the claims of each individual in the group, from one year to the next. This means that the existence and size of a claim in a given period (such as an upcoming policy year) is independent of the claims which occurred in a prior period. This may be more or less true for some coverages, such as non-occupational accidental death. It is definitely not always true with others, such as medical expense coverages. For this reason, many of the theoretical models used in the past to develop credibility levels may understate the relevance of past experience. This fact at least partially justifies the competitively-based experience rating formulas which have commonly been in use for many years.

The extent to which a group's experience in a year depends on its experience in prior years can be measured by the statistical measure called *autocorrelation*. The above assumption of temporal independence is equivalent to an assumption of zero autocorrelation.

Rigorous development of credibility factors today requires recognition of non-zero auto correlation[1].

Practical: Let us examine the competitive pressures which an insurer might feel in setting the credibility levels which it will use in its experience rating formulas.

If an insurer erroneously pools the experience of groups which actually have their own statistically valid experience, then groups with higher than average claim expectations will be subsidized by groups with lower than average claim expectations. If the carrier's competitors are not making the same error, they will be validly quoting lower premiums on the low-claim groups, inducing those groups to migrate away from the insurer's pool. The high-claim groups will be left behind in the pool, where they will no longer have the low-claim groups to subsidize them, causing the average claims in the pool to rise. This antiselection is an important reason why an insurer cannot afford to pool credible groups.

---

[1] Fuher, Charles S., "Some Applications of Credibility Theory to Group Insurance." *Transactions*, Society of Actuaries, Volume XL, 1988.

There have been instances described where a policyholder will believe their experience to be credible where it is not, and will then move the coverage to a basis where its costs are based on actual claims, such as a self-insured plan. Unfortunately, when the occasional large claim does occur, the policyholder suddenly understands the value of pooling.

APPLICABILITY – COVERAGES AND GROUP SIZES

Experience rating can be applied to any coverage where there is reason to believe that future claim experience will be reliably altered from the otherwise expected level by past claim experience. In group insurance, this is usually applied where the individuals belonging to a group, where the size of that group is larger than some chosen level, are believed to have characteristics which make that group have reliable claim expectations which might differ from the average represented by manual rates. (These characteristics might be demographic characteristics, lifestyle, employee turnover rates, average income, industry, or many others. However, since the question of *why* a group's experience is credible is usually fairly immaterial, what truly matters is *whether* it is credible, and *how credible* it is.)

The minimum size chosen for experience rating is an expression of the minimum credibility which an insurer chooses to recognize, whether for theoretical or practical reasons.

Some of the theoretical considerations entering into the choice of credibility levels for experience rating are the following:

- Coverages with low frequency of claim are more volatile, and will require a larger exposure base for a given credibility level than coverages with a high frequency of claim.

- Coverages with widely varying claim sizes will tend to be more volatile.

- The statistical confidence interval chosen by the insurer, whether explicitly or implicitly, and whether knowingly or unknowingly. (A confidence interval can be thought of as the level of credibility where you can be $X\%$ sure that the claim level will fall within $Y\%$ of the observed value. When explicitly set, X is often chosen to be 90 or 95.)

- The portion of experience due to statistical fluctuation has historically been treated as varying inversely to the square root of the number of claims or exposed lives. In nontechnical terms, this could be interpreted as saying that it will take four times the exposure to double the credibility.

- The typical measure of credibility is the number of lives covered. Coverages with stochastically independent claims, however, can increase credibility by using longer experience periods, rather than simply more lives. The measure then becomes the number life-years, rather than lives.

These theoretical considerations must be examined in the light of practical considerations, including the following:

- Competitive pressures.
- Administrative and managerial units within the company, and their ability to cope with experience rating.
- The trade-off between the added cost of applying experience rating and the potential added gains in the volume and quality of new business.
- The effect on any existing business of a change in the credibility level.
- Management philosophy regarding experience rating.
- The need for internal self-consistency between classes of business.

These factors must be synthesized by the group insurer into a unified approach to experience rating, both prospective and retrospective – one which reflects an understanding of both theoretical and practical considerations.

PROSPECTIVE EXPERIENCE RATING

The setting of prospective premium rates for individual groups, based on each group's own experience, can be considered a part of the underwriting process – the process of evaluating and quantifying the risk associated with particular cases. The pricing actuary's most valuable tool for this purpose in the prospective rating arsenal is the evaluation of past experience of the group. This evaluation of past experience for prospective rating will generally take place regardless of whether retrospective experience rating will apply, and regardless of the funding method.

The estimation of future claim costs based on the nature of specific past claims of individuals is more of an underwriting function than an experience rating one, and is beyond the scope of this paper. (Interestingly, the existence of this underwriting function is a demonstration of the lack of stochastic independence of claims from one time period to the next.) Rather, this chapter is concerned with the analysis of group claims from a statistical and algebraic point of view. Underwriting plays a critical role in the rating process, however, and should be considered along with experience rating concerns in any company's or plan sponsor's management decisions.

DEVELOPMENT OF CLAIM EXPERIENCE

The starting point for prospective experience rating is the past claim experience for the group. For the claim experience to be useful and appropriate, there are certain adjustments and calculations which must be made.

Most claim data starts with the dollar amount of claims paid over the experience year. As an example, let us consider the experience year for a sample group contract to be $1/1/Z$ through $12/31/Z$. Our paid data would then be all claims paid in this period.

Since the purpose of our analysis is to evaluate the contractual claim liability during the experience period, we would like to derive claim figures which express that liability. Since some of the claims paid in year Z were actually incurred in Z minus 1 or earlier, and since some of the claims incurred in Z have not yet been paid as of $12/31/Z$ (or perhaps even reported yet), it is necessary to make an adjustment in the paid claims figure to remove claims paid in Z but incurred prior to Z, and to include an estimate for claims incurred in Z but not yet paid. This process of adjustment results in the figure incurred claims, which represents (at least theoretically) all claim payments, regardless of when paid, which became liabilities during the experience period.

Since premium rates must, as a practical matter, be known in advance of the policy anniversary, it follows that the experience of the immediately preceding policy year will not be available at the time of the rating process. The experience year used will thus usually end a few months in advance of the renewal date or the re-rating date.

The common formula for incurred claims is

Incurred Claims

    =   Paid Claims + Ending Reserve − Starting Reserve

    =   Paid Claims + Increase in Reserve (which might be negative).

For prospective rating, it is also fairly common to restate the reserve values to the level which we later believe *should* have been held, rather than what *was* held.

In most insured group cases, there are conversion policies offered to insureds leaving the group, who are thus losing their group coverage. These conversion policies tend not to be self-supporting, often because of law or regulation, creating an unfunded liability for the insurer arising out of the conversion. When this is the case, or when there are any other miscellaneous, recurring liabilities arising out of the insurance contract, such liabilities should be included in the incurred claims figure. (An alternative to this is to make an explicit charge for these liabilities later in the rating process, outside the incurred claim calculation. The important thing is that such charges be included somewhere in the rating calculations.)

POOLING METHODS

At this point, the insurer will often apply some techniques which will dampen the random statistical fluctuations which might cause a particular group's experience to be unusual. These techniques are called pooling methods, meaning algebraic methods whereby the group's experience is combined with that of other groups in an averaging process.

Keep in mind that the purpose of this procedure is to develop premium rates to be charged in the future – the guiding principle for the insurer is to choose methods which will make the rates resulting from this exercise as attractive as possible to the policyholder, while still meeting the insurer's related corporate objectives. It is not part of the contractual relationship between the insurer and the policyholder.

Regardless of the pooling method used, it is important to remember that, over time, the pooling charge included in the experience analysis of all groups must be large enough to equal the average cost of claims modifications made through the pooling process.

Catastrophic Claim Pooling

This method of pooling typically takes the form of "forgiveness" of exceptionally high claims on individuals within the group. This is accomplished by removing the portion of paid or incurred claims due to individual claims above a certain limit. (Such claims are often called catastrophic, stop-loss, or shock claims.) In return for this feature, an average charge is made to all groups participating in this feature, regardless of whether a particular group actually had a catastrophic claim.

Theoretically, we are talking about two expected claim distributions:

- A claim distribution for individuals, such as the comprehensive major medical claim distribution shown in Figure 35.1 on page 735.
- A distribution of the total claims expected by a group whose individuals are each subject to the individual claim distribution. This is the random variable on which experience rating is based, and which is modified by the various pooling methods.

Figure 35.2, shown on page 736, illustrates the results of a Monte Carlo simulation repeated 1000 times, of a group of 50 lives. If this procedure were continued, the results would gradually tend toward the limiting distribution of aggregate group claims. Figure 35.2 thus represents the probabilities of fluctuation of a group's claims which can be expected to happen due to purely random fluctuation.

Figure 35.3, shown on page 737, is similar to Figure 35.2, but shows a simulation of 1000 groups of size 50,000. This illustrates how the group claim distribution changes with the size of the group. As the group size increases, the distribution has lower variance and is less skewed.

Figure 35.4, shown on page 738, illustrates the effect of applying an individual stop-loss limit to the claims composing the aggregate group claim distribution for 50 life groups. The specific stop-loss curve demonstrates what would happen if individual claim amounts exceeding a particular catastrophic claim limit were removed from each group's total claims.

In long-term disability insurance, the catastrophic claim limit often takes the form of claims continuing more than X years, while in medical insurance it is usually expressed as a dollar amount.

Loss Ratio/Rate Increase Limits

Another pooling mechanism which is used is to put an upper limit on the loss ratio which will be used in setting future rates. This is essentially equivalent to two other mechanisms which are used far more often: (a) setting an upper limit on the percentage rate increase which a group will be charged, and (b) setting an upper limit on the aggregate claim dollars a group will be charged (called aggregate stop-loss). The results of this technique, on our hypothetical pool of 50 life groups, are illustrated in Figure 35.5 on page 739, where the limit is set at 125% of expected claims.

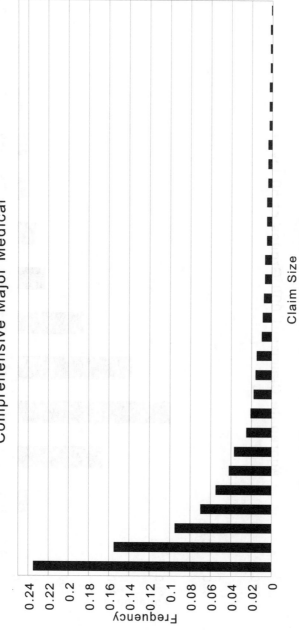

INDIVIDUAL CLAIM DISTRIBUTION

Comprehensive Major Medical

Figure 35.1

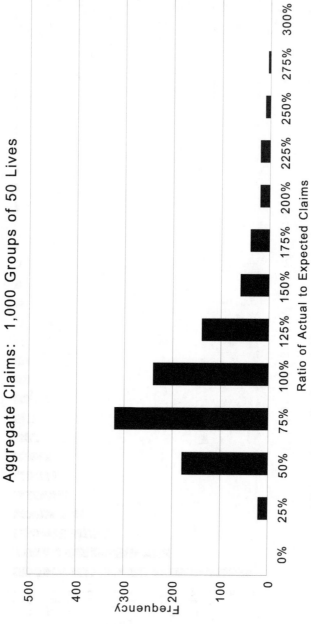

Figure 35.2

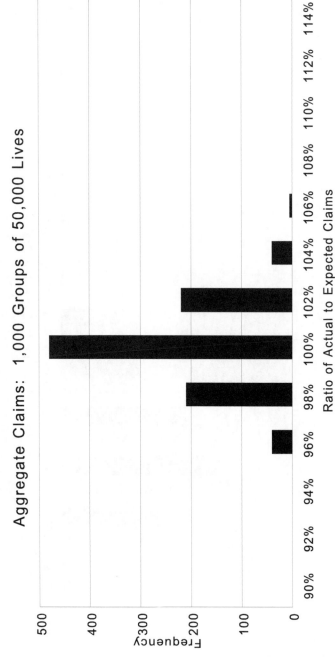

Figure 35.3

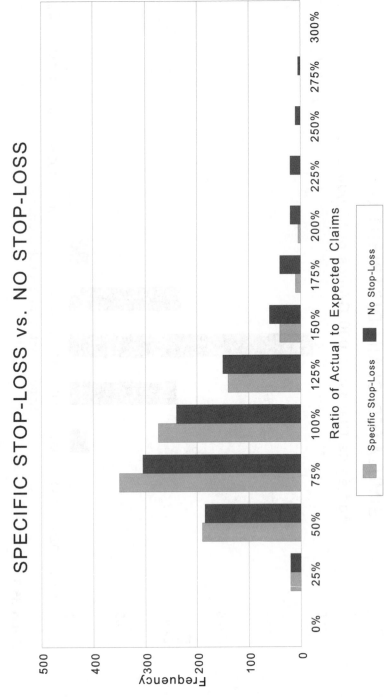

Figure 35.4

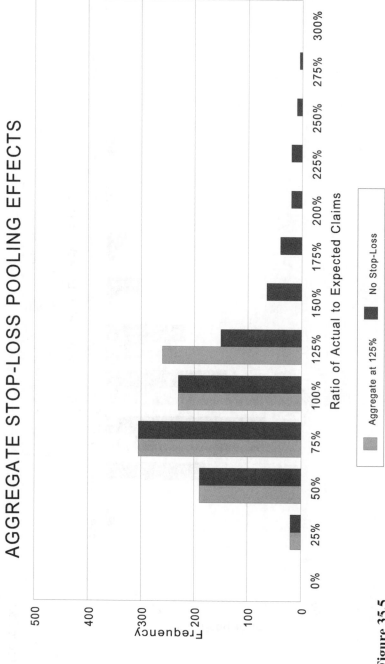

Figure 35.5

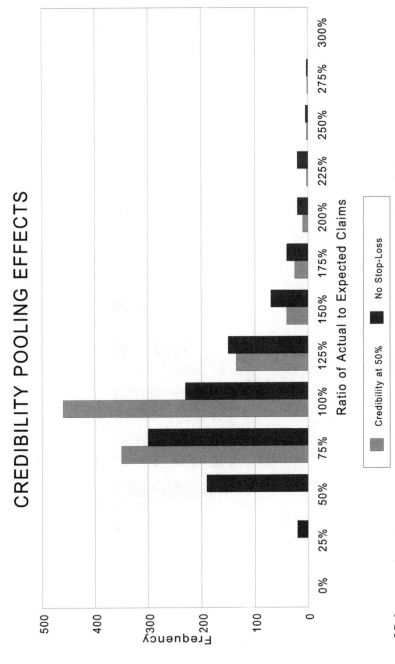

Figure 35.6

As was true in the catastrophic claim pooling case, and as is true for all pooling mechanisms, any lost income resulting from the pooling technique must be recouped through an average charge over all groups in the pool. Conceptually, this pool is not a collection of identical risks, but rather all risks participating in this particular pooling mechanism. It can be made up of a variety of different risks, each partly pooled, perhaps at differing pooling levels.

Credibility Weighting

Credibility weighting is accomplished be imbuing groups in each of various size categories with a credibility factor. This factor can be zero (equivalent to no credibility, meaning that the group's own experience is not to be believed at all), one (meaning the group's experience is fully credible, and therefore will not be pooled at all under this method), or some value in between. The standard formula used in this method is

Incurred Claims after Pooling
$$= (C)(\text{Incurred Claims before Pooling})$$
$$+ (1-C)(\text{Expected Incurred Claims}),$$

where C is the credibility factor, and "Expected Incurred Claims" is the claims which would have occurred if the group had experienced claims at the average level of the pool. The effect of this pooling method (using credibility factor $C = .50$) on our illustrative pool is shown in Figure 35.6 on page 740.

This pooling method is often equivalently expressed as the credibility weighting of loss ratios, rather than of incurred claims. This can be easily seen by dividing both sides of the above formula by the same earned premium figures. The formula then becomes

Loss Ratio after Pooling
$$= (C)(\text{Loss Ratio before Pooling})$$
$$+ (1-C)(\text{Pooled Loss Ratio}).$$

Multi-Year Averaging

One other pooling method, which can be used as a modification to other methods or by itself, is to combine several years of experience, in order to smooth out the statistical fluctuations inherent in the experience of a single year. This will often take the form of a weighted average, such as

Pooled Loss Ratio in Year Z
$$= \{(5 \times (Z\text{'s unpooled ratio})) + (3 \times (Z-1)\text{'s}) + (1 \times (Z-2)\text{'s})\}/9.$$

This method will be less useful when there is high turnover in the group, and in medical insurance, or in any other case where older experience is of limited use.

Combination Methods

Most of the pooling methods described above are not mutually exclusive methods. They can be and are used simultaneously. For example, specific stop-loss pooling might be applied to a group's claim experience to derive a needed rate increase. That increase might then be lowered because it exceeded a given limit, constituting aggregate stop-loss pooling.

AFTER POOLING

Since most insurers have group portfolios with renewal dates spread throughout the year, prospective experience rating is an ongoing process, and it is very difficult to look at the aggregate experience of the whole pool at one time. Most insurers therefore assume the experience underlying their manual rates to represent the aggregate experience of the pool, and rely on updates to the manual rates to keep them in line with the pooled experience.

If the pooled or manual level of claims (or loss ratio) is correctly set at the average level for the whole pool, the aggregate result of applying a pooling formula to all groups will be that the total of all "post-pooling" incurred claims, including pooling charges, will be equal to the total "pre-pooling" incurred claims. With respect to credibility-weighting pooling, if the manual level is incorrectly set to a level not equal to the true average, the result of pooling will be pooled claims or loss ratios which average somewhere between the true average and the manual level. Similar results occur with the other pooling methods when the value of pooled claims is not correctly estimated.

The result of the pooling process produces a figure which is sometimes called charged claims. This term is more meaningful in the retrospective case, where there is an actual charge against a refund or dividend. In the prospective case, the charge is against future premiums which are contingent upon the policyholder accepting and paying the rates.

As in most actuarial analyses of experience, it is necessary to look at the exposure base which corresponds to the charged claims. This can be either earned premium or a measure of the number of people covered. The jargon for the people covered depends upon the type of insurer being analyzed: commercial insurers and employers usually refer to employees, Blue Cross / Blue Shield plans refer to subscribers, HMOs refer to members. These are not necessarily different names for the same thing – care should be taken to ensure that the measurement of exposure is consistent with the rate basis. For example, if rates are charged per employee, it would be inappropriate to apply those rates based on a per member exposure basis.

When claims and exposure have been derived on a consistent basis, their ratio provides a unit cost, the cost per unit of exposure. This historical unit cost forms the starting point for projected unit costs.

One word of caution is in order. Frequently a block of business is analyzed in this way, which may involve the commingling of claims and exposure for two populations which have different expected unit costs. (Two medical plans with different deductibles, or disability coverage for salaried and hourly groups, for example.) Care should be taken to be sure the mix of business in the historical period is representative of the business in the projected rating period, or additional analysis is justified.

The next step in the experience rating process is the translation of historical experience to expected future experience. This involves the trending of the experience, to account for changes in claim cost due to time. Some of the factors influencing future expected costs are group-specific, and some are environmental, applying to all groups. Both are important.

Some of the factors which might have an impact on the expected costs in the prospective rating period include the following:

- Changes in government programs, affecting the cost of benefit intended to supplement them.
- Secular or cyclic trends in rates of disablement or length of disability.
- Mortality trends.
- Utilization or cost trends in medical care, including the effects of changes in negotiated provider agreements and the impact of benefit design on those trends.
- Changes in the demographic characteristics of the group be analyzed.
- Changes in benefits in the plan itself.

- Antiselection opportunities by insureds, whether on-going, due to changes in benefits or premiums, or due to changes in the insured environment, such as increased competition in a multi-option environment.
- Other changes in the insured, economic, or financial environment.
- Any other factors which could be expected to have an effect on the expected costs of the group.

Extreme care should be used in the application of trends. One specific area needing special concern is the choice of appropriate endpoints for the trend period. Although the endpoints are typically the midpoints of the experience period and the future rating period, there may be reasons, such as the following, why this choice is not correct:

- If a group grew rapidly during the experience period, the average exposure date may be well beyond the midpoint of the experience period.
- If the group is an MET (multiple employer trust) where rates change on an employer's anniversary, the average effective date of the rates may extend beyond the midpoint of the rating period.

Many such examples are possible, and the wise analyst will always examine possible reasons for adjusting the trend period.

Another point to keep in mind is that some trends are one-time events (such as benefit changes or open enrollment periods), while others are continuous (such as inflation or changes in practice patterns.)

The result of this trending process is the expected cost in the rating period for the group, per unit of exposure. This is variously called claim cost, net premium (commercial insurers), cost per member per month (HMOs), or pure premium (Blue Cross / Blue Shield plans). It represents the expected cost of the claims themselves in the rating period, but nothing else, although some carriers, particularly those in a casualty insurance environment, tend to include claim administration expense with incurred claims in their illustrations.

One further note is in order. Many times carriers will perform the described calculations on an aggregate level, without dividing by exposure. This simplifies some of the calculations, and makes others more difficult. If done correctly, however, the calculation is equivalent, and should result in the same level of aggregate "needed income," a term sometimes used to describe the product of expected claim cost (perhaps increased for retention) and expected exposure. One major consideration in choosing which of these methods to use is the relative usefulness of the methods in marketing situations. Exhibits given to policyholders are generally more understandable if stated in aggregate terms, rather than in unit costs.

CALCULATING GROSS RATES FROM NET RATES

Gross premiums, the premiums actually charged, must account for expected claims as well as a number of other items. Such items are generally referred to as loadings on the net premium. The generic term for such items is the retention of the insurer, although the term is not well defined and will be discussed more later. Some of the most common retention items are the following:

- *Expense Loadings.* This is usually the largest part of retention, and is generally included as a number of separate charges. Expenses can be expressed as a percentage of net premiums, gross premiums, expected claims, or other retention items; they can be per certificate (or contract), per expected claim, per unit of coverage, per premium billing, or in other ways. Each company generally allocates expenses by line of business, and then each line develops unit expenses, expressed in one or more of the above ways, at levels which would theoretically reproduce overall expenses for the line when applied to all business.

- *Deficit Recovery Charge.* If a policyholder has incurred losses in prior years which have not yet been recovered, the insurer may build in a deficit recovery charge intended to recoup past losses within a reasonable period of time. Of course, such charges will increase premiums, and thus increase the chance that the rates will become noncompetitive. It is not necessary that the policyholder be subject to retrospective experience rating in order to have such a charge be built into the prospective rates; it is only necessary that the insurer is keeping a policyholder account and wishes to recover deficits.

- *Termination Risk Charge.* Occasionally, a policyholder in a deficit position will terminate its contract, leaving the insurer no means to recover the losses from that policyholder. For this reason a risk charge is made in advance on all policyholders to finance this business risk. The size of this charge will depend not only on the policyholder's accumulated surplus position, but on any other policyholder money, such as premium stabilization reserves or contingency reserves, which are held by the insurer and at risk under the contract to pay for unexpected losses.

The termination risk charge should reflect any aspect of the group, its coverages, and its funding arrangements, which affect the likelihood and size of possible deficits under the contract.

- *Pooling Charges.* While pooling charges will generally be included in the development of the net premium figure, occasionally they are not. If not, they should appear as a separate retention item.

- *Profit Charge.* This is the profit that the insurer chooses to include in its pricing formula, generally not including, however, profit arising from the investment of assets. (Nonprofits call this contributions to free reserves, and mutual insurance companies call it contributions to surplus. While the size of the charge will tend to vary between types of insurers, the nature of the factor will not.) To the extent that all other retention items represent true expected costs, this figure, in combination with any margin built into investment income activities, represents true expected profit. Often, however, there are margins built into any or all the other assumptions used in deriving gross premiums, and there may not be an explicit loading for profit in the retention calculation. (This is a particular helpful technique for nonprofit corporations.) It is important that the pricing actuary understand the level and the effect of any such margins, and compare their effect with that of an explicit profit margin.

- *Investment Income.* Many insurers will provide for the crediting of investment income on reserves or other monies held, and treat this income as an offset to other retention items. This should be kept in mind when comparing retention levels between insurers. Investment income is usually separated from other retention items in evaluating retention levels. The investment income credited will usually be net of investment management costs, and may be net of income taxes if such taxes are not included as an expense item.

  The investment credit may also be negative, actually creating an investment charge, if the policyholder has a negative fund balance. There may also be such an investment charge due to the investment income lost on premiums paid beyond the grace period. In this case, it is common to use a higher interest rate on charges than is used for investment credits.

- *Explicit Margin.* Many times an insurer will include a specific margin in the retention calculation. This is essentially a comfort factor built into the rates. It will reduce the insurer's risk, since it will reduce the probability of a policyholder experiencing a deficit during the contract year. For this reason, there can be a reflection of this risk reduction in the termination risk charge.

Once all retention items have been identified, it is a relatively easy exercise to develop the rate per unit of exposure using standard techniques. At this point the insurer may wish to limit the size of an implied rate increase to a particular percentage. It should be kept in mind that such limitations carry with them a reduction in expected profit which should be accounted for (to the extent possible) in the retention formula.

In some coverages, rate guarantees for periods longer than one year may occur. Where such a guarantee exists, the actuary should be sure to take into consideration the changes in the nature of the risk which occur because of the guarantee. These include the following:

- *Misestimation Risk.* Since the insurer is locked into rates for a longer period, the potential impact of misestimation of any of the costs under the contract (claim, expense, or risk) is relatively greater than for a one-year guarantee for any given group. This tends to argue for higher margin and/or higher risk charges.

- *Trend Risk.* One specific rating aspect, that of claim trends, is particularly dangerous, for two reasons: (a) the effect of trend is magnified over time, as is the effect of misestimation of trend, and (b) the longer a trend must be estimated into the future, the more risk there is of inaccuracy due to changing conditions. This argues for extreme caution in the use of long rate guarantees for trend-sensitive coverages.

FINAL ADJUSTMENTS

There may be reasons why the insurer will wish to make a final adjustment in the rates which have nothing to do with premium adequacy. For example, the policy may be with a politically sensitive policyholder.

Whatever the reason, such a decision should not be made without consideration and measurement of its financial impact on the corporation. It is therefore important that the pricing actuary be able to provide such measurements to senior management, in order to provide a balanced response to such marketing or political pressures.

MULTI-OPTION CONSIDERATIONS

In medical or dental insurance, an employer may well provide his employees with the choice of a number of plans; perhaps a health maintenance organization (HMO), a preferred provide arrangement (PPO), and a conventional indemnity (major medical) program. When a single carrier is not the source of all plans being provided, a comprehensive pricing strategy is not possible, and the carrier needs to be aware of the implications of the multi-option situation.

It has been frequently observed that insureds choosing a managed care program tend to have lower average costs than those in an indemnity program. This is especially true with regard to HMOs. The indemnity carrier in such a situation needs to be aware of this, and account for the higher average cost of those who are left behind by the HMO enrollees. (There is an ongoing debate as to whether the difference in average cost is due only to different demographics, or whether the health status of those choosing an HMO tends to be better than those who remain with the indemnity program. At this point, the latter argument tends to have more adherents, including the author of this chapter. This argues that the pricing actuary needs to consider this "going in" anti-selection in the pricing of any plans involved in the multi-option situation.)

The effect of antiselection on the experience of an indemnity program, assuming the above antiselection takes place, is that experience in the first year of the multi-option situation will be worse than would be otherwise expected, creating an artificial one-time increase in claim levels. The extent to which antiselection continues to rear its ugly head in renewal years depends upon many factors, most of which involve various incentives to enrollees, and is beyond the scope of this chapter.

SMALL GROUP CONSIDERATIONS

The use of prospective experience rating for small groups presents another unique set of problems. (The definition of "small" will depend on the coverage. For medical coverage, this level might loosely be set at under 50 lives, while being set at under 500 lives for life and accidental death coverage.)

In the small group medical market, successful companies have generally found it necessary to recognize a group's experience in some way in its prospective rating. The method used may be either formula-based or based on case-by-case reunderwriting of the risk at renewal.

A typical formula-based method might work as follows. Eleven rating categories are created, representing rates at 50%, 60%, ...140%, and 150% of average. Each group will be assigned to a rate category, based initially on the underwriting department's evaluation of the risk, and thereafter on its own experience. That assignment will be reexamined at each policy anniversary, and will be changed by one or more categories if the recent experience deviates by more than a specified amount from the level expected for the category. The number of years' experience used, the maximum number of rate categories of movement used, and the definition of the specified amount will depend on the coverage, the group's size, and the number of years' experience available. (This method of rating is sometimes called band rating or tier rating.) These rules implicitly apply credibility and pooling methods.

Formula-based methods in use today are generally not based on rigorous theory, but rather are shaped on market forces and the need to retain good risks in light of competitors' practices. Generally, when such formulas are applied, they will be used only for groups larger than a certain size, such as ten lives.

The reunderwriting method involves examining the causes of an individual case's experience to determine prospective rates. For carriers with any significant volume of business, this is impractical unless used selectively, usually with those cases with the highest ratio of actual to expected loss ratios. For example, groups with 2-5 lives and actual to expected claims over 150% might be examined on a case-by-case basis, while groups of 25-49 lives might be examined at a ratio of 120% or higher. The cost-effectiveness of these activities is a significant question, however, and should be analyzed before investing any significant resources in implementing them.

Some carriers have successfully combined band rating with the reunderwriting method. In such a scheme, the insurer will generally apply formula-based band rate changes up to a specified level. Beyond that level, the groups are reunderwritten, just as in the pure reunderwriting method.

RETROSPECTIVE EXPERIENCE RATING

THE RETROSPECTIVE PROCESS AND ITS CHARACTERISTICS

When carriers insure a group of substantial size, it has become a common practice to reflect the claim levels resulting from that group's own unique risk characteristics in rating for future years (prospective experience rating). It has also become common practice to give the group the financial benefit of good experience, and hold them financially accountable for bad experience, in the year that such experience emerges from the insurance contract. This practice is called retrospective experience rating.

When experience turns out to be better than was expected in the prospective rating assumptions, the excess can either be accumulated in an account held on behalf of that policyholder or it can be refunded. If it is accumulated in an account, the account is generally called a premium stabilization reserve, claim fluctuation reserve, or contingency reserve. If it is refunded, it may be called either a dividend (by mutual insurance companies) or an "experience rating refund" (by everyone else), depending on the corporate structure of the insurer. In all cases, the calculation involves an evaluation of historical experience under the policy, in ways very similar to prospective rating methods.

It should be noted that dividends are generally set by action of a mutual company's Board of Directors. Experience rating refunds are usually set as part of the insurance contract.

TYPICAL EXPERIENCE REFUND FORMULA

If a refund formula applies to the policyholder, either through contractual agreement or Board of Directors' action (such as a dividend formula by Board resolution), the amount of any refund will be the positive balance, if any, resulting from the formula. If a retrospective premium arrangement is in effect, the amount of additional premium due would be all or part of any negative formula balance.

Retrospective refund formulas are composed of some or all of the elements in the generic formula.

Formula Balance = (Prior Formula Balance carried forward)
+ (Premiums)
+ (Investment earnings on money held)
− (Claims charged)
− (Expenses charged)
− (Risk charge)
− (Rate stabilization reserve addition)
− (Profit).

The result of the retrospective rating formula, also called the formula balance, is often referred to as the policyholder account balance, representing the fund balance attributed to the individual policyholder, and which is refunded following its calculation. Each element of the formula balance will be examined individually.

PRIOR FORMULA BALANCE CARRIED FORWARD

If the prior years' formula balance has not been eliminated, the remaining balance is usually carried forward into the next year's formula.

A positive balance can be eliminated by either paying out the balance as a refund or dividend, by taking the balance out of the individual policyholder's account into the company's general surplus (or free reserves, as nonprofits would say), or by a combination of the two.

A negative balance can be eliminated by a retrospective premium payment, if applicable, or by the company writing off the balance, thus funding it out of company surplus, or by a combination of both. Generally, however, a negative balance is carried forward, hopefully to be offset by emerging future positive surplus.

Thus, the final balance in one year's calculation must be adjusted by such additions and subtractions to the policyholder account before being carried forward into the next year's formula calculation.

PREMIUMS

The premium figure will generally be just the premium paid by the policyholder for the contract year, possibly adjusted with interest charges or credits for the timing of premium payments.

INVESTMENT EARNINGS ON MONEY HELD

If any significant balances are held by the insurer, such as claim reserves, the crediting of investment income earned on those balances needs to be considered. On coverages with significant balances, such as claim reserves for LTD coverage, investment earnings can be a significant source of income to the policyholder's account, and may be one of the significant factors used in choosing a carrier. Generally, the larger and more sophisticated a policyholder is, the more pressure there is to credit investment income which reflects the cash flow of, and amounts held for, that policyholder.

Investment income will generally be credited using either (a) the portfolio method or (b) the investment year method. The investment year method accounts for the timing of cash flows into or out of the policyholder's account, and gives credit for earnings on the particular assets acquired or divested at the point in time the cash flow took place. The portfolio method does not account for the timing of cash flows, and essentially throws all cash flows into one big account, using an average interest rate.

The calculation of investment earnings involves the application of an investment rate of return (calculated using one of the methods mentioned above) to one or more average amounts on deposit. It is usual to treat the earnings on existing amounts on deposit which are carried forward from one year to the next as having accrued linearly (or proportionately) over the course of the experience year. On the other hand, earnings credited on monies accruing out of the experience of a given year may take into account the actual timing of cash flows, since the timing of premium deposits are generally under the control of the policyholder, and are thus subject to the intelligent use of investment timing.

Typically, the amount credited is equal to $r \times MF$, where r is the rate of return, and MF is the mean fund over the period, usually taken as the average of the starting and ending fund amounts over the month or year.

The rate of return will be either pre- or post-income tax, depending on whether the carrier paid income tax on the investment income. This will depend upon the nature of the fund being held, and upon the tax laws of the country having jurisdiction.

CLAIMS CHARGED

The development of this element of the formula involves several steps, as described in the following paragraphs.

Determining Historical Claims Experience

Just as in the case of prospective experience rating, it is necessary to be sure the claims experience used for retrospective rating purposes is on an incurred basis. While paid basis approximations might be used for prospective rating, this is far more uncommon and dangerous in the retrospective situation. The danger arises from the fact that retrospective calculations are usually considered final accountings for the year, and any refunds paid out may not be recoverable if the paid basis approximation should prove to be erroneous.

Since the retrospective calculation does not involve projections of future results, the financial calculation does not require measures of exposure for use as denominators. Also, the policyholder and the insurer are both primarily interested in the actual bottom line – the dollars of gain or loss which occurred. For these reasons, retrospective claim calculations are usually done on an aggregate basis, rather than a per unit of exposure basis.

Managed-care health coverages cause some unique considerations in the retrospective calculation. Quite often, deviations of actual utilization from expected is a risk that is taken by neither the policyholder nor the insurer. Rather, it is taken by the provider of services, under a capitation agreement, perhaps with experience refunds (or withholds) payable to the provider after the close of his contract year as an incentive to keep utilization down. Frequently, such refunds represent some percentage of the savings due to utilization, with the remainder flowing to the insurer. To the extent such refunds are made to providers, they obviously cannot be paid to policyholders. In addition, U.S. HMOs which are federally qualified currently cannot experience rate, although there has been some regulatory movement in that direction. For these reasons, HMO experience included in a retrospective premium calculation is rarely adjusted for deviations of actual from expected experience.

Just as in the prospective situation, incurred claims form the basis for the rating process, and calculation of claim reserves is necessary to derive incurred claims. However, reserves for retrospective calculations tend to include larger margins than for prospective calculations. This is true for the following reasons:

- The competitive pressure of prospective rating is far weaker in retrospective calculations.

- For continuing policyholders, any conservatism resulting in excess monies being held will be released in future retrospective calculations, so there will likely be less policyholder scrutiny of the reserve level.

- For terminating policyholders, conservatism translates into an added margin of comfort to the insurer that the policyholder's claims can be paid out of the policyholder's money. In this situation, the excess can become an added source of profit to the insurer.

Modifications to Claims Experience

Contractual or administrative guarantees made to the policyholder must be reflected, and are generally treated as adjustments to incurred claims. These adjustments take the following forms:

- Specific stop-loss claims are removed from the experience. That is, the portion of individual claims in excess of the pooling level (whether a dollar amount, as for life and medical coverages, or a duration of claim, as for long-term disability) are subtracted from the incurred claims.

- Incurred claims in excess of the aggregate stop-loss pooling level are removed from incurred claims, following the specific stop-loss adjustment.

- The stop-loss pooling charge, representing the average expected cost of claims in excess of stop-loss limits, is often added back into incurred claims at this point, although it might just as easily be a separate charge in the retrospective rating formula. (The theory underlying the stop-loss pooling charges is identical to that described earlier.)

- Occasionally, a company will replace a percentage of actual claims (being the pooled portion of claims) with a percentage of expected claims (being the pooling charge). This is one example of credibility pooling.

- If the insurer provides conversion privileges to insureds leaving the group, the excess claim cost usually experienced in such situations is generally passed along to the policyholder. This is done by another adjustment to incurred claims. Typically in the U.S., conversion privileges exist on life and health coverages. In Canada, they typically exist only for life coverages.

- Charges to incurred claims for life coverage conversion are made on a per conversion basis, with the charge a function of the amount of coverage converted, and perhaps policyholder's age. Health conversion charges may be on a per conversion basis or based on an average charge made to all policyholders. Health per conversion charges are rarely based on employee age, although there is a theoretical basis to do so. (In the U.S., changes in federal law have made group medical conversions far less frequent by requiring groups to allow employees and dependents to voluntarily continue as part of the employer group for two or three years after they would otherwise terminate coverage. Since most insureds have found other, adequate coverage by that time, relatively few are left to convert.)

Any other policy provisions or administrative practices which would affect how an employer will be held liable for the financial effects of incurred claims are reflected at this point. The result is a figure referred to as charged claims or claims charged. This refers to the claims for which the policyholder will be charged in the retrospective calculations.

Thus, a generic formula for charged claims is

$$
\begin{aligned}
\text{Claims Charged} = \ & \text{(Claims paid)} \\
& + \text{(Increase in claim reserves)} \\
& - \text{(Pooled claims)} \\
& + \text{(Pooling charges)} \\
& + \text{(Conversion charges)} \\
& + \text{(Claim margins, if any)}.
\end{aligned}
$$

EXPENSES CHARGED

Here, again, the level of sophistication used in charging the expenses due to an individual policyholder depends upon the size and sophistication of the policyholder, as well as the abilities of the carrier.

Expenses for an insurance company are generally allocated to lines of business, based upon corporate-wide expense studies. Each line of business then chooses unit expenses which are intended to closely reflect the costs attributable to those lines of business. These unit expenses may vary by coverage, size of policyholder, or other factors. They are usually expressed as some combination of percentage of premium, percentage of paid or incurred claims, per claim processed, per policy, or per certificate. (Expenses related to investment income have generally already been deducted from the investment rate of return, and need not be included.)

Expense charges may be broken out into various levels of detail, showing, for example, commissions and agency expenses, premium taxes or other assessments, conversion charges (if not already included in claims charged), corporate overhead, services to certificate holders, claim administration, risk charges, pooling charges (if not already included in claims charged), or others. There is normally a catchall grouping which is intended to summarize a number of expenses which are not large enough individually to justify a separate line of the experience report.

Expenses in the first year, or first few years, may be higher than in renewal years, reflecting initial acquisition costs. They are typically charged to policyholders in this way, using factors which vary by policy year. They can also be averaged by the use of factors which don't vary by duration, although this increases the termination risk to the insurer.

Certain types of groups will require special handling, and the actuary should always be alert for such situations. Jumbo groups, for example, will often have dedicated administrative units, where expenses can be charged directly, independently of the carrier's expenses due to other business. Multiple-employer trusts, as another example, may require separate billing of individual employers, causing billing expenses to resemble those of a small group block of business, rather than those of a single large group.

RISK CHARGE

This is a generic term which may be used to cover charges for a multitude of risks. Usually, however, it refers to the charge made by the insurer to cover the risk that the policyholder will cancel or nonrenew the contract before the carrier has had a chance to recover any existing account deficits. While this charge may be based upon the judgment of the carrier, a theoretical development is necessary to know the appropriate rate.

Risk charge development will take into consideration the expected statistical variance of a group the policyholder's size, as well as the size of any existing deficits. It will generally also account for any monies on deposit with the carrier which can be used to offset losses, such as a contingency reserve, premium stabilization reserve, or claim fluctuation reserve, which serve to lower the probability of a deficit. Known margins in the rates on the financing arrangement have a similar effect.

Although becoming less common, some carriers attempt to recoup losses under a contract in subsequent years. A risk charge can be made to prefund the average losses expected due to groups lapsing before their losses can be recovered. In practice, the ability to recoup past losses is limited.

RATE STABILIZATION RESERVE ADDITION

Most carriers will try to reduce their risk of being in a deficit position by accumulating a portion of policyholder surplus in a reserve which can be used to offset experience fluctuations. The larger such a reserve becomes, the larger would have to be a policyholder's deficit before exhausting it; thus, the carrier's risk would be less. This relationship between the size of the reserve and the carrier's risk is generally reflected in the size of the risk charge. This relationship is generally well quantified for life insurance coverage, somewhat less for LTD, and even less for health coverages. This is due to the existence and relative importance of other risks in the LTD and health lines which are difficult to separate from the statistical risk.

Some insurers require that the policyholder surplus accumulate in such a reserve, up to a particular limit, before the surplus can be paid out as experience refunds to a policyholder. (In some cases, there may be two such reserves for the policyholder – a mandatory one required by the insurer, and an optional one created at the request of the policyholder to reduce risk charges and premium fluctuations.) If the group policy terminates, the reserve may or may not be payable to the policyholder.

When a policyholder's rate stabilization reserve is exhausted by adverse experience, substantial rate increases can result. This results from the need to rebuild the reserve while simultaneously adjusting rates to an adequate level.

PROFIT

Most carriers are reluctant to show an explicit profit charge on experience exhibits which are shown to policyholders. Rather, profit margins are often built into other assumptions, such as expenses, risk charges, or even claims charged.

Stock insurance companies are openly profit-making organizations. Mutual companies, theoretically owned by their policyholders, do not pay out earnings to stockholders, but nevertheless generally require a contribution to surplus by policyholders. Nonprofit corporations (mainly Blue Cross / Blue Shield plans) are limited in the surplus they can accumulate, but will generally make charges to certain lines of business (such as group) in order to fulfill political/moral/social obligations to subsidize other lines (such as "non-group," the Blues' name for individual insurance).

Regardless, then, of company's corporate structure, the group actuary needs to address the question of contributions to surplus.

APPLICABILITY

Retrospective experience rating formulas will not apply to all group policyholders. Their application will depend upon the following considerations:

- *Group Size.* A certain level of resources is needed to compile, analyze, and communicate the experience specific to a particular policyholder. This argues that there is a critical mass below which it is not cost effective for the insurer to apply such a formula.

Further, a minimum size is needed to obtain some degree of statistical credibility in the first place. Otherwise, there is a risk of large swings in experience from year to year.

While prospective experience rating is often used as a tool for management of a block of business, retrospective experience rating requires an insurer to put its money where its credibility formula is, and take the financial risk connected with such calculations.

For these reasons, retrospective formulas will generally apply to groups with a larger minimum size than the minimum for prospectively-experienced rated groups.

- *Contract Provisions Regarding the Funding Arrangement.* As will be seen in the final section of this chapter, the choice of funding methods will have an impact on whether a retrospective formula will apply. A retrospective premium arrangement, for example, substantially changes the risks under an insurance contract, and such an arrangement will replace the normal experience rating formula.

- *Company Policies and Practices.* Regardless of the theoretical reasoning, a carrier's policies and practices will be an overriding factor. Hopefully, senior management has taken the theoretical side into consideration in choosing those policies. Some carriers, such as some nonprofit corporations, will only provide for refunds in special circumstances. Others, such as mutuals, must generally have a contract clause providing for participation by almost every policyholder.

- *Company Financial Situation.* Unless a specified refund formula is guaranteed by the terms of the contract, which is rare, the carrier's overall financial health is an overriding factor in any refund situation. This is a relatively small concern for carriers with substantial surplus, but for those with little surplus this can be a significant concern. Blue Cross plans in the U.S., for example, with their limitation on unallocated surplus (called free reserves) and with their vulnerability to sudden inflationary increases in claim costs, generally keep such concerns foremost in their minds when determining refund policies.

Small groups, to whom the retrospective formula does not apply, must then live or die with their prospective rates, since they must be charged premiums in advance, with no recourse should they prove inadequate. Larger groups will generally have both prospective and retrospective formulas applied.

SPECIAL FUNDING ARRANGEMENTS

The term special funding arrangement (or alternative funding arrangement) is used to describe contracts, or riders which modify contracts, that create special financial arrangements outside the classical insurance arrangements described earlier. This can refer either to how and at what time cash will flow, or to the transfer of financial risk between the carrier and the policyholder.

RESERVELESS PLANS

In recent years (generally the 1960's and later), policyholders began to be aware that claim reserves being held by insurers on an ongoing basis might be put to a better use by the policyholder until needed to actually fund claim payments at contract termination. In response to policyholder concerns, insurers began to find ways in which such monies could be returned to policyholders without creating undue risk to the carrier.

In a typical reserveless agreement, the insurer will forego premium payments up to a specified level intended to equal part or all of the claim reserves, in return for a contractual promise by the policyholder that they will pay the needed amount if and when the contract terminates – a terminal premium. This creates an added risk to the insurer that the policyholder will be unable to pay the premium when it comes due. For this reason, prudence suggests that the carrier financially underwrite the policyholder on an ongoing basis, to ensure the ability to pay the terminal premium.

The reserveless agreement is sometimes structured to "lag" premium payments, meaning that each month's premium is effectively given a 90-day or 120-day grace period. At termination of the policy, all unpaid premiums would immediately come due. This financial structure of the reserveless plan is the source of many of its pseudonyms, such as deferred premium or premium drag plans.

If the policyholder does set up its own reserve for the terminal premium, the investment options available for those funds can be enhanced. Such investments will no longer be limited by insurance company investment limits, but rather by the rules governing welfare benefit plans. This is often perceived as a significant advantage by large employers, although actual investment results may not live up to expectations.

Since the insurer must set up the claim reserves as a financial liability, due to its legal liability to pay claims incurred but not yet paid at contract termination, there must be an offsetting financial asset. This is typically accomplished by structuring the contract to make the terminal premium due and unpaid on statement dates. As long as the premium is due within 90 days of the statement date, the U.S. NAIC statement blank allows it to be called an admitted asset. (If it were not an admitted asset, the company would be forced to set aside assets which would otherwise be surplus, thus reducing the company's unallocated surplus.) A similar 90-day rule exists in Canada.

Less sophisticated policyholders sometimes fail to understand that switching to a reserveless plan provides only a one-time premium reduction, and that renewal premiums in the second year of such a plan will most likely be substantially higher than those in the first year.

FULLY-INSURED PLANS

In a fully-insured plan, all cash paid out by the policyholder is paid to the insurer, and treated as premium. Claims paid by the insurer are paid out of the insurer's accounts, with the insurer's money. Such a plan might be reserveless, or might not.

Following are some of the considerations in using this type of arrangement.

- The insurer bears the immediate risk of adverse experience, as well as the potential profit of favorable experience.

- Insureds have the security of the insurer being claim guarantor.

- Premium tax will be payable on all money flowing to the insurer.

- In the United States the contract will be subject to the insurance laws, rules, and regulations of the state of delivery of the contract. Most significantly in recent years this will include all mandated coverages in that state. (While ERISA rules will generally apply to employers and their plans, insurance laws apply to the insurers and insurance contract, rather than to employers. Insurers will normally modify their contracts where necessary to meet employer needs but are not obligated to, except out of their own self-interest.)

This is the traditional, classical funding arrangement of insurance coverage, and is therefore not strictly an alternate arrangement. It is the arrangement to which all the other methods are "alternates."

SELF-INSURED PLANS

Sometimes an employer will choose to create a self-insured plan, and take on the role of primary risk-taker. Claim payments and all plan-related expenses become the responsibility of the employer, and benefit payments are not guaranteed by an insurance company.

The normal funding vehicle for such a plan is a trust, created for just this purpose. Employer and employee contributions are deposited to this fund, and benefits are paid out of it. The rules governing such plans generally arise out of ERISA (in the U.S.), employment regulations (Canada), or the applicable trust law.

Although some very large employers may administer benefits themselves, most self-insured plans will contract with an insurance company or independent administrator to administer the plan. Services may include enrollment, eligibility, claim, and other administrative services, as well as sometimes consultation on plan design, actuarial and financial services, or others. Such a contract is often called an Administrative Services Only (ASO) agreement. Since the insurer bears no insurance risk, there will not be any risk charges in the charges for the ASO agreement.

In a fully self-insured plan, any investment income earned by the fund on trust assets is earned directly, rather than on an insurer's portfolio of investments. Latitude in the choice of investments is increased significantly over the fully-insured case, but is still bound by the governing laws and regulations.

Since the employer will generally wish to provide conversion rights to plan members, the ASO agreement is often modified to provide for individually issued conversion contracts through the insurer, usually in exchange for a charge to the employer representing some or all of the excess mortality and morbidity expected under a conversion contract. This is quite common in medical coverages, and less so in life and LTD coverage.

The employer may wish to insure against unusual claim fluctuations, and contract with an insurer (not necessarily the administrator) to do so. Such insurance is referred to as stop-loss coverage, and may cover excess claims on individuals (specific stop-loss), in the aggregate (aggregate stop-loss), or both. The premiums paid for such coverage are the self-insured equivalent to stop-loss pooling in an insured situation.

Some of the considerations in choosing a self-insured plan, other than those already mentioned, including the following.

- Premium tax is avoided on the money flowing through the plan, since it is not channeled through an insurer and hence does not become premium.

- State or provincial mandates on insurance contracts will not apply, since there is no contract of insurance, only of administrative services.

- The employer's plan becomes the sole bearer of the insurance risk, unless there is stop-loss coverage or, in medical plans, capitation or similar agreements with providers. This argues that the plan sponsor should carefully evaluate its ability to absorb claim fluctuations in planning its funding mechanisms.

- Different coverages require varying degrees of expertise in specialized areas to successfully manage them. For this reason, the plan sponsor may wish to evaluate the advisability of self-funding, the details of the funding mechanism, and the choice of administrator or advisor separately by coverage. The cost-effectiveness of this will obviously depend on the size of the plan, and is an important (but often overlooked) consideration.

MINIMUM PREMIUM CONTRACTS

A hybrid of insured and self-insured plans was developed in the 1960's, called a minimum premium plan (sometimes also called a splitfunded plan). In this arrangement, a minimum premium rider is usually attached to a fully insured contract, which modifies the funding mechanism to have most or all of the expected claims portion of the premium be used to fund claims directly without becoming premiums. This is accomplished by having the policyholder deposit funds directly to an account on need by them for a trust. Sometimes the arrangement will be for funds to be transferred by wire to the account on a weekly basis, upon notification by the insurer of the amount required. Claims are paid from this account by the insurer, up to the amount in the fund. The insurer will generally pay the claims on drafts which draw on the fund directly, and thus do not become premium. The premium amount then becomes the fully-insured premium minus the contributions paid into the fund and less the premium tax on the self-insured portion. (Not-for-profit insurers, who are generally exempt from premium tax, have not had to be as careful to keep the pre-attachment point dollars from flowing through accounts owned by them. In fact, there may be an advantage to have the dollars flow through the insurer's account, if that will allow the employer to enjoy the benefit of reduced reimbursement levels.)

If claims exceed the expected amount, the insurer is liable for the excess amount, subject to any retrospective premium arrangements which might exist. The arrangement is thus very similar to stop-loss coverage, described later.

The original major advantage to this arrangement is that, in most jurisdictions, state premium tax is avoided on the contributions made to the fund. California is a noticeable exception to this rule. The California Supreme Court has ruled as follows:

> ... *Accordingly, we hold that the entire cost of an employee benefit plan, whether paid from the employer's fund or financed by deductions from the salaries of employees, is taxable as gross premiums inuring to the benefit of the insurer. Applying this rule to the facts of the instant case, we hold that Metropolitan is taxable on the sum of the premium payments it received from the employers and the pre-trigger point (pre-attachment point) claims paid from the employer funds in the tax years in question.*[2]

New York, on the other hand, has long considered the pre-attachment point claims to be nontaxable. It remains to be seen how large the ripples of the California decision will be. The importance of the matter has shrunk considerably since the case was first begun, however, since essentially the same financial arrangement can be reached by issuing an aggregate stop-loss policy to a self-insured plan with an ASO contract.

The New York Insurance Department has developed the following specific rules governing rate filing for minimum premium plans:

- The liability for all runoff claims must be kept by the insurer. This must be stated in the rider. Termination of the rider should occur immediately when the policyholder fails to make the necessary payments for the underlying plan.

- Notice must be given to employees if and when the insurer becomes liable for runoff claims. We (the Department) will accept a rider provision which requires the employer to pass along material provided by the insurer for such a purpose.

- The insurer should maintain full runoff reserves. If the policyholder holds his own reserves (i.e., "reserveless" minimum pre-

---

[2] *Metropolitan Life Insurance Co. v. State Board of Equalization*, 32 Cal, 3d469, 186 cal. Rptr. 578 (1982).

mium plan) the insurer's claim reserves are to be replaced by a terminal premium payable immediately upon termination. This terminal premium may reflect the entire liability for claims owing by the policyholder, but only that portion equal to 90 days of conventional premium may be taken as an admitted asset. The balance of the required reserve is to be offset by non-admitted assets, which therefore requires a charge against surplus.

- The plan should in no way restrict the rights of the insured with respect to conversion and mandated benefits.

- The rate filing as required by Section 52.40(c) or Regulation 62 must be submitted.[3]

Most other states have not formalized rules such as these for regulation of minimum premium plans.

Because of the California decision, and with the advent of stop-loss contracts, minimum premium plans have begun to decline in popularity.

STOP-LOSS CONTRACTS

Stop-loss contracts, used with self-insured plans, provide for the insurance of claims in excess of particular levels, usually substantially in excess of the expected claim level. The chosen level beyond which claims are insured is generally called the attachment point.

Specific stop-loss insures the claims of individuals covered under the contract. Attachment points are usually stated as a round number, such as $50,000 or $100,000. They will generally be larger for larger plans, since a large plan will be able to absorb a given single large claim more easily than a small plan, everything else being equal. The equivalent of a specific stop-loss agreement is sometimes used for LTD plans, where the employer will self-insure disabilities for some period such as twelve months. Insured LTD coverage would then wrap around the self-insured coverage, and have an elimination period of twelve months.

Aggregate stop-loss attachment points are usually expressed in terms of a multiple of expected claims, such as 110% of expected claims. The net cost of this benefit (or pure premium, or claim cost) is based upon the expected value and variance of the group's aggregate claims. Since the group is composed of (relatively) independent claims of individuals, large groups

---

[3] Actuarial Information Letter (Unnumbered), State of New York Insurance Department, May 11, 1983.

will have a smaller probability of aggregate claims exceeding a given attachment point. Another way of saying this is that larger groups will have more predictable and stable claims than smaller groups, so the theoretical cost of stop-loss insurance will be relatively less.

When specific stop-loss insurance is combined with aggregate stop-loss insurance, the specific coverage will be applied first, thus potentially lowering the expected aggregate claims, and thus the cost of the aggregate insurance.

Stop-loss insurance can be purchased on either an incurred or paid basis. On an incurred basis, claims which are incurred during the contract period will be covered, regardless of when they are paid out.

On a paid basis, the insurer will apply the attachment point to claims paid during the contract period. Suppose, for example, an insured is hospitalized for a long period, and reaches the attachment point prior to the end of the contract period. The employer's plan must once again begin paying at the beginning of a new contract period, and must reach the attachment point again before the stop-loss insurance will pick up the claim. A variant on the paid basis is the incurred-and-paid basis, where only claims which are both incurred and paid during the contract period will be covered, thus excluding payments on prior incurrals.

A danger of stop-loss on a paid basis is that, should the self-insured plan go bankrupt, claims which are incurred during the contract term might be covered by the insurer if paid before the end of the term, but identical claims might go unpaid if payable after the end of the term.

Some insurers and some jurisdictions consider stop-loss insurance to insure the employer's liability to the plan, rather than the health benefits themselves. Under this logic, stop-loss insurance is a liability coverage, rather than a health coverage, and must follow the laws, rules, and regulations governing liability insurance. The safest way for an insurer to proceed is to determine the position in the jurisdictions in which it intends to do business.

An important aspect regarding the rating of stop-loss coverages (as well as stop-loss pooling, which is theoretically similar) involves the risk of bad estimation of expected claims. If, for the sake of illustration, an aggregate attachment point is set at 105% of expected claims for a large group, the premium for such insurance might be relatively small, since the expected value of the group's claims exceeding that limit is relatively small. If the insurer has actually underestimated the expected claims level by that same 5%, the true probability is 50% that claims will exceed the expected level, a significant impact for such a small misestimation. Thus, accurate projections and appropriate margins are far more important than in the normal insured situation.

The risk of misestimation of claims can be magnified if care is not taken to accurately estimate claim reserves in the experience period, even if the contract is on a paid basis.

Another unique danger to stop-loss coverage (both specific and aggregate) is the effect of leveraging on trends. The concept is similar to leveraging of trends by deductible, but is more critical in stop-loss situations, because of the much lower premium amounts.

The frequency histogram of the individual claim distributions (as shown earlier in Figure 35.1) can be thought of as being elastic. Claim cost trends stretch that curve horizontally to the right, with the left endpoint of the curve being fixed at zero. If all the fixed values connected with the coverage such as attachment points, stretch with the curve, then the claim cost under the curve will increase proportionately to the trend. If the attachment point remains a fixed amount, as is usually the case in specific stop-loss, then the curve will stretch while the attachment point does not, causing a higher proportion of the curve to exceed the attachment point. This causes the effective claim cost trend to be higher than the underlying cost trend. (Aggregate stop-loss attachment points are usually expressed as a percentage of expected claims and therefore will stretch with the curve, eliminating the leveraging effect.)

To translate this theoretical treatment into real life, we can think of the leveraging effect as having two components. To do so, let a hypothetical attachment point be called A, the expected dollars of claims in the untrended individual distribution which exceed A be called C, and the trend which will occur to the distribution be called t. If t applies for one year, then all claims in the distribution which were A/t or greater before trends applied will now be A or greater. Thus, there will be new claims reaching the attachment point which did not reach it prior to the application of t. This is the first component of leveraging. The second component is the effect of t on the claims which already exceeded A. Since the coverage pays only for the portion of claims exceeding A, the expected payments for the coverage is $(x-A)$ for an aggregate claim amount x. When t is applied, the new claim amount is $(tx-A)$, which is larger than just t applied to $(x-A)$. (Mathematically, the expected claims in excess of A is the integral of $(x-A)$ times the density function, from A to infinity.)

This leveraging effect argues for the importance of accurate and conservative trend assumptions for stop-loss coverage, even if the trend used in the associated total claim projection is not as conservative. A similar leveraging effect occurs if the initial estimated claims are inaccurate.

Specific changes in medical care and other environmental factors should also be kept in mind when pricing stop-loss coverage.

RETROSPECTIVE PREMIUM ARRANGEMENTS

In the retrospective premium arrangement, or "retro," the policyholder takes over some or all of the aggregate claim risk, in exchange for reduced risk charges and often lower up-front premium payments.

For example, a policyholder and a carrier might agree that the policyholder would pay 90% of the otherwise applicable premium in the normal way. After the close of the experience year, if experience is worse than that anticipated in the rating, there would be an additional premium due (which might be payable in cash or out of the policyholder's rate stabilization reserve (RSR)), up to an agreed-upon limiting amount. This limiting amount is conceptually similar to aggregate stop-loss, the major difference being the timing of premium payments and the risk of non-payment.

If experience is better than expected, there might be a refund payable to the policyholder or its RSR (under a modification of the experience rating formula), or the policyholder might just keep the initial 10% reduction.

The actuary should be careful in evaluating risk charges and premiums for a retro agreement, being sure that the premium charged for the retro itself is adequate to cover expected claims, taking leveraging into account. If refunds are made of claim amounts less than that used in the rating, this money will not be available to cover higher claim amounts on other groups.

The retro agreement usually takes the form of a rider attached to a standard group policy. It is often used by some carriers as a back-door means of creating a reserveless plan, described earlier.

When a retro is in effect, it may be more difficult than otherwise for a carrier to accumulate a contingency reserve or rate stabilization reserve. This should be considered in setting retention levels for the retro rider.

FINAL CONSIDERATIONS

From all points of view, the choice of a funding mechanism depends on many things, including the following

- The effect on retention items, including expenses (premium tax, claim administration, and others), risk charges, and profit charges.
- The ability to unbundle aspects of the financial and insuring agreement, and potentially to shop around for services and coverages.
- The nature and size of the insurance risks assumed by each party.
- Possible policyholder or insurer bias about particular funding methods.

As this chapter illustrates, the use of any alternate funding method suggests careful consideration of the risks involved, and each party's ability to absorb them.

CONCLUSION

The interrelationship between prospective experience rating, retrospective experience rating, and various funding methods become more obvious the more they are studied. And well they should, since a comprehensive approach to ratemaking requires these relationships be recognized.

While the practicalities of life in an insurance company environment today may preclude simultaneous revision in all three areas, it is critical that all three at least be considered when revising any one of them. Without this comprehensive view, unintended incentives will be created within the insurer's product line, which will dilute the effectiveness of the insurer's marketing strategy. With it, the company can pursue its financial strategy in the most efficient way possible.

Understanding of the financial impact of these rating and funding matters is important to both parties of the insurance contract. There are often misunderstandings which could be easily avoided if appropriate education and explanation were to take place. For this reason, simplicity and ease of explanation become important aspects of successful financial arrangements.

SECTION SEVEN

ACTUARIAL MODELS

36 MEDICAL CLAIM COST TREND ANALYSIS

John P. Cookson
Peter K. Reilly
Peter L. Perkins

Measuring and setting trends in the health insurance industry is a key determinant of financial results, and is a crucial element in pricing the insurance product. In the insurance field, trend is generally considered in reference to the rate of growth in incurred claim cost per member per month (PMPM), but can also refer to growth in sales, expenses, premium, or other factors. The purpose of this chapter is to discuss the various issues surrounding trends in health insurance.

Trend analysis has been typically performed by analyzing a company's claim costs in isolation, attempting to use historical claims experience data to estimate future trends. This approach has serious limitations. Using statistical techniques, historical trends can be modeled effectively, relating them to external economic factors or other independent measures of medical cost increases. These relationships can be used to generate forecasts that are likely to show improved accuracy over historical methodologies.

We will first introduce some common trend concepts and definitions, to establish a common framework, and then discuss the analysis of trends.

CONCEPTS AND DEFINITIONS

TREND ANALYSIS AND HEALTH INSURANCE OPERATIONS

The analysis of historical claim trends and the forecasting of future trends is a key component in the health insurance business. Typically, trend analysis has been approached by analyzing rates of change in claim costs, but the goal has always been to predict future claim costs for rating purposes. If future claim costs can be predicted accurately, rating a block of business (independent of competitive issues) is a matter of determining administrative, profit, risk and other loadings necessary to produce a final rate level.

The modeling and prediction of claim costs also plays a key role in incurred but not reported reserve (IBNR) calculations. The majority of medical claim reserves stem from the most recent months of experience where traditional completion factor techniques are most unreliable. Reserves are typically set by attempting to forecast claim cost levels or trends. Increasing the accuracy of these estimates would also help stabilize reported financial results.

Finally, analysis of historical experience as part of the trend analysis process can lead to substantial insights in the following areas:

- Competitive analysis;
- Measuring the impact of changes in provider reimbursement methods; and
- Determining the impact of changes in managed care initiatives.

GENERAL ISSUES CONCERNING MEDICAL TRENDS

Medical claim cost trends are generally considered to be composed of two major components – a trend in price (cost per unit) and a trend in utilization (number of units). However, in practice there is often not a clear distinction between price and utilization trends, because other factors, such as mix and intensity of services, may obscure these differences. Trend can also be measured per insured life, per certificate, or per person (including dependents), or in other ways. These differences can cause additional confusion. Thus, when referring to trends, it is important to distinguish the exposure base and other factors to assure comparability and understanding.

This comparability issue is one that often causes confusion because trends may be used for different purposes. It will be useful to standardize the definition of trends on a consistent basis by discussing a number of these issues.

Confusing the picture further is the practice of using the term "trends" to refer to claim cost, premium, and rating trends. Trends may also be considered either before or after issues such as geographic, product, demographic, or benefit mix change. The interaction between cost and premium trends is crucial to understanding fluctuations in financial results. Premium trends are typically driven by either past cost trends, which is usually the case, or anticipated future cost trends. Rating trends are the trend factors used to increase manually and experience rated premiums. These trends often do not match actual premium trends due to the application of underwriting judgment, biases in experience rating systems, and other factors such as changes in demographics and benefit levels.

COMPONENTS OF MEDICAL TREND

The rate of increase in claim costs can be conceptually (and ultimately in practice) split into a number of distinct components. The two major distinctions are between general macro-economic factors that drive medical costs and the factors that cause trends to vary from one health insurer to another. These general macro-economic factors will be referred to as the "force of trend" and are described below. Many of the factors affecting cost trends are related to rating variables (such as demographics, plan design, and risk selection), and should be isolated, if appropriate and feasible, during the trend analysis process.

THE FORCE OF TREND

The force of trend is defined for our purposes as the average per capita reimbursement trends of payments to providers of medical care services, for all types of private payers of health benefits. It is not intended to measure all of the cost effects that are likely to be experienced by the many disparate insurers, employers, and claims payers. In contrast, trends of payments from charge-based payers may be higher than the force of trend, because they must typically absorb higher price increases. Trends of managed care organizations may be lower than those of charge based payers, because they may have immunized themselves from provider cost shifting.

Estimates of the force of trend can be developed from a number of public sources and other data bases. One such example is Health Cost Index™, which was developed to measure the force of trend for the non-Medicare population. Medicare was excluded from this index to adjust for the effects of this major program, which dictates through legislative and regulatory initiative how and what will be reimbursed to providers for Medicare enrollees. Since other payers usually cannot hope to match this level of Medicare legislated cutbacks through free-market forces, it was deemed appropriate to incorporate the effects of Medicare cost shifting in the base, and use the non-Medicare force of trend as a standard for all other insurers.

Antiselection and Demographic Changes

Usage of medical care differs by age, gender, access to care, health status, available supply, and disposition to use health services. Although individuals and families cannot predict their health care needs precisely, they often have a relatively good idea of their near term needs. Once individuals are given a choice of plans that have differing out-of-pocket costs or differing levels of benefits, they begin to gravitate to the program of their perceived optimum economic value. This is a decision based on imperfect knowledge of both the value of the benefits and the actual need. Furthermore, it is not generally a decision based on some desire to abuse or take unfair advantage of the system, but rather is a simple exercise in economic self-interest. However, as individuals strive to optimize their own situations, overall benefit program costs will inevitably rise. This situation, or rather its result, is generally referred to as antiselection.

Many different situations can lead to antiselection. They can be characterized by the insured being given a choice among benefit options and financial arrangements. In this context, antiselection will specifically refer to having a disproportionately high number of adverse risks within a defined risk cell. It does not include demographic and other mix changes, where the impact is due to changes in the mix of those characteristics.

The effects of antiselection can make observed health insurance trends appear much greater than the underlying force of trend. The following is a relatively simple example.

Consider a health benefits program with a high and low cost option with half the employees in each option. The high option represents a 10% greater actuarial value in benefits than the low option. Each option has been rated to stand on its own claim experience. The high option program covers 100 employees, at an average cost of $213 per month. These 100 employees can be segmented into two groups – 80 employees at an average monthly cost of $225, and 20 employees at an average cost of $165. The low option program covers 100 employees at an average cost of $104 per month. These employees also can be segmented into two groups – 95 employees at an average cost of $100 per month, and 5 employees at an average cost of $180 per month. These two smaller subgroups of each option represent the employees who are prone to change options during the next open enrollment, because the other option may be perceived as a better economic value.

If the two smaller subgroups shift enrollment to the other option, the enrollment shift in the high option plan will result in a 4.4% increase in the average claims per high-option employee. Similarly, the average low option claims per employee will increase by 7.0%.

If the overall health care trends are 10%, exclusive of antiselection, then the low option will show a trend of 17.7% $[(1.100 \times 1.07) - 1.000]$ and the high option will show a trend of 14.8% $[(1.100 \times 1.044) - 1.000]$. This is despite the fact that the benefit-adjusted trend for both options combined is still 10%. Thus, the impact of antiselection is to distort the observed trends from the true level of underlying health care trends due to observed shifts of population sub-segments

Cost Shifting

Another major trend issue is the effect of cost shifting resulting from reduced or negotiated payments to providers by Medicare, Medicaid, HMOs, and PPOs, and uncompensated care.

Negotiated provider contracts primarily affect the price component of trend, although providers sometimes try to offset price concessions through increased utilization. Trends are also affected by utilization control programs. However, these would tend to show a one-time only effect on trends.

Price discounts can result from a number of different reimbursement mechanisms. However, utilization, intensity, and mix make a much bigger contribution to trends on the physician side, and can often easily be increased to make up price shortfalls. Medicare experienced such utilization increases during its physician fee freezes in the mid-1980's. The following discussion of price discounts is in the context of hospital reimbursement.

A constant discount from charges will have no impact on average trend after the first year of implementation, unless growth is occurring in the percentage of business subject to discount. For example, in the initial year of obtaining a 10% discount, if charge trends are increasing by 15%, the observed trend to the payer with the discount will be .035, which is $(1.15 \times .9) - 1$. However, in subsequent years if charges increase by 15% then discounted charges also increase by 15%. Indirectly, the effect of such a discount is likely to be an increase in charges (trends) to compensate for the shortfall. This is commonly referred to as cost shifting.

When the market share subject to price discounts grows over time, this has a similar impact on trends as the initial year of price discounts. By increasing the actual charge levels slightly, the providers can compensate for these shortfalls, and maintain total revenues.

Over the long-term, hospital costs have trended very closely with overall hospital revenue. However, for some payers, such as Medicare (under Prospective Payment using DRGs), reimbursements for some periods after 1985 increased less than the actual cost increases each year; therefore, hospitals tried to make up this shortfall to balance revenue. Hospitals balance their revenue by increasing their charges by a higher rate than their costs.

A primary benefactor of hospital price discounts is Medicare. Other common beneficiaries of price discounts include Medicaid, HMOs, PPOs, some Blue Cross plans, some employers, and some commercial insurers. The market penetration of the payers and the nature of their reimbursement mechanisms in a given area will determine the ultimate impact of discounts on trends. Because of the expansion of PPO and HMO networks, very few payers reimburse on a full charge basis except for out-of-area or non-network claims and under provider high charge outlier provisions. Many discounted reimbursements are still based on a percentage of charges, especially for outpatient hospital services.

MANAGED CARE

Various insurers (especially managed care organizations) use techniques to either directly manage the delivery of medical care or to financially influence the providers of care to do so. These activities can cause experienced claim costs trends to differ substantially from the force of trend for a period after the implementation of these managed care techniques, or even on an ongoing basis. Initiatives that lead to a one-time savings will have a transitory impact on trends, whereas other initiatives, such as paying providers a capitation, may have longer term impacts.

BENEFIT DESIGN

Changes in the mix of covered lives with differing benefits can cause observed trends to be different from the market force of trend. This is due to shifts both in cost sharing levels or covered benefits.

Trends can also vary due to benefit design itself. This can occur through specific sentinel effects which hold down utilization, shifts in risks selecting particular benefit levels over time, or via fixed cost sharing leverage.

Cost sharing leverage is principally what leads to certain types of medical coverage, such as individual and aggregate stop loss, having substantially higher observed trends than first dollar or rich HMO style plans. Trend leveraging and its relative impact on differing type of coverage can be illustrated with two simple examples.

EXAMPLE 1

Year 1:

First dollar claim cost in Year 1 = $200 PMPM

Force of trend = 10% (assumed to be all cost per service)

Cost sharing = $20 PMPM

Insurer claim cost in Year 1 = $180 PMPM

Year 2:

First dollar claim cost in Year 2 = $200 × 1/10 = $220 PMPM

Insurer claim cost in Year 2 = $220 − $20 = $200 PMPM

Effective trend = $\frac{\$200}{\$180} - 100\% = 11\%$

Trend leverage = 11% − 10% = 1%

Leverage is not part of the force of trend per se, but will typically be measured as part of trend, as it is difficult to remove unless allowed charges are analyzed. This may be difficult to do where capitations are used extensively or where data is unavailable. Trend leverage is typically desirable to include in the underlying measure of trend for most rating applications, as it represents the actual change in the insurers costs.

RANDOM FLUCTUATION

Random variation is a major source of variation between observed claim cost trends and the market force of trend. Smaller blocks of covered lives will have inherently larger fluctuations in PMPM claim cost levels and trends. Thus, when calculating rates of change, whether smoothed through moving averages or not, these trends will often vary from the market force of trend solely due to randomness. This is a crucial point, as a literal use of measured trends may lead to over or under trending, and thus lead to greater variability in financial results.

For example, suppose recent observed trends are 2% higher than the market force of trend, solely due to random fluctuation. If this higher trend becomes embedded in future trend expectations, then the block of business will be over rated. This may lead to short term higher profits but will also encourage portfolio turnover and antiselection. A trend analysis methodology that isolates the effects of random fluctuations is highly desirable.

Trends by Type or Place of Service

Trends can vary by type or place of service (such as hospital inpatient, hospital outpatient, professional services, or pharmacy.) Depending on the application, these may need to be analyzed and projected separately. For example, changing practice patterns can shift services from inpatient to outpatient settings. Changing medical technologies can allow for tests and procedures to be done in an office setting, when historically they had been performed elsewhere. When viewed in aggregate (across all categories), these shifts simply show up as part of the force of trend. When attempting to analyze trends at a finer level of detail, the impact can be substantial. In addition, there may be dynamics affecting particular types of benefits that may add to the accuracy of projections, while it would be difficult to identify and account for them in aggregate.

Pharmacy trends are a good example of where this may occur. Pharmacy trends have long experienced trend levels are in excess of other medical benefits. A recent driving force has been direct-to-consumer advertising, which is thought to spur consumer demand for certain classes of drugs. Other specific factors that may affect pharmacy trends are: expected drug approvals, block buster drugs, drugs losing patent protection, transition of drugs to over the counter status, changes in formularies, and benefit designs which may alter consumption patterns.

EXTERNAL SOURCES OF TREND/INFORMATION

Most insurers have sufficient information to analyze trends from their own data. However, carrier-specific data is often atypical and subject to significant fluctuations. Furthermore, smaller or new insurers and newer blocks of business do not have sufficient data to rely on. As a result, external data sources may prove useful as supplemental information. Four different external measures of medical care trends are discussed below. Proprietary databases also exist or can be developed.

Medicare trends, Nation Health Expenditures (NHE) of the Gross Domestic Product (GDP), the Consumer Price Index – Medical Care (M-CPI), and trend surveys all represent public or quasi public data sources. Each of these trend measures represents different sources, objectives, and component characteristics and, consequently, produces different results. It is important to understand the differences between these measures in order to properly interpret what has happened to health trends in the past, and to predict what is likely to happen in the future. Examining these external sources can provide supplemental information to those trying to interpret the results of their own trend experience.

MEDICARE

Medicare trends provide a good measure of the history of cost increases for its covered population which is over age 65 and disabled under age 65. However, distortions occur because of eligibility expansions and other significant legislative changes that have been made over time. For example, Medicare claim trends increased dramatically with the addition of the disabled and End Stage Renal Disease enrollees. They were also affected in 1989 and 1990 by the adoption and subsequent repeal of the Medicare Catastrophic Program. Furthermore, Medicare benefits are generally different from most other insured populations, because drugs are not covered, and maternity and pediatric care are at a low utilization level because of the age of the covered population.

GROSS DOMESTIC PRODUCT (GDP) – NATIONAL HEALTH EXPENDITURES (NHE)

The National Health Expenditure (NHE) portion of GDP demonstrates the significant impact of medical care on the economy. Current levels of NHE have reached about 14% of GDP as of the late 1990s.

The official Medical Care GDP expenditure estimates are produced by the Centers for Medicaid and Medicare Services (CMS) Office of National Cost Estimates. CMS publishes its estimates annually in considerable detail.

The CMS data is split along two dimensions: by providers of services and by sources of funds. Several layers of expenses are also developed, including national health expenditures (total), health services and supplies, personal health care expenditures, and government public health activity. A major focus is on personal health care expenditures, which exclude program administration, research and construction, and government public health activity. The annual data release by CMS is published after a significant lapse of time and is subject to retroactive revisions. This data is generally not helpful for current monitoring purposes.

MEDICAL CPI/PPI

The M-CPI (services plus commodities) and its various components (Hospital and Related Services, Physician Services, and so forth), which are published monthly, are probably the most commonly known statistics related to medical care cost trends. Beyond the fact that the M-CPI represents a measure of medical care prices, few of the details about this index are widely understood. But since this index is timely and widely followed, it is important to understand the history and definition of the M-CPI and how it relates to health care costs. Unless otherwise noted, all specific references in this section are to the medical components of the CPI-W for Urban Wage Earners and Clerical Workers.

The CPI and all of its components are constructed to measure the increase in prices for a fixed market basket of consumer-purchased goods and services. The weights of the market basket are developed from consumer expenditure surveys that are updated periodically to reflect changing buying habits. Services covered include a range of hospital, physician, vision and dental services, drugs, and health insurance. Other periodic changes in the CPI have included improvements in statistical techniques and sampling procedures, and expansions of covered populations, cities, and priced items.

The M-CPI is intended to measure the price increase of out-of-pocket costs (those not covered by third-party payments) and the proportion of health insurance paid for by consumers (not employer or government contributions). As a result, compared to a typical health insurance policy, hospital and physician charges are under-weighted and services not included or less significant in a typical health insurance policy, such as nursing home, vision and dental care, are over-weighted. Furthermore, because the intent is to measure out-of-pocket costs, originally the CPI measured billed charges. The CPI was adjusted in the late 1980s to recognize physician discounts, and in the 1990s for hospital discounts. This creates some discontinuity in these CPI series. Also, the CPI ignores the effects of provider capitations.

In 1993 the Bureau of Labor Statistics began publishing a Producer Price Index for hospital (and later for physician) services. This index was intended to alleviate some of the shortcomings of the M-CPI, by capturing the cost of producing a unit (an admission) of hospital services. These series contained substantial detail, including data by type of payer. Early data was somewhat volatile, and recently some of the detail has been eliminated. However, tracking and analyzing this data going forward may prove useful.

TREND SURVEYS

Trend surveys are a common source of medical trend information relied on to help set pricing trend assumptions. These surveys are typically compiled by consultants, and are an easy and attractive source of competitive data points. However, caution should be used in using these sources, as they are typically compiled with differing degrees of statistical rigor, may be compiled for differing purposes, and may therefore be measuring different things. They may also be based on a company's assessment of future trends that may be completely inaccurate. And finally, these surveys rarely produce data that is appropriate for the statistical analysis of trends. More commonly, the results of these surveys are applied as a second opinion to be compared to internal views of trends.

These various public data sources have limited usefulness. However, with a proper understanding of their limitations a skilled technician can use such information to enhance their understanding of private data sources.

ECONOMIC ISSUES IN TREND ANALYSIS

The consumption of health care is a complex process, driven by such diverse factors as the health status and demographics of the population, inflation, the prevalence and level of medical insurance, the financial incentives of providers, and more recently, intervention by third party payers. While some of these factors impact the micro-economic decisions affecting the individual consumption of health care, other factors affect the macro-economic aspects of health care. Such factors include: increases in wealth, price inflation, physician supply, level of benefits, and the specialization of physicians. In fact, increases in wealth (income) appear to be a leading indicator of health care consumption. Econometric models can be designed to forecast health care trends further into the future and with greater accuracy, once this lagged relationship is properly understood.

Many of the factors normally considered to drive individual consumption are unimportant in pursuing a macro-economic approach to model building. This is because the inherent volatility and unpredictability of individual health care consumption obscures the more stable nature of aggregate demand decisions. Micro-economic determinants of health care consumption include health status of the individual, availability and scope of insurance, access to care, and actions of primary care physicians.

The set of variables to model consumption from a macro-economic perspective will be proxies for supply and demand effects. A variable to measure the "wealth effect" is required. Other variables are chosen to test hypotheses that are presented regarding other determinants of health care spending. Among these are: physician supply and composition, general inflation, cost shifting, managed care impact and comprehensiveness of benefits. And finally, the effect of demographics must be considered. Some of these variables are briefly described below.

• As the wealth of the population increases through economic growth, each marginal dollar of income is allocated to some form of savings or consumption. As wealth increases, health care consumption should increase. This variable may also reflect increases in investment in health care research, in both the public and private sectors, which occur as the nation's wealth increases.

• Regular market factors driving general prices higher are reflected in economy-wide inflation. The same market forces also affect the health care sector. Thus, higher general inflation leads to higher health care inflation.

• As physician supply grows, this should impact price, quantity and quality of health care consumption. Increasing physician supply should theoretically work to hold down prices (although it does not appear to have happened) but increase quantity and quality of care by improving access to and usage of medical technology. The net impact of physician growth appears to be increased health care consumption.

• The increasing proportion of physicians in specialty fields appear to have led to, or at least is coincident with, the greater use of technology and more medically intense therapies, thereby raising health care costs.

• As the population ages, more health care is consumed due to the natural physical deterioration of the aging process. The demographic effects tend to be picked up in modeling by some of the other variables, such as physician supply.

• As individuals are required to pay a smaller share of their direct health care bill (excluding insurance premiums), their sensitivity to price is reduced. As a greater percentage of dollars is covered by third-party payers, health care consumption should rise at the margin.

• The growing impact of managed care on the population should affect health care consumption. Due to low market penetration in the past, it may be only recently that managed care has had sufficient impact on National Health Expenditures to be statistically measurable. Or alternatively, effectiveness may have increased once sufficient volume was achieved to exert leverage to change practice patterns.

ANALYSIS OF TREND

In order to project future trends, past experience trends must not only be measured, but the driving factors and special circumstances behind the movements must be better understood. Use of simple regression tools is often inappropriate because of the cyclical patterns of trends. Raising the level of technical sophistication in this area, using Auto Regressive Integrated Moving Average (ARIMA) techniques that adjust for serial correlation in the error terms of statistical models, transfer function models which measure the predictive effects of independent variables on the variable to be modeled, intervention (discontinuities or outliers in the data series) detection, and other statistical techniques, is clearly desirable.

Industry trend setting techniques do not generally attempt to statistically identify causal factors such as the effects of antiselection, regional mix, cost shifting, benefit mix change (such as changes in deductible and copay), and special one-time effects. It would be helpful to isolate these factors so they can be examined separately, and forecasts or informed judgments can be developed about their future applicability.

There are probably as many approaches to analyzing claim cost trends as there are health actuaries but the approaches can be categorized. While there is no definitive or universally applied approach, a statistical-based approach will be presented here as the recommended one.

Approaches to trend analysis can generally be separated into those that do not use external data or indicators and those that do.

TECHNIQUES NOT USING EXTERNAL DATA

Historical Averages/Graphs: This typically involves calculating rates of change in the claim cost, and smoothing them. Various levels of detail can be used, but highly aggregated data are not uncommon in practice, particularly for straightforward situations. These trends are typically shown in tables and graphs. Judgment, experience, and often competitive information are then used to anticipate future trends. These trends are typically heavily influenced by recent experience, and are often dampened with smoothing techniques. This approach is, in this author's opinion, one of the root causes of the "cyclical" nature of industry financial results.

Actuarial Models: One common approach is to develop a detailed cost estimate from basic components. Claim cost experience is broken into detailed benefit categories, and further into cost per service and number of services. A combination of future assumptions and "known" impacts (such as changes in contracted provider reimbursement rates) are then used to build up to a claim cost projection. While this approach may appear reasonable due to the level of detail involved, the end results are often similar to the historical average approach. Recent experience still heavily influences the choice of assumptions, and many of the "known" impacts turn out to be more complex and less predictable at this level of detail than originally anticipated.

The study of unit costs is one area where future information is known with some degree of certainty. Facility contracts are typically negotiated with some lead time, and often have multi-year cost of living adjustments (COLAs) that allow unit costs to be predicted with reasonable accuracy. Unfortunately, unit costs are only one piece of the force of trend and the other components defy prediction within this framework.

Linear Regression: This approach builds a linear (usually after taking logarithms, representing an exponential model) regression model of historical claim costs. This is tantamount to using the historical average trend. It has one advantage, in that recent random fluctuations in claim costs are adjusted for implicitly. It also has the major failing that everything except the average trend, including cyclical factors, are treated as random fluctuation and essentially ignored.

Auto-Regressive Integrated Moving Average (ARIMA) Models: Box-Jenkins ARIMA models use only the past series values in an attempt to fit past experience and extrapolate that experience into the future. Unfortunately this approach does not deal well with changes in trend levels (cyclical changes) that affect medical trends. This limits the forecasting accuracy of this technique over longer periods, but may add value beyond linear regression models.

TECHNIQUES USING EXTERNAL INDICATORS

These techniques are typically statistical in nature, and rely on causal modeling techniques, such as multiple regression analysis or Box-Jenkins transfer function models. The application of these techniques is predicated on the assumption that external indicators (preferably leading ones) are available to model past experience. Another alternative is to use a coincident indicator that has future values specified in some fashion, such as the Health Cost Index.

The basis of the statistical modeling approach is that the observed claim cost trends are the result of a number of complex factors, and that these factors can be modeled and their impact isolated in a linear fashion, using standard statistical techniques. One modeling paradigm that is sufficiently flexible and robust for both the identification of model forms and the robust estimation of the model parameters is the Box-Jenkins transfer function.

As the subject matter can be quite technical, an example of trend analysis using external indicators is presented below using standard regression analysis. Implicitly assumed in the example is that an external indicator, the Health Cost Index (HCI), is an appropriate proxy for the market force of trend, and that the sample carrier data is contemporaneously correlated with the HCI.

EXAMPLE

Background: This example is based on a set of actual observed claim costs. The costs have been altered to disguise the actual nature of the data. The claim costs are for all benefits combined for the insurer's non-Medicare lines of business. Monthly claims are available for sixty months. The more recent months have been adjusted for claim reserve.

Graphical Analysis: A sound first step is to perform a graphical analysis of the claim cost versus the HCI. Figure 36.1 illustrates the sample claim cost and the HCI indexed to 1.0 at a common time period. In this case, April of 2001 was chosen, as it provides a clear view of the series relationship. This index graph allows the slope of the two lines to be compared independently of scale considerations.

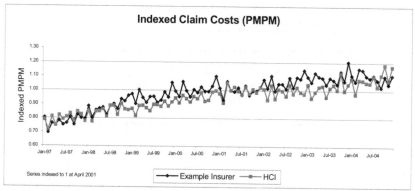

Figure 36.1

While this graphical comparison in no way proves correlation or the nature of any relationship, it does provide for a useful and easy summary of the data and how they relate. From this graph it is clear that the slopes of the lines are at least similar. Furthermore, there was a period during 2001 where this carrier's claim costs dropped below the HCI. This period lasted 12 months, and then the deviation ceased. Again, in July, 2004, the claims appear to drop below the HCI and this persists to the end of the example.

Statistical analysis: Before building a statistical model between the sample claims and the HCI, the two identified periods of discontinuities must be considered. How these periods are handled in the model can have a substantial impact on the results and future forecasts. Often in these situations, it is not clear which is the most appropriate approach. There may be competing ways of modeling the phenomenon that have similar statistical characteristics, yet produce substantially different results. In these cases, the model builder should present the alternate models for consideration and judgment must be used to determine which model to use. An understanding of the cause of the deviations should help in choosing the appropriate method

A multiple regression model relating the sample claim costs and the HCI was constructed, to illustrate a possible approach to modeling this data. The model uses the HCI, seasonal dummy variables and two specially con- structed dummy variables to account for the possible periods where the sample carrier's experience deviates. The two variables are defined as such:

Intervention 1	
Time Period	Series Value
Jan 1999 - Dec 2000	0
Jan 2001 - Dec 2001	1
Jan 2002 - Dec 2004	0

Intervention 2	
Time Period	Series Value
Jan 1999 - Jun 2004	0
Jul 2004 - Dec 2004	1

By including these two variables in the regression, we are testing the hypotheses that the conditional mean (or level) of the series changed temporarily, in the case of intervention 1, and permanently in the case of intervention 2. The inclusion of these variables, if statistically significant, will allow for the estimate of the relationship between the HCI and the sample claim costs to be estimated independently of the two periods of deviation. This is not to say that this is the most appropriate manner of modeling the periods – only that it is one way.

The appropriateness of the model is ultimately determined by the root cause of the deviations and the reasonableness of the results. Note also that the assumption that intervention 2 is permanent will have a profound impact on any forecasts, as we are assuming that the lower level of claim costs continues out into the future.

The regression results are presented below:

Sample Carrier Regression Results	
Regression Output	
Constant	4.4153
Std Err of Y Est	0.0354
R-Squared	0.9299
No. of Observations	96
Degrees of Freedom	81

Variable:	Ln(HCI)	Jan	Feb	Mar	Apr	May	Jun	Jul
X-Coefficient(s)	1.22	−0.05	−0.02	−0.04	−0.05	−0.08	−0.05	−0.07
Std Err of Coef.	0.041	0.018	0.018	0.018	0.018	0.018	0.018	0.018
t-statistic	29.68	−2.59	−1.21	−2.50	−2.93	−4.41	−2.92	−3.83

	Aug	Sep	Oct	Nov	Intervention 1	Intervention 2
X-Coefficient(s)	−0.07	−0.06	−0.07	−0.05	−0.06	−0.07
Std Err of Coef.	0.018	0.018	0.018	0.018	0.011	0.017
t-statistic	−4.06	−3.46	−4.13	−2.81	−5.31	−3.85

The sample claim cost slope (or trend) is approximately 22% higher than the HCI, adjusted for the two periods of deviation, over the period 1999-2004. The t-statistic for this variable is 29.68, indicating a strong relationship. This key relationship will be used to forecast he carrier's future claim costs based on the forecasts of the HCI that were provided. Of course, this forecast assumes that past relationships between the HCI and observed claim costs will hold into the future.

The seasonal dummies measure the differences in seasonality between the two series, relative to the December time period. The statistics for the two interventions indicate that the hypotheses that the level of the sample carrier claim costs changed at those time periods could not be rejected. In fact, both variables were strongly significant.

In applying this type of analysis, residual diagnostic checks should be performed, including residual auto-correlation and partial auto-correlation analysis to determine whether the model is sound. Evidence of residual problems usually indicates that the model is not correctly specified, and one or more variables could be missing from the model. Often missing variables can be modeled using intervention variables, such as those we used, above.

The actual, fitted and forecasted claim values are shown in Figure 36.2.

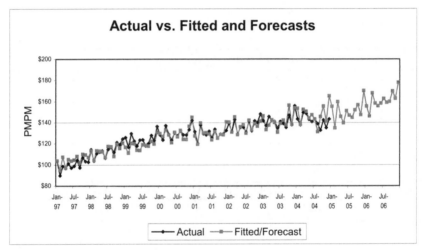

Figure 36.2

<u>COMMON PROBLEMS IN TREND ANALYSIS</u>

Given the issues identified above and the many facets of trends, it is not surprising to find the trend measurement and analysis process subject to a number of challenges. These include changes in claim processing and payment patterns and the lag required to understand and reflect them in claim analysis. Also, the sale and termination of insured groups can change the benefit mix of a business segment between experience periods.

Other challenges may arise from the methods used to analyze trends. The most common technique has been the use of twelve-month moving average trends to smooth out the seasonality effects and to minimize random volatility of claims during the year. Three-month moving average trends are also commonly used; however, they are often considered to be too volatile. The trade-off between the longer and shorter period is the ability to detect recent changes in the trend patterns vs. the higher volatility due to random fluctuations.

Analysis of one-month moving average trends and the time series of relative monthly claim costs, when compared to an external index, can add significant information and identify factors that might be obscured using 12-month or 3-month moving average trends.

Two common statistical reasons for trend interpretation problems are (a) pulse outliers and (b) level shifts (discontinuities). Even when catastrophic claims are adjusted for, pulse outliers are still a significant problem. Furthermore, level shifts appear to be the rule rather than the exception in many samples of actual experience.

Pulse outliers are one or more scattered points (either high or low) in a series of monthly claim costs that exceed the normal statistical ranges. A level shift is an abrupt step (either up or down) in a series of monthly claim costs. By definition, the pulse outliers are temporary. However, the level shift may be either permanent or temporary. If the cause behind an intervention can be understood, it may shed light on whether it is permanent, or temporary and/or reversible, and may help improve forecasting ability.

Figure 36.3, illustrates the impact of a hypothetical 12-month moving trend relative to an external trend standard.

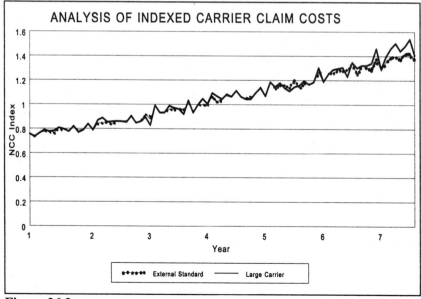

Figure 36.3

It appears as though the trend reasonably follows the standard, with several periods of trends reaching above the standard, and then compensating with a corresponding period below the standard. Toward the end of the data, the trend appears to be in an "above standard" phase. However, based on past history it might be expected to drop "below standard" in the near future.

In turning to Figure 36.4, however, a different interpretation could be made.

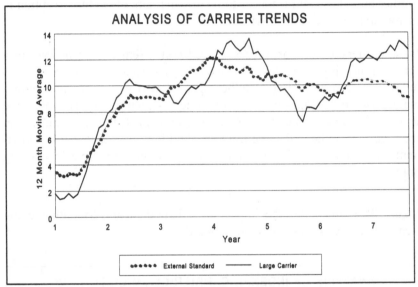

Figure 36.4

This figure compares the relative claim costs month by month to the corresponding index of the external trend standard. This shows a very close correspondence over time, but with short-term random fluctuations which result in the trend deviations noted above. However, at the end of the period there appears to be a clear divergence in the two series. This could be due to loss of a major group, or some other underlying change in the data. As such, the change might be permanent, and the 12-month moving trends may not drop below the standard, but may return to average after this impact is fully factored into the trend base. It would be important to try to identify the cause of this divergence before selecting future trend assumptions. This illustrates the kinds of information that could be masked by relying solely on 12-month moving trends.

Using such a benchmark analysis has many advantages to relying solely on the actual experience of a single data series. As already mentioned, this technique provides the ability to identify statistical or other anomalies that may be having an effect on a single insurer. In addition, a benchmark provides information on the force of trend being experienced by competitors. Finally, a benchmark analysis provides a greater opportunity for sophisticated statistical analysis and forecasting.

TREND ISSUES IN THE MANAGED CARE ENVIRONMENT

Analyzing experience trends in the managed care environment has raised new issues not previously encountered in traditional health insurance environments. While the same macro-economic forces affect health care costs delivered in this environment, new methods of provider reimbursement have changed the nature of risk assumption and therefore the importance of trend to the managed care organization (MCO). Furthermore, the proactive intervention in the medical care delivery process practiced by MCOs leads to greater and more frequent deviations from the market force of trend over the short to medium term.

RISK SHIFTING AND TRENDS

The use of capitation, per diems, DRGs and percent of premium deals (among others) has changed the nature of the risks assumed by an MCO. In many cases trends are more stable than they were under older health insurance models. These arrangements may also change the timing of the relationship between economic factors and an MCOs cost trends. This may occur due to the insertion of a risk transfer mechanism between the MCO and the provider of care. For example, in a capitated reimbursement arrangement the underlying medical costs might rise at the same rate as in the past, but now the provider accepts that risk by agreeing to a flat capitation. The MCO has now been immunized against the market force of trend. However this immunization may only be temporary, as the providers may seek increases commensurate with the costs they have borne. This process may only serve to distort and delay the realization of the force of trend to the MCO. It may also serve to change the fundamental economic relationships driving historical cost trends through the simple act of the risk transfer. Ultimately, the market force of trend may be very different under this environment, and may be de-coupled from the traditional drivers. There is some evidence that this process did occur during the 1990's, a period of rapid growth in managed care. Prior to the late 1980's health care costs grew substantially in excess of real economic activity. Subsequent to this time period, and coincident with the explosion of MCOs, this excess growth rate has shrunk. During the late 1990's there has been a substantial rethinking of the traditional managed care model in response to a market and politically driven backlash. This appears to be leading to a reversion to a more historical relationship of trend relative to economic indicators.

The impact of provider reimbursements, financial incentives, direct patient care initiatives, and other managed care techniques will not affect all insurers uniformly. The impact can vary, depending on what the insurer has done, how they are implemented, and what other health insurers are doing in their local market.

THE IMPACT OF MANAGED CARE ON THE FORCE OF TREND

The changes that managed care has begun have had an impact beyond those covered under MCOs. As providers have changed the way that care is delivered in response to the new economics of health care, they have also applied these new paradigms to patients covered under less aggressive, or even unmanaged, delivery systems. Thus, it is likely that medical cost trends across all types of insurers are influenced by managed care.

CHANGES IN TREND ANALYSIS UNDER MANAGED CARE

Analyzing trends in a managed care environment requires additional preparation and forethought. Data may need to be analyzed at different levels of detail. Whereas analyzing aggregate claim costs may have been sufficient before, benefits which are capitated may need to be excluded and analyzed separately. The analysis of interventions becomes more important as disruptions of trend from market forces are more likely. Analysis of the impact of the changes in costs due to managed care initiatives using intervention or dummy variables can be quite useful.

Impact of Company-Specific Care Management Initiatives on Trend

"Managed care" is a broad term that may encapsulate delivery models that vary from a closed panel model to an open access model. Managed care initiatives that can affect trends of costs are the same ones that impact cost levels in the first place. When these items are implemented, stopped, or changed, they can result in changes in cost levels that are measured as trend. These programs, or the lack of them, can result in trends that are persistently above or below the prevailing force of trend.

One useful measure of the historical trend impact of is the approval percentage of dollars of claims. One could calculate the ratio of paid charges to those that were submitted, and measure this over time. As this percentage rises, it may indicate a less restrictive form of managed care.

Managed care companies that are loosening their care management may experience higher trends, which must then be adjusted for.

Changes in the degree of care management may also affect external behavior. Rigorous application of pre-certification, pre-authorization, and utilization review may create a sentinel effect, limiting the types and number of services that a provider may perform and submit. Therefore, an MCO can be very tightly managed and have a high approval percentage. Conversely, when some of the policies are relaxed this sentinel effect may go away over time, leading to periods of sustained utilization increases in excess of that experienced in the force of trend.

LONG-TERM MEDICAL TRENDS

For most medical insurance, only two or three years of future trends are necessary for managing the business. However, employers' post-retirement liabilities for medical benefits, and Medicare Trust Fund analyses, must project trends out from fifty to seventy years or more. Obviously, for projections of this duration, actual year to year variation in trends are relatively unimportant, but good estimates for average trends in the short, intermediate and long-term horizons are desired. These long-term liabilities and projected cost levels are very sensitive to differences in the long-term trend assumptions. Furthermore, simply extrapolating from historical trends could produce unreasonably high liability estimates.

For the past 60 plus years, the real (inflation adjusted) growth rate of the health portion of Gross Domestic Product (GDP) has risen at a faster rate than the overall GDP, and consequently faster than the non-health portion of the GDP. From the mid-1960's to the early 1990's, the excess growth rate in real National Health Expenditures (Health GDP) has been 3-4%. Part of this growth is due to aging and other demographic shifts, but these impacts are relatively small (0.2-0.4% per year.)

The Technical Advisory Committee to the Trustees of the Medicare Trust Fund considered the issue of the long-term excess health care growth trend. The conclusion of the Advisory Committee in 2004 was that long-term excess growth trend of 1% is appropriate. Such growth would produce Health GDP proportions of around 40%.

37 FORECASTING

Doug Fearrington

INTRODUCTION

This discussion focuses on forecasting as a modeling exercise, rather than as a reporting exercise. Issues and considerations in construction of a forecasting model are outlined. To achieve this end, the discussion divides a forecasting model into two components: (1) content and structure, and (2) methodology. Content and structure refers to choosing forecasting "cells," data inputs, and outputs. Methodology refers to the techniques actually employed for the projection of values.

We will begin by expanding on fundamental concepts, with discussion of the goals of a forecast, and guidelines in forecast development. More detailed content and structure is then addressed. Then, specific forecasting methodologies are described and evaluated.

The context of the discussion is the production of a corporate forecast for group health insurance business, but many of the statements have applicability to different products and different types of forecasts, such as renewal pricing or trend analysis. The primary concern will be on forecasting premium income and claim expenses.

There can be little argument that a corporate forecast is one of the most important reports generated by an organization. In practice, an actuary is likely to spend significant and valuable time in tracking down pieces of information from multiple departments and sources, to make sure all components of a reporting template are accurate and appropriate.

However, in assembling all of these elements, it can be easy to lose sight of the true nature and significance of what's being done. A forecast is

779

more than a mere statement of prospective income or future assessment of balances between assets and liabilities. At its core, a forecast is a statement of the future condition of a block of business. It is the template for how a company will attempt to understand and monitor the marketplace in which it participates. And, through its very existence, a forecast is both a reflection of and a driving force behind the organization of a company's analytical functions.

GOALS

What does a company hope to gain by producing a forecast? The purposes are many, and might include:

- *A forecast serves as a basis for developing company strategy.* Today's pricing, product development, marketing and sales strategy are all dependent upon having an understanding of what revenue, expense and income scenarios are likely tomorrow.

- *A forecast can give guidance for assignment of resources.* A company's resources for implementing strategies are obviously limited. A forecast can guide management in prioritizing its initiatives.

- *A forecast provides metrics for monitoring performance.* A forecast serves as a tracking device for significant deviations from a company's expectations.

- *A forecast is a key component for capital management and reporting.* Forecasted values for operating gain and net income help in targeting and monitoring risk-based capital levels, surplus allocation to lines of business for ROI and ROE reporting, and overall asset liability management activities.

- *A forecast can be used to assist in assigning bottom-line responsibility.* To the extent a company bases its management compensation on results, a forecast is a valuable tool for establishing the targets.

- *A forecast provides guidance to a company's public.* The public can be a company's Board of Directors, investors in a public company, or policyholders in a mutual company. All of these audiences generally prefer being presented with some evidence that a company's senior management has a vision of the company's future.

Spending time to consider the goals of a forecast is a valuable first step in building a model.

PROCESSES TO BE MODELED

When developing a forecasting model, it can be all too tempting to adopt an attitude of "have data, will forecast," and simply select a method that readily incorporates whatever information is at hand. However, before selecting that the first input parameter, it is important to define the processes being addressed.

The healthcare marketplace is a complex one. The individual actions of millions of individuals are involved, and the conditions and events affecting the decisions of each of these individuals changes daily. So it is probably infeasible to create a model at a level of detail that attempts to make statements about each of these millions of decisions.

While complex, the market is not impenetrable. There are a few basic processes that underlie the varying dynamics of the group insurance marketplace. We choose to separate these processes into six fundamental categories:

1. The illnesses and medical conditions experienced by a population

The morbidity of a covered population represents the basic demand of the healthcare marketplace. If we view morbidity as a process, then over any given time horizon existing illnesses and conditions will continue or end, while new illnesses and conditions will emerge. A company will observe this process to the extent that a given member remains under coverage, care is sought, and claims are submitted.

Given a large enough population and no extenuating circumstances (such as a closed pool), most forecasts generally assume that the distribution or mix of conditions will be stable (or, at the very least, that the mix will be stable with respect to cost).

However, determining what constitutes "large enough" and a "stable mix" are not trivial exercises. It's important to consider whether a forecasting model adequately addresses issues such as low frequency conditions and changing trends in disease emergence.

With advances in technology, improvements in data collection and accuracy, and the influence of clinical knowledge on the managed care industry, it's possible that new forecasting methodologies may be able to model changes in disease states directly. Use of proprietary risk assessment software may be a first step in this direction.

This process reflects not only changing medical conditions of a population, but also changes in that population itself.

2. The diagnosis and treatment of illnesses and conditions

This process represents the practice of medicine within a marketplace. For a given condition over a given timeframe, there is a course of utilization that incorporates likely drug therapies, likely specialists to be involved, prevailing settings for treatment, expected hospitals to be visited, equipment, supplies, and other costs.

In common practice the diagnosis and treatment process is addressed with utilization measures by claim type, such as physician claims or facility claims. Using such measures is a place to start for reflecting expected changes in practice, but without adequate provision for differences in population mix (Process 1, above), estimation can be difficult.

3. Insurer payments for reimbursement of diagnosis and treatment

Services provided under Process 2 normally will be reimbursed according to a carrier's contracts in place at the time of service. With the current movement in the market toward more scheduled payments, and therefore more predictability in contracting, it is desirable for a forecasting model to directly incorporate anticipated contractual changes. This can be difficult for several reasons:

- The sheer number of contracts a company of even moderate size has negotiated can be staggering. This can be mitigated to the extent that there's standardization of structure across contracts, or concentration of services at a few larger providers;

- The timing of contractual changes is not always orderly. Providers whom the carrier assumed were pleased with a current contract can suddenly demand changes; a negotiation can drag on and on; or, a provider can simply drop out of the network; and

- "Predictable" terms often leave a measure of uncertainty. This is the case of a hospital per diem arrangement that includes a stop loss provision if charges exceed a threshold (length of stay could change, charges could change), a fee schedule that pays under "lesser of" terms, or any payment arrangement where substantial incentives are involved.

In fact, estimates of the value of changes in a reimbursement arrangement are mini-forecasts in and of themselves, subject to the same process dynamics outlined here. When using independently developed estimates by contract or provider, the actuary should consider the assumptions in each and question consistency and thoroughness.

4. Company actions related to marketing, sales, and enrollment

A projection or statement of future enrollment is one of the most basic and important pieces of information to be incorporated by a forecasting model. Too often, however, a company's enrollment forecast is merely a sales force's "feel" for what is achievable. To the extent that such feel represents expert judgment, this may be a valid approach. However, enrollment estimates developed in such a manner usually provide little guidance as to which specific employer groups or markets will be retained or targeted for new sales.

5. Company actions concerning rating and benefits

Premium income is a function of a company's strategy on pricing trends, rate relationships among products, and product offerings. To the extent past rates were inadequate, observed experience, too, can influence future premiums (depending on rating methodology).

Knowledge of strategy and claim experience for a given segment of business, though, does not guarantee a realistic projection of premium. Realized premiums are determined at a group and individual level, based on circumstances unique to each (see the next section). Historical studies of rate elasticity, product migration, or other factors may provide some additional guidance in formulating a model.

6. Consumer and provider behavior in the presence of financing (payment) for diagnosis and treatment

Consumers and providers will certainly react to rate increases, benefit changes, and reimbursement changes. This set of behaviors represents one of the most important and one of the most difficult processes to model.

Examples of such behavior abound:

- In light of significant premium increases or a changing economic environment, consumers tend to switch ("buy down") to lower cost plans to reduce their premiums.

- Changes in provider billing practices may be observed when reimbursement arrangements or medical management policies change. For example, lower reimbursement levels may result in unbundling of services.

- Changes in visit patterns, such as frequency of referrals or of follow-ups. A capitated payment arrangement with a professional provider may encourage that provider to refer cases to a specialist, due the volume independent nature of a capitation payment.

- Changes in technology investment or capital expenditures. When a facility purchases a piece of equipment, thereby increasing availability of a service, utilization of that service usually increases.

- Partnering among providers. When providers align with other providers, they are likely to modify their referral patterns to take advantage of the new arrangement.

- Changes in treatment settings. This behavior often reflects technological changes. For example, surgical technology has allowed more procedures to be done in a physician's office rather than in a facility setting.

- Changes in patient utilization of services (due to changes in benefits). This behavior is an essential element in insurance in which the provision of coverage for a service increases the utilization of those services.

Many would argue that, in the interest of completeness, the regulatory environment should be listed as a separate process. We choose here merely to point out that regulation has the potential to affect all aspects of the group health insurance marketplace, and to significantly alter the dynamics of all the above processes by limiting company actions. For example, rate regulation can limit a company's ability to adjust premiums. Minimum benefit restrictions, such as a minimum length of stay for maternity hospital admissions, limit a company's ability to manage cost and quality of care.

The real point of listing these distinct processes is to highlight that these are the underlying process that a forecast is really trying to reflect. Thus, in developing a forecasting model, it is important to continually ask the question "How does the model address all of these fundamental processes? What's explicit? What's implicit? What's ignored?"

CONTENT AND STRUCTURE

All forecasting models start with at least some historical or observed data. The choice of such data, and the level of detail selected, is a significant step in the modeling process. We label this step "content and structure"; by this, we are referring to the level of detail the forecast addresses, the layout and types of inputs into a forecasting model, and the types of estimates generated or output by the model.

There are two extremes which illustrate the choices in level of detail. All such models produce enrollment and per member per month estimates of premium and claims. The simple model makes an enterprise-wide projection of these values. The detailed model makes projections separately for groupings (cells) of data defined by employer size and by provider network and other variables, with claims split into unit cost and utilization per 1,000, by provider type and place of treatment.

Even though both models use the same technique, due to the structure and content of the data used, they make different statements about the six fundamental processes described above and how they vary by grouping.

FORECASTING CELL

Defining the cells for modeling is the first step in developing the structure of a forecasting model. By "cell," we mean the segmentation of a company's covered population into distinct units, for which distinct output will be produced.

In general, there are many possibilities for grouping the model's universe: enterprise-wide, by area, by network, by product, by rating methodology, by group size, by product, group-by-group, or even person-by-person. The level of detail assumed in a forecast is often imposed by a company's reporting requirements or management structure. For example, a company may have managers responsible for certain products or market segments and therefore need forecasts for those products or markets. However, such requirements may not be conducive to forecasting techniques due to size of population covered, mixing of rating methodologies, or for other reasons.

Nonetheless, a choice must be made. There are a number of general considerations in choosing these model parameters.

First, segmentation by type of revenue stream is generally desirable, as an efficient means of matching income with expenses. As an example, developing separate forecasts for fully insured, minimum premium, and self insured lines of business allows for better matching of the revenue and obligations inherent in the different types of risk arrangements.

"Homogeneity" of a cohort or covered population generally assists with making consistent statements about the six processes described earlier. Thus, the more a covered population is similar with respect to morbidity, access to care, persistency of enrollment, and financial behaviors, the easier it is to analyze them and make generalizations about them. As an example, smaller employers and their employees tend to exhibit different behavior than large employers and their employees, with respect to price points, benefit options, and expected service levels. As another example, cohorts with a large degree of turnover and low persistency, such as some individual lines of business, warrant separate consideration from those with high persistency and low turnover.

Available historical data will influence choices for segmentation. In general, the more data available, the better position the underwriter will be in to evaluate the experience. However, this usually means less product or market specific detail, and more heterogeneity. Longer time series of data will provide more guidance towards seasonal patterns, inflection points in trends, and the impact of business cycles. At a minimum, more data points will allow for testing the performance of models. On the other hand, new products with little to no previous experience may be best handled with separate treatment, and are probably best not lumped in with existing lines of business.

The more detailed a forecast becomes, the greater the risk for both increased bias and increased computational complexity. What's more, some of the robustness of common forecasting techniques can be lost as a forecast becomes more detailed.

ENROLLMENT

Once segmentation of the company's covered population has been determined, projected enrollment becomes the next most important piece of information.

An enrollment forecast that can describe the specific groups or types of groups that will be targeted is desirable. If possible, it can be helpful to split this projection by retained business versus new sales and also by marketplace. These types of splits can give guidance as to how morbidity, diagnosis, and treatment are likely to change relative to observed experience.

It's also desirable to have some information as to which products and benefit designs will be sold, in order to gauge potential changes in consumer utilization behavior, as well as the potential differences in cost-shifting.

In actual practice, most enrollment forecasts are constructed simplistically, and usually go through a couple of iterations. As an example, a simple percentage increase is usually negotiated between a sales force and a finance department, with little detail provided as to how the growth will occur. In such cases, it may be useful to employ a forecasting methodology that at least makes some provision for scenarios where morbidity and treatment patterns change.

CLAIMS

Current practice usually involves summarizing claim data by claim type (facility, physician, drug, and so forth), by place of treatment (inpatient, outpatient, office), and by type of service (surgery, radiology, emergency, and so forth). Utilization per 1,000 and unit cost measures (and resulting claim costs) are typically gathered historically as far back is as feasible. These breaks serve as a basis for incorporating prospective changes to treatment patterns (adjustments to utilization measures) and anticipated contractual changes (adjustments to unit cost measures).

As these are *summarized* measures, there is a degree of estimation or judgment that occurs with respect to making explicit statements about many of the processes. For example, outpatient facility diagnostic visits could change due to:

- An increase in the number of patients requiring colonoscopies (Process 1),

- Capital investments in office-based equipment by physicians for performing colonoscopies, causing a shift in settings (Process 2), or

- Reductions to a facility fee schedule for colonoscopies, resulting in an increase in utilization (Process 6).

Furthermore, historical data will reflect, of necessity, old market conditions. Certain benefit designs may no longer be offered, reimbursement methodologies may have changed significantly, or a substantially different mix of business may have been sold. Depending on the forecasting technique used, adjustments should be made to the extent possible, either directly to the historical data (prior to applying the technique) or incorporated within the technique itself.

PREMIUMS

As rate changes are closely linked to claims, close matching of that relationship in the model is preferred. This applies not only to the structure of data used by a forecasting model, but also to the methodologies employed for projection. For example, if a market segment being forecasted has a significant proportion of the business renewing in a certain month, then the premium forecast would have to consider this timing of rate actions.

Furthermore, in times of large rate increases, benefit reductions and policy cancellations are likely to increase. This will affect both premium and enrollment projections (to the extent that the enrollment forecast does not assume such behavior). Ad hoc studies of historical rate elasticity can provide some guidance to the actuary in establishing appropriate relationships between a premium projection and a claim projection.

In addition, it is prudent to recognize the potential for plan sponsors to switch funding arrangements in different rating environments, as well as the resulting potential antiselection. As a crude example, large rate increases in a fully insured market may cause some groups to move to self-insured arrangements, potentially hurting the operating gains from each of the two blocks of business.

CONSIDERATIONS FOR OUTPUTS

Beyond point estimates of premium, claims, and resulting gross margin, it may be desirable to make statements about confidence levels or probability of adequacy. This can be handled in a number of ways, depending on the level of rigor and sophistication available from the data and models being employed.

At the more simplistic end of the spectrum, subjective ranges can be constructed around each of the outputs. These can be based on the actuary's judgment of likely variability or based on experiences with previous forecast error.

If the selected forecasting technique supports it, formal statistical distributions of outputs can be created. Generally these will require either parametric fitting from empirical data or will be generated through Monte Carlo simulation, where input distributions are sampled repeatedly and outputs are calculated with each iteration.

The danger in adopting an output structure where "one distribution fits all" is that these tend to be considered independent of each other, while real life correlations of events normally create clustering around certain scenarios. Thus, it is often more effective to establish specific alternative scenarios, and then apply probabilities of occurrence to each. As a starting point, written descriptions of worst, most likely, and best case scenarios can be constructed. Each description should address the key events or underlying assumptions that identify the scenario, to facilitate tracking against actual experience. Simply writing in words what a given forecast "says" or "means" can be a valuable exercise in and of itself, regardless of the degree of variability incorporated.

METHODOLOGIES

There are numerous methods or techniques that have been developed for forecasting, certainly too many to list comprehensively here. Rather, we discuss a few more commonly employed in group health practice, with an eye towards the conceptual framework previously developed.

The content and structure of a forecasting model will affect the range of techniques available. Some methods are more data-intensive than others; some methods perform better when a fair amount of aggregation has occurred, while others require data to be separated into homogenous processes. Picking the appropriate method requires consideration of many factors.

Before detailing specific methods, we will more fully describe the criteria by which different techniques can be compared and evaluated along key dimensions:

- Degree of precision in timing of events. Does the technique allow accurate recognition of the timing of changes, or is some degree of smoothing imposed? As an example, consider a physician fee schedule change scheduled for July of the forecast year. The actuary should decide whether the effect of the change should be reflected beginning in July, or whether annualizing the change and spreading over all months is acceptable.

- Degree of Stochastic Treatment of Variables. Does the method treat inputs and outputs as random variables or as deterministic estimates? If the former, does the method make statistical estimates of the moments of the random variables, or are more general ranges used?

- Degree of balance between historical data and prospective information. Does the technique project solely on the basis of historical data, or is provision made for adjustments which incorporate knowledge the actuary has of future events?

- Degree of judgment involved. How much does the technique rely on statistical estimates based on empirical data, and how much comes from the opinions or experience of the actuary?

- Degree of integration/consistency. How well does the methodology reflect correlation of elements of the forecast? Does the method prevent potentially contradictory statements? This is especially important to consider in the matching of premium and claims.

- Overall level of complexity. How easy is the method to update or modify?

This brings us to actual forecasting techniques typically used in current practice. We'll start with descriptions, and then move on to comparison across the above dimensions.

REGRESSION AND SMOOTHING TECHNIQUES

This approach typically uses historical data in the form of monthly, rolling-3 month, or rolling-12 month values. The practice can range from simply fitting a line to the data, to more complex exponential smoothing.

Seasonal effects can be reflected in these methods, but usually no direct assumptions about correlation across time periods or among components of the model are made.

As these methods are almost completely dependent upon the information content of historical data, the actuary should make adjustments for nonrecurring events. This dependence on past experience can actually make the methods valuable when little is known about the future of a process. The simplicity of the approach also makes updates straightforward.

These techniques can also be used to create a "baseline" forecast around which adjustments are made. As an example, an initial forecast might be done using seasonal exponential smoothing on five years' data. Then somewhat subjective adjustments can be made, for known future events that are not reflected in the experience, such as a substantial change to a large provider contract, or a benefit design that's never been offered before. The danger of such an approach lies in the phrase "events that are not reflected in the experience." If the input data used in the forecast is not in sufficient detail, it can be difficult to say definitively whether an event is just a "normal" change or if it is truly something previously unseen.

STOCHASTIC TIME SERIES METHODS

These methods are an extension of regression techniques, incorporating serial correlation. This can provide for more realistic and accurate projections. Most health insurance data will require logarithmic or other transformations to satisfy the linear conditions assumed by these models. (Taking the logarithm of time series data transforms an exponential function into one which can be analyzed using standard linear regression models.)

If enough care is given to segmenting data in the content and structure phase of forecast construction, methods such as seasonal auto regressive integrated moving average (ARIMA) models can produce fairly accurate results (given some stability within the marketplace). It is also possible to construct confidence intervals for the outputs of such models.

The same comments as above with respect to using such models as a "baseline" forecast also apply here.

Judgmental Methods

Judgmental methods normally start with the most recent observed values, and apply a simple, assumed annual percentage change to each input value. Assumptions are based on a mixture of historical data, knowledge of upcoming company actions within the marketplace, and expert opinion.

These methods provide ample opportunity to incorporate prospective information not contained within observed experience. In fact, in the extreme, observed experience is ignored except for use as a starting point for multiplication.

Judgmental methods tend to work best when coupled with a detailed structure of starting data. Such detail can help to isolate those assumptions which have a good deal of uncertainty around them, separately from those which are more concrete.

Simulation

Simulation models can be constructed with almost any degree of complexity and stochastic treatment.

As a starting point, simulation can be employed around subjectively defined probability distributions of annual increases. Correlation among inputs can be defined to guide sampling; such information can come from past data or can be based on judgment.

Monte Carlo techniques are frequently used for sampling. For long-tailed distributions, however, stratified sampling may be preferred, to ensure extreme values are reflected in results.

Simulation approaches can be built directly around scenarios the actuary wishes to test, which makes it easy to translate numerical results into verbal descriptions.

Comparison between Models

The table below gives a rough assessment of how each of the above models performs across the dimensions outlined earlier.

	Regression & Smoothing	Stochastic Time Series	Judgmental Models	Simulation
Accuracy of Timing	low	low	medium to high	high
Stochastic Treatment	low	medium	low	high
Allowance for	low	low	high	high
Judgment	medium	low	high	medium to high
Integration/Consistency	low	low	varies	high
Overall Complexity	low	medium	low to medium	high

As a final dimension for comparison, we can consider how each of the methodologies speaks to the fundamental processes described earlier.

Methods which do little more than fit aggregated observed data and then project them make no significant explicit statements about each of the underlying processes. Instead, the implicit statement is that "things will continue to behave and change as they have before." These methods may produce an acceptable level of accuracy, but will provide little in the way of causal explanations or meaningful monitoring.

Both the judgmental and simulation methods allow explicit statements about underlying process; success in accurately doing so is largely dependent on the level of detail in the content and structure of the model. Judgmental methods may struggle more with allowing for interactive effects of processes, where simulation methods can incorporate such relationships directly.

CAPITAL AND RISK MANAGEMENT APPLICATIONS

Once forecast models and assumptions have been established for the distinct lines of business within an enterprise, an additional level of modeling can be performed, to evaluate risk-based capital levels, manage allocations of surplus, or identify opportunities for improving overall risk volatility through investment, sales, or other strategies.

In general, these activities fall within the domain of capital and risk management. A forecast supports these activities by providing projected income and exposure by product, line of business, legal entity, or other breakdowns.

Capital and risk management exercises seem to have some common characteristics. First, there are assumptions as to the distribution of income or cash flow by line of business or entity. To the extent that a stochastic forecasting methodology has been used in the basic forecast, this can be readily supported. If a deterministic approach has been used in the build-up, subjective or judgmental techniques as outlined in the previous section may be used.

Most capital or enterprise-wide forecasting models involve a governing covariance structure that accounts for inter-relationships among lines of business or entities.

Finally, most modern capital models involve Monte Carlo simulation techniques, to test a vast number of scenarios and outcomes.

This additional level of modeling can be useful in of itself to the forecasting process. Examining the interdependencies of separate line of business forecasts can allow the modeler to test the implications of assumptions on a much broader scale.

As an example, an enrollment forecast for self-insured group business might be adjusted, to allow for pursuit of a riskier (and potentially more rewarding) line of business. Through a stochastic process, the modeler can examine the risk profile of the resulting distribution of income under the new scenario. Such exercises also emphasize the iterative and strategic uses of a forecast used to develop and set prospective initiatives.

There are a number of technical details which must be addressed in performing the type of modeling described in this section. Such details are beyond the scope of this chapter, but are described in numerous articles available from the archives of both the Society of Actuaries and the Casualty Actuarial Society.

PUTTING IT ALL TOGETHER

Regarding population trends, an insurer may assume that their largest blocks of business are stable and have no emerging morbidity trends. For newer or smaller blocks, the company may assess these blocks' morbidity relative to the company average and project specific morbidity changes for the blocks.

For the diagnosis and treatment of illnesses process, a company will want to assess variability and trends in the practice of medicine. This may suggest forecasting cells that focus on geography, since medical practices are known to vary by locality. The process of how the company contracts to pay for care may suggest focusing on categories of providers, such as hospitals or physicians, and on geography since these are the common·distinctions for this process.

The last three processes relate to benefits, rating and sales. In terms of sales, the company will likely begin with current enrollment statistics. It will then determine what initiatives will drive new sales, and how rates, service, the competitive environment and other considerations will impact the renewal of current business. These processes will likely be done separately by market segment and geography, since these are usually reflective of the rate and competitive environment. Rating and premiums will reflect company experience and profit targets, which will iteratively impact sales projections.

Consumer behavior resulting from insurance is the most challenging process to reflect in a forecast. If premiums are expected to increase significantly, then lower levels of benefits are to be expected. If deductibles increase, then utilization will likely decrease. If providers are paid more for outpatient surgery than for inpatient surgery, then outpatient surgery can be expected to grow at a faster pace than inpatient surgery.

With these processes understood and modeled, the company will choose a structure that focuses on the key drivers. The methods chosen will reflect the data and knowledge available. For example, judgmental models may be used in setting enrollment forecasts, while simulation models might be developed to model consumer purchasing behavior in light of various premium increase environments.

Finally, the outputs might include a projection of premiums and claims, as well as judgment based best case and worst case scenarios. Additionally, if statistical techniques have been employed, some information about the confidence level of the forecast may be available.

SUMMARY

Constructing a forecasting model involves choices about data to be used, outputs to be generated, and methods to be employed for describing change. In making such choices, an actuary should seek to fully address the fundamental processes of the marketplace, rather than being guided by a corporate template, available data, or a whiz-bang statistical technique. Only when such consideration has been given can a company truly use a forecast for the purposes of determining position in the market and strategy going forward.

Current practices in forecasting provide much opportunity for developing new approaches, that will more realistically handle the dynamics of the group health insurance market. With advances in technology and improvements in data capture and quality, it is exciting to see what the future holds.

38 APPLIED STATISTICS

Robert B. Cumming
Stuart A. Klugman

This chapter provides a brief summary of applied statistics for the practicing actuary. The exposition relies on a number of real-world examples. The intent is to show actuaries what are possible statistics applications and to introduce some basic concepts and considerations. Given the focus and space limitations, this chapter is not a how-to document nor does it provide in-depth theoretical background. There is a bibliography at the end of this chapter for further, more detailed information on theory and methods.

This chapter covers the following topics:

- Group Insurance Data
- Stochastic Simulation
- Regression
- Parametric Modeling
- Credibility Theory
- Confidence Intervals
- Central Limit Theorem

GROUP INSURANCE DATA

Group insurance data, especially group health data, exhibits ~vio-
of a 2-year old child. It can be easy to deal with and unde~ods so
come inconsistent and uncooperative in the blink of an e~ly inde-
lates many of the standard assumptions that make s~ y 1 obser-
powerful. For example, group insurance data is n~
pendent nor identically distributed. Also, many t~

vation available per event so there is no way to get a random sample to use in developing distributions or estimators. Even applying time series techniques can be difficult due to the level of correlation. Finally, this type of data can be subject to varying levels of trend.

Most actuaries opt to use actual claims data instead of trying to develop parametric models. There are two reasons for this. First, overcoming the data issues mentioned above is time consuming, and may not provide any more precision. Second, the data already contains many important factors, so instead of developing complicated models that take these factors into account, the data is used directly.

These characteristics of the data help explain why many of the models used by group actuaries have not been very sophisticated. Using a lot of analytical horsepower on messy data just gives the illusion of better estimates.

Given the complicated nature of our business, we need better analytical tools. More computing power and inexpensive statistical software make these methods more accessible to the practicing actuary. As mentioned above, it is important to know what the underlying assumptions are for a given technique, how the data complies with these assumptions, and what happens when some of the assumptions are not met.

Stochastic Simulation

Stochastic simulation is a useful technique for modeling a wide variety of complex insurance systems. Stochastic simulation, also known as Monte Carlo simulation, has been used to model many actuarial applications, including the following:

- Financial and utilization projections for continuing care retirement communities (CCRCs),
- ₁ital requirements for risk based capital models,
- ₂ate claim distributions,
- ₃fices of life insurance and annuities, and

Befor₄nd asset allocation strategies.
backgr₅

₆t stochastic simulation, it is useful to cover some
₇ic versus deterministic models.

STOCHASTIC VS DETERMINISTIC MODELS

It is useful to distinguish between *deterministic* and *stochastic* models. Generally speaking, deterministic models provide information regarding the expected or average value of a random variable. In contrast, stochastic models are used to provide information regarding the statistical distribution of a random variable. The random variable might be the surplus of an insurance company, the number of people in the nursing facility at a CCRC, or the aggregate medical claims for a group of 1,000 people. For example, a deterministic model can be used to estimate the expected surplus of an insurance company after five years. However, it doesn't tell us what the likelihood is of that expected value, nor of other possible values. In particular, it doesn't tell us the likelihood of negative surplus, which constitutes insolvency of the company. To examine the likelihood of insolvency, we need a stochastic model.

Before performing a simulation, we must construct a stochastic model for our insurance system. In general, a stochastic model differs from a deterministic model in that some of the input are probability distributions rather than point estimates. For example, we might input a probability distribution for medical trend rather than a single point estimate. After the stochastic model is constructed, we can perform the simulation. Often times, the most difficult part of constructing a stochastic model is developing probability distributions for the various input parameters.

Other topics of interest in performing stochastic simulation include: (1) how many simulations are necessary to accurately estimate results, and (2) computer generation of random numbers. These topics are discussed in some of the references listed at the end of this chapter.

SIMULATION

Stochastic models of real-world insurance systems are often so complex that it is practically impossible to determine exact analytical solutions. In such situations, stochastic simulation becomes the only practical approach to obtain results.

The major advantage of simulation, and it is a considerable one, is that there is virtually no restriction on the setting to which it can be applied. In particular, it is not necessary that the random variables be identical or independent, as long as the nature of the departure is known. Also, there is no limit on how accurate the results can be. The disadvantage is that it can be slow.

A stochastic simulation is composed of many "runs" or "trials." For each trial, each time we encounter a random variable in the stochastic model, a random number is generated. This random number is used to determine the outcome for that random variable. For example, the random variable might be the level of medical claims for an individual or group, or it might be the living status (independent living, living in a nursing facility, or deceased) of an individual in a CCRC. For each trial, we calculate the financial or population quantities in which we are interested. Using the results of many trials, we can develop a probability distribution for those quantities.

The following illustrates the stochastic simulation process through examples.

SIMPLE EXAMPLE

This example illustrates the general process of performing a stochastic simulation. We start with the following insurance system:

- Number of people insured at start of period = 5
- For each person, the probability of lapse is 20% and the probability of death is 20% during the period.

Deterministic Model: The deterministic model for this insurance system would give us the following results:

Time	Number Lapsed	Number Dead	Number Alive	Total
Start	0	0	5	5
End	1	1	3	5

In the deterministic model, we calculate the expected value for the number of people lapsing and dying. The expected value is calculated as the number of people (5) times the probability of lapse (.2) or death (.2). This model doesn't tell us anything about the likelihood of different outcomes. For example, what is the likelihood that two people die or that everyone is still alive at the end of the period? To answer these questions we must construct a stochastic model.

Stochastic Model: The key input in our stochastic model is a probability distribution for the status of each person at the end of the period. Given the above information, the probability distribution for the status of a person at the end of the period is as follows:

Status at End of Period (x)	Probability [f(x)]
Lapsed	0.2
Dead	0.2
Alive	0.6

Stochastic Simulation: The stochastic simulation process involves the following steps: (1) determine the cumulative probability distribution (cpd) for each random variable in our model, (2) for each trial, generate a random number for each random variable, (3) based on the random numbers, determine the value for each random variable, and (4) calculate quantities of interest and summarize results of the trials.

Step 1: The cumulative probability distribution is:

Status at End of Period	cpd
Lapsed	0.2
Dead	0.4
Alive	1.0

Step 2: Generate random numbers using a $U(0,1)$ distribution:

The following shows the random numbers for two trials. For each trial, we generate a random number for each of the five people.

Trial	Person				
	1	2	3	4	5
1	.783	.280	.561	.467	.989
2	.506	.392	.101	.875	.370

Step 3: Based on random numbers, determine value for random variables in stochastic model:

Each random number in the table above corresponds to a particular status at the end of the period for that person. We compare the random number against the cumulative probability distribution in step 1 to determine the status. If the random number is between 0.0 and 0.2, then that person lapses. If the random number is between 0.2 and 0.4, then that person dies. If the random number is between 0.4 and 1.0, then that person stays alive. Given this relationship, the following table shows the status of each person for each trial:

Trial	Person				
	1	2	3	4	5
1	alive	dead	alive	alive	alive
2	alive	dead	lapsed	alive	dead

Step 4: Calculate quantities of interest and summarize results:

For each trial, the following table summarizes the number of people who lapse, die, and remain alive.

Trial	No. Lapsed	No. Dead	No. Alive	Total
1	0	1	4	5
2	1	2	2	5

If we count up the number of trials where a particular outcome occurs and divide this by the total number of trials, this tells us the probability outcome. For example, the following table shows the probability distribution for the number of people who die based on a 1000 trial simulation.

Number of Deaths	Probability based on 1000 Trial Simulation	Actual Probability (based on binomial)
0	.334	.3277
1	.423	.4096
2	.192	.2048
3	.045	.0512
4	.006	.0064
5	.000	.0003
Average	.966	1.00

For this simple model, we can analytically determine the exact answer using a binomial distribution. The actual probabilities are shown in the last column in the table given above.

The above table shows results for a 1000 trial simulation. In practice, we typically perform anywhere from 100 to 10,000 trials. As we increase the number of trials, the results from the stochastic simulation should become closer and closer to the expected outcome.

EXAMPLE: CCRCs

Continuing Care Retirement Communities (CCRCs) provide housing and nursing home care to the elderly in return for an entrance fee plus monthly fees. Many CCRCs have an insurance component which includes pooling of risks and prefunding of future costs. Due to the small size of the typical CCRC, there can be significant fluctuations in populations and financial results from year-to-year.

To assist in modeling these fluctuations a stochastic simulation model for CCRCs was developed.[1] (This project was sponsored by the Society of Actuaries.) The model provides stochastic results for various population and financial variables, including sample-based averages and variances.

In the CCRC model, each person or couple can undergo a change in living status on an annual basis. The living status must be one of the following: residing in an independent living unit, residing in the nursing care facility, residing in the personal care facility, withdrawal, or dead. The living status for each person or couple represents a random variable. In the stochastic simulation, we generate a random number for each person/couple for each year of the projection. We then use these random numbers to determine what the living status is at the end of each year for each person/couple.

The following figures show some results from the model. Figures 38.1 and 38.2 show the number of nursing home beds needed over time. This information can be useful when CCRCs are determining how many nursing care beds they should build.

Figure 38.1 shows the impact of the number of trials on the results of the stochastic simulation. When we perform 200 trials the mean results are fairly smooth. When we perform just 1 trial, the results fluctuate significantly. Note that this single trial represents how things might actually turn out for a single CCRC.

---

[1] Bluhm, William F., Robert B. Cumming, and Stanley A. Roberts, *CCRC Population and Financial Model* (pamphlet and program disk). Itasca, Ill.: Society of Actuaries, 1991.

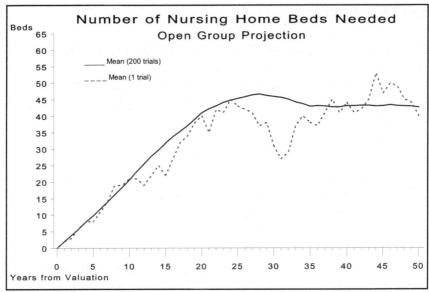

Figure 38.1

Figure 38.2 shows the mean values from the 200 trial simulation, along with the 95% confidence interval (mean ± 2 standard deviations assuming a normal distribution).

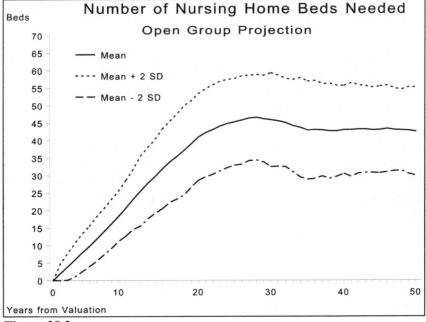

Figure 38.2

EXAMPLE: Ruin Theory Model

A ruin theory model was used in the development of the NAIC Risk Based Capital formula for health organizations. This is discussed in more detail in the chapter on "Risk Based Capital."

REGRESSION

This section discusses regression analysis and the method of least squares. Regression analysis is used to study the relationship between two or more variables. In one common situation, we use regression to fit a line to actual data points. The line might then be used to: (1) predict the outcome for the dependent variable given values for the independent variables, or (2) determine a parameter of interest, such as the average trend in medical costs. The method of least squares is a commonly used technique to determine the best fitting line for a collection of data points.

SIMPLE LINEAR REGRESSION

Suppose we have two random variables, X and Y. The basic problem of regression analysis is to estimate the expected value of Y given a particular value of X. The regression is linear if the expected value of Y given $X = x$ can be expressed as

$$E[Y \mid x] = a + bx.$$

The constants a and b are referred to as the regression coefficients. The regression equation shown above is referred to as simple or bivariate since there is only one independent variable. If there is more than one independent variable, the regression is referred to as multiple or multivariate.

If the regression of Y on X is linear, then

$$E[Y \mid X] = E[Y] + (x - E[X]) \times \frac{Cov(X,Y)}{Var(X)}.$$

If the $Cov(X,Y) = 0$, then X and Y are said to be uncorrelated. Note that if two random variables are independent, they are also uncorrelated. However, two random variables that are uncorrelated are not necessarily independent.

METHOD OF LEAST SQUARES

Least squares is a method of curve-fitting which can be used to estimate the a and b coefficients in the linear regression equation shown above. Suppose we are given a set of paired data (x_i, y_i), for $i = 1, 2, \ldots, n$. We can express each y_i as

$$y_i = a + bx_i + e_i.$$

The e_i variable is called the "error" term. The e_i term represents the error between the actual value (y_i) and the fitted value $(\hat{y}_i = a + bx_i)$. One way to measure how well a particular line fits the data is to calculate the sum of the squared errors. The lower this sum, the lower the cumulative error, and the better the fit. The method of least squares gives the values of a and b that minimize the sum of the squared errors. That is, the a and b least squares coefficients result in the lowest possible value for the quantity $\sum_i e_i^2$.

The least squares coefficients can be calculated as

$$b = \frac{\sum_i [(x_i - \overline{x}) y_i]}{\sum_i (x_i - \overline{x})^2}$$

$$a = \overline{y} - b\overline{x}.$$

The sum of the squared errors can also be written as

$$\sum_i (y_i - \overline{y})^2 = \sum_i (\hat{y}_i - \overline{y})^2 + \sum_i (y_i - \hat{y}_i)^2$$

(Total Variation) = (Explained Variation) + (Residual Variation)

Thus, we can partition the total variability of y into a portion explained by movement of y with x (the explained variation) and a portion that is not due to the movement of y with x (the unexplained or residual variation). The fraction of the total variation that is explained by the linear relationship of y and x is called the coefficient of determination and is often denoted as R^2.

TRANSFORMATIONS

The use of least squares is not limited to situations where there is a linear relationship between two variables. In situations where the hypothesized relationship is non-linear, it is often possible to transform the relationship into a linear form. This allows use of the standard formulas given above for calculating the regression coefficients. The most common transformations involve taking the logarithm, reciprocal, or square root of both sides of the mathematical relationship between the dependent and independent variables. For example, suppose that $Z = c \cdot W^d$. If we take the natural logarithm of both sides of this equation, we can transform it into $\ln(Z) = \ln(c) + d \cdot \ln(W)$. This is the standard linear equation with $Y = \ln(Z)$, $a = \ln(c)$, $b = d$, and $X = \ln(W)$.

WEIGHTED LEAST SQUARES

The least squares approach described above minimizes the sum of the squared errors with *equal weight* on each error term. In situations where the data points do not have equal levels of credibility, it may be desirable to weight the error terms differently. For example, suppose we have been tracking loss ratios (LR_t) by policy duration (t) for a block of health insurance business. This gives us a series of data points (LR_t, t) for $t = 1, 2, \ldots, n$. In such situations we might have much more premium volume or exposure for the early durations than for the later durations. In these situations we might want to put more weight or credibility on the early duration data points.

For weighted least squares, we wish to select a and b so as to minimize the quantity

$$Weighted\ Error\ =\ \sum_i w_i [y_i - (a + bx_i)]^2$$

where w_i is the weight or credibility placed on the ith data point.

EXAMPLE: Selection Factors

This example illustrates the use of least squares to fit a curve to a series of data points. In this example, we use a transformation to convert the underlying relationship into a linear form. Also, due to different levels of credibility for different data points, we use the weighted least squares approach.

We have summarized the actual experience for a block of individual major medical coverage by policy duration. Policy duration is measured in calendar quarters since time of issue. (Before summarizing the data by duration, we: (1) removed the effects of inflation by trending all the claims to the same point in time and (2) adjust the earned premium to a common rate basis.) The durational experience is shown in the following Table 38.1:

Table 38.1

Quarterly Policy Duration (t)	Trend Adjusted Claims	Earned Premium (EP)	Loss Ratio (LR)
1	1,427,208	6,105,064	23.4%
2	2,460,583	8,313,219	29.6
3	3,127,488	7,390,382	42.3
4	3,180,396	6,668,387	47.7
5	2,622,893	6,045,283	43.4
6	3,008,615	5,491,767	54.8
7	2,745,605	5,065,495	54.2
8	3,028,875	4,579,158	66.1
9	2,291,655	4,226,507	54.2
10	2,429,329	3,911,945	62.1
11	2,127,282	3,451,455	61.6
12	1,893,402	2,475,416	76.5
13	1,091,865	1,724,905	63.3
14	641,909	1,218,075	52.7
15	662,507	919,120	72.1
16	495,989	581,130	85.3
17	280,048	312,557	89.6
18	131,357	134,925	97.4
19	1,312	25,651	5.1
Total	33,648,318	68,640,441	49.0

The loss ratios (LR_t) by duration (t) represent a set of (x, y) data points where $y = LR_t$ and $x = t$. We used the method of least squares to fit a curve to these data points. The wear-off of initial underwriting causes the loss ratios by duration to rise steeply at first. Cumulative antiselection at the later durations can cause the loss ratios to continue to rise, but generally at a slower rate than during the early durations. Thus, the selection factors by duration tend to have a concave down shape rather than linear.

This non-linear shape is the reason we assumed that $LR_t = \ln(a+bt)$. Thus, if we exponentiate each side, we get $exp(LR_t) = a+bt$, which is in a linear form.

As can be seen in the above table, the amount of exposure or earned premium varies dramatically by policy duration. For example, the amount of earned premium for duration 2 is over 300 times as great as the earned premium for duration 19. Due to the limited amount of premium for the later durations, we certainly would not want to put as much credibility on the later durations as on the early durations. Thus, we decided to use the method of *weighted* least squares. For weights, we used earned premium by duration.

Using the method of weighted least squares, we get the fitted loss ratios shown in the following table.

Quarterly Policy Duration (t)	Fitted Loss Ratio	Actual Loss Ratio
1	30.7%	23.4%
2	34.8	29.6
3	38.7	42.3
4	42.5	47.7
5	46.1	43.4
6	49.6	54.8
7	53.0	54.2
8	56.2	66.1
9	59.4	54.2
10	62.5	62.1
11	65.5	61.6
12	68.4	76.5
13	71.2	63.3
14	73.9	52.7
15	76.6	72.1
16	79.2	85.3
17	81.7	89.6
18	84.2	97.4
19	86.6	5.1

The fitted loss ratio is calculated using the equation:

$$Fitted\ loss\ ratio\ =\ \ln(a+bt)$$

where a = 1.302796 and b = .05652. The equations for calculating the a and b coefficients are shown below:

$$b = \frac{\sum_{t} EP_{t} \cdot \sum_{t} EP_{t} \cdot t \cdot \exp(LR_{t}) - \sum_{t} EP_{t} \cdot t \sum_{t} EP_{t} \cdot t \cdot \exp(LR_{t})}{\sum_{t} EP_{t} \cdot \sum_{t} EP_{t} \cdot t^{2} \left(\sum_{t} EP_{t} \cdot t\right)^{2}}$$

$$a = \frac{\sum_{t} EP_{t} \cdot \exp(LR_{t}) - b \cdot \sum_{t} EP_{t} \cdot t}{\sum_{t} EP_{t}}$$

Figure 38.3 shows a plot of the actual and fitted loss ratios by policy duration

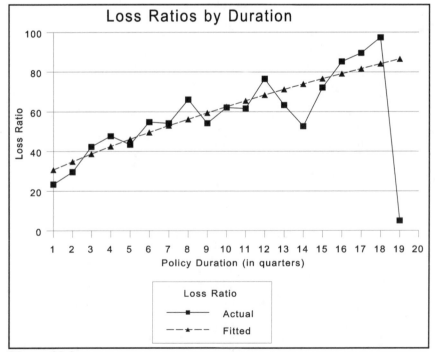

Figure 38.3

ADVANCED REGRESSION TECHNIQUES

There are a variety of more advanced regression techniques. These include the use of more than one independent variable (multiple regression), stepwise regression, and neural networks.

Multiple regression is useful when there are a number of variables that impact the quantity in which we are interested. An example of this is diagnosis based risk assessment models. These models are designed with many independent variables (commonly 100+). In these models, each independent variable represents the presence or absence of a particular medical condition, such as diabetes, skin cancer, or hypertension. For each variable, there is a parameter or coefficient that represents the marginal cost of having that medical condition. Multiple regression techniques are used to determine an appropriate set of parameters based on actual claim data for a set of members. (For more information, refer to the research study sponsored by the Society of Actuaries titled "A Comparative Analysis of Claims Based Methods of Health Risk Assessment for Commercial Populations" by Robert B. Cumming, David Knutson, Brian A. Cameron, and Brian Derrik.)

The main idea behind stepwise regression is to take a set of independent variables and to pare it down to those that make a significant contribution to the regression model. This can be done in a variety of ways such as starting with the entire set of independent variables and discarding those that are not statistically significant. Also, the opposite procedure can be used where the analysis starts with the individual variable that makes the greatest contribution and then adds to the set. There are many ways to set the criteria for including independent variables in the model. This methodology is covered in most textbooks on regression.

An application of this technique is in forecasting incurred fee-for-service non-drug health claims. This can be a very difficult task especially if the forecast is for more than one or two months. The level of claims depend on a variety of factors such as claims inventories, the level of paid claims for the current and prior months, and drug claims. There may be other factors such as the severity of the flu season or changes in a therapeutic regimen. Assuming that the data is available, all of these factors can be fed into a stepwise regression analysis. One of the benefits of this technique is that there are confidence intervals for each estimate. There are some inexpensive software packages that include an option to do stepwise regression.

Neural networks are mentioned here because they are a nonlinear extension of linear regression. This tool takes inputs like those mentioned in the discussion of stepwise regression and constructs a predictive model. There are pros and cons to the use of neural networks. The main advantage is that a model does not need to be specified. The program uses the data to construct the appropriate model. This is also one of the greatest drawbacks to this methodology since there is no straightforward way to determine how the independent variables flow through the calculations. This makes it difficult to explain the results. Neural networks have not made inroads into actuarial calculations yet. However, this is a powerful technique that is worth exploring. There are many good books on this topic and there are some inexpensive software packages that will enable the actuary to experiment with this methodology

PARAMETRIC MODELING

Parametric methods are typically not used in modeling group insurance. When statistical distributions are needed, most often actuaries will rely on stochastic simulations based on empirical data. (Simulations address many of the issues mentioned regarding empirical methods.) However, parametric techniques have some desirable properties and should be part of any practicing actuary's arsenal.

The material in this section is a brief summary of some of the considerations involved when using parametric models. This information is taken from the text *Loss Models: From Data to Decisions*, 2nd Edition by Klugman, Panjer, and Willmot [2004].

THE EMPIRICAL APPROACH

If we have a sample of size n from a population, the empirical distribution is a model that assigns probability $1/n$ to each observed value. We then proceed by pretending the model accurately describes the population and then compute quantities of interest from the model. The following example illustrates this process.

Example: Individual Dental Claims[2]

Claims on basic dental coverage were recorded for a period of time. The policy has a deductible of $25, no limit, and no coinsurance. In a one week

---

[2] All the numerical values used in the remainder of this chapter are artificial. Context is provided to make them more readable, but no conclusions regarding appropriate models for actuarial practice should be drawn.

period, there were 10 claims, which resulted in the following 10 payments (arranged in increasing order):

$14 $63 $88 $101 $104 $150 $178 $248 $259 $292

The following questions are of interest:

- What is the expected payment?
- What will be the expected payment if the deductible is removed and how many extra payments will there be?
- What will be the expected payment if the deductible is increased to $50 and how many fewer payments will there be?
- How will the answers to these questions change if there is 10% inflation?

The empirical model assigns probability 0.1 to each of the ten numbers. The mean is computed by multiplying each payment by 0.1 to yield an expected claim payment of $149.70.

If the deductible is removed, $25 must be added to each claim payment. The empirical estimate of the mean is $174.70, but removing the deductible will bring additional payments in the $0 to $25 range. Normally, insurance companies have data on payments below the deductible in order to determine when the deductible is reached. As a result, adjustments can be made to the empirical distribution for claims below the deductible. If, on the other hand, the deductible is raised to $50, the ten payments become nine (the covered expense of $39 does not produce a payment):

$38 $63 $76 $79 $125 $153 $223 $234 $267

The empirical estimate of the expected payment per payment is the sample mean, $139.78 and the empirical estimate of payment frequency is that 10% of the payments will be eliminated. Note that if the deductible is raised to $60, the empirical estimate of the expected payment will be reduced by 10, and the estimated reduction in the number of payments remains at 10% (one of the ten original claims no longer meets the higher deductible). This lack of continuity is a drawback of the empirical approach.

USING PARAMETRIC MODELS

Construction of a *parametric model* follows three steps. The first is to postulate a model. This consists of a named distribution family such as gamma or Weibull. Such families consist of the probability density function (*pdf*) of the random variable that defines the distribution of claims in the population. The function has one or more unspecified quantities, called *parameters*. By changing the value(s) of the parameter(s) we can obtain various distributional shapes that are somewhat similar (in the sense that a family has certain general characteristics) but allow some flexibility to provide a match to the data.

The second step is to use the data to estimate the value of the parameter. While many methods are available, in the absence of a compelling reason to do otherwise, maximum likelihood estimation is the preferred method.

The third step is to validate the choice of model by verifying that it adequately represents the data. This is often done with the chi-square goodness-of-fit test.

EXAMPLE: Basic Dental Coverage, Continued

By using the covered expense for x (what the casualty actuaries call the 'loss'), rather than the claim payment, the resulting model is for covered expenses. We are concerned with the probability (or probability density function) of observing a particular claim value, given the parametric model. With a continuous model and a deductible of $25, the contribution of an observation of x is $f(x)/[1-F(25)]$.

Suppose we have already found that a Weibull model is an appropriate choice for these claims. That is,

$$f(x) = \tau\theta^{-\tau}x^{\tau-1}e^{-(x/\theta)\tau}, \quad F(x) = 1-e^{-(x/\theta)\tau}, \quad x, \quad \theta > 0.$$

The likelihood function is maximized at $\tau = 2.11526$ and $\theta = 197.566$.

When using parametric models, once the model is determined, the data are discarded and all future calculations are done under the assumption that the population of claims follows the estimated parametric distribution. One drawback of the parametric method is that, to the extent the chosen model is not a perfect fit for the data, there is some information being lost.

When the deductible is removed, the expected claim payment value is the mean of the Weibull distribution, $174.98. The probability of a claim being below $25 is 0.0125 and so the number of payments could be expected to increase by $1/0.9875 - 1$ or 1.3%. Similarly, the probability of a claim being below $50 is 0.0532 and so raising the deductible will eliminate 1 − 0.9468/0.9875 or 4.1% of the payments.

Each of the above numbers can be calculated directly, either from the distribution itself, or from known characteristics of the Weibull distribution. It is possible to answer many other questions, but that will not be done here.

PARAMETRIC VS. EMPIRICAL MODELS

Parametric models are more tractable mathematically. However the ability to manipulate data with today's computes mitigates this advantage somewhat. Empirical models do not have the nice mathematical properties but they reflect the actual experience of a population covered by a specific set of benefits.

One important byproduct of parametric models is the ability to construct confidence intervals.

Both methods are capable of reflecting inflation. This involves adjusting the empirical distribution for claims under the deductible as mentioned above. Also, trends will take this into account if inflation has been fairly stable over the past several years.

Since claims data changes due to trends, mandated benefits, and a variety of other influences, there is no guarantee that a parametric distribution that fits the data one year will be adequate the next even if it is adjusted for these outside influences. As a result, there could be discontinuities in premium rates, capitation rates, and reserves. Also, inferences drawn from one distribution may not be true under another distribution.

Sometimes, it is necessary to use actual data. For example, it is easier to convince various audiences (e.g., corporate management, regulators, and customers) that reserves or premium rates are appropriate if the actuary uses actual experience data. Also, there are times when the actuary is required to use actual claims data in his/her calculations.

If we were to choose a parametric model, and compare the results with original empirical data, we have two sets of answers to the same problem. Aside from the smoothness provided by the parametric solution, is there any reason to believe that those numbers are more accurate? We can never know the true value (else we would not need these statistical approaches), and so the best we can do is ask which procedure, over the long run, tends to produce better answers.

There are two quantities of interest when evaluating an estimation procedure. *Bias* refers to the extent by which, on average, the process over- or under-estimates the true value. In particular, an *unbiased* estimation method has errors that cancel over the long run, yielding an average error of zero. *Variance* refers to the degree to which the estimation method produces values that vary from its long-run average. This is the usual variance measure and is often called sampling error or sampling variation. The ideal situation is to have a method that is unbiased, and among unbiased methods has the smallest variance. It turns out we almost have such a method. For large samples, maximum likelihood estimators will be unbiased and have the smallest variance. (Maximum likelihood estimators are described in most undergraduate statistics textbooks. Much is known about the maximum likelihood estimators for many well-known parametric families, which allows for computational ease in choosing parameters.)

Another advantage of the parametric method is that, via the likelihood ratio test (also available in most mathematical statistics texts), various statements about the population can be tested. One example would be to see if the deductible affects the distribution.

An additional benefit of a parametric model, the ability to smooth grouped observations is demonstrated in the next example.

EXAMPLE: Grouped Dental Expenses

Covered expenses on dental coverage were recorded and grouped. The coverage had a deductible of $50. The results were 57 claims between $50 and $100, 42 between $100 and $150, 65 between $150 and $250, 84 between $250 and $500, 45 between $500 and $1,000, 10 between $1,000 and $1,500, and 14 above $1,500.

A histogram describing the claims up to $1,500 appears in Figure 38.4. When constructing a histogram from grouped data, the height of each bar is the number of claims in the interval divided by both the sample size and the width of the interval. The first bar has a height of $\frac{57}{(317)(50)} = 0.003596$. Empirical estimates can be obtained by treating the histogram as a probability density function. Parameters can be estimated by maximum likelihood.

Assuming a lognormal distribution, where $F(x) = \Phi[\ln x - \mu)/\sigma]$ and $\Phi(x)$ is the standard normal cumulative density function, we can calculate the values of μ and σ that will give us a maximum likelihood function. The texts referenced at the end of this chapter provide additional and related formulas.

In this case, we find that the likelihood function is maximized at $\mu = 5.32037$ and $\sigma = 1.09285$. This then defines our model for dental claim costs. Now that we have a model, questions about inflation or deductible changes can be answered. The quality of the model can be checked by comparing the density function of the lognormal model to the histogram. Figure 38.4 demonstrates that the model provides an excellent fit.

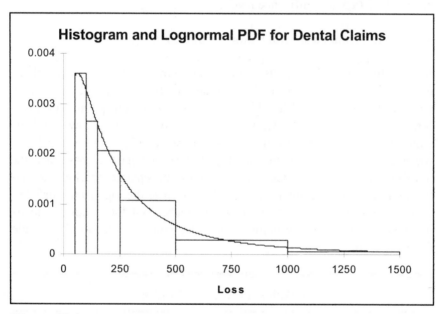

Figure 38.4

DETERMINING AN ACCEPTABLE PARAMETRIC MODEL

Once it has been decided to use a parametric model, the search begins for one that will do the job. (We glossed over this part of the process in earlier examples when we picked the Weibull distribution.) There are a large number of parametric families. Motivation for many of these in an actuarial context is given in Venter [1984]. One feature of many of these families is that some are special or limiting cases of others. For example, when one of the parameters of the Burr distribution is set equal to 1, a Pareto distribution is obtained. Because few of the models have a direct physical motivation, it is usually not possible to postulate a model in advance. A reasonable strategy is to try them all.

For each model, the chi-square goodness-of-fit test can be constructed. As a hypothesis test, it can be used to determine which models are acceptable. The p-value from the hypothesis test can also be used to rank the models from best (highest p-value) to worst. Another way to rank models is by the value of the likelihood function at its maximum. The model which maximizes the likelihood function at the highest value would seem to be the best. However, adding an extra parameter guarantees a higher likelihood value. The likelihood ratio test suggests that to justify an additional parameter, the natural logarithm of the likelihood function should increase by at least 1.92 (a 5% significance level).

Example: Grouped Dental Claims, Continued

In the following table, results from fitting 10 models by maximum likelihood are presented. All pass the goodness-of-fit test. The best (smallest negative logarithm) likelihood value belongs to the four parameter transformed beta distribution. However, it is only 0.6136 below the Burr value and so the extra parameter cannot be justified. The same holds when comparing Burr to the paralogistic. With regard to p-values, the transformed beta scores best, but the clearly acceptable paralogistic distribution is a much simpler choice. Also, because the lognormal distribution is well-known, the comparison in Figure 38.4 looks good, and its likelihood and chi-square numbers are very good, a case could be made for using it for the model.

Results of Fitting 15 Models				
Model*	$-\ln L$**	Chi-square	*df*	*p*-value
Paralogistic(2)	564.1091	1.50	4	0.8271
Loglogistic(2)	564.5449	2.38	4	0.6667
Pareto(2)	564.6012	2.44	4	0.6555
Lognormal(2)	564.6048	2.44	4	0.6555
Inv. Paralogistic(2)	565.2276	3.72	4	0.4448
Inv. Gaussian(2)	565.4414	4.02	4	0.4031
Weibull(2)	566.7777	6.72	4	0.1512
Burr(3)	564.0751	1.43	3	0.6996
Generalized Pareto(3)	564.2134	1.69	3	0.6395
Transformed beta(4)	563.4615	0.24	2	0.8879

* Number of parameters is in parentheses.
** Negative of the logarithm of the likelihood function.

FREQUENCY MODELS

All the discussion to this point involved continuous models for the amount of a claim or payment. Another random variable of interest in insurance modeling is the number of claims in a given period for a given block of business (which again may be a single policy, a single group, a line of business, or the entire company). The only difference is that the model should place probability only on non-negative whole numbers. The methods of analysis (maximum likelihood estimation, likelihood ratio test, chi-square goodness-of-fit test) are the same. We will therefore focus on the few differences.

A collection of frequency models can be found in Panjer and Willmot [1992] and in Klugman, Panjer, and Willmot [2004]. It begins with the three best-known models, the Poisson, binomial, and negative binomial distributions. Unlike the loss distributions, these can be motivated by requiring the physical process to have certain attributes. They can be generalized by allowing the probability of zero claims to be an arbitrary number and then multiplying the remaining probabilities by a constant so that all the probabilities sum to 1. These are called zero-modified models.

Frequency distribution analysis is helpful for casualty coverages, where there may be relatively few, large claims. Since most group coverages involve many, relatively small, claims, it is unusual for group actuaries to separately model the frequency of claims. Rather, they tend to work with compound distributions, which are claim distributions that include the probability of a zero claim. Unfortunately, the use of parametric methods for compound distributions is much more difficult than in the cases above. The actuarial profession continues to progress toward finding applications for these models.

CREDIBILITY THEORY

Credibility theory has a number of practical applications in group insurance, including experience rating and rate making. This section provides some background on credibility theory and suggests some further reading for those interested in group insurance applications.

BÜHLMANN'S CREDIBILITY MODEL

Bühlmann's credibility model is commonly expressed as

$$C = ZA + (1-Z)E,$$

where Z is the credibility factor, A represents the actual outcome (for example, the actual incurred claims for a particular employer group), E represents an estimate of the outcome (for example, an estimate of incurred claims based on the experience of other employer groups), and C is the compromise estimate. In Bühlmann's model, the credibility factor is defined as

$$Z = \frac{n}{n+k}.$$

In this equation, n is the number of trials or exposure units, and

$$k = \frac{\text{expected value of the process variance}}{\text{variance of the hypothetical means}}.$$

If we are considering group health insurance, the *expected value of the process variance* would be the variance in incurred claims for a typical or average employer group. The *variance of the hypothetical means* would be the variance of the expected level of incurred claims among the employer groups.

APPLICATIONS OF CREDIBILITY THEORY

Fuhrer [1989] develops and applies credibility formulas specifically designed for group health insurance. The formula development recognizes the group health insurance dynamics of varying group size, group member turnover, large claims, high deductible plans, competitive requirements and varying experience periods by modifying the credibility factor or other elements of the basic credibility formula.

For large claims, there is an approach suggested to limit the impact that one insured's large claim has on the A in the formula above. In general, these large claims are removed, or pooled, from the actual experience and replaced with an expected amount. Fuhrer suggests that the credibility formula can be used to determine the optimum pooling level.

The selection of Z, the credibility factor, should be sensitive to the underlying experience data. Fuhrer develops some approaches to determining Z that are sensitive to the size of the group and the coverage they have as well as the degree of turnover in the group.

CONFIDENCE INTERVALS

Confidence intervals are used to communicate information regarding the range of possible outcomes, as opposed to just the average or expected outcome. For example, we might estimate that the 80% confidence interval for actual claim runout is plus or minus 10% from a best estimate of the claim liability. This means that, on average, four out of five times the actual claim runout will be within 10% of the estimate. The 80% probability is referred to as the degree of confidence for this confidence interval.

The endpoints of the confidence interval are referred to as the confidence limits. There may be confidence limits on both sides of the estimate, as in the above example, or on just one side of the estimate. This will depend on the purpose of the confidence interval. For example, a one-sided evaluation is more common when analyzing the adequacy of a statutory claim reserve estimate since the key issue is the degree of confidence that the reserve estimate plus margin will exceed the actual runout.

EXAMPLE: Claim Liability Margin

Suppose an insurance company wishes to determine an appropriate margin to use with their statutory claim liability for medical insurance. In particular, the company wishes to add an explicit margin to their best estimate of the claim liability so that there is a 75% to 95% probability that the resulting claim liability will be sufficient to cover the actual claim runout. This company has been using a substantially unchanged process during the last four years to determine a best estimate of the claim liability.

For each month-end, we have compared the actual claim runout with the original claim liability estimate. Figure 38.5 summarizes the percentage difference between the actual claim runout and the original best estimate claim liability based on results for 43 month-ends. The percentage difference is referred to as the "required margin" and is ranked from low to high in the figure. Figure 38.5 also shows the sample mean and sample standard deviation for this set of data points.

Ranking of Required Margin		
Rank	**Required Margin**	**Cumulative Probability***
1	−18.18%	1.2%
2	−15.78%	3.5%
3	−10.45%	5.8%
4	−10.23%	8.1%
5	−9.25%	10.5%
6	−9.18%	12.8%
7	−8.48%	15.1%
⋮	⋮	⋮
37	9.68%	84.9%
38	10.00%	87.2%
39	12.13%	89.5%
40	19.91%	91.9%
41	21.02%	94.2%
42	21.95%	96.5%
43	27.55%	98.8%
Sample Mean	0.50%	
Sample Standard Deviation	9.89%	

Figure 38.5   * Probability = (rank −.50)/43.

Using the data in Figure 38.5 we determined confidence intervals using two approaches. The first approach uses the raw data shown in the figure. The second approach uses a normal distribution fitted to this data. The benefit of using the raw data is that we don't need to make an assumption regarding the underlying distribution. Such an assumption may introduce a bias or error if it is incorrect. The benefit of using a normal (or other parametric) distribution is that it tends to smooth out the results.

Figure 38.6 summarizes the results. It shows the margin needed to have a given confidence level that the reserve estimate plus margin will exceed the actual claim runout. The required margin levels based on the normal distribution are determined using the following one-sided confidence intervals:

Upper Confidence Limit = *Sample Mean*

$$+X \times Sample\ Standard\ Deviation,$$

where X depends on the desired confidence level and is shown in the following table.

One-Sided Confidence Level	X = Number of Standard Deviations
50%	0.00
75%	0.68
80%	0.84
85%	1.04
90%	1.28
95%	1.64

For example, there is an 85% probability that the value of a normally distributed random variable will be less than the mean plus 1.04 times the standard deviation.

Note that this analysis assumes that the distribution of the required margin has not changed significantly over time and that the required margin at each point in time is independent. If there has been a trend over time in the level of required margin or if there is some correlation between the level of required margin over time, it may be possible to develop a more accurate confidence interval by taking these factors into account.

Probability of Claim Reserve Plus Margin Being More than Actual Runout	Required Margin Level (Based on Actual Experience)	Required Margin Level (Based on Normal Curve Using Historical Standard Deviation)
75%	6.17%	7.23%
80%	8.91%	8.81%
85%	9.70%	10.79%
90%	13.69%	13.17%
95%	21.34%	16.73%

Figure 38.6

CENTRAL LIMIT THEOREM

A discussion of applied statistics would not be complete without covering the central limit theorem. The central limit theorem can be stated as follows:

If $x_1, x_2, \ldots, x_n$ constitute a random sample from an infinite population having mean μ and variance σ^2, then the limiting distribution of

$$z = \frac{\sum_i \frac{x_i}{n} - \mu}{\frac{\sigma}{\sqrt{n}}}$$

as n approaches infinity, is the standard normal distribution.

This theorem is sometimes misunderstood when analyzing the level of risk associated with populations of different sizes. This is illustrated in the example of the next section.

EXAMPLE: Orthopedic Capitation

Suppose a group of orthopedic surgeons is evaluating a specialty capitation reimbursement arrangement and want to know how "risky" it is. They might want to know the minimum number of members that should be covered under the arrangement so as to reasonably limit their risk. The orthopedic surgeons believe that as the number of covered lives increases, the risk decreases. For this situation, we define the orthopedic surgeons gain/loss on this reimbursement arrangement as follows:

$(Gain/loss)$ = *(Total capitation revenue for the covered members for a given period of time)*

less

(The value of the services actually provided to the covered members valued using a discounted fee schedule)

To evaluate statistical risk levels, it is useful to distinguish between relative risk and absolute risk. (Of course, there are other risks besides statistical risk, such as misestimation or pricing errors.) For this situation, absolute risk can be viewed as the probability that the orthopedic surgeon group will lose $10,000 or more for given period of time. Relative risk can be viewed as the probability that the orthopedic surgeon group will have claims equal to 10% or more of the capitation revenue.

Based on the central limit theorem, the relative risk decreases as the number of covered members increases. However, the absolute risk still increases as the number of lives increases. That is, the greater the number of covered lives the greater the probability that the orthopedic surgeon group will lose a given amount of money. Of course, if the capitation covers only professional services and the orthopedic surgeon group has excess capacity, the "risk" is not necessarily a financial risk but more of a time risk. That is, the orthopedic surgeon's revenue stream is fixed, but the amount of time that will be spent providing services is uncertain.

Figures 38.7 and 38.8 illustrate the dispersion of the resulting gain/loss. Figure 38.7 shows the dispersion expressed as a percentage deviation from expected. Figure 38.8 shows the dispersion expressed in absolute dollar terms.

The type of information shown above can be used to help evaluate the level of statistical risk associated with different capitation arrangements. (Of course, there are other risks besides the statistical risk.) In generating the above results, we assumed no specific stop loss. In practice, most arrangements have a stop loss built in or the physician group will purchase stop loss from a third party. (The graphs shown in Figures 38.7 and 38.8 on the following page were produced using the Milliman & Robertson, *Risk Simulator*.)

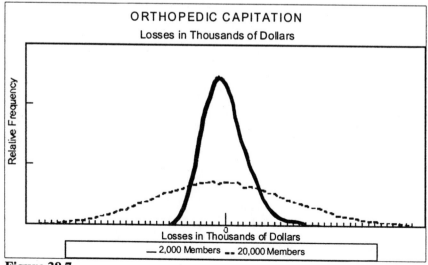

Figure 38.7

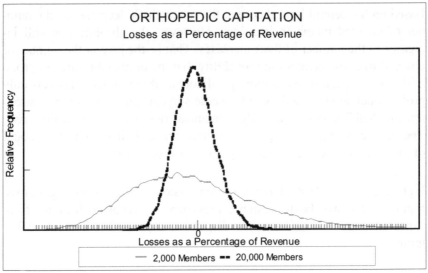

Figure 38.8

REFERENCES

Bowers, N., H. Gerber, J. Hickman, D. Jones, and C. Nesbitt, *Actuarial Mathematics*, 2nd Edition, Chicago: Society of Actuaries, 1997.

Bühlmann, H., "Experience Rating and Credibility," *The ASTIN Bulletin* 4 (1967), 119-207.

Daykin, C., T. Pentikäinen, and M. Pesonen, *Practical Risk Theory for Actuaries*. London: Chapman and Hall, 1994.

Fuhrer, C., "Some Applications of Credibility Theory to Group Insurance," *Transactions of the Society of Actuaries*, XL (1988), 387-404.

Granger, C.W.J., *Forecasting in Business and Economics*. San Diego: Academic Press, 1980.

Heckman, P. and G. Meyers, "The Calculation of Aggregate Loss Distributions from Claim Severity and Claim Count Distributions," *Proceedings of the Casualty Actuarial Society*, 70 (1983), 22-61.

Herzog, T.N., *An Introduction to Stochastic Simulation* (Course 130 Study Note). Chicago: Society of Actuaries, 1983.

Herzog, T.N. with Lord, G., *Applications of Monte Carlo Methods to Finance and Insurance*. Winsted: Actex Publications, 2003.

Hogg, R. and S. Klugman, *Loss Distributions*. New York: John Wiley and Sons, 1984.

Hosler, V.R., "The Application of Fuzzy Sets to Group Health Underwriting," *Actuarial Research Clearing House*, 1992.2 (1992), 1-63.

Hossack, I., J. Pollard, and B. Zehnwirth, *Introductory Statistics with Applications in General Insurance*. Cambridge: Cambridge University Press, 1983.

Klugman, S., H. Panjer, and G. Willmot, *Loss Models: From Data to Decisions*, 2nd Edition: John Wiley & Sons, 2004.

Longley-Cook, L.H., "An Introduction to Credibility Theory," *Proceedings of the Casualty Actuarial Society*, 49 (1962) 194-221.

Miller, R.B. and D. Wichern, *Intermediate Business Statistics*. New York: Holt, Reinhart and Winston, 1977.

Ostaszewski, K., *Fuzzy Set Methods in Actuarial Science*. Chicago: Society of Actuaries, 1993.

Panjer, H., "The Aggregate Claims Distribution and Stop-Loss Reinsurance," *Transactions of the Society of Actuaries*, XXXII (1981), 523-535.

Panjer, H. and G. Willmot, *Insurance Risk Models*. Chicago: Society of Actuaries, 1992.

Rao, C., *Linear Statistical Inference and Its Applications*. New York: John Wiley and Sons, 1965.

Robertson, J., "The Computation of Aggregate Loss Distributions," *Proceedings of the Casualty Actuarial Society*, 79 (1993), 57-133.

Society of Actuaries Committee on Actuarial Principles, "Principles of Actuarial Science," *Transactions of the Society of Actuaries*, XLIV (1992), 565-628.

Venter. G., "Transformed Beta and Gamma Distributions and Aggregate Losses," *Proceedings of the Casualty Actuarial Society*, 71 (1984), 156-193.

39 DATA SOURCES AND STRUCTURES

Randall P. Herman
Kent Sacia

The group actuary requires data for many essential analytical functions, including premium rating, trend analysis, new product development, reserve calculation, network management, and special studies.

Actuarial standards of practice (ASPs) address issues regarding the use of data. *ASP No. 23, Data Quality* applies to all areas of practice and provides guidance regarding selecting, reviewing, and disclosing data.. *ASP No.5, Incurred Health Claim Liabilities* requires that the actuary check the reasonability of data and "make appropriate efforts to obtain" accurate data from claim processing and accounting systems.

This chapter focuses on identifying both internal sources and external sources of data which may be useful in a number of routine and special study situations, and the role of data structure in obtaining information from internal company sources. While the focus of this chapter is on the group medical line of business, many of the general issues apply to other group and individual lines as well.

EXTERNAL DATA SOURCES

The group actuary will often be required to consult external data sources in attempting to price new benefits, expand into new geographic markets, or develop new product lines. External data may also be required when a company's volume of business is insufficient to produce credible experience or as a check for reasonableness against internal company data.

Whenever external data are used, it is important to understand the characteristics of the population that would affect mortality and morbidity and the time period from which experience is gathered. It is also important to understand any limitations which may be inherent in the data collection mechanism, such as over or under reporting, or simplifying assumptions. How the information will be used is an important consideration when evaluating the appropriateness of external data or the accuracy required. For example, if external data are to be used as a reasonableness check, extreme accuracy may not be essential. If the external data are used as the primary source of claim costs underlying a premium rate development, accuracy may be critical. External data source providers are typically not as adept as internal sources at understanding the how these population characteristics can affect accuracy. It is therefore essential for the actuary to analyze and understand the credibility of the data source used for any particular assignment.

The following are a number of sources of data, external to company records, which the group actuary may find useful. Since the Internet has become a primary means of finding data of all kinds, we have included web site addresses, where possible, of established sites.

FEDERAL GOVERNMENT PUBLICATIONS

There are many sources of data compiled by the federal government relating to causes of morbidity, mortality and disability as well as price trends and demographics. Some government studies are published on the Internet, while many are available electronically from the national Technical Information Service, a division of the U.S. Department of Commerce[1]. Useful other sources include:

- *The National Ambulatory Medical Care Survey (NAMCS)*. Centers for Disease Control and Prevention[2] sponsors this detailed annual survey of physicians on the ambulatory medical care rendered at physicians' office visits. A number of detailed analyses are published from this survey (these include encounter rates by physician specialty, drug and lab test prescribing patterns, and reason for encounter). Since the survey has been performed over a number of years, historical information and trends are also available. Survey results are presented by age and sex, which can facilitate the extrapolation of results to the insured population.

- *The National Hospital Discharge Survey (NHDS)*. This is an annual DHHS survey which focuses on the experience among hospitalized individuals in the general population. Patient discharge records from a sample of hospitals are compiled. As with the NAMCS, a number

---

[1] www.ntis.gov

[2] www.cdc.gov

of specific analyses are published from this survey, including hospitalization frequency by diagnosis and region, and length of stay by diagnosis. This survey has also been performed over a number of years, which allows for analysis of trends. As with the NAMCS, the NHDS is a general population survey rather than a survey of the insured population, so some adjustments in results may be appropriate.

- *The National Health Interview Survey (NHIS)*. This is an annual survey of individuals which covers demographic characteristics, illnesses, impairments, chronic conditions and utilization of health care services. The survey can be found at Center for Disease Control website[3].

- *Consumer Price Index (CPI)*. The Bureau of Labor and Statistics[4] publishes CPI information monthly. This index examines the cost of fixed "market baskets" of goods and services nationally and in specific localities. Medical, dental, prescription drugs, and other health care services are included in the analysis. Since this is a market basket analysis, it reflects inflationary trends only, not trends in utilization of services.

There are many other surveys and studies performed by the federal government which are useful to the group actuary. Exhibit I, at the end of the chapter, lists many such sources and is organized according to the governmental body producing the data. Many of these sources can be found in medical school libraries or public libraries. The DHHS or NTIS web sites will contain instructions for downloading or purchasing copies of most studies.

ACTUARIAL PUBLICATIONS

A number of actuarial publications can provide useful data for pricing or analyzing all group lines. These data usually cover insured populations, which can be an advantage over the more general population data available through federal sources.

Even though data may cover insured populations, it is still necessary to examine the underlying population from which data is derived, particularly underwriting source (medically underwritten, guaranteed issue, and so forth) and product (individual or group; indemnity, PPO or HMO).

---

[3] www.cdc.gov
[4] www.bls.gov/cpi

Some of the primary sources of actuarial data are briefly described below. More detailed descriptions can be found in the Society of Actuaries year-book, or at the Society web site[5].

- *Serials.* The Society of Actuaries sponsors a number of periodicals which can provide useful data. The *Transactions Reports* of Mortality and Morbidity Experience include studies of interest such as group long-term disability morbidity and group annuity mortality. The *Transactions* and the *Records* of the Society of Actuaries and the *Actuarial Research Clearing House* all contain many articles and useful studies.

- *Reports.* The Society of Actuaries sponsors reports on areas of special interest. Of particular interest to the group actuary are the reports on "Variation by Duration in Small Group Medical Insurance Claim Costs" and the AIDS and HIV reports.

- *Tables.* Certain mortality and disability tables are available from the Society. Some programs and data are available electronically, including the Group Long-Term Disability (GLTD) Valuation Tables published in *TSA* Vol. XXXIX and the data from the "Variation by Duration in Small Group Medical Insurance Claim Costs" report.

- *Society of Actuaries Research Department and Foundation.* The Society of Actuaries sponsors research activities and projects in the area of Health, as well as in Knowledge Extension Research, Finance, Life Insurance and Retirement Systems. Questions regarding research projects can be directed to the SoA Research Management Coordinator, or the web site can be searched for specific projects[6].

OTHER EXTERNAL SOURCES

Depending upon the need, the group actuary may look to many other sources of data. As always, the actuary must carefully consider the population source of data and the applicability to the problem at hand. Some particularly useful data sources are as follows:

- *State Health Data Organizations.* Most states sponsor health data organizations which capture and compile hospital discharge data and ambulatory care data. An excellent reference which describes the available state data can be obtained from the National Association of Health Data Organizations in Washington, D.C[7].

---

[5] www.soa.org.
[6] www.soa.org/research/
[7] www.nahdo.org

These sources generally do not include exposures, therefore the actuary must look to other sources, such as census data and other demographic statistics, to develop claim cost estimates. The migration of patients from one area to another must be considered when this is done.

- *HMO and PPO Data Sources.* Data on the usage of services in HMOs is available from several sources, including the American's Health Insurance Plans (Washington, D.C.), HealthLeaders-InterStudy (Nashville, TN), and the American Association of Preferred Provider Organizations (Louisville, KY).

- *HEDIS.* The National committee for Quality Assurance[8] (NCQA) is an organization formed for assessing and reporting on the quality of Managed Care plans. NCQA has designed the Health Plan Employer Data and Information Set (HEDIS), a set of 86 standardized measures used to compare health plans' performance. HEDIS is updated annually to reflect advancements in the science of performance measurement and information systems technology, as well as changes in the managed care industry.

- *Hospital, Medical and Other Periodicals and Sources.* The American Hospital Association (Chicago, IL) and the American Medical Association (Chicago, IL) publish directories of hospital and physician resources and other items of interest. There are numerous other medical publications which may be useful, including the *Journal of the American Medical Association*[9] and the *New England Journal of Medicine*[10]. In addition, useful statistics can be found at the American Association of Health Plans' website[11]: www.ahipresearch.org.

- *Major Actuarial Consulting Firms.* A number of firms, such as Milliman, Inc.[12], publish pricing manuals and guidelines that include extensive data on health care utilization and costs. Organizations such as Medstat[13] provide detailed data sources that can be used for analysis.

INTERNAL DATA SOURCES AND STRUCTURE

Internal data sources represent the most important source of information for most actuarial analysis. Detailed, or atomic, data analysis of internal

---

[8] www.ncqa.org
[9] www.ama-assn.org
[10] www.nejm.org
[11] www.ahipresearch.org
[12] www.milliman.com
[13] www.medstat.com

data is becoming an increasing common part of an actuary's daily work. Technology advancements and industry trends have dramatically increased the availability of credible data to the actuary. Most health plan and insurance organizations can readily provide detailed claim and enrollment data. Many can also provide data on premium and capitation payments.

Many organizations today utilize third-party pharmacy benefit managers (PBMs) for the management and payment of prescription drug claims. As a result, it is often necessary to collect PBM data as a distinct source from medical claims data.

Much of the data required for group medical analysis is compiled and maintained to support either the premium billing and collection process or the claim payment process. As group medical coverages have evolved and grown more complex, other processes have developed, such as utilization management and provider contracting, which require additional data systems.

The expanding complexity of group medical coverages has greatly increased the volume and type of data captured. Yet, it is often difficult to extract accurate data and produce meaningful and timely reports. Much of the difficulty relates to the inherent conflict between the data and data structure needs of processing systems (such as claim payment systems) versus data analysis and reporting systems. To understand this conflict it is useful to understand the factors influencing data structures.

TYPES OF DATA STRUCTURES

A data structure is the format used for the storage of a group of data elements. The type of data structure used in a computer system will depend upon the manipulation desired and the storage media chosen. Conversely, the efficiency of the manipulation will depend upon the appropriateness of the data structure.

Computer Systems may employ the following types of data structures:

- *Sequential Files.* In this structure, each individual data record contains all the data elements needed for a specific processing application. Records for premium billing would contain enrollment and coverage information, with associated rates, and all information necessary for mailing the bills and updating the Accounts Receivable. This is the oldest structure used for data processing.

- *Indexed Sequential Files.* The sequential data records are stored in a direct access media (disk), and indices would be attached to the key elements by which records could be selected (group, member, coverage, etc.). These early database structures were a major improvement in data accessibility.

- *Relational Databases.* In these direct access structures, data elements relative to specific processing functions are grouped into separate tables, with indices for quick access of specific records and indices pointing to tables containing other related elements not needed for the specific process. For example, a membership table would contain records for each member's coverage by effective dates. A premium billing system would read this table, and calculate premiums from a rate table, which contained the rates for each coverage and effective dates.

- *Dimensional Databases.* These are a form of relational databases in which the numerical measures associated with the subject (*"facts"*) are aggregated by various attributes (*"dimensions"*) and then the facts and dimensions are stored in separate tables, which are indexed to provide for fast query access. Dimensional database models are particularly effective for ad hoc report or query access to data. They are most useful when processing data files on an ongoing, regular basis.

Computer systems store data in three types of physical media:

- *On-line.* This is disk storage that is immediately available to the application and may be used for any of the data structures described above.

- *Near-line.* Near-line storage is on-line data which has been compressed for more efficient storage, but which can be recalled by the processing application to on-line storage.

- *Off-line.* Off-line storage utilizes peripherals such as magnetic tape or removable disk. It is less expensive, but is slower to access. It is usually used for sequential data structures due to their large size.

The choice of data structure for a particular problem depends upon the following factors:

- *Volume of Data.* When storing small amounts of data, the structure used does not significantly affect the speed at which the data can be accessed. Most health insurance databases contain large volumes of data, and it must be structured to minimize processing time and storage costs. Historical data, which is not needed for daily processing, will generally be purged from the active data files on a periodic basis and placed in off-line storage.

- *Dynamic Nature and Frequency of Use.* Data that are updated frequently or are queried often will need to be stored on-line and structured in a way that allows quick and efficient access of the desired elements. When large volumes of data must be accessed frequently and in many complex ways, they will generally be stored in fully relational databases. Data that need not be accessed frequently can be accessed sequentially and stored in an off-line media.

- *Retrieval Time.* Magnetic tape stores data sequentially which makes it difficult and time consuming to search for particular elements. On-line disk storage allows direct access to physical records without processing all preceding records, making searches easier and retrievals faster. Near-line disk storage is a compromise between the two.

- *Ease of Programming.* When results are required immediately, an easy-to-program data structure may be chosen, although it might require a long execution time. At the other extreme, a complex structure may be more difficult to program and maintain, but may provide greater speed and flexibility of access.

ACTUARIAL INFORMATION SYSTEMS

The fundamental differences between the needs underlying processing systems and those underlying reporting and analytical systems have led most insurance companies to develop data warehouses and data marts that are distinct from their daily processing systems. These database systems contain historical extracts of data and are typically refreshed on a periodic basis (often weekly or monthly). The data structure used for these systems is designed to facilitate reporting and analysis rather than processing. When these warehouses and marts are developed, it is important that information contained in them are reconciled to the underlying financial records of the company.

Data warehouses and data marts may be housed on mainframe, minicomputer, personal computer or server platforms. The processing speed and storage capacity of the latter platforms continue to increase dramatically, allowing analysis of extremely large databases. These subsystems allow more "hands on" manipulation of data and do not interfere with ongoing production systems.

Many health carriers have developed actuarial or managed care information systems. These systems allow greater flexibility in terms of "slicing & dicing" the data and allow users to run ad hoc reports with quick turnaround. These actuarial information systems, which are often under the management control of the actuarial department, or shared with the underwriting and medical management areas, allow greater familiarity with the database and often better data integrity. The systems are often designed for some or all of the following tasks:

- Reserving
- Trend analysis
- Experience monitoring
- Rating
- Persistency studies
- Provider and network analysis
- Analysis of provider reimbursement agreements

SPECIFIC INTERNAL DATA SOURCES

MEDICAL CLAIM SYSTEMS DATA

Much of the actual analysis required by the group actuary centers around claim experience. Claim systems used by group insurers have grown to be incredibly sophisticated and complex. To appreciate the complexity of the systems, consider the following six high-level steps which must be performed before authorizing a claim payment:

- Eligibility of the claimant must be determined, requiring a query of the billing/eligibility files.
- The claim must be analyzed to determine if a preexisting condition exclusion or waiver is applicable.
- Coordination of benefits must be examined, which may require an examination of past claim history as well as subscriber files for indication of other coverage.
- Proper authorization for medical care must be verified. Many modern managed care systems require pre-authorization for high cost services, requiring query of the utilization review or pre-authorization system.

- The appropriate payment rate must be determined. Physician claims may be compared to usual and customary limits. Provider identifier may need to be verified. Specific contractual rates for hospitalization or physician payment also may be applied, requiring interface with the provider contract files. If a provider is covered under a capitation arrangement, there may be no claim payment made.

- Benefit plan provisions must be applied. This requires not only the calculation of deductible and coinsurance amounts, but also checking for exclusions due to preexisting condition clauses, elimination riders, non-covered services, and duplicate claims.

A tremendous amount of data is required to perform this process with many different data files. These data, if retained and accurate, present a wealth of analytical possibilities.

<u>CLAIM FORM DATA</u>

In order to understand the types of analyses which can be performed with claim system data, it is important to understand the data sources and how they are compiled.

Data captured by the claim systems comes primarily from electronic or paper claims filed by health care providers or patients, for care rendered to covered individuals. These electronic or paper claims are often completed by hospital, clinic or physician office personnel, particularly where the insured has authorized direct payment to the provider or where a paperless claim system is used, such as in a Preferred Provider Organization (PPO) or Health Maintenance Organization (HMO).

The information entered onto the claim record comes from medical and financial records of the provider. Office personnel analyze the medical records and code the events related to those medical records into the proper diagnosis and procedure codes for the care given. This process is important as payment for services is usually tied to the specific procedure (or diagnosis in the case of Medicare hospitalization claims).

Claim forms provide most of the information required to pay claims for hospital and physician services. While many insurance companies and payors originally designed their own claim forms to meet their specific needs, there was a strong movement towards standardization of claim forms. This movement resulted in two major standardized claim forms; the Uniform Bill UB-92 (CMS 1450) and the Health Insurance Claim Form (CMS 1500). The former is used for hospital and institutional claims, and the latter for physician and other provider claims. In addition, there is a standardized dental claim form (the ADA form).

In 1996, Congress passed the Health Insurance Portability and Accountability Act (HIPAA), which covered two areas, Portability of Health Insurance Coverage and Administrative Simplification. The purpose of Administrative Simplification was to improve the Medicare and Medicaid programs in particular, and the efficiency and effectiveness of the health care system in general, by encouraging the development of a health information system through the establishment of standards and requirements to facilitate the electronic transmission of certain health information. In August, 2000, the Standards for Electronic Transactions final rule was adopted, which mandated the use of a format designed by the Accredited Standards Committee X12. This form, ASC X12N 837 (X12 837) is now required for all claim records transmitted electronically.

HOSPITAL CLAIMS (UB-92)

The uniform hospital claim form, known as the UB-92 or CMS 1450 form, was used by hospitals and institutions for claims filed with most payors including Medicare, Medicaid, private insurance companies and Blue Cross and Blue Shield service plans. Many states had enacted laws mandating the acceptance of the UB-92 by payors. Most hospital claims are now transmitted electronically in the X12 837 format.

Data Components of the UB-92 Claim Form

The major data components collected on the UB-92 claim form are the following:

- *Patient/Insured Data*
    - Patient name, address, date of birth, sex
    - Insured's name, relationship to patient, employer
    - Payor name (Medicare, Blue Cross, and so on)
- *Hospital or Institution Data*
    - Listing of services rendered and charges
    - Allocation of charges between payor and insured
    - Attending physician
    - Codes of principal and other diagnoses
    - Codes of principal and other procedures performed
    - Dates of admission and discharge

The UB-92 must also be signed by a provider representative who attests to both the correctness of the information provided and that a signed patient authorization to release information is on file.

Uses of UB-92 Data

The primary use of the UB-92 data by the insurance industry has been for claim payment and adjudication. Data pertaining to the diagnoses, procedures performed, the detailed listing of charges and provider identification often have not been captured by an insurer unless it was needed for claim payment.

Recently, both insurers and employers have been performing detailed studies of costs by diagnoses, comparisons of costs for different facilities and summaries of the specific types of services used by their insureds. Results of these studies may point to benefit design changes, indicate those providers with whom discounts should be negotiated, and determine the effectiveness of cost containment programs.

Many HMOs will track UB-92 data to analyze the relative costs of participating facilities and the appropriateness of the services provided.

HEALTH INSURANCE CLAIM FORM (CMS 1500)

The Health Insurance Claim Form, commonly referred to as the CMS-1500, was been developed for the reporting of physician and other provider services, other than hospitals and institutions. The form was developed in conjunction with the American Medical Association and, as with the UB-92, is designed to provide all data needed by the payor and to eliminate the need for supporting information. It was used for Medicare, Medicaid, other government programs and private insurance programs.

The CMS-1500 form may also be electronically scanned by payers using optical character reading (OCR) equipment.

Data Components

The data contained in the CMS-1500 claim form included the following:

- *Patient/Insured Data*
  - Patient name, address, date of birth, sex, relationship to insured
  - Insured's name, address, policy group
  - Payor name (Medicare, Medicaid, other)

- *Physician or Supplier Information*
  - Date of illness or disability
  - Name of referring physician or other source
  - Admission date, if hospitalized
  - For each procedure performed:
    - Date of service
    - Place of service
    - Type of service
    - Procedure code
    - Diagnosis code
    - Charges
    - Total charges

The CMS-1500 may also include the signatures of the patient authorizing release of medical records, the insured authorizing direct payment to the physician, and the physician certifying to the correctness of the claim data and the medical necessity of care provided.

Uses of CMS-1500 Data

As with the UB-92 data, the primary use of the information provided in the CMS-1500 has been for the adjudication of claims. Certain data relating to other insurance and the circumstance surrounding the injury (at workplace, in accident) can facilitate coordination of benefits and subrogation activities.

Additional analyses of charges by procedure, site of care and usage of services by age and sex can also be developed using the CMS-1500 data. Many health plans use data provided by the CMS-1500 to analyze the performance of participating physicians.

ANSI ASC X12N 837 –
PROFESSIONAL AND INSTITUTIONAL HEALTH CARE CLAIM

This electronic format was mandated by HIPAA for all electronic claims transmissions for both Professional and Hospital claims. It contains all the elements included in the UB92 and CMS-1500 records, in addition to many additional fields designed to facilitate filing of claims by hospitals and professionals, as well as coordination of benefits among Insurance payers. The use of a common format for both types of claims, and national standardized codes and identifiers, are the main improvements over the old forms. The X12 837 contain placeholders for many more data elements than paper claim forms. As the use of this form becomes prevalent, organizations are using these placeholders to transmit additional information on the claim and the nature of the medical care. The X12 837 format also contains requirements for standardized coding of data elements. This results in more consistent transmission of electronic data among varying provider and payor sources.

X12 837 is a very complex data format. In order to read and process data from the X12 837 format, most organization purchase translation software. This software allows the user to read X12 837 and translate the data elements into a format that can be used in data warehouse or sequential file systems.

PREMIUM BILLING AND ELIGIBILITY SYSTEM

One of the other essential systems required for group insurance is the premium billing and eligibility system. This system is used to develop the group billing and to keep track of eligible enrollees. The claim system interfaces with the premium billing and eligibility system through eligibility verification, which is performed before each claim is paid. In HMOs and other Managed Care Organizations, the provider capitation system also interfaces with the eligibility system to tabulate the number of members attributable to each provider and the appropriate capitation rate to apply for each.

Because group billing and provider capitation are often characterized by many retroactive additions and subtractions of covered employees, the group billing and eligibility system performs the complex task of maintaining appropriate reconciliations and accounting.

Data Components of Premium Billing and Eligibility Systems

The group billing and eligibility systems will typically contain the following data:

- *Group Level Data.* Data will be accumulated that will facilitate the billing of the group. This will include a group identifier, benefit plan identification, agent or broker identification, listing of rating factors (geographic factor area, industry factor, and so forth) or the actual premium rates on rating formula.

- *Subscriber Level Detail.* The second hierarchy of data maintained in the system is usually subscriber and dependent data, which contain information regarding each individual who is covered. This information will often include the age, sex and dependency status of an individual. In addition, the employee class (hourly or salaried, or other determinant), starting eligibility, and termination dates will be maintained along with coordinator of benefit (COB) indicators and underwriting flags to indicate preexisting or excluded conditions

- *Benefit Detail. Contains information about the benefit plan of the covered enrollee including base benefits, cost sharing arrangements, riders, exclusions, and other relevant information.*

- *Additional Member Level Detail.* For HMOs and other Managed Care Organizations, PCP information will also be maintained.

Uses of Premium Billing/Eligibility System Data

Data from the premium billing and eligibility system will provide the exposure counts needed for claim analysis and trend studies. In addition, the age, sex, industry, and other characteristics can be computed from this system. Historical extracts from the file can be used to perform lapse studies and other demographic trend analyses.

OTHER INTERNAL DATA SOURCES

There are many other systems and subsystems within the insurance company which could provide data which may be useful to the group actuary. These include the following:

- *Commission Payment System.* This data file is used to process commission payments and can be used to examine the underwriting experience and persistency of coverage for specific brokers.

- *Utilization Review (UR) or Pre-Certification System.* Many managed care systems require pre-certification for high cost services. Most UR systems log the requests for pre-certification and provide authorization for the type of service to be performed. Often data available from these systems can be useful in developing unpaid claim reserve estimates based on open authorizations which have not yet been paid.

- *Provider Contract System.* Managed care medical products often pay providers according to fixed contractual rates. If contracting is done directly by the group insurer, or if discounts are applied automatically through the claim system, a file must be maintained of the appropriate reimbursement rates. Also, special systems are often set up for processing capitations, financial settlements, withholds, bonus payments, and other forms of provider risk-sharing.

Summary

As group products have become more complex, particularly in the group medical area, the information captured and the processing requirements have become more complex. The increasing availability of this information however supports more complex, complete, and powerful analysis.

In order to obtain information from the various systems, it is important to understand the purposes for which the systems were established and the structure of the data contained on the systems. Occasionally, the reporting needs of the group actuary will conflict with the processing needs for which systems were established. In this case, the group actuaries should be aware of any shortcomings which might exit in the system, such as historical limitations on data. They may also need to change the existing systems or develop ancillary systems, such as data warehouses and data marts, to better meet reporting needs.

EXHIBIT I

Federal Government Surveys and Studies

I. DEPARTMENT OF HEALTH AND HUMAN SERVICES

   A. Public Health Service

      1. Center for Disease Control and National Center for Health Statistics
- National Vital Statistics Systems
- National Survey of Family Growth
- National Health Interview Survey
- National Health and Nutrition Examination Survey
- National Master Facility Inventory
- National Hospital Discharge Survey
- National Nursing Home Survey
- National Ambulatory Medical Care Survey

      2. Center for Infectious Diseases
- AIDS Surveillance

      3. Epidemiology Program Office
- National Notifiable Diseases Surveillance System

      4. Center for Chronic Disease Prevention and Health Promotion
- Abortion Surveillance

      5. Center for Prevention Services
- U.S. Immunization Survey

      6. National Institute for Occupational Safety and Health
- National Occupational Hazard Survey
- National Occupational Exposure Survey

   B. Health Resources and Services Administration

      1. Bureau of Health Professions
- Physician Supply Projections
- Nurse Supply Estimates

C. Alcohol, Drug Abuse, and Mental Health Administration

    1. National Institute on Alcohol Abuse and Alcoholism
       ● National Survey of Drinking

    2. National Institute on Drug Abuse
       ● National Household Surveys on Drug Abuse
       ● The Drug Abuse Warning Network

    3. National Institute of Mental Health
       ● Survey of Mental Health Organizations

D. National Institutes of Health

    1. National Cancer Institute
       ● Surveillance, Epidemiology, and End Results Program

E. Centers for Medicaid and Medicare Services

    1. Office of the Actuary
       ● National Health Expenditures and Indicators
       ● Monthly Trend Report for Medicare, Medicaid and SCHIP

II. DEPARTMENT OF COMMERCE

A. Bureau of the Census

    1. U.S. Census of Population

    2. Current Population Survey

    3. Population Estimates

    4. Statistical Abstract of the United States

III. DEPARTMENT OF LABOR

A. Bureau of Labor Statistics

    1. Consumer Price Index

    2. Employment and Earnings

40 SHORT-TERM RESERVES

Mark E. Litow
Doug Fearrington

This chapter presents basic principles, considerations and methods for developing claim reserves for life and accident and health insurance. Appropriate estimation of claim reserves is extremely important in establishing profitability or solvency of companies, as well as estimating earnings and determining appropriate rating strategies. Poor methodology in determining claim reserves, in conjunction with a lack of understanding of principles, is a major reason why some companies have been unable to recognize poor or deteriorating experience, and have subsequently suffered high losses.

This chapter is broken into the following sections:

- Definition of claim reserves and component parts
- Considerations in establishing claim reserves
- Reserve methods
- Standards of Practice

DEFINITIONS OF CLAIM RESERVES AND COMPONENT PARTS

In defining claim reserves, a number of terms must be understood. These include the following:

- *Valuation Date.* This is the date at which reserves are estimated.
- *Incurral or Loss Date.* This is the date at which the event which establishes a reserve or liability occurs. This can be the date of death, disability, hospitalization, or other insured event. (In some cases,

the incurred date for a maternity claim may be the date of conception.) Any claim incurred on or before a valuation date represents an item which must be reserved for if benefits have not been paid for such a claim.

- *Service Date.* This is the date a service is actually rendered or performed, and each service date must be assigned an incurral date. However, many different methods exist of assigning incurral dates to a service date, and this can impact claim reserves significantly.

- *Reporting Date.* This is the date at which the claim is reported. Claims unreported as of the valuation date are referred to hereafter as unreported claims, while known claims are labeled reported claims.

- *Payment Date.* This is the date at which payment is made on a claim. Payment of a claim necessarily moves that amount paid from reserve status to paid status.

- *Lag.* This is the period of time between two dates. Typical lags include the following:

  ○ Reporting lag, between the incurral date and reporting date

  ○ Service lag, between incurral date and service date

  ○ Payment lag, between incurral date and payment date

  ○ Accrual lag, between service date and payment date

Each of these various lags can be used to help establish claim reserves, particularly through development type methods, as discussed later.

A claim reserve can be defined as an estimate of the amount remaining to be paid on a claim for an event that has as its loss (incurral) date any date on or before the specified valuation date. The term "claim reserve," as used in this chapter, includes both claim reserves and claim liabilities. Strictly speaking, based on statutory accounting definitions, a claim reserve is an amount set aside to pay for a service that will be rendered in the future, which is related to a loss event that has already occurred. In contrast, a claim liability is an amount set aside to pay for a service that has already been rendered. Such unpaid claims include the following:

- Due and unpaid, meaning they are reported and a dollar amount has been assigned to it by the company, but no payment has been made.

- In course of settlement, meaning that a claim has been reported but is still under investigation and no dollar amount has been assigned.

- Incurred and reported, meaning that a claim has been submitted, but hasn't been paid. The incurred and reported amount consists of the in course of settlement amount and the due and unpaid amount.

- Incurred but unreported, meaning that the claim has a loss date on or before the valuation date but is unknown to the company at the valuation date.

- Unaccrued, which means that the actual services are after the valuation date, but are still tied or related to a loss date on or before the valuation date. (Such unaccrued losses can be for a reported or unreported claim. Long-term disability and long-term care typically have a high proportion of the claim reserve in this category.)

- Deferred maternity or other extended benefits, which essentially means that while a loss date is triggered on or before the valuation date, benefits tied to that loss date are deferred into the future by contractual provisions.

- Other special reserves, such as disability claims under group life insurance, where premium is waived in the future due to a disability occurring on or before the valuation date.

The consistent use of the principles underlying claim reserves and other factors involved in the development of premiums should be maintained to the extent possible. In other words, if incurral dates or other definitions underlying claim reserves are used in developing company reserves and liabilities, the same principles should be used in developing premiums. Otherwise, financial results will show inconsistent revenues and disbursements as of the valuation date which, in turn, will produce a misleading financial picture.

CONSIDERATIONS IN ESTABLISHING CLAIM RESERVES

The level of claim reserves established is highly dependent on the incurral dating methods used, the basis of the reserve calculations, and many other influences. The important consideration is that once the company becomes responsible for payment, as determined by the contract, the liability or reserve must be established. Differences due to incurral dating methods occur because some methods reserve for services only as they occur (pay as you go), while other methods establish reserves for services in the future.

Reserves may also vary depending on whether calculations are on a statutory, GAAP, tax, or other basis. These reserve bases may differ in terms of the required or commonly used margins, interest rates, morbidity tables, and methodologies. Regulatory and professional standards require that statutory claim reserves include some margin for unforeseen fluctuation or adverse experience. Due to this, medical claim reserves are often set by adding a small percentage margin to a best estimate. For example, for statutory medical claim reserves, this margin is often 5% to 15% of the best estimate amount. Periodic tests of the liabilities will help determine how much of a margin is needed to cover unexpected results.

On reserves where the payout may take longer than six months to a year, a discount factor can be used as prescribed by regulation or determined by interest earned by the company. On reserves where the payout is typically much quicker, such as major medical, usually no discount is applied.

Other items which may affect claim reserve values are discussed in the following paragraphs.

CONTROLS AND RECONCILIATION

It is important for the actuarial department to communicate closely with the accounting department, to ensure that the data being used by the actuary reconcile and are consistent with the data and reporting practices used by the accounting department. Inventory counts, reported hospital admissions, and other information relied on should also be tested for accuracy periodically.

INTERNAL COMPANY PRACTICES

Many organizations have their own internal practices, which may cause lags to be faster or slower than normal. Also, fluctuating payment patterns can be caused by staffing practices and staffing events (such as vacations and layoffs, or unusual weather such as snow storms or floods), changes in computer systems, and other company specific practices. The impact of these factors, where significant, should be examined by analyzing the various lags, as applicable.

The impact of such fluctuations can be significant. For example, a change in computer systems may be preceded by a speed up in claims processing time as the processing area "cleans up" their inventory of unpaid claims in anticipation of the computer change. During the system change itself, unanticipated bugs or errors may emerge that slow processing time and create claim backlogs. This fluctuation in payment patterns will create experience data that is not as reliable in estimating incurred claims as data from a stable payment situation.

Many companies keep inventory logs where claims are tracked that have been received but are unpaid. Claims that are "pended" for more information may also be tracked. The available claim inventory information should be reviewed over time, and appropriate adjustments made if claim inventories have changed significantly. Some companies have processes where providers file claims electronically. As more providers gain this capability, the reporting lag can shrink dramatically. These are examples of why it is important to know if and when payment processes change.

Also, practices can differ dramatically for different companies. For example, different companies use different claims dating practices which can significantly affect lag patterns and claim reserves.

EXTERNAL INFLUENCES

Company lags can also be affected significantly by environmental influences, such as epidemics, governmental mandates, or new laws. For instance, a government induced slow down of payments for Medicare at the end of 1989 and 1990 caused many companies to experience slow-downs in Medicare payments. This was later followed by a flood of claims once the induced slow down subsided. Also, some medical care providers will file claims more quickly at the end of their fiscal year, in preparation for tax reporting.

POLICY PROVISIONS

The types of benefit, utilization incentives or disincentives, claim sizes in general, and other policy provisions can dramatically affect the pattern of claim payments. In evaluating such factors, one must consider the frequency of claim payment, as well as the severity of claims. For instance, disability claims will have a long runout due to the month by month payment pattern and general duration of disabilities; these claims represent a continuing contingent benefit where each payment is made only if the individual is still disabled. On the other hand, major medical claims will have a faster runout, since most of the services will occur closer to the date of accident or illness. For life insurance, claims are typically paid within a few months of death, thus producing an even more predictable runout than for A&H claims.

Insurance Characteristics

Claim reserves will also vary depending on the type of risk covered. In general, new plans will typically have long lags initially, because of the insured being unfamiliar with plan benefits and claims filing procedures, impact of pre-existing provisions, and the company's lack of familiarity with a new type of benefit (resulting in longer investigation times). However, once this initial period after issue has passed, lags will usually become shorter, meaning that reserves will become a lower portion of incurred claims for a while. Still later, lags may eventually increase over time, due to the severity of the claim increasing over time. This phenomenon is particularly noticeable on major medical or other A&H types of coverage where underwriting is particularly important. Such a result occurs because larger claims generally take longer to process and investigate, and also take longer periods of time before they are paid off. In fact, some companies will identify and reserve for large claims separately.

Reserve Cells

Typically, separate reserves are estimated for each homogenous category of business, and sometimes for each type of claim. This reflects that different types of claims may exhibit different claim lags and trends.

For medical benefits, reserves for hospital benefits may be estimated separately from those for physician benefits due to different trends as well as the claim lag. On occasion, hospital claims are submitted more quickly via electronic means than physician claims. Drug claims may be processed by an outside vendor, and may have very different trends and lags than hospital or physician.

In addition, since the data and information used for reserving may also be used to help analyze changes in claim costs, many companies reserve in detail to stay apprised of emerging changes in claim costs. Similarly, some companies reserve at the same level of detail that is used to analyze profitability and rate levels. For example, reserve cells can be set up for small groups, large groups, medically underwritten versus guaranteed issue, over 65 versus under 65, by network, or by region. HMOs might be interested in reserving for Medicare vs. non-Medicare members.

The drawback of increasing the number of reserve cells is that the estimation error may be increased for cells that are too small. In addition, there is the practical consideration of what detail the data is kept, and the time and resources involved in estimating numerous reserve cells. Understanding the nature of the benefits and the business will help decide what reserving cells make sense.

MANAGED CARE

Use of managed care initiatives or discounts in providing health care may also alter the level of claim reserves. If managed care results in changes in utilization levels, particularly relating to large claims that have longer lags, the lag factors may change. Changes over time in the discount levels may further affect reserve calculations, for the simple reason that, as charge levels move, the claim cost level will change, and with it the level of necessary claim reserves.

Managed care programs such as large case management and pre-admission certification may provide an early warning of unreported large claims. Information such as the number of approved hospital days or admissions can be used in setting claim reserves and is generally available prior to claim payment information.

Managed care programs often involve provider risk sharing arrangements such as withholds, settlements, or bonus or incentive payments. When estimating claim reserves, the type and scope of these arrangements should be reflected in the claim reserves. These risk-sharing arrangements often depend on the number or dollar value of the medical services provided. Because of this, the level of claims and claim reserves can affect estimates of payouts and recoveries related to provider risk-sharing arrangements. Further reserves may be needed to recognize payout of provider risk-sharing amounts. Also, it is critical to understand what risk arrangement amounts are and are not included in the claim data used to estimate claim reserves.

TRENDS

This influence is generally a factor only in medical care reimbursement plans, and can have a significant impact on experience. However, trends will not often have a dramatic impact on lag factors unless the trends change dramatically over a short period of time, so that they impact lags differently from one period to the next. More importantly, the trends resulting from the reserve calculation will be used to test the reasonableness of the results, and will be of interest in and of themselves.

SEASONALITY

Claims may increase or decrease significantly at various times of the year. If this is the case, lags should be studied by seasonal and not calendar year periods. Examples of benefits that may produce strong seasonal patterns are prescription drug plans, calendar year plans with high deductibles and plans where incurral dating is based on assigning loss dates to the earliest date or time period within a calendar year.

ECONOMIC CONDITIONS

Recession will impact claims for elective treatments, such as dental and cosmetic surgery, but cause an increase in incidences and durations of claim where people fear the loss of coverage.

CLAIM ADMINISTRATIVE EXPENSES

Actuarial Standards of Practice require recognition of a liability for the administrative expenses related to the incurred but not paid claims. It is common to determine this liability as a percentage of the claim reserve.

Many of these considerations are important and should be recognized as part of the methods, as described in the next section. Omission of such factors can, in come cases, lead to estimates which are inaccurate, even where all other parts of the method are applied properly.

RESERVE METHODS

This section describes the methods typically used to develop claim reserves for group insurance products, including data requirements and recognized tables applicable for each method.

In using various claim reserve methods, the differences between types of business and runout patterns must necessarily be recognized. Long-term disability claims will not have the same type of runout as major medical claims, and neither have the same type of runout as group life insurance claims. Thus, some of the methods noted below are appropriate for certain types of business, but not for others.

The types of methods generally used in estimating group claim reserves are presented in the following paragraphs.

FACTOR METHOD

This method is generally used for reserves which are easily estimated due to a short lag or run off period. An example would include group life insurance, where reserves are often established as a percentage of premium (a typical percentage for group life insurance might be 7% to 10% of annual premium in force on a valuation date). The percentage used under this method is usually based on an analysis of reserves from past valuation dates, comparing the annual premium in force at those dates with claims paid after the valuation date on claims incurred on or before the valuation date. For example, if a company had $10,000,000 of annual premium in force on December 31, and paid death claims of $700,000 after December 31 on claims incurred on or before December 31, a reasonable estimate of the claim reserve for next year might be 7% of current in force premium. Thus, if annual premium in force is $15,000,000 at any year end, the corresponding claim reserve established might be $1,050,000.

LAG OR DEVELOPMENT METHOD

The data necessary to utilize a development method are typically (a) claim payments split by period of incurral and period of payment, and (b) earned premiums or exposed lives, for the same incurral periods. The incurred periods should preferably be of small duration, such as monthly or quarterly, especially for products vulnerable to significant fluctuation in experience because of inflation or other influences.

The underlying principle of a development method is that contingencies affecting the progression of claim payments for a particular claim are inherently and properly modeled by an assumed runoff pattern; this includes probabilities of claim termination estimated from past experience, and adjusted to properly reflect the current environment and administrative practices of a company.

The minimum volume of claim payments normally needed to use this method will vary depending on the benefits covered, duration since plan inception, and the growth rate of business. Major medical plans, whether indemnity, managed care or some blend, may require roughly $350,000 or more (in 1998 dollars) of claim payments in a year to obtain credible results. Various types of policy forms should be combined for analysis only if the runoff pattern of claims is expected to be similar and the relative distribution of plans included remains unchanged.

The following steps describe the general lag or development method. Unless otherwise noted, "lag" as used here refers to the payment lag or lag between incurral month and payment month. Many modifications exist to this approach, but the underlying principles are the same.

Step 1. Develop paid claims by period of incurral and payment. Table 40.1 below shows a month by month runoff for a period of one year. In practice, Table 40.1 would be maintained for a number of years (up to 4 or 5) of incurred and paid claims, in order to be able to examine any changes in the payment pattern for this block of business.

Step 2. Develop a claim runout or lag chart, for which several similar methods exist. One method involves calculating the percent of ultimate claims that are paid after one month, two months, and so on for a given incurral month. This process is used to develop completion percentages and corresponding incurred claims, where incurred claims are determined from payments to date (in Step 1) divided by the appropriate completion percentage. Starting with the Table 40.1 data, these calculations produce the results shown in Table 40.2.

Table 40.1

CLAIMS BY PAYMENT MONTH (in thousands)												
Month of Incurral	Jan	Feb	Mar	Apr	May	Jun	Jul	Aug	Sep	Oct	Nov	Dec	Total
January	50	200	200	100	50	25	0	0	0	0	0	0	625
Febuary	N/A	60	250	200	150	75	30	0	0	0	0	0	765
March	N/A	N/A	50	220	300	130	80	10	0	0	0	0	790
April	N/A	N/A	N/A	50	200	200	100	100	50	10	0	0	710
November	N/A	N/A	N/A	N/A	N/A	N/A	N/A	N/A	N/A	N/A	70	230	300
December	N/A	N/A	N/A	N/A	N/A	N/A	N/A	N/A	N/A	N/A	N/A	75	75

Table 40.2

CLAIM COMPLETION PERCENTAGES (Proportion of ultimate total paid through month of payment)												
Month of Incurral	Jan	Feb	Mar	Apr	May	Jun	Jul	Aug	Sep	Oct	Nov	Dec
January	0.08	0.400	.0720	0.880	.0960	1.000	1.000	1.000	1.000	1.000	1.000	1.000
Febuary	N/A	0.078	0.405	0.667	0.863	0.961	1.000	1.000	1.000	1.000	1.000	1.000
March	N/A	N/A	0.063	0.342	0.722	0.886	0.987	1.000	1.000	1.000	1.000	1.000
April	N/A	N/A	N/A	0.070	0.352	0.634	0.775	0.916	0.986	1.000	1.000	1.000
November*	N/A	N/A	N/A	N/A	N/A	N/A	N/A	N/A	N/A	N/A	0.088	0.375
December**	N/A	N/A	N/A	N/A	N/A	N/A	N/A	N/A	N/A	N/A	N/A	0.088

* Assumes incurred claims of $800. ** Assumes incurred claims of $850.

From Table 40.2 we observe that payments for November and December incurrals are still quite incomplete. However, earlier months, such as January through April, can be used to estimate what total incurred claims for these months of incurral might be. For example, November has $300 of claim payments through December, and months January through April of incurral suggest a completion factor of around 35-40% (the ratio of paid to estimated incurred claims at any valuation date). Thus, November incurrals might be estimated at $750 to $800 (the example uses $800, for a reserve of $500). For December, incurred claims of $850 has been estimated, based on the following factors:

- The fact that December payments are a little higher than previous months.

- The estimated level of incurrals for earlier months.

- The completion percentages attained for each incurred month has always been under .09.

Generally, months with completion factors lower than a chosen percentage are seen as non-credible estimates of claim reserves for those periods. That percentage may vary by benefit type, and is somewhat subjective. Typically, the percentage will be in the 35%-70% range. In that case, claim reserves are often based on an estimate of the average cost per contract or member (which underscores the important of being able to estimate the trend in claims cost PMPM) or a loss ratio estimate (ratio of incurred claims to earned premium). The known claim payments are subtracted from these estimates to determine the claim reserve. In estimating the average cost per member, it is important to consider changes in demographics, benefits, provider contracts (fee levels and what services are being capitated), and care management programs over time.

When using development methods, many of the considerations mentioned in the previous section can cause dramatic changes in completion factors. For that reason, use of other methods to confirm results from a lag method is necessary. Further, where strong seasonal influences impact a block of business, completion factors should be analyzed for corresponding time periods in earlier calendar years. Thus, where loss ratios differ significantly by calendar quarter, completion factors should be analyzed separately as they relate to each calendar quarter.

Another approach using a development type method is the development of paid loss ratios by incurral period. For instance, for any incurral quarter, paid loss ratios can be tracked relative to incurral quarter. Thus, for quarters of incurral during calendar years Z and $Z+1$, the following Table 40.3 might be applicable as a separate illustration (unrelated to the earlier examples).

Projecting from the pattern in this table, the ultimate loss ratio for the third quarter of $Z+1$ would be based on the current value of 22% divided by the relative completeness of earlier quarters at the same point in time. For quarter 1/Z, the completeness and completion factor (CF) is 0.20÷.50 = 0.40; for 2/Z the CF is 0.22÷.48 = 0.458; for 3/Z the CF is 0.23÷.53 = 0.434. The average of these ratios is 0.43, producing a final loss ratio of roughly 0.52, or 0.22÷.43.

Table 40.3

Loss Ratios Paid To Date Through Each Quarter								
Quarter of Incurral	1/Z	2/Z	3/Z	4/Z	1/Z+1	2/Z+1	3/Z+1	4/Z+1
1/Z	0.04	0.20	0.35	0.43	0.48	0.50	0.50	0.50
2/Z	—	0.08	.022	0.35	0.42	0.47	0.48	0.48
3/Z	—	—	0.09	0.23	0.40	0.48	0.53	0.53
4/Z	—	—	—	0.07	0.26	0.45	0.55	0.58
1/Z+1	—	—	—	—	0.10	0.27	0.48	0.60
2/Z+1	—	—	—	—	—	0.09	0.25	0.45
3/Z+1	—	—	—	—	—	—	0.07	0.22
4/Z+1	—	—	—	—	—	—	—	0.08

Development methods can also estimate claim reserves by component, analyzing each of the various lags noted earlier in this chapter. The techniques are generally the same, but the detail is greater, and each component part must be accounted for in producing the aggregate claim reserve.

The development method does present problems where claim payment patterns involve a long payout period with considerable fluctuations, such as long-term disability insurance. An uneven payment pattern, such as a large settlement made on occasion, could make the development method unreliable. In such cases, other methods are used, such as the tabular or average size claim methods discussed below.

TABULAR METHOD

This method applies factors to individual claims or waived premiums to estimate the remaining claim or waiver payments. Usually, this method is used for long-term disability claims where regulatory standards have established minimum reserves, for claims incurred more than two years prior to the valuation date. Under this method, factors representing the present value of remaining claim payments are calculated either by use of annuity values, or disability continuance probabilities. Minimum standards in many states are based on the 1964 CDT or 1987 CGDT disability tables with an interest discount at the maximum interest rate allowed for life insurance reserves as of the issue date. Generally, disabled life annuity values are based on the age of disablement, length of disability as of the valuation date, and the remaining benefit period at that time. More recently, tables have begun to include sex and elimination period as variables.

AVERAGE SIZE CLAIM METHOD

Under this method, the claim reserve for reported claims is estimated by reviewing claim sizes for previously closed claims. The total reported reserve is then the estimated average size multiplied by the number of reported claims, less any payments made on these claims prior to the valuation date. This method works well if closed claims to date accurately represent a fully developed block of business. If a block of business is new, and the data does not yet represent a credible estimate of the average size, this method should not be used.

With this method, a reserve is also needed for unreported claims or the incurred but not reported (IBNR) reserve. In this case, the IBNR reserve can be based on loss ratio estimates or the average number of IBNR claims incurred but not reported as of prior valuation dates, adjusted for exposure differences.

LOSS RATIO METHOD

Consistent with reserves for unreported claims, the reserve under this method is based on earned premium times an estimated loss ratio minus paid claims. This method is generally used only where sufficient information is not available to use other methods, such as for new blocks of business or periods of time when experience is not credible. Also, this method can be used for confirming estimates under other methods. Similarly, a claim cost per month or year of exposed life can be substituted for loss ratios by using exposure instead of earned premium.

EXAMINERS METHOD

Under this method, claims department personnel or qualified personnel are asked to estimate the remaining claim payments expected on known claims, based on the characteristics of each claim. Generally, these estimates are based on doctors' statements and past history for such claims. This method is often used to estimate the liability arising from claims subject to law suits. The legal department should be involved in the process.

As with the average claim size method, this method produces a reserve only for reported claims, and a separate reserve (the IBNR) must be set aside for unreported claims.

STOCHASTIC APPROACHES

General Comments

Almost any of the deterministic methods outlined above can be given a stochastic treatment, with varying degrees of rigor and sophistication. As a general definition in this context, a "stochastic" method simply refers to any approach which allows us to make probabilistic statements about the level and adequacy of the reserve amount. In practice, most stochastic methods explicitly treat some component of the reserve as a random variable, and then model these components, as opposed to directly adopting an overall distributional form (typically parametric) for the total reserve. The reserve is then calculated as a function of these random components, and the variability of the reserve becomes a reflection of the variability of the components.

The benefits of adopting a stochastic approach are several. First, it provides explicit guidance for establishing provision for adverse deviation in statutory filings. It provides explicit guidance to management on potential variability in reported earnings and reserve levels. It allows for quantification of variability in internal processes, such as payment systems, and external processes, such as seasonality and claim trend.

Further, a stochastic approach allows for improved evaluation of separate reserve estimates for alternate lines of business. While both reserves may represent "best estimates," the uncertainty associated with one may greatly exceed that of the other. (In other words, not all best estimates are created equally.)

In short, stochastic methods provide a means to quantify uncertainty around reserve estimates. Notably, a reserve that is developed and booked from a stochastic method does not necessarily provide any more accuracy than a reserve developed and booked from a deterministic method; after all, under both approaches, only a single number is recorded. Instead, an appropriately developed stochastic method provides up-front guidance as to the nature and size of the statistical error associated with the financial entry.

Indeed, there are drawbacks and complicating issues to consider when adopting a stochastic methodology. To start with, it is important to consider the sophistication of the audience. An advanced statistical method, producing what we deem to be a rigorous prediction interval, may instill a false sense of confidence in an audience unfamiliar with such approaches. What's more, there is the potential for surprise and confusion when future adjustments are made to past reserves. For example, the statement "The reserve level which last month represented an 80th percentile, now only has a 20% chance of being adequate" is not necessarily inconsistent, but is likely to be frustrating.

The complexity of the methodology may be an issue. Pursuit of rigor must be balanced with time constraints and logistical feasibility. What's more, a methodology that only one or two people on staff can fully understand might create problems in training, communication, and interaction with other actuarial functions such as the financial forecast or renewal pricing.

It is important to understand the limits of the approach. Not every stochastic model can be applied to every set of data or line of business, and it's important to know how to identify such cases. Not every process can be modeled rigorously, and knowing when can be valuable—the analyst can then say, "Here is an estimate for which I can, at best, provide only a subjective range."

MODELING TECHNIQUES

This section outlines some general modeling techniques that are useful when adopting a stochastic approach.

As mentioned earlier, most stochastic approaches for estimating short term reserves involve actually modeling *components* of the reserve, then *combining* the individual model results in some fashion. As an example, consider a loss ratio method that projects an estimated loss ratio for each reporting month. One possible stochastic approach would be to:

1. Specify each monthly loss ratio as an independent normal random variable, each with its own mean and variance. So, the monthly loss ratios are the "components."

2. From each of the monthly loss ratio distributions, take a large number of samples. With each sample selected, calculate the product of the loss ratio and the matching monthly premium.

3. Sum this product across all months for each sample realization, and subtract any payments made to date. (This is the "combining" step, producing an estimated reserve from each set of samples.)

4. After sampling is completed, compute statistics about the set of all realized reserve estimates.

This example leads to us a more detailed discussion of potential techniques available for building stochastic models. None of the techniques is meant to be viewed only in isolation; employing a combination of methods is more likely to be of value than rigidly adhering to only one approach.

- Parametric Distribution-Fitting: Much like the example above, this technique involves fitting a parametric distribution directly to data, or, when there is no data to work with, specifying a distributional form based on professional judgment. The technique works best when the process being modeled is stationary over time.

For example, consider a claim reserve calculation using the development method, where we might be attempting to fit a lognormal distribution to the run-out pattern from the claim triangle. If the same parameter estimates (the mean and variance of the lognormal form) fit well for each incurred month being analyzed, and we expect the fit to be valid going forward, we may have success with this technique. If, however, trends or cyclical patterns are present in the data, indicating that the mean or variance may not be constant, an alternate technique which addresses these patterns may be preferable.

- Ordinary Least Squares Regression: Multivariate regression models represent a straightforward approach to handling situations where we want to investigate the effects of specific explanatory variables, such as a time trend or seasonality. For example, as a continuation of the example above, suppose we believe the mean of the lognormal distribution is subject to a linear time trend with a significant seasonal effect occurring in January of each year. Then, we could model the mean of the distribution with

$$\mu_t = A \times t + B_t \times (\text{January indicator}) + C + e$$

Where t represents time and e represents the error term.

Alternately, linear regression models can be used as simple forecasting models for future values of either loss ratios, development factors, incremental payments in a claim triangle, or other factors.

Use of regression models can be limited by their assumptions of normality and constant variance.

- Generalized Linear Models: True to their name, general linear models represent a more generalized form of multivariate linear regression. Specifically, these models allow for occasions where the dependent variable being modeled is either bounded (for example, required to be strictly greater than zero) or not normally distributed (as would be the case if the variable were bounded). A detailed description of these types of models is beyond the scope of this chapter, but several references included in the bibliography illustrate their application to actuarial reserve estimation.

- Stochastic Time Series Models: Time series models are useful for handling situations where values are correlated across time. For example, suppose we had hoped to use the above linear regression model, but had noticed that the residuals from fitting such a model seemed to have a cyclical pattern present. In that case, an ARIMA (autoregressive moving average) model fit to the residuals may be of value. The form would then be:

$$\mu_t = A \times t + B_t \times (\text{January indicator}) + ARMA(p,q) + C + e$$

- Monte Carlo Sampling / Simulation: Monte Carlo sampling techniques are of significant practical value when attempting to combine results from any of the techniques described above. While certain model forms lend themselves to analytical solutions, in practice it can be much more efficient to combine results through sampling techniques. Many commercial packages are available as well as the freely distributed WinBUGS.

MODELING CONSIDERATIONS

There are some preliminary considerations to be made when developing a stochastic approach to reserve estimation. In general, these issues will play a significant role in determining the set of feasible stochastic techniques, the degree of sophistication possible, and the amount of actuarial judgment involved in interpreting results:

- Availability of data: The amount of available data will affect the extent of historical validation that can be performed, and the degree to which any model assumptions can be tested or confirmed. This will directly impact the validity of model results and the degree of care that is needed in communicating results.

- Appropriateness of data: Consideration should be given to whether the processes reflected in the historical data are likely to be representative of the processes being modeled going forward. This involves looking at the maturity of the block of business being modeled, as significant changes in size may limit the range of stochastic techniques available. Also, any changes in the payment processes, whether one-time or permanent, are an important element to be examined.

- Access to statistical software: In general, it's advisable not to reinvent the wheel when it comes to implementing more advanced models. Obviously, lack of access to modeling software, or a lack of understanding of its application will limit the choices available.

In addition to these considerations, there are some more advanced issues which should be addressed. The first is that it bears repeating that specifying an *appropriate* model for the data at hand is one of the most important parts of the modeling process. It can be all too tempting to blindly apply a technique developed in a paper or publication without considering appropriateness. What's more, for stochastic approaches, validation is all the more necessary since the results are predicated directly on the model's assumptions. Common techniques in such validation include goodness-of-fit testing, residual analysis, and hold-out sample evaluation.

Another important issue is that, to the extent that a reserve estimate is broken down into "component" model estimates, covariance between those components becomes a primary modeling concern. While it can be tempting to simply assume independence, potential covariance should be evaluated both within a component model and across models.

To illustrate the covariance issue, suppose we are projecting incremental payments to be made within a claims triangle using time series models (a variation of a development method). The diagram below illustrates the potential covariance that may need to be addressed:

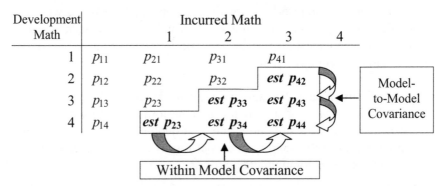

Development Math	Incurred Math			
	1	2	3	4
1	p_{11}	p_{21}	p_{31}	p_{41}
2	p_{12}	p_{22}	p_{32}	*est* p_{42}
3	p_{13}	p_{23}	*est* p_{33}	*est* p_{43}
4	p_{14}	*est* p_{23}	*est* p_{34}	*est* p_{44}

Est p_{42} produced from Model 1
Est p_{33} and p_{43} produced from Model 2
Est p_{23}, p_{34}, p_{44} produced from Model 3

Within Model Covariance:
  Covariance of *est* p_{33}, p_{43} in Model 2
  Covariance of *est* p_{23}, p_{34}, p_{44} in Model 2

Model-to-Model Covariance:
  Model 1 to Model 2
  Model 1 to Model 3
  Model 2 to Model 3

Not only are the reserves produced by stochastic approaches estimates, it's important to remember that, with many techniques, the parameters specified are estimates themselves. It may be necessary to reflect associated uncertainty of any parameters in producing prediction intervals for reserves. This additional uncertainty will typically widen the interval.

FINAL COMMENTS

As with any modeling exercise, it bears repeating that continual monitoring and evaluation are advisable. Despite our best efforts at historical validation of a technique, the true test of the reliability of the ranges produced falls to subsequent monitoring as future values are realized.

STANDARDS OF PRACTICE

Many guidelines and standards of practice now exist and apply to calculation of claim reserves. These guides and standards provide discussion of definitions, methods, and considerations in calculating claim reserves. Such guidelines or standards include the following:

- The Guides to Professional Conduct of the Academy of Actuaries, as they relate to methodology and assumptions

- The Actuarial Standards Board's Actuarial Standard of Practice (ASOP): No.5, "Incurred Health and Disability Claims," No. 16 "Actuarial Practice Concerning Health Maintenance Organizations and Other Managed-Care Health Plans," No. 18 "Long-Term Care Insurance," No. 22 "Statements of Opinion Based on Asset Adequacy Analysis by Actuaries for Life or Health Insurers," No. 28 "Compliance with Statutory Statement of Actuarial Opinion Requirements for Hospital, Medical and Dental Service or Indemnity Corporation, and for Health Maintenance Organizations," and No. 42 "Determining Health and Disability Liabilities Other Than Liabilities for Incurred Claims." Actuarial Compliance Guideline #4, "Statutory Statements of Opinion Not Including An Asset Adequacy Analysis By Appointed Actuaries for Life or Health Insurers"

- NAIC guidelines and model regulations relative to reserve standards and opinions, in particular, The NAIC Health Reserves Guidance Manual. At the end of this manual there is a comprehensive list of reference documents.

- Statement of Statutory Accounting Principles (SSAP) No. 54, Individual and Group Accident and Health Contracts, National Association of Insurance Commissioners, and No. 55 – "Unpaid Claims, Losses and Loss Adjustment Expenses," effective January 1, 2001

- Literature published in textbooks and by the actuarial profession

ASOP 5 directly discusses the calculation of incurred claims for health and disability claims, and this chapter is intended to be consistent with it. This ASOP discusses the considerations and analysis that are done to develop an incurred claim estimate, as well as the methods used in estimating incurred claims. The standard also includes a reference to ASOP 23, Data Quality, which suggests that data used to estimate incurred claims must be reviewed for accuracy and completeness.

ASOP 16 discusses estimating incurred claims in a managed care environment. It discusses the impact of capitation, risk sharing, and utilization and cost management may have on the estimation process. With managed care being common in the marketplace, managed care impact on actuarial practice has been incorporated in other ASOPs. Therefore ASOP 16 may be withdrawn by the Actuarial Standards Board. This is an example of practice maturing and actuarial standards keeping pace with change.

ASOP 42 discusses liabilities other than claim reserves such as contract reserves, premium deficiency reserves, claim settlement expense reserves, and various reserves related to provider contracts. Some of these are short term reserves that must be established when appropriate.
While this chapter briefly mentions claim expense reserves, these reserves do need to be established. Expense reserves can be calculated as part of the claim reserve (as described herein), but are often calculated separately from claim reserves (consistent with experience or pricing assumptions as appropriate).

REFERENCE

Litow, M.E. 1989. "A Modified Development Method for Deriving Health Claim Reserves." *TSA* 41:89.

41 CLAIM RESERVES FOR LONG-TERM BENEFITS

Daniel D. Skwire

The two primary forms of long-term health benefits are long-term disability (LTD) insurance and long-term care (LTC) insurance. Detailed discussions of these benefits are provided in other chapters of this text. Although LTD and LTC plans insure different risks, their similar structure and long-term nature mean that they share many of the same concerns in the calculation of claim reserves.

There are several aspects of LTD and LTC contracts that are particularly important with respect to claim reserves:

- *Periodic Benefits*: Unlike most short-term health products, LTD and LTC plans typically have a benefit equal to a specified monthly or daily amount. LTD plans generally specify a monthly indemnity amount. LTC plans generally reimburse actual expenses up to a specified daily benefit amount.

- *Long-Term Benefit Periods*: LTD and LTC plans have maximum benefit periods that are quite long relative to other health benefits. The maximum benefit period for LTD is often To Age 65 (or other normal retirement age). LTC plans often specify a lifetime dollar maximum benefit, which determines the maximum length of time for which benefits may be paid.

- *Elimination Periods*: The elimination period is the period of time after someone becomes eligible for benefits under the policy, but before benefits begin to accrue. LTD and LTC plans offer a variety of elimination periods, often 90 days or more.

- *Optional Benefits*: Both LTD and LTC plans offer a variety of optional benefits that may affect the timing or the amount of monthly payments. Examples of optional benefits include partial disability benefit (which pay an amount less than the monthly benefit if the person is able to work part time while disabled) and cost of living adjustments (which increase a benefit for inflation while a person is disabled).

- *Integration of Benefits*: LTD plans often contain provisions that reduce the amount of benefits paid to reflect social insurance benefits received while disabled (such as Social Security or Worker's Compensation). LTC plans typically integrate with Medicare long-term care benefits.

- *Limitations and Exclusions*: Certain types of claims, such as intentionally self-inflicted injuries are excluded from coverage altogether, and need not be considered in claim reserves. Other types of claims may be subject to limited pay periods, which should be reflected in the reserving process. One common example consists of mental and nervous claims, which are often limited to a payment period of two years under LTD policies.

The product features discussed above affect the beginning date, the ending date, or the amount of benefits paid under LTD and LTC plans. They therefore have a significant impact on the value of the benefits, and they must be explicitly considered in the calculation of claim reserves.

COMPONENTS OF LONG-TERM CLAIM RESERVES

Long-term claims may be divided into three primary categories, each of which is treated separately for the purpose of claim reserve calculations:

- *Open Claims*: These are claims that have benefits currently being paid. These benefits will be paid no longer than the benefit period (BP).

- *Pending Claims*: These are claims that have been reported to the company but payments have not yet begun. Payments may be held up waiting for approval from a claim manager, or they may still be within the elimination period (EP).

- *Incurred but not Reported (IBNR) Claims*: These are claims for which the loss has already occurred (the person has become disabled or satisfied the LTC benefit requirements), but which have not yet been reported to the company.

The three categories of claims can be illustrated by a timeline. For claims that are reported during their elimination period, the timeline typically

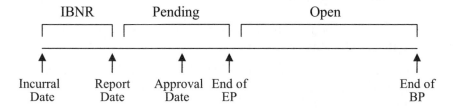

For claims that are reported after the completion of the elimination period, the timeline looks like the following:

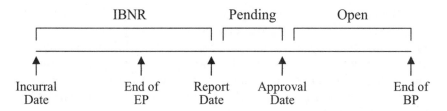

A separate reserve calculation is performed for each of the three claim categories. The type of calculation for each category reflects the amount of information that is available. Open claims have the most detailed information, so the most precise methodology can be used. For pending claims and IBNR claims, less information is available, so there is a greater need for estimation. The following sections describe the reserving methodology for each category of claims.

RESERVE METHODOLOGY FOR OPEN CLAIMS

Reserves for open claims are the largest component of claim reserves for LTD and LTC plans. They are often called "tabular reserves," because the calculation method involves using tables of expected claim termination rates. The formula for a tabular claim reserve at claim duration n may be written in simplified fashion as follows:

$$V_n = \sum_{t=n}^{BP} Benefit_t \cdot Continuance_t \cdot InterestDiscount_t$$

This formula expresses the tabular claim reserve as the sum, for each month from the current claim duration until the end of the benefit period, of the product of three items:

- *Benefit*: The monthly benefit, which may vary from month to month based on the product provisions.

- *Continuance*: The probability of a claim continuing to receive payments in a future time period (the probability that the individual will not recover or die).

- *Interest Discount*: The time value of money, reflecting the fact that the payment will not be made until some time in the future.

The calculation of the benefit term in the claim reserve formula may be quite simple or quite complex, depending on the product provisions. Some plans may pay a flat amount each month, while others may increase or decrease for a variety of reasons, including optional benefits, benefit integration, or cost of living adjustments. Any expected increases or decreases in the benefit amount should be considered as part of the claim reserve calculation.

The calculation of the continuance factor is generally performed by using data contained in a continuance table, which may be based on either industry experience or company-specific experience. A sample continuance table is shown below:

Table 41.1

Sample Continuance Table			
Claim Duration	**Age At Claim**		
(months)	**35**	**45**	**55**
0	1000	1000	1000
1	975	950	900
2	950	900	800
3	925	850	700
4	900	800	600
5	875	750	500
6	850	700	400
7	825	650	300
—	—	—	—

This sample continuance table, which is designed for illustrative purposes only, allows the calculation of continuance factors for the first seven months of claim for people who become disabled at ages 35, 45, or 55. The number at the top of each column, for claim duration 0, is the radix, or the initial number of disabled individuals. The chance that an individual who becomes disabled at a certain age will remain disabled for a certain number of months can be computed as the ratio of the value in the table for that month, divided by the radix. So the chance that a 35-year-old who has just become disabled (at time 0) will remain disabled until the end of 3 months can be computed as 0.925, or (925/1000). Similarly, the chance that a 55 year-old who has already been disabled for two months will remain disabled for an additional two months, may be computed as 0.75, or (600/800).

In order to perform a sample claim reserve calculation, the simple formula for tabular claim reserves provided above may be restated in actuarial notation as follows:

$$V_n = \sum_{t=n}^{BP-1} Benefit_{t+1} \cdot \frac{l_{t+0.5}}{l_n} \cdot (1+i)^{-(t-n+0.5)/12}$$

Where:

n = Claim duration at the valuation date, in months (the claim reserve is computed as of the end of duration n)

$Benefit$ = Benefit paid in month t. The first benefit occurs in the month immediately following the valuation date.

t = Claim duration, in months from claim incurral date

BP = Final claim duration in which benefits may be paid

l_x = Value from continuance table at claim duration x for the appropriate age at disability

i = Annual interest rate

This formula assumes that claim payments are made in the middle of a month, so the continuance and interest discount terms reflect a mid-month assumption. Continuance table values for the middle of a month are computed through averaging:

$$l_{x+.50} = \frac{l_x + l_{x+1}}{2}$$

EXAMPLE:

Using the continuance table above, and an interest rate of 5%, compute the tabular claim reserves at the end of months 3, 4, and 5 for a 45-year-old claimant who has a policy with a 3 month elimination period, a 3-month benefit period, and a flat monthly benefit of $1000.

End of Month 3:

$$V_3 = 1000 \cdot \frac{825}{850}(1.05)^{\frac{-1}{24}} + 1000 \cdot \frac{775}{850}(1.05)^{\frac{-3}{24}}$$
$$+ 1000 \cdot \frac{725}{850}(1.05)^{\frac{-5}{24}}$$

$$V_3 = 968.62 + 906.22 + 844.32 = 2719.16$$

End of Month 4:

$$V_4 = 1000 \cdot \frac{775}{800}(1.05)^{\frac{-1}{24}} + 1000 \cdot \frac{725}{800}(1.05)^{\frac{-3}{24}}$$

$$V_4 = 966.78 + 900.74 = 1867.52$$

End of Month 5:

$$V_5 = 1000 \cdot \frac{725}{750}(1.05)^{\frac{-1}{24}}$$

$$V_5 = 964.70$$

RESERVE METHODOLOGY FOR PENDING CLAIMS

The reserve calculation for a pending long-term claim is similar to the calculation for an open long-term claim, but it involves an additional factor reflecting the likelihood that the claim will eventually receive a payment. This factor, called the pending factor, includes the probabilities that a claim will remain disabled through the elimination period and that it will be approved for payment, as well as including any necessary interest discounting.

For pending claims that are still in the elimination period, the claim reserve may be computed as the product of the pending factor and the tabular claim reserve at the end of the elimination period. (Discounting for interest between the valuation date and the end of the elimination period might be conservatively ignored.)

For pending claims that have completed the elimination period, the claim reserve may be computed as the product of the pending factor and the sum of (a) the tabular reserve at the current claim duration, and (b) the accumulated value of past claim payments that have not yet been made since the claim is not yet approved.

The pending factor is developed by each company based on its own experience. Theoretically, a different pending factor could be used for claims within the elimination period than for claims that have completed the elimination period. In practice, however, most companies use a single pending factor that reflects the combined probability of a claim completing the elimination period and being approved for payment, along with any margin for conservatism that the actuary feels is appropriate. Pending factors often range from 60-80%, although the values can vary significantly for different companies. As discussed in the section on IBNR claim reserves, some companies may combine the pending claims with IBNR claims in the development of an IBNR reserve.

EXAMPLE:

- Monthly Benefit of $1000, paid at the end of each month of disability.
- Elimination Period of 3 months

- Interest Rate of 5%

- Tabular Reserves of $25,000, $28,000, and $32,000 at the end of months 3, 4, and 5, respectively.

- Pending factor of 75% for all claims.

Compute the pending reserve, assuming the claim is reported at the end of month 2.

$$V_2 = 75\% \cdot \$25,000 = \$18,750$$

Compute the pending reserve, assuming the claim is reported at the end of month 5.

$$V_5 = 75\% \cdot \left[\$32,000 + \$1,000 + \$1,000 \cdot (1.05)^{1/12} \right] = \$25,503$$

Note that this second reserve calculation includes the payment from month 5 (which is due at the end of month 5 and therefore has no accumulated interest) and the payment from month 4 (which was due at the end of month 4 and has one month of accumulated interest). No payments are included from months 1 through 3, since the policy has an elimination period of 3 months.

RESERVE METHODOLOGY FOR IBNR CLAIMS

Because IBNR claims are not known at the time of valuation, the reserve calculation typically involves an estimation process based on historical experience trends and the size of the current block of business. The two most common methods used for computing IBNR claim reserves for long-term benefits are the lag method and the loss ratio method. These methods are similar to the methods described in the chapter on computing claim reserves on short term health benefits.

THE LAG METHOD

Where credible historical data is available, the lag method is preferable for computing IBNR reserves, because it reflects a company's actual claim development patterns as accurately as possible. For the purpose of this calculation, "lag" refers to the time period between the incurral date of a claim and the date that the claim is reported to the company. Due to their long elimination periods, which may exceed 12 months in some cases, LTD benefits often have very long reporting lags, and it may sometimes take 2 years or more past the incurral date for a claim to be reported to the company. LTC benefits typically have somewhat shorter reporting lags, since their elimination periods are 12 months or less, and since a plan of care is generally established shortly after the commencement of a claim.

Suppose a company is interested in using the lag method to determine an IBNR reserve factor for use in computing an IBNR reserve at the end of 2005. It performs a lag study to determine how many claims were incurred but not reported at a previous valuation date. The company decides to study the valuation date 12/31/2003, which is two years prior to the current valuation date, so that it can be reasonably certain that any claims which were incurred but not reported at that time have since been reported.

To conduct the study, the company creates a list of all claims that were incurred *prior to 12/31/2003*, and that were reported to the company *after 12/31/2003*. These are the IBNR claims as of 12/31/2003. It then computes a tabular reserve for each of these claims *as of 12/31/2003*. The total of the tabular reserves for each of these claims equals the claim reserve that the company would have held for its IBNR claims on 12/31/2003 had those claims been reported. This amount is then expressed as a percentage of the earned premium for the business during the year 2003 (assuming the volume of business didn't grow or shrink significantly during the year.) This percentage is the IBNR reserve factor. To compute the IBNR reserve as of 12/31/2005, the company simply multiplies the 2005 earned premium by the IBNR reserve factor.

IBNR reserves are typically expressed as percentage of premium because the premium reflects the size of the block and is not distorted by the amount of reported claims in a particular year. If the IBNR reserve factor were expressed as a percentage of tabular reserves, a company might find itself in the counter-intuitive position of setting up a larger IBNR reserve in years when more claims were reported, and a smaller IBNR reserve in years when fewer claims were reported. The IBNR reserve factor should be reviewed and updated on a regular basis to ensure that it reflects recent trends in claim lags.

When computing IBNR reserves based on a lag method, some companies elect to include pending claims by defining the lag as the time period from claim incurral to the first claim payment (as opposed to the reporting date.) This methodology, which is more common for LTC claims than for LTD claims, eliminates the need for a separate pending claim reserve.

THE LOSS RATIO METHOD

IBNR reserves may also be computed using a loss ratio method. This approach is most often used for new lines of business, or by companies with very small blocks of business who do not have sufficient data to develop an IBNR reserve factor by the lag method. Under the loss ratio method, the company computes its IBNR reserve at the end of a year by assuming that the incurred loss ratio for that year will be a target amount, generally tied to pricing assumptions or recent experience. It then computes its actual loss ratio for that year by dividing the incurred claims for that year (the paid benefits plus the change in claim reserves for reported claims) by the earned premium for that year. Finally, it subtracts the actual loss ratio from the target amount, resulting in an IBNR reserve factor as a percentage of earned premium. This factor is then multiplied by the earned premium for the year to compute the IBNR reserve.

Under this method, the company's experience for the year will equal the target loss ratio, unless the actual loss ratio exceeds the target loss ratio. In that case, some IBNR reserve should still be established since there are very likely to be unreported claims. One drawback to the loss ratio method is that the company's financial statements may not accurately reflect underlying changes in experience. For this reason, the loss ratio method should be used cautiously, and only when the lag method is impractical.

CONSIDERATIONS IN CALCULATING CLAIM RESERVES

MORBIDITY ASSUMPTIONS

The selection of an appropriate morbidity basis (continuance table) is essential in computing claim reserves for long-term health benefits. The determination of the appropriate basis depends on the type of benefit being reserved, and on the purpose for which the reserves are being computed. Different tables are needed for LTD plans than for LTC plans. In many cases, it is also necessary to use different tables for reserves that are computed for statutory, GAAP, and tax financial reporting, as well as for experience analysis and management reporting.

Continuance tables for LTD benefits commonly vary by the following factors:

- Sex,
- Elimination Period,
- Age at Disability, and
- Claim Duration.

Some more recent tables for LTD insurance also vary by the cause of disability and by the definition of disability.

According to the NAIC model law, which has been adopted in most states, statutory reserves for LTD claims with a duration of less than two years may be based on the insurer's own experience, if it is credible. Reserves for claims in later durations should be based on the 1987 Commissioner's Group Disability Table (1987 CGDT), except that companies with very large blocks of business may request permission to use their own experience basis for claims in durations two through five. The 1987 CGDT is based on industry experience from the early 1980's, and is generally felt to be quite conservative (that is, it results in excessively high reserves) for early claim durations.

During the 1990's, the Society of Actuaries conducted an experience study of LTD claims that resulted in the development of the 1995 Basic Experience Table. Subsequent modifications to that table resulted in the development of the 2000 Basic Experience Table. This table currently provides the most accurate reflection of recent industry experience. Two interesting characteristics of this table are: (1) the fact that it has separate termination rates for claims due to mental and nervous conditions (which tend to recover more slowly than other claims), and (2) that it has adjustment factors based on the own occupation period of the claim (since recoveries tend to increase in the month immediately following the end of the own occupation period). It is important to note, however, that this table has not been accepted by the NAIC for statutory reserving purposes, and it is believed to be somewhat aggressive (it results in somewhat understated reserves) in some claim durations. Companies who use this table for reserving or other purposes may need to adjust the claim termination rates in order to develop adequate reserves.

LTC continuance tables are similar in structure to LTD tables, and they may also be based on published industry data. Continuance tables for nursing home care were created by the Society of Actuaries (SOA) from the 1985 National Nursing Home Survey (NNHS), and published in the Transactions of the Society of Actuaries. These tables are commonly referred to as the "Wilkins Tables." The NNHS is conducted by the National Center for Health Statistics, and is periodically updated, but is based on population, not insured data. The SOA Long Term Care Experience Committee publishes periodic reports of LTC experience on lives insured under private LTC plans in the United States. The most recent report was published in 2004.

LTC experience for specific companies has been shown to vary widely from the morbidity rates contained in population studies, and from the composite data from the experience committee, and the NAIC has not specified a table for use in computing statutory reserves for LTC benefits. Therefore, most LTC insurers compute claim reserves based on their own experience, if it is credible, or on a morbidity basis that is consistent with the pricing basis for the policy, though often with an added margin for conservatism. The selection of the appropriate morbidity basis for reserving LTC claims is a complex question that should be carefully considered by the actuary responsible for computing reserves.

For both LTD and LTC claim reserves, it is essential for companies to regularly compare their actual morbidity experience to the assumptions used in claim reserves (see the section on "Evaluating Claim Reserve Adequacy" later in this chapter).

INTEREST RATES

Interest rates for statutory reserves are generally specified by law, and are most often equal to the maximum interest rate permitted for the valuation of whole life insurance contracts. Interest rates for tax reserves are specified by the Internal Revenue Service. Interest rates for GAAP reserves are generally equal to a company's expected investment income rate on the assets backing its claim reserves, less a margin for conservatism.

POLICY PROVISIONS

Claim reserve calculations must make explicit allowance for many policy provisions. In some cases, such as the own occupation period for LTD or home care benefits for LTC, the impact of these provisions is seen in the choice of a morbidity basis. In other cases, however, these policy provisions affect the amount and the timing of benefit payments.

Common policy provisions that should be considered in claim reserving include the following:

- *Cost of Living Adjustments (COLA)*: COLA benefits increase the amount of claim payments for inflation. The increasing pattern of benefits must be explicitly reflected in the calculation of reserves.

- *Partial and Residual Benefits*: Partial and residual benefits are common on LTD policies. These benefits pay between 20-80% of the monthly benefit if the claimant is able to work part-time during a period of disability. The fractional portion of the benefit that is paid should be reflected in the reserve calculation.

- *Survivor Benefits*: Survivor benefits may pay a death benefit equal to a few months of payments to a designated beneficiary if a claimant dies while receiving benefits. The expected cost of this benefit, while often small, should be reflected in the claim reserve calculation.

- *Benefit Integration*: Many LTD and LTC plans are integrated with benefits for social insurance, meaning that the benefit must be reduced for amounts received from these other sources. This reduction must be reflected in the reserve calculation. Some companies also estimate the impact of future offsets for social insurance benefits not yet being received by the claimant.

- *Benefit Limitations*: Many LTD benefits have a limited benefit period, such as two years, for some specified conditions. This limited benefit period must be reflected in the reserve calculation.

- *Waiver of Premium*: Some LTD and LTC benefits contain a provision that waives premiums if the insured is on claim, or (in the case of survivor waiver benefits on LTC), if a person's spouse has passed away. For LTD claim reserves, it is usually not necessary to hold an additional reserve for waiver benefits, due to the term structure of the premiums. On the other hand, for LTC claim reserves waived premiums are most often treated as an additional monthly benefit, since group LTC policies have level issue-age premiums and the coverage is usually guaranteed renewable.

- *Non-Level Daily Benefits*: Many LTC claimants do not receive a level benefit from day to day, because they receive different levels of care on different days of the week. This means that they are eligible for different levels of reimbursement on a day-by-day basis. The pattern of daily benefits can affect both the amount that is paid each day and the length of time for which benefits may be paid (under policies that have specified lifetime dollar maximum benefits.) In computing reserves for policies with non-level daily benefits, it is necessary to reflect the actual payment patterns, through specific calculations or averaging techniques.

CLAIM EXPENSES

In reserving for long-term health benefits, insurers must also make provision for the expenses that are related to the management and payment of these claims. Claim expenses are often expressed as a percentage of claim payments, such as 3-7% of paid claims. Therefore, the claim expense reserve is equal to that percentage times the tabular claim reserve.

The NAIC requires companies to hold claim expense reserves for statutory purposes, and these reserves are computed for GAAP purposes as well. The IRS does not permit the deduction of claim expense reserves, however, so no such reserve is computed for tax purposes.

DIAGNOSIS-BASED TABULAR RESERVES

Claims arising from different causes may have different patterns of expected recoveries. An LTD claimant with a broken arm, for example, may be expected to return to work within a matter of weeks, while a claimant with a chronic and debilitating disease may be unlikely ever to return to work. The most common industry practice for LTD is to compute reserves for all causes of disability using the same morbidity basis, assuming that the aggregate reserve will appropriately reflect the underlying mix of different causes of disability.

In recent years, some companies have begun developing different morbidity bases for different causes of disability. Although this approach has the advantage of generating claim reserves that are more closely aligned with each individual claim, there are several challenges to this approach:

- *Lack of credible data*: The total number of claims for any specific cause of disability may be quite small, making it difficult to develop a credible morbidity basis.

- *Complexity of calculation*: The use of a large number of different morbidity bases may complicate the reserve calculation process.

- *"All or nothing" approach*: This method must be used consistently for all claims, if it is used at all. For example, it would not be appropriate to use a table assuming very rapid claim terminations for some claims expected to recover quickly, and a table based on aggregate industry experience for all other claims. This method would understate the reserves for the "all other" claims, since this category does not include any of the claims expected to recover quickly.

For these reasons, care should be taken in the use of diagnosis-based claim reserves for LTD benefits.

LTC CASE RESERVES

Some LTC companies who have small claim blocks may elect to compute "case reserves" for some claims, meaning that their reserves are based on an evaluation of a specific claimant's medical condition and plan of care, rather than on aggregate morbidity assumptions contained in a published table. This approach is very labor intensive, and is most often used on blocks of claims that either do not have sufficient size to develop credible morbidity assumptions, or have a large enough reserve amount involved to justify it.

DATA INTEGRITY

Unlike the aggregate reserves computed for short-term health benefits, tabular reserves for long-term benefits are heavily dependent on the underlying seriatim claim data. Seemingly small errors in a claim data file can have an enormous impact on the tabular reserve that is computed for a particular claim. The failure to recognize a two-year benefit limitation on a specific claim, for example, may result in a reserve that is too high by several hundred percent.

Common errors in claim data include the following:

- Missing data,
- Misstated age or sex,

- Inaccurate elimination periods or benefit periods,
- Incomplete or inaccurate information on benefit integration,
- Inaccurate information on cause of disability, and
- Incorrect coding of claim status (open, closed, or pending).

Companies should conduct regular audits to ensure that their claim data is being captured accurately and interpreted properly in reserve calculations.

EVALUATING CLAIM RESERVE ADEQUACY

RUNOFF STUDIES

Frequent testing of claim reserves is necessary to ensure the adequacy of the reserves. One method to test reserve adequacy is a claim runoff study, in which previous reserve balances are compared to subsequent claim payments and reserve balances, with appropriate adjustments for interest. The object is to determine whether the previous reserve balance was adequate to cover the subsequent payments and reserves.

Table 41.2 contains an example of a runoff study to test the tabular reserves computed at 12/31/2003, relative to payments and reserve balances for the year 2004:

Table 41.2

Claim Runoff Study					
Incurral Year	12/31/2003 Reserve	2004 Payments	12/31/2004 Reserve	12/31/2003 Runoff	12/31/2003 Margin
2001	900,000	100,000	800,000	859,495	40,505
2002	800,000	75,000	750,000	787,478	12,522
2003	700,000	80,000	700,000	744,739	(44,739)

In Table 41.2, the 12/31/2003 runoff is computed as the present value (at 5% interest as of 12/31/2003) of the 2004 payments, plus the present value of the 12/31/2004 reserve. The 2004 payments are assumed to occur in the middle of 2004. The 12/31/2003 margin is computed as the 12/31/2003 reserve less the 12/31/2003 runoff.

Table 41.2 presents runoff experience by claim incurral years, which is a common approach for long-term health benefits. Companies can use the results of this type of runoff study to identify areas where their claim reserve basis appears to be weak or strong. For example, the results in Table 41.2 show a negative margin for claims incurred in 2003, which were in their first duration as of 12/31/2003. This suggests that the morbidity basis used to compute claim reserves may be weak in the first duration. Table 41.2 also shows a positive margin for claims incurred in 2002 and 2001, suggesting that the morbidity basis is adequate in the second and third claim durations.

A/E CLAIM TERMINATION RATE STUDIES

Claim runoff studies provide a high-level indication of the adequacy of claim reserves, with detail by claim duration. The results of runoff studies can be somewhat difficult to interpret, however. For example, a basis that produces reserves of increasing weakness by claim duration may appear to generate positive margins, because the runoff is significantly understated.

For companies that have sufficient data, further information on reserve adequacy may be obtained through the development of an actual to expected (A/E) claim termination rate study. This type of study uses a company's actual claims as an exposure base, and then compares the actual claim terminations experienced by the company to the expected claim terminations based on the table used for reserving. A/E ratios of greater than 1.00 indicate that more claims are terminating than assumed in the reserve basis, meaning that the reserve basis is adequate. A/E ratios of less than 1.00 indicate that fewer claims are terminating than assumed in the reserve basis, meaning that the reserve basis is inadequate.

Table 41.3 contains an example of an A/E claim termination rate study:

Table 41.3

Claim Termination Rate Study			
Claim Duration	Actual Terminations	Expected Terminations	A/E Ratio
1	80	120	0.67
2	120	130	0.92
3	100	75	1.33
4+	250	200	1.25
Total	550	525	1.05

Claim termination rates vary significantly by claim duration, so it is essential to look at results by claim duration when conducting a claim termination rate study. The study in Table 41.3 shows overall claim termination rates that are 105% of expected, but also reveals lower-than-expected claim terminations in durations 1 and 2, and higher-than-expected claim terminations in durations 3 and higher. Even though the overall claim termination rates may appear adequate, a company might wish to use the information in Table 41.3 determine adjustments to its morbidity basis that would result in more accurate reserving by claim duration.

There are several important considerations in preparing a claim termination rate study:

- *Credibility*: It is important to ensure that there is sufficient data in the study before drawing conclusions about the experience.

- *Types of terminations included*: Generally speaking, only those terminations due to recovery and death should be included since most morbidity tables reflect only these types of terminations. Claims that terminate due to the end of the benefit period or the presence of a benefit limitation should not be counted as terminations.

- *Exposure characteristics*: A company should be aware of any characteristics of its claim exposure that may not be reflected in the morbidity basis used to determine expected claims. For example, if a company's expected morbidity basis did not vary by type of disability, and if its exposure had a large number of claims for short-term causes of disability such as maternity, it might expect to see very high A/E termination rates. In this case, rather than adjust its overall morbidity basis, it might want to consider performing separate studies for maternity claims and all other claims, and developing two separate A/E results.

A/E claim termination studies can be used in combination with claim runoff studies to modify the claim reserve morbidity basis. For example, a company may identify deficiencies in its reserve basis through a runoff study. It may then perform an A/E claim termination rate study to determine specific adjustments to its morbidity basis by claim duration. The adjusted morbidity basis can then be used to compute a new set of claim reserves, which can be tested against recent payment experience by repeating the claim runoff study. In this manner, a company can demonstrate that a proposed new claim reserve morbidity basis will produce reserves with an adequate runoff.

CONSIDERATIONS FOR SELF-INSURED PLANS

Some employers may offer LTD benefits to their employees on a self-insured basis (this is quite rare for LTC). In this case, the claim reserve liability must be computed and held by the employer, rather than by an insurance company. The considerations in calculation claim reserves for a self-insured plan are generally the same as for an insured plan. There are certain accounting guidelines related to the reporting of these liabilities, however, that must be considered by employers.

Of particular note is the recent publication of new accounting standards for public employee benefit plans and public employers. These standards, published by the Government Accounting Standards Board (GASB), and known as GASB43 and GASB45, apply to post-employment benefits other than pensions, a category that includes disability benefits. The standards require employee benefit plans and employers, respectively, to make certain disclosures about the financial status of the plan, including current funding levels. They also require the use of certain pension accounting methods in the creation of the required reports. These standards, which were published in 2004, become effective in staggered fashion, depending on the type of plan or employer, between 2005 and 2008.

FURTHER INFORMATION AND RESOURCES

Many guidelines and standards of practice now exist and apply to the calculation of claim reserves for LTD and LTC benefits. These guidelines and standards include the following:

- The Guides to Professional Conduct of the American Academy of Actuaries, as they relate to methodology and assumptions.
- Actuarial Standards of Practice (ASOPs) developed by the Actuarial Standards Board including ASOP No. 5, "Incurred Health and Disability Claims"; ASOP No. 18, "Long-Term Care Insurance,"

and ASOP No. 42, "Determining Health and Disability Liabilities Other Than Liabilities for Incurred Claims."

- Health practice notes issued by the American Academy of Actuaries.

- NAIC guidelines and model regulations relative to reserve standards and opinions

- NAIC Accounting Practices and Procedures Manual

- GAAP accounting standards, including SFAS60 and SFAS112 (insurers and private employers), and GASB43 and GASB45 (public employers)

- Canadian Office of the Superintendent of Financial Insurance (OFSI) and the Canadian Institute of Actuaries publications and papers

- Literature published in textbooks and by the actuarial profession.

These guidelines require appropriate review, methods, and assumptions, and suggest that mere mechanical calculations performed without actuarial judgment and analysis are not appropriate. It is not generally accepted actuarial practice to use factors and values directly from published tables or computer programs (such as those supplied by the Society of Actuaries or commercial vendors) without performing the proper analysis to determine whether the reserves developed in this manner are reasonable and adequate.

42 UNDERWRITING GAIN AND LOSS CYCLES

John P. Cookson

The presence of a regular group health underwriting cycle for over thirty years, from the 1960's to 1990's has been well-known and discussed in many venues. This pattern has clearly changed since the mid-1990's. These results are evident in the diagram shown in Figure 42.1. This diagram illustrates the total reported underwriting gains and losses as a percentage of Earned Premium/Revenue of the Blue Cross and Blue Shield (BCBS) system from 1965 through 2004[1]. This long history of under writing gains and losses had exhibited a consistent pattern of three successive years of gain followed by three successive years of loss through 1991.

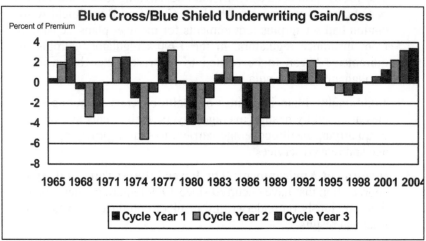

Figure 42.1

Since 1989, the pattern has been less regular and greatly muted. These financial results shown in Figure 42.1 are as initially reported by the plans,

---

[1] This information has not been made public for the last few of these years. Our data for these years are estimates inferred from Blue Cross and Blue Shield Association press releases.

and are not recast for reserve restatements. They also are affected by accounting changes over time. Recast financial results would likely show a somewhat different pattern. However, it is not the absolute numbers that are relevant here, but the general pattern of results. Similar patterns were apparent in the historical results of commercial health insurers, but summarized results have not been available since 1993.

While the fundamental risks associated with providing health coverage remain, there are several reasons for the change in the pattern of results beginning in the mid-1990's. Additional discussion of this change can be found in [1] and [2]. These reasons include:

1. **Severe Financial Stress in the late 1980's:** The bankruptcy or near bankruptcy of several large plans in the late 1980 generated a critical examination of the underwriting cycle, and a greater awareness of its importance, by both insurers and regulators.

2. **Risk-Based-Capital (RBC):** The formalization and adoption of health RBC levels by the National Association of Insurance Commissioners and the various states beginning in the mid- 1990's. The 1980s' produced a significant underwriting losses and a number of carrier insolvencies. The Blue Cross and Blue Shield Association had set surplus requirements for member plans, separately from insurance regulators. In the 1990's regulatory surplus requirements began to be related to the risks taken by insurers, through an RBC formula

   Additionally, financial ratings of health coverage by rating agencies are used by health coverage buyers, their agents and brokers in qualifying health coverage carriers to bid on providing coverage and related services[2].

3. **Investment Environment: The lower interest rates and** equity appreciation that have occurred since 1999 require greater reliance than previously on underwriting results to produce equivalent net financial results.

4. **Federal Income Tax:** After initially becoming effective in 1987 for not-for-profit plans, even though phased in, this gradually built up to a substantial charge against net income. This increased the underwriting income needed to yield the same rate of return on capital.

---

[2] The reader may also want to review the 1995 Society of Actuaries Research Report "Analysis of Health Carrier Insolvencies."

5. **Investment Analysts and Debt Ratings: Both** for-profit and not-for-profit health carrier activities are heavily scrutinized by financial analysts. Not-for-profit health carriers look to raising capital via debt instruments, which are rated. Additionally, there are many for-profit plans, including some former not-for-profit Blue Cross and Blue Shield Plans. The omni-presence of investment analysts, and the need for publicly held companies to answer to shareholders, puts extra pressure on avoiding the underwriting swings of the past.

6. **Capital Investments:** Health carriers have had to make significant capital investments in claim systems, Y2K (as with all computer dependent corporations), and modifications resulting from the Health Insurance Portability and Accountability Act (HIPAA). Currently health carriers are making significant investments in health information technology infrastructures, and will have to expend considerably with conversion to ICD-10 (International Classification of Diseases).

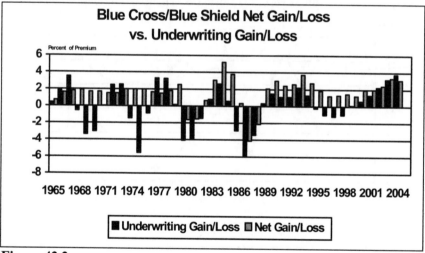

Figure 42.2

The results shown in Figure 42.1 are exclusive of investment income. A corresponding history that includes investment income and the impact of income tax is shown in Figure 42.2. Investment income has followed its own course during the period, sometimes adding significantly to gains, and sometimes not.

In an inflationary environment, insurers cannot prosper with net operating gain consistently at only a break-even level. Health insurers have surplus and return-on-equity requirements that must be met, and which must allow for growth. Most of the aggregate growth in non-governmental health insurance in recent decades has come from trends and consolidation, and not from new business. Therefore, growth in aggregate surplus and RBC targets has been due to the trend of claim costs per member, rather than in the number of members.

The impact of this fact on profit targets can be seen with the following illustration. If we assume 25% of claims as target surplus, and a 5-15% rate of growth in claims (doubling every 5 to 7 years or so), it is necessary to generate an average net operating gain (contribution to surplus) of 1.1% to 3.3% per year just to maintain the target surplus level. To have shareholder returns or capital for expansion, additional operating gains would be needed.

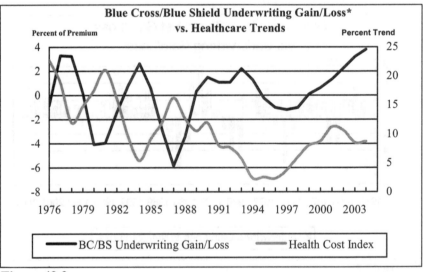

Figure 42.3

Historically, the high negative correlation between underwriting results and health care cost trends, as shown in Figure 42.3, was a major contributor to the underwriting cycle. This pattern has clearly changed since the mid to late 1990's. (The trends in this figure are from the Health Cost Index™, a measure of average underlying health cost trends for the non-Medicare population.)

NATURE OF THE UNDERWRITING CYCLE

The underwriting cycle is a normal economic phenomenon. It is the end result of many factors and decisions operating within the health insurance environment. However, the cycle does not represent a predestined result. In fact, the underwriting results of the industry are a stochastic phenomenon, with a range of outcomes, which may change over time based on many variables.

This is similar to the effects of typical business cycles, which represent fluctuation in business activity of many individual businesses that often tend to expand and contract at roughly the same time. However, most business cycles do not exhibit the regularity that health insurance did from 1965-1991.

As illustrated in Figure 42.3, to a large extent, past underwriting cycles have been caused by unanticipated upswings in health insurance trends. Trends are so often associated with the underwriting cycle because trends are a crucial factor in determining premium rate increases, which, in conjunction with actual claim trends, ultimately determine financial results.

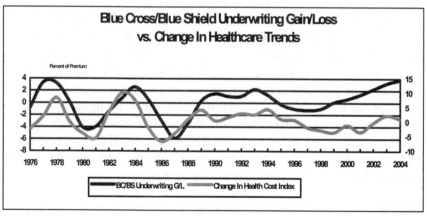

Figure 42.4

* As a Percent of Net Premiums
HCI data reflects change in 12-month trends 18 months apart

Past trends determined the cost of claims in the historical experience on which the projection is based.

Assumed claim trends for rating, plus a correction for the difference between recent actual trends and those assumed in past rating, will largely
determine the current level of rate increases. If actual experience trends are
higher than assumed for the period, lower underwriting results occur, and
future rate increases will be higher than the corresponding future trend assumptions to return profitability to the previously desired target. This is
true even without an explicit effort to recoup past losses, or increase the
profitability target. Similarly, if actual experience trends are lower than
assumed, underwriting gains above the target level will result, and upcoming rate increases will be lower than current trend assumptions, assuming
the previous target profitability is not reduced.

CAUSES OF THE UNDERWRITING CYCLE

The relationship between trends and the underwriting cycle is further illustrated in Figure 42.4 for the period 1976-2004. This compares the change
in trends 18-months apart using data from the Health Cost Index™ (HCI)
vs. Blue Cross and Blue Shield underwriting gains and losses as a percentage of premiums.

Since the trend change and underwriting results are inversely correlated, the
negative of the trend change is shown to more clearly illustrate that decreases in trend correspond to increasing underwriting gains and that increases in trend correspond to reduced underwriting gains. The use of the
18-month lag reflects the time between the latest actual trend information
that would be available at the time of rate renewals and the endpoint of the
rating period to which actual trends will apply. This also implicitly assumes
that the most recent actual trends form the basis for rating assumptions. The
impact of improved technology in estimating claim liabilities and trends
and the speed up in claims payments which reduce uncertainty about recent
results help to reduce the miss-estimation of trends and forecasts.

Keep in mind that the Health Cost Index™ represents underlying population trends, exclusive of factors such as adverse selection and deductible
leverage. Thus, actual incurred trends are likely to be higher and more
volatile than the HCI and the trend change between time periods are also
likely to be slightly greater. These factors would most likely increase the
relationship between trends and underwriting gains and losses, since carriers' financial results can be significantly affected by antiselection due to
large rate increases.

A number of typical health insurance pricing practices tend to exacerbate the cycles, including the following:

- Health insurance pricing must be performed with incomplete information as to the level of current experience trends. A reaction delay naturally occurs, as carriers tend to rely on measurements of past experience in developing current pricing assumptions. Historically, the delay has been as much as 12 months or more after trends begin to change; as a result, carriers were often unknowingly increasing their rating trends when actual experience trends had begun to decline, and decreasing their rating trends when actual trends were increasing. Even if trends are predicted accurately, the impact of individual underwriting decisions on many case renewals can result in a different effective trend actually being applied in rates. This tends to produce a cycle of gains followed by losses. The increases in electronic submissions of claims, the speed of processing and summarization of data, and more powerful computer resources has helped to reduce this effect.

- The industry has exhibited periods of unwarranted optimism and pessimism with respect to their financial results. These attitudes have generally occurred in response to what has happened in the recent past rather than in anticipation of what is likely to happen in the near future. For example, most carriers were optimistic in their pricing and marketing strategies in 1985 and 1986, as a result of the favorable experience (increased profitability due to lower trends) that developed in 1984 and 1985. This appears to have been a major contributor to widespread underwriting losses during 1987 and early 1988. However, the increased intensity of financial surveillance and more effective management have helped reduce this effect.

- Health insurance operates in a commodity-like market which does not allow a carrier to significantly increase rates without loss of market share, unless the market is moving in the same direction. Further, when rate increases are nominal, the number of groups seeking alternative quotes is reduced. Also, shifting between plan options by insureds is likely to be reduced. In the past, in order to gain market share insurers have sometimes had successive price-cutting, in an effort to induce groups and covered lives to change carriers.

- In contrast, when rate increases are high, requests for competitive rate quotes becomes more common. Purchasers tend to comparison shop, and the marketplace becomes increasingly price-sensitive. This makes a carrier vulnerable to any weak spots in its rating structure. That is, an insurer is more likely to enroll those groups for which the rates it quotes are too low due to imperfect rating factors. As a result, a carrier may experience losses from its new mix of business, even though its rating structure would have been adequate for its previous mix of business. Again, the greater discipline of more professional management (perhaps intensified by consolidation in the market), and a for-profit orientation, has reduced the prevalence of this risk. Consolidations within the industry may also be mitigating this factor somewhat.

- During high trend periods, trend assumptions are likely to ultimately overshoot actual values. Also, in this environment more groups tend to move to self-funding. Both of these effects may reduce future underwriting results and the ability to recoup previous losses. It also reduces needed RBC levels.

- Accounting conventions tend to further exaggerate the underwriting cycles through loss carry-forward provisions and retrospective refunds in experience rated business. When deficits are accumulated, the full loss is recorded at the time it occurs, even though a large percentage of deficits may be recouped in the future. Following the loss period, when deficits are being recouped, these recoveries are shown as additional underwriting gains.

Thus, to a large extent, historical cycles have been influenced by a succession of management decisions that reflect the ebb and flow of the internal corporate emphasis between favorable financial results and market share, interacting with the imperfect forecasting of future trends. This can be visualized as a pendulum that swings back and forth between the focus on financial results and market share, always reacting too late and overshooting the mark. A more knowledgeable and professional level of management overall in the industry has helped produce a more stable progression of results.

HISTORICAL UNDERWRITING CYCLES

The reason that past cycles lasted approximately three years in each phase is due to the combined effects of (a) one-year rate guarantees, although many now have the capability (but seldom used) of off-anniversary changes, (b) pricing changes that must be phased-in over a full year of renewals once a change is implemented, (c) marketplace inertia which causes delays for competitive considerations, and (d) the effects of incurred vs. paid claim lags which tend to obscure changes in financial results for some time and further delay management reaction time.

The change in the duration and amplitude of the cycle since 1992 is probably due to a several factors. The first is a prolonged decline in trends from 1987 through 1996. During this period insurers using recent experience trends for their projections would always be overstating their future trends. Second, there was much discussion within the Blues early in this period concerning the underwriting cycle and how to control it. This was given further impetus by imposition of Risk Based Capital (RBC) Requirements. And third, conversion of a number of Blue Cross/Blue Shield Plans to for profit status, or consolidation over multi-state areas as mutual insurance companies, which has further increased the emphasis on profitability.

For decades, health care trends have been significantly higher than the growth rate of the overall economy. Beginning in the early 1990's, it appears that this excess health growth rate was significantly reduced, leading to a consistent pattern of lower trends. This change was attributed by some to attainment of critical mass in managed care, which had forced trends lower than they might otherwise have been. However, in the late 1990's and early 2000's higher trends re-emerged. As of the middle of the 2000 decade, health cost trends are still much higher than the overall growth of the economy. The question is whether this is a temporary phenomenon resulting from managed care backlash, or if we have returned to a more permanent high excess health care growth rate. In the long run, the excess health care growth rate will have to decline, or health care will ultimately become the vast majority of our economic activity.

In the past, certain precipitating factors have been significant contributors to the negative cycles. The following represent such factors in past loss cycles:

- **1968-1970**
  - The maturing of the health insurance market

- **1974-1976**
  - Removal of Wage and Price Controls
  - Recession and high unemployment rates

- **1980-1982**
  - Double-digit inflation (oil shock)
  - Recession and high unemployment rates

- **1986-1988**
  - Cost shifting by providers to compensate for pricing concessions to government, HMOs, and PPOs
  - Aggressive marketing of HMOs and PPOs at unrealistic premium rates
  - Complacency and unrealistic expectations resulting from historically low trends in 1984-1985
  - Unrealistic pricing expectations for hospital utilization review
  - Antiselection resulting from HMO, PPO, and multiple option programs
- **1995-1997**
  - Slowing of the continuing decline of trends.
  - Extremely competitive environment.
  - Legislation at the state and federal level that increased costs to insurers.

MANAGING THE UNDERWRITING CYCLE

The first step to managing the underwriting cycle for a health insurance carrier is to recognize it in its financial goals. This means that a carrier needs to realize underwriting gains during the favorable portion of the cycle, that, together with investment income, will be sufficient to offset losses from the unfavorable portion, maintain adequate capital levels, and (if publicly held) provide appropriate return to investors. Achievement of these financial goals over the full underwriting cycle is not easy. It requires adequate financial resources, disciplined management, and pricing and marketing strategies that may, at times, be deliberately out-of-sync with the market. (See [2] for additional discussion). Traditional but essential ingredients for a successful long-term financial strategy include the following:

- **Strategies for Targeted Market Segments.** Both marketing and financial objectives will vary at different points in the underwriting cycle. For example, during periods where the market is underpricing certain products due to delays in recognizing trend increases, it is not logical to establish objectives for increasing market share in these areas unless the carrier is willing to suffer corresponding financial losses or lower margins.

- **Risk Objectives.** Assuming that the underwriting cycle in some form and degree will probably repeat indefinitely (although perhaps more irregularly than historically), a health insurer must make crucial policy decisions defining the level of risk it is willing to assume in such an environment. These decisions regarding risk should recognize that, even with strong corporate attempts to minimize loss, it is unlikely that a carrier will be able to avoid periodic reductions in underwriting gains (or even losses) and still maintain their desired market share. However, it may be possible to dampen the extremes through explicit recognition of the cycles.

- **Timely Evaluation of Experience and Trends.** Proper management of health insurance calls for timely, tempered responses to economic influences of both the health and the non-health sectors. Responses that are entirely market-driven can be counterproductive in their effect on financial results. The ability to respond appropriately requires meaningful management information, which in turn depends on extensive information systems and a strong analytical capability. This also requires much more investment on the part of insurers than they have been willing to make historically.

- **Counter-Cyclical Marketing.** A carrier cannot expect to operate in a vacuum. There are, nevertheless, advantages to using counter-cyclical strategies (including price concessions) at times, provided they are part of a deliberate management plan, and are backed by adequate financial resources. This requires adequate information regarding developing trends, as well as appropriate long-term strategies that allow for pulling back at some points and being aggressive at others, even when the marketplace is behaving differently. Adequate contingency reserves can compensate for deficiencies in trend analysis. Conversely, without adequate contingency reserves, the need for adequate trend information becomes more critical.

- **Cost-Effective Administration.** Competitive forces in the market have reduced the level of margins available for expenses. At the same time, however, the health insurance business has grown in complexity, requiring an increasing level of resources and greater expertise. It is essential that these resources be managed in an efficient manner. This may be particularly significant for the many companies that have pursued high volume or high risk diversifications, in an effort to cover fixed expenses.

- **Consistent Management Compensation Goals.** After recognizing the effects of underwriting cycles, and developing strategies to survive them safely, the next logical step is to tie management compensation incentives to carrying out those strategies and establishing appropriate accountabilities.

The objectives discussed above highlight the relationship between adequate surplus and the ability of a company to satisfy it's financial and marketing objectives, within the context of health insurance underwriting cycles. Adequate surplus may afford the ability to implement counter-cyclical strategies that serve to dampen the effects of such cycles on underwriting results.

REFERENCES

[1]   Grossman JM, Ginsburg PB, "As The Health Insurance Underwriting Cycle Turns: What Next?" *Health Affairs*, Volume 23 Number 6.

[2]   Rosenblatt A, "The Underwriting Cycle: The Rule of Six," *Health Affairs*, Volume 23 Number 6.

[3]   Ross JB, Woodruff C, "Analysis of Health Carrier Insolvencies," *Transactions of Society of Actuaries*, 1995, Volume XLVII, http://library.soa.org/library/tsa/1990-95/TSA95V4717.pdf

SECTION EIGHT

MANAGEMENT

43 ANALYSIS OF FINANCIAL AND OPERATIONAL PERFORMANCE

Douglas B. Sherlock

Life must be lived forward, but it can only be understood backward.
Søren Kierkegaard

This chapter concerns financial and operational performance and analysis of health plans. An underlying premise in this discussion is that the responsibility of the insurance enterprise is to maximize its owners' value, even in the case of non-profit or mutual plans. Earnings and its growth are the drivers of value, and the factors influencing them provide a systematic framework for the analysis of a health plan.

MAXIMIZATION FRAMEWORK

All enterprises, including health plans, can be analyzed based on how they maximize their owner's value. While most health plans have public shareholders, the "publicly held stock company" corporate model is also a convenient paradigm for understanding not-for-profit enterprises, whose primary obligation is to benefit the public, and for mutuals, whose obligation is to their policyholders, even though the accounting systems that apply to these other organizations may be different.

Investors measure maximization of value based on the stock price of an enterprise. However, stock price generally is only indirectly affected by the actions of the management team. Moreover the enterprise may be privately held (and therefore not have a public market for its stock), or it may be non-profit or mutual.

Managements seek to maximize value by achieving superior performance, which is hopefully recognized and rewarded by investors through share price improvement. To connect the value of ownership with corporate performance, investors often employ valuation models that capture and quantify performance of the enterprise. Unlike stock prices, such models can more directly reflect management performance, being based on the company's financial statements. GAAP reporting is designed to inform the owners of an enterprise of management's progress in achieving this maximization objective.

The classic analysis for estimating value (or valuation analysis) is the discounted future cash flow model. This model is based on the notion that the value of the corporation is determined by the amount and timing of the cash available for distribution to its owners. Such cash available for distribution are often termed 'dividends,' although the real cash flow available to owners may in fact be realized in other ways.

Thus, value depends on things that managements can affect, such as dividends distributed to investors and their long-term growth rate. Value is also affected by something on which managements have relatively little influence – the discount rate in the valuation, reflecting the riskiness of the activities of the enterprise. This hypothesized link between value and free cash flows is broadly accepted by investors in the price/earnings multiples found in most major daily newspapers, and also in the commonly used PEG ratios. (A PEG ratio is a stock's P/E ratio divided by the annual growth rate of the underlying company's earnings).

This can be seen mathematically, as well. The **Gordon** Constant Growth Model, rearranged, illuminates that the P/E ratio relates to the discount rate and the growth of earnings.

$$P = \frac{D}{k - G},$$

where

P = Price per share

D = Expected dividend per share one year from now

k = Required rate of return for equity investor

G = Growth rate in dividends (in perpetuity)

Dividing by D, then

$$\frac{P}{D} = \frac{1}{k - G}$$

Therefore, an enterprise with a growth rate of 3.0% merits a P/E of 8.33 times while an enterprise with growth of 6.0% merits a P/E of 11.11 times, holding constant the discount rate of 15.0%. In essence, maximizing value means maximizing growth. (We have made the simplifying assumption of substituting earnings for dividends.)

Classically, financial statements measure financial performance as it relates to the objective of maximization. In other words, financial statements are designed for external readers, mainly owners, and they reflect the fact that equity shareholders are paid after creditors. By contrast, other financial statements, such as those using statutory accounting, are designed to measure solvency, for an audience of creditors or their advocates. So the significance of GAAP financial statements is that they capture the overall performance of the enterprise, which can, if owners choose, be translated into valuation models that measure the owners' value.

At any point in time, few health plans are generally contemplating business changes for which valuation models would be necessary. However, valuation models provide a starting point for a systematic look at performance metrics, measuring contributions to value maximization.

GROWTH AND RETURN ON EQUITY

Given the essential role of earnings growth in maximization of value, what then do reported financials tell users about earnings growth? Return on Equity (ROE) is a key growth metric from an owner's perspective. It measures how fast the enterprise's net worth is growing, assuming zero dividends, plus it reflects the limits of such growth without external capital sources. For this reason, Return on Equity is the same thing as Sustainable Growth Rate in cases in which no dividends are paid. (The sustainable growth rate is calculated as the product of the Earnings Retention Rate, 1 – (Dividends/Earnings), and ROE.)

Return on Equity is calculated as Net Income Divided by Shareholders' Equity, as shown below.

$$\text{ROE} = \frac{\text{Net Income}}{\text{Shareholder Equity}}$$

ROE is linked to growth. Suppose, in year 1, an enterprise earns $15 when it has $100 in equity at the beginning of the year, for a 15% ROE. Suppose, then, that it reinvests all its earnings into the equity of the enterprise, making it $115 by year end. If it is able to earn the same 15% return on equity in year 2, earnings will be $17.25, a 15% increase from year one. Thus ROE is the growth rate if no dividends are paid and the ROE is sustainable.

By the same token, ROE can measure the *limits* on growth. The amount of equity required by an enterprise is a result of its technical requirements. For instance, a health plan may require investment in real estate and desktop computers in which to serve the customer services function, which in turn requires a certain level of equity capital. Thus, for the health plan to grow faster than the Return on Equity would require it to access external equity.

FACTORS OF GROWTH

The venerable warhorse known as the Dupont Formula is a convenient way of understanding the factors of a business that contribute to its growth. In other words, as shown in the following schedule, return on equity is explained as the product of various technical elements that are quantified in these metrics.

Dupont Formula:

$$(\text{Total Asset Turnover}) \times (\text{Net Profit Margin}) = (\text{Return on Assets})$$

Each of these values can be seen to be composed of:

$$\left(\frac{\text{Revenues}}{\text{Total Assets}}\right) \times \left(\frac{\text{Net Income}}{\text{Revenue}}\right) = \left(\frac{\text{Net Income}}{\text{Total Assets}}\right)$$

Similarly, taking the return on assets as a starting point,

$$(\text{Return on Assets}) \times (\text{Total Leverage Ratio}) = (\text{Return on Equity})$$

Restating each of these, in turn:

$$\left(\frac{\text{Net Income}}{\text{Total Assets}}\right) \times \left(\frac{\text{Total Assets}}{\text{Shareholder Equity}}\right) = \left(\frac{\text{Net Income}}{\text{Shareholder Equity}}\right)$$

The factors affecting ROE can be decomposed into a series of questions, such as the following:

Total Asset Turnover This is defined as the net sales of the enterprise, divided by the assets. In other words, how much *total* investment (equity and debt) is required to meet the requirements of this business?

Profit Margin: What return on sales does this business achieve?

Return on Assets: What return on all invested assets can be earned by this enterprise?

Total Leverage Ratio: To what degree can the business be operated using other peoples' money? That is, to what degree can trade and other creditors' (including long term creditors) money be employed to magnify returns on assets?

This decomposition is important in the understanding business strategies, which can be radically different from company to company, even if in the same business, and even if ROE is the same. A low profit margin can actually maximize growth, if it has a high total asset turnover or a high total leverage ratio.

Figures 43.1 – 43.4 represent three prototypical health plans, although the staff and IPA plans are loosely based on actual enterprises. Figure 43.1 contains the income statements; Figure 43.2 contains the related balance sheets; Figure 43.3 provides certain key ratios; and Figure 43.4 provides a Dupont Formula analysis for these enterprises.

As shown in Figure 43.4, all have the same return on equity, but they achieve it in far different ways. The staff model plan has a higher profit margin than the IPA, which is necessary since it has a lower total asset turnover. Moreover, financial leverage is employed to magnify returns to meet the benchmark ROE. Administrative Services Only (ASO) business has the highest profit margins, on much lower total asset turnover: Its ROE is driven upward as financial leverage is used to increase return on equity.

Financial and Operational Performance and Analysis

Income Statements

	Staff	IPA	ASO
Insured			
Insured Member Months	9,500,000	5,600,000	
Insured Revenues PMPM	$ 209	$208	
ASO			
ASO Member Months	2,600,000	200,000	5,800,000
ASO Revenues PMPM	$ 20	20	$ 20
Total Member Months	12,100,000	5,800,000	5,800,000
Revenues			
Premium Revenues	$1,987,000,000	$1,167,000,000	$ —
Other Revenues	52,000,000	4,000,000	116,000,000
Total Revenues	$2,039,000,000	$1,171,000,000	$ 116,000,000
Expenses			
Health Benefit Expenses	$1,672,000,000	$ 985,000,000	$ —
Administrative Expenses	267,000,000	103,000,000	103,000,000
Total Expenses	1,939,000,000	$1,088,000,000	$ 103,000,000
Operating Profits	100,000,000	$ 83,000,000	$ 13,000,000
Non-Operating			
Investment Income	$11,000,000	$ 5,000,000	$ —
Interest Expense	5,000,000	1,000,000	1,000,000
Total Non-Operating	$6,000,000	$ 4,000,000	$ (1,000,000)
Pretax Income	$106,000,000	$ 87,000,000	$ 12,000,000
Income Taxes		32,000,000	4,000,000
Net Income	$106,000,000	$ 55,000,000	$8,000,000

Figure 43.1

Financial and Operational Performance and Analysis

Balance Sheet

	Staff	IPA	ASO
Assets			
Current Assets			
Cash and Equivalents	$ 511,000,000	$ 327,000,000	24,000,000
Accounts Receivable	69,000,000	65,000,000	10,000,000
Inventories	23,000,000	—	
Prepaid Expenses	11,000,000	8,000,000	
Other Current Assets	—	4,000,000	
Total Current Assets	$ 614,000,000	$ 404,000,000	$ 34,000,000
Fixed Assets	$ 316,000,000	$ 26,000,000	$ 26,000,000
Other Assets	65,000,000	19,000,000	19,000,000
Total Assets	$ 995,000,000	$ 449,000,000	$ 9,000,000
Liabilities			
Current Liabilities			
Claims Payable	$ 122,000,000	$ 160,000,000	$ —
Other Accounts Payable	135,000,000	23,000,000	23,000,000
Prepaid Premiums	11,000,000	—	
Other Current Liabilities	—	9,000,000	9,000,000
Total Current Liabilities	$ 268,000,000	$ 192,000,000	$ 32,000,000
Long-Term Debt	116,000,000	2,000,000	2,000,000
Other Liabilities	136,000,000	9,000,000	9,000,000
Equity or Fund Balance	474,000,000	246,000,000	36,000,000
Total Liabilities and Net Worth	$ 994,000,000	$ 449,000,000	$ 79,000,000

Figure 43.2

Financial and Operational Performance and Analysis

Key Ratios

	Staff	IPA	ASO
Fixed Asset Turnover	6.45	45.04	4.46
Fixed Assets Per Member	$ 26.12	$ 4.48	$ 4.48
Long-term Debt to Fixed Assets	36.7%	7.7%	7.7%
Long-term Debt to Total Capital	19.7%	0.8%	5.3%
Days of Accounts Receivable	12.4	20.3	31.5
Days of Claims Payable	26.6	59.3	NM
Health Benefits Ratio (Unadjusted)	84.1%	84.4%	NM
Administration to Revenues (Unadjusted)	13.1%	8.8%	88.8%
Operating Profit Margin	4.9%	7.1%	11.2%

Figure 43.3

Financial and Operational Performance and Analysis

Dupont Formula

	Staff	IPA	ASO
Return on Equity	22.4%	22.4%	22.4%
=			
Total Leverage Ratio	2.10	1.83	2.19
×			
Return on Assets	10.7%	12.2%	10.1%
=			
Net Profit Margin	5.2%	4.7%	6.9%
×			
Total Asset Turnover	2.05	2.61	1.47

Figure 43.4

TOTAL ASSET TURNOVER

Total asset turnover is defined as the net sales of the enterprise, divided by the assets, a technical metric used to describe health plan operations. It is one of the better differentiators of model designs. Changes in this ratio tend either to: (1) take a long time to implement, or (2) require a major acquisition or divestiture.

Assets required by health plans are the tools necessary to perform the functions required to serve the membership, either directly or indirectly. These generally include office space and information systems, but can also include intangible assets emerging from business combinations ("Other Assets" in the case of the IPA) and health care delivery assets.

As shown in Figure 2, the size and nature of assets vary by model design. Staff model health plans that deliver health care have substantial investment in health care delivery capability, classified in balance sheets as *fixed assets*. These may range from ownership of clinics to, in some cases, ownership of multiple hospitals. Staff models have a relatively high amount of fixed assets per member, as shown in Figure 3. Over the past several decades, there has been a trend away from vertically integrated prepaid group practices. This has meant that, for the health plan industry, there has been a resulting significant change in the character of the assets-- in favor of cash and equivalents, and away from fixed assets.

On the other hand, unlike IPA models (meant to include most commercial and Blue Cross/Blue Shield insurers, as well), staff models are less likely to require investments in liquid assets to pay for care that they have incurred but for which they have not yet paid (IBNP or IBNR reserves), since they are providing this care internally. Enterprises that are focused on ASO services have neither health care delivery investment requirements, nor do they have to retain cash equivalents to satisfy the payment of claims.

All health plans have accounts receivable, which typically represent a few weeks of revenue. Prepaid expenses are also common, including for the health plan's own insurance. In addition, cash and other liquid investments are held to honor claims by external providers. Levels of highly liquid assets have the beneficial property of being preferred by state health insurance departments in order to protect health care providers and members from exposure to failure of the health plan.

The size and nature of cash equivalents also vary with the organizational structure. Non-profit Blue Cross Blue Shield Plans often possess higher levels of investment assets and greater mixes of equities than do publicly traded enterprises. The higher need for capital probably stems from the need to meet BCBS Association licensure requirements (normally higher than state requirements), as well as the heightened riskiness of the portfolio (resulting naturally from the ability of the portfolio to sustain higher volatility of returns).

A complication in quantifying the capital intensity of health plans is that some plans "rent" information systems or provider capacity, so they do not have to own them. In effect, both the liabilities and assets are kept off balance sheet, with the cost reflected in higher operating expenses.

PROFIT MARGINS

Profit margins are probably the most common metric employed by financial analysts. Interpretation of profit margins is most meaningful in short term periods, when one can assume a stable level of assets and leverage. This analysis can be thought of as part of a family of income statement based performance metrics.

THE MARGINS THEMSELVES

In general, profit margins are expressed as a percent of total revenues, as shown in Figures43.3 and 43.4. Revenues are most illuminating if they include premiums and ASO fee income, but exclude investment income. (Insurers often refer to this as "underwriting income." Income with investment income included is "operating income"). Premium and ASO fee income derive from the relationships between vendors and customers, investment income relates to the investment portfolio, and doesn't depend on commercial relationships. (Notably, the staff and IPA model enterprises used in our examples had actually classified their investment income as operating revenues. For illustrative purposes we considered it more meaningful to restate these financials.)

The two most common margins employed by financial analysts are 'operating profit margin' and 'net margin', shown in Figures 43.3 and 43.4 respectively. Operating margin is operating profits divided by revenues, and net margins is net income divided by revenues. The difference between them is that non-operating income and income taxes (if any) are included in net margins.

Profit margins for insured businesses are less than meet the eye, since they imply a level of profitability that excludes statutory reserves. A presentation more reflective of health insurers would increase expenses by the increase in reserves.

RELATED RATIOS

The most common income statement ratios are the health benefit ratio and the administrative expense ratio, shown in Figure 43.3. In a simple insured business, this ratio relates directly to the profit margin, since 1 minus the health benefit ratio, minus the administrative expense ratio, equates to the operating profit margin.

Administrative Expense Ratio

The administrative expense ratio is administrative expenses divided by revenues. Care should be taken to properly treat non-premium revenues-- they should be excluded from both expenses and revenues so that the ratio could be expressed in an intuitive way. Depending on how much information is available to the analyst, this adjustment can be made in several ways as illustrated in Figure 6:

- Subtract the fees from the administrative costs;
- Calculate the administrative expenses on a PMPM basis for all members, then reduce the cost of administration for the ASO portion; or
- If the enterprise discloses administrative expenses for its ASO products, reduce it directly.

Health Benefit Ratio

The health benefit ratio is often called the medical loss ratio, but the former description may be a better reflection of the fact that these costs are often actively managed. It should be calculated as a percent of the associated premiums, not total revenues, in order to match expenses with revenues.

Capitated health care expenses can affect the apparent margins, and must be accounted for carefully. Capitation is the payment of a fixed per capita amount to a health care provider, in exchange for an agreed upon set of services. A capitated provider is a subcontractor to the health plan, and the recognition of capitation as an expense implies that the plan has completely satisfied its requirements to its members served by the capitated provider. However, if the capitated entity loses money on the relationship, there is a risk that the provider's resulting insolvency would require the plan to cover the losses of the capitated entity. In such circumstances, it may be appropriate for the plan to consolidate the performance of the capitated entity for analytical purposes. This can be difficult if the entity is unwilling to provide financials, or if the entity also is the subcontractor for other enterprises.

The calculation of health benefit expenses (or claims) is discussed estensively elsewhere in this text. Suffice it to say, health benefit costs are booked on an accrual basis, that is, they are booked when incurred rather than when reported.

Medical management costs can be considered either health care expenses or administrative expenses. However, considering them as administrative expenses helps to highlight the potential benefits of these expenses. The exclusion of medical management costs from health benefits is also in accordance with the requirements of the National Association of Insurance Commissioners (NAIC). However, this becomes more complex if some of the medical management is outsourced, as in the example of mental health care provided under a capitated arrangement. Under such arrangements, medical management expenses associated with this health benefit are often invisible to the plan, and are, in effect, reported as if converted into health benefits. To the degree that a particular plan manages all of this internally, it can improve comparability by backing out these expenses.

Quirks in Both Ratios due to Capitation

Capitation of specialty health services can affect comparability of financial statements, especially respecting the segmentation of expenses into administrative and health benefit components. For instance, all things being equal, a health plan with a capitated arrangement will have a higher health benefit ratio and a lower administrative ratio than one without. This is solely due to administrative expenses associated with mental health being included with the capitation, thus excluded from total administration. For this reason, it can be helpful to remove such capitated services from both administrative expense and from health benefits. This is not only true for mental health, but may also be true for pharmaceutical benefits and disease or case management.

THE SAME-SIZE-INCOME STATEMENT

Because profit margins are expressed as a percent of revenues, they can also be considered as a component of a financial analysis exercise called a "same size" income statement. In this exercise, all relevant financial components are similarly expressed as percents of revenue. In this way, profit margins can be divided into relative components, all of which are expressed in a way that is not a (direct) function of the size of the enterprise.

The same-size-income statement expresses all income statement items as a percent of revenues, permitting comparisons between health plans and year-over-year comparisons of the same enterprise. (Only the operating items in the Figure 5 income statement have been included for brevity and relevance.) This approach can be more useful than raw income statement information. Changes in expense items reflected in this way can be immediately understood in their impact on profit margins.

Financial and Operational Performance and Analysis

Same Size Income Statement, Unadjusted

	Staff	IPA	ASO
Revenues			
Premium Revenues	97.4%	99.7%	0.0%
Other Revenues	2.6%	0.3%	100.0%
Total Revenues	100.0%	100.0%	100.0%
Expenses			
Health Benefit Expenses	82.0%	84.1%	0.0%
Administrative Expenses	13.1%	8.8%	88.8%
Total Expenses	95.1%	92.9%	88.8%
Operating Profits	4.9%	7.1%	11.2%

Figure 43.5

As previously discussed, it is helpful to adjust for the presence of capitated mental health and other benefits that would otherwise lead to distortions.

A key drawback of this approach is that interpretation can be a challenge. For instance, the staff model plan has health benefit expenses of 82.0% of revenues, yet its health benefit ratio is really 84.1%, as shown in Figure 6. It can be confusing to compare plans of different models. For instance, despite its much higher profit margins (shown in Figure 5), it is not clear that the ASO has the best performance. Also, as shown later, segmenting the business into lines can be helpful.

ADJUSTMENTS FOR REVENUE REPORTING DIFFERENCES

The same-size-income statement has many virtues but there are also several revenue reporting challenges that should be considered by the analyst, to make the best use of this analytical tool. Treatments of revenue that may be unique to the enterprise include classifications of reinsurance, investments, ASO revenue, and commissions.

Reinsurance. Some enterprises include reinsurance recoveries as a revenue item. It is more useful to consider reinsurance premiums paid as health expenses, and reinsurance recoveries as offsets to health care costs. This is particularly helpful when including very large health plans (that do not purchase reinsurance) in the comparison.

Commissions. Payments to brokers are sometimes excluded from premiums. As an expense of the health plan, it is better to view this as an administrative expense.

Investment Income. Health plans have a financial "float," stemming from customer payments happening in advance of claim incurrals, while claim payments can take two months from when claims care incurred. Plans earn interest on this float, which is sometimes considered to be part of operating revenue.

It is true that this float results from the terms of trade with vendors and customers. However, since many health plans are also active in capital markets, it is not possible to separate investment returns realized through terms of trade from investment returns that result from capital market activity. For instance companies using the debt markets incur interest expense, which is considered to be non-operating. Moreover the investment returns themselves are subject to only limited managerial influence, since external capital markets set rates of return.

Accordingly, as previously discussed, it is more helpful to group investment returns with capital costs as non-operating income. The alternative, of counting investment income as operating and capital costs as non-operating, is hard to defend.

Administrative Services Only Products. Increasingly, health plans offer products that require health benefit plan sponsors, as opposed to the health plans, to absorb variances in health care costs. In that instance, the only revenue that is received is payments for administrative services, such as claim processing, customer service inquiries, and so forth.

If one calculates administrative expenses relative to revenues, the ratio seems artificially high, since the (revenue) denominator does not include the cost of health care cost risk. Recall that health care costs are typically 80-90% of premium revenue.

One way of normalizing ratios for this product line is to make this calculation based on "premium equivalents." That is, estimating what the premiums would have been in the event that the health plan actually bore health care cost variance risk. However, this treatment is not appropriate in the actual financial reports, because it would imply that the plan assumes risk that it does not in fact assume. This approach also disregards that the level of administrative expenses may be different between ASO and fully insured products, for instance in rating and medical management.

To get a better understanding of the enterprises that offer such products, it is helpful to look at financial reports for each product separately, or to make adjustments to back out both fee revenue and associated administrative expense from comparisons. The former approach can be limited by unavailable data, since many plans are not capable of presenting financial information in this detail. The latter approach can be approximated as shown in Figure 43.6. The "Similar Administrative Cost Assumption", shown in the far right columns, does this by assuming a similar per member per month administrative expense across the products. The "ASO Breakeven Assumption" deducts ASO revenues from the administrative expenses, and is similar to the assumption often employed in statutory statements.

PMPM Income Statement, Unadjusted

Financial and Operational Performance and Analysis

	Staff	IPA	ASO
Revenues			
Premium Revenues	$ 164.21	$ 201.21	$ —
Other Revenues	$4.30	$ 0.69	$ 20.00
Total Revenues	$ 168.51	$ 201.90	$ 20.00
Expenses			
Health Benefit Expenses	$ 138.18	$ 169.83	$ —
Administrative Expenses	$ 22.07	$ 17.76	$ 17.76
Total Expenses	$ 160.25	$ 187.59	$ 17.76
Operating Profits	$ 8.26	$ 14.31	$ 2.24

Figure 43.6

PMPM ANALYSIS

Another challenge of the same-size-income statement is that it confounds two somewhat independent relationships-- the competitive pressures on health plan pricing and the challenges of actually managing the operations themselves. In other words, on a day-to-day basis, managers have pressure to manage operations independently of the pricing pressures faced by the plan in the market.

The traditional solution is to divide each of the expense items by the membership to which the expenses apply, rather than by the revenues. Corresponding with how many health plans bill for such insurance, the metrics are stated in terms of their units of "Per Member Per Month" (PMPM), as shown in Figure 43.7.

Adjusted Same Size Income Statement, Staff Model

Financial and Operational Performance and Analysis

	ASO Breakeven Assumption			Similar Administrative Cost Assumption	
	Total	Insured	ASO	Insured	ASO
Revenues					
Premium Revenues	97.4%	100.0%		100.0%	0.0%
Other Revenues	2.6%		100.0%	0.0%	100.0%
Total Revenues	100.0%	100.0%	100.0%	100.0%	100.0%
Expenses					
Health Benefit Expenses	82.0%	84.1%		84.1%	0.0%
Administrative Expenses	13.1%	10.8%	100.0%	10.5%	110.3%
Total Expenses	95.1%	95.0%	100.0%	94.7%	110.3%
Operating Profits	4.9%	5.0%	0.0%	5.3%	−10.3%

Figure 43.7

By isolating costs in this standardized form, this approach has the advantage of providing more actionable information. For example, a change in administrative costs, when reported in a same-size-income statement, can be obscured by changes in revenues. The PMPM approach clearly isolates such changes.

A drawback to the PMPM approach is in communications with generalists, including board members or other external audiences. Since ratios similar to those from the same-size-income statement are more familiar, this approach is sometimes disorienting to some users of financial analysis. Other drawbacks parallel those of the "same size" income statement, including the applicability of health benefits for calculating benefit ratios and comparability across plan design.

The same issues of reinsurance, commissions, investment income, and ASO products pertain to the PMPM income statements as they do to the same-size-income statements. As previously stated, it is advisable to segment ASO products, ideally with high quality segment cost breakouts. However, as shown in Figure 43.8, this can be estimated through either the assumption that ASO has similar per member costs to the insured line, or that it operates at breakeven.

Adjusted PMPM Income Statement, Staff Model

Financial and Operational Performance and Analysis

	Total	ASO Breakeven Assumption		Similar Administrative Cost Assumption	
		Insured	ASO	Insured	ASO
Insured					
Insured Member Months	9,500,000	9,500,000		9,500,000	
Insured Revenues PMPM	209				
ASO	—				
ASO Member Months	2,600,000		2,600,000		2,600,000
ASO Revenues PMPM	20				
Total Member Months	12,100,000	9,500,000	2,600,000	9,500,000	2,600,000
Revenues					
Premium Revenues	$ 164.21	$ 209.16	$ —	$ 209.16	$ —
Other Revenues	4.30		20.00		20.00
Total Revenues	$ 168.51	$ 209.16	20.00	$ 209.16	$ 20.00
Expenses					
Health Benefit Expenses	$138.18	$ 176.00		$ 76.00	
Administrative Expenses	22.07	22.63	20.00	22.07	22.07
Total Expenses	$160.25	$ 198.63	20.00	$ 198.07	$ 22.07
Operating Profits	$ 8.26	$ 10.53	$ —	$ 11.09	$ (2.07)

Figure 43.8

DECOMPOSING PMPMS

Costs expressed in PMPMs can be made even more actionable if they are decomposed into factors that drive these costs. For this, it is helpful to break expenses into functional areas rather than natural accounting categories, since accounting categories do not identify the activities that the plan undertakes. Figure 43.9 lists functions commonly performed by health plans in which costs can be grouped.

Administrative Functional Areas of Health Plans

Financial and Operational Performance and Analysis

Rating and Underwriting
Product Development / Market Research
Sales and Marketing (except Advertising and Promotion)
Commissions (external)
Advertising and Promotion
Enrollment / Membership / Billing
Customer Services
Provider Network Management and Services
Medical Mgmt. / Quality Assurance / Wellness
Claim and Encounter Capture and Adjudication
Total Information System Expenditures (as expensed)
HIPAA
Finance and Accounting
Actuarial
Corporate Services (HR, Facilities, Legal, Regulatory)
Corporate Executive / Governance
Association Dues and License/Filing Fees

Figure 43.9

RETURN ON ASSETS

Return on Assets (ROA) is defined as net income divided by total assets. It is a measure of how profitable a business is relative to the capital deployed, regardless of whether the capital is equity or debt. Debt, in this instance, includes not just traditional long-term debt but other "trade" obligations including claims payable and obligations to employees. It is based on technical constraints of the required investment needed to operate as a health plan.

The IPA example happens to be based on a publicly traded health plan. This enterprise has an ROA of 12.2%. This seems low but it can provide an acceptable return to investors if the enterprise is leveraged, especially if the debt is trade-related, in which capital costs may not be present. The analogy might be that if the expected appreciation on one's home is merely 5% but 75% of its value is debt, then the return on one's equity is the more exciting 20%.

The assets typically required by health plans are described in Section IV, Total Asset Turnover. However, there are environmental conditions faced by the health plan that affect assets required, but are not separately identified. These include statutory requirements and the access of the plan to capital markets.

Statutory requirements typically increase capital needs above and beyond what the enterprise's owners may deem necessary for the success of the health plan. State insurance departments' interest in such capital levels are intended to protect health care providers and customers from the risks of insolvency. Thus, certain types of assets, such as information systems, are not accorded value commensurate with their cost. For this reason, this additional required capital tends to be based on liquid assets, since such assets are less likely to be discounted by regulators.

While various chapters discuss this in some detail, suffice it to say that due to statutory accounting and capital requirements, the capital (and thus the assets) needed to offer health insurance are higher than would otherwise be the case. By the same token, to achieve the same ROA, profit margins must be higher than would otherwise be the case without these requirements.

Another environmental factor is the availability of external sources of capital. In many cases, it appears that publicly traded companies, which have greater access to equity than other enterprises, tend to operate with thinner capital structures. This may reflect both access to external sources of capital as well as capital market discipline. Management preferences can also require more capital to be retained. This may not be optimal from the standpoint of capital efficiency, but it may preserve scarce management time from the need to regularly consult with insurance regulators or external sources of capital.

TOTAL LEVERAGE RATIO

The total leverage ratio is total assets divided by equity. The difference between assets (which equal total liabilities plus equity) and equity is debt (including reserves), both short and long term.

Like the asset side of the balance sheet, the liability side's characteristics relate to the model design, as shown in Figure 43.2. Long-term debt is relatively unusual, and when it exists, tends to be related to, or even collateralized by, fixed assets. The "debt to fixed asset" ratio and the "fixed assets per member" ratio are both high, as seen in Figure 43.3. Long-term debt is commonly employed by vertically integrated plans with provider-related assets, such as hospitals or clinics. (A complete discussion of the cost of debt, and associated ratios such as debt-to-equity, fixed charge coverage and debt-to-EBITDA is not presented here, since traditional long-term debt is relatively unusual. When it does exist, it typically represents a small proportion of a health plan's total capitalization.)

More frequently, liabilities are current (due within a year) and relate to the terms of trade with providers. The most important current liability is claims payable, which stems from the length of time between when the claim is incurred and when it is finally paid. (This is the Incurred But Not Paid, or IBNP reserve.) The IPA has days of claims payable [(((Claims Payable) / (Annual Health Benefits)) × 365] that are typical for third party payers. The actuarial process used to derive these estimates is described elsewhere in the text. The administrative cost of processing those claims are also typically included as a liability. The time required to submit the claim, to process the claim and the timing of payment all impact the actual time to process the claims. By contrast, the lower apparent days of claims payable in the staff model plan reflects its direct provision of care.

Prepaid premiums are common in plans that serve Medicare Advantage members, in cases in which month's ends occur on weekends – payments in this case are made on the Friday prior. Accounts payable and compensation payable resemble similar liabilities in enterprises in other industries.

KEY QUALIFICATIONS TO THE ANALYSIS

To execute a meaningful analysis, it is often necessary to make adjustments in reported financials to counteract the effects of unusual or nonrecurring items. This is called normalization. Such items may include: (1) those that qualify as extraordinary for accounting purposes, (2) disputed items resolved after the fact but reported in a later period, (3) expenses discovered after the fact, (4) significant IBNR adjustments, and (5) others. Depending on the purpose for which the analysis is used, these may also include legal settlements and start-up costs for new products.

CONTEXT OF THE ANALYSIS

This chapter began with a discussion about the underlying financial framework, noting that the maximization goal, combined with the central importance of growth, provides the global context for this analysis. There are also a number of practical applications including year over year analyses, comparisons with other enterprises, and financial planning and analysis.

Year-over-Year. This is a "personal best" approach that has the virtue of near perfect comparability. The approach is better than the successive quarter approach, in that it is not sensitive to seasonal patterns. Marketing and medical management may exhibit seasonal patterns.

Changes should be analyzed in a deconstructed way, such as separating membership and premium rate growth rates, rather than only using revenue growth. Such parsing of growth should be interpreted in light of any changes in the nature of the product, such as the increasing acceptance of low premium, high deductible products.

One risk of an enterprise's use of such longitudinal comparisons is that the historical results can cause the bar to be set too high or too low. The industry has historically been cyclical. While such cycles may no longer be as regular, due to superior information on health care costs or changing managerial behavior, it is nevertheless an aspect worth considering.

Comparisons with Other, Similar Enterprises. This sort of comparison is intended to reflect similar environmental and capital cost conditions, ranging from price pressures to investments in new product development. Free data is available, through www.naic.org, www.sec.gov, or commercial sources. It is important to be careful concerning the quality of data, especially in the case of subsidiaries. Many health plans that report to state regulators are subsidiaries of large multi-state plans. Their income statement information in naic.org may reflect intersegment charges whose purpose is repatriation of cash, rather than actual costs. Also, as discussed elsewhere, the analyst should be careful of product mix differences.

Financial Analysis and Planning. Financial planning involves objectives designed to improve shareholder value. This occurs prospectively, in an annual or long-term budget, and then retrospectively, through a review of how performance compares to these objectives. In this way, financial planning complements financial analysis.

If one of the tasks in planning is determining the attractiveness of specific potential endeavors, then a discount rate should be applied reflecting the riskiness of that business. The time horizons should reflect the needs of the planning process. Some believe that the horizons for such projections should be limited by the ability to have confidence in their reliability. Three to five years is a common time horizon.[1]

In addition to estimating membership, prices and costs, it can make sense to estimate the effect on Risk Based Capital (RBC) requirements. For instance, the sale of an insured business line not only provides proceeds, but it may enhance shareholder value beyond this as a result of freeing up capital from RBC requirements.

Interim results can be measured against long-term projections. Similarly, performance can be compared with peers, through statutory statements, SEC documents, or commercial services.

EXTERNAL MANIFESTATIONS OF SHAREHOLDER VALUE

While maximization of owners' value is a useful paradigm for financial analysis of health plans, there can be major differences between this objective and its recognition by the stock market. Accordingly, while stock prices sometimes reflect short-term phenomena, planning should be for the long term. First, investment analysts may not understand the market realities, and it may be impossible to clearly communicate detailed aspects of strategies to them. Second, while the impact of an errant decision may ultimately lead to a change in management, there are few, if any, examples of hostile takeovers. (This may change if the health plan industry becomes more of a transaction oriented business.)

Stock prices, over the long term, should reflect performance of the plan. But it may also in part reflect the transparency of information provided to shareholders, since the credibility of management may be a risk factor implicit in earnings multiples.

---

[1] Editor's note: There is some controversy over this. Some feel that failure to complete any projection is equivalent to saying there will be zero impact from such future activity. In that case, we may be better off with a not-so-great best estimate than an even worse estimate of zero. Some actuaries segregate this element of their projection, so the user can do with it as they please.

CONCLUSION

Successful health plans operate to maximize their value over the long term, regardless of whether the plan is owned by public shareholders or is "owned" by the public at large. Achieving maximum value involves maximization of growth, which is in turn dependent upon efficient capital deployment, high long-term profitability, and prudent use of financial leverage. Numerous financial metrics can help to measure how successfully the plan is achieving these subsidiary goals, and many metrics can measure the operating performance that determines financial performance.

44 PRODUCT DEVELOPMENT

Irwin J. Stricker
Janet M. Carstens

Developing and bringing a product to market involves many facets of a group insurance operation. The product development process can be viewed as consisting of three major steps. The first step is to identify and understand the need for the product. The next step is the design of the product and all of the systems and procedures to support it. The third step is taking the product to market.

In the first step, the need for a product can be identified and understood by obtaining and assimilating information from customers, producers, competitors, group sales people, providers of medical care (for medical coverage), regulators, and home office staff. In identifying the need for a product, it is important to review how the product matches the company's mission, strategic goals, capacity for risk, and market segments. Administrative and operational capabilities and resources must be considered, and the regulatory environment must be assessed.

In designing the product, benefit structures, networks, rate structure, policy forms, marketing materials, administrative systems and processes must be developed and priced, to reflect expected claim costs, administrative costs, sales compensation, selection of risk, and profit goals.

Finally, training and communication plans must be in place for a successful market introduction.

PRODUCT NEED

In developing and bringing a product to market, it is important that the driving force for the product be identified and understood. The focus is, "Who wants the product?"

To answer this question, product ideas and needs can be drawn from sources external and internal to the company. Product ideas are then compared against similar products already in a company's portfolio or in the market. The new product is then assessed in light of a company's strategy and strengths. A product idea that has passed all of these considerations is ready to have outlines prepared on how the product will be sold and serviced. Finally, with this detailed understanding of the product, consideration is given to the profits to be expected from the product.

EXTERNAL PRODUCT DRIVERS

There are, of course, multiple users or customers for any product, each with their own needs and priorities. Some users are external, such as plan holders, producers, and regulators. Others are internal, such as group salespeople and home office staff.

Plan Holder

The primary reason for most employers to have a plan of benefits is to attract and retain good employees. Additionally, there are tax advantages in providing coverage on a group basis. For different industries or regions, employees have varying expectations and, traditionally, different types of benefits. This can vary with economic conditions, especially as they affect the employer's industry, as well as with the increasing cost of providing benefits. The successful employer would be sensitive to the need for keeping up with, and at times, improving upon the benefits provided by his competitors. Therefore, even minor benefit enhancements such as health screenings or other wellness benefits, or minor administrative enhancements such as online Web accessibility for employee benefit information, may be important to the sale.

Once the employer has satisfied the security needs of his employees, his focus is likely to turn to cost. While it may be too much to ask for a reduction in costs, a plan of benefits that promises to control the employer's costs can be very attractive. Increasingly, employers are concerned about health care cost increases and are interested in benefit designs that address this concern. They may consider consolidation of health plan options, changes in plan design and cost sharing features, emerging medical management techniques such as focused disease management, or integrated disability and medical plan alternatives. They may also consider alternatives with increased patient involvement in the medical care decision making process, a characteristic of consumer driven health plan products. In addition, alternative and flexible funding arrangements may have distinct cash flow advantages to many employers.

Brokers/Agents/Employee Benefit Consultants

To succeed in a broker-driven market, it is important to develop products that keep up with the company's major competitors. Since brokers see and sell many competitors' products, they are a valuable source of product advice. For companies that rely on a captive agency force or an internal sales staff, such as some managed care companies, the agents or internal sales staff can often provide valuable commentary on the competitive market. Additionally, employee benefit consultants may develop an approach or theory to benefit design that they will use in many sales or bid situations. Their input can therefore be extremely valuable.

Competitive product features are important if a company is to have a market presence, but thereafter, product cost becomes a key element. Despite cost concerns, many companies feel that a competitive commission scale is critical to maintaining broker/agent loyalty, and these companies have developed additional commission payments for their best producers.

The advent of certain legislation, such as guaranteed issue requirements for small employer medical coverage, has lessened the involvement of brokers in certain markets. In these instances, the company must rely on employee benefit consultants and other forms of external market intelligence.

Direct Market Input

Market research can be used to discern what products consumers want. Some well-planned market research can go a long way towards developing a better product, and possibly cut short a product development project that is not likely to succeed.

Through the use of surveys of group insurance purchasers and their employees, an unmet product need may be identified. For example, by surveying group benefit managers an insurer may find that there is a need for a new product or service to solve a cost concern, or an issue related to compliance with an employee benefit law or regulation.

Focus group research is another technique in which current or potential customers are gathered for a discussion on a new product. These discussions usually present several versions of the product, and seek the group's reaction on whether they would buy the product and at what price.

A focus group can be helpful in giving insight into market opportunities. They can also provide useful information as to how the company is perceived and the degree of receptivity towards selling or buying the proposed product. A focus group may also be helpful in ferreting out weaknesses in competitors' products. These may be in plan design, ease of administration, sales compensation, price, customer service, or something else not previously considered.

Productive focus groups can be comprised of brokers, employers, or even employees. For medical products, a focus group of health care providers might discuss product enhancements to address quality of care issues, such as including health and wellness education benefits, or providing fitness club discounts.

Legislation and Regulations

In looking externally for product needs, emerging legislation and regulations should be monitored. The Medicare Prescription Drug, Improvement, and Modernization Act of 2003 created the need for employers to make critical decisions regarding prescription drug insurance coverage under their retiree health benefit plans, leading to a product development opportunity for several insurers.

In addition, regulations on rating, benefit mandates, and other government requirements or limitations should be monitored and reflected in product planning

INTERNAL PRODUCT DRIVERS

Group Sales Force

The group sales force will tend to reflect the requirements of the brokerage community, and will indicate what products are missing from the portfolio. To encourage this feedback, a well-designed and competitive incentive compensation arrangement is important.

It is desirable to find out who may currently be successfully marketing the product. If it is a major competitor, this will not go unnoticed by the sales force. Group sales representatives can and should be used as an outpost of market intelligence. Details of a new product's plan design and other point of sale material can often be obtained from them. They will also be able to provide pricing information. It is particularly important that rate comparisons be examined with an understanding of the demographic and other assumptions used to develop the rates. The company's field force should be directly questioned as to the amount of sales expected from any new product. This should be reinforced through a commitment to specific sales goals.

Home Office Staff

It is important that new products have a strategic and operational fit within the corporate business plan. For example, a corporate aversion to fluctuations in financial results may suggest that medical care is not a desirable product line. Alternatively, if a company has efficient and low cost medical claim processing, they may consider a dental product that could use similar operational processes and take advantage of the efficiencies and low costs.

Some internally-driven products are developed in response to perceived public needs. Living benefits (a rider to a life insurance policy, providing payment of a portion of the face amount prior to death in the event of certain terminal illnesses), is one such example of an insurance company-driven innovation that matches the product to a perceived public need.

A product variation may be intended to rectify underwriting and actuarial concerns that would otherwise limit profitability or competitiveness. Variations may also be in response to product innovations by competitors. Long-term disability benefits, for example, are as often sold on the features of the contract as on the rate being offered. It is critical in developing product enhancements to understand the nuances and cost implications of the benefit. Copying a provision from a leading edge competitor may be simple. If, however, it is difficult to effectively market, administer, pay claims properly or evaluate the product, the ensuing results may be undesirable.

Products with innovative benefits may take the competitive focus away from price and permit a greater profit margin.

EVALUATING THE PRODUCT

It is important to be aware of which competitors may actually be marketing the product, and their strengths and weaknesses. Knowing the competitive product features will allow for greater predictability of success.

One important consideration is whether the product fits into a particular market segment. If so, it is important to identify the segment as to size of case, industry or occupation, and geographic area. These segments should fit into the company's market strategy, relate well to the distribution channels that are employed, and possibly contribute to market awareness of the company's brand. Existing market segments should not necessarily be absolute constraints, and in the right circumstance may be expanded. If so, variations in the product may be required. An example would be expanding dental coverage to smaller groups. Concerns about antiselection may be alleviated by not permitting certain benefit features, and requiring longer waiting periods for others.

It is desirable to have experience data from which to fully understand and price the product, including any available published data. If at all possible, company experience should be used. It is also important to be aware of the administrative rules and underwriting standards of the competitors currently writing the product, and to determine if the company can achieve or exceed these standards, given the company's strengths and weaknesses.

Product innovation is intended to provide or maintain a marketing edge over competitors. It does, however, present additional challenges to properly rate, underwrite and administer the benefit. Without direct product experience, alternate means must be developed to do the evaluation such as analogies with similar products, and extrapolations or interpolations from existing data. As an example, following the introduction of the Medicare Prescription Drug, Improvement and Modernization Act of 2003, many companies had little or no directly relevant experience data to price prescription drug coverage for the individual senior market. Therefore, to price the coverage, any prescription drug experience data that was available needed to be adjusted.

It is important to be aware of what makes this product distinct from other products the company markets, and whether this is a major product variation or a minor change to an existing product. In most situations, the company will want to highlight distinctions. In these instances, the product variations should not be too subtle. Taking advantage of the product distinction will allow the product to be perceived as more competitive than what the competition is offering. It is obviously a positive if the product distinction creates internal advantages such as administrative simplicity, increased cash flow, or greater profit margin. If the variation requires changes in administrative rules or underwriting standards, it is important that these changes be communicated to the underwriting and administrative staff.

STRATEGIC FIT

A key marketing issue is to determine if the product fits the company's traditional market segments. If so, it is more likely to achieve quick success. If not, it may provide an opportunity to expand. There may also be an opportunity to be innovative, by offering the product to groups that do not currently find the product readily available. In this case, however, it is critical to understand why the product is not usually offered in this market segment, and how to overcome any potential pitfalls.

It is important to understand how the administrative requirements of the product match the company's capabilities. This includes pre-sale quoting, issue, premium administration, and benefit payment. If something is lacking, it may be desirable to have a product manager to sort through the required changes and see that the necessary systems effort is carried out.

It is equally important, for medical insurance products, to understand how the company's network size, provider payment, and provider incentive structures will support the product being considered. For example, an HMO that pays physicians through capitation arrangements would need to modify those arrangements if they were going to develop a product that allows the insured to see a physician outside the network. This would be necessary to prevent paying once through the capitation payment for a service and then again when the insured went to a non-capitated physician outside the network.

If the company has stated profit objectives, the company should determine whether the market will allow for the same level of profit for the new product. Profit objectives are often tempered by the associated risks, so it is important to understand the risks and evaluate the appropriateness of the expected profit in light of these risks, as well as to determine if the risk is consistent with the company's risk tolerance. Another consideration is the amount of capital to be consumed by the product. A product that requires significant capital to support it will require a higher return than a product with low capital demands. Products that are risk intensive, such as aggregate stop-loss, require greater profit margins to support the chance of adverse swings in earnings.

If there are federal tax issues regarding this product, and if a potential tax liability exists, it is important that this be understood. One frequent issue is whether the reserves required to sustain the product are deductible from net income. If so, this will have to be factored into the pricing formula. The cost of the product may also be affected in some geographic areas by variations in state and local premium taxes.

Market receptiveness to the product may be affected by whether or not employer contributions are fully deductible from income for tax purposes. This should be appropriately reflected in the plan design and marketing material. Employee concerns are also critical. It is important to know whether employer contributions or benefits received are taxable to the employee as income.

Tax strategies that may be followed by the company, the employer or the employee that would minimize their respective tax liabilities, both currently and in the future, are often an important issue. In regard to the company, this might help in pricing the product. In regard to the employer and employee, it might be critical at point of sale.

CLARIFYING THE PRODUCT

The company's traditional market segments might be based on size of case, industry or occupation, or geographic area. It is important that there be an understanding of how the new product will be marketed and how well this fits in with the company's current or anticipated market segment strategy.

The company need not be limited to the current market segments. If the market is expanded, however, it is especially critical to understand all the ramifications of the expansion. This would include taking account of the administrative requirements, potential sales, and the distribution system.

It is critical for the field force to understand the product. If the product is similar to other products they are marketing, there may be no problem. If not, they must have understandable descriptive material. Sales training classes may also be desirable. If the product is highly technical, specialists may be required to market it.

Some products are inherently simpler to administer than others. It is important to keep in mind that a relative degree of administrative efficiency, compared to the competition, will help maintain a competitive cost and perhaps service edge. It is also important to realize that there may be an investment required in a new product. Break-even analyses are required to determine how long the investment period may last, and when the product is expected to become profitable.

Required changes to current systems should be planned in advance. While products may be brought to market without crossing every "t" and dotting every "i," there should be an understanding of what is ultimately required for proper rating, administration, underwriting, compliance, renewal, and evaluation of the product. It is desirable at the outset to develop an implementation schedule that suggests under what conditions, and when, the various pieces will be in place.

If the product is subject to significant potential deviations from assumptions, an economic cycle, or other elements outside the company's control, there may be earnings fluctuations. If a steady stream of earnings is expected from the product, this may present a problem. The problem will be exacerbated if the potential earnings swings affect overall profits. In some cases, there may be great uncertainty about future benefit costs (for example, utilization of home health care benefits under a long-term care policy). Senior management should be made aware of the risk environment early on, so that any potential effect on the company may be evaluated.

In some instances, reinsurance will be an important adjunct to launching a new product. It can be helpful when there is a concern regarding risk capacity such as with a high limit long-term disability policy; when there is uncertainty as to the emerging experience such as with long-term care products; or to smooth out annual experience fluctuations.

In addition, for some companies, reinsurance may encompass the entire product development process by providing a turnkey product, meaning a product that is so fully developed that, to get started, you merely "turn the key". This would be useful when there is limited in-house experience, or an inability to assign enough resources towards developing the product. In some instances, reinsurance may provide capacity for underwriting and rating following product introduction.

For some group products, concerns regarding extreme events (such as acts of terrorism, hurricanes, earthquakes and pandemics) may limit the availability of reinsurance. Reinsurers may be concerned about concentration risk in high visibility geographic locations such as New York City and Washington DC, and may include exclusions for extreme events, limit benefit coverage, or increase premium rates for certain coverages. Product introduction that relies on reinsurance should be evaluated in terms of the current environment for reinsurance coverage.

EXPECTED PROFIT MARGINS

If the company has articulated profit objectives, the product should be evaluated in relation to these objectives. If there is a change in profit expectation from standard goals, it may be justifiable by any of the following:

- Additional sales of other profitable products,
- An enhanced ability to amortize fixed expenses,
- A less risk intensive product,
- Low capital outlay, or
- A requirement to offer the product so as to remain competitive in the company's core business.

It is useful to know if there are any peer companies that are financially successful with this product. Perhaps more importantly, are there any that are not doing too well? If there is a critical mass required to achieve the expense assumptions used in pricing, achieving sales goals on schedule may be important.

One thing to consider is the time frame needed to generate a profit. This may vary depending upon the type of accounting to be used, for example, statutory or GAAP.

DESIGNING THE PRODUCT

Once the need for a product has been identified and understood, the product design process begins. The elements of designing a product include determining the legal and market requirements for the product and for its sale. The degree of product flexibility to be offered and antiselection concerns must be addressed in the design of the product. How the product will be administered and what systems changes are required for support are significant considerations. Finally, for medical coverage, benefit payment, and managed care issues (such as provider relations) drive many product design decisions.

LEGAL REQUIREMENTS

Before much effort is expended, it should be determined whether the product meets the statutory and regulatory requirements of the state of domicile and the states where it will be brought to market. It is important to understand what mandated benefits may apply in each jurisdiction. If this is a medical care product to be sold to groups of less than 50, then it will likely be subject to small group market legislation.

In some instances, the product may be designed to meet specific state legislation, such as the mandated offering of a limited benefit policy intended to make medical insurance more affordable to all or some small group employers in a specific state. Alternatively, the product may be designed to respond to employer needs as a result of federal legislation, such as prescription drug coverage under retiree health plans, as a result of the Medicare Prescription Drug, Improvement and Modernization Act of 2003.

Policy forms must be filed in the state of domicile as well as in all states where the product will be marketed. Many states require prior approval from the state of domicile. The usual procedure, therefore, is to file in the state of domicile first. If the product will not be marketed in the home state, it may be filed there for out-of-state use only. This will often speed up the approval process. Some states have a deemer provision. In these states, a policy is deemed to be approved after a fixed number of days, usually 30 or 60, if the insurance department has not responded within that time. They may, however, require withdrawal of the form for further sales at a later date if they subsequently disapprove the form.

In some states, premium rates must be filed with policy forms. Depending on the state and the type of carrier, the rates may require regulatory approval, may be file-and-use, or need not be filed. When rates must be filed, an actuarial memorandum describing the development of the rates, along with a statement that the rates enable the product to be self-sustaining may be required. In some states, the expected loss ratio may be required. In these instances, there usually will be a minimum loss ratio requirement. In any case, a first step in preparing the filing should be a review of the pertinent Actuarial Standards of Practice. Standards of Practice cover such topics as risk classification, HMO and managed care pricing, data quality, and small group rate regulation.

An important principle to remember is that policy forms and rates should be as flexible as possible. It is, therefore, desirable to give some thought at the outset as to what constitutes flexibility for this product. It may take the form of variable language whenever a number is involved, such as the length of time that defines a preexisting condition. Other variations for medical insurance coverage might include deductibles, coinsurance, and managed care options.

Some products are specifically designed to conform to state legislation, such as mandated benefits. In many instances, when the product variation is minor, the actuary will have to determine whether or not to change the rates to reflect the benefit. If the actuary views the cost to be minor, it may be incorporated through the emerging experience base that is used as a basis for pricing the product.

Some products will require various levels of approval from entities other than state insurance departments. Products involving securities, for example, will require approval from the Securities Exchange Commission for the product, as well as licensing of agents to sell securities. Developing an HMO product may require approval from the state Department of Health.

PACKAGED VERSUS TAILOR-MADE

An important point to consider is the degree of flexibility in product design. This can run the gamut from a packaged product – a locked-in product design for the very smallest groups, to tailor-made products – virtually unlimited flexibility for the very largest groups. More often, there will be some choices available to the plan holder, with the amount and type of choice dependent upon the employer desires and the size of group. There are a number of considerations in determining what options to offer.

For certain specific benefits, antiselection will add an additional element of cost to some plan variations, especially for smaller groups. Mental and nervous benefits and prescription drug benefits are particularly vulnerable to antiselection, and need to be carefully designed.

Simplicity of plan offerings is desirable for small groups. When the proposal is contained within a brochure, plan variations should be limited, easily understood and simple to rate. Fewer plan variations will reduce issue expenses and allow you to maintain a more competitive expense level for small groups. Larger groups can and do demand more complexity in their plans.

ANTISELECTION AND CLAIMS VOLATILITY

Traditional methods of addressing antiselection concerns are through the initial plan design and underwriting (front end) and through provisions restricting payment of claims (back end). Participation requirements are the most widely used vehicle in group insurance. Underwriting rules also address antiselection, and are an important part of the product development process. These are discussed further in other chapters.

It is important to understand the competitive environment for each product in each market segment. Product introduction may be either a response to a competitor's offerings or to achieve a competitive advantage by being first in the market. A well-organized group operation will coordinate its entry into new markets and products with an understanding of what will be its competitive strengths and weaknesses. This would include field compensation, field understanding of products, and premium rate competitiveness. All of these can influence which groups buy or which employees choose the products and therefore what costs will ultimately be incurred.

Claim volatility is a function of both the inherent degree of fluctuation in the benefit and the volume of business. Products that have low frequencies and high payouts, such as accidental death and dismemberment, stop-loss coverage and high limit life and long-term disability, for example, require a critical mass to avoid significant swings in experience. In addition, an extreme event (such as hurricane Katrina) can have a significant impact on claim experience. When using data subject to such volatility, caution must be taken to make sure the data are relevant to the benefit being priced and that the likely variations in experience have been understood and reflected.

ADMINISTRATIVE AND SYSTEMS ISSUES

It is important to understand at the outset what systems, both manual systems and information support systems, must be modified to allow for an orderly implementation of the new product. The cost of issuing a proposal, the proper adjudication of benefits, and the issuance of correct policy and certificate pages must be determined.

In bringing products to market as soon as possible, shortcuts may be taken that will impair the systems effort required to maintain the product. To be successful, it is important not only to charge the proper rate at the outset, but also to be able to renew policies properly. This requires that the data for rating pass through the renewal rating system as well as to the experience evaluation system.

It is often helpful to have the rate calculation modules designed, to the extent possible, with table driven flexibility where the tables are under the control of the rating actuaries. This reduces the necessity of queuing up for allocation of systems resources whenever modifications are made. It is especially critical to understand the data required to monitor emerging experience for the product. Managed care products, for example, brought a whole array of new data requirements into play. The aggregate experience evaluations of the past were not adequate to initially price, track or re-price these products, evaluate negotiated provider arrangements, or handle withhold arrangements for physicians.

It is also critical to know what data will be retrievable from the benefit payment system. Certain data elements that are necessary to evaluate future experience may not be required to process claims. Nevertheless, they may be required for the future success of the product.

MANAGED CARE ISSUES

Managed care products provide comprehensive benefits with a focus on coordinated care and cost control. Managed care plans strive to achieve these objectives by establishing, among other things, a provider network that includes negotiating reimbursement arrangements which emphasize control of utilization through care management. Since there are substantial differences between managed care products and traditional medical insurance products in the ways they are priced, underwritten, marketed, sold and administered, it is important to recognize these differences in the product development process. For example, network development, administration of managed care protocols, and negotiation of provider reimbursement and incentive arrangements, are examples of managed care plan features that are usually not included in traditional medical plans. These features add a layer of expense to the plan that will likely be offset by claim cost savings. The interaction between expenses and claim cost savings is a unique and critical element to be considered in managed care product development and pricing.

Managed care does not mandate a unique set of plan benefits, insured requirements, or provider arrangements. (These features are described in the chapter on Medical Benefits in the United States.) Rather, managed care represents an array of options, reflecting various degrees of individual choice of providers. These options include PPOs, EPOs and HMOs. However, increasingly, benefit features exist that blur the distinction between these options. For example, an HMO may market a plan limiting non-emergency services to participating providers affiliated with their network, and who are accessed through the primary care physician. The HMO may at the same time also have a Point-of-Service (POS) benefit to pay for services provided outside of the network at a reduced rate. This feature may be attractive to plan holders wanting more freedom of choice in their benefit program.

The dynamics of managed care are rapidly changing. Continued cost increases, headline articles questioning the effectiveness of managed care, reluctance on the part of providers to negotiate contracts, and class action lawsuits have resulted in managed care losing favor in certain markets. Protocols that were effective in reducing costs last year may not work next year. The effectiveness may even vary by geographic area, reflecting local standards of medical practice. In this environment, it is critical to have periodic reevaluations of expected costs and savings if you are to maintain sound premium rates and competitive products.

Network Development

The managed care network will be a critical factor in successful marketing, as well as in achieving financial goals from the managed care product. It is more difficult to impact patient care management in an open and expansive network.

Success in marketing the network includes ensuring sufficient representation in the geographic areas where the insureds reside – this includes ensuring sufficient specialty representation. Certain key facilities may need to be included to give the network credibility such as centers of excellence, or hospitals that dominate the local health care delivery market. As providers continue to consolidate, and as they become less willing to negotiate at historic discounted levels, it may become harder for a health plan to achieve sufficient representation. Prior to investing too much time in the product development process, the health plan should be confident in their ability to successfully contract with a network under a reimbursement methodology that will achieve competitive reductions in cost.

The perceived "quality" of the network is also an important competitive issue. Quality can be somewhat assured through the credentialing process. However, to ensure ongoing quality, the health plan may need to conduct ongoing provider profiling. Provider profiling information is increasingly being made available to consumers via the Web.

It is especially important to incorporate local understanding of the medical care environment into the provider selection process. A good understanding of the number of competitors, the types of managed care products offered, the acceptance level of managed care protocols by the provider community and consumers, the types of provider networks currently in place, and the regulatory environment, is essential to managed care product development. Because of this, local health plans may be more successful in establishing an effective managed care network than large national carriers.

Most companies make sure they have put significant thought into how they will access networks in each of their markets, early in the planning process for a new managed care product. As part of the process, it might be desirable to model a realistic projection of anticipated membership, to develop the economics of various alternatives. The three major alternatives for accessing networks include: build or buy, participate in a joint venture, or rent a network.

- *Build or Buy.* If a company wishes to have a proprietary interest in the network, it must decide whether to develop one from scratch or buy into an existing network. Things to consider in reaching a decision are: the time necessary to bring a product to market, the importance of an exclusive versus non-exclusive provider network, knowledge of the local market, local culture and acceptance of managed care, administrative and system capabilities, relative cost, and compatibility with any existing networks the company is already using. This strategy may be most successful for companies with a local market presence.

- *Joint Venture.* Joint ventures may take a variety of forms, ranging from marketing and distributing someone else's product, to a full partnership including underwriting a portion of the product, participating in the design, pricing and administration, and sharing profits.

The nature of the arrangement may depend on the maturity of the market in regard to managed care penetration, what is brought to the table in regard to market presence, current business in force, and the managed care state of development of each potential partner. A point to consider is that when risk is shared, it may be desirable to include insureds from all plan options (indemnity, PPO, and HMO) within the agreement. This can avoid concern about selection against one segment of the plan. This strategy could be successful for small local carriers or national carriers.

- *Rent.* Many PPOs permit access to their network for a fee. In these arrangements, the insurance carrier underwrites the overall risk. Benefits may be administered by either the insurance carrier or the PPO. In some instances, the insurer may administer benefits after the PPO establishes the amount to be paid on the claim. This strategy might be most successful for large national carriers interested in expanding marketing of managed care products in new geographical regions.

- *"Passive" Networks.* Some insurers have created non-contractual PPOs. In these arrangements, sometimes called "passive" networks, the insurer selects low cost providers in an area from its database, and includes them in a PPO policy. Even though fees are not being discounted, costs may be significantly reduced by redirection to low cost providers. This strategy requires continual monitoring of provider costs and outcomes.

Provider Reimbursement Methods

With a network product, the method of determining provider reimbursement can have a significant impact on total claim dollars paid and, therefore, should be considered in developing and pricing the product. For example, fee-for-service or discounted fee-for-service may be the preferred reimbursement method from the provider's viewpoint, and will enhance provider relationships and contracting ability. However, under fee-for-service, there is limited cost benefit from redirecting care to alternative settings. Additionally, capitation and other forms of risk sharing arrangements may stabilize health plan costs and help ensure coordinated care for an individual, but capitation may create concern for providers and consumers and may create additional administrative requirements (such as assigning of members to certain providers).

An important issue to consider in developing and pricing the product is whether the method of reimbursement for the product will be different from that in the claim experience.

Carve-Out Networks and Services

Certain benefits may be carved out of the network and administered separately, usually by a third-party vendor. The most typical carve-outs are mental health, including substance abuse, and prescription drugs. The rationale for carving out benefits is that by having a specialty vendor focus on the benefits, the benefits may be more easily controlled and managed, and delivered at a lower cost. The arrangement may be capitated or fee-for-service. If the arrangement is fee-for-service, the health plan should be comfortable that the vendor has sufficient medical management controls in place to achieve pricing objectives.

Prescription benefit managers (PBMs) have programs to help achieve a company's objectives. They can provide prescription drug plan management services at a lower cost through negotiated discounts with pharmaceutical manufacturers. They have programs that steer usage to generic drugs and a specified list of drugs known as a formulary. They may also be able to achieve lower costs through larger discounts and by limiting the number of participating pharmacies. This must be evaluated relative to the effect that limited access has on marketability.

PBM programs may also help address quality of care objectives through monitoring current prescription use and potentially avoiding adverse reactions to a new prescription. It is essential for the actuary to understand the details associated with any prescription drug program. It is also important to monitor these costs, and desirable to have a base with which to compare them. Sorting out the pluses and minuses requires considerable actuarial review.

Increasingly, health plans are facing the decision of whether to outsource care management services or develop these services internally, as they develop new managed care products. For instance, there are many vendors that offer disease management programs. Whether or not a health plan decides to outsource these programs or develop them internally depends on several factors, such as: ability of the health plan to identify individuals needing care, ability of the health plan to communicate with individuals on a one-on-one basis, the number and types of programs needed, consumer acceptance of the health plan and/or vendor, and the cost of the programs.

Finally, high cost surgical procedures may be carved out and directed to a single hospital or medical group. These arrangements are often referred to as "centers of excellence." The goal of such an arrangement is to direct care to a high quality facility and physician, and to negotiate a lower cost as a result of the higher volume of services being delivered by these providers.

Managed Care Data Requirements

In addition to the usual array of aggregate data that actuaries need to price medical care products, there are significant additional data required to properly price managed care products. This would include items such as the following:

- *Who Goes Where.* To which provider, including both physicians and facilities, did the insured go before the introduction of the managed care benefits? This may be of significance during provider negotiations. In addition, pricing assumptions require projections of who will go where when the managed care plan is introduced. On-going monitoring of utilization changes will be of help in renegotiation, as well as in re-pricing.

- *Efficiency of Providers.* A key element in developing an effective low cost managed care network is the ability to identify those providers who are providing high quality and coordinated care that fits within the health plan objectives. This entails profiling providers against community norms for their peers. Significant savings may be achieved if outliers are identified, and then educated or culled out. Consumerism and the Web are leading to greater acceptance of provider profiling.

- *Provider Charges.* Provider charges and procedures should be understood in great detail. This requires significant additional coding of charges by procedure, greater attention to diagnosis, and all in all, much more in the way of claim coding.

SELF-INSURED ISSUES

With risk shifted to the employer, ASO plan competitiveness focuses on the various services that are being supplied. The product represents the services to be delivered, such as benefit administration, plan administration, actuarial and consulting services, and in the case of managed care products, access to managed care networks. These may be purchased independently by the employer. It is therefore necessary to fully understand the nature of the expense charges, to be as competitive as possible while still maintaining desired profit margins, regardless of what configuration of services are purchased. It is also important to consider that additional administrative services are often requested by plan holders for no additional charge. To the extent the company accommodates these plan holders, the costs of these additional services must be anticipated and factored into plan charges. Some companies believe that, because there is no insurance risk, reduced profit margins should be applicable to ASO business. Other companies may write ASO business at little or no profit margin, to attract large prestigious employers. While these items are something for each company to decide, it does make for a more competitive environment.

Cash flow concerns, increasing medical insurance costs, and an overall desire to participate directly in plan experience are some of the reasons why partially self-funded medical plans are growing in appeal to more and more plan holders of modest size. These plans are being marketed to groups with as few as 25 lives. Typical plans being sold include high dollar deductible (usually with an aggregate stop loss) minimum premium, and specific and aggregate stop-loss. Specific and aggregate plans also have the added benefit of being non-insured programs, and therefore are exempt from potentially costly state-mandated benefits. This is because state mandates only apply to insurance contracts. In this situation, the plan benefits are non-insured. The contract between the employer and the company does not call for any direct payments to employees by the insurer. Rather, the employer is reimbursed when his non-insured benefits exceed some specified level known as the attachment point.

In developing these partially self-funded medical products, it is important to be particularly aware of the impact of the benefit structure on cost trends. Higher deductibles will have a stronger leveraging effect on trends. For self-insured managed care products, it is important to recognize that the benefits associated with reductions in utilization will flow directly to the policyholder. It is also important to the product development of such shared funding products that financial underwriting rules be established. This will usually require the assistance of an outside credit service, such as Dun and Bradstreet, and may involve financial instruments such as letters of credit. The purpose of financial underwriting is to reduce the insurer's risk in those situations where the company is advancing the plan holder significant amounts of money.

If there is a lesser premium for similar benefits than would be the case in a fully-insured program, special arrangements may be required for field compensation. This is both for brokers and agents as well as for the company's own group sales representatives. If the goal is to approximate the compensation of a fully-insured plan, the method may depend on the limitations of the administrative systems. Some standard approaches are (a) a flat amount per employee per month, (b) a decremental scale of monthly payments based on the number of employees, and (c) a percentage of total premium equivalencies. For some products, at least in some geographic areas, the prevailing practice is to make brokers compensation a function of the insured premium only. This will result in reduced commissions.

Prevailing market practices are critical, as the commission scale you choose will have a significant effect on pricing.

ORGANIZATIONAL CONSIDERATIONS FOR BLUE CROSS / BLUE SHIELD PLANS AND HMOS

While Blue Cross and Blue Shield plans have a national accounts capability to handle groups with exposure in two or more Blue Cross and Blue Shield operating areas, and while there has been significant consolidation of several Blue Cross and Blue Shield plans, by and large their focus is local. Depending on the plan, this will either be a portion of or an entire state. Despite the presence of a few large national HMOs, HMOs are even more localized and usually cover a fairly limited geographic area. The regional nature of these health carriers can be advantageous, in that it allows a more ready concentration on the critical local issues when bringing products to market. It cannot be overemphasized that medical care is organized locally and not nationally.

Both the nature of and the degree to which Blue Cross and Blue Shield plans and HMOs receive discounted fees vary significantly from state to state. These arrangements require a thorough understanding, and as indicated in the section on managed care, they represent a critical part of the rate making process.

In order for an HMO product to be viable, it must have the capability to provide for out-of-area and out-of-network benefits in appropriate circumstances. Blue Cross and Blue Shield plans usually handle this through reciprocal arrangements with each other. HMOs generally must project the expected cost for these benefits and include it in their premium rate. Circumstances permitting, these benefits are tightly defined, and would include emergency care while traveling, and coverage of college students away from home.

Underwriting Requirements

In its original role as a carrier of last resort for small groups, Blue Cross and Blue Shield plans accepted all groups and applicants that met their size and participation requirements. Increasingly, however, Blue Cross and Blue Shield plans have been underwriting groups of all sizes to the extent that regulations allow them to do so. As a product is developed, it is important to focus on what underwriting safeguards are necessary to preserve the integrity of the pool, and balance that with the mandate for providing broad levels of coverage. This has led to developing rules and policy provisions that vary based on the size of the group.

Usually operating in a dual choice environment, HMOs have unique concerns. At the start of each plan year, employees select the benefit program of their choice. The plan features that will influence their decision are the strength of provider network (especially in regard to primary care physicians), the level of benefits being offered compared to that of the competing program, and the comparative employee contributions of each. Perhaps the most significant element in the decision-making process for many individuals, however, is whether or not there are previously established relationships with physicians and whether they are inside or outside the HMO network. The interplay of all these factors is important to the product development process. In certain situations, HMOs may institute a sole carrier requirement to avoid the antiselection associated with dual choice.

Some HMOs have encountered other problems in dual choice situations that affect their ability to market. One is the indemnity carrier terminating coverage for lack of participation. Another is a growing employer concern about spiraling medical care costs from the indemnity plan, coupled with favorable experience on the HMO plan, not accruing to the employer. This may make it advantageous for the HMO to develop a joint marketing arrangement, or even a joint risk-sharing arrangement with a commercial carrier. The legal and regulatory issues surrounding these arrangements vary by state, and in general are not well-defined. It may be prudent to get legal advice before proceeding.

Special Regulations and Statutes

Blue Cross and Blue Shield plans and HMOs across the country vary in their approach towards community versus demographic rating. The dialogue tends to be one of public policy. There is no actuarial rationale for charging all groups the identical rate regardless of their expected morbidity. Blue Cross and Blue Shield plans and HMOs that community rate must be cognizant of potential financial and marketing difficulties that can arise from this practice in an environment where competitors demographically rate. In developing and pricing new products, the actuary should take account of the rating basis and its impact on the cost structure.

GOING TO MARKET

Once a product is designed, priced and capable of being serviced, it is ready to be marketed. The key steps to introducing a product to market are training the field and home office staffs, and advertising the product. Test marketing may be an approach to refine both the product and its introduction. In any product introduction, it is essential that the company review whether there are any governmental restrictions on how the product can be marketed and sold. It is also essential that the advertising, promotion and sale of the product be consistent with the methods assumed in developing and pricing the product. For example, if the product was developed and priced to be sold through an alliance with health clubs, it is critical to the adequacy of the rates that this is done.

TRAINING AND IMPLEMENTATION

If the product is new to the field force, or has features that are technical and complex, it is critical to arrange training programs prior to the product's introduction. If this is not done, some representatives not comfortable with the product are less likely to make an effort to present it. As important, if they do present it, it may be misrepresented.

The methods you use for field training will depend upon such issues as the field training staff, home office facilities for field training, geographic dispersion of the field force, and the local or regional nature of the product. Some methods for consideration are the following:

- *Training Manual.* A product manual can be useful to reinforce product knowledge after the training sessions are over. It may also be used by the more experienced sales representatives to train new sales representatives, or those not attending formal training sessions.

- *Home Office and/or Regional Training Sessions.* These formal sessions will bring in sales representatives from a number of regional group offices. They often include classroom style lectures as well as role-playing presentations. The product manual will be valuable in providing an agenda and leading the instructors through the sessions.

- *Other Methods.* Telephone conferencing, videos, and product bulletins may be effectively used to introduce and explain product updates. Web based training methods are perhaps the newest and one of the most effective ways to conduct interactive training at relatively low cost.

Home office support functions include rating, underwriting, issue, and plan administration and benefit payment. Some of these may require systems modification as well as staff training. While a smooth product introduction requires having all administrative and technical backup in place, the pressure of bringing the product to market quickly may require that some things be done manually, on a temporary basis. When this is the case, it is even more important to have a well-trained home office staff.

From the outset, the ability to prepare a proposal and quote rates is necessary. While not as apparent to the outside world, it is equally important to be able to analyze the developing experience as quickly as possible. It will, of course, be some time before a credible block of business emerges. Initial data gathering should therefore concentrate on the amount of business written. This may provide an early indication of rate adequacy.

Once a case is sold, it must be issued, have premium statements prepared and, in the not too distant future, benefit payments made. All these actions should be integrated so that similar plan information passes through to each administrative area. This would be facilitated by seeing that any automated systems are updated to accommodate the new product.

Advertising and Sales Promotion

The extent to which a new product is advertised and the medium used will depend on already established company patterns as well as the nature of the product. It is important to initiate a campaign to communicate with direct producers. This could be accomplished by brokerage or agency meetings, informational releases, and perhaps, advertising in the trade press. It is also important to provide producers with descriptive brochures and other point-of-sale material.

Sales materials must be developed to communicate the desired message to potential plan holders. With the recent increase in class action litigation, particular attention must be given to sales and marketing practices, to ensure they can not be construed as misleading.

TEST MARKETING

Prior to bringing the final product to market, it may be desirable to test market it in a limited and more controlled environment. This will allow evaluation and fine-tuning of various product features, and testing of benefit and plan administration. In addition, it may give needed insight into the receptivity of the benefit design by plan holders and employees.

Regional test marketing may provide the opportunity to "debug" the product and to fine-tune the administration prior to developing the systems that would be required for it to be marketed nationally.

In some instances, the company's own employees may be able to provide a marketing laboratory. If the product fits in with the corporate benefit program this could be advantageous to everyone.

CURRENT TRENDS IN MEDICAL PRODUCT DESIGN

The group insurance market is continually evolving. Employers are responding to rapidly rising medical costs by changing plan design, changing employee contribution strategies and introducing Web based enrollment and communication tools. They are also limiting their number of benefit plan offerings. Managed care enrollment is declining as consumers demand provider choice.

Competing in the medical insurance market has become increasingly difficult. Factors such as persistent health care cost increases, disenchanted employers, industry consolidation, consumer and provider hostility, consumerism, litigation and regulation, and technical advances such as the Internet have contributed to the introduction of new products and changes to existing products.

NEW PRODUCTS

Consumer Driven Health Plans

Consumer driven health plans (CDHPs) have developed in response to employers looking for more predictability in budgeting their health costs. They are viewed as a way to help educate employees about the true cost of health care and to get employees more involved in the decision making process. They represent a shift in responsibility from employers to employees in the selection and cost of health care services. The plans are generally high deductible benefit plans ($1,000 to $5,000) combined with a health savings account (HSA) or health reimbursement account (HRA) to cover medical costs under the deductible. With both an HSA and an HRA, the employer generally funds a fixed allowance (such as $500) per employee to cover the cost of benefits under the deductible. CDHPs have been growing in popularity in recent years.

Internet Based Products

The Internet is driving the evolution of health care by providing widespread access to health related information. Consumers now have direct access to information that was previously only available to providers. Internet based products, which often include CDHPs, provide health information on line. Individuals can perform on-line health risk assessments and have access to nurse coaches. Provider information is also generally available on-line, including price and quality information.

Personal Network Products

With these products, the employee chooses their own provider network including specialist physicians as well as a primary care physician. If the employee chooses expensive providers as part of their network, they are responsible for the additional cost of those providers. These products may be a component of CDHPs.

CHANGES TO EXISTING PRODUCTS

Open Access

While open access products are not new, they have become increasingly popular as a result of health insurers responding to employees' demands for provider choice. In addition, continual cost increases in the managed care arena have brought into question traditional approaches to care management such as use of gatekeeper models and pre-certification of hospital stays. Many health plans have questioned the effectiveness of these traditional approaches in light of the additional costs to administer these programs. As a result, PPO products continue to increase in popularity. Product development of open access products needs to consider the provider network, selection issues, and cost sharing differentials.

Tiered Networks

At the same time that insurers are focusing on providing open-access medical insurance products, some are introducing tiered networks. Under a tiered network product, individuals have lower cost sharing when they use a select group of (presumably lower cost) providers. There may be two tiers or multiple tiers. Individuals continue to have the highest cost sharing when they use out-of-network providers.

Focus on Disease Management

Disease management programs are thought by many to improve the quality of health care provided to an individual, and r educe costs for certain diseases. They often focus on chronic diseases (such as diabetes) or diseases where there may be an immediate return on investment following implementation of the program (such as for cardiac diseases). Disease management programs may be developed internally or may be outsourced to an outside vendor.

SUMMARY

Whether considering new products or changes to existing products, multiple and sometimes unique factors must be considered in the product development process. For example, product development associated with open access and tiered networks must consider the provider network, cost sharing differentials, selection issues, and overall marketability. In addition, the overall acceptance level of the provider community needs to be considered. New products need to be evaluated for market acceptance and for the start-up costs associated with the product. Product development associated with disease management needs to consider which diseases to include, whether to outsource, how to identify individuals and how to communicate.

The medical plan design of the future is hard to predict. Continual consolidation of the health insurance industry will limit the number of players in the short term. The traditional HMO model will probably survive as a closed network product, with a carefully selected provider network and provider incentives structured to produce efficient care delivery. This design will focus on building relationships with providers and the consumers of health care. Continual cost increases will likely result in a reintroduction of traditional managed care features (such as gatekeepers and active medical management) in some markets.

Open access products will continue to be available but will emphasize consumer education and consumer sharing in the decision making process. The Internet will be used to ensure patient access to information, including information on provider quality measures.

Consumer driven health plans and consumer oriented disease management strategies will become more prevalent, and technology will continue to play an increasing role.

45 Planning and Control

Francis G. Morewood

This chapter will focus primarily on planning and control for a group insurance business unit which constitutes a separate profit center.

To quote loosely from Lewis Carroll's Cheshire cat, "If you don't know where you want to go, it doesn't much matter which route you take." Planning is important for a group insurance business unit because it provides the framework for the unit's future business activities. Planning starts with an assessment of the environment in which the group insurance products and services will be marketed, and an assessment of the group operation's current strengths and weaknesses. The next stage is to define what the group insurance operation is to become, and plan how it will be changed from what it is now to what management wants it to become. Taking into account the current and projected environment, it will be necessary to decide how to capitalize on the unit's strengths and to prioritize the elimination of its weaknesses. Long-term goals and the strategies to achieve those goals will be determined. These will appear in summary form in the group insurance operation's mission and vision statements. The next step is to break these down into bite-size pieces with interim goals. These will constitute the annual plans.

Control enters the picture after the plans have been developed and after the implementation of the plans has begun. Of course, the planning process will include an annual review of the environment and an annual reassessment of the business unit's strengths and weaknesses. Hence, the annual planning activity has a secondary function of exerting a form of control over the long-term strategies and goals.

A measurement system will be used to produce timely and accurate comparisons of actual results to planned results. Deviations will be scrutinized in order to determine their causes. Management can then make assessments of the need for changes in the plans or changes in the operations. Finally, control includes the implementation of any required changes.

It should be noted that many of the aspects of planning and control for a group insurance business unit are equally applicable to any other kind of business. At the same time, it should be noted that the application of the general principles must take into account the specifics of the business unit's particular product and service offerings.

PLANNING CYCLES AND CONTENT

COMPETITIVE STRATEGIES

Every group insurance operation has a variety of competitors: other insurance companies, third-party administrators, health maintenance organizations, self-insured employers, and service organizations such as Blue Cross Blue Shield and Delta Dental plans. In this environment, in order to grow and prosper, the organization must have some way of attracting customers. The more successful the competitive strategy, the more the organization will grow and prosper.

The possible strategies for gaining competitive advantage can be summarized under three headings: price, differentiation, and niche marketing.

Price

Companies who seek to gain competitive advantage with a low price must have a method of operating with a lower cost base than their competitors. Otherwise, they will not achieve a satisfactory profit. Possible avenues for developing a lower cost base include the following:

- Using a lower cost distribution system than the competition.
- Utilizing technology more effectively than the competition.
- Out-performing competitors in claims cost containment for pooled risks.
- Relocating all or part of the work force geographically to take advantage of areas with cheaper labor costs.
- Otherwise improving productivity.

From time to time, some companies have reduced prices for a period of time resulting in reduced profits or even losses in order to gain market share. This type of approach might be adopted in order to get started in the group insurance business or to build the critical mass necessary for running a viable group insurance operation. It is emphasized that this type of strategy can only be sustained for a short period of time. Furthermore, this type of strategy is disruptive to the marketplace as a whole, because it creates customer expectations that cannot be satisfied over the longer term.

Differentiation

The possible avenues for gaining competitive advantage through differentiation are the following:

- The development of a unique product.
- The provision of superior service.
- The development of a higher quality product than the competition.
- Out-performing the competition in cost containment for experience rated risks.
- Continuous development of improved product features.
- Offering a full product line with a capacity for wide distribution of products and services.

Niche Marketing

The niche marketer gains competitive advantage through specialized product knowledge and specialized knowledge of the customer base. The customer base could be defined in terms of a specific geographical area, or case size, or in terms of the users of a specialized product (such as group creditor insurance).

TIME FRAME

The mission and vision are intended to deal with the long-term and to provide a degree of stability and continuity to the operation. A five-year time frame should be viewed as a minimum for these elements of the plans. Environmental conditions could change drastically between one year and the next, forcing changes in the mission and vision, but this is unlikely. If it does happen, the redrafted mission and vision will also have a time frame of at least five years.

The annual plans will normally focus primarily on a one-year period, but should include some reference to the longer term.

OBJECTIVES

Objectives, some more easily measurable quantitatively (which we'll call 'quantitative') and some less ('qualitative'), are essential elements of the annual planning process as well as the strategic planning process.

Qualitative

Qualitative objectives for the longer term will relate to such things as the following:

- Developing a reputation as a provider of quality products and services.

- Developing or maintaining a reputation for fair dealing and integrity.

- Developing a highly skilled work force that is rewarded for excellence and exceptional results.

- Developing a new management information system.

- Developing a new distribution channel.

- Developing a system for electronic claims submission.

Qualitative objectives for the annual plans might represent one or more steps in the development of a longer term objective. For example, if the business unit has an objective of developing a reputation as a provider of quality products and services, it might decide that this could best be accomplished if the group insurance organization structure emphasized business units built around product lines. The product lines might be group life, medical, dental and disability. The product lines might be split further by market segment (small group, large group, jumbo group) and/or geographic region. Each of these product units might be headed up by a product manager whose staff members are responsible for product development, pricing, profit, growth, underwriting and claims processing. The first set of annual plans following the establishment of the long-term objective (developing a reputation as a provider of quality products and services) might provide for the selection of the personnel for each of the product line business units and their physical relocation. The next set of annual plans might involve the development of specific in-depth product knowledge among the members of each team through a combination of training programs and on the job experience. The same set of annual plans may call for a customer survey to ferret out new ideas for product enhancement. The third set of annual plans might involve the development of a gain-sharing program to foster the development of teamwork among the members of each team. The annual plans, as mentioned earlier, break down the long-term objectives into bite-size pieces that permit focused attention on specifics.

Quantitative

The quantitative objectives relate to growth and profit. Longer term quantitative objectives might relate to the attainment of a specific market share percentage at some future date. From the profit viewpoint, the group insurance business unit might plan to ensure that each year's operations are profitable, or define the average profit margin to be realized over a given period of time.

The growth objectives included in the annual plans would normally include such items as new business premium, premium on lapsed policies, and increase in premium in force. Since many health coverages are now delivered on a non-insured basis, reference must also be made to the equivalent premium or the administrative fees for the non-insured products. New business and persistency are the growth factors over which management has some control. The total business in force will increase or decrease in response to the combined impact of new business, lapses, premium rate or fee changes, minor changes in the group insurance benefit details which are not classified as new business or lapses, as well as changes in the number of employees and the payroll of each policyholder's workforce.

The annual plans should include total new business objectives and persistency objectives, but effective planning requires more detail. Quantitative objectives, which set out the new business objectives by case size and by product line as well as the planned ratios of sales to quotations for each case-size/product-line cell, will permit effective analysis of results, and will provide focus for remedial action if there are deviations. Similarly, the details of expected lapses should be set out by case size and product line. The plans may focus on particular target industries for new business or particular types of intermediary as sources of new business. Indeed there are many possibilities. The point is that the objectives should be in line with the focus and should be detailed enough for the business unit to know just what is going wrong, if actual results differ from the plans.

Profit objectives for the group insurance division may relate to earnings before or after income tax. The key determinant here is whether or not the group insurance business unit is responsible for the income tax implications of their business activities. As is the case for growth objectives, it is not sufficient to set out a single figure for earnings from the group insurance operation. For effective analysis of results and appropriate remedial action when deviations occur, the objectives must include some detail on the planned sources of profit.

One year growth objectives may have implications on the profits for more than a single year. Hence, it is prudent to set objectives which cover a longer period. A three-year period is suggested but the major emphasis should be on the objectives of the first of these three years.

Another factor is the group insurance underwriting or pricing cycle. This problem results from inadequate pricing by companies who, for one reason or another, are trying to gain market share. Other companies, in order to defend existing policies, and in order to attempt to meet new business objectives, will tend to follow suit, with the result that profitability for the industry as a whole tends to drop off. Eventually a semblance of order will return to the market as companies decide that they can no longer afford to sell business at inadequate premium rates in order to enhance or maintain their share of market. During these self-imposed cyclical downturns it may be extremely difficult to meet short-term profit and growth objectives.

ANNUAL PLANS

The annual plans represent a route map or itinerary for the group insurance business unit for the coming year. Typical contents of the annual plans include the following:

- Profit objectives for the year for each of the group insurance product lines.
- New business objectives for the year for each of the group insurance product lines.
- Expected or target lapses for the year for each of the group insurance product lines.
- Objectives for the overall increase in premium in force for each of the group insurance product lines.
- Outline of the specific projects for the year in respect of the long term qualitative objectives for the group insurance operation.
- Outline of the specific projects for the year which are known to be required as a result of changes in the regulatory (or market) environment.

An example has already been given of the way a long-term objective might be broken down into projects for inclusion in the annual plans. The annual plans might include other projects which would help to satisfy the long-term objectives for the shorter term. A further example might help to illustrate the form of this type of project.

To illustrate, assume that senior company management has decided that the group insurance profit picture must be improved. Long-term goals have been set and long-term strategies (such as a new computer system, a different kind of distribution channel, or a new emphasis on delivering quality service at a fair price) have been identified. Work has commenced on the projects which will ultimately result in implementation of these long-term strategies. The annual plans include a clearly defined work plan for the current year's activities on the development of these long-term plans. While these goals and strategies are designed to improve profitability over the longer term, they will do little or nothing for the short term. Senior management is happy with the long range remedial strategies, but they are insistent that results should be improved in the near term as well. In response, the annual plans also include a variety of programs that are designed to improve profitability over the short run.

For example, the annual plans might specify a target claims to premium ratio and a target lapse ratio for renewals. The underwriters would have the responsibility of setting renewal premium rates that satisfy the target claims ratio. They would also have the responsibility, in those cases where a policyholder's premium rates are being increased, of providing the group representative with an explanation of the need for the rate increase. The group representative would have the responsibility of convincing the policyholder that the renewal premium rate is fair, reasonable and necessary. The annual plans might also call for the development of an incentive program to reward the underwriters and the group representatives for attaining or exceeding the targets.

For new business the annual plans might specify a target closing ratio (ratio of sales to quotations) as well as a target profit margin. As in the case of renewals, the plans might call for an incentive program to reward the underwriters and the group representatives for attaining or exceeding the targets.

Cost containment is everybody's business, but unless specific targets are identified, included in the annual plans and incentives provided, it often works out to be nobody's business. The annual plans might focus on improved claims handling costs as a means of controlling expenses, utilizing a target for performance measures such as administrative costs per claim. The annual plan might also provide for the inauguration of an employee suggestion box, a mechanism for acting on the suggestions and a reward program for suggestions that are adopted.

Annual plans for a group insurance operation can take many different forms, and the ingredients of a particular plan will depend a great deal upon the circumstances.

Major Factors Affecting Results

No matter what reason a company has for being in the group insurance business, one of the key result areas will be the operating profit. If a life insurance company is in the group insurance business strictly to assist its agency force, the primary concern will be the effectiveness of the group insurance unit in its support role for the individual sales force. Under this scenario, management is likely to consider that the group insurance operation can be supported through a shifted expense charge, as the existence of the group products permit the individual side of the business to operate more effectively. If this is the case, the desired result may be that the shifted expense charge should be no larger than the gains from the offsetting benefit to the individual agency force. The dollar value of this benefit may be very difficult to measure, but, if the business is to be managed effectively, some sort of measurement must be made.

If the group insurance operation is a strategic business unit in its own right, the key result areas will be growth and profit. We will now examine these two key result areas and consider the effect of the various factors that have an impact on them.

Growth

The major factors affecting growth have already been considered above, in the section entitled Objectives. The factors are new business, lapses, and other growth (minor changes in benefit details, changes in the number of employees and changes in the payroll of each policyholder's workforce). Some companies treat premium rate or fee increases as new business while other companies treat these as other growth. The growth factors over which management has a measure of control are new business, renewal premium rates, fee increases or decreases and lapses. New business depends upon the following:

- The extent to which premium rates or fees are competitive in the market place.
- The relative quality of the product.

- The company's reputation for service quality.
- A number of qualitative and quantitative aspects about the activities of the distribution system.
- The effectiveness of the various techniques that are used to promote the product.

Renewal rate increases or decreases are the result of a variety of influences, including the following:

- The adequacy of the rates when the policy was issued.
- The rate of inflation in claims costs.
- Changing claims frequencies.
- The company's skill at controlling expenses.
- Other trend factors.
- The underwriter's skill at setting revised rates based on these factors.
- The company's skill at selling the revised rate structure to the client.

Persistency depends upon the following factors:

- The level of activity in the marketplace.
- The policyholder's perception of the service he/she is receiving.
- The policyholder's perception of the fairness of the price established by the insurer at each renewal date.
- The cost to the policyholder of changing to a new insurance carrier.

PROFITS

The profit or operating gain for a single year consists of the excess of income over expenditure. The income items are premiums, fees and investment income. The expenditure items are claims, expenses, dividends or experience rating refunds, and taxes. In order to plan for and control profit, it is necessary (but not sufficient) to analyze and understand the items of income and expenditure, and to establish a system for monitoring these items on a periodic basis. The business unit must also understand the factors which will influence the income and expenditure items. Effective underwriting and adequate pricing will have an effect on premium income. So will the extent of new business income, and so will persistency. It appears, then, that the major factors affecting growth will also be major factors affecting profits.

It has already been mentioned that growth and persistency will be affected by such factors as the following:

- The price of the company's products and services compared to those offered by competitors. It is noted that this relationship will have a bearing on the number of group premium dollars the company receives and on which it will generate profits (or losses), whereas the relationship between the price and cost of the company's products will determine the profit per dollar of premium.
- Quality, or more accurately, customer perceptions of the quality of products and services offered by the insurer.

Marketplace perceptions, in turn, will be determined by such things as product quality, product innovation, quality of service, effectiveness of advertising and other promotional tools, interpersonal relationships with intermediaries, and effective use of technology.

SETTING GROWTH AND PROFIT OBJECTIVES

Profit and growth are not independent of each other. Hence, it is essential that the two be considered jointly when the objectives are being formulated. The interdependence of profit and growth is partly due to the effects of acquisition strain and valuation strain, but a more fundamental influence is the inverse relationship between rapid growth and large profit margins in the premium rates.

In order to plan for profits from a group insurance operation it is essential to consider the various potential sources of profits. If the insurance is fully pooled, these sources include gains from mortality/morbidity, expenses (including taxes and commission), investment income, and contingency or explicit profit charges.

If the insurance is retrospectively experience rated, the incurral and recovery of deficits becomes a fifth source.

The premium can be looked upon as consisting of a number of different components, or sources of income corresponding to the sources of profit. The largest part of the premium is the mortality/morbidity element. The expected gain (or loss) from mortality/morbidity will depend on whether the business is fully pooled, fully experience rated or partially experience rated. Assuming that premiums, retention charges and fees are adequate, the gain or loss on expenses tends to be a function of policy duration because acquisition expense is incurred in the first policy year, and recovered by amortizing the costs over subsequent years. The gain or loss on investment income tends to be small for most group insurance policies because most of the products are sold on a one-year renewable term basis and there is very little asset accumulation. The principal items of asset accumulation result from claim reserves and surplus or risk fluctuation reserve.

Long-term disability tends to have more asset accumulation than other benefits because the claims have a potentially long payment period, which means that a sizeable reserve must be set up when a claim is incurred.

Company practices as to recognition of investment income by the different lines of business may also vary, and this would impact the gain or loss on investment income. The charge for contingencies tends to be a function of the probability of claims fluctuation. The explicit profit charge is usually expressed as a percentage of premium with perhaps some variation by size of policy. Hence, the expected profit from a group insurance operation depends not only upon the adequacy of premiums, retention charges and fees but also upon the amount of new business in relation to the amount of business in force, the kind of products sold, the size of policy, and the persistency.

For a proper analysis of the expected profits from a given group insurance operation for a given year, all these factors must be taken into account. Once the analysis has been done, it may be expedient to express the profit objective as a percentage of premium.

MAINTENANCE OF SURPLUS FUNDS AS A PERCENTAGE OF PREMIUM

Of a more fundamental nature is the question "What constitutes a satisfactory profit or operating gain from a group insurance business unit?" In considering this question, it should be noted that operating gain is basically a short-term measure. Over the long run, in order for the business to be self-supporting, it must generate enough surplus to fund its own risk fluctuation reserve or required surplus, as discussed in another chapter of this book. A second consideration is the question of whether or not there is a different answer for a mutual or not-for-profit company than for a stock company. If the company is a stock company, the owners will be looking for some return on their investment from every aspect of the company's business, including the group insurance lines.

The required size of the risk fluctuation reserve is a function of quite a number of variables. Among these are the following:

- The size of the company.
- The other product lines written.
- The company's underwriting philosophy in writing experimental or highly fluctuating kinds of coverage.
- The product mix.
- The contingency and/or profit margins included in rate levels.

Once a company has decided on the required size of the risk fluctuation reserve and any additional profit requirements, it has to consider the interaction between the growth rate, the operating gain as a percentage of premium and the longer term surplus requirements.

RETURN ON CAPITAL OR SURPLUS

Another way of looking at the question of setting profit and growth objectives is from the return on capital or surplus point of view. Under this approach, management determines the return on capital or surplus that is considered satisfactory for the businesses the company chooses to conduct. The group insurance operation would have the designated return on capital or surplus as its starting point for setting profit and growth objectives. It would then plan for the above-mentioned variables in such a way that the required return on capital or surplus will be met.

Under this approach to objective setting, it is first necessary to determine the amount of capital or surplus that will be attributed to each of the company's businesses, and on which the required rate of return is to be calculated. The suggested approach is to determine the amount of capital or surplus that is required to support the business, rather than any amounts of capital or surplus that result from the financial history of the business. Required capital or surplus can be thought of as the minimum required surplus or the amount of the required risk fluctuation reserve. This approach results in the need for an annual calculation of the required surplus.

The required rate of return will take into account the rate at which the risk fluctuation reserve must be built up to support the projected rate of growth, as well as the desired rate of return for the owners of the business.

PLANNING TO MEET OBJECTIVES

The preceding section considered the question of setting objectives from the point of view of what is to be accomplished. This section will consider the question of how it is to be accomplished. At the most fundamental level, growth is achieved by attracting and retaining customers, while profit is achieved by charging the customer more for the product or service than its costs to produce and deliver. If the product or service is offered by only one firm and if there are customers who must have that product of service, the company can grow and make the required profits without a great deal of planning. It is the element of competition that results in the need for planning. In order for a particular firm to grow it must attract customers that other firms are also trying to attract. The planning function must answer the question of how this is to be done.

The planning function provides the framework for the future activities of the business unit, and this framework is based on an assessment of the business environment in relation to the business unit's strengths and weaknesses. This process starts with a definition of the business focus and its boundaries. The business unit must decide what customer functions it will try to satisfy and the customer segments on which it will focus.

For example, a group insurance business unit may choose to offer only group life insurance, or only group long-term disability insurance. It might decide to offer group life insurance in conjunction with administrative services only for group health benefits, or it might choose to offer the entire gamut of group insurance benefits. There are many possibilities. A company might decide to offer its chosen products in a limited geographic area or it might choose to offer them nationwide.

Whatever the product focus is to be and whatever customer segments are to be addressed, the choice should be based upon a marriage of the opportunities that exist in the group insurance marketplace and the existing strengths of the business unit. Going one step further, the business unit may determine that there are certain strengths which it lacks, but which it must acquire in order to take advantage of the opportunities that exist in the group insurance marketplace.

In order for the business unit to gain a sustainable competitive advantage, the product and service offerings must be of benefit to the customer. Equally important, the customer must be made to perceive the advantages of acquiring the product or service from this supplier and he or she should be willing to pay the required price.

Regardless of which competitive strategy (price, niche marketing, differentiation, or a combination of some or all of these) is chosen, the business unit will do well to focus on three fundamentals of gaining competitive advantage. First is the need to minimize operating costs. Second is the need to offer up-to-date products and services. Third is the need to provide quality service. Quality service is defined as meeting customer expectations by doing the right things, doing them right the first time, doing them on time, at the right cost and with the right attitude. Developing a quality service orientation in the business unit may be the most difficult of the three fundamentals. It involves a continuing customer research program, communication and training programs for the employees, delegation of decision-making, and employee recognition and reward programs.

The Role of the Product Manager

There are probably as many definitions of the product manager's role as there are organizations which use product managers. Indeed, the definitions range all the way from that of coordinators who have no line responsibility whatsoever to the heads of business units built around product lines whose staff members are responsible for all aspects of product management, including product development, pricing, profit, underwriting and claims processing. There are, however, certain essential ingredients which will be discussed here. In the simplest terms, the product manager is in some way responsible for the growth and profitability of their product line. The role, then, will include direct or indirect responsibility for the following:

- Monitoring the growth and profitability of the product line. While the tracking of results will usually fall outside the responsibilities of the product manager, effective use of the results of the tracking is expected.

- Planning and managing the product range within the product line, including the development of new products, the modification and enhancement of existing products, the withdrawal of redundant products and the development of new ways of using the existing product range.

- Monitoring market developments, what competitors are doing, where the products stand in relation to the market and in relation to the characteristics of the buyers.

- Developing and maintaining effective promotional material and for ensuring the development of adequate training material for effective distribution of the product.

- Being a major player in the development of the annual plans as they relate to all aspects of the product range.

Clearly, the product manager cannot operate effectively without the support of any essential functions which do not report directly to the manager. Depending on the organization structure and the manager's job description, this may include such functions as sales promotion, distribution, investment, information systems, publicity, administration, pricing, underwriting, and so on. Whether the product manager's role is a line or a staff function, some or all of these functions will not report directly to the product manager. The job, therefore, will require the incumbent to liaise with and co-ordinate the activities of many different disciplines. The successful performance of the job depends upon the successful performance of many other jobs.

Regardless of the organization structure, personal accountability and appropriate incentives are universal elements for successful performance, not only with respect to the product manager, but also with respect to the functions with whom the product manager liaises. Personal accountability and incentives are the subject of the final section of this chapter.

TRACKING RESULTS, SOURCES OF INFORMATION, AND CORRECTING DEVIATIONS

A method for tracking results against objectives is required to assess the success in implementing the plans. The quantitative objectives relate to growth and profit and these will be the main subject of discussion here. It should be noted, however, that for effective control of all aspects of plan implementation, there must be a tracking system for the qualitative aspects of the annual plans as well. For example, plans to develop or implement a new information system should be accompanied by detailed scheduling of project tasks, followed by regular reporting of progress compared to schedule. The purpose of such reporting is to note deviations from the plans, to assess the reasons for the deviations and to decide on a course of remedial action.

Reports tracking growth may include reports of new business and new business closing ratios by segment, such as by size of case, geographical area, insurance intermediary, type of industry, or branch office. Similar analyses of lapses and lapse ratios may also be prepared.

Companies who carefully track sources of profit are in a position to control their growth and profit results much more effectively than those companies who do not.

It is now common to have a separate set of books which are geared towards financial management of the business. The principal differences between the statutory reports and the corresponding internal statements for the company as a whole stem from differences in the liabilities, surplus and capital. The liability items will, for internal management purposes, be based on most likely assumptions instead of the conservative assumptions that are appropriate to solvency considerations. The surplus or capital will be the sum of the required surplus or capital for each of the strategic business units, instead of the historical accumulation of capital contributions and surplus earnings. These balance sheet changes will affect the investment income and the reserve changes in the income statement.

The figures for the profit center may be segregated, so that each business unit can exercise some measure of control over the investment strategy for the assets which generate its earned investment income. Similarly, it is possible to track and use the direct expenses attributable to the business unit. Unfortunately, indirect expenses are still, and probably always will be, subject to allocation techniques that are sometimes relatively crude. The problem is that many indirect expenses are inherently unallocable by any scientific method. In spite of the deficiency on the indirect expense side of the picture, it is now possible to produce meaningful profit or operating gain figures for the business unit as a whole on a monthly basis. These figures are sufficient to show whether the group insurance profit results are in line with the planned results, but they are not sufficient to show where the operation has gone wrong if there is a deviation from planned results.

The question of where the operation has gone wrong is addressed by subdividing the group insurance income statement. As is the case for growth measurements, there are a great many useful ways of subdividing (by product, by case size, by geographical area, by branch office, by type of intermediary, and so on). The subdivisions must be large enough to produce meaningful results and they should be geared towards action. The business, then, should be subdivided into segments which show where the deviations are occurring and, hence, where remedial action is required. The tracking mechanism, also, should indicate what sort of remedial action needs to be taken. One approach to this question is to analyze the operating gain for each subdivision by source of profit or loss (gain from mortality/morbidity, gain from expenses, gain from investment income and gain from contingency and/or explicit profit charges).

CONTROL MECHANISMS FOR MAJOR FACTORS

Given that the principal quantitative objectives relate to growth and profit, it follows that the factors to be controlled are the revenue and expenditure items, such as new business premium, renewal premium, investment income, claims, and expenses.

NEW BUSINESS AND RENEWAL PREMIUM

New business and renewal premium are controlled by managing the elements of the marketing mix. The potential for acquiring new business and retaining existing business is higher when the following conditions hold:

- Products and services are designed to meet customers' expectations. Products and services can be so designed through effective use of customer research, the product manager concept, and programs to develop a quality service orientation throughout the organization.

- The price is lower than the price offered by the competition. A low price policy can be sustained only if it results from a low cost operation. Hence the control mechanisms for claims and expenses constitute the appropriate control mechanisms for a low price policy.

- Customers *perceive* that products and services will meet their expectations and that the price is favorable. Promotional tools and personal contact are the mechanisms that will influence customers' perceptions.

INVESTMENT INCOME

In a life insurance company, the group insurance business unit is most unlikely to have the responsibility for actually investing the assets arising from their own operations. However, the group insurance area can exercise a measure of control if their assets are segmented from the rest of the company's assets, and if they are involved in determining the investment policy for the group insurance assets. Control might be exercised through a committee consisting of representatives from the business unit and from the investment department. The committee would meet on a periodic basis and the agenda would include items such as the following:

- An overview of the current investment market.
- A review of the business unit's asset and liability activity since the last meeting.

- A review and updating of the business unit's investment strategy including objectives, asset mix targets and liquidity requirements.

For other types of group insurers, such as health plans, investment functions don't tend to receive the same attention and focus as for life insurers. This is because group medical and other term products tend to have much lower levels of invested assets, relative to life insurance.

CLAIMS

Mechanisms to control the level of claims will depend upon the type of benefit. In general, these mechanisms take on the following characteristics.

- Verifying that the individual was eligible for coverage;
- Verifying that the event insured against actually occurred;
- Promoting activities to prevent or delay the event insured against, such as support for healthy lifestyles;
- Clear contractual language that defines what is and what is not covered;
- Contractual language and underwriting to avoid duplicate coverage and overinsurance; and
- Claim amelioration activities to shorten the intensity or the duration of the claim.

EXPENSES

Typically, salaries and wages represent about fifty percent of general expenses (expenses other than commissions and taxes) for a group insurance operation. Many of the other expense items (employee benefits, rent, telephone, furniture, travel) are a function of the number of employees or their earnings. It follows that expense control is largely a matter of controlling the number of employees and their salaries and wages.

Control mechanisms for these expense items may be direct or indirect. A direct approach would be to move all or part of the business unit to a location where salaries and wages are low. This might be combined with one or more indirect control mechanisms.

Effective use of technology, over the longer term, should reduce the required number of staff. Over the shorter term, developmental expense for new applications of technology will have the opposite effect.

Productivity improvements result from an environment in which the entire work force is totally involved in the operation, so that everyone is thinking about how to improve the business and everyone is making the changes that result in the necessary improvements.

Total involvement stems from recognizing all workers as true co-partners in the operation. The partnership arrangement means that management and workers share common goals, all partners are encouraged to develop and implement ideas for improvement and rewards are related to performance. Fulfillment of common goals is best accomplished when there is joint commitment, joint training, jointly devised allocation of rewards, joint examination of feedback, and joint diffusion of the process throughout the organization.

PERSONAL ACCOUNTABILITY AND INCENTIVES

According to Dr. Frederick Herzberg, noted behavioral scientist, the growth and health of any organization depends on the healthy growth of its individual members. True personal accountability will only happen in a partnership environment, one in which the following conditions apply:

- Business goals are clearly defined.
- Employees have helped to shape the business goals.
- Each employee has a strong sense of ownership for his or her job and feels responsible for it.
- Employees are rewarded through opportunities for understanding, recognition, influence, power and increased financial rewards through the achievement of personal and team goals.

A variety of programs have been used to implement these ideas. The list includes quality of work-life, participative management, employee involvement, work-place democracy, quality circles, job enrichment, project teams, entrepreneuring, problem-solving groups, gainsharing and incentive compensation programs. While these programs differ in detail, they all have in common the goal of achieving success through people. The essential ingredients of such a program include focusing employee attention on key business needs and objectives, encouraging employees to work "smarter," not just harder, and rewarding employees for their efforts as a group.

If group insurance management can establish the necessary degree of trust and credibility with employees, personal accountability and incentive programs can result in increased output as well as improved cost control and improved quality.

The financial incentives built into the program must be incorporated into a formal document detailing such things as eligibility, calculation of rewards, performance period (monthly, quarterly, yearly) and targeted payout levels. Employees need to understand and support the plan. For this to happen, employees must have complete information about the purpose and objectives of the plan and the performance measures that will be used to calculate their financial rewards.

CONCLUSION

The group insurance market is extremely competitive, and has been so for many years. An article entitled "The Group Insurance Myth" by Peter Walker of McKinsey & Co. Inc., written in 1977, started out by stating that one of the widely accepted beliefs in the group insurance business was that a company could either grow faster than the industry or achieve above-average profit margins, but it could not do both.[1] The author disproved the myth by analyzing the experience of the fourteen largest group insurers for 1971-1976 and by demonstrating that a number of these companies had consistently done both. Based on his analysis of the successful companies' performance, he outlined a general approach to improving group insurance performance through strategic and operational means. Planning and control were very much a part of the approach he outlined.

He recommended planning for a superior product/market mix of business by skewing the book of business toward the more attractive markets defined in terms of risk characteristics, products and geographic areas. He also recommended improving operating performance by taking advantage of the computer's potential for management information systems, by exercising strong control over expenses and claim settlement practices and by improving service to producers.

His recommendations for improving the mix of business involved the following four steps:

---

[1] Walker, P.B., *The Group Insurance Myth, Best=s Review,* Vol. 78, No. 2, June 1977.

- The company must decide why it is in the group business, then set goals for the business and articulate them to the employees and producers.

- The company must assess the profit and growth potential of the major markets (defined by risk characteristics, products and geographic area), and relate this assessment to its own group insurance goals. The long term influence of external factors in each major market must be identified, as well as the requirements (in respect of product, expense control, management information, producer plant, claims capability and underwriting) for competing effectively in each.

- Next, the company must assess its own strengths and weaknesses and match these against the requirements to determine whether the company can compete effectively with the industry leaders.

- Based on the analytical foundation of the first three steps, the company must then determine the shifts in the product and geographic mix of business required to achieve the corporate goals for group insurance and it must make the necessary decisions to effect those shifts.

Under the management information heading, he recommended the following:

- Analyzing experience by risk characteristic in order to identify prime marketing opportunities and to target marketing efforts.

- Analyzing premium growth by source (geographic area, risk characteristics, number of quotes, closing ratios, new business premium, casual growth, lapses) in order to exercise greater control over group sales operations.

- Monitoring pricing activity to determine whether prices are keeping pace with inflation.

- Developing the data base needed to price a wide range of benefit and cash flow options.

Six years later Peter Walker revisited the "Group Insurance Myth" by analyzing the 1977-1981 performance of the same fourteen companies.[2] The analysis reconfirmed his earlier conclusions.

---

[2] Walker, P.B., *The Group Insurance Myth Revisited, Best=s Review*, Vol. 83, No. 11, March 1983.

There is still a great deal of room in the marketplace for improvement in group insurance performance and in the planning and control process. Key elements include the following:

- Knowing about the company's competitive position.

- Having critical knowledge about customer values and caring about customers.

- Having a vision of the future and moving towards that vision.

- Knowing about the past, particularly as it relates to profitability, and projecting from this knowledge base into the future.

- Having critical knowledge about employee values, caring about them and creating an environment which permits them to make a real contribution to the success of the operation.

- Exploiting technology.

Future success of group insurers may depend on their ability to achieve these goals.

46 MANAGEMENT OF PROVIDER NETWORKS

Robert B. Cumming

This chapter provides an introduction to the management of health care provider networks, from the perspective of a health care insurer. Provider networks are an integral part of many health insurance products, and significant efforts are expended in contracting with and managing provider networks. Actuaries, in particular, often play a key role in analyzing various financial aspects of provider networks.

This chapter will first describe different types of healthcare providers, including how they operate and organize. It will then describe various dimensions of network performance, including techniques and strategies employed to maximize performance.

The frame of reference for most of the discussions in this chapter is in terms of U.S. practices for providers of medical services. Many of the general concepts and management techniques discussed also apply to dental providers. A short section at the end of this chapter discusses the situation in Canada.

TYPES OF HEALTHCARE PROVIDERS

There are a variety of entities directly involved in the delivery of health care services. These provider entities include healthcare professionals as well as healthcare facilities. Health insurers that develop their own provider networks need to either work directly with these entities or with organizations that represent a collection of these entities. The following provides some general background information on healthcare professionals and healthcare facilities.

HEALTHCARE PROFESSIONALS

Healthcare professionals are the people who together with patients decide what medical care will be delivered and who assist in delivering that care. Healthcare professionals include physicians, nurses, pharmacists, chiropractors, podiatrists, and others. Physicians, and other practitioners, are generally involved in the diagnosis of medical problems and in deciding what treatment is appropriate. Nurses, pharmacists, and others assist in carrying out the treatment decisions.

Physicians are considered the key element in managing health care costs and quality due to their control over the use of the vast majority of health care services. Typically, physicians' direct services account for less than half of medical spending. However, physicians also decide when and for how long a person should be admitted to a hospital, which diagnostic tests should be performed, and which drugs should be prescribed. Thus, they control or strongly influence the use of hospital and ancillary services and prescription drugs.

In managing provider networks, it is important to recognize the key role played by physicians. This is critical in designing successful reimbursement arrangements.

Physician Specialties

As a group, physicians deliver a broad array of complex and important services. Due to the complexity of these services, many physicians specialize in a particular area. The American Medical Association categorizes physicians into about 40 different specialties and subspecialties.

Managed care plans often distinguish between "primary care" and "specialist" physicians. Sometimes, each member in a managed care plan must select a primary care physician to act as a case manager or "gatekeeper." Primary care physicians typically include general practitioners, family practitioners, pediatricians, and general internists (internal medicine). Obstetricians and gynecologists are sometimes included as primary care. The remaining specialties and subspecialties comprise "specialist" physicians.

Specialists can be categorized as: (1) surgical specialists, (2) medical specialists, and (3) hospital-based specialists. The surgical specialties include orthopedics, general surgery, cardiovascular/thoracic surgery, otolaryngology, neurosurgery and others. The medical specialties include allergy, hematology, oncology, rheumatology and others. The hospital-based specialists include, for example: anesthesiologists, radiologists, pathologists, and emergency medicine.

Ultimately, networks must include access to physicians from all the major specialties. If this is properly integrated, reimbursement savings will be maximized. Proper integration will also help assure efficient patient flow so that patients are evaluated and treated by the most appropriate type of specialist.

Physician Employment and Group Practices

The vast majority of physicians are directly involved in providing patient care. Other professional activities include medical teaching, research, administration, consulting, and sales. Of the physicians directly involved in patient care, most are self-employed or work in physician-owned group practices. Thus, many physicians can be considered, and operate much like, small business owners. Other patient care physicians may work for a hospital or HMO as an employee.

Medical group practices are important contracting entities for health insurers due to: (1) their ability to act for a large number of physicians with a single contract, (2) their ability to develop and employ practice protocols, internal peer review, and profiling, and (3) their ability to accept and spread significant insurance risk (although healthcare providers taking insurance risk has become less common than it was a decade ago). Also, medical groups are sometimes easier to contract with, since they often have a professional administrator to assist in working through the details of a managed care contract.

HEALTHCARE FACILITIES

Healthcare facilities are the places where medical and surgical care is provided. Healthcare facilities include hospitals, ambulatory surgical centers, imaging centers, skilled nursing facilities, rehabilitation centers, long-term care facilities (nursing homes), and similar facilities. Ambulatory surgical centers and imaging centers may be free-standing or may be part of a hospital's outpatient operation. (Although medical care is provided in a physician's office, this is not generally considered to be a "healthcare facility" since no separate amount beyond the physician's fee is charged.) Hospitals represent the vast majority of facility claim costs in a typical commercial insurance plan and in Medicare.

Role of Hospitals

The primary purpose of hospitals is to care for patients who are too ill to be treated elsewhere. As a result, hospitals are the site of the most complex and expensive care. Hospitals also serve physicians by providing various ancillary services, particularly capital-intensive services. Examples of such capital-intensive services include diagnostic testing such as CAT scans and MRIs. Historically, hospitals have used such state-of-the-art ancillary services to attract their medical staff. In return, physicians admitted patients, ordered ancillary services, and performed procedures, all of which generated revenue for the hospital in a fee-for-service environment.

Hospitals vary in terms of the types and complexity level of inpatient care they provide. Inpatient care can be categorized into three different levels of complexity: (1) primary, (2) secondary, and (3) tertiary. Tertiary care is the most complex and expensive, and would include, for example, organ transplants and special burn units. Most smaller community hospitals do not have the capability to deliver such tertiary care and send these patients to regional or university hospitals.

Impact of Managed Care on Hospitals

Managed care has had a sometimes dramatic affect on the use of hospital services in the U.S. Over the long term, hospital inpatient admissions and days have declined significantly. As inpatient care has declined and shifted to the outpatient setting, the use of hospital outpatient facilities has increased. Many hospitals have focused their capital expenditures on building outpatient facilities and buying physician practices.

PROVIDER NETWORKS

A provider network is a collection of healthcare providers that have various common attributes. The common attributes include: (1) the providers within a network have satisfied whatever selection criteria are being used to determine which providers should be invited to join, and (2) the providers within the network have signed a contract agreeing to various financial and operational requirements. The major financial and operational requirements may include reimbursement levels, accessibility requirements, quality standards, and patient satisfaction.

GOALS OF PROVIDER NETWORKS

Provider networks may be established by health insurers, non-insurance organizations such as third party administrators (TPAs), and by healthcare providers themselves. Health insurers and TPAs establish provider networks to help achieve particular goals, such as the following:

- Lower the *cost* of health care
- Increase the *quality* of health care
- Increase *member satisfaction*

Each of these goals can be viewed as one dimension of network performance. In developing a network, the overall objective is to *maximize these performance measures while keeping the network as broad (i.e. marketable) as possible.* Networks established by healthcare providers may be organized with other goals in mind, such as to preserve market share or to provide negotiation leverage through size and a united front.

MEASURING NETWORK PERFORMANCE

In order to judge the performance level of a network, we need to define and measure cost, quality, and member satisfaction. Of these three measures, cost is often the primary focus in evaluating performance. Cost performance is more objective and is relatively easy to measure.

Measuring Cost Performance

Cost performance is intended to measure the level of financial savings generated by a particular network. Savings may be generated in two ways: (1) negotiating lower per unit prices for health care services, and (2) reducing the number of health care services performed. The combined effect of these two factors gives the overall level of savings for the network. Commonly used measures of cost performance include the following:

- *Price Level Measures.* Percentage discount from billed charges, price levels expressed on a standard scale (such as physician fee levels expressed as a conversion factor using RBRVS relative values), or the average fee for a category of medical services (such as average charge per hospital inpatient day or admission, or the average fee for all office visits.);

- *Utilization Measures.* Utilization rates per 1000 covered members per year (such as hospital inpatient admits and days, office visits, prescriptions, emergency room visits), utilization rates per patient (such as the percentage of patients referred to a specialist, or the number of diagnostic tests per office visit), hospital inpatient average length of stay, or estimates of the percentage of hospital days and admissions that are unnecessary based on clinical chart reviews; and

- *Claim Cost Measures.* Claim cost per member per month or claim cost per episode of care.

When comparing providers and networks, these cost measures should be adjusted, to the extent possible, for demographic factors and health status.

When evaluating the overall performance of one network versus another, it is common to use measures such as the risk adjusted claim cost per member per month. In this scenario, the risk adjustment is commonly performed using diagnosis based health risk assessment tools such as the Diagnostic Cost Groups (DCGs). These tools provide an overall risk score for the population covered under each network. When evaluating the performance of specific health care providers (for example, orthopedic group A versus orthopedic group B) it is common to use claim cost per episode of care. The episode based approach allows the measure to be based on the specific types of services delivered by each health care provider. Also, given the growth of open access products, it is less common to have membership assigned to specific health care providers. Without assigned membership, it is not possible to use a population-based health risk assessment tool.

Clinical measures, such as hospital inpatient chart reviews, directly account for severity and, so, do not need adjustment for health status.

In order to monitor performance, utilization and claim cost measures may be compared to various benchmarks. Typical benchmarks include prior performance, the performance level of competitors in the same geographic area, and optimal performance. Optimal performance reflects utilization levels consistent with best observed health care management practices and results.

In judging the cost performance of a network, it is important to look at utilization as well as price levels. In networks where utilization is not carefully monitored, utilization may increase as providers seek to recover revenue lost due to price discounts.

Measuring Quality

There has been increased emphasis on measuring quality and comparing quality across provider networks. This tends to be driven by the desires and requirements of influential payers such as government, large employers, and employer coalitions. Financial incentives for providers to reduce services have heightened concern about maintaining quality and have resulted in efforts to better measure it. However, there are still many issues related to defining meaningful and objective measures of quality.

Classical quality assessment looks at three dimensions of health care delivery: structure, process, and outcome. Structural measures of quality focus on various attributes of the care delivery system, such as the qualifications of the physicians and hospital. Process measures focus on the administration of care and often involve measuring conformity to standard protocols through case audits and peer review. Outcome measures focus on the end effects of the care that was delivered. An example of an outcome measure is mortality levels. Although each dimension of quality is important, relevance increases as one progresses from structure to process to outcome. However, so does the difficulty of measurement.

One may divide the measurement of outcomes into two categories: administrative and clinical. Examples of administrative measures are access to services, member satisfaction, and member disenrollment rates. Clinical outcome measures tend to be more complex to deal with. There are a variety of outcomes that might be measured, including mortality, morbidity, disability, discomfort, and a sense of "well-being." Furthermore, there may be trade-offs between different types of outcomes when evaluating the efficacy of a procedure. For example, operating on an arthritic knee can greatly improve long-term disability. However, short-term disability is worsened, and there is a small risk of surgical mortality.

In assessing the quality of particular providers, it is possible to build on the requirements of other payers. For example, hospitals that care for Medicare patients must be accredited by the Joint Commission on the Accreditation of Healthcare Organizations (JCAHO) or be certified by the Health Care Financing Administration. The JCAHO is a private body that accredits hospitals and other institutional providers. The measures used by the JCAHO largely focus on structure and process.

The National Committee for Quality Assurance (NCQA) has developed a set of standards which are used to evaluate quality management and improvement programs. A managed care organization (MCO) can hire the NCQA to perform a review their quality management and improvement programs for a fee. The review process also looks at utilization management, credentialing, members' rights and responsibilities, preventive health services, and medical records. A MCO that receives NCQA accreditation may publicize it in advertising and marketing. It is worth noting that NCQA accreditation does not indicate that a MCO has high quality outcomes, rather that the MCO is committed to the principles of quality and is continuously improving the clinical care and services it provides.

A highly publicized effort directed at standardizing quality of care measures is the Health Plan Employer Data Information Set (HEDIS). HEDIS uses a variety of process and outcome measures to assess quality of care and provides various benchmarks for the measures. The process measures assess utilization of certain preventive care services (childhood immunizations, cholesterol screening, mammography screening, cervical cancer screening, prenatal care in the first trimester, diabetic retinal examination) and mental health care services (ambulatory follow-up after hospitalization for a major affective disorder). The outcome measures assess the percentage of babies that are low birth weight and the percentage of members with asthma-related inpatient admissions.

There are also many other quality initiatives that may focus on particular specialties, be used in certain regions, or evaluate selected aspects of health care delivery.

Measuring Member Satisfaction

Regardless of quality assurance programs and clinical outcome studies, managed care organizations need to attract and retain members to be viable. Thus, member satisfaction is an important aspect of quality for health plans and successful providers.

There are two types of measures of member satisfaction. The first type focuses on how members feel about various aspects of the medical care they receive, such as access, friendliness, continuity of care, communication, and perceived quality. It also includes how members feel about the health plan itself. The second type focuses on behavioral indicators of satisfaction, such as disenrollment rates and use of out-of-network providers.

Closely related to member satisfaction are direct measures of member access to care. This includes measures such as: average waiting time for non-urgent office visits, average waiting time in the doctor's office, average waiting time for telephone access to a nurse or physician, and percentage of members who have visited a primary care physician within the past three years.

HEDIS, mentioned above, has defined a standard set of measures related to member satisfaction. The HEDIS measures include responses to the following types of questions:

- Overall evaluation of health plan
- Access to medical care whenever the member needs it

- Thoroughness of examinations
- Ease of seeing the doctor of choice
- Personal interest in the member and their medical problems,
- Outcomes of medical care and how much the member is helped
- Whether the member would recommend health plan to others
- Intent to switch plans

For some HEDIS measures, members subjectively rank the health plan using a five point scale with the rankings ranging from "poor" to "excellent." However, as noted above, HEDIS measures also include many other aspects of quality including clinical outcomes.

TO BUILD OR NOT TO BUILD?

A health plan may have the option of building its own network or renting an existing network. This decision often needs to be evaluated market by market. Building your own network often involves greater upfront costs but lower ongoing costs as compared with renting. Also, building often involves a longer lead time but provides more control over the network than renting.

Key factors which impact the decision of whether to build or rent include: (1) number of members in the market (this impacts the health plan's ability to spread the fixed costs of developing a network), (2) percentage market share (this impacts the health plan's ability to negotiate competitive discounts), and (3) access to competitive rental networks for a reasonable access fee. The decision to build or rent may also vary by type of service or provider. For example, most large health plans have their own physician and hospital networks but often rent networks for pharmacy or certain specialty care services (such as mental health and chiropractic).

CONSIDERATIONS IN ESTABLISHING A PROVIDER NETWORK

There are a variety of factors that should be considered when establishing a provider network. These factors include the following:

- Population to be served,
- Type of product,
- Accessibility of providers,
- Trade-off between size of network and level of discounts,

- Trade-off between size of network and level of medical efficiency,
- Entities with which to contract,
- Target reimbursement levels and methodology,
- Current referral patterns, and
- Specialty networks.

Each of these considerations is discussed below.

Population to be Served

Insurers often form unique networks for different populations or markets. For example, a Blue Cross / Blue Shield plan may establish different provider networks for its commercial business, Medicare Risk business, managed Medicaid business, and Workers Compensation business. Each network should be designed to match the population to be served. The networks may differ in terms of the proportion of providers who participate, the type and specialty mix of the providers, the geographic location of the providers, and the reimbursement methodology and level.

Networks designed for Medicare and Medicaid populations often have fewer providers participating than a network designed for a commercial population. This may be due to a variety of factors. One reason is that broad access to providers in general may be more important for marketing a commercial product to employers than to individuals covered under Medicare and Medicaid. Also, reimbursement rates may be lower, particularly for Medicaid, and therefore acceptable to fewer providers. In addition, Medicare contracts often involve greater provider risk-sharing which may be acceptable to fewer providers.

The mix of provider specialty types in a network should be tailored to the population to be served. Typical AFDC medical populations require significant access to mother and child care. Medicare networks require more specialty services. For example, a network designed for a workers compensation product should focus on healthcare providers that treat accidents and injuries, such as occupational specialists, orthopedic surgeons, and physical rehabilitation centers.

The location of the providers that participate in a network may depend on the population to be served. For example, Medicaid populations are often concentrated in inner-city areas and have limited means of transportation. In order to have accessible providers, it is critical to sign-up the hospitals and physicians located in the inner-city that serve these populations.

Type of Product

The type of product will affect various aspects of the provider contracts, which will impact provider selection and decisions regarding participation. For example, is the network being designed for a referral based product or non-referral product? A referral based product often imposes additional administrative and care management responsibilities on the primary care physicians.

Accessibility of Providers

The geographic accessibility of providers is often measured in terms of the distance between a covered member's home or place of work and the location of the physician's office and the hospitals. Networks should have as wide a geographic spread as possible to maximize the proportion of the population that can readily access a provider within a short distance. Accessibility also depends on the providers' ability to take on new patients and their office hours. Increased accessibility will increase the marketability of the product and will increase the reimbursement savings generated on point-of-service and PPO products.

Trade-Off between Network Size and Discounts

In developing a provider network, there is typically a trade-off between the size of the network and the level of discounts that can be negotiated. Generally speaking, an insurer can achieve lower negotiated fee levels if they are willing to accept fewer providers participating in the network. This reflects that, as fee levels are lowered, fewer providers are willing to sign-up for the network. A smaller network is more likely to result in an increase in business for a provider and, so, the provider will be more willing to accept a large discount. In addition, if an insurer is willing to leave some providers out, it provides greater negotiation leverage.

Some insurers develop an array of networks which vary in terms of size, level of provider discounts, and therefore, premiums. For example, some larger plans may have three or more networks in order to meet the diverse needs and desires of their commercial customers. This might include a "par" or participating network, including nearly all the providers in the service area, a PPO network including perhaps about two-thirds of the providers, and an HMO network including perhaps about one-third of the providers.

A recent hot topic is the multi-tier network. In these networks, providers are slotted in 2 or more tiers, as opposed to either being "in" or "out" of the network. The member premium or, more commonly, the member cost sharing will vary based on the provider or provider system selected by the member. For example, hospitals may be slotted into three tiers: (1) tier 1 – no-copayments, (2) tier 2 – $500 co-pay per admit, and (3) tier 3 – $1000 co-pay per admission.

The advantages of a multi-tier network include: (1) more providers – they can include nearly all providers, as long as there are enough tier levels and enough variation among the tier levels, and (2) more choices – they provide more choices to the member. The disadvantages include that multi-tier networks are more complicated.

Trade-Off between Network Size and Medical Efficiency

A smaller network also allows an insurer to be more selective with respect to picking providers who demonstrate efficient practice patterns. This can generate significant savings through lower utilization levels, if medical efficiency criteria are used in the selection or building process.

Medical efficiency can be evaluated using either clinical reviews or analytical methods. Clinical reviews involve health care professions, such as physicians or nurses, reviewing the treatment decisions and care provided to individual patients as documented in the hospital or clinic patient charts. These types of reviews can be expensive, time consuming, and, some argue, subjective.

Due to the drawbacks of clinical reviews, there has been a dramatic growth in the use of analytical methods. A key issue when trying to compare the medical efficiency levels of different providers is the need to adjust for differences in health status or severity in the patients they treat. Analytical methods often involve the use of risk assessment models or episode grouping software. Diagnosis based risk assessment models, such as the Diagnostic Cost Groups (DCGs) or Adjusted Clinical Groups (ACGs), adjust for differences in the health status of the members. (These models are discussed in more detail in the chapter on health risk adjustment.) Episode grouping software groups together all the care provided to a patient that related to a particular episode of treatment. These models then classify the episodes into clinically distinct groups.

Contracting Entities

Increasingly, health care providers are forming various types of organizations for the purpose of sharing risk and contracting with insurers. Insurers are often faced with decisions regarding whether they should contract through such an organization or contract and negotiate directly with the individual providers.

These organizations may bring together providers with various characteristics, such as type of provider, physician specialty, level of care, and geographic area. These organizations may include only hospitals, only physicians, or both hospitals and physicians. For example, a hospital consortium represents a collection of hospitals that band together for purposes of contracting with health plans and to coordinate care. The consortium may bring together similar hospitals to cover a particular geographic region, or it may bring together dispersed primary care hospitals with a centrally located tertiary hospital. Physician networks may include primary and specialty physicians, or may represent only selected physician specialties. An integrated delivery system is a physician-hospital organization (PHO) that has the capability to deliver comprehensive medical services within their network.

There are advantages and disadvantages in contracting with such provider organizations. Advantages may include the ability to sign up a large number of providers with a single contract, a ready made set of providers that are coordinated geographically or by type of service, greater ability to shift risk if the provider organization is set up to accept and share risk, and perhaps better coordination of care.

Disadvantages may include less negotiation leverage (with lower discounts) since it is a larger organization, the possible need to pay an access fee for use of a ready-made network, and the inability to sub-select only the most efficient and high quality providers. Furthermore, the provider organization may have limitations on its ability to negotiate on behalf of its constituent providers, and it may be difficult for the provider organization to reach a decision due to the diverse interests of their members. If thinly capitalized, the provider organization may have solvency problems if it accepts risk without passing it on to the actual entities that provide the care, such as the hospital. Also, in the future, the provider organization could switch to a different insurer or may form its own insurance company, taking the membership with them. Frequently, such provider organizations rely on the health plan to perform special reporting and analysis in order for the provider organization to perform its own provider reimbursement and analysis.

Provider organizations vary dramatically in terms of their level of integration and their cohesiveness. The degree of financial and operational integration may affect whether an insurer decides to negotiate with the provider organization or with each individual provider separately. For example, a hospital which owns a series of primary care clinics may be much easier to negotiate with than a physician-hospital organization (PHO) where the physicians own their own practices and the only thing that binds them together is a relatively modest capital investment in the PHO. Similarly, a physician group practice is typically much more cohesive than a network of independent physicians.

Health plans may contract directly with individual physicians, or indirectly through intermediary entities. The intermediary entities include group medical practices, independent physician associations (IPAs), physician-hospital associations (PHOs), and other arrangements.

Target Reimbursement Levels

An insurer should have a clear idea of their target reimbursement levels when setting up a network. Two opposing factors affect the choice of the target reimbursement levels. First, higher reimbursement levels may endanger competitive premium rates. Second, there is a need to pay a competitive reimbursement level to providers, in order to have a reasonable portion of the providers sign-up for the network.

Two types of analyses are typically done in setting the target reimbursement levels. The first analysis is a study of existing regional managed care reimbursement levels in the particular geographic area. The source data for this may come from provider fee surveys, regulatory filings, consultants, experience reports for employers used in underwriting new groups, and brokers. Second, is a projection of premium rates, and the resulting enrollment, based on various scenarios for reimbursement levels. The relationship of the projected premium rates to those of the competitors will affect the marketability of the product and the expected enrollment.

Current Referral Patterns

Health care providers have existing relationships, formal and informal, with other providers. These determine where they send their patients for care that they can not provide directly. For example, physicians may have admitting privileges at one or more hospitals, which essentially limit the hospitals to which they can admit their patients. Also, many primary care physicians may have established informal referral patterns, recommending particular specialists for their patients.

It is advantageous for a network to incorporate or build on existing referral and admission patterns. The advantages include less operational hassles, a higher proportion of utilization in-network, and greater physician satisfaction with the health plan and its operation. This must be counterbalanced by the need to limit the number of hospitals and specialists that are in the network in order to assist negotiating competitive reimbursement levels.

MANAGING NETWORK PERFORMANCE

The three dimensions of network performance are cost, quality, and member satisfaction. Managed care plans use various techniques to try to maximize these performance measures. The techniques include the following:

- Selection and retention of providers
- Negotiated reimbursement levels and methods
- Utilization management

Each of these techniques is discussed below.

SELECTION AND RETENTION OF PROVIDERS

Health plans seek to select and retain high quality, efficient providers. Most health plans consider physician selection and retention as a critical factor in the success of the health plan. We shall outline some criteria used by health plans in selecting providers, information used to decide which providers should be renewed, and strategies for selecting a network. Of course, the selection and retention of providers should also reflect the various overall considerations listed earlier under the section on "Considerations in Establishing a Network."

Selection Criteria

In selecting physicians, health plans review a variety of qualitative and quantitative information. The review process may include credentialing, office evaluation, medical record review, and analysis of utilization or cost data. Each of these steps is described below, as they are applied in the selection of physicians. Similar steps and processes are used in selecting other health care professionals and in selecting hospitals.

Credentialing involves reviewing and verifying the credentials of the physician, such as their training, licensure, specialty certification, hospital privileges, and malpractice insurance history. Nearly all health plans perform basic credentialing which includes verifying that the physician is licensed and has the appropriate credentials to practice. Many health plans also check for disciplinary actions or substance abuse problems.

An *office evaluation* typically involves a visit to the physician's office to evaluate the ambiance of the office, accessibility for patients, and in-office service capabilities. This might include looking at office hours and the appointment book to check the capacity to take on more patients and ability to provide timely appointments. An office evaluation tends to be more commonly used by HMOs than PPOs.

Some health plans review a sampling of *medical records*. This might be done by the medical director or by an outside clinical consultant. The purpose of the review is to analyze the physician's practice pattern with respect to quality and cost-efficiency. Issues concerning confidentiality must be clarified before examining patient records.

Some health plans *review utilization or cost data* in selecting physicians for a network. However, this approach is limited in that many health plans do not have access to a credible volume of data for a given provider. Also, there is some controversy regarding such "economic credentialing" due to its limitations and the potentially negative impact on quality of care. Due to these factors, most health plans put a minor importance on utilization and cost data during the *initial* selection process. Health plans tend to put more emphasis on subjective, qualitative information in judging practice patterns and focus on selecting physicians who are flexible and receptive to managed care principles.

Also, if the appropriate data is available, health plans may review what portion of their inforce members currently are utilizing the provider.

Renewal of Contracts

Health plans use a variety of information in deciding whether to renew contracts with providers. For physicians, the renewal process typically involves recredentialing and review of performance information. The sources for the performance information include: quality review, consumer complaints, profiling, and consumer surveys.

Health plans like to keep physician turnover as low as possible. Large employers often look at physician turnover rates in judging the performance of a health plan. High rates of turnover tend to indicate that physicians are unhappy with the plan or that the plan did not do a very good job in selecting physicians in the first place. High rates of turnover also result in problems with member relations since most members do not like to change physicians.

Strategies for Selecting a Network

There are a variety of strategies employed in constructing provider networks. The strategies may be referred to as "careful selection," "prune later," and "broad as feasible."

Many plans prefer to carefully select physicians from the outset in order to achieve a cohesive and reasonably small network that the health plan can work with efficiently. Also, it tends to be more difficult to non-renew a provider than just not to select that provider in the first place. The "prune later" approach is typically coupled with a broad initial selection. This strategy reflects that careful selection at the outset can be very time consuming and useful data very limited. A broad network initially will also help encourage rapid enrollment growth. However, if a significant number of physicians are "pruned" later, there may be significant member and customer dissatisfaction. Furthermore, providers may be litigious when involuntarily removed from a network.

Health plans may employ different strategies for physicians versus hospitals or by type of physician specialty. For example, a health plan may use the "broad as feasible" approach for selecting primary care physicians due to their marketing value and a "careful selection" approach in setting up an oncology or cardiac care network, due to efficiency and quality concerns.

Specialty Networks

The development of networks for specialty providers is similar in concept and involves similar considerations. However, the relative importance of different considerations can vary depending on the type of provider, which we mean to include chiropractors, mental health providers, and dentists. The factors that drive this variation include local supply and demand, as well as the amount of variability in treatment protocols.

The impact of local supply and demand can vary significantly by type of provider. For example, in many locations, the supply of dentists is considered to be low given the demand. This makes it more difficult to develop dental networks with significant fee discounts. (This can differ significantly from the dynamics for some types of physicians and hospitals where the supply might exceed demand.) Due to difficulty in negotiating significant discounts for dental services, a dental network often does not add as much relative value as a physician network.

Some of the specialty providers listed above are involved in providing care that, in some people's opinion, involves more discretion, more variability in practice patterns, and more difficulty in assessing the value of the care provided. Due to these considerations, as part of the network development it can be worthwhile to put more effort into the selection and profiling of these providers.

Negotiated Reimbursement

Health plans use negotiated reimbursement arrangements to help control costs and to improve quality and member satisfaction. Cost control comes through negotiating discounts from current payment levels and through financial incentives to deliver cost-effective care. Increasingly, quality and member satisfaction measures are also being emphasized with financial incentives for providers.

Cost Control

Provider networks typically involve negotiated fee arrangements, including the following types of arrangements:

- Discounted fee-for-service
- Fee schedule
- Variable fee schedule (fee schedules move up or down for each provider, based on actual experience versus target, sometimes called "retrospective capitation")
- Bonuses and withholds
- Per diem
- Per case (per admission or per visit to emergency room, for example)
- Global rates (incorporate hospital and physician charges in one rate)
- Case rate per episode of care (sometimes called "encounter capitation")
- Capitation

Some of these fee arrangements are described in more detail in the chapter entitled "The Pricing of Managed Care Plans and Capitation Programs."

In designing the reimbursement approach for a network, there are a number of important factors that should be considered, including the overall impact and interplay of the financial incentives, the need for risk adjustment, and acceptable levels of risk for providers.

It is important that the financial incentives be coordinated and monitored to avoid cost shifting and other perverse incentives which don't encourage lower *overall* costs and which may impair quality.

As providers assume greater risk, there is greater need for risk adjustment that goes beyond age and gender. Some health plans are implementing risk adjustment which recognizes health status.

Provider entities that are capitated but don't provide all the required services themselves may have significant solvency risk.

Traditionally, capitation and similar risk sharing approaches were limited to systems where the member chose a primary care physician (PCP) or clinic. Some innovative health plans have developed techniques to assign members to a "virtual" PCP for members in non-gatekeeper products. This facilitates performance analysis and provider risk sharing that was previously impossible for such products and networks.

Negotiation Strategies

Health plans achieve leverage in their negotiations through their willingness to leave some providers out of the network and through their ability to direct members to particular providers for care. Providers accept discounted fee levels in order to maintain their market share or to gain market share by being part of the network. Providers accept risk because they perceive themselves to be more efficient than the average provider and, therefore, able to increase their reimbursement by accepting risk.

Health plans use a variety of contracting approaches. Depending on the type of provider or size of the provider, these may include reimbursement offers made on "accept or reject" basis, negotiated reimbursement levels, and requested bids from providers. Generally speaking, when dealing with individual physicians or small groups, the approach is often "accept or reject." When dealing with large medical groups, hospitals, or certain key providers, the health plan often must negotiate or request proposals.

An example of a unique approach is that of a coalition of large employers in Minnesota. The idea was to push competition beyond the level of health plans (which often had overlapping networks and were limited in number) to the level of the providers. First, the coalition requested bids directly from provider-based integrated delivery systems, rather than from the health plans. Primary care physicians could only be part of one delivery system, but hospitals and specialists could be in more than one system. Each member could select any one of the delivery systems. However, the member's employee contribution rate directly depended on which delivery system they picked. Thus, delivery systems were incented to bid as low as possible in order to capture more members.

MANAGEMENT OF PROVIDERS IN CANADA

In Canada, the government provides and finances universal health insurance for all citizens. Each province has its own health insurance program, however, the provincial programs must include some standard features in order to receive the federal subsidy. The provinces use a variety of techniques to manage providers and health care costs, including the following:

- Global hospital budgets
- Physician fee schedules
- Physician utilization controls
- Control of physician supply

Each of these techniques is briefly discussed below.

Note that the process of negotiating hospital and physician reimbursement tends to be very different in Canada than in the U.S. since the provinces are the sole payer. As a result, there is no competitive marketplace with multiple payers each independently negotiating with health care providers. In general, the health care providers must accept whatever the provincial governments are willing to pay.

Global hospital budgets are negotiated each year between the provincial governments and each individual hospital. These budgets cover the operating expenses of the hospital, which are kept separate from capital expenditures. Since the government must approve the funds required to operate any new facility or equipment, the government also controls capital expenditures by hospitals. As a result, highly advanced equipment is much less prevalent and tends to be concentrated in selected hospitals, such as university hospitals. Operating under a fixed budget is similar to being capitated. However, due to the global nature of the budgets, Canadian hospitals have had to face other economic consequences. For example, a hospital may budget for a certain number of elective surgeries. If more than a predetermined number of patients need the procedure, queues result, and patients are ranked according to need. Some policymakers and providers are concerned about adequate capital replenishment.

Physician fee schedules are negotiated between the provincial governments and the provincial medical associations. Physicians are then paid on a fee-for-service basis using the negotiated schedule. Since the government is the only payer, a monopsony exists and the negotiations are somewhat one-sided. If medical associations feel the fee levels are inadequate, they have the option of striking. Due to the use of a fee-for-service payment mechanism, utilization controls are important in controlling overall health care costs.

Utilization controls on physician services are employed by some of the provinces. The most common approach involves setting utilization targets and then adjusting fee levels downward if the utilization targets are exceeded. While this mechanism does not control utilization itself, it does control the impact of higher utilization on overall claim costs. Quebec uses a unique approach to control utilization by setting billing caps for physicians. If the physician exceeds the cap in a particular quarter, the physician's fees are reduced by 75% for the remainder of the quarter. Such low fee levels financially discourage providing more services than necessary to reach the cap.

The *physician supply* is controlled by provinces through their control over the funding of medical schools. Also, the provinces have emphasized primary care educational programs rather than specialty training.

REFERENCES

Graig, Laurene A., *Health of Nations: Second Edition.* Washington D.C.: Congressional Quarterly Inc., 1993.

47   MEDICAL CARE MANAGEMENT

Alison Johnson

INTRODUCTION

The medical management of healthcare has been an important part of insurance company functions since the advent of HMOs. There are a variety of opinions about the effectiveness and even the appropriateness of this kind of care management by insurers. An understanding of medical management methods and their likely impacts can help actuaries as they analyze and model aspects of healthcare cost and utilization.

This chapter begins by describing the history of medical management practices. Descriptions of medical management practices such as utilization and case management are next, including checks lists of key parts of various programs.

A discussion of current topics and trends, including the rising prevalence of chronic illness, concern over medical errors, return on investment (ROI) for medical management activities and behavioral health and pharmacy issues complete the chapter.

HISTORY OF MEDICAL MANAGEMENT

Medical management of patient care is rooted in early arrangements which combined insurance financial risk and medical care delivery. In the 1930's, physicians offered prepaid medical care to groups of people, primarily construction, mining, railroad and utility workers and their families.

Eventually unions, granges, cooperatives and benevolent societies took over the organizing function from physicians. They collected dues from

993

members, and assumed the administrative functions of membership management, such as establishing eligibility and tracking enrollment. These organizations also began to formalize relationships with doctors and hospitals through contracts.

Insurance companies began hiring nurses in the 1970's to review claims. Their charge was to review claims for correct billing, and for the medical necessity of tests and procedures. This function has evolved to include assisting health plan members manage their health issues and promoting healthy lifestyle choices.

Studies are currently underway to accurately measure the clinical and financial impact of medical management activities. Measuring return on investment (ROI) has become increasingly important as health care costs continue to rise.

Medicaid programs in the U.S. offer medical management services through a variety of state initiatives. Managed care is now the dominant delivery system in Medicaid, offered in 47 states. In addition, Medicare, the federal health insurance program for US citizens over age 65 and certain other classes of citizens, has offered managed care programs for many years. These managed care programs continue to evolve.

MEDICAL MANAGEMENT

Medical Management is comprised of a set of activities and programs the health plan delivers or administers to control the cost and assure the quality of the health care members receive. Typical programs include:

- Utilization Management,
- Case Management,
- Disease Management. and
- Wellness

The first medical management programs were developed to contain rising medical costs. These programs were labeled "Utilization Management" or "Utilization Review." These programs include precertification, admission notification, concurrent review, referral management and retrospective review. They were helpful in standardizing care and expectations among the provider and member communities.

The next wave of medical management programs included Case Management (CM). These programs paired a Registered Nurse (RN) with a high cost member to help the member make health care choices and stay healthy. Programs include catastrophic CM, maternity management and transitional CM.

Disease Management programs are a newer form of case management, concentrating on the care of people with chronic illness such as cardiac disease, diabetes and end stage renal disease.

Prevention Programs, such as immunization drives, healthy diet programs and cancer screening focus on preventing illness or promoting early detection of disease.

Demand Management Programs provide immediate services to members when they need them. Nurse phone lines are the most familiar form of demand management programs.

Wellness programs identify health risk factors such as smoking and obesity and work directly with members to reduce these risks factors before disease and illness develop.

UTILIZATION MANAGEMENT

Utilization Management (UM) or Utilization Review (UR) are the best know types of medical management programs and have the longest history. Physicians and hospitals are required to call the insurance company prior to a member receiving certain high cost services; services that may not be medically necessary, or services that may be excluded from insurance coverage. The insurance company checks to be sure that the member is currently enrolled, checks available benefits and, if warranted, established the medical necessity for the procedure. Typical areas for utilization review include:

- Hospital admissions
- Referral to a specialist physician
- Expensive Durable Medical Equipment (DME)
- Expensive scanning technology (PET and MRI)
- Cosmetic surgery
- Alternative therapies

Two things fueled the move to utilization review:

- Observable differences in utilization patterns across physicians and across hospitals
- Insurance company certificates of coverage that included 'medical necessity' as requirement for coverage.

PRECERTIFICATION

Precertification Programs require providers (hospitals, physicians and others) to obtain approval for services from the insurance company before those services are provided to members. Some common forms of precertification include referral to a specialist physician, elective surgery, and expensive Durable Medical Equipment.

SPECIALTY REFERRALS

Treatment by a physician who specializes in one area of medicine is generally more expensive than treatment by primary care physicians. Specialists are able to contract with insurance companies for higher rates. There may also be additional expenses associated with the transfer of medical records and redundancy if tests needed for diagnosis are repeated at the specialist's office. For these reasons, insurance companies may require physicians' offices to receive authorization before sending a member to a specialist.

For example, a physician may notify the insurance company of his/her intention to refer a patient to a dermatologist for treatment of a persistent rash. It is rare for insurance companies to deny payment for specialty visits. However, they may note how often primary care doctors make referrals and encourage them to obtain training and provide more services in their own office.

ELECTIVE SURGERY

If a hospital admission is pre-planned, such as elective surgery, the doctor's office will initiate a call or fax to the insurance company. They will identify the member and the type of surgery that is planned. The insurance company nurse will check that the patient is still a member of the health plan, and that the requested surgery is covered by their policy. She may also be required to determine if the requested surgery is medically necessary. This can be a few simple questions on the telephone or an extensive review of the patient medical records. Here are a few examples:

A doctor's office faxes to the insurance company a referral for a patient to obtain a wheel chair. The insurance company clerk check to see if the patient's policy includes coverage for wheel chairs. The doctor's office and the member are notified in writing of the coverage, including any specified vendors from whom the wheel chair must be purchased.

A doctor's office calls the insurance company because they want to schedule a patient for breast reduction surgery. This type of surgery can be performed for medical reasons, such as back and shoulder pain, or for cosmetic reasons only. The nurse requests medical records from the clinic. She reviews the records, comparing them to the insurance company guidelines for this procedure. She has the authority to approve the surgery, if it meets the guidelines. If the proposed surgery does not meet medical necessity guidelines, she will refer the case to the insurance company medical director, who will call the surgeon and discuss alternatives for this patient.

For cosmetic surgery, such as breast reductions, the insurance company nurse will gather information that will help her determine if there is a medically justifiable reason for the surgery, such as a history of back or shoulder pain likely caused by overly large breasts. The history of medical problems and the amount of breast tissue to be removed are frequently used to determine if the surgery is medically required or cosmetic. The patient's past medical records, sometimes including photographs are sent to the insurance company for review.

DURABLE MEDICAL EQUIPMENT (DME)

DME includes medical equipment intended for use more than once or twice. Items for home use such as wheel chairs, scooters, crutches, hospital beds and artificial limbs are considered durable. Bandages, syringes and colostomy supplies, because they are used once are non-durable medical equipment. Issues in utilization management for DME include:

Rent vs. Purchase

The insurance company may need to decide whether it is best to rent or lease equipment, or to purchase it for members. Some items, such as hospital beds are typically used for a short time and so are rented or leased. Other items such as artificial limbs are used for a very long time, and are purchased.

Review List

Some DME items are of such low cost that it does not make sense, from a business perspective to review these items. Most companies establish a minimum dollar threshold, and do not review equipment purchases below that amount.

Timing

This controversial issue deals with when items are purchased. Insurance companies are reluctant to purchase or lease equipment in anticipation of member needs, as those needs may change, the member may change insurance plans, or the member may die. Typical items for DME review include:

- Wheel chairs
- Electric scooters
- Oxygen equipment
- Hospital beds
- Insulin pumps
- Orthotics over $300

EXPENSIVE SCANNING TECHNOLOGY (MRI AND PET SCANS)

A variety of less invasive but very expensive scanning technologies have become available in recent years. All of these technologies allow physicians to obtain a detailed look at the inside of the human body without a surgical incision, an important advance in diagnosing diseases and disorders without the need for exploratory surgery.

X-ray-based computerized tomography (CT) Scans were the first of this type of imaging to be introduced in the early 1970's. Magnetic Resonance Imaging (MRI) became widely available in the late 1980's and 1990's. The newest technology is Positron Emission Tomography (PET) scans. They have been available as a diagnostic tool since the late 1990's.

These scans are expensive, and health plans frequently add the most recent (and most expensive) technology to their utilization review lists. They may require prior authorization of the use of these procedures, or may review and discuss overuse with individual physicians. MRIs are about twice the cost of CT scans, and Pet scans can be two or three times more expensive than MRIs.

ADMISSION NOTIFICATION

Admission notification systems require that the hospital or member notify the insurance company when the member is unexpectedly hospitalized. Since most hospitalizations are not pre planned, these programs are an important source of information for the health plan. Typically, a clerk at the hospital notifies the health plan Utilization Management Department by leaving a voice mail or faxing a list of all health plan members who have been hospitalized each day, including Saturday and Sunday. Utilization Management nurses from the health plan can then work with the hospital to assure that members receive efficient care, and help arrange for any needed medical services after discharge.

ADMISSION AVOIDANCE

Health Plan admission avoidance programs focus on preventing the need for hospital admissions among their members. Typically, the first step in developing such a program is analysis of admission rates per 1000, and comparison of those actual rates to expected rates. This analysis is used to identify diagnoses that are suitable targets for admission avoidance. The types of diagnoses identified direct the strategies the health plan chooses. Here are some examples:

Surgical Diagnoses

Analysis may indicate that many more hysterectomies are performed than would be expected for the population. The health plan can review evidence based literature about indication for surgery, and share this information with physicians. Pre-certification programs for selected elective surgeries reinforce the need to assure that members have met surgical need criteria before surgery is scheduled.

Chronic Conditions

Some chronic conditions, such as diabetes and congestive heart failure, may result in frequent visits to the emergency department and hospital admissions. Better outpatient support by nurse call lines, patient education, and other clinic based programs help patients achieve control over their disease, and avoid hospital admissions.

Social Admissions

Patients are sometime admitted to the hospital because a relatively minor health issue cannot be safely handled, due to special social circumstances, such as homelessness or mental illness. Strengthening the Emergency Department's ability to assist with social issues can also avoid hospital admissions.

CONCURRENT REVIEW

Nurses who perform concurrent review follow the patient's care while they are in the hospital. They review the care the patient is receiving, compare that care to national benchmarks and encourage, or sometimes insist on efficient care and timely discharges. This is perhaps the most controversial of all utilization management activities. Table 47.1 summarizes some of the issues in concurrent review programs.

These competing interests can cause friction between insurance companies, hospital administrators and doctors. In the best situations, all three groups work together to assure that patients receive safe and efficient care.

Table 47.1

	Issues in Concurrent Review of Hospital Stays
Insurance Company Perspective	• Services – Hospital care may duplicate diagnostic testing or other services that the member has already received as an outpatient.
	• Efficiency – Services to members may be delayed due to hospital scheduling choices. For example, non emergent surgery may not be available as the hospital is reluctant to incur overtime costs for bringing in a surgical crew after hours.
Hospital Perspective	• Services – It can be difficult or impossible to obtain timely information from doctor's office and labs that are not open after hours or on weekends. Many hospitals deliver most of the diagnostics tests in their area. Labs and clinics should be coordinating with them.
	• Efficiency – Overall hospital efficiency is more important than efficient case by case management.
	• Discharges – Timely patient discharge may depend on factors outside the hospital's control, such as the availability of nursing home beds or home health care.
Physician	• Services – Hospital services are provided according to the physician's orders. Typically, however, the physician has no financial interest or liability for those services.
	• Efficiency – The physician's personal efficiency is more important than hospital efficiency, or the efficient delivery of care for just one case. The physician delivers most care in the clinic, visiting the hospital patients once or twice each day.
	• Coordination of Care – The physician typically cares for the patient across all settings (clinic, hospital, nursing home)

Example

A hospital faxes a list to the insurance company of all members admitted to their hospital in the past 24 hours. The insurance company nurse reviews the list and calls the utilization review nurse at the hospital, asking for an update on the clinical status of all patients. The nurses discuss the cases, reviewing any barriers to safe and efficient care, and make plans for care delivery, communication with the patient and family, and for coordination of the next phase of care. Clinical guidelines often form the basis for this conversation.

The insurance company nurse checks the member's benefits and may suggest referral to special case management or disease management services offered by the plan. If needed, she will advise the hospital nurse of providers such as home care agencies and nursing homes that are in the insurance company network. The hospital nurse then handles communication with the physician, patient and family.

RETROSPECTIVE REVIEW

Retrospective review is a review of medical records after services have been delivered to the patient. Insurance companies and government agencies such as Medicare and Medicaid perform these reviews to search for quality of care issues, billing errors or unnecessary services. Retrospective reviews are often a cornerstone of fraud and abuse detection. Computer analysis of billing and claims patterns may be used to select charts for retrospective review.

The provider may be required to copy the medical record and send it to the reviewing agency, or the provider may be required to provide space for an on site review of records.

CASE MANAGEMENT

Case Management programs help members manage their own heath and navigate the health care system. Case Management can be an informal system, as when a clinic RN helps members with complex problems, or a very formal system implemented by an organ transplant program.

Case Management means delivering a set of personalized services to a person to improve their health. It's not a random event, delivered when a patient in trouble is 'discovered,' but a planned approach to finding and helping people that would fall through the cracks without some special attention.

There are four steps in case management:

1. *Screen* for people appropriate for the program.
2. *Plan and deliver care*, using standard approaches.
3. *Evaluate the plan's effectiveness* for each person, and rework it as necessary.
4. *Evaluate the overall program effectiveness*, and make necessary changes.

SCREENING

The purpose of screening is to find the people who will benefit from the case management program.

The usual problem with screening programs are that they identify people who will benefit only marginally from case management, or identifying people too late, after a preventable hospitalization, or other serious medical event.

A screening program must be easy to administer, and should screen 1% to 5% of the population for case management. Some screening programs rely on a questionnaire, completed after enrollment or at the first doctor's visit. Other screening programs review claims data, searching for specific diagnosis or utilization patterns.

PLAN AND DELIVER CARE

The case manager does not deliver care directly, but assures that the patient is receiving efficient and effective care. One key tool is a standard set of guidelines that help the case manager determine the ideal treatment for each patient. Another tool is exceptional knowledge of community and health plan resources. Telephone assessment skills are also essential.

EVALUATE THE PLAN'S EFFECTIVENESS

An effective plan balances outcomes in four areas:

- Cost and utilization
- Clinical outcomes
- Functional outcomes
- Customer satisfaction

These four areas should be balanced to achieve optimal outcomes for the patient. Many patient chose to trade off clinical outcomes for better functional outcomes. The case manager is usually the one who keeps an eye on the finances, communicating with the member's health plan about covered benefits. Many case managers take a 'total financial picture' approach, helping the member view their personal finances, health plan benefits and community resources together, so that wise choices can be made.

A Return on Investment (ROI) analysis is frequently performed during program evaluation. The use of the term "ROI" in this context can mean a different measure than what is typically used by actuaries in profitability analysis. In this context, the total cost of the program (mostly nurses' salaries) is compared to the program's savings. It is difficult to measure the financial return of case management, because changes in health care costs over time cannot be assumed to be the result of only the case manager's intervention. Consequently, there is no standard, accepted method for calculating the savings from case management. Typically, the case management department manager and the finance department will develop an agreed upon method for counting savings that includes assumptions about the case manager's impact on the members' use of emergency department, hospital inpatient, and other medical services. The nursing shortage has resulted in increased nursing salaries, driving up the cost of Case Management. Case Management programs are receiving close financial scrutiny as a result.

EVALUATE THE PROGRAM'S OVERALL EFFECTIVENESS

This last step is an annual event, meant to examine the case management steps together. The program manager assesses the outcomes to identify:

- Is your screening program finding people appropriate for your program?
- What has been learned from planning and delivering care? What kind of aggregate patient results are being produced?

Program evaluation is followed by planned program changes in a continuous improvement cycle.

Case Managers are usually Registered Nurses, but may also be social workers or occupational health professionals. Case Managers can become certified in case management as a specialty by passing a certification exam.

Case Managers may work for a heath insurance company, for a hospital or clinic or for an employer.

Insurance case managers generally focus on coordinating a variety of services for members, and are frequently charged with managing the member's benefits in a manner that conserves the health plan dollars and assures that the members receive the care they need. Typical work includes:

- Checking benefit coverage levels.
- Negotiate special rates with non-contracted providers, if possible.
- Recommend exceptions to current coverage in lieu of more expensive services.
- Coordinating referrals to specialty care so that all or most care is delivered within the insurance company network.
- Suggesting and arranging for special services.
- Coordinating insured care with community services.
- Coordinating payment with other payers, such as Medicaid and Automotive insurers.

Hospital and clinic case managers coordinate services for people while they are seeking services at the clinic or hospital. Their duties include:

- Checking coverage with the insurance company to assure appropriate payment for the clinic or hospital.
- Coordinate the services needed immediately to affect a safe hospital discharge or return home from the clinic.
- Education of the patient about their medical condition and how to better care for themselves.
- Follow-up telephone calls after the patient has received services at their hospital or clinic.
- Close coordination of services among various providers, as care is being delivered.

Employer based case managers are present when large groups of people work together and services can be delivered on site. The focus of their work is to promote health among the worker, reducing work absences. Clinic and industrial health nurses may also work at the site of employment, providing basic medical services to ill or injured workers. The case manager's work includes:

- Monitoring reasons for employee work absences.
- Follow-up with workers after health related work absences.

- Education programs for groups and individuals.

- One-on-one assistance for people with chronic illnesses or special conditions.

- Work site wellness programs.

CATASTROPHIC CASE MANAGEMENT

These case management programs focus on people who have experienced catastrophic health care changes, or who's claims expense have reached stop loss thresholds. Many times both of these events have happened.

Typical diseases include End Stage Renal Disease (ESRD), conditions that require organ transplantation, some cardiac conditions, some cancer treatments and many terminal illnesses.

During this time, a person may be very ill, bewildered by the treatment choices, overwhelmed by the possible consequences, and having to travel long distances to receive specialty care. Catastrophic case managers can help people make choices, receive emotional support, conserve resources and return to independence. These case managers generally work closely with family members, as catastrophically ill people may be unable to participate fully in all of these activities.

MATERNITY CASE MANAGEMENT PROGRAMS

These programs are generally aimed at getting pregnant women, especially women at risk for poor pregnancy outcomes into prenatal care as early in their pregnancy as possible.

The Case Manager's role in maternity case management is:

- Identify pregnant women early, generally through reporting from physician offices and member outreach.

- Telephone contact with women to ask them questions that may identify a high risk pregnancy.

- Periodic telephone calls to encourage medical care, smoking cessation, good nutrition and attendance at prenatal classes.

- Closer follow-up and physician office coordination for women with high risk pregnancies.

Table 47.2 summarizes some key points about maternity case management.

Table 47.2

Key Points about Maternity Case Management
• Better birth outcomes are generally defined as less prematurity, less neonatal mortality, fewer neurologic and developmental problems, and fewer cognitive capacity problems (adaptive skills and scholastic performance)
• Low birth weights are closely linked to negative birth outcomes.
• The effectiveness of standard prenatal care in preventing poor birth outcomes is not entirely clear from prior research, but some studies do show a strong positive link.
• The quality of prenatal care (medical tests, type and amount of education, continuity of care) may be more important than the quantity (number and timing of visits)
• The main risk factors for low birth weight babies are previous late term abortion, previous live birth that died, and current unwanted pregnancy.
• Women at higher risk for poor birth outcomes already are higher users of prenatal care.

TRANSITIONAL CASE MANAGEMENT

Transitional case managers specialize in helping people navigate specific cross roads in health. They generally operate in two types of programs:

• Disease focused
• Nursing home or extended care placements

Disease focused case managers support people newly diagnosed with a disease that will require life style modifications, such as diabetes or arthritis. They assist people by providing intense support and education so that people can once again become self sufficient in caring for themselves.

Transitional case managers can also step in when there is a need for a person to be temporarily or permanently placed in a rehabilitation or nursing facility. They can help the patient and family select a facility and make all necessary arrangements. They can also set realistic expectations about if and when a person may be able to return to their former living arrangement.

DISEASE MANAGEMENT

Disease management is one of the recent trends in the managed health care industry. People with some chronic illnesses incur greater health care expenses for diagnostic and monitoring tests, medication and other treatment, and emergency care when their chronic illness is not well controlled.

As a financial risk management tool, health care managers have been seeking ways to reduce the costs and to improve the health status of this group. Disease management varies from handing out a pamphlet to aggressive individual patient management. Table 47.3 summarizes some important aspects for a successful disease management program.

Table 47.3

Important Aspects of Disease Management Programs
• Population Identification process
• Evidence-based practice guidelines
• Collaborative practice model to include physician and support-service
• Risk identification and matching of interventions with need
• Patient self-management education (may include primary prevention, modification programs, and compliance/surveillance)
• Process and outcomes measurement, evaluation, and management
• Routine reporting/feedback loop (may include communication with patient health plan and ancillary providers, and practice profiling)
• Appropriate use of information technology (may include specialized registries, automated decision support tools, and call-back systems)

Disease management is frequently used in chronic disease situations particularly diabetes, asthma and heart disease.

Most disease management programs involve more than simply mailing patient brochures. They include continued coordination and follow up with the primary physician and patient. It can involve telephone, mail and e-mail visits between the disease manager and the patient and physician. For most patients with chronic conditions, there is behavior coaching to help improve medication adherence, diet, risk avoidance (e.g. stop smoking) and exercise.

Many insurance companies contract with vendors to provide disease management services to their members. Other companies develop their own programs.

Here are some of the key aspects of disease management programs.

Population Identification Process

Programs may use a combination of health risk appraisals, claims information, predictive models, member questionnaires and phone calls, referrals from case managers and physicians and other methods for identifying patients for inclusion.

Process for Enrolling, Re-Enrolling, and Dis-Enrolling, and Risk Stratifying Members in the Program

This includes sorting members by severity, age or geographic region, and obtaining member agreement to participate. Enrollment may be annual or continuous, and members may need to be re-assessed and moved between severity groups. If members are likely to recover, a dis-enrollement process will be necessary.

Clinical Information Sources

Information is needed to manage cases. This may include clinical practice guidelines, reference material, access to disease experts, and other clinical information sources. A Disease Management program will also have tools to measure functional status, change readiness, quality of life, compliance or other clinical aspects of care.

Care Delivery Model

Components of the model may include phone calls, visits, telemonitoring, educational materials and other methods for working with enrolled members. Days and hours of service must be established, as well as staff qualifications and case loads. Interventions should be matched with member risk levels, and the program must have a process for managing co-morbid conditions, and for managing primary and secondary risk factors.

Collaborative Practice Model to Include Physician and Support-Service

The program must have methods for interaction and involvement with community primary care physicians and specialists. This may include physician educational efforts, and physician satisfaction and/or complaint data. The program may also have relationships with physicians, hospitals, home care agencies and other providers.

Patient Self-Management Education

This will consist of primary prevention, modification programs, compliance/surveillance process, and automated reminder systems.

Process and Outcomes Measurement, Evaluation, and Management

The program should measure cost and utilization outcomes, member and provider satisfaction, and functional status and quality of life measures. Programs typically include some type of quality assurance and quality improvement process, and may be URAC or NCQA accredited. Internal audit processes are common.

Disease management programs do improve the clinical outcomes of care, but the financial ROI for disease management is difficult to measure. As with case management, it may not be possible to separate the impact of the disease management program from other external factors. Measurement of ROI for disease management programs is discussed in more detail in the section titled "Measuring Return on Investment (ROI)."

Information Technology

An advanced information technology base is required for disease management programs, including specialized registries, automated decision support tools and call-back systems.

Privacy and Confidentiality

Programs must maintain member and provider confidentiality.

Medicare Demonstration Project

Medicare launched a large scale disease management demonstration project in 2004. Medicare members with advanced congestive heart failure, diabetes, and coronary artery disease are offered disease management services and prescription drugs. This project is expected to enroll 300,000 people in three areas of the US. The evaluation of this program is expected to offer significant contributions to the debate about the financial and utilization impact of disease management over time.

WELLNESS

Wellness programs (sometimes also called 'prevention' programs) identify health plan members or employees with higher than average risk factors for the eventual development of illness or disease. Those people are then encouraged, coached, and counseled to adopt healthier life styles. Employers and health plans hope that the reduction of risk factors will result in lower healthcare costs, less missed work time and greater productivity. Modifiable risk factors include lack of regular exercise, smoking, high cholesterol, obesity, high blood pressure, and high alcohol use. The medical costs of people with risk factors can be as much as a third higher than the general population.

It can take a long time for medical cost savings to be realized by the health plan, sometimes many years. Some believe that employers can realize earlier cost savings, when worker absenteeism decreases and productivity increases. Reports from large employers indicate cost savings in the range of $3 to $4 for every $1 invested in wellness programs.

RECENT DEVELOPMENTS AND TRENDS

Several topics have emerged as 'hot topics' in medical management recently. These are areas likely to shape the delivery and financing of care in the near future.

CHRONIC ILLNESS AND THE AGING POPULATION

As the baby boomer population becomes older, reaching 50 and 60 years old, their needs and desires are influencing care delivery and management. Chronic illnesses such as arthritis and diabetes now affect a larger portion of the overall population, as this group ages. New methods to treat and control these chronic illnesses are being developed. This trend is most apparent in the development of drugs and medical devices for chronic ailments.

Many new medications have been developed to treat cardiac conditions, and to treat precursors to heart disease, such as elevated lipid (fat) levels in the blood, or to treat high blood pressure. People may be on these medications for decades.

Medical devices such as insulin pumps for diabetics and implantable defibrillators for certain cardiac patients add to the cost and complexity of medical care.

Chronic illness among the baby boomer generation is expected to continue to fuel the development and marketing of new drugs and medical devices, and the consumer movement in health care that demands more convenient and personalized care.

MEDICAL ERRORS

Errors by medical professionals (primarily doctors and nurses) were highlighted in a report "To Err is Human" by the Institute of Medicine, published in 1999, and their follow-up report "Crossing the Quality Chasm" published in 2001. The first report found that medical errors were a leading cause of death and injury. Projections from two large scale studies estimate that between 44,000 and 98,000 people die in American hospitals as a result of medical errors each year.

These reports have been picked up by the media and widely reported, causing concern by regulatory bodies, consumer groups and the medical profession. The Quality Chasm report offers pointed advice for improving the safety of care, including ten simple rules for care delivery professionals and a list of obstacles and policy remedies. Accreditation bodies such as the Joint Commission on Accreditation of Heathcare Organization (JCAHO) and the National Committee for Quality Assurance (NCQA) are concerned about these issues, as are Hospitals and Integrated Delivery System and doctors and nurses. Many new initiatives have been started as a result of the findings are recommendations of the Institute of Medicine.

MEASURING RETURN ON INVESTMENT (ROI)

Medical Management activities have come under increased financial scrutiny as the overall cost of medical services and the concomitant cost of health insurance, have increased. Actuaries have been called on to help with the measurement of cost savings.

The program cost side of the equation is relatively easy to calculate. This is typically done by combining the nursing costs with department and overhead expenses. The program savings side of the equation, however, is challenging.

Two general methods are used to measure the cost savings due to medical management programs and activities. Control group methods divide a population into a group that is managed and a group that is not. The financial results of the two groups are compared. A second method is the pre/post method. In this method costs for medical care are compared before and after management.

Both methods have strengths and weaknesses. The pre/post method is more popular. This is because populations in need of management are much smaller than the general population. The pre/post method provides a larger group for analysis, as the entire group is compared in two time frames. The other reason is that clinicians and insurers, who are aware that some medical management activities such as disease management, improve the clinical health of members, and they do not want to withhold these services from people in the control group.

Measurement issues with disease management include: (1) regression to the mean, (2) selection bias, (3) statistical validity of the population size, and (4) technological advances or benefit design changes over time.

Disease members may be identified and enrolled in management programs when medical expenses are high. Chronic illness follows a natural course of exacerbation and recovery. Costs are higher during an illness exacerbation. This natural cycle of fluctuating costs can result in the overstatement of savings attributable to the program, if members are identified at the high point of utilization, and recovery would have occurred even without the program.

Diseased people who elect to join a disease management program may have a significantly different utilization pattern than people with the same disease who do not join. If the program's impact is measured by comparing the enrollees to non-enrollees, results may reflect this selection bias.

Only a small portion of the general population has a chronic illness. If the overall population is small, there may not be enough people in the disease management program to allow for a statistically valid analysis.

As costs continue to climb, methods for measuring the impact of medical management programs will continue to be examined, and it is reasonable to expect that standardized methods for financial measurement will emerge.

BEHAVIORAL HEALTH ISSUES

Behavioral health problems include mental illness and alcohol and drug abuse problems. There are several issues developing in the behavioral health area, including:

Treatment for these conditions has not always been covered at the same level as coverage for medical problems. This, in part has lead the U.S. Congress to consider mental health parity legislation that would assure the same coverage for behavioral health treatment as is available for medical treatment.

The medical community has long recognized that medical and behavioral health are related. Treatment for behavioral health conditions is frequently "carved out" and managed by a separate company and a separate group of providers. Sensitivity to the need for confidentiality can mean that the provider groups are not sharing information about the patient and coordinating care. Lack of treatment for behavioral health conditions, such as substance abuse can result in serious and expensive medical conditions, for example, liver failure.

Certain behavioral health diagnoses seem to be increasing. Conditions include attention deficit disorder, Bipolar (Manic Depressive) illness, Depression and Autism. It is unclear whether this is an actual rise in illness, or better diagnosing on the part of physicians.

A variety of new behavioral health treatment have become available, including new potent medications, residential treatment facilities and many intensive and lengthy treatments, sometimes lasting many hours several days per week.

The expectation is that costs for behavioral health problems will increase a result of these many factors.

REFERENCES

A Brief History of Managed Care. Tufts Managed Care Institute.

Altman, Drew E. and Larry Levitt, "The Sad History of Health Care Cost Containment As Told In One Chart," *Health Affairs*, January 23, 2002.

Berwick, Donald M., "A User's Manual for the IOM's 'Quality Chasm' Report," *Health Affairs*, Vol. 21, No. 3, May/June 2002.

Crossing the Quality Chasm: A New Health System for the 21ˢᵗ Century. Washington, D.C.: National Academy Press, 2001.

Disease Management Accreditation and Certification. NCQA, 2001.

History of Managed Care. NCMIC Chiropractic Solutions. http://www.ncmic.com/cmicins/doctorsofchiro/practicetools/ managedcaresln/ history.asp [05/30/2002].

Medicare Medical Review Program: Pay it Right. Medicare Medical Review. http://www.hcfa.gov/medicare/mr/[06/14/2002].

Peeno, Linda, MD. *Presentation to the Romanow Commission on the Future of Health Care in Canada.* Louisville, KY, May 31, 2002.

Reeder, Linda, RN, CM, CNA, MBA. *Anatomy of a Disease Management Program.* Nursing Management, April 1999. http://www.nursingmanagement.com

To Err Is Human: Building a Safer Health System. Washington, D.C.: National Academy Press, 2000.

"Disease Management Programs: What's the Cost?" *Issue Brief, American Academy of Actuaries* [April 2005].

ABOUT THE PRINCIPAL EDITOR

WILLIAM F. BLUHM, FSA, MAAA, FCA

The principal editor of *Group Insurance*, Bill Bluhm, is a Principal and Consulting Actuary with Milliman USA in Minneapolis. Bill joined that firm in 1983, when he opened the Albany office with a new practice, and has been in Minneapolis since 1987.

Bill works with healthcare providers, insurers, governments, and others, on matters relating to health care management and group and individual health insurance. He is particularly well-known for his work in antiselection, regulatory matters, and risk-based capital.

Bill's prior publications include a number of papers, including the two award-winning papers "Cumulative Antiselection Theory" (winner of the Society of Actuaries triennial prize in 1980-82, and one of seven papers honored as 'seminal works' in the Society's 50th anniversary monograph), and "The Minnesota Antiselection Model" (winner of the Actuarial Education and Research Fund Practitioners Award in 1991). He is author of another Actex textbook, "Individual Health Insurance," scheduled to be published in 2007. Bill is an active speaker, and serves on many professional committees and Boards of Directors. He has served as President of the Conference of Consulting Actuaries, and is currently President-Elect of the American Academy of Actuaries.

Bill lives in Minnesota with his wife, Christine, and their children, Samantha and Joseph. His interests include cooking, fishing, guitar, and volunteer work for The Mankind Project.

ABOUT THE ASSOCIATE EDITORS

ROBERT B. CUMMING, FSA, MAAA

Bob is Senior Vice President, Actuarial & Underwriting at HealthPartners and President of HealthPartners Insurance Company and HealthPartners Administrators Inc. HealthPartners is an integrated health plan with both medical and dental clinics and a hospital. HealthPartners has about 10,000 employees, 750,000 members and $2 billion in annual revenue. Bob focuses on market and product strategy, process improvement, and sales efforts.

Prior to joining HealthPartners, Bob was a Principal at Milliman USA. His area of expertise is managed healthcare programs. He assisted clients in the areas of risk analysis and predictive modeling, underwriting process improvement, Medicaid rate setting, product development and network evaluation, and regulatory filings. Bob has advised Blue Cross/Blue Shield plans, HMOs, healthcare providers, governmental agencies, insurance companies, and employers.

Bob is a graduate of the University of Minnesota; is a Fellow of the Society of Actuaries and a Member of the American Academy of Actuaries.

ALAN D. FORD, FSA, MAAA

Al Ford, Fellow of the Society of Actuaries and Member of the American Academy of Actuaries, is an independent consultant in Hampton, New Jersey. Al has extensive experience in the health insurance industry, having served as Senior Vice President and Chief Actuary for a major health insurance company.

Al has been a member of the American Academy of Actuaries Health Practice Council, the Actuarial Standards Board and the Society of Actuaries Research Committee. He is also the chairperson for the Fellowship portion of the Society of Actuaries' education redesign program.

Al is a graduate of Bucknell University with a BS degree in Mathematics. He has worked on the Society's Education and Examination Committee, serving as the General Chair in 1996-97. He has also served as a faculty member for the Society's Fellowship and Associate Admissions Courses.

JERRY E. LUSK, MAAA, FCA

Jerry Lusk is Chairman of the Board at Blue Cross Blue Shield of Montana. Jerry was previously a consulting actuary with the Atlanta office of Milliman USA, Inc. He joined Milliman originally in 1977 and again in 1989, after serving as Chief Financial Officer and Chief Actuary at Blue Cross Blue Shield of Georgia. He has more than 30 years of actuarial experience. Jerry was also the Principal responsible for the Health Insurance Consulting Practice in the Atlanta office from 1989 to 2004.

Jerry is a Member of the American Academy of Actuaries, and a Fellow of the Conference of Consulting Actuaries. He is a graduate of the University of Colorado with BS degrees in Applied Mathematics and Business Administration. He also received an MBA from the University of Dayton.

PETER L. PERKINS, FSA, MAAA

Peter Perkins retired from the actuarial profession in 2004. Prior to his retirement, he was Vice President and General Manager for Anthem Blue Cross and Blue Shield, previously Trigon Blue Cross Blue Shield, in Richmond, Virginia. Previously Peter was employed by CIGNA and worked in several areas including group health insurance and group pensions.

Peter is past President of the American Academy of Actuaries. He has served as the Academy's Secretary-Treasurer and has been a member of the Academy's Health Practice Council and State Health Committee. He chaired the American Academy of Actuaries Health Organizations Risk-Based Capital Simplification Task Force. He also chaired the Work Group that authored the American Academy of Actuaries Monograph, "Medicare Managed Care Savings, Access and Quality." Peter was a Fellow in the Society of Actuaries and has served on the Society's Group Benefits Examination Committee.

Peter is now a worship leader sharing the gospel of Jesus Christ in song. He also serves on the Older Adults Action Council of the United Way of Richmond Virginia.

Peter is a graduate of the University of Illinois with a B.S. degree in Actuarial Science, Summa cum Laude.

ABOUT THE AUTHORS

KEITH M. ANDREWS

Keith Andrews, President of Andrews Consulting Services, Inc., has been a Compliance Specialist since 1965, and was the group Compliance Officer of a major mid-west insurance company for over 15 years prior to starting his own firm in 1989. ACS is a broad-based life-health and property-casualty compliance consulting firm which provides insurers with product development, research, drafting and filing serves as well as TPA licensing and policy and certificate issue services.

In addition, ACS publishes: Compliance Updates, an annual publication that analyzes state laws, rules, and regulations; Product Filing Guide, a subscription publication that provides comprehensive information on policy filing requirements; and Filing Wizard, a fully automated online filing service.

JOHN C. ANTLIFF, FSA, MAAA, EA

John Antliff is a retired Consulting Actuary in Tucson, Arizona who specializes in Group Long-Term Disability Insurance and other welfare benefits. He served as Chairman of the Preliminary Examination Committee of the Society of Actuaries, and Chairman of the Group Officers Round Table and the Disability Insurance Committee of the Health Insurance Association of America.

JOHN W. BAUERLEIN, FSA, MAAA

John W. Bauerlein is a Principal and Consulting Actuary with Milliman USA in Atlanta, GA. He has 20 years of professional actuarial experience, primarily in the group insurance and employee benefits field. His consulting work focuses on health plan profitability, product strategies, and provider network evaluation. Prior to joining Milliman, John served as the Director of Actuarial Services for PacifiCare Health Systems. Earlier in his career, he worked for a group insurance carrier and a national employee benefits consulting firm. He graduated in 1983 from the University of

1023

California at Los Angeles with a Bachelor of Arts Degree in Applied Mathematics. John earned his FSA designation in 1986.

John has a broad range of group insurance actuarial expertise, specifically in healthcare. He consults regularly with health insurers, HMO's, hospitals, and physician organizations. John also consults to large employers on their health and welfare benefit programs. His recent work has focused on benchmarking provider reimbursement, and communicating network performance to current and potential purchasers of health plan services and products. John is a frequent speaker on these and other related actuarial topics.

ROWEN B. BELL, FSA, MAAA

Rowen Bell is an Actuarial Advisor in the Chicago office of Ernst & Young LLP's Insurance and Actuarial Advisory Services practice. His professional interests center around health insurance financial reporting and solvency management issues. Prior to joining Ernst & Young, Rowen served as Director of Financial Regulatory Services for the Blue Cross Blue Shield Association, and as an officer in the Corporate Actuarial department at Trustmark Insurance.

Rowen has been very active in the activities of the American Academy of Actuaries and currently sits on the Academy's Board of Directors. He has represented the Academy on multiple occasions in discussions with the NAIC, FASB, and AICPA on financial reporting and solvency issues. Rowen is a former Chair of the Academy's Health Practice Financial Reporting Committee and a former Vice-Chair of the Academy's Health RBC Task Force.

Rowen has in an MBA in Finance and Accounting from the University of Chicago's Graduate School of Business. He also has a master's degree in mathematics from the University of Chicago, and a bachelor's degree in mathematics from Queen's University in his native Canada.

GERALD R. BERNSTEIN, FSA

Gerry is a Principal with the Milwaukee office of Milliman USA, Inc. He has been with the firm since 1981.

Gerry's area of expertise is group health care programs, with emphasis on all forms of managed care. He has assisted clients with plan design, pricing, provider reimbursement, experience analysis, financial projections, liability estimation, underwriting, retiree medical projections, and Medicare/Medicaid contracting. Gerry has advised HMOs, PPOs, provider groups, state and local governments, and insurance companies.

Gerry also has extensive experience working with state Medicaid programs, assisting with the development of managed care programs for TANF, SOBRA, SSI elderly, disabled, and at-risk youth populations.

Gerry is a Fellow of the Society of Actuaries and a Member of the American Academy of Actuaries. He earned a bachelor's degree in actuarial science from the University of Wisconsin - Madison.

JAMES T. BLACKLEDGE, FSA, MAAA

James Blackledge is a Senior Vice President with Mutual of Omaha Insurance Company. He manages the Group Financial and Product Management Division within the company's Group Benefit Services strategic business unit. His responsibilities currently include accounting, budget, cost accounting, financial reporting, financial analysis, valuation, reinsurance, strategic business planning and development, business information management, strategic systems development, and product management for certain group health products. James serves on the Board of Directors of the company's HMO, TPA, and health-related holding company subsidiaries. He joined Mutual of Omaha in December of 1989, following a brief stint with Mercer's Kansas City office as a Group Actuarial Analyst.

James is a 1988 graduate of the University of Nebraska at Lincoln with a Bachelor's degree in Finance/Actuarial Science. He became a Member of the American Academy of Actuaries in 1991, and a Fellow in the Society of Actuaries in 1993. He received his Master's degree in Business Administration from Creighton University in 1998.

SHELLY S. BRANDEL, FSA, MAAA

Shelly is Manager of Analytics at Bowers & Associates, Inc. She joined the company in 2006. Shelly is a Fellow in the Society of Actuaries and a Member of the American Academy of Actuaries. She has over ten years of healthcare experience. Shelly received her Bachelor of Science in Mathematics & Statistics from Miami University.

J. HARVEY CAMPBELL, FSA, FCIA, MAAA

Harvey Campbell is the Appointed Actuary for Optimum Reassurance Company and Optimum Re Insurance Company, both subsidiaries of the Optimum Group based in Montreal. His previous experience was with Optimum Life in Paris and with Montreal Life, as a Valuation Actuary.

Harvey is a graduate of the University of Manitoba and McGill University.

JANET M. CARSTENS, FSA, FCA, MAAA

Jan is an Actuary and Consultant with J Carstens Consulting, LLC. She has 25 years of experience in the healthcare industry, with significant experience consulting to a variety of health plans including insurance companies, Blues plans and managed care sponsors on indemnity, PPO, POS and HMO products. Jan has consulted on actuarial, underwriting, financial and other operational aspects to mature health plans as well as start-up operations. She has consulted on commercial coverages, Medicaid, and Medicare. Her specific consulting expertise includes benefit plan design, provider reimbursement and risk sharing arrangements, pricing, rating and underwriting strategies, premium rate filings, reserve adequacy, financial forecasting and reporting, and financial and operational risk assessment.

In addition, Jan has conducted operations reviews to ensure consistency with health plan objectives and industry norms; she has audited segments of a health plans' operations to ensure compliance with regulatory requirements; she has appraised the economic value of health plans for merger or acquisition purposes; she has assessed the competitive market environment for new and existing product offerings; and she has helped health plans analyze cost and utilization trends to assess the effectiveness of various clinical programs and managed care protocols. Jan's prior work experience included managing the Minneapolis and San Francisco health practices of an international consulting firm. During the mid-1990's Jan spent a year in Europe consulting to insurance companies on pricing and rating strategies and managed care concepts. She is a frequent speaker at health industry meetings and has authored several health articles.

STEPHEN T. CARTER, FSA, MAAA, EA, FLMI

Stephen Carter is Vice President of Actuarial Services for Companion Life Insurance Company, a subsidiary of Blue Cross and Blue Shield of South Carolina. Previously, he was Vice President of Product Management for Provident Life and Accident Company. He has been Chairman of the Committee on Health and Group Insurance for the Society of Actuaries, Vice President of the Health Section Council, and President of the Southeastern Actuaries Club.

He holds the degrees of Bachelor of Industrial Engineering from Georgia Institute of Technology and Master of Actuarial Science from Georgia State University.

FRANK CASSANDRA, FSA, MAAA

Frank Cassandra is a Vice President and Actuary with the Metropolitan Life Insurance Company. He currently is the planning officer for MetLife's Institutional Business. In this position, he is responsible for financial plan development, financial analysis, and earnings projections for the division.

Frank joined MetLife in 1986 as an Actuarial Assistant in the Group Insurance Department. He advanced through positions of increasing responsibility, and in 1999 was appointed Vice President and Actuary with responsibility for all pricing and underwriting policy for MetLife's group life insurance and group dental product lines. He has also served as financial officer for MetLife's group disability line. In 1996, Frank was awarded MetLife's Alexander J. Bailie Award for actuarial professionalism and dedication.

Frank received his B.S. degree in Applied Mathematics (summa cum laude) from Polytechnic University, Brooklyn, New York in 1986. He currently resides in Staten Island, New York and Tuckerton, New Jersey.

MALCOLM A. CHEUNG, FSA, MAAA

Malcolm is Vice President of LTC Product & Risk Management for the Prudential Insurance Company of America in Livingston, NJ. His responsibilities include pricing, product development, medical underwriting, claims, regulatory compliance and financial reporting for Prudential's group and individual long term care insurance products.

Prior to joining Prudential, Malcolm worked for John Hancock Mutual Life Insurance Company, where he had more than eight years of experience in their Group Long Term Care division, first as their senior actuary, and then as the vice president of the division. Previously, Malcolm had worked for Metropolitan Life, Phoenix Mutual Life, and Towers-Perrin.

Malcolm received a BA degree in statistics from Princeton University and an MS in statistics from Stanford University. He is a Fellow of the Society of Actuaries, where he is Vice Chairman of the LTC Section Council, and is a member of the American Academy of Actuaries, where he serves on the Federal Long Term Care Task Force. Malcolm is also the Chairman of the ACLI's LTC Policy Committee and a member of AHIP's LTC Committee. He is a frequent public speaker on long term care insurance issues and has twenty-five years of group insurance and employee benefits consulting experience.

KARA L. CLARK, FSA, MAAA

Kara Clark is a Managing Director at the Society of Actuaries, responsible for leading and managing the SOA's Actuarial Marketplace Solutions department in the identification and development of actuarial business solutions to address market challenges and to enable the SOA to best serve its members and stakeholders. She first joined the SOA as the Staff Fellow, Health Benefit Systems, and was then responsible for providing health actuarial content staff support across the organization and specifically to the SOA's Health and Long-Term Care Sections. In her Staff Fellow role, Kara partnered with professional volunteers to develop health actuarial content, promote health actuarial knowledge, and build professional relationships between the health actuarial community and other related disciplines.

Prior to joining the SOA, Kara was an Employee Benefits Consultant with Hewitt Associates. She also has experience with Ernst & Young LLP as a Health Insurance and Health Plan Consultant and in CIGNA's employee benefits division.

JOHN P. COOKSON, JR. FSA, MAAA

John is a principal with the Philadelphia office of Milliman. He joined the firm in 1973.

John's areas of expertise include all aspects of group health insurance and statistical methods for solving actuarial problems. He has substantial experience in trend forecasting, dental insurance, stop loss, and risk analysis. He has also dealt extensively with clients' market strategy problems. John has advised Blue Cross and Blue Shield plans, commercial insurers, HMOs, and PPOs. Recent projects have included the application of risk adjusters to both Medicare/Medicaid risk and commercial experience.

John has experience working with large self-funded employers in areas such as strategic planning, benefit design and pricing, IBNR, financial forecasting, establishment of contingency reserves, and catastrophic claims analysis.

John has written numerous articles and has spoken on a number of insurance topics. He is the publisher of the *Health Cost Index Report*™ and is responsible for the development of the *Health Cost Index Database*™ — tools used by a number of insurers to project their healthcare trends. John also developed the *LOS Efficiency Index* and the *Admission Appropriateness Index*—methods for evaluating the efficiency of hospital utilization. He is also responsible for the initial development of Milliman's *Dental Cost Guidelines* and *Aggregate Stop Loss Net Claim Cost Guidelines*.

John is a Fellow of the Society of Actuaries and a Member of the American Academy of Actuaries. He is past chairman of the Health Section Council and member of the Health Benefits Systems Practice Advancement Committee of the Society of Actuaries, he is also current Chair of Health Section Research Team.

John is a graduate from LaSalle University with a B.A. in mathematics.

PATRICK J. DUNKS, FSA, MAAA

Pat is a Principal with the Milwaukee office of Milliman, Inc. He joined the firm in 1985.

Pat's area of expertise is managed health care programs with emphasis on managed Medicare products. He has assisted clients with Medicare contracting, liability estimation, risk adjustment, medical cost estimates and projections, provider reimbursement strategies, product development, risk-sharing arrangements, provider negotiations, experience analysis, trend analysis, Medicaid contracting, e-health product development, mergers and acquisitions, and managed workers' compensation programs. Pat has advised HMOs, PPOs, hospitals, medical groups, PHOs, Blue Cross / Blue Shield plans, and insurance companies. He is a frequent speaker at managed care industry meetings.

Pat has assisted many managed care organizations with their managed Medicare products. His assistance has ranged from the initial stages of development through successfully managing the products. His extensive Medicare product experience includes assisting many HMOs and provider organizations with Medicare Advantage start-up issues and in understanding and adjusting to CMS' risk-adjusted payments. Pat has also provided input to CMS regarding managed Medicare product issues. His experience includes an actuarial review of the health status risk adjustor methodology for Medicare Advantage organizations as an active participant on an American Academy of Actuaries task force.

Pat is a Fellow of the Society of Actuaries and a Member of the American Academy of Actuaries. He earned a bachelor's degree in mathematics from Saint Norbert College and a master's degree in mathematics from Purdue University.

DOUG FEARRINGTON, FSA, MAAA

Doug serves as Staff Vice President and Actuary with Wellpoint, Inc. He currently leads the Advanced Analytics and Innovation team within Wellpoint's Commercial and Consumer Business Actuarial Division.

Doug has served in a variety of positions spanning many actuarial functions, including pricing & product development, valuation and forecasting, provider network management and evaluation, and data mining.

Doug graduated from the University of North Carolina with a B.S. in mathematical sciences with honors. He lives with his wife Stefanie and sons Asa and Graham in Richmond, VA.

BRUNO GAGNON, FSA, FCIA

Bruno Gagnon is a Consulting Actuary with the Montreal Office of Eckler Ltd. He has been working as a Consultant in the field of actuarial services for more than 25 years, mainly in the areas of group insurance, employee benefits, and social security programs. Prior to consulting, he worked for a life insurance company.

Over the years, Bruno has done consulting for corporate clients regarding the design, implementation, and funding of group insurance plans, including post-retirement benefits. He currently does consulting for employee benefit programs, insurance companies and governments, mainly in the areas of plan design and funding, communications, pricing strategies and rate manuals, reinsurance, social program and legal aspects of group insurance programs.

Bruno has served on the Education and Examination Committees of both the Society of actuaries and the Canadian Institute of Actuaries for the group insurance track. He is currently teaching on the Practice Education Course of the CIA. He also teaches at the Université du Québec á Montréal.

RICHARD J. GLATZ, FLMI

Dick Glatz is an Actuarial Supervisor in the St. Louis office of Milliman, Inc. Since joining the firm in 1990, Dick has assisted clients in designing, pricing, reserving, and financial modeling for a variety of group life and group health products. In addition, he has provided support to insurers in their financial reporting as well as to state departments of insurance in their financial examinations. Prior to joining Milliman, Dick worked for a group of life and property/casualty insurers, focusing on pricing, reserving, and financial reporting for group products. Dick started his career with a life insurer, working on pricing, state compliance, and financial reporting.

Dick holds a BS degree in Statistics from the University of Illinois in Springfield, and also holds the Fellow, Life Management Institute (FLMI) designation.

ERIC P. GOETSCH, FSA, MAAA

Eric is an Actuary with the Milwaukee office of Milliman. He joined the firm in 1994. Eric's area of expertise is managed healthcare programs with an emphasis on Medicare Advantage. He has assisted clients in the areas of strategic analysis, premium and capitation rate development, experience analysis, evaluation of provider reimbursement and risk sharing arrangements, liability estimation, and other actuarial projections. He has worked with managed care organizations, state government agencies, insurance companies, employers, and other organizations.

Eric is a Fellow of the Society of Actuaries and a Member of the American Academy of Actuaries. He earned his Bachelors degree in Mathematics from Marquette University and his Masters degree in Actuarial Science from the University of Wisconsin-Madison.

ROY GOLDMAN, FSA

Roy Goldman was named Senior Vice President and CFO of Geisinger Insurance Operations (GIO) in February 2006. GIO is part of Geisinger Health System in Danville, PA. He is responsible for all financial, actuarial, underwriting, and reporting activities. In his position Roy also plays a key role in establishing strategic direction and goals for the Health Plan as well as helping to integrate the Health Plan with the rest of the Geisinger Health System.

He was previously Vice President and CFO and Chief Actuary of Mercy Health Plans based in St. Louis, MO (1997-2006). From 1995 to 1997, he was Corporate Vice President and Actuary at The Prudential Insurance Company of America. From 1987 to 1995 he served as Senior Vice President/Chief Financial Officer/Chief Actuary for The Prudential HealthCare Group where he was responsible for providing direction and oversight for all strategic, financial, and capital functions for the $11 billion business unit.

Roy holds a Ph.D. in mathematics from Rutgers University and a B.A., Cum Laude, Phi Beta Kappa from Franklin and Marshall College. He is a Fellow of the Society of Actuaries and a member of the American Academy of Actuaries.

Roy has served nearly continuously since 1980 in various capacities in the Society's Education and Examination (E&E) system including serving as General Chairperson in 1994 and on Board task forces for the 2000 and 2005 syllabi revisions. He is co-chair of the 2007 redesign of the Fellowship curriculum for health and group actuaries. He has also served on Society committees dealing with credibility, group and individual disability, and health benefit practices. In 1990 he won the L. Ronald Hill prize for his paper "Underwriting and Pricing Group Disability Income Coverages."

DEBORAH A. GRANT, FSA, MAAA

Deborah is a Principal & Consulting Actuary with Milliman, Inc. She joined the Chicago office of Milliman USA in 1990 after two years as an actuarial student with Benefit Trust Life Insurance Company, now Trustmark.

Deborah specializes in individual health and small-employer group health insurance, with special emphasis in long-term care insurance. She has experience in pricing and plan design, marketing and administrative management, financial reporting and strategic planning and acquisitions. Recently her focus has been in the plan design and valuations for long-term care insurance, both group and individual, with special emphasis on claims adjudication and underwriting for this product line. She was a Physician Assistant before changing careers to become an actuary.

Deborah is a Fellow of the Society of Actuaries and a Member of the American Academy of Actuaries.

AUDREY HALVORSON, FSA, MAAA

Audrey Halvorson joined Premera Blue Cross in July 2000, as Vice President Actuarial, and was promoted to Senior Vice President and Chief Actuary in April 2002. Her position with Premera follows sixteen years with Milliman & Robertson, where she held the position Principal and Healthcare Management Consultant.

While at M&R, Audrey specialized in analyzing the strategic risk arrangements of group healthcare programs to achieve actuarially sound financial arrangements that are integrated with clinically appropriate care programs.

Her current role includes the responsibility of overseeing reserving, financial planning and analysis, pricing, LOB and MBS monitoring, vendor financial modeling, knowledge services, data warehouse stewardship, healthcare economics, and other functions, as needed. She is key in driving Premera's corporate initiative on Knowledge Management.

Audrey is a Fellow of the Society of Actuaries and a Member of the American Academy of Actuaries. She has served on the American Academy of Actuaries' Continuing Care Retirement Communities Standards Committee, the Academy's Health Liquidity Work Group, the Society's

Continuing Education Committee, and the Society of Actuaries' Futurism Section Council.

P. ANTHONY HAMMOND, ASA, MAAA

Tony is VP Health Services and Chief Actuary for Senior Products for Humana, Inc. Mr. Hammond is also Chief Actuary of Humana's Puerto Rico companies.

Prior to joining Humana, Tony was Principal and Senior Actuary with Greenwood Consultants, an independent actuarial consulting firm. Tony has also held positions as Vice President or Chief Actuary of several health plans throughout his career.

Tony has been very involved in health insurance policy issues over the years, working extensively with the American Academy of Actuaries, the Health Insurance Association of America, the Institute for Health Policy Solutions and as a private consultant. In that regard, he has testified, analyzed and commented on a range of health insurance issues, especially Medicare products and prescription drug costs, health risk adjusters and the impact of health policy alternatives on employer-sponsored group, individual and child health insurance coverages. Tony has authored various papers on health policy issues.

Tony is an Associate of the Society of Actuaries and a Member of the American Academy of Actuaries. He has served on numerous Society and Academy health insurance committees and work groups.

TIMOTHY HARRIS, FSA, MAAA

Tim is a Principal with Milliman, Inc., a firm of consultants and actuaries, in their St. Louis, MO office. He has been with the firm since 1987. Prior to that time he held senior positions with several insurance companies.

Tim built and manages a Life and Health related actuarial consulting practice in St. Louis. Consulting projects include assignments for Insurers, State and Federal agencies, HMOs, healthcare providers, and employers.

Tim is a Fellow of the Society of Actuaries and a Member of the American Academy of Actuaries. He has served on many professional committees. He was a member of the Life Committee of the Actuarial Standards Board from 1988 to 1995, is a past member of the Society of Actuaries' Board of Governors, and was also a member of the Medicare Cost Containment Work Group of the Academy of Actuaries which was established at the direction of Congress. Tim is well published as a co-author of several texts and many articles. He has been on a large number of professional panels as panelist, moderator and/or facilitator.

RANDALL P. HERMAN, FSA

Randall, is one of the founders of Patient Choice Healthcare and serves as chairman and chief executive officer. A nationally known leader in the health care industry, he has over twenty years of managed care experience and has participated in more than 75 HMO startups. He is a founder and chairman of EvergreenRe, a managed care reinsurance brokerage firm covering more than 1.5 million lives. Prior to Patient Choice, Randall co-founded and served as president and managing principal of Reden and Anders, an actuarial consulting firm. While at Reden and Anders, he served as the key consultant to the Buyers Health Care Action Group in the development and assessment of their purchasing initiative. Prior to Reden and Anders, Randall was senior vice president of Ingenix, a United Health Group company, where he was responsible for strategic business development and acquisitions. Before that, he served as the CEO of Certitude, a healthcare data and technology firm sold to Ingenix in 1997.

Randall has a bachelor of science degree from the University of Minnesota. He is a fellow of the Society of Actuaries and a member of the American Academy of Actuaries.

ALISON JOHNSON, RN, MBA

Alison Johnson is the Director of Clinical Consulting with Halleland Health Consulting, a subsidiary of the Minneapolis law firm Halleland, Lewis, Nilan and Johnson. She joined the firm after seven years as a Health Care Management Consultant with Milliman, working with government agencies, health plans and large employers, particularly in the automotive industry.

Alison specializes in disease and case management, assisting clients with the development, implementation and evaluation of these and other care management programs, evolving them to care management program that boost quality and contain medical costs.

She began her nursing career at the University of Washington Hospital system and has held position s in Washington (Group Health Cooperative of Puget Sound), Alaska (Kodiak Island Hospital), Oregon (Bay Area Hospital) and Minnesota.

Alison's nursing, financial and consulting career spans more than 30 years, including 16 years of hospital nursing and administrative work, and 14 years of finance and consulting experience. She is a frequent industry speaker on medical management and healthcare finance topics.

STUART A. KLUGMAN, FSA, PH.D.

Stuart is the Principal Financial Group Professor of Actuarial Science at Drake University in Des Moines, IA, a position he has held since 1988. For the 14 previous years he held the same position at The University of Iowa.

Stuart's area of expertise is statistical models for insurance processes. This is reflected in numerous publications and presentations, including co-authorship of the textbooks Loss Distributions and Loss Models: From Data to Decisions. He has taught modeling seminars for the CAS and has been heavily involved in the SOA Course 7 seminar on applied modeling. For 2001-2003 he was the SOA Vice President for Education.

DARRELL D. KNAPP, FSA, MAAA, CPA

Darrell Knapp is Executive Director in the Kansas City office of Ernst & Young LLP. He specializes in managed care consulting including provider capitation analysis, product development, and financial reporting. He has also been Head of the financial area of a major insurer's group insurance division.

Darrell received his Bachelor of Science Degree in Business Administration, majoring in Actuarial Science and Accounting, from Drake University in 1981. He coauthored the paper "A Model for Evaluating a Multiple Option Plan Package" and has spoken at numerous industry meetings.

He is a Member of the American Academy of Actuaries State Health Committee, and chairs the Health Practice Financial Reporting Committee. He also served many roles in the Society of Actuaries Education and Examination Committee including General Chairperson.

MICHAEL D. LACHANCE, FSA, MAAA

Mr. Lachance is Co-President of Core, Inc., having joined Core's senior management team in 1998 when Core acquired, Disability RMS a Maine-based disability reinsurance underwriting manager of which Mr. Lachance was one of the founders.

Mike began his insurance career at The New England, and has over 20 years of experience in life, pension, and disability insurance. Prior to forming Disability RMS, Mike was with UNUM and Duncanson & Holt where he spent over 11 years in a variety of Individual Disability and Group Reinsurance management positions. His responsibilities included financial reporting, product development, and, subsequently, overall management of the finance, actuarial, and marketing functions. Upon UNUM's acquisition of Duncanson & Holt, Mike was Vice President in charge of the newly merged Finance and Actuarial Reinsurance operations with over $200 million of LTD premium under management.

A graduate of the University of Maine at Orono with a BA in Mathematics, Mike later did graduate work in Business Administration at the University of Maine and Ball State University. He earned his FSA designation in 1986.

WILLIAM R. LANE, FSA, MAAA

Mr. Lane is a Fellow of the Society of Actuaries (1978) and a Member of the American Academy of Actuaries (1980). He is Chairman of the Health Benefits Research Committee for the Society of Actuaries and chaired the Task Force on Risk Adjustors.

Mr. Lane has been Principal for Heartland Actuarial Consulting, LLC for the past five and a half years. He spent eleven years with Mutual of Omaha, at positions starting as a Second Vice President and ending as Senior Vice President. From 1986 to 1993, he was the Group Actuary with responsibility for a block of medical insurance of over a billion dollars in premium. He actively participated in the lobbying efforts when Health Care Reform was being discussed in Congress. Mr. Lane has been Group Actuary for several other companies including Guarantee Life, Protective Life, and Time Insurance.

MARK E. LITOW, FSA, MAAA

Mark is a Principal with the Milwaukee office of Milliman, Inc. and past International Health Steering Director for Milliman Global. He joined the firm in 1975. Mark has been on the Board of Governors for the Society of Actuaries, and a member of numerous Committees for ASB, American Academy of Actuaries and SOA.

Mark has been involved with various projects concerning health care reform, managed care, disease management, and regulatory issues world wide. A well respected speaker on health topics, Mark frequently provides testimony on controversial issues and has authored numerous papers. He has been a dominant force in the development of the Medical Savings Account concept in the U.S. and South Africa, and has performed health care reform analyses related to financial issues for numerous countries.

Mark's areas of expertise include the projection of health costs for medical care and long term care products and special risk accident and health products, evaluation of health care reform proposals, development of Medical Savings Accounts, reform of Medicare, Medicaid, and other government programs, estimation of reserves and liabilities, new product development, appraisals of accident and health business as part of a life insurance company, expense and persistency studies, rating and re-rating of individual and group insurance products, and analysis of various risk sharing arrangements. He has assisted clients with troubleshooting, pricing and valuation of reserves, and analysis of risk-sharing arrangements.

JAMES T. LUNDBERG

Jim Lundberg is group Dental Underwriting Head for Aetna, Inc. working out of Blue Bell, PA. He has 30 years' experience in various underwriting and financial roles. His most recent prior assignments involved underwriting group health plans for national accounts with Aetna and Prudential Health Care. His career path included a stint as a Senior Account Manager in an employee benefits consulting firm.

Jim has a B.S. degree in Psychology from North Park College (Magna Cum Laude). His leisure activities include golf, tennis and kayaking. He lives in Newtown, PA with his wife, Mary Anne, and their two children.

FRANCIS G. MOREWOOD, FSA, FCIA

Frank Morewood retired from the Sun Life Assurance Company of Canada in 1999. He obtained a Bachelors Degree in Commerce (Honours Actuarial Mathematics) from the University of Manitoba in 1957, following which he spent two years as a Lecturer in Actuarial Mathematics at the same university. He joined the Sun Life in 1959, and was involved with group insurance in various capacities from 1962 until his retirement date. In 1981, he assumed overall corporate responsibility for Group Life and Health Insurance. In 1988, his responsibility was expanded to include Group Pensions.

He has served as Chairman of LIMRA's Group and Pension Marketing Committee and as Secretary of the SOA Health Section Council. His current activities include serving on Rotary International and church committees, studying the piano and recording his family history. He also enjoys golf, tennis, skiing, bridge, hiking, and collecting wild mushrooms.

JAMES T. O'CONNOR, FSA, MAAA

Jim is a Principal and Consulting Actuary with the Chicago office of Milliman. He joined the firm in 1987 after nine years of actuarial experience with Bankers Life and Casualty Company.

Jim has considerable experience consulting in individual health and small group insurance. He has assisted a variety of clients with pricing and plan design, marketing and administrative management, provider network evaluation, regulatory compliance issues, financial reporting, strategic planning, and acquisitions. More recently, he has assisted clients with the development of HSA qualified insurance programs. Clients also seek his expertise regarding voluntary worksite insurance programs.

Jim has been active in the Society of Actuaries and the American Academy of Actuaries, serving on subcommittees and frequently speaking on issues related to small group insurance. He has been a Fellow of the Society and a Member of the Academy since 1982. He received his Masters degree in Mathematics from Loyola University of Chicago.

NICOLA PARKER-SMITH, FSA, FCIA

Nicola Parker-Smith is Assistant Vice-President, Group Underwriting, Central Region at Sun Life Assurance Company of Canada. She is accountable for the financial underwriting of Sun Life's Group Benefit business in their Central Region. Before joining the underwriting team, Nicola was AVP, Group Creditor Business where she was accountable for Sun Life's creditor insurance business. Prior to Sun Life's acquisition of the Clarica Life Insurance Company of Canada, Nicola was Actuary, Group Insurance Pricing at Clarica. She joined Mutual Life (now Clarica) in 1986 and has experienced various work assignments in actuarial valuation and pricing in Group Benefits, Group Pensions and Individual Insurance.

Nicola became a Fellow of the Society of Actuaries and a Fellow of the Canadian Institute of Actuaries in 1992. She received a Bachelors degree in Mathematics from Queens University in Kingston, Ontario.

AMY PAHL, FSA, MAAA

Amy is a Principal and Consulting Actuary in the Minneapolis office of Milliman. She has been with the firm since 2001. Previously Amy was employed by LifeCare Assurance Company and Allianz Life Insurance Company of North America. She specializes in long term care insurance products with experience in plan design and pricing, implementation and development, state insurance department filings, inforce management, and financial reporting.

Amy is a Fellow of the Society of Actuaries and a Member of the American Academy of Actuaries. She speaks regularly at industry meetings and has authored several articles on long term care insurance.

Amy is a graduate of Macalester College with a B.A. degree in Mathematics and Economics, cum Laude.

JULIA T. PHILIPS, FSA, MAAA

Julia Philips is an Actuary with the Minnesota Department of Commerce. She reviews insurance rates and forms for compliance with state law, reviews reserve levels and financial stability of life and health insurance companies, reviews actuarial statements for compliance with actuarial standards, provides technical advice to state policy-makers on insurance reform proposals, and participates in model law and regulatory guidance development for the National Association of Insurance Commissioners.

Julia is a Fellow of the Society of Actuaries, a Member of the American Academy of Actuaries, and a graduate of UCLA. She also received a Master of Arts degree from the University of Minnesota in Mathematics. She chairs the Editorial Advisory Board of Contingencies magazine, and is a former Member of the Board of Governors of the Society of Actuaries. She is currently serving on the Actuarial Board for Counseling and Discipline.

EDWARD P. POTANKA, JD

Edward P. Potanka is an Associate Chief Counsel in the Legal & Public Affairs Division of CIGNA Corporation. He has been an attorney in a variety of roles with CIGNA and its predecessor, Connecticut General Life Insurance Company, for thirty three years. In his current position, Mr. Potanka is responsible for counseling CIGNA HealthCare's insurance, managed care and third party administration operations. He has written and spoken extensively on the legal and regulatory aspects of group health insurance and managed care. Mr. Potanka is an honors graduate of Amherst College and the Cornell Law School, and is a member of the Connecticut Bar Association.

WILLIAM A. RAAB

Mr. Raab is currently Regional Sales Manager of the Philadelphia/Delaware Valley Market for CIGNA Dental. During a 30-year career in the group insurance industry, he has held a variety of sales, management, and executive positions. Among them is Vice President of Sales and Marketing for AH&L Insurance Company in Piscataway, New Jersey, where he was responsible for overseeing all marketing and communications, advertising, field operations, product development, and sales training functions for the company.

Active in the industry, Raab is currently a Director of the Greater Philadelphia Association of Health Underwriters, and the Pennsylvania Association of Health Underwriters. He served for a number of years on the Dental Relations Committee of the Health Insurance Association of America, including two years as Chairman. He also served on the Group Insurance Marketing Committee of LIMRA.

In addition to his insurance industry responsibilities, Raab is also active in his community. He was elected to the local Board of School Directors, where he served as the Vice President. He is also former Director of the Lions Club, and a member of the school district's Long Range Planning Committee.

Raab is a graduate of Allegheny College in Meadville, Pennsylvania. Father of three, he and his wife Nina reside in East Greenville, Pennsylvania.

HERSCHEL REICH, FSA, MAAA

Herschel Reich is Senior Consultant for Reden & Anders and manages their New York Office. In this capacity, he works with his clients on strategic pricing, underwriting, marketing, acquisition and product positioning strategies. He has worked extensively in the actuarial healthcare and managed care arena for over 20 years. Prior to joining Reden & Anders, Herschel held actuarial and executive leadership roles in group healthcare, dental and vision for The Guardian Life Insurance Company of America. He is a frequent speaker at both actuarial and healthcare industry meetings. Herschel received a Bachelor of Arts degree in mathematics from the Bernard M. Baruch College and is a Fellow of the Society of Actuaries since 1989 and a Member of the American Academy of Actuaries since 1987.

PETER K. REILLY, FSA, MAAA

Peter is an Actuary with Aetna, Inc. in Blue Bell, PA. He has been with Aetna since 1998. From 1985 through 1998 Peter was an actuary with Milliman & Robertson and was elected principal in 1997. While at Milliman and Robertson Peter was instrumental in developing the Health Cost Index and specialized in modeling and forecasting health care trends. Peter is a graduate of LaSalle University with a B.A. degree in Mathematics and Indiana University with a M.A. degree in Economics.

JAY C. RIPPS, FSA, MAAA

Jay is a consulting actuary with the San Francisco office of Milliman. He joined the firm in 2001, after 26 years as an actuary and senior executive at

Aetna, 2 years as a public school teacher, and 10 years of actuarial consulting work with other firms.

Jay assists healthcare providers, health maintenance organizations, and insurance companies with the development and management of their managed care activities and risks. He has also assisted state government agencies in New York, Florida, Arizona, and California regarding insurance and managed care issues, including drafting of regulations and public testimony. He has also served as an expert witness regarding group insurance and managed care, including litigation with high visibility and national scope.

Jay is a Fellow of the Society of Actuaries and a Member of the American Academy of Actuaries. He chaired the American Academy of Actuaries Medicare Reform Task Force and Committee on Risk Classification, and he was a contributing author to the following Monographs of the American Academy of Actuaries: Medicaid Managed Care: Savings, Access, and Quality; Actuarial Perspectives on Regional Health Alliances Under Health Care Reform; Medicare Reform: Evaluating the Fiscal Soundness of Medicare, Medicare Reform: Using Private-Sector Competition Strategies; and Medicare Reform: Providing Prescription Drug Coverage for Medicare Beneficiaries

Jay is a graduate of the Princeton University with an A.B. degree in Mathematics, Cum Laude.

KENT SACIA

Kent Sacia is a Principal and Healthcare Management Consultant with the Seattle office of Milliman. He joined the firm in 1996.

Kent has designed technology systems and operational procedures to increase efficiencies and gain strategic advantages for over 100 insurance and healthcare entities. He has led the redesign of business processes, developed strategic systems plans, and managed the migration of systems from mainframe to client/server environments. He has also managed the development and implementation of several, large Internet-based systems and created two Internet-based software products.

Under Kent's direction, clients have achieved productivity improvements as high as 300% in the processing of medical and dental claims. He has also developed a well-known set of industry benchmarks for evaluating and measuring the performance of healthcare operations. Kent's technical expertise is centered in the design and development of client/server and Internet-based systems. He has experience with enterprise Internet systems and associated privacy and security issues.

Kent is a graduate of the University of Washington and has a Masters Degree from Carnegie-Mellon University.

PIERRE SADDIK, FSA, FCIA

Pierre Saddik, FCIA, FSA, is President of Saddik International Consulting, a specialized actuarial consulting firm in the areas of Group Insurance, health insurance, travel insurance, and international reinsurance.

His previous experience encompassed 26 years of insurance and reinsurance experience in group insurance, mainly in underwriting, pricing, development and actuarial with major Canadian insurers and reinsurers.

Pierre has also served from 1999 to 2003 as an Elected Member of the Canadian Institute of Actuary's Board of Directors, and on various Canadian Institute of Actuaries Committees as well as on the Canadian Life and Health Insurance Association (C.L.H.I.A.)'s Health Strategy Group. Pierre graduated at McGill University in 1979

BRUCE D. SCHOBEL, FSA, MAAA, FCA

Bruce Schobel is Vice President and Actuary with New York Life Insurance Co. He joined New York Life in 1990, after two years with William M. Mercer, Inc. During 1979-88, Mr. Schobel held various actuarial and policy related positions with the Social Security Administration.

A graduate of Massachusetts Institute of Technology, he is a Fellow of the Society of Actuaries and the Conference of Consulting Actuaries, a Member of the American Academy of Actuaries, a Chartered Life Underwriter, a Certified Employee Benefit Specialist and a Founding Member of the National Academy of Social Insurance. He serves on the Boards of the AAA, CCA and SOA, and will be president of the Society of Actuaries for a 1-year term beginning October 2007. Mr. Schobel is a frequent speaker on social insurance topics, and his papers and articles have appeared in a number of actuarial and non-actuarial publications.

SHEILA SHAPIRO

Sheila Shapiro is a Senior Vice President and the Chief Operations Officer at Blue Cross Blue Shield of Montana. She has also served in similar capacities at Premera Blue Cross in Seattle and Molina Healthcare, Inc. in Long Beach California. She has over 20 years of experience in managing diverse operations for health insurance plans and HMOs.

Sheila has a BS in Business Administration from Arizona State University and an MA in Management from the University of Phoenix.

DOUGLAS B. SHERLOCK

Douglas B. Sherlock is President of Sherlock Company, which assists health plans, their business partners and their investors in the treasury, strategic and control functions of finance. Now in its twentieth year, Sherlock Company provides benchmarking data and analysis for the management of administrative functions, performs valuation and due diligence for business combinations and other capital transactions and offers research publications concerning the financial affairs of health plans.

Prior to founding Sherlock Company, Sherlock was Vice President of Financial Analysis of U.S. Healthcare, Inc., a predecessor to Aetna Inc., where he directed the company's merger and joint venture activity, its investor relations program and its Medicare Advantage business. Previously, Sherlock was a Vice President of Salomon Brothers, Inc where he wrote financial research concerning publicly traded health plans and hospital systems for institutional investors.

Sherlock is a Chartered Financial Analyst and holds an M.B.A. in finance from Loyola College in Maryland. He received his bachelor's degree in economics from Franklin and Marshall College, Lancaster, Pennsylvania.

DANIEL D. SKWIRE, FSA, MAAA

Dan is a Principal and Consulting Actuary with the Portland, Maine office of Milliman, Inc. He joined the firm in 1998 after 7 years with UNUM Life Insurance Company. Dan specializes in the areas of group and individual disability insurance and group life insurance. He has assisted clients with projects including product design, pricing, valuation, reinsurance, actuarial appraisals, and compliance.

Dan is an active Member of the Society of Actuaries. He has served on the SOA Health Section Council and Health Practice Advancement Committee, and he is currently the Chairperson of the SOA Disability Special Interest Group and of the International Actuarial Association's Income Protection Topic Team. He is a regular speaker at industry meetings, and he has published articles in a variety of professional publications, including the North American Actuarial Journal, Contingencies, and Best's Review. Dan is a graduate of Williams College.

CLARK E. SLIPHER, FSA, MAAA

Clark is a Principal and consulting actuary with the Milwaukee office of Milliman, Inc. He joined the firm in 1994.

Clark assists healthcare plans and providers to be successful in a competitive and volatile environment. Trained as an actuary, most of his current projects involve using his actuarial perspective to solve practical business problems. Clark also has extensive experience in helping large employers manage their employee benefit plans. Clark's clients span the public and private sectors. He assists organizations of all sizes in the areas of plan design, health cost projection, consumer directed plans, liability valuation, experience analysis, risk analysis, utilization benchmarking, plan administration, network evaluation, provider reimbursement, medical management, and strategic planning.

Clark is a Fellow of the Society of Actuaries and a Member of the American Academy of Actuaries. He earned a bachelor's degree in actuarial science from Ball State University - Indiana.

JEFFREY L. SMITH, MAAA, MCA

Jeff is a Senior Consultant with the Columbus, Ohio office of Milliman USA. He joined the firm in 1999.

Jeff has over 35 years of health actuarial experience. His experience includes work with insurance companies, managed care organizations, regulators, providers and employers. Prior to joining Milliman, Jeff had his own practice in Columbus and was affiliated with Rector & Associates, Inc. and First Health Associates, Inc. Jeff previously served as Vice President with United HealthCare Corporation, where he was named its first Actuarial Officer. Jeff also served as Vice President of finance and administration for United HealthCare of Ohio. He spent 19 years with Blue Cross and Blue Shield Plans in Ohio, serving as Vice President and Chief Actuary, as well as Chief Financial Officer.

Jeff is a Member of the American Academy of Actuaries and the Conference of Consulting Actuaries. He received a BS in Mathematics from Ohio State University and an MBA from the University of Dayton.

IRWIN J. STRICKER, FSA, MAAA

Irwin Stricker recently retired from the Guardian Life Insurance Company of America after 27 years of service there and a total of 40 years of experience in the group insurance field. His last position at The Guardian was Vice President for Group Pricing and Standards. In that capacity, he was responsible for overseeing the pricing of all group insurance products, establishing and coordinating underwriting standards throughout the Company's regional home offices, supervising the Group Planning and Control and Group Contract and Compliance Divisions and served as the Company's Appointed Actuary for its group insurance products.

Irwin has served on various committees relating to group insurance of the Health Insurance Association of America, the Society of Actuaries, and the American Academy of Actuaries.

MICHAEL J. THOMPSON, FSA, MAAA

Michael J. Thompson is a Principal with PricewaterhouseCoopers. He has over 25 years of experience in healthcare and employee benefits strategy development and implementation, design, financing, pricing, operations and analysis. Mike consults with major employers and health plans on integrated health, wellness and consumerism, defined contribution retiree health, vendor performance management, human capital effectiveness and healthcare supply chain management strategies.

Mike serves as one of PwC's national thought leaders for healthcare consumerism strategies for the health industries practice, participates on the steering board of the World Economic Forum "Working for Wellness" initiative as well as a delegate to the Montage Group focused on cross-sector collaborative solutions and is a frequent speaker on next generation health strategies. In the past few years, Mike has served as a leader promoting health industry efforts based on the principals of Six Sigma.

Mike is a Fellow of the Society of Actuaries (SOA) and serves on the Federal Health Committee, Disease Management Committee, Medicare Committee as well as chairman of the Quality Initiatives Subcommittee of the American Academy of Actuaries (AAA). Mike also serves on boards of the New York chapter of the National Alliance on Mental Illness and the New York Business Group on Health.

Mike is a primary author of multiple articles and publications including "Employer Driven Consumerism – Integrating Health into the Business Model" (Employee Benefits Quarterly), "The Factors Fueling Rising Healthcare Costs 2006" (AHIP Publication), "Pay for Performance - Rewarding Improvements in Quality of Healthcare" (AAA Issue Brief), "Healthcare Transformation, Leadership and the Evolution of Consumerism" (WELCOA), "The Healthcare Balancing Act: Aligning Objectives, Intentions and Incentives" (View).

WILLIAM J. THOMPSON, FSA, MAAA

Bill Thompson is a Principal and Consulting Actuary in the Hartford office of Milliman, Inc. He directs that practice, which he established when he joined the firm in 1988. His clients include several major insurance companies, HMOs, healthcare provider organizations, Medicare Prescription Drug Plan Sponsors, medical device manufacturers, employers, and regulators.

Prior to joining Milliman, Bill held several actuarial positions at John Hancock and at Aetna. In total, he has over 37 years of actuarial experience, virtually all of it in healthcare.

In addition to serving terms on his firm's Health Steering Committee and Public Relations Committee, Bill served as Chairman of the Society of Actuaries Program Committee and served on the Academy of Actuaries State Health Committee and Task Force on Health Risk-Based Capital. He is Chairman of Milliman's Marketing Committee and is a facilitator for the Society of Actuaries Fellowship Admissions Course and Associate Professionalism Course. He is also a faculty member for the American Academy of Actuaries Life & Health Qualifications Seminar.

CORI E. UCCELLO, FSA, MAAA, MPP

Cori Uccello is the Senior Health Fellow at the American Academy of Actuaries. In this role she serves as the actuarial profession's chief policy liaison on health care issues. She promotes the formulation of sound health care policy by providing nonpartisan technical assistance to legislators and regulators. Cori has prepared testimony and has authored or co-authored several Academy publications on Medicare and other health policy issues.

Before joining the Academy, she was a senior research associate at the Urban Institute, where she focused on health care and retirement issues. Prior to moving to the public policy arena, she was an actuary with John Hancock. Her tenure there included work on pensions and long-term care insurance.

Cori holds an MPP from Georgetown University.

LEIGH M. WACHENHEIM, FSA, MAAA

Leigh is a Principal and Consulting Actuary with Milliman in Minneapolis. She joined the firm in 1994. Her project work has focused on the development and effective management of health insurance plans, including: product design, rate development and management, regulatory compliance, financial forecasting and experience monitoring, and financial reporting. She has worked with insurance companies, Blues plans, HMOs, government agencies, and trade groups. Other work has included the evaluation of blocks of business for potential sale or acquisition, financial modeling to evaluate the impact of proposed legislation, development of benchmarks for experience evaluation and resource allocation, and litigation support.

Leigh has also been active with the American Academy of Actuaries and the Society of Actuaries. She currently chairs the Medicaid Work Group of the Academy and formerly chaired the Health Section Council and the Seminars Committee of the Health Benefit Systems Practice Advancement Committee. She has also authored articles that appear on the Society exam syllabus and has been a frequent speaker at Society and other industry meetings.

JOHN WATKINS, RPH, MPH, BCPS

John has managed the formulary process at Premera Blue Cross since 2000 and is currently leading Premera's Biotechnology Initiative and participating in the New Medical Technology Initiative. His responsibilities include health technology assessment, formulary process development, formulary reviews, clinical guidelines development and medical policy review. He also provides drug information support to medical and case management staff. John is Clinical Associate Professor of Pharmacy at the University of Washington, where he teaches medical literature evaluation methods. His areas of interest include health policy and the application of evidence-based medicine, economics and ethics to formulary and coverage decision-making processes.

After graduating from the University of Washington and working as a community pharmacist, John served as a hospital pharmacy director, medical supplies director and pharmacology instructor for 7 years in Kathmandu, Nepal. He completed a combined MPH degree in Pharmacy and Health Services at the University of Washington (1993) with a residency at Group Health Cooperative, where he later worked as a clinical and drug information pharmacist. Before coming to Premera, he was an Associate Pharmacy Director at Regence BlueShield.

John's interest in formulary systems goes back to Nepal, where he established the first formal P&T committee and developed a combined formulary and drug procurement system serving 30 projects under two separate NGOs. It was there that he first became interested in the problem of managing scarce resources to maximize the value of pharmacotherapy at the patient level.

RICHARD S. WOLF, FSA, MAAA

Richard has a BA degree from Washington & Lee University and a Masters Degree from the University of Iowa. He has served as President of both the Southwestern and Atlanta Actuarial Clubs, and the Board of the North Central Georgia Health Systems Agency, and the Board of the Georgia High Risk Medical Plan. He is now retired after serving a number of years as Vice President and Group Actuary of Life Insurance Company of Georgia.

ANN MARIE WOOD

Ann Marie Wood is a Regional Vice President for Large Group Underwriting for Wellpoint, Inc. working out of the Richmond, Virginia office. She has 34 years experience in the health insurance industry including underwriting, sales, client reporting, underwriting systems and operations. She has been with the Blue Cross and Blue Shield organization since 1973 participating in due diligence operations, the conversion from mutual to public company and several mergers and acquisitions. Her most recent assignment involved leading the large group underwriting activities for Virginia and Georgia. She has led enterprise-wide initiatives on reinsurance and underwriting best practices. She has served on state and national boards, currently serving as the Secretary of the Group Underwriters of America Association. Ann Marie is a graduate of Westhampton College of the University of Richmond where she served a term on the Board. Her leisure activities include golf and travel. Ann Marie currently resides in Richmond, Virginia with her husband, Reggie.

ROBERT E. WORTHINGTON

Robert E. Worthington has been in IS/IT for thirty-three years, and in management for twenty-one years. He has worked in manufacturing, education, healthcare, and insurance industries. Currently, Mr. Worthington is Senior Vice President, Business Operations, for Blue Cross / BlueShield of Tennessee.

Mr. Worthington is active as a speaker and contributing writer regarding business and information technologies. He serves as an advisor to the College of Engineering and Computer Science at the University of Tennessee, Chattanooga, and is a topical speaker for the Owens School of Business, Vanderbilt University.

INDEX

A

Access 47-49
Accelerated benefits provision 59
Accidental Death and
  Dismemberment 65-66, 214, 608-609
Accounting Practices and
  Procedures Manual 394-399
Activities of daily living (ADL) 188
Actuarial certification 391-407, 679
Actuarial cost models 627-629
Actuarial practice notes 406-407
Actuarial soundness 416, 423-424
Actuarial standards of practice
  401-402, 683, 865-866
Actuaries 54, 355
AD&D 65-66, 214, 608-609
Adequacy of reserves 882-885
Adjusted clinical groups 576-577
Administrative service agreements
  344-346
Advertising 259-260
Affiliate rule 410-211
Affordability 42-46
Agent 23
Alternative funding methods 340-343
American Academy of Actuaries 41
American Marketing Association 17
Americans with Disabilities Act
  306-307
Analysis of trend 755-777
Annual statement blanks
  Canada 362-367
  health 352-354
  life 349-352

B

Bed reservation benefit 195
Behavioral health issues 1014
Benefit amounts
  LTD 80-85
    OASDI 221-222
    offsets (LTD) 83-84
Benefit triggers 187-188
Between class testing 422-423
Blue Cross / Blue Shield 11, 26,
  942-943
Bonus pools 107
Broker 23, 686
Brokerages 25
Bühlmann's credibility model 819-820

C

Cafeteria plans 217-218
California Medicaid managed care
  243
Canada Health Act 5, 117-119
Canada Pension Plan 323
Canadian integration 639
Canadian Institute of Actuaries studies
  595
Canadian network providers 989-991
Canadian private medical plans
  127-135

Anti-selection 533, 758-759, 934
Antitrust Laws 279-280
Any willing provider 289
ASO contracts 11, 559-560
Asset adequacy analyhsis 356
Asset shares 689
Associations 7, 494-495

1049

Q

R

S